FIRST CANADIAN EDITION

P9-CPY-544

Marriages and Families

AGNES RIEDMANN
California State University, Stanislaus

MARY ANN LAMANNA
University of Nebraska at Omaha

ADIE NELSON
University of Waterloo

THOMSON
★
NELSON

Australia   Canada   Mexico   Singapore   Spain   United Kingdom   United States

Marriages and Families
First Canadian Edition

by Agnes Riedmann, Mary Ann Lamanna and
Adie Nelson

Editorial Director and Publisher:
Evelyn Veitch

Executive Editor:
Joanna Cotton

Acquisitions Editor:
Brad Lambertus

Marketing Manager:
Karen Howell

Publisher's Representative:
Pamela Armstrong-Duprey

Senior Developmental Editor:
Edward Ikeda

Production Editor:
Julie van Veen

Production Coordinator:
Hedy Sellers

Copy Editor/Proofreader:
Alex Moore

Creative Director:
Angela Cluer

Interior Design Modifications:
Katherine Strain

Cover Design:
Peter Papayanakis

Cover Image:
Photo Disc

Compositor:
Janet Zanette

Indexer:
Belle Wong

Printer:
Transcontinental Printing Inc.

COPYRIGHT © 2003 by Nelson, a division of Thomson Canada Limited.

Printed and bound in Canada
1   2   3   4   05   04   03   02

For more information contact Nelson Thomson Learning, 1120 Birchmount Road, Scarborough, Ontario, M1K 5G4. Or you can visit our internet site at http://www.nelson.com

Statistics Canada information is used with the permission of the Minister of Industry, as Minister responsible for Statistics Canada. Information on the availability of the wide range of data from Statistics Canada can be obtained from Statistics Canada's Regional Offices, its World Wide Web site at http://www.statcan.ca, and its toll-free access number 1-800-263-1136.

ALL RIGHTS RESERVED. No part of this work covered by the copyright hereon may be reproduced, transcribed, or used in any form or by any means—graphic, electronic, or mechanical, including photocopying, recording, taping, Web distribution or information storage or retrieval systems—without the written permission of the publisher.

For permission to use material from this text or product, contact us by
Tel 1-800-730-2214
Fax 1-800-730-2215
www.thomsonrights.com

Every effort has been made to trace ownership of all copyrighted material and to secure permission from copyright holders. In the event of any question arising as to the use of any material, we will be pleased to make the necessary corrections in future printings.

National Library of Canada Cataloguing in Publication Data

Riedmann, Agnes Czerwinski
Marriages and families

1st Canadian ed.

Includes bibliographical references and index.

ISBN 0-17-616887-7

1. Marriage. 2. Family. 3. Single people. 4. Choice (Psychology) I. Lamanna, Mary Ann II. Nelson, Adie, 1958–

III. Title.

HQ734.R54 2002   306.8
C2001-904316-3

Brief Contents

Table of Contents

Chapter 2 **Exploring the Family   33**

Part II   Becoming Partners   87

Part III   Defining Your Marriage and Family 177

Chapter   8   Marriage: A Unique Relationship   221

Chapter   9   Communication and Conflict Management in Marriages and Families   253

Chapter   10   Power and Violence in Marriages and Families   279

Part IV   Experiencing Family Commitment 319

Part V   Family Change and Crisis   447

Preface

MAKING CHOICES

Making decisions about one's marriage and family, either knowledgeably or by default, begins in early adulthood and lasts into old age. People choose whether they will adhere to traditional beliefs, values, and attitudes about gender roles or will adopt more androgynous roles and relationships. They may clarify their values about sex and become more knowledgeable and comfortable with their sexual choices.

Women and men may choose to remain single or to marry, and they have the option today of staying single longer before marrying. Single people make choices about their lives, ranging from decisions to engage in sex for recreation to decisions to abstain from sex altogether. In the courtship process people choose between the more formal custom of dating and the less formal "getting together."

Once individuals choose their partners, they have to decide how they are going to structure their marriages and families. Will the partners be legally married? Will theirs be a dual-career marriage? Will they plan periods in which just the husband or just the wife works interspersed with times in which both work? Will they have children? Will they use the new reproductive technology to become parents? Will other family members live with them—parents, for example? They will make these decisions not once but over and over during their lifetimes.

Within the marital relationship, couples choose how they will deal with conflicts. Will they try to ignore conflicts and risk devitalized relationships? Will they vent their anger in hostile, alienating, or physically violent ways? Or will they practise bonding methods of communicating and fighting—methods that emphasize sharing and can deepen intimacy?

How will the partners distribute power in the marriage? Will they work toward a no-power relationship in which the individual is more concerned with helping and supporting the other than with gaining a power advantage? How will the partners allocate work responsibilities in the home? What value will they place on their sexual lives together? Throughout their experience family members continually face decisions about how to balance each one's need for individuality with the need for togetherness.

Parents also have choices. In raising their children, they can assume the role of martyr or police officer, for example, or they can simply present themselves as human beings who have more experience than their youngsters and who are concerned about developing supportive, mutually cooperative relationships as they exercise their parental responsibilities.

Many spouses face decisions about whether to divorce. They weigh the pros and cons, asking themselves which is the better alternative: living together as they are or separating? Even when a couple decides to divorce, there are choices to make: Will they try to cooperate as much as possible or insist on blame and revenge? What living and economic support arrangements will work best for themselves and their children? How will they handle the legal process?

The majority of divorced individuals eventually face decisions about remarriage. In the absence of cultural models, they choose how they will define step-relationships.

When families meet challenges—and every family will face some—members must make additional decisions. Will they view each crisis as a challenge to be met, or will they blame each other? What resources can they use to handle the crisis?

An emphasis on knowledgeable decision making does not mean that individuals can completely control their lives. People can influence but never directly determine how those around them behave or feel about them. Partners cannot control each other's changes over time, nor can they avoid all accidents, illnesses, unemployment, deaths, or even divorce. Society-wide conditions may create unavoidable crises for individual families.

Families can control how they respond to such crises, however. Their responses will meet their own needs better when they refuse to react automatically and choose instead to act as a consequence of knowledgeable decision making.

The Book's Themes

Several themes are interwoven throughout this text: People are influenced by the society around them as they make choices; social conditions change in ways that may impede or support family life; there is an interplay between individual families and the larger society; and individuals make family-related choices throughout adulthood.

MAKING CHOICES THROUGHOUT LIFE The process of creating and maintaining marriages and families requires many personal choices, and people continue to make decisions, even "big" ones, throughout their lives.

PERSONAL CHOICE AND SOCIAL LIFE Tension frequently exists between the individual and the social environment. Many personal troubles result from societal influences, values, or assumptions, inadequate societal support for family goals, or conflict between family values and individual values. By understanding some of these possible sources of tension and conflict, individuals can perceive their personal troubles more clearly and can work constructively toward solutions. They may choose to form or join groups to achieve family or individual goals. This may include involvement in the political process to shape federal or provincial social policy. The accumulated decisions of individuals and families may also shape the social environment.

A CHANGING SOCIETY In the past, people tended to emphasize the dutiful performance of social roles in marriage and in the family structure. Today people are more apt to view marriages as committed relationships in which they expect to find companionship, intimacy, and support. This book examines the implications of this shift in perspective.

Individualism, economic pressure, time pressures, social diversity, and decreasing marital permanence are features of the social context in which personal decision making takes place today. And as fewer social guidelines seem fixed, personal decision making becomes even more challenging.

The Themes Throughout the Life Course

The book's themes are introduced in Chapter 1, and they reappear throughout the text. We developed these themes by looking at the interplay between findings in the social sciences and experiences of the people around us. Ideas for topics arose from the needs and concerns we perceived. We observed many changes in the roles people play and in the ways they relate to each other. Neither the "old" nor the "new" roles and relationships seemed to us as stereotyped or as free of ambivalence and conflicts as is often indicated in books and articles. The attitudes, behaviour, and relationships of real people have a complexity that we have tried to portray in this book.

Interwoven with these themes is the concept of the life course—the idea that adults may change through reevaluation and restructuring throughout their lives. This emphasis on the life course creates a comprehensive picture of marriages and families and enables this book to cover many topics that are new to marriage and family texts. This book makes these points:

- Many people reexamine the decisions they have made about marriage and family not once or twice but throughout their lives.

- People's personal problems and their interaction with the social environment change as they and their marriages and families grow older.

- People reevaluate their relationships and their expectations for relationships as they and their marriages and families mature.

- Because marriage and family forms are more flexible today, people may change the style of their marriage and family throughout their lives.

Key Features

We have three goals in mind for student readers: first, to help them better understand themselves and their family situations; second, to make students more conscious of the personal decisions that they will make throughout their lives and of the societal influences that affect those decisions; and, third, to help students better appreciate the variety and diversity among families today. We highlight the theme of making choices with a group of theme boxes ("As we make choices ...") throughout the text. These boxes emphasize human agency and are designed to help students through those moments of crucial decisions. In order to accomplish our third goal we have presented the latest research and statistical information on diverse family forms, lesbian and gay male families, and on families of diverse races and ethnicities. We consciously integrated these materials throughout the textbook, always with an eye toward avoiding stereo-

typical, simplistic generalizations and, instead, explaining data in sociological and sociohistorical context. Besides integrating information on ethnic diversity throughout the text proper, we have a series of boxes entitled, "A closer look at family diversity." These boxes focus on the latest theory of research as it applies to some area of family diversity.

In addition, this text is designed to be especially text–student interactive: Students are asked to think critically and answer questions about what they think family values are and the relationship between these and social policy.

Case Studies Agnes Riedmann talked with individuals of all ages about their experiences in marriages and families. These interviews appear as boxed excerpts, balancing and expanding topics presented in the chapters. Some student essays also appear as case study boxes. We hope that the presentation of individuals' stories in their own words will help students to see their own lives more clearly and will encourage them to discuss and reevaluate their own attitudes and values.

Enrichment material Boxed material on making choices and on family diversity, drawn from classic research, new studies, popular social science, and newspaper and journal articles, supports and expands the chapter content.

Pedagogical aids An outline of topics to be covered introduces each chapter. A large number of charts and diagrams present current data in easily understood form. End-of-chapter study aids include a summary, a list of key terms, study questions, and annotated suggested readings. A comprehensive glossary defines and illustrates important terms.

ANCILLARY MATERIALS AVAILABLE The *Instructor's Manual/Test Bank* offers the instructor a wide range of resources to help them teach their course including Chapter Contents, Lecture Outlines, Lecture Suggestions, Student Activities, and Review Worksheets.

The *Instructor's Manual/Test Bank* also includes 45 multiple-choice questions and 40 true-false questions for each chapter, all with page references. It also includes 10 short-essay questions and five extended essay questions for each chapter.

The Computerized Test Bank is a test-generating software supplement that allows instructors to create, edit, store, and print exams quickly and efficiently using the questions taken from the Test Bank.

The text's Web site (www.marriagesandfamilies. nelson.com) offers students and instructors alike access to practice quizzes, chapter-specific Web links, study tips, and information on degrees and careers in sociology.

A free four-month subscription to InfoTrac College Edition, an extensive online library, is enclosed with every new copy of the book, giving students access to the latest news and research articles. This easy-to-use database features thousands of reliable, full-length articles from hundreds of top academic journals and popular sources.

There is a continuously updated selection of videos available to help support classroom teaching. Please contact your sales representative for more information.

Acknowledgments

We would like to thank some of the many people who helped in the publication of this edition.

At Statistics Canada, we would like to thank Tina Chui, Jennifer Chard, and Sylvie Bourbonnais for their assistance with the Canadian statistical data. At The Vanier Institute of the Family, we would like to thank Robert Glossop. For some of the photos, we would like to acknowledge Ronald and Marilyn Lambert and their family.

At Nelson, the professionalism, guidance, and support provided by the editorial team of Joanna Cotton, Edward Ikeda, Toni Chahley, and Julie van Veen are gratefully acknowledged. We also wish to express our enormous gratitude for the talent, hard work, and inimitable wit of our copy editor, Alex Moore.

Reviewers gave us many helpful suggestions for revising the manuscript. And although we have not incorporated all of their suggestions, we considered them all carefully and used many. The reviewer insights and evaluations have enhanced this text, and we list them below with our thanks:

Tami Bereska, Grant MacEwan College
Barbara Mitchell, Simon Fraser University
Vappu Tyyska, Ryerson Polytechnic University
James White, University of British Columbia
Helene Cummins, Brescia University College

Agnes Riedmann
Mary Ann Lamanna
Adie Nelson

To our families, especially
Bill, Beth, Chris, and Natalie
Larry, Valerie, Sam, Janice, and Simon
Ronnie and Josh

Family Commitments: Making Choices in a Changing Society

HUMAN NATURE IS NOT A MACHINE
TO BE BUILT AFTER A MODEL, AND
SET TO DO EXACTLY THE WORK PRE-
SCRIBED FOR IT, BUT A TREE, WHICH
REQUIRES TO GROW AND DEVELOP
ITSELF ON ALL SIDES, ACCORDING TO
THE TENDENCY OF THE INWARD
FORCES WHICH MAKE IT A LIVING
THING.

JOHN STUART MILL, 1859

WE ARE NEITHER TOTALLY VICTIMS
OF SYSTEMS NOR TOTALLY CAPTAINS
OF OUR OWN SOULS.

CATHERINE CHILMAN

Today's Canadians are cautious and apprehensive—and at the same time creative and hopeful—about marriages and families. On the one hand, most of us still hope to experience ongoing happiness in committed unions and families (Bibby 2001). And there are long-term, happy marriages (Wallerstein and Blakeslee 1995). Yet we have reason to wonder about the chances of finding such happiness. For one thing, our divorce rate has called into question the stability of marriage. Beginning in the 1980s, some sociologists began to speak of "the reconceptualization of marriage as a nonpermanent relationship" (Safilios-Rothschild 1983, p. 306); they claimed that the family had been so shaken up that "all bets are off" (Wiley 1985, p. 2).

Meanwhile, we remain hopeful about family commitment because families are central to society as an institution, and to our everyday lives. While Canadian adults are more likely than Canadians teens to identify the family as "very important" to them (85 percent

and 59 percent, respectively) Canadian teens "have high hopes when it comes to family life. Most plan to marry and stay with their partners for life. Almost all plan to have children" (Bibby 2001, p. 155). Families are commissioned with the pivotal tasks of raising children and providing continuing intimacy, affection, and companionship to members. But hoping alone won't make enduring or emotionally satisfying families, although faith and dedication to the possibility of committed happiness and stability would seem an essential precondition. Maintaining a family requires both commitment and knowledge of what you're doing. That theme is a good part of what this book is about. We will return to it later in this chapter and throughout this text. Right now, though, we need to explore what a family is.

DEFINING FAMILY

What is a family? (To think about this question, examine Box 1.1, "Which of These Is a Family?") In everyday conversation we make assumptions about what families are or should be. Traditionally, both law and social science specified that the family consisted of people related by blood, marriage, or adoption. Some definitions of the family specified a common household, economic interdependency, and sexual and reproductive relations (Murdock 1949). Changes to the Canadian Census alert us to some of the changes that have occurred in relation to thinking about the family. For example, the 1981 Canadian Census was the first to report on common-law marriages. More recently, the 2001 Canadian Census included two questions that recognize same-sex partners (Box 1.2, "Questions #5 and #6 from the 2001 Canadian Census"). You should note that Question #6 in the 2001 Census also explicitly recognizes children being raised in same-sex households, even in jurisdictions where provincial or territorial laws do not permit same-sex couples to formally adopt or share guardianship of their children. According to Statistics Canada, a **census family** is "a now married couple (with or without never-married sons and/or daughters of either or both spouses), a couple living common-law (again with or without never-married sons and/or daughters of either or both parents), or a lone parent of any marital status, with at least one never-married son or daughter living in the same dwelling."

Which of These Is a Family?

BOX 1.1

A husband and wife and their offspring.

A single woman and her three young children.

A 52-year-old woman and her adoptive mother.

A man, his daughter, and the daughter's son.

An 84-year-old widow and her dog, Fido.

A man and all of his ancestors back to Adam and Eve.

Three adult sisters living together.

Two lesbians in an intimate relationship and their children from a previous marriage of one woman and a previous relationship of the other woman with a male friend.

Two children, their divorced parents, the current spouses of their divorced parents, and the children from previous marriages of their stepparents.

A child, his stepfather, and the stepfather's wife subsequent to his divorce from the child's mother.

Two adult male cousins living together.

A 77-year-old man and his lifelong best friend.

A childless husband and wife who live 1000 km apart.

A widow and her former husband's grandfather's sister's granddaughter.

A divorced man, his girlfriend, and her child.

Both sets of parents of a deceased married couple.

A married couple, one son and his wife, and the latter couple's children, all living together.

Six adults and their 12 young children, all living together in a communal fashion.

Source: Klein and White 1996.

In their modern classic, *The Family: From Institution to Companionship* (1945), Burgess and Locke defined the family as "a group of persons united by the ties of marriage, blood, or adoption; constituting a single household; interacting and communicating with each other in their respective social roles (husband and wife, mother and father, son and daughter, brother and sister); and creating and maintaining a common culture" (p. 8). This definition goes beyond earlier ones to talk about family relationships and interaction. Burgess and Locke saw the family as a **primary group**—a term coined by sociologist Charles Horton Cooley (1909, p. 23) more than 80 years ago to describe any group in which there is a close, face-to-face relationship.[1] In a

primary group, people communicate with one another as whole human beings. They laugh and cry together, they share experiences, and they quarrel, too, because that's part of being close. Primary groups can give each of us the feeling of being accepted and liked for what we are.

Burgess and Locke gave us a definition of the family that described some family relationships. But their view of family interaction was more limited than our current ones. It assumed that interaction occurred primarily in the context of traditional (heterosexual, married-couple) social roles, rather than emphasizing spontaneity, individuality, and intimacy. Social scientists today are still studying the family's responsibility in performing necessary social roles, such as child rearing. But many social scientists (including us) reject Burgess and Locke's limited definition of family. Family members are not necessarily bound by legal marriage, by blood, or by adoption.

1. Another example of a primary group relationship is a close friendship. A **secondary group**, in contrast, is characterized by more distant, practical relationships, as, for example, in a professional organization or business association.

5. Is this person living with a common-law partner? Common-law refers to two people of the opposite sex or of the same sex who live together as a couple but who are not legally married to each other.

[X] Yes

[X] No

6. Relationship to Person 1

For each person usually living here, describe his/her relationship to Person 1.

Mark "X" or specify one response only.

Stepchildren, adopted children and children of a common-law partner should be considered sons and daughters.

If none of the choices apply, use the "Other" box to indicate this person's relationship to Person 1. Examples of "Other" relationships to Person 1:

[X] grandparent

[X] cousin

[X] niece or nephew

[X] lodger's husband or wife

[X] room-mate's daughter or son

[X] employee

[X] husband or wife of Person 1

[X] common-law partner (opposite-sex) of Person 1

[X] common-law partner (same-sex) of Person 1

[X] son or daughter of Person 1

[X] son-in-law or daughter-in-law of Person 1

[X] grandchild of Person 1

[X] father or mother of Person 1

[X] father-in-law or mother-in-law of Person 1

[X] brother or sister of Person 1

[X] brother-in-law or sister-in-law of Person 1

[X] lodger or boarder

[X] room-mate

[X] other—Specify _____

Source: from the Statistics Canada publication "2001 Canadian Census Questionnaire."

Burgess and Locke also specified that family members "constitute a household." We would expand this definition to include, for example, commuter couples, noncustodial parents, parents with adult children living elsewhere, extended kin such as aunts and uncles, and adult siblings and stepsiblings. In other words, the term family does not necessarily include only partners, parents, and any children in one household.

Throughout much of this century, the traditional **nuclear family** (husband, wife, and children in one household) has been considered the **modern family**. The progressively increasing family diversity that we see now has led some scholars to refer to today's family as the **postmodern family**. Indeed, a few postmodern theorists (e.g., Stacey 1990, 1996; Edwards 1991) now argue that the concept of "family" no longer has any objective meaning of any sort.

This liberalization of the definition of family has affected others besides social scientists. For example, in 2000, the federal government of Canada enacted the *Modernization of Benefits and Obligations Act*, "recognizing same-sex couples equally with opposite-sex couples in some 68 federal laws. Similar initiatives have been undertaken by a number of provinces and private employers" (EGALE 2001). Furthermore, to be a family not all the roles mentioned—husband, wife, children—need be included. Single-parent households and childless unions are families. And roles may be nontraditional: Social scientists no longer assume that a family has a male breadwinner and a female homemaker; and dual-career and reversed-role (working wife, househusband) combinations are also families. As the Canadian Minister of Citizenship and Immigration noted in a 1998 report, the "development of more flexible definitions reflects the diversity of family arrangements and connections in this country."

As families have become less traditional (see Box 1.3, "Some Facts About Families in Canada Today"), the legal definition of a family has become much more flexible and nonspecific and is not necessarily limited to people linked by legal marriage, blood, or adoption. The term "family" has become an increasingly fluid concept.

Canada has a divided jurisdiction in matters of family law. Under the *Constitution Act*, the provinces and the federal government share the responsibility for marriage and marriage-like relationships. While marriage and divorce (including custody and maintenance upon divorce) are under federal jurisdiction, provincial laws govern such matters as adoption, matrimonial property disputes, guardianship, and the licensing and formation of a valid marriage ceremony.

Outside of the province of Quebec, Canadian family law, or the body of law that governs relations between spouses and between spouses and their children, derives from the English *common law* system. Common law is a system of dispute resolution that evolved from decisions arrived at within the English courts of justice from the time of the Norman Conquest in 1066. This system of law relies on case-setting precedents. In contrast, the legal system of Quebec is based on *civil law* and has its origins in the French and Roman codification of law tradition. Historically, family law in that province was also heavily influenced by the teachings of the Catholic Church, which prohibited divorce and made separation or annulment of marriage exceedingly difficult to obtain.

In the past, both systems of law were informed by a vision of the family in which the role of the husband/father was pivotal and in which the labour and

services of a wife belonged to her husband as a right. Under common law wives did not exist as independent beings: "By marriage, the husband and wife are one person in law; the very being or legal existence of the woman is suspended during the marriage, or at least is incorporated and consolidated into that of the husband: under whose wing, protection and cover, she performs everything" (Blackstone 1805, p. 442). Matrimonial law decreed that a husband assumed control or ownership of his wife's personal property and that a wife was not entitled to compensation for her labour. "The one recompense allowed the wife was a 'dower'" (Grey 1998, p. 816)—that is, a life interest in a portion of the land owned by her deceased husband. Upon separation, children were held to be the "natural property" of their fathers and mothers had no legal right of either custody or visitation. Similarly, the Quebec Civil Code "consecrated a notion of 'paternal authority,' which made the husband the head of the family and gave him considerable powers over his wife and children" (Grey 1998, p. 816).

The concept of wives as property also found expression in loss of consortium actions. Common law decreed that a husband had a right to a wife's company and service and that he could sue a third party who interfered with his enjoyment of this right. The underlying assumption here was that "since wifely services could easily be equated with those of any servant, legal liabilities for interference with the master-servant relationship was easily extended to cases of injury to the husband-wife relationship" (Steel 1987, p. 159). In addition, English Common Law recognized the wrongful act of criminal conversation—defined as one man having sex with another man's wife—and permitted a cuckolded husband to sue his wife's lover and claim compensation for his loss of honour and the loss of his monopoly over his wife's services.

Following the passage of the *Married Women's Property Act* of 1882 in England, an act that reinstated the legal existence of the married woman, similar Acts permitting wives to hold property separate from their husbands were passed in common law jurisdictions in Canada and the United States. Since that time, and with gaining momentum since the 1970s, reforms have altered the formerly harsh legal position of married women. In general, "[t]he thrust of legal reform has been on ensuring that both men

What do Canadian marriages and families look like today? Statistics can't tell the whole story, but they are an important beginning.

1. *Canadians come from a variety of ethnic backgrounds.*[2] In the 1996 Canadian census, 5.3 million individuals (19 percent of Canada's total population) reported their ethnic origin as simply "Canadian."[3] Almost all of the people who reported "Canadian" were Canadian-born and had French or English as their first language.[4] In this census, 4.9 million people (17 percent of Canada's total population) reported British-Isles-only ancestry while 2.7 million (9 percent) reported French-only ancestry. Approximately 2.9 million (10 percent) reported some combination of British Isles, French, or Canadian origin in that year. About 4.6 million people (16 percent of the population) reported an ethnic ancestry of either British Isles, French, or Canadian, in combination with some other ethnic origin. Among those who reported origins other than the British Isles, French, or Canadian (8.1 million or 28 percent of Canada's total population), 3.7 million reported European single origin, 1.3 reported single East and Southeast Asian origins, and 590 000 reported single South Asian origins.

2. *The majority of Canadians (84 percent) live in a family setting.* In 1996, the once-dominant family form—married couples with children—represented 45 percent of all families. In that year, 29 percent of families were married couples without children, 15 percent were lone-parent families, 6 percent were common-law couples with children, and 6 percent were common-law couples without children. While married couple families still constitute the majority of Canadian families, the proportion of married couple families has declined from 80 percent of all families in 1986 to 74 percent in 1996 (Figure 1.1).

3. *Common-law couple families account for a growing proportion of first unions and of all Canadian families.* Particularly among those whose language is French—regardless of where they live in Canada—an increasing proportion of first unions in Canada are common-law unions. While in 1970–74, 17 percent of all first unions were common-law unions, this rose to 41 percent in 1980–84 and 57 percent in 1990–95. "In Quebec, 80 percent of all first unions are common-law" (Ambert 1998, p. 7). However, for many Canadians, "common-law union is not only a prelude to marriage,

2. "Ethnic origin," as defined in the 1996 Canadian census, refers to ethnic or cultural ancestry and should not be confused with place of birth, citizenship, or nationality. Before 1996, the census question,"To which ethnic or cultural group(s) did this person's ancestors belong?" was accompanied by a list of the 15 most frequent ethnic origins. Respondents, in turn, were asked to mark as many from this list as applicable and were provided with two blank spaces in which they could indicate other ethnic origins that were not included on the list. However, for the 1996 census, the format of the ethnic origin question was modified. Rather than providing respondents with a list of answer categories, respondents were given blank spaces in which to indicate single or multiple ethnic origins. In recognition of the fact that "Canadian" was the fifth most frequently reported ethnic origin in the 1991 census, "Canadian" was included, for the first time, among the examples given of how this question might be answered.

3. In 1991, when "Canadian" was not listed as an option, only three percent identified their ethnic origin solely as Canadian, with an additional one percent listing it in combination with one or more other ethnic origins.

4. Evidence also suggests that those who identified themselves as Canadian in 1996 were those who had, on earlier censuses, identified their ethnic origins as English or French. The highest proportion of people who reported their ethnic origin as Canadian occurred in places where comparatively little recent immigration has occurred and in regions of Canada that had been settled the earliest. For example, 21 percent of those in the Atlantic provinces and 38 percent of those living in Quebec gave "Canadian" as a single response.

Because of intermarriage, there has been an increase in the number of persons reporting more than one ethnic origin. In 1996, more than one in three (36 percent) reported more than one ethnic origin, with the highest proportion of multiple responses occurring in Prince Edward Island (52 percent) and the lowest proportion occurring in Quebec (17 percent). In general, groups that settled more recently in Canada (i.e., persons with, for example, Caribbean, African, Arab, or Latin American origins) were less likely to report multiple origins than those of Aboriginal, British Isles, French, or other European origins.

	1981	1996
Married couples with children	55.0%	45.1%
Married couples without children	28.1%	28.6%
Lone-parent families	11.3%	14.5%
Common-law families without children	3.7%	6.2%
Common-law families with children	1.9%	5.5%

FIGURE **1.1**

Changing family structures. (Source: from the Statistics Canada publication "Canada Year Book 1999," Cat. No. 11-204, p. 188.

but also an alternative to marriage and remarriage" (Statistics Canada 1996). Indeed, between 1991 and 1996, the rate of increase in common-law families was about 16 times that for married couple families (Statistics Canada 1997).

"Between 1981 and 1995, the number of couples living in common-law unions tripled" (Ambert 1998, p. 7). While in 1991, one Canadian couple in nine was living common law, by 1996, one couple in seven was doing so. Almost two-thirds of the individuals in common-law unions were never-married, while more than a quarter were divorced. Consistent with earlier findings for over a decade, in 1996, common-law families were by far more prevalent in the province of Quebec than in any other province. In Quebec, almost one couple in four (24 percent) was in a common-law relationship in 1996. Over four in ten (43 percent) of Canada's common-law families reside in Quebec.

Approximately half of the common-law couple families in 1996 included children from either the current or previous unions. In 1996, 7.9 percent of all Canadian children were living with parents in common-law families. Young children, under the age of six, were especially likely to be doing so. In that year,

14 percent of all Canadian children under the age of six and almost one in three children (31 percent) in this age group in the province of Quebec were living in common-law couple families.

4. *People have been postponing marriage in recent years.* Although the average age at first marriage reached an all-time low, in 1972, of 22.2 years for brides and 24.7 years for grooms (Nelson and Robinson 1999, p. 284), by 1997, the average age at first marriage for Canadian brides and grooms was 27.4 years and 29.5 years, respectively (Statistics Canada 1999).

On the surface, the increase in the mean age at first marriage may seem to suggest that Canadians are increasingly reluctant to enter marriage and that marriage is weakening as a social institution. However, taking a broader, historical view, sociologist Zheng Wu (1998) points out that it was the postwar period of youthful marriages that was anomalous and that, "[t]he sharp decline in the mean age after World War II through the 1950s and 1960s may reflect the events occurring in a unique historical period" rather than a "'traditional' norm." (p. 4). Observing that, "if current patterns of first marriage persist, close to 90 percent

(continued)

(continued)

of Canadian women and men are likely to marry eventually," he concludes that "there is no indication that marriage is going out of style soon" (p. 4).

5. *The total fertility rate (which represents the number of children born to a hypothetical, typical woman during her childbearing years) has generally declined.* Although Canada experienced a high fertility rate during the period of the baby boom (which is generally considered to have occurred in this country from 1946 to 1959), the birth rate in Canada has been declining since the 1970s with the fertility rate remaining around 1.6 children per woman for several years. The 1997 fertility rate, at 1.552 live births per 1000 women, is less than half the peak reached in 1959, when there were 3935 births per 1000 women. Reasons for this decline include: (1) fewer children born to women of childbearing age following the baby boom (the "baby bust" years), (2) the decline in the size of large families, (3) the increase in the average age of women giving birth for the first time, and (4) the increasing popularity of sterilization as a method of contraception (Canadian Global Almanac 2000).

In 1995, all Canadian provinces reported figures below the replacement rate of 2.1 children that is theoretically necessary to ensure the renewal of generations. In Newfoundland, for example, the reported rate of 1.25 children per woman was the lowest level ever reported by any Canadian province (Statistics Canada 1998). While Quebec has tried to aggressively reverse its plunging birth rate through baby bonuses and, more recently, family-friendly policies, total births in Quebec have also decreased 25 percent since 1990. At present, the birth rate in Quebec has plummeted to its lowest since 1908, with the drop particularly abrupt among women aged 20 to 29 (Peritz 1999). In 1997, the total fertility rate in Canada reached a record low at 1552 births per 1000 women aged 15 to 49; in that year, the Northwest Territories had the highest fertility rate, with 2.583 live births per 1000 women (Statistics Canada 1999).[5]

While the pregnancy rate among every other age group of fertile women is decreasing, *the teenage pregnancy rate is increasing.* From 1985 to 1993, pregnancy rates for Canadian teenagers 15 to 19 increased from 41 to 48 per 1000. In 1994, there were 48.8 pregnancies for every 1000 women aged 15 to 19, a rate that had not been witnessed in Canada since the 1970s. In contrast to the situation among teen mothers in the 1970s, however, teen mothers in the 1990s were more likely to be single (25 percent in 1974 versus 81 percent in 1994). By 1997, the teen pregnancy rate had increased to 59.2 (Crawford 1997). However, the number of live births to teenagers is down because the proportion of pregnancies ending in abortion is up. This proportion almost doubled between 1974 and 1994 from 26 to 45 percent.

6. *First-time mothers are getting older.* In 1997, almost one-third (31 percent) of first births were to mothers who were 30 years of age or over. One decade ago, only 19 percent of first births were to women in this age group. While women in their 20s continue to account for the majority of first births, their share of the total dropped from 70 percent in 1987 to 58 percent in 1996. In 1997, teenagers accounted for 11 percent of first births.

5. Although the fertility rate among Canada's Aboriginal population has also declined, the Aboriginal population is growing more rapidly than the general population. According to census data, while there were 290 children per 1000 women of childbearing years in the total population, the comparable figure for the Aboriginal population (at 491 children aged under five for every 1000 women of childbearing years) "was about 70 percent higher than the ratio for the total population." It is projected that, over the next decade, large increases will occur in the Aboriginal youth population aged 15 to 24 and that the associated increase in Aboriginal women of childbearing age "will result in continued large numbers of Aboriginal children being born" (Statistics Canada 1998c).

From 1987 to 1997, women 30 years of age or over also increased their share of all live births (from 31 percent to 44 percent). During this time period, the proportion of births to mothers 30 years of age and over increased in every Canadian province and territory. In British Columbia, for example, the proportion of births to women aged 30 and over rose from 34 percent in 1987 to 47 percent in 1997, while in Ontario, the proportion of births to women in this age group was higher than the proportion of births to mothers in their 20s (50 percent versus 45 percent, respectively). Nationally, the proportion of live births to women in their 20s declined during this time period, from 63 percent to 50 percent. The proportion of births to teenagers remained at six percent throughout this decade (Statistics Canada 1999).

7. *Lone parent families are more common and more often the result of divorce and births to unwed mothers than due to widowhood.* The proportion of lone-parent families has doubled over the past 35 years in Canada, from 11 percent of all families to 22 percent (Canadian Council on Social Development 2000). Between 1991 and 1996, lone-parent families increased at four times the rate of husband-wife families; in 1996, there were 1.1 million lone-parent families, the vast majority of which were headed by women (Statistics Canada 1997). While in the 1950s and 1960s, the death of a spouse was the major cause of lone parenthood (with over 60 percent of all lone parents widows or widowers), by 1996, divorce, separation and births outside of marriage had become the primary factors of lone parenthood with widowhood accounting for only 20 percent of lone-parent families. The proportion of never-married lone parents increased from 14 percent in 1986 to 22 percent in 1996. About one-third of lone parents were divorced in 1996, while about one-fifth were separated. In that year, just under one-quarter of all female lone parents had never been married. Regardless of cause, however, poverty is particularly likely to occur in lone-parent families. In 1999, almost one-third (32 percent) of single parents (versus 13 percent of couples with children) felt that their income was inadequate to meet their family's basic needs (Canadian Council on Social Development 2001, p. 2).

8. *More and more lesbians and gay men are establishing families with children.* While findings from the 2001 Census were unavailable at the time that this book was written, it has been suggested that approximately 444 000 families in Canada have gay or lesbian parents (Nelson and Robinson 1999).

9. *More mothers are employed.* Over the past two decades, the employment rate of women with school-aged children and, in particular, preschool-aged children, has grown dramatically. In 1999, almost 80 percent of mothers with school-aged children were in the labour force. In that year, "61 percent of women with children less than age 3 were employed, more than double the figure in 1976" (Statistics Canada 2000a; Canadian Council on Social Development 2001). Of the 387 000 employed Canadian women who gave birth in 1993 or 1994, 86 percent had returned to work within a year's time of giving birth and, by two years after, over nine out of ten (93 percent) had returned to paid employment (Marshall 2000, p. 20). However, even when employed, mothers remain responsible for the bulk of housework and childcare. In 1998, for example, married women employed full-time with at least one child at home under the age of 19 spent an hour and a half more per day on unpaid work activities than their male counterparts (Statistics Canada 2000).

10. *Parents are increasingly time-stressed.* "Between 1991 and 1998, the proportion of workers with dependents

(continued)

Some Facts About Families in Canada Today

(continued)

who reported excess tension due to work/family conflicts increased from 38 percent to 44 percent" (Canadian Council on Social Development 2001). During this time period, married parents aged 25 to 44 who were employed full-time increased the amount of time they spent on both paid and unpaid work. An additional two hours a week were spent on paid work activities, while unpaid work hours increased from 33.6 hours to 34.3 hours per week for employed mothers (up two percent) and from 22.4 hours to 23.1 hours per week for employed fathers (up three percent). Among full-time employed parents, slightly more than one-quarter of married fathers (26 percent), and over one-third of married (38 percent) and single mothers (38 percent) report severe time stress. About two out of three parents who are in full-time employment say that they are dissatisfied with the balance between their job and family life. About one parent in eight (13 percent) reports feeling very guilty about the time they devote to work away from their children; among those parents with children under the age of 12, nearly one in five (18 percent) reports feeling very guilty (Canadian Council on Social Development 2001; Schlesinger 1998).

11. *Young adults are increasingly likely to be living with their parents.* In 1996, 33 percent of men and 23 percent of young women aged 20 to 34 were still—or again—living with their parents. These percentages were up from 26 percent for men and 16 percent for women in 1981. The growing tendency to live at home with one's parents was common for young adults who were unmarried (including divorced, separated, widowed, and never-married) and married (including common-law relationships) (Boyd and Norris 2000). Compared to their counterparts in 1981, young adults living with their parents in 1996 were older; while in 1981, about one-quarter of unmarried women and men were age 25 or older, by 1996, 33 percent of unmarried women living

with their parents and 40 percent of unmarried men living at home were 25 years of age or over. "Changes were even more pronounced for young adults who were married, jumping from 52 percent of women and 64 percent of men in 1981, to 69 percent and 78 percent in 1996" (Boyd and Norris 2000, p. 158). This trend reflects economic difficulties, the lengthening of education (and the period of dependency on adults and/or the state) and changes in marital patterns.

12. *Canada experienced a five-fold increase in divorce from 1968 to 1995.* However, divorce rates peaked in 1987 and have generally declined since that time (Ambert 1998; Statistics Canada 2000). While the 1998 crude divorce rate of 228 divorces for every 100 000 people was slightly higher than the 1997 rate of 225 divorces per 100 000 Canadians, it was still far below the peak obtained in 1987, following amendments to the Divorce Act, of 355 divorces per 100 000 people. Based on 1998 divorce rates, projections are that 36 percent of marriages will end in divorce within 30 years of marriage (Statistics Canada 2000).

13. *Remarriages are common following divorce.* Remarriage remains the most common aftermath following divorce, with about 75 percent of divorced men and 65 percent of divorced women remarrying. However, because of the increasing tendency to cohabit, particularly among younger divorced persons and among divorced men, remarriage is less common now than in previous years (Ambert 1998). For example, based on data from the 1995 General Social Survey, women in their 30s and 40s whose first marriage had dissolved were twice as likely to live common-law as to remarry for their second union (Le Bourdais, Neill and Turcotte 2000).

14. *Stepfamilies represent a growing phenomenon.* In 1995, there were about 430 000 stepfamilies in Canada, about 10 percent of all couple families with children. Slightly

more than half of these families involved couples that were currently married, while the remainder were common-law couples. In that year, slightly more than half of all Canadian stepfamilies consisted of a mother, her children, and a stepfather; 13 percent were composed of a father, his children, and a stepmother; and more than a third were recombined or "blended" families composed of remarried spouses with a mix of children that both parents brought to the family from previous unions or a mix of children from previous unions and the most current one (Statistics Canada 1996).

15. *Because people are living longer and fertility has declined, the population of Canada is "greying," that is getting older.*[6] During the "baby boom" period of our history, Canadian families averaged four children—resulting in more boomers per capita than in the United States, Australia, or New Zealand (Nikoforuk 1999)—and these 10 million baby boomers are getting older. Combined with increased life expectancy (the result of better medical care, sanitation, nutrition and so on) and lowered birthrates, the proportion of our population that is elderly has increased. It is estimated that by 2041, almost one-quarter of the Canadian population will be aged 65 or older, nearly double the proportion in 1995 (Statistics Canada 1998b).

6. Compared to the general population in 1996, a smaller proportion of the Aboriginal population was aged 65 and over (12 percent versus four percent, respectively). In that year, the average age of the Aboriginal population (25.5 years) was almost 10 years younger than the general population (35.4 years). While children under the age of 15 accounted for 20 percent of Canada's total population, children in this age group represented 35 percent of all Aboriginal people. Similarly, young people aged 15 to 24 accounted for 18 percent of the Aboriginal population, compared with 13 percent of the general population. Due to the concentrations of Aboriginal people within the younger age groups, the Aboriginal population is much younger than the general population. In consequence, although large proportional increases are also expected for the Aboriginal population aged 65 and over, the numbers are smaller and other segments of the Aboriginal adult population are expected to exhibit significant growth, particularly those aged 34 to 54. It is expected that, by 2016, this age group will experience a 62 percent increase (Statistics Canada 1998c).

 Focusing on Children

16. *More children live in lone-parent families.* In 1996, about one in every five children lived with a lone parent. Between 1990 and 1999, the number of lone-parent families with school-aged children increased by 35 percent. During this time period, lone-parent families with school-aged children accounted for an increasing proportion of all families with school-aged children (from 22 percent to 27 percent) (Canadian Council on Social Development 2001). Aboriginal children are especially likely to live with a lone parent, particularly if they live in one of Canada's Census Metropolitan Areas such as Winnipeg, Regina, and Saskatoon. In these cities, about half lived in single-parent families in 1996. "Almost one-third (32 percent of Aboriginal children under the age of 15 in Census families lived in a lone-parent family in 1996, twice the rate within the general population" (Statistics Canada 1998).

17. *Increasing numbers of young Canadians live in families that speak a non-official language (i.e., neither English nor French).* "Between 1991 and 1996, the proportion of children aged 14 and under in families speaking a language other than English or French rose from 6.5 percent to 7.5 percent. The most commonly used non-official language was Chinese" (Canadian Council on Social Development 2001).

18. *Among school-aged Canadian children, one in eight lives in a family with a very low average income.* "Between 1993 and 1998, children under age 18 living in the poorest families got poorer while the most affluent were increasingly better off. In the same period, persistent poverty affected 12 percent of children" (Canadian Council on Social Development 2001, p. 2). According to

(continued)

(continued)

UNICEF, among the 16 industrialized nations, Canada has one of the worst rates of child poverty; in 1998, almost one in five (19 percent) Canadian children lived in poverty.

In Canada, Aboriginal and visible minority children are especially likely to be poor (Figure 1.2). In 1995, three out of five Aboriginal children under the age of six were in low-income families, compared with a national rate of slightly more than one in four. Among Aboriginal children aged six to 14, the incidence of low income was 48 percent, more than double the national average. In that year, 45 percent of children under the age of six in the visible minority population were in low-income families (compared with 26 percent for all Canadians) (Statistics Canada 1998b). In addition, over one third (37 percent) of children with disabilities[7], 0–14 years, lived in poverty in 1996 (National Report Card on Child Poverty-Campaign 2000).

Findings from the 1996 Canadian Census indicate that over half a million Canadian families with children live in housing that is in need of major repair, overcrowded, or consumes more than 30 percent of their pre-tax income, in communities where no affordable alternative is available (Canadian Council on Social Development, p. 3). Consider as well that while children under the age of 18 make up just over one-quarter of the Canadian population, they account for 39 percent of food bank recipients. While we might not normally associate child hunger with Canada, "62 000 children went hungry at least once in 1996. Of those, 22 percent went hungry at least once a month" (Canadian Council on Social Development 2001, p. 3).

7. Persons with disabilities are identified as such on the basis of their responses to questions on activity limitations or long-term physical or mental conditions or health problems at home, work or school.

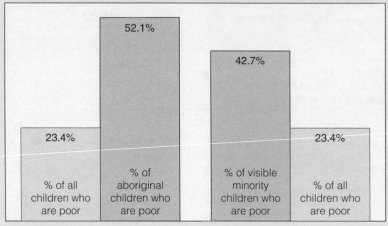

FIGURE **1.2**

Aboriginal and visible minority children (0–14 Years) most likely to be poor. (Source: National Report Card on Child Poverty, Campaign 2000)

Statistics Canada Census 1996, custom tabulation for Canadian Council on Social Development. Aboriginal refers to those persons who identified themselves with being North American Indian, Metis or Inuit. Visible minority persons are defined under the Employment Equity Act (1986) as those (other than Aboriginal persons) who are non-Caucasian in race or non-white in colour. Persons with disabilities are identified based on their responses to questions regarding their activity limitations or disabilities.

and women have equality of opportunity. Legal rules have been made gender neutral, so much so that there are no more wives or husbands in family law, only spouses" (Steel 1987, p. 160). In Quebec, the revised *Civil Code* (1980) also now insists on absolute equality of spouses.

Other aspects of family life have also been subject to legal reforms in recent decades and in later chapters we will examine various reforms in relation to such areas as parental employment, divorce, child custody, and remarriage. However, as simply one example, one may consider that many rights and obligations that were once exclusively associated with marriage (e.g., the right to spousal support) have now been extended to couples living in marriage-like relationships. In response to the increased social acceptance of same-sex relationships and unmarried cohabitation, "courts have 'rewritten' legislation to include same-sex couples or opposite-sex couples into the definition of 'spouse' for various purposes. As well, courts have creatively applied non-family laws, including the law of contract, property and restitution, to cohabiting couples who were excluded from family law regimes" (Bailey 2000, p.3). As might be expected, however, the "test for extending marital rights and obligations to cohabiting couples varies from jurisdiction to jurisdiction, and within each jurisdiction according to the purpose of the legislation" (Bailey 2000, p. 4).

As Martha Bailey (2000, p. 42) observes,

> There have been hundreds of Canadian cases over the past several years dealing with issues of the rights and obligations of unmarried opposite-sex and same-sex couples, and these cases have contributed to the declining legal significance of marriage. The result of the hundreds of court decisions and some statutory reform is a patchwork of laws that do not represent a consistent or coherent approach to regulation of marriage or cohabitation. "Spouse" is defined in various manners for different purposes, resulting in arbitrary rules that do not always protect posited social goals. The periods of cohabitation and other requirements for meeting the definition of "spouse" vary, and the various requisite elements of spousal status are not clearly linked with accepted social goals or legitimate state objectives.

Nevertheless, it is increasingly believed, that as Judge Vito J. Titone has remarked, the definition of the family "should not rest on fictitious legal distinctions or genetic history, but instead should find its foundation in the reality of family life." Rather, "it is the totality of the relationship as evidenced by the dedication, caring and self-sacrifice of the parties which should, in the final analysis, control" (in Gutis 1989b, p. C-6).

In this text, we have adopted a definition of the **family** that combines elements of some of the definitions discussed here. A family is any sexually expressive or parent-child or other kin relationship in which people—usually related by ancestry, marriage, or adoption—(1) form an economic unit and care for any young, (2) consider their identity to be significantly attached to the group, and (3) are committed to maintaining that group over time. This definition combines some practical and objective criteria with a more social-psychological sense of family identity. Ultimately, there is no one correct answer to the question "What is a family?" We hope our definition and the others presented here will stimulate your thoughts and discussion.

To a significant extent, the diversity that we see in families today is a result, over time, of people making personal choices. We turn now to a discussion of such choices.

THE FREEDOM AND PRESSURES OF CHOOSING

This text is different from others you may have read. It is not intended specifically to prepare you for a particular occupation. Instead, it has three other goals: first, to help you understand yourself and your family situations; second, to help you appreciate the variety and diversity among families today; and third, to make you more conscious of the personal decisions you must make throughout your life and of the societal influences that affect those decisions. As families have become less rigidly structured, people have made fewer choices "once and for all." Many people reexamine their decisions about family throughout the course of their lives, continually reassessing and reevaluating their relationships. Thus, choice is an important emphasis of this book.

The best way to make decisions about our personal lives is to make them knowledgeably. It helps to know something about all the alternatives; it also helps to know what kinds of social pressures affect our decisions. As we'll see, people are influenced by the beliefs and values of their society. In a very real way, we and our personal decisions and attitudes are products of our environment.

But in just as real a way, people can influence society. If you don't agree with something in this text, you can write us; your opinion may influence ours. Similarly, every time you participate in class discussions, you help to shape the content of the class. Individuals create social change by continually offering new insights to their groups.[8] Sometimes this occurs in conversation with others. Sometimes affecting social change requires forming social organizations and becoming politically involved. Sometimes creating social change involves many people living their lives according to their principles, even when these fly in the face of accepted group or cultural norms.

We can apply this view to the phenomenon of living together, or cohabitation. Thirty years ago, it was widely accepted that unmarried couples who lived together were immoral. But in the seventies, students challenged restrictions on cohabitation, and many more people than before—students and non-students, young and old—chose to live together. As cohabitation rates increased, societal attitudes became more favourable toward living together outside marriage. Consequently, it is now easier for people to choose this option. (At the same time, many religions today still object to cohabitation outside marriage.) While we are influenced by the society around us, we are also free to influence it. And we do that every time we make a choice.

Moreover, if people are to shape the kinds of family living they want, they must not limit their attention to their own marriages and families. Making knowledgeable decisions about one's family increasingly means getting involved in national, provincial and local political campaigns, finding out what candidates have in mind for families, and writing and phoning government representatives once they are in office. One's role as a family member, as much as one's role as a citizen, has come to require participation in public policy decisions. Although no family policy, of course, can guarantee "ideal" families, such a policy may contribute to a good foundation for family life.

Personal Troubles and Societal Influences

People's private lives are affected by what is happening in the society around them. Many of their personal troubles are shared by others, and these troubles often reflect societal influences.[9] When a family breadwinner cannot find work, for example, the cause may not lie in his or her lack of ambition but rather in the economy's inability to provide a job. Moreover, racism may make employment in general, and good jobs and promotions in particular, elusive for many visible minority and Aboriginal men and women in Canada (Figure 1.3). For example, in their 2001 "report card" on racism in Canada, the Canadian Race Relations Foundation noted that while "in times of economic prosperity, it is not difficult to find a job...for men and women who are members of minority groups, it is still difficult to find jobs that match their qualifications." Among their findings:

- Despite their higher educational attainment compared to non-racialized groups, visible minorities trail behind in terms of their employment and income.

- Foreign-born visible minorities experience greater discrepancies between their education levels and their occupations, compared to other groups. Less than half of foreign-born visible minorities who have a university education work in jobs with a high skill level.

8. We have drawn this theme from Peter Berger and Thomas Luckmann, *The Social Construction of Reality* (1966). According to these social scientists, people externalize their own ideas, impressions, opinions, and ways of doing things (that is, they voice them or act them out). In the process of externalization, things may come to seem real, to become part of assumed common knowledge. At the same time, individuals often internalize externalized impressions or points of view. They thus begin to believe that commonly held opinions are true.

9. This theme is drawn from C. Wright Mills, *The Sociological Imagination*. In Mills' words, people must begin to grasp the "problems of biography, of history and their interactions within a society" ([1959], 1973, p. 6).

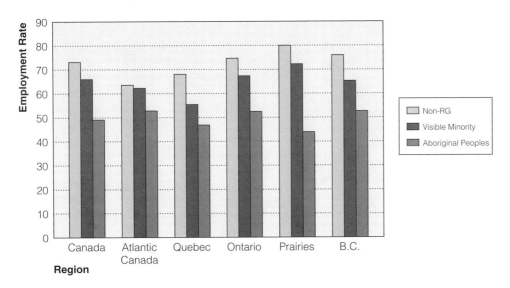

FIGURE **1.3**

Employment rates by racial groups, people aged 25–64, 1996. (Source: Kunz, Milan and Schetagne 2000, p. 2)

- Compared to non-racialized groups, members of visible minority groups and Aboriginal people with a university education are less likely to hold managerial or professional jobs. For those who do obtain managerial jobs, more than half are self-employed, compared to only one-third among non-racialized groups.

- Aboriginal peoples and foreign-born visible minorities are over-represented in the bottom quintile (or bottom 20 percent) of the income scale. Even when they have a university education, they are still less likely than non-racialized groups to have incomes in the top 20 percent of the income scale (Kunz, Milan and Schetagne 2000).

Andrew Jackson (2001) points out that unemployment rates for visible minority immigrants "were significantly higher than the average in 1995, and the gaps were largest among the most highly educated groups." Noting that poverty rates among visible minorities in Canada, particularly those who are recent visible minority immigrants, are "unacceptably high—greater than 50 percent for some groups, such

as recent black immigrants," he argues that the fundamental problem is not lack of skill—"as a group, foreign-born visible minorities are more highly educated than the Canadian average across all age groups"—but "barriers to equal participation in the job market and lack of access to permanent, skilled and reasonably well-paying jobs."

This text assumes that people need to understand themselves (and their problems) in the context of the larger society. Individuals' choices depend largely on the alternatives that exist in their social environment and on cultural values and attitudes toward those alternatives. Moreover, our ability to make good choices in response to changing alternatives depends to a degree on how quickly societal changes occur.

Demographer Paul Glick notes that when changes come suddenly, as they have over the past three decades, the problem of adjustment is "especially great" and leads to increasing signs of personal and family stress. In that individual choices are shaped by the social context in which they are made, we'll examine some social factors that influence adult decisions.

SOCIAL INFLUENCES AND PERSONAL CHOICES

Social factors influence people's personal choices in three ways. First, it is always easier to make the common choice; norms about appropriate behaviour make the alternatives psychologically and socially difficult. For example, in the 1950s and early 1960s people tended to marry earlier than they do now. In consequence, it was more difficult to remain single after graduation, and women in their last year of college or university sometimes became panicky enough to marry men they did not really care for. Now, staying single longer is much more acceptable in our society and, consequently, a more comfortable choice for individuals. Second, social factors can expand people's options. For example, the availability of effective contraceptives makes limiting one's family size easily possible, if desired. While birth control measures have been legal in Canada since 1969, prior to that time, such measures "were illegal if practiced for birth control rather than for an acceptable 'medical' reason—to prevent venereal disease or to deal with problems of menstrual irregularity" (Conway 1990, p. 213). Third, social factors can also limit people's options. For example, we are presently watching how federal and provincial courts and legislatures may affect individuals' options concerning gay male or lesbian unions.

Historical Events

Specific historical events, such as war, depression, inflation, and social change, affect options, choices, and the everyday lives of families (see Box 1.4, "Life for People Born Before 1945"). The work of sociologists Glen Elder (1977) and Stephanie Coontz (1992) reminds us that family life has been a different experience in the Great Depression, in the optimistic fifties, in the tumultuous sixties, in the economically-constricted eighties, and in the time-crunched nineties.

In the affluent fifties, young people could better afford to get married and they did so, at increasingly young ages. The average age at first marriage in Canada dropped from 24.4 years for brides and 27.6 for bridegrooms in 1941, to 23.4 and 26.1 years, respectively, by 1956 (McVey and Kalbach 1995, p. 225). By and large, families did not limit themselves to having only one child and "from 1946 to 1961, the average Canadian woman had between 3.4 and 3.9 children" (Nelson and Robinson 1999, p. 91). In marked contrast to the situation today, married men were significantly more likely than married men to be working for pay. For example, in 1951, 90.0 percent of married men but only 11.2 percent of married women were in the labour force.

Today, one person is far less likely to earn a "family wage." More and more wives seek employment, regardless of their preference to be employed or not. Real wages have deteriorated, making it difficult to make ends meet even with two incomes.

This family portrait reminds us that individuals are freer to make personal choices today than in the past. These men can be more open than in the past about choosing a same-sex relationship.

In the following paragraphs, sociologist Reginald Bibby (2001, p. 211) provides a light-hearted summary of how the everyday life of Canadians differed for those born before 1945. As you read, consider how family life has been altered by the various changes he describes.

You were born before television, before penicillin, before polio shots, frozen foods, Xerox, contact lenses, Frisbees, and the Pill. You were born before radar, credit cards, split atoms, laser beams, and ballpoint pens. You were born before panty hose, dishwashers, clothes dryers, electric blankets, air conditioners, drip-dry clothes, and before man walked on the moon. Fast food, pizza, Kentucky Fried Chicken, and instant coffee were unheard of. You were born before househusbands, gay rights, computer dating, dual careers, nursing homes, FM radio, artificial hearts, and yogurt.

You got married first and then lived together. Closets were for clothes. Bunnies were small rabbits and rabbits were not Volkswagens. You were not before differences between the sexes were discovered, but you were before the sex change; you made do with what you had. And you were the last generation to think you needed a husband to have a baby.

Time-sharing meant togetherness, not jobs or condominiums; a "chip" meant a piece of wood; hardware meant hardware, and software wasn't even a word. You hit the scene when five and ten-cent stores sold things for five and ten cents. Cigarette smoking was fashionable, grass was mowed. Coke was a cold drink, pot was something you cooked in. Rock music was a grandma's lullaby and aides were helpers in the principal's office. But you survived. What more reason do you need to celebrate?

Historical change involves not only specific events but also short- or long-term change in basic indicators of human life. While men and women born in (what was to become Canada) in 1831 lived an average of 40 and 42 years respectively (Lavoie and Oderkirk 2000, p. 3), Canadians can now expect to outlive citizens in almost every country except Switzerland, Sweden, and Japan.[10] In Canada, a girl born in 1995 can realistically hope to celebrate her 81st birthday, a boy his 75th (Statistics Canada 1998). Among the consequences of this increased longevity are more years invested in education, longer marriages for those who do not divorce, a longer period during which parents and children are both adults, and a long retirement.

We will increasingly be influenced by the age structure of our society. More of us will have longer relationships with our grandparents and aging parents than in previous generations, and increasing numbers of elderly people must be cared for by a smaller group of middle-aged and young adults, for example. This impact will be felt not only economically but also at the level of personal care for kin. The smaller family sizes of today will result in fewer adults who can share intergenerational family responsibilities in the future (Treas 1995).

10. In Australia and Iceland, men have a slightly longer life expectancy than Canadian men do; in France, the life expectancy of women is slightly greater than among their Canadian counterparts (Statistics Canada 1998).

Race and Ethnicity

The historical moment shapes people's options and decisions, but so does their place within our culturally diverse society. Marriage and family patterns vary among racial and ethnic groups. For example, a greater proportion of Aboriginal families confront difficulties with housing and food affordability than Canadians as a whole. Moreover, despite major improvements since the 1970s, infant mortality rates in First Nation communities remain twice as high as those in Canada as a whole (Health Canada 1999, p. xiv). In general, Aboriginal families experience a heightened risk of confronting issues of poor health and the early death of a family member. The life expectancy of Aboriginal people is significantly lower than non-Aboriginal Canadians. High rates of suicide and fatal unintentional injuries among First Nations and Inuit young people account for part of the difference in life expectancy. Moreover, the prevalence of such major chronic diseases as diabetes, heart problems, cancer, hypertension, and arthritis/rheumatism is not only significantly higher in Aboriginal communities than in the general population, but also appears to be increasing (Health Canada 1999, p. 14).

The growth of immigration in recent decades may increase the impact of ethnicity on family life because first-generation immigrant families retain more of their ethnic culture than do later generation families (Dhruvaraja 1993). Traditionally, first-generation immigrants to Canada and the United States have tended to settle in communities made up of others who have emigrated from the same or neighbouring countries (Kazemipur and Halli 2000). Additionally, they usually maintain most of their cultural customs and traditions, as well as their native language. For those who have experienced oppression in their country of origin because of their "race" or ethnicity, immigration to Canada may provide an opportunity to celebrate a status that was previously devalued by others.

For example, Marjorie Lambert's (1998) study on Kurds who have immigrated to Canada from Turkey noted that the celebration of such family events as weddings and births allowed new Canadians to "discover" or reclaim their ethnic identity. She reports that, among her respondents, there was a common sequence upon immigration to Canada, beginning with a tending to the importance of being Kurdish, a consciousness of themselves as such, and an often eager attempt to learn the culture, heritage and history of the Kurdish people both in Turkey and elsewhere. Her respondents commonly sought out other Kurds and attended Kurdish cultural centres—activities that often promoted a heightened sense of "being Kurdish and the celebration of Kurdish events" (Lambert 1998, p. 173).

However, she notes that attempts to learn one or both of Canada's official languages, find a job and be self- or other-supporting, establish friendships or find an intimate partner could act "as centrifugal forces encouraging the person to decrease the amount of time and attention that their ethnicity, which had brought them to Canada, commanded" (p. 174). As well, she observes that while her older repondents stressed the importance of in-group marriage, giving children Kurdish names, and teaching them the history, culture, and language of the Kurds, respondents in their late 20s to late 30s tended to be "less categorical over the desirability of pursuing activities or associations that marked them as Kurdish." Young respondents, she notes, were more likely to stress that their children were being raised to be "100 percent Canadian."

Second-generation immigrants may come into conflict with their parents' culture in a variety of ways (Noivo 1993; Swanson 1986). For example, it is reportedly not uncommon for members of second-generation immigrants to change or anglicize their last names in an attempt to conceal what may be perceived as a devalued ethnicity (Lambert 1998, p. 15). Second-generation youth may also clash with their parents in relation to such issues as dating (Seifeddine 1994) and arranged versus free-choice marriages (Basran 1993; Haddad and Smith 1996). The concept of "choice" itself may be alien or incompatible in cultures in which family life is experienced as carrying on tradition and accepting the decisions of family heads.

Some research suggests that marriages of recent immigrants seem less egalitarian than do those of couples of similar ethnic background whose families have been in the United States or Canada for longer periods (Pozzetta 1991). While first-generation immigrant families may find it necessary, due to financial necessity, for wives to engage in paid labour (Basavarajappa and Halli 1997; Kazemipur and Halli 1997; Reitz 1997), unemployed or underemployed husbands may feel resentful or challenged in their role as family breadwinners. Attempts by employed wives to renegotiate the division of labour within the home may also result in marital stress and conflict if husbands perceive doing housework as "unmanly" or as "women's work" (Gilanshah 1994; Espiritu 1997; Gill and Matthews 1995). In addition, one study of Hong Kong families suggested that wives may hesitate to even suggest that such changes are necessary for fear that they will be seen as less than admirable wives and mothers (Mann 1995).

Ethnic identity is a dynamic concept that consists of cultural, social, and psychological elements that overlap and make many different permutations possible (Darroch and Marston 1987; Roosens 1991). Immigration does not necessarily entail a linear process in which the importance of ethnic identity invariably declines with each successive generation. For example, research on French Canadians reports that most evidence equal attachment to both French and English Canadian culture (Laroche et al. 1996). In addition, it has been suggested that rather than being extinguished among third-generation immigrants, an "ethnic" revival may occur as a result of "renewed interest in the national fate of their countries of origin," or as a way to explain "scepticism associated with discontent and racial confrontation" (Rose 1976, pp. 29–30).

People's racial/ethnic heritage affects their options and decisions. Box 1.5, "Family Ties and Immigration," examines how immigration policies, in the past and present, have contributed to Canada's mosaic of families. In taking account of racial and ethnic differences, it is important not to rely on assumptions about differences that may not exist.[11]

Social Class

Social class may be as important as race or ethnicity in affecting people's choices. Clearly, the distribution of wealth in Canada is skewed. Since the 1960s, income inequality has remained roughly stable in Canada, with the top 20 percent of households receiving over 40 percent of the nation's total income and the poorest 20 percent, less than five percent (Statistics Canada 1996, 2000). Figure 1.4 indicates the notable stability of income over the past few decades. Although our politicians have made frequent reference to Canada's identification, for a five-year period beginning in 1995, as the first-ranked nation in which to live (as measured by the United Nation's Human Development Index)[12], our country fared more poorly over the same time when ranked under the United Nations Poverty Index for our treatment of the poor (Campaign 2000). For example, as Figure 1.5 indicates, in terms of child poverty, Canada is ranked 17th among 23 of the "'rich nations club,' those countries belonging to the Organization for Economic Co-operation and Development (OECD)" (Campaign 2000).

Money may not buy happiness, but it does afford a myriad of options, from sufficient and nutritious food to eat to comfortable residences to better health care to keeping in touch with family and friends through the Internet to education at prestigious universities to vacations, household help, and family counselling. Consider that, among two-parent Canadian families with children aged four to 11:

• Nearly 30 percent of poor children have changed school three times before they were 11 years of age, in contrast to about 10 percent of children in upper-income families. Children experiencing frequent transitions tend to have lower math scores, more grade failures and more behaviour problems than children who remain in the same school.

• One-third of poor children (four–five years of age) display delayed vocabulary development, while less than 10 percent of children from high income families are behind in vocabulary development.

• Organized and unorganized sports are less likely to be part of a poor child's activities than an advantaged child. About 25 percent of poor children participate in organized sports in contrast to 75 percent of children in high-income families. (Campaign 2000)

11. It is equally important not to assume that "all immigrants are alike." One of the most common ways of discussing racialized and ethnic groups is to talk about them in wide sweeping ways, i.e., as "immigrants" or "visible minorities," without regard to the distinctions between and within ethnic and racialized minority groups.

12. The Human Development Index measures national development using indicators of longevity (based upon life expectancy), knowledge (based on adult literacy rates) and income or "purchasing power parity"—the per-capita Gross National Product (GNP) adjusted for local cost of living.

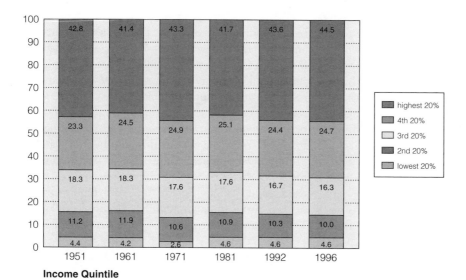

FIGURE **1.4**

Percentage distribution of total incomes of families and unattached individuals by quintiles, Canada, 1951–1996. (Source: Reproduced by authority of the Minister of Industry, 1996. Statistics Canada, from *Income Distribution by Size in Canada*, Cat. no. 13-207, Centre for International Statistics at the Canadian Council on Social Development, Statistics Canada, *Income Distribution by Size in Canada, 1996*, Cat. no. 13-207 XPB; Kendall et al., 2000, p. 255)

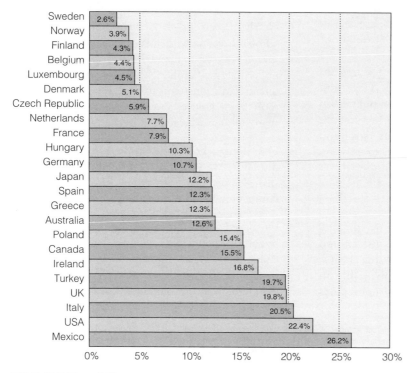

FIGURE **1.5**

Child poverty in selected OECD countries. (Source: Campaign 2000)

The effects of social class can be subtle, yet far-reaching. Regarding marriage, for example, working-class couples tend to emphasize values associated with parenthood and job stability, whereas middle-class partners are more inclined to value companionship, self-expression, and communication. Middle-class parents value self-direction and initiative in children, whereas parents in working-class families stress obedience and conformity (Luster, Rhoades, and Haas 1989).

Besides distinguishing families on the basis of income and/or assets, social scientists have often focused on status differences, as represented by supposed differences between white- and blue-collar workers. White-collar workers include professionals, clerical workers, salespeople, and so forth that have traditionally worn white shirts to work. Working-class people, or blue-collar workers, are employed as mechanics, truckers, police officers, machine operators, and factory workers—jobs typically requiring uniforms. Social scientists do not agree on whether blue- and white-collar workers have become increasingly alike in their values and attitudes in recent decades. But white- and blue-collar employees may continue to look at life differently even at similar income levels (Henslin and Nelson 1996, p. 75).

Other Social-Group Memberships

Other social-group memberships, including religion, region, rural-urban residence and **age expectations** can also influence family life. For example, the family heritage of major religious groups is a significant influence. Muslim and Jewish families, among others, celebrate holidays that are different from more well-known Christian holidays such as Christmas. Catholics appear to have shifted from the traditional church teachings to modern conceptualizations of the family and sexuality (D'Antonio et al. 1996). But studies still find contemporary Catholics to be different from Protestants in their more communal, rather than individualistic, worldview (Greeley 1989). As a second example, rural families are more likely to be married-couple families with more children than urban families (Albrecht and Albrecht 1996).

In the same way that historical events and social location influence choices, so do age expectations.

When individuals shop for clothes, they sometimes wonder whether they are too old or too young to wear something they like. They are at least unconsciously aware that society views some attitudes and behaviours as appropriate for a given age and others as inappropriate. Despite growing diversity and broader time frames, there is still a sense of a "right time" to have children or to "slow down" or retire, for example.

In sum, social factors such as historical events and social location limit people's options. (We will discuss the impact of socially defined gender roles in Chapter 3.) Even though individuals may be limited in their choices by social conditions in ways that they do not realize, becoming conscious of social influences permits a more knowledgeable choice. It also minimizes self-blame for what may be a socially structured lack of options and can inspire collective effort to alter social conditions.

Let's look more closely at two forms of decision making—choosing by default and choosing knowledgeably—along with the consequences of each.

MAKING CHOICES

All people make choices, even when they are not aware of it. One effect of taking a course in marriage and the family may be to make you more aware of when choices are available and how a decision may be related to subsequent options and choices, so that you can make decisions more knowledgeably.

Choosing by Default

Unconscious decisions are called **choosing by default**. Choices made by default are ones people make when they are not aware of all the alternatives or when they pursue the proverbial path of least resistance. If you're taking this class, for example, but you're unaware that a class in modern dance (which you would have preferred) is meeting at the same time, you have chosen not to take the class in modern dance, but you have done so by default because you didn't find out about all the alternatives when you registered.

Another kind of decision by default occurs when people pursue a course of action primarily because it seems the easiest thing to do. Many times university students choose their courses or even their majors by default. They arrive at registration only

Family Ties and Immigration

The growing racial and ethnic diversity in Canada is largely attributable to immigration. However, the history of Canada's immigration policies is far from exemplary.

In the 1870s and 1880s, the active attempt to recruit immigrants to Canada for labour-intensive industries was accompanied by the emergence of regulations that sought to preserve Canada's "English stock" by restricting or denying entry to certain groups who were depicted as "coming in swarms" and "breeding like insects" (Green 1986). These regulations reflected the sentiment that, while useful as labourers, certain groups were "undesirable" as permanent residents of Canada. For example, hostility towards Asians is clear in the sentiment by Sir John A. Macdonald, Canada's first prime minister, that "a Mongolian or Chinese population in our country... would not be a welcome element...At present it is simply a question of alternatives—either you have this labour or you cannot have the railway" (in Sher 1983, p. 33). The 1885 *Chinese Immigration Act* barred virtually all Chinese through a variety of discriminatory rules. In 1907, the federal government "obliged Japan to sign a 'voluntary' agreement" restricting emigration to Canada. In 1908, the federal government enacted a regulation which made it "nearly impossible" for East Indians to enter this country (Sher 1983, p. 33). Canada's 1910 *Immigration Act* was later to give the government the formal power to "prohibit for a stated period, or permanently, the landing in Canada...of immigrants belonging to any race unsuited to the climate or requirements of Canada."

Illustrating the "climate" of this time, when rumours spread that a group of black people were preparing to immigrate to Canada from the United States,

> federal authorities initiated an ingeniously simple scheme. Nothing in the *Immigration Act* specifically barred black Americans, but any immigrant could effectively be denied access to Canada for health reasons under the Act's medical provisions. The government merely instructed immigration inspectors and their medical aides along the American border to reject all

blacks as unfit for admission on medical grounds. There was no appeal. Blacks were warned they should not waste their time and money by considering immigration to Canada. (Troper 1999, p. 1140)

Canada's *Chinese Immigration Act* of 1923 completely barred the Chinese from entering Canada and Chinese persons already in Canada were not allowed to sponsor family or relatives. In the same year, the federal government listed Poland, Yugoslavia, Hungary, and Romania as "non-preferred" countries for the purposes of immigration. In addition, the pervasive anti-Semitism of pre-war Canada is well-illustrated by Canada's refusal to accept Jewish refugees from Hitler's Europe. At that time, when journalists asked a senior Canadian official how many Jewish refugees would be admitted after the war, his response was "None is too many." "It is perhaps no surprise, therefore, that Canada had by far the worst record of any Western country for providing sanctuary to the Jews of Europe in the 1930s and 1940s" (Abella 1999, p. 90).

In 1947, Prime Minister William Lyon Mackenzie King pledged to remove "objectionable discrimination" from the *Immigration Act*. While certain blatantly discriminatory features of the *Act* were removed, Canada's immigration policy still included "selective restriction" and preferred candidates were those who were British, Irish, French, or American. The Ministry of Citizenship and Immigration was to determine the suitability of other would-be immigrants in light of "the climate, educational, social, industrial, labour and other requirements in Canada." A person applying to immigrate to Canada could be declared "undesirable" because of "his peculiar customs, habits, modes of life, methods of holding property or his general inability to assimilate."

In the 1950s, under pressure from other countries of the Commonwealth, Canada began to relax its immigration policies. Some of the changes were simply cosmetic: for example, southern and eastern European countries were renamed "traditional sources" rather than "non-preferred."

However, other changes were more substantive. The White Paper of 1966 and the Regulations of 1967 called for the abolishment of discrimination based on race, colour, religion, national origin, or gender. Immigration was to respond to Canada's need for workers and cultural enrichment was added as part of Canada's immigration objectives. In addition, the White Paper noted Canada's commitment to the plight of international refugees.

Currently, our *Immigration Act* specifies three major objectives of immigration: (1) family reunification; (2) the fulfillment of Canada's international legal obligations and the compassionate and humanitarian treatment of refugees, and; (3) the promotion of a strong and viable economy in all of Canada's regions. *Family-class* applicants are those who are sponsored by a family member already in Canada who agrees to assume responsibility for providing the sponsored immigrant with the necessities of life for as many as 10 years. Sponsors or anyone other than a spouse or dependent children must meet minimum income requirements. *Independent or skilled workers* are assessed by a point system that looks at such factors as age, education, knowledge of one or both of Canada's official languages, specific vocational preparation, job training, occupation, arranged employment (in which case employers must show that there are no Canadians qualified to do the job and demonstrate that the working conditions and proposed wages are adequate), and designated occupations (a listing of occupations for which workers are in short supply in either specific provinces or regions). Canada also admits "business immigrants"—investors and entrepreneurs—based on either an approved investment or the applicant's ability and resolve to start a business that will create jobs for Canadians.

The selection criteria used in assessing potential immigrants to Canada are subject to the Canadian Charter of Rights and Freedoms and immigrants are to be selected without discrimination. Under the Canada-Quebec Accord on Immigration, Quebec holds sole selection powers for both refugees who are to be resettled from abroad and independent immigrants who desire to immigrate to Quebec.

In 1996, approximately five million persons (17 percent of the Canadian population) were immigrants and the largest proportion of immigrants was born in the United Kingdom (13 percent) or Italy (seven percent). However, Asia and the Middle East are increasingly furnishing greater numbers of Canada's immigrants. Between 1991 and 1996, 57 percent of those who immigrated to Canada were from either Asia or the Middle East, with high immigration from Hong Kong, the People's Republic of China, and India. In contrast to the 1960s, when "close to 90 percent of new arrivals originated in the traditional (and primarily Caucasian) source countries of Europe and the United States that had dominated immigration every year since Confederation" (Ley and Smith in Harvey et al. 1999, p.1), currently, about 80 percent of all immigrants coming to Canada are visible racial minorites "with increasing numbers of blacks, South Asians and East Asians making up each successive cohort of immigrants (Harvey et al. 1999; Jackson 2001, p. 1).

The majority of Canada's immigrants in 1996 were independent class immigrants (56 percent), followed by family immigrants (30 percent). Approximately one in six immigrants in 1996 was classified as a refugee. Canada's major urban areas attract the vast majority of recent immigrants and in 1996, approximately 85 percent lived in a census metropolitan area[13] with high concentrations in Toronto, Vancouver, and Montreal.

The increase in immigrant families has led policymakers and others to consider many issues. For one

---

13. Statistics Canada (1998, p. 117) defines a "census metropolitan area" or CMA as "a very large urban area, together with adjacent urban and rural areas that have a high degree of economic and social integration with that urban area." In 1996, Canada had 25 CMAs which ranged in size from Toronto with approximately 4.4 million people to Saint John, with 129 000.

(continued)

(continued)

thing, of the nearly 200 000 immigrants who enter Canada each year, about 45 000 are school-aged children who subsequently enroll in Canada's elementary and secondary schools. About two-thirds of all school-aged immigrant children arrive in Canada speaking neither English nor French, a situation "which puts pressures on the educational system for such programs as English as a Second Language (ESL) and for course materials and curricula that reflect the diversity of...beliefs and backgrounds" (Canadian Council on Social Development 1999, p.4). How to best educate children in a multicultural society is a matter of public debate.

Another issue is whether, on balance, immigrant families are an asset or a liability to the nation's economy. According to the Vanier Institute of the Family (1998), immigrants are neither "a fiscal liability" nor a "drain on the public purse" and "may have a small but *positive* impact on economic activity in Canada." They point out that most econometric models of immigration fail to consider the economic contributions of immigration, including the unpaid labour that some immigrants, such as grandparents or older children, provide through childcare or helping out in small family-owned businesses.

to find that the classes they had planned to take are closed. So they register for something they hadn't planned on, do pretty well, and continue in it just because that seems easier than rearranging their curriculum programs.

Many decisions concerning marriages and families are also made by default. Spouses may focus on career success, for example, to the neglect of their relationship simply because this is what society expects of them. Although most of us have made at least some decisions by default, almost everyone can recall having the opposite experience: choosing knowledgeably.

Choosing Knowledgeably

Today, society offers many options. People can stay single or marry; they can choose to live together outside legal marriage; they can form communes or family-like ties with others; they can decide to divorce or to stay married. One important component of **choosing knowledgeably** is recognizing as many

options or alternatives as possible. This text is designed in part to help you do that.

A second component in making knowledgeable choices is recognizing the social pressures that may influence personal choices. Some of these pressures are economic, whereas others relate to cultural norms that have been taken for granted. Sometimes people decide that they agree with socially accepted or prescribed behaviour. They concur in the teachings of their religion, for example. Other times, though, people decide that they strongly disagree with socially prescribed beliefs, values, and standards. Whether they agree with such standards or not, once people recognize the force of social pressures they are free to choose whether to act in accordance with them.

An important aspect of making knowledgeable choices is considering the consequences of each alternative rather than just gravitating toward the one that initially seems most attractive. A couple deciding whether to move so that one partner can be promoted, for example, may want to list the consequences, both positive and negative. In the positive column, that partner may have a higher position and earn more money, and the region to which they would move may have a friendlier climate. In the negative column, the other spouse may have to give up or disrupt his or her career, and both may have to leave relatives. Listing positive and negative consequences of alternatives—either mentally or on paper—helps one see the larger picture and thus make a more knowledgeable decision.

An element in this process is personally clarifying your own values. In recent years, counsellors and others have given considerable attention to values clarification—becoming aware of your values and choosing to act consistently with those values. Society today holds up contradictory sets of values. For example, there are varied standards of nonmarital sex ranging from abstinence to sex for recreation only, without personal affection. Contradictory values can cause people to feel ambivalent about what they want for themselves.

Clarifying one's values involves cutting through this ambivalence in order to decide which of several orientations are more strongly valued. To do this, it is important to respect the so-called gut factor—the emotional dimension of decision making. Besides rationally considering alternatives, people have subjective, often almost visceral feelings about what feels right or wrong, good or bad. Respecting one's feelings is an important part of making the right decision.

One other component of decision making should be mentioned, and that is rechecking. Once a choice is made and a person acts on it, the process is not necessarily complete. People constantly recheck their decisions, as Figure 1.6 suggests, throughout the entire decision-making cycle, testing these decisions against their own subsequent feelings and against any changes in the social environment.

An assumption underlying this discussion has been that individuals cannot have everything. Every time people make an important decision or

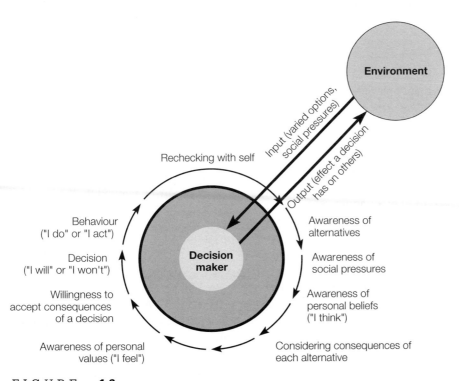

FIGURE **1.6**

The cycle of knowledgeable decision making. (Source: Adapted from O'Neill and O'Neill 1974.)

While families are composed of individuals, each seeking self-fulfillment and a unique identity, they also offer a place to learn and express togetherness, stability, and loyalty. Families also perform a special archival function: events, rituals, and histories are created and preserved and, in turn, become intrinsic parts of each individual.

commitment, they rule out alternatives—at least for the time being, and perhaps permanently. People cannot simultaneously have the relative freedom of a child-free union and the gratification that often accompanies parenthood.

In some respects, though, people can focus on some goals and values during one part of their lives, then turn their attention to different ones at other times. Four decades ago, we used to think of adults as people who entered adulthood in their early 20s, found work, married, had children, and continued on the same track until the end of the life course. That view has changed. Today we view adulthood as a time with potential for continued personal development, growth, and change.

Meanwhile marriage and other domestic partnerships involve two or more adults. Family living becomes a situation in which multiple life courses must be coordinated, often including those of children. Moreover, life in Canadian families reflects a tension in our culture between family solidarity and individual freedom.

A FAMILY OF INDIVIDUALS

Family values (familism) permeate our culture. These values, such as family togetherness, stability, and loyalty, focus on the family as a whole. Many of us have an image of the ideal family in which members spend considerable time together, enjoying one another's company. Togetherness, in other words, represents an important part of family life. For many of us, the family is a major source of stability; we are disturbed when it is disrupted. Then, too, the group most deserving our loyalty, we believe, is often our family. Most of us who are married today vowed publicly to stay with our partners as long as we live. We expect our partners, parents, children, and even our more distant relatives to remain loyal to the family unit. Because of familism, home is sometimes considered "the place where you can scratch anywhere you itch."

Families as a Place to Belong

Whether families are traditional or newer in form (such as communes or cohabiting partnerships), they create a place to belong in at least two ways. First, families create *boundaries*, both physical and psychological, between themselves and the rest of the world. Whether in multiple- or single-family dwellings, families in virtually all cultures mark off some physical space that is private and theirs alone (Boulding 1976). Family members determine "what kinds of things are allowed to enter the family space and under what conditions and what kinds of items are simply not permitted admission" (Kantor and Lehr 1975, p. 68).

With an idea of how the external world resembles and differs from the family interior, family members screen off certain aspects of the larger, outside culture. They put up fences so that they can barbeque or sunbathe in privacy, for example, and they prevent certain people, books, pictures, words, and topics of conversation from entering the family interior. Family members may patrol one another's activities, so that a child or a spouse is accompanied by another family member when leaving the family home, in order to provide safety from the real or imagined hazards of the outside world.

A second way families create a place to belong is by performing an **archival family function**. That is, families create, store, preserve, and pass on particular objects, events, or rituals that members consider relevant to their personal identities and to maintaining the family as a unique existential reality or group. The archives contain a variety of symbols:

> These are snapshots of happy times, posed and unposed (apparently never snapshots of sad times); family movies of celebrations or rites of passage or vacations; ... artifacts from infancy or childhood transmuted into relics of lost and sweet identities; symbols of recognition and achievement such as diplomas; ... pointed anecdotes about infancy or youth which reinforce a particular identity as the reckless one, the always helpful one, or the unlucky one ("Remember the time you accidentally broke two of Mr. Jones's porch windows!"); and various ... symbols which function almost like debts binding one to past relationships with the implication of potential future obligations ("Here is part of the plaster cast from your left leg which you broke in sixth grade, when I had to care for you at home for six weeks—remember that when I am unable to walk around by myself anymore"). (Weigert and Hastings 1977, p. 1174)

But just as family values permeate our society, so also do **individualistic (self-fulfillment) values**. Individualistic values encourage people to develop an **individualistic orientation**: that is, persons think in terms of seeking primarily personal—as opposed to communal, or group—happiness and goals. An individualistic orientation can lead us to maximize our options and choices. However, an individualistic orientation can also put great stress on family relationships, when there is little emphasis on contributing to other family members' happiness or postponing personal satisfactions in order to attain communal goals (Dion and Dion 1993; Triandis 1995). Expressing our individuality within the context of a family requires us to negotiate innumerable day-to-day issues. How much privacy can each person be allowed at home? What things and places in the family dwelling belong just to one particular individual? What family activities should be scheduled, how often, and when? What outside friendships and activities can a family member have?

Family Rhythms of Separateness and Togetherness

In every family, members regulate personal privacy (Kantor and Lehr 1975). Members come together for family rituals, such as playing games or watching television, but they also need and want to spend time alone. Being shortchanged on privacy is associated with irritability, weariness, family violence, poor family relationships, and emotional distance from one's spouse.

Time represents another important dimension of family life. Each family member has personal feelings about timing. Staying at a party until the wee hours might feel good to one spouse, but the other might prefer to call it quits earlier. Working out a common rhythm for dialogue, sexual expression, and joint activities can be difficult for spouses, for example, when a "night person" marries a "morning person."

In all intimate relationships, partners alternately move toward each other, then back away to reestablish a sense of individuality or separateness. The needs of different individuals vary, of course, and so do the temporary or permanent balances that couples and families strike between togetherness and individuality.

"Family life in any form has both costs and benefits.... Belonging to any group involves loss of personal freedom" (Chilman 1978). The juxtaposition of opposing values—familism and individualism—creates tension in society and in ourselves that we must resolve. Where are our solutions leading us?

Family "Decline" or Family Change?

Sociologist Lynn White (1987), among others, believes that "the pendulum between freedom and constraint has swung so far toward freedom that it has altered the family in basic and undesirable ways" (p. 470). Family sociologist David Popenoe (1988, 1993) similarly warns that self-interest has led to "family decline" over the past three decades, the consequences of which—particularly for children—are "cause for alarm" (1993, p. 539). More recently, Popenoe (1996) has argued that research gives "compelling new evidence that fatherhood and marriage are indispensable for the good of children and society." Other family advocates agree that the family is in "decline," write of the "war against the family" (Gairdner 1992), of a "fatherless" society (Blankenhorn 1995) and of "posterity lost" (Gill 1997).

Not every family expert concurs, however. John Edwards (1987) posits that the situation is not necessarily this bleak. He suggests that we may be putting too much emphasis on the weakening of the nuclear husband-wife family without recognizing that other structural arrangements may be equally capable of raising children well. Similarly Edward Kain (1990) analyzes what he calls "the myth of family decline" and argues that today's families must be understood as one component in a culture of rapid social change. Finally, Judith Stacey (1993, 1996) sees the concept of "family decline" as unfairly value-laden and argues that there are many ways to define the word family besides that of husband, wife, and children: "The point is there isn't one kind of family anymore; there are numerous kinds of families: blended families, gay families, single-parent families" (Stacey, in Hagar 1997, p. 6). Moreover, according to Stacey, "Short of exhorting or coercing people to enter or remain in unequal, hostile marriages, family decline critics offer few social proposals to address children's pressing needs" (1993, p. 547).

Morley and Edith Lambert were married in 1934 and are shown here at their 50th wedding anniversary. The Lamberts learned to balance individualism and familism over the course of their marriage.

Providing something of a middle ground, sociologist Norval Glenn states his position:

I believe that marriage should be satisfying to the spouses.... [However,] I do not give the spouses' needs and desires priority over the needs of their children or over the social need for the proper socialization of children. Second, I do not believe that each spouse's giving priority to his or her own needs, deemphasizing duty and obligation in marriage, and giving up the ideal of marital permanence will maximize the happiness and satisfaction of... adults. (Glenn 1987a, pp. 350–51)

Glenn (1993) has made a plea for objective assessment of the notion of family decline through research. Meanwhile, Paul Amato and Alan Booth (1997) see children "at risk"—a generation "growing up in an era of family upheaval"—but refuse to place blame solely on individuals' supposedly self-centred choices. Responsible social science research requires careful analysis, not only of individualism but also of social forces, such as poverty and the cultural encouragement of violence—particularly violence toward women—as causal factors in family "decline" or change.

Individualism, Familism, and Partners

Shifts in the balance of individuality and familism have meant that family members have become less predictable than in the past. The course of family living results in large part from the decisions and choices two adults make, both moving in their own ways and at their own paces through their own lives. Assuming that partners' respective beliefs, values, and behaviours mesh fairly well at the point of marriage, any change in either spouse is likely to adversely affect the fit. One consequence of ongoing developmental change in two individuals is that a marriage is no longer as likely to be permanent, as we'll see in Chapter 14. If one or both change considerably over time, the danger exists that they will grow apart instead of together. A challenge for contemporary relationships is to integrate divergent personal change into the relationship and to nurture any children involved at the same time.

How can partners make it through such changes and still stay together? Two guidelines may be helpful. The first is for people to take responsibility for their own past choices and decisions rather than blaming previous "mistakes" on their mates. The second is for individuals to be aware that married life is far more complex than the traditional image commonly portrayed. It helps to recognize that a changing spouse may be difficult to live with for a while. A relationship needs to be flexible enough to allow for each partner's individual changes—to allow family members some degree of freedom. At the same time, we must remind ourselves of the benefits of family living. Research shows that a supportive marriage has a significant positive impact on individual well-being, for example (Waite 1995). Throughout this text we will return to the theme of individualism and familism—"the two great cultural values that appear to conflict most flagrantly with one another in the area of the family" (Popenoe 1988, p. 305).

We have defined the term *family* and discussed decision making and diversity in the context of family living. We can now state explicitly the four themes of this text.

MARRIAGES AND FAMILIES: FOUR THEMES

Throughout this book, we will develop the following four themes.

1. Personal decisions must be made throughout the life course. Decision making is a trade-off; once we choose an option, we discard alternatives. No one can have everything. Thus, the best way to make choices is knowledgeably.

2. People are influenced by the society around them. Cultural beliefs and values influence our attitudes and decisions. And societal or structural conditions can limit or expand our options.

3. We live in a changing society, characterized by increased ethnic, economic, and family diversity; by increased tension between family and individualistic values; by decreased marital and family permanence; and by increased recent political and policy attention to the needs of children. This can make personal decision making not only more difficult than in the past but also more important.

4. Personal decision making feeds back into society and changes it. Making personal decisions in order to effect family-related social change can mean choosing to become politically involved. But we affect our social environment every time we choose, so it's best to choose according to our thought-through principles whether or not these agree with what's accepted.

IN SUM

This chapter introduced the subject matter for this course and presented the four themes that this text develops. The chapter began by addressing the challenge of defining the term family. In Box 1.3, "Some Facts About Families in Canada Today," we have pointed to much evidence that we live in a changing society, characterized by increasing ethnic, economic, and family diversity. Family diversity has progressed to the point where there is no typical family form today.

It is now widely recognized that change and development continue throughout adult life. People make choices, either actively and knowledgeably or by default, that determine the courses of their lives. These choices are influenced by a number of factors, including age expectations, "race" and ethnicity, religion, social class, gender, and historical events. People must make choices or decisions throughout their life courses, and those choices and decisions simultaneously are limited by social structure and are causes for change in that structure.

Marriages and families are composed of separate, unique individuals. That uniqueness stems partly from the fact that human beings are able to make choices. They have creativity and free will: Nothing they think or do is totally programmed.

At the same time, all of the individuals in a particular society share some things. They generally speak either or both of our official languages and have some common attitudes about work, education, and marriages and families. Moreover, within a socially diverse society such as ours, many individuals are part of a racial, ethnic, or religious community or social class that has a distinct family heritage.

Our culture values both familism and individualism. Whether individualism has gone too far and led to an alarming family decline is a matter of debate. Even though families fill the important function of providing members a place to belong, finding personal freedom within families is an ongoing, negotiated process.

Adults change, and because they do, marriages and families are not static: Every time one individual in a relationship changes, the relationship changes, however subtly. Throughout this text we will discuss some creative ways in which partners can alter their relationship in order to meet their changing needs.

Remembering, then, that no two people are exactly alike—and that in many ways every adult continues to change—we begin our study by looking at choices in the context of individual development and social change.

Key Terms

age expectations
archival family function
census family
choosing by default
choosing knowledgeably
family
family values (familism)
individualistic orientation

individualistic (self-fulfillment) values
modern family
nuclear family
postmodern family
primary group
secondary group

Study Questions

1. Has marriage in Canada been reconceptualized as a nonpermanent relationship, as sociologist Constantina Safilios-Rothschild says? If not, give examples to support your point. (Are your examples from personal experience or scientific investigation?) If you agree with Safilios-Rothschild, explain how you think this has happened, giving examples.

2. Without looking to find ours, write your definition of the family. Now compare yours to ours. How are the two similar? How are they different? Does your definition have advantages over ours? If so, what are they?

3. What important changes in family patterns do you see today?

4. In what ways does personal decision making involve pressures? In what ways does it involve freedom? Give concrete examples.

5. This chapter gave the example of a person's being unemployed as a personal problem that can result from societal influences. What are some other examples of this concept? In general, do the beliefs in our society reflect this concept—or do they put responsibility for personal problems on the individual? Give examples to support your position.

6. When might a personal problem not result from societal influences?

7. What are some of the social factors that influence people's choices? How do these factors operate? Does the fact that social factors limit people's

options mean that important life decisions are pre-determined? Why or why not?

8. What are the components of knowledgeable decision making? How does knowledgeable choosing differ from choosing by default? How might the consequences be different? Give some examples of the two forms of decision making.

9. What is the archival function of families? How important is it?

10. Do you agree with sociologist David Popenoe that "family decline" today is cause for alarm? Why or why not? How might this issue be objectively researched and assessed?

11. Do you want your family life to be similar to or different from that of your parents? In what ways?

Suggested Readings

Bradbury, Bettina (ed.) 1992. *Canadian Family History: Selected Readings*. Toronto: Copp Clark Pitman. A fascinating collection of articles on Canadian family life, with particular attention given to the challenges faced by the marginalized.

Lynn, Marion (ed.). 1996. *Voices: Essays on Canadian Families*. Scarborough, ON: Nelson Canada. As the title suggests, a rich and inclusive collection of articles on Canada's many different ethnocultural groups.

Mandell, Nancy and Ann Duffy (ed.). 2000. *Canadian Families: Diversity, Conflict and Change,* 2nd ed. Toronto: Harcourt Brace Canada. An anthology that takes into account the growing diversity in our society and culture today. Among the topics addressed are family histories, children's roles in the parent-child relationship, contemporary diversities, lesbians and gay men inside and outside of relationships, families of native people, immigrants, and people of colour, divorce, family violence and change and diversity in aging families and intergenerational relations.

Popenoe, David. 1996. *Life without Father: Compelling New Evidence that Fatherhood and Marriage are Indispensable for*

the Good of Children and Society. New York: Martin Kessler Books. Treatise for the traditional husband-wife family in direct opposition to Stacey's views, below.

Stacey, Judith. 1996. *In the Name of the Family: Rethinking Family Values in the Postmodern Age*. Boston: Beacon Press. Stacey argues that there is no longer such a thing as "The Family"—rather there are many and diverse families.

Stone, Elizabeth. 1988. *Black Sheep and Kissing Cousins: How Our Family Stories Shape Us*. New York: Penguin. The shaping of family identity and family "rules" through the medium of tales told about the family's history.

Weston, Kath. 1997. *Families We Choose: Lesbians, Gays, Kinship*, Rev. ed. New York: Columbia University Press. The premise of this work is we create our own families; families are those persons whom we actively choose to include as members. This theme is specifically applied to lesbians and gay men as they create families through involved decision making.

On the Net

1) Vanier Institute of the Family
   A wealth of information on all aspects of Canadian families can be found at the Web site
   http://www.vifamily.ca

2) Statistics Canada
   http:www.statcan.ca

3) Ancestry Search
   http://www.ancestry.com

4) The Department of Heritage
   http://www.pch.gc.ca/multi/html/english.html

5) Adoptive Families Magazine
   http://www.adoptivefam.org/

6) One Parent Families Association of Canada
   http://www.tcn.net/~oneparent/

7) Canada's Families: A Mini-Quiz
   http://www.cfc-efc.ca/docs/vanif/00000913.htm

Exploring the Family

THEORETICAL PERSPECTIVES ON THE FAMILY

STUDYING FAMILIES

THERE IS NOTHING SO PRACTICAL AS

A GOOD THEORY.

KURT LEWIN

When we begin a course on the family, we are eager to have our questions answered, including:

- "What's a good family?"

- "How do I make that happen?"

- "Whom should I choose?"

- "What do I need to know to be a good parent?"

Perhaps the most important question of all is:

- "What's happening to the family today?"

Box 1.3, "Some Facts About Families in Canada Today," outlines some trends in family life, including some changes and developments you may have learned about from the media or deduced from observing life around you. But what these trends mean—how to interpret them—is not always so easy to determine. There are many visions of the family, and what an observer reads into the data depends partly on his or her perspective.

For some social commentators, these trends mean that the family is "declining" or "vanishing," whereas for others it is simply "changing." But in forming their interpretations, social scientists often use the more formal vocabulary of social theory and research methodology to characterize marriage and family patterns.

This chapter invites you to share this way of seeing families. We look at some theoretical perspectives that shape our thinking about families and at the knotty problem of studying a phenomenon as close to our hearts as family life.

THEORETICAL PERSPECTIVES ON THE FAMILY

Theoretical perspectives are ways of viewing reality, lenses through which analysts organize and interpret what they see. A theoretical perspective leads researchers to identify those aspects of families that are of interest to them. There are several different theoretical perspectives on the family. We shall see that what is significant about families varies from one perspective to the next. Sometimes the perspectives complement one another and appear together in a single piece of research. In other instances the perspectives compete, a situation that can lead analysts and policymakers to heated debate. All this can be frustrating to students who grope for the one "correct" answer. Instead, it is useful to think of a theoretical perspective as a point of view. As we move around an object and see it from different angles, we have a better grasp of what it is than if we look at it from a single fixed position.

In this chapter, we describe seven theoretical perspectives on the family: family ecology, family development, structural-functionalism, the interactionist perspective, exchange theory, family systems theory, and feminist perspectives. Each of these perspectives will be further explored in subsequent chapters. In actual research, two or more of these perspectives may come together. We will see that each perspective not only illuminates our understanding in its own way but also emerged in its own social and historical context.

The Family Ecology Perspective

The **family ecology perspective** explores how a family influences and is influenced by the environments that surround it. Every family is embedded in "a set of nested structures, each inside the next, like a set of Russian dolls" (Bronfenbrenner 1979, in Bubolz and Sontag 1993, p. 423). The neighbourhood in which a family lives includes components of these environments (see Figure 2.1). All parts of the model are interrelated and influence one another. We use the family ecology perspective throughout this book when we stress that society does not determine family members' behaviour but does present limitations and constraints, as well as possibilities and opportunities, for families.

This perspective emerged in the latter part of the nineteenth century, a period marked by social concern about the health and welfare of families. After losing ground to the family development and structural-functional perspectives (discussed below), the family ecology model resurfaced in the 1960s with increased societal awareness of the interdependence between families and their political and economic environments (Bubolz and Sontag 1993). In our current unpredictable economy, the family ecology model is again prominent in research and in political discussion and debate. Furthermore, today's family ecologists, in an increasingly global society, stress the interdependence of all the world's families—not only with each other but also with our fragile physical-biological environment (Bubolz and Sontag 1993). While crucial, this last focus is beyond the scope of this text. Here our interest centres on families enmeshed in their socio-cultural environments.

The ecology model leads researchers to investigate how various socio-cultural environments impact families. Put another way, the family ecology model is concerned with family policy—how to influence the effects that circumstances in the broader society have on families. For instance, family ecologists would point to poverty as a real problem for many Canadian families (see items 17 and 18 in Box 1.3).

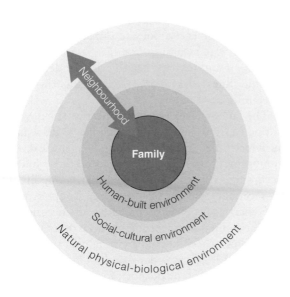

FIGURE   **2.1**

The family ecology perspective. The family is embedded in the natural physical-biological, social-cultural, and human-built environment. (Adapted from Bubotz and Sontag 1993, p. 432.)

More and more Canadians worry about making ends meet: How will we support ourselves, find comfortable housing, educate (or feed) our children, finance our old age? Meanwhile, economic and political developments over at least the last 15 years, as well as changes in government programs, have resulted in declining and inadequate government resources and spending for social services (Canadian Council of Social Development 2001; National Council of Welfare 1999).

FAMILY POLICY   In a narrow sense, **family policy** is all the procedures, regulations, attitudes, and goals of government that affect families. For simply one example, family reunification is one of the three major objectives to Canada's *Immigration Act* (See Box 1.5, "A closer look at family diversity: Family Ties and Immigation"). Family ecologists might point out that in comparison to our closest neighbour, the United States, Canada offers many examples of a successful partnership between government and families in the interests of family support.

To appreciate society's impact on the family, one need only consider how Canadian families have been affected by such legal reforms as the introduction of no-fault divorce; the legal equality of husband and wife in relation to marital and parental rights and obligations; decriminalization of homsexuality; decriminalization of abortion; prohibition of discrimination on the basis of sex or sexual orientation under the Canadian Charter of Rights and Freedoms; recognition of heterosexual cohabiting couples for both positive reasons (e.g. government or employee benefits) as well as negative reasons (e.g., disqualification of an individual for government benefits); and extension of government or employee benefits as well as some marital or parental rights and obligations to same-sex couples (Bailey 2000, pp. 43–44).

In addition to noting society's impact on families, the ecology perspective encourages researchers and policymakers to investigate what families might do to create environments that improve their quality of life. How can families become activists for the kinds of changes they want? This, of course, is a thorny issue. Some argue, for example, that only heterosexual, nuclear families should be encouraged, whereas others believe in supporting a variety of families—single-parent or gay and lesbian families. Ultimately, policies will provide answers to such questions as, "Should marital rights and obligations be further extended to same-sex couples?" or "Should same-sex marriages be legalized?" or "Should Canada follow the lead of Denmark, Norway, Sweden, Iceland and the Netherlands, and introduce registered partnership legislation?" However, given the diversity of the Canadian population, it is obviously difficult to develop policies that satisfy all Canadians equally.

As evidence of the controversies that abound in the formation of policies related to the family, one may consider that in June, 2001, the nine justices of the Supreme Court of Canada attempted to rule, for the first time, on the questions of "What role should race play in decisions regarding custody of children of mixed race relationships?" and "What principles ought to be applied?" As we note in Case Study 2.1, "Not Just Black and White: Child Custody and Bi-Racial Children," these questions defy easy answers.

A strength of the family ecology perspective is that it sensitizes us to significant politico-economic and socio-cultural issues that may not be addressed in other theories. A weakness is that the perspective is so broad and inclusive that virtually nothing is left out. As a result, it can be difficult for analysts to focus on specific causes for particular circumstances or problems.

The Family Development Perspective

Whereas family ecology analyzes the family and society (and even the physical-biological environment) as interdependent parts of a whole, the **family development perspective** emphasizes the family itself as its unit of analysis. The concept of the *family life cycle* is central here. Typical stages of family life are marked off by (1) the addition or subtraction of family members (through birth, death, and leaving home), (2) the various stages the children go through, and (3) changes in the family's connection with other social institutions (retirement from work, for example). These stages of family development are termed the **family life cycle**. They succeed one another in an orderly progression and have their requisite developmental tasks. For example, in our dominant culture newly established couples are expected to make homes of their own. If the developmental

tasks of one stage are not successfully completed, adjustment in the next stage will be more difficult.

Various versions of the stages of the family life cycle have been offered, but there is some convergence on a seven-stage model (Duvall 1957; Aldous 1978; Rodgers and White 1993). In this view, the *newly established couple* stage comes to an end through a dramatic change occasioned by the *arrival of the first baby*.

Entry of the oldest child into school brings about further changes in family life as the *parents of school-children* need to coordinate schedules with another social institution (education). Here parents are faced with the task of helping their children meet the school's expectations. *Parents of secondary-school children* may be dealing with more complex problems involving adolescent sexual activity or drug and alcohol abuse, for example. Children become increasingly expensive during this stage, while anticipated university costs add to parents' financial pressures.

Parents of young adults help their offspring enter into the adult world of employment and their own family formation. Later, *families in the middle years* return to a couple focus with (if they are fortunate!) the time and money to pursue leisure activities. Still later, aging families must adjust to retirement and perhaps health crises or debilitating chronic illness. *Death of a spouse* marks the end of the family life cycle.

The family development perspective emerged and prospered from the 1930s through the 1950s—an era in which the "natural" family was nuclear, two monogamous heterosexual parents and their children. Accordingly, the model assumed that family life follows certain conventional patterns: Couples marry, and marriage precedes parenthood; families are nuclear and reside independently from other relatives; all families have children; parents remain together for a lifetime. Of course today—and, in fact, in the past as well—many of us do not proceed so predictably along these well-marked paths.

Furthermore, critics have noted the white, middle-class bias of the family life cycle perspective (Hogan and Astone 1986). Due to economic, ethnic, and cultural differences, two families in the same life cycle stage can still be very different from one another in many respects. For these reasons, the perspective is less popular now than it was once. Meanwhile, family

Not Just Black and White: Child Custody and Bi-Racial Children

What role, if any, should race play in child custody determinations in Canada, the world's first and only officially multicultural country? If the guiding rule of law for the courts is, "What is in the child's 'best interests,'" the complexity of this seemingly simple concept was made apparent in the case of Van de Perre vs. Edwards and Edwards in 2001.

The following summary of the case, by journalist Julian Beltarame, originally appeared in Maclean's, *June 25, 2001, p. 33. For additional information on this case, you might wish to review the summary of this case on the Web site of the Supreme Court of Canada http://www.scc-cse.gc.ca/ information/hearings/spring/spring_e.html or read The Honourable Madam Justice Newbury's written reasons for the B.C. Court of Appeal's decision at http://qsilver.queensu.ca/ law/restrict/bala/law520/vandeperrevedwards.htm.*

Even by the often-nasty standards of custody cases, Kimberly Van de Perre vs. Theodore (Blue) Edwards has been vicious and destructive. As each side has staked its claim to a playful four-year-old named Elijah, the charges and countercharges have run the gamut—starting with mutual accusations of promiscuity. Then there's Edward's wealth and notoriety as a former NBA player for the Vancouver Grizzlies—and his claim the mother is a "gold digger." Still, there's no doubt the most incendiary issue in the mix is race—Van de Perre is white, Edwards black. It's a case so contentious two different courts have reached opposite conclusions about who should be Elijah's primary custodian.

Last week, Canada's Supreme Court became the third and final court to get involved. In February, 1999, a B.C. Supreme Court judge gave custody to Van de Perre, a part-time receptionist at a Vancouver hotel.[1] A year later, the B.C. Court of Appeal reversed the custody to Edwards, who is now retired from pro-ball and lives with his wife, Valerie, and twin 11 year-old girls in Charlotte, N.C.[2] Lawyers for both sides, who presented their arguments last week, say the key issue before the Supreme Court is which parent would be best for Elijah—the 27-year-old mother, whom the Edwardses accuse of being an irresponsible party-goer, or the 36-year-old father, who, by his own admission, has had three extramarital affairs, including the one with Van de Perre in 1996.

But the court, which is expected to rule later this summer, has a rare opportunity to also offer guidance on the role race should play in custody cases. "This has the potential of setting a very important precedent," says Sheena Scott of the African Canadian Legal Clinic,[3]

---

1. Although primary emphasis in this case was placed on race, some headlines directed at least partial attention to the differing socio-economic statuses of the two parents. For example, in a June 13, 2001 article appearing in the *Toronto Star*, the headline read: "Top court to decide custody of mixed-race boy: White, single mother fighting rich, black father" (MacCharles 2001).

2. The Honourable Madam Justice Newbury, in her written reasons for this decision opinioned: "If it is correct that Elijah will be seen by the world at large as 'being black,' it would obviously be in his interests to live with a parent or family who can nurture his identity as a person of colour and who can appreciate and understand the day-to-day realities that black people face in North American society—including discrimination and racism in various forms. It would certainly be naive to assume that Elijah would not encounter problems of racial prejudice at some point in his life in this

country. The Supreme Court of Canada has found that there is 'systemic discrimination against black and Aboriginal people' in Canada....[citations deleted]....It would also be naive to think that Elijah would not encounter racial prejudice growing up in the southern United States, where Mr. and Mrs. Edwards plan to settle in the long term. However, it seems to me likely that being raised in an Afro-American family in a part of the world where the black population is proportionately greater than it is here, would to some extent be less difficult than it would be in Canada. Elijah would in this event have a greater chance of achieving a sense of cultural belonging and identity and would in his father have [a] strong role model who has succeeded in the world of professional sports."

3. The Association of Black Social Workers and the Jamaican Canadian Association also received intervener status in this case.

(continued)

Not Just Black and White: Child Custody and Bi-Racial Children

(continued)

which is intervening in the case.[4] To date, says Scott, Canadian courts have been "all over the map" on the issue. Some have viewed photographs of the child and, all things being equal, ruled in favour of the parent the offspring most resembled. Other courts have dismissed physical characters as a factor. Adoption agencies, for the most part, now attempt to place children in families sharing similar birth cultures, says Peter Ferrish, director of services with the Weechi-it-te-win Family Services, an Aboriginal child-care agency in Fort Frances, Ont. "Love and nurturing is one element," he says. "But if you're an Ojibwa Indian being raised in a culture that's totally different, yes, I think something important is lost."

But just what is the child losing? Edwards says since society will regard Elijah as black, he is best able to teach him how to make his way in a predominantly white culture (a point the B.C. appeals court also made). That is doubly true for Elijah, he says, because he suspects Van de Perre or others around her of denigrating his African-American makeup.... Van de Perre denies she has disparaged blacks and notes her son would remain in contact with his father should she win custody. Beside, she adds, the race issue is a saw-off since Elijah is as much white as he is black.

4. In their factum to the Supreme Court, the clinic's lawyers wrote, "To ignore the issue of race may have consequences that are potentially discriminatory and will impose disadvantages on children from racialized groups that are not imposed on others. Biracial children have been and are classified by society on the basis of colour. In the case of a biracial child of African parentage, he will be treated as a black child in Canadian society."

If the parents agree on one thing, it's that the tug-of-war is not healthy for Elijah, who, of late, has been jetting back and forth between Vancouver and Charlotte every three weeks....

Yet weighing the race factor will be a task even the biblical Solomon would not relish, never mind the nine Supreme Court justices, all of whom are white. An out the court may take, says Barbara Bulmer, one of two lawyers representing Edwards, is that there was no expert testimony at trial dealing with the race factor. "The court would always like a record in the court below and some expert opinion and there was very little evidence," she notes. That would allow the court to render a ruling on more typical custody issues. But with interracial matches on the rise in Canada, the court would only be leaving the tough question for another day.

On September 28, 2001, the Supreme Court of Canada ruled 9–0 that the British Columbia Court of Appeal judgment that had awarded joint custody to Edwards and his wife should be overturned and upheld the decision of the trial judge, who had awarded custody to Van de Perre. The high court dismissed the suggestion that Elijah would be best raised by the Edwards family in North Carolina. "In this case, there absolutely no evidence adduced (at trial) which indicates that race was an important consideration," wrote Justice Michel Bastarache on behalf of the Supreme Court (in Bailey 2001:A12). In your opinion, was this judgment in the "best interests of the child"? Why or why not?

development theorists continue to see the model as useful (Mattessich and Hill 1987, p. 445), and some have modified it to recognize racial/ethnic and other social variations, such as child-free unions, single parenthood, divorce (Rodgers and White 1993) and/or lesbian families (Slater 1995). In sum, family development theory can sensitize us to important family transitions and challenges. But its usefulness is limited by the implied assumptions that families are essentially similar, that they share a fairly traditional way of life, and that they change according to conventional time-of-life transitions.

The Structural-Functionalist Perspective

The **structural-functionalist perspective** sees the family as a social institution that performs certain essential functions for society. When social scientists use the term *institution*, they are not referring to a university, a hospital, or a prison. In the social sciences, the term has an abstract meaning: **Social institutions** are patterned and predictable ways of thinking and behaving—beliefs, values, attitudes, and norms—that are organized around vital aspects of group life and serve essential social functions. In the structural-functionalist perspective (as well as others), the family is the institution, or structure commissioned to perform some very basic social functions. In preindustrial or traditional societies, the family structure was extended to involve whole kinship groups and performed most societal functions. In industrial or modern societies, the typical family structure is more often nuclear (husband, wife, children) and has lost many functions (Goode 1963). Nevertheless, in contemporary society, the family remains principally accountable for at least three important functions: to raise children responsibly, to provide economic support, and to give emotional security.

FAMILY FUNCTION 1: TO RAISE CHILDREN RESPONSIBLY   If a society is to persist beyond one generation, it is necessary that adults not only bear children but feed, clothe, and shelter them during

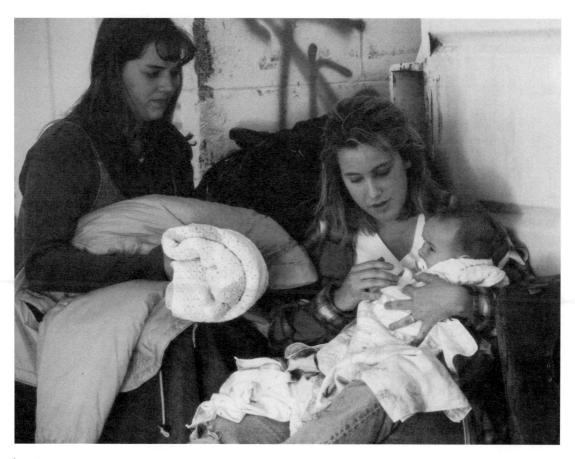

If a society is to persist beyond one generation, it is necessary that adults not only bear children but feed, clothe, and shelter them during their long years of dependency. Doing all this is an important function of families. Despite the fact that they are homeless, these parents are obviously trying to fulfill that function.

their long years of dependency. Furthermore, a society needs new members who are properly trained in the ways of the culture and who will be dependable members of the group. All this requires that children be responsibly raised. Virtually every society places this essential task on the shoulders of families—either extended or nuclear. Accordingly, a related family function has traditionally been to control its members' sexual activity. Although there are several reasons for the social control of sexual activity, the most important one is to ensure that reproduction takes place under circumstances that guarantee the responsible care and socialization of children. Even though the proportion of births to unmarried mothers has increased dramatically in Canada since the 1960s and, by 1991, 27 percent of births occurred outside of marriage (Belle and McQuillan 2000, p. 115), the universally approved locus of reproduction remains the married-couple family. Today, for this reason, there is renewed, concerted effort on the part of politicians and others to keep married couples together. But today the child-rearing function is often performed by divorced or never-married parents. For example, in 1996, about 22 percent of single mothers in Canada were never-married women (Statistics Canada 1998d).

FAMILY FUNCTION 2: TO PROVIDE ECONOMIC SUPPORT   A second family function involves providing economic support. For much of history, the family was primarily an economic rather than an emotional unit. The family was the unit of economic production in societies with agriculture, craft, and earlier industrial or commercial economies (Shorter 1975; Stone 1980). Although the modern family is no longer a self-sufficient economic unit, virtually every family engages in activities aimed at providing for such practical needs as food, clothing, and shelter.

The broader family network, or extended family—grandparents, aunts and uncles—is often an important source of security. Extended families meet most needs in a traditional society—economic and material needs and reproduction and child care, for example—and they have strong bonds. In urban societies, specialized institutions, such as factories, schools, and public agencies, often meet practical needs. But extended families may also help each other materially in urban society, especially during crises.

Family economic functions now consist of earning a living outside the home, pooling resources, and making consumption decisions together. In assisting one another economically, family members create some sense of physical security. For example, mates can offer each other a kind of unemployment insurance. They reciprocally ensure that if one is not employed—because of long illness, the inability to find work, the wish to change jobs, or to stay home with children—the other will support both of them. And family members care for each other in additional practical ways, such as nursing and transportation during illness. Chapter 13 explores how individuals integrate work and family today.

FAMILY FUNCTION 3: TO GIVE EMOTIONAL SECURITY In today's world, the family has grown more important as a source of emotional security (Berger, Berger, and Kellner 1973; Popenoe 1993, 1996). This is not to say that families can solve all our longings for affection, companionship, and intimacy. They cannot. (Frequently, in fact, the family situation itself is a source of stress, as we'll discuss in Chapters 9 and 10.) Neither is it true that family members or intimate partners never experience loneliness—nor that they can fill all of one another's emotional needs. But families and committed intimate relationships can offer important emotional security. The broader family network—grandparents, grown sisters and brothers, aunts and uncles—is often an important source of emotional security. Family can mean having a place where you can be yourself, even sometimes your worst self, and still belong.

In anthropology, the structural-functionalism perspective calls attention to cross-cultural variation in family structure. Box 2.1, "Marriages and Families Across Cultures," gives some examples. As it dominated family sociology in both Canada the United States during the 1950s, however, the structural-functionalist perspective emphasized the heterosexual nuclear family as "normal," "good," or "functional" (Parsons and Bales 1955). Furthermore, the perspective gave much attention to arguing the functionality of specialized gender roles: the "instrumental" husband-father who makes the living and wields authority, and the "expressive" wife-mother whose main function is to enhance emotional relations at

home (Parsons and Bales 1955). (Gender roles and issues are discussed in detail in Chapter 3.) The shared values of society, which are a given in structural-functionalist theory, would lead to family members' performance of these conventional and functional roles. Deviance from them would likely result in "family disorganization" as measured by divorce and juvenile delinquency. These views fit nicely in a post-World War II society, characterized by an expanding economy and widespread attitudes specifying husbands as providers and wives as homemakers. While many women had been gainfully employed during World War II as well as during the preceding Depression years, a return to "normal" after the war meant an emphasis on traditional husband-wife roles (Kingsbury and Scanzoni 1993).

Much of the current debate over family "decline" can be better understood once one has a grasp of the structural-functionalist perspective. Those who argue that the family is in decline or "breaking down" generally come from this perspective and see the nuclear family as the structure for performing necessary social functions (Popenoe 1993, 1996). Their opponents refuse to view the nuclear family as "normal," "natural," or best. Both sides would agree, however, that many families in our contemporary society do depart from the nuclear family structure. As you can see in Figure 2.2, less than half of Canadian families in 1996 took the form of the typical nuclear family (married-couple families with children).

The structural-functional perspective has been criticized for giving us an image of smoothly working families characterized by shared values while overlooking such issues as power disadvantages, spousal or parent–child conflict, and even family violence. The perspective has been further criticized because it generally fails to recognize that what is functional for one group or category of people may not be so for others. For instance, structural-functionalism does not take into consideration racial/ethnic or class variation in family structures. Nonetheless, virtually all social scientists assume the one basic premise underlying structural-functionalist: that families comprise an important social institution (however they might be defined or structured) with essential social functions to be performed.

The Interactionist Perspective

Unlike the three theoretical orientations that we have already described, the **interactionist perspective** looks within families, at internal family dynamics. This point of view explores the interaction of family members—that is, the back and forth talk, gestures, and actions that go on in families. Members respond to what other members say (verbally or nonverbally) and do. These interchanges take on a reality of their own; they construct or create a family. Put another way, something called "family" emerges from the relationships and interactions among family members. Unlike structural-functionalism, which posits a standard family form, the interactionist perspective refuses to identify a "natural" family structure. The family is not a stock social unit but the creation of its participants as they spontaneously relate to one another.

Based on the work of Charles Horton Cooley (1909) and George Herbert Mead (1934), the interactionist perspective was the principal theoretical orientation in sociology during the 1920s and 1930s when the family studies field was establishing itself as a legitimate social science. The orientation remains a popular and fruitful one. Interactionists are keenly interested in the two concepts, "self" and "identity." They assume that an individual develops concepts of self (**self-concept**: the basic feelings people have about themselves, their abilities, and their worth) and **identity** (a sense of inner sameness developed by individuals throughout their lives) through social interaction. The self, in turn, is able to assess and assign meaning and value to ongoing family activities. Families shape the identities and self-concepts of all their members, including adults. Family identities and traditions emerge through interaction as the family identifies itself with the growth of relationships and the creation of rituals (Bossard and Boll 1943; Fiese et al. 1993).

Thinking about families in this way leads interactionists to investigate questions like the following: How do two separate individuals interact in a marriage or otherwise committed partnership to fashion a couple identity (Berger and Kellner 1970)? Conversely, how is the couple identity dismantled through divorce (Vaughan 1986)? How do families define the appropriateness of feelings (Hochschild 1979)? How do family members communicate intimacy? How are family roles constructed and learned (LaRossa and Reitzes 1993)? By what processes exactly do parents socialize children—and children, their parents? What mechanisms underlie family power dynamics? By what process do family members arrive at more or less shared goals, beliefs, values, and norms (LaRossa and Reitzes 1993)? If, as structural-functionalists assume, family members

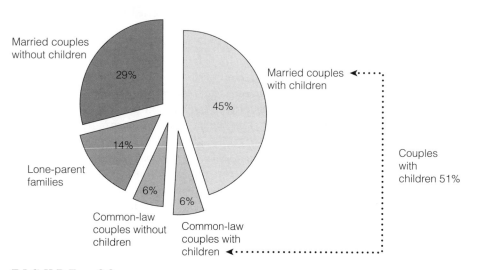

FIGURE **2.2**

Family structure, 1996. (Source: Statistics Canada, "Canadian Families: Diversity and Change," Cat. no. 12F0061XFE.)

BOX 2.1

Marriages and Families Across Cultures

Some features of family life that many of us take for granted in Canada do not necessarily occur in all cultures—nor among immigrant groups arriving from other cultures. This box describes some cross-cultural variations in family life and illustrates the wide range of family practices that societies consider normal. How many of the following five statements have you assumed to be characteristic of what is normal or universal?

1. *Marriage is monogamous.* When we think of marriage, we often think of **monogamy**: the sexually exclusive union of one woman and one man. Actually, only a minority of the world's cultures insist on monogamous marriage. Many societies permit **polygamy** (a person having more than one spouse) and practise both polygamy and monogamy. The Quaran, the traditional holy book in Muslim cultures, allows polygamy. But the Quaran also emphasizes that if practising polygamy causes anyone pain or suffering, then polygamy abuses Allah's (or God's) law. ("Polygamy, the Quaranic Way" 1997). In some societies adultery is accepted, though often limited to males.

2. *Spouses form an economic unit.* We assume that a wife and husband buy necessities as a couple and work together to support their nuclear family. However, some cultures expect the husband and the wife each to be economically self-sufficient. Among the Hopi Indians, for example, only the wife owns farmland, orchards, livestock, and water holes; they are not joint property (Stephens 1963).

3. *The nuclear family lives in a separate household.* We might assume that nuclear family members, but not other relatives, ordinarily share housing, income, property, and expenses. In many societies, however, an **extended family** shares one household. In a **vertically extended family** three or more generations share housing and resources; in an **horizontally extended family**, family members from the same generation or other related lines such as uncles, brothers, sisters, and aunts, live and work together (Ruggles 1987).

Cross-cultural researchers (researchers who compare cultures around the world) often contrast societies in terms of whether they have more individualistic or more collectivist values. In **individualistic societies** the main concern is with one's own interests and those of one's immediate family. In **collectivist societies** people identify with and conform to the expectations of their relatives or clan, who look after their interests in return for their loyalty (Hofstede 1980). Individualistic societies such as Canada, the United States, and Western European countries, favour nuclear families. Other, more collectivist societies, are more likely to see extended families as normative or fully acceptable (Kamo and Zhou 1994). Recent increases in three-generation households in Canada have occurred, at least in part, from rising numbers of Asian immigrants, and from economic and practical concerns as well as from cultural preferences (Che-Alford and Hamm 2000, p. 162).

4. *Young people select their own marriage partners.* Historically, few traditional societies allowed young people to choose partners without the approval of parents or other relatives. Today arranged marriages persist in parts of the world, although the practice is diminishing as more and more cultures become westernized (Levine et al. 1995; Dugger 1998). In contemporary arranged marriages the child's preference is often, though not always, deferred to—at least somewhat. For example, traditional Indian culture has favoured marriages arranged by parents (Nyrop 1985), with parents often hiring an astrologer to make sure that the prospective spouses have compatible astrological charts. Arranged marriage is discussed further in Chapter 7.

(continued)

(continued)

5. *Love is universal and provides the basis for marriage.* Most Canadians believe that falling in love is a prerequisite for marrying someone. But love is not thought to be a necessity for a happy marriage in all societies. Individualistic cultures assign much greater importance to love in decisions about marriage partners than do more collectivist cultures such as India, Pakistan, Thailand, the Philippines, or Mexico, for example (Levine et al. 1995). As we will see in Chapter 4, the romantic love individualistic cultures focus upon is not necessarily the same type of love that people in collectivist cultures focus on.

In what ways do you think expectations concerning marriage in other cultures are more or less realistic than in most parts of Canada? What possible changes and conflicts do you imagine could arise or have arisen in your own experience when families immigrate to Canada?

For additional examples of cross-cultural variations in family life, see Stuart A. Queen, Robert W. Habenstein, and Jill Quadagno (eds), *The Family in Various Cultures*, 5th edition, New York: Harper and Row, 1985; and Lorne Tepperman and Susannah J. Wilson (eds), *Next of Kin: An International Reader on Changing Families*, New York: Prentice Hall, 1993.

---

share common values, interactionists would want to know how this situation develops.

An often-voiced criticism of the interactionist perspective is that (similar to family ecology) interactionism makes intuitive sense but is difficult to test empirically. A related criticism is that, because it is qualitative and relatively subjective, the research connected with the interactional perspective lacks rigour.

Interactionists have not always been sensitive to cultural variation, taking interaction to be the same in all settings. This theoretical perspective needs to be expanded to consider: "how do geography, race/ethnicity, class, gender, age, and time relate to family groups?" (LaRossa and Reitzes 1993:136). As another example within our own society, how are rural families in poverty dissimilar to their urban counterparts? How do families change—or avoid changing—in the wake of general social upheaval or more personal crisis (LaRossa and Reitzes 1993)?

Perhaps a more serious criticism is that interactionism overestimates the power of individuals to create their own realities, ignoring the extent to which humans inhabit a world not of their own making.

Exchange Theory

Exchange theory grew out of the application of an economic perspective to social relationships, beginning around 1960 and flourishing during the 1960s and 1970s. This orientation focuses on how individuals' various personal resources affect their relative positions in families or other groups (Thibaut and Kelley 1959; Nye 1979). The basic premise here is that people use their resources to bargain and secure advantage in relationships. Exchange theorists pay attention to the exchange of rewards and costs between participants in a relationship or family unit. Such transactions form and stabilize a relationship or group.

Relationships based on equal or equitable (fair, if not actually equal) exchanges thrive, whereas those in which the exchange balance feels consistently one-sided were more likely to dissolve or be unhappy (Walster and Walster 1978; Van Yperen and Buunk 1994; Sprecher and Schwartz 1994). Whether an unhappy couple divorces or remains married can be analyzed in exchange terms (Walster and Walster 1978; Van Yperen and Buunk 1990).

Exchange theory must fight the human tendency to see family relationships in far more romantic and emotional terms. Yet, dating relationships, marriage and other committed partnerships, divorce, and even parent–child relationships show signs of being influenced by the relative assets of the parties. Money is power, and the children of wealthier parents are more likely to share their parents' values (Luster, Rhoades, and Haas 1989). Marriages tend to take place between people of equal status (see Chapter 7). Decision making within a marriage, as well as decisions to divorce, are affected by the relative resources of the spouses. People without resources or alternatives to a relationship defer to the preferences of others and are less likely to leave it (see Chapter 10).

Family Systems Theory

Family systems theory, like interactionism, is an umbrella term for a wide range of specific theories. Growing out of psychotherapy, this theoretical framework looks at the family as a whole (Kantor and Lehr 1975). Even though they are like interactionism in being concerned with the interaction among family members, systems theories have some unique concepts and propositions.

Systems theory uses the model of—a system! Like an organic system (the body), a mechanical or a cybernetic system (a computer), the parts of a family make a whole that is more than the sum of the parts (Laing 1971).

A family functions regularly in a certain way; emotional expression and behaviour of family members tend to persist. Put another way, systems tend toward equilibrium. Like a computer program directing a space vehicle, information about behaviour provides feedback to the system, which then adjusts itself. Change in the external environment or in one of the internal parts sets in motion a process to restore equilibrium. What this means in a family is that there is pressure on a changing family member to revert to his or her original behaviour within the family system. For change to occur, the family system as a whole must change. Indeed, that is the goal of family therapy based on systems theory.

Without therapeutic intervention, families may replicate problem behaviours over the generations. Similarly, it might be unrealistic for a spouse to attempt to resolve marital difficulties by leaving the family (by divorcing). An individual may recreate or enter a family system similar to the one she or he left. Then too, family systems can survive divorce.

Systems theory and family therapy overlap. But social scientists have moved systems theory away from its therapeutic origins to use it in a more general analysis of families. They have been especially interested in how family systems handle information, deal with problems, respond to crises, and regulate contact with the outside world. Boundaries of the family, as well as closeness or distance of family members from one another, are important issues.

Criticism of the family systems perspective relates to its nonspecificity: So the family is a system—then what? In working concretely with families in therapy, it can be very useful to both therapists and clients. If family members come to understand how their family system operates, they can use this knowledge to achieve desired goals.

Systems theory does not take note of social structure (the class system or race/ethnicity), but presumes instead that families are families the world over. Transactions with a particular family's external world of work, school, religious affiliation, and extended family may be addressed, but the structure of economic opportunity and other features of the larger society are not analyzed. Systems theory tends to diffuse responsibility for conflict, by attributing dysfunction to the system. This makes it difficult to extend social support to victimized family members while establishing legal accountability for others, as in incest or other domestic violence (Stewart 1984).

But systems theory often gives family members insight into the effects of their behaviour and is a good analytic tool. It can make visible the hidden benefits or costs of certain family patterns. For example, doctors were puzzled by the fact that death rates were higher among kidney dialysis patients with supportive families. Family systems theorists attributed the higher rates to the unspoken desire of the patients to lift the burden of care from the close-knit family they loved (Reiss, Gonzalez, and Kramer 1986).

Feminist Perspectives

For decades, sociologists talked about how traditional family roles were functional for society, ignoring in the process the politics of gender. Directly and indirectly, functionalists have suggested that a specialized division of labour, whereby men mainly perform roles within the public sphere and women mainly perform roles within the private sphere, produces an efficient and complementary social and family life. By compartmentalizing the domestic and extra-domestic worlds, functionalists ignored issues of significant sex differences in power, property, and prestige or, if they acknowledged them, implied that they were necessary for the efficient functioning of the social world.

Feminist sociological theories challenge the mainstream assertions that such a division of labour is necessarily sex-linked, functional, and complementary. Moreover, they argue that the "myth of separate worlds" (Kanter 1989) denies the interlinkages between roles played within the family and within the labour market and renders invisible the work of women. What is generally referred to as **feminist theory** was formulated in large part in reaction to the perceived limitations of traditional or mainstream social science theories (and related methodologies).

While all feminist theories begin from the premise that men and women are not evaluated similarly in a society such as Canada and therefore that women live under conditions of oppression that are neither natural nor inevitable, that are many types of feminist theory. While it is beyond the scope of this book to fully discuss all the many variants of feminist theorizing, we will briefly discuss four major types: liberal feminism, Marxist feminism, radical feminism, and socialist feminism.

The most moderate, **liberal feminism**, identifies its goal as "a just and compassionate society in which freedom flourishes" (Wendell in Tong 1989, p. 13). Liberal feminists maintain that women are valued less in societies such as Canada in terms of social rewards because of their unequal participation in institutions outside the family and domestic sphere—in particular, the economic institution. Liberal feminism is sometimes derisively referred to as "assimilationism" (Williams 1991, p. 95), both for its focus on providing opportunities for women in areas that were traditionally reserved for men and for its focus on "sameness"—that is, on how women are like men or would be, if given the chance.

This theory is described as moderate because it does not propose to radically restructure the nature of basic institutions in Canadian society, but rather stresses the need to restructure the distribution of individuals within these institutions. For liberal feminists, women's unequal distribution within the economic institution stems from a combination of discrimination based on sex and a lack of equal-quality education. The solution to women's oppression, they argue, requires that such obstacles be eliminated and equality of opportunity for both women and men assured.

In contrast to the liberal feminist viewpoint, Marxist feminists insist that the entire structure of our society must be changed before true gender equality can be attained. This orientation traces its intellectual roots to Karl Marx, who analyzed disparate power in terms of wealth, or capital. Marx viewed industrialized workers, because they were required to sell their own labour, as fundamentally exploited by industry-owning capitalists. Engels (1942 [1884]) elaborated a Marxist theory of the family that emphasized capitalism's failure to pay a living wage; exploitative reliance on the family to maintain the labour force through reproduction of children and maintenance of workers' morale; and the corruption of the couple relationship by the economic dependency of women. Engels expected a communist revolution to bring about a more satisfying marriage, based on personal attachment rather than property relations.

Marxist feminism has focused particular attention on women's work-related concerns: "how the institution of the family is related to capitalism; how women's domestic work is trivialized as not real work; and finally, how women are generally given the more boring and low-paying jobs" (Tong 1989, p. 51). However, for Marxist feminists, once the fundamental economic oppression inherent in capitalism is eliminated, the oppression of women will necessarily disappear. From the Marxist perspective, the unequal status of women is analogous to that of any other disadvantaged group in our society. Sexual, racial, and class inequalities are all believed to be byproducts of the same underlying cause—the capitalist economic system.

In contrast, **radical feminists** do not identify the capitalist economic system of production as the source of gender inequality. Rather, they suggest that women live under conditions of inequality in most systems of economic production, whether they be capitalist, socialist, or communist. They argue that the oppression of women is ultimately based on a system of ideas, referred to as **patriarchy**, which promotes the belief in male superiority, and therefore supports, and justifies, the domination of women by men. According to radical feminists, patriarchy pervades not only the public world of the formal economic production process but also, and perhaps more oppressively, the private world of family or domestic relations. Accordingly, radical feminists maintain that patriarchal ideology must be eliminated before any meaningful change in women's oppression can occur.

Some proponents of the radical feminist perspective maintain that women must also be liberated from the limitations of their bodies, which form the foundation of patriarchy. Specifically, it is argued that as long as women's roles and rewards are tied to reproductive differences and the beliefs associated with them, true gender-equality cannot be realized. For radical feminists, the ultimate goal is to eliminate biological sex as a basis for any social action and social response.

The **socialist feminist** analysis combines that of the Marxist and radical feminists. Socialist feminists seek to eliminate both class and sexual oppression, that is, both capitalism and patriarchy. From the socialist feminist viewpoint, it is the historical combination of the capitalist economic and political system and the patriarchal ideology that leads to the oppression of women in so many ways. For socialist feminists, not only must the organized system of producing goods and services be restructured, but also the systems of sexuality, child bearing, and child rearing in order to promote a truly egalitarian society for men and women.

In the 1960s and subsequently, the application of feminist perspectives to families has permitted us to see some things about families that had been overlooked before. Social scientists discovered child abuse, wife abuse, marital rape, husband abuse, elder abuse, child sexual abuse, parent abuse, and sibling abuse, for instance.[5]

Although we have noted that there are many variations within the feminist perspective, in general, this perspective focuses on how male dominance in the family and society is oppressive to women. Moreover, and unlike the perspectives already described, which emerged primarily among academic researchers, feminist theories developed from political and social movements over the past 30 years. As a result, the feminist perspective is fairly unique: Its mission is using knowledge to confront and end the oppression of women and related patterns of subordination based on social class, race/ethnicity, age, or sexual orientation.

Feminist theorizing has contributed to political action regarding families in the following ways, among others:

1. Changes in policies that economically weaken households headed by women (for example, efforts to end gender and race discrimination in wages)

2. Changes in laws that reinforce the privileges of men and heterosexual nuclear families versus other family types (for example, divorce laws that disadvantage women economically or laws that exclude nontraditional families from economic and legal supports offered to marrieds)

3. Efforts to stop sexual harassment and sexual and physical violence against women and children

4. Advances in securing women's reproductive freedom (for example, through abortion rights)

5. New recognition and support for women's unpaid work, by involving men more fully in housework and child care and by efforts to fund quality day care and paid parental leaves

6. Transformations in family therapy so that counsellors recognize the reality of gender inequality in family life and treat women's concerns with respect (Goldner 1993)

Feminist perspectives are currently under fire from conservative talk-radio hosts, politicians, and religious leaders. For some family sociologists as well (e.g., Blankenhorn 1995, Popenoe 1996), feminism may have taken women's rights too far, resulting in too many children alone after school because their mothers are employed outside the home, too high divorce rates, too many single-parent families—in short, "family breakdown." Meanwhile, from the feminist perspective, championing the traditional nuclear

---

5. Actually, a physician "discovered" child abuse. He published an article on the "battered child syndrome," based on the hidden injuries to children revealed by X-rays (Kempe et al. 1962). Social scientists then pursued their interest in child abuse and other forms of domestic violence.

family at the cost of women's equality and well-being is unconscionable. In Judith Stacey's analysis

> the family values campaigns have an antifeminist tinge.... There was a lot of emphasis on the selfish career woman,... the self-indulgent woman or the promiscuous woman.... At first, it was all about the decline of motherhood.... It's a huge movement now... [and] it's really about restoring the father to his rightful place as head of the household, the center of authority. That's what I have a problem with.... and restoring sharply differentiated roles of mothers and fathers. (in Hagar 1997, pp. 9, 12)

Moreover, Stacey and others argue, there is not just one effective way to structure family life.

There Is No Typical Family

It is important to emphasize as we close this section that diversity exists not only among family theorists but also among families themselves. Despite its functions, the structure of the family institution is remarkably flexible. Until recently, Judeo-Christian tradition, the law, and societal attitudes converged into a fairly common expectation about what form the North American family should take. This expected model (nuclear family with children, breadwinner father and homemaker mother) is often called "traditional," but it is also called "modern" because it emerged with modern industrial society. Over the past three decades, however, the predominance of this "modern" pattern has disappeared and has been replaced by a proliferation of different family forms: two-earner, single-parent, cohabiting, blended, gay families. Increasingly social scientists refer to this situation as the "**postmodern family** condition" and to contemporary families, in all their diversity, as "postmodern." *There is no typical Canadian family today.* As sociologist Pat Armstrong (1999, p. 813) has pointedly observed, "There is no such thing as 'the Canadian family.'"

Canadians' response to this change is the stuff of talk radio, serious political debate, and academic analysis and debate. Critics have labeled this shift in family structure as "family breakdown." Others argue that today's "postmodern family condition" is the newest development in the historical evolution of family life (Stacey 1996). We, the authors, have worked to balance in this text an appreciation for flex-ibility and diversity in family structure and relations—and for freedom of choice—with the increased concern of many social scientists about what they see as diminished marital and child-rearing commitment. Still, in varied circumstances, chosen or not, we find that families are made of people: committed people who are married or in otherwise committed intimate relationships, people trying to raise their children or contribute to the rearing of others' children, and people providing material and emotional support to each other in relationships they identify as "family."

STUDYING FAMILIES

The great variation in family forms and the variety of social settings for family life mean that few of us can rely on firsthand experience alone in studying the family. Although we "know" about the family because we have lived in one, our **experiential reality**—beliefs we have about the family—may not be accurate. We may also be misled by media images and common sense—what everybody knows. Everybody knows, for example, that the Canadian family is a nuclear one—or else that it is dying. This **agreement reality**—what members of a society agree is true—may misrepresent the actual experience of families (Babbie 1992, p. 17).

We turn now to consider the difficulties inherent in studying the family and then to a presentation of various methods used by social scientists. Although imperfect, the methods of scientific inquiry can bring us a clearer knowledge of the family than either personal experience or speculation based on media images. Scientific methods represent a form of agreement reality that sets special standards for the acceptance of statements about the family.

The Blinders of Personal Experience

Most people grow up in some form of family and know something about what marriages and families are. But while personal experience provides us with information, it can also act as blinders. We assume that our own family is normal or typical. If you grew up in a large family, for example, in which a grandparent or an aunt or uncle shared your home, you probably assumed (for a short time at least) that everyone had a big family. Perceptions like this are usually outgrown at an early age, but there may be more subtle, not-yet-apparent differences between your family experiences and those of others. For instance, the members of your family may spend a lot of time alone, perhaps reading, whereas in other families it may be cause for alarm if a family member—adult or child—is not talking with others around the kitchen table.

Personal experience, then, can make us believe that most people's family lives are similar to our own when often this is not the case. We may be very committed to the view of family life shaped by our experiences and our own choices: "The search for regularities and generalized understanding is not a trivial intellectual exercise. It critically affects our personal lives" (Babbie 1992, p. 25).

In looking at marriage and family customs around the world (see Box 2.1, "Marriages and Families Across Cultures"), we can easily see the error of

Traditional Muslim families follow the Islamic code of sharia. In this photo of a Saudi family, the Western dress and uncovered hair suggest that cultural beliefs and norms concerning dress and behaviour have been privately negotiated within this family—a conclusion that reflects the interactionist perspective.

assuming that all marriage and family practices are like our own. But not only do our assumptions about family life not hold true in other places, they also frequently don't even describe our own society. For example, **heterosexism**, the tendency to see heterosexual or straight families as the standard, can lead us to ignore lesbian or gay male families. However, the tendency to use the most familiar yardstick for measuring things is a strong one; even social scientists fall victim to it. (See Box 2.2, "Studying Ethnic Minority Families," for a look at how social scientists have begun to address the problems of cultural bias.)

Scientific Investigation: Removing Blinders

Seeing beyond our personal experience involves learning what kinds of families other people are experiencing, and with what consequences. To do this, we rely on data gathered systematically from many sources through techniques of **scientific investigation**, from which it often is possible to generalize. The techniques—surveys, laboratory observation and experiments, naturalistic observation, case studies, longitudinal studies, and historical and cross-cultural data—will be referred to throughout this text, so we will briefly describe them now.

SURVEYS **Surveys** are part of our everyday experience. When conducting scientific surveys, researchers either engage in face-to-face or telephone interviews or distribute questionnaires to be answered and returned. Questions are often structured so that after a statement, such as "I like to go places with my partner," the respondent has answers from which to choose. The possible responses might be: Always, Usually, Sometimes, Not very often, Never. Researchers spend much energy and time wording such *close-ended* questions so that, as much as possible, all respondents will interpret questions in the same way.

Interview questions can also be *open-ended*. For example, the question might be, "How do you feel about going places with your partner?" or "Tell me about going places with your partner." Many social scientists and respondents alike believe that open-ended questions give those answering more opportunity to express how they really feel or what they actually believe than do more structured survey questions, which require people to choose from a predetermined set of responses.

Studying Ethnic Minority Families

Just a few decades ago, white, middle-class (and male) scholars conducted the preponderance of theorizing and research on families. But beginning about 30 years ago, men and women from diverse ethnic backgrounds began to study families scientifically. One of the first contributions they made was to point out how limited, and hence biased, our theoretical and research perspectives have been. In this chapter, for example, we note the white, middle-class bias in family development theory. (And it becomes obvious from our text discussion that the structural-functionalist perspective can be seen as biased against women.) To begin to understand this question of bias, we might think of theory and research on ethnic minority families as falling into one of three frameworks: cultural equivalent, cultural deviant, and cultural variant (Allen 1978). The **cultural equivalent** approach emphasizes those features that minority families have in common with mainstream white families. An example would be the finding that middle-class black parents treat their children much the same way as do middle-class white parents (Taylor et al. 1991). The **cultural deviant** approach views the qualities that distinguish minority families from mainstream families as negative or pathological. An example would be analyses that lament the high incidence of Aboriginal children under the age of 15 who live with a single parent (32.1 percent) compared with non-Aboriginals (16.4 percent).

The **cultural variant** approach calls for making culturally and contextually relevant interpretations of minority family lives. A classic example is Carol Stack's (1974) participant observation in a black community; her resulting book, *All Our Kin*, emphasized previously ignored strengths in extended African-American families. In the first two approaches, white mainstream families are considered the standard against which "other" or "less valid" families are compared, either favourably or unfavourably—a situation conducive to bias. In the third and preferred approach, minority families are studied on their own terms, and comparisons are made *within* those groups (for example, comparing parenting styles of First Nations peoples on and off reserves).

Besides pointing out bias in theory and research, some scholars have introduced new, more culturally relevant, theoretical concepts. One of these is the **kin scripts framework** for studying ethnic minority families. This theoretical framework includes three culturally relevant family concepts: kin-work, kin-time, and kin-scription. *Kin-work* is the labour families must accomplish in order to survive. *Kin-time* refers to family norms concerning the temporal and sequential nature of such transitions as parenthood, marriage, and grandparenthood. *Kin-scription* is the active recruitment of family members to do kin-work. Besides helping to make family theory and research less biased and more relevant to minority families, thinking like this is potentially an example of reverse theorizing. That is, although the kin scripts framework was derived from research on black extended families, the concepts might be used to study nonminority mainstream families as well (Dilworth-Anderson, Burton, and Johnson 1993).

Once the returns are in, survey responses are tallied and statistically analyzed, usually with computers. After the survey data have been analyzed, the scientists conducting the research begin to draw conclusions about the respondents' attitudes and feelings. Then the scientists must decide to whom their conclusions are applicable. Do they apply *only* to those whom they interviewed directly, for example, or to other people similar to the respondents? In order to ensure, moreover, that their conclusions can be *generalized* (applied to people other than those directly questioned), survey researchers do their best to ensure that their respondents constitute a *representative sample* of the people they intend to draw conclusions about. Popular magazine surveys, for example, may tell us more about the demographics of their readership and are unlikely to be drawn from a representative sample. It is evident, for example, that a survey on attitudes about premarital sex in *Penthouse* or *Playboy* will likely yield different findings than one in *Family Circle* or *Reader's Digest*. It would not be scientifically accurate to generalize from a set of conclusions drawn from a *Chatelaine* survey about how Canadian adults feel about premarital sex. In the same way, results from a survey in which all respondents are white, middle-class university students cannot be considered representative of Canadians in general. Researchers and political pollsters may instead use random samples, in which households or individuals are randomly selected from a comprehensive list (see Babbie 1998 for a more detailed discussion). A random sample is considered to be representative of the population from which it is drawn. A national random sample of approximately 1500 people can validly represent the Canadian population.

Survey research has certain advantages over other inquiry techniques. The main advantage is uniformity. Presumably, all respondents are asked exactly the same questions in the same way. Also, surveys are relatively efficient means of gathering large amounts of information. And, provided the sample is designed to be accurately representative, conclusions drawn from that information can be applied to a large number of people.

Surveys have disadvantages, too. Because they ask uniform or standardized questions, surveys may miss points respondents consider important. Surveys neither tell us about the context in which a question is answered nor guarantee that in a real-life situation a person will act in a manner consistent with the answer given to the interviewer (Babbie 1998).

Other disadvantages of surveys result from respondents' tendency to say what they think they *should* say, rather than what they in fact believe. Social scientists refer to this problem as the tendency of respondents to give *normative answers*. If asked whether or how often physical abuse occurs in the home, for example, those who often engage in family violence might be especially reluctant to say so.

Another disadvantage of surveys, closely akin to the tendency of respondents to say what they think they should, is the tendency of respondents to forget or to reinterpret what happened in the past. (Because of this, social scientists recognize the value of longitudinal studies—studies in which the same group of respondents is surveyed or interviewed intermittently over a period of years.) For this reason, most researchers agree that asking about attitudes or events that occurred in the past seldom yields valid results. Another disadvantage of surveys, again closely related to respondents' tendency to give normative answers, is a problem specific to interviewer surveys. Depending on the sex, age, race, and style of the person questioning you, you might tend, even without knowing it, to give a certain response. Scientists call this tendency *interview effects of an interviewer*. Certain characteristics of the interviewer—age, sex, clothing style, hair length—may tend to elicit a certain kind of response. A 45-year-old male, for example, asked about his experience concerning sexual impotence, can be expected to reply differently to a male interviewer of 20 than he would to one of 60—or to a female of any age. Perhaps the most significant disadvantage of every research survey is that what respondents say may not accurately reflect what they do.

LABORATORY OBSERVATION AND EXPERIMENTS Because of the relative ease of conducting surveys, the flexibility of the format, and the availability of samples (even a classroom sample can provide useful information), surveys have been the primary source of information about family living. Other techniques are also used, however. In a laboratory observation or **experiment**, behaviours are carefully monitored or measured under controlled conditions. These methods are particularly useful in measuring physiological changes associated with anger, fear, sexual response (as discussed in Chapter 5), or behaviour that is difficult to report verbally. In family problem solving, for example, families may be asked to discuss a hypothetical case or to play a game, while their behaviour is observed and recorded.

In an experiment, subjects from a pool of similar participants will be randomly assigned to groups (experimental and control groups) that will be given different experiences (treatments). Families whose child is undergoing a bone marrow transplant may be asked to participate in an experiment to determine how they can best be helped to cope with the situation. One group of families may be assigned to a support group in which the expression of feelings, even negative ones, is encouraged (Experimental Group 1). Another set of families may be assigned to a group in which the emphasis is on providing factual information about transplantation and maintaining a positive, cheerful outlook (Experimental Group 2). A third group of families may receive no special intervention (Control Group).

If at the conclusion of the experiment the groups differ in attitudes and behaviour according to some explicit measures of coping behaviour, mental health, and family functioning, then this outcome is presumed to be a result of the experimental treatment. Put another way, because no other differences are presumed to exist among the randomly assigned groups, the results of the experiment provide evidence of the effects of the therapeutic interventions.

A true experiment has these features of random assignment and experimental manipulation of the important variable. Laboratory observation, on the other hand, simply means that behaviour is observed in a laboratory setting, but it does not involve random assignment or experimental manipulation of a variable.

The experiment just described takes place in a field (real-life) setting, but experiments are often conducted in a laboratory setting because the researcher has more control over what will happen. He or she has more chance to plan the activities, measure the results, determine who is involved, and eliminate outside influences. In the previous example, families might have obtained additional personal counselling on their own, which would affect the results, or they may have attended the group only infrequently.

Experiments, like surveys, have both advantages and disadvantages. One advantage of experiments is that social scientists can observe human behaviour directly, rather than depending, as they do in surveys, on what respondents tell them about what they think or do. The experimenter can control the experience of the subjects and can ensure, to some extent, the initial similarity of subjects in the two groups. A disadvantage of this research technique is that the behaviours being observed often take place in an artificial situation, and whether an artificial or simulated testing situation is analogous to real life is virtually always debatable. A family asked to solve a hypothetical problem through group discussion may behave very differently in a formal laboratory experiment than they would at home around the kitchen table discussing a real problem.

The fact that in social research the subject pool is often drawn from university classrooms and is not very representative of the general population is another limitation. Sometimes "volunteer" participants are really draftees or subjects who have responded to financial incentives; in such cases the authenticity of results is often in question. And volunteer subjects may be very different from their peers who decide not to participate.

NATURALISTIC OBSERVATION Many aspects of human behaviour and interaction just don't lend themselves to study in laboratory settings, so social scientists use another technique in an attempt to overcome virtually all artificiality (or as much as possible). In **naturalistic observation**, the researcher lives with a family or social group or spends extensive time with family or group members, carefully recording their activities, conversations, gestures, and other aspects of everyday life. Sometimes the researcher is a member of the family. The researcher attempts to discern family interrelationships and communication patterns and to draw implications and conclusions from them for understanding family behaviour in general.

The principal advantage of naturalistic observation is that it allows us to view family behaviour as it actually happens in its own natural—as opposed to artificial—setting. The most significant disadvantage of this tool is that findings and conclusions may be highly subjective. That is, what is recorded, analyzed, and assumed to be accurate depends on what one or very few observers think is significant. Another drawback to naturalistic observation is that it requires enormous amounts of time to observe only a few families. And these families may not be representative of family living in general. Perhaps because of these disadvantages, relatively few studies use this technique.

Still, Fred Davis' (1991) study of the families of polio victims, first published in 1963, remains an important piece of observational research that provides useful insights into family dynamics. It may become even more relevant because as medical science has enabled more and more children to survive serious illness, they and their families will live with crisis and chronic disease for an extended period.

An especially important use of naturalistic observation has been in research on racial/ethnic communities or in other settings not easily accessible to survey or experimental research. Studies such as anthropologist Carol Stack's (1974) participant observation of families in a lower-class black community and sociologist Arlie Hochschild's (1997) study of family members at work give us the context in which families live their lives. They often reveal that families play an active role in using the resources of their social environment to shape their destinies.

CLINICIANS' CASE STUDIES   A fourth way that we get information about families is from **case studies** compiled by clinicians—psychologists, psychiatrists, marriage counsellors, and social workers who counsel people with marital and family problems. As they see individuals, couples, or whole families over a period of time, these counsellors become acquainted with communication patterns and other interactions within families. Clinicians offer us knowledge about family behaviour and attitudes by describing cases to us or by telling us about their conclusions based on a series of cases.

The advantages of case studies are the vivid detail and realistic flavour that enable us to experience vicariously the family life of others. The insights of clinicians can be helpful.

But case studies also have weaknesses. There is always a subjective or personal element in the way the clinician views the family. Inevitably, any one person has a limited viewpoint. Clinicians' professional training may also lead them to over- or underemphasize certain aspects of family life and to see family behaviour in a certain way. For example, as a group, psychiatrists used to assume that the assertiveness or career interests of women caused the development of marital and sexual problems.

Furthermore, people who present themselves for counselling may differ in important ways from those who do not. Most obviously, they may have more problems. For example, throughout the fifties psychiatrists reported that gays and lesbians in therapy had many emotional difficulties. Subsequent studies of gay males not in therapy concluded that gays were no more likely to have mental health problems than were heterosexuals.

LONGITUDINAL STUDIES   **Longitudinal studies** provide long-term information about individuals or groups, as a researcher or research group conducts follow-up investigations (by means of interviews or questionnaires), most often for several years after the initial study. Observational or experimental studies could be repeated, but this is rarely done.

Booth and White's ongoing research, in which adults who were married at the time of the first survey in 1980 were reinterviewed three more times during the 1980s and 1990s, is a good example of longitudinal research. The researchers traced the demographic and relationship patterns affecting marital quality and stability, divorce, and remarriage (Booth, Johnson, and White 1984; White and Booth 1985a, b; White, Booth, and Edwards 1986; Booth and Johnson 1988; White and Keith 1990; White and Booth 1991).

A difficulty encountered in longitudinal studies, besides the almost prohibitive cost, is the frequent loss of subjects due to death, emigration, or loss of interest. Social change occurring over a long period of time can make it difficult to ascertain what, precisely, has influenced family change. Yet cross-sectional data (one-time comparison of different groups) cannot show change in the same individuals over time.

HISTORICAL AND CROSS-CULTURAL DATA   Analyzing historical records is a research approach that is becoming more and more common in the study of the family. Some interesting work by social historians in France (Ariès 1962) and in England (Laslett 1971) began to attract the interest of sociologists about 30 years ago, affecting current generations of scholars and teachers.

Historical research, whether done by historians or sociologists, has had a powerful influence on the study of the family. Zelizer's (1985) study of insurance documents and other historical materials conveys the changing status of the child from economic asset to emotional asset. Linda Gordon's (1988) research using social agency files from the early twentieth century reveals how lower- and working-class women used social agencies to cope with domestic violence, child sexual abuse, and other family problems.

Drawbacks to historical research are the unevenness and unavailability of data. Scholars must rely on only those data to which they have access. Typically, the upper classes, that had both the leisure and resources to record their activities, are overrepresented. But historical scholars have been very creative. Hanawalt (1986) constructed a rich picture of the medieval family from an examination of death records. Demographic and economic data and legal records, among the most reliable sources, are especially useful for analyses of the family institution (see Glendon 1989). Scholars are on less solid footing in describing intimate family matters because they must rely on materials such as individuals' diaries, which may not be representative of the period.

Sociologists, especially those who place more emphasis on cross-cultural comparison than we are able to do in this text, continue to look to anthropological fieldwork for information on family life and structure in societies in both developed and developing nations. Many make use of anthropological data that have been compiled in a systematic way, such as the Human Relations Area Files, in which various features of a multitude of societies are described in a standard format. Since the former Soviet Union fairly recently became open to social scientists from around the world, scholars have analyzed families in Russia (Maddock et al. 1993).

The Application of Scientific Techniques

All research tools represent a compromise. Each has its special strengths and weaknesses. The strengths of one research tool, however, can make up for the weaknesses of another. Findings that result from direct observations, for example, supplement survey reports in an important way. Whereas the former allow scientists to observe actual behaviours among a limited number of people, surveys provide information about attitudes and reported behaviour of a vast number of people. To get around the drawbacks of each technique, social scientists may combine two or more tools in their research. Ideally, a number of scientists examine one topic by several different methods. In general, the scientific conclusions in this text result from many studies and from various and complementary research tools. Despite the drawbacks and occasional blinders, the total body of information available from sociological, psychological, and counselling literature provides a reasonably accurate portrayal of marriage and family life today.

IN SUM

Different theoretical perspectives—family ecology, family development, structural-functionalism, interactionist, exchange, family systems, and conflict/feminist—illuminate various features of families. Just as there is no one correct family theory, there is no typical Canadian family today.

Structural functionalism leads us to see families as a social institution commissioned to perform basic functions for society—responsible child rearing, economic support, and emotional security.

How do we know what families are like? We can call upon personal opinion and experience for the beginning of an answer to this question. But everyone's personal experience is limited. Scientific investigation—with its various methodological techniques—is designed to provide a more effective way of gathering knowledge about the family.

Key Terms

agreement reality
case studies
collectivist society
cross-cultural researchers
cultural deviant
cultural equivalent
cultural variant
exchange theory
experiential reality
experiment
extended family
family development perspective
family ecology perspective
family life cycle
family policy
family systems theory
feminist theory
heterosexism
horizontally extended family
identity

individualistic society
interactionist perspective
kin scripts framework
liberal feminism
longitudinal studies
Marxist feminism
monogamy
naturalistic observation
patriarchy
polygamy
postmodern family
radical feminism
scientific investigation
self-concept
social institutions
socialist feminism
structural-functionalist perspective
surveys
theoretical perspectives
vertically extended family

Study Questions

1. Choose one of the major theoretical perspectives on the family and try to explain how you might use it to understand something about life in your family.

2. Choose a magazine photo and analyze its content from a structural-functionalist perspective. (Hint: Together the people in the photo can constitute the group under analysis, with each person meeting certain of the group's needs, or functional requisites.) Then analyze it from one or more other perspectives. How do your insights differ?

3. Why is the family a major social institution? Does your family fulfill each of the functions identified in the text? How?

4. How do the concepts *individualistic culture* and *collectivist culture*, described in Box 2.1, correspond with the discussion of *individualism* and *familism* in Chapter 1?

5. How is your family structured? That is, is it a traditional nuclear family, or does it represent the diversity of Canadian families? How would you apply the current debate over family values to your own family experience?

6. Review the techniques of scientific investigation, and discuss why science is often considered a better way to gain knowledge than is personal experience alone. When might this not be the case?

Suggested Readings

Babbie, Earl. 1998. *The Practice of Social Research*. 7th ed. Belmont, CA: Wadsworth. Respected textbook in sociological methods. Recommended for those who would like additional information or clarification.

Boss, Pauline G., William J. Doherty, Ralph LaRossa, Walter R. Schumm, and Suzanne K. Steinmetz, eds. 1993. *Sourcebook of Family Theories and Methods: A Contextual Approach*. New York: Plenum. Don't let the size of this book scare you off! It is filled with very readable essays on all the theoretical perspectives and methods described in this chapter and more.

Klein, David M., and James M. White. 1996. *Family Theories*. Thousand Oaks, CA: Sage. Excellent general text, summarizing and discussing family theories.

Mandell, Nancy and Ann Duffy. 2000. *Canadian Families: Diversity, Conflict and Change (2nd edition)*. Toronto: Harcourt Brace Canada. Highlight the many conflicts and contradictions that surround discussion of the family today.

On the Net

1) Theory
Links to home pages on social theory
http://www.pscw.uva.nl/sociosite/TOPICS/theory.html

2) Research Methods
Resources for qualitative researchers
http://www.ualberta.ca/~jrnorris/qual.html

3) Family Connections
A site for researchers, families and those in the helping professions
http://www.bccf.bc.ca/

4) Canada's Changing Families: Challenges to Public Policy
http://www.vifamily.ca/pubs/ccf.htm

5) Sources for Aboriginal Families with Children
http://www.infocan.gc.ca/children-enfants/08_e.htm

6) Investing in Children & Families
http://www.hrdc-drhc.gc.ca/arb/publications/research/investing.shtml

Our Gendered Identities

WOMEN ARE CREATING A NEW WORLD, RESTRUCTURING AND REINVENTING SOCIAL INSTITUTIONS AROUND THE GLOBE.

NANCY FELIPE RUSSO, PSYCHOLOGY OF WOMEN QUARTERLY

IF THE POLITICAL FORCES CURRENTLY PROMOTING MODERN SEXISM CONTINUE TO GAIN STRENGTH, OLD-FASHIONED SEXISM MAY ALSO BE ON THE RISE.

JANET T. SPENCE AND EUGENE D. HAHN, PSYCHOLOGY OF WOMEN QUARTERLY

Would you agree or disagree with the following statements?

- Swearing and obscenity are more repulsive in the speech of a woman than a man.
- A woman should be careful not to appear smarter than the man she is dating.
- When there's an important job to be done, I'd prefer to have a man as leader than a woman.
- Women who are very assertive and independent don't have the concern about other people that most women have.

The above statements are some examples that researchers (Spence, Helmreich, and Stapp 1973; Spence and Hahn 1997) have developed to measure attitudes about what's appropriate for women and men. If you agree with these statements, researchers might classify you as "conservative" regarding what's appropriate for men and women. If you disagree, you might be classified "liberal." Research shows that since about 1986, attitudes have grown more liberal regarding men's and women's roles in both Canada

and the United States (Bibby 1995; Twenge 1997a). At the same time, even among today's college and university students, men are more conservative than women, especially when preferring other men in leadership roles—and a significant proportion of coeds admit to acting "feminine" when with guys (Spence and Hahn 1997; Sherman and Spence 1997).

Regarding gender attitudes and behaviours, this is an ambivalent time. On the one hand, women (including Canadian Roberta Bondar) have gone into space as astronauts and lead nations (in 1993, Kim Campbell became Canada's first woman prime minister). On the other hand, as recently as June 2000, when *Maclean's* reported that, at Ontario's York University, five out of eight senior positions including the presidency were held by women, the article was mockingly entitled "Gender Bender 101: Life in the Ovary Tower" (Deziel 2000, p. 19). Although gender expectations have changed and continue to change, they have obviously not done so completely. It's still

In 1992, physician and astronaut Roberta Bondar became the first Canadian woman in space.

true that living in our society remains a different experience for males and females.

Gender influences virtually every aspect of people's lives and relationships. Put another way, we are all **gendered**. In this chapter we will examine various aspects of gender, especially those that more directly affect committed relationships and families. In doing so, we'll consider personality traits and cultural scripts typically associated with masculinity and femininity. We'll describe male dominance, discuss the possible influence of biology, and examine the socialization process, the study of which helps us discover whether people learn to behave as either females or males, or whether they are born that way. We'll discuss the lives of adults as they select from options available to them and speculate about what the future is likely to hold.

GENDERED IDENTITIES

We are using the term *gender* rather than *sex* for an important reason. The word **sex** refers only to male or female anatomy and physiology. Sex includes the different chromosomal, hormonal, and anatomical components of males and females that are present at birth. We use the term **gender** (or **gender role**) far more broadly—to describe societal attitudes and behaviours expected of and associated with the two sexes. Another concept, **gender identity** refers to the degree to which an individual sees her- or himself as feminine or masculine based on society's definitions of appropriate gender roles (Burke and Cast 1997). Gender, as distinguished from sex, involves socially constructed roles regarding what it means to be masculine or feminine.

The first two chapters pointed out that our personal decisions, attitudes, and behaviours are influenced by our social environment, which we in turn influence and shape. The interactionist perspective (Chapter 2) encourages us to recognize that our culture and the social arrangements surrounding us are neither God-given nor natural but rather are socially constructed. Hence gender roles, or attitudes and behaviours, are socially constructed as well. People **internalize** others' expectations regarding gender; by acting accordingly, they reinforce those expectations for themselves, for others around them, and for all who will follow them in subsequent generations. People who refuse to act accordingly precipitate change.

Let's examine the predominant gender expectations in our culture.

Gender Expectations

You can probably think of some characteristics typically associated with being feminine or masculine. Stereotypically masculine people are often thought to have *agentic* (from the root word *agent*) or **instrumental character traits**—those that enable them to accomplish difficult tasks or goals. A relative absence of agency characterizes our expectations of women, who are thought to embody *communal* or **expressive character traits**: warmth, sensitivity, concern about others' needs, and the ability to express tender feelings (Best and Williams 1998).

Talcott Parsons, a prominent structural-functionalist in the 1950s, helped to establish these gender expectations when he wrote

> The masculine personality tends more to the predominance of instrumental interests, needs, and functions, presumably in whatever social system both sexes are involved, while the feminine personality tends more to the primacy of expressive interests, needs, and functions. We would expect, by and large, that other things being equal, men would assume technical, executive, and "judicial" roles, women more supportive, integrative, and "tension-managing" roles. (Parsons and Bales 1955, p. 101)

Gender Expectations and Diversity

This view of men as instrumental and women as expressive is based primarily on people's images of white, middle-class heterosexuals. But subcultural variations exist (Blee and Tickamyer 1995). Compared with white men, black men are viewed as more emotionally expressive. Compared with white women, black women are viewed as less passive and less dependent (Dill 1999). Asian women are stereotyped as being more submissive than white women (Chow 1985; Yee 1993). "Native women face unique problems among women stemming from stereotypes of them perpetuated by European men since the earliest contacts. The image of the Indian princess gave way to that of the promiscuous "squaw," which renders indigenous women vulnerable to violence and mistreatment, and vindicates their violators" (McNab 1999, p. 1599).

In addition, there are age, class, and sexual-orientation differences in gender expectations. We may think of elderly men as less aggressive, for example. Working-class women are expected and thought to be more hostile, inconsiderate, and irresponsible than middle-class white women (Cazenave 1984). Gays are stereotyped as possessing feminine traits, whereas lesbians are stereotyped as possessing masculine ones (Fiske 1998; Kite and Deaux 1987; Twenge and Zucker 1999).

Cultural Messages

The particular ways in which men are expected to show agency and women expressiveness are embedded in the culture around us. Let's examine some of our cultural messages about masculinity and femininity in turn.

MASCULINITIES In writing about men and gender, we need to state the obvious: Men are not all alike. Recognizing this, scholars have begun to analyze **masculinities** in the plural, rather than the singular—a recent and subtle change meant to promote our appreciation for the differences among men. Anthropologist David Gilmore (1990), having examined expectations for men cross-culturally, argues that what is common among the world's concepts of "masculinity"—and what separates these from cultural messages regarding women—is that a man must somehow prove that he is a "real man" (versus "no man at all") whereas a women is allowed to take gender for granted.

How do men go about demonstrating their manhood? Twenty years ago, sociologists Deborah David and Robert Brannon (1976) pointed to four masculine "scripts" that our culture provides as guidelines. The first was no "sissy" stuff, according to which men are expected to distance themselves from anything considered feminine. In a second cultural message, a man should be occupationally or financially successful, a "big wheel." Third, a man is expected to be confident and self-reliant, even tough—a "sturdy oak." A fourth cultural message emphasizes adventure, sometimes coupled with violence and or the need to outwit, humiliate, and defeat. Adult men

"give 'em hell" or "kick ass" in barroom brawls, contact sports, and war. If a male finds that legitimate avenues to occupational success are blocked to him because of, for example, social class or racial/ethnic status, he might "make it" through subcultural standards, such as physical aggression or striking a "cool pose." The latter involves dress and postures manifesting fearlessness and detachment, adapted by some minority group males for emotional survival in a discriminatory and hostile society (Majors and Billson 1992). During the 1980s, another cultural message emerged and was lauded by many as the preferred option for men. According to this message, the "new" or "liberated" male is emotionally sensitive and expressive, valuing tenderness and equal relationships with women (Kimmel 1989). These divergent cul-

Traditional stereotypes of children define boys as aggressive and competitive, and girls as sensitive and concerned for others. Real behaviour is far more varied than these stereotypes, however.

tural messages—coupled with the male's need to prove his manhood—contribute to men's ambivalence and confusion in today's changing society (Gilmore 1990; Gerson 1993), a point explored later in this chapter.

FEMININITIES   The pivotal expectation in **femininities** for a woman requires her to offer emotional support. Traditionally, the ideal woman was physically attractive, not too competitive, a good listener, and adaptable. Considered fortunate if she had a man in her life, she acted as his helpmate, facilitating and cheering his accomplishments. In addition to caring for a man, a woman has been expected to be a good mother and put her family's and children's needs before her own.

A feminine expectation that has emerged over the past twenty years is the "professional woman"—independent, ambitious, self-confident. This cultural message may combine with the traditional one to form the "superwoman" message, according to which a good wife and/or mother also efficiently attains career success or supports her children by herself. An emerging female expectation is the "satisfied single"—a woman (either lesbian or heterosexual and usually employed) who is quite happy not to have a serious relationship with a male.

A theme that has wound through cultural images of femininity is the good girl/bad girl or virgin/whore theme. Women have traditionally been stereotyped as either sexually conservative or sluts.

To What Extent Do Individual Women and Men Follow Cultural Expectations?

It is one thing to recognize cultural messages but another to choose to live accordingly. Consequently, we can ask to what extent actual men and women exhibit gender-expected behaviours. The first thing we need to recognize here is that gender traits are sometimes *thought* to be opposite and mutually exclusive; that is, we may think that a person cannot be both masculine and feminine. But this is not the case. Indeed, descriptions by university students of "typical" men and women overlap considerably (De Lisi and Soundranayagam 1990).

For one thing, acting according to cultural expectations may be situational (Wagner and Berger 1997). The same woman may speak forcefully when in a job interview and demurely when on a date, for example. A man who suffers pain without wincing on a football field may cry in a less public or less competitive situation. Then too, beginning in the 1970s (Bem 1975, 1981; Best and Williams 1998; Swim 1994) researchers have found that individuals actually see themselves as having both agentic/instrumental and communal/expressive traits: "[G]ender stereotypes do not always 'copy' directly onto the self concepts of young women and young men; often times one finds only a 'weak echo' of the stereotypes in the self concepts" (Williams and Best 1999, p. 524).

We can visualize the extent to which females and males actually differ on a trait as two overlapping normal distribution curves (see Figure 3.1). For example, although the majority of men are taller than the majority of women, the area of overlap in men's and women's heights is considerable. Furthermore, the shaded area in Figure 3.1 indicates that some men are shorter than some women and vice versa. It is also true that differences among women or among men ("within-group variation") are usually greater than the differences between men and women ("between-group variation").

Although some research finds women more concerned about others' well-being than men and men more competitive than women (Beutel and Marini 1995), generally the gendered expectations we've discussed fit an overlapping pattern (Basow 1992). An exception is male dominance, although this may be changing.

Male Dominance

On an interpersonal level, **male dominance** describes a situation in which the male(s) in a dyad or group assume authority over the female(s). On the societal level, male dominance is the assignment to men of greater control and influence over society's institutions. Sociologist Clyde Franklin II cited both mixed-gender play situations in which boys take over playground equipment "whenever they want" and men harassing women on jobs as evidence that male dominance "seems ubiquitous" (1988, p. 30).

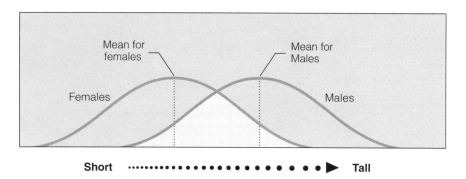

Short ••••••••••••••••••••••• ▶ Tall

FIGURE **3.1**

How females and males differ on one trait, height, conceptualized as overlapping normal distribution curves.

Research shows that on an interpersonal level, males in groups tend to dominate verbally. Men talk louder and longer and interrupt other speakers and control conversational topics more than women do. Also, females restrict themselves more in claiming personal space, smile more when smiling is not related to happiness, and touch others less in groups but are touched more. Although these findings may reflect personality differences, they also indicate male–female status differences (Henley and Freeman 1995). On an institutional level, male dominance is evident in politics, religion, and the economy.

MALE DOMINANCE IN POLITICS   Before June 1993, when Kim Campbell was elected Conservative Party leader and, by ascension shortly after, became prime minister (for an admittedly limited term of six months), there had never been a woman prime minister in Canada. In December 1989, the election of Audrey McLaughlin as leader of the New Democratic Party signalled the first time a woman had been elected to head a federal political party in Canada and North America. During the November 2000 elections, 375 women ran for office and 62 were elected to the House of Commons (39 Liberal, 10 Bloc Quebecois, 7 Canadian Alliance, 5 New Democratic Party and 1 Progressive Conservative. Women currently account for 21 percent of all MPs and occupy 33 of the 104 seats in the Senate (22 Liberal, 10 Progressive Conservative, 1 Independent) (Nelson 2001, "Women Federal Political Representation").

In general, the more important the political office, the lower the probability that a woman will hold it. Moreover, minority women have been especially underrepresented in political office. While Mary Ellen Smith became, in 1918, the first woman to be elected to the Legislative Assembly in British Columbia (and the first woman in the British Empire to serve as a cabinet minister) it was not until 1972 that a black woman, Rosemary Brown, won a seat in that province. Brown was also the first black woman elected to any Canadian legislature. In 1991, Zanana Akande was the first black woman to be elected to the Ontario legislature and also the first black woman to become a cabinet minister in that province (Mandell 1995, p. 347). In 1993, Ethel Blondin-Andrew became the first Aboriginal woman appointed to a senior political level as Secretary of State (Training and Youth) and also the first Aboriginal woman to ever sit in the House of Commons (Canadian Women's Issues Network 2001).

MALE DOMINANCE IN RELIGION   Religion evidences male dominance as well. Even though women are more likely to attend religious services than men (Statistics Canada 1998) and, in the role of mothers, are most influential in the religious identification of children (Bibby, 1997), in virtually all religions, men more often hold positions of authority (Baril and Mori 1991, McQuire 1992). Some signs of change are apparent. For example, since the 1970s, Reform and Reconstructionist Judaism have allowed women rabbis and, in 1985, the Conservative denomination of Judaism followed suit. In addition, "[a] growing number of Protestant denominations—including the Church of England—have overturned historical policies and now ordain women" (Macionis et al. 1997, p. 489). However, while a large majority of Catholic lay persons (Reese 1992) and theologians (Woodward 1997), believe the Catholic Church should ordain women priests, the Vatican disagrees.

The Plan of Action document, resulting from the 1995 United Nations Fourth World Conference on Women, in Beijing, declares women's rights as human rights to be actively endorsed by the world's governments. But the document's insistence on women's right to control their bodies and sexuality angered the Vatican, Muslim Iran, and various Christian fundamentalist groups in North America (Chen 1995).

The effects of personal religious involvement on women's daily lives are complex. On the one hand, the phenomenal growth of fundamentalist Islam religions, evangelical Protestantism, and the similar charismatic renewal in the Catholic Church have fostered a traditional family ideal of male headship and a corresponding rejection of feminist-inspired redefinitions of family roles. On the other hand, some feminist evangelicals mingle the two movements, as other evangelical and charismatic women redefine male family authority to foster greater male involvement in the household, more open communication, and shared decision making (Stacey 1990). There is also a feminist movement among Arab women, who seek to combine their religio-cultural heritage with equal rights for females (Tucker 1993).

MALE DOMINANCE IN ECONOMICS Although the situation is changing, men as a category have been and continue to be dominant economically. When data were first collected in 1967 in Canada on female-to-male earnings, the ratio stood at 58.4 percent. Since that time, it has increased notable, For example, during 1989 to 1993, the ratio increased from 66 percent to 72 percent because of both an increase in average female earnings and a stalling in average male earnings. In 1994, men's earnings improved significantly as the result of a surge in employment in the higher-wage goods-producing industries and the earnings ratio fell to 69.8 percent. "In short, recent variations in the ratio have been due more to improving or faltering earnings for men than to changes in the earnings for women" (Statistics Canada 1997a). In 1997, employed women earned, on average, 80 percent of what employed men did: female workers earned an average of $15.10 an hour while male workers received $18.80 an hour (Statistics Canada 1999g).

The hourly wage gap between men and women is widespread among individuals of all ages, educational levels, occupations, and industries. However, it varies for different groups. For example, in 1997, single women who had never been married earned 96 cents for every $1 earned by their male counterparts. Women with a university education earned 85 cents for every dollar earned by their male counterparts, and women without a high school diploma earned only 69 cents for every $1 earned by comparably educated men (Statistics Canada 1999e). Table 3.1 illustrates the persistence of the gender wage gap in the average earnings of full-year, full-time workers in the 25 highest paying and 25 lower-paying occupations in Canada in 1995.

In addition, work is highly gendered. Men's and women's employment remains segmented into dual labour markets, with women in a narrower range of jobs offering fewer benefits and advancement opportunities. Investigating the gender gap in organizational authority in seven countries (Australia, Canada, Japan, Norway, Sweden, the United Kingdom, and the United States), Wright et al. (1995, p. 419) conclude that in every country, "women are less likely than men to be in the formal authority hierarchy, to have sanctioning power over subordinates, or to participate in organizational policy decisions." Women of colour, First Nations women, and women with disabilities may be even less likely to hold positions of power. For example, in contrast to visible minority men, who are found concentrated in either professional occupations or service jobs (in both cases at higher proportions than Canadians overall), visible minority women are more likely than Canadian women as a whole to be concentrated in manual labour work (Moreau 1991, p. 28). In 1995, women of colour earned just over half (51 percent) of what white men earned and only 60 percent of what men of colour earned (Das Gupta 1996, p. 7). Consider as well that while differently-abled women aged 15 to 64 are less likely than differently-abled men (41 percent versus 56 percent) to be employed (Shain 1995, p. 10), when differently-abled women do obtain full-time, full-year employment, they typically earn less

TABLE   3.1

Average Earnings of Full-Year, Full-Time Workers in the 25 Highest-Paying and 25 Lowest-Paying Occupations, by Sex, Canada, 1995

	Average Earnings ($)		
	Both Sexes	Men	Women
All Occupations	37 556	42 488	30 130
Total: 25 highest-paying occupations[1]	**80 206**	**86 139**	**58 943**
Judges	126 246	128 791	117 707
Specialist physicians	123 976	137 019	86 086
General practitioners and family physicians	107 620	116 750	81 512
Dentists	102 433	109 187	71 587
Senior Managers: Goods production, utilities, transportation, and construction	99 360	102 971	58 463
Senior Managers: Financial, communications carriers, and other business services	99 177	104 715	71 270
Lawyers and Quebec notaries	81 617	89 353	60 930
Senior managers: Trade, broadcasting, and other services	79 200	84 137	48 651
Primary production managers (except agriculture)	76 701	78 421	48 479
Securities agents, investment dealers, traders	75 911	90 391	47 323
Petroleum engineers	72 543	73 657	56 506
Chiropractors	68 808	71 032	56 764
Engineering, science, and architecture managers	68 235	69 792	53 138
University professors	68 195	72 532	55 909
Senior managers: Health, education, social, and community services, and membership organizations	68 187	78 012	56 190
Air pilots, flight engineers, and flying instructors	67 581	68 219	43 991
Geologists, geochemists, and geophysicists	66 210	68 116	51 151
Utilities managers	64 816	66 239	52 564
School principals, and administrators of elementary and secondary education	64 513	66 837	60 394
Optometrists	64 419	73 920	48 337
Insurance, real estate, and financial brokerage managers	64 197	73 419	46 070
Commissioned police officers	63 518	64 865	50 011
Senior government managers and officials	63 195	69 477	49 667
Supervisors: mining and quarrying	62 537	62 768	0
Information systems and data processing managers	62 387	64 999	53 140

[1] Although athletes were in the 25 highest paying occupations and trappers and hunters were in the 25 lowest paying occupations, their very small numbers rendered their income statistics unreliable. Hence, the individuals in these occupations were excluded from this table.

Source: Adapted from Statistics Canada 1998i.

	Average Earnings ($)		
	Both Sexes	Men	Women
Total: 25 lowest-paying occupations[1]	**17 729**	**20 238**	**16 564**
Inspectors and testers, fabric, fur, leather products manufacturing	20 001	25 396	18 507
Light duty cleaners	19 991	23 829	18 125
Early childhood educators and assistants	19 772	25 074	19 586
Pet groomers and animal care workers	19 716	24 467	17 398
Taxi and limousine drivers and chauffeurs	19 664	19 845	16 756
Visiting homemakers, housekeepers, and related occupations	19 607	24 751	19 063
Hotel front desk clerks	19 220	20 364	18 575
Cooks	19 054	20 224	17 607
Maitre d'hotel and hosts/hostesses	18 873	24 649	17 336
Kitchen and food service helpers	18 799	17 320	19 697
Hairstylists and barbers	18 292	22 867	16 755
Painters, sculptors and other visual artists	18 188	20 421	14 982
Tailors, dressmakers, furriers, and milliners	17 850	24 686	16 026
General farm workers	17 756	19 990	13 825
Estheticians, electrologists, and related occupations	17 658	22 889	17 462
Sewing machine operators	17 613	20 664	17 340
Cashiers	17 553	20 557	16 977
Ironing, pressing, and finishing occupations	17 322	19 297	16 499
Artisans and craftpersons	16 943	20 555	13 565
Bartenders	16 740	18 899	14 940
Harvesting labourers	16 426	18 683	14 465
Service station attendants	16 203	16 520	14 947
Food service counter attendants and food preparers	15 487	17 912	14 681
Food and beverage servers	14 891	18 192	13 861
Babysitters, nannies, and parents' helpers	12 713	15 106	12 662

than either non-disabled women or differently-abled men. Their situation is especially bleak because they are also more likely than other groups to live as lone parents. In 1996, almost 1 in 10 (9.7 percent) differently-abled women was a lone parent (compared with 7.6 percent of women without a disability, 2.8 percent of differently-abled men, and 1.1 percent of non-disabled men) (Fawcett 1999).

Women's roles have changed—some would say dramatically changed—over the past 20 years. Meanwhile, male dominance persists in major social institutions such as politics, religion, and the economy. This situation has led scholars to talk about "old-fashioned" and "modern" sexism. (Other researchers [Glick and Fiske 1997] discuss "hostile" and "benevolent" sexism, described in Chapter 10.)

Old-Fashioned and Modern Sexism

Sexism involves prejudice and discrimination based on gender. Old-fashioned, or traditional, sexism refers to believing that women's roles should be confined to family roles (wife, mother) and that women should exercise leadership positions neither at home nor elsewhere. "Modern" sexism denies that gender discrimination persists and believes that women are probably asking too much now—a situation that results in resistance to women's demands (Swim et al. 1995). Relatedly, some social psychologists refer to "neosexism" as the "manifestation of a conflict between egalitarian values and residual negative feelings towards women" (Tongas et al. 1995, p. 843).

When researchers study people's attitudes toward women's and men's roles, they often use several statements together that comprise a measurement scale. The statements at the beginning of this chapter are from various measurement scales. Following are some statements designed by social psychologists to measure old-fashioned sexism:

- Swearing and obscenity are more repulsive in the speech of a woman than a man.

- It is ridiculous for a woman to run a locomotive and for a man to darn socks.

- In general, the father should have greater authority than the mother in bringing up the children.

- Women are generally not as smart as men.

- It is more important to encourage boys than to encourage girls to participate in athletics (Spence et al. 1973; Swim et al. 1995; Swim and Cohen 1997).

Agreeing with statements like these would likely define you as an "old-fashioned" or "traditional" sexist. Researchers have generally found that, since about 15 years ago, fewer and fewer respondents agree with statements like these (Twenge 1997). For example, while 34 percent of Canadians in 1975 agreed with the statement that "Married women should not be employed if their husbands are capable of supporting them," in 1995, only 10 percent of Canadians expressed this sentiment. In like fashion, while in 1975, 22 percent of Canadians agreed that "Women should take care of running their homes and leave running the country up to the men," in 1995, only 10 percent agreed with the statement (Bibby 1995). Nevertheless, many Canadians continue to agree, and some see these issues as religious ones.

Meanwhile, a larger proportion of all Canadians is likely to agree with statements designed to measure neo- or modern sexism. Some statements measuring "neosexism" are the following (Tongas et al. 1995; Campbell, Schellenberg, and Senn 1997):

- Discrimination against women in the labour force is no longer a problem.

- Women shouldn't push themselves where they are not wanted.

- Universities are wrong to admit women in costly programs such as medicine, when in fact a large number will leave their jobs after a few years to raise their children.

- In order not to appear sexist, many men are inclined to overcompensate women.

- Due to social pressures, firms frequently have to hire underqualified women.

Agreeing with these statements would classify you as a neo- or modern sexist. What is your response to this?

We have been discussing male dominance in Canada today. Cross-culturally and historically, it appears that virtually all societies have been characterized by some degree of male dominance. This leads us to ask whether the cause might be genetic. Put another way, is what Sigmund Freud once proposed true—that "anatomy is destiny"?

IS ANATOMY DESTINY?

We need to ask which aspects of gender-associated behaviour depend on physiology and which have people learned. For example, about 80 percent of adult North American females shave their body hair (Basow 1991). Is this behaviour genetic in females, or learned? More seriously, are males biologically destined to be more agentic, instrumental, and dominant than females? Or do men and women learn and enforce their different behaviours and statuses?

Genetics-Based Arguments

Advocates of the genetic basis for gender-related differences invoke various arguments to support their contentions. Some find "proof" for inborn differences in religious works such as the Bible or the Quran (Koran)—the sacred text of Islam; various religions see aspects of male dominance as sacred and ordained by God. In science, arguments for genetics as the basis of gender differences have been provided by sociobiologists (Udry 1994) and by ethologists, primatologists who study human beings as an evolved animal species (Tiger 1969; Goldberg 1973). Ethologists such as Tiger, who studied baboons primarily, found males to be dominant and argue that *Homo sapiens* inherited this condition through evolution. Attributing masculine instrumentality and dominance to testosterone, characteristically present at higher levels in males, they hold that the prehistoric male's greater size and musculature let him better perform instrumental tasks, such as hunting and defense. Because these roles were functional to the species, the argument continues, they were the basis of male political and familial controls that became genetically established in humans.

In the 1980s, much of this "baboons-with-briefcases" reasoning (Sperling 1991) was scientifically debunked. Newer data on nonhuman primates have challenged these conclusions as socially constructed myths—as "politics by other means" (Haraway 1989)—or as biased science at best.[1] Although male baboons are dominant and very aggressive, not all monkeys behave that way. Males are much less dominant and aggressive among chimpanzees than among baboons, and the former may be more closely related to humans (McGrew 1981). Female dominance seems typical of lemurs and bonobos; gibbons manifest no sex difference in dominance (Hrdy 1981; Wrangham and Peterson 1996).

Most social scientists refuse to impute animal behaviour to that of humans. Humans share ancestry with the apes, but we did not descend directly from them; the two families have evolved separately for millions of years. Moreover, gender-expected behaviours have "clearly followed no logical pattern based on biological differences. Even though men possessed the requisite skills, for example, they were much less likely than women to bottle-feed babies" (Huber 1989, p. 111). Demographer Richard Udry's theory also relies on differences in male and female levels of testosterone and other hormones and posits a "primate model" for some sex differences in behaviour. But this theory attempts to integrate sociocultural explanations with biological ones, rather than extrapolating directly from animal behaviour to human gender differences.

Society-Based Arguments

Sociologists stress that stratification and the division of labour in society (how necessary tasks are divided by gender, age, and social class) shape gender roles. In addition, cultural ideas enforce gender stratification.

FORAGING AND HOE SOCIETIES In both foraging (hunting and gathering) and hoe societies, food production was relatively compatible with pregnancy, childbirth, and breast-feeding; women thus played an important part. Among foragers, for example, 60 to 80 percent of the food comes from gathering activities, performed predominantly by women, and both sexes may hunt small game (Linton 1971). With women fully participating economically, males are less dominant than in agricultural or industrial societies (Chafetz 1988).

First Nations peoples, members of what were once hunting and gathering and hoe cultures, have a complex heritage that varies by tribe but may include a matrilineal tradition in which women owned, and may still own, houses, tools, and land (Wagner 1990; Weaver 1993). Prior to the colonization of the Americas, women in most Aboriginal societies also enjoyed a large amount of status and power. For example, among the *Haudenosaunee* (Iroquois for "People of the Longhouse") women "occupied prominent positions in all aspects of indigenous life" and the *Kaianerekowa* (Great Law of Peace) "clearly stated that women choose the *Oyaneh* (Clan Mothers), who had a large amount of power in each clan, including the power to remove chiefs, to decide

1. As Cynthia Fuchs Epstein (1988) points out, "biological explanations have been used to support inequality between the sexes, as they have been used to support inequality between the races and other dominant and subordinate groups" (p. 51).

on matters of inter-tribal disputes, and determine distribution of resources" (Sunseri 2000, pp. 145–146). But the political power of indigenous women declined with the spread of Europeans into their territories and the subsequent reorganization of Aboriginal life, including the legal categories imposed by the Government of Canada's Indian Act.

The Indian Act, designed to assimilate Native peoples, was passed in 1868 as an "Act for the gradual civilization of Indian peoples," and defined who could be classified as Indian and to which band they belonged. From 1869 to 1985, the Act required women to follow their husbands into or out of legal status as an "Indian." Native women who married non-natives or non-status Indians lost their treaty and Aboriginal rights and their children were not recognized as Indian. In contrast, native men kept their "Indian" status if they married non-Indians and their wives and children were conferred with this legal status.

In 1973, in the case of A.G. (Can) v Lavell, the Supreme Court of Canada ruled that this statutory rule did not discriminate against women and stated that the 1960 Canadian Bill of Rights did not prohibit this form of racial-sexual discrimination nor invalidate the Indian Act. In 1985, Bill C-31 amended the Indian Act to remove this legal discrimination and bring the Act in line with Canada's Charter of Rights and Freedoms. Bill C-31 allowed women who "married out" (as well as their children) to apply for the restoration of their Indian status and accompanying rights and benefits and "to pass native status on to their children just as men always have" (McNab 1999, p. 1599). However, the resulting increase in the number of individuals entitled to be registered as status Indians under the Indian Act has reportedly "incited resentment and backlash toward these 'Bill C-31s' by First Nations members" (McNab 1999, p. 1599). Moreover, "[w]hile many native women share goals for the advancement of their people, their voices are often ignored by the Aboriginal leadership and male-dominated political organizations" (McNab 1999, p. 1599).

In 1998, for example, there were approximately 82 women chiefs out of 623 First Nations across

Although many Aboriginal women share goals for the advancement of their people, few hold leadership roles within regional and national political organizations. In 1996, Angela Neveau was elected the first female chief in the history of the Batchewana First Nation band of Sault Ste. Marie.

Canada, with the majority of these women elected in Ontario and British Columbia. Although more Aboriginal women currently serve as councillors in First Nations governments, few hold leadership roles within regional and national political organizations.

AGRICULTURAL SOCIETIES Agricultural (agrarian) societies, based on plow cultivation, the domestication of animals, and laying claim to land, developed about 5000 years ago. Plow agriculture requires greater physical strength and full-time labour, conditions less compatible with pregnancy and nursing (Basow 1992, p. 108). Although women continued to contribute significantly to the family economic enterprise (Huber 1986), men may have taken over plow and other heavy work, thereby making women's productive labour less visible. About this time, patriarchy—a societal organization based on the supremacy of fathers and inheritance through the male line—became firmly established. As it became possible to accumulate wealth through large landholdings, concern with property inheritance—and hence with legitimacy of offspring—increased the social control exerted over women, particularly in non-European areas.

INDUSTRIAL SOCIETIES With industrialization, beginning about 200 years ago in Europe, economic production gradually shifted from agriculture to mechanized production of manufactured goods.[2] The status of women declined further as industrialization separated work from home and family life, transferring work traditionally done by women (such as clothing production) from homes to factories. Owners organized factories in such a way that industrial work could not easily be combined with domestic tasks and the supervision of children. Thus, women at home no longer contributed directly to economic production; their indirect contribution to the economy through domestic support and reproduction of the labour force became virtually invisible.

In the middle and upper classes, an ideology of "separate spheres" arose to support this separation of men's and women's roles. Men came to be seen as possessing the instrumental traits referred to earlier, as being more comfortable than women with the competition and harshness of the world outside the home. Middle- and upper-class white women were "angels of the house" whose delicacy and passivity were appropriate to their more sheltered lives.[3] White women's submissiveness and emotional sensitivity, the expressive qualities described earlier, supposedly enabled them both to provide a haven for their wage-earner husbands and to bring up innocent children (Cancian 1987).[4]

These breadwinner and housewife roles applied mainly to middle- and upper-class white men's and women's work—and for only a brief period, from the late nineteenth century to the mid-twentieth century. Most immigrant, visible minority, and working- and lower-class women did not have the housewife option but instead needed employment in domestic service, factories, or in home-based activities such as piece-work performed for money. Nevertheless, although the idealized portrait of men, women, work, and personality is changing, we have retained remnants of it to the present.

We have seen that sociobiologists and ethologists stress genetics, whereas most social scientists stress the importance of society in the formation of gender roles and expectations and stratification. Very probably, biology and society interact to create **gender-linked characteristics and roles**. For example, men's greater average physical strength, a result of higher testosterone levels, may have resulted in force and/or threats of force to effect some degree of male dominance in virtually all societies. But, as we have seen, the various forms of economic organization either mitigated or exaggerated male dominance.

3. According to Winona Stevenson (1999, p. 58):
The European ideal of womanhood was projected on Aboriginal women throughout the colonized world where it functioned as "the single most important criterion for contrasting savagism with civility" (Smith 1982, 298). Victorian morality was the severe standard against which Aboriginal women were judged. They were ultimately found wanting because almost everything about their being—their appearance, their social, economic, political and spiritual positions, activities, and authority—was a violent affront to the European ideal. Compared to European women, Aboriginal women appeared "antithetical to the presumed natural condition of women" (Weist 1983, 39).

4. We should note that some women were able to use the moral authority given to them by a separate spheres ideology to lead anti-slavery and temperance crusades and suffrage movements. During this era some women advocated far more radical changes in society and the family (Rossi 1973).

2. Men who had been peasants, serfs, or slaves became urban wage workers. Men's responses to changed work lives produced the socialist and labour movements of nineteenth-century Europe. Sociologist Joan Huber (1986) labels those movements "men's movements" because, as responses to changed forms of economic participation, they parallel the later women's movements.

CHAPTER 3   Our Gendered Identities

The Interaction of Culture and Biology

Strong support exists for the proposition that gender-linked characteristics result from the interaction of cultural learning and biological hormones.[5] Sex hormones influence sexual dimorphism: sex-related differences in body structure and size, muscle development, fat distribution, hair growth, and voice quality. Male fetuses are exposed to relatively large amounts of testosterone at about mid-pregnancy, resulting in the masculinization of their genitals as well as dimorphic brain structure. Testosterone levels peak in adolescence and early adulthood, then slowly decline throughout the rest of a man's life. Testosterone and other "male hormones" called androgens exist in females as well, although at lower average levels than in males.

Reviewing the literature on the effects of androgen levels in women, demographer Richard Udry (1994) concludes that females exposed to unusually high androgen levels evidence more masculinized behaviour than the average for their sex.[6] Udry's own research suggests that women (and probably men too) differ from one another in their biological propensity to sex-typed behaviour, due to disparate amounts of androgens in their blood, both prenatally and as adults.

Money and Ehrhardt also found evidence for genetic influence. Androgynized females (female infants who had been exposed prenatally to a greater amount of the male sex hormone androgen through drugs taken by the mother) were much more apt than

normal girls to be tomboys. Taller and stronger than average, they were more likely to be athletic, play with boys, assert themselves, compete, and reject feminine adornment. They tended to be uninterested in either dolls or babies. As adult women, they were oriented much more toward careers than marriage. Such masculinization, the researchers concluded, probably results from the action of male sex hormones on the developing fetus.

Udry's research also suggests that, as groups, females and males differ in their average biological propensity (or inclination) to some behaviours. But Udry is quick to point out that biological propensity, or predisposition does *not* mean that a person's behaviour cannot be influenced or changed by social structure. Working together with biology, our culture continues to influence human behaviour (Udry 1994).

Moreover, in Udry's theory, biology does not explain *change* in gender roles. What it does explain are certain cross-cultural regularities in gendered behaviour (greater male aggressiveness, for example), as well as within-sex differences in gendered behaviour. That is, given a certain cultural pattern, variations among individuals within that culture are shaped by the differences in hormonal levels produced by the prenatal environment and adolescent development.

AGGRESSIVENESS Various researchers report findings that testosterone levels correlate positively with tendencies toward physical and verbal aggression, although not necessarily with desire for achievement or competitiveness (Bardwick 1971; Goleman 1990a). About 25 years ago, psychologists Eleanor Maccoby and Carol Jacklin (1974) reviewed all of the research on sex differences through the early 1970s. The only difference between girls and boys that clearly seemed to Maccoby and Jacklin to be biologically based was aggressiveness. The term *aggressiveness* here refers to physical or verbal hostility and attempts to injure another, not simply competitiveness. Researchers continue to find sex differences in aggression, which may or may not be biologically based (Maccoby 1990; Feingold 1994; Eagly 1995; Hyde and Plant 1995).

More recent studies have investigated the relationship between testosterone levels (often determined from saliva samples) and gender-related behaviours. In one study (Baucom and Besch 1985), 84 female

---

5. **Hormones** are chemical substances secreted into the bloodstream by the endocrine glands; they influence the activities of cells, tissues, and body organs. Sex hormones are secreted by male or female gonads, or sex glands. The primary male sex hormones are androgens. Testosterone, produced in the male testes, is an androgen. Female secrete testosterone also, but in smaller amounts. The primary female hormones are estrogen and progesterone, secreted by the female ovaries.

6. Early research in this regard is that of John Money and Anke Ehrhardt. Money and Ehrhardt (1974) studied **hermaphrodites**, people whose genitalia cannot be clearly identified at birth as either female or male. Their research supported arguments for both socialization and genetics as influences on behaviour. For the argument for socialization, Money and Ehrhardt found that the most crucial factor in these infants' ultimate self-perception as girls or boys, and later as women or men, was their assignment (at birth or shortly after, hermaphrodites are often arbitrarily assigned a sex identity and are then treated accordingly). While this finding is now disputed, Money and Ehrhardt concluded that hermaphrodites assigned *male* grow up to think and behave as men, whereas those assigned *female* grow up to think and behave as women.

students completed masculinity and femininity scales (questionnaires identifying one's personality traits as either mainly instrumental or mainly expressive). The researchers found that women with "the stereotypic feminine personality" had relatively low levels of testosterone and that those with more stereotypically masculine traits had somewhat higher levels. Other research among males (Booth and Dabbs 1993) suggests that those with more testosterone may be less likely to marry and more likely to divorce. When married, they may experience a lower quality of spousal interaction, are more likely to report hitting or throwing things at their wives, and may be more likely to have extramarital sex.

But what's happening in one's environment can influence hormone secretion levels. For example, hormone levels regulating a new mother's ability to produce milk are influenced by her culturally learned attitudes toward nursing (Bardwick 1971, p. 80). Similarly, when a husband batters his wife—at least partly because he lives in a society and a culture that condone violence—the action may stimulate increased secretions of testosterone (which may in turn result in a greater tendency to act aggressively in the future). We might conclude that even though evidence for an intrinsic sex difference in aggressiveness continues to build, society and socialization still play a significant—if not a major—role.

VERBAL AND SPATIAL SKILLS Many researchers have found girls to be better at verbal skills (Crawford 1995) and boys to be better at math and visual–spatial tasks (Hedges and Nowell 1995; Signorella and Jamison 1986). The suggestion associated with such findings is that these differences are genetic. Today some research on brain lateralization supports that conclusion (for example, see Gorman 1992; Kimura 1992; Wade 1994; Shaywitz 1995). Brain lateralization refers to the relative dominance and the synchronization of the two hemispheres of the brain. Some scientists have argued that male and female brains differ due to greater amounts of testosterone secreted by a male fetus. Different sides of the brain may be dominant in males and females, or males and females may differ in the degree to which the two brain halves work together (Moir and Jessel 1991; Springer and Deutsch 1994). Overall, however, lateralization studies have produced conflicting evidence concerning sex differences or their connection to various cognitive activities such as verbal tasks or spatial relations (see, for example, Ankney 1995; Richardson 1997).

Moreover, girls' consistently observed disadvantage in math is arguably a consequence of social expectations and opportunities (Marecek 1995). Test scores in this and other areas appear to be converging. An analysis of research done through 1988 found girls and boys to be equivalent in mathematical ability, with comparable performance through middle school. Although boys performed better in high school and university, this difference was limited to the university-bound population rather than all high school students, and it has declined over the years (Hyde, Fennema, and Lamon 1990).

These facts point to what sociologist Alice Rossi (1984) has called the interactive influence of both "nature" (genetics) and "nurture" (learning) on sex-linked attitudes and behaviours. In Rossi's words,

> It makes no sense to view biology and social experience as separate domains contesting for election as "primary causes." Biological processes unfold in a cultural context, and are themselves malleable, not stable and inevitable. So too, cultural processes take place within and through the biological organism; they do not take place in a biological vacuum. (p. 10)

Beginning at birth, however, and throughout their lives, males and females learn and negotiate sex-appropriate attitudes and behaviour (Brannon 1995; Buss and Kendrick 1998). It's important to recognize that cultural learning can either exaggerate (as seems to be the case in our society) or minimize whatever genetic tendencies exist (Kagan 1994; Wright 1998).

GENDER AND SOCIALIZATION

Societal attitudes influence how we behave. As people in a given society learn to talk, think, and feel, they internalize cultural attitudes; that is, they make the attitudes their own. Besides attitudes, people internalize cultural expectations about how to behave. The process by which society influences members to internalize attitudes and expectations is called **socialization**. The socialization process is an important concept in the interactional theoretical perspective (Chapter 1). Interactionists point out that individuals do not automatically absorb, but rather negotiate, cultural attitudes and roles.

Therefore, gender identity varies from individual to individual. Nevertheless, in various ways society encourages people to adhere, often unconsciously, to culturally acceptable gender roles. We'll examine in detail how language, family, and school function in gender socialization.

The Power of Cultural Images

Our cultural images in language and in the media convey the gendered expectations described earlier in this chapter. You are no doubt aware of the many—and sometimes controversial—efforts to make our language less gender-oriented over the past two decades. A recent edition of *Webster's College Dictionary*, for example, defines new words such as "waitron" (gender-neutral for waiter) and "womyn," meant to avoid the perception of sexism in the word *men*. But our language also continues to accentuate male–female differences rather than similarities (Adams and Ware 1995). Soon after birth, most infants receive either a masculine or a feminine name. From that day on, gender identity is stamped on the individual so thoroughly that people who want to avoid gender identification (for instance, through the mail, e-mail or in phone-book listings) must replace their first names with initials.

Besides first names, titles, adjectives, nouns, and verbs remind people that males and females differ—and in stereotypic ways. A new mother may be told that she has either a "*lovely* girl" or a "*sturdy* boy." In her book about the differences in masculine and feminine communication styles, linguist Deborah Tannen writes:

> If I wrote, "After delivering the acceptance speech, the candidate fainted," you would know I was talking about a woman. Men do not faint; they pass out. And these terms have vastly different connotations that both reflect and affect our images of women and men. Fainting conjures up a frail figure crumpling into [rescuing arms].... Passing out suggests a straightforward fall to the floor. (Tannen 1990, pp. 241–42)

The media promote gender stereotypes as well. Children's programming more often depicts boys than girls in dominant, agentic roles. Beginning in 1991, all Saturday morning children's programs deliberately began to feature dominant males as lead characters (Carter 1991). This was a deliberate marketing decision by television executives based on the finding that girls will watch shows with either male or female lead characters, but boys will watch only shows with male leads. On music videos such as those on MuchMusic, females are likely to be shown trying to get a man's attention. Some videos contain violent misogynist (hatred of women) messages.

Television sitcoms convey "mixed messages about being feminist yet feminine" (Douglas 1995, p. 79). In TV commercials, men predominate by about nine to one as the authoritative narrators or voice-overs, even when the products are aimed at women. Daytime ads, targeted for women, portray men in family and/or dominant roles, but weekend ads, aimed more toward men, emphasize male escape from home and family (Craig 1992; Kilbourne 1994).

Cultural images in the media and language help to socialize individuals to expected gender attitudes and roles. They do so by portraying what is "normal" and by influencing socializing agents, such as our parents, peers, and teachers. We turn now to a brief examination of socialization theories.

Theories of Socialization

How do cultural ideas about gender get incorporated into personality and behaviour? We don't have a definitive answer to that question. There are a number of competing theories of gender socialization, each with some supporting evidence.

SOCIAL LEARNING THEORY Much of what we have just described fits a **social learning theory** in which children learn gender roles as they are taught by parents, schools, and the media. In general, children imitate models for behaviour and are rewarded by parents and others for whatever is perceived as sex-appropriate behaviour.

As children grow older, toys, talk of future careers or marriages, and admonitions about "sissies" and "tomboys" communicate parents' ideas about appropriate behaviour for boys and girls. The rewards and punishments, however subtle, that parents assign to gender roles are sometimes seen to be the key to behaviour patterns. Other theorists emphasize the significance of parents as models of masculine and feminine behaviour, although researchers have found little association between children's personalities and parents' characteristics. Fathers seem to have stronger expectations for gender-appropriate behaviour than mothers (Fivush 1999; Losh-Hesselbart 1987; Andersen 1988).

SELF-IDENTIFICATION THEORY Some psychologists think that what comes first is not rules about what boys and girls should do but rather the child's awareness of being a boy or a girl. In this **self-identification theory**, at least by age three, children categorize themselves. They then identify behaviours in their families, in the media, or elsewhere appropriate to their sex, and they adopt those behaviours. In effect, children socialize themselves from available cultural materials. This perspective, developed by psychologist Lawrence Kohlberg (1966), can account for the fact that boys without a father in the home may be just as masculine as boys in intact families (Vander Zanden 1981; Anderson 1988).

GENDER SCHEMA THEORY Somewhat similar to self-identification theory, gender schema theory posits that children develop a framework of knowledge (a **gender schema**) about what girls and boys typically do (Bem 1981). Children then use this framework to organize how they interpret new information and think about gender. Young children internalize information relevant to their gender schema and build their own gender roles accordingly. Once a child has developed a gender schema, the schema influences how she or he processes new information, with gender-consistent information remembered better than gender-inconsistent information. For example, a child with a traditional gender schema would be more likely to remember seeing a female baking cookies than one chopping wood. As another example, a child with traditional gender schema might remember her or his pediatrician as a man even though the doctor was actually a woman. Overall, gender schema theorists see gender schema as maintaining traditional stereotypes.

CHODOROW'S THEORY OF GENDER Sociologist Nancy Chodorow (1978) has constructed a theory of gender that combines psychoanalytic ideas about identification of children with parents with an awareness of what those parents' social roles are in our society.

According to **Chodorow's theory of gender**, infants develop a "primary identification" with the person primarily responsible for their early care. Later, as young children, they must distinguish between "self" and "other." Put another way, developing children must learn to differentiate psychologically and emotionally between themselves and their primary caregiver.

Cross-culturally and historically, children's primary caregivers are virtually always female. Both daughters and sons make their primary identification with a female; as a result, the task of separation is more difficult for a boy. Because a daughter is developing a gender identity similar to her principal caregiver's (that is, an identity similar to her mother's), she can readily model her mother's behaviour. And her feeling of oneness with her caregiver is not sexually threatening. But a boy cannot model his mother's behaviour and also develop a culturally consistent gender identity. He learns instead that he is "not female." Also, he must suppress "feelings of overwhelming love, attachment, and dependence on his mother that are charged by the sexual current between mother and son" (Thurman 1982, p. 35). The stress of separation is heightened for boys in cultures such as ours where open grieving is discouraged as inappropriate for males (Pollack 1998; Kantrowitz and Kalb 1998).

Chodorow attributes commonly held beliefs about the differences between men and women to this divergence in the early socialization experiences of boys and girls. Boys are disappointed and angry at the necessary but abrupt and emotionally charged detachment from their mother. Gradually, however, they come to value their relatively absent fathers as models of agency, independence, and "the superiority of masculine… prerogatives" (Thurman 1982, p. 35). Conversely, "relatedness" or expressiveness is allowed and fostered among girls.

As with other theories we are discussing, research does not always support Chodorow. Because gender socialization theories are abstracted from empirical observations, each seems plausible. We'll turn now to some empirical findings regarding gender socialization.

Girls and Boys in the Family

Most studies on gender socialization beliefs and practices have been conducted on white families. One study of black families indicated that both sons and daughters are socialized toward independence, employment, and child care (Hale-Benson 1986). Still, because most of the research presented in this section has focused on middle-class whites, findings may or may not apply to other racial/ethnic or class categories.

At least among middle-class whites, parents rear female and male infants differently. From the 1970s on, parents have reported treating their sons and daughters similarly (Maccoby and Jacklin 1974; Antill 1987), but differential socialization exists and typically is subtle and not deliberate (Shapiro 1990). Even parents who support nonsexist child rearing for their daughters are often concerned if their sons are not aggressive or competitive "enough"—or are "too" sensitive (Pleck 1992).

Research shows that parents handle infant sons more roughly and respond more quickly to crying baby girls (Lips 1995). As a toddler, Patricia will probably have a doll; Patrick, a truck. A study of 120 babies', and toddlers' rooms found that girls had more dolls, fictional characters, children's furniture, and the colour pink; boys had more sports equipment, tools, toy vehicles, and the colours blue, red, and white (Pomerleau et al. 1990). The majority of parents, especially fathers, discourage their children, especially sons, from playing with other-sex toys (Lytton and Romney 1991).

Boys have toys that develop spatial ability and creative construction; girls have toys that encourage social skills (Hughes 1994; Leaper 1994; Lips 1995). Toys considered appropriate for boys encourage physical activity and independent play, whereas "girls' toys" elicit closer physical proximity and more talk between child and caregiver (Etaugh and Liss 1992; Martin et al 1995; McAninch et al 1996). As children get older, Patrick is more likely to have computer software designed to appeal to him than is Patricia (Breidenbach 1997; Tanaka 1996). *Game Boy* wasn't given this name for nothing; 92 percent of video games have no female characters (O'Neal 1998).

Beginning when children are about five and increasing through adolescence, parents allocate household chores—both the amounts and kinds—to their children differentially, that is, according to their sex. Patricia will more likely be assigned indoor cooking and laundry tasks; Patrick, outdoor activites such as painting and mowing (Burns and Homel 1989; McHale et al. 1990).[7] Because typically girls' chores are daily and boys' sporadic, girls spend more time doing them—a fact that "may convey a message about male privilege" (Basow 1992, p. 131). Some parents unconsciously allow (even expect) sons to be inconsiderate, rude, and interrupting while their sisters are reminded to be a little quieter and less argumentative (Orenstein 1994, pp. 46–47).

Parents also model different behaviours. As Chodorow notes, most children are cared for by mothers primarily. This situation may convey to children the idea that child care (and nurturance in general) is "women's work." Meanwhile, fathers may appear to be involved with "more important" and prestigious things (Burns and Homel 1989).

Gender socialization in early childhood begins a continuing process whereby females and males are channeled into different spheres of skills and interests (Nelson and Robinson 2002). This situation is changing for girls because they increasingly are allowed or encouraged to develop instrumental attitudes and skills. Boys, meanwhile, are still discouraged from developing attitudes and skills of tenderness or nurturance (Kindlon and Thompson 1998; Pollack 1998). Although relations in the family provide early feedback and help shape a child's developing identity, play and peer groups become important as children try out identities and adult behaviours. We turn our attention now to research on differences in boys' and girls' play.

7. The number of girls and boys in a family apparently influences how chores are distributed. Families with all girls, for example, more readily assign traditional male-child tasks to girls than do families with at least one boy. And the age and gender of siblings are important. Research has also found that when an older sibling is of the same sex, play activities tend to be gender-stereotyped; if the older sibling is of the other sex, cross-sex play is common (Brody and Steelman 1985).

Play and Games

Girls play in one-to-one relationships or small groups of twosomes and threesomes; their play[8] is relatively cooperative, emphasizes turn taking, requires little competition, and has relatively few rules. In "feminine" games like jump rope or hopscotch, the goal is skill rather than winning (Basow 1992). Boys more often play in fairly large groups, characterized by more fighting and attempts to effect a hierarchical pecking order. From preschool through adolescence, children who play according to traditional gender roles are more popular with their peers; this is more true for boys (Martin 1989). Sex segregation at play and leisure begins in preschool and intensifies in elementary school. When boys and girls do interact on school playgrounds, their games (for example, "girls chase the boys" or "chase and kiss") emphasize the differences and cultural boundaries between them (Thorne 1992).

Furthermore, from about second grade, boys' play begins to incorporate the cultural message, "no sissy stuff"—as in "girls have cooties." "In societies where men's higher status is obvious and differential treatment of male and female children pronounced, boys' struggle to disassociate themselves from females is particularly strong" (Whiting and Edwards 1988, p. 12). The tendency to degrade whatever is feminine increases into adolescence—and for some males, into adulthood—when males are expected to put "the guys" first in their priorities. Peer status for adolescent girls, in contrast, more often rests on being popular

with boys (Basow 1992, p. 139). These differences in childhood play and games work to teach boys and girls divergent attitudes, skills, and gendered identities. The process is reinforced in schools.

Socialization in Schools

School organization, classroom teachers, and textbooks all convey the message that boys are more important than girls. Indeed, there is considerable evidence that the way girls and boys are treated differentially in school is detrimental to both genders (AAUW 1998; Gurian 1996; Hoff Sommers 2000; Kindlon and Thompson 1998; Pollack 1998). Let's consider each element of the educational system in turn.

SCHOOL ORGANIZATION   Although the composition of Canada's student population is becoming increasingly multicultural, this is less true of Canada's teachers. According to the Canadian Council of Social Development (1999), "[r]esearch suggests that teachers will continue to be mainly white, middle-aged women." In 1996, women outnumbered men in elementary and kindergarten teaching positions by approximately four to one.[9]

The predominance of women at the kindergarten and elementary school levels may refurbish notions that caring for young children is "women's work." With men in positions of authority (coordinators, principals, superintendents) and women in positions of service (teacher's aides, secretaries), school organization itself models male dominance.

TEACHERS   Research shows that, at least among white children, teachers pay more attention to males than to females, and males tend to dominate classroom environments from nursery school through university (Lips 1999). Compared to girls, boys are

---

8. The role of play is an important concept in the interactionist perspective, particularly symbolic interactionist theory, developed by philosopher/social psychologist George Herbert Mead (1934). This theory argues that gender identity, like other aspects of self-identity, is developed by and anchored in social relations. One's self-concept, including one's sense of masculinity and femininity and adult gender roles, depends on the responses of significant others (emotionally important people such as parents). A boy or a girl begins to see himself or herself as competent or as delicate and nurturing, depending on the comments of parents and others.

Those others may be other children at play. Play, in Mead's theory, is not idle time but rather a significant vehicle through which children develop appropriate conceptions of adult roles, as well as images of themselves. His theory distinguishes two stages: "play," one-to-one role playing, and "game," in which children must take multiple positions and roles into account, as in a baseball game with two teams and many positions. (A third stage is that of the "generalized other," in which the norms of the society as a whole are taken into account.)

9. While women were approximately equal in number to male teachers at the postsecondary level, they were outnumbered by men as university professors by about two to one (Statistics Canada 1998). In 1998/99, women made up 13.7 percent of Full Professors (the highest rank) and 29.1 percent of Associate Professors in Canada. Women's higher concentration in the lower ranks was reflected in their lower average salaries. In that year, the average salary of women faculty was 85.7 percent of men (Statistics Canada 2001).

more likely to receive a teacher's attention, to call out in class, to demand help or attention from the teacher, to be seen as a model student, or to be praised by teachers. Boys are also more likely to be disciplined harshly by teachers (Gurian 1996; Kindlon and Thompson 1998; Pollack 1998).

Researchers who observed more than 100 fourth-, sixth-, and eighth-grade classes over a three-year period found that boys consistently and clearly dominated classrooms. Teachers called on and encouraged boys more often than they did girls. If a girl gave an incorrect answer, the teacher was likely to call on another student; but if a boy was incorrect, the teacher was more likely to encourage him to learn by helping him discover his error and correct it (Sadker and Sadker 1994).[10] Psychologist Hilary Lips observes, "teachers seem to be guided by the idea that boys do not work hard enough, but that girls (always such well-behaved, good little workers) are already doing their best" (1999, p. 113).

In subtle ways teachers may reinforce the idea that males and females are more different than similar. There are times when boys and girls interact together relatively comfortably—in the school band, for example. But especially in elementary schools, many cross-sexual interaction rituals are based on and reaffirm boundaries and differences between girls and boys. Sociologist Barrie Thorne (1992) calls these rituals **borderwork**. Between 1976 and 1981, Thorne spent 11 months doing naturalistic or participant observation (see Chapter 2) in two elementary schools. She found several types of borderwork both on playgrounds (for example, "boys chase the girls") and in the classroom. In classrooms, for instance, teachers often pitted girls and boys against each other in spelling bees or math contests. On one occasion, the teacher wrote two scorekeeping columns on the board: "Beastly Boys" and "Gossipy Girls." In thinking about this research, remember that Thorne's participant observation was done over two decades ago. It would be interesting to research the number of teachers who use designations like those today. However, it seems likely that borderwork still persists in schools.

10. For a critique of this research and its conclusions see Hoff Summers 2000.

WOMEN IN COLLEGE AND UNIVERSITY   In Canada, the proportionate number of women enrolled full-time at universities has increased noticeably over the past decades. In 1964–65 less than one-third (31 percent) of full-time undergraduates were women; in 1994–95 women accounted for 54 percent of full-time university undergraduates and 53 percent of full-time college students (Normand 1995; Statistics Canada 1998). While some traditionally male-dominated fields are no longer male-dominated (e.g., in 1994–95, 70 percent of the students in veterinary medicine were women and equal numbers of men and women were studying medicine), women's participation levels in mathematics, engineering, and the physical and applied sciences remain relatively low. For example, in 1994–95, male computer science students outnumbered women by more than four to one at Canadian universities, and only one in five full-time undergraduate engineering students was a woman (Statistics Canada 1999a, pp. 157–8). In addition, while women's proportional participation remains constant at the master's degree level, the proportion drops noticeably in most fields of study at the doctoral level with the exception of the social sciences. It is only within the traditionally female-dominated field of education that women constitute the majority of doctoral students.

Of all full-time enrolments at Canadian community colleges, women constitute the primary student component in programs such as secretarial services (96 percent), educational and counselling services (90 percent), and nursing (89 percent). Women remain underrepresented in programs related to the natural sciences (32 percent), mathematics and computing sciences (30 percent), and engineering and related technologies (12 percent) (Normand 1995).

Although women now account for over half of the full-time community college and university undergraduate enrolment in Canada, this does not necessarily mean that women have assumed equality on campus. For instance, with the exception of women's studies, females are relatively absent from college and university texts (Peterson and Kroner 1992). Furthermore, even though women faculty members serve as role models for female students, in certain fields such as physics or engineering, women faculty are relatively rare. Aboriginal and visible minority women have even fewer available role models and may confront both racism and sexism at predominantly white colleges and universities (Guy-Sheftall and Bell-Scott 1989; Nieves-Squires 1991). Men's harassment of campus women is also fairly common (Alvi et al. 1999; McDaniel and Roosmalen 1992; Paludi 1990). Some of the unwanted sexual attention comes from male faculty members, but other sources of this problem exist as well. Sexual harassment and sexual assault on campus may be associated with both fraternity and sorority membership (Copenhaver and Grauerholz 1991). Among male students, attitudes of dominance are associated with fraternity membership (Kalof and Cargill 1991).

Biology and socialization interact throughout infancy, childhood, and adolescence to produce the adult women and men we see around us. But socialization continues throughout adulthood as we negotiate and learn new roles—or as those already learned are renegotiated and sometimes, though assuredly not always, reinforced. The varied opportunities we encounter as adults influence the adult roles we play. In the next section we examine various aspects of gender in adults' lives today.

GENDER IN ADULT LIVES

Old patterns can be difficult to alter. This is true for women and men, both of whom may be torn between what they have learned to value from the past and newer ideas. But new roles promise some rewards.

Gender and Stress

Traditional gender roles result in some characteristic stresses. Oriented to others at the expense of self, many women have felt depressed, bored, empty, dissatisfied with life, inadequate, and excessively guilty. Suicide attempts are more common among women than men (although men are more likely to succeed in suicide efforts and therefore have a higher suicide rate). Women also experience higher rates of mental illness and eating disorders and are particularly prone to depression (Bower 1995; Health Canada 1999). Traditional sex roles are hazardous to women's health.

Traditional gender expectations are hazardous to men as well. Overemphasis on productivity, competition, and achievement creates anxiety or emotional stress, which may contribute to men's shorter life expectancy. Undue, physically dangerous behaviour and violence shorten men's lives as well.

The masculine role not only requires that men experience pressure to "prove it" but also encourages them to discount or ignore their anxiety and physical symptoms of stress. Men also learn to hide emotions of vulnerability, tenderness, and warmth when they are in public. When hiding tender feelings, men cannot share their inner selves, a situation that can lead to hidden depression, which, in turn, can be acted out with violence (Real 1997). Following traditional gender role expectations, men may block avenues to intimacy, isolating themselves. Meanwhile, psychological and other research tells us that both agency (instrumental roles) and communion (expressive roles) are required for optimum well-being (Helgeson 1994).

Gender and Personal Change

Sometimes in response to these stresses—and also in response to available options—adults reconsider earlier choices regarding gender roles. For example, a small proportion of men choose to be full-time fathers and/or househusbands. More may effect more subtle changes, such as breaking through previously learned isolating habits to form more intimate friendships.

That choices in adult development and social roles are contingent on opportunity and, to some degree, chance, is illustrated by Kathleen Gerson's research on women's and men's role choices. Gerson (1985) studied 63 women who were between ages 27 and 37 when interviewed in 1978–79. Extensive and repeated interviews enabled Gerson to construct life histories and to trace gender-related decisions made in adulthood, particularly decisions about work and motherhood.

The women fell into four groups: Two groups of women made role choices early in life and held to them. The other two groups are more interesting for our purposes here. These women had entered young adulthood with clear expectations for their lives. One set planned a rather conventional marriage and family; work would be an interim activity. The other group gave high priority to careers, regardless of any hopes for marriage and children.

But their lives turned out to be quite different from their expectations. Sometimes women who had planned careers met obstacles, often overt or covert discrimination. They became dissatisfied and pessimistic about their chances of realizing their original goals. Or they fell into very satisfying relationships and may also have found children more enjoyable than they had expected. These circumstances combined to channel their movements into a more traditional family lifestyle. Here is one example:

Vicki was never especially oriented toward motherhood. Instead, since she was old enough to know who the police were, she wanted to be a policewoman.... Forced to take the best job she could find after high school, Vicki became a secretary-clerk. She also took the qualifying exam for police work and passed with high marks. No jobs were available, however.... In the meantime, she met and married Joe.

... She ultimately grew to hate working, for it usually involved taking orders from bosses she did not respect.... After the birth of her first child, Vicki discovered that staying at home to rear a child was more important than her succession of boring, deadend jobs. By her mid-thirties, she was a full-time mother of two. Today she has given up hope of becoming a policewoman, but in return for this sacrifice she feels she has gained the secure home life she never knew as a child. (Gerson 1985, pp. 18–19)

Vicki's story illustrates a point we made earlier: Individuals can choose only options that are available in their society. At the time Vicki sought a job as a police officer, probably few women were being hired, so she was not able to have the career she wanted. Other women may have been discouraged from working by the lack of child care or inadequate maternity or parental leave policies. In recent years, women have been hired as policewomen in growing numbers, partly as a consequence of the 1986 proclamation of the Employment Equity Act in Canada; this change indicates that it is possible to create wanted options through changes in public policy (Nelson 1993). Making choices about family life may include political activity directed toward creating those choices.

Some of the women in Gerson's study who planned to marry and start families did not develop permanent relationships or were unable to have children. Women also chanced into career opportunities, particularly as women began to be included in formerly male-dominated positions. Other women found themselves very involved in their careers and perhaps not married or not wanting to become a parent.

Several years later, Gerson (1993) turned her attention to men's changing lives. She interviewed 138 men, mostly in their 30s, and found that, like women, they were reexamining choices made when they were younger. Subsequent changes often involved the family roles they played, a point we will return to throughout this text. But some of these men had also changed their attitudes toward masculinity in general. In one example, Carlos, a social worker, recalled his earlier days:

When I was in high school, I was more of a traditional Hispanic male—sort of macho. At least, I was playing with that idea. A relationship started that was more of a traditional relationship. I expected that person to give to me more than I gave them. It was almost like a fetch-me type of relationship. I think if we had lived together, she would have cooked, cleaned the house, raised the kids.

A growing sense of discomfort led Carlos to later reject this cultural message:

I felt that I wouldn't want to be treated that way, and I shouldn't treat someone else that way. I saw there could be an abuse of the traditional male role, and also I saw limitations in that type of relationship. The woman is limited within the family, and the man gets locked into an image I didn't enjoy. At that point, I pretty much decided that the type of person I wanted to be did not match with the traditional Hispanic role model. (Gerson 1993, p. 159)

The import of Gerson's two studies for our understanding of change over the course of life is that childhood socialization and early goals do not necessarily predict adult lifestyles. The adult life course is determined by the interaction of the individual's goals, values, abilities, and motivation with the opportunities that present themselves. Throughout adulthood, individuals made a series of choices about their lives, and different individuals respond differently to those options that are the product of a particular time. The development of adult life is a process of ongoing decision and choice, early choices shaping later ones, within the possibilities of a particular historical time.

Both men and women may rethink gender roles in adulthood. Today that rethinking takes place in a society changed considerably by the women's movement.

Options and the Women's Movement

The first wave of the women's movement in Canada occurred from about the nineteenth century until about the 1920s. Arguably the most prominent public achievements of this movement in Canada were the right to vote and the right (granted in 1929) to be considered persons, and not chattels, under Canadian law. Women over the age of 21 were granted the right to vote in provincial elections in 1916 in Alberta, Manitoba and Saskatchewan; in 1917 in British Columbia and Ontario; in 1918 in Nova Scotia; in 1919 in New Brunswick; in 1922 in Prince Edward Island; in 1925 in Newfoundland (initially only for free women over the age of 25); and in 1940 in Quebec (Whitla 1995, pp. 320–332). These rights were first granted to white women; women from certain other ethnic groups did not receive the franchise until later years.

The separate spheres ideology of gender retained its power into the fifties and early sixties, as media glorification of housewife and breadwinner roles made them seem natural despite the reality of increased women's employment. But contradictions between what women were actually doing and the roles prescribed for them became increasingly apparent. As women pursued higher education, they often perceived a significant gap between their abilities and the housewife role assigned to them (Friedan 1963; Huber 1973). Employed women chafed at the unequal pay and working conditions in which they laboured and began to think that their interest lay in increasing equal opportunity. Economic change precipitated a social movement, the second wave of the women's movement, which challenged the heretofore accepted traditional roles in favour of increasing gender equality.

Women vary in their attitudes toward the women's movement (Buschman and Lenart 1996; Myaskovsky and Wittig 1997; Twenge and Zucker 1999; Williams and Wittig 1997). Some women deplore the rise of feminism and encourage traditional marriage and motherhood as the best path to females' self-fulfillment (Marshall 1995; Enda 1998). Others view the contemporary feminist movement as a white middle-class creation, with origins in the historical experience of educated upper middle-class homemakers (Friedan 1963) and New Left activists. Some women of colour and white working-class women find the women's movement irrelevant to the extent that it focuses on psychological oppression or on professional women's opportunities. Working-class women have always laboured in the productive economy under duress or out of financial necessity and did not experience the enforced delicacy of women in the Victorian period. Nor were they ever housewives, so much of the feminist critique of that role seems irrelevant to them (Terrelong 1995; Hunter and Sellers 1998).

It has also been acknowledged that the second wave of the women's movement did not always nor consistently champion the needs of all Canadian women equally. For example, women with disabilities often found their needs excluded or marginalized (Driedger 1993). It has also been noted that even though women's organizations "provided some support,...[t]he activist work of Native women to change section 12(b) of the Indian Act, and its denial of treaty rights to Native women who married non-Native men...[was a] battle fought almost entirely by Native women" (Wine and Ristock 1991, p. 13). As Barbara Cassidy, Robina Lord and Nancy Mandell (1998, p. 26) point out in their discussion of "silenced and forgotten women"—First Nations women, black women, immigrant women, women with disabilities, and poor women—it is only recently that the second wave of the women's movement "has finally begun to address criticisms that white, middle-class feminists have denied, dismissed, and denigrated the experiences of differently raced, abled, and classed women." Box 3.1 discusses Aboriginal women and feminism.

Despite its deficiencies, the women's movement has caused changes in society and, consequently, in people's options and decisions. Nevertheless, against a backdrop of highly publicized expanding options for women over the past two decades, both men and women who choose nontraditional roles can still experience discrimination and negative sanctioning. Men, for example, often face prejudice when they take jobs traditionally considered women's, such as day-care workers. Because the pay and prestige are so low, people assume male day-care workers might be child molesters (Campbell 1991). In professions that are traditionally men's, such as politics, the military (Gleick 1996; Thomas and Vistica 1997), police work, law, and medicine, men may harass women who challenge boundaries.

Some research suggests that the number of incidents of sexual harassment is inversely proportional to the number of women in an occupational category (Fitzgerald and Shullman 1993). For example, female doctors (Schneider and Phillips 1997) and lawyers (Rosenberg et al. 1997) report high rates of sexual harassment, in the first case by male patients and in the second by male colleagues. Sexual harassment may result in feelings of isolation and estrangement from one's colleagues (*The Chilly Collective* 1995). Feeling "unwelcome" in one's chosen profession may also cause individuals "to doubt their own abilities and effectiveness" (Hayes, 1991b).

Negative sanctions (punishments for breaking norms) can also effectively close off opportunities. For example, Sheila McIntyre has chronicled the "patterns of stereotyping, sexualization, overt harassment, exclusion, and devaluation" (*The Chilly Collective*, 1995 p. 1) she experienced during her first year of teaching law at Queen's University. When she attempted to use gender neutral language in the classroom, she was accused of "shoving my politics down students' throats"; she was also informed by the student president that he and others "knew" that she had only been hired because the hiring process was "stacked" by a "feminist conspiracy." Her name and image showed up in pornography on the walls of the men students' bathrooms where she was depicted as the "wife" of another female professor and described with captions such as "Sheila McIntyre sucks clits and tits" (p. 233). When she reported being berated and insulted by a male colleague, she was treated as an "over-reacting female." She observes,

Perhaps nothing can ensure it stops, but at least we could name this pattern of conduct for what it is—bullying, rank-pulling, cowardly abuse of hier-

archy, and intimidation—and take an institutional and public stand that such conduct is unacceptable. (p. 237)

We caution our readers against inferring that sexual harassment and "gender insensitivity" only occur in settings in which men and women pursue nontraditional work roles. For example, in 1996, a woman who had come to Canada from the Philippines to work as a live-in nanny for a B.C. couple, looking after their one-year daughter, became the first foreign domestic worker in Canada to successfully bring forward a complaint of sexual harassment in the home and receive damages. In this case, incidents of sexual harassment began approximately two months after the nanny began working for the couple. "[The husband] made suggestive remarks to the complainant when she dressed up for church, touched her knees, suggested that she work as a prostitute, pulled her bra strap, referred to his past sexual experiences and fondled himself in the bedroom in her presence" (Daisley 1996, p. 21). Although the woman repeatedly told the husband that his "suggestive comments and sexual advances were unwelcome," she initially feared that filing a complaint of sexual harassment would affect her immigration status. Immigration regulations allowing domestic workers into Canada stipulates that they work as nannies and live in the home of their employer. Should they wish to obtain landed immigration status, they must work for two years as a live-in domestic worker.

In awarding the woman $8000 in damages, the B.C. Council of Human Rights noted that the conduct of the husband had "interfered with the complainant's work performance and created an intimidating, hostile, and offensive working environment contrary to [the *Human Rights Act*]...The complainant was effectively forced to terminate her employment because [the man's] unwelcome conduct was so intolerable" (in Daisley 1996, p. 21).

Some observers point to a backlash against women's continuing gains in self-awareness and political and economic power (Faludi 1991). Talk shows rant about "feminazis," for example, and conservative women and men argue now that "noisy feminists" are ill-informed because today's "women have all the rights as men have" (Schlafly, in Enda, 1998, p. 4A). Meanwhile, feminist scholars, such as Kimberly Christensen, urge men to:

listen carefully to the diverse experiences and writings of feminists—and to take our words seriously. Taking our words seriously would mean acting to change the material reality of women's lives: fighting to increase funding for battered women's shelters, working to eliminate sexual harassment by their colleagues, fighting to make true reproductive freedom available to all women, doing their fair share of the housework and child care in heterosexual relationships.... I want men to read and listen to feminist analyses of why and how women are oppressed and to use their very real gender power to help change the material reality of our oppression. (1997, p. 620)

The Men's Movement

As the women's movement encouraged changes in gendered cultural expectations and social organization, some men responded by initiating the men's movement. The focus of the men's movement is on changes men want in their lives and how best to get them. One goal has been to give men a forum—in consciousness-raising groups, in men's studies courses, and, increasingly, on the Internet—in which to air their feelings about gender.

Kimmel (1995) divides today's men's movement into three fairly distinct camps: antifeminists, profeminists, and masculinists. *Antifeminists* believe the women's movement has caused the collapse of the natural order that guaranteed male dominance, and they work to reverse this trend. Some antifeminists' responses emphasize men's rights, especially fathers' rights, and no guilt in relationships with women. According to Mark Kann, men's self-interest may reasonably lead to an antifeminist response:

I would suggest as a rule of thumb that men's immediate self-interest rarely coincides with feminist opposition to patriarchy. Consider that men need money and leisure to carry out their experiments in self-fulfillment. Is it not in their immediate interest to monopolize the few jobs that promise affluence and autonomy by continuing to deny women equal access to them? Further, men need social space or freedom from constraints for their experiments. Why should they commit themselves to those aspects of feminism that reduce men's social space? It is one thing to try out the joys of parenting, for example, but quite another to assume sacrificial responsibility for the pains of parenting. Is it not in men's immediate self-interest to strengthen the cultural presumption that women are the prime parents and thus the ones who must diaper, chauffeur, tend middle-of-the-night illnesses, launder, and so forth? (Kann 1986, p. 32)

Profeminists support feminists in their disdain for patriarchy. They analyze men's problems as stemming from a patriarchal system that privileges white heterosexual men while forcing all males into restrictive gender roles. In the United States, profeminist men formed the National Organization for Changing Men in 1983 (changed in 1990 to the National Organization for Men Against Sexism, or NOMAS), whose purposes are to transcend gender stereotypes while supporting women's and gays' struggles for respect and equality (Doyle 1989). In Canada, there are also many profeminist men's organizations, such as Montreal Men Against Sexism and the Men's Network for Change (MNC), a coast-to-coast, "pro-feminist, gay affirmative, anti-racist, male positive" group.

The newer *masculinists*, who emerged in the early 1990s, tend not to focus on patriarchy as problematic (although they might agree that it is). Instead, masculinists analyze their own gendered expectations and behaviours. They work to develop a positive image of masculinity, one combining strength with tenderness. The path to this is through therapy, consciousness-raising groups, and rituals. The latter encourage men to release the "wild man" from within the socialized or "civilized" man. Through rituals men are to get in touch with their inner feelings and heal the buried rage and grief caused by the oppressive nature of corporate culture, the psychological and/or physical absence of their fathers, and men's general isolation due to a learned reluctance to share their feelings. Robert Bly's *Iron John* (1990) is a prominent example of the ideas of this camp. Retreats ("wildman gatherings") encourage men to overcome the barriers to intimate friendships with each other (Kimmel 1995).

Gloria Steinem (1992) suggests the more inclusive term "Wild Child" and encourages both women and men to release the child within by getting in touch with buried feelings of rage and resentment. Steinem argues that both women and men, having been socialized as children to limiting gender roles, experience grief over the loss of "a part of myself" (p. 160). Finding and developing that other part of oneself is discussed next.

Aboriginal Women and Feminism

The following is an extract from a discussion paper written by Madeleine Dion Stout entitled Aboriginal Canada: Women and Health. *The full version of this paper can be found on the World Wide Web (http://www.hc-sc.gc.ca/ canusa/papers/canada/english/indigen.htm). Dion Stout, a Cree originally from the Kehewin First Nations in Alberta, is an Assistant Professor of Canadians Studies and Coordinator of the North and Native Studies Program at Carleton University in Ottawa.*

Most Aboriginal women reject the term "feminist" because it is loaded and foreign. As Patricia Monture-Okanee puts it, "I want to understand why feminists continue to believe in the universality of male dominance, the universality of sisterhood and why they strive so hard to convert Aboriginal women. I want feminists to know why Aboriginal women do not identify as feminist" (Jackson, 1993, p. 190). In short, mainstream feminism does not sit easily with Aboriginal women's sense of social reality based upon subsistence and balanced men/women relationships (Emberley 1993, p. XV). In addition, Aboriginal women shun mainstream feminism for philosophical reasons such as those found in the passage below:

> Aboriginal women, eight out of ten of whom are survivors of abuse relationships, often reject majoritarian feminist 'solutions' for these problems, preferring a community healing approach, which keeps abusers out of white jails. This difference in philosophy has limited practical interaction between Aboriginal women and most majority feminists. (Vickers 1993, p. 266)

Of course, this is not to say that there is no such thing as Aboriginal feminism, for clearly there is. However, our feminism differs from that of many of our mainstream counterparts in that we reject the over-emphasis upon personal success and achievement that is embodied in such sayings as "it will all be because of me," focusing our attention instead upon the ways in which women's oppression is linked to the wider domination of all men and all women. Still, given the pain that Aboriginal women have suffered at the hands of Aboriginal men, it is unlikely that the practice of Aboriginal feminism will be free of contradiction and conflict, and indeed Aboriginal women are often told that, by challenging women's oppression, we are betraying our womanhood, and diverting attention away from the larger, and by implication more important, struggle for self-government.

In that "gender is clearly not one identity but a set of relations," (Razack 1993, p. 39), a more "inclusive feminism" (Nelson and Robinson 1999, p. 107) must address and "render comprehensible the interactive or multiplicative impacts" of sexism, racism, classism, heterosexualism, ableism and so on. "The challenge is to develop an understanding of the commonality of women's subordination, without asserting that this subordination is necessarily more fundamental than other forms of subordination women confront....In some instances, issues of gender transcend issues of race, ethnicity, class, sexuality, or ability. In other instances, gender is a background issue" (Nelson and Robinson 1999, p. 108).

Sources cited: Emberley, J. (1993). *Thresholds of Difference: Feminist Critique, Native Women's Writings, Postcolonial Theory.* Toronto: University of Toronto Press.

Jackson, M. (1994). "Aboriginal women and self-government." In J. Hylton (ed.) *Aboriginal self-government in Canada: current trends and issues.* Saskatoon: Purich, pp. 180–198.

Vickers, J. (1993). "The Canadian women's movement and a changing constitutional order." *International Journal of Canadian Studies,* 7–8, pp. 261–284.

Ambivalence, Confusion—and Hope

In the 1970s, some feminist social scientists proposed **androgyny** as an answer to the stresses and inequalities that result from traditional masculine and feminine expectations and conditions. Androgyny (formed from the Greek words *andro,* meaning "male," and *gyne,* meaning "female") is the social and psychological condition by which individuals think, feel, and behave both instrumentally and expressively (Bem 1975). In other words, androgynous persons evidence the positive qualities traditionally associated with both masculine and feminine roles. An androgynous man or woman could be achievement-oriented *and* emotionally nurturing, for example. More recently, feminists have disagreed about androgyny as a model for women. Probably the majority continue to emphasize equal treatment of men and women and to encourage nonsexist child rearing that would produce similarity in personality between men and women. Others seek to acknowledge biological differences and celebrate a "women's culture" that mitigates individual ambition to emphasize communitarian values and women's nurturing capacity (Mitchell and Oakley 1986; Fox-Genovese 1991). Nevertheless, the fact remains that in a modern, complex society such as ours, people need to be assertive and self-reliant and also to depend on one another for intimacy and emotional support (Helgeson 1994). Allowing people both to develop their talents fully and to be emotionally expressive can greatly expand the range of behaviours and possibilities open to everyone.

Ironically, however, that very expansion in the range of people's opportunities has led to new ambivalences, or mixed feelings and conflicts, both within ourselves and between men and women. Although women's attitudes and behaviours began to change appreciatively more than 25 years ago, women continue to experience a great deal of ambivalence and conflict. Stay-at-home moms may feel stigmatized for not being employed, for instance. Others, who are employed, may wish they could stay home full-time with their families. Moreover, a wife's career success may push her into renegotiating gender boundaries at home. Today's women are typically expected both to assume primary responsibility for nurturing others and also to pursue their own achievement—goals that can conflict. This conflict is more than psychological. It is in part a consequence of our society's failure to provide support for all employed mothers in the form of adequate maternity (and parental) leave or child care, for example. More than women in many other industrialized societies, such as those in western Europe, women in Canada and the United States continue to deal individually with problems of pregnancy, recovery from childbirth, and early child care as best they can. Adequate job performance, let alone career achievement, is difficult under such conditions regardless of a woman's ability. These points are further developed in later chapters.

Currently, however, it is men's ambivalence and confusion (even anger) that receives the most attention. For one thing, husbands are still expected to succeed as principal family breadwinners—even in an economy that makes this increasingly difficult (Marin 1991). Declining economic opportunities, coupled with criticisms of patriarchy sparked by the women's movement, can lead a man to feel unfairly picked on. Recently a male student in co-author Agnes Riedmann's family course wrote this, for example: "Why is it that when the male 'good provider' fails to achieve his duties, he is considered a failure, but if the woman (mother) fails in completing her duties or job, she and others will push the blame on the father? It seems no matter what, the male will be downgraded for failures of his family!"

Not all men are angry, of course. Nonetheless, today's society offers them copious opportunities for ambivalence and confusion (Gerson 1993). Currently, varied cultural messages no longer provide clear-cut guidelines for men's behaviour. The "new" man is expected to succeed economically and to value relationships and emotional openness. Although women want men to be sensitive and emotionally expressive, they also want them to be self-assured and confident. And they may want male leadership to relieve them of minor, or even major, choices. Taken together, today's "masculinities" are not only multifaceted but also paradoxical (Gerson 1993).

Furthermore, today's men, like women, find it increasingly difficult to have it all. If women find it difficult to combine a sustained work career with motherhood, men face a conflict between maintaining their privileges and enjoying supportive relationships. In the face of societal changes and new options, some men will choose to opt out of family living altogether, a topic discussed in Chapters 6 and

7. But others "will find that equality and sharing offer compensations to offset their attendant loss of power and privilege" (Gerson 1993, p. 274).

IN SUM

Roles of men and women have changed over time, but living in our society remains a different experience for women and for men. Gendered messages and social organization influence people's behaviour, attitudes, and options. Women tend to be seen as more expressive, relationship-oriented, and "communal"; men are considered more instrumental or agentic.

Generally, traditional masculine expectations require that men be confident, self-reliant, and occupationally successful and engage in "no sissy stuff." During the 1980s the "new male" (or "liberated male") cultural message emerged, according to which men are expected to value tenderness and equal relationships with women. Traditional feminine expectations involve a woman's being a man's helpmate and a "good mother." An emergent feminine role is the successful "professional woman"; when coupled with the more traditional ones, this results in the "superwoman."

The extent to which men and women differ from one another and follow these cultural messages can be visualized as two overlapping normal distribution curves. Means differ according to cultural expectations, but within-group variation is usually greater than between-group variation. An exception is male dominance, evident in politics, in religion, and (although this is changing for many men) in the economy.

Biology interacts with culture to produce human behaviour, and the two influences are difficult to separate. Sociologists give greater attention to the socialization process, for which there are several theoretical explanations. Overall, however, sociologists stress socialization in the family, in play and games, and in school as encouraging gendered attitudes and behaviour.

Turning our attention to the actual lives of adults, we find women and men negotiating gendered expectations and making choices in a context of change at work and in relationships. Change brings mixed responses, depending on class, racial/ethnic membership, religion, or other social indicators. New cultural ideals are far from realization, and efforts to create lives balancing love and work involve conflict and struggle.

Key Terms

androgyny	gender schema
borderwork	hermaphrodites
Chodorow's theory of gender	hormones
expressive character traits	instrumental character traits
femininities	internalize
gender	male dominance
gendered	masculinities
gender identity	self-identification theory
gender-linked characteristics and roles	sex
gender role	socialization
	social learning theory

Study Questions

1. What are some characteristics generally associated with males in our society? What traits are associated with females? How do these affect our expectations about the ways men and women behave?

2. How are our role expectations for men and women related to changes in the larger society?

3. What evidence is used to demonstrate the influence of heredity on gender-linked behaviour? To show the influence of the cultural environment? Describe the research and findings of Money and Ehrhardt on this issue.

4. How are people socialized to adhere, often unconsciously, to culturally acceptable gender roles? Can you give some examples of how you were socialized into your gender role?

5. Discuss Chodorow's theory of gender. How does it help to explain how and why men tend to develop autonomy and women a capability for relatedness?

6. How have traditional gender roles been stressful for men and women? How have changing roles altered the stresses on men and women?

7. Women and men may renegotiate and change their gendered attitudes and behaviours as they progress through life. What evidence do you see of this in your own or others' lives?

8. Describe the women's movement and the men's movement. What evidence is there of a backlash against the women's movement?

9. Explain the concept of "androgyny" as an alternative to traditional gender roles. Why might people in our society feel ambivalent about androgyny?

10. What do we mean by "masculinities" and "femininities" today?

Suggested Readings

Gerson, Kathleen. 1993. *No Man's Land: Men's Changing Commitments to Family and Work.* New York: Harper Collins, Basic Books. Readable and convincing analysis of the changing options and expectations for men in today's society, along with the various choices they make.

Hamer, Dean and Peter Copeland. 1998. *Living With Our Genes.* New York: Doubleday. One of several recent books supporting the broad area of biosociology, this one examines research on human genes as influential in human attitudes and behaviour, including (among other things) gender behaviour.

Kimmel, Michael S. 1995. *Manhood in American: A Cultural History.* Berkeley: University of California Press. This exploration of how manhood has been historically defined in U.S. culture argues that it was not until about the 1890s that manhood became masculinity—something that had to be proven through sports, fraternities, and fashion.

Mandell, Nancy (ed.). 2001. *Feminist Issues: Race, Class, and Sexuality, 3rd edition.* Toronto: Pearson Education Canada, Inc. A valuable collection of original writings by many of Canada's leading feminist scholars.

Nelson, Adie and Barrie W. Robinson. 2002. *Gender in Canada, 2nd edition.* Don Mills, Ontario: Pearson Education Canada, Inc. A comprehensive treatment of how gender is constructed and reconstructed through socialization, work, and the family.

On the Net

1) Feminism Links
http://www.feminist.org

2) Men's Net
http://www.magi.com/~mensnet/

3) The History of Gender in Canada
http://www.hartford-hwp.com/archives/44/index-eb.html

4) Children's Literature: Gender Roles and Stereotyping
http://www.indiana.edu/~eric_rec/ieo/bibs/childgen.html

5) Children's Advertising and Gender Roles
http://www.mediaandthefamily.org/research/fact/childgen.shtml

6) Gender.Org
http://www.gender.org.uk

Loving Ourselves and Others

LOVE IS NOT CONSOLATION, IT IS

LIGHT.

SIMONE WEIL

North Americans love love. We marry and remarry for love. Because it involves the will, "love implies choice. We do not have to love. We choose to love." But when asked what love is, most of us have trouble answering. Love is difficult to define; in attempting to do so, we "toy with mystery" (Peck 1978).

In this chapter we'll discuss the need for loving in today's society and describe one writer's view of some forms love takes. We'll examine what love is (and isn't). We'll explore the idea that self-esteem—as distinguished from narcissism—is a prerequisite to loving others. We begin by looking at what love means in impersonal, modern society.

PERSONAL TIES IN AN IMPERSONAL SOCIETY

We say that modern society is impersonal because so much of the time we are encouraged to think and behave in ways that deny our emotional need to be cared for and to care for others (Bellah et al. 1985). An impersonal society exaggerates the rational aspect of human beings and tends to ignore people's feelings and their need for affection and human contact.[1] We expect people to leave their friends and relatives to move to job-determined new locations because it is an economically efficient way of organizing production and management. Salespeople and service employees (flight attendants, for example) may be required to display certain emotions and repress others as part of their job (Hochschild 1983).

In the context of this impersonality, most people search for at least one caring person with whom to share

their private time. Some find love and nourish it; some don't discover loving at all. But we all need it (Gold and Rogers 1995). Physicians point out that loving enhances physical health, and many psychologists insist that loving is essential for emotional survival. It helps confirm a person's sense of individual worth.

WHAT IS LOVE?

Love exists between parents and children, and between people of the same and opposite sexes. Love may or may not involve sexuality. When it does involve sexuality, "romantic" love can be heterosexual or homosexual. Psychoanalyst Rollo May defines love as "a delight in the presence of the other person and an affirming of his [or her] value and development as much as one's own" (1975, p. 116). We include this definition here because we like it and think it complements ours. But for our purposes we will define love in more detail. **Love** is a deep and vital emotion that satisfies certain needs, coupled with a caring for and acceptance of the beloved and resulting in an intimate relationship. We'll discuss each part of this definition.

Love is a Deep and Vital Emotion

An **emotion** is a strong feeling, arising without conscious mental or rational effort, which motivates an individual to behave in certain ways. Loving parents, for example, are motivated to see what is wrong if their child begins to cry. Anger, reverence, and fear are other emotions that also evoke certain behaviours. When people get angry, for instance, they may feel like screaming or throwing things. Emotions are sometimes difficult for social scientists to come to grips with. Yet, even the most careful of researchers are able to find the poetry of love in their psychological data. The part of the brain associated with fantasy rather than rationality is most closely connected with emotional response and spontaneous behaviour toward others (McClelland 1986).

Love Satisfies Legitimate Personal Needs

Human beings need recognition and affection, and a second element of love is that it fills this basic need. Loving enables people to fulfill their needs for nurturance, creativity, and self-revelation.

---

1. This impersonality of modern society has been a principal concern of sociologists (see Durkheim 1893; Weber 1948; Simmel 1950; Berger, Berg, and Kellner 1973) since sociology first appeared as a distinct discipline in the Western world, roughly at the time of the Industrial Revolution.

It's all very well to state that a person's emotional needs can be fulfilled by love, but what kind of—and how many—needs can we expect to be satisfied? Psychologists stress that love cannot fulfill all needs, and they distinguish between legitimate and illegitimate needs.

LEGITIMATE NEEDS   Sometimes called "being needs," **legitimate needs** arise in the present rather than out of deficits accumulated in the past (Crosby 1991, pp. 50–51). Ongoing social and emotional support is certainly a legitimate human need (Wills 1991; Strobe and Strobe 1996; Uchino and Cacioppo 1996). People who have a healthy self-concept expect emotional support and understanding, companionship, and often sexual sharing from their partners. But they do not expect their partners to make them feel lovable or worthwhile; they already take those things for granted. Achieving a sense of individuality and personal identity is a step that best precedes relationship formation (Vannoy 1991). People's legitimate need in loving becomes the desire to share themselves with loved ones to enrich their lives (Maslow 1943).

ILLEGITIMATE NEEDS   Sometimes called "deficiency needs," **illegitimate needs** arise from feelings of self-doubt, unworthiness, and inadequacy. People who feel deficient often count on others to convince them they are worthwhile (Crosby 1991, pp. 50–54). "If you are not eternally showing me that you live for me," they seem to say, "then I feel like nothing" (Satir 1972, p. 136). They strive to borrow security from others.

To expect others to fill such needs is asking the impossible: No amount of loving will convince a person that he or she is worthwhile or lovable if that person doesn't already believe it. Hence, illegitimate needs for affection are insatiable. Love does satisfy legitimate needs, however.

Love Involves Caring and Acceptance

A third element of love is the acceptance of partners for themselves and "not for their ability to change themselves or to meet another's requirements to play a role" (Dahms 1976, p. 100). People are free to be

Love is a deep and vital emotion, coupled with a caring for and acceptance for the beloved, and resulting in an intimate relationship.

themselves in a loving relationship, to expose their feelings, frailties, and strengths.

Related to this acceptance is caring: the concern a person has for the partner's growth. Rollo May defines this caring as a state "in which something does matter.... [It is] the source of eros, the source of human tenderness. It is a state composed of the recognition of another; a fellow human being like one's self; of identification of one's self with the pain or joy of the other" (1969, p. 289). Ideally, lovers support and encourage each other's personal growth. If a loved one wants to join a softball league or spend some evenings studying, for example, he or she is encouraged to do so. At the same time, partners respond to each other's needs for affection by recognizing budding feelings of insecurity or jealousy in each other and trying to be reassuring: "Just because I want to play softball doesn't mean I don't still love you," they explain; or "I love you, but I want to study now; let's get ice cream later."

Do Men and Women Care Differently?

Note also that experiencing feelings and expressing them may not be entirely the same thing. Sociologists have observed that in our society women verbally express feelings of love more than men do. Various writers have explored how girls' and boys' differing socialization experiences affect male–female relationships later in life (Levinson 1996; Thompson 1993). Men are encouraged to develop independence, and by extension to give autonomy priority over intimacy. They bring a sharper sense of self to relationships, but at the expense of interdependence.

Research indicates that women today do not believe that they should be more self-sacrificing in relationships (Heiss 1991). But their socialization has been directed more strongly to attachment than to autonomy. Women have been raised to be more aware of both their feelings and ways of communicating them. Men tend to be more often baffled by questions about inner feelings.

During the twentieth century, seeking emotional satisfaction in marriage has been part of a general trend toward self-development and the cultivation of emotional intimacy for both sexes. Before the nineteenth century, men's and women's domestic activities involved economic production, not personal inti-

macy. With the development of separate gender spheres in the nineteenth century, love and *feeling* became the domain of women, whereas *work* was seen to be the appropriate masculine mode. Men consequently felt estranged from the "female world of love and ritual" (Smith-Rosenberg 1975), the social world of women that is anchored in the family and close friendships between women. We have come to see men, as a result of this historical legacy, as inadequately equipped for the emotional relatedness considered essential to the companionate model of marriage that emerged in the twentieth century (Cancian 1987).

Sociologist Francesca Cancian maintains that men are equally loving, but that love is expressed in our society on feminine terms and women are the verbal sex. Nonverbal expressions of love such as men may make through doing favours, reducing their partners' burdens, and so on, are not credited. This is especially true for middle-class as opposed to working-class people. Moreover, women tend to view sex as one of several means for communicating an already established emotional closeness. Men, on the other hand, tend to view sex as *the* emotional communication (Rubin 1983; Cancian 1985; Critelli, Myers, and Loos 1986; Vannoy 1991).

Cancian argues that in our society women, not men, are made to feel primarily responsible for love's endurance or success. This situation results in both partners feeling manipulated and powerless. When there are problems in a relationship, the woman is likely to propose discussing them. But for a man, "talking about the relationship, like she wants, feels like taking a test that she made up and he will fail." Probably he won't refuse to talk outright because he, like she, has been taught that verbal intimacy is good. So his typical response is withdrawal or passive aggression, behaviour that will "probably make her feel helpless and controlled" (Cancian 1985, p. 260). "The consequences of love would be more positive if love were the responsibility of men as well as women and if love were defined more broadly to include instrumental help as well as emotional expression" (p. 262).

Cancian also argues that a more balanced view of how love is to be expressed—one that includes masculine as well as feminine elements—would find men equally loving and emotionally profound. Less abstractly, a lover could consider the possibility that the partner expresses love differently and accept such differences, or else negotiate change openly. It is possible that as gender roles change generally, men and women will develop more balanced capacities for autonomy and intimacy, "the very capacities necessary for sustaining the loving relationships on which marriages now depend" (Vannoy 1991, p. 262).

Love and Intimacy: Commitment to Sharing

Love involves **intimacy**, the capacity to share one's inner self with someone else and to commit oneself to that person despite some personal sacrifices. We'll look more closely at two elements of that definition: first, the experience of sharing intimacy; and second, the **commitment** involved in intimacy. Then we'll look at the triangular theory of love, which tries to put it all together.

PSYCHIC AND SEXUAL INTIMACY Intimacy involves sharing. This sharing can take place on two often overlapping planes. At one level is **sexual intimacy**. In popular terminology, people who have a sexual relationship are "intimate" with each other. At another level is **psychic intimacy**: people engage in self-disclosure. That is, they share their thoughts, feelings, and goals. This is the sense in which we use the term in this book. Although sexual intimacy can either result from or lead to psychic intimacy, the two concepts are not synonymous. Strangers and people who like each other can enjoy sexual intimacy. Those who share with and accept each other experience psychic intimacy. They engage in the "work of attention": making the effort to set aside existing preoccupations in order to listen to each other (Peck 1978, pp. 120–21). Research on married couples indicates that partners who are self-disclosing and openly express feelings of love to each other perceive their marriages to be more intimate and score high on measures of marital adjustment (Davidson, Balswick, and Halverson 1983; Waring, Schaefer, and Fry 1994; Rotenberg et al. 1993). Psychic and/or sexual intimacy enhances feelings of attachment, which in turn strengthens the will to commit (Lopez 1995; Holmes 1997).

COMMITMENT In love, committing oneself to another person involves the determination to develop a relationship "where experiences cover many areas of personality; where problems are worked through;

Love involves intimacy, the capacity to share one's inner self with someone else and to commit oneself to that person despite some personal sacrifices. But love—and commitment—aren't meant to be all work. Love needs to feel supportive and fun, at least sometimes, as well.

where conflict is expected and seen as a normal part of the growth process; and where there is an expectation that the relationship is basically viable and worthwhile" (Altman and Taylor 1973, pp. 184–87). Case Study 4.1, "Sharon and Gary: Discovering Love After 25 Years," illustrates commitment.

Committed lovers have fun together; they also share more tedious times. They express themselves freely and authentically. Committed partners do not see problems or disagreements as indications that their relationship is over. They view their relationship as worth keeping, and they work to maintain it in spite of difficulties. Commitment is characterized by this willingness to work through problems and conflicts as opposed to calling it quits when problems arise. In this view, commitment need not include a vow to stay together exclusively for life or even for a certain period of time. But it does imply that love involves effort: Committed partners "regularly, routinely, and predictably attend to each other and their relationship no matter how they feel" (Peck, 1978, p. 118).

THE TRIANGULAR THEORY OF LOVE Psychological research expands upon these notions but presents a more complex picture. Psychologist Robert Sternberg believes that the qualities most

Sharon and Gary: Discovering Love After 25 Years

Married at ages 16 and 18, respectively, Sharon and Gary were together nearly 25 years and had four children before separating for ten months. After the separation they got back together, publicly restating their wedding vows in a religious ceremony. Here they talk about what commitment to loving means to them.

Interviewer: How did you guys get back together?

Sharon: Connection. For me it was that I had to be connected. I just need someone regular to check in with, to have dinner with, to care where you are and what you are doing.

Gary: For me it was just love. For a long time I didn't love Sharon after we got married, and then I grew to love her very much. Then when we separated—it was both of our idea to separate—I think once she moved out it was an empty place. I knew that I just needed her back. I needed to have her there to share my love with her. It kinda took her moving out to really find that, to determine that was what I wanted.

Sharon: I think our troubles started when we got married. I was pregnant, our parents didn't approve, and we both thought we were doing the right thing. We tried for years to do the right things, and it wasn't quite right. A lot of things we never talked about and buried, they got deep...he told me he didn't love me when we first got married...I got married because I loved him like crazy and I knew I could make it work. I tried really hard. I did all the right things. I thought if we had a child it would tie us together.

Gary: I got married because it was the honourable thing to do. I don't regret being married. I don't regret being married as young as I was...It took a few years and I ended up loving her.

Interviewer: You got to know Sharon?

Gary: I don't know if I've ever got to know Sharon. Probably the last year I have got to know Sharon more than I had up until then.

Interviewer: Why's that?

Gary: That's because we didn't say nothing. We could argue and neither one of us would tell why we were mad or what the problem was.

Sharon: We didn't argue that much either.

Gary: No.

Sharon: Just glaring, that kind of stuff....We were young, and I used to cry for his attention. And when I cried, he left. A few of those and you think, "What good is this doing me?" So I quit crying.

Gary: Well, if I had known what else to do, I probably would have done that. Today I give her a hug and try to hold her. Back then, you know, laughter was easier.

Sharon: I don't remember if I ever told him what I needed then or not. I don't think so. I just wanted comfort and understanding, I guess. I think I usually cried over something—lack of money or fears.

Gary: We had plenty of all that.

important to a lasting relationship are not so visible in the early stages. In his research on relationships varying in length from one month to 36 years, he found three components of love: intimacy, passion, and commitment.

According to **Sternberg's triangular theory of love**, **intimacy** "refers to close, connected, and bonded feelings in a loving relationship. It includes feelings that create the experience of warmth in a loving relationship ... [such as] experiencing happiness with the

Sharon: I found out with the separation, though, finally I realized that Gary loved me. The turning point was when Gary made a commitment to help me get into the apartment. It made me look at him differently. It was the commitment; it was obvious that he cared—and not for his own personal thing. He wasn't just saying to get out. He was saying, "I want you to be well." He came to help me do that.

Interviewer: What did he do?

Sharon: Painted, laid carpet and ripped wall paper, those things.

Gary: I was doing that because I cared about her. It surprised me that it was the turning point because I was helping her get out. We had set this date that she had to be moved, but where she was moving to—it was next to impossible to move in there at that date. So we set another week, and we cleaned and got the place ready for her. That was the time that she decided that I cared for her.

Sharon: I remember it was a Sunday that I first got into the apartment where I was going to move to. It was pretty awful. I called Gary and said could I have another week, and he came over and brought breakfast...

Interviewer: Why did you guys have a public ceremony when you got back together?

Gary: I think one of the reasons that I wanted it was because there were a lot of our friends who knew what had gone on between us. I just wanted them to be part of our getting back together....It was very touching to me, very emotional. We never had anything like this. We got married by the justice of the peace—very cold, very. I don't know who was the witness now, just some person in the courthouse at the time. That wasn't emotional; it was cold. It was just: "Let's get this over with so people can start counting the months." And hoping that the baby would come up a month late or something.

Sharon: This time we invited our whole church and our whole square-dance club and our whole group of people that we both work with....We called our parents and asked for their blessing.

Gary: What they wanted to do was to make believe that we had already done this 25 years ago.

Sharon: But it was important that they came this time.

Gary: [At this ceremony] I felt a lot of love. We had it taped. I've watched the tape lots of times already. In the tape I see it. Sharon's trying to hold this thing together. She doesn't want to cry. She is just trying to hold a stiff lip, you know, and keep this thing going. You can see every once in a while, when I would break down and cry, she would try to stiffen up for the whole bunch.

Sharon: Sometimes I do that too well.

How does Gary and Sharon's story illustrate the idea of commitment in loving? How does it illustrate Francesca Cancian's (1985) view that men love differently than women do and that a more balanced view of what loving is would find men equally loving?

loved one; ... sharing one's self and one's possessions with the loved one; receiving ... and giving emotional support to the loved one; [and] having intimate communication with the loved one." **Passion** "refers to the drives that lead to romance, physical attraction, sexual consummation, and the like in a loving relationship." **Commitment**—actually, the "decision/commitment component of love" consists of "two aspects, one short-term and one long-term. The short-term one is the decision that one loves someone. The long-term aspect is the commitment to maintain that love" (Sternberg 1988, pp. 120–21).

Sternberg used these three dimensions to create a typology of "love" (see Figure 4.1). (The word is in quotes because many types of love would not meet our definition of love for romantic partners.) **Consummate love**, composed of all three components, is "complete love, ... a kind of love toward which many of us strive, especially in romantic relationships. Attaining consummate love can be difficult, but keeping it is even harder. We do not seek consummate love in all our loving relationships or even in most of them. Rather, we tend to reserve it for those loves that mean the most to us and that we want to make as nearly complete as possible" (Sternberg 1988, p.129).

The three components of consummate love develop at different times, as love grows and changes. "Passion is the quickest to develop, and the quickest to fade.... Intimacy develops more slowly, and commitment more gradually still" (Sternberg, quoted in Goleman 1985). Passion peaks early in the relationship but continues at a stable lower level and is important to the long-term maintenance of the relationship. Intimacy, which includes understanding each other's needs, listening and supporting each other, and sharing common values, becomes increasingly important. In its most emotional form, intimacy may not always be visible, but it emerges when the relationship is interrupted—for example, by travel, sickness, or death. Commitment is essential, but a commitment without intimacy and passion is hollow. In other words, all these elements of love are important. Because these components each develop at a different rate and so exist in various combinations of intensity, no relationship is stable but rather will be always changing (Sternberg 1988).

The triangular theory of love has been explored further in research (Chojnack and Walsh 1990; Acker and Davis 1992). Sternberg developed a scale measuring the three dimensions. Researchers have found a good deal of overlap in measurements of the three dimensions, and modifications of the scale have improved it. Social scientists find the theory conceptually appealing, and reviews of a number of theories of love and their measures identify similar elements. Generally, commitment has been found to be the factor that is most predictive of happiness in

relationships. Initial research finds passion to decline over time, as Sternberg theorizes, but only for women. Intimacy did not decline in longer relationships (Hendrick and Hendrick 1989; Acker and Davis 1992).

Of course, the triangular theory of love is not the only way of looking at love. One interesting typology developed by Canadian sociologist John Alan Lee looks at the wide individual variation in love styles.

Six Love Styles

Loving relationships can take many forms or personalities, just as the individuals in a relationship can.

John Alan Lee (1973) classified six love styles, initially based on interviews with 120 respondents, half of them male and half female. All were heterosexual, white, and of Canadian or English descent. Lee subsequently applied his typology to an analysis of gay relationships (Lee 1981). Researchers have developed a Love Attitudes Scale (LAS)—42 specific questions to measure Lee's typology (Hendrick and Hendrick 1986). Although not all subsequent research has found all six dimensions, this typology of love styles has withstood the test of time and has proven to be more than hypothetical (Borello and Thompson 1990; Hendrick and Hendrick 1989).

Love styles are distinctive characteristics or personalities that loving or lovelike relationships can

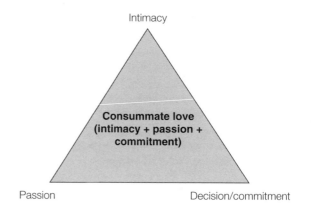

FIGURE **4.1**

The three components of love: triangular theory. (Source: Adapted from Sternberg 1988, p. 21.)

take. The word *lovelike* is included in this definition because not all love styles are genuine loving as we have defined it. Moreover, people do not necessarily confine themselves to one style or another; they may incorporate different aspects of several styles into their relationships. In any case, these love styles tell us that people can love passionately, quietly, pragmatically, playfully, self-sacrificingly, and crazily.

EROS **Eros** (pronounced "AIR-ohs") is a Greek word meaning "love"; it forms the root of our word *erotic*. This love style is characterized by intense emotional attachment and powerful sexual feelings or desires. When erotic couples establish sustained relationships, these are characterized by continued active interest in sexual and emotional fulfillment, plus the development of intellectual rapport. Romeo and Juliet, who fell in love on first meeting, were erotic lovers; so are the older couple you know who seem endlessly fascinated by each other. A sample question on the Love Attitudes Scale designed to measure Eros asks the respondent to agree or disagree with the statement, "My partner and I have the right chemistry between us." Agreement would indicate erotic love (Hendrick and Hendrick 1986).

STORGE **Storge** ("STOR-gay") is an affectionate, companionate style of loving. This love style focuses on deepening mutual commitment, respect, friendship over time, and common goals. Whereas eros emphasizes emotional intensity and sexual passion, storge does not. Sexual intimacy comes about as partners develop increasing understanding of one another. The storgic lover's basic attitude to his or her partner is one of familiarity: "I've known you a long time, seen you in many moods" (Lee 1973, p. 87); "my partner is my friend." Storgic lovers are likely to agree that, "Genuine loving involves caring for awhile," and that, "I always expect to be friends with the one I love" (Hendrick and Hendrick 1986).

PRAGMA **Pragma** ("PRAG-mah") is the root word for *pragmatic*. Pragmatic love emphasizes the practical element in human relationships, particularly in marriages. Pragmatic love involves rational assessment of a potential partner's assets and liabilities. Here a relationship provides a practical base for both economic and emotional security. The arranged marriages of royalty or the pairing of the children of business partners or rivals are visible examples of pragma. But so is the person who decides very rationally to get married to a suitable partner. LAS questions that measure pragma are, "A main consideration in choosing a partner is/was how he/she would reflect on my family," and, "I tried to plan my life carefully before choosing a partner" (Hendrick and Hendrick 1986).

AGAPE **Agape** ("ah-GAH-pay") is a Greek word meaning "love feast." Agape emphasizes unselfish concern for the beloved's needs even when that means some personal sacrifice. Often called altruistic love, agape emphasizes nurturing others with little conscious desire for return other than the intrinsic satisfaction of having loved and cared for someone else. The sexual component of love seems less important in agape. Agapic lovers would likely agree that they "would rather suffer myself than let my partner suffer" and that, "I try to always help my partner through difficult times" (Hendrick and Hendrick 1986).

LUDUS **Ludus** ("LEWD-us") focuses on love as play or fun. Ludus emphasizes the recreational aspects of sexuality and the enjoyment of many sexual partners rather than searching for one serious relationship. Of course, ludic flirtation and playful sexuality may be part of a more committed relationship based on one of the other love styles. LAS questions designed to measure Ludus include the following: "I enjoy playing the game of love with a number of different partners"; "I try to keep my partner a little uncertain about my commitment to him/her" (Hendrick and Hendrick 1986).

MANIA **Mania**, a Greek word, designates a wild or violent mental disorder, an obsession or craze. Mania rests on strong sexual attraction and emotional intensity, as does eros. It differs from eros, however, in that manic partners are extremely jealous and moody, and their need for attention and affection is insatiable. Manic lovers alternate between euphoria and depression. The slightest lack of response from the love partner causes anxiety and resentment; any small sign of warmth evokes enormous relief. It is probably safe to say that manic lovers lack self-esteem, discussed later in this chapter. Manic lovers would be likely to

Agape is a love style that emphasizes unselfish concern for another's needs. Often called altruistic love, agape emphasizes nurturing. This love style exists between partners, and also between and among other family members.

say that, "When my partner doesn't pay attention to me, I feel sick all over;" or that, "I cannot relax if I feel my partner is with someone else" (Hendrick and Hendrick 1986).

We may learn of manic love in the newspaper or on TV when a relationship ends violently. But more humdrum versions of mania exist. Many of us have experienced the would-be or former lover who just won't quit or have been appalled at our own jealousy or obsessiveness in love.

These six love styles represent different ways people can feel about and behave toward each other in love-like relationships. In real life a relationship is never entirely one style, and the same relationship may be characterized, at different times, by features of several styles. Lovers can be erotic or pragmatic. Loving can assume qualities of quiet understanding and respect, along with playfulness.

Psychologists Marilyn Montgomery and Gwendolyn Sorell (1997) administered the LAS to 250 single undergraduate students and married adults of all ages. They found that singles were more likely than marrieds to have ludic and manic love attitudes, and less likely to favour agapic love. The researchers also found that erotic love attitudes existed throughout marriage and were related to high marital satisfaction. Agapic attitudes were also positively associated with relationship satisfaction. Ludus did not affect satisfaction with a relationship among singles. However, at least as measured by the LAS (which emphasizes ludic lovers' lack of commitment), ludic attitudes are associated with diminished marital satisfaction. We turn now to an examination of two things love isn't.

TWO THINGS LOVE ISN'T

Love is not inordinate self-sacrifice. And loving is not the continual attempt to get others to feel or do what we want them to—although each of these ideas is frequently mistaken for love. Next we'll examine these misconceptions in detail.

Martyring

Love isn't martyring. **Martyring** involves maintaining relationships by consistently ignoring one's own legitimate needs while trying to satisfy virtually all of a partner's needs, even illegitimate ones. Martyring differs from agapic love, described above. Agapic love involves giving much attention to the needs of a beloved—but not ignoring one's own legitimate needs at the same time. Martyrs usually have good intentions; they believe that loving involves doing unselfishly for others without voicing their own needs in return. Consequently, they seldom feel that they receive genuine affection. Martyrs may

- Be reluctant to suggest what they would like (concerning recreation or entertainment, for example) and leave decisions to others.

- Allow others to be constantly late for engagements and never protest directly.

- Work on helping loved ones develop talents and interests while neglecting their own.

- Be sensitive to others' feelings and problems while hiding their own disappointments and hurts.

Although it may sound noble, there's a catch to martyring. Believing that they're not receiving much emotional support, martyrs grow angry, even though they seldom express their anger directly. (In Chapter 9 we will discuss how unexpressed anger can damage a loving relationship.) Psychologists tell us that martyrs often think "it is better to be wanted as a victim than to not be wanted at all" (Szasz 1976, p. 62). The reluctance of martyrs to express legitimate needs is damaging to a relationship, for it prevents openness and intimacy.

Martyring has other negative consequences. Social psychologists have been researching the concept of equity, the balance of rewards and costs to the partners in a relationship. In love relationships and marriage, as well as in other relationships, people seem most comfortable when things feel generally fair or equitable—that is, when, over time, partners are reasonably well balanced in terms of what they are giving to and getting from the relationship.

Manipulating

Manipulators follow this maxim: If I can get him/her to do what I want done, then I'll be sure he/she loves me. **Manipulating** means seeking to control the feelings, attitudes, and behaviour of your partner or partners in underhanded ways rather than by assertively stating your case. Controlling behaviours (whether subtle manipulation or overt dictation and use of force) are not to be confused with love. Manipulators may

- Ask others to do things for them that they could do for themselves, and generally expect to be waited on.

- Assume that others will (if they "really" love them) be happy to do whatever the manipulators choose, not only regarding recreation, for example, but also in more important matters.

- Be consistently late for engagements ("if he [or she] will wait patiently for me, he [or she] loves me").

- Want others to help them develop their interests and talents but seldom think of reciprocating.

Manipulators, like martyrs, do not believe that they are lovable or that others can really love them; that is why they feel a continual need to test their partner. Aware that they are exploiting others, habitual manipulators often experience guilt. They try to relieve this guilt by minimizing or finding fault with their loved one's complaints. "You don't really love me," they may

accuse. Manipulating, along with the guilt that often accompanies it, can destroy a relationship.

You may already have noticed that martyring and manipulating complement each other. Martyrs and manipulators are often attracted to each other, forming what family counsellor John Crosby (1991) calls **symbiotic relationships** in which each partner depends on the other for a sense of self-worth. Often, such symbiotic relationships are quite stable, although at the same time they can be unhappy—maybe even dangerously violent. Should one symbiotic partner learn to stand on his or her own feet, the relationship is less likely to last.

Manipulating and martyring are both sometimes mistaken for love. But they are not love, for one simple reason: Both relationships share a refusal to accept oneself or one's partner realistically—a quality we'll examine in greater detail now. The next section examines a necessary prerequisite for loving: self-esteem.

SELF-ESTEEM AS A PREREQUISITE TO LOVING[2]

I'm more interested," writes Leo Buscaglia, "in who is a loving person.... I believe that probably the most important thing is that this loving person is a person who loves him [or her] self" (1982, p. 9).

According to many psychologists, high self-esteem is a prerequisite for loving others because, among other reasons, loving requires self-disclosure—sharing who each of us is and how we feel. Individuals who are

---

2. The concept, *self-esteem*, is controversial among psychologists and others today. Some "postmodern" philosophers and psychologists argue that there is no such thing as a constant self, and hence, there can be no such thing as global self-esteem (Cravens 1997). Other critics see the self-esteem movement, which began in Canada and the United States after World War II, as too individualistic and leading to self-absorption, which in turn discourages people from taking any real interest in social or political issues (Bellah et al. 1985). Most recently, psychologists who mainly study violence have argued that parents' and teachers' efforts to promote self-esteem in children can actually foster its opposite, narcissism, and that narcissism can lead to violent outbursts (Bushman and Baumeister 1998; Johnson 1998). Nevertheless, much research has been done on self-esteem, and the majority of psychologists, especially counselling psychologists, continue to research and find use in the concept (Roberts and Bengston 1993; Jezl, Molidor, and Wright 1996; Jacobvitz and Bush 1996; Page, Stevens, and Galvin 1996; Durm, Giddens, and Blakenship 1997). Having considered the arguments, we continue to present and explore the concept, *self-esteem*, in this edition.

higher in self-esteem more frequently reported that they experience romantic love and report rich love experiences (Dion and Dion 1988). Chapter 5 discusses the importance of self-esteem to pleasurable sex.

Self-esteem is part of a person's self-concept; it involves feelings people have about their own worth. Social psychologist Stanley Coopersmith defines self-esteem as an evaluation a person makes and maintains of her- or himself. "It expresses an attitude of approval or disapproval, and indicates the extent to which the individual believes himself [or herself] to be capable, significant, successful, and worthy" (Coopersmith 1967, pp. 4–5). More recently, psychologist Nathaniel Branden has defined self-esteem as "the disposition to experience oneself as competent to cope with the basic challenges of life and as worthy of happiness" (1994, p. 21).

Branden (1994), as well as other contemporary psychologists, argues that self-esteem is a consequence, not simply an uncontrollable condition. Healthy self-esteem results from actual, real accomplishments, not simply from hearing or telling oneself that one is, for example, "special" (Bandura 1986; Begley 1998; Johnson 1998). Because self-esteem is a consequence of all the things we do, we can enhance it purposefully by working to develop our talents and by doing things that we believe contribute to our communities (Katz 1998). Accordingly, Branden identifies six "pillars" of self-esteem:

1. The practice of living consciously, or aware of what's going on

2. The practice of self-acceptance

3. The practice of self-responsibility

4. The practice of self-assertiveness

5. The practice of living purposefully

6. The practice of personal integrity

Individuals have a "global," or general sense of self-esteem, but they also have more "situated" experiences of self-esteem. One situation would be taking a test. Getting an A on a test, for instance, will probably increase your self-esteem markedly for a while. Flunking a test will likely lower it, at least temporarily. You can evaluate your own self-esteem by answering questions in Box 4.1, "A Self-Esteem Checklist."

Self-Love Versus Narcissism

In defining self-esteem we need to also explain a related concept (actually, a synonym in this book's context), that of *self-love*. Self-love is the same as high self-esteem, and it enhances a person's capacity to love others. People commonly confuse self-love with conceit—a self-centred, selfish outlook (Katz 1998). But psychologists point out that self-love and narcissism are opposites. **Narcissism** is characterized by an exaggerated concern with one's own self image and how one *appears* to others, not with one's own or others' true feelings. That is, narcissism is concerned chiefly or only with oneself, without regard for the well-being of others. Narcissists may act as if and try to convince themselves that they are superior, but such attitudes and behaviours actually result from low self-esteem. Disregarding others' needs results from preoccupation with one's own feelings of insecurity, together with the desire to compensate for such feelings (Lowen 1985; Emmons 1987; Begley 1998).

Whether people genuinely love themselves—as opposed to being narcissistic—affects their personal relationships.

Self-Esteem and Personal Relationships

Research indicates that self-esteem does a lot to influence the way people respond to others (Rugel and Martinovich 1997; Jezl, Molidor, and Wright 1996; Longmore and Demaris 1997).

In personal relationships, people with very low self-esteem often experience a persistent and insatiable need for affection. As psychologist Erich Fromm puts it, "If I am attached to another person because I cannot stand on my own two feet, he or she may be a life saver, but the relationship is not one of love" (Fromm 1956, p. 112).[3] We will explore the difference between loving and dependency in the next section.

3. Fromm chastises North Americans for their emphasis on wanting to *be loved* rather than on learning *to love*. Many of our ways to be loved or make ourselves lovable, he writes, "are the same as those used to make oneself successful, 'to win friends and influence people.' As a matter of fact, what most people in our culture mean by being lovable is essentially a mixture between being popular and having sex appeal" (Fromm 1956, p. 2)

A Self-Esteem Checklist

In this brief self-test you can broadly evaluate your own level of self-esteem.

- Do you believe strongly in certain values and principles, so that you are willing to defend them?
- Do you act on your own best judgment, without regretting your actions if others disapprove?
- Do you avoid worrying about what is coming tomorrow or fussing over yesterday's or today's mistakes?
- Do you have confidence in your general ability to deal with problems, even in the face of failures and setbacks?
- Do you feel generally equal—neither inferior nor superior—to others?
- Do you take it more or less for granted that other people are interested in you and value you?
- Do you accept praise without pretense of false modesty and accept compliments without feeling guilty?

- Do you resist the efforts of others to dominate you, especially your peers?
- Do you accept the idea—and admit to others—that you are capable of feeling a wide range of impulses and desires, ranging from anger to love, sadness to happiness, resentment to acceptance? (It does not follow, however, that you will act on all these feelings and desires.)
- Do you genuinely enjoy yourself in a wide range of activities, including work, play, creative self-expression, companionship, and just plain loafing?
- Do you sense and consider the needs of others?

If your answers to most of these questions are "yes" or "usually," you probably have high self-esteem.

Sources: Hamachek 1971, pp. 248–51; Hamachek 1992, especially pp. 355–6; see also Branden 1994.

Self-esteem affects love relationships in other ways. For instance, people with high self-esteem are more responsive to praise, whereas men and women with low self-esteem "are forever on the alert for criticism ... and remember it long afterward." People high in self-esteem are better at picking up signs of interest from other people and responding to them genuinely, whereas people low in self-esteem often miss such cues and, in general, are "set for rejection" (Walster and Walster 1978, pp. 54–55; Duck 1998, 1999). Psychologist Brad Bushman, who has conducted a recent study of what he calls "unjustified and unstable self-esteem" (i.e., narcissism), argues that "narcissists are supersensitive to criticisms or slights because deep down they suspect that their feeling of superiority is built on quicksand" (Begley 1998; Bushman and Baumeister 1998).

Emotional Interdependence

Besides self-esteem, or self-love, a quality necessary for loving is the ability to be emotionally interdependent. Interdependence is different from both dependence and independence. **Dependence** involves reliance on another or others for continual support or assurance, coupled with subordination—being easily influenced or controlled by those who are so greatly needed. **Independence**, on the other hand, involves self-reliance and self-sufficiency and may imply that the individual functions in isolation from others. It emphasizes separation from others.

Loving is different from both dependence and independence as we have defined them. Loving is **interdependence**, a relationship in which people with high esteem make strong commitments to each other. Therapist John Crosby has distinguished

Learning to Love Yourself More

We all feel inadequate at times. What can you do with feelings of inadequacy besides worry about them? People can work in many ways to improve their self-esteem. For example, you may choose to

- Pursue satisfying and useful occupations that realistically reflect your strengths and interests ("Young children make me nervous, but I'd like to teach, so I'll consider secondary or higher education")

- Work to develop the skills and interests you have rather than fret about those you don't

- Try being more honest and open with other people

- Make efforts to appreciate the good things you have rather than focus on the more negative things in your life

- Avoid excessive daydreaming and fantasy living ("Boy, things would be different if only I were a little taller," or "If only I had not gotten married so young, things would be better")

- "Keep on keeping on"—even when you are discouraged, realizing that one little step in the right direction is often good enough

- Reevaluate the standards by which you have learned to think of yourself as inadequate—you try to be satisfied to be smart enough, slender enough, or successful enough rather than continue to impose unrealistic standards on yourself

- Relax ("If I feel this way, it means this is a human way to feel, and everybody else has probably felt this way too at one time or another")

- Decide to be your own good friend, complimenting yourself when you do things well enough and not criticizing yourself too harshly

- Try to lighten up on yourself, remembering that you don't have to be perfect ("Easy does it")

Sources: Hamachek 1971, 1992.

between A-frame (dependent), H-frame (independent), and M-frame (interdependent) relationships. **A-frame relationships** are symbolized by the capital letter A: Partners have a strong couple identity but little individual self-esteem. They think of themselves as a unit rather than as separate individuals. Like the long lines in the letter A, they lean on one another. The relationship is structured so that "if one lets go, the other falls" (Crosby 1991, p. 55). And that is exactly what happens—at least for a while—when one partner outgrows his or her dependency in a martyr–manipulator relationship.

H-frame relationships are structured like a capital H: partners stand virtually alone, each self-sufficient and neither influenced much by the other. There is little or no couple identity and little emotionality: "If one lets go, the other hardly feels a thing" (Crosby

1991, p. 55). Research supports the notion that high levels of individualism are associated with a more detached style of loving (Dion and Dion 1991).

M-frame relationships rest on interdependence: Each partner has high self-esteem (unlike in the A-frame relationship), and partners experience loving as a deep emotion (unlike in the H-frame relationship). The relationship involves mutual influence and emotional support. M-frame relationships exhibit a meaningful couple identity: "If one lets go, the other feels a loss but recovers balance" (Crosby 1991, p. 55).

EMOTIONAL INTERDEPENDENCE AND ATTACHMENT STYLES Psychology, counselling psychologists, and relationship therapists often analyze an individual's relationship in terms of that person's attachment style. This perspective, known as **attachment**

theory, holds that during infancy and childhood a young person develops a general style of attaching to others. Once a youngster's attachment style is established, she or he unconsciously applies that style to later, adult relationships.

An individual's primary caretakers (usually parents and most often mother) exhibit a "style" of attachment with the young child. The three basic styles are **secure**, **insecure/anxious**, and **avoidant**. Children who can trust that a caretaker will be there to attend to their practical and emotional needs develop a secure attachment style. Children who are, or feel, uncared for or abandoned develop either an insecure/anxious or an avoidant attachment style. In adulthood a secure attachment style involves trust that the relationship will provide necessary and ongoing emotional and social support. An insecure/anxious attachment style entails concern that the beloved will disappear, a situation often characterized as "fear of abandonment." An adult with an avoidant attachment style dodges closeness and genuine intimacy either by evading relationships altogether or establishing considerable distance in intimate situations (Benoit and Parker 1994; Hazen and Shaver 1994). Individual or relationship therapy can help persons change their attachment style (Fuller and Fincham 1997; Furman and Flanagan 1997).

Correlating attachment theory with Crosby's relationship typology, described above, a secure attachment style would characterize partners in an emotionally interdependent, or M-frame relationship. An insecure/anxious attachment style would likely be evidenced in partners engaged in an A-frame, or dependent relationship. An avoidant style would characterize partners in an independent, or H-frame relationship. We turn now to a final quality associated with genuine loving—acceptance.

Acceptance of Self and Others

Loving partners need to have another quality besides self-love and interdependence—that of acceptance or empathy. Love "requires the ability to have empathy with the other person, to appreciate and affirm his [or her] potentialities" (May 1975, p. 116).

Each partner must try to understand and accept how the other perceives situations and people. If a loved one tells you he or she dislikes a friend of yours, for example, the accepting response is not "That's impossible!" but "Tell me why." Accepting relationships rest on unconditional positive regard. This doesn't mean that you, too, have to decide to dislike your friend. But even when loved ones do not share or condone specific attitudes and behaviour, they accept each other as people (Dahms 1976, pp. 100–101). This, in fact, is the hallmark of a committed relationship.

Only people with high self-esteem can accept others as people. Because they accept their own feelings, anxieties, and frailties, they do not fear seeing these emotions in others. In other words, the more that people can accept themselves the more they can accept others. We will now discuss how love happens.

LOVE AS A DISCOVERY

Love is discovered, not just found. The words *discover* and *find* have similar meanings. But to discover involves a process, whereas to find refers to a singular act. One definition of *discover*, for example, is to reveal or expose through exploration; *finding* more often means to attain or succeed in reaching. Loving is a process of discovery. It is something people must do—and keep doing—rather than just a feeling they come upon. In Erich Fromm's words, love is "an activity, not a passive affect; it is a 'standing in,' not a 'falling for'" (1956, p. 22).

Discovering Love

It's fine to say that love is a process of discovery. But that doesn't answer the question of how love happens. Don't people fall in love when least expecting it? Do they find they're in love after knowing each other a while? Or do they work at learning to love each other? The answer to all these questions is "sometimes."

Some people know what kind of social characteristics they want in a partner before they find one, as Chapter 7 explores further. He or she must be the right age, for example, and have the appropriate occupation, area of residence, or education. These people often find partners by joining organizations in which they think it most likely to meet fitting mates.

Other people report that they fell in love on an accidental first meeting. Typically, their partners also fit well-defined images of those whom they could love, but these images emphasize physical attractiveness and potential for emotional and intellectual rapport.

Still others do not have any clear image or specific demands regarding potential love partners. Not actively looking for love, they choose activities for their own sake rather than as a means to meet a partner. In these activities, however, they meet other people with the same interests.

People can find love in any of these ways and often in any combination. Psychologists warn, however, that romantically inclined individuals who insist on waiting for their ideal lover to come around the next corner may wait forever—and miss opportunities to love real people. George Bach and Ronald Deutsch counselled many single adults who hoped to find love. Often, they reported, clients ask where to meet potential partners. "Ironically, the questioner is [frequently] in the presence of some of the people he is looking for" (Bach and Deutsch 1970, p. 31). These psychologists pointed out, too, that waiting for accidental meetings to occur can be a barrier to discovering love. A more realistic alternative is simply to introduce oneself to others who seem appealing.

Once a person meets the right partner, love can begin to develop. To describe this process of development, social scientist Ira Reiss has proposed what he calls the "wheel theory of love."

The Wheel of Love

According to Reiss' theory, there are four stages in the development of love, which he sees as a circular process—a **wheel of love**—capable of continuing indefinitely. The four stages—rapport, self-revelation, mutual dependency, and personality need fulfillment—are shown in Figure 4.2, and they describe the span from attraction to love.

RAPPORT   Feelings of rapport rest on mutual trust and respect. People vary in their ability to gain rapport with others. Some feel at ease with a variety of people; others find it hard to relax with most people and have difficulty understanding others.

One factor that can make people more likely to establish rapport is similarity of background—social class, religion, and so forth, as Chapter 7 will discuss. The outside circle in Figure 4.2 is means to convey this point. But rapport can also be established between people of different backgrounds, who may perceive one another as an interesting contrast to themselves or see qualities in one another that they admire (Reiss and Lee 1988).

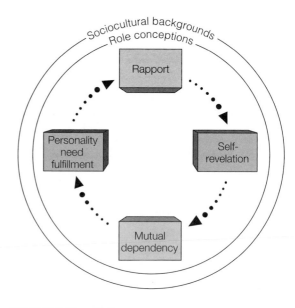

FIGURE   **4.2**

Reiss' wheel theory of the development of love. (Source: Reiss and Lee 1988, p. 103.)

SELF-REVELATION   Self-revelation, or **self-disclosure**, involves gradually sharing intimate information about oneself. People have internalized different views regarding how much self-revelation is proper. Men, for example, are socialized to be less self-disclosing than women. The middle circle, Role conceptions, signifies that ideas about gender-appropriate behaviours influence how partners respond to each other's self-revelations and other activities. In addition, as we saw earlier in this chapter, people with low self-esteem will likely find it difficult to share themselves fully.

Even for people with high self-esteem, however, loving produces anxiety. They fear their love won't be returned. They worry about being exploited. They are afraid of becoming too dependent or of being depended on too much. One way of dealing with these anxieties is, ironically, to let others see us as we really are and to share our motives, beliefs, and feelings.

Altman and Taylor (1973) see the self as having penetrable layers (see Figure 4.3). People's "outer layers" are easily accessible to many others. We are willing to share with the general public such information as our middle name, for example. But the inner layers are progressively more private: These are revealed to fewer and fewer people and only after knowing them over time. As the figure shows, the self can be visualized as being opened in the shape of a wedge, gradually penetrating to the centre. At the outer layers the symbolic wedge makes a wide space, allowing room for many others. As the wedge penetrates, the space gradually narrows, allowing increasingly fewer people into the centre. As reciprocal self-revelation continues, an intimate relationship may develop while a couple progresses to the third stage in the wheel of love: developing interdependence or mutual dependency.

MUTUAL DEPENDENCY   In this stage of a relationship, the two people desire to spend more time together and thereby develop the kind of interdependence or, in Reiss' terminology, mutual dependency, described in the discussion of M-frame relationships. Partners develop habits that require the presence of both partners. Consequently, they begin to depend on or need each other. For example, a woman may begin to need her partner as an audience for her jokes. Or watching evening television or videos may begin to seem lonely without the other person because enjoyment now depends not only on the program but on sharing it with the other. Interdependency leads to the fourth stage: a degree of mutual personality need fulfillment.

PERSONALITY NEED FULFILLMENT   As their relationship develops, two people find they satisfy a majority of each other's emotional needs. As personality needs are satisfied, greater rapport is developed, which leads to deeper self-revelation, more mutually dependent habits, and still greater need satisfaction. Reiss uses the term *personality need fulfillment* to describe the stage of a relationship in which a stable pattern of emotional exchange and mutual support has developed. The relationship meets basic human needs, both practical and emotional.

Returning to Reiss' image of this four-stage process as a wheel, then, the wheel turns indefinitely in a lasting, deep relationship. Or the wheel may turn only a few times in a passing romance. Finally, the wheel can reverse itself and turn in the other direction. As Reiss explains: "If one reduced the amount of self-revelation through an argument, ... that would affect the dependency and need-fulfillment processes, which would in turn weaken the rapport process, which would in turn lower the revelation level even further" (1988).

Keeping Love

The wheel theory suggests that once people fall in love, they may not necessarily stay in love. Relationships can "keep turning," or they may slow down or reverse themselves. We need to point out

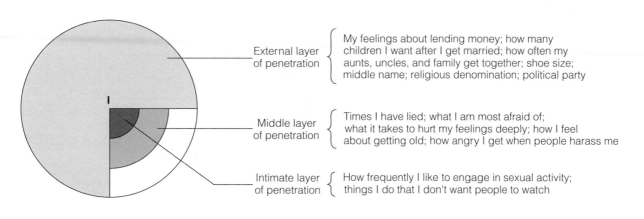

External layer of penetration: My feelings about lending money; how many children I want after I get married; how often my aunts, uncles, and family get together; shoe size; middle name; religious denomination; political party

Middle layer of penetration: Times I have lied; what I am most afraid of; what it takes to hurt my feelings deeply; how I feel about getting old; how angry I get when people harass me

Intimate layer of penetration: How frequently I like to engage in sexual activity; things I do that I don't want people to watch

FIGURE   **4.3**

Social penetration. (Source: Adapted from Altman and Haythorn 1965, pp. 411–26.)

that sometimes this reversal, and eventual break up, is a good thing. "Perhaps the hardest part of a relationship is knowing when to salvage things and when not to" (Sternberg 1988, p. 242). Chapter 7 explores this issue more fully. But here we need to point out that being committed is not always noble—as in cases of physical violence or consistent verbal abuse, for example.

How do people stay in love? Keeping love requires continual discovery of both oneself and one's partner through mutual self-disclosure. As partners penetrate deeper toward the centre of each other's personalities, they continually discover the remarkable and unique.

Love, then, is a continual process. Partners need to keep on sharing their thoughts, feelings, troubles, and joys with each other, an effort that will receive much more of our attention later in this text.

In a marriage relationship a vital dimension of this sharing is sexual intimacy. In Chapter 5 we'll turn to the physical expressions of love.

IN SUM

In an impersonal society, love provides an important source of fulfillment and intimacy. Genuine loving in our competitive society is rare and difficult to learn (May 1975, p. 115). Our culture's emphasis on self-reliance as a central virtue ignores the fact that all of us are interdependent. We rely on parents, spouses or partners, other relatives, and friends far more than our culture encourages us to recognize (Cancian 1985, pp. 261–62). Loving is one form of interdependence.

Despite its importance, love is often misunderstood. It should not be confused with martyring or manipulating. There are many contemporary love styles that indicate the range that lovelike relationships—not necessarily love—can take. John Lee lists six love types: eros, or passionate love; storge, or friendship love; pragma, or pragmatic love; agape, or altruistic love; ludus, or love play; and mania, or possessive love.

We *can* learn to love, even if it's difficult. A first step is knowing what love and loving are. Love is a deep and vital emotion resulting from significant need satisfaction, coupled with caring for and acceptance of the beloved, and resulting in an intimate relationship. Loving is a caring, responsible, and

sharing relationship involving deep feelings, and it is a commitment to intimacy. Intimacy involves disclosing one's inner feelings, a process that is always emotionally risky. For this reason, the people who are most capable of intimate loving are those who first love themselves or have high self-esteem (self-love). Loving also takes the ability to be emotionally interdependent, an acceptance of oneself as well as a sense of empathy, and a willingness to let down barriers set up for self-preservation.

People discover love; they don't simply find it. The term *discovering* implies a process, and to develop and maintain a loving relationship requires self-disclosure. This mutual self-disclosure requires time and trust.

Key Terms

A-frame relationships	love styles
agape	ludus
attachment theory	mania
avoidant	manipulating
commitment	martyring
commitment (Sternberg's theory)	M-frame relationships
consummate love	narcissism
dependence	passion (Sternberg's theory)
emotion	
eros	pragma
H-frame relationships	psychic intimacy
illegitimate needs	secure
independence	self-disclosure
insecure/anxious	self-esteem
interdependence	sexual intimacy
intimacy	Sternberg's triangular theory of love
intimacy (Sternberg's theory)	
legitimate needs	storge
love	symbiotic relationships
	wheel of love

Study Questions

1. Do you agree that loving is essential for emotional survival today? Why or why not?

2. What kinds of needs can a love relationship satisfy? What needs can never be satisfied by a love relationship?

3. Discuss the characteristics necessary for a fully loving relationship. Do you agree or disagree with

what the text says? Which characteristics seem most important to you as you observe the world around you?

4. Sternberg offers a very specific triangular theory of love. What are its components? Are they useful concepts in analyzing any love experience(s) you have had?

5. What are some misconceptions of love? Why is each of them not love?

6. Explain the distinction between martyring and agapic love, and give examples of each.

7. What is the difference between self-love and narcissism? How is each related to a person's capacity to love others?

8. Describe A-frame, H-frame, and M-frame relationships.

9. Describe attachment theory. Can you apply the perspective to your own life? Why or why not?

10. Describe Reiss' wheel theory of love. Compare it with your idea of how love develops.

11. How do the two outer circles (Role Conceptions and Sociocultural Background) move Reiss' theory from a purely social–psychological one to a theory with commonalities with the family ecology perspective discussed in Chapter 2?

Suggested Readings

Bellah, Robert N., et al. 1996. *Habits of the Heart: Individualism and Commitment in American Life* (updated, with a new introduction). Berkeley: Univ. of California Press. Bellah and his colleagues argue that a preoccupation with self-esteem is actually detrimental to society because this preoccupation encourages excessive individualism.

Berne, Eric. 1964. *Games People Play: The Psychology of Human Relationships*. This classic book examines how people may play games in their relationships in order to avoid reality or genuine intimacy.

Cancian, Francesca. 1987. *Love in America: Gender and Self-Development*. New York: Cambridge University Press. A look at how ideas about love have changed; a consideration of feminine love, masculine love, and androgynous love.

Duck, Steve. 1999. *Relating to Others*, 2nd ed. Philadelphia, PA: Open University Press. This well-known social psychologist explores many topics in this chapter, such as self-esteem and attachment theory.

Fromm, Erich. 1976. *The Art of Loving*. New York: Harper & Row. A classic, this book talks about love as an active choice to care for another person.

Sternberg, Robert I. and Mahzad Hojjat (eds.) 1991. *Satisfaction in Close Relationships*. NY: Guilford. Explores Sternberg's model of love as it relates to relationship satisfaction. Research by a number of scholars.

On the Net

1) Romantic versus Compassionate Love
http://www.mentalhelp.net/psyhelp/chap10/chap10c.htm

2) Styles of Loving
http://www.scrippscol.edu/~home/kwong/www/lovestyles.html

3) Love Thyself: Resources for Improving Self-Esteem
http://www.webheights.net/lovethyself/home.htm

4) The Personal Link
http://www.marywood.edu/departments/psychology/students/love/personal_link.htm

5) Singles Can Develop Self-Esteem and Self-Worth
http://www.solosingles.com/ssesteem

6) Self-Esteem Inventory Test
http://www.psychtests.com/tests/personality/self_esteem_r_access.html

Our Sexual Selves

I HAVE A FANCY BODY.

MR. ROGERS, "MR. ROGERS' NEIGHBOURHOOD"

THE REAL ISSUE ISN'T MAKING LOVE; IT'S FEELING LOVED.

WILLIAM H. MASTERS AND VIRGINIA E. JOHNSON, THE PLEASURE BOND

From childhood to old age, people are sexual beings. Sexuality has a lot to do with the way we think about ourselves and how we relate to others. It goes without saying that sex plays a vital role in marriages and other relationships. Despite the pleasure it can give, sexuality can be one of the most baffling aspects of ourselves. In our society sex is both exaggerated and repressed; rarely is it treated naturally. For this reason, people's sexual selves may be sources of ambivalence, even discomfort. Finding mutually satisfying ways of expressing our sexuality can be a challenge.

This chapter discusses the sexual and reproductive aspects of people's lives. Here we will define sexual orientation and examine various cultural messages regarding men's and women's sexuality. We will discuss sex as a pleasure bond that requires open, honest, and supportive communication, then look at the role sex plays throughout marriage. We will consider the impact of HIV/AIDS on relationships. Finally, we will examine ways that politics and religion have combined to influence sexual expression in our society today.

Before we begin, we want to point out our society's tendency to reinforce the differences between women and men and to ignore the common feelings, problems, and joys that make us all human. The truth is, men and women aren't really so different. Many physiological parts of the male and female genital systems are either alike or directly analogous. Furthermore, the patterns of sexual response are very similar in men and women. Space limits our ability to present much detail on the various possibilities of sexual expression (kissing, fondling, cuddling, even holding hands); but we want to point out that intercourse, or coitus, is not the only mode of sexual relating.

SEXUAL DEVELOPMENT AND ORIENTATION

Humans' development into sexually expressive beings begins in childhood (Friedrich 1998). Between ages two and five, children become interested in their own genitals, often touching themselves. They may also try to look at others who are nude or undressing. These behaviours may continue until sexual attraction first manifests itself, often by about fourth grade (Friedrich 1998; Marano 1997). As we develop into sexually expressive individuals, we manifest a sexual orientation.

Sexual Orientation

Sexual orientation refers to whether an individual prefers a partner of the same or opposite sex. **Heterosexuals** are attracted to opposite-sex partners and **homosexuals** to same-sex partners. A person's sexual orientation does not necessarily predict his or her sexual behaviour. Abstinence is a behavioural choice, as well as sexual expression with partners of the non-preferred gender. Everyday terms are *straight* (heterosexual), *gay,* and *lesbian*. Technically, the term *gay* is synonymous with homosexual and refers to males or females. But often "gay" (or "gay male") is used in reference to men; "lesbian" is used to refer to gay women. The Commission on Lesbian and Gay Concerns of the American Psychological Association (1991) prefers the words *gay male* or *gay man* and *lesbian* to *homosexual* because it thinks that the latter term may perpetuate negative stereotypes. All these terms designate one's choice of sex partner only, not general masculinity or femininity or other aspects of personality.

We tend to think of sexual orientation as a dichotomy: One is either gay or straight. Actually, sexual orientation may be a continuum. Freud and many contemporary psychologists and biologists maintain that humans are inherently bisexual; that is, we all may have the latent physiological and emotional structures necessary for responding sexually to either sex. From the interactionist point of view (Chapter 2), the very concepts "bisexual," "heterosexual," and "homosexual" are social inventions. They

emerged during the nineteenth century when a new category of scientists (sexologists) first began to examine sexual behaviour (Weeks 1985). Put another way, conceptual categories—along with the notion of sexual orientation itself—were created by social interaction, not by nature. Hence, developing a sexual orientation may be influenced by our tendency to think in dichotomous terms: Individuals may sort themselves into the categories and behave accordingly. In time, social pressures to view oneself as either straight or gay may inhibit latent bisexuality (Beach 1977; Gagnon 1977).

The Development of Sexual Orientation

Deciding who is to be categorized as gay or lesbian, along with possible concealment by survey respondents, precludes any accurate calculation of how many gays and lesbians there are in our society. Until fairly recently, it was generally stated that about 10 percent of adult individuals are gay or lesbian. However, evidence published in 1994 suggests that the incidence of exclusively same-sex behaviour is probably lower than this and may be about four percent (Laumann et al. 1994). Much gay or lesbian activity is episodic, rather than ongoing or consistent, and the majority of gay men also report male–female sexual contact (Rogers and Turner 1991). Conceptual problems—that is, deciding who is to be classified as homosexual (How much experience? How exclusively homosexual?)—preclude any really accurate count.

Amid this uncertainty, the origins of both heterosexual and gay identities remain a puzzle. The existence of a fairly constant proportion of gays in virtually every society—in societies that treat homosexuality permissively as well as those that treat it harshly—suggests a biological imperative (Ford and Beach 1971; Bell, Weinberg, and Hammersmith 1981). Some anatomical and genetics research has found a possible relationship between physiology and sexual orientation (Gelman 1992; LeVay and Hamer 1994; Hamer and Copeland 1994, 1998; Pillard and Bailey 1998). However, no clear genetic differences between heterosexuals and gays have been conclusively established (Byrne 1994; Peele and DeGrandpre 1995; Reagan 1999; Rice et al. 1999). It may not be clear to what extent, if at all, sexual orientation is genetic, but nonetheless we each make choices regarding it and many other aspects of sexuality. As we have seen, we negotiate decisions within the parameters established by society. The next section takes a look at how sexuality and society interface.

THEORETICAL PERSPECTIVES ON HUMAN SEXUALITY

We saw in Chapter 2 that there are various theoretical perspectives concerning marriage and families. The same is true for theoretical approaches to human sexuality. Here we discuss three of these.

The Interactionist Perspective: Negotiating Cultural Messages

"*That* we are sexual is determined by a biological imperative toward reproduction, but *how* we are sexual—where, when, how often, with whom, and why—has to do with cultural learning, with meaning transmitted in a cultural setting" (Fracher and Kimmel 1992).

As with gender roles (Chapter 3), the way people think and feel about sex has a lot to do with the messages society gives them (Longmore 1998). Cultural messages give us legitimate reasons for having sex, as well as who should take the sexual initiative, how long a sexual encounter should last, how important it is to experience orgasm, what positions are acceptable, and whether it is appropriate to masturbate, among other things. We, the authors, take primarily an **interactionist perspective on human sexuality** (generally described in Chapter 2). In this context, an interactionist theoretical perspective holds that women and men negotiate and are influenced by the "sexual scripts" (Laumann et al. 1994) they learn from society. There is a competing point of view, however, called evolutionary psychology, and we will examine it now.

Evolutionary Psychology—Once Again: Is Anatomy Destiny?

Chapter 3 asked whether gendered behaviour is due mainly to biological factors (genetics). The question can also be raised regarding human sexuality. **Evolutionary psychology** argues that humans have an evolutionary biological origin that affects their

sexual relations (De Lameter and Hyde 1998). This perspective has its roots in Charles Darwin's *The Origin of the Species,* first published in 1859. Darwin proposed that all species evolve according to the **survival of the fittest** principle: Only the stronger, more intelligent, and adaptable of a species survive to reproduce, a process whereby the entire species is strengthened and prospers over time.

According to evolutionary psychologists, humans—like the species from which they evolved—are designed for the purpose of transmitting their biological hereditary material (genes or chromosomes) to the next generation. They do this in the most efficient ways possible. Human sexual attitudes and behaviours are best understood in this context. Like males in other primate species, men are inclined toward casual sex with many partners while women are more discriminating. (After all, male gorillas keep a harem, while female gorillas do not.) In this view, the basic source for this difference is as follows: A woman, regardless of how many sex partners she has, can generally have only one offspring a year. Compared with men, a woman's anatomy limits her ability to pass on her genes, and so she must be more discriminating when choosing a partner. For a man, each new mate offers a real chance for carrying on his genetic material into the future. Evolutionary psychologists also assume, and attribute to biology, men's association of sex with power. Some of their evidence for this is that among baboons, the higher a male ranks in the social hierarchy, the more sex he has (Wright 1994a).

Even proponents of the biosocial perspective, of which evolutionary psychology is a part, recognize that biosocial influences are *both* genetic and social in character (Udry 1988; Troost and Filsinger 1993; Money 1995; Hamer and Copeland 1998). As we concluded in our discussion of gender in Chapter 3, at best, genetics has an interactive influence with society on human behaviour. In contrast to evolutionary psychology, the social–historical perspective shows us that in North America (and elsewhere), societal messages about sex have changed over time.

An Historical Perspective

From colonial times until the nineteenth century, the purpose of sex in Canada was reproduction; the sociocultural attitudes were patriarchal. A new definition of sexuality emerged in the nineteenth century and has flourished in the twentieth. Sex became significant for many persons as a means of couple communication and intimacy (D'Emilio and Freedman 1988). We will explore the cultural messages of several historical periods in Canada in more detail.

EARLY CANADA: PATRIARCHAL SEX In a patriarchal society, descent, succession, and inheritance are traced through the male genetic line, and the socioeconomic system is male dominated. **Patriarchal sexuality** is characterized by many beliefs, values, attitudes, and behaviours developed to protect the male line of descent. Exclusive sexual possession by a man of a woman in monogamous marriage ensures that her children will be legitimately his, and men control women's sexuality. Sex is defined as a physiological activity, valued for its procreative potential. Men are thought to be born with an urgent sex drive, while women are naturally sexually passive; orgasm is expected for men but not for women. Unmarried men and husbands whose wives do not meet their sexual needs can gratify those needs outside marriage. Sex outside marriage is wrong for women, however; only tainted or loose women do it.

While it has been significantly challenged, the patriarchal sexual script persists to some extent in our society and corresponds with traditional gender expectations (see Chapter 3). If masculinity is a quality that must be achieved or proven, one arena for doing so is sexual accomplishment or conquest. A "real" man performs (Zilbergeld 1992). A 1995 national survey conducted on a representative sample of 1713 Canadians found that from about age 30 onward, men were more likely than women to report having sex at least weekly (Bibby 1995, p. 67). Another Canadian survey (*Maclean's* 2000, p. 52) based on telephone interviews with 1400 adult Canadians, randomly selected from all 10 provinces, reports that 36 percent of Canadian men—compared with 13 percent of women—say they have had six or more sexual partners in a lifetime; in this survey, the largest grouping of women (30 percent) maintained that they had had only one partner (p. 40). A summary of surveys conducted in Canada over the past three decades additionally finds that young-adult men are more likely than young-adult women to endorse a casual, recreational, "fun" orientation towards hetero-

sexual involvement (51.9 percent of francophone men and 36.4 anglophone men versus 37.1 percent of francophone women and 19.7 percent of anglophone women) (Hobart 1996, p. 149).

One Canadian study conducted on a sample of 292 (148 women and 144 men) heterosexual undergraduate students reports that men report more frequent and more diverse sexual fantasies than women (Renaud and Byers 1999). A Canadian survey, based on 569 respondents living in the Greater Toronto Area, also notes that men were three times as likely to fantasize about sex with more than one partner than were women (37 percent versus 11 percent) (Mandel 1999).

A 1992 national survey, by the National Opinion Research Center (NORC) and based on a representative sample of 3432 Americans aged 18–59 additionally found that three times as many men as women report masturbating at least once a week. Three-quarters of the men reported always reaching orgasm in intercourse, while the fraction for women was nearer to one-quarter. Men are also much more likely to think about sex (54 percent of men and 19 percent of women said they think about it at least once a day) and to have multiple partners and more of them. Men are also more excited by the prospect of group sex. These differences are less pronounced among the youngest cohort, a trend that holds out the possibility of more convergence between men's and women's sexual experiences (Laumann et al. 1994).

THE TWENTIETH CENTURY: THE EMERGENCE OF EXPRESSIVE SEXUALITY A different sexual message has emerged as the result of several societal changes, including the decreasing economic dependence of women and the availability of new methods of birth control. **Expressive sexuality** sees sexuality as basic to the humanness of *both* women and men; there is no one-sided sense of ownership. Orgasm is important for women as well as for men. Sex is not only, or even primarily, for reproduction, but is an important means of enhancing human intimacy. Hence, all forms of sexual activity between consenting adults are acceptable. Because of the emphasis on couple intimacy in recent decades, women's sexual expression has been more encouraged than it had been earlier (D'Emilio and Freedman 1988).

THE SEXUAL REVOLUTION: SEX FOR PLEASURE Although the view of sex as intimacy continues to predominate, in the 1920s an alternative message began to emerge wherein sex was seen as a legitimate means to individual pleasure, whether or not it played a role in serious couple relationship. Probably as a result, the generation of women born in the first decade of the twentieth century showed twice the incidence of nonmarital intercourse than those born earlier (D'Emilio and Freedman 1988; Seidman 1991). This liberalization of attitudes and behaviours characterized the sexual revolution of the mid-1960s.

Although these changes have often been attributed to the invention of oral contraceptives, various forms of contraception were available and used in the past without initiating similar changes in attitudes. For example, the condom was invented over 150 years ago, when the vulcanization of rubber made the mass production of condoms possible, but this device had no liberalizing effect on Victorian attitudes towards sexual self-expression. It is also obvious that "an inert object—a pill—cannot by itself, bring about significant changes in behaviour. Behaviour itself must first change, including, at the very minimum, creating the behaviour of actually taking the pill" (Nelson and Robinson 1994, p. 116). These sociologists note that "among the many other changes occurring during this time were women's growing financial independence from men and a growing female sense of empowerment that has continued to this day." They argue that women's "growing economic independence, coupled with a more effective form of contraception that permitted greater control over reproduction," weakened the previous necessary link between sexuality, legal marriage, and reproduction (Nelson and Robinson 1994, p. 117). Since 1969, birth control measures have been legal in Canada.

Definitions of what is acceptable and what is unacceptable have changed in recent decades with laws becoming increasingly more liberal. Until relatively recently, for example, the language of various sections of the Canadian Criminal Code harkened back "to a time when chastity and virginity were the paramount considerations and preoccupations" (Rozovsky and Rozovsky 1982, p. 12). As recently as two decades ago, Criminal Code provisions set out that it was a crime for a man over 18 to seduce a woman between 16 and 18 years of age who was—prior to the seduction—of "chaste character" and specified a penalty of up to two years' imprisonment. This penalty was also specified for a man who engaged in the offence of "seduction under promise of marriage of an unmarried female person of previously chaste character who is under the age of 21."

Prime Minister Pierre Trudeau's famous comment that the "state has no place in the bedrooms of the nation" was linked to the 1969 decriminalization of homosexual acts, committed in private, between two consenting adults of at least 21 years of age (Sanders 1999, p. 159). Although the age of consent for homosexual acts was later lowered to 18, a higher age of consent for anal sex than for vaginal and oral sex (age 14) remained in effect until a 1995 ruling that this distinction unlawfully discriminated against homosexuals. We have rapidly come to take it for granted that sexual and reproductive choices are ours to make.

Attitudes (and information) also changed regarding female orgasm as it became clear that there is no such thing as a purely vaginal orgasm. Rather, the clitoris is involved in virtually all female orgasms; "Think clitoris" was how feminist writers of the 1960s redefined female—hence, heterosexual couples'—sexuality (Segal 1994, p. 36).

Not only did attitudes become more liberal, but behaviours (particularly women's behaviours) changed as well. Research conducted on college and university undergraduate students pointed to the steady increase in the proportion of women who were experiencing premarital sexual intercourse as well as oral and anal sex, with no intention of marrying their current sexual partner (see Rubin 1990). In Canada, the most dramatic increases in female premarital sexual behaviour occurred during the period from the mid-1960s through the 1970s. The rate of nonmarital sex and the number of partners rose, while age at first intercourse dropped. The median age at first intercourse has not only declined in the last 40 years, it is now almost the same for females and males (Maticka-Tyndale et al., 2000).

By the mid-1970s, surveys reported that the majority of unmarried adults had experienced intercourse (Darling, Kallen, and VanDusen 1984; DeBuono et al. 1990). The trend toward higher rates of nonmarital sex has continued, especially among women (men already had high rates) (Fisher et al., 1999; Robinson et al. 1991). Today, sexual activity often begins in the teen years. Surveys show that teenagers in the 1970s were twice as likely to have had sex as were teens in the early 1960s.[1] According to one national Canadian survey, about 55 percent of 15 to 19 year-old say that they are sexually active (Bibby 1995, p. 70). Findings from the four-province Atlantic Student Drug Use Survey (Nova Scotia Department of Health 1998) also indicate that 26 percent of Grade 9 students, 37 percent of Grade 10 students and 58 percent of Grade 12 students had sexual intercourse during the previous year. Among sexually active students, 40 percent had more than one sexual partner. This study additionally found that condoms were inconsistently used, particularly among older students (Health Canada 1999, p. 127). The related issue of unmarried childbirth is addressed in Chapter 11.

The attitudes and behaviour of Canadians regarding sex have continued to become more permissive. For instance, in 1975 about one-third of Canadians tended to disapprove of premarital sex; by 1995, that figure had dropped to one in five (Bibby 1995, p. 69). Sociologist Reginald Bibby suggests that, based on current trends, "by about the year 2010, close to 85 percent of Canadians will approve of nonmarital sex, while a durable core of some 15 percent will continue to be opposed to such behaviour" (p. 70). Over the same time period, the percentage of Canadians who viewed homosexual relations as either "almost always wrong" or "always wrong" decreased from 72 percent to 52 percent (Bibby 1995, p. 72). Canadians living in the province of Quebec evidence the most liberal sexual attitudes in general towards premarital, homosexual, and extramarital sex. Currently, people living in the prairie provinces are more likely than other Canadians to disapprove of premarital sex and, along with those in the Atlantic region, express the greatest disapproval of homosexuality (Bibby 1995, p. 76).

1. Surveys based on the self-reports of young people must be interpreted with care. For example, one should be wary of young males' reports of their sexual activity because they are known to exaggerate. In addition, the social acceptability of being a virgin may have decreased so much that this, more than any change in behaviour, has led to the higher reported rates of sexual experience (Besharov 1993).

But perhaps the most significant change in sexuality since the 1960s, among heterosexuals at least, has been in marital sex. Today spouses are engaging in sexual activity more frequently than in the 1950s and in more varied and experimental ways. More married women are experiencing orgasm, and they're doing so more often (Hunt 1974; Jasso 1985; Laumann et al. 1994). Today's marrieds report taking baths or showers together (30 percent), buying erotic underwear (20 percent), swimming together nude (19 percent) (Schmidt 1990); and videotaping their sexual escapades for later viewing (Toufexis 1990). In a recent study of 3432 Americans by the University of Chicago's National Opinion Research Center (NORC), 88 percent of married partners said they enjoy great sexual pleasure (Laumann et al. 1994). If the sexual revolution of the 1960s focused on freer attitudes and behaviours among heterosexuals, more recent decades have expanded that liberalism to encompass lesbian and gay male sexuality.

INTO THE NEW MILLENNIUM: CHALLENGES TO HETEROSEXISM In 1995, *Newsweek* ran a story titled "Bisexuality." In large print, the author proclaimed that being "bi" was becoming noticeable "in pop culture, in cyberspace and on campus" (Leland 1995). The story quoted a man who said he had identified himself as gay since he was 16, even though he'd slept with both men and women. Now he is "proud to say I'm a recovering bi-phobe" (in Leland 1995, p. 49). "Bi-phobe" is a take-off on "homophobe," slang for a person who demonstrates **homophobia** (fear, dread, aversion to, and often hatred of homosexuals).

Until about two decades ago, most people thought about sexuality almost exclusively as between men and women. In other words, our thinking was characterized by **heterosexism**—the taken-for-granted system of beliefs, values, and customs that places superior value on heterosexual behaviour (as opposed to homosexual) and denies or stigmatizes nonheterosexual relations (Neisen 1990). However, since "Stonewall" (a 1969 police raid on a U.S. gay bar) galvanized the gay community into advocacy, gay males and lesbians have not only become increasingly visible but also have challenged the notion that heterosexuality is the one proper form of sexual expression.

Lesbian and gay male partnerships and families have become increasingly visible over the past decade. Meanwhile, discrimination and controversy persist.

Although the percentage of gay men and lesbians in our society is relatively small, political activism has resulted in gays' greater visibility (Sullivan 1995). Furthermore, gay men and lesbians have won legal victories, new tolerance by some religious denominations, greater understanding on the part of some heterosexuals, and sometimes positive action by government. Sociologist John Alan Lee (1999 p. 1095) observes that "By 1996, the majority of Canadian provinces had legislated against discrimination, as is also the case in the internal rules of numerous public and private institutions ranging from churches to universities to Canada Post to major banks." He also notes that the Canadian military "has gone much further than the American military's 'Don't ask, don't tell' policy by banning discrimination on the basis of sexual orientation." "Sexual ori-

entation" has been added to the *Canadian Human Rights Act* and to legislation imposing harsher penalties for such "hate crimes" as gay-bashing. Gay and lesbian domestic partners have also increasingly gained access to numerous social, financial and legal benefits formerly available only to legally married couples. However, unlike the Netherlands, which in March of 2001 became the first jurisdiction in the world to allow same-sex couples to legally marry (EGALE 2001) at present, no province or territory in Canada sanctions marriage between individuals of the same sex.

In June of 1999, the Canadian House of Commons voted overwhelmingly in favour of a motion, introduced by MP Eric Lowther, the then-Reform Party critic on "Children and Families," opposing same-sex marriages. The motion, which signalled the first time same-sex marriage was the subject of a vote in the House of Commons, affirmed the exclusion of gays and lesbians from the institution of marriage and committed Parliament to "take all nececessary steps" to preserve legal marriage as an opposite-sex institution.

A 1999 Angus Reid survey of a national random sample of Canadians found that, when asked if gay couples should be able to legally married, younger Canadians were more likely to support the suggestion than older Canadians. Two-thirds of those 18 to 34 years of age versus just over half (52 percent) of those 35 to 54 and slightly less than a third (32 percent) of those 55 and older agreed with the idea of same-sex marriage. Support also varied with education; almost six out of 10 (59 percent) who possessed a university degree, versus 38 percent of those who had not completed high school, supported same-sex marriages (EGALE 1999). Support for gays being able to legally married was highest among those living in Quebec (63 percent), followed by those in British Columbia (54 percent), and Ontario (53 percent). Support was lowest in Alberta (43 percent), Saskatchewan (42 percent), and Manitoba (42 percent) (McIvoy 1999). Those Canadians who identify themselves as supporting the Bloc Quebecois, the NDP, or the Liberal Party are more likely to say that gay marriages should be recognized by the state, while those who report that they are Canadian Alliance (formerly Reform) and Conservative Party supporters are the least likely. In addition, people who see being gay as a choice are less sympathetic to lesbians or gay men, regarding job discrimination and other rights (Schmalz 1993).

In 1999, the landmark *M. v. H.* ruling by the Supreme Court of Canada held that the *Charter of Rights* requires governments to recognize gay and lesbian relationships equally with opposite-sex married couples in 68 federal laws. In the 1990s, various provincial governments also grappled with the issues presented by same-sex marriages. In May 1999, the Supreme Court of Ontario ruled that an Ontario law that excluded gays and lesbians from a definition of common-law couples was unconstitutional. Shortly after, the Ontario government passed an omnibus bill that amended 67 of its laws to include same-sex couples. Although the Supreme Court's ruling was only binding on the Ontario government, several other provinces quickly announced plans to make similar changes.

In June of 1999, when the Quebec National Assembly unanimously passed Bill 32, the Quebec government became the first Canadian province to ensure that same-sex couples would receive all the benefits and responsibilities of opposite-sex couples. Bill 32 changed the definition of "spouse" within the province and committed the Quebec government to making changes in 39 provincial laws and regulations. A month later, the British Columbia government introduced the "Definition of Spouse Amendment," which expanded the definition of "spouse" in that province to include "a person who has lived and cohabited with another person, for a period of at least two years immediately before the other's death, in a 'marriage-like' relationship, including a marriage-like relationship between persons of the same gender." As in Quebec, this change sought to ensure that same-sex couples would be treated the same as opposite-sex couples in relation to such matters as, for example, wills, estates, and inheritance.

In introducing the changes into law, B.C. Attorney General Ujjal Dosanjh stated that, "the legislation is proof that this government is committed to supporting stable family relationships, whether they involve traditional families, common law families, or same-sex relationships.... All British Columbians deserve the same rights and benefits in life and death" (EGALE 1999d). Omnibus provincial initiatives have also taken place in Nova Scotia while some limited laws to extend equality to same-sex couples have been enacted in New Brunswick (addressing spousal support) and Alberta (in relation to step-parent adoptions). However, it may be noted that in October 2001, the Supreme Court of British Columbia ruled that the rights of same-sex couples to marry under the equality provisions of the Canadian Charter of Rights and Freedoms were secondary to the "main purpose of marriage, which is to provide a structure within which to raise children" (Arnold 2001). In concluding that marital discrimination against same-sex couples was justified, Judge Ian H. Pitfield maintained that "same-sex and opposite-sex relationships are, at their core, demonstrably different" and that, "[t]he objective of limiting marriage to opposite sex couples is sufficiently important to warrant infringing the rights...[of same-sex couples]. The gain to society from the preservation of the deep-rooted and fundamental legal institution of opposite-sex marriage outweighs the detrimental effect of the law" (in Arnold 2001).

It is evident that while we are currently experiencing a challenge to heterosexism, the goals of this challenge—equal treatment and acceptance for lesbians and gay males—have not yet been accomplished. A majority (an estimated 70 percent in one poll) of gay men and lesbians report feeling free to be open about their sexual preferences with other family members today, although telling family members can result in reactions ranging from violence to support (Berke 1998; Savin-Williams and Dube 1998). Moreover, according to a 2001 report prepared by Amnesty International, over 70 countries currently consider homosexuality to be a crime and 30 of those violate the human rights of homosexuals. According to Ignacio Sainz, one of the authors of the report, "All over the world gays, lesbians, bisexuals, transsexuals and transvestites are at risk, especially of being victimized by human rights violations because of their sexual identity" (in Reuters 2001).

Constructing Gay Male and Lesbian Identities Amid Homophobia

One result of homophobia is that gay males and lesbians often negotiate, or construct their sexual identities amid hostility and maintain them within the context of a deviant subculture. According to one model (Troiden 1988, pp. 42–58), this process occurs in four stages: sensitization, identity confusion, identity assumption (acceptance and "coming out"), and commitment to homosexuality as a way of life.

Sensitization occurs before puberty. At this time most children assume they are heterosexual (if they think about their sexuality at all). But future homosexuals, feeling sexually marginal, have experiences that sensitize them to subsequent definitions of themselves as lesbian or gay: "I wasn't interested in boys (girls)"; "I didn't express myself the way other girls (or boys) would."

Identity confusion occurs in adolescence as lesbians and gays begin to see that their feelings, fantasies, or behaviours could be considered homosexual. Because the idea that they could be homosexual goes against previously held self-images, identity confusion (inner turmoil and uncertainty) results. Some assume antihomosexual postures or establish heterosexual involvements to eliminate their "inappropriate" sexual interests: "I thought my homosexual feelings would go away if I dated a lot and had sex with as many women as possible," or "I thought my attraction to women was a passing phase and would go away once I started having intercourse with my boyfriend" (Troiden 1988, p. 48).

Identity assumption, which occurs during or after late adolescence, involves developing both a self-identity and a presented identity—presented, that is, among other homosexuals at least—as homosexual. In one writer's description of this stage,

> you are quite sure you are a homosexual and you accept this fairly happily. You are prepared to tell a few people about being a homosexual but you carefully select whom you will tell. You adopt an attitude of fitting in where you live and work. You can't see any point in confronting people with your homosexuality if it's going to embarrass all concerned. (Cass 1984, cited in Troiden 1988, p. 53)

The final stage, commitment, involves the decision to accept homosexuality as a way of life. Here the costs are less and the rewards greater for remaining a homosexual than for trying to function as a heterosexual. Having "come out," even to nonhomosexuals, "you are happy about the way you are but feel that being a homosexual is not the most important part of you. You mix socially with homosexuals and heterosexuals [with whom] you are open about your homosexuality" (Cass 1984, cited in Troiden 1988, p. 57).

The above analysis treats the development of gay male and lesbian sexual identities as similar processes. Nevertheless, lesbian and gay male behaviours are different from one another.

Comparing Gay Male and Lesbian Sexual Behaviours

In a large national sample of 12 000 American volunteers from the Seattle, San Francisco, and Washington, D.C. areas, sociologists Philip Blumstein and Pepper Schwartz (1983) compared four types of couples: heterosexual marrieds, cohabiting heterosexuals, gay male, and lesbian couples. Among other things, they found that gay male and lesbian relationships differ. The fact that lesbian couples consist of two women and gay couples of two men is significant. Gay men tend to have considerably more transitory, or casual, sex than do lesbians (or heterosexual men, whose union with a woman may require compromise on this issue), while casual sex among lesbians is relatively rare. That is, gay male sexuality is more often "body-centred" (Ruefli, Yu, and Barton 1992) and lesbian sexuality, person-centred. Blumstein and Schwartz (1983), in fact, described lesbian relationships as the "least sexualized" of the four kinds of couples compared. (Box 5.1, "Lesbian 'Sex'," addresses this finding.) Interestingly, meanwhile, lesbians report greater sexual satisfaction than do heterosexual women, including more frequent sexual expression and orgasms. "Their greater tenderness, patience, and knowledge of the female body are said to be the reasons" (Konner 1990, p. 26). Many—though assuredly not all—women and men today have internalized divergent sexual messages.

NEGOTIATING (HETERO)SEXUAL EXPRESSION

Today heterosexuals negotiate sexual relationships in a context in which new expectations of equality and similarity coexist with a heritage of difference. Studies in the 1970s found that, compared to before the sexual revolution, men are more interested in communicating intimately through sex while women show more interest in the physical pleasure involved in sex (Pietropinto and Simenauer 1977). Nevertheless, studies continue to show that women are more interested than men in romantic foreplay (Purnine and Carey 1998). Women may feel lonely and emotionally separated from task-oriented, emotionally reserved male partners, whereas men feel that their female partners ask too much emotionally (Tannen 1990; Gray 1995).

Moreover, if a man continues to equate sex with performance in a culture that now expects women to reach orgasm, he may feel undue pressure to sexually satisfy his partner. "So the knowledgeable man ... instead of doing something to his [partner] sexually, was prepared to do something for her sexually.... Unfortunately, in the role of doing for rather than just doing to he had to assume even more sexual responsibility" (Masters and Johnson 1976, p. 6). In a society that allows both males and females multiple partners, he may also fear his mate's comparing him with other lovers (Boyer 1981).

Masters and Johnson argue nonetheless that more equal gender expectations facilitate better sex. "The

most effective sex is not something a man does to or for a woman but something a man and a woman do together *as equals*" (Masters and Johnson 1976, p. 88). From this point of view the female not only is free to initiate sex but also is equally responsible for her own arousal and orgasm. The male is not required to "deliver pleasure on demand," but can openly express his spontaneous feelings.

This discussion points again to the fact that cultural messages, both about gender (Chapter 3) and about sexual expression, are negotiated. Recognizing this, sociologist Ira Reiss has developed a fourfold classification of societal standards for nonmarital sex. We should note that these are standards, or cultural prescriptions, not research reports of what people actually do.

Four Standards of Nonmarital Sex

Sociologist Ira Reiss' (1976) four standards—abstinence, permissiveness with affection, permissiveness without affection, and the double standard—were originally developed to apply to *premarital* sex among heterosexual couples. However, they have since been more generally applied to nonmarital sexual activities of divorced and separated heterosexuals, as well as to those who do not plan to marry.

ABSTINENCE   The standard of **abstinence** maintains that regardless of the circumstances, nonmarital intercourse is wrong for both women and men. Some women and men have withdrawn from nonmarital sexual relationships entirely, advocating celibacy, or "the right to say no" (Goodstein and Connelly 1998; Johnson 1990; Stark 1997). Many contemporary religious groups, especially the more conservative or fundamentalist Christian and Islamic congregations, encourage abstinence (Runkel 1998). In one national survey, conservative Protestants who attend church regularly were more likely than other Protestants or Catholics to endorse nonmarital abstinence (Petersen and Donnenwerth 1997). A 1987 Gallup poll found that the most common reason given for opposing sex outside marriage was religious or moral beliefs (83 percent), followed by the risk of sexually transmitted diseases or STDs (20 percent) and of pregnancy (13 percent) and the belief that women should be virgins until marriage (9 percent) ("Gallup Poll Shows"

1988). With tongue only partly in cheek, one writer suggests that cybersex (sexual talk on the Internet, with or without masturbation) is a preferable "new abstinence": You can't get diseases from computers (Gerhard 1994).

Abstinence, or celibacy, at least for teens and young adults, receives support from counsellors and feminists as a positive choice (Whitman 1997). These experts are concerned about pressures on young people to establish sexual activity before they're ready, or about pressures for men and women to engage in sexual relationships when they don't want to. They maintain that celibacy, much devalued in the context of sexual liberation, ought to remain a valid and respected option.

PERMISSIVENESS WITH AFFECTION The standard **permissiveness with affection** permits nonmarital intercourse for both men and women equally, provided they have a fairly stable, affectionate relationship. This standard may be the most widespread sexual norm among unmarrieds today (Darling, Kallen and VanDusen 1984; Whitman 1997). In a 1997 national U.S. poll by *U.S. News & World Report,* a majority of respondents under the age of 45 said that adult, nonmarital sex "generally benefits people" in addition to offering sexual pleasure. A majority also felt that having had a few sexual partners makes it easier for a person to choose a sexually compatible spouse (Whitman 1997). The NORC survey, (described in detail later in chapter), concluded that we have sex mainly with people we know and care about. In this survey, over seven in ten respondents said that they had only one sexual partner in the course of a year (Laumann et al. 1994).

PERMISSIVENESS WITHOUT AFFECTION Sometimes called recreational sex, **permissiveness without affection** allows intercourse for women and men regardless of how much stability or affection there is in their relationship. Casual sex—intercourse between partners only briefly acquainted—is permitted. This standard reminds us of historians D'Emilio and Freedman's (1988) argument that, from about the 1920s, sex began increasingly to be seen as an avenue for individual pleasure. But removed from its relationship context, sex could and did become a "commercial product." That is, in the extreme, the interests and preferences of a partner

could be discounted (D'Emilio and Freedman 1988). (The authors of this text do not consider this attitude to be an example of acting with sexual responsibility, a topic addressed in detail later in this chapter.) In recent class discussions on this topic, co-author Agnes Riedmann's marriage and family students worried that too much permissiveness without affection led people to think of sex as "no big deal." And if sex is no big deal, what is there to define a committed or marital relationship as special? Efforts by various religious denominations, coupled with the fear of HIV/AIDS and other sexually transmitted diseases, meanwhile, may have caused some decline in the popularity of this standard (Ku et al. 1995; Sengupta 1997). However, as we shall discuss later, surveys suggest that even those Canadians who voice concern about HIV/AIDS and/or who participate in high-risk sexual behaviour (e.g., sex with multiple partners, a failure to practise "safe sex") have not, generally speaking, changed their behaviour to reduce their level of risk (Fisher et al., 1999; Misovich et al., 1999; Myers et al., 1999)

THE DOUBLE STANDARD According to the double standard, women's sexual behaviour must be more conservative than men's. In its original form, the **double standard** meant that women should not have sex before or outside of marriage, whereas men could. More recently, the double standard has required that women be in love to have sex, or at least have fewer partners than men have.

Throughout the 1980s, researchers found the double standard to be declining and reported expectations to be similar for men and women (Sprecher, McKinney, and Orbuch 1987; Sprecher et al. 1988; Sprecher 1989; Williams 1989). Masters and

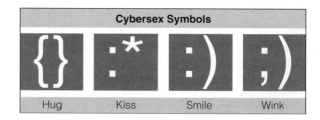

Cybersex. Is it sex—cyberstyle—or is it abstinence? From an interactionist perspective, we might say that society is still constructing the answer. But we've already constructed the beginnings of a cybersex language.

Lesbian "Sex"

This essay is by lesbian theorist Marilyn Frye. It has as much to say about scientific research methods as about sexual expression.

[T]he word "sex" is in quotation marks in my title... [because] the term "sex" is an inappropriate term for what lesbians do....

Recent discussions of lesbian "sex" frequently cite the findings of a study on couples by Blumstein and Schwartz [1983, and cited by Lamanna, Riedmann and Nelson in this chapter] which is perceived by most of those who discuss it as having been done well, with a good sample of couples—lesbian, male homosexual, heterosexual non-married and heterosexual married couples. These people apparently found that lesbian couples "have sex" far less frequently than any other type of couple, that lesbians are less "sexual" as couples and as individuals than anyone else. In their sample,...47 percent of lesbians in long term relationships "had sex" once a month or less, while among heterosexual married couples only 15 percent had sex once a month or less. And they report that lesbians seem to be more limited in the range of their "sexual" techniques than are other couples....

The suspicion arises that what 85 percent of heterosexual married couples are doing more than once a month and what 47 percent of lesbian couples are doing less than once a month is not the same thing. And if they are not doing the same thing, how was this research done that would line these different things up against each other to compare how many times they were done?

I remember that one of my first delicious tastes of old gay lesbian culture occurred in a bar where I was chatting with some other lesbians.... One was talking about being busted out of the Marines for being gay. She had been put under suspicion somehow, and was sent off to the base psychiatrist to be questioned.... To this end [the psychiatrist] asked her, "How many times have you had sex with a woman?" At this, we all laughed and giggled: what an ignorant fool he was!

What does he think he means by "times"? What will we count? What's to count?...

If what the heterosexual married couples do that the individuals report under the rubric "sex" or "have sex" is something that in most instances can easily be individuated into countable instances, this is more evidence that it is not what long-term lesbian couples do...or, for that matter, what short-term lesbian couples do....

How did the lesbians figure out how to answer the questions "How frequently?" or "How many times?" My guess is, for starters, that different individuals figured it out differently, to some degree. Some might have counted a two- or three-cycle evening as one "time" they "had sex"; some might have counted that as two or three "times." Some may have counted as "times" only the times both partners had orgasms; some may have counted as "times" occasions on which at least one had an orgasm; some may not have orgasms or have them rarely and may not have figured orgasms into the calculations; perhaps they counted as a "time" every episode in which both touched the other's vulva more than fleetingly and not for something like a health examination....

We have no idea how individual lesbians individuated their so-called "sexual acts" or encounters; we have no idea what it means when they said they did it less than once a month....

So, do lesbian couples really "have sex" any less frequently than heterosexual couples? My own view is that lesbian couples "have sex" a great deal less frequently than heterosexual couples: I think, in fact, we don't "have sex" at all. By the criteria that I'm betting most of the heterosexual people used in reporting the frequency with which they have sex, lesbians don't have sex. There is no male partner whose orgasm and ejaculation can be the criterion for counting "times." (I'm willing to draw the conclusion that heterosexual women don't have sex either, that what they report is the frequency with which their partners had sex.)

(continued)

Lesbian "Sex"

(continued)

What does "have sex" mean to you? Is the term, as Frye suggests, defined principally according to the male's experience? What does this say about heterosexual women's sexual expression? What does this say about the research findings of Blumstein and Schwartz? How might Blumstein and Schwartz have asked about what they wanted to know in a better, more effective way?

Source: Frye 1992.

Johnson's (1966) work on human sexual response probably contributed to the sense that men and women are equally sexual creatures, similar in their sexual capacity and needs. Nevertheless, there is also new evidence that, at least among some young people, the double standard remains alive and well.

In his research on male athletes' friendships, sociologist Michael Messner (1992) found that a "Big Man on Campus" was expected to be considerably (hetero)sexually active. Other males were envious of the ease with which he could "get women." Even among high schoolers, being a "real" guy meant "you get 'em into bed" (p. 96). Messner laments that this cultural conditioning encourages men to separate sex from intimacy: Male friendship is defined as intimate but not sexual, while relationships with women are defined as sexual but not intimate. Among women, on the other hand, sexual expression more often symbolizes connection with a partner and communicates intimacy.

Peggy Orenstein (1994) conducted naturalistic observation (see Chapter 2) in a middle school of mostly white, middle-class students. She describes an episode in an eighth-grade sex education class on STDs:

"We'll use a woman," [Ms. Webster, the teacher] says, drawing the Greek symbol for woman on the blackboard. "Let's say she is infected, but she hasn't really noticed yet, so she has sex with three men."

Ms. Webster draws three symbols for man on the board, and as she does, a heavyset boy in a Chicago Bulls cap stage-whispers, "What a slut," and the class titters.

"Okay," says Ms. Webster, who doesn't hear the comment. "Now the first guy has three sexual encounters in six months." She turns to draw three more women's signs, her back to the class, and several of the boys point at themselves proudly, striking exaggerated macho poses.

"The second guy was very active, he had intercourse with five women." As she turns to the diagram again, two boys stand and take bows.

"Now the third guy was smart—he didn't sleep with *anyone*." She draws a happy face and the boys point at each other derisively, mouthing, "You! You!"

During the entire diagramming process, the girls in the class remain silent. (p. 61)

The more restrained sexual standards of women are usually attributed to a legacy of differential socialization, such as this example illustrates and perhaps to greater religiosity as well (Tanfer and Cubbins 1992). One observer argues that women are more likely to have less control over a sexual encounter; hence gender differences in permissiveness may reflect differences in social power and vulnerability (Howard 1988). Meanwhile, two social scientists (Robinson and Jedlicka 1982) have proposed an emergent new double standard, according to which both sexes feel more permissive about their own sex but expect more conservative behaviour from the opposite sex. According to these researchers, men expect stricter morality of women and women expect stricter morality of men.

We turn now to a brief discussion of cultural diversity and sexual expression.

Cultural Diversity and Sexual Expression

Social customs may reinforce the message that while sexual pleasure is acceptable for men, it is unacceptable for women. This may be more pronounced in some ethnic cultures than others. At the risk of exaggerating the homogeneity of different ethno-religious cultures, sociologist Lloyd Saxton (1996), for example, observes that "it is culturally unacceptable for a Muslim woman to feel sexual pleasure or to experience orgasm. This culture teaches that sexual responsiveness in a woman is unseemly or shameful; a woman who does experience erotic sensations or pleasure is expected to conceal this from her husband" (p. 124). An extreme form of the sexual double standard is evidenced in the practices referred to by Westerners as **female genital mutilation (FGM)**. FGM is also known as *female circumcision* or, more precisely, *excision* (the removal of the clitoris and part or all of the labia minora), *clitoridectomy* (the scarring or partial or complete removal of the clitoris), *infibulation* (the complete removal of the clitoris and labia minora, partial removal of the labia majora and stitching together of the vulva, leaving a small hole for urine and menstrual blood to pass), and *labiadectomy* (removal of the labia). Although FGM is often associated with the religion of Islam, FGM is a *social custom* and *not* a religious practice (*Religious Tolerance*, 2000a).

Although the specific reasons given for FGM vary by culture, the most common justifications include the assumption that a woman who does not undergo the procedure is "unclean," "masculine" (in that she retains a vestige of a male sex organ), and/or sexually aggressive (and therefore less likely to remain a virgin before marriage or faithful within marriage). "The

justification for the operation appears to be largely grounded in a desire to terminate or reduce feelings of sexual arousal in women so that they will be much less likely to engage in pre-marital intercourse or adultery" (*Religious Tolerance*, 2000b). For example, the 1995 Report on the Ottawa consultations on female genital mutilation, based on a limited, non-representative sample of members of the Somali community in Ottawa, noted that "in the Somali society the cultural and traditional pressures to continue FGM still exist, because most believe that it is a means of sustaining virginity and marriageability, and therefore the potential for having a family" (Hussein 1995).

In Canada, FGM techniques are illegal. "[A] doctor can legally open an infibulated woman to facilitate intercourse or childbirth, but cannot legally resew the genitals" (Scott 2000). Section 273.3 of the Canadian Criminal Code additionally protects children who are ordinarily resident in Canada (as citizens or landed immigrants) from being removed from this country and subjected to FGM. Nevertheless, it has been asserted that "[f]emale genital mutilation is taking place in Canada and young girls are also taken outside the country to be mutilated" (in Scott 2000).

In addition, certain cultures may still place considerable emphasis upon women remaining virgins until marriage. In some cases, "[a] woman's future can hang, literally, by a membrane," and, without an intact hymen, women may be "shunned as whores—in extreme cases, even murdered by male relatives to restore family honour" (Oh 2000, p. 44). Perhaps in consequence, plastic surgery to reconstruct hymens has recently emerged as a specialty offered by some Canadian plastic surgeons. For example, a Toronto woman from a Middle Eastern Muslim culture recounted how, prior to her arranged marriage, she "searched desperately" for a plastic surgeon who would perform the $2000 operation. Her hymen had been damaged in an erotic encounter with a boyfriend with whom she had been meeting, without her family's knowledge, for two years. "My first thought was that I'd have to kill myself to avoid hardship and shame for myself and my family" (in Oh 2000, p.43).

At least one sex researcher (Belcastro 1985) has recommended that priority be given to "research describing the sexual development and behaviour patterns, across the life cycle, for diversified cultural groups in diversified geographic regions" (p. 56). However, it is only recently that such research has been published. One example is a Canadian study comparing undergraduates of Asian ancestry with those of European descent. In an admittedly small, nonrepresentative sample, the researchers found Asian-Canadian undergrads to have more conservative sexual attitudes and behaviours as well as less knowledge about sex. The longer Asian-Canadians were in North America, the more they resembled Canadians of European descent with regard to sex (Meston, Trapnell, and Gorzalka 1998).

We turn now to a consideration of sex in marriage.

SEXUALITY THROUGHOUT MARRIAGE

It might surprise you that various aspects of nonmarital sex are more likely to be studied than are those within marriage (Call, Sprecher, and Schwartz 1995). One aspect of marital sex that has consistently been researched is sexual frequency: How often do married couples have sex and what factors affect this frequency? Before we get to the answers, we need to say something about how the information is gathered.

How Do We Know What We Do? A Look at Sex Surveys

Chapter 2 points out that a *Playboy* magazine survey about sex would yield different results from one in *Family Circle*. Because the readers of these two magazines differ from each other as categories, their answers would hardly be the same. In serious social science, however, researchers strive for **representative samples**—survey samples that reflect, or represent, all the people about whom they want to know something.

The pioneer research surveys on sex in North America were the Kinsey reports on male and female sexuality (Kinsey, Pomeroy, and Martin 1948, 1953) in the 1940s and 1950s. Kinsey believed that a statistically representative survey of sexual behaviour was impossible, because many of the randomly selected respondents would refuse to answer or lie. This issue remains a problem for researchers today. For instance, footnote 1 in this chapter points out that sex surveys among teenagers need to be interpreted with caution because, among other things, young men are likely to exaggerate their sexual activities. In the Kinsey era,

however, the worry was that people would minimize their sexual behaviours. Hence the Kinsey reports were conducted with volunteers. But people who volunteer information about their sex lives very probably do not represent all North Americans. They may be more sexually permissive and/or active, for example, or have a particular axe to grind.

Since the Kinsey research, other scientific studies on sexual behaviour have used random samples. For example, the 1998 Canadian Contraception Study was designed to examine knowledge, attitudes, and behaviour of Canadian women with respect to contraception and related sexual and reproductive health issues. The study was conducted by a marketing research firm that used a panel of 60 000 Canadian households, pre-recruited for participation in survey research (and balanced against census data for age of female head of households, household income, city size, household size and number of children). From this panel, a sample of 2893 women aged 15–44 (with a maximum of one per household) was randomly chosen. Of the 2893 surveys mailed out, 1599 responses were eventually returned (a response rate of 55 percent). Responses were then weighted to approximate the Canadian census profile by region and age, within marital status, based on the 1996 Canadian census.

In 1992 in the United States, the National Opinion Research Center (NORC) at the University of Chicago conducted interviews with a random and representative sample of 3432 Americans, ages 18 to 59 (Laumann et al. 1994). These respondents were selected using sophisticated sampling techniques developed through decades of political and consumer polling. NORC can be reasonably certain the respondents did not lie (at least not any more than subjects lie on surveys about other topics, always a concern for social scientists) because they were questioned in 90-minute face-to-face interviews. Furthermore, 80 percent of the randomly selected persons actually agreed to be interviewed—an impressively high and statistically viable response rate for social science research. NORC's findings can be generalized to the U.S. population under age 60 with a high degree of confidence. Indeed, the results have been welcomed as the first-ever truly scientific nation-wide survey of sex in the United States. The NORC data, however, included only people under 60. As a result, the findings really cannot be generalized to the United States as a whole, nor do they tell us anything about the sexual activities of older Americans.[2]

Conclusions based on survey research on sensitive matters such as sexuality must always be qualified by an awareness of their limitations—the possibility that respondents have minimized or exaggerated their sexuality or that people willing to answer a survey on sex are not representative of the public. Nevertheless, we have far more reliable information than ever before. Appreciating both the strengths and weaknesses of the data, let us examine what we know about sexuality in Canadian and American marriages.

How Often?

Social scientists are interested in sexual frequency because they like to examine trends over time and to relate these to other aspects of intimate relationships, such as communication styles or feelings of satisfaction. For the rest of us, "How often?" is typically a question motivated by curiosity about our own sexual behaviour compared to that of others. Either way, what do we know?

In the NORC survey, described above, the average frequency of sex for sexually active, married respondents under age 60 was seven times a month, or 1.6 times a week. About 40 percent of marrieds said they had intercourse at least twice a week (Laumann et al. 1994). If we take into consideration that none of these findings include older Americans, we might conclude—along with various experts in the field—that American couples average having sex about once a week. Of course, this is an *average*. "People don't have sex every week; they have good weeks and bad weeks" (Pepper Schwartz in Adler 1993). So does the ratio of good to bad weeks change over the course of a marriage? Yes: You have fewer good weeks (sorry).

FEWER GOOD WEEKS To examine sexual frequency throughout marriage, Call, Sprecher, and Schwartz (1995) looked at 6785 marrieds with a spouse in the household (and also at 678 respondents who were cohabiting, or living together). Like researchers before them (for example, Blumstein and Schwartz [1983]), they found that sexual activity is highest among young marrieds. About 96 percent of spouses under age 25 reported having had sex at least once during the previous month. The proportion of sexually active spouses gradually diminished until about age 50 when sharp declines were evident. Among 50- to 54-year-olds, 83 percent said they had sex within the previous month; for those between 65 and 69, the figure was 57 percent; 27 percent of respondents over age 74 reported having had sex within the previous month.

Figure 5.1 shows the mean average frequency of sexual intercourse during the month prior to the interview by age (and marital status). When examining Figure 5.1, note that the researchers report separate mean averages for all the marrieds in the sample and also for the sexually active spouses only. (The figure also shows frequency rates for cohabitors, and we will address these findings below.) The average number of times that married persons under age 25 had sex is about 12 times a month. That number drops to about eight times a month at ages 30–34, then to about six times monthly at about age 50. After that, frequency of intercourse drops more sharply; spouses over age 74 average having sex less than once each month.[3]

---

2. One study of sex among marrieds (Call, Sprecher, and Schwartz 1995) used in this section seeks to remedy the NORC study's deficiencies by using another U.S. national data set, the National Survey of Families and Households (NSFH). In 1987–88 the NSFH staff, affiliated with the University of Wisconsin, personally interviewed a representative national sample of 13 000 respondents aged 18 and over (Sweet, Bumpass, and Call 1988). The NSFH survey asked far fewer questions concerning sexual activity specifically, but some information on sexual behaviour is included. Considered very reliable, the NSFH data are often used as a basis for analysis regarding many topics discussed in this text.

3. These researchers found no significant differences in this pattern that were due to gender, race, or region of the country. While higher education levels had a positive effect on sexual frequency, very low and very high educational levels had a significant negative impact on sexual frequency. In contrast, in Canada, the POLLARA survey found that frequency of sex relations did vary by region of the country with the highest reported levels occurring in eastern Canada and declining as we move west. Canadians in the Atlantic provinces report frequencies above the national average of 7.33 times per month. "Ontarians are the next busiest at 7.18, followed by Prairie residents at 7.09 and Albertans who stirred themselves 6.91 times. British Columbians were up to the task just 6.57 times a month" (Cobb 1997). People in the Atlantic provinces were also the ones most satisfied with their sex lives, followed by those living in Quebec. Individuals earning $100 000 a year or more reported having sex more than most. This survey additionally reported that relatively few university-educated Canadians "are members of the 11-times-or-more club. Community college education seems to be the recommended qualification for 11-plussers" (Cobb 1997).

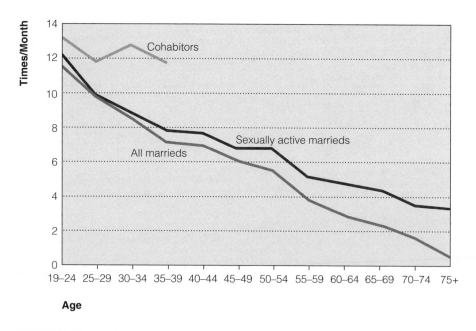

FIGURE **5.1**

Frequency of sex last month by age and marital status. (Source: Call, Sprecher, and Schwartz, 1995, p. 646.)

It used to be that describing sexuality over the course of a marriage would be nearly the same issue as discussing sex as people grow older. Today this is not the case. Many couples are remarried so that at age 45, or even 70, a person may be newly married. Nonetheless, we can logically assume that young spouses are in the early years of marriage.

Young Spouses

Why do young spouses have sexual intercourse more frequently than do older mates? The most important answer is simply age. On average, as people get older they have sex less often (Call, Sprecher, and Schwartz 1995). For example, the national *Citizen*-Global survey of 1410 adult Canadian adults conducted by the national polling firm POLLARA (Cobb 1997) found that the frequency of sexual relations per month declines with age: age 18 to 24, 8.6 times per month; 25 to 34, 8.6 times; 35 to 44, 8.0 times; 45 to 54, 7.3 times; 55 to 64, 5.6 times; and 65 and older, 3.5 times. But aging does not explain the decline entirely. Young married partners, as a rule,

have fewer distractions and worries, such as mortgage payments or small children. The high frequency of intercourse in this age group may also reflect a self-fulfilling prophecy: These couples may have sex more often partly because society expects them to.

After the first year, couples can expect sexual frequency to decline (Jasso 1985). Why so? It seems that a frequency pattern is set the first year. And "from then on almost everything—children, jobs, commuting, housework, financial worries—that happens to a couples conspires to reduce the degree of sexual interaction while almost nothing leads to increasing it" (Greenblatt 1983, p. 294).

Spouses in Middle Age

Despite declining coital frequency, respondents in one study emphasized the importance of sexuality. They pointed to the total marital relationship rather than just intercourse, however—to such aspects as "closeness, tenderness, love, companionship and affection" (Greenblatt 1983, p. 298)—as well as other forms of physical closeness such as cuddling or lying in bed together. In other words, with time, sex may become more broadly based in the couple's relationship. During this period, sexual relating may also become more sophisticated, as the partners become more experienced and secure. Greenblatt's was a small study (30 men and 50 women), though a random sample. But similar to her results, the NSFH study (whose results are illustrated in Figure 5.1) found that, after age, marital satisfaction was the second largest predictor of sexual frequency. Unhappy marriages were associated with a lower sexual frequency (Call, Sprecher, and Schwartz 1995). A more recent study (Young et al. 1998) also reports that the "overall marital satisfaction" variable had the highest correlation with sexual satisfaction.

We should be clear that it is impossible to determine which factor is cause and which is effect here: Does a lower level of marital satisfaction cause a couple to have sex less often, or is it the other way around? Another point: Middle-aged couples are apt to be more sexually active now than in the past. Over the past several decades, each age cohort has been somewhat more active than its predecessor. What appears to be declining frequency of sex with age is in part a generation-by-generation change toward heightened sexual activity (Jasso 1985).

Older Partners

In our society, images of sex tend to be associated with youth, beauty, and romance; to many young people, sex seems out of place in the lives of older adults. Sociologist Andrew Greeley goes further, finding "the image of passionate love between older people as grotesque" dominant in our society. "It may be that the last great...taboo is passion among the elderly," he asserts (in "Happiest Couples in Study ..." 1992). About 25 years ago, public opinion was virtually uniform in seeing sex as unlikely—even inappropriate—for older people. With Masters and Johnson's work in the 1970s indicating that many older people are sexually active, public opinion began to swing the other way. Then in the 1980s, researchers began to caution against the romanticized notion that biological aging could be abolished—that "old people are (or should be) healthy, sexually active, engaged, productive, and self-reliant" (Cole 1983, pp. 35, 39). Of course, biological aging cannot be eradicated, and physical changes associated with aging do affect sexuality

(Marsiglio and Donnelly 1991). The 1997–98 spurt of publicity surrounding Viagra, a new drug to treat male impotence (Leland 1997; Cowley 1998a) illustrates at least two points: 1) aging does affect sexual performance, and 2) many older people want to continue to be sexually active. Consider as well, in this context, that in the first year following its approval for use by Health Canada on March 8, 1999, Canadians spent more than $41 million on Viagra. Almost 535 000 prescriptions were written for this drug (with Ontario leading the nation with over 215 000 prescriptions, followed by Quebec with 110 500 and British Columbia with just over 80 000) and over 375 000 Canadian men sought treatment for erectile dysfunction—about double the number seeking help before Viagra's launch (Canadian Press 2000).

Health concerns that may particularly affect sexual activity include prostate problems, diabetes and vascular illnesses, the need to take pain-killing drugs, and—contrary to the reassuring statements we sometimes read—hysterectomies. Sexual functioning may also be impaired by the body's withdrawal of energy from the sexual system in order to address any other serious illness. Some older partners shift from intercourse to petting as a preferred sexual activity.

On the other hand, sexual intercourse does not necessarily cease with age. Analyzing data from a U.S. national survey conducted by the National Opinion Research Center, Greeley found that over one-third of marrieds, over age 60, have sexual intercourse once a week or more; 16 percent do so several times a week. Among the sexually active, 90 percent said they found their mates "very attractive physically." Some reported undressing each other, having sex outdoors, and/or swimming together nude (Woodward 1992). You can see in Figure 5.1 that for older respondents, among whom the proportion of sexually inactive couples is large, the mean average frequency seriously understates what is happening in sexually active marriages. For example, sexually active spouses over age 74 have sex about four times a month. Indeed, retirement "creates the possibility for more erotic spontaneity, because leisure time increases" (Allgeier 1983, p. 146).

When health problems do not interfere, both women's and men's emotional and psychological outlooks are as important as age in determining sexual functioning. Factors such as monotony, lack of an understanding partner, mental or physical fatigue, and overindulgence in food or alcohol can all have a profound negative effect on a person's capacity for sexual expression. Another important factor is regular sexual activity (Masters and Johnson 1966)—as in use it or lose it.

What About Boredom?

Jokes about sex in marriage are often about boredom. Among social scientists, an explanation for the decline in marital sexual frequency (after aging) is **habituation**—the decreased interest in sex that results from the increased accessibility of a sexual partner and the predictability in sexual behaviour with that partner over time. There is some evidence that habituation occurs in that sexual frequency declines sharply after about the first year of marriage, no matter how old (or young) the partners are. The reason for "this rather quick loss of intensity of interest and performance" appears to have two components:

> a reduction in the novelty of the physical pleasure provided by sex with a particular partner and a reduction in the perceived need to maintain high levels of sexual behaviour. From this perspective, the legitimization or institutionalization of sex through marriage may affect early diminution of interest, whereas the reduction in novelty is subtler. (Call, Sprecher, and Schwartz 1995, p. 649)

To study this theory, researchers examined the effects on coital frequency of remarriage and of cohabiting—living together in a (hetero)sexual relationship without being legally married.

FIRST-MARRIEDS COMPARED WITH REMARRIEDS AND COHABITORS Remarried respondents reported somewhat higher rates of sex frequency, compared with people in first marriages who were the same age, and this was particularly true for those under age 40. Because people who remarry do renew the novelty of marital sex with a new partner, this finding is evidence for the habituation hypothesis, although it could also be true for other reasons (Call, Sprecher, and Schwartz 1995).

Unfortunately, the NSFH sample did not have enough cohabiting respondents over age 35 to allow for statistical analysis of older partners. Among those ages 35 and younger, however, it is clear that cohab-

iting respondents had considerably higher intercourse rates than did legal spouses of the same age (see Figure 5.1). In Canada, the *Citizen*-Global survey, referred to earlier, found that individuals in common-law marriages have sex more often (an average of 11 times per month) than those in traditional marriages (7.8 times per month) (Cobb 1997). A second Canadian survey (Bibby 1995, p. 66) also observes that "Canadians who are cohabiting and unmarried, who tend to be somewhat younger, claim to be having sex more often than any category" (See Figure 5.2). These findings support the idea that legal marriage lessens a person's interest in sex by legitimating it, or making it "perfectly okay," even expected. However, this difference could also be at least partly explained by cohabitors' generally more permissive sexual attitudes and values (Call, Sprecher, and Schwartz 1995).

All this discussion of coital frequency can tempt us to forget that committed partners' sexuality is essentially about intimacy and self-disclosure. In other words, sex between partners—heterosexual partners and gay and lesbian partners as well—both gives pleasure and reinforces their relationship.

SEX AS A PLEASURE BOND

Masters, Johnson, and Kolodny (1994) view sex as a **pleasure bond** by which partners commit themselves to expressing their sexual feelings with each other.

In sharing sexual pleasure, partners realize that sex is something partners do with each other, not to or for each other. Each partner participates actively, as an equal in the sexual union. Further, each partner assumes **sexual responsibility**, that is, responsibility for his or her own sexual response. When this happens, the stage is set for conscious mutual cooperation. Partners feel freer to express themselves sexually. Such expression may not be as easy as it seems, for it requires a high degree of self-esteem, the willingness to transcend gendered expectations, and the ability to create and maintain an atmosphere of mutual cooperation. We'll look at each of these elements in turn.

Sexual Pleasure and Self-Esteem

Research shows a correlation between sexual satisfaction and self-esteem (Wiederman and Hurst 1998; Larson et al. 1998). High self-esteem is important to

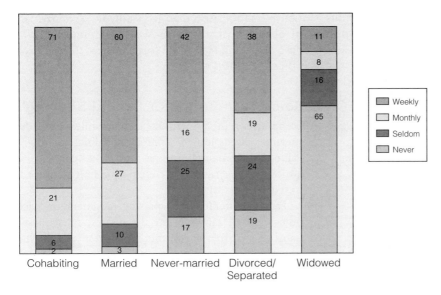

Weekly
Monthly
Seldom
Never

	Cohabiting	Married	Never-married	Divorced/Separated	Widowed
	71	60	42	38	11
					8
					16
	21	27	16	19	65
			25	24	
	6	10	17	19	
	2	3			

FIGURE **5.2**

Sexual activity by marital status. (Source: Bibby, 1995, p. 56.)

pleasurable sex in several ways. First, self-esteem allows a person the freedom to receive pleasure. People who become uncomfortable when offered a favour, a present, or praise typically have low self-esteem and have trouble believing that others think well of them. This problem is heightened when the gift is sexual pleasure. People with low self-esteem may turn off their erotic feelings because unconsciously they feel they don't deserve them.

Self-esteem also allows individuals to acknowledge and accept their own tastes and preferences. This is vital in sexual relationships because there is a great deal of individuality in sexual expression. An important part of sexual pleasure lies in doing what one wants to—not necessarily doing things the ways others do them.

Third, self-esteem provides us the freedom to search for new pleasures. As we've seen, some individuals let their sexual relationship grow stale because they do not accept or appreciate their own sexuality and their needs to experiment and explore with their partner.

Fourth, high self-esteem lets each of us ask our partner to help satisfy our preferences. In contrast, low self-esteem can lead a person to be defensive about her or his sexuality and reluctant to express valid human needs. In fact, people with low self-

esteem may actively discourage their partners from stimulating them effectively (Burchell 1975; Piche et al. 2000; Scheffler and Naus 1999).

Finally, high self-esteem allows us to engage in **pleasuring**: spontaneously doing what feels good at the moment and letting orgasm happen (or not), rather than working to produce it.

Masters and Johnson (1976), who initiated contemporary sex therapy, point out that trying too hard can cause sexual problems. They use the term **spectatoring** to describe the practice of emotionally removing oneself from a sexual encounter in order to watch and judge one's productivity, and they state that this practice can be self-inhibiting.

Sexual Pleasure and Gender

A second important element in making sex a pleasure bond is the ability to transcend gender stereotypes. For instance, a man may reject tender sexual advances and activities because he believes he has to be emotionally unfeeling or "bad" or be the initiator of sexual activity (Dubois 1997; Garcia 1999).

Likewise, women may have trouble in receiving or asking for pleasure because they feel uncomfortable or guilty about being assertive. Many women have been culturally conditioned to put their partners' needs first, so heterosexual women may proceed to coitus before they are sufficiently aroused to reach climax. Such women are less likely to enjoy sex, which can detract from the experience for both partners.

Sex can be more effective as a pleasure bond when the relationship both appreciates any real gender differences that may exist, and also transcends restrictive gender stereotypes (Money 1995). To do this, partners must be equal and must communicate in bonding rather than alienating ways (McCabe 1999).

Communication and Cooperation

A third element in sharing sex as a pleasure bond is communication and cooperation (MacNeil and Byers 1997; Young, Luquis and Young 1998). Partners can use conjugal sex as an arena for power struggles, or they can cooperate to enrich their sexual relationship and to nurture each other's sexual self-concept. To create a cooperative sexual atmosphere, partners must be willing to clearly communicate their own sexual needs and to hear and respond to their partners' needs and preferences as well.

When conflicts arise—and they do in any honest sexual relationship—they need to be constructively negotiated. For example, one partner may desire to have sex more frequently than the other does, which could cause the other to feel pressured. The couple might agree that the partner who wants sex more often stops pressing, and the other partner promises to consider what external pressures such as workload might be lessening his or her sexual feelings.

Other couples might have conflicts over whether to engage in oral-genital sex. It is important to communicate about such differences. Sometimes a couple can work out a compromise; in other cases, compromise may be difficult or impossible. Therapists generally agree that no one should be urged to do something he or she finds abhorrent. (And labeling partners "perverted" or "prudish" obviously does not contribute to a cooperative atmosphere.)

Open communication is important not only in resolving conflicts but also in sharing anxieties or doubts. Sex is a topic that is especially difficult for many people to talk about, yet misunderstanding about sex can cause genuine stress in a relationship. Good sex is not something that just happens when two people are in love. Forming a good sexual rela-

tionship is a process that necessarily involves partners in open verbal and nonverbal communication. To have satisfying sex, both partners need to tell each other what pleases them.

Some Principles for Sexual Sharing

Some important principles can be distilled from the previous discussion to serve as guidelines for establishing and maintaining a nurturing, cooperative atmosphere even when a couple can't find a compromise that suits them both.

Partners should avoid passing judgment on each other's sexual fantasies, needs, desires, or requests. Labeling a partner or communicating nonverbally that something is disgusting or wrong can lower a person's sexual self-esteem and destroy the trust in a relationship. Nor should partners presume to know what the other is thinking or feeling, or what would be good for the other sexually. In a cooperative relationship, each partner accepts the other as the final authority on his or her own feelings, tastes, and preferences.

Another principle is what Masters and Johnson (1976) call the "principle of mutuality." Mutuality implies that "all sexual messages between two people, whether conveyed by words or actions, by tone of voice or touch of fingertips, be exchanged in the spirit of having a common cause." Mutuality means "two people united in an effort to discover what is best for both" (p. 53).

An attitude of mutuality is important because it fills each partner's need to feel secure, to know that any sexual difficulties, failures, or misgivings will not be used against him or her. "Together they succeed or together they fail in the sexual encounter, sharing the responsibility for failure, whether it is reflected in his performance or hers" (pp. 57, 89).

A final principle of sexual sharing is to maintain a **holistic view of sex**—that is, to see sex as an extension of the whole relationship rather than as a purely physical exchange, a single aspect of marriage. One woman described it this way:

> I don't quite understand these references to the sex side of life. It is life. My husband and I are first of all a man and a woman—sexual creatures all through. That's where we get our real and central life satisfactions. If that's not right, nothing is. (in Cuber and Harroff 1965, p. 136)

Researchers John Cuber and Peggy Harroff found that among the couples they interviewed, those who saw sex holistically were "remarkably free of the well-known sexual disabilities" (1965, p. 136).

Recognizing its holistic emotional value is one way to keep marital sex pleasurable. Another is a commitment to discovering a partner's continually changing fantasies and needs. For, as one writer put it, besides a partner's fairly predictable habits and character,

> there is also a core of surprises hidden in us all that can become an inexhaustible source of freshness in life and love.

> The Greek philosopher Heraclitus once said that it is impossible to step into the same river twice. By the same token, it is actually impossible to make love to the same person twice—if we let ourselves know it....

> Often it is enough simply to go to bed in a different, more attentive state of mind—giving and listening. (Gottlieb 1979, p. 196)

Deepening the commitment to sharing and cooperation can make sex a growing and continuing pleasure bond. This does not mean that a couple regularly has great sex by some external standard. It means that each partner chooses to try—and keep on trying—to say and to hear more. Box 5.2, "Communicating About Sex," gives tips on how to do that.

Intimacy and sexuality require communication—physical as well as verbal—from both partners. Each generation finds itself reevaluating sexual assumptions, behaviours, and standards.

Making the Time for Intimacy

Just as it is important for families to arrange their schedules so that they can spend time together, it's also important for couples to plan time to be alone and intimate (Masters, Johnson, and Kolodny 1994).

Planning time for intimacy involves making conscious choices. For example, partners can choose to set aside at least one night a week for themselves alone, without work, movies, television, the VCR, the computer, another couple's company, or the children. They do not have to have intercourse during these times: They should do only what they feel like doing. But scheduling time alone together does mean mutually agreeing to exclude other preoccupations and devote full attention to each other. Two sex therapists advise couples to reserve at least 25 minutes each night for a quiet talk, "with clothes off and defenses down" (Koch and Koch 1976, p. 35). This last suggestion may be easier for parents with young children who are put to bed fairly early. A common complaint from parents of older children is that the children stay up later, and that by the time they are teenagers, the parents no longer have any private evening time together even with their clothes on. One woman, after attending an education course for parents, found a solution. She explains:

> Our house shuts down at 9:30 now. That doesn't mean we say "It's your bedtime, kids. You're tired and you need your sleep." It means we say, "Your dad (or your mom) and I need some time alone." The children go to their rooms at 9:30. Help with

Communicating About Sex

Negotiating our own sexuality and sexual expression in face-to-face relationships can be tricky. (Maybe that's why cybersex is so popular!) Sexual expression carries the promise of "transcending the limits of the individual and relating intimately... to other persons" (Francoeur 1987, p. 531). At the same time, sharing our sexuality makes us tremendously vulnerable. Both women and men need clear and positive feedback to know what brings their partners the greatest joy and fulfillment. One popular seminar leader on relationship communication and sex recommends that couples take a half hour every so often, particularly when they are not feeling negative about sex, and talk about it.

Here are some questions to stimulate an informative conversation:

- What do you like about having sex with me?
- How did you feel when I did _____?
- Would you like more sex?
- About how much sex would you like each week (or month, or day)?
- Would you like for us to spend more (or less) time when we have sex?
- Is there something specific you would like me to do in the next month during sex?
- Is there a new way you would like me to touch you? If yes, would you show me?

- Is there anything new you would like me to try?
- Is there anything you would like to try that we've never done?
- Is there anything I used to do that you would like me to do more of or again?

Note that a conversation like this needs to be mutual and reciprocal: Both partners ask and answer these questions—and they accept each other's answers without judgment either of themselves or of their partner.

What makes it difficult to talk about our sexual desires is that we don't want to hurt our partner's feelings and, conversely, we would hate to hear that we are disappointing our partner in any way at all. Meanwhile, we don't want to feel pressured to do anything that would not feel comfortable to us. So when answering these questions, it is important that you make it clear that you are not demanding more. The dialogue works best if its only purpose is to share information.

Then, too, you should not do things that do not feel right to you. But if your partner wants something that doesn't seem important to you or seems unpleasant, you might consider keeping an open mind. And when your partner does not seem open to things you favour, try to accept that at least for now. "A secret of great sex is to build on the strengths you have and not focus on the problems or what you are missing" (Gray 1995, pp. 53–55).

homework, lunch money, decisions about what they'll wear tomorrow—all those things get taken care of by 9:30 or they don't get taken care of. We allow interruptions only in emergencies—and I'm redefining what an "emergency" is too. (personal interview)

Boredom with sex after many years in a marriage may be at least partly the consequence of a decision

by default. Therapists suggest that couples can avoid this situation, perhaps by creating romantic settings—a candlelit dinner or a night away from the family at a motel—by opening themselves to new experiences, such as describing their sexual fantasies to each other, reading sex manuals together, or renting an erotic movie. (The important thing, they stress, is that partners don't lose touch with either their sexuality or their ability to share it with each other.) Therapists also point out that just because spouses find they don't desire sex together much anymore does not mean they no longer love each other.

We have been talking about human sexual expression as a pleasure bond. It is terribly unfortunate that today sexuality can also be associated with disease and death. Indeed, the fact that it is so difficult to make this transition here points to the multifaceted, sometimes even contradictory, nature of human sexual expression in the new millennium.

SEXUAL EXPRESSION AND HIV/AIDS

HIV/AIDS was identified as such in 1981, and it is an understatement to say that our lives have not been the same since. **HIV/AIDS** is a viral disease that destroys the immune system—hence the name acquired immune deficiency syndrome. The virus that causes HIV/AIDS—called HIV, or human immunodeficiency virus—is transmitted through the exchange of infected body fluids. With a lowered resistance to disease, an HIV-infected person becomes vulnerable to infections and diseases that noninfected people easily fight off; the immediate cause of death from AIDS is often a rare form of pneumonia or cancer. Not everyone who has been infected with HIV will develop full-blown AIDS. Part of the public

health problem is that a carrier of the virus can be unaware of its presence for perhaps as long as nine or more years and can infect others during that time if precautions are not taken.

In 1996, a combination of new drugs, called protease inhibitors, promised hope for living more comfortably and longer with AIDS (Leland 1996; Gorman 1996a). By 1998, however, hope had diminished somewhat as the new drugs proved less potent and had more toxic side effects than was expected. Also, researchers reported that the HIV virus had mutated into new, drug-resistant strains (Cowley 1998b; Kalb 1998).

Who Has HIV/AIDS?

As of December 31, 1999, 16 913 HIV/AIDS cases had been confirmed in Canada, all but 15 percent of them among adults. Since the disease was first diagnosed in Canada in 1992, 11 046 Canadians have died due to HIV/AIDS infection (Figure 5.3) (Statistics Canada, 1998b). According to Health Canada, those who undergo HIV testing and test positive account for only a fraction of the HIV population. By 1999, an estimated 50 000 people were living with HIV in Canada—including an estimated 15 000 who remained unaware of their HIV infection (HIV/AIDS *Epi Update*, April 2000).

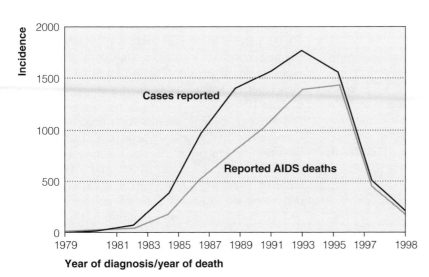

FIGURE   **5.3**

Reported AIDS cases and reported AIDS deaths in Canada, 1978 to 1998.
(Source: Bureau of HIV/AIDS, STD and TB, LCDC. December 1998.)

PRIMARY RISK GROUPS   In Canada, men who have sex with other men (MSM) are the group most at risk for developing HIV/AIDS, representing two-thirds of all AIDS cases reported among males in 1997. Although infections decreased among MSM during the first half of the 1990s, in 1999, MSM accounted for 38 percent of the 4200 new infections diagnosed in Canada (Health Canada 2000). Worldwide, however, the predominant mode of HIV transmission is through heterosexual contact (Inciardi and Harrison 1997). In Canada, the number of HIV/AIDS cases attributed to heterosexual contact rose from three percent to 19 percent between 1987 and 1995, and by 1999 had increased to 21 percent. Prior to 1995, adult women represented less than 10 percent (9.6 percent) of all positive HIV test reports with known age and gender in Canada. By 1995, this proportion had increased to 18.5 percent and in 1996, to 20.4 percent. As well, the number of HIV/AIDS cases attributed to the sharing of needles by intravenous drug users climbed from two percent of cases diagnosed before 1992 to almost 20 percent in 1998. In British Columbia, intravenous drug users now constitute the group with the highest number of new HIV/AIDS infections. Among Aboriginal peoples, injection drug use accounts for 54 percent of reported HIV/AIDS cases among women and 17.8 percent of reported cases among men (Statistics Canada 1998b).

Safer Sex

Safer sex, for heterosexuals as well as in the gay community, refers to the use of latex (they *must* be latex) condoms ("rubbers") and to the limiting of partners in number and selectivity. Latex condoms—contraceptive sheaths that fit over the penis—reduce the likelihood that HIV will be transmitted to a sexual partner during genital or anal intercourse (Hawa et al. 1998). Latex condoms can also be used for protection during oral sex.

According to the 1998 Canadian Contraception Study, the vast majority of Canadian women (91 percent) are aware of condoms as a birth control method and three-quarters (75 percent) regard them favourably (Figure 5.4). However, this survey found that condom use is often inconsistent and that about one in four Canadian women mistakenly believes that monogamy and getting to know and trust a sexual partner eliminates the need to use condoms to protect against HIV or other sexually transmitted diseases (STDs). As indicated in Table 5.1, less than one in five women respondents in this survey who had engaged in sexual intercourse during the six months prior to the survey had always used condoms, with married women even less likely than unmarried women to do so (13 percent versus 26 percent). Among unmarried women, condom use was reported as "always" engaged in by merely 40 percent of those aged 15 to 17, 22 percent of those aged 18 to 24, 28 percent of women aged 25 to 29, 35 percent of women aged 30 to 34, 32 percent of women aged 30 to 34, 32 percent of women 35 to 39 years old, and 15 percent of women 40 to 44 years old (Fisher et al. 1999).

"Safe sex" remains a misnomer, however, because condoms can be broken, although rarely, and HIV can still be transmitted. Nevertheless, latex condoms do substantially reduce the risk (Centers for Disease Control 1993b; Davis and Weller 1999; Hatcher et al. 1998).

Young adults are the age group at greatest risk of acquiring a sexually transmitted disease because they are more likely to engage in intercourse without using condoms and to have multiple sex partners. According to the 1996–97 National Population Health Survey, among those Canadians aged 15 to 59 who were in a relationship of less than one year's duration, 16 percent reported that they had not used a condom the last time they had sex; eight percent reported never using a condom. Among sexually active individuals aged 15 to 19, 51 percent of females and 24 of males reported having sex without a condom; among those 20 to 24 years of age, 53 percent of women and 44 percent of men reported having sex without a condom (Health Canada 1999b).

Moreover, evidence suggests that beliefs about the effectiveness of a pregnancy prevention method may be generalized to beliefs about its efficacy for disease prevention. The Canadian Youth and AIDS study reported that only 27 percent of contraceptive pill users reported concurrent use of condoms. A secondary analysis of the college and university subset of the Canadian Youth and AIDS study (mean age 19.7 years) reported that those students with a greater number of sex partners were more likely to use oral contraceptive pills but less likely to use condoms. Of those who had 10 or more lifetime partners, only 21 percent of males and 7.5 percent of females reported

TABLE 5.1

Frequency of Partner Condom Use Among Women Aged 15–44 Having Intercourse in the Previous Six Months (n=872)

	Total	Married	Unmarried
Always	18%	13%	26%
Usually	10%	8%	14%
Sometimes	19%	12%	30%
Never	50%	64%	27%
Not Stated	2%	2%	2%

Source: William A Fisher, Richard Boroditsky and Martha L Bridges. 1999. "Condom Use Among Canadian Women: Practices and Opinions." *The Canadian Journal of Human Sexuality*, 8 (3), Fall, p. 190.

regular condom use. Overall, 24.8 percent of men and 15.6 percent of women reported regular condom use (Boroditsky et al 1996). For this reason, it is not perhaps surprising that, in 1997, 69 percent of all reported cases of chlamydia and almost 50 percent of all reported cases of gonorrhea in Canada occurred among individuals aged 15 to 24. In that year, the reported incidence of chlamydia, the most common sexually transmitted infection in Canada, was highest among females aged 15 to 19 years (971.6 per 100 000). The reported incidence of gonorrhea was also highest among this age group of women (73.3 per 100 000) (Statistics Canada 1999).

How HIV/AIDS Affects Relationships, Marriages, and Families

A theme of this text is that sociocultural conditions affect people's choices. We can examine how HIV/AIDS, as a societal phenomenon, has changed and will continue to change attitudes, options, the consequences of decisions, and, thereby, personal decision making or choices.

HIV/AIDS AND HETEROSEXUALS The NORC survey concluded that "sporadic aborted breakouts of the AIDS virus into the general public are the exception, not the rule ... we are convinced that there is not and very unlikely ever will be a heterosexual AIDS epidemic in this country" (quoted in Freeman 1994). But William Freeman, Executive Director of the

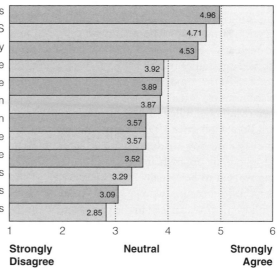

FIGURE 5.4

Opinions about condoms from the 1998 Canadian Contraception Study. (Source: Fisher, Boroditsky and Bridges, 1999, p. 91.)

National Association of People with AIDS, has responded that the NORC researchers' "implication that there is very little risk in having unprotected sex is appalling" (Freeman 1994). It is difficult to strike a balance between alerting North Americans to the AIDS risk and generating unwarranted anxiety. (See Box 5.3 "HIV/AIDS: Some Precautions.")

Although men can contract HIV/AIDS from coitus with infected women, transmission from men to women is higher because of anatomical differences (The Boston Women's Health Book Collective 1998). Still, the risk is only about one in 500 for a woman to become infected from any single sexual contact with an infected man (Laumann et al. 1994, citing the Centers for Disease Control). Repeated encounters result in about a third of the female sexual partners of infected men becoming infected. Because sexually transmitted diseases, or STDs, such as syphilis, herpes, or chancroid cause open sores on the genitals, HIV/AIDS is more easily transmitted to STD-infected women.

Heterosexual adults—although not necessarily teens (Sangi-Haghpeykar et al. 1997; Santelli et al. 1997)—may be responding to the threat of AIDS with changed behaviour (Hawa, Munro and Doherty-Poirier 1998; Ku, Sonnenstein, and Pleck 1995; Mosher and Pratt 1993; Rye 1998). Sexually active singles may now expect to have a longer period of acquaintance before initiating sexual contact, hoping to experience greater attraction, security, or commitment before deciding sex is worth it. Some opt for periods of celibacy. Dating clubs whose members are required to be regularly tested for HIV/AIDS have developed in some larger cities (Geist 1987).

A side issue of safer sex among heterosexuals has become the placement of sexual responsibility, once again, on women (Mosher and Pratt 1993; The Boston Women's Health Book Collective 1998). Forty percent of condom purchases are now made by women, who are encouraged to prevail upon their partners to use them. Requiring women to be sexually assertive is not always easy, especially because women have been encouraged to follow men's sexual lead in the past. Men sometimes resist the use of condoms because folk wisdom holds that condoms cut down on sensation.[4]

4. In fact, some women's shelters have reported violent reactions from men when their partners ask them to use condoms. "With the coming of AIDS, the age-old battle of the sexes is literally becoming a life and death struggle for women" (Maria Maggenti, in Halpern 1989a, p. 85).

Also, "the maintenance of power over women, in and of itself, can lead to resistance to using condoms" (Lever 1995, p. 173). But "if you say 'safe' and 'no' often enough, it will start to sink in," said a participant in a women's AIDS workshop (Dunning 1986).

A recent Canadian study assessed attitudes toward young adults who initiate condom use in the context of exclusive dating relationships (Davidson-Harden and Fisher 2000). In this research, 120 male and female undergraduate students were randomly assigned to read one of three scenarios in which a university-aged couple engaged in sex for the first time with each other; they were then asked to rate their perception of the characters described. One scenario did not mention condom use, the second described the female as initiating condom use, and the third had the male initiate condom use. In all three cases, the female partner was described as using oral contraception. The researchers report that, in general, the undergraduate student raters looked favourably on individuals of either sex who initiated condom use in the context of an exclusive dating relationship and rated both the initiator and his/her partner as more sexually knowledgeable (but not more sexually experienced) than in the no condom condition. Ratings of commitment to partner, kindness, and social attractiveness were not adversely affected by condom initiation or use (Davidson-Harden and Fisher 2000).

To what extent various groups are using latex condoms, asking for their partners' sexual histories, and being selective of sexual partners is uncertain. Moreover, prospective partners may lie about their sexual history or even about their HIV/AIDS status, especially if they don't know you well (Payn et al. 1997; "Sex Partners Often Silent..." 1998). So the best bet—next to abstinence—is using a latex condom.

HIV/AIDS AND GAY MEN   Many gay men modified their sexual behaviour in the 1980s (Kantrowitz 1987). Multiple, frequent, and anonymous sexual contacts had been common elements of the lifestyle and sexual ideology for many gays (Blumstein and Schwartz 1983). But attitudes and behaviour have changed somewhat, at least among men in their 30s and over.

Still, recent research indicates that many gays continue to engage in risky sex (Rogers 1994) or have returned to unsafe sex, called "barebacking" (Gillis et al 1998; Myers et al. 1999; Peyser 1997). For

DO YOU RECOGNIZE THE FACE OF AIDS?

YOU MIGHT NEED A CLEARER PICTURE.

The sharper image: AIDS doesn't discriminate. HIV

Louise Binder, a Toronto woman living with HIV/AIDS, is seen here during a Canadian AIDS Society news conference.

example, a Canadian study asked a nonrandom sample of gay and bisexual men—recruited through community groups, gay bars, and bath houses—to complete a questionnaire on their sexual practices with primary and casual same-sex partners. The study found that 40 percent reported at least one episode of unprotected sex during the previous three months. Moreover, while there was a tendency for men to refrain from risky activities with their casual partners, this was not a consistent pattern of behaviour among the men sampled (Myers et al. 1999).

Ironically, AIDS education programs may have backfired among gays in their teens and 20s. According to one San Francisco area gay activist and psychologist with a largely gay practice, "A lot of younger men have grown up from the time they were eight years old hearing on television about gay men and HIV. They have seamlessly integrated being gay with having HIV. When you ask them if it's important not to get infected they shrug their shoulders and say, 'I guess so'" (Walt Odets, in Hagar 1995, p. 10). Then too, so much attention has gone to "HIV posi-

tives" (people who are infected) within gay communities such as San Francisco's Castro district that young gay men, especially adolescents, may feel "left out" when they test negative for the disease (Odets, in Hagar 1995; Dunlap 1996; Peyser 1997). According to one AIDS activist and community worker, "There's also an assumed fidelity that's not always the case" (Dunlap 1996).

A recent Canadian study reports that the increasingly prevalent belief that HIV infection can be cured through highly active antiretroviral therapy (HAART) regimens may also be associated with greater HIV risk behaviour among HIV positive men who have sex with men (Misovich et al. 2000). This research sought to determine the extent to which a sample of HIV seropositive men who have sex with men believe that HIV is currently or will shortly be curable. The researchers report that belief in a cure for HIV was significantly positively related to levels of HIV-risk behaviours (including unprotected insertive and receptive anal sex, and unprotected oral sex to ejaculation) and significantly positively related to levels of behavioural intention to perform such behaviours in the future. The authors note that, "[a]s advanced treatments for HIV become more widespread, the potential exists for individuals to decide that HIV preventive behaviours may no longer be necessary" (Misovich, Fisher and Fisher 2000, p. 241).

Many in the gay community have experienced the frequent loss of friends and intimate partners. It is difficult for the majority of us to imagine losing as many as five—or 20—dear friends and acquaintances to death from disease over the course of just a few years. This situation can lead a gay man to wonder whether he himself wants to go on living (Hagar 1995). Indeed, there have been a substantial number of AIDS-related suicides: the bereaved, along with the ill, and sometimes those reacting to positive results from having been tested for HIV/AIDS ("Suicides Tied" 1990).

WIVES OF GAY MEN   Perhaps 20 percent of gay men marry at least once (Buxton 1991), sometimes to camouflage their homosexuality (Schmitt 1993). Consequently, some heterosexual women may be regularly exposed to the virus themselves. Although some knowingly married gays, 85 percent of a sample of wives in a support group were not aware of their husbands' homosexuality at the time of marriage.

HIV/AIDS: Some Precautions

AIDS has changed sex, relationships, and life choices. Readers will want to keep updating their information; precautions that at present seem reasonable are:

1. Sexually active individuals who are not in long-term, securely monogamous relationships predating the identification of AIDS in 1981 should use latex condoms (perhaps with spermicide) when having sex. Explicit information about protective practices is available on the Canadian Health Network Web site www.canadian-health-network.ca.

2. Inquiry about a potential sex partner's health, HIV status, and previous partners is useful and may produce information on which to base a decision about having sex. It is entirely possible, however, that a prospective partner will not be honest. Consequently, experts argue that use of latex condoms with any partner is the most protective approach. Moreover, antibodies to HIV do not develop for up to six months or longer after infection with the virus, so an infected person who may appear virus-free in tests will report the possibly erroneous results in good faith.

   Communication about sex and disease is going to be necessary in a way that it never was before. Canadians used to risk pregnancy without discussion; the stakes are higher now.

3. It would be prudent to confine sexual activity and relationships to those worth the risk. This can mean decisions about individuals or it can mean categorical decisions about multiple partners or sex with members of high-risk groups such as homosexual and bisexual men, individuals who have multiple partners, intravenous drug users, or people known to have AIDS or HIV.

4. Decisions to take risks may involve others: your current or future sex partners, your children, and your family. A responsible sexually active individual will be voluntarily tested, and, if the test is positive, will either refrain from sex or inform the partner beforehand and use latex condoms during sex. Informing partners about one's AIDS-risk status must include discussion of sexual history—that is, of past sexual activity with infected or high-risk individuals. An individual's failure to be forthcoming may also result in criminal sanction; as early as 1995, a Canadian man who ignored public health warnings after his HIV diagnosis and knowingly infected 19 women was sentenced to 11 years and three months for criminal negligence causing bodily harm (*Toronto Star*, May 13, 1995).

5. Women planning to become pregnant or not taking precautions against pregnancy should be sure that they are free of HIV by being tested and perhaps retested over a six-month period of time. Sources of possible infection include not only sexual contacts but also past blood transfusions before the implementation of screening programs.

6. Health-care workers should take the precautions recommended by guidelines for their occupation.

7. Citizens should support sex education designed to prevent the spread of AIDS. Appropriate AIDS education should be encouraged for children (because even young children can be exposed to AIDS through sexual abuse), teenagers, and adults. Videotapes intended for home viewing are available from schools, libraries, public health departments, and commercial sources (Rye 1998).

Keep yourself informed by consulting your local public health department, the Canadian Red Cross, student services, gay activist groups, churches, and other sources, including newspapers, radio, television, and the Internet.

Most of these women denied concern about infection, claiming that their husbands practised safe sex or had only one male partner. Counsellors, however, are alarmed that an unknown but possibly large number of women are knowingly or unknowingly exposed to HIV through marriage to men who have homosexual contacts. Revelation of husbands' homosexual activity through development of AIDS or through his protective revelation of risk is likely to change the dynamics of these marital relationships—and possibly end them (Dullea 1987d). One writer has pointed out that straight spouses of gays (or lesbians) have been left out of discussions and research about gay lifestyles. When a partner's coming out begins a divorce process, "straight wives and husbands experience the pain of any marital rupture, plus the anguish of being rejected as a woman or a man" (Buxton 1992).

HIV/AIDS MEANS NEW FAMILY CRISES Some families will face unprecedented crises because of AIDS. Telling one's family members that one has HIV/AIDS is a crisis in itself (Serovich, Kimberly, and Greene 1998; Travers and Paoletti 2000). AIDS sufferers and their friends and families often experience loss and grief. Some relatives grieve amid a shroud of secrecy, due to shame associated with the disease, thereby isolating themselves.

In addition, HIV/AIDS victims, their families and friends are living with the burden of community and personal care for friends, lovers, or family members with AIDS. Especially in geographically distinct gay/lesbian communities, this situation applies to lesbians as well as to gay men. Lesbians often have close ties with gay men and may consider them members of their families. In some cases gay men, who years later test positive for HIV, have donated sperm for lesbian mothers.

Some married heterosexuals have lost partners to the disease or are helping infected partners fight health battles. AIDS contracted from a blood transfusion means a prolonged medical battle for the partner, and perhaps children who may be infected. But it is a tragedy that can be shared. AIDS resulting from drug use frequently occurs in transient relationships, but in marital settings it often indicates a family that has many problems. In cases in which a partner (more often, the husband) develops AIDS from sex outside the relationship, the marriage may break down. As

more senior citizens develop AIDS, grandparents may worry that they will be stigmatized by their grown children, maybe even isolated from their grandchildren (Stock 1997).

A related issue, when focusing on HIV/AIDS and children, is that we will begin to see orphaned children whose parents have died of AIDS (Gorman 1993). Some, but not all, of these children are being raised by grandparents and other relatives. To what extent we will see community responses to the needs of orphaned children, resulting from the HIV/AIDS epidemic, is in question.

HIV/AIDS and other sexually transmitted diseases are more than a medical or a family problem—they are conditions imbued with social meanings and consequences.

As we will see in the next section, politics influences individuals' decisions about HIV/AIDS—and about sexuality in general.

PLATFORM AND PULPIT

Political and religious conflict over sexuality has characterized recent decades. For some people, HIV/AIDS is primarily a pragmatic problem requiring pragmatic solutions. Strong gay activism, as well as the fact that AIDS has spread to the adult heterosexual population and to children, has increased societal commitment of resources to combat AIDS, although some remain convinced that not enough is being done. But others argue that, given other serious health threats, the Canadian government is spending enough on HIV/AIDS—more per death, for example, than on heart disease or cancer (Hoy, 1995; Stout 1992).

There is also some evidence that North Americans generally have tired of hearing about AIDS (Krieger 1995).

Meanwhile, some spokespersons see HIV/AIDS as evidence of God's judgment against "sinful" lifestyles. One of the most striking changes in the political climate over the past two decades has been the emergence of a loose coalition of religious fundamentalists and political conservatives who believe that our government and social institutions must be made to operate according to what they see as Christian principles. For example, on April 30, 2001, the Web site of the Canada Family Action Coalition (CFAC) asked:

Public education and AIDS organizations wants to continue promoting sexual activity that costs you huge money, loss of life and irreparable social damage....Do we really want to incite the population to choose homosexuality? (http://www.familyaction.org/Articles/education.htm)

The movement stresses specific "family" values; heterosexuality, sex only in marriage, monogamy, anti-abortion, and traditional female gender roles, both in and outside the (heterosexual) nuclear family. Some fundamentalist religious spokespersons who for religious reasons oppose nonmarital sexual relationships or homosexuality, may cast the AIDS epidemic into this framework. They may also rule out certain preventive measures such as condoms and explicit sex education. Other religious leaders stress compassion and work with AIDS victims.

Politics, Research and Sex Education

Although the need for more comprehensive and current data, particularly in light of HIV/AIDS is self-evident, obtaining the necessary funding for large-scale projects on sexual behaviour may be difficult. For example, the NORC survey, described above, was originally meant to sample 20 000 adults, not 3400. But the U.S. Congress first insisted that questions on masturbation be omitted, then canceled the pilot study altogether on the grounds that a sex survey would be too controversial. NORC conducted the much smaller survey without federal funds. A survey of 24 000 teens in grades 7 to 11 was also scrapped for the same reason ("U.S. Scraps" 1991). The U.S. Congress did, however, decide to "set aside $50 million in grants each year in teaching sexual abstinence. Combined with the addition of non-federal matching funds nearly half a billion dollars have been earmarked for teaching abstinence" (Larson et al. 2000, p. 151).

Even providing explicit information on how Canadians can avoid becoming infected with HIV/AIDS may become controversial. For example, in April 2000, a federal AIDS-prevention pamphlet, which carried the logos of Health Canada and the Canadian AIDS society and was distributed at health clinics, schools, and libraries sparked considerable debate. The pamphlet, which provided detailed instructions for safe sex and the cleaning of needles, additionally contained comments such as, "Just because we've made the choice that we don't want AIDS doesn't mean the party's over. We can still fool around with sex and have a great time. Still shoot up if that's what we're into." Various social critics denounced the pamphlet, suggesting that it should be viewed as "immoral" and as encouraging of intravenous drug use. However, while Richard Garlick of the Canadian Centre on Substance Abuse acknowledged the approach taken "hits people pretty forcefully," he defended its use: "The here and now is, that people are becoming infected everyday because they don't know how to inject safely. Getting someone off drugs by having them die is not viewed as the ideal solution. If you want to reach these people you have to talk to them in their own language" (Canadian Press 2000b).

People today are making decisions about sex in a climate characterized by evident conflict over sexual issues. Premarital and other nonmarital sex, homosexuality, abortion, contraception, and reproductive technology represent political issues as well as personal choices.

Both public and private communication must rise to a new level, as potential sexual partners talk about sex and disease, precautions and risk, sexual history and sexual practices. If such communication in fact develops, it would be the realization of one of the few hopeful comments about AIDS—that "out of the peril of the plague could rise a strong new ... ethic of sexual responsibility" (Rosenthal 1987, p. A-23).

SEXUAL RESPONSIBILITY

Our changing society offers divergent sexual standards, from casual sex to abstinence. In such a climate, making knowledgeable choices is a must. Because there are various standards today concerning sex outside of marriage (as well as sexual orientation itself), each individual must determine what sexual standard he or she values, which is not always easy. Moreover, today's adults may be exposed to several different standards throughout the course of their lives because different groups and individuals adhere to various standards. Even when people feel they know which standard they value, decisions in particular situations can be difficult. People who believe in the standard of sexual permissiveness with affection, for example, must determine when a particular relationship is affectionate enough.

Making these choices and feeling comfortable with them requires recognizing and respecting your own values, instead of just being influenced by others.

Whether it is due to having—or fear of contracting—a sexually transmitted disease, or due to living in a culture characterized by conflicting and mixed messages, anxiety can accompany the choice to develop a sexual relationship, and there is considerable potential for misunderstanding between partners. This section addresses some principles of sexual responsibility that can serve as guidelines for sexual decision making.

It's easy to see that even though sexuality is a natural part of ourselves, it is more complex than just being a part of our bodily functions. The AIDS epidemic has brought the importance of sexual responsibility to our attention in a dramatic way. We will suggest a few guidelines that may help make sexual choices clearer.

Nelson Foote (1954), a social scientist, once observed that because sex was becoming increasingly dissociated from procreation, it was also becoming more recreational. Alex Comfort, in his book *The Joy of Sex*, called sexual expression "the most important form of adult play" (Comfort 1972, p. 85).

If we use this terminology to describe sexual expression, we should stress that it is adult play, not child play. People must take responsibility for the consequences of their behaviour. Certain rules and responsibilities are important.

One obvious responsibility concerns the possibility of pregnancy. Both partners should responsibly plan whether and when they will conceive children and use effective birth control methods accordingly. (Chapter 11 provides more information on this subject.)

A second responsibility has to do with the possibility of contracting sexually transmitted diseases (STDs) or transmitting them to someone else. Individuals should be aware of the threat and the facts concerning HIV and other serious STDs. They need to assume responsibility for protecting themselves and their partners. They need to know how to recognize the symptoms of an STD and what to do if they get one. Guidelines pertaining to AIDS are presented in the preceding section of this chapter.

A third responsibility concerns communicating with partners or potential sexual partners. In one study, 35 percent of men reported lying to a partner in order to have sex with her, while 60 percent of women thought they had been lied to. Such lies involved overstating love and caring, denying other simultaneous relationships, and reporting fewer sex partners than was true (Goleman 1988c).

People should be honest with partners about their motives for wanting to have sexual relations with them. As we've seen in this chapter, sex can mean many different things to different people. A sexual encounter can mean love and intimacy to one partner and be a source of achievement or relaxation to the other. Honesty lessens the potential for misunderstanding and hurt between partners. People should treat each other as people rather than things—as people with needs and feelings. Sex should never consciously be used for exploitation or degradation.

A fourth responsibility is to oneself. In expressing sexuality today, each of us must make decisions according to our own values. A person may choose to follow values held as a result of religious training or put forth by ethicists or by psychologists or counsellors. People's values change over the course of their lives, and what's right at one time may not be satisfying later. Despite the confusion caused both by internal changes as our personalities develop and by the social changes going on around us, it is important for individuals to make their own decisions about relating sexually.

IN SUM

Social attitudes and values play an important role in the forms of sexual expression people find comfortable and enjoyable. This point applies to many aspects of sexuality, including even our sexual orientation—whether we prefer a partner of the same or opposite sex. Despite decades of conjecture and research, it is still unclear just how sexual orientation develops, or even whether it is genetic or socially conditioned. The 1980s and 1990s have witnessed political and other challenges by gay activists (and a few others) to heterosexism and one of its consequences, homophobia.

Whatever one's sexual orientation, sexual expression is negotiated with cultural messages about what is sexually permissible, even desirable. In both Canada and the United States, these cultural messages have moved from one that encouraged patriarchal sex, based on male dominance and reproduction as its principal purpose, to a message that encourages sexual expressiveness in myriad ways for both genders equally. Four standards of nonmarital sex are abstinence, permissiveness with affection, permissiveness without affection, and the double standard—diminished somewhat since the 1960s, but still alive and well.

Marital sex changes throughout life. Young spouses tend to place greater emphasis on sex than do older mates. But, while the frequency of sexual intercourse declines over time and the length of a marriage, some 27 percent of married persons over age 74 are sexually active and having sex about four times a month. Making sex this kind of pleasure bond, whether married or not, involves cooperation in a nurturing, caring relationship. To fully cooperate sexually, partners need to develop high self-esteem, to break free from restrictive gendered stereotypes, and to communicate openly.

We also discussed HIV/AIDS in this chapter, with some focus on how the disease affects relationships, marriages, and families. We noted that the New Christian Right advocates "family" values that include celibacy outside marriage, traditional roles for women, and heterosexism. Whether or not one agrees with the major agenda of the New Christian Right, there are certain guidelines for personal sexual responsibility that we all should heed.

Key Terms

abstinence
double standard
evolutionary psychology
expressive sexuality
female genital mutilation (FGM)
habituation
heterosexism
heterosexual
HIV/AIDS
holistic view of sex
homophobia
homosexual
interactionist perspective on human sexuality

patriarchal sexuality
permissiveness with affection
permissiveness without affection
pleasure bond
pleasuring
representative sample
safer sex
sexual orientation
sexual responsibility
spectatoring
survival of the fittest

Study Questions

1. Give some examples to illustrate changes in sexual behaviour and social attitudes about sex. What do you think future attitudes and behaviour will be? Why?

2. How has the sexual revolution affected marital sex? Why?

3. Do you think that sex is changing from "his and hers" to "theirs"? What do you see as some difficulties in making this transition?

4. How do you account for the fact that younger spouses engage in coitus more frequently than older partners?

5. Discuss the relationship between sexual pleasure and (a) self-esteem, (b) gendered expectations, and (c) cooperation and communication.

6. Discuss the principles for sexual sharing that are suggested in this chapter. Are there any you would add?

7. What do we know about how sexual orientation develops? What kinds of relationships and families do gays and lesbians create in today's society?

8. Describe the process by which a lesbian or gay man constructs that self-identity. How is this process a result of homophobia in the surrounding culture?

9. How do you think AIDS will change sex and relationships? Do you anticipate that it will have a major impact on Canadian family life or not?

10. This book stresses that people must take responsibility for the consequences of their sexual behaviour. What responsibilities does the book list? Do you agree with the list? What would you add or subtract?

Suggested Readings

Adams, Mary Louise. 1997. *The Trouble with Normal: Postwar Youth and the Making of Heterosexuality*. Toronto: University of Toronto Press. An important work which challenges many taken-for-granted assumptions about heterosexuality and its privileging.

Bibby, Reginald W. 2001. *Canada's Teens: Today, Yesterday and Tomorrow*. Toronto: Stoddart Publishing Company Ltd. Examines and compares the views and experiences of Canadians teens on many issues, including sexuality, with that of previous generations. Written by a prominent

Canadian sociologist who has been conducting surveys of Canadian teens and adults since the 1970s.

Francoeur, Robert. T., ed. *Taking Sides: Clashing Views on Controversial Issues in Human Sexuality,* 6th ed. New York: Guilford, CN: Dushkin, 1998. Presents both sides of controversies in various areas of human sexuality. Lots of attention to values, attitudes and norms and to the outcomes and impact of sexual behaviour.

Zahn-Waxler, Carolyn, ed. 1995. *Sexual Orientation and Human Development. Special issue of Developmental Psychology.* Vol. 31. Academic journal articles including biosocial perspectives and social construction of homosexuality; articles on pressures and problems of gay youth; gay and lesbian relationships and parenthood, as well as some integrative essays.

On the Net

1) Dr. Ruth Here to Answer Your Questions on Site
   Dr. Ruth Westheimer, noted expert on sexuality, answers questions on sex.
   http://www.drruth.com

2) EGALE
   A national organization dedicated to promoting the full acceptance of gays, lesbian, bisexual and transgendered Canadians
   http://www.egale.ca

3) "The Social Construction of Male Homosexuality and Related Suicide Problems: Research Proposals for the Twenty-First Century" by Pierre J. Tremblay and Richard Ramsey, University of Calgary
   http://www.sws.soton.ac.uk/gay-youth-suicide/c-gay-male-youth-suicide.htm

4) For a discussion on sex and marital satisfaction:
   http://www.hope.edu/academic/psychology/335/webrep/marital.html

5) Sex Information and Educational Council of Canada (SIECCAN)
   http://www.sieccan.org/

6) Homosexual (Same-Sex) Marriages in Canada
   http://www.religioustolerance.org/hom_marb.htm

7) The Business of Sex
   http://www.canada.com/national/features/businessofsex/

Unmarried: Alone and with Others

TODAY MARRIAGE AND PARENTHOOD ARE RARELY VIEWED AS NECESSARY, AND PEOPLE WHO DO NOT CHOOSE THESE ROLES ARE NO LONGER CONSIDERED AS DEVIANTS.

ELIZABETH DOUVAN, 1979

POSSIBLY, YOU THOUGHT THAT IN THIS MODERN, ENLIGHTENED AGE, WOMEN NO LONGER MOPE ABOUT NOT GETTING MARRIED.

ROSE DEWOLF, 1982

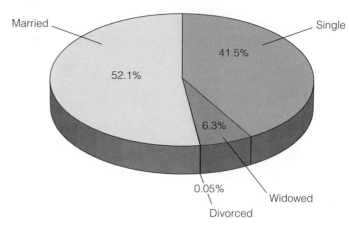

FIGURE **6.1**

Marital status of Canadians aged 15 and over (1901). (Source: based on data from the Statistics Canada Census of Population 1901.)

Being other than "legally married" is common among Canadian adults today. While in both 1901 and 1996, about half of Canadians 15 years of age and over were married (52.1 percent and 51.5 percent, respectively), some significant differences exist among those who were not legally married in Canada at the start and at the end of the twentieth century.

In this chapter we will examine what social scientists know about those who are currently unmarried. We'll look at reasons why people are not legally married and discuss changing cultural attitudes towards the unmarried. We will also look at the variety of lifestyles among those who are not legally married. Many individuals who are not legally married live with partners. Many are parents. In various ways, the distinction between those who are legally married and those who are not has become increasingly blurry in recent years.

To begin, we examine some statistics on those who are legally unmarried today.

THE UNMARRIED: MARITAL STATUS

Figures 6.1 and 6.2 show the marital status of Canadians in 1901 and 1996. As we have already noted, in both years, just over half of Canadians, 15 years of age and over, were legally married. However, reflective of Canada's younger population in 1901, a larger proportion of the population at that time was single (never-married) (41.5 percent) than in 1996 (27.0 percent). While in both years, the proportion of the widowed is markedly similar (6.3 percent in 1901 and 6.2 percent in 1996), the proportion of those who were formerly married but have separated or divorced has increased. In 1996,[1] 6.7 percent of the Canadian population, 15 years of age and over, were separated or divorced. In addition, it is evident that a growing proportion of Canadians have decided to, at least temporarily, forego legal marriage and live within a **common-law relationship,** with individuals in the province of Quebec especially likely to do so (Table 6.1) (Vanier Institute of the Family 2000, p. 20).

Sometimes when we discuss reasons for being legally unmarried, we will consider only those who have never married; other times we will consider factors applying to all those who are legally unmarried, whether divorced, widowed, or never-married. Because Canadian law has increasingly extended the rights and privileges associated with marriage to those in cohabiting relations, we also consider common-law relationships in Chapters 7 and 8.

1. Prior to the 1991 census, those who were married but separated were not tabulated "separated" but rather, submerged within the status category of "married."

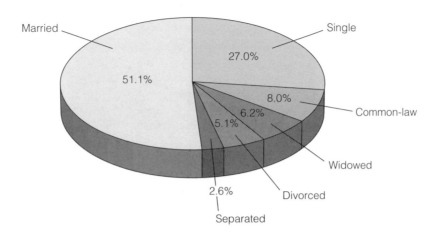

Married — 51.1%

Single — 27.0%

Common-law — 8.0%

Widowed — 6.2%

Divorced — 5.1%

Separated — 2.6%

F I G U R E   **6.2**

Marital status of Canadians aged 15 and over (1996). (Source: based on data from the Statistics Canada publications "Population by five-year age groups", Catalogue 93F0022, October 1997, and 1992, and "Population 15 years and over living in common-law unions by five-year age groups", Catalogue 95F0188, January 1998.

Next we explore some categories of the legally unmarried, beginning with the divorced and the widowed.

The Divorced and Widowed

The growing divorce rate throughout the last quarter of the twentieth century has contributed to the increased number of formerly-married persons who are now unmarried. According to the Vanier Institute of the Family,

> Of the Canadian couples who married in 1968/69, eleven percent were divorced before their 10th wedding anniversary. Fourteen percent of those who married in 1973/74 had divorced before their marriage was ten years old and of those who married in 1983/84, 18 percent did not stay married long enough to mark their 11th anniversary. Based on 1996 divorce rates, 37 percent of marriages were expected to end in divorce. (Vanier Institute of the Family 2000, p. 48)

In 1997, 5.0 percent of men and 7.5 percent of women age 15 and over were divorced (*Canada Global Almanac* 2000, p. 72). While the divorced account for a smaller percentage of those in their twenties and early thirties, with increasing age,

"divorced" becomes a more common marital status (Table 6.2). For example, you will note that at age 55 to 59, 9.0 percent of men and 12.0 of women are divorced. Although the divorce rate peaked in 1987 in Canada, the divorced will continue to be a substantial component of the single population. (Divorce is discussed at length in Chapter 14.)

In 1997, the widowed accounted for 2.2 percent of Canadian men and 9.9 percent of Canadian women, 15 years of age and over. Death rates declined throughout the twentieth century, reducing the likelihood of widowhood for the young and middle-aged. However, the proportion of older people in the population has increased, and they are at risk of losing a spouse.

At all ages, Canadian women are much more likely to be widowed than men (Table 6.2). This difference is due to women's greater longevity and their lower likelihood of remarrying after the death of a spouse. (Chapter 14 discusses the experience of widowhood.)

Except in very rare cases involving the intentional killing of a spouse, widowhood is not a status of choice, even though those who are widowed may experience some positive aspects of independent living. We turn now to the never-married.

TABLE 6.1

Marital Status of Canadians Aged 15 and Over by Province (1996)

	Can	NF	PE	NS	NB	QC	ON	MB	SK	AB	BC	YT	NT
Never married (single)	27.0%	28.0%	27.7%	26.5%	26.3%	28.4%	26.5%	27.0%	26.3%	26.3%	26.4%	28.7%	33.3%
Married (including common-law)	59.1	61.6	59.1	59.2	60.4	57.5	59.6	58.8	60.0	60.8	59.0	59.0	58.5
Total common-law	8.0	5.9	5.3	6.6	7.5	13.9	5.3	5.8	5.8	6.9	6.9	15.8	18.7
Total married (without common-law)	51.2	55.7	53.8	52.6	52.8	43.7	54.3	53.1	54.3	54.0	52.1	43.2	39.8
Separated	2.6	1.6	2.7	2.6	2.8	2.0	2.9	2.5	2.2	2.4	2.9	3.6	2.4
Divorced	5.1	2.8	3.6	4.7	3.9	5.8	4.7	4.5	4.1	5.4	5.9	6.0	2.9
Widowed	6.2	6.1	7.0	7.1	6.7	6.2	6.3	7.2	7.4	5.1	5.8	2.7	2.8

Sources: based on data from the Statistics Canada publications "Population by five-year age groups", Catalogue 93F0022, October 1997, and 1992, and "Population 15 years and over living in common-law unions by five-year age groups", Catalogue 95F0188, January 1998.

The Never-Married

There is a growing tendency for young adults to postpone marriage until they are older. By 1996, almost one-quarter of women and just over a third of men marrying for the first time did so after the age of 30. While a half a century ago, in the 1950s, over four out of ten women were married by the age of 22, by 1996, only about one in ten Canadian women had married for the first time by the age of 25 (Vanier Institute of the Family 2000, p. 45).

As a consequence, the number of singles in their 20s has risen dramatically. In 1997, 76.8 percent of women and 89.5 percent of men ages 20–24 were single (see Table 6.2). Although this rate of singlehood is striking when compared with the 1950s, it is not so unusual in a broader time frame—that is, compared with the behaviour of Canadians earlier in the twentieth century (Figure 6.3) (Vanier Institute of the Family 2000; Oderkirk 2000).

A theme of this text is that cultural values influence individual choices. Historical and demographic factors influence cultural values as well. The availability of education and jobs shaped twentieth-century marriage rates in complex ways (Cooney and Hogan 1991). A major historical event that affected people's decisions about marriage and families during the 1950s was the Great Depression of the 1930s.

During the Depression, individuals postponed marriage—if they married at all. "Among those born from 1906 to 1914, the average age at first marriage was 28 for men and 25 for women" (Oderkirk 2000, p. 95). With its extensive unemployment and poverty, the Depression wreaked havoc on the traditional family pattern—breadwinner husband, homemaker wife, and moderate-to-large family size. World War II saw an upswing in marriages in 1940 to 1942, at least partially the result of pragmatic reasoning. As Jillian Oderkirk (2000, p. 95) observes,

Canada entered the war in 1939, but was geographically far from the battlefield, and thus initially sent only career soldiers and volunteers. Conscription was extensively debated and was not

TABLE 6.2
Marital Status of the Canadian Population by Age, 1997

Age Group	Total Population Male (000s)	Total Population Female (000s)	Single Male (%)	Single Female (%)	Married Male (%)	Married Female (%)	Widowed Male (%)	Widowed Female (%)	Divorced Male (%)	Divorced Female (%)
Total Population 15+	11 927.7	12 385.6	32.0	34.5	78.7	58.9	2.2	9.9	5.0	7.5
15–19	1 051.1	996.7	99.7	98.7	0.3	1.2	...	...	...	...
20–24	1 039.0	997.7	89.5	76.8	10.3	22.6	...	0.1	0.2	0.5
25–29	1 076.4	1 052.9	56.7	38.9	41.6	58.4	0.1	0.2	1.6	2.5
30–34	1 225.6	1 202.3	32.2	21.1	63.9	74.5	0.1	0.3	3.8	5.1
35–39	1 353.0	1 340.0	21.3	14.0	72.8	78.2	0.2	0.6	5.8	5.1
40–44	1 259.5	1 262.5	21.3	14.0	72.8	78.2	0.2	0.6	5.8	7.2
45–49	1 095.1	1 100.2	14.6	10.4	77.5	78.8	0.3	1.2	7.7	9.7
50–54	933.4	940.7	10.3	8.1	80.3	78.2	0.6	2.2	8.9	11.5
55–59	711.5	726.6	7.6	6.4	82.5	77.4	1.0	4.2	9.0	12.0
60–64	594.6	618.7	6.1	5.2	83.3	70.8	3.4	15.0	7.2	9.0
65–69	547.0	594.7	6.2	5.4	82.0	62.6	5.8	24.7	6.0	7.3
70–74	439.3	543.7	6.2	5.7	79.7	51.8	9.6	37.2	4.4	5.2
75–79	312.5	447.3	5.7	6.3	75.9	38.9	15.2	51.1	3.2	3.7
80–84	175.1	295.8	5.7	7.3	68.1	24.3	23.7	65.8	2.4	2.3
85–89	83.2	172.9	6.3	8.9	56.7	13.0	35.2	76.7	1.8	1.4
90+	31.5	92.7	6.8	10.1	40.1	5.1	51.7	84.1	1.3	0.7

Note: (...) = Less than 0.1 percent.
Source: adapted from the Statistics Canada publication "Incidence of low income," Cat. 93F0029, The Nation Series 1996 Census, May 1998.

decided upon until a 1942 referendum. During these years of uncertainty, the prospect of being drafted into the armed forces was a potent stimulant to marriage for young single men, since they would be called first to go to war. Among those born during the last half of the 1910s and early 1920s, the average age at first marriage dropped to 27 for men and 24 for women.

However, World War II also disrupted family life by separating married couples; some wives were left widowed. In 1946, in the immediate aftermath of men's return from war, the divorce rate shot up to three times its pre-war level. "Marriages entered into too quickly and too young ended, promoting some 'experts' to lament the collapse of marriage and the decline of 'family values'" (Vanier Institute of the Family 2000, p. 48).

One legacy of the Depression was a high cultural valuation of that threatened family form, a large family. With the end of World War II and the growing prosperity of the postwar era, an expanded family life became possible. Children born during the Depression, who came to maturity in the 1950s,

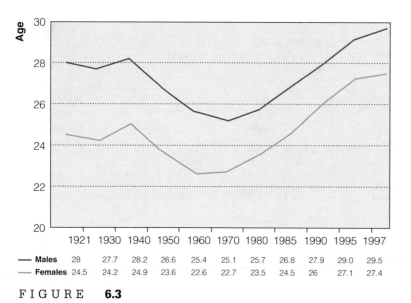

	1921	1930	1940	1950	1960	1970	1980	1985	1990	1995	1997
Males	28	27.7	28.2	26.6	25.4	25.1	25.7	26.8	27.9	29.0	29.5
Females	24.5	24.2	24.9	23.6	22.6	22.7	23.5	24.5	26	27.1	27.4

FIGURE   **6.3**

Average age at first marriage.
(Source: Statistics Canada (1992), *Current Demographic Analysis: Marriage and Conjugal Life in Canada*. Cat. 91-534, Statistics Canada, The Daily, October 28, 1999 and January 29, 1998.)

appear to have acted on this high commitment to traditional family values: They married unusually early and began families soon after (Elder 1974). Expanding economic opportunity characteristic of the 1950s facilitated such choices (Easterlin 1987) because young men could get jobs easily and be relatively confident that their real income would increase substantially. They were able to support stay-at-home wives and more children than their parents had been able to support and could afford better housing.

We may be tempted to think of the fifties as typical of Canadian marriage patterns, partly because of the images of family life presented by popular television shows during this period and partly because many adults can remember this era but not previous decades. The fifties were *not* typical, however, and the recent trend toward later marriage simply brings us back toward the pattern. The percentage of never-married men and women ages 20–24 today is comparable to the proportion of young adults never married at the turn of the twentieth century (Haines 1996).

At least four social factors may encourage young people today to postpone marriage or not to marry at all. First, changes in the economy may make early marriage less attractive or simply less feasible (Lloyd and South 1996). For example, the lengthening period of dependency of young people on their parents and/or on the state (while getting educated or trained) can lead to postponement of marriage or couple formation. The fact that many youth jobs are poorly paid, part-time, or transient may also discourage youthful marriages.

Second, improved contraception may contribute to the decision to delay getting married. With effective contraception, fewer couples may find that they "have to" get married as a result of pregnancy (Cherlin 1981).[2]

A third reason for the growing proportion of singles is demographic—that is, is related to population numbers. The **sex ratio** is the ratio of men to women in a given society or subgroup of society.[3] Historically, Canada had more men than women, mainly because

2. One can also argue, however, that contraception could facilitate early marriage by offering the possibility of marriage without pregnancy.

3. The sex ratio is expressed in one number: the number of males for every 100 females. Thus a sex ratio of 105 means that there are 105 men for every 100 women in a given population. More specialized sex ratios can be calculated for specific race/ethnic categories or at various ages, for example, or of unmarried people only.

more men than women migrated to this country, and, to a lesser extent, because a considerable number of young women died in childbirth (McVey and Kalbach 1995). However, since 1921, the sex ratio in Canada gradually declined and shortly after the 1971 census, the sex ratio was 100, or "even." However, as a result of the "greying" of Canada's population and women's greater life expectancy, as well as the increasing proportion of women among immigrants, the sex ratio by 1981 had reached 98 and, in 1996, there were only 94 males for every 100 females.[4]

The shortage of men becomes especially notable when we focus on the ratio of males per 100 females by age group. While sex ratios at birth favour males (with about 106 males per 100 females), this declines with increasing age. Focusing on sex ratios among the *general population*, in 1996, among Canadians aged 30 to 49, the sex ratio was 98.1 and 97.8 for those aged 50 to 64 (Larson et al. 2000, p. 123). "For the population 75 years of age and over, there were only 59 males per 100 females and for those over 85 years, females outnumbered males more than 2 to 1" (Kalbach 1999, p. 1868).

Of course, the sex ratio for society *as a whole* does not tell the entire story. To get a better picture of how the sex ratio impacts one's odds of marrying, we need to examine sex ratios within certain age groups—and more specifically, sex ratios for "single" (i.e., never-married, divorced and widowed) persons within certain age groups. In the 1980s, the popular press made much of the idea that there weren't enough single, eligible men to go around. There still are far more women than men in older age groups (Nelson and Robinson 2002). In Chapter 7, we will look more closely at how sex ratios influence the quest for an intimate partner.

A fourth reason is changing attitudes toward marriage and singlehood. We can speculate about what impact cultural change may have had on choices and feelings about singlehood. As the value of personal autonomy is emphasized (Bellah et al. 1985, 1996), many find singlehood more desirable.

4. Sex ratios vary by area of the country. Until 1986, a slight "excess" of males still existed in Canada's more rural populations and in its West and North. In 1996, the highest sex ratio occurred in the Yukon and Northwest Territories, where there were 107 males per 100 females. In contrast, an "excess" of women characterizes Canada's large urban centres—a "trend...already noticeable in 1961, when the sex ratio had declined in 6 of the 11 metropolitan areas. (Kalbach 1999, p. 1868).

The increase in the number and proportion of singles in our society is the result of many factors, including changing attitudes towards marriage and singlehood.

CHANGING ATTITUDES TOWARD MARRIAGE AND SINGLEHOOD

Social scientists used to discount changing attitudes as a serious reason for increased singlehood. They pointed out that both Canada and the United States have always been highly married societies, with about 90 percent of each cohort marrying at least once. This contrasts with Europe, where considerably higher proportions of adults never marry (U.S. Bureau of the Census 1998, Table 1346). Sociologists also argued that although people marry at older ages now, this situation is similar to a century ago when presumably attitudes toward marriage were wholly favourable (Cherlin 1981). In other words, social scientists generally believed that Canadians had not soured on marriage; they were just postponing it.

Sociologist Peter Stein (1976) was one of the first to argue otherwise. Stein identifies "a shift in attitudes about the desirability of marriage...: people are moving away from marriage and family norms as these norms conflict with the potentials for individual development and personal growth" (pp. 5, 6). Sociologist Zheng Wu (2000, pp. 65–66) has observed that, when asked the question, "In order for you to be happy in life, is it very important, important, not very important, or not at all important to be married?" just over 70 percent of Canadian women in 1984 and 67 percent of Canadian women in 1995 rated marriage as "very important" or "important." While the difference is slight, women in 1995 also placed less emphasis on the importance of marriage than Canadian men. Younger Canadians were less likely than older Canadians to place emphasis on marriage. Those living in the province of Quebec were considerably less likely to rate marriage as very important or important. In Quebec, just over 53 percent of women and 59 percent of men did so.

Based on his multivariate analysis of data collected in the 1984 Canadian Fertility Survey and the 1995 General Social Survey, Wu (2000, p. 71) reports that "[t]here is clear evidence that people now place less emphasis on marriage than they did a decade ago." In particular, he notes that a

> reduced emphasis on the importance of marriage is found among those with high SES [socio-economic status], an unhappy childhood, and who are middle-aged, unmarried, Canadian-born, non-Protestant, less religious, and/or residing in Quebec.

At the same time, however, he cautions that "we should not lose sight of the broader picture: a majority of Canadians feel that it is *very important*, or *important*, to be married....Marriage is not going out of style soon" (p. 66).

Although the vast majority of Canadians both expect to marry and do marry (Bibby 1995, 2001), some will not. Why?

First, compared with married people, singles hold more individualistic than familistic values. For example, we saw in Chapter 4 that young, never-married singles are more likely to have ludic or playful love styles and less likely to have agapic or unselfish love styles than were marrieds (Montgomery and Sorell 1997). In another study, interviewers asked singles and marrieds what was important to their happiness. Perhaps not surprisingly, marrieds tended to place a higher value on marriage, children, and love, whereas singles valued friends and personal growth more (Cargan and Melko 1982, pp. 166–70).

In addition, singles may intensify their individualistic attitudes the longer they remain unmarried. In an study conducted on 2075 never-married American men and women ages 19 to 35 who were not cohabiting, sociologist Scott South found that of those under age 26, 12.6 percent did not want to marry. However, when singles up to age 35 were included, the proportion rose to 17.2 percent (South 1993). Furthermore, the spectre of divorce has left many gun-shy. As one 28-year-old single woman explained, "If marriage is so good, why are so many people divorced?" (in Kantrowitz 1992, p. 52).

Sociologists have applied the exchange theoretical perspective (see Chapter 2) to this question of less favourable attitudes about marriage. They argue that singles weigh the costs against the benefits of marrying. At least some people see the benefits of marriage as decreasing while the costs of being single have simultaneously declined.

One reason for the declining perceived advantages of marriage is that today society views being single as an optional rather than a deviant lifestyle. During the 1950s, both social scientists and people in general tended to characterize singles as neurotic or unattractive (Kuhn 1955, cited in Stein 1976, p. 521). That view changed so that by the late 1970s, three-quarters of those interviewed in one poll considered it "normal" to be unmarried (Yankelovich 1981, p. 95). Virtually socially accepted alternatives to permanent marriage—being divorced, cohabiting, and permanent singlehood—have emerged.

It is also true that getting married is no longer the principal way to gain adult status. As Monica Boyd and Doug Norris (2000, p. 157) point out, while "[l]eaving high school, going to college or university, getting a full-time job, becoming economically self-sufficient, getting married....are commonly accepted indicators of being an adult...[t]oday, these changes are not one-time only events that occur in sequence." Increasingly, twentysomethings leave their parental home for reasons other than marriage. As more and

BOX 6.1

Three Never-Married Singles Speak Out About Their Lives and Concerns

More than ten years ago, social scientist Arthur Shostak noted that there was a prejudice against singles, but that it was lessening. "One thing that could help," he suggested, was for "proud singles" to "speak out and defend themselves" (1987, p. 366). We don't know of a current study that addresses whether discrimination against singles still exists, or to what extent. However, we present here the voices of three singles who, in their own words, speak of their experiences and concerns. The first is from a letter we received from a female student several years ago. The second is from a single man, who Agnes Riedmann interviewed for an early edition of this text. The third is from a student essay written in 1997.

1. *Excerpt from a letter to the authors from a single student*
   I prefer [being single] and am very happy being single. I even like myself! I do what I want, when I want, things are my way. Perhaps this is a selfish attitude, but I've earned the right to be somewhat selfish. I work very hard at a high pressure job, am going to school, have two homes and money in the bank, I'm saving/planning for retirement, have a few good friends, am always going to seminars, meetings, or classes at the local park district—so I keep myself busy. I couldn't imagine sharing all this with another. A lot of people would not have the time or energy to keep up. Many people would not even want to! I would not want my life any other way....

   I am not totally self-centred. I am an eternal volunteer and did volunteer work with handicapped/retarded kids and adults for 6 1/2 years and loved every minute of it. It was very difficult and emotionally draining, but I'm glad I had the opportunity to share with these people. If I had been married, I would never have been able to give the amount of time I did to that organization.

2. *Excerpt from an interview with a single young man*
   Some buddies and I have a car we race. Weekends we take it to different towns around the circuit....Racing takes up most of the weekends. Friday night is getting ready, drive all day Saturday, figure out what isn't right with the car, work on it all Saturday night, and get in the elimination Sunday morning. Then put the car back up on the trailer and get back in time to go to work on Monday morning....

   I had a girlfriend. We used to make the circuit together. This was back in high school and probably a year beyond. We were planning to get married. But then one time I cracked up pretty bad, and she was there. She wanted me to quit after that. She kept saying, "You are going to get yourself killed."... But freak accidents happen, it's just one of those things. She couldn't take me for what I did or what I was. She had her things she wanted to do. I wanted to run my life the way I wanted. I suppose, looking back, I could have been a little more flexible.... There are times that I think I should have quit. But racing is the way it is, that's just the way it is. Lots of things you do in the single life, it's just doing it and taking it for granted. If I don't like you and you don't like me, we go our separate ways.

3. *Excerpt from a 1997 young female student's essay*
   As we get closer to graduation and to our lives beyond college, many issues come to mind that we will have to deal with in the near future. We have to start looking for good jobs, or least ones with potential, searching for where we want to live, whether or not to get married, and so on.... I have a steady boyfriend and we have discussed marriage and family. I have a great job with opportunity for advancement, and although it's not exactly what I want to do for the rest of my life, it's good experience and decent money.

   It's the marriage and family part of my future that scares me. I have worked hard for the last four-and-one-half years at college to secure my degree. I have a job

(continued)

(continued)

where I can quickly advance and have more responsibility. Am I ready or will I want to get married? I know that the decision to get married will alter my life drastically.... [Once I graduate] I will have a job where I get offered regular promotions. I will probably move up quickly with the experience I have and with my degree, but in five years, since I already make nearly four dollars less an hour than my boyfriend, will I have to quit?...The common vision of a housewife from the fifties is of a woman who sacrificed her desires in the best interest of the family. But many young women who have been directed toward college by their parents will not want to be a housewife with a degree.

Each of these singles touches on points raised in this chapter. The first argues that singles are not unduly individualistic and points out that she does considerable volunteer work. However, the second illustrates the fact that, as a category, singles do exhibit more individualistic values than do marrieds. The third depicts the concerns of more and more educated single women—whether and how to combine career with family life.

more young people choose to claim independence simply by moving out of their parental homes, marriages loses its monopoly as the way to claim adulthood (Goldscheider and Goldscheider 1994).

While "the chance to fly solo was quite high from the 1960s to the 1980s, a time of prosperity, and a social easing of the pressure to marry" (Boyd and Norris, 2000, p. 183) difficult economic times in the 1990s caused many young adults to remain in or return to their parental homes. The struggles entailed in attempts to meet the educational/training demands of a "credential society" (Collins 1979) or establish oneself in a time of high youth unemployment and underemployment[5] (Rossi 1997) may well discourage the formation of intimate relationships.

Moreover, there is less parental pressure to marry than in the past. Although one researcher states that many parents "remain vexed when their offspring approach a thirtieth birthday without at least one marriage in the record" (Shostak 1987, p. 355), one important survey found that only half of never-marrieds in their late 30s perceived parental pressure to marry (Bumpass, Sweet, and Cherlin 1991).

Feminist social scientist Barbara Ehrenreich (1983) traced the historical development of what she called the "breadwinner revolt" among men from the 1950s through the 1980s. She argued that through the 1940s men demonstrated their masculinity through family breadwinning—that is, by establishing and providing for a family. Beginning in the 1950s, divergent cultural factors, from the *Playboy* mystique to the counterculture, have legitimated singlehood for men. More recently, sociologist Kathleen Gerson (1993) has argued that changes in our economy have made family breadwinning more difficult, hence less attractive, to a growing number of men. Also, the fact that men's earning potential is declining may make marriage less attractive to women (Oppenheimer 1994). Moreover, women have increasingly challenged men's privileges in marriage. Men differ in their responses to these changes.

5. Young people in Canada often find it difficult to obtain employment. In 1996, more than one out of every five Canadians between the ages of 15 and 24 had never held a job and the unemployment rate for this group was approximately 16 percent. A high rate of youth unemployment is not unique to Canada but part of an international trend, with young people in European countries finding it as difficult or more difficult to obtain work (Statistics Canada 1998).

Many will marry, but others will eschew commitment, either permanently or at least "for now."

Simultaneously, expanded educational and career options for women and, consequently, their growing commitment to paid work has given women increased economic independence (Waite, Goldscheider, and Witsberger 1986; Oppenheimer 1994; Lloyd and South 1996). Sociologist Frances Goldscheider has called women's growing lack of interest in marriage a revolution. In particular, middle-aged, divorced women with careers tend to look on marriage skeptically, viewing it as a bad bargain once they have gained financial and sexual independence. A 49-year-old divorced female executive, for example, says she loves eating popcorn for dinner rather than cooking like she used to when she was married. Once divorced, she said, "I could do anything I wanted for the first time in my life" (in Gross 1992). "The higher an older woman's income, the more likely she is to live alone, presumably because she has the means to support her independence" (Statistics Canada 1998, p. 183). Box 6.1, "Three Never-Married Singles Talk about Their Lives and Concerns," illustrates several of the points in this section. At the same time, however, Box 6.2, "Obstacles to Intimacy for Persons with Visible Disabilities," reminds us that single status is not always self-imposed or freely chosen.

In sum, it appears that being unmarried (1) represents a return to long-term patterns of late marriage from which the 1950s deviated; (2) results from the low sex ratio and economic disadvantage, which prevent a portion of the population from marrying; and (3) results from changing attitudes toward marriage and singlehood. Other reasons include the high likelihood of and tolerance for cohabitation (Axinn and Barber 1997), and for divorce in our society (see Chapter 15), and the relatively new possibilities for parenting—by means of artificial insemination, for example—for single women (see Chapter 11). Experts are divided on the likely futures of singlehood and marriage. Some research suggests that today marriage has regained some ground as a favoured status (Lee, Seccombe, and Shehan 1991). On the other hand, researchers point out that the long periods of nonmarried living that now characterize young adult life may result in a less familistic orientation and a permanent shift toward a preference for the independence and autonomy of singlehood (Waite, Goldscheider and Witsberger 1986).

In our society, whether or not people marry—and the timing of marriage for those who do—will probably remain unsettled for a while. Says Robert Willis, economics director of the National Opinion Research Center at the University of Chicago:

> A lot of people are trying different ways of sequencing—marriage first, then babies, then career, or getting established in a career first, then marriage or babies.... It seems to me until people have found a right way to travel through this, it'll be very difficult to predict how these statistics are going to change. (in Barringer 1992c, p. A-19)

THE VARIETY OF SINGLES

Factors such as age, sex, residence, religion, and economic status contribute to the diversity and complexity of single life. An elderly man or woman existing on Social Security payments and meagre savings has a vastly different lifestyle from, for example, two single professionals living together in an urban area. Single life in small towns differs greatly from that in large cities.

Types of Singles

Robert Staples developed a typology of singles based largely on whether their status is freely chosen. He designated five singles types.[6] The first type is the *free floating,* unattached single who dates randomly. The second type is a person in an *open-coupled relationship*: "This person has a relatively steady partner but the relationship is open enough to encompass other individuals in a sexual or romantic relationship." Staples warns that "sometimes it is an open-coupled relationship in a unilateral sense, with one of the partners pursuing other people; this may be a matter of deception or merely rest on the failure of the couple to define the relationship explicitly." In the third type—the *closed-couple relationship*—partners look only to each other for their romantic and sexual needs. Fidelity is expected. The fourth type consists of *committed singles* living in the same household and either engaged or having an agreement to maintain a permanent relationship. The fifth type is an *accommodationist,* one who either temporarily or permanently lives a solitary

---

6. Although Staples' typology was developed in the course of his work on African-Americans, these types can be applied to other "races" and ethnic groups.

Obstacles to Intimacy for Persons with Visible Disabilities

The author of the following extract, Harlan Hahn (1981/1990) writes, "I have been a 'participant-observer' concerning this subject for more than 35 years. As a result of polio, I have walked with crutches and braces since the age of six. In some respects, I have found my life as a disabled person to be a more useful source of concepts and propositions regarding physical disability than much of the published literature on the subject" (p. 344).

In his classic work of stigma, Goffman [1963] not only notes that a physical disability is a discrediting attribute which may induce others to believe that such a person "is not quite human," but he also concludes by pointing out that "the devaluation of those with bodily disfigurements can perhaps be interpreted as contributing to a ... narrowing of courtship decisions." The perceptibility of a stigmatized physical characteristic may vary along a continuum which reflects the severity of a disability and which may be enhanced by increasing degrees of intimacy. But, for some disabled men and women, the effects of stigmatization may be so powerful that they may pose a seemingly insurmountable obstacle to love or marriage.

Some support for this proposition can be derived from studies of visibly disabled persons. One study of veterans with spinal cord injuries, for example, found that one-half did not expect to be married, and an earlier study of 437 former polio patients disclosed that only 27.7 percent of the men and 41.1 percent of the women had either married or contemplated marriage after their release from the hospital. Another study revealed that, even in countries such as Columbia where strong social traditions support the institution of marriage and the family, more than 85 percent of the physically disabled women and 69 percent of the disabled men were single...

[R]esearch not only has demonstrated a correlation between the visibility of physical disabilities and the disruption of conjugal and family relationships, but it also has revealed the existence of widespread and deeply rooted attitudes of aversion and prejudice which effect the personal or social acceptability of disabled persons. Studies utilizing social distance measures have discovered an unwillingness to accept visibly disabled partners in a close personal or intimate relationship. As a result, several writers have observed that the disabled frequently are regarded as "asexual objects" and as unacceptable candidates for marriage. Safilios-Rothschild [1970], for example, in suggesting that "the main type of aversion (to disabled persons) is 'esthetic-sexual'" concluded that the likelihood of intermarriage between visibly disabled and nondisabled persons is "very small" and that "while the nondisabled tend to be cooperative and understanding when it comes to the occupational world, they close their ears to the disabled's attempts to gain social acceptance and marriage eligibility." This, of course, does not imply an absolute prohibition on relationships between disabled and nondisabled individuals; but it does suggest the possibility that, among many nondisabled people, the mere thought of an intimate relationship with a disabled person may be an offensive idea which conjures up feelings of disgust or repugnance. For some indeterminate portion of the nondisabled population, the barriers against sexual relationships with disabled persons almost amount to a taboo which few are willing to defy...

Social Conventions

...[T]here are many social customs which regulate the formation of intimate relationships and which impose a significant disadvantage upon disabled persons. Physical attractiveness, for example, often has been considered of paramount importance in the development of such relationships. This emphasis may reflect traditional values which were attached to physical strength and power as well as to physical beauty or grace...

Visibly disabled persons also may confront unique problems in their efforts to initiate social interactions with nondisabled people...[T]he symbols of a physical disability may be so prominent that they overshadow a disabled person's personality or intellectual traits. Such factors may affect both those with communications impairments such as blindness or deafness and persons with orthopedic disabilities which may restrict their movements. According to Davis [1961], informal encounters between disabled and nondisabled individuals usually are characterized by a stage of "fictional acceptance," in which no reference is made to an obvious physical disability, and by a subsequent attempt of the disabled person to "break through" the initial perception of the disability and to demonstrate other aspects of her or his personal characteristics. In many respects, this effort may reflect the desire to overcome conventional patterns of "paternalism" which place disabled people in a child-like (asexual) position of defencelessness, dependency, and inferiority and which often permeates interactions between disabled and nondisabled persons. Since superficial considerations seldom can sustain a personal relationship, the ability to "break through" may be an especially crucial concern of visibly disabled persons...

[I]f a visibly disabled person succeeds in "breaking through" to allow another individual to perceive human qualities that are unrelated to the disability, (s)he may confront unusual obstacles in attempting to determine whether or not the possible interest of the other party might extend to a physical or a sexual relationship. The language of sexuality often is conveyed by subtle unspoken cues such as eye contact, gestures, seemingly casual movement, and physical contact. While the interpretation of such ambiguous cues also is a concern of nondisabled people, they present particular problems both for disabled individuals who must not misperceive the nature of the encounter and for others who may find the mannerisms of disabled persons both awkward and difficult to translate. As a result, a disproportionate number of contacts between disabled and nondisabled individuals are terminated without explanation before they have an opportunity to explore the potential of the interaction.

For a variety of reasons, relations between disabled and nondisabled persons frequently are confined to a platonic realm. Disabled young people often serve as "good friends," "valued confidants," or even as "mascots" to their non-disabled peers... In a society dominated by physical standards and conventions which visibly disabled persons seldom can hope to approximate, they are frequently compelled to assume a role that denies the sexual aspect of their being... If a disabled person should attempt to venture beyond a simple friendship by suggesting the possibility of a close or intimate relationship, (s)he may be forced to confront an increased likelihood of rejection....[T]he cumulative effects of repeated rejections of visibly disabled individuals may result in a lowering of their sense of self esteem and in an unfavourable perception of their bodily images. Although some writers have urged disabled persons to become more assertive in their efforts to initiate personal relationships, there might also be a need for an awareness that they face increased probabilities of rejection.

If a disabled man or woman should succeed in forming a social or personal relationship with a nondisabled person, (s)he still may face major pitfalls in the courtship process. Most interactions between disabled and nondisabled individuals are conducted "as if" the disability were not present; and they may be severely tested by unanticipated architectural or other obstacles. Many common social or recreational patterns in courtship involve physical skills or activities which are beyond the capacity of the disabled person. Disabled and nondisabled persons also may face intensive resistance from

(continued)

Obstacles to Intimacy for Persons with Visible Disabilities

(continued)

others, including parents and friends of both parties as well as casual onlookers, who often regard the relationship as inappropriate or inadvisable....

Suitability of Marriage or Sexual Partners

The personal vulnerability of visibly disabled persons also may have a strong effect upon the types of individuals with whom they might engage in sexual relationships. Hicks [1980], for example, has pointed out, "All types of handicap restrict one's range of potential partners." Although the task of identifying an appropriate mate among those who might be willing to enter into a relationship with a disabled person is a critical problem, relatively little attention has been devoted to this subject. DeLoach and Greer [1981], in noting that "lack of available sexual partners doesn't always concern the disabled as much as lack of suitable sexual partners," offered a typology of "persons unusually attracted to the disabled" which includes the "walking wounded," the "would-be dictators," the "unsolicited missionaries," and the "gallant gestures." Similarly, Odgers [1979] described "five types of men disabled women should avoid"...

Disabled individuals, therefore, may confront significantly reduced probabilities in forming and in maintaining relationships with the nondisabled... Although nondisabled people may claim that their ability to find a compatible partner also is a "one in a million" experience, I believe that this analogy serious distorts reality because it underestimates the vast discrepancy between the social and sexual problems faced by disabled and nondisabled individuals.....

Source: Abridged from Hahn (1981/1990, pp. 343–48).

---

life, "except for friendships, refusing all dates and heterosexual contacts" (Staples 1981a, pp. 44–45).

Staples' discussion here reminds us that singles' lives differ due to many factors. Staples makes a further point: Singlehood may be temporary or permanent. Peter Stein has grouped "the heterogeneous populations of singles according to whether singlehood is voluntary or involuntary and stable or temporary" (1981, pp. 10–12).

As you can see in Table 6.3, voluntary singles may be single either temporarily or permanently; the same is true for involuntary singles.

Voluntary temporary singles are younger never-marrieds and divorced people who are postponing marriage or remarriage. They are open to the possibility of marriage, but searching for a mate has a lower priority than do other activities such as career.

Voluntary stable singles are singles who are satisfied to have never married, divorced people who do not want to remarry, cohabitants who do not intend to marry, and those whose lifestyles preclude marriage, such as priests and nuns.

Involuntary temporary singles are singles who would like, and expect, to marry. These can be either younger never-marrieds who do not want to be single and are actively seeking mates or older people who had not previously been interested in marrying but are now seeking mates.

Involuntary stable singles are older divorced, widowed, and never-married people who wanted to marry or to remarry, have not found a mate, and have come to accept being single as a probable life situation.

You may already have realized that throughout their lives people can move from one category to another. For example,

as younger never-marrieds who regarded singlehood as a temporary state become older, some

TABLE   6.3
Typology of Singlehood

	Voluntary	Involuntary
Temporary	Never-marrieds and former-marrieds who are postponing marriage by not currently seeking mates, but who are not opposed to the idea of marriage	Those who have been actively seeking mates for shorter or longer periods of time but have not yet found them
		Those who were not interested in marriage or remarriage for some period of time but are now actively seeking mates
Stable	Those choosing to be single (never-marrieds and former marrieds)	Never-marrieds and former-marrieds who wanted to marry or remarry, have not found a mate, and have more or less accepted singlehood as a probable life state
	Those who for various reasons oppose the idea of marriage	
	Members of religious orders	

Source: Stein 1981, p.11.

marry. Others, unable to find an appropriate mate, remain single involuntarily and become increasingly concerned about the possibility that they will never find a mate. Others may enjoy their single state and begin to see it as a stable rather than a temporary condition. The same person can identify singlehood as a voluntary temporary status before marriage, then marry and divorce and become single again. This person may then be a voluntary stable, involuntary stable, or involuntary temporary single, depending on his or her experiences and preferences. (Stein 1981, pp. 11–12)

Then, too, singles may feel ambivalent about whether they would rather be married. Even involuntary singles may find much to enjoy in being unattached. In short, single individuals' experiences and feelings about being single, in addition to changing throughout their lives, may differ based on whether their status is voluntary and whether it is permanent.

INCOME AND RESIDENTIAL PATTERNS OF SINGLES

Satisfaction with single living depends to some extent on income, for financial hardships can impose heavy restrictions. Many single women, especially those with children, just do not make enough money. These women head single-parent families rather than engaging in the stereotypical singles lifestyle characterized by personal freedom and consumerism. Many work two relatively low-paying jobs, one full-time and one part-time, then take care of their homes and children. For them "career advancement" means hoping for a small annual raise or just hanging on to a job in the face of growing economic insecurity. Pursuing higher educational opportunities means rushing to class one evening a week after working all day and making dinner for the children. For reasons that we will examine in detail throughout this book, many women's experiences as heads of single-parent households can be aptly described, in

Those called to religious orders, such as nuns and priests, are voluntary stable singles.

TABLE 6.4
Incidence of Low Income for Selected Types of Families, 1997

Economic families, two persons or more[1]	14.0
Elderly families[2]	6.8
Married couples only	6.0
All other elderly families	9.2
Non-elderly families[3]	15.3
Married couples, no children	10.6
One earner	13.9
Two earners	4.2
Two-partner families with children[4]	12.0
One earner	25.6
Two earners	6.6
Three or more earners	4.1
Married couples with other relatives[5]	5.3
Lone-parent families[4]	51.1
Male lone-parent families	23.5
Female lone-parent families	56.0
No earner	95.7
One earner	42.6
All other families	18.3
Unattached individuals	39.6
Elderly	45.0
Male	33.3
Female	49.1
Non-elderly	37.5
Male	35.1
Female	40.9

1. An economic family is a group of individuals sharing a common dwelling unit who are related by blood, marriage (including common-law relationships) or adoption.

2. Head aged 65 or over.

3. Head aged under 65.

4. With single children less than 18. (Children 18 or over and other relatives may also be present.)

5. Children less than 18 are not present, but children over 18 may be present.

Source: adapted from the Statistics Canada publication "Incidence of low income," Cat. 93F0029, The Nation Series 1996 Census, May 1998.

social scientist Sylvia Hewlett's words, as "a lesser life" (1986). (The problems of single-parent families are addressed in Chapter 14.)

There is evidence that occupation and income are related to marital status. As you can see in Table 6.4, the incidence of low income is considerably lower among married couples than singles, and this is true even if both spouses are not in the paid labour force. Singles who are not living with any other relatives earn significantly less, with single women earning the least. Married people are more likely to have white-collar jobs and higher incomes than are singles, regardless of age and education. Income and employment needs affect singles' residence patterns.

Urban and Suburban Singles

In the past, most of the singles population became concentrated in specific areas of larger cities. Today, singles move from small towns to medium-sized cities and from medium-sized cities to larger metropolitan areas not only for employment but for other reasons as well. Often, they move because they want to be near others who are like themselves.

Singles with money to spend on leisure activities migrate to larger cities because there is more to do there. More and more cities have singles-oriented special interest clubs (book, bird-watching, chess, opera, and so on) as well as singles-oriented restaurants, dance halls, travel agencies, and lecture/study groups. Reflecting their urban residential pattern, singles have been more likely than marrieds to complain to pollsters of urban discontents—traffic congestion, lack of parks, air and noise pollution, and so on (Shostak 1987).

Partly because of these dissatisfactions with city life, singles are now moving to the suburbs (Cobb 1997). At the same time, suburbs are changing. Employers, services, and cultural activities have relocated from cities to suburbs. Singles can feel at home because of the "citification" of suburbs while enjoying the outdoors and the lower cost of housing: "There's a lot of calmness here and birds chirping. It's not as stressful," says one single suburbanite (Nemy 1991, p. B–8).

DOMESTIC ARRANGEMENTS OF SINGLES

Wherever singles live, they must make choices about whom (if anyone) to live with. We see again the variety of singles' lives: Some live alone; some live with parents; some live in groups or communally; some cohabit with partners of the same or opposite sex; some women share a man in an ongoing relationship. We look now at this variety of domestic arrangements. In the process we will find that the distinction between being single and married is not that sharp, for people who are legally single tend to be embedded in families of one form or another.

Living with Parents

A growing proportion of young adults are living with one or both parents. In 1940 the proportion of adults under age 30 living with their parents was quite high. Sociologists Paul Glick and SungLing Lin suggest why:

The economic depression of the 1930s had made it difficult for young men and women to obtain employment on a regular basis, and this must have discouraged many of them from establishing new homes. Also, the birth rate had been low for sev-

eral years; this means that fewer homes were crowded with numerous young children, and that left more space for young adult sons and daughters to occupy. (Glick and Lin 1986a, p. 108)

Some of these same reasons apply to young people today. Although the proportion of young Canadian adults that lived in their parental homes declined between 1971 and 1981, "following the general twentieth century trend toward non-familial family arrangements for the young and the older generations," (Boyd and Norris 2000, p. 157) young adults are now increasingly likely to be living with their parents. Table 6.5 lists the percentages of young adults living with their parents in 1981, 1986, 1991 and 1996; the term "unmarried" here is used to refer to a young adult who was not married and includes those who were divorced, separated, widowed as well as those who were never-married. The term "married" within this table refers to those who were either legally married or living in a common-law relationship.

Although Table 6.5 indicates that "the growing propensity to live at home was common to both unmarried and married young adults" (Boyd and Norris 2000, p. 158), the postponement of marriage discussed earlier in this chapter has meant a longer period of singlehood.

In addition, housing in urban areas can be so expensive that singles and young marrieds cannot maintain their own apartments. Difficulty in finding adequate employment is also a factor in the proportion of young adults living with parents today. Others are trying to minimize expenses as they complete graduate or undergraduate education. Unmarried women who have babies, especially those who became parents in their teens, may be living with parents. Others may return after divorce, as may divorced men as well. Singles are less likely to return home when their parents have been divorced or remarried (Goldscheider and Goldscheider 1998).

Table 6.5 also reveals that smaller percentages of young adult women than young adult men live in their parental home. This finding, which has been noted in other studies that have looked at the living arrangements of young adults in Canada as well as the United States (e.g., Boyd and Pryor 1989; Ward and Spitze 1996a, 1996b), has led to speculation about male domestic dependency that is not always flattering:

TABLE 6.5

The Proportion of Young Adults Living at Home Has Been Rising Over the Past 15 Years

| | Percentage living with parents | | | | | | | |
| | Unmarried | | | | Married* | | | |
	Total	20–24	25–29	30–34	Total	20–24	25–29	30–34
Women								
1981	44	60	27	18	1	3	1	1
1986	46	64	32	18	2	3	2	1
1991	44	63	33	19	2	5	2	1
1996	47	67	36	19	3	7	4	2
Men								
1981	55	69	40	28	2	3	2	1
1986	57	72	45	30	2	4	2	1
1991	53	71	44	29	3	6	3	1
1996	56	74	48	32	4	9	5	3

*Married inclues legal marriages and common-law relationships.

Source: Statistics Canada, "Canadian Social Trends," Cat. No. 11-008, Sept. 1995, No. 38.

The rent is low and utilities are free. There is hot food on the table and clean socks in the drawer. Mom nags a little and dad scowls a lot [fathers are often not enthusiastic about the arrangement, particularly if it is because of the son's unemployment], but mostly they don't get in the way. And there's money left at the end of the month for a car payment. (Gross 1991c, p. 1)

Parents do "get in the way" of women who live at home. They are more likely to try to limit daughters' freedom to come and go or to be suspicious of suspected sexual activity. Men, on the other hand, may find living with parents a stigma when dating women who expect them to live independently (Gross 1991c).

Just as economic considerations or the need for emotional support or the need for help with child rearing may lead young singles to choose living with parents, similar pressures may encourage singles to fashion group or communal living arrangements.

Group or Communal Living

Groups of adults and perhaps children who live together, sharing aspects of their lives in common, are known as **communes**. In some communes, such as the Israeli kibbutz (Spiro 1956), some nineteenth-century American groups such as the Shakers and the Oneida colony (Kephart 1971; Kern 1981), and contemporary Canadian groups such as the Hutterites (Ryan 1999), emphasis is placed on communal living and communal ownership of property. Work is organized by the commune, and commune members are fed, housed, and clothed by the community. Other communes may have some private property; even some Israeli farming cooperatives that superficially resemble kibbutzim have private land plots, although members share a communal life (Schwartz 1954).

There is also variation in sexual arrangements among communes, ranging from celibacy to monogamous couples (the kibbutz, the Hutterites) to the open sexual sharing found in the Oneida colony and to the polygamy-endorsing United Effort Order, a commune of dissident Mormons located outside of Creston, B.C. Children may be under the control and supervision of a parent, or they may be more communally reared, with a de-emphasis on biological relationships and responsibility for discipline and care vested in the entire community.

Living communally has declined in both Canada and the United States from its highly visible and idealized status in the 1960s. But new small scale and nonideological versions of communal living have surfaced as singlehood has increased, and as our population ages. Communal living, either in single houses or in cohousing complexes that combine private areas with communal kitchens (Ravo 1993), may be one way to cope with some of the problems of aging, singleness, or single parenthood. In a small but growing number of cohousing complexes, people of different sexes and diverse ages may choose to reside together as a solution to economic and other practical concerns, such as in-home child care ("Communal Living ..." 1998).

As does any living arrangement, communal living has positives and negatives. Single mothers may get help, but may also relinquish some parental control. And, as one might expect, agreeing on standards for privacy, housekeeping, and noise may be a source of conflict among members. Still, communal living represents an attempt to provide people with greater opportunities for social support, companionship, and personal growth.

Financial considerations and the need for social support may also encourage dating singles to share households. We explore cohabitation, or living together, next.

Cohabitation

Singles engaging in **cohabitation**, or living together, gained widespread acceptance over the past few decades. Although we may associate cohabitation with university students of the 1960s, the trend actually began much earlier. "Although non-marital cohabitation has been practised for centuries in Western and other civilizations, the rapid increase in cohabitation in recent years caught most of us, academe and public alike, by surprise" (Wu 2000, p. 4). Since

the Canadian census first began to collect information on cohabitation in 1981, the number of cohabiting persons, 15 years of age and older, has increased from 713 210 to 1.84 million in 1996—a 158 percent increase[7]. In Quebec, the number of cohabiters 15 years of age older rose by 231 percent over this time period (Figure 6.4) (Wu 2000, p. 43).

Although only about eight percent of the population is currently cohabiting, heterosexual cohabiting unions (also known as common-law unions in Canada) grew from six percent to 14 percent of all unions between 1981 and 1996. In Quebec, cohabitation is particularly popular. "Currently, nearly one out of four heterosexual couples in Quebec is not married, compared to one out of nine elsewhere in Canada. In fact, almost one-half (43.4 percent) of all heterosexual cohabiting couples in Canada are now residing in the province of Quebec" (Wu 2000, p. iv). Cohabitation is particularly common among the young and among those who are separated and divorced (Bumpass and Sweet 1995).

Many cohabiting relationships are relatively short-term. A national U.S. survey of cohabiting women found that just over one-half of their relationships ended in marriage, 37.2 percent broke up, and 10 percent were still ongoing at the time of the survey (London 1991). Research conducted in Canada reports that while more than half of cohabiting relationships end within three years, they are more likely to end in marriage: "about one-third of cohabiting couples marry each other within three years of cohabitation, while another quarter dissolve their relationships through separation" (Wu 2000, p. 1).

Living together is a way of life that more and more people are choosing for many reasons. Increasingly, people from all social, educational, and age groups have at least experimented with this family form. Although cohabitation is particular common among the young[8], older retired couples have also found that living together without being legally married can be an agreeable living arrangement. Table 6.6 provides the percentage of persons in cohabitations by age group, for selected years.

7. When Quebec is excluded from consideration, the number of cohabiters increased by "only" 121 percent between 1981 and 1996 (Wu 2000, p. 43).

8. In 1996, 37 percent of Canadian women and 28 percent of Canadian men who cohabited were under the age of 30 (Wu 2000, p. 1).

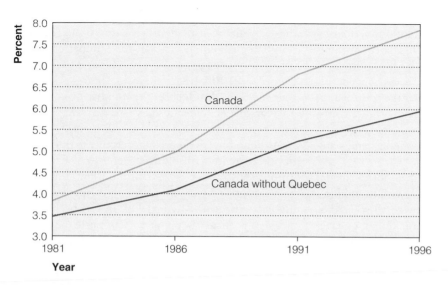

FIGURE **6.4**

Percentage of persons 15+ in cohabitations. (Source: Census of Canada, various years; Wu 2000, p. 42.)

Many cohabitants have been previously married, then divorced, or (less often) widowed. For this group, living together may provide a respite from the singles scene and a return to the domestic lifestyle to which they are accustomed; or it may be, as for many never-marrieds, a way station on the road to marriage.

About half of cohabiting couples' families contain children. While cohabiting couples are significantly less likely to stay together than marrieds, having children in the household stabilizes unmarried couples somewhat (Wu 1995).

Unmarried couples are somewhat more likely than married couples to be interracial (see Chapter 8). "A reasonable speculation is that interracial couples violate strongly held social norms; and, therefore, some of them may be reluctant to formalize their relationship by marriage" (Glick and Spanier 1980, p. 26). They may also receive more social support for their relationship if it is not formalized.

Some cohabitants may consider their lifestyle a means of courtship, as discussed in Chapter 7. For other cohabitants, living together can be a long-term alternative to legal wedlock. People's reasons for living together outside of legal marriage include the wish not to make the strong commitment that marriage requires and the belief that legal marriage can stifle

communication and equality between partners (Watson and DeMeo 1987; Steinhauer 1995).

Whether an early beginning to marriage or an alternative lifestyle, "cohabitation is very much a family status, but one in which the levels of certainty about commitment are less than in marriage" (Bumpass, Sweet, and Cherlin 1991, p. 913). This uncertainty about commitment may be one reason why, compared to marrieds, cohabitants say they are less satisfied with their relationships (Nock 1995). There is also evidence of considerable domestic violence in cohabiting relationships, perhaps due to conflict over "rights, duties, and obligations" (Magdol et al. 1998, p. 52). Cohabitants express "little concern with cohabitation being a moral issue or with the disapproval of parents or friends" (Bumpass, Sweet, and Cherlin 1991, p. 921; Steinhauer 1995). Indeed, they are more likely than others to be nontraditional in many ways, including attitudes about gender roles, and to have parents with nontraditional attitudes (Axinn and Thornton 1993; Booth and Amato 1994).

Although in responding to surveys people are articulate about their reasons for cohabitation, accounts of how cohabitation begins suggest that cohabiting does not always result from a well-considered choice (Macklin 1983). Like some of the decisions previously discussed,

TABLE 6.6
Percentage of Persons in Cohabitation by Age Group, 1981–1996

Age	15–19	20–24	25–29	30–34	35–39	40–44	45–49	50–54
Year								
1981	1.7	8.2	7.6	5.7	4.2	3.2	2.4	1.9
1986	1.6	9.5	10.4	7.8	5.9	4.8	3.7	2.1
1991	1.8	11.6	14.0	10.9	8.5	6.8	5.8	4.4
1996	1.6	11.8	16.9	14.1	11.2	9.0	7.3	6.1

Source: *Census of Canada,* various years; Wu 2000, p.44.

it can also happen by default. As one university student explained, "It just got to be too much bother to go home every morning." Compared to postmarital cohabitation, the "tempo" of entry into premarital cohabitation is much slower (Wu 2000, p. 87).

Counsellors and others stress the importance of clarifying motivations and goals for cohabiting before taking the step. For individuals who are not prepared, living together can lead to "misunderstanding, frustration, and resentment" (Ridley, Peterman, and Avery 1978, p. 129). Counsellors also stress the importance of individuals being relatively independent before they cohabit, having clear goals and expectations, and being sensitive to the needs of their partners. (Chapter 7 discusses the useful advice of these researchers in more detail.)

As people choose cohabitation, the legal aspects of living together outside of marriage are simultaneously coming into focus and changing. Box 6.3, "The Legal Side of Living Common-Law," outlines some important considerations for cohabitants.

Gay and Lesbian Partners

Because the results of the 2001 Canadian census were unavailable at the time that this book was written, we are unable to provide national statistics on the domestic arrangements of gays and lesbians. Moreover, at the time of writing, homosexual marriage was not legal in Canada.

In consequence, while attempts to legalize such marriages continue, for now, lesbians and gay male couples are legally single. (The issue of gay and lesbian legal marriage is addressed in Chapter 8.)

Nevertheless, many gay and lesbian couples live together and share sexual and emotional commitment. They may consider themselves married as a result of personal ceremonies in which they exchange vows or rings or both, or they may form more public unions, religiously recognized by the Metropolitan Community Church or the Unitarian Universalist Church, for example. Some newspapers have begun to announce gay and lesbian partnerships on the society page. Some gays and lesbians are also establishing families with children, becoming parents through adoption, foster care, planned sexual intercourse, or artificial insemination.

The growing social and legal recognition of gay and lesbian families challenges all of us to reexamine our understanding of what a family is. As Eric W. Sager, the Director of the Canadian Families Project at the University of Victoria has so eloquently remarked,

We know family by what it does, not by any single "traditional" form. Think, for a moment of one of English-Canada's most famous families. A fictional family, to be sure, but a very believable one. It consists of an elderly spinster, her brother, and a nonkin child named Anne of Green Gables. By

Statistics Canada's definition of "census family," this small group is not a family. It is certainly not a traditional nuclear family. Yet we all know it to be a family, not by its form but by what these three people did with and for each other. There were many such families in the past and there are many today. (Sager 2000, p. xi)

Psychologist Lawrence Kurdek has conducted considerable research on gay and lesbian couples. In one study comparing cohabiting gay male, lesbian, heterosexually married, and dating couples, Kurdek concluded that the gay and lesbian couples experienced relationship quality similar to that of the marrieds (Kurdek 1995). One earlier study directed by Letitia Peplau (1981) based on questionnaires administered to 128 gay men, 127 lesbians, and 130 unmarried heterosexual women and men found that both heterosexuals and gay people struggle to balance "the value placed on having an emotionally close and secure relationship" with that of "having major interests of ... [one's] own outside the relationship [and] a supportive group of friends as well as ... [one's] romantic sexual partner" (Peplau 1981, p. 33). Regarding gay people's similarities with—or differences from—heterosexuals, Peplau concluded:

We found little evidence for a distinctive homosexual "ethos" or orientation toward love relationships. There are many commonalities in the values most people bring to intimate relationships. Individual differences in values are more closely linked to gender and to background characteristics than to sexual orientation. (Peplau 1981, p. 33)

Blumstein and Schwartz's study (1983) of married heterosexual couples, unmarried heterosexual cohabitants, and gay male and lesbian couples reached a similar conclusion: Gender is a more important determinant of the nature of couple relationships than sexual orientation is (see also Chapter 5).

Kurdek's study of a nonrandom, convenience sample of 74 gay male and 45 lesbian couples found lesbian couples to have "enhanced relationship quality" (Kurdek 1989b, p. 55). Like the other researchers, he attributes the lesbian couples'

greater relationship satisfaction, stronger liking of their partners, greater trust, and more frequent

shared decision making ... to both partners having been socialized to define themselves in terms of relationships with others, to regulate interactions with others on the basis of care and nurturance, to be sensitive to the needs and feelings of others and to suppress aggressive and competitive urges which may result in social isolation. (Kurdek 1989b, p. 55)

More recent research on gay male couples found that, for older couples, relationship satisfaction was related to sexual satisfaction. However, for younger men, relationship satisfaction was more often related to psychological intimacy (Deenen, Gijs, and van Naerssen 1994).

Although there may be no distinct homosexual "ethos," gay male and lesbian relationships do differ from others in two important ways. First, gay male and lesbian partners tend to be more autonomous than heterosexual spouses (Kurdek 1998). Second, gays and lesbians are less likely to adopt traditional masculine and feminine roles in their relationships (Reimann 1997). Instead, couples assume a pattern characterized by more equality and role-sharing than in heterosexual marriages (Rosenbluth 1997). One reason many gay relationships are relatively egalitarian is that pairings of two men or two women generally provide members of the couple with similar incomes, whereas a heterosexual couple tends to be characterized by higher income, and therefore more power, for males (Harry 1983). (Chapter 10 addresses the association of income equality with egalitarian decision making.)

Same-sex partners, like singles in other situations, search for a community of friends and neighbours. Some find community in urban areas with concentrations of other gays and lesbians and strong activist organizations. But like some heterosexual singles, gay people are moving to the suburbs. "There are still people who clearly want to live in the gay ghettoes.... But a whole lot more ... want to lead their lives like other people lead their lives" (Tom Nolan in Gross 1991b, p. E–16).

Our discussion of heterosexual cohabiting couples and gay and lesbian relationships presumes partners who identify themselves as a couple. Even should they have a nonexclusive sexual relationship, their primary commitment is to each other. But if we look closely at intimate relationships in our society, we find other

BOX 6.3

The Legal Side of Living Common-Law—Some Advice

When unmarried lovers decide to move in together, they can encounter regulations, customs, and laws that cause them problems, especially if they're not prepared for them (Rowland 1994). What follows is not intended to replace consultation with a lawyer in your area. Laws and policies vary across Canada. However, the general information provided in the following extract, by Canadian lawyer Linda Silver Dranoff, may be helpful.

Legal Rights and Responsibilities

As recently as 15 years ago, I was able to write that Canadian law "took little notice of a union known as 'common-law' marriage." This is no longer; more and more rights and obligations of marriage are being visited upon couples who may have thought they were avoiding all that by living together "without benefit of clergy." ....

It is getting more difficult even to define a common-law relationship because definitions differ for different purposes. Traditionally, this relationship was legally defined as an alliance between parties who passed themselves off in the community as married, consummated their union by living together in a sexual relationship and were free to marry each other. Although they did not possess a marriage licence, they did have a commitment akin to traditional marriage.

Today, the laws vary. For example, the support laws in some provinces have been extended from common-law partners to include live-in partners, when there is no pretence of a long-term relationship.... Since the trend in law is toward greater recognition of the rights of common-law spouses, and legal treatment of the couple as married partners, the law in this area is subject to particular change....

Here [are only a few examples of]...how cohabitation may affect a person's interests.

The Home. If the partners live in a home owned on title by the two of them, they are protected by their registered interest, just as anyone would be; in fact, a name on the title is the best assurance of ownership. A person who lives with the registered owner but is not registered as owner has no ownership interest. However, if the non-titled partner makes a contribution to purchase, renovate, pay off the mortgage or participate in some other way with work, money or money's worth (labour) to the home, then he or she may make a claim in court for a share of the value of the home. The non-titled partner will be required to prove his or her claim with evidence of contribution, and will not be able to secure his or her rights until the lawsuit is over...

Support. Most provinces provide for a mutual obligation of support between unmarried couples if certain criteria are met. For example, in Ontario, Saskatchewan, New Brunswick and Prince Edward Island, a man and woman who live together continuously for three years or more are entitled to claim support from each other, particularly if a dependency has been created by the relationship, or if they live in a relationship that is defined as having "some permanence" because they are the natural or adoptive parents of a child. In Nova Scotia, support obligations only apply after one year (or it the couple have a child together). Most other provinces have varying minimum periods.

But the definition of cohabit was stretched by an Ontario judge in 1996 to rule that a man was still a "spouse" to a woman with whom he had never lived, although they spent four of five nights a week together. According to him, they had a seven-year "affair;" according to her, he had made promises of permanence and fidelity. The judge ruled that "he had given the woman every reason to believe that she was in a permanent relationship with him. He told her he loved only her and intended to be faithful. He never told [her] she was just a girlfriend and it was his intention to be free, independent and carry on affairs with a number of other women... The court cannot condone fraud and deceit." ...

Children. The children of a common-law relationship normally use their mother's surname, unless she wants

(continued)

(continued)

to register them in the father's name and he agrees in writing, or (in Alberta, Newfoundland, Nova Scotia) a court declares him to be the father of the children. All provincial laws oblige both parents to support their children.

Pension Plans. A common-law spouse may be able to receive the benefit of a spouse from certain private pension plans and the Canada Pension plan, provided that the partner has no legal mate to take priority. The Canada Pension Plan now defines spouse generally to include a person of the opposite sex who has been cohabiting in a conjugal relationship with the contributor for a continuous period of at least one year.

Spousal Benefits. More and more benefit plans are being extended to common-law couples on the same basis as married partners...

Income Tax Laws. Income tax law has caught up to common-law spouses, who used to pay tax as if they were single. Since January 1, 1993, the law gives common-law spouses a new status for tax purposes:

They have the same rights and are subject to the same liabilities as legally married spouses...

Inheritance Rights. Live-in partners have no automatic right to inherit each other's property upon death.... But support is possible if one partner was dependent on the other financially at date of death, and the will failed to provide adequately for the dependent person... Generally speaking, if a couple wants to ensure that they have rights not provided by law, or ensure that they agree on the mutual rights and expectations they do want, then they should have a cohabitation contract...

To sum up the legal side of living together, individuals must decide how they want to live, based on their needs, values and goals. In so doing, they will do well to be aware of the laws of their country as well as their province. The burden is on individuals to keep informed. At the same time, laws and policies seem to be in the process of changing to meet the needs of today's variety of families.

Source: Abridged from Dranoff 2001, pp. 99–103.

situations in which the parties in a relationship know that one of them has another primary partner. We look now at women sharing men.

Women Sharing Men

One response to women's declining chances to marry is represented by single women's sexual relationships with married men (Salamon 1984). For the woman who would like to marry but hasn't, or for the woman who values independence and career over conventional domesticity, a partial (but often

lengthy) sexual and companionate relationship seems preferable to autonomous singlehood or a series of temporary relationships.

Sociologist Laurel Richardson (1985) explored this increasingly common phenomenon in interviews with 55 women from varied social backgrounds: high school graduates and women with postgraduate degrees; skilled workers and professional and managerial women; traditional women and feminists. For the most part, the woman did not intend to have the affair; it developed inadvertently out of sustained work or social contact. Once begun, it seemed a rational solution to the woman's dilemma: how to meet her emotional, sexual, and companionship needs in the absence of marriage. Women whose work demanded a great deal of time and energy found the married man an appealing alternative. Furthermore, married men were perceived as more stable, attractive, and willing to express feelings than were unmarried men.

Women entered the relationship with a sense of personal efficacy. But over time the structure of the relationship gave most of the power to the man, and women felt this dependency and lack of control keenly. Meetings and other contacts had to depend on the man's initiative. The classic limitation of an unsanctioned relationship, holidays spent alone, was more depressing than expected. Although some women were able to integrate their relationship with the rest of their lives, those who maintained secrecy felt cut off from family, friends, and work colleagues. Richardson believes that in the long run the new other woman phenomenon supports male privileges while being a disadvantage to both lover and wife (see also Nelson 1994).

In a similar vein, sociologist Joseph Scott (1980, 1999) has studied what he terms "polygamy"[9] among African-Americans. In the African-American polygamous family, two (or more) women maintain separate households and are independently "pair-bonded to a man whom they share and who moves between ... households as a husband to both women" (Scott 1980, p. 43). In view of the particularly unbalanced sex ratio among American blacks, Scott suggests "the only way many black women may have men permanently in their lives would be to share them with women who already have them as husbands or friends" (1980, p. 48).

Polygamy has been very common throughout history as a permissible pattern in many cultures. Where permitted, though, it is not always that frequent, for many men cannot afford multiple wives. Polyandry is rare and tends to exist in very poor societies in which female infanticide is practised to reduce the number of mouths to feed, with the result that there are not

enough women to go around for marriage in adulthood. It is also practised when brothers share a wife, again, often because of economic constraints. Group marriage is rarer still because of the obvious difficulties in balancing rights and duties and in working out conflicts and loyalties in this system (Stephens 1963).

Scott interviewed 22 African-American women who either were or had been in a polygamous relationship. Half the women were single (consensual wives), and half were married (legal wives). Their relationships varied in length from two to 12 years. These women tended to be young, of low socioeconomic status, and to have experienced premarital pregnancies for which they were ill-prepared. They believed men to be polygamous by nature and resigned themselves to sharing. Consensual wives saw the single black men available to them as unreliable compared to those already married. "Married men, the women say, were generally more emotionally stable, more knowledgeable about family life, and very importantly, more financially able to assist them" (Scott 1980, p. 53; 1999). Most of the legal wives became involved in polygamy because their husbands had other close female companions before marriage and kept them. Generally, they accepted their situations as inevitable, "given the scarcity of what they call 'good men.' ... They all shared the view that if their husbands maintained their economic priorities to their legal families, this was evidence of their giving priority to the legal marriages themselves" (Scott 1980, p. 60; 1998).

Critics question whether polygamy among African-Americans is freely chosen or imposed on the women by circumstance and men's behaviour (Staples 1985). Scott replies to the critics that, in fact, the polygamy is consensual (that is, agreed to by the women) and that these unions are socially recognized as legitimate family constellations in the black community. Even though polygamy may be a logical solution to the lack of adult black males in urban settings, "many are concerned about the vulnerability of the mother/child units in 'man sharing' and see the pattern as one more instance of the exploitation of poor women" (Peters and McAdoo 1983, pp. 302–303).

Looking at singles who live with parents, in communal groups, with common-law partners, or in polygamous arrangements, we realize that the distinction between married and single is no longer very

---

9. The term *polygamy* means more than one spouse at a time for a partner of either sex. *Polygyny* refers to multiple wives for a man, and *polyandry* to multiple husbands for one wife. *Group marriage* indicates a marriage of more than one woman to more than one man.

clear. Most singles are embedded in families. There are also married couples who live apart in commuter marriages (see Chapter 13), postdivorce families in which no longer married individuals still function as a couple, and married couples who are emotionally or sexually estranged.

Keeping that in mind, we turn now to look at the question of marital status and life satisfaction.

ALONENESS, LONELINESS, AND LIFE SATISFACTION

The number of one-person households has increased dramatically since 1941 (Figure 6.5). There is disagreement over whether "flying solo" should be viewed as "one of the most profound changes to occur in Canada's history, a reflection of our evolution towards more independent and individual lifestyles" or, alternatively, explained "in terms of family or economic factors that don't necessarily mean we have fundamentally changed our thinking" (Statistics Canada 1998, p. 183). Nevertheless, whether as the result of divorce, widowhood, or simply personal choice, in 1996 approximately 2.6 million Canadians lived alone. "Of all the living arrangements that can be found in private households in Canada, fully 24 percent consist of just one person" (Statistics Canada 1998, p. 183).

Among men who live alone, approximately half are between 30 to 54 years old. These men "often represent the fall-out from divorce, given that child custody is typically granted to women" (Statistics Canada 1998, p. 183). Among women who lived alone in that year, many were older widows.

Older Single Adults: The Double Standard of Aging

While the majority of Canadian men aged 50 and 89 are married, the proportion of married females drops dramatically with age (see Chapter 7). Because of differences in death rates and a greater likelihood of previously widowed men remarrying, older women are more likely to be widowed and to retain this marital status.

The elderly's living alone results to a significant extent from values of independence (Kramarow 1995). Meanwhile, while some observers have suggested that people create group marriages (Kassel 1966), others forward the idea that women of any age who are left without partners due to the imbalanced sex ratio might begin to explore lesbian relationships (Doudna 1981). But a study of change in preferred sexual activity from young adulthood to old age found few older adults shifting to homosexuality (Turner and Adams 1988). In a society that condemns homosexuality and encourages exclusive sexual

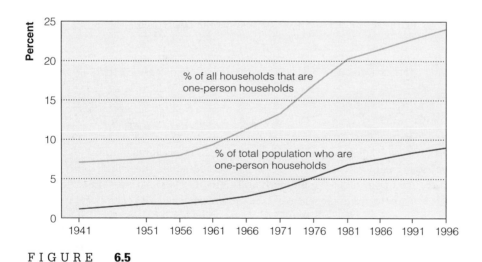

FIGURE   **6.5**

| Living alone. (Source: Statistics Canada, "Canada Year Book 1999," Cat. No. 11-204, p. 183.)

relationships between one man and one woman, many older women are left without partners.

Moreover, as they grow older, women are adversely affected by the **double standard of aging** (Sontag 1976); that is, men aren't considered old or sexually ineligible as soon as women are. In our culture, being physically attractive is far more important in attracting a mate for women than for men. Beauty, "identified, as it is for women, with youthfulness, does not stand up well to age" (Sontag 1976, p. 352). So in our society women become sexually ineligible much earlier than men do. An attractive man can remain eligible well into old age and is considered an acceptable mate for a younger woman. For older single women this situation can exacerbate more general feelings of loneliness. A recent study of 3390 Dutch older women found that they were lonelier when not in a partnership and were lonelier the more—and the more recent—union dissolutions they had experienced (Peters and Liefbroer 1997).

Aloneness and Loneliness Are Different

Although living alone can be lonesome, we need to remember that aloneness, being by oneself, and loneliness, a subjective sensation of distress, are different (Shahan 1981). One can feel lonely in the presence of others, even a spouse, and happy alone. Moreover, living alone does not necessarily imply a lack of social integration or meaningful connections with others. In one national American survey, 3692 respondents were asked how many neighbours they knew by name, the number of relatives and friends living close by, and how often they saw them. They were also asked the number of "good friends" that could be counted on in "any sort of trouble" and the number of confidants—people with whom they could discuss just about anything—they had. Those living alone had fewer relatives living close by, and were less familiar with neighbours, than the married respondents; but they generally had more contact with friends and confidants. The researchers concluded that

> contrary to conventional wisdom, we find that many persons who live alone are not socially isolated relative to others. Indeed, under most (although not all) life circumstances, they seem to show signs of an active "compensation" phenom-

enon, so that they visibly exceed persons living with others in their magnitude of contact with persons outside the household. (Alwin, Converse, and Martin 1985, p. 327)

Despite the "compensation phenomenon," however, singles have tended to report feeling lonely more often than do marrieds (Shostak 1987). Poor and older singles were especially likely to be lonely, perhaps because the low incomes and ill health that tend to accompany old age make socializing very difficult.

Besides age and income, being single as a result of divorce apparently affects loneliness. The newly divorced tend to suffer from depression (Menaghan and Lieberman 1986). One study found the divorced to be depressed by being alone about twice as often as other people. After expressing some surprise at these findings, the researchers explained that, "The never-married may not be lonely because they have not experienced marriage, and therefore have not experienced the implications of loneliness" (Cargan and Melko 1982, p. 128). Moreover, as a group the never-married are younger, and, among singles, being older is related to loneliness.

Looking more broadly at life satisfaction among adults, U.S. surveys through the 1970s generally found that singles of both sexes were less likely to say they were happy with their lives. But nationwide survey data show a steady decline from the early seventies through 1986 in the positive relationship between being married and reported life satisfaction or happiness. In 1972 only about 15 percent of singles said they were "very happy," while nearly 40 percent of the marrieds did. By 1986, the percentage of singles who said they were "very happy" had nearly doubled to almost 30 percent while the proportion of marrieds who said they were "very happy" declined to just over 30 percent (Glenn and Weaver 1988).[10] Since that time, however, further research (Lee, Seccombe and Shehan 1991) has indicated a return to more divergence between the married and single states. According to sociologists Susan McDaniel and Lorne Tepperman (2000, p. 84), "[o]n average, never-married people are less satisfied than married people....but more satisfied than divorced or separated people."

I   10. For a contrary view, see Greeley (1991).

To sum up the research on the differences in happiness between married and unmarried individuals, the never-married are still less likely to say they are "very happy," but the difference has declined in the past 25 years.[11]

Social scientists Norval Glenn and Charles Weaver, who conducted one of these studies, explain these changes as follows:

> In many respects, differences in the circumstances of married and unmarried persons have lessened. For instance, for at least a substantial proportion of unmarried persons, regular sexual relations without stigma have become available, and now that a divorce can rather easily be obtained by any spouse who wants it, marriage no longer provides the security, financial or otherwise, that it once did. (Glenn and Weaver 1988, pp. 322–323)

Still, at least some researchers maintain that married living has some benefits when compared to singlehood (Waite 1995). Married people are less likely to abuse alcohol, for example, or to commit suicide (Stack and Wasserman 1993).[12] Speaking largely about marriage, sociologist Walter Gove and colleagues, who have examined the relationship between sex, marital status, and mental health over a period of two decades, conclude:

> The type of interaction that occurs in the family is particularly well suited to the development, maintenance, and enhancement of the self.... [F]amily interaction is based on a very direct and deep concern with the individual.... [F]amily members have a considerable investment in giving the individual support and an accurate appraisal of his or her strengths and weaknesses.... [T]he family [also] serves as a "back region" where the individual can

expound, ponder, and complain about the characteristics of his or her [nonfamily] ... roles. (Gove, Style, and Hughes 1990, p. 18)

Marriage seems to have physical health benefits as well (Lillard and Waite 1995; Trovato and Laurin 1989; Waite 1995; Wickrama et al. 1997; Murphy, Glaser, and Grundy 1997). In the words of demographer Linda Waite, "There's something about being married that makes people work better. We're group-living animals, and we're hard-wired to bond" (in Angier 1998). Cohabitants are midway between singles and marrieds in mental and physical well-being (Kurdek 1991b).

However, not all researchers agree that married people are healthier than single people (McDaniel 1998; White 1992). For example, James White (1992) has suggested that a reliance on American data may lead us to overestimate the health benefits of marriage. In particular, he emphasizes the differences that exist between our two health care systems. Unlike the Canadian health care system that is premised on universality, health care in the United States "is not the right of citizens, but a commodity to be sold at the highest price" (Henslin and Nelson 1996, p. 567). In that country, being married may increase the likelihood that one will be able to afford superior care or, at least, obtain medical coverage through a spouse's employer. Rather than marriage, it may be increased accessibility to superior health care that accounts for the mental and physical benefits that have been observed for those who are married in the United States.

In addition, sociologists in both Canada and the United States have increasingly focused on the negative as well as the positive aspects of marriage and family life.

In this vein, Gove, Style, and Hughes (1990) call attention to family violence (which we will discuss extensively in Chapter 10). Gove and colleagues also point out that marriage includes a set of obligations and the responsibility of coping with both the burdens of other family members and the disappointments and tragedies that come with family life. Increasingly, individualistic individuals may find these obligations more emotionally stressful than in the familistic past (Gove, Style, and Hughes 1990). Hughes and Gove (1989) note that social scientists have tended to focus on the benefits of social integra-

11. Exact comparisons of these studies are impossible because whereas Glenn and Weaver combined all unmarried individuals, Lee, Secombe and Shehan (1991) looked only at never-married singles. Age categorizations also differ. Because the most recent study (Lee and colleagues) emphasizes the never-married category of singles, it is important to note that the formerly married are typically less well-off than the never-married (Kurdek 1991b).

12. We need to caution, here, that association between two variables does not necessarily prove causality. Marriage may be associated with lower alcohol abuse, not because being married encourages moderation, but because alcoholics are more likely to be divorced and/or less likely to get married in the first place. Bottom line: Marrying a person who abuses alcohol or other drugs is very unlikely to sober up him or her.

tion and ignore its costs and that there are some areas in which those living alone are consistently better off than the married. They point to less irritation; widowed people living alone have higher self-esteem, and the never-married report a greater sense of control over their lives.

An Israeli sociologist, Ofra Anson, has offered a somewhat different response to the fact that marrieds have consistently been found healthier than non-marrieds. This analysis (Anson 1989) suggests that it is important to bear in mind that not all singles live alone. Living with another adult (as in group living or cohabitation) could serve as a functional alternative to marriage; that is, living with another adult, whether spouse or not, may provide the social ties and social control required for mental and physical well-being.

In this line of thinking, sociologist Catherine Ross (1995) suggests that we need to reconceptualize marital status as a **continuum of social attachment**. You can think of a continuum as a line between two opposites; the property on a continuum is not simply black or white but has many shades of gray. When we think of singlehood this way, we realize that not all singles are socially unattached, disconnected, or isolated. Her research, based on telephone interviews with 2031 adults, reported that people in close relationships—whether married or not and whether living alone or not—were significantly less depressed than those with no intimate partner at all. Moreover (and this is important!), the relationship between being involved and not being depressed only held for those in happy, or supportive, arrangements (see also Wickrama et al. 1997). Research biologist Ingrid Waldron found that marriage was related to better overall health for women who were not employed outside their homes, though not for employed women. "We suspect that it's a matter of social support," Waldron explained. "You can get that support from your husband, or you can get it from being around other adults at work, but having it seems to be the key" (in Angier 1998). *Being alone and without a partner is less depressing than being in an unhappy relationship.*

Choice and Singlehood

Whether a person is single by choice affects satisfaction with singlehood. In 1983 and 1984, Barbara Levy Simon interviewed 50 never-married women born between 1884 and 1918. When she categorized them according to Staples' classification scheme presented earlier in this chapter, she found 36 voluntarily stable singles. All said they were happy and satisfied. Thirty-four expressed antimarriage sentiments. As one woman put it:

> Men? Men have been important to me all my life. I have had friendship and love and sex with men since I was a young thing ....

> You see, dear, it's *marriage* I avoid, not men. Why would I ever want to be a wife? ... A wife is someone's servant. A woman is someone's friend. (in Simon 1987, pp. 31–32)

Predictably, the 12 women who were single involuntarily gave a less rosy picture of never-married life. Of these, seven said conflicts between caring for elderly parents and the demands of finances ended their marriage plans. These women remained somewhat bitter, resenting siblings' failure to help out and/or the inflexibility of their suitors (Simon 1987, p. 51).

Put another way, being single voluntarily must be qualitatively different from being single involuntarily. And moving from temporary to stable or permanent singlehood represents a major shift in self-identity. As one self-reported unhappy 39-year-old woman (with a master's degree in music and self-employed as a freelance musician) put it, "I have always been brought up to believe that I would be taken care of by a husband. I just assumed that it would happen and it is not happening" (in Holmes 1983, p. 115). A voluntary temporary singlehood might gradually become either a voluntary or an involuntary stable one.

Single Women Compared with Single Men

Research indicates that men are more affected than women by social isolation (Nelson and Robinson 1999; study by House, Landis, and Urberson, reported in Goleman 1988a). Unmarried men may not cultivate intimate relationships, feeling they shouldn't bother others when they feel low (McGill 1985). Heterosexual men may fear that intimate sharing with another man might be interpreted as "gay" behaviour (Monroe, Baker, and Roll 1997). Gay men may also find it difficult to obtain support from others in their community (See Case Study 6.1,

Reflections of A Visible Minority Gay Man.") "The thinness of men's friendships with each other [compared to women's] and the ways that they seem to be constantly undermined through competition and jealousy are distinctive features of modern society" (Seidler 1992, p. 17). Such isolation increases feelings of unhappiness, depression, and anxiety (Umberson et al. 1996). "It's the 10 to 20 percent of people who say they have nobody with whom they can share their private feelings or who have close contact with others less than once a week who are at most risk" (James House, quoted in Goleman 1988a, p. 21).

Maintaining Supportive Social Networks

People's self-concepts depend greatly on other people's responses to them. People who have only secondary relationships know no one who understands them as a whole, unified person. Consequently, they may begin to feel fragmented. Moreover, human beings need others who can help confirm and clarify the meaning of situations and events. In marriage and other primary relationships, people discuss and agree on daily events and interpretations of those events. This process may be taken for granted, but it is an important source of stability for individuals (Berger and Kellner 1970, p. 5).

Social networks involve more than simply a series of dating partners or casual acquaintances to do things with. Social scientists stress that even singles who are in love and involved in an exclusive dating relationship need a supportive network of intimate friends.

Perhaps the greatest challenge to unmarried individuals of both sexes is the development of strong social networks. Maintaining close relationships with parents, brothers and sisters, and friends is associated with positive adjustment and satisfaction among singles.

A crucial part of one's support network might be valued same-sex friendships. Other sources of support for singles involve opposite-sex friendships (either sexual or nonsexual), group-living situations, and volunteer work.

Singles may also reach out to their families of origin. Barbara Simon studied 50 never-marrieds old enough to be retired and found that they received a great deal of support from their families, especially in middle and old age. Families helped in crises, whether of health and disability or economic loss.

In later life, single women were likely to set up joint living arrangements with siblings, something they would have been reluctant to do earlier. Twenty-three of 50 women Simon studied were living with a brother or sister in retirement. One of the women explains:

"I lost my three most intimate buddies in the space of five years. Those three were the people whom I had shared everything with since I was first employed.... Then I took stock of my situation.... The next-best thing to those friends were my sisters. They were each widows who were delighted with the prospect [of sharing an apartment]. We lived together as a trio for twelve years [until death and disability separated them]. The three of us did pretty well." (Simon 1987, p. 71)

But ties outside the family remained important. Simon (1987, pp. 53–54) found among the 50 elderly women she interviewed that "perhaps the most common thread of identity" these women shared was "their view of themselves as members of a group *larger than* their own families." Asked what had given their lives meaning, 45 emphasized religious, political, or humanitarian volunteer work. One woman who had been a Big Sister to 16 children over the past 23 years explained proudly that "Of those 16 children I have been a buddy to over the years, not one of them has gotten into trouble" (in Simon 1987, p. 54). Contributing an average of 18 hours weekly, these women

have acted throughout their lives as people with twentieth-century versions of a "calling," a term Robert Bellah has recently reframed in *Habits of the Heart*. These single women think of themselves as members of an integrated moral world in which their commitments to their work, their family, their friends, their neighborhood, and their society flow from one passion—the desire to be a responsible and responsive actor in the world. (Simon 1987, p. 56)

Although individuals may be single for many reasons, they cannot remain happy for long without support from people they are close to and who care about

Reflections of a Visible Minority Gay Man

There are many misconceptions about what it means to be queer. For instance, when you picture the average gay or lesbian, you imagine him flouncing with a limp wrist or her as an athletic butch. And when you think of them, you visualize white people. But not all homosexuals are Caucasian. There are queer East Indians, African-Americans, Inuit, and even Asians. Here's my study, a story of one gay Asian.

Being gay and of colour sets me apart from others and makes me feel like an outsider. I grew up with the white world outside, the Asian world at home, and the gay world inside me. All my worlds still clash to this day. Being gay has always been normal to me, but....I never told anyone because I was taught to keep my opinions to myself, a by-product of an Asian rearing.....

I also learned to keep quiet and obey those higher in the chain of command. By learning to be so quiet, I mastered the art of listening. I listened to people brutalize every one of my worlds. White people told me to go back to my own country and that I've taken away their jobs. People also used to pull their eyes back at me and yell, "Chinky!" What about support from the gay community? You would think that gay people, being oppressed and all, would be open-minded and accepting. Sadly, that's not the case....

I have trouble meeting other queer people, so a friend suggested the Internet to me. After two days of failure, I figured out that the only way to get any decent conversation was to describe myself as white.... If I mentioned the word "Asian," it was like, "Oops, sorry. Gotta wash my hair!" It's uncomfortable for gay people to admit that, as oppressed people, they themselves can be oppressors. There is also plenty of internal racism. Most of my gay Asian friends refuse to date anyone who is Asian.... Gay Asian men can literally be called a brotherhood, since nobody dates each other.

Bombarded by the ideal image of beauty, thanks to *GQ* and the plethora of other fashion guides, I hated all my oriental features. When I first came out, I learned very quickly that being white was advantageous. It was easier for a white person to find support for his gay lifestyle than it was for me. It took years of deprogramming to erase the notion of white being better. I had to do that by myself, as there aren't many people out there who are gay, Asian and proud of it.

North American society is undergoing changes, dealing with all sorts of isms, religion, and homosexuality. It is far from being perfect, people are talking, yelling and even fighting. At least there is plenty of dialogue, but in Asian culture, there is none. Many Asians feel that homosexuality is a disease, or something you get when you are sexually abused. Even Dr. Laura would blush, if she listened to what Chinese radio talk-show hosts say about homosexuality....

I am fortunate, as my parents love me. At home all that mattered was family, education, and money. These are very Asian goals. It was this utmost importance of family, the core value of all Asian culture, that saved me. My family had always been particularly close to me and when I came out, they knew that nobody could have turned me gay. They had confidence that I wasn't high on drugs nor was I trying just to spite them. It was difficult at first, but being a close-knit family made it easier to communicate. Initially, being gay was a big concern for my parents because they were concerned about AIDS, the family name not being continued, and the family losing face. Many of my Asian friends' parents told their kids to stay away from me, until they found out that I didn't turn their children gay. What a shocker. I can laugh about this now, but I shouldn't.

As a result of all this, I feel that I don't belong anywhere. I am a minority within a minority.

Source: Abridged from Tsang 2001, pp. 24–25.

them (Kraus, et al. 1993). This support is necessary for feeling positive about and generally satisfied with being single. Feeling satisfied with being single, of course, probably also depends on whether one is voluntarily single. At the same time, though, people who find themselves involuntarily single may feel better about their status as they choose to develop supportive networks.

IN SUM

Since the 1960s the number of singles has risen. Much of this increase is due simply to rising numbers of young adults, who are typically single. Although there is a growing tendency for these young adults to postpone marriage until they are older, this is not a new trend but rather a return to a pattern that was typical early in the twentieth century.

One reason people are postponing marriage today is that increased job and lifestyle opportunities may make marriage less attractive. Also, the low sex ratio has caused some women to postpone marriage or put it off entirely. And attitudes toward marriage and singlehood are changing so that now being single is viewed not so much as deviant but as a legitimate choice.

Singles can be classified according to whether they freely choose this option (voluntary singles) or would prefer to marry but are single nevertheless (involuntary singles). Singles can also be classified according to whether they plan to remain single (stable singles) or marry someday (temporary singles).

Singles used to live in cities, often because employment and leisure opportunities drew them there, but recently more singles have moved to the suburbs. More and more singles are living in their parents' homes; this is usually at least partly a result of economic constraints. Some singles have chosen to live in

For singles, it's important to develop and maintain supportive social networks of friends and family. Single people place high value on friendships, and they are also major contributors to community services and volunteer work.

communal or group homes. A growing number of unmarrieds are cohabiting or living common-law. Some are heterosexual couples, and some are gay and lesbian couples; we compare the interpersonal patterns of these relationships. Finally, some women share a man in a polygamous arrangement.

Although research consistently finds marrieds physically and psychologically healthier and happier than singles, this situation is slowly changing as singlehood allows the sexual expression once reserved for marriage and as marriage fails to guarantee the security that it once did. The limits that marriage puts on individuality seem more constraining to today's Canadians.

However one chooses to live the single life, maintaining supportive social networks is important.

Key Terms

cohabitation
common-law relationship
communes
continuum of social
    attachment
double standard of aging
involuntary stable singles

involuntary temporary singles
sex ratio
voluntary stable singles
voluntary temporary singles

Study Questions

1. How do economics and income affect a single person's life?

2. Individual choices take place within a broader social spectrum—that is, within society. How do social factors influence an individual's decision about whether to marry or remain single?

3. What are the particular circumstances constraining the visibly disabled who are single and would like to marry?

4. What do you see as the differences—advantages or disadvantages—of cohabitation compared to marriage?

5. Should the law treat married and unmarried partners alike?

6. Do you consider a relationship with a married man to be a satisfactory alternative to marriage for the single woman? Why or why not?

7. What problem do older unmarried adults face that are not faced by their younger counterparts? How are these problems different for men and women?

8. How is the relationship between marital status and general happiness changing? Why?

9. What are some components of a satisfying single life?

Suggested Readings

Clements, Marcelle. 1998. *The Improvised Woman: Single Women Reinventing Single Life.* New York: W. W. Norton. Based on research, an upbeat look at various options and decisions single women can and do make to fashion satisfying lifestyles.

Nardi, Peter M., ed. 1992. *Men's Friendships: Research on Men and Masculinities.* Newbury Park, CA: Sage. Essays and research reports by social scientists on this topic.

Simon, Barbara Levy. 1987. *Never Married Women.* Philadelphia: Temple University Press. A qualitative study of 50 elderly, never-married women; includes honest talk about how being single feels to them now and how it has felt over the years; addresses their experiences as never-married women: their work, families of origin, sexual intimacy, and aging.

Werking, Kathy. 1997. *We're Just Good Friends: Men and Women in Non-Romantic Relationships.* New York: Guilford. Analysis of cross-sexual friendships and the support and challenges they offer.

On the Net

1) Parents Without Partners
   http://www.parentswithoutpartners.org

2) Cybersociology Magazine Issue Six: Cybersex and Love Online
   http://www.socio.demon.co.uk/magazine/1/issue1.html

3) Digital Dating in Canada
   www.nelson.com/nelson/harcourt/sociology/newsociety3e/socplus.htm

Committing to Each Other

MARRIAGE: WHEN AND WHY

IF LOVE IS THE BEGINNING,

LET US BEGIN TO UNDERSTAND THE

END;

THEN LOVE CAN LIVE HAPPILY EVER

AFTER.

LEN GASPARINI

"SEPARATED"

People want to love and be loved. Although we can maintain close relationships with several others, many Canadians value having one special relationship with a person they love best. This often means selecting someone, usually of the opposite sex, with whom to become both emotionally and sexually intimate. In Western culture this relationship is supposed to have a romantic quality. It may lead to marriage.

Many people in the world, however, expect love to develop after marriage. As we'll see, only recently in history have people even begun to equate the two concepts of love and marriage. Although love is usually an important ingredient, successful marriages are also based on such qualities as the partners' common goals and needs, their maturity, and the soundness of their reasons for marrying.

You'll recall that Chapter 4 examines developing a loving relationship with an intimate partner. In the following pages we'll examine patterns by which the majority of individuals in our society develop commitments to each other. We'll also look at some social variables that may influence choice of partners and marital stability. First, we'll explore the idea that love and marriage go together and look at different ways that spouses can be selected for marriage.

LOVE—AND MARRIAGE?

That marriages should involve romance and lead to personal satisfaction is a uniquely modern—and Western—idea. (By *Western* we mean the culture that developed in Western Europe and now characterizes not only that region but also Canada, the United States, and Australia.) According to an old song, "love and marriage go together like a horse and carriage." The obvious meaning in this phrase, of course, is that love is a necessary factor in marriage. You may also notice a second assumption: Love, the horse, goes before marriage, the carriage. Not all cultures adhere to these assumptions about "love marriages," however—as Box 7.1, "Arranged Marriages: A True Family Affair," illustrates.

Arranged Marriages

In much of the world, particularly in parts of southeastern Europe, Asia, and Africa that are less westernized, parents arrange their children's marriages. In **arranged marriage**, there are various ways that future spouses can be brought together. Typically, the parents of both prospective partners (often with other relatives' help) will work out the details and then announce the upcoming marriage to their children. The children may have little or no say in the matter, and they may not meet their future spouse until the wedding (Tepperman and Wilson 1993; Ingoldsby 1995a); or they may have a veto over the parents' choice, marrying only when they themselves accept the parents' choice. Although not in the majority of cases today, the prospective partners may be young children when they are betrothed. "In some cases, two couples who have been good friends commit to the marriage of their children even when their children are not yet born" (Ahmed 1993, p. 76).[1]

The fact that marriages are arranged doesn't mean that love is completely ignored by parents. Indeed marital love may be highly valued. However, in arranged marriages couples are expected to develop a loving relationship after the marriage, not before (Tepperman and Wilson 1993). In some societies, such as India, for example, parents typically check prospective partners' astrological charts to assure future compatibility (Ingoldsby 1995a, p. 149).

Arranged marriage developed in collectivist societies based on strong extended family ties.[2] In these societies, marriage unites, not just two people, but two kinship groups. Because a marriage joins two families, selecting a suitable mate is a "huge responsibility," not to be left to the young people themselves (Tepperman and Wilson 1993, pp. 73–74). Analyzing arranged marriage in Bangladesh, sociologist Ashraf Uddin Ahmed (1993) notes that, "Love marriage is thought to be disruptive to family ties, and is viewed as a children's transference of the loyalty from a family orientation to a single person, ignoring obligations to the family and kin group for personal goals" (p. 76). Then too, it is often assumed that an infatuated young person may choose a partner who will make a poor spouse. ("Smoke Gets in Your Eyes," warns another old song.)

Taking a functional perspective (see Chapter 2), Ahmed concludes that arranged marriage performs the following functions, among others. Arranged marriage:

1. affirms and strengthens parents' power over their children,

2. helps keep the family traditions and value systems intact,

3. helps consolidate and extend family property,

4. enhances the value of the kinship group,

5. helps young people from getting into the uncertainty of searching for a mate (1993, p. 74).

Despite its functions, arranged marriage is changing as the world's cultures become increasingly westernized—that is, adopt Western beliefs, values, and norms. For example, in Thailand most young

---

1. In some arranged marriages a traditional pattern for mate selection developed, such as marriage between cousins. Some cultures practise *sororate* and/or *levirate* arrangements. These terms refer to remarriage practices after a first spouse's death. In sororate cultures, a sister replaces a deceased wife. More widely practised has been the levirate. Under this system, a woman's brother-in-law replaces her deceased husband.

There are various reasons for the sororate and the levirate. For one thing, these practices assure that any property arrangements made by the two families in the first marriage continue. In the case of the levirate, a wife was typically the property of her husband, and therefore, she would be inherited, with other possessions by her brother-in-law. Also, it was understood that women needed to be taken care of and that a brother-in-law should assume that responsibility. It has been reported that the levirate has been practised by Afghans, Abyssinians, Hebrews, Hindus, and some Native peoples among others (Ingoldsby 1995a).

2. You may recall that Box 2.1 contrasts individualistic and collectivist societies. In individualistic societies the main concern is with one's own self-actualization and interests. In collectivist societies people identify with and conform to the expectations of their extended kin. Western societies are characterized as individualistic (Hofstede 1980), and individualism is positively associated with valuing romantic love (Dion and Dion 1991).

Arranged Marriages: A True Family Affair

The following article, written by a University of Western Ontario student, Leena Kamat, originally appeared in The Gazette, *the daily student newspaper at that university, on November 7, 2000. Her article challenges some popular stereotypes about arranged marriages and reminds us that, even within a "free choice system," a series of structurally and personally imposed constraints operate upon our selection of an intimate partner.*

While many Western students assume they will marry someone of their own choice for love, there are some people who may not marry for these same reasons. Arranged marriages are quite common in many faiths around the world. Marriages are often not only between the husband and wife, but between both families. Therefore, the entire family is involved in the marriage preparation right from the beginning.

Love marriages are common in Canada among Islamic people, said Nina Karachi-Khaled, correspondence secretary for the National Executive of the Canadian Council of Muslim Women. Arranged marriages are more common in other countries, like Pakistan and India and in rural communities. Karachi-Khaled said her parents had an arranged marriage, but her own was a love mar-

riage. For many Muslim women living in Canada, the love aspect of marriage is paramount....

"People have a very stereotypical view on arranged marriages," said Fariha Tayyeb, a third-year honours economics student at Western. "What an arranged marriage is, is an introduction to a guy through your parents. It's like a blind date." But the definition given to love today greatly differs from what is needed to keeping a marriage successful. "We're given the implication that love is all sex," Karachi-Khaled said, "love is also working on communication skills and raising a family."

Some cultures accept arranged marriages because the family is involved in the decision Karachi-Khaled explained. "People say your parents know you the best," Karachi-Khaled said, adding parents may know their child's likes and dislikes, personal habits and preferences.

In the Islamic faith, the family's support is critical. "If family wants this marriage, then we're not alone," she said. "You need your family and friends' help." Being introduced by family members ensures parental approval of the husband. "I wouldn't mind marrying someone who my parents introduced me to," Tayyeb said.

Arranged marriages have become a topic of discussion with the recent trial of Saskatoon dentist Alpna

people choose their own spouse, but at the same time they need their parents' approval in order to have the traditional wedding ceremony. If their parents are not supportive, the couple may elope, and there is an institutionalized method for elopement:

> This elopement pattern often follows its own elaborate ritual, in which the couple runs away to a nearby village only to return after a short stay of a few days or weeks. Then the young man begs forgiveness from the young woman's parents. The parents nearly always agree to forgive, and typically

an abbreviated ceremony is held. (Cherlin and Chamratrithirong 1993, p. 86)

With global westernization, "love marriages" are replacing arranged marriage as the preferred way to select mates throughout the world. For instance, in the 1980s in Sri Lanka, an island nation off the coast of India, researchers asked respondents whether they were in arranged marriages. Among those who were wed before 1940, 80 percent of the marriages had been arranged. Of those married in the early 1980s, only about one-quarter were arranged (Caldwell et al. 1993).

Patel, who was found guilty of manslaughter in the stabbing death of her husband. The couple had an arranged marriage and the unhappiness in their marriage was brought out as a defence during the trial. Peter Chimbos, professor of sociology at Brescia College, said one case should not imply arranged marriages are more violent than others and the couples are more unhappy. "I cannot make that assumption on one or two cases. There is no data indicating arranged marriages are more lethal than individual mate selection," Chimbos said.... In the Patel case, there could have been many incidents which led to the unhappy marriage and it cannot be assumed the arranged marriage played a significant role, he explained.

Arranged marriages have been criticized because most times the couple does not know each other well. However, Karachi-Khaled said she did not think people who marry for love always know each other really well before the wedding either. Even living together before marriage does not ensure a happy and successful union, she said. Ping-Chun Hsiung, a professor of sociology at the University of Toronto, said people cannot assume an arranged marriage is one without love. Also, a non-arranged marriage does not guarantee love.

Other criticisms surrounding arranged marriages centres on the woman in the relationship having no say in her future. Karachi-Khaled said this is not a concern in Islamic marriages as the woman has to agree she wants to marry the man. During the wedding ceremony itself, the bride is asked three times for confirmation she wishes to marry the groom....The freedom associated with non-arranged marriages should also be looked at more closely. "Even in non-arranged marriages, how much freedom is there?" Hsiung asked. "When people are dating, there is so much pressure to either continue or not continue the relationship. There is so much pressure after marriage." Hsiung explained even in "love" marriages, people tend to marry within their background. The criteria used to find mates are generally the same in both types of marriages. "You cannot deny that people use criteria when finding their spouse."

"Even love marriages are arranged," Karachi-Khaled said. "Look at want ads." People specify everything they are looking for, including the possible mate's height, skin colour, religion, likes, education, and job.

What are some advantages of arranged marriage? Some disadvantages? How do you think arranged marriage is changing, as a result of westernization?

In another study (Levine et al. 1995), researchers asked 497 male and 673 female urban university undergraduates in ten countries and in Hong Kong the following question: If a man (woman) had all the qualities you desired, would you marry this person if you were not in love with him (her)? The results are presented in Figure 7.1. As you can see from that figure, of the 11 societies sampled, students in Pakistan were most likely to answer yes; 50.4 percent of them did so. Japanese students were least likely to say yes, but more than one-third (35.7 percent) said they were undecided. In the United States, often considered the most individualistic society in the world, only 3.5 percent of the students said they would marry someone with whom they were not in love, and the highest proportion (85.9 percent) said that no, they would not.

Both Canada and the United States are examples of what cross-cultural researchers call a **free-choice culture**: People freely choose their own mates. Immigrants who come to Canada from more collectivist cultures, in which arranged marriages have been the tradition, face the situation of living with a divergent set of expectations for selecting a mate. Some

CHAPTER 7   Committing to Each Other

immigrant parents arrange for a spouse from their home country to marry their offspring. This is one type of cross-national marriage. Either the future spouse comes to Canada to marry the child, or the child travels to the home country for the wedding ceremony, after which the newlyweds usually live in Canada (Ahmed et al. 1993; Dugger 1998). In this case, the marriage is typically characterized by one partner's (the child who has lived in Canada) greater westernization and one spouse's need simultaneously to adjust to an entirely new culture and to marriage (Cottrell 1993).

Some children of immigrant parents will follow their parents' expectations and participate in arranged unions. Others will not. Arranged marriage was practised throughout most of the world into the twentieth century—and in Western Europe well into the eighteenth century. The following section explores how the idea of love before marriage developed in Western Europe.

"Love" Marriages

How did our notion of romantic love come about, and why is it assumed to be the basis for weddings in our society?

Courtly love (or romantic love) flourished during the Middle Ages. Most marriages in the visible upper levels of society during this period were based on pragmatic considerations involving property and family alliances (Stone, L., 1980). Tender emotions were expressed in nonmarital relationships in which a knight worshipped his lady, and ladies had their favourites. These relationships involved a great deal of idealization, were not necessarily sexually consummated, and certainty did not require the parties to live together. In time the ideology of romantic love was adapted to a situation for which it was probably much less suitable—marriage.

As urban economies developed and young people increasingly worked away from home, arranged marriages gave way to marriages in which individuals

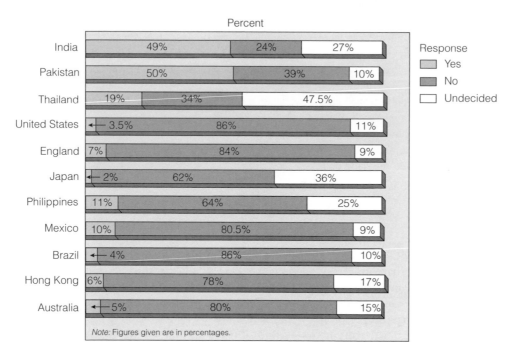

FIGURE **7.1**

Responses to question: "If a man (woman) had all the other qualities you desired, would you marry this person if you were not in love with him (her)?" (Source: Levine et al. 1995, p. 561.)

selected their own mates. Sentiment rather than property became the basis for unions (Shorter 1975). The strong emotional and personal qualities of romantic love were in keeping with the individualism and introspection characteristic of the evolving Protestant capitalistic society of Western Europe (Stone 1980).

In the absence of arranged marriages, love provided motivation for choosing mates and forming families and thereby served important social functions. This continues to be true. The connection between love and marriage serves to harness unpredictable feelings, to the service of society (Goode 1959; Greenfield 1969).

Intense romantic feelings may serve to get a married couple through bad times (Udry 1974; Wallerstein and Blakeslee 1996). However, the idealization and unrealistic expectations implicit in the ideology of romantic love can also cause problems. Many Canadians expect romance to continue not only through courtship but in marriage, too. Combining the practical and economic elements of marriage with developing intimacy and love is, historically speaking, a new goal.

Falling in love in a society such as ours, that emphasizes individualism and free-choice of marriage partners usually involves developing an intimate relationship and establishing mutual commitment. The next section examines these ideas.

COURTSHIP IN A FREE-CHOICE SOCIETY

As romantic love has come to be associated with marriage and parents are less likely to arrange their children's unions, responsibility for finding marital partners has fallen to individuals themselves (Basran 1993). Typically, a wedding takes place only after a relationship has developed.

Developing the Relationship

Sociologists and social psychologists have been interested in how relationships develop during courtship. What first brings people together? What keeps them together?

AT FIRST MEETING: PHYSICAL ATTRACTIVENESS AND RAPPORT Why is that we can be so drawn to one person and so indifferent to another? One reason is physical attractiveness (Buss 1994; Cowley 1996). Deny it as we might, our evaluations of others, even in our early years, are influenced by their appearance. Research shows that cute children are perceived by adults as less naughty, as well as brighter, more popular, and more likely to attend university, than are less attractive children. The same assumptions influence adults' perceptions of one another. Both women and men tend to see more socially desirable personality traits in people who are physically attractive than in those who are less attractive (Saks and Krupat 1988; Hatfield and Sprecher 1986).

To find out how important physical appearance is in a situation in which two people meet for the first time, several social psychologists planned an experimental university dance. Students who came to the dance were under the impression that a computer had selected their dates on the basis of similar interests. In fact, they were assigned at random. During the dance intermission the students were asked how they liked their dates. For both females and males, physical attractiveness seemed to determine whether these students were satisfied with their dates (Walster et al. 1966). Physical attractiveness is especially important in the early stages of a relationship.

Physical appeal and other readily apparent characteristics serve to attract people to each other, to spark an interest in getting acquainted, which leads to an initial contact (Buss 1994). But whether this initial interest develops into a prolonged attachment depends on whether they can develop rapport: Do they feel at ease with each other? Are they free to talk spontaneously? Do they feel they can understand each other? When two people experience rapport, they may be ready to develop a loving relationship. Common values appear to play an important role here, though whether in early stages only or throughout courtship is not clear. Couples also seem to be matched on sex drive and interest in sex (Murstein 1980), as well as on what sex means to them (Lally and Maddock 1994), suggesting that this is an important sorting factor.

AS THE RELATIONSHIP PROGRESSES The wheel theory of love (Reiss and Lee 1988), described in Chapter 4, explains the role of rapport in the development of a relationship. It suggests that mutual disclosure, along with feelings of trust and understanding, are necessary first steps. As you may recall, this theory also posits that an important step in developing love is "mutual need satisfaction." Along this line, social scientist Robert Winch (1958) once proposed the **theory of complementary needs**, whereby we are attracted to partners whose needs complement our own. Sometimes this is taken to mean that, psychologically, opposites attract. This idea makes intuitive sense to many of us, and social science researchers have found some evidence to support complementary needs theory (McLeod 1995). Some "needs theorists" argue that we are attracted to others whose strengths are harmonious with our own so that we are more effective as a couple than either of us would be alone (Epstein, Evans, and Evans 1994).

ASSORTIVE MATING—A FILTERING PROCESS

Whatever the case regarding complementary or harmonious needs, individuals gradually filter out those among their pool of eligibles who, they think, would not make the best spouse that they could find. Social psychologists call this process **assortive mating**. Studies have consistently shown, for example, that people are willing to date a wider range of individuals than they would become engaged to or live with, and they are willing to live with a wider range of persons than they would marry (Schoen and Weinick 1993; Forste and Tanfer 1996). Some social scientists have proposed that people go through a three-stage filtering sequence, called **SVR**—for **stimulus-values-roles** (Murstein 1986).

In the *stimulus stage*, interaction depends upon physical attraction. In the values stage, partners compare their individual values and determine whether these are appropriately matched. For instance, they might explore their views on marital fidelity, abortion, racism, the value of a university education, the environment, personal ambition, and work. If a couple finds a satisfactory degree of values consensus, they proceed to the final stage, that of exploring role compatibility. Here the prospective spouses test and negotiate how they will play their respective marital and leisure roles (Houts, Robins, and Huston 1996). It is possible, of course, that the courtship process will break down at either the values or the role compatibility stage; if it does not, however, the assumption is

that the filtering process ends with one chosen marriage partner.

Relationships leading to marriage do not always show these rational characteristics, however. In lengthy interviews with 116 individuals in "premarital relationships," two social scientists examined the process by which these partners gradually committed to marriage (Surra and Hughes 1997). From the interviews, the researchers classified the respondents' relationships in two categories: *relationship-driven* and *event-driven*. Relationship-driven couples followed the rationally evolving pattern described above. Partners evaluated their mutual values and goals, likes and dislikes; the more these matched, the more the couples grew in commitment.

In event-driven relationships, partners vacillated between commitment and ambivalence. Often they disagreed on how committed they were as well as why they became committed in the first place. Event-driven couples more often had separate friends and did not necessarily agree on what they liked to do together; their satisfaction with the relationship fluctuated over time. The researchers called this relationship type event-driven because events—fights, discussing the relationship with one's own friends, and making up—punctuated each partner's account.

Event-driven couples often recognize their relationships as rocky, but they do not necessarily break up because positive events (for example, a discussion about getting married or an expression of approval of the relationship from others) typically follow negative ones. The researchers describe event-driven courtships as more "dramatic" than relationships-driven ones. They go on to speculate that:

> Over the long run, we expect that the negative qualities of event-driven relationships will overshadow the attractions of a dramatic courtship and that the stronger bases of relationship-driven commitments will lead to more satisfying interaction and more positive outcomes ... (p. 19).

Some social scientists have wondered to what extent our courtship process encourages such patterns as event-driven relationships. In the next section, we more generally discuss **courtship**, the process through which the couple develops a mutual commitment to marry. We contrast getting together and cohabitation.

Getting to Know Someone and Gaining Commitment

The courtship pattern that has evolved has two apparent purposes: (1) for romantic partners to try to get to know one another better, and (2) to gain each other's progressive commitment to marriage.

These two purposes can be at odds. On the one hand, courtship is supposed to lead to self-disclosure and intimacy. On the other hand, gaining a partner's commitment to marriage often involves marketing oneself in the best possible package. Before we look at the most frequent patterns of courtship in our society today, we will examine this potential contradiction.

IMAGING VERSUS INTIMACY

Whom shall I marry? That question seems obviously to be about my choice, about one of the most important controls I shall establish over my life. The more researchers probe that question, however, the more they find a secret question, more destructive, more insistent, that is asked as well: Am I the kind of person worthy of loving? This secret question is really about a person's dignity in the eyes of others, but it involves self-doubt of a peculiar kind. (Sennett and Cobb 1974, p. 63)

Many people fear not being worthy of love—a fear that is often associated with low self-esteem, as we saw in Chapter 4. As courtship progresses, these people may feel anxious, and in response they may avoid self-disclosure rather than develop it. They may "put their best foot forward," in a process called **imaging**—projecting and maintaining a facade as a way of holding the other person's interest. It is likely that everybody practices imaging to some degree.

Psychotherapists George Bach and Ronald Deutsch (1970, pp. 43–44) have illustrated how this happens, using conversations between "Susan" and "Paul" (who have dated twice in the last two weeks). Here they are making themselves comfortable in Susan's apartment:

PAUL: Say, this is neat. (He looks around.) And I like that Van Gogh print. He's one of my favourite artists.

SUSAN: Is he? Mine too. I don't know just what it is. The colour and vitality, I guess.

PAUL: Yes, that's what it is.

SUSAN: (She starts to put [CDs] on her [CD player].) What do you like, Paul? ...

PAUL: Either one. (The music begins.) Why, I have that same [CD]! (He beams with the discovery.)

SUSAN: Really? ... [I really like them.]

PAUL: Right. [Me too.]

Clearly, Paul and Susan are intent on selling themselves. Both are imaging, but neither seems to realize that the other is doing so. "To both, the constantly appearing bits of likeness seem amazing" (Bach and Deutsch 1970, p. 44). When they do discover important differences, the way they handle them is worth noting:

SUSAN: Well, I don't think I want any [children]. You know, with all the overpopulation and that....

PAUL: No children at all? ...

SUSAN: Well, I saw what it did to my mother, how dependent it made her, how—helpless, and I don't know....

PAUL: The right man wouldn't let that happen....

SUSAN: I guess it really is an experience any woman would want to have.... (Bach and Deutsch 1970, pp. 46–47)

Here a basic difference in values and a source of potential marital conflict have been smoothed over in a matter of minutes, in order that courting (which is intended to uncover such differences!) can proceed.

People are tempted to image in any courtship process. Social scientists agree, however, that some courting practices encourage more imaging than others. In the next few sections we will contrast three styles of courtship that are familiar to Canadians today: the traditional ritual of dating, getting together, and cohabitation.

DATING AND "GETTING TOGETHER" The dating system emerged in our society at the beginning of the twentieth century, prevailed through the 1950s and early 1960s, became less popular in the late 1960s and early 1970s, and appears to have become somewhat popular again in the 1980s and 1990s.

Dating consists of an exclusive relationship developed between two people through a series of appointed meetings. Of course, dating can be just for fun! Dating relationships develop into marriage through evolving, progressive commitment, along with greater emphasis on sexual exclusivity.

By the 1970s, an alternative to dating had emerged—"getting together" (Libby 1976). **Getting together** is a courtship process in which, unlike dating, groups of women and men congregate at a party or share an activity. Getting together deemphasizes relating solely to one member of the opposite sex. In getting

The dating tradition that began in the early twentieth century has been ritualized in the high school prom. Some dating norms are changing, however, as more women share the expense of dating, as more couples and friends get together in groups, and as more individuals have less conventional ideas about appropriate partners. All these changes help create alternatives to more traditional dating practices.

together, females play a similar role to males, initiating relationships and suggesting activities. Meetings are often less formal than in the traditional date.

These changes in how women and men relate to each other are associated with changing attitudes toward marriage itself. In one significant change the pattern of getting together is not as closely oriented to marriage as dating was in the 1950s. We've seen that remaining single, at least for a good part of one's 20s, is a more attractive alternative for many people today. As a result, people who are freed somewhat from the pressure to date and to marry can be more casual and spontaneous with each other. They are less likely to focus so intensely on their physical appearance and more likely to see each other in a variety of settings and moods (Murstein 1986, p. 67).

As a courtship process, getting together places less emphasis on the end result, marriage, than dating does. Ironically, this deemphasis may be effective, as it allows people to choose partners whom they really know and could be happily married to.

MARGARET MEAD'S CRITICISMS OF DATING AS COURTSHIP In 1949 anthropologist Margaret Mead severely criticized the Western tradition of dating as a competitive game in which individuals try to be the most popular and have the most dates rather than try to genuinely get to know their dating partner(s). Sociologist Willard Waller (1937) had earlier termed this "rating and dating."

Mead saw at least two major problems in dating. First, it encourages men and women to define heterosexual relationships as situational, rather than ongoing. "You 'have a date,' you 'go out with a date,' you groan because 'there isn't a decent date in town'" (Mead 1949, p. 276). Because dating is formalized, women and men—even as they approach marriage—see each other only at appointed times and places. Partners look and behave their best during a date; they seldom share their "backstage behaviour."[3]

3. From the interactionist theoretical perspective (Chapter 2), sociologist Erving Goffman (1979), in *The Presentation of Self in Everyday Life*, differentiates between people's front- and backstage behaviour. Frontstage behaviour is what we show the public, backstage behaviour is more private. We can think of individuals' grooming rituals—shaving, doing their hair, applying makeup—as taking place backstage. They are preliminary preparations for meeting one's audience. Developing intimacy involves gradually allowing another person to see more of one's backstage behaviour.

Second, sex becomes depersonalized and genitally oriented, rather than oriented to the whole person; that is, the salient question becomes whether a couple "went all the way"—or whether the male is "getting any"—rather than how much emotional and sensual rapport partners share. Taking Mead's criticisms seriously, some fundamentalist Christian writers propose a different courtship pattern. Here, "If a young man is interested in a young woman, he starts by praying about the relationship. With a go-ahead from the Lord and his parents, he then approaches the girl's parents." Before the couple begins spending time together, the young woman's father and the interested young man spend time, getting to know one another. Parents of both parties would focus on their child's prospective partner's "spiritual depth, strong biblical character, financial responsibility, sexual and emotional purity, and the ability to lead a simple practical life." Courtship activities often would involve family, not just couple, activities (Ryan and Ryan 1995, p. 12). Meanwhile, Mead's criticisms of dating might lead one to consider issues of power in courtship.

Power in Courtship

Chapter 10 examines power in marriages and families. Here we will look at power issues in courtship. Sociologists Naomi McCormick and Clinton Jessor (1983) comment in an essay that

> students sometimes balk when we suggest that nice people, not just sadists, use power during courtship.... [But] not everyone sees dating and mating in the same romantic light as these ... students.... Power, the potential to influence another person's attitudes or behaviour, may be an essential component of any romantic attraction or sexual relationship. (pp. 66–67)

McCormick and Jessor point out that "the development of skills and knowledge, being perceived as attractive and likeable, and even acting helpless or 'needed' can all be used to influence someone else" (p. 67).

These same sociologists researched, among other things, whether the rules for courtship had changed since the 1950s. What they concluded has some bearing on discussions of both gender roles and power. According to their research findings, the courtship game has changed in three ways:

First, thanks to the weakening of the double standard and encouragement from feminists, women are freer to make the first move in a flirtation and to have premarital sex than in the past. Second, men seem to be encouraging women to be more assertive in initiating sexual relationships. Third, given the opportunity, men would reject sex and women would try to have sex with the same strategies that are characteristically used by the other gender.

Despite these changes, the courtship game continues to follow gender-role stereotypes. Men ask women out more than vice versa. Men are more likely to influence a date to have sex; women are more likely to refuse sex. (p. 85)

Some research on how flirtations and sexual encounters proceed suggests that, at least with beginning flirtations, "both genders have equal power"; that is, "each person takes a turn at influencing the partner and at signaling that the other's influence attempts are welcome" (McCormick and Jessor 1983, p. 76).

But such "equal power" may not last as courtship continues. In fact, popular magazines for young people, along with school counsellors and others, have just begun to recognize that power struggles play a part in dating and courtship—sometimes to the point of violence. The feminist movement and other social changes have transformed dating into a somewhat more egalitarian experience with some features of the pattern we call getting together. But research indicates considerable confusion, mistrust, and uncertainty about what rules and preferences are operating in a given situation. Such misunderstanding may contribute to date rape (Gibbs 1991a)—although we do not want to understate the force and coercion very often characterizing date rape. Date rape is addressed later in this section. We first turn to the more general topic of courtship violence.

COURTSHIP VIOLENCE   Research evidence suggests that physical violence occurs in from 20 to 40 percent of dating relationships (Makepeace 1981; White and Koss 1991; Simons, Lin, and Gordon 1998). One national survey of Canadian university and college students found that about 14 percent of male students reported abusing a dating partner during the previous year while almost 23 percent of female students identified themselves as victims of dating violence (DeKeseredy and Ellis 1995). While both genders engage in physical aggression, women are apt to report pushing or slapping a man, whereas men are more likely to report beating up a date or threatening her with a weapon (Makepeace 1981; Riggs 1993; Totten 2001). Dating violence tends to occur over jealousy, with a refusal of sex, after excessive drinking of alcohol, or upon disagreement over drinking behaviour (Makepeace 1981, 1986). Due to stereotypes, research on courtship violence is neglected for certain ethnic groups, such as Asians for example, although it does exist (Yoshihama, Parekh, and Boyington 1991).

Researchers have found it discouraging that about half of relationships continue after the violence rather than being broken off (Levy 1991). Given that the economic and social constraints of marriage are not as applicable to courtship relationships, researchers have wondered about the reasons these relationships continue. Some evidence suggests that having been physically abused by one's father is highly related to men's—but not women's—verbal and physical abuse of dating partners (Alexander, Moore, and Alexander 1991). In a longitudinal study of 116 teenage boys, social scientists found that boys who experienced little involvement or support from their parents were more likely to begin abusing illegal drugs. The drug abuse then led to violence on dates. Also, boys who often had received physical or corporal punishment from their fathers were more likely to be violent on dates (Simons, Lin, and Gordon 1998). Then too, the study described next suggests some answers.

TRADITIONAL AND EGALITARIAN COURTSHIP PATTERNS Two models of power coexist in dating relationships: the traditional and the egalitarian. Psychologist Letitia Peplau surveyed 231 university-age dating couples about their courtship behaviour and attitudes. These students were asked about power in general and with respect to specific matters, such as recreation, conversation, sexual activity, amount of time spent together, and activities with other people (Peplau and Campbell 1989). Most of those questioned had *attitudes* favouring equality. Ninety-five percent of the women and 87 percent of the men agreed that "dating partners should have 'exactly equal say.'" But only 49 percent of the women

and 42 percent of the men reported actually having equal power. (Forty-five percent of the men and 35 percent of the women reported more male power; 13 percent of the men and 17 percent of the women reported more female power.)

Many students pointed out that a simple "his power or her power" dichotomy did not reflect their real decision-making process. Instead, they told of taking turns, being sensitive to a partner's moods, or making concessions freely. A sense of trust of the partner was significant to feeling one had equal power in the relationship (Grauerholz 1987). Still, fewer than half the couples in the Peplau studies believed they had an equal power relationship, although most wanted to. Reasons for that, according to Peplau, appear to be, first, that many still had traditional gender role attitudes. Moreover, the "principle of least interest" (discussed in Chapter 10) was operating. Those who said they had alternatives to the relationship had greater power than their partners. Finally—and perhaps at the root of these students' failure to establish egalitarian relationships, according to Peplau—is the fact that few of them had egalitarian parental relationships as models.

Some of these dynamics probably operate to influence battered partners to maintain violent courtship relationships. A recent study (Ronfeldt, Kimerling, and Arias 1998) for example, found that men who were dissatisfied with the power they felt they had in their dating relationships were more likely to be verbally or physically violent toward their dates. We turn now to the issue of date rape.

DATE RAPE **Date rape** or **acquaintance rape**—being involved in a coercive sexual encounter with a date or other acquaintance—has emerged as an issue in high schools and on university and college campuses over the past several years. Psychologists who deal with the problem agree that although we have only recently acknowledged it, the phenomenon has plagued the dating scene for a long time—probably decades (Friedman, Boumil, and Taylor 1992).

Most victims know their rapists (Warshaw 1995). Often excessive use of alcohol is involved (Cue, George, and Norris 1996). However, since the late 1990s, growing concern has been expressed in relation to the so-called "date-rape drugs" such as Lorazepam, Rohypnol, GHB (Gabba-Hydroxybutrate), Robaine, Chloral Hydrate, Ketamine, GBL (Gamma-Butyrolactone); "the street names for some of these drugs are mind erasers, party poppers, liquid ecstasy, 'special k' or roofies" (CFS 2001). Although when slipped into a drink, such drugs are typically colourless, odourless, and tasteless, they cause blackouts, disorientation, and memory loss (BC Ministry of Women's Equality, April 1999). The first major Canadian seizure of Rohypnol occurred in January 1999, when 3500 doses were seized in a raid on a home in North Vancouver, B.C. Following this seizure, a RCMP spokesperson remarked, "[The RCMP] had been under the impression, up till now, that there wasn't any Rohypnol [problem] in Canada....Guess what—it's here, so we need to be concerned." (*Vancouver Sun*, January 26, 1999:A1).

Not all date rapes, however, involve the use of drugs. One study (DeKeseredy and Kelly 1993) found that 20.2 percent of female Canadian university and college students said they gave into unwanted sexual intercourse because they were overwhelmed by a man's continued arguments and pressure; 6.6 percent of female students said that they had unwanted sexual intercourse because a man threatened or used some degree of physical force; and 13.6 percent of female students reported that, when they were drunk or high, a man attempted unwanted sexual intercourse. An American study found that half of the freshmen and sophomore college women interviewed reported unwanted attempts at intercourse by males of their acquaintance. These were usually (83 percent) men they knew at least moderately well. One-third of these attempts were accompanied by "strong" physical force, and another third by "mild" physical force. The women seemed constrained by traditional roles in their responses, which were largely passive and accepting; 37 percent did nothing. Only a minority gave a strong verbal (26 percent) or a physical response (14 percent). Half of the attacks succeeded; the stronger the victim's response, the less likely it was that the attempted rape was completed. None of the women reported the attack to the authorities and half talked to no one about it; the remainder told friends. Only 11 percent ended the relationship, whereas almost three-quarters either accepted or ignored the attack. Fifty percent continued to be friends (25 percent) or dating or sex partners (25 percent). Most blamed themselves at least partially (Murnen, Perot, and Byrne 1989).

According to psychologist Barry Burkhart, the phenomenon is prevalent because of "hidden norms" in society that condone sexual violence; that is, people have internalized gender roles according to which male aggression is acceptable. Even though rapists have typically been thought of as psychotics or criminals, Burkhart argues that research on acquaintance rape demonstrates that "normal" men are capable of rape (Meyer 1984; Senn et al 2000). Over the past decade, college and university administrations as well as other groups have begun to deal with this serious hazard of dating. For example, the Canadian Federation of Students (CFS 2001), representing 400 000 students attending 60 college and universities across Canada, has a long-standing "No Means No" campaign, distributing a fact sheet on date rape and, more recently, on the use of date rape drugs. The aim of the campaign is to send the message that, "when it comes to sex, 'no means no' and there is no excuse for not understanding 'no.'"

We turn now to what sometimes has been considered another form of courtship—**cohabitation**.

Cohabitation and Marriage

Critical of the dating tradition, Margaret Mead proposed instead what she called the **two-stage marriage**. As the name suggests, it consists of two sequential types of marriage, each with a different license, different ceremonies, and different responsibilities. The first stage, called *individual marriage*, involves "serious commitment...in which each partner would have a deep and continuing concern for the happiness of the other" (Mead 1966, p. 50). It limits responsibilities, however, for the couple agrees not to have children during this time. The second stage, parental marriage, would follow only if a couple decides that they want to continue their relationship and to share the responsibility of children.

Akin to Mead's proposal, some couples today decide to live together to test and further develop their relationship before marrying. While cohabitation can be an alternative to marriage, it can also be a prelude to marriage. Cohabitation is also discussed in Chapter 6; this section addresses cohabitation as courtship.

FOUR COHABITATION TYPES   In their review of research and clinical observation, Carl Ridley and his colleagues detected four common patterns of cohabitation: "Linus blanket," emancipation, convenience, and testing, all of which vary in their utility as training grounds for marriage. The **"Linus blanket"** relationship develops from the dependence or insecurity of one of the partners, who prefers a relationship with *anyone* to being alone. **Emancipation** as a motive involves using cohabitation to gain independence from parental values and influence. The **convenience** relationship involves partners who live together sexually more for practical reasons than for intimacy.

The **testing** mode of cohabitation is what we think of when we view cohabitation as trial marriage. Two partners, relatively mature and with a clear commitment to test their already satisfying intimate relationship in a situation more closely resembling the marriage they tentatively anticipate, move in together. If all goes well, they get married. If all doesn't go well, they separate, but because of their preparation and skills in communication they are able to understand and assimilate the experience. It becomes a beneficial experience in their development and contributes to the success of any marriage they ultimately formalize.

Ridley and his colleagues stressed the importance of clarifying motivations and goals for cohabiting before the step is taken. They stated that cohabitation could be an experience of some value as a preparation to marriage, either to test a particular relationship or to help the individual mature and become better able to sustain intimate relationships. On the other hand, cohabitation for the wrong reasons or for individuals who are not prepared can lead to misunderstanding, frustration, and resentment.

Ridley and his associates also stressed the importance of individuals being fairly independent before they decide to cohabit, having clear goals and expectations, and being sensitive to the needs of their partners. Table 7.3, on pp. 198-9, presents some "good" signs and some "concern" signs that, although intended for use by counsellors, can serve as guidelines for individual decision making regarding cohabiting (Ridley, Peterman, and Avery 1978).

Cohabitation does not necessarily lead to marriage, of course.

WHO COHABITS? As Box 7.2, "The Changing Face of Conjugal Relationships," indicates, cohabitation has become increasingly common with growing numbers of Canadians electing to enter into common-law relationships. While the number of legally married couples in Canada increased by less than one percent over the last decade, the number of people living in a common-law relationship increased by 26 percent. Figure 7.2 provides life table estimates of the cumulative experience of cohabitation for Canadian men and women.

As you will see in Figure 7.3, among the provinces Quebec currently has the highest proportion of couples living in a common-law relationship (24 percent) while Prince Edward Island and Ontario have the lowest (9 percent). Francophones in the province of Quebec are most likely to enter a common-law union and least likely to select marriage for a first union (Dumas and Belanger 1997). Francophone men and women are also more likely than anglophones to view cohabitation as an alternative to marriage (Hobart and Grigel 1992). The high proportion of common-law families in Quebec would seem to reflect the continuing legacy of the "Quiet Revolution" during the 1950s and 1960s, Quebec's increasing urbanization, and in particular, the significant changes in female gender roles.

However, residents of Quebec are clearly not alone in their changed attitude towards unmarried cohabitation. Recent research finds that a majority of Canadian women aged 18–49 approve of both premarital sex and of non-marital cohabitation when couples intend to marry at some point in the future, with younger women and women in the province of Quebec particularly likely to voice such approval. In addition, 55 percent of women outside of Quebec and 73 percent of Quebec women believed it acceptable for couples to live together when they had no intention of making a long-term commitment and were simply sexually attracted to each other. Once again, the approval rate was higher among younger women and women living in Quebec (Wu 2000, p. 59).

Not all Canadians, of course, approve of cohabitation or choose to cohabit. In general, young adult Canadians are more likely to approve of cohabitation and to cohabit than are older adults. Among those who cohabited at the time of the 1996 Canadian Census, 37 percent of the women and 28 percent of the men were under the age of 30 (Wu 2000, p. 1). "Young adults account for the greatest increase in the number and proportion of common-law unions. One in five persons aged 20 to 24 were members of a

The Changing Face of Conjugal Relationships

Drawing upon a sample of 4656 female respondents living in the 10 Canadian provinces,[4] Celine Le Bourdais, Ghyslaine Neill and Pierre Turcotte (2000) analyzed how the types of conjugal unions Canadian women enter into have changed over time and if starting life together in a common-law union as opposed to a marriage influences the chances of breaking up or predicts the types of relationships that may follow. Although their analysis focused on women, they note that their results "generally apply to men as well."

The vast majority of Canadian women form conjugal relationships at some point in their lives. Whether born in the 1920s, the mid-1960s or any decade in between, nearly all women have been in a marriage or common-law relationship at least once. In 1995, over 94 percent of women ranging in age from 30 to 69 reported that they had entered at least one such union. Although the proportion was somewhat lower for the 20- to 29-year-old group (87 percent), it is likely to rise for these women as they grow older.

While the tendency for women to form unions has remained consistently high over the years, the nature of these unions has changed fundamentally. Although marriage still accounts for the majority of relationships, its one-time near-universal appeal has given way to ever more popular common-law unions....The proportion of women who started their first conjugal union in a marriage fell from 95 percent of those in their 60s and 56 percent of those in their 30s and to a still lower 35 percent of those in their 20s. Clearly, common-law has become younger people's favoured arrangement for a first conjugal relationship [see Table 7.1]....

4. Data for their analysis were collected in the 1995 General Social Survey, which interviewed approximately 11 000 respondents aged 15 and over, living in private households, in the ten provinces. Using interviews, the 1995 GSS collected information on all marital and common-law unions, separation, divorce, widowhood, and a broad range of background characteristics.

Of course, having chosen one type of arrangement for a first union does not preclude the eventual possibility of the other. Many women who started their relationship through common-law have subsequently married, while those who married first and then separated are increasingly deciding to live in a common-law relationship in their subsequent union. However, compared with their older counterparts, young women are less inclined to marry their first partner and, instead, are more likely to continue living common-law, thus increasing the average duration of these common-law unions.

Women enter common-law arrangements at different stages in their lives, depending on the generation they belong to. The vast majority of women aged 20 to 29 who lived common-law did so as their first conjugal union. These women grew up in times when living together without marriage had been accepted by most people as a legitimate way of settling into a relationship. In contrast, women in the 50- to 59-year-old group—most of whom came of age in an era when common-law relationships were frowned upon—were nearly three times as likely to enter a common-law relationship after their first marriage ended than for their first conjugal union....

Starting conjugal life in a common-law relationship, as opposed to a marriage, sharply increases the probability of this first union ending in separation. And whether the common-law partners eventually marry or not makes little difference; the risk of separation is just as high. In the 30 to 39-year-old group, for example, almost two-thirds (63 percent) of those who first relationship was common-law had separated by 1995, compared with one-third (33 percent) of women who had married first....

The increase in the break-up of couples has resulted in more women being potentially available to enter a second relationship. Indeed, the proportion of women

(continued)

The Changing Face of Conjugal Relationships

(continued)

who had experienced at least two unions (marital or common-law) nearly tripled from the older to the younger generations....It appears that separation, followed by subsequent conjugal relationships, has become a common experience for many women in the last three decades of the 20th century.

Women whose first marriage had dissolved were very likely to form another union.... In all age groups, previously-married women were more likely to chose to live common-law in their second relationship than to remarry. And if they were in their 30s or 40s, they were twice as likely to do so.

Women who had started their conjugal life in a common-law relationship were just as likely to form new relationships if their union collapsed as those who had married first. However, they were substantially more likely to prefer common-law for their second relationship than were married-first women. While married-first women in their 30s were twice as likely to choose common-law as marriage for their second union, women whose first relationship was common-law were six times more likely to do so....

People today have more options in choosing the types of conjugal relationships they wish to have. While women born in the 1920s and 1930s had little choice but to marry, common-law unions are now accepted and they have become increasingly popular with young Canadians. However, the instability of many common-law arrangements, and the rising rate of dissolution of all unions, suggest that more people may spend more time living alone or alternatively, may be involved in more short-term relationships.

couple, but more than half of them (56 percent) were living common-law" (Vanier Institute of the Family 2000, p. 36). As Figure 7.4 indicates, at younger age and stages of their lives, Canadians are more likely to live in a common-law union. Among those under the age of 30 who were cohabiting, 95 percent had never been married; this was also true of the majority (72 percent) of those under the age of 40. Among those between the ages of 40 and 64 who were living common-law, almost two-thirds were divorced or separated (Figure 7.5).

In his analysis of the determinants of *premarital cohabition*, Wu (2000, p. 81) reports that the likelihood of cohabitation is higher among those who are:

- employed
- low-educated (women)
- non-students
- have no religious orientation
- Canadian-born
- Quebecers
- are pregnant (or their partners are pregnant)
- entering into parenthood (men)
- had a less happy childhood
- come from a broken family or a low social class family background (women)

In general, those who choose to cohabit tend to hold less conventional views towards marriage or view themselves as poor risks in terms of a long-term relationship (Wu 2000, p. 3).

COHABITATION AND THE LIKELIHOOD OF MARRIAGE   Cohabitations tend to be temporary and short-lived, with over half of cohabiting unions ending in three years (Wu and Balakrishnan 1995).

TABLE   7.1

Proportion of All Women Experiencing....

	Age in 1995				
	60–69	50–59	40–49	30–39	20–29
			Born in		
	1926–1935	1936–1945	1946–1955	1956–1965	1966–1975
Proportion of all women experiencing					
At least one union	96	97	96	94	87
At least one marriage	96	95	92	84	66
First union starts with marriage	95	91	78	56	35
At least one common-law union	8	22	35	49	59
First union starts with common-law union	1	6	18	38	52
At least one separation	25	32	40	43	—
At least two unions	14	27	34	39	—
At least two separations	8	13	16	—	—

— Sample too small to produce reliable estimates.

Source: Statistics Canada, "Canadian Social Trends," Cat. No. 11-008, March 2000, No. 56.

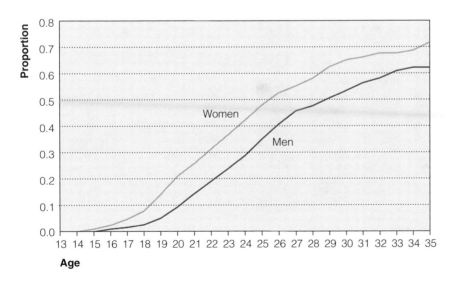

FIGURE   **7.2**

Life table estimates of cumulative proportion of premarital cohabitation.
(Source: Wu 2000, p. 77.)

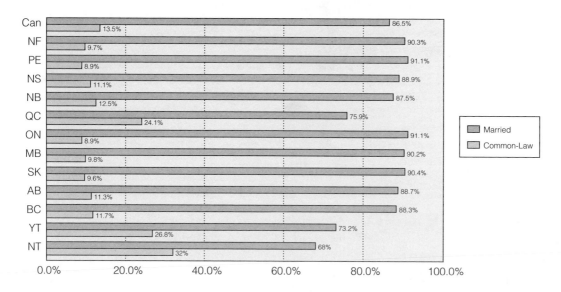

FIGURE   **7.3**

Marriage and common-law unions as percentage of all conjugal unions (1996).
(Source: based on data from the Statistics Canada publications "Population by
five-year age groups....", Catalogue 93F0022, October 1997, and 1992, and
"Population 15 years and over living in common-law unions by five-year age
groups....", Catalogue 95F0188, January 1998.)

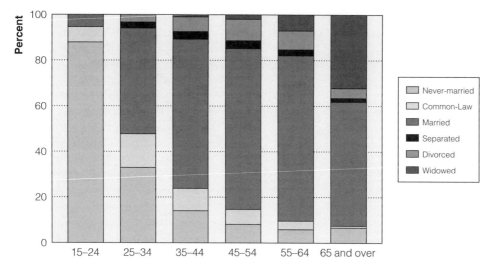

FIGURE   **7.4**

Marital status by age group (1996). (Source: based on data from the Statistics
Canada publications "Population by five-year age groups....", Catalogue 93F0022,
October 1997, and 1992, and "Population 15 years and over living in common-
law unions by five-year age groups....", Catalogue 95F0188, January 1998.)

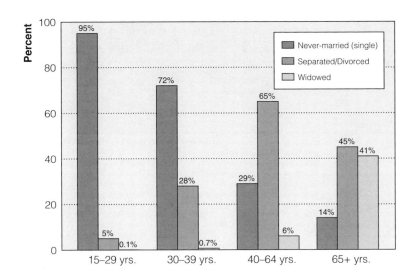

FIGURE **7.5**

Legal marital status of persons living common-law, by age group (1996)
(Source: based on data from the Statistics Canada publication "Population 15 years and over
living in common-law unions by five-year age groups....", Catalogue 95F0188, January 1998.)

"However, these unions are more likely to end in marriage than in separation; about one-third of cohabiting couples marry each other within three years of cohabitation, while another quarter dissolve their relationships through separation" (Wu 2000, p. 1).

Not all persons who cohabit desire marriage. As Table 7.2 indicates, those who have never been married and are cohabiting are far more likely than those who are divorced and cohabiting to express an intention to marry. Outside of Quebec, and regardless of whether they are cohabiting premaritally or postmaritally, women are more likely than men to desire to marry. This is also the case for women in Quebec who are cohabiting postmaritally. However, women in Quebec who are cohabiting premaritally "have lower desire to marry than their male counterparts" (Wu 2000, p. 115). While the desire for marriage is "conspicuously lower in Quebec than elsewhere in Canada," considerable levels of uncertainty exist, both inside and outside of Quebec, in relation to future intentions.

Certain factors increase the likelihood of marriage following cohabitation. Specifically:

The rate of marriage is particularly high among non-student women, individuals affiliated with Christian religions, and people outside of Quebec.

The rate of marriage also increases with a decrease in age at entry into cohabitation, in cohabitations involving never-married men and women, and when men cohabit with women 10 or more years younger than themselves. However, the rate decreases when children are involved (either brought or born into the relationship) and when people entered into cohabitation prior to 1970. (Wu 2000, pp. 119–120)

In addition, research (Pollard and Wu 1998) finds a strong association between a couple's economic circumstances and the likelihood that their union will end or be transformed into marriage. Specifically, the better a woman's economic position, the less likely it is that she will marry her common-law partner and the more likely it is that she will leave the common-law union. For example, among semi-professional and skilled women, common-law unions are more likely to result in separation than marriage. It would seem that the lower the woman's financial need to depend on her partner, the lower the perceived necessity to transform her common-law union into a marital relationship. However, in similar circumstances, men react differently. In contrast to their female counterparts, professional and semi-professional men are more likely to marry their common-law partners.

TABLE 7.2

Marriage Intentions among Cohabitors by Marital Status, Sex, Region (%)

	Women		Men	
Intent to marry	Premarital Cohabitation	Post-marital Cohabitation	Premarital Cohabitation	Post-marital Cohabitation
Quebec				
Yes	35.5	26.5	40.8	14.3
Uncertain	12.2	10.9	11.3	19.6
No	52.3	62.6	47.9	66.1
Total	100	100	100	100
Non-Quebec				
Yes	74.1	38.7	64.6	29.8
Uncertain	14.8	21.9	19.3	15.2
No	11.2	39.4	16.1	55.0
Total*	100	100	100	100

* May not total to 100 percent due to rounding.

Source: The 1995 General Social Survey.

COHABITATION AND MARITAL QUALITY
Evidence accumulated in the past ten years suggests that, contrary to Margaret Mead's hopes, "trial marriage" may have a negative effect on marital success (Ambert 1998; Lillard et al. 1995; Teachman and Polonko 1990). One American study found that cohabitation was negatively related to supportive marital interaction and was associated with marital disagreement and increased probability of divorce (Booth and Johnson 1988). The researchers thought that what some cohabitants bring to marriage might explain the negative relationship between cohabitation and successful marriage. Drug, money, legal, and unemployment problems; risk taking; parental disapproval; and lesser commitment to marriage were more characteristic of cohabitants than noncohabitants. Still, much remained unexplained by the data, suggesting that further research might find the cohabitation process itself to be contributing to marital weakness.

In a subsequent study, Thomson and Colella (1992) analyzed the relationship between prior cohabiting and the likelihood of divorce among 714 American couples in first marriages. Researchers classified these couples according to whether and for how long they had lived together before marrying. Respondents were also asked the following question: "It is always difficult to predict what will happen in a marriage, but realistically, what do you think the chances are that you and your husband/wife will eventually separate or divorce?" Response options included "very low," "low," "about even," "high," or "very high." Whereas 61 percent of those who had not cohabited said the likelihood of divorce was "very low," only 39 percent of those who had cohabited for two years or more said so. Generally, those who had cohabited were less satisfied with their marriages and less committed to the institution of marriage; their dissatisfaction increased with the length of time they had lived together before marrying. Wives who had cohabited had more individualistic views (as opposed to family-oriented views; see the discussion of free-choice and arranged marriages on pp. 178–183) than those who had not.

Thomson and Colella (1992) did not disagree with explanations offered by Booth and Johnson (1988) but rather added to them. It is possible, they suggested, that the experience of cohabiting adversely affects subsequent marital quality and stability inasmuch as the experience actually weakens commitment because "'successful' cohabitation (ending in marriage) demonstrates that reasonable alternatives to marriage exist" (Thomson and Colella 1992, p. 266). Put another way, experiencing cohabitation may lead to more individualistic attitudes and values (see also Axinn and Thornton 1992).[5]

Research conducted in Canada which used data collected from the 1995 General Social Survey also confirms the relationship between premarital cohabitation and subsequent marital instability.

Specifically, for women, five percent of marriages preceded by cohabitation experienced marital disruption within two years, compared to 1.5 percent of the marriages that were not. After five years, the comparable figures grow to 14 percent and 5 percent for cohabitators and non-cohabitors, respectively. After 10 years, the figures are 30 percent and 12 percent. Overall, the risk of marital disruption for premarital cohabitors is about two or three times higher than for non-cohabitors. A similar pattern is also observed for men. (Wu 2000, pp. 131–132)

This study also found that while cohabiting couples faced an increased risk of marital disruption, simply being coupled with a spouse who had previously cohabited with someone else elevated the risk of marital disruption to a similar level. "This 'spousal' effect remains whether or not the couple themselves cohabited premaritally, reinforcing the notion that living together as a form of trial marriage

---

5. Another analysis of data from the same survey (Schoen 1992) compared first marriages of women who had married their first cohabiting partner with first marriages of women who had never cohabited. This analysis looked at effects for separate age categories and found that among the younger cohorts (women born between 1948 and 1957) the differential risk of divorce associated with cohabitation was insignificant. Because people born between 1948 and 1957 had the highest incidence of cohabitation, these results "suggest that the less select nature of those cohabiting played a significant role in lessening the risk of marital disruption" (Schoen 1992, p. 284). Yet another analysis of this survey found that only *serial cohabitation* (cohabiting with a series of partners) was associated with higher subsequent divorce rates, at least during the first ten years of marriage (DeMaris and MacDonald 1993).

has a detrimental impact on subsequent marital stability" (Wu 2000, p. 143).

However, not all Canadian researchers agree that cohabitation increases the likelihood of marital instability (White 1987; 1989). For example, while a Statistics Canada study released in 2001 found that parents who cohabited prior to marriage were almost twice as likely to separate as those who had not, the authors of this study remained hopeful about the stability of such relationships in the future. According to one of the co-authors of the study, Heather Juby, "As common-law becomes more institutionalized it attracts more of the stable committed couples. There is some evidence in Quebec, where common-law is the norm, that there is not such a gap between the stability of common-law and marriage unions" (in Levine, 2001).

We have looked at dating, getting together, and cohabiting as courtship processes. Of course, in many real-life instances there are likely to be elements of each. A couple's courtship experience and their reasons for marrying make a difference in their long-term happiness. For this reason, when couples find themselves drifting into a default decision to marry—through dating, cohabiting or any other form of formal or informal courtship—they are wise if they stop, reconsider, and weigh the pros and cons. Box 7.3, "How to Tell When He or She is Wrong for You," provides some guidelines. Making a conscious decision about marrying increases the chances of not marrying, however, and of letting go of a special relationship, and that can be a painful experience. We'll look briefly at the experience of ending courtship by breaking up.

Breaking Up

Psychologist Lawrence Kurdek (1995) has applied exchange theory to whether couple relationships continue. (Exchange theory is described in detail later in this chapter.) According to the exchange perspective, couples choose either to stay committed or to break up by weighing the rewards of their relationship against its costs. As partners go through this process, they also consider how well their relationship matches an imagined, ideal one. Partners also contemplate alternatives to the relationship, the investments they've made in it, and barriers to breaking up. (We will see in Chapter 14 that this perspective also is used when examining people's decisions about divorce.)

TABLE 7.3

Should You Live Together?

Counsellor's Questions	"Good" Signs and "Concern" Signs
1. Could you talk a little about how each of you came to the decision to live together?	*Good signs:* Each partner has given considerable thought to the decision, including the advantages and disadvantages of living together. *Concern signs:* One or both partners have given little thought to the advantages and disadvantages of living together.
2. Perhaps each of you could discuss for a minute what you think you will get out of living together?	*Good signs:* Each individual is concerned about learning more about self and partner through intimate daily living. Both wish to obtain further information about each other's commitment to the relationship. *Concern signs:* One or both partners desire to live together for convenience only or to show independence from parents or peers.
3. Could each of you discuss what you see as your role and your partner's role in the relationship (e.g., responsibilities, expectations)?	*Good signs:* Each individual's expectations of self and partner are compatible with those of partner. *Concern signs:* One or both individuals have given little thought to the roles or expectations of self and/or partner. Individuals disagree in terms of their expectations.
4. Could each of you identify your partner's primary physical and emotional needs and the degree to which you believe that you are able to fulfill them?	*Good signs*: Each individual has a clear understanding of partner's needs and is motivated and able to meet most of them. *Concern signs*: One or both individuals are not motivated or able to meet needs of partner.
5. Would each of you identify your primary physical and emotional needs in your relationship with your partner? To what degree have these needs been met in the past? To what extent are these needs likely to be met if the two of you were to live together?	*Good signs:* Each partner clearly understands his or her needs. Most of these needs are presently being met and are likely to continue to be met in a cohabiting relationship. *Concern signs:* One or both partners are not fully aware of their needs. Needs are not being met in the present relationship and are not likely to be met if the individuals live together.
6. Could each of you discuss what makes this relationship important to you? What are your feelings toward your partner?	*Good signs*: Partners care deeply for each other and view the relationship as a highly significant one. *Concern signs*: One or both individuals do not care deeply for their partner or do not view the relationship as a highly significant one. Partners have an emotional imbalance, with one partner more involved in the relationship than the other.

Counsellor's Questions	"Good" Signs and "Concern" Signs
7. Could each of you explore briefly your previous dating experiences and what you have learned from them?	*Good signs:* Both individuals have had a rich dating history. Individuals have positive perceptions of self and opposite sex and are aware of what they learned from previous relationships. *Concern signs:* One or both partners have had minimal dating experience. Individuals have negative perceptions of self and/or of the opposite sex and do not seem aware of having learned from their previous relationships.
8. Perhaps each of you could talk for a minute about how your family and friends might react to the two of you living together?	*Good signs:* Each individual is aware of the potential repercussions from family and friends should they learn of the cohabiting relationship. Family and friends are supportive of the cohabiting relationship, or couple has considered how they will deal with opposition. *Concern signs:* One or both individuals are not fully aware of family and friends' possible reactions to their living together. Family and friends are not supportive of the cohabiting relationship.
9. Could each of you discuss your ability to openly and honestly share your feelings with your partner?	*Good signs:* Each individual is usually able to express feelings to partner without difficulty. *Concern signs:* One or both individuals have difficulty expressing feelings to partner or do not believe expressing feelings is important.
10. Could each of you discuss your partner's strengths and weaknesses? To what extent would you like to change your partner, relative to his or her strengths or weaknesses?	*Good signs:* Each individual is usually able to accept feelings of partner. Individuals are able to accept partner's strengths and weaknesses. *Concern signs:* One or both individuals are unable to understand and accept partner or have difficulty accepting partner's strengths and weaknesses.
11. How does each of you handle relationship problems when they occur? Can you give some examples of difficult problems you have had and how you have dealt with them?	*Good signs:* Both individuals express feelings openly and are able to understand and accept partner's point of view. Individuals are able to solve problems mutually. *Concern signs:* One or both partners have difficulty expressing feelings openly or accepting partner's point of view. Couple frequently avoids problems or fails to solve them mutually.

Source: Ridley, Peterman, and Avery, 1978, pp. 129–136.

Using this scheme, Kurdek developed a questionnaire to measure a couple's relationship commitment. The following are some questions from Kurdek's measure (respondents could strongly agree, agree, remain neutral, disagree, or strongly disagree):

Rewards:

One advantage to my relationship is having someone to count on.

Costs:

It takes a lot for me to be in my relationship.

Match to Ideal Comparison Level:

My current relationship comes close to matching what I would consider to be my ideal relationship.

Alternatives:

As an alternative to my current relationship, I would like the freedom to do what I want to do whenever I want to do it.

As an alternative to my relationship, I would like to date someone else.

Investments:

I've put a lot of energy and effort into my relationship.

A part of me is tied up in my relationship.

Barriers to breaking up:

It would be difficult to leave my partner because of the emotional pain involved.

I would find it difficult to leave my partner because I would feel obligated to keep the relationship together. (p. 263)

When a partner's rewards are higher than the costs, when there are few desirable alternatives to the relationship, when the relationship comes close to one's ideal one, when one has invested a great deal in the relationship and the barriers to breaking up are perceived as high, an individual is likely to remain committed. However, when costs outweigh rewards, when there are desirable alternatives to the relationship, when one's relationship does not match one's ideal, when little has been invested in the relationship by comparison to rewards, and when there are fewer barriers to breaking up, couples are more likely to do so.

Although breaking up is hard to do any time, breakups before marriage are generally less stressful than divorce.

Research has suggested that men tend to fall in love more readily than women, and women tend to fall out of love more readily than men (Bradsher 1990). Social scientists suggest two explanations for women initiating breakups more often. First, a married woman's income and status are far more dependent on her husband than his are on her. Consequently, women must be especially discriminating, whereas men can afford to be more romantic. Second, women are more sensitive than men to the quality of interpersonal relationships. Hence, their standards for developing love may be higher than men's. A woman may experience lack of rapport or self-revelation in a relationship, for example, while the man does not. As a result, women may evaluate and reevaluate their relationships more carefully.

Whatever the end results may be, the act of breaking up can be an ordeal. Sociologists and counsellors offers the following guidelines for ending a relationship:

1. Decide that terminating the relationship is what you really want to do.

2. Assuming you have definitely determined to break up, prepare yourself for wavering—but don't change your mind.

3. Plan the breakup discussion with your partner in person, but at a location from which you can readily withdraw.

4. Explain your reasons for breaking up in terms of your own values, rather than pointing out what you think is wrong with the other person.

5. Seek out new relationships.

Item 5 is also good advice for those who have recently been broken up with (Knox 1975, pp. 143–45).

In the past, counsellors usually recommended making the breakup final without expectations for friendship afterward. They reasoned that trying to develop a post-dating friendship would almost always be painful because one or both partners would expect too much from the continued contact. Today, however, former partners are more likely to take classes or work together, and to have mutual friends. A few recent studies have found that some ex-partners do forge supportive post-dating relationships that satisfy legitimate needs, such as friendship and shared history (Foley and Fraser 1998).

Until this point in the chapter we have been discussing the way relationships develop as they proceed (or don't proceed) to marriage. But falling in love, especially when we expect that it could lead to marriage, may be a more practical or pragmatic process than we think. Social scientists use the analogy of the marketplace to describe how people select spouses.

THE MARRIAGE MARKET

Imagine a large marketplace in which people come with goods to exchange for other items. In nonindustrialized societies a person may go to market with a few chickens to trade for some vegetables. In modern societies, people attend hockey equipment swaps, for example, trading outgrown skates for larger ones. People choose marriage partners in much the same way: They enter the **marriage market** armed with resources—their (or their children's, in the case of arranged marriages) personal and social characteristics—and then bargain for the best buy they can get.

We saw at the beginning of this chapter that in many other cultures, parents arrange their children's marriages. Parents go through a bargaining process not unlike what takes place at a traditional village market. They make rationally calculated choices after determining the social status or position, health, temperament, and, sometimes, physical attractiveness of their prospective son- or daughter-in-law. In such societies the bargaining is obvious. Professional matchmakers often serve as investigators and go-betweens, just as we might engage an attorney or a stockbroker in an important business deal.

Sometimes the exchange involves a **bride price**, money or property that the future groom pays the future bride's family so that he can marry her. More often a **dowry**, a sum of money or property brought to the marriage by the female, accompanies the exchange. A woman with a large dowry can expect to marry into a higher-ranking family than can a woman with a small dowry, and dowries are often increased to make up for qualities considered undesirable (Kaplan 1985, pp. 1–13). Parents in eighteenth-century England, for instance, increased the dowries of daughters who were pockmarked.

The difference between arranged marriages and marriages in free-choice cultures seems so great that we are inclined to overlook an important similarity: Both involve bargaining. What has changed in modern society is that the individuals, not the family, do the bargaining.

Exchange Theory

The ideas of bargaining, market, and resources used to describe relationships such as marriage come to us from **exchange theory**, described in Chapter 2. Recall that the basic idea of exchange theory is that whether or not relationships form or continue depends on the rewards and costs they provide to the partners. Individuals, it is presumed, want to maximize their rewards and avoid costs, so when there are choices, they will pick the relationship that is most rewarding or least costly. The analogy is to economics, but in romantic and marital relationships individuals are thought to have other sorts of resources to bargain besides money: physical attractiveness, personality, family status, skills, emotional supportiveness, cooperativeness, intellect, originality, and so on. Individuals also have costly attributes: irritability, demandingness, ineptitude, low social status, geographic inaccessibility (a major consideration in modern society), and so on. If each individual adopts a strategy of maximizing outcomes, then stable relationships will tend to exist between people who have like amounts of resources because they will strike a fair balance or bargain.

One weakness of exchange theory is its assumption of absolute rationality. Are people actually so calculating about rewards and costs, even at an unconscious level? Further, in an exchange analysis, what is rewarding and what is costly? It varies with the individual.

Descriptions of exchange behaviour are reminiscent of traditional arranged marriages. Nevertheless, even for the majority of Canadians who choose their own partners, we present an exchange perspective as a useful tool. In fact, the basic structures of Canadian life channel men and women into roles that have certain consequences for marital partnerships. We need to be aware of an underlying exchange structure of intimate relationships and marital ties. Let us look now at an exchange version of marital choice.

The Traditional Exchange

Individuals may bargain such characteristics as social class, age, physical attractiveness, and education, but

How to Tell When He or She is Wrong for You

Sometimes, people pretend to themselves that sexual desire, the fear of being alone, or the hope for financial and other social advantages can be turned into feelings of love. Before marrying, people need to ask themselves the following questions about their partners:

1. *Does he or she have several close friends?* A person who has learned to enjoy and foster intimate friendships can put this talent to work in a marriage relationship. But if no one likes him or her well enough to be a close friend, shouldn't you wonder why you like him or her?

2. *Do you keep putting off introducing him or her to your friends and relatives?* Does he or she put off introducing you to his or her friends and relatives? Why? A hesitancy to show off a partner to those people who are most important to you may be a sign of uncertainty: Will the family and friends think it is a mistake?

3. *If the love relationship folded, would you still want to keep each other as friends?* For some lovers, this seems impossible. But the question here is whether the two people share enough respect and interests to want to be together even if no longer sexually intimate. Marriage involves companionship as well as sexual attraction.

4. *Do you spend most of your time trying to stay out of his or her bed?* A yes to this question can point up one of two problems: Either the chemistry just isn't there for you—and probably never will be—or your partner's emphasis on the importance of sex in an intimate relationship is considerably different from yours.

5. *Are you happy with the way he or she treats other people?* If he or she is condescending or rude—even physically violent—to others, you'll get the same treatment eventually. Watch how he or she deals with employees, food servers, salesclerks, parking lot attendants, telephone operators, and so forth. Also, study his or her behaviour with family members and close friends. If he or she doesn't treat them the way you want him or her to treat you, he or she is wrong for you. You may be an exception now, during courtship, but you won't be later.

6. *Do you know what he or she is like sexually?*

7. *Was your life stimulating and satisfying before you met her or him?* "Never, never bind yourself to someone because you need him or her to transform your unsatisfactory life into a super one."

8. *Do you often feel apprehensive about your future happiness together?* Little panics are normal, but they should be few and far between. If you are apprehensive more often than optimistic, this should serve as a warning signal.

9. *Are there taboo topics that you cannot discuss with each other?* Good relationships are built on trust, respect, spontaneity, and lack of stress. People are free to talk about almost anything. Even though they may hold very different views, not many subjects are taboo. Topics that have a bearing on the relationship are never taboo.

Source: "J" (Joan Garrity) 1977.

the basic marital exchange is traditionally related to gender roles. Historically, women have traded their ability to bear and rear children and perform domestic duties, along with sexual accessibility and physical attractiveness, for masculine protection, status, and economic support (see Figure 7.6) (Sprecher, Sullivan, and Hatfield 1994). Even though more and more women are gaining status by means of their own careers or professions, many of them continue to expect greater success from their future hus-

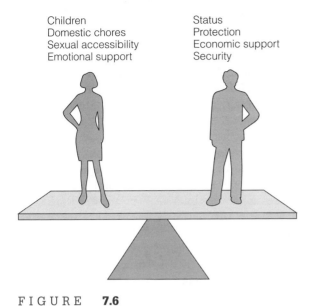

Children
Domestic chores
Sexual accessibility
Emotional support

Status
Protection
Economic support
Security

FIGURE 7.6

| The traditional exchange.

bands than vice versa (Ganong and Coleman 1992; Sprecher, Sullivan, and Hatfield 1994) and perhaps to attain a higher status by marrying than they would have as single individuals supporting themselves (Twenge 1997b). Being a doctor's wife may offer a higher status, for example, than being a teacher or nurse. Recent evidence from classified personal ads shows that the traditional exchange still influences heterosexual relationships. Men are more likely to advertise for a physically attractive woman; and women, for an economically stable man (Yancey and Yancey 1998). Then too, the traditional exchange characterizes marriages in many recently arrived immigrant groups to Canada.

Women have had some disadvantages in the traditional exchange. For one thing, men can bargain on their potential, taking their time to shop for a partner, whereas women lose an important advantage with time. A woman's traditional bargaining assets of physical attractiveness and childbearing capacity are given less value as she ages. Men, meanwhile, can exchange promises of anticipated occupational success and power for marital security.

Sociologists point to a related bargaining advantage for men. In the traditional exchange, young men and women bargain for spouses with different degrees of available information. The man can more easily assess the woman, observing whether she offers emo-

tional support and empathy as well as responding to her physical attractiveness. But the occupational abilities of many young men have generally not yet been tested. In this traditional exchange, then, a woman must therefore base her appraisal on such cues as a young man's grades in school and his father's occupation. Older men and women may more easily evaluate prospective partners because personal and economic characteristics are more established.

Bargaining in a Changing Society: The Optimistic View

As society changes, so does the basic exchange in marriage. Social scientists predict that, should true androgyny emerge (as was discussed in Chapter 3), exchange between partners will no longer depend greatly on practical or economic resources but instead will include "expressive, affective, sexual, and companionship resources" for both partners. As women gain occupational and economic equality with men, the exchange will become more symmetrical, with women and men increasingly looking for similar characteristics in each other (see Figure 7.7a).

Marriage based on both partners' contributing roughly equal economic and status resources should be more egalitarian. Current changes in men's roles toward greater emotional expressiveness may improve marriage. Furthermore, as gender roles change, even those exchanges that are complementary (that is, based on unlike resources) can be individualized. For example, an ambitious career woman might be comfortable bargaining for a nurturant husband, and vice versa. This is the bargaining we would anticipate in an egalitarian and androgynous society.

Bargaining in a Changing Society: The Pessimistic View

Another view pays more attention to the substantial inequalities that remain, particularly women's marginal position in the economic system (Wax 1998). Although women have entered the labour market in large numbers, their jobs and incomes are inferior, on the average, to those of men.

Even though social expectations may be moving toward androgyny, women are still at a disadvantage in the marriage market. While this is changing, men continue to hold the advantage regarding access to financial security and status. Meanwhile, many of the bargaining chips women have traditionally brought to the basic exchange—children, domestic services, sexual accessibility—have been devalued because they are now available to unmarried men as well as husbands (see Figure 7.7b).

It may have been true for our grandparents, for example, that "the way to a man's heart is through his stomach." Today, however, cooking and other domestic skills and services are no longer monopo-

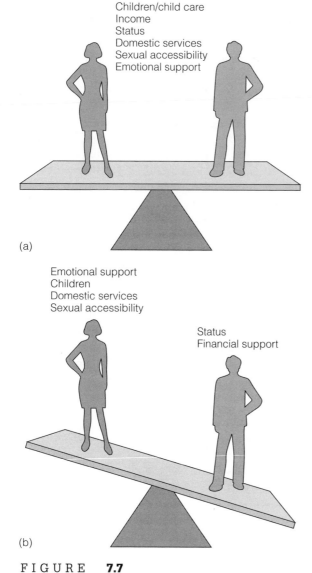

(a)

(b)

FIGURE   7.7

Two interpretations of the changing traditional exchange (a) the optimistic, egalitarian view; and (b) the more pessimistic view.

lized by potential wives, and many men have discovered that they like to cook. The increased acceptance of nonmarital sex (however satisfying this may be to many women as well as men) has weakened women's traditional bargaining position, decreasing the possibility of trading sexual accessibility for marriage. And finally, even the ability to have children may be less vital than in the past, as some people are questioning the value of having children. Moreover, with today's divorce rate and custody of children usually going to mothers, marriage no longer assures men ongoing access to their children (Gerson 1993). In this analysis the wife's primary remaining resource in the marital exchange consists of the promise of lifelong affection and encouragement (Scanzoni 1970).

Besides cultural expectations, certain demographic features of the current marriage market can negatively affect the bargaining position of women. Of particular importance is how an unequal sex ratio limits choice of marriage partners.

Sex Ratios and Bargaining for a Spouse

Chapter 6 explored the impact of **sex ratios** on singlehood. The obvious flip side of the discussion is that sex ratios affect bargaining for a spouse.

Calculation of the availability of mates is complicated by both the tendency of men to be two to three years older than the women they marry and by the fact that individuals seek mates within local markets (Lichter, LeClere, and McLaughlin 1991). Based on an assumption of an average two-year age difference, Adie Nelson and Barrie Robinson (1995) calculated sex ratios for selected age groups of marital eligibles (never married + widowed + divorced)[6] derived from

6. The identification of whom, precisely, qualifies as an "eligible" must be considered problematic and these authors acknowledge that the actual eligible population may be much larger than their calculation by these components would suggest. Noting Farber's (1964) argument that we are moving towards a condition of "'permanent availability' in which every adult, outside of the incest taboo, can or will be considered to be potentially available as a mate," regardless of their current marital status, Nelson and Robinson (1995, p. 233) point out that, "Being currently married does not necessarily remove one from circulation, as evidenced at the very least by the existence of extramarital affairs some of which lead to divorce and the subsequent marrying of former lovers." In addition, they note that their calculation assumes that everyone is interested in forming a heterosexual relationship, "a questionable assumption at best but one that must be made nonetheless given the general unreliability of estimates of the gay/lesbian population distributed across different age-sex categories."

Although the arranged marriage of this Indian couple may be a world apart from the freely chosen marriage of this Waterloo, Ontario couple, bargaining has occurred in both of these unions. In arranged marriages, families and community do the bargaining, based on assets such as status, possessions, and dowry. In freely chosen marriages, the individuals perform a more subtle form of bargaining, weighing the costs and benefits of personal characteristics, economic status, and education.

estimates of the Canadian population for 1991 (Table 7.4). They point out that in sharp contrast to the situation of women born at the beginning of the "baby boom" who confronted a deficit of older men of the appropriate age for marriage (what demographers at the time referred to as a "**marriage squeeze**"), there were more eligible men than women at the younger ages (i.e., under age 35).

However, they note that "[r]egardless of whether one examines the 1960s, the 1980s, or even the early 1990s, a group of females exists for whom the problem has always been one of an imbalance between the eligible sexes—namely, females over 55 (Table 7.5) (Nelson and Robinson 1994, p. 85). As the combined result of differential mortality (particularly at older ages) and the greater likelihood of divorced and widowed men remarrying, they observe that older women in Canada who ask the question, "'Where have all the good men gone?' must confront the answer: 'They are either confirmed bachelors, gay, currently in relationships of some form, or dead'" (Nelson and Robinson 1995, p. 238).

The Marriage Gradient

The **marriage gradient** is the traditional tendency for women to marry "up" with regard to age, education, occupation, and even height. But this process takes place within culturally accepted limits. Regarding age, for example, most marriages are characterized by an age difference of no more than three or four years (Surra 1990, p. 847).

The same is true for education. University-educated women and men tend to marry each other; so do people without university educations (Albrecht et al. 1997; Qian 1998). Researchers suggest that this situation is due to "increasing competition in the marriage market for wives with good prospects in the labour market" (Mare 1991, p. 15)—hence a weakening of the traditional marriage gradient with respect to education. However, "[p]artial confirmation of the problems associated with our society's emphasis....[on the marriage gradient] can be found in the fact that....women located at the top of their professions tend to be unmarried" (Nelson and Robinson 1999, p. 315). In addition, where the marriage gradient does

TABLE 7.4

Sex Ratios for Marital Eligibles, Selected Age Groups, Canada, 1991

Female's Age	Male's Age	
15 years	17 years	102.4
16 years	18 years	104.6
17 years	19 years	110.1
18 years	20 years	113.8
19 years	21 years	111.4
20 years	22 years	102.2
21 years	23 years	101.8
22 years	24 years	107.4
23 years	25 years	116.0
24 years	26 years	127.3
25 years	27 years	127.5
26 years	28 years	119.6
27 years	29 years	114.7
28 years	30 years	117.7
29 years	31 years	116.8
30 years	32 years	109.8
31 years	33 years	108.3
32 years	34 years	108.1
33 years	35 years	103.1
34 years	36 years	99.6
35 years	37 years	97.9
36 years	38 years	92.3
37 years	39 years	89.0
38 years	40 years	89.0
39 years	41 years	88.0
40 years	42 years	85.6
41 years	43 years	85.3
42 years	44 years	84.1

Note: Eligibles = Never Married + Divorced + Widowed

Source: Adapted from Wayne W. McVey and Warren E. Kalbach, *Canadian Population*. Toronto: Nelson, 1995.

TABLE 7.5

Sex Ratios for Marital Eligibles, Selected Age Groups, Canada, 1991

Age	Sex Ratio	Age	Sex Ratio
45–49 years	78	60–64 years	49
50–54 years	70	65–69 years	37
55–59 years	60	70–74 years	29

Note: Eligibles = Never Married + Divorced + Widowed

Source: Calculations based on Table 3, "Population by Marital Status and Sex showing Five-year Age Groups for Canada, Provinces, Territories, and Census Metropolitan Areas, 1986 and 1991 — 100% Data" in *Age, Sex and Marital Status: The Nation*. (Catalogue 93–310) Ottawa: Minister of Industry, Science and Technology, 1992.

Besides the marriage gradient and sex ratios, an additional factor shaping marital choice is the tendency of people to marry others with whom they share certain social characteristics. Social scientists term this phenomenon *homogamy*.

HOMOGAMY: NARROWING THE POOL OF ELIGIBLES

Not everyone who enters the marriage market is equally available to everyone else. Canadians, like many other peoples, tend to make marital choices in socially patterned ways, viewing only certain others as potentially suitable mates. The market analogy would be to choose only certain stores at which to shop. For each shopper there is a socially defined **pool of eligibles**: a group of individuals who, by virtue of background or birth, are considered most likely to make compatible marriage partners.

Canadians tend to choose partners who are like themselves in many ways. This situation is called **homogamy**: People tend to marry people of similar race, age, education, religious background, and social class. Traditionally, the Protestant, Catholic, and Jewish religions, for example, as well as Muslim and Hindu religions, have all encouraged **endogamy**: marrying within one's own social group. (The opposite of endogamy is **exogamy**, marrying outside one's

exist, the practice sets the stage for greater marital power for husbands than wives, because husbands have greater educational and/or financial resources. Issues of marital power are explored in Chapter 10.

group, or **heterogamy**, marrying someone dissimilar in race, age, education, religion, or social class.)

Social scientists point out that although today people are marrying across small class distinctions, they still are not doing so across large ones. For instance, individuals of established wealth seldom marry the poor. All in all, an individual is most likely to marry someone who is similar in basic social characteristics (Kalmijn 1998). Let's look at a hypothetical case to see why this may be so.

Reasons for Homogamy

Laura is attracted to Jeremy (and vice versa) who is a university student (like herself), two years older, and single. Laura's parents are upper middle class. They live in the expensive section of her hometown, have a housekeeper, drink wine with their meals, and frequently have parties by their pool with a live band. Catholic, they go to Mass every Sunday. Jeremy's parents are upper lower class. They are separated. His mother lives in an apartment and works as a checker in the supermarket. The family drinks iced tea at mealtime, then watches TV. They believe in "being good people" but do not belong to any organized religion.

How likely is it that Laura and Jeremy will marry? If they do marry, what sources of conflict might occur? We can help to answer these questions by exploring four related elements that influence both initial attraction and long-term happiness. These elements—propinquity, social pressure, feeling at home, and a fair exchange—are important reasons why many people are homogamous.

PROPINQUITY   Propinquity (or geographic closeness) has typically been a basic reason people tend to meet others much like themselves. Geographic segregation, which can result from discrimination and segregation or from community ties, contributes to homogamous marriages.

Propinquity also helps account for educational (Stevens 1991) and social class homogamy. Middle-class people live in neighbourhoods with other middle-class people. They socialize together and send their children to the same schools; upper- and lower-class people do the same. Unless they had met in uni-

versity, it is unlikely that Jeremy and Laura would have become acquainted at all. The effort expended in associating with, or even meeting, people who are outside one's physical circle of friends encourages homogamy.

However, as psychologist Bernard Murstein (1986) points out, more and more people today choose spouses from open fields. An open field encounter refers to a situation in which the man and woman do not yet know each other well. A closed field encounter, on the other hand, is one in which partners are forced to interact by reason of their environment—in a small town, for example. Today, open field encounters occur in cyberspace as people meet on the Internet in various "chat rooms." Still, though, their mutual ability to access the Internet assures some degree of educational and/or financial homogamy. Box 7.4, "Today's Matchmakers in a Free-Choice Society: Formal Intermediaries in the Marriage Market," addresses cyberspace courtship.

SOCIAL PRESSURE   A second reason for homogamy is social pressure. Our cultural values encourage people to marry others socially similar to themselves and discourage marrying anyone too different: Laura's parents, friends, and siblings are not likely to approve of Jeremy because he doesn't exhibit the social skills and behaviour of their social class (Blackwell 1998). Meanwhile, Jeremy's mother and friends may say to him, "Laura thinks she is too good for us. Find a girl more like our own kind." Sometimes, social pressure results from a group's concern for preserving its ethnic or cultural identity. When young Jews, particularly students, began to intermarry more often in the 1960s, for example, Jewish leaders became concerned.

From pulpits across the country rabbis lamented the disintegrating Jewish family and the "demographic holocaust" that threatened the community. Federations rushed to form task forces on intermarriage; Hillel directors sought new ways to cement the group loyalties of Jewish ... students so they would not intermarry; and a spate of "how-to-stop-an-intermarriage" books appeared. (William Petschek National Jewish Family Center 1986b, p. 2)

While ethnic intermarriage has become increasingly common in Canada (Kalbach 1983, 2000), parents may still encourage their children to marry within their

Today's Matchmakers in a Free-Choice Society: Formal Intermediaries in the Marriage Market

Historically, matchmaking has long claimed a commercial niche in the marriage market. Today, a modem, phone line, or advertisement might bring potential partners together....Social scientists have long seen mate selection as occurring in a marriage market where both economic and interpersonal assets are exchanged. Commercial dating services, by making these assets explicit, further emphasize the relevance of market theory....

A market intermediary is any organization, event, or institution that takes on work that otherwise would be performed by the provider or consumer of the good. For example, help wanted advertising is an intermediary in the labour market that takes on some of the [searching and matching] tasks needed for employee selection. Searching is the process of gaining information essential for exchange (e.g., what products are available, where they can be found, how much they cost). Matching is the process of bringing together compatible exchange partners....

[In] the marriage market...searching consists of information acquisition (learning about who is available as a potential mate). Matching is the process of using information on eligible others to determine which relationships will be pursued....

The vast majority of singles meet their dating partners through social networks, such as mutual friends or parties that function as informal marriage market intermediaries (MMIs). [But today's singles also use formal MMIs such as singles ads, video dating, and electronic/phone communication networks.]....

Video Dating

....Video dating firms usually operate by having a client first read the written descriptions of other members. At many video dating services these written descriptions contain a photograph of the single, which is often placed on the back of the information sheet.... [But] clients tend to read the forms from the back to the front, doing an initial screening on the basis of the photo. If the client finds someone whose form piques his or her interest, then he or she is shown that person's video. Usually the video lasts 2 to 10 minutes and shows the client responding to a series of questions. If the suitor is still interested after seeing the video, the prospective date is contacted and then views the suitor's video. If the parties agree to meet, they are given each other's phone numbers and the rest is up to them....

own ethnic group in order to preserve their unique culture (Bhargava 1988; Kitano and Daniels 1995).

FEELING AT HOME People often feel more at home with others from similar education and backgrounds; couples from different social groups may struggle to communicate and may feel uncomfortable (Blackwell 1998). With regard to social-class differences, Jeremy is likely to have different attitudes, mannerisms, and vocabulary from Laura. Laura won't know how to dress or behave in Jeremy's hangouts

and among his friends. Each may feel uncomfortable and out of place in the surroundings the other considers natural.

STRIKING A FAIR EXCHANGE As previously noted, exchange theory suggests that people tend to marry others whose social currency—social class, education, physical attractiveness, and even self-esteem— is similar to their own (Murstein 1986).

The questions people ask on first meeting point up their concern with each other's exchange value. They

Electronic/Phone Communication Networks

One of the most recent innovations in MMIs is the development of electronic communication networks, such as computer-based networks....[There are] two kinds of computer-based networks: computer-accessed singles ads in which singles leave messages on computer bulletin boards, and on-line networks....

Like computer networks, telephone-based MMIs can also be divided into those that allow for interactive contact (i.e., party lines) and bulletin board systems (i.e., telephone singles ads) which allow singles to leave short taped messages or hear the messages left by others. As with computer networks, these systems may facilitate relationship formation by allowing people to get to know each other before screening on the basis of physical appearance takes place, but they may also cause singles to waste time and energy on a relationship that they later reject due to lack of physical attraction.... (Ahuvia and Adelman 1992, pp. 452–463).

Today there are books (Capulet 1998) and popular magazine articles (Astor 1996; Nign 1995) that give advice about Internet courtship. Many of us know someone who has met her or his spouse through a classified ad or on the Net. We also might know someone who had a bad experience in this regard. When the relationship does work, it typically evolves from meeting on the Net, to talking over the telephone, to sending photographs (if the relationship is a long distance one), to arranging to meet physically. Counsellors and others warn that the first few physical meetings should be arranged in the daytime and in a public place, such as a restaurant or coffee shop, in order to protect oneself against possible physical danger.

The verdict is still out on whether Internet courtships result in happy, stable unions any more or less often than more traditional courtship patterns; this topic is a focus of debate on the Internet itself (Hering 1994; Hyman 1997; Pitman 1997).

How do MMIs support the view in social science that mate selection takes place in a marriage market? How do formal MMIs differ from informal ones? According to one estimate, a 5–20 percent marriage rate is typical for formal MMIs. In what ways do you think MMIs might decrease marital homogamy? In what ways do you think they might continue or even increase marital homogamy?

want to know whether their prospective dates are married or single, where they are employed, whether they attend university and what they are studying, what they plan to do upon graduation, where they live, and perhaps what kind of car they drive. If prospective partners are single, they will be asked whether they are divorced or still single and, especially in the case of women, whether they have children and how many.

If meeting in the marriage market can sound like a job interview, maybe that's because in at least one important way it is: The goal is to strike a fair exchange. And even without the benefit of interviews, people learn to discern the social class of others through mannerisms, language, dress, and a score of other cues.

We've discussed some reasons for homogamy, but, as we pointed out earlier in this chapter, not all marriages are homogamous. *Heterogamy* refers to marriage between those who are different in race/ethnicity, age, education, religious background, or social class.

Examples of Heterogamy

How does marrying someone from a different religion, social class, or race/ethnicity affect a person's chances for a happy union? In answer to this, we first examine interfaith marriages, then look at interclass partnerships, and finally at interracial unions.

INTERRELIGIOUS MARRIAGES Between 1981 and 1990, the number of interfaith marriages increased from 21.8 percent to 48.6 percent. Over this time period, religious homogamy was "highest among the Jewish and non-Christian faiths, and lowest among mainline Protestant religions" (Larson et al. 2000, p. 120;). Being highly educated seems to lessen individuals' commitment to religious homogamy (Petersen 1994).

Marriages are generally considered to be religiously homogamous if both spouses identify the same religious affiliation at the time of marriage. However, marriages are less homogamous if we consider couples' religion before the wedding. Many partners who originally differed in religion switch to make their religion the same as their future spouse's (Glenn 1982; Shatzmiller 1996). Some of this switching may be due to one partner's strong methods of persuasion. Religions that see themselves as the one true faith and people who adhere to a religion as an integral component of their ethnic/cultural identity (for example, some Catholics, Jews, and Muslims) are more likely to press a prospective spouse to convert (Smits, Ultee, and Lammers 1998).

Often they are concerned that children born into the marriage will not be raised in their religion (Adler 1997). A Web site for Muslims considering interreligious unions questions how children would be raised, along with other concerns such as appropriate dress and demeanour of non-Muslim wives (http://www.pakistanlink.com/religion).

Some switching, no doubt, also takes place because partners agree with the widely held belief that interreligious marriages tend not to be as successful as homogamous ones—a belief supported by research (Lehrer and Chiswick 1993; Ortega, Whitt, and Williams 1988; Heaton and Pratt 1990; Maneker and Rankin 1993). Exploring this question by means of statistical analysis, Glenn (1982) found that religious heterogeneity lessened marital satisfaction for husbands but not for wives. Glenn specu-

lated that a husband's marital happiness might be more affected because religious heterogeneity is more likely to result in religious differences between father and children; "persons who are not disturbed by their spouse's being of a different religion frequently may be disturbed by their children's being of a different religion, if only because it may relegate them to a kind of outsider or minority status in their own family" (Glenn 1982, p. 564). If the spouses are traditional, the husband may see a wife's refusal to change her religion to match his as a threat to his authority, whereas the wife does not expect this concession. The sex role ideologies of the spouses were not investigated in this study, however.

One probable reason that religious homogeneity improves chances for marital success involves value consensus. "Religious orientations may come into play when deciding about leisure activity, child rearing, spending money, and many other facets of marital interaction." Then too, religious homogamy may "create a more integrated social network of relatives, friends, and religious advisors" (Heaton and Pratt 1990, p. 192). However, if intramarried couples appear to experience greater personal similarity and mutual understanding that aids the development of intimacy, intermarried couples may find that the process of negotiating differences leads to greater mutual understanding and intimacy (Heller and Wood 2000; Cogan 2000).

One research team has attributed differences in marital happiness associated with religious homogeneity almost entirely to the positive effect of church attendance: Homogamously married partners go to church more often and at similar rates and, as a result, show higher marital satisfaction and stability (Heaton and Pratt 1990). Another American study (Sheehan, Bock, and Lee 1990), which compared Catholics in heterogeneous marriages with those in homogamous ones, found that while heterogamously married Catholics went to Mass less frequently, this did *not* reduce marital satisfaction. These researchers concluded that

the effect of church attendance on marital satisfaction in the general population may be due more to the integrative properties of couple-centred organizational participation than to the religious nature of the activity. Heterogamous couples in which one spouse is Catholic are unlikely to attend church together, and may compensate for this by engaging in other couple-centred activities that are equally effective in promoting marital solidarity. (p. 78)

Glenn concluded that

some of the problems encountered by interreligious couples evidently [had] grown out of the disapproval of family and friends; and as such disapproval diminishes, so should some of the disruptive influences on interreligious marriages. (Glenn 1982, p. 564)

This is also true, as is pointed out later in this chapter, for interracial marriages.

INTERCLASS MARRIAGES What about the marital satisfaction of partners in interclass unions? Researchers have tended to ignore this question in recent decades, focusing instead on interracial and interethnic unions (Kalmijn 1991, 1998). They have, however, defined the concept of **hypergamy**—improving one's social and/or economic status by marrying up. The opposite, **hypogamy**, involves marrying down.

One early study of marriage (Pearlin 1975) found that partners experienced more stress in these class-heterogamous unions. Moreover, the spouse who had married down was more stressed than the one who had married up. It is important to note, however, that the relationship between stress and marrying down existed only when status striving was important to the individual. Those people for whom status was important and who had married down perceived their marriages more negatively—as less reciprocal, less affectionate, less emotionally supportive, and with less value consensus—than those who had married up. In an exchange framework, the partner who had married down had not struck a good bargain in an important matter. For people for whom status was not important, neither marrying up nor down produced any difference in their evaluation of their marriages.

Within Canada,

the most frequently occurring scenario....involves female hypergamy wherein a woman marries, or becomes involved in a relationship with a man of slightly higher social characteristics....[However], [t]he "Cinderella-Prince Charming" myth of two people from vastly different backgrounds being drawn to one another to form a mystical relationship is just that—a myth. Mates come from generally similar backgrounds with only slight, but often important, differences in the status characteristics they each possess. (Nelson and Robinson 1999, p. 314)

INTERRACIAL MARRIAGES Sociologist Enakshi Dua (1999, p. 244) argues that the historical discouragement of **interracial marriages** in Canada and other British, white settler colonies such as Canada, South Africa, Australia, New Zealand, and the United States, emerged as part of "the project of creating a white settler colony with political power in the hands of white settlers."

Nationalists and eugenicists pointed out that the inclusion of colonized people made race deterioration an immediate threat....As eugenicists linked miscegenation to the deterioration of the race and nation, sexual purity became a controlling metaphor for racial, economic and political power.... (pp. 252–253)

While the United States enacted a series of laws specifically prohibiting marriages between white settlers and those of African descent (Mare 1991; Haney-Lopez 1997; Sollors 2000), "[i]n Canada the regulation of interracial sexuality took place through other legal mechanisms," including the 1876 Indian Act which was "employed to govern marriage and sexual relations between white settlers and First Nations people" (Dua 1999, p. 256).

In addition, in his historical analysis of the status of black American fugitive slaves to Canada between 1830 and 1860, Jason Silverman (1981) writes that "at its worst, white Canadian prejudice was founded on the pervading fear of miscegenation," or interracial marriage (p. 207). Sociologist Tanis Das Gupta (2000, p. 159) also observes that in the early part of the twentieth century, single male Chinese workers were seen as posing "a threat of miscegenation to white Canadians" and villified in newspapers as sexual predators who lusted after white women. Such inflammatory, racist stereotypes were consequential and galvanized Protestant moral reformers, middle-class white women's groups, the owners of small businesses and trade unionists to jointly campaign for legislation which prohibited Asian employers from hiring white women as employees.

Fearful of the implications of the pronounced sexual imbalance within the Asian-Canadian community [an imbalance created by restrictive immigration policies, see Chapter 1], these groups decried racial intermarriage and fretted over the potential for coercive sexuality that suffused the employment relationship. White women were called into service as the 'guardians of the race,' a symbol of the most valuable property known to white society, to be protected at all costs from the encroachment of other races. (Backhouse 1999, p. 5)

Towards the end of "protecting" white womanhood and keeping the "races" "pure," a Saskatchewan statute, colloquially referred to as the "white women's labour law'" was enacted in 1912. It specified that "No person shall employ in any capacity any white woman or girl or permit any white woman or girl to reside or lodge in or to work in or, save as a bona fide customer in a public apartment thereof only, to frequent any restaurant, laundry or other place of business or amusement owned, kept or managed by any Japanese, Chinaman or other Oriental person."[7] Similar statutes were also passed in 1913 in the province of Manitoba (where indications are that it was never actually proclaimed), in 1914 in Ontario[8] and in 1919 in British Columbia[9] and remained in force for many years. Manitoba was the first province to repeal its Act (in 1940); Ontario followed in 1947 and British Columbia in 1968. The Saskatchewan statute, "veiled in racially neutral language, was not repealed until 1969" (Backhouse 1999, p. 15).

There is no doubt that interracial marriages have become more acceptable in Canada. Based on a secondary analysis of data collected in four national surveys in 1968, 1973, 1978 and 1983, Lambert and Curtis (1984) found a substantial drop in disapproval for black–white marriage. While in 1968, 59.8 percent of English-speaking Canadians expressed opposition, this dropped to 24.2 percent in 1983. Among French-speaking Quebeckers, the level of opposition also dropped from 38.2 percent in 1968 to 10.6 percent in 1983. In each of the four years, English-speaking Canadians expressed more opposition to interracial marriages than did French-speaking Quebeckers. The Project Canada national surveys of adults, which has examined intergroup attitudes in Canada since 1975, also reports a growing pattern of tolerance and acceptance of racial minorities, including increases in the percentages of those expressing approval towards racial intermarriage (Table 7.6) (Bibby 2001, p. 216).

Data from the 1996 census, however, suggests that the vast majority of Canadian couples, whether married or living common-law, with or without children, are racially homogeneous (Table 7.7).

---

7. The "White Woman's Labour Law" was amended in 1913 to delete all references to "Japanese" or "other Oriental persons" and further amended in 1919 and 1926. However, it was not repealed in Saskatchewan until the passage of the "Labour Standards Act, 1969."

8. In Ontario, "An Act to amend The Factory, Shop and Office Building Act" (Statutes of Ontario 1914, chapter 40, Section 2(1), specified: "No Chinese person shall employ in any capacity or have under his direction or control any female white person in any factory, restaurant or laundry." In response to strenuous objections from the Chinese Consulate General, it was amended in 1929. However, it was not repealed until 1947.

9. In British Columbia, "An Act to amend the 'Municipal Act,'" of 1919 was patterned after the initial amendment of the Saskatchewan Act and "prohibited the employment of 'any white woman or girl' in restaurants, laundries, places of business or amusement owned, kept, or managed by 'any Chinese person'" (Backhouse 1999, p. 18). In 1923, specific reference to Chinese employers was deleted and police officials were to use their discretion in determining whether or not white women should be allowed to work in a particular restaurant or laundry. The 1923 "Act for the Protection of Women and Girls in certain Cases" "also included 'Indian' women and girls as 'protected' categories of employees" (Backhouse 1999, p. 18). In British Columbia, the statute stood on the books until 1968.

TABLE 7.6

Approval of Intergroup Marriage: 1975 Through 1995

	1975	1980	1985	1990	1995
Whites and Natives	75%	80	83	84	84
Whites and Asians (Orientals)	66	75	78	82	83
Whites and East Indians/Pakistanis	58	66	72	77	80
Whites and Blacks	57	64	72	79	81

Source: Bibby 1995, p. 54.

TABLE 7.7

Racially Homogenous and Heterogeneous Couples, Canada, 1996

	Total Couples N=6 700 355	Married Couples, with children N=3 535 635	Common-law partners, with children N=434 950	Married Couples, without children N=2 244 085	Common-law partners, without children N=485 685
Racially homogeneous*	95.1%	96.3%	93.1%	96.3%	92.5%
Racially heterogeneous**	4.9%	3.7%	6.9%	3.7%	7.5%

*Includes: "Both visible minority same group" + "Both White" + "Both Aboriginal."

** Includes: "Both visible minority, different groups" + "One visible minority, one White and visible minority" + "One visible minority, one Aboriginal"+ "One visible minority, one Canadian, European or non-European" + "Both White and visible minority, same groups" + "Both white and visible minority, different groups" + "One White and visible minority, one White"+ "One White and visible minority, one Aboriginal" + "One White and visible minority, one Canadian, European or non-European" + "One White, One Aboriginal" + "One White, one Canadian, European or non-European" + "One Aboriginal, one Canadian, European or non-European (only)."

Source: Census Families by Population Group of Couple (Detailed) with Aggregations (1) and Census Family Structure for Couples (9) for Canada, 1996 Census (20% Sample Data).

Much attention has been devoted to why people marry interracially. One apparent reason among racial groups that are relatively small in number is simply that they are more likely than larger groups to interact with others of different "races" (Hwang, Saenz, and Aguirre 1997). Similarly, black–white marriages may be more numerous today in the United States simply because the races are interacting more ("Why Interracial ..." 1996; Yancey and Yancey 1998; Staples 1999c).

Psychoanalytic and psychological hypotheses suggest that whites marry interracially because of rebellion and hostility, guilt, or low self-esteem. Such explanations smack of racism and are not supported by research (Davidson 1992). Another theory is hypergamy: marrying up socioeconomically on the part of a white woman who, in effect, trades her socially defined superior racial status for the economically superior status of a middle- or upper middle-class non-white partner. It is important to note that empirical research provides little support for the theory of hypergamy.

Meanwhile, some African-American sociologists, worried about the unequal sex ratio among blacks and about black females' relatively small pool of "desirable" black men (Staples 1994, 1998) have expressed concern about black men's—especially educated black men's—choosing spouses from other races. For example, Robert Davis, who has been President of the Association of Black Sociologists, believes that black men are inclined to see white women as "the prize." In fact, he told a reporter for *Jet* magazine, "Some Black men will jump over three successful Black women just to be with a White woman." (Davis, in "Why Interracial ..." 1996). Meanwhile, some African-American women view black males' interracial relationships as "selling out"—sacrificing allegiance to one's racial heritage in order to date someone of higher racial status (Paset and Taylor 1991).

Having said all this, we note that at least one study of 40 black–white interracially married couples found, simply, that "with few exceptions, this group's motives for marriage do not appear to be any different from those of individuals marrying ... within their own race" (Porterfield 1982, p. 23).

INTERETHNIC MARRIAGES Karol Krotki and Colin Reid (1994, p. 21) refer to ethnic intermarriage, somewhat apocalyptically, as "the route to the melting pot and assimilation." Ethnic intramarriage, or ethnic endogamy, occurs when a person marries another of the same ethnic or cultural origin as him/herself. Those who marry exogamously are said to be more assimilated than those who do not (Richard 1991).

An analysis of ethnic intermarriage using census data for 1871 and 1971 found that the overall level of ethnic intermarriage increased from 17.1 percent in 1871 to 24 percent in 1971 (Richard 1991). While husbands were overwhelming endogamous in 1871 and 83 percent married spouses of the same ethnic origin, only 63 percent did so in 1971. Native-born Irish, Scottish, and German husbands went from being "overwhelmingly endogamous in 1871 to being overwhelmingly exogamous by 1971" (Kalbach 2001, p. 113). While increases in marital assimilation did occur among French husbands during this time span, they remained largely endogamous.

More recently, Madeline Kalbach (2000) has examined "ethnicity and the altar" in Canada from 1871 to 1991. She reports that over this time period, ethnic intermarriage has increased both overall and for specific ethnic-origin groups. The highest proportions of ethnic exogamy are exhibited by those of Northern, Western, and Eastern European origins, followed by the more recent immigrant groups such as the Greeks, Italians, Portuguese, Latin/Central/South Americans, and Blacks/Carribeans. Asians have the lowest proportions of ethnic exogamy.

Kalbach's analysis found that in 1991, husbands were generally more likely than wives to ethnically outmarry, regardless of ethnic origin. In addition, foreign-born husbands and wives had significantly lower levels of ethnic exogamy than their native-born counterparts. More specifically, her research observes that:

> Germans exhibit the highest rates of ethnic exogamy, followed by Blacks/Carribeans and Italians. The more recent immigrant groups, that is, East Indian and Chinese, have the lowest rates of ethnic exogamy. Charter-group husbands and wives have relatively low rates of ethnic exogamy compared with most of the other groups because they are dominant numerically and culturally, and so do not have a shortage of potential mates to choose from. (p. 116)

Consistent with earlier research (Hurd 1964; Richard 1991), Kalbach reports that British- and French-origin individuals continue to be "most popular choices for a marriage mate" (p. 117). Among those who did not marry someone of the same ethnic or cultural origin as themselves, wives and husbands selected mates who were British or French, followed by those of other European groups (e.g., Italian, Ukrainian, Dutch, Polish). However, those who were Chinese, East Indian, Arab, Latin/Central/South American and Black/Caribbean, selected other visible minorities (e.g., Filipinos, West Asians, Indo-Pakistanis) as their spouse when they married outside of their ethnic or cultural group.

Kalbach points out that although ethnic intermarriage has demonstrably increased over the course of the twentieth century, "it is not known whether the sons and daughters of husbands and wives in Canada who chose to ethnically intermarry will be influenced by either parent's ethnocultural identity" (p. 119). While some studies conducted in the United States suggest that this is the case (Lieberson and Waters 1988), others report that low levels of ethnic identity characterize children in mixed marriages.

Heterogamy and Marital Stability

Marital success can be measured in terms of stability—whether or how long the union lasts—and the happiness of the partners. Marital stability is not synonymous with marital happiness because in some instances unhappy spouses remain married, whereas less unhappy partners may choose to separate. In general, social scientists find that marriages that are homogamous in age, education, religion, and race are most stable (Heaton, Albrecht, and Martin 1985; Kalmijn 1998).

We can offer at least three explanations for any differences in marital stability that may exist. First, significant differences in values and interests between partners can create a lack of mutual understanding, resulting in emotional gaps. One in-depth study of 17 married interracial couples concluded that from the view of outsiders, the union is interracial. From the inside, however, the spouses themselves may see their union as "cross-cultural" (Johnson and Warren 1994).

Second, such marriages are likely to create conflict between the partners and other groups, such as parents, relatives, and friends. Then too, continual discriminatory pressure from the broader society may create undue marital stress. As one interracially married husband put it, "People's heads almost whiplashed off their necks when we walked down the street together" (in Romano and Trescott 1992, p. 91). Deprived of a social network of support, partners may find it more difficult to maintain their union in times of crisis.

Finally, a higher divorce rate among heterogamous marriages may reflect the fact that these partners are likely to be less conventional in their values and behaviour. Such unconventional people may divorce more readily if things begin to go wrong, rather than remain unhappily, though stably, married.

Heterogamy and Human Values

It is important to note the difference between scientific information and values. Social science can tell us that the stability of heterogamous marriages may be lower than that of homogamous marriages, but many people do not want to limit their social contacts—including potential marriage partners—to socially similar people. Although many people may retain a warm attachment to their racial or ethnic community, social and political change has been in the direction of breaking down those barriers. People committed to an open society find intermarriage to be an important symbol, whether or not it is a personal choice, and do not wish to discourage this option.

From this perspective we can think of the negative data on heterogamy and marital stability not as a discouragement to marriage, but in terms of its utility in helping couples be aware of possible problems. Intermarrying couples such as Jeremy and Laura may anticipate and talk through the differences in their lifestyles rather than becoming prematurely defeated.

The data on heterogamy may also be interpreted to mean that it is common values and lifestyles that contribute to stability. A heterogamous pair may have common values that transcend their differences in background. Furthermore, some problems of interracial (or other heterogamous) marriages have to do with social disapproval and lack of social support from either race.

But individuals can choose to work to change the society into one in which heterogamous marriage will be more accepted and hence will pose fewer problems. Then, too, to the degree that ethnic, religious, or economically heterogamous marriages increase in number, they are less likely to be troubled by the reactions of society. Again we see that private troubles—or choices—are intertwined with public issues; social changes are needed to make heterogamous marriages work. Finally, "it seems untenable ... to assume that heterogamy can lead only to negative consequences for the marital relationship" (Haller 1981, p. 786). If people are able to cross ethnic, class, or religious boundaries and at the same time share important values, they may open doors to a varied and exciting relationship.

Until this point in the chapter we have been discussing some of the events and motivations that bring a couple to marry or not to marry. The final section of this chapter will lay some of the groundwork for later chapters of this text by looking ahead to see how these factors influence the long-term happiness and stability of marriage.

MARRIAGE: WHEN AND WHY

A couple's happiness in marriage frequently depends on when and why they married. In this section we will look first at the relationship between marital stability and age at marriage. Then we will discuss some reasons for marrying that are less likely than others to lead to happiness.

The Stability of Early and Late Marriages

Statistics show that marriages are more likely to be stable when partners are in their 20s or older. Marriages that occur when women are over 30 may be slightly more stable than those that take place in their 20s, but the most significant distinction is between teenage and all other marriages.

Teenage marriages are twice as likely to end in divorce as marriages of those in their 20s (Norton and Moorman 1987). Social scientists generally maintain that people who marry young are less apt to be emotionally or psychologically prepared to select a mate or to perform marital roles. Low socioeconomic origins, coupled with school failure or lack of interest in school, are associated with early marriages. Higher fertility and economic deprivation are also associated with early marriages (Hayes 1987; Teti and Lamb 1989).

Age itself is probably not the key variable in determining the likelihood of a marriage succeeding. Rather, it seems likely that one's age at marriage is associated with other elements contributing to marital instability, such as parental dissatisfactions accompanying precocious marriage, social and economic handicaps, lowered educational achievement (South 1995), premarital pregnancy or the female's attitude toward the pregnancy condition, courtship histories including length of acquaintance and engagement, personality characteristics, and the rapid onset of parental responsibilities. According to one study (Booth and Edwards 1985), however, marrying before age 20 remained a significant predictor of divorce even after all of these factors were statistically controlled for or taken into consideration. Respondents often mentioned sexual infidelity as a reason for conflict. As a result, the researchers hypothesized that teens who marry do so when their unmarried peers are experimenting sexually with more than one partner and before they are emotionally ready or willing to relinquish this behaviour. In the words of the researchers:

> It is striking that the role performance variable which best accounts for instability has to do with a lack of sexual exclusiveness. What is intriguing is that this perceived problem coincides with the peak in sexual interest, especially among males, hinting at the possibility that part of the instability experienced may have a biosocial origin. Perhaps individuals constrained to limit their sexual activity to a single individual at a time in their life when variety is important develop a pattern of acting out their impulses throughout much of their life. (p. 73)

Although one's age at marriage is only one factor contributing to marital stability or instability, age still is associated with maturity, and sociologist David Knox (1975) has isolated four elements of maturity that he considers to be critical: emotional, economic, relationship, and value maturity.

EMOTIONAL MATURITY The emotionally mature person has high self-esteem, which permits a greater degree of intimacy and interdependence in a relationship, as we saw in Chapter 4. Emotional maturity allows people to respond appropriately to situations. When conflict arises, emotionally mature

people aim to resolve it, rather than becoming defensive or threatening to end the relationship.

ECONOMIC MATURITY Economic maturity implies the ability to support oneself and a partner if necessary. Especially for teenagers who have had little formal training or other job preparation, economic problems can put heavy strains on a marriage. Without a decent wage, people's physical and emotional energy can be drained as they try to scrape together enough to live on. Developing a loving relationship under these conditions is extremely difficult.

RELATIONSHIP MATURITY Relationship maturity involves the skill of communicating with a partner. People with this kind of maturity are able to (1) understand their partner's point of view, (2) make decisions about changing behaviour a partner doesn't like, (3) explain their own points of view to their partner, and (4) ask for changes in their partner's behaviour when they believe this is appropriate. Without the willingness and skills to understand each other and to make themselves understood, it is difficult or impossible for a couple to maintain intimacy.

VALUE MATURITY Value maturity allows people to recognize and feel confident about their own personal values. By their mid-20s most people have developed a sense of their own values. A high school senior or a first-year university student, however, may still have a number of years of testing and experiencing before he or she reaches value maturity.

Age, then, is an important variable in determining a relationship's potential for success. We can measure age objectively; that is, statistics can tell us how age relates to marital stability. Other factors are more subjective; they have to do with the explanations people give for marrying a certain person. But these reasons are also associated with the success of a relationship.

Reasons for Marrying

The reasons people give for marrying are far more complex than "because we are in love." A combination of many complicated situations and needs motivates people to marry. We'll look at several common reasons why people marry—first, those that are less likely to lead to a stable marriage, and second, more positive reasons—and see how each relates to the probability of a marriage's success.

PREMARITAL PREGNANCY   One problematic reason for marriage is premarital pregnancy. Recent research suggests that nonmarital pregnancy today may actually thwart a woman's opportunities for later marriage, because some potential husbands may view her as stigmatized or as requiring undue financial support, and also because the time and activities of child care limit her activities in the marriage market (Bennett, Bloom, and Miller 1995). When premarital pregnancy does lead to marriage, research has identified a consistent relationship between premarital pregnancy and unhappiness in marriage (see, for example, Norton and Moorman 1987). Ironically, teenage women who marry to avoid single parenthood often become single parents after all. Research indicates that a premarital birth is most associated with subsequent marital breakup, followed by premarital pregnancy and no premarital pregnancy, in that order (Teachman 1983; Teti and Lamb 1989).

There are several reasons for this. First, the marriage is forced to occur at a time not planned. Second, babies are expensive, and a couple not financially prepared for the costs can be overwhelmed. Third, "babies shatter goals": Teenage parents, for example, are less likely to attain educational goals, whether high school or beyond; and they are more likely to have lower incomes and occupational status, to have more children than they would like, and to go on welfare (Hayes 1987). Fourth, the in-law relationship may be marred if parents resent their child's marital partner for having brought about a marriage they did not want or viewed as too early. Finally, the couple may not ever have decided they were compatible enough for marriage and may resent each other, either overtly or subconsciously, during the marriage. Of course, other options—abortion, giving the child up for adoption, or raising the child as a single parent—also have an impact on the lives of the young couple. And values and emotions may vary widely among individuals. Still, it is difficult to be encouraging about young, pregnancy-inspired marriages, and some churches have been reluctant to sanction them unless the young couple is unusually mature.

There are certainly exceptions to this scenario. Factors that reduce the damaging effects of pregnancy-inspired or teenage marriage include having a supportive family (giving both financial and emotional support), being able to remain in school and then become steadily employed, controlling further fertility and being older when the pregnancy occurs (Furstenberg, Brooks-Gunn, and Morgan 1987).

Whether for better or for worse, when compared to their counterparts in the 1970s, Canadian teenagers who became pregnant in the 1990s were less likely to carry their pregnancy to term. While in 1974, two-thirds of pregnant teenagers gave birth, in 1994, only half did so. Canadian teenagers who became pregnant at the end of the twentieth century were also less likely to be married or to get married prior to the birth of their child. In contrast to the situation among teen mothers in the 1970s, teen mothers in the 1990s were more likely to be single (25 percent in 1974 versus 81 percent in 1994). Moreover, when compared to Canadian teenagers in the 1970s, Canadian teenagers in the 1990s who were unmarried were also less likely to give up their child for adoption (Vanier Institute of the Family 2000, p. 74).

REBOUND   People may tend to fall in love more easily when they're on the rebound. Sociologist Elaine Walster (1965) experimented with the concept of love on the rebound. She concluded that when people have low self-esteem, due to having been broken up with, they may be less discriminating in choosing love partners and may fall in love more easily.

Marriage on the rebound occurs when a person marries very shortly after breaking up in another relationship. To marry on the rebound is undesirable because the wedding occurs as a reaction to a previous partner, rather than being based on real love for the new partner.

REBELLION   Marriage for the sake of rebellion occurs when young people marry primarily because their parents disapprove. Social-psychological theory and research show that parental interference can increase feelings of romantic attraction between partners (Katz and Liu 1988); this has been called the *Romeo and Juliet effect*. As with marriage on the rebound, the wedding is a response to someone else (one's parents) rather than to one's partner.

ESCAPE   Some people marry to escape an unhappy home situation. The working-class male who hasn't gone on to higher education, for instance, may reason that getting married is the one way he can keep for himself any money he makes instead of handing it over to his parents. Or, denied the opportunity to go to college or university, working-class youths may use marriage as an escape from parental authority (Katz and Liu 1988).

PHYSICAL APPEARANCE Marrying solely because of the physical attractiveness of one's partner seldom leads to lifelong happiness. For one thing, beauty is in the eye of the beholder, and if the beholder finds he or she really doesn't like the partner, that beauty is certain to diminish. Second, the physical beauty of youth changes as partners age. The person who married for beauty often feels she or he has been cheated. After a time, there is less to be attracted to.

LONELINESS Sometimes people, especially older adults, marry because they don't want to grow old alone. Marrying is not always the solution, for people can be lonely within marriage if the relationship isn't a strong one. In other words, it is the relationship rather than the institution that banishes loneliness.

PITY AND OBLIGATION Some partners marry because one of them feels guilty about terminating a relationship: A sense of pity or obligation substitutes for love. Sometimes this pity or obligation takes the form of marrying in order to help or to change a partner, as when a woman marries a man because she believes that her loyal devotion and encouragement will help him quit drinking and live up to his potential. Such marriages don't often work: The helper finds that his or her partner won't change so easily, and the pitied partner comes to resent being the object of a crusade.

SOCIAL PRESSURE Parents, peers, and society in general all put pressure on singles to marry. Approval (or disapproval) of a partner from family and friends may be important in a relationship's stability, especially for women (Cate and Lloyd 1992, pp. 79–80). This may be particularly true for ethnic minority groups, especially recent immigrant groups, whose cultures are more collectivist than individualistic.

The expectations built up during courtship exert a great deal of social pressure to go through with the marriage. As engagements are announced or as people become increasingly identified as a couple by friends and family, it becomes more difficult to back out. In most cases, such a situation will not be problematic. Still, breaking an engagement or a less formal commitment is probably less stressful than divorcing later or living together unhappily.

ECONOMIC ADVANCEMENT Marrying for economic advancement occurs in all social classes. Young divorced mothers may consider remarriage primarily because they are exhausted from the struggle of supporting and caring for their small children; and working single women often associate marrying with the freedom to stay home at least part of the time. Men, too, can marry for reasons of economic advancement. This can be especially true in some professions in which social connections provide important business ties.

Is marrying for economic advancement the right reason? The answer depends on the individuals. Certainly the thrust of this book is to encourage intimacy and a strong emotional relationship as a basis for marriage. A person going into a marriage mainly for economic reasons should be very honest with her or his partner, so that both know what the marriage means to the other.

MORE POSITIVE REASONS FOR MARRYING
What are some positive reasons for marrying? Knox (1975) lists three: companionship, emotional security, and a desire to parent and raise children.

Marriage is a socially approved union for developing closeness with another human being. In this environment, legitimate needs for companionship— to love and to be loved by someone else—can be satisfied. Marrying for emotional security implies that a person seeks the stable structure of marrying to help ensure the maintenance of a close interpersonal relationship over time. Although most people do not marry only to have children (and this alone may not be a positive reason for marrying), many regard children as a valuable part of married life. "The benefits of love, sex, companionship, emotional security, and children can be enjoyed without marriage. But marriage provides the social approval and structure for experiencing these phenomena with the same person over time" (Knox 1975, p. 143).

In Chapter 8 we will examine marriage as an institution and an intimate relationship. It seems to us that the most positive motivation toward marriage involves the goal of making permanent the relationships of love and intimacy, discussed in Chapter 4. This theme will be repeated throughout this section of the text.

IN SUM

The Western association of love and marriage is unique to our modern culture. Historically, marriages were often arranged in the marriage market, as business deals. Many elements of the basic exchange (a man's providing financial support in exchange for the woman's childbearing and child-rearing capabilities, domestic services, and sexual availability) remain.

What attracts people to each other? Two important factors are homogamy and physical attractiveness. Some elements of homogamy are propinquity, social pressure, feeling at home with each other, and the fair exchange. Three patterns of courtship familiar in our society are dating, getting together, and cohabitation.

Besides homogamy and the degree of intimacy developed during courtship, two other factors related to the success of a marriage are a couple's age at marriage and their reasons for marrying. People who marry too young are less likely to stay married; and there are several negative reasons for marrying that can lead to unhappiness or divorce.

If potential marriage unhappiness can be anticipated, breaking up before marriage is by far the best course of action, however difficult it seems at the time. A certain number of courting relationships will end in this fashion.

But many couples will go on to marry. Chapter 8 describes what form the marriage is likely to take and some choices the couple makes in setting up their marriage.

Key Terms

arranged marriage
assortive mating
bride price
cohabitation
convenience
courtly love
courtship
date rape (acquaintance rape)
dowry
emancipation
endogamy
exchange theory
exogamy
free-choice culture
getting together
heterogamy
homogamy

hypergamy
hypogamy
imaging
interracial marriage
"Linus blanket"
marriage gradient
marriage market
marriage squeeze
pool of eligibles
sex ratio
stimulus-values-roles (SVR) theory of courtship
testing
theory of complementary needs
two-stage marriage

Study Questions

1. Explain how our notion of romantic love came about.

2. How are modern marriages similar to arranged marriages? How are they different?

3. Compare the way we choose marriage partners with the process at a marketplace. Why do women in the marriage market tend to be more serious shoppers than men?

4. Give four reasons people are likely to be homogamous. What difficulties are people in heterogamous relationships likely to face?

5. Why do you think homogamous marriages are more stable than heterogamous marriages? Does this necessarily mean that homogamous marriages are more successful? Why or why not?

6. Explain why the two aspects of courtship—getting to know each other better and gaining commitment to marriage—are potentially contradictory.

7. What problems did Margaret Mead think were caused by dating? Do we still face these problems today?

8. What does the idea that "normal" men are capable of date rape or acquaintance rape say about gender scripts today and whether, how, and how much they are changing?

9. Differentiate the four common patterns of cohabitation put forth by Ridley and his associates. Which are more useful as training grounds for marriage? Why?

10. If possible, talk to a few married couples you know who lived together before marrying, and ask them how their cohabiting experience influenced their transition to marriage. How do their answers compare with survey findings presented in this chapter?

11. Do you agree that age itself is not the key variable in determining a marriage's likelihood of succeeding? Describe what you think to be critical.

12. Discuss some problematic and more positive reasons for marrying, and point out how each relates to the probability of a marriage's success.

Suggested Readings

Buss, David M. 1994. *The Evolution of Desire: Strategies of Human Mating.* New York: Basic Books. Analysis of human courtship and mating from an evolutionary psychology, or biosociological, perspective.

Cate, Rodney M. and Sally A. Lloyd. 1992. *Courtship.* Newbury Park, CA: Sage. This readable book, one in the Sage series on close relationships, reviews the social scientific literature on courtship.

Crohn, John. 1995. *Mixed Matches: How to Create Successful Interracial, Interethnic, and Interfaith Relationships.* New York: Fawcett Columbine. Crohn is a psychologist and therapist who gives good advice based on his clinical experience.

Kaplan, Marion A., ed. 1985. *The Marriage Bargain: Women and Dowries in European History.* New York: Harrington Park. This collection of five essays by social and family historians explores the relationships between dowries and economic conditions, and between dowries and women's rights and position in society. It offers significant insights into the historical functions of marriage.

Wu, Zheng, 2000. *Cohabitation: An Alternative Form of Family Living.* Don Mills, Ontario: Oxford University Press. A comprehensive examination of cohabitation in Canadian society which also considers the legal and public policy implications of this demographic shift.

On the Net

1) Marriage Customs
http://womensissues.about.com/cs/marriagecustoms/

2) Marriage
http://marriage.about.com/msubxul.htm?once=trve&

3) Colorful Couples
Organization of interracial couples for heterogamous couples of all backgrounds
http://www.kudoku.com/colorful/

4) Why do some relationships last and others do not? Read an article that discusses these questions at
http://www.apa.org/releases/relation.html

5) A guide on Love, Respect and Abuse in Dating Relationships
http://www.dvirc.org.au/whenlove

Marriage: A Unique Relationship

MARRIAGE IS NOT AN ANSWER, BUT A

SEARCH, A PROCESS, A SEARCH FOR

LIFE, JUST AS DIALOGUE IS A SEARCH

FOR TRUTH.

SIDNEY JOURARD

You'll recall that in Chapter 1, we defined families as kin relationships in which people form an economic unit and care for their young, consider their identity to be significantly attached to the group, and are committed to maintaining that group over time. Although certainly not always, marriage is often the gateway to family life. Being married is a unique relationship. Despite wide variations, all marriages have an important element in common: the commitment that partners have made—and made publicly—to each other. This is the subject of this chapter.

In the discussions that follow we'll look especially at how getting married announces a personal life-course decision. In keeping with one of the themes of this text, we'll discuss how marrying is a decision-making trade-off. Brides and grooms discard prior alternatives and are no longer available in the marriage market. This is one expectation inherent in the marriage premise, described in this chapter. We'll look at how relationships throughout marriage reflect spouses' personal choices, either made actively or by default, for the kind of relationship a couple shares is a product of the values, expectations, and efforts partners invest in it. One way to design and retain the kind of relationship spouses want, as we will see, is to write a personal marriage agreement. To begin, we explore the relationship between marriage and kinship.

MARRIAGE AND KINSHIP

Who are your kin? Anthropologists have defined kinship as the social organization of the entire family, including blood, or **consanguineous** relatives, and **conjugal** relationships acquired through marriage. (The word *consanguineous* comes from the Latin prefix *com*, which means "joint," and the Latin word *sanguineus*, which means "of blood." The word *conjugal* comes from the Latin word *conjugere*, which means "to join together.") Parents and grandparents are consanguineous relations; spouses and in-laws are conjugal relatives; aunts and uncles may be either. Certain rights and obligations accompany one's kinship status. For example, you may expect your grown sister or brother to attend your wedding or graduation.

As you may have already noticed, the concept of kinship is closely related to that of *extended family*. An extended family includes parents and children, along with other relatives, such as in-laws, grandparents, aunts and uncles, and cousins. Some groups, such as gay male and lesbian families (Aulette 1994; Bould 1993; Weston 1991), also have "fictive" or "virtual" kin (a *compadrazo* in Hispanic families)—friends who are so close that they are hardly distinguished from actual relatives.

Meanwhile, it may be the case that every society has a **dominant dyad**—a centrally important twosome, or dyad, that symbolizes the culture's basic values and kinship obligations (Hsu 1971). Lord Hyde's 1886 definition of marriage as "the voluntary union for life of one man and one woman to the exclusion of all others" suggests how the husband–wife dyad is expected to take precedence over any and all others. According to sociologist Talcott Parsons (1943), our kinship system is generally not based on vital extended family ties but, instead comprised of "interlocking conjugal families" in which married people are common members of their **family of orientation** (the family they grew up in) and of their **family of procreation** (the one formed by marrying and having children). Parsons sees the husband–wife bond and the resulting family of procreation as the most meaningful "inner circle" of kin relations, surrounded by decreasingly important outer circles. However, he noted that his model was not equally applicable to all families and that, for example, lower socioeconomic classes rely on meaningful ties to their extended kin.

In the majority of non-European countries, the extended family (as opposed to the married couple or nuclear family) is the basic family unit (Murdock 1949; Ingoldsby and Smith 1995). Sociologist Maureen Baker (1996, p. 6) observes that in both Europe and North America, nuclear families have always been the most common living arrangement and that at no time in Canadian history "has it been a widespread practice for married couples to live with parents." However, while noting that "[e]xtended family living was... more typical among certain cultural groups such as some First Nations people, Asians, South Europeans, Africans, and Caribbeans," she emphasizes that the "extended family remains important in Canada and elsewhere as a living arrangement as well as a support group."

> Many Southern Europeans, Middle Eastern people, and Asians living in Canada and abroad maintain close ties with siblings and parents after marriage. Even when they do not share a residence, relatives may live next door or in the neighbourhood, visit regularly, telephone daily, assist with childcare, provide economic and emotional support, and help find employment and accommodation for one another. (Baker 1996, p. 6)

Research on French Acadians in Ste. Marie, New Brunswick also suggests the enduring importance of the extended family in Canada (Davis 1985).

Recent Asian immigrants are also likely to emphasize extended kin ties over the marriage relationship (Glick, Bean, and Van Hook 1997). Among Chinese and Japanese immigrants, *hsiao* defines the dominant dyad—that of adult child (especially son) and aging parent (especially father). *Hsiao* requires that an adult child provide aid and affection to parents even when this might conflict with marital obligations (Lin and Liu 1993). However, Nancy Howell (1996, p. 134) notes that immigration often results in the "reduction of extended family to nuclear family."

Members of ethnic groups who live in and expect extended multinuclear families as units of production, consumption, and household composition in the old country often find themselves effectively living in a nuclear family after immigration, due to distance from extended kin and the high cost of the kinds of accommodations in Canada which would permit joint households.

In the following passage, a Vietnamese refugee describes his reaction to housing patterns that reflect nuclear family norms and husband-wife as the dominant dyad:

> Before I left Vietnam, three generations lived together in the same group. My mom, my family including wife and seven children, my elder brother, his wife and three children, my little brother and two sisters—we live in a big house. So when we came here we are thinking of being united in one

place. But there is no way. However, we try to live as close as possible. (in Gold 1993, p. 303)

Housing architecture is similarly discouraging to many Muslim families—from India, Pakistan, or Bangladesh, for example—who would prefer to live in extended households (Nanji 1993).

Kinship Obligations and Marriage Relationships

Thirty years ago, family sociologist Jesse Bernard noted what she called a **parallel relationship pattern** among spouses in the working class; she distinguished this pattern from the **interactional pattern** of middle-class marriages. In a parallel relationship, the husband was expected mainly to be a hard-working provider and the wife, a good housekeeper and cook. "Companionship in the sense of exchange of ideas or opinions or the enhancement of personality by verbal play or conversation is not considered a basic component in this pattern" (Bernard 1964, p. 687). In the interactional pattern which dominates Canadians' goals for marriage today, partners expect companionship and intimacy as well as more practical benefits.

Depending on individual preferences and socioeconomic backgrounds, however, Canadian spouses can emphasize either practical or emotional benefits in marriage. The more practical style has been called **utilitarian marriage**; the more emotional, **intrinsic marriage** (Cuber and Harroff 1965). In intrinsic unions, the husband–wife relationship is "interactional" and an end in itself. Intrinsic marriages rest on intimacy and mutual affection between partners. Mates strive to fulfill as much as possible of each other's personal needs for sexual expression and companionship. In utilitarian marriages, the emphasis is not necessarily on the husband–wife dyad as centrally important: probably the relationship is "parallel." Marriage may be a means to other ends, such as satisfying one's parents' wishes according to *hsiao* or uniting two distinct kinship networks of similar ethnicity. Over time, however, recent immigrants may gradually assume (that is, become acculturated to) norms that more highly value intrinsic marriages (Chilman 1993; Wilkinson 1993). We should not forget, meanwhile, that even for fifth- or sixth-generation Canadians, utilitarian marriage may provide material luxuries or career advancement or simply basic economic security.

Moreover, in real life very few marriages are either completely utilitarian or completely intrinsic. Rather, these two types represent polar opposites of an imaginary line or continuum. Real-life marriages fall somewhere on the continuum, combining elements of pragmatism and emotional sharing in various degrees. Between the two extremes is an almost limitless variety of types of marriage relationships. Recognizing the variety of marriage types (that is, that there are not just two polar opposites, intrinsic and utilitarian) sociologist Stephen Marks (1989) has created a more elaborate model for understanding couple dynamics.

Family, Outside Interests, and Marriage Relationships

Marks developed a model that depicts the self as a triangle (see Figure 8.1). One corner of the triangle is called the inner-corner and represents a person's private self. The second is the partnership-corner of the self and represents a person's interest in his or her spouse. The third-corner represents interest in something outside the couple's relationship. The third-corner "may be anything—God or a guru, parenting, work, fishing, TV, sports, friendships, psychoanalysis, and so on" (p. 20).

Marks analyzed couple relationships according to how each individual's triangular self relates to that of their partner. For example, in **romantically-fused couples**, both individuals focus only on their partnership-corner. "Enormous energy" fuses the couple together (p. 19). In **dependency-distancing couples**, one partner focuses on the marriage; however, the other partner puts most energy outside the relationship—into the third-corner. The partner focused on the partnership becomes "dependent" on the union while the other distances him or herself from the relationship. "There is maximum dynamic tension in this arrangement: the more the dependent one pursues the distancer, the more the distancer pulls away, and vice versa" (p. 19). In a third couple type, the **separate couple**, both individuals are focused outside the marriage and distance themselves from their spouses. In Marks' words,

> Despite the scant energy flowing from either one's partnership-corner to the other's, this arrangement may foster more comfort than the dependency-distancing pattern, so long as there is symmetry in

the strength of their respective third-corner pulls.... Separate partnerships can be very stable and durable while remaining rather low on marital quality. (pp. 19–20)

Having established these three basic relationship models, Marks went on to elaborate four varieties of couple connectedness (see Figure 8.2). Here, Marks recognizes that each partner's focus actually rotates around his or her triangular self. Marks sees each of these four as valid options for a satisfying marriage relationship. Partners with a **balanced connection** move their focus from one corner of each individual's triangular self to another. Sometimes a spouse is focused on her or his private self and needs quiet time. At other times the partners focus on each other; at still other times, on some outside interest. Each partner brings what he or she gains from an outside interest to the couple relationship, making the marriage more interesting.

> Specifically, in a high-quality marriage, part of what makes our partner more 'attractive' is his or her 'alternative attractions' ...; a partner without them would be fused to the partnership, insufferably dependent, and lacking sufficient opportunity either to stimulate and develop him/herself or to stimulate the other partner. (p. 24)

In a more **couple-centred connection**, the spouses retain elements of all three corners of the self but the couple is more romantically fused, focusing mainly on their relationship. We can think of the couple-centred marriage as highly intrinsic. In a **family-centred connection,** spouses focus on a joint or shared third-corner, such as parenting and/or relations with extended kin. In a couple with a **loose connection**, both partners focus mainly (although not exclusively) on their individual third-corners— their separate careers, hobbies, or friends, for example.[1] With an appreciation for the variety of

---

1. You might recognize that Marks' concept of romantically-fused couples is somewhat similar to Crosby's A-frame relationship, described in Chapter 4. Marks' concept, separateness, resembles Crosby's H-frame relationship. Crosby (Chapter 4) did not elaborate a relationship that can be compared to Marks' dependency-distancing couple. Meanwhile, Marks' ideas of balanced, couple-centred, family, and loose connection might all be thought of as versions of Crosby's M-frame relationship. Going further with this comparison of Marks' and Crosby's ideas, we might think of a loosely connected couple as having an M-frame relationship with aspects of an H-frame relationship.

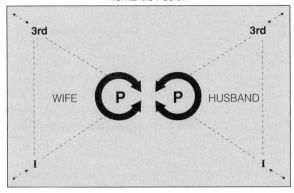

Romantic Fusion

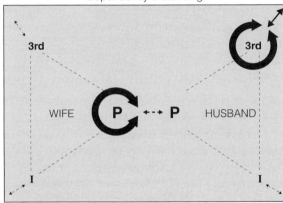

Dependency-Distancing

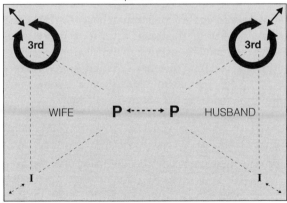

Separateness

Note: P = partnership-corner; I = inner-corner; 3rd = third-corner

FIGURE **8.1**

Three Relationship Types with Each Partner's Self Conceptualized as a Triangle. (Source: Stephen R. Marks. "Toward A Systems Theory of Marital Quality." *Journal of Marriage and the Family* **51 (February) 1989: 15–26.)**

ways that couples can be connected—and for the concepts *utilitarian* and *intrinsic unions*—we turn now to some characteristic relationship patterns in Canadian marriages.

FIVE MARRIAGE RELATIONSHIPS

We can't look at every possible kind of relationship, but we can look at a few representative types based on the research of Cuber and Harroff, who conducted extensive interviews with upper middle-class married couples. From their interviews with 107 men and 104 women, Cuber and Harroff (1965) classified five kinds of marital relationships that act as useful prototypes. Two are closer to the utilitarian pole on the continuum; two are intrinsic; and one (conflict-habituated) is difficult to define as either utilitarian or intrinsic.

Although this classic study was done in the 1960s, the interactional qualities of marriage, which are its focus, are not so timebound. This research continues to be useful in the study of marriage and other long-term relationships. It is possible that gay and lesbian couples could recognize themselves in one or more of these relationships.

In identifying five types of marriage—conflict-habituated, devitalized, passive-congenial, vital, and total—Cuber and Harroff emphasize that their findings represent "different kinds of adjustment and conceptions of marriage, rather than degrees of marital happiness" (1965, p. 61). In other words, couples living in any of these relationships might or might not be satisfied with them. The relationships differ according to how spouses feel about their marriages. Some researchers also have found these relationship types among cohabitants (Clatworthy 1975, p. 77ff).

Conflict-Habituated Marriages

Couples with a **conflict-habituated marriage** experience considerable tension and unresolved conflict. Spouses habitually quarrel, nag, and bring up the past. As a rule, both spouses acknowledge their incompatibility and recognize the atmosphere of tension as normal.

Conflict-habituated relationships differ from those in which conflicts arise over specific issues. In conflict-habituated relationships, the subject of the argument

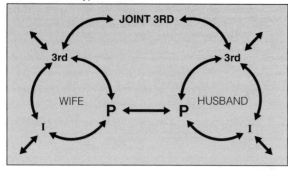

Type 1: Balanced Connection

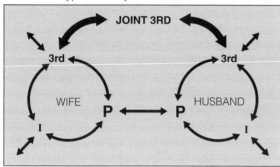

Type 2: Couple-Centred Connection

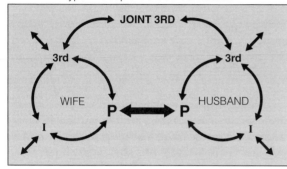

Type 3: Family-Centred Connection

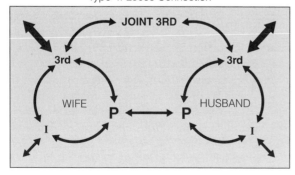

Type 4: Loose Connection

hardly seems important, and partners generally do not resolve, or expect to resolve, their differences. "Of course we don't settle any of the issues," said a veteran of 25 years of this type of marriage. "It's sort of a matter of principle not to. Because somebody would have to give in then and lose face for the next encounter" (Cuber and Harroff 1965, p. 45).

These relationships do not necessarily end with divorce. In fact, it has been suggested by some psychiatrists that for some partners this kind of marriage fulfills a need for conflict. In this sense, conflict-habituated relationships are intrinsic relationships, for they fulfill partners' emotional needs. Such relationships cannot be called intimate, however, for they are not based on mutual acceptance and support or on honest self-disclosure. And evidence suggests that such relationships have a negative impact on the couple's children (see Box 8.1, "Growing Up in a Conflict-Habituated Household.")

Devitalized Marriages

Partners in a **devitalized marriage** have typically been married several years, and over the course of time the relationship has lost its original zest, intimacy, and meaning. Once deeply in love, they recall spending a great deal of time together, enjoying sex, and having a close emotional relationship. Their present situation is in sharp contrast: They spend little time together, enjoy sex less, and no longer share many interests and activities. Most of their time together is "duty time" spent entertaining, planning and sharing activities with their children, and participating in community responsibilities and functions. Once an intrinsic union, the marriage has become utilitarian.

Cuber and Harroff found devitalized marriages to be exceedingly common among their respondents. They also found several reactions among devitalized partners. Some were accepting and tried to be "mature

FIGURE **8.2**

Four Types of Couple Connection with Each Partner's Focus Rotating Around His/Her Triangular Self. (Source: Stephen R. Marks. "Towards a Systems Theory of Marital Quality," *Journal of Marriage and the Family* 51 (February), 1989: 15–26.)

about it." As one wife explained, "There's a cycle to life. There are things you do in high school. And different things you do in college. Then you're a young adult. And then you're middle-aged. That's where we are now" (in Cuber and Harroff 1965, pp. 47–48). Others were resentful and bitter; and still others were ambivalent. From his study of a group of 50 marriages, psychoanalyst George Bach provides this description:

> Essentially they had resigned themselves to ... ritualized routines.... They were mutually protective associations who looked on their marriage as pretty much of a lost cause but felt it would be disloyal and ill-mannered to complain about it, especially since the loneliness of being unmarried would probably be worse. (Bach and Wyden 1970, pp. 47–48)

Emotional emptiness does not necessarily threaten the stability of a marriage. Many people, like the accepting wife just quoted, believe that the devitalized mode is appropriate for spouses who have been married several years. Devitalized partners frequently compare their relationship with others who have similar relationships, concluding that "marriage is like this—except for a few oddballs or pretenders who claim otherwise" (Cuber and Harroff 1965, p. 50).

Passive-Congenial Marriages

Partners in a **passive-congenial marriage** (utilitarian), like devitalized partners, emphasize qualities other than emotional closeness. These qualities may be different for different groups. Upper middle-class couples tend to emphasize civic and professional responsibilities and the importance of property, children, and reputation; working-class people focus on their need for economic security, the benefits of the basic exchange, and their hopes for their children.

Unlike the devitalized marriage, passive-congenial partners never expected marriage to encompass emotional intensity. Instead, they stress the sensibleness of their decision to marry. There is little conflict, but that does not mean there are no unspoken frustrations. And while there is little intimacy, these unions fulfill partners' needs for more casual companionships.

Passive-congenial marriages are less likely to end in divorce than are unions in which partners have unrealistic expectations of emotional intensity. Partners may decide to terminate passive-congenial unions, however, if they feel the marriage is not adequately fulfilling their more practical needs such as for economic support or professional advancement. Or one partner may discover that he or she wants greater intimacy from a relationship or may inadvertently fall in love with someone else.

Vital Marriages

In a **vital marriage**, a type of intrinsic marriage, being together and sharing are intensely enjoyable and important. As one husband said:

> The things we do together aren't fun intrinsically—the ecstasy comes from being together in the doing. Take her out of the picture and I wouldn't give a damn for the boat, the lake, or any of the fun that goes on out there. (Cuber and Harroff 1965, p. 55)

This statement should not lead you to believe that vital partners lose their separate identities, or that conflict does not occur in vital marriages. There is conflict, but it is more apt to centre on real issues rather than the "who said what first and when" and "I can't forget when you ..." that characterize conflict-habituated marriages. And vital partners try to settle disagreements quickly so they can resume the relationship that means so much to both.

Typically, vital partners consider sex important and pleasurable. "It seems to be getting better all the time," said one spouse, age 55. Instead of being dutifully performed as a ritual, sexuality pervaded vital partners' whole lives. A grandmother spoke about it this way:

> You can't draw the line between being in bed together and just being alive together. You can touch tenderly when you pass; you wait for the intimate touch in the morning. Even the scents you make in bed together are cherished. (in Cuber and Harroff 1965, pp. 135–36)

Enduring vital marriages may be a minority. Those in Cuber and Harroff's research often reported feeling

Growing up in a Conflict-Habituated Household

When Cuber and Harroff described the five relationship types in their data, they refused to make value judgments about one marital style as any better or worse than another. However, many social scientists have found that conflict-habituated parental relationships have a negative impact on the couple's children. Researchers divide children's behaviour problems into two categories: externalizing (aggression, lying, cheating, running away from home, disobeying at school, delinquency) and internalizing (withdrawal, depression, and anxiety). At least since the 1980s, researchers consistently have found a link between marital conflict and both types of behaviour problems in children (Erel and Burman 1995).

One study (Buehler et al. 1998) sampled 337 sixth-through eighth-grade girls and boys, aged ten through 15. Most families were white (three-quarters) and middle-class; 85 percent of the children had their own bedroom, for example. The parents of 87 percent of the children in the sample were married. The parents' average education level was somewhere between high school graduation and some university.

The youth were asked to fill out questionnaires that assessed their behaviour and any conflict between their parents. Externalizing behaviour problems were measured by students' agreeing or disagreeing with statements such as "I cheat a lot" or "I tease others a lot." Internalizing behaviour problems were measured by students' agreeing or disagreeing with statements such as "I am unhappy a lot" or "I worry a lot." The children were also asked how often their parents disagreed on certain topics. Then they were asked about the style of their parents' conflict. Overt parental conflict styles involved such things as the parents calling each other names, telling each other to shut up, or threatening one another in front of the child. Covert parental conflict styles included such things as trying to get the child to side with one parent, or asking the child to relay a message from one parent to the other because the parents didn't want to talk to each other.

The researchers found that conflict between parents was far from the only cause of children's behaviour problems. Nevertheless, for both girls and boys the

that their lifestyles were neither experienced nor understood by their associates. Even rarer than vital marriages are total marriages.

Total Marriages

Total marriages are also intrinsic. They are like vital marriages, only more multifaceted. "The points of vital meshing are more numerous—in some cases all of the important life foci are vitally shared" (Cuber and Harroff 1965, p. 58).

Spouses may share work life (similar jobs, same employer, or projects such as writing a book, making a film, or running a family business) and friends and leisure activities, as well as home life. They may orga-

nize their lives to make it possible to be alone together for long periods. Both vital and total marriages are emotionally intense, but the total marriage is more all-encompassing, whereas the vital marriage leaves areas of individual activity to each partner. Total marriages are rare, but they do exist and can endure.

On the negative side, total marriages are vulnerable to rapid disintegration if marital quality changes. They foster a mutual dependency that makes it difficult for the remaining partner to adjust in case of death or divorce. On the positive side, they provide a wide range of fulfillment focused on the couple as a unit.

This discussion points up three important facts. First, marriage is different from other sexual relation-

researchers did find a strong correlation between interparental conflict and behaviour problems. This relationship held true regardless of whether the parents were married or divorced. When parents displayed an overt conflict style, the youth were more likely to report externalizing behaviour problems; this relationship was stronger for fifth graders than it was for eighth graders. When parents displayed a more covert conflict style, the youth were more likely to report internalizing behaviour problems. In the researchers' words, "The results of our study confirm previous findings that hostile and sometimes violent ways of managing interparental disagreements place youth at risk for problem behaviours" (p. 130).

In another study of 55 Caucasian middle- and upper-middle-class five-year-olds (26 girls and 29 boys) and their married mothers, the mothers completed questionnaires on parent–child relations and interparental arguing that were mailed to them at home. Later, the mothers took their children to be observed in a university laboratory setting. The researchers found that marital discord was positively related both to children's externalizing and internalizing behaviour problems. However, this research also showed that the interparental conflict influenced the child's behaviour indirectly: Marital discord negatively affected the mother's relationship with her child, and the resultant poor parent–child relationship negatively affected the child's behaviour. The researchers concluded that, "if parents are able to maintain good relations with children in the face of marital conflict, the children may be buffered from the potential emotional fallout of the conflict" (Harrist and Ainslie 1998, p. 156).

Generally, these two studies and others show that choices about one's marital relations, conflicts, and conflict styles impact not only the spouses but their children. Whether children are better off in two-parent conflict-habituated households or in single-parent households is explored at length in Chapter 14.

ships, even cohabiting. Second, partners expect marriage to offer certain advantages, such as companionship, psychic and sexual intimacy, and emotional support. Third, marriage involves more responsibilities than do other sexual relationships.

THE MARRIAGE PREMISE

By getting married, the majority of Canadian partners accept the responsibility to keep each other primary in their lives. All married individuals vow to work hard to ensure that their relationship continues. Essentially, this is the **marriage premise**. We can look more closely at the two important elements of this definition: permanence and primariness.

Expectations of Permanence

A wedding is a community event marking a bride and groom's passage into adult family roles. Whether spouses love each other has only recently been considered important, as we saw in Chapter 7. And with few exceptions, marriages were always thought of as permanent, lifelong commitments. Partly, this definition of marriage as permanent was related to the assumed need for spouses to stay together in order to effectively raise any children born to the union.

Although it is statistically less permanent now than it has ever been in our society, marriage, more than any other relationship, holds the **expectation of permanence**. Standing on the outside, looking in, the vast majority of Canadian teenagers, regardless of family background, "say they expect—not *hope*" to marry and to stay with the same partner for life (Bibby 2001, p. 144) (Table 8.1).

The marriage contract remains a legal contract between two people that cannot be broken without permission of society or the state. Most religions urge permanence in marriage. In our society, couples usually vow publicly to stay together "until death do us part" or "so long as we both shall live." People enter marriage expecting—hoping—that mutual affection and commitment will be lasting.

Expectations for permanence derive from the fact that, historically, marriage has been a practical social institution. Economic security and responsible child rearing required marriages to be permanent, and even at the turn of the twentieth century parents only occasionally outlived the departure of their last child from home to become a couple household again.

Today, as we've seen in earlier chapters, marriage is somewhat less important for economic security. However, as we saw in Chapter 1, some social scientists are concerned that while marriage is important for responsible child rearing, individuals are too quick to reconsider their vow of permanence (Popenoe 1996, Blankenhorn 1995). Then too, another function of marriage has become more important for most people. They expect marriage to provide emotional support and love. It might be said that we are coming closer to realizing a prediction, made by social theorist Herbert Spencer in 1876, that some day "union by law" would no longer be the essential part of marriage. Rather, "union by affection will be held of primary moment" (Spencer, H., 1876, cited in Burgess and Locke 1953, p. 29).

Today, marriages of intimacy are usually held together by more than mutual affection, and that is why marriages remain more permanent than do other intimate relationships. If there were no legal contract, marriage would be no different from living together. Today's marriages continue to be bolstered by mores (that is, by strongly held social norms), public opinion, and the law, although less so than in the past. Tradition, religious beliefs, and social pressure from family and friends all encourage couples to spend considerable time and energy working to improve their relationship before they contemplate divorce. As a result, marriages, more than other intimate relationships today, last for life.

TABLE 8.1
Family Expectations and Family Background

	Nationally	Parents together	Parents not together
"I expect to …"			
Marry	88%	89	86
Have children	92	91	92
Stay with same partner for life	88	91	83
"I want to have …"			
A home like the one I grew up in	70	75	60

(*Source:* Bibby 2001, p. 144.)

As far back as 1949, Margaret Mead pointed out that "all the phraseology, the expectation of marriage that would last, 'until death do us part,' has survived long after....[the passage of] laws permitting cheap and quick divorces" (1949, p. 334). The result is "great contradictoriness" in our culture. People "are still encouraged to marry as if they could count on marriage being for life, and at the same time they are absorbing a knowledge of the great frequency of divorce" (Mead 1949, p. 335). The recognition of this cultural contradiction is a step toward self-understanding and a help in making personal choices about permanence in marriage. Today "marriage may be for life, can be for life, but also may not be" (Mead 1949, p. 338).

Marital relationships can more often be permanently satisfying, counsellors advise, when spouses learn to care for the "unvarnished" other, not a "splendid image" (Van den Haag 1974, p. 142). In this regard, psychoanalyst Sidney Jourard addressed an audience about his own marriage of 26 years. Here is part of what he said:

Marriage is not for happiness, I have concluded after 25 ½ years. It's a many splendored thing, a place to learn how to live with human beings who differ from oneself in age, sex, values, and perspectives. It's a place to learn how to hate and to control hate. It's a place to learn laughter and love and dialogue. (Jourard 1979, p. 234)

Getting married, then, can encourage partners to continue to commit themselves to learning how to live with each other, to developing, through the course of their individual life cycles, an ongoing love relationship. Some U.S. policymakers, concerned about the high divorce rate in that country, advocate "covenant marriage" to encourage marital permanence.

COVENANT MARRIAGE   **Covenant marriage** is a new type of legal marriage in the United States in which the bride and groom agree to be bound by a marriage contract that will not let them get divorced as easily as is allowed presently. In 1997, Louisiana became the first U.S. state to enact covenant marriage. Before their wedding, Louisiana couples are now required to choose between two marital contracts, conventional or covenant. Under no-fault divorce laws (discussed at length in Chapter 14), which apply to conventional marriages in all 50 American states, either spouse can divorce the other at relatively short notice, without showing that anyone was "at fault" for causing the marriage relationship to deteriorate. Under a covenant marriage contract, couples are required to get premarital counselling and may divorce only after being separated for at least two years or if imprisonment, desertion for one year, adultery or domestic abuse is proved in court. In addition, a covenant couple will have to submit to counselling before a divorce (Olson 1998). In 1998, Arizona became the second state to enact a covenant marriage law (Munsil 1998), and other states are considering doing so.

Proponents, many of whom are members of conservative Christian organizations, explain that a basic reason for covenant marriage is concern for the welfare of any children born to the union. Proponents also argue that too much individualism and too little familism (see Chapter 1) are destroying the family ("Covenant Marriages Ministry" 1998; Hafen 1998). Covenant marriage is an attempt in the United States to legislate people's options so that they can publicly choose familism over individualism.

Critics warn that covenant marriage could result in emotional blackmail: A partner could be pressured into the contract and later regret it ("Covenant Marriages Tie a Firm Knot" 1997; Olson 1998). They also point out that the "premarital counselling that it mandates is too shallow to alert couples to their incompatibilities, and forced marital counselling for married couples in marital difficulties has, in the past, proven unable to forestall divorce" (in Bailey 2000, p. 58). In addition, proving adultery or domestic abuse in court can be difficult and expensive—and living in a violent household can be deadly.

Some religious authorities have expressed concern that covenant marriage laws, in effect, set up a two-tiered marriage structure that makes a non-covenant marriage second class, however valid and sacramental it may be. For example, the institutional Catholic Church in the United States has declined to endorse covenant marriage for this reason. "It should also be pointed out that the drafters of the covenant marriage law gave little consideration to private international law issues, and it is doubtful that the restrictions on divorce would be enforced by a sister state or by a foreign country with jurisdiction to grant a divorce" (Bailey 2000, p.58).

A central theme of this text is that society influences individuals' options and thereby impacts people's decisions. Covenant marriage gives some American couples an option that may encourage them to keep their union permanent, even through difficult times. However, in her analysis of the covenant marriage law adopted by Louisiana, Martha Bailey (2000, p. 58) concludes that it is "unlikely" that this law "will be effective in reducing divorce rates or in improving conditions for children."

Expectations of Primariness

Marriage involves the expectations of **primariness**: the commitment of both partners to keeping each other the most important people in their lives. Usually couples agree that primariness will include expectations of **sexual exclusivity**, in which partners promise to have sexual relations only with each other. "Many people still feel that the self-disclosure involved in sexuality symbolizes the love relationship and therefore sexuality should not be shared with extramarital partners" (Reiss 1986a, pp. 56–57).

Sexual exclusivity emerged as a cultural value in traditional society to maintain the patriarchal line of descent; the wedding ring placed on the bride's finger by the groom symbolized this expectation of sexual exclusivity on her part. Although historically polygamy was common (remember the Old Testament patriarchs), the Judeo-Christian tradition extended expectations of sexual exclusivity to include both husbands and wives. For example, the Book of Common Prayer asks both partners to "forsake all others."

POLYGAMY   Polygamy has been illegal in Canada since 1878, with the prohibition specifically aimed at Mormons who had established settlements in British Columbia and Alberta. Under Section 293 of the Criminal Code,

> Every one who (a) practices or enters into or in any manner agrees or consents to practise or enter into (i)... any form of polygamy or (ii)...any kind of conjugal union with more than one person at the same time, whether or not it is by law recognized as a binding form of a marriage; or (b) celebrates, assists or is a party to a rite, ceremony, contract or consent that purports to sanction a relationship mentioned in subparagraph (a)(i) or (ii) is guilty of an indictable offence and liable to imprisonment for a term not exceeding five years.

Although the Mormon Church no longer permits polygamy, there are dissident Mormons (i.e. not recognized as Mormons by the mainstream church), such as the United Effort Order, based in Colorado City but with a commune near Creston, B.C., who follow the traditional teachings and take multiple wives. There are also non-Mormon polygamous Christian sects and families who call themselves "Christian polygamists" and who generally advocate a strong patriarchal family structure. Occasionally members of such polygamous families have talked to the media to explain and advocate their lifestyle. Some multiple wives have argued that polygamy is a feminist arrangement because the sharing of domestic responsibilities benefits working women (Johnson 1991; Joseph 1991).

Polygamy has not received the public acceptance that heterosexual and even homosexual cohabitation have. In 1996, when a Canadian MP proposed a polygamy bill, allowing men to marry up to three women, his suggestion was ridiculed and attacked. Similarly, those in polygamous marriages who have sought permanent residence in Canada have had their applicants denied where evidence suggested that they intended to continue the practice of polygamy in

Canada. For example, in the 1998 case of *Ali v. Canada (Minister of Citizenship and Immigration)*, Bahig Mohamed Skaik Ali, a Palestinian national residing in Kuwait, who was married twice in Kuwait (where both marriages were recognized as valid), made an application with his first wife for permanent residence in Canada. The application included the three children born of his first marriage as well as the two children born of his second. On the same date, his second wife also applied for permanent residence in Canada. In this case, the applications were denied because the immigration officer believed that they intended to practise polygamy in Canada (i.e., that he would have more than one wife) since there was no evidence that Ali or either of his wives had any intention to divorce.

However, recent developments suggest that, at least in the province of B.C., plural marriages are illegal in theory but legal in practice. In that province, the Attorney General declined to charge two leaders of United Effort Order commune under S. 293, noting that his review of the research had led him to conclude that the law banning plural marriage "unconstitutionally restricts religious freedom." In consequence, crown counsel Herman Rohmoser announced that "Section 293 is invalid and will not be enforced in B.C." (Associated Press 2000).

Another exception to the marital expectation of primariness involves deliberately sexually nonexclusive marriages, such as swinging and sexually open marriages.

SWINGING AND SEXUALLY OPEN MARRIAGE
Swinging is a marriage arrangement in which couples exchange partners in order to engage in purely recreational sex. Swinging gained media and research attention in the late sixties and seventies. Since then, little research has been done on swinging.

What we do know is that active swingers emphasized its positive effects—variety, for example. Former swingers who had given up the lifestyle pointed to problems with jealousy, guilt, competing emotional attachments, and fear of being discovered by other family members, friends, or neighbours (Macklin 1987).

Like swinging, sexually open marriage received considerable publicity in the late sixties and seventies. In a **sexually open marriage**, spouses agree that each may have openly acknowledged sexual relationships with others while keeping the marriage relationship primary. Unlike in swinging, one or both spouses go out separately, and outside relationships can be emotional as well as sexual. Partners in sexually open unions tend to be highly independent, willing to take risks, nonconforming, and committed to nonpossessiveness and personal growth. Couples usually establish limits on the degree of sexual and/or emotional involvement of the outside relationship, along with ground rules concerning honesty and what details to tell one another (Macklin 1987, p. 335).

Spouses in sexually open marriages often say that the arrangement has many personal and relationship benefits. They also report complications: jealousy, guilt, difficulty in apportioning time and attention, pressure from the extramarital partner, need for continuous negotiation and accommodation, and loneliness when the spouse is not home. This is a tall order and may be why many sexually open marriages have unanticipated difficulties (Masters, Johnson, and Kolodny 1994) or apparently become monogamous after a period of time.

Advocacy of sexually nonexclusive marriage, as well as research on such unions, is largely a product of the pre-AIDS era. All of us realize that the advent of AIDS means that sexual adventurousness can have potentially lethal consequences, for children as well as for consenting adults. The willingness to consider a consensual agreement to have a sexually nonexclusive marriage now must take into account more than personal values and relationship management challenges, for it involves the risk of disease and even death. (See Chapter 5 for a more detailed discussion of AIDS and marriage.) Meanwhile, the majority of husbands and wives today feel that extramarital sex for either partner is wrong (Macklin 1987).

How closely do the actions of married couples support these beliefs? Although monogamy remains the cultural ideal, it is not as widespread in practice as many people think.

Extramarital Sex

Taboos against **extramarital sex** are widespread among the world's cultures, but the proscription against extramarital sex is stronger in Canada and the United States than in many other parts of the world.

This is probably due to the emphasis, discussed earlier, on the marital dyad as the seminal relationship in these countries. Currently, about 70 percent of Americans believe that extramarital sex is "always harmful to a marriage" (Adler 1996a). In Canada, survey research by sociologist Reginald Bibby (2001, p. 250) reports that "[a]bout 90 percent of teens and 85 percent of adults give thumbs-down to extramarital sex."

Although a large majority of Canadians publicly disapprove of extramarital sex, in practice the picture is somewhat different. Statistics are probably less than totally accurate because they are based on what people report: Some spouses hesitate to admit an affair; others boast about affairs that didn't really happen. In a recent national survey on sexuality in the United States conducted by the National Opinion Research Center (see Chapter 5), one-quarter of all husbands and 15 percent of wives ages 18 through 59 reported having had at least one affair. Among men in their 50s, the figure was 37 percent (Laumann et al. 1994). Others suggest the figures are even higher. While one researcher claims that 37 percent of couples experience affairs (Spring 1997), a second maintains that the "current acceptable statistic is roughly half of all men and women get involved in extramarital affairs" (Layton-Tholl 1998). Indeed, a recent book suggests that 60 percent of husband and 40 percent of wives will have an affair and that no fewer than 80 percent of marriages will experience the adultery of at least one spouse (Vaughan 1998). According to sexologists Masters, Johnson, and Kolodny, "Extramarital sex hasn't disappeared in the 1990s. In fact, there is little evidence that participation in extramarital sex has even slowed down a bit in the age of AIDS" (1994, p. 483).

Gender differences are evident in any discussion of extramarital sex. More husbands (about 23 percent according to one national survey) than wives (about 12 percent) have had an affair sometime during their marriage (Wiederman 1997). If a wife has an affair, she is more likely to do so because she feels emotionally distanced by her husband. Men who have affairs are far more likely to do so for the sexual excitement and variety they hope to find (Masters, Johnson, and Kolodny 1994, pp. 494, 499). Although gender roles are changing, there is evidence that the sexual double standard persists. In one survey of midwestern college students whose mean age was 19 years, males were generally more tolerant of a man's infidelity than a woman's. Also, males were more tolerant of men's affairs than females were of women's (Margolin 1989).

REASONS FOR EXTRAMARITAL AFFAIRS

You may recall that Chapter 5 discussed evolutionary psychology's argument that human sexual behaviour may be partly genetically influenced. From this point-of-view, men are genetically more likely to be unfaithful because of an evolutionary predisposition to fertilize as many female eggs as possible. Women, on the other hand, because pregnancy and delivery are far more time- and energy-consuming than the act of conception, are genetically more reluctant to engage in casual sex (Buss 1994a, Wright 1994b). This biosocial perspective of affairs is highly contro-versial. The remainder of our focus here is on social causes for affairs. After reviewing the literature on extramarital sex, Macklin (1987) concludes that having an affair depends on the following factors:

- Opportunity—whether there is sufficient privacy and a potential partner is available.

- Willingness to take advantage of the opportunity. Generally, spouses who are less satisfied with or dependent on their marriages and have more lib-eral values regarding monogamy are more likely to have affairs.

- Expectations for satisfaction—influenced by role models and past experiences, as well as attraction to the potential partner.

- Expectations about negative consequences—based on the perceived likelihood of being found out or rejected by one's spouse or friends if found out.

Some extramarital affairs are short term; others are more enduring. Many *short-term affairs* are "situation specific": a fling while attending an out-of-town con-vention or business meeting, a sexual encounter at an office holiday party, a surprise telephone call from a former boy- or girlfriend that leads to sex but ends as abruptly as it began, a cruise-ship romance that occurs when spouses take separate vacations (Masters, Johnson, and Kolodny 1994, pp. 483–86).

Other short-term affairs are motivated by the need for conquest (a new "notch on his or her belt") or to get revenge for a spouse's real or imagined injustices.

Husbands are more likely to engage in conquest affairs while wives are more likely to have anger/revenge affairs. Another type of short-term affair precedes a possibly anticipated divorce; predivorce affairs are "like test flights—transient forays into the world of sex outside marriage as a prelude to making the final decision to terminate a relationship that is already on a shaky foundation" (Masters, Johnson, and Kolodny 1994, p. 489).

A final type of short-term affair is the male bisexual affair. While a wife's bisexual affair is more likely to be long term, a husband's bisexual affair(s) is/are much more likely to be quick and anonymous. Male bisexual affairs can occur among husbands who are predominantly heterosexual but occasionally are drawn to the danger, variety, or intrigue of same-sex relations as a means of experiencing a different form of sexual excitement. On the other hand, there are married men who might appear to be heterosexual but who are really closeted gay men using marriage to hide their sexual orientation (Masters, Johnson, and Kolodny 1994, p. 489). One small study on college students found that women would be more intolerant of a male partner's homosexual infidelity than hetero-sexual infidelity. However, the reverse was true for the male students: Men would be more intolerant of a female partner's heterosexual infidelity than lesbian infidelity (Wiederman and LaMar 1998).

Long-term affairs tend to be more complex than short-term liaisons. Among others, Masters, Johnson, and Kolodny list the following types, depending on their purpose: hedonistic, marriage maintenance, intimacy reduction, and reactive affairs.

Hedonistic affairs rarely lead to emotional entan-glements:

> The affair is an indulgence, a creative act of play-fulness, an oasis of sensual energy in a world fogged over by trivial details of everyday life.... The participants often have happy and sexually fulfilling marriages of their own. (Masters, Johnson, and Kolodny 1994, p. 492)

Marriage maintenance affairs are convenient arrangements that provide something that is missing from the marriage, such as kinky sexual experimenta-tion. By supplying this element, the affair actually sta-bilizes the marriage and makes it less likely that a marital breakup will occur. "Although common wisdom has it that affairs often lead to marital dissolution, we have encountered hundreds of marriages that were held together and solidified by affairs" (Masters, Johnson, and Kolodny 1994, p. 491).

Intimacy reduction affairs are undertaken by spouses who are ambivalent about the intimacy demanded by their husband or wife. Creating a safety zone of emotional distance within the marriage, the affair serves as a buffer against too much closeness:

> When tension and anxiety over too much intimacy mount, it can be defused by more involvement with the affair. In contrast, when enough emotional space has developed in the marriage for it to feel comfortable, rather than smothering, the affair may be ignored for awhile, since there is at least temporarily safe harbour at home. (Masters, Johnson, and Kolodny 1994, p. 492).

Reactive affairs are motivated by a spouse's desire to be reassured amid changing life circumstances. For instance, a middle-aged husband who is feeling over the hill may seek to prove his youthfulness by having an affair with a younger woman. Or a wife may rediscover her sexuality once her children have left home and opt for the excitement of extramarital sex. A wife's bisexual affair often fits this category (Masters, Johnson, and Kolodny 1994, p. 493).

CYBER-ADULTERY The 1990s saw the emergence of a new brand of marital infidelity—adultery on the Internet, or **cyberadultery**. In a typical scenario, a spouse wanders into a computer chat room, becomes enamored with a cyberpartner, and may—or may not—eventually meet the cyberpartner in person. According to Canadian research conducted by Robert Brym and Rhonda Lenton, based on 1200 random phone interviews as well as a separate online survey of 6500 people who had previously dated someone they had met online, almost 18 percent of online daters are married or living common law (Canadian Press 2001).

Experts and spouses are now trying to define just what is sexual infidelity in today's computer age. Does it have to be physical? Or is cybersex, or cyberromance, really not adultery? Meanwhile, there is evidence that cyberinfidelity has resulted in the break up

of at least some marriages (Toufexis 1996; Campbell 1996; Craig 1996; "The Dark Side ..." 1997).

EFFECTS OF EXTRAMARITAL AFFAIRS
Extramarital sex can have positive effects (Cano and O'Leary 1997). As we have seen, an affair can sometimes help keep a marriage together by providing some missing need or reducing intimacy anxiety. Because an affair does not necessarily offer better sex, a spouse might find renewed appreciation for the marriage. But recognizing that affairs can have a positive side is hardly the whole story: "We are firmly convinced that the downside of extramarital sex usually looms larger than any potential benefits" (Masters, Johnson, and Kolodny 1994, p. 502).

First, an affair that is nonconsensual involves deceit and can be considered a form of theft: "What is stolen is the bond of trust and its attendant consent to mutual vulnerability between spouses. Such vulnerability is based largely on the assumption that neither partner is out to hurt the other" (Masters, Johnson, and Kolodny 1994, p. 503). Breaking that trust can result is unanticipated—and unwanted—complications. For one thing, the discovery of a spouse's affair (which happens in a large number of cases) is likely to seriously undermine marital trust and intimacy. The reaction is often shock and outrage, setting off a series of negative consequences that reverberate over time through the course of the marriage. Anger over a spouse's affair may linger and undermine the relationship for years. To some partners, extramarital sex is such a profound violation of moral and religious principles that it shatters a fundamental marital pillar that can never be fully repaired. In other unions the problems have nothing to do with moral or religious beliefs but are grounded in what the affair takes from the marital relationship. Sometimes an affair becomes known to the entire family, including the children. Clearly, this situation is not good (Masters, Johnson, and Kolodny 1994, p. 502).

Moreover, affairs victimize the uninvolved partner without giving her or him prior warning or any way to avoid being injured (Cano and O'Leary 1997). Not only has trust been eroded and feelings been hurt, but the uninvolved spouse may have been exposed to various sexually transmitted diseases—not a rare occurrence. For many spouses, concern about

AIDS heightens anger and turmoil over affairs (Adler 1996). The uninvolved spouse is often exploited financially as well, because what were thought to be joint funds have been unilaterally spent on dinners, gifts, hotel rooms, or weekends away.

JEALOUSY **Jealousy** is strong emotional pain, anger, fear, and uncertainty arising when a valued relationship is threatened or perceived to be threatened. Sociologist Ira Reiss sees a spouse's jealousy as "a boundary-setting mechanism." When boundaries are violated (in this case, those circumscribing the married couple as primary), "jealousy occurs and indexes the anger and hurt that are expected to be activated by a violation of an important norm" (1986a, p. 47).

Research has found differences in how men and women experience and react to jealousy. Men are more reactive to the sexual threat, whereas women are more anxious about losing a primary relationship. Women, being more likely to monitor relationships, are more apt to try to change to please their partner so as to avoid the threat of another relationship. Men, meanwhile, are more likely to seek solace or retribution in alternative relationships (White and Mullen 1989; Cano and O'Leary 1997). Several research projects suggest that those who feel insecure already or have poor self-images are more inclined toward jealousy (Macklin 1987; Buunk 1991; Cano and O'Leary 1997).

We tend to equate feeling jealous with sexual threats to a relationship, but other threats also evoke jealousy. Friends, colleagues, work, education or leisure commitments, and even a couple's children can be perceived as "trespassers" (McDonald and Osmond 1980, p. 4). Box 8.2, "Marriage and Opposite-Sex Friends," addresses marriage and opposite-sex friends.

Even though marital jealousy can probably never be completely eliminated, mutually supportive encouragement may lessen feelings of insecurity and jealousy. Nurturing one's self-esteem can allay what may indeed be unwarranted jealousy (Cano and O'Leary 1997). In sum, jealousy, like pain, needs to be viewed as a warning signal. Jealousy may mean that one or both partners' interests in outside activities need to be counterbalanced with activities within the relationship.

RECOVERING FROM AN EXTRAMARITAL AFFAIR Given that affairs do occur, a good number of people will perhaps rethink the issue when they discover that their spouse has had (or is having) one. The uninvolved mate will need to consider how important the affair is relative to the marital relationship as a whole. Can she or he regain trust? In some cases, the answer is "no"; trust never gets reestablished and the heightened suspicion gets incorporated into other problems the couple might have (Levine 1998).

Whether trust can be reestablished depends on several factors. One is how much trust there is in the first place. One researcher (Hansen 1985) has suggested that for this reason new marriages may be especially vulnerable to breaking up after an affair. Many marriages can and do recover from affairs, however (Cano and O'Leary 1997). Therapists suggest that doing so requires the following:

- The offending spouse needs to apologize sincerely and without defending her or his behaviour.

- The offending spouse needs to allow and hear the verbally vented anger and rage of the offended partner (but never permit physical abuse).

- The offending spouse needs to allow for trust to rebuild gradually and to realize that this may take a long time—up to two years or more.

- The offending spouse needs to do things to help the offended partner to regain trust—keep agreements, for example, and calling if he or she is running late.

- The offended spouse needs to decide whether she or he is committed to the marriage and, if so, needs to be willing to let go of resentments as this becomes possible.

- The couple should consider marriage counselling.

On the one hand, data on extramarital affairs suggest that lifelong fidelity is far from universal; on the other hand, specific acts of infidelity may not be routine or continual. The contrasting data on extramarital sex suggest that today, as in the past, many spouses are torn between lifelong commitment to a sexually exclusive marriage and desire for outside sexual relationships (Levine 1998). For the majority of mates, however, the decision to marry involves the promise to forgo other sexual partners. If we interpret fidelity to mean a primary commitment to one's partner and the relationship, then maintaining emotional intimacy becomes essential to being faithful. Without continued intimacy and self-disclosure, partners may not remain in love or keep a central place in each other's lives. Emotional commitment, in this view, is the essential element of primariness, as much or more than sexual fidelity per se. This ideal of primariness can make marriage relationships more satisfying.

To sum up, marriage entails making ongoing choices about permanence and primariness. In the next section, we'll examine whether same-sex couples should marry legally.

SHOULD SAME-SEX COUPLES MARRY?

Many gay male and lesbian couples live together in long-term, committed relationships (Allen and Demo 1995). Partners may exchange vows, or rings, or both (Mackey 1997). Couples may publicly declare their commitment in ceremonies among friends or in some congregations and churches, such as the Unitarian Universalist Association or the Metropolitan Community Church, the latter expressly dedicated to serving the gay community. In Canada, the first publicized gay "marriage" occurred in 1974, when two gay men were married by a Unitarian-Universalist minister in Winnipeg (Jackson and Persky 1982). Catholics have access to a union ceremony designed by Dignity, a support association. (The Catholic Church does not recognize these unions.) However, as we noted in Chapter 5, same-sex marriage is not legally recognized in Canada. At present, both the *Civil Code* in Quebec and the common law in the other provinces restrict marriages to opposite-sexed persons.

Under the *Constitution Act, 1867, s. 91(26)*, the federal Parliament is given the power to make laws in relation to "marriage and divorce," with exclusive jurisdiction over all aspects of marriage including authority over the essential validity of marriage (i.e., the capacity of persons to marry), and the recognition of foreign marriages. However, an exception exists in relation to the rules regarding the "solemnization of marriages," which under s. 92(12) of the *Constitution*

Act, is given to provincial legislatures. In consequence, this means that in Canada, the provinces and territories have exclusive jurisdiction over the formal validity of marriage.

Because of this division of responsibilities, complications may arise in the future. For example, in the event that a gay couple in Quebec successfully challenges the restriction of marriage to same-sex couples, one might well ask whether this marriage would be recognized elsewhere in Canada? According to Martha Bailey (2000, p. 29), it is likely that

> any apparent difference....[between the laws in Quebec and the rest of Canada] would be short-lived, because any ruling in favour of same-sex marriage would be appealed to the Supreme Court of Canada, which has general appellate jurisdiction and deals with cases of federal law and provincial law. A Supreme Court of Canada ruling on same-sex marriage would undoubtedly enunciate the law of Canada on this issue, regardless of whether it was an appeal from a common law jurisdiction or from Quebec....Because of the constitutional division of power, the federal government has the exclusive jurisdiction to enact legislation allowing same-sex marriage.

Given that the Netherlands legalized same-sex marriage in 2001, it is possible that foreign same-sex marriages would be recognized under our current laws. However, Canada's Parliament has yet to enact comprehensive legislation governing recognition of foreign marriages.

As we have previously noted in Chapter 5, the greater recognition and acceptance of same-sex couples in Canada has been accompanied by some responsive legal changes. At the same time, gay rights activists maintain that existing legal restrictions on their freedom to marry pose an unreasonable limit on their freedom of choice. The argument for challenging the restriction of legal marriage to same-sexed persons has found at least some degree of support in Canadian courtrooms. Although in the case of *Layland v. Ontario* (1993) the applicant was unsuccessful in challenging the exclusion of same-sex couples from marrying, a dissenting opinion on this case, written by Justice Greer, agreed with this freedom-of-choice argument. She wrote:

Marriage and Opposite-Sex Friends

In a society publicly dedicated to monogamy, spouses may be wary of opposite-sex friendships because of their potential for sexual involvement. Moreover, the absence of clear role expectations for an opposite-sex friend of a married person makes it difficult to know what to say and do in such a situation.

Partners need to negotiate carefully and discuss openly their feelings about the nature of the activities and degree of emotional and physical intimacy they find acceptable in their spouse's friendships. Couple boundaries should be clarified. What confidential information can be shared? Can the couple's sex life be discussed with others?

Same-sex friendships can present the same emotional threat to gay and lesbian couples that cross-sex friendships do to heterosexuals. Yet they are different in that same-sex friendships are culturally acceptable, even encouraged. There may be more social support and less self-consciousness in same-sex friendships among gays and lesbians, but there is also an ambiguity that can give rise to insecurity. Lesbian and gay couples are frequently embedded in a larger gay or lesbian community, occasioning frequent contact with same-sex friends who are potential partners. As with heterosexual couples, open discussion, agreement, and clarification of boundaries between a couple and their friends may prevent misunderstandings and conflict.

The following ten statements can help clarify what you believe is appropriate in opposite-sex friendships for heterosexual partners and in same-sex friendships for homosexual partners. Answer "always," "sometimes," "occasionally," or "never" to the following statements as they apply to someone of the sex from which you also choose sexual partners:

A wife/husband/female partner/male partner should be able to:

1. go to lunch with a work colleague to discuss business

2. go to lunch with a work colleague just because they are friends

3. go to lunch with a friend, not a work colleague

4. go to dinner with a work colleague

5. go to dinner with a friend, not a work colleague

6. go to a movie with a friend

7. go dancing with a friend

8. spend a full day with a friend

9. vacation with a friend

10. have sex with a friend

To evaluate your responses, look first at where you draw the line. Although you may have said "always" to all ten statements, it is more likely that you did so with those listed earlier than later. Examine if and how your responses differ according to whether a partner is married, is heterosexual or gay, or female or male. If you are in a relationship now, you might ask your partner to respond to these statements and then compare answers. Doing so will let you know where opinions differ and might stimulate communication and negotiation on these topics.

The *Charter* cases show that our courts have found that "choice" is a benefit of the law. In the case at bar, the applicants have been denied their right to choose whom they wish to marry. In my view, the right to choose is a fundamental right and it applies to the context of marriage in our society. It is a basic theory in our society that the state will respect choices made by individuals and the state will avoid subordinating these choices.

However, the majority rejected the argument in favour of same-sex marriages on the grounds that:

One of the principal purposes of the institution of marriage is the founding and maintaining of families in which children will be produced and cared for, a procedure that is necessary for the continuance of the species....That principal purpose of marriage cannot, as a general rule, be achieved in a homosexual union because of the biological limitations of such a union. It is this reality that is recognized in the limitation of marriage to persons of opposite sex. It is true that some married couples are unable or unwilling to have children, and that the incapacity or unwillingness to procreate is not a bar to marriage or a ground for divorce. Despite these circumstances in which a marriage will be childless, the institution of marriage is intended by the states, by religions and by society to encourage the procreation of children. (*Layland v. Ontario, 1993*)

The Supreme Court of Canada expressed a similar view, identifying procreation as the "ultimate purpose of marriage," in the case of *Egan v. Canada* in 1995. Justice La Forest, writing for the majority, wrote that the "ultimate *raison d'etre* of marriage....is firmly anchored in the biological and social realities that heterosexual couples have the unique ability to procreate, that most children are the product of these relationships, and that they are generally cared for and nurtured by those who live in that relationship."

However, in her analysis of these judgments, Martha Bailey (2000, p. 20) observes:

Although opposite-sex couples have a unique capacity to procreate, same-sex couples may have a child together by means of assisted reproductive technology, adoption or otherwise. As well, in some same-sex relationships there are children of former marriages or relationships....In any case,

extending marital rights and obligations, or even marital status, to same-sex couples will not derail the state objective of encouraging procreation.

Quoting Justice Iacobucci, she remarks, "it eludes me how according same sex couples the benefits flowing to opposite-sex couples in any way inhibits, dissuades or impedes the formation of heterosexual unions" (p. 21).

It is evident that, although attitudes toward gay rights have generally become more liberal, some continue to voice militant opposition to same-sex marriage. For example, for religious fundamentalists and other conservative groups, the case against gay marriage is unambiguous: Marriage is intrinsically a union of opposite-sexed persons. From this point of view, any move to legalize marriage is an "attempt to deconstruct traditional morality." Indeed, in June 1999, an American Baptist preacher from Topeka, Kansas, announced that he and a group of his followers would be leading a demonstration on the steps of the Supreme Court of Canada to protest its decision to extend the definition of "spouse" to same-sex couples and referred to Canada as the "sperm bank of Satan" (Anderssen 1999). Others have wielded posters proclaiming, "God made Adam and Eve, not Adam and Steve" (Salholz 1993; Gross 1994; Smolowe 1996a).

The Response of Other Countries

Other western countries have responded to the issue of gay marriages in a number of ways. **Registered partnership** legislation has been enacted in Denmark, Norway, Sweden, Iceland, the Netherlands, and Hawaii. In other countries such as Belgium and Spain, similar initiatives have been or are currently being considered before their parliaments. According to this concept, unmarried couples may register their partnership and then receive some of the legal benefits of marriage, such as joint health or auto insurance or bereavement leave, for example. Besides practical benefits, registering as domestic partners has emotional significance for some same-sex couples, who do so as a way of publicly expressing their commitment (Ames 1992). But registering as domestic partners lacks the deep symbolism of marriage. "Gays and lesbians were raised in the same culture [as] everyone else," notes gay historian Eric

Marcus. "When they settle down they want gold bands [and] legal documents" (in Salholz 1993).[2]

Registered Partnerships

Denmark was the first country in the world to enact, in 1989, registered partnership legislation for same-sex couples. By the end of December 1997, more than 7000 persons had entered into registered partnerships (Bailey 2000, p. 46). In 1993, Norway enacted a registered partnership law modelled on Denmark. In both of these countries, registered partnership carries with it almost all of the same rights and obligations as marriage. However, in both countries, registered partners are prohibited from adopting a child or from adopting the child of a registered partner.

In the Netherlands, registered partnership law came into effect on January 1, 1998; as noted above and in Chapter 5, the Netherlands became, in 2001, the first country in the world to legalize same-sex marriage. Prior to that time, registered partnership legislation (available to both same-sex and opposite-sex couples) made partnership and marriage virtually identical in relation to rights and obligations. Almost 4000 couples registered their partnerships in the first ten months following the passage of the Netherlands' domestic partnership legislation. Of these partnerships, 1198 were between women, 1507 between men, and 1291 between opposite-sexed persons (Bailey 2000, p. 50).

In Spain, the *Stable Couples Act*, enacted in July 1998, extends partial marital rights and obligations to same-sex couples as well as to registered opposite-sex couples.

In the United States, legislative reactions to the issue of same-sex marriage have been mixed. In 1998, both Hawaii and Alaska held constitutional referenda on whether or not to amend their state constitutions to continue the exclusion of same-sex couples from legal marriages. In both cases, voters elected to do so. However, in what seems an attempt to arrive at a compromise position, Hawaii enacted a "reciprocal beneficiaries" law that came into effect on July 1, 1997 and granted same-sex couples, as well as others (excluding heterosexual couples) who are not legally allowed to marry (e.g., two sisters; a widowed mother and her unmarried son) to register as a domestic partnership and entitles them to a limited range of marital rights and obligations. These include "rights and obligations in relation to health insurance, hospital visitation, health care decisions, insurance policies, death benefits, and bereavement leave" (Bailey 2000, p. 57).

In itself, a court ruling in Hawaii would not affect other states. However, in order to allow states not to follow the principle of reciprocity regarding same-sex marriages, the U.S. Congress passed and President Clinton signed the Defense of Marriage Act in September, 1996. This federal statute, declaring marriage to be a "legal union of one man and one woman," denies gay couples many of the civil advantages of marriage, and also relieves states of the obligation to grant reciprocity, or "full faith and credit" to marriages performed in another state (Hatfield 1996; Purdum 1996). As a result of the Defense of Marriage Act, at least 28 states have passed laws that would block out-of-state marriage licenses obtained by gay or lesbian couples. Twenty-three other states tried to pass such legislation but failed (Partners Task Force for Gay & Lesbian Couples 1998).

Highly motivated activists are organizing, lobbying, and agitating on both sides of this issue ("ACLU Blasts ..." 1996; Kaplan and Klaidman 1996; Smolowe 1996). Meanwhile, gays and lesbians themselves are divided somewhat on the desirability of legalized same-sex marriage.

Views of Gay Rights Activists on Same-Sex Marriage

Lesbians and gay men who favour legalized same-sex marriage argue that legal marriage yields economic and other practical advantages (Wyman 1994; Zicklin 1997; Bryon 1998). Moreover, unlike heterosexual couples, homosexual couples receive little social support for continuing long-term relationships. As Mary

---

2. Justice L'Heureux-Dubé emphasized the symbolic value of being legally treated as a couple in *Egan v. Canada*. In Justice L'Heureux-Dube's words, "Official state recognition of the legitimacy and acceptance in society of a particular type of status or relationship may be of greater value and importance to those affected than any pecuniary gain flowing from that recognition....Given the marginalized position of homosexuals in society, the metamessage that flows almost invariably from excluding same-sex couples from such an important social institution is essentially that society considers such relationships to be less worthy of respect, concern and consideration than relationships involving members of the opposite sex."

Mendola, author of the *Mendola Report* (1980), explains:

> The major difference separating us as heterosexual and lesbian couples: our lesbian marriage had none of the support systems Mr. and Mrs. Next Door enjoyed. I have not had a bridal shower or a bachelor party, depending on how one looks at it.... Aunts and uncles did not come to visit and admire our home. We never received anniversary cards. As trivial as these things may seem, they represent something vitally important: heterosexual couples are encouraged to stay together.... Lesbian and homosexual couples have no such support systems. Rather than being encouraged to stay together, we are conditioned to believe there is no future for us as couples. (p. 4)

Being able to marry legally could help to change this situation.

Furthermore, denying lesbians and gay men the right to marry implies that they are not as good or valuable as heterosexuals. The right to marry legally could remedy this. Some lesbians and gay men believe that legal marriage would be their "most important civil rights victory" yet; related successes would follow.

Gay and lesbian opponents of legal same-sex marriage, such as gay rights attorney Paula Ettelbrick, object to mimicking a traditionally patriarchal institution based on property rights and institutionalized husband–wife roles. As one lesbian explained,

> Within my home I feel married to Frances, but I don't consider us "married." The marriage part is still very heterosexual to me. One of the reasons I don't like to associate with marriage is because heterosexual marriage seems to be in trouble. It's like booking passage on the *Titanic*. Frances is my life partner; that's how I'm accustomed to thinking of her. (in Sherman 1992, pp. 189–90)

More generally, opponents object to giving the state power to regulate primary adult relationships (Johnson 1996). They stress that legalizing same-sex unions would further stigmatize any sex outside marriage, with unmarried lesbians and gay men facing heightened discrimination ("Monogamy: Is it ...?" 1998).

Whether one's commitment is same-sex or heterosexual, being—and staying—married involves choices. The following section examines some of these.

A MATTER OF CHOICES THROUGHOUT LIFE

Our theme of making choices throughout life surely applies both to early years of marriage and to couples preparing for marriage. Surprisingly, there is less social science research on these topics than on divorce! Along with the available social science data, we will incorporate our own ideas, those of other family sociologists, and information available in the media.

Preparation for Marriage

Clergy, teachers, parents, policymakers, and others have grown increasingly concerned that individuals be better prepared for a marital relationship. Conventional dating in which the focus is on the enjoyment of social events does not prepare couples for dealing with practicalities, decisions, and problems. Yet, as we also saw in Chapter 7, living together does not seem to prepare couples well either; at least, the marital success rates of couples who cohabited before marriage are no higher, and are often lower, than those of couples who did not cohabit premaritally.

Family life education courses, which take place in high school and university classrooms, are designed to prepare individuals for marriage. Premarital counselling, which generally takes place at churches or with private counsellors, is specifically oriented to couples who plan to be married. Many Catholic dioceses, for example, require premarital counselling before a couple may be married by a priest. Catholic dioceses have also organized weekend engagement encounters during which couples who plan to marry learn about and discuss various aspects of married life. Such programs are designed and generally conducted by professionally trained people. Other churches have adopted these programs, and some couples may seek premarital counselling on their own initiative.

Premarital counselling has two goals: first, to evaluate the relationship with the possibility of deciding against marriage; and second, to sensitize partners to potential problems and to teach positive ways of communicating about and resolving conflicts. Even though common sense suggests that these kinds of programs help, they have seldom been scientifically evaluated in terms of their impact on subsequent marriages. Nevertheless, family experts see these programs as important, especially for adult children of troubled, dysfunctional, or divorced families (Spanier 1989; Markman, Stanley, and Blumberg 1994; Russo 1997). Premarital education or counselling may help make the first years of marriage go more smoothly.

The First Years of Marriage

In the 1950s marriage and family texts characteristically referred to the first months and years of marriage as a period of adjustment, after which, presumably, spouses had learned to play traditional marital roles. Today we view early marriage more as a time of role *making* than of role *taking*.

Role making involves issues explored fully in other chapters of this text. Newlyweds negotiate expectations for sex and intimacy (Chapter 5), establish communication (Chapter 9) and decision-making patterns (Chapter 10), balance expectations about marital and job responsibilities (Chapter 13), and come to some agreement about childbearing (Chapter 11) and how they will handle and budget their money (Knudson-Martin and Mahoney 1998; Burke and Cast 1997). When children are present, role making involves negotiation about parenting roles (Chapter 12). Role-making issues peculiar to remarriages are addressed in Chapter 15. Generally, role making in new marriages involves creating, by means of communication and negotiation, identities as married persons (Rotenburg, Schaut, and O'Connor 1993). One aspect of this process involves decisions about keeping or changing one's last name. This issue is explored in Box 8.3, "Getting Married—And Changing Your Name?" The time of role making is not a clearly demarcated period but rather continues throughout marriage.

Even though the early stages of marriage are not a distinct period, sociologists continue to speak and write about them as such. One thing we know is that this period tends to be the happiest, with gradual declines in marital satisfaction afterward. (Perhaps this is where we get the popular expression, "The

honeymoon's over.") Why this is is not clear. One explanation points to life-cycle stresses as children arrive and economic pressures intensify; others simply assume that courtship and new marriage are periods of emotional intensity from which there is an inevitable decline (Whyte 1990, pp. 190–95).

We do know something about the structural advantages of early marriage, and it is likely that these contribute to high levels of satisfaction. For one thing, partners' roles are relatively similar or unsegregated in early marriage. Spouses tend to share household tasks and, because of similar experiences, are better able to empathize with each other. One recent qualitative study of 12 white, middle-class newlywed couples found that even when not entirely egalitarian or equal, the new spouses thought and talked about their marriage as equal by using a "language of equality" (Knudson-Martin and Mahoney 1998). Early marriage may also be less vulnerable to stress arising from dissatisfaction with finances. Typically, both partners are employed, and though their salaries may be relatively low, so are their expenses.

But early marriage is not characterized only by happiness. Couples must also accomplish certain tasks during this period. In general, "the solidarity of the new couple relation must be established and competing interpersonal ties modified" (Aldous 1978, p. 141; Rotenberg, Schaut, and O'Connor 1993). The couple constructs relationships and interprets events in a way that reinforces their sense of themselves as a couple (Wallerstein and Blakeslee 1995).

Changing friendships is one indication that getting married changes—sometimes subtly, sometimes surprisingly—what people expect from themselves and their partners. Marriage changes a couple's relationship. To some extent this is true for all newlyweds, even those who lived together before marrying. One reason for this change is that weddings usher in a host of conscious and unconscious beliefs about wives' and husbands' roles. One husband, for example, said that before his wedding he and his partner ate out regularly. He enjoyed this and had expected it to continue. His wife, however, felt that married people ought to eat at home. Some spouses (both husbands and wives) said they became more possessive. They felt they should now go out as a couple rather than separately, for example. One new husband surprised both himself and his wife by getting angry when his wife refused to vote his way in an election (Arond and Pauker 1987).

Because being married is a different relationship from dating or living together, the wedding may begin a new cycle of adjustment and change even for couples who have lived together for some time. Newlyweds may feel as if they're falling in love all over again. Subsequently, they may find themselves disappointed about both old and new issues. The increased security of marriage can encourage partners to let their hair down. Sometimes this comes as a shock to a spouse and raises new problems. Said one young husband, "I never knew my wife could be so sloppy." Getting through this stage requires making requests for change and negotiating resolutions, along with renewed acceptance of one another. Indeed, recent research by psychoanalyst John Gottman shows that communication as newlyweds tend to influence later happiness—and even permanence—of the marriage (Gottman et al. 1998).

For spouses who previously lived together, an unexpected problem may arise. One may define the wedding and honeymoon as ho-hum events; to her or him nothing has changed. The mate, meanwhile, may see the wedding as important, marking the advent of a different relationship. One wife described her honeymoon as frustrating for this reason. The couple went separate ways because she wanted to shop and he wanted to see the sights. This would have been acceptable to her, she said, had they not been on their honeymoon. Although they had travelled together before, she had expected increased togetherness this time; but he behaved as if it were just another trip. Similarly, a groom reported being upset on his honeymoon when his wife, with whom he had lived for three years, "jumped out of bed at 7:00 A.M." each day to jog. "I wanted her to lounge around with me in bed," he explained. "I wanted to play the romantic honeymoon image up more" (Arond and Pauker 1987, p. 219).

Newlyweds typically reported heightened feelings of responsibility, along with increased expectations for responsible behaviour from their mates. A woman explained that before marriage she was reluctant to challenge her partner's habit of taking off alone on motorcycle trips. As his wife, however, she felt "entitled to a more predictable and stable life" (Arond and Pauker 1987, p. 13). As one wife put it, "I don't feel like such a kid anymore" (p. 26). One man (who said he felt a lot closer to his wife than before the wedding) said being married meant feeling "rooted in a community" and "a lot more settled and future-directed" (p. 12).

Creating Couple Connection

Would you prefer a balanced-couple-centred, family-centred, or loose couple connection? Put differently, would you choose a more utilitarian or a more intrinsic marriage? It is important to keep in mind that utilitarian and intrinsic marriage types are poles on a continuum. A couple's relationship lies somewhere along that continuum (between these

The early states of marriage tend to be the happiest, as couples have time to enjoy each other and to pursue common interests. During this time, couples also need to establish a sense of solidarity and to modify competing interpersonal ties.

Getting Married—and Changing Your Name?

If you're married, did you change your last name on your wedding day? If you're not married but plan to marry someday, do you think you'll change your name? If you have answered "yes" to either of these questions, there's a good chance you're female (and live outside Quebec where Quebec's Civil Code says that husbands and wives keep their own surnames after marriage). Nevertheless, the norms in our society continue to encourage brides to change their names, despite changing gender roles (Scheuble and Johnson 1993; Twenge 1997b). Even stronger norms discourage grooms from changing (or "giving up") their surnames.

Meanwhile, it is not only custom and gender roles that affect individuals' choices about married names. Changing—or not changing—one's name is also symbolic of what marriage means to people. In a study at the University of Michigan (Twenge 1997b), 153 young women enrolled in an introductory psychology course were questioned about their preferences for married last names. Virtually all were middle- or upper-middle class. Ninety-eight percent identified themselves as heterosexual, and ninety-eight percent were unmarried. The women were asked to choose one of seven options for their own name after marriage and one of six options for their future children's names. Table 8.2 shows the results.

Nearly 60 percent said that they would take their husband's name, compared with about 10 percent who said they planned to keep their own name for all purposes. Another 4 percent thought that both spouses should hyphenate their names. More than twice as many young women (9.2 percent) planned to hyphenate their name but did not expect their husband to hyphenate his. With regard to future children's names, nearly 80 percent of the coeds expected their children to have their husband's name while 12 percent said their children would have a hyphenated name.

The researcher asked the students to explain in their own words the reason for their choices. Those who said

they would take their husband's name often gave tradition as a reason: for example, "Traditionally, that's the way it is supposed to be." These women also indicated that taking their husband's name symbolized romantic conjugal bonding: "...The same last name would symbolize this 'two becoming one' idea"; "I think that we will be together as one now and I can share his last name" (p. 424).

The women who said they would do something other than take their husband's last name often explained their need to retain a sense of personal identity. Typical responses included: "My last name is important to me, because that represents me and everything I worked for and accomplished in my life, and I will not entirely give up my identity for a man"; "It makes no sense to give up my identity just because I marry. It is sexist, archaic, and illogical." Some women who preferred to keep their names explained that the decision was related to their ethnicity and culture. As one Latina wrote, "I want to keep my last name because it reflects my culture, which is part of who I am" (p. 424).

As Table 8.2 shows, the students were more likely to choose their husband's last name for their children than for themselves. Those who said that their children should have their husband's last name explained that this was traditional and would generally be easier and avoid confusion. A woman who hopes to give her children hyphenated names explained that, "Their names should be a combination of our last names, since that is what they are, a combination of the two of us" (p. 425).

An earlier study surveyed both female and male students in a small midwestern American college in 1990. In that study, the women students thought of more good reasons for the bride to keep her name than the men did. Probably not surprisingly, women who planned to marry later and/or to have a professional career were more likely not to want to change their names. Women who planned to marry earlier and have larger families

TABLE   8.2

Young Women's Preferred Name Choice at Marriage (Sample n = 153)

Choices for Own Last Name	Percentage Choosing Option
Take husband's name	59.5
Keep own name for all purposes	9.8
Use my name for professional purposes, husband's for social	13.7
Hyphenate my name, but not expect him to hyphenate his	9.2
Hyphenate my name, and he will hyphenate his	3.9
Husband and I will choose new name and both use	0.7
Other	3.3

Choices for Children's Last Name	
Husband's name	79.6
My name	0.7
Hyphenated name	12.1
Daughters will have my name, sons my husband's	0.7
New name	0.7
Other	3.9

Source: Jean M. Twenge. 1997. "'Mrs. His Name': Women's Preferences for Married Names." Psychology of Women Quarterly 21: Table 1, p. 422.

were more likely to plan to change their name (Scheuble and Johnson 1993).

If you are single and plan to marry, what do you want to do about your last name at the wedding? If you are presently married, did you keep or change your surname? What does doing so symbolize, do you think? Do you think that changing one's name has anything to do with the marriage premise? Why or why not?

poles) and combines utilitarian with intrinsic characteristics. In Chapter 4 we saw that sociologist Francesca Cancian (1985) views love as combining both instrumental and affectionate qualities. Similarly, a marriage relationship fulfills both practical and intimacy needs. Where partners place their relationship on the utilitarian-intrinsic continuum depends on choices they make throughout their lives—and on societal conditions that limit or expand their options as well.

Some couples choose to emphasize the utilitarian functions of their marriage. For example, a passive-congenial union can be a deliberate arrangement for spouses who want to direct their creative energies outside of their relationship—into obligations to parents or other kin, raising children, or careers.

Working-class marital relationships are likely to be more utilitarian because spouses are less free to develop according to their personalities and lifestyle choices. They seem channeled by restricted childhoods and current economic pressures into a preoccupation with day-to-day survival and with attaining a minimum of order and stability, and they seem handicapped by the spiral of alienation likely to develop out of their early struggles. Many working-class couples have the desire but not the skills, models, or freedom from worry to sustain a more intrinsic relationship (Rubin 1976; Hughes and Perry-Jenkins 1996).

Among middle-class partners, however, more utilitarian unions can be chosen mainly by default. Couples allow themselves to drift, ignoring their initial commitment to keep each other primary in their lives. Earlier in this chapter we saw that each partner's having outside interests of their own can enhance a relationship. "When we 'bargain' for marriage, our partner's independent third-corners are always part of the bargain, and how we handle those third-corners (both our partner's and our own)" affects the quality of our union (Marks 1989, p. 24). Nevertheless, increased emphasis on other matters, such as career advancement or children, can result in slow emotional erosion (Sternberg 1988b, p. 273). Among Cuber and Harroff's devitalized couples, husbands who were promoted grew busier, came home later, and brought with them "bulging briefcases." The nonworking wives of "organization men" busied themselves with children and community organizations. Today both partners may be concentrating on careers rather than building intimacy. And there is new concern that preoccupation with the Internet can erode marital and family communication and companionship (Hamilton and Kalb 1995).

Although many utilitarian marriages are chosen by default, successful intrinsic couples often shape their relationship "deliberately, consciously, sometimes even ruthlessly" (Cuber and Harroff 1965, p. 134). At different times throughout their marriage, a couple's relationship may be more (or less) couple-centred, parenting-centred, or relatively loosely connected as one or both partners pursue careers or other personal interests (Marks 1989). We have seen that the first years of marriage are often more couple-centred than are later years. Spouses who desire enduring, more intrinsic relationships must keep the primariness of their mate and marriage as a high priority. For example, a spouse or partner may choose to turn down career opportunities that could threaten the relationship. In one instance reported by Cuber and Harroff, a husband married for 22 years had passed up two promotions because one would have required some traveling and the other would have taken evening and weekend time away from his wife.

Keeping one's marriage vital requires that partners consciously and continuously strive to maintain primariness and intimacy, which can entail personal sacrifice in career goals or other areas of life. As a result, intrinsic partners see their relationship as the product of an enormous investment: in time, effort, and priorities. In other words, an emotionally meaningful relationship does not often develop "by drift or default" (Cuber and Harroff 1965, pp. 142–45).

Clearly, the nature and quality of a marital relationship has a great deal to do with choices partners make. They risk disillusionment less when they make their choices consciously and knowledgeably. Partners are freer today to design their own unions, both the form their marriages and families will take and the kind of relationship they will develop. They therefore need to be as honest as they can be with each other (and with themselves) about their expectations and goals, both before and throughout a marriage. We saw in Chapter 1 that as people change throughout life, the kind of relationship they need also changes. Thus, marriages need to be flexible if they are to continue to be satisfying to changing partners. In the next section we'll see what this flexibility entails.

STATIC VERSUS FLEXIBLE MARRIAGES

For years, writes Sidney Jourard,

spouses go to sleep night after night, with their relationship patterned one way, a way that perhaps satisfies neither—too close, too distant, boring or suffocating—and on awakening the next morning, they reinvent their relationship *in the same way.* (1976, p. 231)

Spouses who choose to behave in this way are shaping **static (closed) marriages** (O'Neill and O'Neill 1972). Partners in static marriages rely on their formal, legal bond to enforce permanence, strict monogamy, and rigid husband-wife role behaviour. Spouses who rely on formal rules to maintain their feelings of intimacy, however, have unrealistic expectations about marriage. They may expect, for example, that their loving relationship will (in spite of the rising divorce rate) last forever. They may falsely believe that marriage guarantees their own and their partner's total commitment. Often they begin to think that their mate belongs to them.

People do change, however, and promises will not prevent change. Partners who vowed never to change may try to hide their personal growth from each other, with the result, of course, that intimacy diminishes. They may be left with a permanent, but stale, relationship.

An option is to actively pursue a **flexible marriage**, one that allows and encourages partners to grow and change. In a flexible marriage, spouses' roles may be renegotiated as the needs of each change (Scarf 1995).

Flexible marriages are more likely to be intrinsic, as partners are freer to reveal their changing selves and the parts of themselves that no longer fit into their established pattern. They can continue to be in touch at a deep emotional level while they alter the outer framework of their lives. Utilitarian marriages are also likely to benefit from flexibility, as utilitarian needs are likely to change over time.

How can marriages remain or become flexible? Some people may have an intuitive knack for achieving this kind of marriage. Others are able to act and react creatively on realizing the need for flexibility, without following any particular pattern. Some partners may object in principle to the idea of consciously and formally considering their marriage arrangements in order to make the marriage more flexible. But again, we want to stress the way in which decisions, in the absence of conscious reflection, often are made by default, and we suggest negotiating a personal marriage agreement. Even for those who do not wish to exercise this option, the following sec-tion outlines some of the issues likely to arise in a flexible marriage.

CONTRACTING FOR FLEXIBILITY—A CONTRADICTION?

How do people design flexible marriages? It may sound contradictory, but one way is purposefully to contract for ongoing flexibility. Partners begin by consciously negotiating personal marriage agreements.

When partners marry, they agree to two contracts: a legal–social one between the couple and the state or society and a personal one between the partners themselves. "The legally married nuclear family has access to this ready-made blueprint for building a family: familiar models, designated roles, and socially approved patterns of behaviour" (Kornfein, Weisner, and Martin 1979, pp. 284–85). But at the same time, the legal–social contract is hidden, or generally outside people's conscious awareness; it is seldom verbalized or evaluated. "It is in many ways an unconscious contract, agreed to by default in the sense that it is unwitting" (O'Neill and O'Neill 1972, p. 51). But that does not make the contract any less binding on how partners think, feel, and behave toward each other. Indeed, the power of the hidden legal-social contract to construct spouses' relationships is tremendous.

One way for couples to develop flexible marriages is to write **personal marriage agreements**, which involve articulating, negotiating, and coming to some agreement on expectations about how you and your partner will behave. Moreover, to develop flexible marriages, partners need to renegotiate their agreements often, to keep the relationship pliable enough to accommodate the changes in two people over time. Static marriage contracts too often lead to disillusionment (Crosby 1985). When the rules begin to seem too rigid or it becomes clear that unrealistic expectations will not be met, closed contracts leave only two alternatives: divorce or a devitalized relationship.

In drawing up a personal marriage agreement, people begin by separately writing down their expectations about their relationship. Even if they are single and not seriously involved in a relationship, thinking about and writing down their expectations about intimate relationships is important for self-understanding. Later they can compare and negotiate the differences in their expectations. The result is a working marital agreement.

The goal of personal marriage agreements is to help partners actively define their relationship. Because unmarried partners can also benefit from this process, such personal agreements could also be termed **relationship agreements**. (Research indicates that the need to resolve such issues as sexual exclusivity, division of labour, and power and decision making is not much different in gay or lesbian pairings than in heterosexual pairings or marriage [Peplau 1981; Harry 1983].)

Writing an agreement may seem rational and cold. Or it may seem to define a commitment that is limited, like a business contract, not one that is open-ended and at least intended to last forever, like marriage. But there are important reasons for defining a marriage with some degree of consciousness and awareness.

Reasons for a Marriage Agreement

One important reason for writing a marriage agreement is that it helps partners to be aware of and avoid choosing closed marriage by default. There are other reasons a contract can be helpful.

First, partners need to articulate the primary focus of their marriage. Will their union be—or is it— mainly utilitarian or intrinsic? Partners who want intrinsic unions need to articulate that, or they may unwittingly allow occupational, household, educational, or other responsibilities to drain their energies.

Second, writing a marriage agreement can allow partners to understand each other's role expectations. Differentiated roles can be satisfying if both partners accept the arrangement. Spouses who wish to develop egalitarian relationships, however, must battle remnants of patriarchal tradition, both in society and in their own previously internalized attitudes. Women who are willing to share the provider role may still expect a husband to do the household repairs and plan the long-term finances. Men who in many ways truly appreciate their wife's achievements may wish they didn't have to worry about the wife's schedule or her need to travel, or they may wish she were more available to play hostess, or run to the cleaners, or deal with the children.

Third, partners may have different ideas of what marriage means and different expectations about how they will behave in marriage. For example, one partner may expect to continue going out alone with his or her separate friends; the other may expect to build a joint social network. Or one partner may assume they share a desire to buy a house and to sacrifice small pleasures to build up a nest egg, whereas the other may place more emphasis on the day-to-day sharing of movies, dinners out, small gifts, and travel expenses.

Discussing and negotiating these differences is important. Writing an agreement before marrying can point up differences, many of which can be worked out. If partners uncover basic values differences and cannot work them out—for example, about whether or not to have children—it would probably be better to end their relationship before marriage than to commit themselves to a union that cannot satisfy either of them. Writing an agreement after having been married for some time can point up previously unrecognized disagreements. Facing these openly and honestly is important in maintaining a mutually supportive relationship.

Fourth, love before and during the early years of marriage is often blind. Courting partners often romanticize each other, creating images and refusing to see anything that contradicts those images. Negotiating personal agreements helps cut through the tendency to overromanticize.

A premarital agreement can also determine division of property between a current spouse and children of an earlier marriage. Prospective remarriage partners are more likely to see a need for a premarital contract to clarify financial obligations because the potential for future conflict is obvious. For example, for those entering a union with a previously married spouse with children, it may be useful to specific what the stepparent's obligations will be in the event of a separation or divorce. As we note in Chapter 15, a stepparent may find him or herself required to provide support to his/her stepchildren because s/he behaved like a parent ("in loco parentis"—literally, in place of a parent) during the course of marriage.

However, we should emphasize that the terms within marriage contracts may not always be enforceable. First, it is probably obvious that Canadian courts will not monitor marriages to ensure compliance with agreements that specify that the wife will mow the lawn and shovel the snow or that the husband carries out the garbage and is responsible for all cooking done outdoors.

Second, rules may vary across jurisdictions. It is not legal in certain provinces (e.g., British Columbia, Alberta, Ontario, New Brunswick, Prince Edward Island, Newfoundland, the Northwest Territories) for couples to agree, in advance of marriage, on matters of child custody or child access in the event of marital breakdown. (The agreement may state, however, that spouses will cooperate in determining that custody decisions will be made in the "best interests of the child" or that the couple will seek mediation in the event that child custody and access become the subjects of dispute). In the province of Quebec, parties are restricted from contracting out of marital property rights. Moreover, "Quebec's Civil Code states specifically the rights and duties of spouses, which apply no matter what a marriage contract says" (Dranoff 2001, p. 89).

Specifically, under Quebec's Civil Code, each spouse possesses the same rights and obligations in marriage as the other and each "owe each other respect, fidelity, succour and assistance." The married couple "are bound to live together...[and] together take in hand the moral and material direction of the family, exercise parental authority and assume the tasks resulting therefrom." The Code also directs that the married couple jointly select the family residence, and contribute to the marriage, in accordance with their means. Each spouse is also responsible for any debts incurred by the other for the current needs of the family (Dranoff 2001, p. 89).

Third, in Canada, "[p]rovisions that limit the right of a spouse to live in the matrimonial home, or consent to the mortgaging or encumbrancing of it" (Dranoff 2001, p. 92) are also unenforceable. There are also limitations in relation to contracting out of rights and obligations relating to spousal support and child support. For example, in the event that a spouse waives all claims to support or agrees to terms of support that originally appeared reasonable but result in "unconscionable circumstances" (e.g., destitution or a reliance upon social assistance), the court can exercise its discretion and disregard such provisions. In Canada, "spouses cannot waive child support, as a matter of public policy" (Dranoff 2001, p. 91).

Increasingly couples have been encouraged to privately negotiate marital rights and obligations, "in part because such matters are now considered more the business of the parties than the state, but also because private negotiation....serves the interest of the state in reducing public expenditure on court proceedings" (Bailey 2000, 16). However, as we have noted, spouses are not entirely free to do as they please.

Sometimes prenuptial contracts about property—usually between an older, wealthy man and a not-so-wealthy woman—are signed in a coercive atmosphere of "sign or stay single" (Dullea 1988b). Such potential for abuse should remind us that negotiation of a premarital contract or relationship agreement should take place in an atmosphere of equality, respect, and full disclosure, with each party free to seek professional legal advice on the matter. In general terms, a properly witnessed and executed marital contract is difficult to set aside. A marriage contract can be set aside if there is evidence that the agreement was signed under duress or that one partner was unduly influenced (e.g., through physical violence or improper pressure) by his or her spouse. The latter, however, is particularly difficult to prove.

The following paragraphs provide an overview of some of the most crucial aspects of a marital agreement.

Some Questions to Ask

An initial marriage agreement can be short or long, general or detailed. Some agreements include such fine points as exactly how spouses will allocate money and household chores. Others are more general, emphasizing marital goals, values, and attitudes. (A general agreement may become more specific in the course of renegotiations or further development.) However it evolves, the agreement should consider the following basic questions, along with any others that are important to particular couples (Crosby 1991, pp. 321–22).

1. *Preliminary statement of marital goals.* Will you aim primarily at developing intimacy? Or do you want to emphasize more practical advantages from marriage, such as economic security or someone to share a household with, for example? What kind of relationship do you and your partner realistically anticipate: conflict-habituated? passive-congenial? vital? total? How do you feel about devitalized relationships? Should partners learn to accept these gracefully, work toward changing them, or divorce?

2. *Provisions for revision and renewal of contract.* Because spouses change, marriage agreements

need to be rewritten often. Couples can plan to discuss and revise their agreement periodically—every six months for example. Ideally, they agree that their contract is a living document to be renegotiated and changed any time one partner feels the need. Is there any part of this contract that you think now you would never, under any circumstances, consider changing?

3. *Provisions for dissolution of the legal marriage.* When should a marriage be dissolved and under what conditions? How long and in what ways would you work on an unsatisfactory relationship before dissolving it?

4. *Decision making and division of labour.* Will decisions be made equally? Will there be a principal breadwinner? Or will partners equally share responsibility for earning money? How will funds be allocated? Will there be his, her, and our money? Or will all money be pooled? Who is the owner of family property, such as family business(es), farms, or other partnerships? Will there be a principal homemaker? Or will domestic chores be shared?

5. *Religious beliefs and practices and educational goals.* What are your religious values? Do you expect your partner to share them? Will you attend church services together? How often? If you are of a different religion from your mate, whose church will you attend on special religious holidays? What about the children's religion?

    What are your educational goals? What educational goals do you expect your partner to have? Under what circumstances could you or your partner put aside wage-earning or housekeeping responsibilities to pursue advanced education?

6. *Relationships with other relatives.* How will you relate to your own and to your spouse's relatives? How do you expect your partner to relate to them? Will you expect to share many or most activities with relatives? Or do you prefer more couple togetherness, discouraging activities with relatives?

7. *Children.* Whose responsibility is birth control, and what kind of contraception will you use?

What is your attitude toward unwanted pregnancy: abortion? adoption? keeping and rearing the child? Do you want children? If so, how many and how would you like to space them? How will you allocate child-rearing responsibilities and tasks? Will either spouse be primarily responsible for discipline? What are some of your values about rearing children?

8. *Expectations for sexual relations.* Can you discuss your sexual needs and desires openly with your partner? Are there sexual activities that you consider distasteful and would prefer not to engage in? How would you expect to deal with either your own or your partner's sexual dysfunction if that occurred?

9. *Extramarital friendships and sexual relations.* How much time and how much intimate information will you share with friends other than your partner? What is your attitude toward friendships with people of the opposite sex? How about Internet (cyberspace) friends? Would you ever consider having sex with someone other than your mate? If so, under what circumstances? How would you react if your partner were to have sex with another person? (Box 8.2 explores some of these questions.)

10. *Privacy expectations.* How much time alone do you need? How much are you willing to allow your partner? Will you buy a larger house or rent a bigger apartment so that each partner can have private space?

11. *Communication expectations.* Will you purposely set aside time to talk with each other? What topics do you like to talk about? What topics do you dislike? Are you willing to try to become more comfortable about discussing these? If communication becomes difficult, will you go to a marriage counsellor? If so, what percentage of your income would you be willing to pay for marriage counselling?

12. *Vacations.* What kinds of vacations will you take? Will you take couple-only vacations? Will you take separate vacations? If so, how often and what kind?

13. *Definition of terms.* What are your own and your partner's personal definitions of *primariness, intimacy, commitment,* and *responsibility?*

Addressing these questions and others like them is important to keeping a marriage relationship vital. In negotiating with each other, people must try to keep an open mind and use their creativity. Creatively negotiating not only an agreement but a working relationship is difficult, if only because two people, two imaginations, and two sets of needs are involved. Differences *will* arise because no two individuals have exactly the same points of view. (Some methods for reconciling these differences, and other conflicts, are discussed in Chapter 9.)

IN SUM

Although marriage is less permanent and more flexible than it has ever been, it is still unique and set apart from other human relationships. Although legal marriage is not possible for same-sex couples in Canada, this situation may change. Meanwhile, the marriage premise includes expectations of permanence and primariness. As both of these expectations come to depend less on legal definitions and social conventions, partners need to invest more effort in sustaining a marriage.

Because few data are available on the period just before marriage, there is much concern about preparation for marriage—is it adequate in today's society? Premarital counselling and family life education in the schools are two approaches that have been developed, but we need more research data on their effectiveness. We need to learn more about the transition into marriage, although it appears that the early years of marriage tend to be a happy time.

Two opposite poles on a continuum of marriage are the utilitarian marriage and the intrinsic marriage. Most marriages fall somewhere in between. Some frequently occurring marital types are the conflict-habituated, the devitalized, the passive-congenial, the vital, and the total marriage.

Partners change over the course of a marriage, so a relationship needs to be flexible if it is to continue to be intrinsically satisfying. Static marriages are usually devitalized. Marriage or domestic partner agreements, which can be renegotiated as the need arises, are one useful way of coming to mutual agreement. Working on a marriage agreement together can help partners develop a couple identity—one of the tasks of early marriage.

Key Terms

balanced connection
conflict-habituated marriage
conjugal kin
consanguineous kin
couple-centred connection
covenant marriage
cyberadultery
dependency-distancing couples
devitalized marriage
dominant dyad
expectations of permanence
externalizing
extramarital sex
family-centred connection
family of orientation
family of procreation
flexible marriages
interactional relationship pattern
internalizing

intrinsic marriage
jealousy
loose connection
marriage premise
parallel relationship pattern
passive-congenial marriage
personal marriage agreements
primariness
registered partnerships
relationship agreements
role making
romantically-fused couples
separate couple
sexual exclusivity
sexually open marriage
static (closed) marriages
swinging
total marriage
utilitarian marriage
vital marriage

Study Questions

1. Discuss the expectation of permanence in a marital relationship. How does it affect a relationship?

2. Partners' expectations of primariness in marriage may be interpreted sexually or emotionally. How do these two interpretations differ? Which do you agree with? Why?

3. Give some reasons why people enter utilitarian marriages. How do these differ from reasons for entering intrinsic marriages?

4. Review footnote 1, and write an essay that compares and contrasts Crosby's A; H; and M-frame relationships (Chapter 4) with Marks' typology of couple connection. Give original examples as often as you can.

5. Describe the five kinds of marital relationships classified by Cuber and Harroff. Which kinds are utilitarian and which are intrinsic? Explain your reasoning.

6. Why do you think that total marriages are rare?

7. Do you think that legalizing same-sex marriage is a good idea? Give evidence to support your opinion.

8. Do you favour or oppose legal marriage for same-sex partners? Give evidence for your answer.

9. Do you think it is easier to develop a utilitarian relationship or an intrinsic relationship? Why?

10. Differentiate static and flexible marriages, and discuss the reasons a marriage agreement can be helpful.

11. This chapter lists thirteen questions that the authors think are important to consider in any marriage agreement. Which do you think are the most important? Which do you think are the least important? Why?

12. Design your own marriage agreement. What does it tell you about your ideas on marriage?

13. What do you think couples should do before marriage to improve their chances of having a happy and stable marriage?

14. What do you think are likely to be the most important issues in the early years of marriage?

Suggested Readings

Mackey, Richard A. 1997. *Gay and Lesbian Couples: Voices from Lasting Relationships.* Westport, CT: Praeger. Even if they cannot presently marry legally, many gay and lesbian couples do forge lasting relationships, and the couples in this book describe their relationships.

Scanzoni, John, Karen Polonko, Jay Teachman, and Linda Thompson. 1989. *The Sexual Bond: Rethinking Families and Close Relationships.* Newbury Park, CA: Sage. A thorough consideration of issues of primariness and permanence in marriage that is anything but conventional. The authors propose reconceptualizing "family," given the pervasive departure from the cultural ideals of permanent marriage and the nuclear family.

Sherman, Suzanne, ed. 1992. *Lesbian and Gay Marriage: Private Commitments, Public Ceremonies.* Philadelphia: Temple University Press. A collection of first-person accounts by lesbian and gay male couples regarding their views on marriage and their various experiences with wedding/marriage ceremonies.

Wallerstein, S. and Sandra Blakeslee. 1995. *The Good Marriage: How and Why Love Lasts.* New York: Houghton Mifflin. These two marriage counsellors and researchers offer their own typology of marriage relationships and list tasks that every couple needs to accomplish in a long-term, successful union.

On the Net

1) For useful links dealing with marital satisfaction see
http://www.gwdg.de/~rbeer/marital/links.html

2) For up-to-date info on the status of same-sex relationships in Canada see
http://www.egale.ca

3) Promise Keepers' Official Home Page
http://www.promisekeepers.org

4) NOW (National Organization of Women on the Promise Keepers
http://www.now.org/issues/right/pk.html

5) Institute for Families in Society
http:www.sc.edu/ifis/

Communication and Conflict Management in Marriages and Families

I KNOW YOU BELIEVE YOU UNDER-
STAND WHAT YOU THINK I SAID, BUT I
AM NOT SURE YOU REALIZE THAT
WHAT YOU HEARD IS NOT WHAT I
MEANT.

ANONYMOUS,

FROM A POSTER

WHEN TWO PEOPLE ALWAYS AGREE,
THERE'S NO NEED FOR ONE OF THEM
ANYWAY.

BEN BROWN, 54,

MARRIED 31 YEARS

Communication between mates is addressed throughout this text. Chapter 4, for example, emphasized the need for self-esteem as a prerequisite to self-disclosure. Chapter 8 discussed negotiating flexible marriage agreements. In this chapter we'll focus on couple communication generally, especially communicating about conflicts. (Domestic violence, which can be the unfortunate, even tragic, result of poorly managed conflict, is addressed at length in Chapter 10.) In this chapter we'll see that the sulking that characterizes unhappiness and boredom in marriage often results from spouses' attempts to deny or ignore conflict, and we'll examine several other outcomes of refusing to deal openly with conflict. We will also explore some alienating attitudes and behaviours that couples should avoid when fighting. We will discuss some healthy attitudes and propose some guidelines for communicating constructively. Finally, we will look at family cohesiveness and see what partners can do to enhance it. To begin, we will address the idea of families as powerful environments.

One important effect of loving is that it provides individuals with a sense of being personally and specially cared for in an impersonal society. Providing emotional security and feelings of belonging is an important function of the family today.

Families are powerful environments. Nowhere else in our society is there such power to support, hurt, comfort, denigrate, reassure, ridicule, love, and hate. For most Canadians, belonging to a family probably yields both positive and negative feelings. At one moment a person feels supported and reassured; at another, unappreciated and misunderstood. How we feel has a lot to do with how we communicate with one another.

The emotional tone of a couple's everyday communication is very important (Noller and Fitzpatrick 1991). Distressed couples tend toward negative exchanges that put these couples' marriages on a downward spiral (Gottman 1998). Conflict is a natural part of every relationship. But research shows that unhappily married couples are distinguished by their failure to manage that conflict. It is very important to think about how we communicate with our loved ones on a daily basis—and also how we communicate about our inevitable conflicts.

FAMILIES AS POWERFUL ENVIRONMENTS

Using the interactionist theoretical perspective (Chapter 2), Charles Horton Cooley (1902) used the term **looking-glass self** to describe the process by which people adopt as their own, and gradually come to accept, the evaluation, definitions, and judgments of themselves they see reflected in the faces, words, and gestures of those around them.

Cooley's description has broad applicability in social environments, but perhaps nowhere is it more evident than in the family, for three reasons. First, people reveal more of themselves in families than they do in superficial relationships; thus, they are more vulnerable to evaluation, encouragement, and criticism. Second, today Canadian nuclear (and single-parent) families are largely separated from the monitoring gaze of extended kin, neighbours, or friends (Nock 1998a). Hence, the opinions of our immediate family members are likely to go undisputed. Third, the opinions of family members have a significant influence on the way people perceive themselves. Family members are **significant others**: people whose opinions about each other are important to each individual's self-esteem.

Attributions

The family has a tremendous influence on self-concept and behaviour. Family members can validate—or refuse to validate—an individual's self-concept (Schafer, Wickrama, and Keith 1996). For example, if you think of yourself as generally capable but temporarily overextended, your family members can either validate that or not. So powerful is the family in shaping people's self-images that psychoanalyst R. D. Laing compares the process to hypnotism. In hypnosis one person gets another not only to *do* but also to *be* what the first person wants. Family members exercise hypnotic power over one another by implying that a member *is* a kind of person—selfish, kind, competent, lazy, and so on. This is accomplished through the process of **attribution**: ascribing certain character traits to people. For example, a person is told she or he *is* intelligent, not directly instructed to *act* intelligently. In fact, attributions can be considered part of a family's archives. Anecdotes reinforce a member's identity as reckless, helpful, or unlucky (Weigert and Hastings 1977).

Attributions are often more powerful in a primary group of more than two: One person says or implies something about a second person to a third person in front of the second. For example, a mother might tell her children in front of their father that he is a skilled "handyman." With repetition, the father may soon have a family reputation, which even he believes, of being able to fix anything—even if he can't.

As the process of attribution occurs again and again, family members unconsciously begin to behave according to their reputations. In a sense, family interaction can be viewed as a play in which the same theme is repeated in scenario after scenario, such as being late for work "again" or becoming flustered before guests arrive. Each member, without thinking, plays out the part attributed to him or her (Laing 1971, pp. 78–80).

Consensual Validation

Families also influence their members' definitions of the world around them. People see things differently from one another, and as a result, they define reality in many different ways. They also depend on others, especially significant others, to help them affirm their definitions. This process is called **consensual validation**, and it is an important dimension of family functioning. Through conversation, members can help one another feel comfortable about how each perceives the world. Husbands and wives may feel stronger in their political convictions—or in their views on social issues such as Canadian unity, free trade or abortion—if their spouse agrees; or a teenager may feel more comfortable when she refuses to drink with her friends if she has a sibling who thinks she's doing the right thing.

Consensual validation also takes place in a much broader sense. In Berger and Kellner's (1970) words, "the reality of the world is sustained through conversation with significant others." Family interaction

> validates over and over again the fundamental definitions of reality once entered into, not, of course, so much by explicit articulation, but precisely by taking the definitions silently for granted and conversing about all conceivable matters on this taken-for-granted basis. (pp. 52–53)

One of the possibly alarming aspects of marital breakup is that the taken-for-granted world is no longer validated by the partner (Vaughan 1986).

Negative Family Power

Even in an ongoing family, interaction does not always validate members' perceptions of situations and events. Significant others in a family have power, if they choose to use it, to make one member feel out of step. One way families do this is by a process Bach and Wyden (1970) have called *gaslighting*. The term comes from the old movie *Gaslight,* in which a husband attempts to drive his wife insane so she can be put in an asylum. He gradually turns down their gaslight over a period of time but tells his wife she's wrong when she perceives that their home is becoming dimmer.

In **gaslighting**, one partner chips away at the other's perception of him- or herself and at the other's definitions of reality. Typically, this occurs through destructive snipes at a partner, sometimes faintly camouflaged as humour. Often the gaslighter uses mixed messages or sarcasm. When a spouse protests or questions, the gaslighter denies everything and insists that the spouse must be crazy. In the movie the husband *wanted* to drive his wife insane; in real families, members can accomplish the same results without intending to.

A related destructive family behaviour is **scapegoating**: consistently blaming one particular member for virtually everything that goes wrong in the family (Vogel and Bell 1960). The power of the family over its members is due partly to the modern definition of the family as a sanctuary and retreat. Ironically, the family's tendency to create boundaries not only gives members a place to belong but also increases family members' power to undermine one another's self-esteem (Pruchino, Burant, and Peters 1994). Family systems theory, described in Chapter 2, represents one way of explaining how this occurs. The whole family, as a system of interacting parts, works together to create complementary roles, or family personalities, for each of its members. Some of these roles, such as family scapegoat, are antithetical to building self-esteem.[1]

In calling attention to the negative power of the family to shape self-concept and behaviour, we do not mean to leave the impression that powerful family forces are invariably malevolent. Rather, we want to balance the "folk concept of the family" (Edwards 1991), which conveys an image of warmth, understanding, support, and happy holiday rituals, with a description of the darker side of family life (Worchel 1984). Some readers may be dealing with this dark side.

Antidotes to Destructive Behaviour

An antidote to destructive behaviour such as gaslighting or scapegoating is for a victim to begin thinking more independently and challenging negative attributions. People do this more readily when they have sources for building self-esteem outside their families. Among adolescents, for example, the peer group is a common resource (Bibby 1995). Other sources are grandparents and other relatives, teachers, work colleagues, or therapists. With such help from the outside, people can more easily resist the temptation to let destructive significant others define their identities.

A second antidote is to begin to foster a family atmosphere of encouragement rather than criticism. This does not mean that families are successful only if

---

1. See Chapter 4, including footnote 2 in Chapter 4, for a discussion of self-esteem as a useful analytic concept.

they are unvarying centres of solidarity, consensus, and harmony—and never of conflict, anger, or fighting.

Our society holds out a **conflict taboo** that considers conflict and anger morally wrong, and it discourages these emotions even (or especially) within the family. The assumption that conflict and anger don't belong in healthy relationships is based partly on the idea that love is the polar opposite of hate (Crosby 1991). But emotional intimacy necessarily involves feelings of both wanting to be close and needing to be separate, of agreeing and disagreeing (Scarf 1995).

CONFLICT AND LOVE

Marital anger and conflict are necessary forces and a challenge to be met rather than avoided. This is especially true in the early years of marriage, when individuals are often still engaged in the process of getting to know each other. (At this point, a complete lack of conflict might even be cause for concern!) It is also true at points throughout a good relationship.

Sociologist Judith Wallerstein (Wallerstein and Blakeslee 1995) conducted lengthy interviews with 50 predominantly white, middle-class couples. The shortest marriage was ten years and the longest, 40 years. In order to participate, both husband and wife had to define their marriage as happy. When discussing what she found, Wallerstein wrote:

[E]very married person knows that "conflict-free marriage" is an oxymoron. In reality it is neither possible nor desirable.... [I]n a contemporary marriage it is expected that husbands and wives will have different opinions. More important, they can't avoid having serious collisions on big issues that defy compromise. (p. 143)

The couples in Wallerstein's research quarreled on issues such as personal autonomy, who should handle the money and how it ought to be spent, how much a spouse should work, and whether the wife should be employed at all. Some fought over smoking and drinking:

In one marriage the husband and wife sat in the car to argue, to avoid upsetting the children. She told him that passive smoke was a proven carcinogen, and while the children were young he could not smoke in their home. He could do what he wanted outside. The man admitted that the request was reasonable, but he was furious. He punished her by not talking to her except when absolutely necessary for three months. Then he accepted the injunction on his smoking and they resumed their customary relationship. (p. 148)

Wallerstein concluded that:

The happily married couples I spoke with were frank in acknowledging their serious differences over the years.... What emerged from these interviews was not only that conflict is ubiquitous but that these couples considered learning to disagree and to stand one's ground one of the gifts of a good marriage. (p. 144)

We don't want to give the impression that communication and loving are *all* or *only* conflict management. (Box 9.1, "Some Rules for a Successful Relationship," gives ideas about communicating more generally.) Crosby points out that people can misinterpret the idea of working *at* marriages and other relationships. "Instead of working *at* marriage we may, with all good intentions, end up making work *of* marriage" (Crosby 1991, p. 287). Along with managing conflicts, being married involves play—humour, spontaneity, fun. Being able to feel playful and behave playfully involves feeling safe in the presence of a partner. But how conflicts, which do necessarily arise, are addressed and resolved has much to do with how secure mates feel in their relationship.

Denying Conflict: Some Results

Many married couples are reluctant to fight. This reluctance can have destructive effects on the partners as individuals and on their relationship. For example, research that examined the communication approaches of 282 newly married couples found that couples who believed in avoiding marital conflict were less happy than others two years later (Crohan 1992). Other longitudinal research reported that disagreement and anger exchange were related to current marital unhappiness but led to measurable improvement in marital satisfaction at the three-year follow-up (Gottman and Krokoff 1989). The implication of this research is that couples may have gone through a painful period in order to deal

with their dissatisfactions, but engaging in conflict enhanced the long-run health of their marriages.

In a later section we'll review some research on marital communication that suggests that the dynamics of conflict or conflict avoidance differs depending on the nature of the marriage. Here we'll look at several potential negative side effects of conflict avoidance: first those that relate to the individual, then those that affect the marriage relationship.

ANGER "INSTEADS"   Most people know when they are angry, but they feel uncomfortable about expressing anger directly. Through years of being socialized in the conflict taboo, people learn not to raise their voices and not to make an issue of things. One result is that many people resort to anger substitutes, or **anger "insteads"** (Kassorla 1973), rather than dealing directly with their emotions.

"Insteads" such as overeating, boredom, depression, physical illness, and gossip are probably familiar to most readers. Even though these "insteads" may be more socially acceptable than the direct expression of anger, they can be self-destructive. Because of this, they are costly, both to the individual who uses them and to any intimate relationship of the individuals. For example, sex therapists report that one of the most common complaints they hear from married couples these days is that "we don't feel much like having sex anymore" (Masters, Johnson, and Kolodny 1994). Repressing one's anger can contribute to this sexual boredom.

PASSIVE-AGGRESSION   The anger "insteads" can be subtle forms of what psychologists call **passive-aggression**. When a person expresses anger at someone but does so indirectly rather than directly, that behaviour is passive-aggression. People use passive-aggression for the same reason they use anger substitutes—they are afraid of direct conflict.

Chronic criticism, nagging, nitpicking, and sarcasm are all forms of passive-aggression. Procrastination, especially when you have promised a partner that you will do something, can be a form of passive-aggression (Ferrari and Emmons 1994). Like overeating, these reactions momentarily relieve anxiety. In intimate relationships, however, they create unnecessary distance and pain. Most people use sarcasm unthinkingly, and they often aren't aware of its effect on a partner. But being the target of a sarcastic remark can be painful; it also can result in partners feeling alienated from each other.

Sex becomes an arena for ongoing conflict when mates habitually withhold it or use it as passive-aggressive behaviour. A partner makes a disparaging comment in front of company. The hurt spouse says nothing at the time but rejects the other's sexual advances later that night because "I'm just too tired." It is much better to express anger at the time an incident occurs. Otherwise, the anger festers and contaminates other areas of the relationship.

Other forms of passive-aggression are sabotage and displacement. In **sabotage** one partner attempts to spoil or undermine some activity the other has planned. The husband who is angry because his wife invited friends over when he wanted to relax may sabotage her evening, for example, by acting bored. In **displacement** a person directs anger at people or things the other cherishes. A wife who is angry with her husband for spending too much time and energy on his career may hate his expensive car, or a husband who feels angry and threatened because his wife returned to school may express disgust for her books and "clutter." Often, child abuse can be related to displaced aggression felt by a parent. Child abuse is discussed further in Chapter 10.

DEVITALIZED MARRIAGES Another possible consequence of **suppression of anger**, the devitalized marriage, was discussed in Chapter 8. The result of suppressing anger over a long period of time can be indifference, as opposed to either love or hate (Crosby 1991). Because partners refuse to recognize or express any anger toward each other, their penalty may be the emotional divorce of a devitalized marriage.

This kind of gradual erosion does not take place only within marital relationships. Unmarried lovers who feel progressively less enthusiastic about their partners may be refusing to accept and voice anger, too. Little irritations build up until finally one decides, "I'm tired of his (or her) always doing _____." If the irritations had been brought into the open, the offending lover could have chosen to change, and the relationship might have continued.

Although the suppression of anger can be a source of boredom and devitalization, partners can go too far in the opposite direction and habitually or violently hurt each other in angry outbursts. Chapter 10 addresses spouse abuse as the extreme of destructive conflict. In this chapter we look at what some social psychologists and family therapists can teach us about communication and conflict management in general. We turn now to what some recent communication research has to say about comparing successful and unsuccessful marriages.

COMMUNICATION AND COUPLE SATISFACTION

In his great novel *Anna Karenina* (1899), Leo Tolstoy characterized happy families as being all alike, while suggesting that unhappy families exhibit infinite variety. Scholars of marital communication find that happy families do share some common qualities, especially the expression of positive emotions and affection (Gottman 1994). However, it also appears that Tolstoy was wrong in presuming that all happy marriages are alike.

One prominent researcher on marital communication, Mary Anne Fitzpatrick (1988, 1995) has found variation among happy couples in their marital ideology—ideas about the roles they should play, expectations for closeness and/or distance, and attitudes toward conflict. Some couples expect to engage in conflict only over big issues. Other couples are more open to conflict and fight more often. Still others, similar to the "separate" couples described in Chapter 8, expect a marital relationship that largely avoids both conflict and demonstrations of affection.

All of these couples can be satisfied with their relationship. What matters is whether the partners' actual interaction matches their marital ideology. For instance, the marital happiness of the more interdependent couples depends on their level of sharing and disclosure, whereas "separates" are more satisfied if they avoid jarring conflicts. Sociologist Stephen Marks (1989), whose work is described in Chapter 8, posits that the pivotal task for all marrieds is to balance each partner's need for autonomy with the simultaneous need for intimacy and togetherness. The happiest couples are those who manage to do this—by negotiating personal and couple boundaries through supportive communication (Scarf 1995).

Some Rules for a Successful Relationship

Research consistently shows that expressions of positive interest and affection are related to happy marriages. Psychologists Nathaniel Branden and Robert Sternberg, both of whom are mentioned in our discussion about love in Chapter 5, have developed some rules for nourishing a romantically loving relationship. Here are ten:

1. *Express your love verbally*. Say "I love you" or some equivalent (in contrast to the attitude, "What do you mean, do I love you? I married you, didn't I?")

2. *Be physically affectionate*. This includes making love sexually as well as hand-holding, kissing, cuddling, and comforting—with a cup of tea, a pillow, or a wooly blanket.

3. *Express your appreciation and even admiration*. Talk together about what you like, enjoy, and cherish in each other.

4. *Share more about yourself with your partner than you do with any other person*. In other words, keep each other primary (see Chapter 8).

5. *Offer each other an emotional support system*. Be there for each other in times of illness, difficulty, and crisis; be generally helpful and nurturing—devoted to each other's well-being.

6. *Express your love materially*. Send cards or give presents, big and small, on more than just routine occasions. Lighten the burden of your partner's life once in a while by doing more than your agreed-upon share of the chores.

7. *Accept your partner's demands and put up with your partner's shortcomings*. We are not talking here about putting up with physical or verbal abuse. But

demands and shortcomings are part of every happy relationship; and so is the grace with which we respond to them. Love your partner, not an unattainable idealization of him or her.

8. *Make time to be alone together*. This time should be exclusively devoted to the two of you as a couple. Understand that love requires attention and leisure.

9. *Do not take your relationship for granted*. Make your relationship your first priority and actively seek to meet each other's needs.

10. *Do unto each other as you would have the other do unto you*. Unconsciously we sometimes want to give less than we get, or to be treated in special ways that we seldom offer our mate. Try to see things from your lover's viewpoint so that you can develop the empathy that underlies every lasting close relationship.

Source: Branden 1988, pp. 225–28; Sternberg 1988b, pp. 272–77).

Meanwhile, Fitzpatrick's research also uncovered "mixed couples." In this case, spouses have dissimilar ideologies of marriage; they differ in their expectations for closeness and attitudes toward conflict (Fitzpatrick 1988, 1995; Noller and Fitzpatrick 1991). Not surprisingly, couples who differ in these ways are unlikely to be very satisfied with their marriages (VanLear 1992). Furthermore, unhappy marriages such as these do tend to have some common features: less positive and more negative verbal and nonverbal communication, together with more reciprocity of negative, but not positive communication (Noller and Fitzpatrick 1991).

The Four Horsemen of the Apocalypse

Social psychologist John Gottman (1979, 1994, 1996; Gottman et al. 1998) has made his reputation in the field of marital communication. In the 1970s, he began studying newly married couples in a university lab while they talked casually, discussed issues that they disagreed about, or tried to solve problems. Video cameras recorded the spouses' gestures, facial expressions, and verbal pitch and tone.

Since he began this research, Gottman has kept in contact with more than 650 of the couples, some for as many as 14 years. Typically the couples were videotaped intermittently. More recently, some couples have volunteered for laboratory observation that monitors shifts in their heart rate and chemical stress indicators in their blood and urine as a result of their communicating with each other (Gottman 1996).

Studying marital communication in this detail, Gottman and his colleagues were able to chart the effects of small gestures. For example, early in his career he discovered that when a spouse—particularly the wife—rolls her eyes while the other is talking, divorce is likely to follow sometime in the future, even if the couple is not thinking about divorce at the time (Gottman and Krokoff 1989).

Gottman's research (1994) showed that conflict and anger themselves did not predict divorce, but four processes that he called **The Four Horsemen of the Apocalypse** did.[2] The Four Horsemen of the Apocalypse are contempt, criticism, defensiveness, and stonewalling. Rolling one's eyes indicates **contempt**, a feeling that one's spouse is inferior or unde-

sirable. **Criticism** involves making disapproving judgments or evaluations of one's partner. **Defensiveness** means preparing to defend oneself against what one presumes is an upcoming attack. **Stonewalling** is resistance, refusing to listen to one's partner, particularly to a partner's complaints. In study after study these behaviours identified those who would divorce with an unusually high accuracy of about 90 percent. Later, after more research, Gottman added **belligerence**, "a behaviour that is provocative and that challenges the spouse's power and authority. For example: 'What can you do if I do go drinking with Dave? What are you going to do about it?' (Gottman et al. 1998, p. 6).

In sum, contempt, criticism, defensiveness, stonewalling, and belligerence characterize unhappy marriages and signal impending divorce. Supportive communication characterizes happier, stable unions. But what exactly is supportive communication?

SUPPORTIVE COUPLE COMMUNICATION AND CONFLICT MANAGEMENT

In recent research, Gottman and his colleagues videotaped 130 newlywed couples as they discussed for 15 minutes a problem that caused ongoing disagreement in their marriage (Gottman et al. 1998). Each couple's communication was coded in one-second sequences, then synchronized with each spouse's heart rate data, which was being collected at the same time. The heart rate data would indicate each partner's physiological stress.

The researchers examined all of the interaction sequences in which one partner first expressed *negative affect:* anger, sadness, whining, disgust, tension and fear, belligerence, contempt, or defensiveness. Belligerence, contempt, and defensiveness (three of Gottman's indicators of impending divorce) were coded as high-intensity, negative affect. The other emotions listed above (anger, sadness, whining, etc.) were coded as low-intensity negative affect.

Next the researchers watched what happened immediately after a spouse had expressed negative

---

2. The word *Apocalypse* refers to the ancient Greek and, later, Biblical idea that the world is soon to end, being destroyed by fire. Gottman used the term to indicate impending divorce.

affect, or raised a complaint. Sometimes the partner reciprocated with negative affect in kind, either low or high intensity. For example, she whines and he whines back; or, he expresses anger and she responds with tension and fear; or, she is contemptuous and he immediately becomes defensive.

At other times, one partner's first negative expression was reciprocated with an escalation of the negativity. For example, she whined and he grew belligerent; or, he expressed anger and she became defensive. Gottman and his colleagues called this kind of interchange *refusing-to-accept-influence*, because the spouse on the receiving end of the other's complaint refuses to consider it and, instead, escalates the fight.

Meanwhile, still other couples were likely to communicate with *positive affect*, responding to each other warmly, with interest, affection, or shared (not mean or contemptuous) humour. Positive affect typically de-escalated conflict.

What did Gottman and his colleagues find? First, they found that, "The only variable that predicted both marital stability and marital happiness among stable couples was the amount of positive effect in the conflict" (p. 17). In stable, happy couples, shared humour and expressions of warmth, interest, and affection were apparent even in conflict situations and, therefore, de-escalated the argument.

Second, the researchers "found no evidence ... to support the [idea that] anger is the destructive emotion in marriages" (p. 16). Instead they found that contempt, belligerence, and defensiveness were the destructive attitudes and behaviours. Specifically, they concluded that the interaction pattern that best predicts divorce is a wife's raising a complaint; followed by her husband's refusing-to-accept-influence; followed, in turn, by the wife's reciprocating her husband's escalated negativity; and the absence of any de-escalation by means of positive affect. Gottman and his colleagues went on to make suggestions for better couple communication, and their advice for wives is different than for husbands.

Gender Differences in Couple Communication

Deborah Tannen's book *You Just Don't Understand* (1990) argues that men typically engage in **report talk**, conversation aimed mainly at conveying infor-

mation. Women, on the other hand, are likely to engage in **rapport talk**, speaking to gain or reinforce rapport or intimacy. The resulting "men and women talking at cross-purposes" (p. 287) Tannen identifies is played out in marital or other relationship communication. "Gender is a category that will not go away," says Tannen (p. 287).

A review of research on couples in counselling over many years (Gottman and Levinson 1988) shows that men and women differ in their responses to negative affect in close relationships. When faced with a complaint from their partner, men tend to withdraw emotionally while women do not. This pattern is so common that some therapists refer to it as the "**female-demand/male-withdrawal pattern**." In distressed marriages, the demand-withdrawal pattern becomes a repeated cycle of negative verbal expression by a wife and withdrawal by the husband (Kurdek 1995); which came first is hard to say. One researcher speculates that wives, being more attuned to the emotional quality of a marriage and having less power, attempt to bring conflict out into the open by initiatives that have an attention-getting negative tone. Husbands try to minimize conflict by conciliatory gestures. Either a healthy problem-solving dialogue may ensue, or, more likely, the husband's minimization of conflict may seem to the wife to be a lack of recognition of her emotional needs and her concern about the marriage (Noller and Fitzpatrick 1991; Canary and Dindia 1998).

Early in his research, Gottman concluded that wives and husbands have different goals when they disagree. "The wife wants to resolve the disagreement so that she feels closer to the husband and respected by him. The husband, though, just wants to avoid a blowup. The husband doesn't see the disagreement as an opportunity for closeness, but for trouble" (in Gottman 1986). "I just don't know what she wants." In one husband's words, "When she comes after me like that, yapping like that, she might as well be hitting me with a bat" (Rubin 1976, p. 113). And as another explained, "I just got mad and I'd take off—go out with the guys and have a few beers or something. When I'd get back, things would be even worse" (p. 77). From his wife's perspective, "The more I screamed, the more he'd withdraw, until finally I'd go kind of crazy. Then he'd leave and not come back until two or three in the morning sometimes" (p. 79). Gottman and his colleagues sought to better understand this female-demand/male-withdrawal pattern.

You'll recall that the researchers monitored spouses' heart rates as indicators of physiological stress during conflict. They found that, while the final word is not yet in, "it is likely that the biological, stress-related response of men is more rapid and recovery is slower than that of women, and that this response is related to the greater emotional withdrawal of men than women in distressed families" (p. 19). That is, when confronted with conflict from an intimate, men may experience more intense and uncomfortable physical symptoms of stress than women do. Therefore, men are more likely than women to withdraw emotionally and/or physically.

An alternative—or complementary—view is that men have been socialized to withdraw. You'll recall that Chapter 3 discussed traditional differences in the ways men and women have been socialized, with men expected to be more instrumental and women, more expressive or relationship-oriented. The cultural options for masculinity described in Chapter 3 include "no 'sissy' stuff," according to which men are expected to distance themselves from anything considered feminine. We guess this could include a wife's complaints. In a recent book on men and communication called *I Don't Want to Talk About It,* therapist Terrence Real (1997) attributes males' withdrawal to a "secret legacy of depression," brought on by men's traditional socialization, particularly society's refusal to let them grieve over losses (e.g., "Don't cry over nothing."). It is likely that physiology and culture interact to create the female-demand/male withdrawal pattern.

In line with the view that social factors influence divergent communication patterns for men and women is research that examines responses to conflict in gay and lesbian relationships. Consistent with feminine socialization, lesbians employ a strategy of talking about tensions to respond to conflict and restore intimacy. At the same time, the emphasis placed on using communication to achieve emotional intimacy may actually discourage partners from expressing discontent. "[W]hile lesbian communication tends to be warm and supportive, it may not always be effective for resolving painful differences of opinion or creating change" (Huston and Schwartz 1996, p. 170). In contrast, gay couples, influenced by male speech patterns,

may attempt to bully their partner to get their own way or, alternatively, end discussion when they become uncomfortable. Michelle Huston and Pepper Schwartz (1996 p. 170) observe that communication between gay males may turn "into a battlefield in which each partner tries to win the upper hand and assert or display his own dominance."

If this is the case, winning is more important than resolution, and simple disagreements can evolve into serious arguments for which there seem to be no answers that satisfy both men's desire to dominate (p. 170).

However, "[w]hat men and women often do in intimate relationships is not necessarily an expression of what they are capable of doing" (Nelson and Robinson 1999, p. 323). For example, laboratory experiments found that when women are confronted with demands for change from men, they are as likely as men to withdraw into silence (Christensen and Heavey 1993; Klinetob and Smith 1996). Findings which indicate that men are more likely than women to withdraw may be "a consequence of the fact that women, charged with the responsibility for maintaining relationships, are most often in the position of asking men to change in order to explore or consolidate some aspect of the relationship" (Nelson and Robinson 1999, p. 323). It would appear that, within the power dynamics of intimate relationships, the "spouse with the most to gain by maintaining the status quo is likely to withdraw" (Klinetob and Smith 1996, p. 945).

WHAT WIVES CAN DO   In the following discussion, the term "soothe" indicates things people do to reduce physical stress symptoms. While both spouses benefit from being soothed, Gottman and his colleagues go so far as to say that, "Marriages will work to the extent that they provide for soothing of the male" (Gottman et al. 1998, p. 20). "Soothing of the male" can involve self-soothing—for example, he takes a time out or tells his wife that, "I just can't talk about it now, but I will later" (and means it). Also, soothing can imply soothing of the male by the female. This process involves two things: (1) using positive affect, such as shared humour and expressions of affection, to de-escalate negativity; and (2) the wife's softening the way she brings up complaints. Gottman does not mean to discourage wives from raising disagreeable topics, but rather to "soften" their confrontations by using less negative communication styles. For example, a wife who often voices complaints by whining or with a tone of contempt might try to speak more gently.

WHAT HUSBANDS CAN DO   Reminding us that fighting per se ("negative affect reciprocity in kind") is not the problem, Gottman and his colleagues argue that the husband's escalation of negativity is the real problem. The researchers view this escalation as a symptom of the husband's refusal to accept influence from, or share power with his wife.

> Usually the wife brings marital issues to the table for discussion, and she usually brings a detailed analysis of the conditions in which this problem occurs, its history, and suggestions for a solution. Some men, those whose marriages wind up stable and happy, accept influence from their wives, and some do not.... Our data suggest that only newlywed men who accept influence from their wives are winding up in happy and stable marriages. (pp. 18–19)

Unfortunately, newspapers publicized this research with headlines such as, "'Honey, just be a yes man,'" and "Marriage lasts if husband gives in." But sharing power is not the same as how one journalist described it: "Just do what your wife says. Go ahead, give in to her" (Maugh 1998). And thinking of oneself as constrained to be a "yes man" is itself contemptuous—one of Gottman's Four Horsemen. The real message to husbands is not to respond to their wife's complaints by escalating the argument with defensiveness, contempt, or belligerence.

IN SUM: WHAT COUPLES CAN DO   The general conclusion of Gottman's research on communication and conflict management among married couples is as follows:

1. Partners, especially wives, need to try to be more gentle when they raise complaints;

2. Partners, especially wives, can help soothe their spouse by communicating care and affection;

3. Partners, especially husbands, can learn self-soothing techniques;

4. Partners, especially husbands, need to be willing to accept influence from their wives.

5. Both partners need to do what they can, perhaps using authentic, shared humour, kindness, and other signs of affection, to de-escalate the argument. (It is important to recognize that this does not mean avoiding the issue altogether.) (Case Study 9.1, "Sharing a Grievance," illustrates many of these points.)

Finally, Gottman and his colleagues (1998) suggest that it probably is important for couples to think about communicating with positive affect more often in their daily living, and not just during times of conflict. (Box 9.1, "Some Rules for a Successful Relationship," suggests ways to do this.) Communicating with positive affect, of course, implies avoiding the Four Horsemen of the Apocalypse.

Avoiding the Four Horsemen of the Apocalypse

Consider the following exchange:

He: I need more socks.

She: What do you mean, you need more socks? Didn't you wash any? Are you accusing me of losing your socks?

He: No, Stupid, I mean I need some new socks.

She: So get some.

He: I thought you could pick them up since you'll be out this afternoon anyway.

She: You're just like your father—always ordering somebody around.

He: So what are you going to do about it? What do you think you can do about it?

She: Your father's a bum.

He: Oh yeah? Well, at least my mother can cook!

She: Well, she's a mess herself! She hasn't had a decent haircut in years.

He: You ought to do something with *your* hair. It's ridiculous.

She: Not that there's room in the bathroom with your stuff scattered all over....

In this scenario, the husband announces that he needs more socks and a fight ensues.

Some might find this couple's exchange humorous. But it is obviously not supportive marital communication, and it's not the kind that helps to bond couples and keep them together. This fight reveals three of Gottman's Four Horsemen of the Apocalypse—contempt, defensiveness, and criticism—along with belligerence, the sign of impending divorce that Gottman added later.

When he says that he needs more socks, she becomes defensive: "What do you mean you need more socks? ... Are you accusing me of losing your socks?" At this point a less distressed couple might stop this negative communication with shared humour or some sign of affection. But he fails to de-escalate the interchange and responds by calling his wife stupid. Name-calling is typically contemptuous; counsellors encourage us to avoid it.

He subsequently explains that he thought she could buy the socks, "since you'll be out this afternoon anyway." Her reply is contemptuous and critical: "You're just like your father—always ordering somebody around." Again, the couple fails to de-escalate the negative affect. This time he responds with belligerence: "So what are you going to do about it? What do you think you can do about it?"

The couple continues to criticize and show contempt for each other, while neither spouse de-escalates the argument. It probably goes without saying that this is the type of couple interaction we are advised to avoid. Moreover, it appears they've forgotten what the fight was about. In fact, one wonders whether they *know* what the fight is about.

Counsellors point out that distressed couples, like the one described here, often do not know what they are really fighting about. Fighting over petty annoyances, such as who should have put gas in the car, is healthy and can even be fun as an essentially harmless way to release tension. But partners sometimes unconsciously allow trivial issues to become decoys, so that they evade the real area of conflict and leave it unresolved. An irate husband, for example, who complains about how his wife treats their children, may really be fighting about his feelings of rejection because he feels that his wife isn't giving him enough attention.

The fight in the above scenario is actually about power and work roles in this couple's relationship. He feels comfortable requesting that she purchase his socks; she feels that she is being ordered around and that buying his socks is not her role in the relationship; he believes that she is not adequately performing her role in the union (he finds her cooking unsatisfactory). These are actually serious underlying issues for this couple—the fight is not about socks! Counsellors suggest that couples need to try to be clear about what they are really fighting about. This may be a tall order, however, and going to marriage counselling or couple therapy might be recommended.

We turn now to take a closer look at Gottman's fourth Horseman of the Apocalypse—stonewalling or refusing to listen to a partner's complaints.

STONEWALLING   Avoiding or evading a fight is an example of stonewalling.

Stonewallers react to their partner's attempts to raise disputed or tension-producing issues by refusing to engage with the partner's initiatives. They fear conflict and hesitate to accept their own and others' hostile or angry emotions.

Fight evaders use several tactics to avoid fighting, such as

1. Leaving the house or the scene when a fight threatens

2. Turning sullen and refusing to argue or talk

3. Derailing potential arguments by saying, "I can't take it when you yell at me"

4. Flatly stating, "I can't take you seriously when you act this way"

5. Using the "hit and run" tactic of filing a complaint, then leaving no time for an answer or for a resolution (Bach and Wyden 1970)

6. Saying, "Okay, you win," giving in verbally, maybe even promising to "Do better next time," but without meaning it

Stonewallers may argue that they avoid conflicts because they don't want to hurt their partners. Often,

Sharing a Grievance

Janet, 28, is married to Joe, who has two sons from a previous marriage. Here Janet talks about her need to share a grievance with Joe and the anxiety that taking such a risk can cause.

Joe's sons live with their mother .... They come to stay with us Christmas, spring break, and summers. Last summer when they were here, I was a wreck. I was jealous of Joe's relationship with the boys. He did so much with them, it seemed, and I was feeling left out. I was so upset, I was feeling sick.

I went to a physician, trying to figure out whether I really was physically ill or whether it was my head. He said, "Just take some time out and think about where you stand. And as time goes by and you feel the time is right, certainly discuss these feelings with your husband." Which is exactly what I did!

It was really kind of tricky though. Joe wanted so desperately for everybody to be happy, for us to have the one great big happy family. It was tricky because I had to find the right moment, the right atmosphere to speak what was on my mind. But I did. And it worked!

I remember so vividly reaching the point where I knew that I had to say something real soon or else it was gonna be bad for everybody. I knew Joe and I had to be away from the boys when we talked. And Joe had to be away from the phone.

So one Saturday afternoon he had to go to his office to pick something up, and I volunteered to go with him. But the atmosphere wasn't right in the car. I didn't

say anything. I thought, "Well, as soon as—when we get to the office—I'll just sit down and kind of open up then."

Well, the janitor that opened up the outside door also had to open the door to Joe's office. He just kept standing there, so I couldn't open up. I can remember the anxiety. My hands were sweating.

Finally, back in the car, before we got home, I said, "We have to stop for a drink because there's something on my mind and I really have to talk to you about it." We did. I think I opened the conversation by saying, "You know, I finally realize what it feels like to be a father when there is a newborn in the house." Because there was this bonding between him and the boys, and you hear all the time about the father's feeling left out with a newborn. And that was just exactly how I felt.

He said, "Well, let's see. How shall we approach this?" He was very open. I laugh now at all my anxiety because there was a tremendous effort on his part to really understand what my feelings were.

Why do you think Janet felt anxiety about sharing her feelings with Joe? What risk did she take in being honest? What did she gain? What did Joe gain?

Suppose Joe had been contemptuous, belligerent, or defensive rather than supportive. In your opinion, would the risk still have been worth it for Janet? What do you believe might have happened in the long run had Janet not risked initiating a fight?

however, the one they are really trying to protect is themselves. "A great deal of dishonesty that ostensibly occurs in an effort to prevent pain actually occurs as we try to protect and shield ourselves from the agony of feeling our own pain, fear, fright, shame, or embar-

rassment" (Crosby 1991, pp. 159–60). Stonewalling can also make partners who want and need to fight feel worse, not better.

Stonewalling can encourage one's partner to engage in **gunnysacking**: keeping one's grievances secret while tossing them into an imaginary gunny-sack that grows heavier and heavier over time. Martyring (see Chapter 4) typically accompanies gunnysacking. When marital complaints are toted and nursed along quietly in a gunnysack for any length of time, they "make a dreadful mess when they burst" out (Bach and Wyden 1970, p. 19).

Now that we've examined attitudes and behaviours that can pull a marriage apart, we turn to a complementary idea—that some fights can actually bring a couple closer together.

BONDING FIGHTS—SOME GUIDELINES

The tactics described previously are likely to alienate partners, but some goals and strategies can help make conflict management productive rather than destructive. This kind of fighting, which brings people closer rather than pushing them apart, is called **bonding fighting**. The key to creating a bonding fight is for partners to try to build up, not tear down, each other's self-esteem while fighting.

Social groups within Canada vary considerably in the endorsement their cultures give to the open expression of emotion, which may make bonding fighting more or less difficult for people within or across cultures. Deborah Tannen's best-selling book *You Just Don't Understand*, which drew wide attention for its comparison of men's and women's communication styles, also points out communication differences among, for example, Scandinavians, Canada's native peoples, and Greeks.

Now we turn to several specific guidelines for constructive fighting. Each of them has as its goals the development of a mutuality in communication and conflict management.

Let Your Partner Know You're Listening

Listening is so basic we often assume we're doing it effectively. But in couple conflict, listening may be forgotten as both partners strive to put forward their points of view. Accuracy in hearing what the speaker intended to communicate is noticeably lower in less well-functioning marriages (Noller and Fitzpatrick 1991; Markman, Stanley, and Blumberg 1994; Klein and Johnson 1997).

Communication involves both a sender and a receiver. Just as the sender gives both a verbal message and a nonverbal metamessage, so also does a receiver give nonverbal cues about how seriously she or he is taking the message. Listening while continuing to do chores, for example, sends the nonverbal message that what is being heard is not very important. Thinking about what listening does may help a person listen as well as talk.

According to sociologist/counsellor Carlfred Broderick, good listening has the following important results:

1. The attitude of listening itself shows love, concern, and respect.... Any act that expresses a positive attitude is likely to trigger a sequence of positive responses back and forth....

2. The avoidance of interrupting and criticism prevents the sending of negative messages such as "I don't care how you feel or what you think." "You're not worth listening to." ...

3. You discover how things actually look from your spouse's or partner's point of view. There's a risk, because what you hear may be surprising and even unsettling. But it is nearly always worth it. In fact, it's hard to imagine how any couple can become close without achieving insight into each other's feelings.

4. You lose your status as chief expert on what your spouse really thinks, wants, fears, and feels. Instead, your spouse takes over as the final authority on his or her own feelings.... [Furthermore] if you listen sympathetically to your spouse, he or she is able to develop greater clarity in areas that may have been confused and confusing....

5. You set an example for your spouse to follow in listening to your ... feelings (Broderick 1979a, pp. 40–41).

WHAT ABOUT "ACTIVE LISTENING?" Over the past several decades, psychologists and marriage counsellors have taught and encouraged the "active listening" communication model. There's a good chance you've already heard that term—maybe even been encouraged to practise it.

Active listening involves paying close attention to what the other is saying, coupled with giving **feed-**

back and **checking-it-out**. When giving feedback, a partner repeats in her or his own words what the other has said or revealed. For example, a wife says, "I don't like it when you're on the computer for a long time in the evenings, when we have so little time together." To give feedback, her husband would respond with something like, "I hear you saying that it irritates you when I'm on the computer instead of visiting with you."

Checking-it-out involves asking the other person whether your perception of his or her feelings or of the present situation is accurate. Studies consistently show that partners in distressed marriages seldom understand each other as well as they think they do (Noller and Fitzpatrick 1991; Zak 1998). Checking-it-out often helps avoid unnecessary hurt feelings. As the following example shows, the procedure can also help partners avoid imagining trouble that may not be there.

He: I sense you're angry about something. (checking it out) Is it because it's my class night and I haven't done the dishes?

She: No, but I am mad—because I was tied up in traffic an extra half hour on my way home.

Interestingly, however, Gottman and his colleagues, in the research described at length earlier in this chapter, found that few couples—including happy couples—used either feedback or checking-it-out. The researchers' general conclusion was that the active-listening model "occurred infrequently in the resolution of marital conflict and was not predictive of different marital outcomes" (Gottman et al. 1998, p. 17). If you are surprised to hear this, you might be interested to know that Gottman and his colleagues were "shocked and surprised" as well. So they reanalyzed all their videotaped data over the past 13 years. They found that couples seldom paraphrased what their partner said. In addition:

We also found that they were not summarizing their partner's feelings (e.g., "Sounds like this makes you pretty mad"), nor even summarizing the content of their spouse's statements (e.g., "You'd like it if we saved more money each month"). Furthermore, they almost never validated their spouse's feelings (e.g., "I can understand why this would make you upset"). (p. 17)

Gottman concluded that the active listening model may be misguided because:

it expects people to be able to be empathetic in the face of negative affect directed at them by their spouses…. [and] may be expecting a form of emotional gymnastics from people who at that moment in the relationship, are somewhat emotionally disabled by conflict. (p. 18)

Meanwhile, Gottman and his colleagues did find that happy couples typically let each other know they were listening. They did this by using what communication researchers call **listener backchannels**—"the usual brief vocalizations, head nods, and facial movements that convey to the speaker that the listener is tracking" (p. 17).

In conclusion, Gottman's research does not suggest that giving feedback or checking-it-out are harmful communication skills, rather that counsellors may be asking too much to expect couples to use them. The alternative suggested by Gottman and his colleagues centres less on communication skills and more on each partner's attitudes and motivation to show caring and affection—"a model of gentleness, soothing, and de-escalation of negativity" (p. 17).

Level With Each Other

Partners need to be as (gently, kindly) candid as possible; counsellors call this **leveling**—being transparent, authentic, and explicit about how one feels, "especially concerning the more conflictive or hurtful aspects" of an intimate relationship (Bach and Wyden 1970, p. 368). Leveling is self-disclosure in action.

Various studies indicate that because of boredom (an anger "instead"), indifference, or the mistaken impression that the partner already knows how the other feels, spouses often overestimate how accurately their partner understands them and then fail to understand their partner. Underlying conflicts often go unresolved because partners fail to voice their feelings, irritations, and preferences—and neither is aware that the other is holding back. The solution to this problem is to air grievances—to candidly explain where one stands and how one feels about a specific situation.

Being candid does not mean the same thing as being mean or unnecessarily critical. Leveling is never intentionally hurtful and is always consistent with the next guideline.

Avoid Mixed, or Double, Messages

In addition to stonewalling and gaslighting, a third **alienating fight tactic** is the use of **mixed, or double, messages**: simultaneous messages that contradict each other.[3] Contradictory messages can be verbal, or one can be verbal and one nonverbal. For example, a spouse agrees to go out to eat with a partner but at the same time yawns and says that he or she is tired and had a hard day at work. Or a partner insists "Of course I love you" while picking an invisible speck from her or his sleeve in a gesture of indifference.

Senders of mixed messages may not be aware of what they are doing, and mixed messages can be very subtle. They usually result from simultaneously wanting to recognize and to deny conflict or tension. Mixed messages allow senders to let other people know they are angry at them and at the same time to deny that they are. A classic example is the *silent treatment*. A spouse becomes aware that she or he has said or done something and asks what's wrong. "Oh, nothing," the partner replies, without much feeling, but everything about the partner's face, body, attitude, and posture suggests that something is indeed wrong.

Besides the silent treatment, other ways to indicate that something is wrong while denying it include making a partner the butt of jokes, using subtle innuendos rather than direct communication, and being sarcastic (also defended as "just a joke" by mixed-message senders).

Sarcasm and other mixed messages create distance and cause pain and confusion, for they prevent honest communication from taking place. Expressing anger is a far better tactic, for it opens the way for solutions. The next section presents guidelines for fighting more constructively.

To Avoid Attacks, Use I-Statements When You Can

Attacks are assaults on a partner's character or self-esteem. We have already seen that "contemptuous remarks or insults" are destructive fighting tactics (John Gottman, research reported in Goleman 1989, p. 1-B).

A rule in avoiding attack is to use *I* rather than *you* or *why*. The receiver usually perceives I-statements as an attempt to recognize and communicate feelings, but you- and why-statements are more likely to be perceived as attacks—whether or not they are intended as such. For example, instead of asking "Why are *you* late?" a statement such as "*I* was worried because you hadn't arrived" may allow more communication.

I-statements are most effective if they are communicated in a positive way. A partner should express his or her anger directly, but it will seem less threatening if he or she conveys positive feelings at the same time negative emotions are voiced. The message comes across, but it's not as bitter as when only angry feelings are expressed.

Making I-statements can be difficult, of course, and may be too much to ask in the heat of an argument. One social psychologist has admitted what many of us may already know: "It is impossible to make an 'I-statement' when you are in the 'hating-my-partner, wanting-revenge, feeling-stung-and-needing-to-sting-back' state of mind" (in Gottman et al. 1998, p. 18). Of course, this is partly the point. Keeping in mind, the possibility of expressing a complaint—at least *beginning* a confrontation—with an I-statement can discourage partners from getting to that wanting revenge state-of-mind in the first place.

Try to Choose the Time and Place Carefully

Fights can be nonconstructive if the complainant raises grievances at the wrong time. One partner may be ready to argue about an issue when the other is almost asleep or working on an important assignment, for instance. At such times, the person who picked the fight may get more than he or she bargained for.

Partners might try to negotiate *gripe hours* by pinning down a time and place for a fight. Fighting by appointment may sound silly and may be difficult to arrange, but it has two important advantages. First, complainants can organize their thoughts and feelings more calmly and deliberately, increasing the likelihood that their arguments will be persuasive. Second,

---

3. Communication scholars and counsellors point out that there are two major aspects of any communication: what is said (the verbal message) and how it is said (the nonverbal "metamessage"). The metamessage includes tone of voice, inflection, and body language. In a mixed message, the verbal message does not correspond with the nonverbal metamessage.

recipients of complaints have time before the fight to prepare themselves for some criticism.

Try to Focus Anger Only on Specific Issues

Constructive fighting aims at resolving specific problems that are happening *now*—not at gunnysacking. To maintain their self-esteem, recipients of complaints need to feel that they can do something specific to help resolve the problem raised. This will be more difficult if they feel overwhelmed.

Ask for a Specific Change, But Be Open to Compromise

Initially, complainants should be ready to propose at least one solution to the problem. Recipients, too, might come up with possible solutions. If they can keep proposed solutions pertinent to the issue at hand, partners might be able to negotiate alternatives.

Resolving specific issues involves bargaining and negotiation. Partners need to recognize that there are

Open communication involves listening—without judgment, without formulating a response while the other talks, and without interrupting. The goal isn't agreement, but acknowledgment, insight, and understanding.

probably several ways to solve a particular problem, and backing each other into corners with ultimatums and counterultimatums is not negotiation but attack. John Gottman found that happily married couples reach agreement rather quickly. Either one partner gives in to the other without resentment or the two compromise. Unhappily married couples tend to continue in a cycle of stubbornness and conflict (Gottman and Krokoff 1989).

Be Willing to Change Yourself

Communication, of course, needs to be accompanied by action. One counsellor team (Jacobson and Christensen 1996) has suggested "acceptance therapy," helping partners accept their spouses as they are instead of demanding change, although they suggest that, paradoxically, acceptance is also the basis for obtaining behaviour change. Meanwhile, the romantic belief that couples should accept each other *completely* as they are is often merged with the individualistic view that people should be exactly what they choose to be. The result is an erroneous assumption that if a partner loves you, he or she will accept you just as you are and not ask for even minor changes. On the contrary, partners need to be willing to change themselves, to be changed by others, and to be influenced by their partner's feelings and rational arguments. Defensiveness and refusing to change are dysfunctional responses that contribute to marital deterioration (Gottman and Krotkoff 1989). Every intimate relationship involves negotiation and mutual compromise; partners who refuse to change, or who insist they cannot, are in effect refusing to engage in an intimate relationship.

Don't Try to Win

Partners must not compete in fights. Our society encourages people to see almost everything they do in terms of winning or losing. Yet research clearly indicates that the tactics associated with winning in a particular conflict are also those associated with lower marital satisfaction (Noller and Fitzpatrick 1991; Holmes and Murray 1996; Klein and Johnson 1997; Zak 1998).

Bonding fights, like dancing, can't involve a winner and a loser. If one partner must win, then the other obviously must lose. But losing lessens a person's self-esteem and increases resentment and strain on the relationship. This is why in intimate fighting there can never be one winner and one loser—only two losers. Both partners lose if they engage in destructive conflict. Both win if they become closer and settle, or at least understand, their differences.

Remember to End the Fight

The happily married couples that Wallerstein (1995) interviewed (described earlier in this chapter) tried to fight only about big issues and knew how and when to stop fighting. However, if a couple cannot designate a winner and a loser, they can be at a loss to know how to end a fight. Ideally, a fight ends when there has been a mutually satisfactory airing of each partner's views. Bach suggests that partners question each other to make sure that they've said all they need to say.

Sometimes, when partners are too hurt or frightened to continue, they need to stop fighting before they reach a resolution. Women often cry as a signal that they've been hit below the "beltline" or that they feel too frustrated or hurt to go on fighting. Men experience the same feelings, but they have learned from childhood not to cry. Hence, they may hide their emotions, or they may erupt angrily. In either case it would help to bargain about whether the fight should continue. The partner who is not feeling so hurt or frightened might ask, "Do you want to stop now or to go on with this?" If the answer is "I want to stop," the fight should be either terminated or interrupted for a time.

CHANGING FIGHTING HABITS

Social scientists Suzanne Steinmetz traced the patterns of how families resolve conflict in 57 intact urban and suburban families. Her research shows not only that individual families assume consistent patterns or habits for facing conflict but also that these patterns are passed from one generation to the next (see also VanLear 1992). Parents who resort to physical abuse teach their children, in effect, that such abuse is an acceptable outlet for tension. In this way the "cycle of violence" is perpetuated (Steinmetz 1977). Irene Kassorla (1973) points out that a similar process takes place as people learn anger "insteads" from their parents.

Generational Change

Even though this generalization about the transmission of marital communication patterns from parents to children is correct, it is important to note variations from this pattern. VanLear (1992) found that young married men tend to rebel against their parents' marital conflict style. (Women are more apt to follow their parents' lead.) VanLear's comparison (in 58 families) of married couples in their late 20s to parental couples in their 50s found that the younger married men tended to choose different conflict styles from their parents. Most often, that meant they evidenced less conflict avoidance. These men also married women very different in conflict style from their own mothers. Moreover, the younger couples also reported more sharing and disclosure than was characteristic of the parental generation (VanLear 1992).

Couple Change

The change in couple communication and conflict management just described is the unplanned outcome of social change and family dynamics. But couples also may consciously act to change marital interaction patterns. Some training programs in communication, conducted by psychologists, have proven quite effective in helping people to change these behaviours. One such program for married couples is ENRICH, developed by social psychologist David Olson (1994). Meanwhile, the following steps are given to help people work for change on their own.

The first step in changing destructive fighting habits is to accept the reality of conflict. Feeling that conflict is wrong or that it should be kept out of the children's sight, for example, can cause dangerous buildups of tension.

A second, related step is to begin to use the guidelines for bonding fighting we have described. But changing can be a confusing and frightening process. For example, partners who have been hardened fight evaders may suddenly need to argue over just about everything. Afraid that they won't like themselves this way, that their family and friends "won't even know me," or that their partners won't understand or cooperate, these spouses will be tempted to return to their old and familiar ways. They need to realize two important things.

First, the feeling that one wants to fight over everything is largely a short-term result of releasing long-harboured resentments. The best way to counteract this tendency is to concentrate on keeping arguments focused only on current and specific issues. Recognizing old resentments is an indication of growth and well-being, but fighting about old resentments isn't necessary. Second, as partners grow more accustomed to voicing grievances regularly, their fights may hardly seem like fights at all: Partners will gradually learn to incorporate many irritations and requests into their normal conversations. Partners adept at constructive fighting often argue in normal tones of voice and even with humour. In a very real sense their disagreements are essential to their intimacy.

When partners are just learning to fight, however, they are often frightened and insecure. One way to begin is by writing letters or using a tape recorder. In this way the complainant is not inhibited or stopped by a mate's interruption or hostile nonverbal cues. Then the mate can read or listen to the other's complaints in privacy when she or he is ready to listen. Letters and tape recorders are no substitute for face-to-face communication, but they don't intimidate either. Once partners become more comfortable with their differences, they can begin to fight face to face.

Another option is to record a fight and play it back later. This exercise can help spouses look at themselves objectively. They can ask themselves whether and where they really listened and stuck to specifics or resorted to hurtful, alienating tactics.

Although all the suggestions made in this text may help, learning to fight fair is not easy. A good number of fights are even about fighting itself. Sometimes one or both partners feel that they need outside help with their fighting, and they may decide to have a marriage counsellor serve as referee. It is important to note that making a Marriage Encounter Weekend work, like that described in Case Study 9.2, may not be a good idea for distressed couples. Marriage Encounter Weekends are designed for couples in generally satisfying relationships. Taking part in a marriage encounter may bring up serious issues among distressed couples that they cannot deal with effectively once the weekend is over.

THE MYTH OF CONFLICT-FREE CONFLICT

By now, so much attention has been devoted to the bonding capacity of intimate fighting that it may seem as if conflict itself can be free of conflict. It can't. Even the fairest fighters hit below the belt once in a while, and it's probably safe to say that all fighting involves some degree of frustration and hurt feelings. After all, anger is anger and hostility is hostility—even between partners who are very close to each other.

Moreover, some spouses are married to mates who don't want to learn to fight more positively. As we saw in Chapter 8, partners can indeed be satisfied with devitalized or even conflict-habituated unions. In marriages in which one partner wants to change and the other doesn't, sometimes much can be gained if just one partner begins to communicate more positively. Other times, however, positive changes in one spouse do not spur growth in the other. Situations like this often end in divorce.

Even when both partners develop constructive habits, all of their problems will not necessarily be resolved. Even though a complainant may feel that he or she is being fair in bringing up a grievance and discussing it openly and calmly, the recipient may view the complaint as critical and punitive, and it may be a blow to that partner's self-esteem. The recipient may not feel that the time is right for fighting and may not want to bargain about the issue. Finally, sharing anger and hostilities may violate what the other partner expects of the relationship.

A study comparing mutually satisfied couples with those experiencing marital difficulties found that when couples are having trouble getting along or are stressed, they tend to interpret each other's messages and behaviour more negatively. Satisfied partners did not differ from distressed ones in how they intended their behaviour to be received by mates. But distressed partners interpreted their spouse's words and behaviour as being more harsh and hurtful than was intended (Gottman 1979; Noller and Fitzpatrick 1991).

Then, too, not all negative facts and feelings need to be communicated. Some psychologists suggest that one characteristic of happier couples is the restraint each uses with regard to expressing negative thoughts and feelings (Lauer and Lauer 1985). Before offering negative information, it is important to ask yourself why you want to tell it (to win?) and whether the other person really needs to know the information. This is particularly true with regard to revealing a past extramarital affair for example.

Moreover, not every conflict can be resolved, even between the fairest and most mature fighters. If an

Making a Marriage Encounter Weekend Work

According to its promotional literature, Marriage Encounter is a weekend for couples "who have a good thing going for them, and who want to make it better." Worldwide Marriage Encounter is a movement devoted to the renewal of the sacrament of matrimony in and for the Catholic Church. However, at least ten other faiths offer similar weekends. The movement began in the New York area of the United States in 1968. Since then, the movement has spread into 55 countries. Here, a woman tells about her Marriage Encounter weekend.

We were going along fine. But I think we both had begun to feel we were maybe taking each other pretty much for granted. So we signed up for a Marriage Encounter weekend. Believe me, it was a big step: finding a babysitter and everything just to go talk!

Marriage Encounter is an extensive 44 hours of uninterrupted togetherness. You do nothing else but eat, sleep, and share with each other. There's virtually no socializing with the other couples. It's just the two of you.

You write letters to one another. You write them alone, privately, and then you exchange them. You aren't using your body language while you're writing this, of course, or being interrupted or interrupting the other person. You have a train of thought. With just trying to talk sometimes, you know, the other person jumps in or tells you what you're saying is positive or negative, and you've gotten off the track. So we would write for ten minutes, picking a topic like, "How do I feel about sex?" Or, "How do I feel about anything really?" And both write.

Then you exchange notebooks and you each read it through twice—once with the heart and once with the head, as they say. And then you what they call dialogue on it for ten minutes. It really leads into neat areas....

I was amazed at how little I had been into feelings, and how much I was into thoughts. And the same for

Jerry. It was just really weird how we both thought we were expressing our feelings before the encounter. But we weren't. Not completely anyway. We thought we'd been letting it all hang out, but we weren't. We were expressing our thoughts and our grudges and our hang-ups. But not our true—not all our true—feelings....

I prayed too. I don't want to leave that out. I don't want to minimize that. I want to have the courage to emphasize that I prayed; I prayed hard that weekend, partly because when I went into the room where I was going to write down my feelings about something, I sometimes found myself surprisingly afraid.

And then when we'd start writing, I'd say to myself, "Do I feel like this?" I would be surprised at how I felt, and I'd be surprised at how he felt too. It's such a revelation—almost as exciting for you alone as it is for your relationship, because you find out a lot of stuff about yourself that you had no idea about. Anyway I did. And Jerry did too.

When we left that weekend, they gave us a list of 90 topics, suggestions for continuing the dialogue. Things like sex, kids, finances. You can think up anything you want to dialogue about, but we've been more or less going by this list. We recognized, though, that for a while we were skipping around on the list. And then we realized that we were avoiding subjects that we were afraid to talk about. So we've decided—and this took courage, believe me—to go just straight down the list and take the topics as they come....

It's really been a revelation. But maybe the very best thing about it is just that we're making the time to do it.

How might weekend encounters such as this one enhance family commitment? What might be some drawbacks or problems with a Marriage Encounter weekend? In what ways does intimacy (described in Chapter 4) affect family cohesion, do you think? Why?

unresolved conflict is not crucial to either partner, then they have reached a stalemate. The two may simply have to accept their inability to resolve that particular issue.

Like love, fair fighting doesn't conquer all. But it can certainly help partners who are reasonably well matched and who want to stay together. Success in marriage has much to do with a couple's gentleness in relating to one another—perhaps much more than the social similarity, financial stress, and age at marriage often emphasized by social scientists in earlier studies of marital adjustment (Gottman et al. 1998; Noller and Fitzpatrick 1991).

We turn now to look at a more general, but related concept—family cohesion.

FAMILY COHESION

A clear implication from the body of research on marital communication is that marriages are held together not only by the successful management of conflict but by positive communication and expression of feelings on a regular or daily basis (Erickson 1993; Langhinrichsen-Rohling, Smutzler, and Vivian 1994).

Yet it is often difficult to know what it is, exactly, that husbands, wives, and other members of the family should do to create **family cohesion**—the emotional bonding of family members. How do people create family cohesion?

In an effort to find out what makes families strong and cohesive, social scientist Nick Stinnett researched 130 "strong families" in rural and urban areas (Stinnett 1979, 1985). Obviously, this limited sample has no claim to representativeness. The concept of "strong family" is equally subjective. Various individuals or groups have their own ideas about family strengths that are likely to vary by religion, ethnicity, and political persuasion. Stinnett (1997) has more recently used the term "good families," by which he largely means "resilient"—able to face crises and stay together. Meanwhile, Stinnett's interest in strong families has been influential in stimulating research on the specifications and correlates of family solidarity and satisfaction (see, for example, Meredith et al. 1989 on holiday celebrations and other family rituals).

Stinnett's suggestions for building positive family bonds have a simplicity that is deceptive because the

common sense that suggests that positive family-building efforts are important often takes second place to the drama of dealing with conflict and crisis. Yet, in the long run, research makes it clear that the existence or nonexistence of positive feelings is the most important determinant of marital and family happiness.

When Stinnett made his observations of family strengths, six qualities stood out. First and most important, members often communicated appreciation for one another. They "built each other up psychologically" (p. 25). In Stinnett's assessment, "each of us likes to be with people who make us feel good about ourselves" (p. 25); thus, the family liked being together.

Stinnett suggests an exercise to help family members express appreciation for each other. Family members sit in a circle. Taking turns, each tells something he or she likes about the person to her or his left. When they have gone around the circle once or twice, each member then shares something he or she likes about himself or herself. After that, the direction is reversed, and members say something they like about the person to their right. The exercise needn't take long, and even when all members are not present, it helps build a sense of family togetherness and appreciation for one another. Studies show that families maintain more supportive interaction patterns for a time after the experience. To create togetherness, then, families might use this technique periodically.

Second, Stinnett found that members of strong families *arranged their personal schedules* so that they could do things, or simply be, together. The members of some families agreed to save Sundays for one another. Or members could agree to reserve every other weekend strictly for family activities. What families do together at home doesn't have to be routine, habitual, or boring: They might have a winter picnic in front of the fireplace, for example.

Religion plays an important role in the formation of attitudes towards marriage and subsequent marital behaviour.

A third characteristic Stinnett found was *positive communication* patterns. Family members took time to talk with and listen to each other, conveying respect and interest. They also argued, but they did so openly, sharing their feelings and talking over alternative solutions to their problems.

Fourth, members of strong families had a *high degree of commitment* to promoting one another's hap-

Religion and Marriage

Statistics Canada's General Social Survey (1995) collected data from a sample of approximately 10 000 Canadians aged 15 and over living in private households in the ten provinces. In this brief extract, sociologist Wayne Clark (2000) reports findings on the influence of religiosity (as measured by attendance at religious services) on the attitudes of Canadians toward marriage and family relationships.

Religion can be viewed as a system of thoughts, feelings, and actions shared by a group that gives members an object of devotion; a code of ethics governing personal and social conduct; and a frame of reference relating individuals to their group and the universe. Most major religions teach compassion and helpfulness, and research has shown that religious attendance is associated with positive social behaviour. Also, those who attend religious services more frequently are more likely to state that they have spiritual needs. This may indicate that frequent attenders at religious services attach more importance to finding purpose and meaning in life than those who do not....

Religion plays an important role in the formation of attitudes to marriage and subsequent marital behaviour. For example, acceptance of biblical teachings about the sanctity of marriage and prohibitions against adultery may act as a barrier against divorce by reducing the likelihood of infidelity. The 1995 *General Social Survey* (GSS) found that the most common reasons why someone might decide to pursue a divorce were unfaithfulness, lack of love and respect, and a partner who drinks too much. While religious people were just as unwilling as those who never attended religious services to forgive a spouse's abusive or unfaithful behaviour, they were less likely to view lack of love and respect, and a partner's drinking too much as grounds for divorce. Religious couples were also more likely to state that they would stay married for the sake of their children....The 1995 *General Social Survey* (GSS) [additionally] asked Canadians to rate several areas of life in terms of their importance to the respondent's happiness...Weekly attenders of religious services—both men and women—placed greater importance on lasting relationships, being married, and having at least one child than those who did not attend [Table 9.1]....

Many things contribute to happy marital or common-law relationships. While religion may sometimes be a source of conflict in some relationships where partners differ strongly in their religious views, it seems that regular attendance at religious services is related to stronger marriages. The odds of having a very happy marital relationship were 1.5 times greater for those attending religious services weekly than for those who didn't attend at all (after accounting for differences in age, education, income, religion, province, employment status, and the decade when the marriage began. Interestingly, income appeared to have no influence on marital happiness, after the other factors were controlled for.).... The 1995 GSS...[found] that compared with those who never attended religious services, the odds that a weekly attender's marriage would break down were less than half. Marriage longevity of weekly attenders was greater than that of non-attenders regardless of which decade they were married. For example, 89 percent of the marriages of weekly attenders who were married in the 1970s lasted at least 10 years, compared with 74 percent of non-attenders' marriages....

TABLE 9.1

Religious People Tend To Place Greater Importance On Marriage, Family, And Children

	Average score	
	Attends religious services weekly	Never attends religious services
Importance to happiness of...	(0=not at all important, 3=very important)	
a lasting relationship	2.60*	2.45*
being married	2.35	1.80
having at least one child	2.27	1.95
being able to have a paying job	1.89	2.10
Agreement with following statement	(0=strongly disagree, 4=strongly agree)	
Employed mothers can establish just as warm a relationship with their children as mothers who do not work for pay	2.26	2.54
Keeping house is just as fulfilling as working for pay	2.60	2.28
A job is alright but what women really want is a home and children	2.32	1.94
A pre-school child is likely to suffer if both parents are employed	2.54	2.22
Having a job is the best way for a woman to be an independent person	2.03	2.28
If a man brings enough money home so his wife and children have a comfortable life, he has fulfilled his role as a husband and a parent	1.62	1.36
A man should refuse a promotion at work if it means spending too little time with his family	2.24	2.01
A woman should refuse a promotion at work if it means spending too little time with her family	2.30	2.05
Both the man and woman should contribute to the household income	2.56*	2.73*
Having a family is alright, but what most men really want is to be successful in their job	2.13*	2.09*
A man does not have to be very involved in sharing the everyday tasks of raising children; this is not primarily a man's responsibility	0.91*	0.81*

*Difference not statistically significant.

Note: Some of the differences between weekly attenders and those who never attended during 1995 is accounted for by age differences between the two groups. Young people have different values than older people; also young people are less likely to attend religious services on a weekly basis. Even after accounting for age differences between the two groups, all differences remained statistically significant except for those marked.

Source: Statistics Canada, "Canadian Social Trends," Cat. No. 11-008, Sept. 1998, No. 50.

piness and welfare and to the family group as a whole. And they "put their money where their mouths were," investing time and energy in the family group. When life got so hectic that members didn't have enough time for their families, they listed the activities they were involved in, found those that weren't worth their time, and scratched them off their lists, leaving more free time for their families. Stinnett comments on the element of knowledgeable decision making in that action:

> This sounds very simple, but how many of us do it? We too often get involved and it's not always because we want to be. We act so often as if we cannot change the situation [but] we do have a choice…. [T]here is a great deal that families can do to make life more enjoyable. (Stinnett 1979, p. 28)

A fifth characteristic of the families Stinnett studied was *spiritual orientation*. The results of a Canadian study described in Box 9.2, "Religion and Marriage," offer some evidence in support of this. Although Stinnett's "strong families" were not necessarily members of an organized religion, they did have a sense of some power and purpose greater than themselves.

And sixth, Stinnett found that strong families were able to *deal positively with crises*. Members were able to see something good in a bad situation, even if only gratitude that they had each other and were able to face the crisis together, supporting one another. (Chapter 16 discusses dealing creatively with family challenges.)

In general, Stinnett's families took the initiative in structuring their lifestyles to enhance family relationships. Instead of drifting into a family relationship by default, they played an active part in carrying out their family commitments (see also, Olson 1998).

IN SUM

Families are powerful sources of support for individuals, and they reinforce members' sense of identity. Because the family is powerful, however, it can cause individuals to feel constrained. Tactics such as gaslighting and scapegoating can be stressful or denigrating to an individual.

Even though such family interaction tactics can reach the point of pathology, family conflict itself is an inevitable part of normal family life. We are socialized to respect a conflict taboo, but both sociologists and counsellors are recognizing that to deny conflict can be destructive to both individuals and relationships.

Although fighting is a normal part of the most loving relationships, there are better and worse ways of fighting. Alienating practices, such as belligerence and the Four Horsemen of the Apocalypse—contempt, criticism, defensiveness, and stonewalling—should be avoided. Bonding fights, in contrast, can often resolve issues and also bring partners closer together by improving communication. Bonding fights can be characterized by attitudes of and efforts at gentleness, soothing, and de-escalation of negativity. In bonding fights both partners win. Still, there is no such thing as conflict-free conflict!

Research on marital communication indicates the importance to marriage of both positive communication and the avoidance of a spiral of negativity. Stinnett's research on "strong" or "resilient" families suggests that what makes families cohesive are expressing appreciation for each other, doing things together, having positive communication patterns, being committed to the group, having some spiritual orientation, and being able to deal creatively with crises.

Key Terms

alienating fight tactics	gaslighting
anger "insteads"	gunnysacking
attribution	leveling
belligerence	listener backchannels
bonding fighting	looking-glass self
checking-it-out	mixed, or double,
conflict taboo	messages
consensual validation	passive-aggression
contempt	rapport talk
criticism	report talk
defensiveness	sabotage
displacement	scapegoating
family cohesion	significant others
feedback	stonewalling
female-demand/male-	suppression of anger
withdrawal pattern	
Four Horsemen of the	
Apocalypse	

Study Questions

1. Explain why families are powerful environments. What are the advantages and disadvantages of such power in family interaction?

2. Do you agree that marital anger and conflict are necessary to a vital, intimate relationship? Why or why not?

3. Discuss the possible negative side effects of denying conflict in a marriage relationship. Include the effects on the individuals and on their relationship.

4. Define passive-aggression and give examples of behaviour that could be passive-aggressive.

5. Describe the Four Horsemen of the Apocalypse. If someone you care for treated you this way in a disagreement, how would you feel? What might you say in response?

6. Discuss your reactions to each of the guidelines proposed in this chapter for bonding fights. What would you add or subtract?

7. Why might it be difficult for people to change their fighting habits? What do you think is necessary for change to occur?

8. In your opinion, when should couples visit a marriage counsellor?

9. Do you agree with psychologist John Gottman's statement that husbands and wives have different goals in marital conflict? Why or why not? Give examples to support your response.

10. Explain the female-demand/male-withdrawal pattern of marital communication, along with Gottman's explanation for it. Do you agree with Gottman? Why or why not?

11. Do Stinnett's suggestions for "strong families" work? Put another way, do they seem realistic; would they really have an impact on family life?

Suggested Readings

Fitzpatrick, Mary Anne. 1995. *Explaining Family Interactions*. Newbury Park, CA: Sage. Reports academic research on marital relationships, including communication.

Lerner, Harriet Goldhor. 1985. *The Dance of Anger*. New York: Harper & Row. A well-written book on anger, its causes, and its consequences for individuals and relationships. Offers practical advice on how to deal constructively with old and current anger.

Scarf, Maggie. 1995: *Intimate Worlds: Life Inside the Family*. New York: Random House. A counselling psychologist, Scarf explores the issues of intimacy, power, and conflict as these affect marital/family communication and levels of health in families.

Tannen, Deborah. 1990. *You Just Don't Understand: Women and Men in Conversation*. New York: Basic Books. This book presents information on common gender differences in communications practices in a way that would be useful to people in any relationship involving any combination of the sexes.

On the Net

1) "Gender Stereotypes, Communciation Styles and Effective Managerial Communication" by Michelle Howe and Warren Weber, California State Polytechnic University, Pomona
http://www.csupomona.edu/~wcweber/resources/slidesho/gndrster/

2) *Journal of Social and Personal Relationships*
http://www.jspr.org/caughlin.html

Power and Violence in Marriages and Families

...ENT THAT POWER IS THE

...VAILING FORCE IN A RELATION-

SHIP—WHETHER BETWEEN HUSBAND

AND WIFE OR PARENT AND CHILD,

BETWEEN FRIENDS OR BETWEEN COL-

LEAGUES—TO THAT EXTENT LOVE IS

DIMINISHED.

RONALD V. SAMPSON,

THE PSYCHOLOGY OF POWER

S arah gets a chance for promotion at work, but accepting it will mean moving to another city; Sarah's spouse does not want to relocate.

- Antonio wants a new stereo for his truck; his partner would prefer to spend the money on ski equipment.

- Marietta would like to talk with her husband about what he does (and doesn't do) around the house, but he is always too busy to discuss the issue.

- Greg feels that he gives more and is more committed to his marriage than his wife.

Each of these situations is about power in a relationship.

This chapter examines power in relationships, particularly marriage. We will discuss some classic studies of decision making in marriage. We'll look at what contemporary social scientists say about conjugal power. We will discuss why playing power politics is harmful to intimacy and explore an alternative. Finally, we will explore one tragic result of the abuse of power in families—family violence, including wife abuse, husband abuse, child abuse, and elderly abuse. We begin by defining power.

WHAT IS POWER?

Power can be defined as the ability to exercise one's will. There are many kinds of power. Power exercised over oneself is personal power, or autonomy. Having a comfortable degree of personal power is important to self-development. **Social power** is the ability of people to exercise their wills over the wills of others. Social power can be exerted in different realms, even within the family. Parental power, for instance, operates between parents and children. In this chapter our discussion of power in families will focus on power between married partners, or **conjugal power**.

What Does Conjugal Power Involve?

Conjugal power is complex and has several components. First, conjugal power involves decision making: Who gets to make decisions about everything, from where the couple will live to how they will spend their leisure time. Second, conjugal power involves the relative division of labour: Who does more work around the house? Third, conjugal power involves a partner's sense of empowerment—feeling free to raise complaints to one's spouse about the relationship (Komter 1989). The division of domestic labour is the focus of Chapter 13, while couple communication is discussed in Chapter 9.

In addition to these three components of conjugal power, the concept involves both **objective measures of power** (who actually makes more important—or more—decisions, does more housework, and/or feels freer to raise complaints) and a **subjective measure of fairness** in the marriage (Sprecher and Schwartz 1994). These two concepts may be, but are not necessarily, related. For example, a spouse who makes virtually all of the important decisions and does relatively little housework may perceive the relationship as fair, while another spouse who actually shares more of the decision making and housework may feel that the relationship is unfair.

For the most part, research shows that it is partners' *perception* of fairness (as opposed to objective measures of *actual* equality) that influences marital satisfaction (Kurdek 1998; Wilkie, Ferree, and Ratcliff 1998). Furthermore, when partners perceive themselves as reciprocally respected, listened to, and supported, they are more apt to define themselves as equal partners (Rosenbluth, Steil, and Whitcomb 1998). They also are less depressed (Longmore and Demaris 1997), generally happier (Steil 1997), and more satisfied with their marriage (Rosenbluth, Steil, and Whitcomb 1998). Understanding that conjugal power is a complex concept, we turn to the question of what are the sources of conjugal power.

Power Bases

Two social scientists (French and Raven 1959) have suggested six bases, or sources, of power: coercive, reward, expert, informational, referent, and legitimate. **Coercive power** is based on the dominant person's ability and willingness to punish the partner either with psychological-emotional or physical violence or, more subtly, by withholding favours or affection. Slapping a mate or spanking a child are examples; so is refusing to talk to the other person—giving the silent treatment. **Reward power** is based on an individual's ability to give material or nonmaterial gifts and favours, ranging from financial support (food, clothing, and shelter) to school tuition to a night out at a concert or the movies.

Expert power stems from the dominant person's superior judgment, knowledge, or ability. Although this is certainly changing, our society has traditionally attributed expertise in important matters, such as finances or career decisions, to men. Consequently, wives have been encouraged to assign expert power to husbands more often than the reverse. **Informational power** is based on the persuasive content of what the dominant person tells another individual. A husband may be persuaded to stop smoking by his wife's giving him information on the health dangers of smoking.

Referent power is based on the less dominant person's emotional identification with the more dominant individual. In feeling part of a couple or group, such as a family, whose members share a common identity, an individual gets emotional satisfaction from thinking as the more dominant person does or behaving as the "referent" individual wishes. A husband who attends a social function when he'd rather not "because my wife wanted to go and so I wanted to go too" has been swayed by referent power. In happy relationships, referent power increases as partners grow older together (Raven, Centers, and Rodrigues 1975).

Finally, **legitimate power** stems from the more dominant individual's ability to claim authority, or the right to request compliance. Legitimate power in traditional marriages involves both partners' acceptance of the husband's role as head of the family. One social scientist (Komter 1989) sees legitimate power as giving "hidden" or "invisible" power to husbands.

Throughout the rest of this chapter, we will see these various power bases at work. The consistent research finding, for instance, that the economic dependence of one partner on the other results in the dependent partner's being less powerful can be explained by understanding the interplay of both *reward power* and *coercive power:* If I can reward you with financial support—or threaten to take it away—I am more likely than otherwise to exert power over you. We turn now to look more specifically at conjugal power.

CONJUGAL POWER AND RESOURCES

Research on marital power began well before the second wave of the feminist movement in the 1970s (see Chapter 3), before the development of family therapy and the identification of family violence as a social problem. In the 1950s, social scientists Robert Blood and Donald Wolfe had an academic interest in conjugal decision making. Their book *Husbands and Wives: The Dynamics of Married Living* (1960) was based on interviews with wives only. Nevertheless, it was a significant piece of research and shaped thinking on marital power for many years.

Egalitarian Power and the Resource Hypothesis

THE RESOURCE HYPOTHESIS   Blood and Wolfe began with the assumption that although our family's forebears were patriarchal, "the predominance of the male has been so thoroughly undermined that we no longer live in a patriarchal system" (Blood and Wolfe 1960, pp. 18–19). On this basis the researchers developed their major hypothesis about what had replaced the system of patriarchy.

They reasoned, in their **resource hypothesis**, that the relative power between wives and husbands results from their relative resources as individuals: The spouse with more resources has more power in marriage. These resources, according to Blood and Wolfe, include education and occupational training. Within marriage a spouse's most valuable resource would be the ability to provide money to the union. Another resource would be good judgment, probably enhanced by education and experience. [Recall the discussion of exchange theory in Chapters 2 and 7 and note that the resource hypothesis is a variation on exchange theory (Sprecher and Schwartz 1994; Van Yperen and Buunk 1994).]

To test their resource hypothesis, Blood and Wolfe interviewed about 900 wives and asked who made the final decision in eight areas, such as what job the husband should take, what car to buy, whether the wife should go to work (or quit work), and how much money the family could afford to spend per week on food. From their interviews Blood and Wolfe drew the conclusion that most families (72 percent) had a "relatively equalitarian" (or equal; a synonym for *equalitarian*, or equal, is *egalitarian*) decision-making structure. However, there were families in which the husband made the most decisions (25 percent) and there were a few wife-dominated families (3 percent).

The resource hypothesis was supported by the finding that the relative resources of wives and husbands were important in determining which partner made more decisions. Older spouses and those with more education made more decisions. Blood and Wolfe also found the relative power of a wife to be greater after she no longer had young children or when she worked outside the home and thereby gained the wage-earning resource for herself. They reported little on black families, except to say that black husbands, when compared with white husbands, had more equal decision-making power with their wives.

CRITICISM OF THE RESOURCE HYPOTHESIS
In all, Blood and Wolfe's study had the important effect of encouraging people to see conjugal power as shared rather than patriarchal. The power of individual partners was seen as resting on their own attributes or resources rather than on social roles or expectations, a perspective that changed the thinking of social scientists. But Blood and Wolfe's study has also been strongly criticized.

One criticism concerns Blood and Wolfe's criteria for conjugal power. Critics stated that power between spouses involves far more than which partner makes the most final decisions; it also implies the relative autonomy of wives and husbands, along with questions about the division of labour in marriages (Safilios-Rothschild 1970). Moreover, Blood and Wolfe came under heavy fire for their assumption that the patriarchal power structure had been replaced by egalitarian marriages.

Resources and Gender

Feminist Dair Gillespie (1971) pointed out that power-giving resources tend to be unevenly distributed between the sexes. Husbands usually earn more money even when wives work, and so husbands control more economic resources. Husbands are often older and better educated than their wives, so husbands are more likely to have more status, and they may be more knowledgeable, or seem so. Even their greater physical strength may be a powerful resource, although a destructive one, as we will see later in this chapter (Collins 1995).

Moreover, women are likely to have fewer alternatives to the marriage than their husbands do, especially if wives cannot support themselves or are responsible for the care of young children. Consequently, according to Gillespie, the resource hypothesis, which presents resources as neutral and power as gender-free, is simply "rationalizing the preponderance of the male sex." Furthermore, women are socialized differently from men so that by the time they marry, women have already been "systematically trained to accept second best," and marriage is hardly a "free contract between equals" (p. 449).

Research tends to support Gillespie's insight that North American marriages continue to be inegalitarian even though they are no longer traditional (Rosenbluth, Steil, and Whitcomb 1998; Wilkie, Ferree, and Ratcliff 1998). True, resources make a difference, and an important factor in marital power is whether or not a wife is working. Wage-earning wives have more to say in important decisions (Blumberg and Coleman 1989) and in the division of household labour (Risman and Johnson-Sumerford 1998).

But resources are gender influenced, and one way in which women come to have fewer resources is through their reproductive roles and resulting economic dependence (Blumberg and Coleman 1989). Wives who do not earn wages, especially mothers of small children, have considerably less power than do women who earn an income. Relationships tend to become less egalitarian with the first pregnancy and birth (Coltrane and Ishii-Kuntz 1992). Just after marriage the relationship is apt to be relatively egalitarian, with the husband only moderately more powerful than the wife—if at all. Often at this point the wife has considerable economic power in relation to her husband; that is, she is working for wages and may even have established herself in a high-paying career.

But during the childbearing years of the marriage, the practical need to be married is felt especially strongly by women (Johnson and Huston 1998). Divorce is likely to mean that the woman must parent and support small children alone. In some cases, expectant mothers lose not only economic power but also "sexual attractiveness" power (Blumberg and Coleman 1989). Moreover, they have fewer alterna-tives and less energy or physical strength to resist dominance attempts, and they may be vulnerable to the manipulative offer or withdrawal of the husband's help with child care. On the other hand, a mother may exert power over her husband by threatening to leave and take the infant with her (LaRossa 1979).

Working, then, contributes to marital power. But even though the working wife is less obliged to defer to her husband and has greater authority in making family decisions, she still does not necessarily partici-pate equally in decision making and is still unequally burdened with housekeeping, child rearing, and caring for her partner (Greenstein 1995; Health Canada 1999). In one study, social scientists Dana Hiller and William Philliber (1986) found that the husband's expectations determine how and whether housekeeping roles will be shared. Even if she is employed, a wife does more housework if her hus-band believes she should than if her husband thinks he too should be involved (Brines 1994). Also, if her husband believes her wages are needed, a wife has more power (Blumberg and Coleman 1989). Hence, working for wages does not necessarily give a wife full

During the childbearing years of marriage, the practical need to be married is felt especially strongly by women.

status as an equal partner (Risman and Johnson-Sumerford 1998). There are a variety of explanations for this continuation of male dominance in a society that, on the whole, articulates an ideology of marital equality.

Resources in Cultural Context

The family ecology theoretical perspective (Chapter 2) stresses that family interaction needs to be examined within the context of the society and culture in which it exists. Accordingly, the cultural context may determine whether or not a resource theory explains marital power. Studies comparing traditional societies, such as in Greece, with more modern ones, such as in France, suggest that in a traditional society norms of patriarchal authority may be so strong that they override personal resources and give considerable power to all husbands (Safilios-Rothschild 1967; Blumberg and Coleman 1989). Put another way, *legitimate power* predominates.

When asked the question, "how do [Indian] women exercise power within the family and elsewhere," sociologist Vanaja Dhruvarajan (1999) responded:

> Exercise of power and control within the family is considered legitimate as long as it is done discreetly and within the accepted role of proper behaviour for a woman—namely, showing respect to husband and elders, even if it is symbolic at times. Many women in fact exert significant influence in day-to-day family life. Making economic contributions to the family does increase the degree of influence in the family, but again, to be deserving of respect, a woman must follow tenets of proper womanhood. (p. 163)

This situation may be equally true for families who have recently immigrated to Canada from traditional societies, such as in Asia or Central and South America. A Sri Lankan woman, whose husband acted in an inflexible and dictatorial way towards her and their children told sociologist Nancy Howell (1996):

> Whether he is good or bad....that's the way he was brought up and that's the way he is. He cannot change. A little bit he is changing. At least we should be happy for that. (p. 132)

Among most Canadians and Americans, we must recognize the continuing salience of tradition and the assumption that it is legitimate for husbands to wield authority in the family (Komter 1989). A study of Japanese-American couples, for instance, found that even though wives actively participated in making countless decisions, they did so by virtue of delegation of power from their husbands (Johnson 1975). The continued importance of traditional legitimations of husbands' authority is apparent in some religious groups. For example, Promise Keepers, an evangelical men's movement, is committed to "do right by women" as well as to the restoration of traditional family norms and roles (Minkowitz 1995).

We must note another way in which cultural context conditions the resource theory; it explains marital power only in the absence of an overriding egalitarian norm as well as a traditional one. Put another way, if traditional norms of male authority are strong, husbands will almost inevitably dominate, regardless of personal resources (see Figure 10.1). Similarly, if an egalitarian norm of marriage were completely accepted, then a husband's superior economic achievements would be irrelevant to his decision-making power because both spouses would have equal power (Cooney et al. 1982). It is only in the present situation, in which neither patriarchal nor egalitarian norms are firmly entrenched, that marital power is negotiated by individual couples and the power of husbands and wives may be a consequence of their resources. We now look at the influence of social class on conjugal power.

Social Class and Conjugal Power

The majority of Canadians, regardless of class, do not see power inequities in their own marriages. Some sociological studies find middle-class husbands to have more power than working-class husbands. This may be because middle-class husbands are more likely than lower-class men to have substantially higher earnings than their wives. However, differences among classes are slight (Peplau and Campbell 1989). Relative economic power of husband and wife is important, however (Blumberg and Coleman 1989). Greater income or other financial resources, such as inherited wealth, provide power because they provide benefits that the other cannot obtain alone.

Husband's resources are greater

	Yes	No
Yes (The culture gives husbands absolute legitimate power)	Husband dominant	Husband dominant
No	Husband probably dominant (unless egalitarian cultural norm for marriage is completely accepted)	Equalitarian marriage or wife-dominant (if she has the greater resources)

FIGURE **10.1**

How resources and legitimate power interact to affect conjugal power.

Love, Need, and Power

Some have argued that a primarily economic analysis does not do justice to the complexities of marital power. Perhaps a wife has considerable power through her husband's love for her:

> The relative degree to which the one spouse loves and needs the other may be the most crucial variable in explaining total power structure. The spouse who has relatively less feeling for the other may be the one in the best position to control and manipulate all the "resources" that he [sic] has in his command in order to effectively influence the outcome of decisions, if not also to dominate the decision making. Thus, a "relative love and need" theory may be ... basic in explaining power structure. (Safilios-Rothschild 1970, pp. 548–49)

This theory is congruent with what sociologist Willard Waller termed the **principle of least interest**. The partner with the least interest in the relationship is the one who is more apt to exploit the other. The spouse who is more willing to break up the marriage or to shatter rapport and refuse to be the first to make up can maintain dominance (Waller 1951, pp.

190–92). We have already seen that dependence on a relationship can be practical and economic as well as emotional. For example, older women have less probability of remarriage after divorce or of significant employment (if they have not already established a career), so they may be reluctant to leave a marriage (Blumberg and Coleman 1989).

Like resource theory, the **relative love and need theory** is a variation of exchange theory. (See Chapter 2.) Each partner brings resources to the marriage and receives rewards from the other partner. These may not balance precisely, and one partner may be gaining more from the marriage than the other partner, emotionally or otherwise. This partner is more dependent on the marriage and thus is more likely to comply with the other's preferences.

The relative love and need theory does not predict whether husbands or wives will generally be more powerful. In other words, it assumes that women are as likely to have power as men are: "The man who desires or values the woman as a mate more than she desires or values him will be in the position of wanting to please him. Her enchantment in his eyes may be physical attractiveness, pleasing personality, his perception of her as a 'perfect' wife and mother" (Hallenbeck 1966, p. 201).

Generally, however, the wife holds the less powerful position. How does the relative love and need theory account for this? One explanation offered is that "love has been a feminine specialty" (Cancian 1985, p. 253). Women are more socialized to love and need their husbands than the reverse. They also tend to be more relationship-oriented than men are (Tannen 1990; Murstein and Adler 1997). In our society, women are encouraged to express their feelings, men to repress them. Men are less likely, therefore, to articulate their feelings for their partners, and "men's dependence on close relationships remains covert and repressed, whereas women's dependence is overt and exaggerated" (Cancian 1985, p. 258). Overt dependency affects power: "A woman gains power over her husband if he clearly places a high value on her company or if he expresses a high demand or need for what she supplies.... If his need for her and high evaluation of her remain covert and unexpressed, her power will be low" (p. 258). According to the principle of least interest, this puts women at a power disadvantage.

Micropolitics: The Private Sphere

In sum, according to Francesca Cancian, "men dominate women in close relationships [and] ... husbands tend to have more power in making decisions, a situation that has not changed in recent decades" (1985, p. 259). But, argue several social scientists, men are far less powerful in the private, intimate sphere than they are in the public world. Therapists, the mass media, and to an increasing degree, the public, support women's desire for more expression of feelings, reducing men's ability to minimize the emotional sphere in which women are deemed more competent. Men's ability to get what they want may also be limited by the very "avoidance of dependence" built into the male role. "He may not even know what he wants or needs from her, and therefore, may be unable to try to get it" (Cancian 1985, p. 259). Men are as likely to feel controlled by women as women believe they are controlled by men:

> Insofar as love is defined as the woman's "turf," an area where she sets the rules and expectations, a man is likely to feel threatened and controlled when she seeks more intimacy. Talking about the relationship, like she wants, feels like taking a test that she made up and he will fail. The husband is likely to react with withdrawal and passive aggression. He is blocked from straightforward counterattack insofar as he believes that intimacy is good. (Cancian 1985, p. 260)

Cancian's view of this dilemma is presented with much empathy for men. Psychotherapist and social scientist Lillian Rubin's work on men and women in intimate relationships (1976, 1983, 1994) looks at the differences between men's and women's styles of expressing love neutrally in terms of the problems they produce for couples. A more critical view is presented by sociologist Jean Lipmen-Blumen (1984) as she discusses women's greater relationship skills from the perspective of conflict theory. In her view, women are oppressed by men and respond with "micromanipulation"—that is, manipulation of interpersonal power in the micro, or private, sphere.

Lipmen-Blumen argues that men dominate the public sphere of work and political leadership, whereas women occupy the private sphere. If men dominate public policy, then women,

as well as other powerless groups, become well versed in interpreting the unspoken intentions, even the body language, of the powerful.... By the various interpersonal strategies of micromanipulation, women have learned to sway and change, circumvent, and subvert the decisions of the powerful to which they seem to have agreed.... Women have also mastered how to "obey without obeying" those rules they find overly repressive. When necessary, they cooperate with men to maintain the mirage of male control. True, a growing minority of women have also consciously rejected the tools of micromanipulation in favour of a more direct assault [by becoming involved in the public arena of work and politics]. The majority, however, continue to operate primarily at the interpersonal level. (Lipmen-Blumen 1984, pp. 30–31)

With Lipmen-Blumen's analysis, we have come back to the question of men's and women's power in the larger society. Sociologists see marital power as affected by position and resources in the larger society, the public world of work and politics (Huber and Spitze 1983; Blumberg and Coleman 1989). If women have relied on micromanipulation, it is primarily because, as we noted in Chapter 3, they are not yet integrated into the higher levels of the occupational structure of political leadership.

Lipmen-Blumen's description reinforces our initial premise: Power disparities discourage an intimacy based on honesty, sharing, and mutual respect. Realization of the current ideal of equality in marriage (Kurdek 1989; Lips 1999; Peplau and Campbell 1989), however, would seem to support the development of intimacy in relationships.

The Future of Conjugal Power

Equalization of the marital power of men and women can occur in a number of ways. First, women can attain equal status in the public world and develop resources that are truly similar to men's. Despite the persistence of occupational segregation, the trend of the times is in this direction (Risman and Johnson-Sumerford 1998; Wilkie, Ferree, and Ratcliff 1998). Women's increase in income should "lead to an increased sense of self, sense of control over [their] lives, and expectation of achieving greater bargaining power within the relationship" (Blumberg and Coleman 1989, p. 239).

Second, society can come to value more highly women's resources of caring and emotional expression. Even though women's care of children, the elderly, and other dependents, their creation of a warm, comfortable home, and their emotional support of family and other social bonds have not been much rewarded with either money or status, feminists forcefully argue the social importance of these contributions. One impact of feminism may be the way that women's values are increasingly incorporated into the culture (Lenz and Myerhoff 1985). Some men's liberation movements now articulate expressive values as well (see Chapter 3). Although there may be more rhetoric than reality to this cultural change, women's traditional assets could increase in worth in such a cultural climate.

And finally, norms of equality can come to be so strong that men and women will have equal power in marriage regardless of resources. Equality is an important value in our culture. Our society could come to legitimate norms of equality in marriage as strongly as it endorsed patriarchal authority in the past.

Power in Four Types of Couples

Having looked at theories and research on conjugal power, we might look more closely now at a study that allows us to observe the workings of power in the everyday lives of four types of couples.

As you may recall from Chapter 5, sociologists Philip Blumstein and Pepper Schwartz (1983) undertook a comparison of four types of couples: heterosexual married couples, cohabiting heterosexual couples, gay couples, and lesbian couples. Twenty-two thousand questionnaires were sent to couples who responded to media advertisements for participants or to the researchers' solicitation for participants at various events and meetings. Over 12 000 questionnaires were returned and some 300 couples were interviewed; data were used only if both parties participated.

The results confirm some of our ideas about power. Gender was by far the most significant determinant of the pattern of power. Composed, by definition, of a male and a female, marital and cohabiting couples tended to be the least egalitarian. As the resource theory suggests, money was a major determi-

nant of power, and two men or two women were far more likely to have similar incomes. But money strongly affected power even in a same-sex couple. High-earning individuals (or the employed partner with an unemployed companion) tended to be excused from tiresome household chores and got to pick leisure activities. The way in which one partner's success in the wider world serves as a basis for claiming relationship benefits is illustrated by the reaction of a gay partner:

> Our biggest arguments are about what I haven't done lately.... I am willing to help out when I can, but my career is not just nine to five and usually I either don't have the time or I'm so tired when I come home that the last thing I'm going to do is clean the kitchen floor.... We had this one discussion where he suggested I get up earlier in the morning to help clean up if I'm too tired at night. I blew up and told him that I was the one with the career here and it was my prospects and my salary that gave us his vacations and you just can't be a housewife and a success all at the same time. (Blumstein and Schwartz 1983, pp. 152–53)

The impact of gender was apparent in a comparison of gay and lesbian couples. Gay men tended to be more competitive, very aware of each other's earning power and other signs of status in the public world. Lesbians, on the other hand, with feminine values of cooperation and pleasing others, worked very hard at their relationship and often deferred to each other (see also Kurdek 1998).

Lesbian couples illustrate another principle of conjugal power: the importance of norms and the cultural context. Committed to egalitarian and cooperative decision making, these couples were the only ones to transcend the principle that economic resources determine decision-making power. Norms of equality were simply so strong that lesbians made strenuous efforts not to let differential earning power or unemployment affect control over the relationship.

Finally, this study tells us that commitment influences power. In marriages, representing the highest level of commitment, low-resource partners (usually the women) felt much freer to spend money earned by the partner than did individuals in a cohabiting relationship. They were likely to view resources as joint ones. The formal commitment represented a barrier to separation that limited the principle of least interest. Because both partners would have found it difficult to leave the relationship, both felt secure in the relationship. They were less apt to believe that money or other resources were divided into "yours" and "mine." As couples in the other relationship types intensified their commitment over time, the partner with fewer resources also gained in power (Blumstein and Schwartz 1983).

Perhaps because of their greater sense of separate identity and need to be economically independent if necessary, maintaining equality was very important to individuals in gay, lesbian, and cohabiting couples. Resources, rather than a commitment bond, ensured their security and power within the relationship. "Only married couples do not rely on equality to hold them together" (Blumstein and Schwartz 1983, p. 317). Married couples took a longer view of the rewards obtained from marriage, which perhaps explains why another study (Schafer and Keith 1981) found that the power inequity perceived by wives diminished over time. Regardless of actual power in the marriage, it seems that as the years pass, spouses develop an increased sense of identity with each other and so are more apt to view marital decisions as joint ones. They also believe, despite periods of inequality, that relative commitment, energy, and marital rewards even out over time.

Blumstein and Schwartz emerged from their project impressed by the advantages of marriage. The stability of a formal commitment enabled couples to survive difficulties and required a sharing and negotiation of conflict that in the long run strengthened the relationship. Still, they noted that, at least into the 1980s, the institution of marriage had been organized around inequality; attempts at change had led to spouses' frustration and unhappiness (1983, p. 324).

Change is hard, Blumstein and Schwartz concluded, because couples "must not only go against everything they have learned and develop new skills, but they have to resist the negative sanction of society" (1983, p. 324). That was almost two decades ago. Since then researchers have consistently come to similar conclusions (Burke and Cast 1997), although some have found a few truly equal or "peer" marriages (Schwartz 1994; Risman and Johnson-Sumerford 1998). We turn now to a discussion of the process of changing power relationships in marriage.

POWER POLITICS VERSUS NO-POWER RELATIONSHIPS

Through the early 1980s, researchers found "very little consistent evidence that egalitarian couples are more satisfied with their marriages than husband dominant couples" (Gray-Little 1982, p. 634; Fitzpatrick 1988, p. 107). But current evidence indicates that equitable relationships are generally more apt to be stable and satisfying (Lennon and Rosenfield 1994; Schwartz 1994; Greenstein 1995; Risman and Johnson-Sumerford 1998), as we argue throughout this chapter.

With a goal for couples of developing relationships best suited to partners' individual needs and assets, marriage counsellors today are virtually unanimous in asserting that greater intimacy takes place insofar as partners are equal. Social scientist Peter Blau terms this situation *no-power*. **No-power** does not mean that one partner exerts little or no power; it means that both partners wield about equal power. Each has the ability to mutually and reciprocally influence and be influenced by the other (Schwartz 1994; Gottman et al. 1998). As we use the term, no-power also implies partners' unconcern about exercising their relative power over each other. No-power partners seek to negotiate and compromise, not to win (see Chapter 9). They are able to avoid **power politics**, a term that relates broadly to the power bases and tactics discussed in this chapter (see Box 10.1, "Disengaging From Power Struggles").

Power Politics in Marriage

As gender norms move from traditional to egalitarian, all family members' interests and preferences gain legitimacy, not only or primarily those of the husband or husband-father. The man's occupation, for example, is no longer the sole determining factor in where the family will live or how the wife will spend her time. Thus, decisions formerly made automatically, or by spontaneous consensus, must now be consciously negotiated. A possible outcome of such conscious negotiating, of course, is greater intimacy; another is locking into power politics and conflict. If the essential source of conjugal power is (as the relative love and need theory suggests) "the greater power to go away," then "politics in marriage has to do with suggesting the use of that power to leave the marriage." A spouse plays power politics in marriage by saying, in effect, "This is

Disengaging From Power Struggles

Carlfred Broderick, sociologist and marriage counsellor, offers the following exercise to help people disengage from power struggles. He begins by pointing out that almost nothing is more frustrating and resentment-inducing than an elaborate, unilaterally developed plan for yourself, your spouse, your children, and your friends. It is frustrating because when you try to live by such a script, or set of rules, you are condemned to seeing yourself as a failure (because neither you nor your children ever measure up) and to feeling rejected (because your spouse and friends never come through). Moreover, you are likely to imagine that you are surrounded by lazy, selfish, unfeeling, stubborn, underachieving, low-quality people.

The object of this exercise is to get you out of the business of monitoring everyone else's behaviour and so free you from the unrewarding power struggles resulting from that assignment. Here is the exercise:

1. Think of as many things as you can that your spouse or children *should do*, *ought to do*, and *would do if they really cared, but don't do* (or do only grudgingly because you are always after them). Write them down in a list.

2. From your list choose three or four items that are especially troublesome right now. Write each one at the head of a sheet of blank paper. These are the issues that you, considerably more than your spouse, want to resolve (even though he or she, by rights, should be the one to see the need for resolution). Right now you are locked in a power struggle over each one, leading to more resentment and less satisfaction all around.

3. In this step you'll consider, one by one, optional ways of dealing with these issues without provoking a power struggle. Place an A, B, C, and D on each sheet of paper at appropriate intervals to represent the four options listed below. Depending on the nature of the issue, some of these options will work better than others, but for a start, write a sentence or paragraph indicating how each one might be applied in your case. Even if

you feel like rejecting a particular approach out of hand, be sure to write something as positive as possible about it.

Option A: Resign the Crown

Swallow your pride and cut your losses by delegating to the other person full control and responsibility for his or her own life in this area. Let your partner reap his or her own harvest, whatever it is. In many cases your partner will rise to the occasion, but if this doesn't happen, resign yourself to suffering the consequences.

Option B: Do It Yourself

There's an old saying, "If you want something done right, do it yourself." Accordingly, if you want something done, and if the person you feel should do it doesn't want to, it makes sense to do it yourself the way you'd like to have it done. After all, who ever said someone should do something he or she doesn't want to do just because you want him or her to do it?

Option C: Make an Offer Your Partner Can't Refuse

Too many interpret this, at first, as including threats of what will happen if the partner doesn't shape up. The real point, however, if you select this approach, is to find out what your partner would really like and then offer it in exchange for what you want him or her to do. After all, it's your want, not your spouse's, that is involved. Why shouldn't you take the responsibility for making it worth your spouse's while?

Option D: Join with Joy

Often the most resisted task can become pleasant if one's partner shares in it, especially if an atmosphere of play or warmth can be established. This calls for imagination and good will, but it can also be effective in putting an end to established power struggles.

Source: Broderick 1979a, pp. 117–23.

how it would be if I were not here" (Blumberg and Coleman 1989; Chafetz 1989).

Both equal and unequal partners may engage in a cycle of devitalizing power politics. Partners come to know where their own power lies, along with the particular weaknesses of the other. They may alternate in acting sulky, sloppy, critical, or distant. The sulking partner carries on this behaviour until she or he fears the mate will "stop dancing" if it goes on much longer; then it's the other partner's turn. This kind of seesawing may continue indefinitely, with partners taking turns manipulating each other. The cumulative effect of such power politics, however, is to create distance and loneliness for both spouses.

Few couples knowingly choose power politics, but this is an aspect of marriage in which choosing by default may occur. Our discussion of power in marriage is designed to help partners become sensitive to these issues so that they can avoid such a power spiral, or reverse one if it has already started.

Alternatives to Power Politics

There are alternatives to this kind of power struggle. Robert Blood and Donald Wolfe (1960) proposed one in which partners grow increasingly separate in their decision making; that is, they take charge of separate domains, one buying the car, perhaps the other in charge of disciplining their children. This alternative is a poor one for partners who seek intimacy, however, for it enforces the separateness associated with devitalized marriages.

A second, more viable alternative to perpetuating an endless cycle of power politics is for the subordinate spouse to disengage from power struggles, as described in Box 10.1. A third, perhaps best, alternative is for the more powerful partner to consciously relinquish some power in order to save or enhance the marriage. We saw in Chapter 9, for instance, that marriage communication expert John Gottman (1998) advises husbands to be willing to share power with their wives if they want happy, stable marriages (pp. 18–19).

THE IMPORTANCE OF COMMUNICATION
Partners who feel free to raise complaints and see themselves as mutually respected, equally committed, and listened to are more likely to see their relationship as egalitarian and are more satisfied overall with their

relationships (Rosenbluth, Steil, and Whitcomb 1998; Langhinrichsen-Rohling, Smutzler, and Vivian 1994). Meanwhile, unequal relationships discourage closeness between partners: Exchange of confidences between unequals may be difficult, especially when self-disclosure is seen to indicate weakness and men have been socialized not to reveal their emotions (Henley and Freeman 1989). Wives, feeling less powerful and more vulnerable, may resort to pretense and withholding of sexual and emotional response (Blumberg and Coleman 1989). Nevertheless, trying to change the balance of conjugal power can bring the risk of devitalizing a relationship, depending on how partners go about it. Subordinate mates who try to disengage from power struggles without explaining what they are doing and why risk estrangement. The reason is that dominant partners may mistake a subordinate mate's acts of deference and compliance as evidence of love rather than fear. If signs of deference are withdrawn, a dominant partner can conclude that "she (or he) doesn't love me anymore." The harder the subordinate partner works to change the balance of power, the more effort will the dominant one invest in regaining control. The result is estrangement. Case Study 10.1, "An Ice-Skating Homemaker in a Me-or-Him Bind," illustrates this pattern.

One wife reported that she had lived 10 years in a husband-dominated marriage before she returned to school, and when she did return, their power relationship changed. Receiving substitute nourishment for her self-esteem in good grades and new friends, she no longer relied totally on her husband's signs of affection. In subtle ways she showed decreasing deference and felt herself growing toward equality in the marriage. But the couple did not discuss these changes. Meanwhile, her husband had begun to drink heavily. The wife remained convinced he would "come along." Four years later, the couple were hardly speaking to each other and began marriage counselling. "I thought she didn't love me anymore," her husband said. "After she went back to school, she stopped doing things for me."

This couple might have avoided estrangement through mutual self-disclosure. The husband could have shared his anxiety. The wife could have explained that, from her point of view, signs of deference—doing things for him—did not show love. Perhaps the couple could have negotiated an agreement whereby he continued to feel loved while she proceeded to gain

An Ice-Skating Homemaker in a Me-or-Him Bind

Joan is a full-time homemaker who has been married 19 years. Recently she began taking courses at a local university and also became involved in learning to figure-skate.

Interviewer: When did you begin ice-skating?

Joan: Well, I took one year when I was a kid, but I had to ride the bus and the streetcar and all that....And then I didn't skate again until last year. I've been skating for two years now and I just love it. I'm getting better. I can do three turns real well and three of the very basic dances....

I try to skate twice a week. But it's created a problem with Chuck. Last year he was working days during the skating season. But now he works midnight to eight and he just hates for me to go there during the day....I don't know whether it's because I like it real well or what. There's nothing there to be jealous of because I skate with the housewives....I don't know whether it's that I enjoy something he can't do well or what it is. But he doesn't like it. When he works midnight to eight, he knows every time I go. When he was working days and I went, as long as my work was done and I had dinner on the table, there was no problem when he came home from work.

Now he knows every time I leave this house. Every place I go he knows. Every time the garage door opens, it wakes him up. It's almost like being in prison without the doors being locked....

One time I stayed too late. I got home at five thirty. My brother was there—I got home at five thirty and no dinner or nothing. He told me, he said, "If you ever do this again—there's no dinner—if you ever do this again, I'm going to cut your skates." Oh boy! So I try to avoid doing that. I come home about four o'clock, so I can get dinner on okay. But the trouble [with the ice-skating] is I can go there and it's almost like on that ice nothing—I just get totally absorbed in it and I forget I'm a mother, forget I'm a wife, I forget everything, I'm just there. I felt that way about golf and waterskiing too, but those things didn't bother Chuck because I was doing them with him I think. Skating excludes him....

At first I thought it was jealousy. No, it's not jealousy. It's possessiveness. He wants to control what I do:..."This is a possession now; I own this person; I can control her mind and her body."

My daughter's starting to want to skate now too. The rink is open for the public this summer and I'm not going to be skating very much because I'd have to go in the evenings and that's just not going to work out with our schedule. But I'll try to go. Like this weekend Chuck will be out of town, so I'm going to go then. Anyway, my daughter's going to go with me when she's out of school. She's getting so she can skate pretty well and she's starting to like it. So she wants a pair of skates. Now he won't buy her the skates. He says, "No, we're not going to spend the money on something like that." Now I think that's terrible....

I could just go buy them because I definitely bought my own skates. I just went out and bought them. And then at first I lied to him—this is awful—I told him, "Oh, these are just my sister-in-law's skates...." Then finally once I told him they were my own. He said, "Oh! You can afford those skates and I can't afford a jacket." I said, "You can afford a jacket. Go buy one if you want...."

A lot of times he'll say, "What are you going to do today?" And I say, "Well, it's Tuesday and I skate on Tuesday." He's known that all year, but every time he wants to take me to lunch or go somewhere, it is always on Tuesday....One time I said, "Why can't we do it on Monday or Wednesday?" He said, "Oh, I never thought about that...."

(continued)

(continued)

He gets mad about everything I really like. Like when I started bowling and I really liked that, he gave me a hard time. It's really not just the skating. If he took the ice-skating away, and I replaced it with something else I liked equally well, that would be the thing he'd be against.

Whether a spouse is free to spend time in self-actualizing pursuits, how much time is allowed, and which pursuits are allowed depend largely on conjugal power. Chuck is exercising coercive power in threatening to cut Joan's skates. Such a threat is psychological abuse, or psychological violence.

equality. As couples assert their interests and bargain in marriage, communication is especially important in establishing and maintaining trust.

THE CHANGE TO A NO-POWER RELATION-SHIP Even when couples discuss power changes, living through them can be difficult (Blaisure and Allen 1995). Changing conjugal power patterns can be difficult, even for couples who talk about it, because these patterns usually have been established from the earliest days of the relationship (Blaisure and Allen 1995). Although partners may not have discussed them directly, they set up unconscious agreements by sending countless verbal and nonverbal cues. As partners experience recurring subtle messages, they build up predictable behaviour patterns. From the interactionist perspective, certain behaviours not only come to be expected but also to have symbolic meaning. For many couples, initiating or responding to sexual overtones, spending holidays in a certain way, or buying favourite foods or other treats symbolizes not just who has how much power but love itself. About two decades ago, sociologist William Goode had an insight that is still relevant for many couples. He wrote that the most important change in men's position, as they themselves see it, is a "loss of centrality," a decline in the extent to which they are the centre of women's attention. According to Goode:

Men have always taken for granted that what they were doing was more important than what the other sex was doing, that where they were, was where the action was. Their women accepted that definition. Men occupied the centre of the stage, and women's attention was focused on them.... [But] the centre of attention shifts to women more now than in the past. I believe that this shift troubles men far more, and creates more of their resistance, than the women's demand for equal opportunity and pay in employment. (Goode 1982, p. 140)

It is possible that spouses have never experienced a no-power man–woman relationship. By experience each knows either the dominant or the submissive role; vicariously, each knows how to play the other's role. When undergoing changes in power, they may be more inclined to reverse roles, moving to behaviour they know vicariously, rather than creating new egalitarian roles.

Husbands may respond to wives' power challenges by abdicating interest in decision making, assuming a submissive rather than an equal stance. Their reaction is "It's up to you" or "Whatever you want. I don't have anything to say around here anymore anyway." They relinquish, along with their authority, their willingness to influence the relationship. Much of this is probably passive-aggressive behaviour.

One small study of 12 fairly equal newlywed couples found that some of them either consciously or unconsciously avoided issues about conjugal power and developed a "myth of equality" (Knudson-Martin and Mahoney 1998). Sometimes this seems to work—but only for a while. The best way to work through power changes is to openly discuss power and to fight about it fairly, using techniques and cooperative attitudes described in Chapter 9. The partner who feels more uncomfortable can bring up the subject, sharing his or her anger and desire for change but also stressing that he or she still loves the other. Indeed, recent research suggests that spouses think of their marital relationship as fair when they feel listened to and emotionally supported (Risman and Johnson-Sumerford 1998; Wilkie, Ferree, and Ratcliff 1998). Meanwhile, partners need to remember that managing conflict about power in a positive way is easier said than done. Attempts at communication—and open communication itself—do not solve all marital problems. Changing a power relationship is a challenge to any marriage and is painful for both partners. One option is to seek the help of a qualified marriage counsellor.

The Role Marriage Counsellors Can Play

Today many marriage counsellors are committed to viewing couples as two human beings who need to relate to each other as equals. In other words, they are committed to helping couples develop no-power relationships. They realize that once both spouses admit—to themselves and to each other—that they do in fact love and need each other, the basis for power politics is gone. On this assumption, counsellors help spouses learn to respect each other as people, not to fear each other's coercive withdrawal.

Couples need to be aware that, like everybody in society, marriage counsellors have internalized masculine and feminine biases. Also, they have personal reactions to and feelings about women's emerging rights. Some counsellors are angry about past injustices. They may be more committed to urging a wife's separate autonomy through divorce, if necessary, than to helping her reach a no-power marital relationship. In the first session (or before, if possible), clients should ask prospective counsellors about their feelings on this issue. One counsellor may assume, for example, that

whenever marriage seriously threatens personal growth, it should be dissolved. Another may assume that partners need to learn to communicate and, only after that, to determine whether they want to stay married or to divorce. Counsellors may also demonstrate racial, heterosexist or other cultural biases (Taylor et al. 1990, pp. 1000–1001).

Choosing an appropriate counsellor can be difficult for reasons other than their differing assumptions. A dominant husband, fearful that "it's going to be two against one," may feel threatened by a female counsellor. On the other hand, a wife may fear that a male counsellor will be too traditional or unable to relate to her. In this situation, counsellors sometimes work as a team, woman and man.

Partners in a no-power relationship work at doing things on equal terms and seek to negotiate and compromise, thus avoiding deadly power games. By not competing with each other, both partners win.

It is important that both partners feel comfortable with a counsellor from the beginning, for two reasons. First, clients will hesitate to be frank with counsellors they mistrust or don't like. Without honesty and openness, marriage counselling is only an expensive hour away from work or home. Second, as counsellors gradually probe deeper into the couple's problems, one or both spouses may begin to feel threatened. Problems they had never recognized emerge into consciousness. As one counsellor put it, "Things get worse before they get better." A common reaction is to dismiss the counsellor's insight as all wrong. If couples quit at this point, they may find themselves more estranged than before they began. Understanding and accepting a counsellor's assumptions from the beginning help to avoid failure. Nevertheless, marriage counselling does not keep all marriages intact.

No marriage, indeed no relationship of any kind, is entirely free of power politics. But together partners can choose to emphasize no-power over the politics of power. One spouse can't do it alone, however. No-power involves both spouses' conscious refusal to be exchange-oriented or to engage in psychological bookkeeping. No-power involves honest self-disclosure and negotiation rather than passive-aggressive maneuvering. As Chapter 9 points out, the politics of love requires managing conflict in such a way that both partners win. When power politics triumphs over no-power, one result can be family violence—psychological (emotional) and/or physical.

FAMILY VIOLENCE

The use of physical violence to gain or demonstrate power in a family relationship has occurred throughout history, but only recently has family violence been labelled a social problem. The discovery of child abuse in the 1960s was followed in the 1970s by growing attention to wife abuse as a widespread problem with roots in assumptions about marital power. With the 1980s came concern about elderly abuse.

Measuring the extent of family violence is not a simple task. Consider, for example, that

The term "family violence" can encompass a wide range of experiences. Definitions vary according to the type of relationships considered under the definition of "family" (e.g., marriage, blood, adoption, foster care, step and blended family arrangements, and same-sex relationships) and the type of experiences to be included under the definition of "violence" (e.g., *Criminal Code* offences, threatening, psychologically controlling and emotionally abusive behaviour, and financial abuse). Clearly, more all-encompassing definitions of family violence will produce higher estimates of the extent of the problem. (Statistics Canada 2000, p. 9).

It is evident that **violence between intimates** can take many forms including, but not limited to physical violence, verbal and emotional abuse and sexual abuse. In Canada, social scientists and others who wish to understand the nature and extent of family violence can draw upon two general categories of data sources: *official statistics* based on incidents reported and thereby known to police, hospitals, child welfare or other social service agencies and coroners, and *victimization surveys*, that ask people if they have been victims of family violence.

The Homicide Survey, for example, provides national, police-reported data on the characteristics of all homicides that become known in a given year. Based on this data source, we can note that from 1979 to 1998, one-third of the 12 767 victims of homicide in Canada were killed by family members (Figure 10.2). The relationship between the perpetrator and victim of these family-related homicides, however, differed by gender. While "[f]emale victims were most likely to be killed by their husbands (66 percent), followed by their fathers and mothers (18 percent), male victims of family homicide were most likely to have been killed by fathers or mothers (28 percent), followed by wives (26 percent) and extended family members such as grandparents, aunts, uncles, cousins and in-laws (20 percent)" (Locke 2000, p. 39). Over the same time period, over three times as many wives as husbands were killed by spouses (Figure 10.3). Among both wives and husbands, those under the age of 25 years were at the greatest risk of being victims of spousal homicide (22 per million couples and 10 per million couples, respectively).

Firearms were the most commonly used weapon in the commission of spousal homicides between 1979 and 1998, followed by stabbings. Consistent with findings reported earlier in Canada and in the United States, husbands were more likely than wives

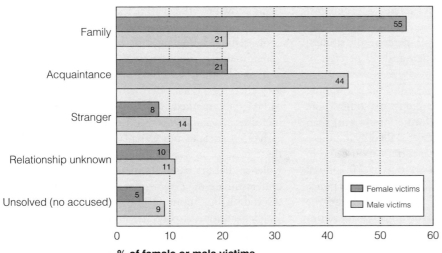

FIGURE   **10.2**

Homicides by type of relationship, Canada, 1979–1998.[r1] (Source: Statistics Canada, "Family Violence in Canada: A Statistical Profile," Cat. No. 85-224, July 2000, p. 39.)

Percentages may not total 100% due to rounding.

[r] revised

[1] Includes only those cases in which the sex of the victim is known.

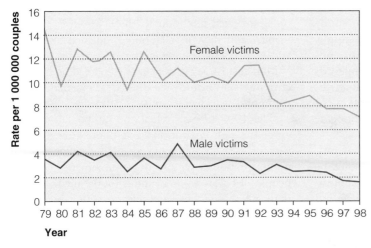

FIGURE   **10.3**

Spousal homicide rate, Canada, 1979–1998. [r1] (Source: Statistics Canada, "Family Violence in Canada: A Statistical Profile," Cat. No. 85-224, July 2000, p. 40.)

[r] revised

[1] Based on revised July 1 population estimates from Annual Demographic Statistics 1999 for men and women legally married, in common-law relationships, divorced or separated.

to use firearms (40 percent versus 25 percent) (Wilson and Daly, 1994). The use of alcohol was reported to be involved in 59 percent of spousal homicides committed by women and 30 percent of those committed by men.

In 1998, a current legal or common-law spouse killed 48 women; women were almost five times more likely to be killed by a spouse (former or current) than a stranger. In that year, 13 men were killed by a spouse; in 12 cases, the perpetrator was a current spouse and in one case, a former spouse. In six out of 10 spousal homicides in that year, the couple was known to police as having a history of domestic violence; this was true for seven out of 10 incidents involving a female victim and half of those incidents involving a male victim. In that year, more than half (55 percent) of female victims and six percent of male victims were killed by someone whom, at some time, they had been involved with in an intimate relationship (Fedorowycz 1999).

The Homicide Survey additionally finds that between 1979 and 1998, the majority of children and youths under 18 years who were victims of homicide were killed by their parents, most commonly, their fathers (Table 10.1). During this time period, the age of greatest risk of being a victim of homicide was during the first year of life. Infant homicides may go unrecorded and be wrongfully attributed to accidents or other causes. For example, a review conducted in Ontario of all deaths of children under the age of two suggested that as many as one in ten deaths prior to 1995 that had been attributed to Sudden Infant Death Syndrome (SIDS) or other causes may have, in fact, been a homicide (Trocme and Brison 1997).[1]

While findings based on official records may provide us with much valuable information, it should be emphasized that violence between intimates is notoriously difficult to measure. It often occurs in private and victims may be reluctant to report incidents of violence because of shame, dependency upon the perpetrator, fear of reprisal, a lack of knowledge about available sources of help, or pessimism about the quality of help that they will receive. In addition, the number of inci-

dents known to official agencies may also be affected by changes in policy, legislation, or levels of resources. "For example, a change in legislation (Bill C-127, amendments to the *Criminal Code* related to assault and sexual assault) and the implementation of mandatory charging policies by many police agencies in the early 1980s, marked the beginning of year-over-year increases in assaults reported to the police through the early 1990s" (Statistics Canada 2000, p. 9). For all of these reasons, it is evident that measures of intimate violence that are based upon agency records may well underestimate the extent of violence among intimates (Ogrodnik and Trainor 1997).

Victimization surveys are another source of information about violence among intimates. "However, these surveys are sensitive to question wording, definitions of victimization, interviewer effects, and the underlying approach (for example, a survey dedicated to violence against women versus one that focuses more generally on all forms of victimization" (Statistics Canada 2000, p. 9). In addition, such surveys may exclude those who speak neither English nor French as well as those households without telephones.

Unlike Statistics Canada's Violence Against Women Survey (1993), which focused exclusively on the experiences of women, the 1999 General Social Survey (GSS) directed attention to the experiences of both women and men in relation to violence by current and/or previous spouses and common-law partners. Within this survey, a person was defined as having a current relationship if s/he was married, living common-law or had a same-sex partner.[2]

The 1999 GSS, a telephone sample survey covering the non-institutionalized population aged 15 year or over in the ten Canadian provinces, drew upon a random sample of approximately 26 000 people (14 269 women and 11 607 men). Rather than ask respondents a single question about "violence" or "assault," respondents were asked whether, "in the past 5 years, your spouse/partner has (1) threatened to hit you with his/her fist or anything else that could have hurt you; (2) thrown anything at you that could have hurt you; (3) pushed, grabbed or

1. In 1995, the majority of the provinces passed legislation that requires a coroner's inquest in all cases involving the death of a child under the age of two.

2. Less than one percent of the sample in this survey identified themselves as living in same-sex relationships. In consequence, reliable estimates of the extent of violence within same-sex relationships could not be provided.

TABLE 10.1

Solved Homicides of Victims Under Age 18 by Accused–Victim Relationship, 1998[r1]

Relationship of accused to victim	Number of victims			
	1998[r]		Average 1988–1997	
	No.	%	No.	%
Total family homicides	**56**	**72**	**46**	**61**
Total fathers	34	44	23	30
Biological fathers	30	38	20	26
Step-fathers	4	5	3	4
Total mothers	18	23	17	22
Biological mothers	17	22	17	22
Step-mothers	1	1	—	—
Other family[2]	3	4	4	5
Sibling	1	1	2	3
Husband	-	-	—	—
Total non-family homicides	**22**	**28**	**30**	**39**
Acquaintance[3]	15	19	21	28
Stranger	7	9	6	7
Unknown	-	-	3	4
Total solved homicides	**78**	**100**	**76**	**100**

Columns may not add up due to rounding.

Percentages may not total 100% due to rounding.

- Nil or zero

— Amount too small to be expressed

[r] revised

[1] Includes only homicide incidents in which there are known suspects. If there was more than one suspect, only the closest relationship to the victim is recorded.

[2] Includes all other family members related through blood, marriage, adoption or foster care.

[3] Includes intimate relationships such as boyfriend/girlfriend as well as business associates, criminal associates and casual acquaintances.

Source: Statistics Canada, "Family Violence in Canada: A Statistical Profile," Cat. No. 85-224, July 2000, p. 43.

shoved you in a way that could have hurt you; (4) slapped you; (5) kicked, bit, or hit you with his/her fist; (6) hit you with something that could have hurt you; (7) beaten you; (8) choked you; (9) used or threatened to use a gun or knife on you; (10) forced you into any unwanted sexual activity by threatening you, holding you down, or hurting you in some way." Although this survey did include questions about emotional abuse, the findings we present here do *not* include emotional abuse within the overall reported rates of spousal violence.

The results of this survey suggest that many Canadian women and men experience violence in their marriages or common-law relationships. Estimates derived from this survey suggest that seven percent of Canadians "who were married or living in a common-law relationship during the past five years experienced some type of violence by their intimate partners" (Bunge 2000, p. 11). Figure 10.4 provides the estimated provincial rates of spousal violence for women and men. While this survey indicates that the five-year rate of violence is relatively similar for women (eight percent) and men (seven percent), it also notes that women are more likely to experience severe forms of violence, and "are three times more likely to suffer injury, five times more likely to receive medical attention, and five times more likely to fear for their lives as a result of the violence" (Bunge 2000, p.11).

[W]omen were more than twice as likely as men to report being beaten (25 percent versus 10 percent), five times more likely to report being choked (20 percent versus four percent), and almost twice as likely to report being threatened by, or having a gun or knife used against them (13 percent versus seven percent). Men in violent relationships were more likely than women to report being slapped (57 percent versus 40 percent), having something thrown at them (56 percent of men versus 44 percent of women) and being kicked, bit or hit (51 percent versus 33 percent). (Bunge 2000, p. 12).

Women were also more likely than men to report multiple incidents of spousal violence. Sixty-five percent of women (versus 54 percent of men) who experienced spousal violence reported being assaulted on more than one occasion; 26 percent of women (versus 13 percent of men) said it happened more than 10 times (Bunge 2000, p.14).

The GSS survey data reveals that women and men from all income and educational levels experience spousal violence. Although statistics compiled by police services suggest that family violence most often occurs in blue-collar and lower-class families, this is at least partly attributable to the fact that middle-class families have greater privacy than lower-class families and hence are better able to conceal family violence (Bachman and Saltzman 1995; Fineman and Mykitiuk 1994). Also, middle-class individuals have recourse to friends and professional counsellors to help deal with their violence; consequently, their altercations are less likely to become matters for the police (Buzawa and Buzawa 1990). According to the 1999 GSS, rates of spousal violence ranged from a high of three percent for those who had a household income below $30 0000 to a low of one percent for those with a household income of $60 000 or more (Bunge 2000).

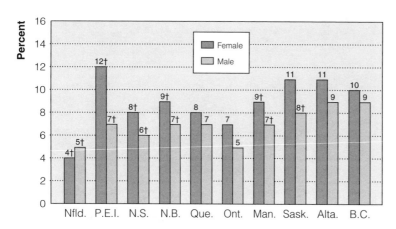

FIGURE **10.4**

Women more likely than men to experience spousal violence in most provinces, past 5 years. (Source: Statistics Canada, "Family Violence in Canada: A Statistical Profile," Cat. No. 85-224, July 2000, p. 12.)
†Coeffiecient of variation is high (16.6% and 33.3%)

This survey additionally found that, in general, younger people face the greatest risk of experiencing spousal violence with the highest rates reported by young women under the age of 25 (five percent). Younger men aged 25–34 also reported higher rates of violence (four percent) than those who were older (one percent).[3] Consistent with earlier studies conducted in both Canada and the United States (Kong 1997; Stets 1991; U.S. Department of Justice 1998a) the 1999 GSS reported that the risk of being a victim of spousal violence was higher for both women and men living in common-law unions (four percent) than in legal marriages (one percent).

We will examine issues of spouse abuse, child abuse, and elderly abuse in some detail in the sections that follow. (Relationship violence is also discussed in Chapter 7.) Often two or more of these forms of domestic violence occur together in the same family.

Wife Abuse

Wife abuse is a serious and significant problem whose most visible manifestation occurs in wife beating.

Other forms of violence, such as kicking, pushing down stairs, and hitting with objects, are also considered abuse. It is difficult to define wife abuse so that it includes all possible acts of serious physical violence while excluding verbal abuse because verbal aggression (threats, foul name calling, and other vocal assaults) virtually always occurs with physical aggression (Stets 1990). Although verbal aggression is of great psychological importance, we concern ourselves here primarily with repetitive, physically injurious acts. The alienating fight practices (along with the "Four Horsemen of the Apocalypse") discussed in Chapter 9 can also be verbal, or emotional abuse.

Physical wife abuse can result in serious injuries, including death (Bachman and Saltzman 1995). In Canada, various indicators suggest at least a slight decline in the severity of violence committed against wives in recent years (Figure 10.5). Assaults on wives in 1999 occurred less frequently than in 1993, were less likely to result in injuries and less likely to require medical attention for injuries sustained. At the same time, however, victims in 1999 were slightly more likely than those in earlier years to report fear that their life was endangered by a violent spouse (Figure 10.6).

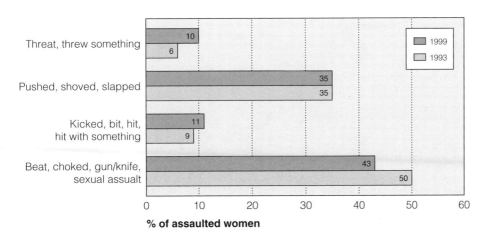

FIGURE **10.5**

Slight decline in the most serious violence against wives.[1,2] (Source: Statistics Canada, "Family Violence in Canada: A Statistical Profile," Cat. No. 85-224, July 2000, p. 21.)
[1]Includes common-law partners.
[2]Counts each victim once according to the most serious type of violence during the 5 years preceding the survey.

3. In this survey, the small samples for men in the under-25 age category who reported spousal violence prohibited making reliable estimates.

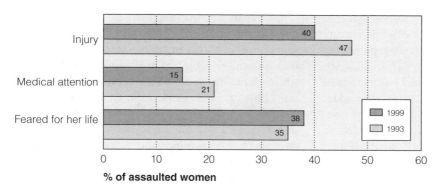

FIGURE   **10.6**

Change in severity of assaults on wives.[1] (Source: Statistics Canada, "Family Violence in Canada: A Statistical Profile," Cat. No. 85-224, July 2000, p. 11.)
[1]Includes common-law partners.

MARITAL RAPE   Wife abuse may take the form of sexual abuse and forced sexual intercourse, or **marital rape**, and sexual abuse is often combined with other physical violence. Ten percent of wives in one study reported that their husbands used physical force or threats to compel sex (Finkelhor and Yllo 1985). Another study found that 35 to 50 percent of marital rapes involved beating, hitting, or kicking (Russell 1982). Incredibly sadistic attacks are reported by many wives.

Prior to 1983 and the introduction of Canada's "sexual assault" laws, it was legally impossible for a man in Canada to rape his wife because the rape law contained a marital exemption. The wife was considered her husband's property and he was entitled to unlimited sexual access. A man could only be found guilty of a rape on his own wife if he was party to someone else raping her (e.g., if he forcibly restrained his wife while another man raped her) (Clark and Lewis 1977).

THE THREE-PHASE CYCLE OF DOMESTIC VIOLENCE   Experts are finding that the initial violent episode usually comes as a shock to a wife, who treats her mate's violence as an exceptional, isolated outburst. He promises it will not happen again; she believes him. She also tries to figure out what she did to cause his reaction so there will be no reason for it to happen again. The likelihood is that it will, however, because of what counsellors call the **three-phase cycle of violence**. First, tension resulting from some minor altercations builds over a period of time. Second, the situation escalates, eventually exploding in another violent episode. Third, the husband becomes gen-

uinely contrite, treating his wife lovingly. She wants to believe that this change in him will be permanent. This cycle repeats itself, with the violence worsening, if nothing is done to change things (Sonkin, Martin, and Walker 1985).

Two questions arise: Why do husbands beat their wives? And why do wives tolerate it? Both can be answered by the relative love and need theory.

WHY DO HUSBANDS DO IT?   Studies suggest that husbands who beat their wives are attempting to compensate for general feelings of powerlessness or inadequacy—in their jobs, in their marriages, or both. This type of family violence has been called **patriarchal terrorism** (Johnson 1995). As Chapter 3 indicated, our cultural images and the socialization process encourage men to be strong and self-sufficient. Husbands may use physical expressions of male supremacy to compensate for their lack of occupational success, prestige, or satisfaction (Anderson 1997). Husbands' feelings of powerlessness may also stem from an inability to earn a salary that keeps up with inflation and the family's standard of living or from the stress of a high-pressure occupation. Put another way, absent the *reward power* base, some husbands resort to *coercive power*. Figure 10.7, from a program for male batterers, illustrates how a male partner's need for power and control can result in both psychoemotional and physical violence.

Men may also use violence in an attempt to maintain control over wives or partners who are trying to become entirely independent of the relationship (Dutton and Browning 1988). Richard Gelles (1994,

1997) lists among "risk factors" for men who abuse women those who are between 18 and 30 years old, unemployed, users of illicit drugs or abusers of alcohol, and high school dropouts. With few legitimate avenues toward personal or social power, such men may resort to coercive power over the women in their lives in an attempt to gain control (Pyke 1997). As we saw in Chapter 7, the use of verbal and/or physical abuse to gain or regain control is also a cause for male violence in dating relationships (Ronfeldt, Kimerling, and Arias 1998).

WHY DO WIVES CONTINUE TO LIVE WITH IT?

Women do not like to get beaten up. They do not cooperate in their own beatings, and they often try to get away. They may, however, stay married to husbands who beat them repeatedly. For the most part, battered wives seek divorce only after a long history of severe violence and repeated conciliation. There are several reasons for this, and they all point to these women's lack of personal resources with which to take control of their own lives.

Fear Battered wives' lack of personal power begins with fear (DeMaris and Swinford 1996). "First of all," reports social scientist Richard Gelles, "the wife figures if she calls police or files for divorce, her husband will kill her—literally" (Gelles, in C. Booth 1977, p. 7). This fear is not unfounded. An estimated 75 percent of murders of women by their male partners occurred in response to the woman's attempt to leave (de Santis 1990). Husbands or ex-husbands have shown enormous persistence in stalking, pursuing and beating or killing women who try to leave an abusive situation (Johann 1994; Kong 1999).

Recognition that the most dangerous time for a victim of intimate violence was after leaving a violent relationship helped fuel the 1993 enactment of a law against "criminal harassment." This Canadian law is directed against "stalking" behaviours. In 1999, 5382 incidents of criminal harassment were reported to 106 police forces[4] in Canada (up 32 percent from 1996) (Greeno 2000).[5] Consistent with earlier

4. In that year, Saskatoon had the highest rate of reported cases of criminal harassment—75 incidents per 100 000 population, followed by Montreal 73, Vancouver 68, Toronto 40, St. Catharines-Niagara 27. In Edmonton, the rate was 11 and in Calgary, 12 (Greeno 2000).

5. Between 1998 and 1999, more than 4000 criminal harassment charges were taken to court, an increase of 43 percent from 1994–95. About half of these charges led to convictions and jail terms were imposed in 35 percent of them (Greeno 2000).

research (Kong 1997), women were the victims in 75 percent of reported cases; in most of these cases, the woman knew the stalker and, in many instances, had been involved with him in a previous relationship. While women were most likely to be stalked by an ex-husband, boyfriend, or current husband, 44 percent of male victims were stalked by a casual acquaintance; few of the male victims of criminal harassment were stalked by an ex-wife or girlfriend. In addition, from 1997 to 1999, there were nine stalking-related homicides reported, each involving a woman being stalked by a former partner (Greeno 2000).

Cultural Norms Furthermore, our cultural tradition historically has encouraged women to put up with abuse. English common law asserted that a husband had the right to physically chastise an errant wife (a legal norm still prevalent in the nineteenth century) (Straus and Gelles 1986; Gelles 1997). A cross-cultural analysis of domestic violence in 90 different societies found family violence to be virtually absent in 16. These 16 societies were characterized by economic and decision-making equality between the sexes, norms encouraging nonviolence generally, and regular intervention by neighbours and kin in domestic disputes (Levinson 1989). Although the legal right to physically abuse women has long since disappeared in our society, our cultural heritage continues to influence our attitudes (Torr and Swisher 1999).

Love, Economic Dependence, and Hopes for Reform Wives may live with abuse, not because they enjoy being battered, but because they love their husbands, depend on their economic resources, and hope they will reform. Battered wives who stay with their husbands fear the economic hardship or uncertainty that will result if they leave. They hesitate to summon police or to press charges not only out of fear of retaliation, but because of the loss of income or damage to a husband's professional reputation that could result from his incarceration. This economic hardship is heightened when children are involved. For mothers, leaving requires either being financially able to take her children—who may also be in danger—with her, or leaving them behind. (Box 10.2, "Family Violence Against Women With Disabilities examines the especial hardships experienced by women with disabilities who experience family violence.) Consequently, even though a dramatic rise in a

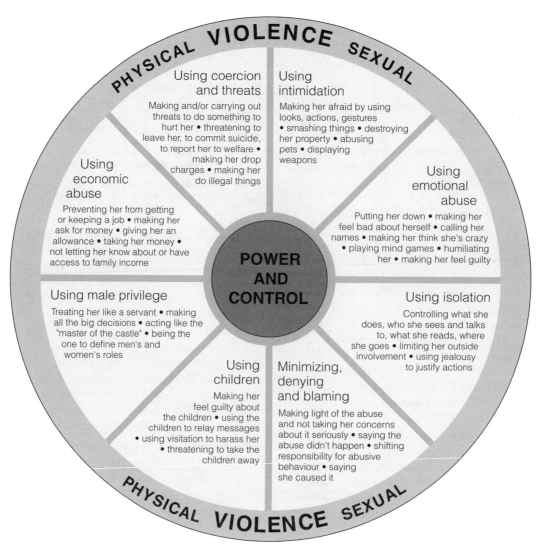

PHYSICAL VIOLENCE SEXUAL

Using coercion and threats

Making and/or carrying out threats to do something to hurt her • threatening to leave her, to commit suicide, to report her to welfare • making her drop charges • making her do illegal things

Using intimidation

Making her afraid by using looks, actions, gestures • smashing things • destroying her property • abusing pets • displaying weapons

Using economic abuse

Preventing her from getting or keeping a job • making her ask for money • giving her an allowance • taking her money • not letting her know about or have access to family income

Using emotional abuse

Putting her down • making her feel bad about herself • calling her names • making her think she's crazy • playing mind games • humiliating her • making her feel guilty

POWER AND CONTROL

Using male privilege

Treating her like a servant • making all the big decisions • acting like the "master of the castle" • being the one to define men's and women's roles

Using isolation

Controlling what she does, who she sees and talks to, what she reads, where she goes • limiting her outside involvement • using jealousy to justify actions

Using children

Making her feel guilty about the children • using the children to relay messages • using visitation to harass her • threatening to take the children away

Minimizing, denying and blaming

Making light of the abuse and not taking her concerns about it seriously • saying the abuse didn't happen • shifting responsibility for abusive behaviour • saying she caused it

PHYSICAL VIOLENCE SEXUAL

FIGURE **10.7**

Coercive power some male partners resort to for power and control.

wife's earnings may prove threatening to a low-earning husband, in the long run mutual awareness of the wife's economic independence may ultimately deter wife abuse (Blumberg and Coleman 1989).

Gendered Socialization   Another factor that helps perpetuate wife abuse is that women accept the cultural mandate that it is primarily their responsibility to keep their marriage from failing. Believing this, wives are often convinced that their emotional sup-

port can lead husbands to reform. Thus, wives often return to violent mates after leaving them (Herbert, Silver, and Ellard 1991).

Childhood Experience   Another frequent factor in women's living with abuse is childhood experience. Research suggests that people who experience violence in their parents' home while growing up may regard beatings as part of married life (Torr and Swisher 1999). One study of 204 recently divorced women concluded that girls subjected to abusive parenting tend to develop a hostile, rebellious personality and are likely to affiliate later with men who are like them. These men, in turn, tend to be violent toward their dates and, later, their wives (Simons et al. 1993).

According to the Violence Against Women Survey (VAWS), children witness violence against their mothers in about 40 percent of violent marriages in Canada, including more than 50 percent of the cases in which the women fear for their lives. The VAWS additionally reports that "women who were exposed to wife battering while growing up had rates of violence directed at them by their own husbands that were almost twice as high as women who grew up in nonviolent environments" (Johnson 1996, p. 176).

Low Self-Esteem   Finally, unusually low self-esteem interacts with fear, depression, confusion, anxiety, feelings of self-blame (Andrews and Brewin 1990), and loss of a sense of personal control (Umberson et al. 1998) to create the **battered woman syndrome**, in which a wife cannot see a way out of her situation (Walker 1988; Johann 1994).

A WAY OUT   A woman in such a position needs to redefine her situation before she can deal with her problem, and she needs to forge some links with the outside world to alter her relationship.

Although there are not enough of them (Health Canada 1999), a network of shelters for battered women provides a woman and her children with temporary housing, food, and clothing to alleviate the problems of economic dependency and physical safety. These organizations may also provide counselling to encourage a stronger self-concept so that the woman can view herself as worthy of better treatment and capable of making her way in the outside world if need be. Finally, shelters provide guidance in obtaining employment, legal assistance, family counselling, or whatever practical assistance is required for a more permanent solution.

This last service provided by shelters—obtaining help toward more long-range solutions—is important, research shows. Two face-to-face interviews with the same 155 wife-battery victims (a "two-wave panel study") were conducted within 18 months during 1982 and 1983. Each of the women interviewed had sought refuge in a shelter. Findings showed that victims who were also taking other measures (for example, calling the police, trying to get a restraining order, seeking personal counselling or legal help) were more likely to benefit from their shelter experience. "Otherwise, shelters may have no impact or perhaps even trigger retaliation (from husbands) for disobedience" (Berk, Newton, and Berk 1986, p. 488). The researchers conclude:

> The possibility of perverse shelter effects for certain kinds of women poses a troubling policy dilemma. On the one hand, it is difficult to be enthusiastic about an intervention that places battered victims at further risk. On the other hand, a shelter stay may for many women be one important step in a lengthy process toward freedom, even though there may also be genuine short-run dangers. Perhaps solutions can be found in strategies that link together several different kinds of interventions. (p. 488)

As with some other decisions discussed in this text, social scientists have applied exchange theory (Chapter 2) to an abused woman's decision to stay or leave (Choice and Lamke 1997). As Figure 10.8 illustrates, an abused wife weighs such things as her investment in the relationship, her (dis)satisfaction with the relationship, the quality of her alternatives, and her beliefs about whether it is appropriate for her to leave ("subjective norm") against questions such as, whether she will be better off if she leaves (Might her husband retaliate, for example?) and whether she can actually do it. The woman's personal resources along with community (structural) resources, such as whether shelters or other forms of assistance are available, further impact her decision. Personal barriers might involve not having either a job with adequate pay or extended family who could help. Structural barriers might include the lack of community systems for practical help.

Husband Abuse

Both wives and husbands sometimes resort to violence. Although men may be more likely to deny using violence (DeMaris, Pugh, and Harman 1992), various surveys show a pattern of mutual violence between spouses (Bunge 2000; Stacey, Hazlewood, and Shupe 1994).

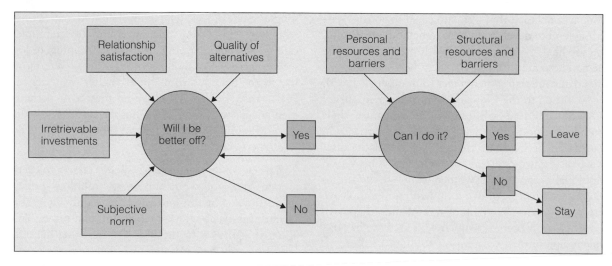

FIGURE **10.8**

| Conceptual model of abused women's stay/leave decision-making processes. (Source: Choice and Lamke 1997, p. 295.)

Whether wives' violence toward husbands is most often in self-defense is debated among experts. Noting that wives often strike out first, Straus (1993) argues that this situation "does not support the hypothesis that assaults by wives are primarily acts of self-defense or retaliation" (p. 76). Others (Kurz 1993; Alvi et al. 2000; Saunders 1988) assert that husband abuse is largely in self-defense or, at least, retaliation. In any case, Straus and Gelles found it "distressing" that, "in marked contrast to the behaviour of women outside the family, women are about as violent within the family as men" (1986, p. 470). They noted that criticism from feminist scholars (see for example, Yllo and Bograd 1988) has led most researchers to avoid publishing articles on battered husbands (Gelles and Conte 1990, p. 1046). Furthermore, battered husbands have fewer community resources, such as shelters, than do battered wives (Cose 1994a). Responding to the controversy, Straus and Gelles have stated their position:

Violence by women is a critically important issue for the safety and well-being *of women*. Let us assume that most of the assaults by women are of the "slap the cad" genre and are not intended to and do not physically injure the husband. The danger to women of such behaviour is that it sets the stage for the husband to assault her. Sometimes this is immediate and severe retaliation. But regardless of whether that occurs, the fact that she slapped him provides the precedent and justification for him to hit her when she is being obstinate, "bitchy," or "not listening to reason" as he sees it. Unless women also forsake violence in their relationships with male partners and children, they cannot expect to be free of assault. Women must insist as much on non-violence by their sisters as they rightfully insist on it by men. (Straus and Gelles 1988, pp. 25–26)

Indeed, it may be that there are two forms of heterosexual violence against women—"patriarchal terrorism" and "common couple violence" (Johnson 1995). **Patriarchal violence** refers specifically to wife abuse and typically follows the cycle of violence described earlier. **Common couple violence** refers to mutual violence between partners and tends to be less severe in terms of injuries. While common couple violence certainly exists and may be more common than patriarchal terrorism, "it would be a great mistake if our new awareness of husband abuse were to deflect attention from wives as victims" (see Yllo and Bograd 1988). This is so for the following reasons, all based on research:

Family Violence Against Women With Disabilities

Probably the single biggest factor affecting the incidence of family violence against women with disabilities is the extent of these women's "families." Women with disabilities must often depend on a variety of people to provide them with assistance in carrying out their everyday lives. For this reason, their "family" is understood to include not only parents, husbands, boyfriends, and other relatives, but also friends, neighbours, and caregivers. Caregivers can include attendants, interpreters, homemakers, drivers, doctors, nurses, teachers, social workers, psychiatrists, therapists, counsellors, and workers in hospitals and other institutions. This large number of people, and the intimate physical and emotional contact involved in the care they provide, greatly increases the risk of abuse to persons with disabilities.

Women who live in institutional settings, and women who are multiply or profoundly disabled, are most vulnerable to abuse because they are more dependent upon even larger numbers of people, and less able to get away. It is estimated that women with disabilities are 1.5 to 10 times as likely to be abused as women without disabilities are, depending on whether they live in the community or in institutions.

While a disability can make it more difficult for a woman to escape or report abuse, social attitudes toward persons with disabilities are probably a bigger factor in her increased vulnerability to violence. The way in which society views persons with disabilities handicaps these women in many ways.

- They tend to be viewed and treated as children, as lacking intelligence.

- They may be trained to be compliant and are sometimes punished for assertiveness or for challenging authority figures. This is in direct contrast to the street-proofing taught to many children in schools.

- Women with disabilities are considered to be non-sexual and are often not given sex-education, which can result in an inability to distinguish between abusive behaviour and normal or necessary forms of touching.

- They may be considered incompetent witnesses by police and the courts, particularly if they have difficulty or require assistance in communicating.

- When they do report abuse, they may not be believed....

Barriers to Obtaining Help

It is extremely difficult for any abused woman to leave a situation....For a woman with a disability, this situation is even more difficult. She may be dependent on her abuser for affection, communication, and financial, physical, and medical support. If she reports the abuse, she may risk poverty and loss of housing. She may fear that she will not be heard or believed if she speaks out. She may face further violence, institutionalization, or loss of her children if she seeks help. She may not have access to information about existing support services for victims of violence. Even if she has this information, many sources of support may not be accessible. She may not be able to contact the police or women's shelters because they do not have communication devices such as Telecommunication Devices for the Deaf (TDDs). She may not be able to physically leave her situation because of a lack of accessible transportation. Her lack of options may leave her feeling so powerless and despairing that suicide seems the only viable choice. And if she seeks help in dealing with suicidal thoughts or attempts, she is unlikely to find counselling that takes account of her own reality....

Source: Abridged from "Family Violence Against Women With Disabilities." 1993. National Clearing House on Family Violence. Ottawa: Minister of Supply and Services Canada.

1. Husbands have higher rates of inflicting the most dangerous and injurious forms of violence, such as severe beatings (Bunge 2000a, 2000b; Johnson 2000; U.S. Department of Justice 1998).

2. Violence by husbands does more damage, even if it is an exchange of slaps or punches, because of a man's generally greater physical strength; the woman, therefore, is more likely to be seriously injured (Brush 1990).

3. Violent acts by the husband tend to be repeated over time, whereas those by wives do not. (As we have earlier noted, violence directed at women by their partners is more frequent and severe than violence directed at men; Bunge 2000a, p. 14.)

4. Husbands are more apt to leave an abusive relationship within a short time. Having more resources, men rarely face the choice women do of choosing between poverty (for their children as well as themselves) and violence (Straus, Gelles, and Steinmetz 1980).

For these reasons, women are rightly concerned about losing public attention and resources to what is perceived as a less drastic need (Dobash et al. 1992). Yet there may be a need for some programmatic support for male victims of spouse abuse. Both needs must be met.

Abuse Among Lesbian and Gay Male Couples

Domestic violence has long been one of the lesbian and gay communities' "nastiest secrets" (Island and Letellier 1991, p. 36; Obejas 1994, p. 53). Lesbians may have denied the issue because they believe in the inherent goodness of lesbian relationships or are afraid of giving fuel to homophobia. As for violence in the relationships of gay men, there may be even more silence and denial:

> After two and one-half years of researching and learning about gay men's domestic violence, we have reached the conclusion that as a community we are responding to domestic violence generally the same way a victim responds to domestic violence when it first happens to him. Our community is minimizing the problem. (Island and Letellier 1991, pp. 36–37)

Research on lesbian and gay male relationship violence is very scanty, but the few studies that have been done suggest that violence between same-sex partners occurs at about the same rate as it does in heterosexual relationships (Chesley et al. 1999; Lockhart et al. 1994). As is also true for heterosexual couples, domestic violence can be found in all racial/ethnic categories, social classes, education levels, and age groups. Among lesbians, neither "butch/femme" roles nor the women's physical size has been found to figure into violence (Obejas 1994).

Some of the relationship dynamics in same-sex abuse partnerships are similar to those in abusive heterosexual relationships (Kurdek 1994, 1998). Alcohol and/or drug abuse are often involved, for instance (Renzetti 1992). And the abusive partner is typically jealously possessive, using violence or threats of violence to keep the partner from leaving him or her. Furthermore, the couple is likely to deny or minimize the violence, along with believing that the violence is at least partly the victim's fault (Island and Letellier 1991; Renzetti 1992).

Meanwhile, there are other relationship dynamics that are specific to same-sex domestic abuse. For one thing, both men and women in same-sex relationships are freer to be either dominant or submissive, so it is more difficult to allocate violence to culturally influenced gender roles. Lesbians as well as gay men may fight back more often than do heterosexual women, a situation that leads to confusion about who is the battered and who is the batterer. Furthermore, some lesbians and gay men who are battered in one relationship may become batterers in another relationship (Island and Letellier 1991; Obejas 1994).

Lesbian violence is different in still other respects. For one thing, according to psychologist Vallerie Coleman, who works with battered lesbians, heterosexual men tend to feel they have a right to abuse their mates, while lesbians do not (Obejas 1994). And a greater proportion of lesbian batterers seek help than do heterosexual male abusers. Lesbians are more likely to go into treatment on their own, according to Coleman. "Heterosexual men go in because they're court-mandated" (in Obejas 1994).

A special problem for lesbian and gay male domestic violence victims is that few resources exist to serve their needs, although some services are beginning to be developed, particularly in major urban areas (Island

and Letellier 1991; Obejas 1994). This is an issue that is just beginning to be discussed and researched; studies should enhance what we know about all the various forms of domestic violence (Renzetti and Miley 1996).

Stopping Relationship Violence and Legal Arrest

Intimate abuse tends to escalate, growing more severe over time. According to one estimate, 32 percent of victimized women will be revictimized within a relatively short time in the absence of intervention (Langan and Innes 1986).

LEGAL ARREST Police protection and arrest of spousal abusers constitute an alternative that may be in the long-term interests of both abuser and abused. If a spouse has an effective means of coping with violence, s/he will not be forced into violent, self-protective acts. There has been little legal protection for battered spouses until fairly recently. In the past, police typically avoided making arrests for assault that would be automatic if the man and woman involved were not married. The laws themselves contributed to police reluctance: policies might require a police officer to witness the act before making an arrest at the scene, or more severe injury (requiring stitches, for example)

might be required for prosecution to take place. In some cases restraining orders required additional court action before they could be enforced.

In the past two decades, both federal and provincial/territorial governments have responded to the problem of family violence with changes in legislation, policies, and programs. For example, in the early 1980s, "mandatory charging policies were implemented across Canada to increase charging by the police and prosecution by the Crown in cases of wife assault" (Bunge 2000a, p. 19). At present, most Canadian provinces have special policies and procedures for responding to spousal violence. Some provinces have specialized courts to deal with these cases. Manitoba was the first jurisdiction in Canada to do so (Ursel 2000).

The majority of Canadian women (93 percent) and men (79 percent) who reported spousal violence to Canadian police departments in 1999 said they did so to stop the violence or to receive protection from the abuser (Figure 10.9). Women were more likely than men to report the incident to police in the hope that their abusive partner would be arrested and punished (48 percent versus 34 percent).

Various researchers (Sherman and Berk 1994; Berk and Newton 1995) have found that mandatory arrests deter new assaults. Mandatory arrest policies,

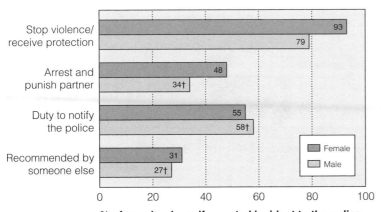

% of people who self-reported incident to the police

FIGURE **10.9**

Motivations for involving the police somewhat different for women and men, past 5 years.[1] (Source: Statistics Canada, "Family Violence in Canada: A Statistical Profile," Cat. No. 85-224, July 2000, p. 11.)

[†]Coefficient of variation is high (16.6% and 33.3%).

[1]Asked only of those respondents who reported the incident to the police.

when publicized, may also deter at least some men from physically assaulting their wives. However, others suggest that arresting an abusive partner or pressing charges will only aggravate the situation and result in escalating violence later. Some suggest that "shaming" an offender may be a more powerful tool in reducing acts of family violence than the formal processes of arrest, conviction, and incarceration (Braithwaite 1989; Mugford and Mugford 1991).

While research continues as to the circumstances in which a mandatory arrest policy can be effective (Sherman 1992), other strategies are being pursued. For example, in response to various studies that have noted elevated rates of spousal abuse and other forms of family violence within Aboriginal communities, over 180 projects, focusing on public awareness, training, community workshops, and research and program development, were conducted in Native communities across Canada in the 1990s. Care was also taken to respect the preferred strategies of intervention within Aboriginal communities.

For example, within Aboriginal communities, an incident of spousal abuse may not be viewed as a problem of an individual offender–victim. Rather, it may be viewed as a symptom of community dysfunction. In consequence, proposed solutions may be framed in terms of a holistic, community-wide healing process that should be planned, developed and implemented by Aboriginal peoples. A workshop dealing with issues of abuse may begin with a prayer and a sharing circle or smudge ceremony using the local root. Communities may also use naming ceremonies and feasts to celebrate different points of healing or encourage those who have experienced abuse to take part in sweat lodges to ask for help for themselves and others. The Medicine Wheel, which explains that a healthy person must use all four parts of himself or herself—physical, mental, emotional and spiritual—may also be utilized as a healing tool with many versions of the Wheel used in counselling programs.

COUNSELLING AND GROUP THERAPY Counselling and group therapy, thought to be ineffective with male abusers, have now been tried with some success. Here we mean not conventional marital therapy but group therapy for abusive men who wish to stop. Many abusing partners have difficulty controlling their response to anger and frustration, dealing with problems, or handling intimacy. Even though many, perhaps most, abusers are not reachable (Hueschler 1989) and may drop out of treatment (Brown, O'Leary and Feldbau 1997), others have a sincere desire to stop. Group therapy reduces stigma and provides a setting in which abusive partners can learn more constructive ways of both coping with anger and balancing autonomy and intimacy, often another area of difficulty. Some men's therapy groups have emerged in which former batterers help lead male abusers toward recovery (Allen and Kivel 1994).

In the past decade, some couples' therapy programs have emerged to treat wife abuse (Johannson and Tutty 1998). Typically, such programs counsel husbands and wives—or just husbands—separately over a period of up to six months. After this first treatment phase, couples are counselled together and are taught anger-management techniques, along with communication, problem-solving, and conflict-resolution skills. Couples' therapy programs designed to stop domestic violence are somewhat controversial because they proceed from the premise that a couple's staying together, without violence after an abusive past, is possible. Many feminist scholars have expressed concern that this is seldom the case (Hansen and Goldenberg 1993). There is also some evidence that negative social sanctions from either partner's relatives or friends can help stop wife abuse (Lackey and Williams 1995).

We will turn now to another family violence issue in which the more powerful members of a family abuse the less powerful—child abuse.

 Focusing on Children

Child Abuse and Neglect

Perceptions of what constitutes child abuse or neglect have differed throughout history and in various cultures. Some of the practices that we currently consider abusive were accepted in the past as the normal exercise of parental rights or as appropriate discipline. While exceptions exist, children have historically had little control over their lives and been regarded as the property of their parents, particularly their fathers. Today, standards of acceptable child care vary according to culture and social class. However, what some consider to be abusive, others may consider right and proper discipline.

Consider that while many mental health professionals and child development experts argue that corporal punishment is ineffective and damaging to children, many parents accept the cultural tradition of spanking as an appropriate form of child discipline. Unlike such countries as Austria, Cyprus, Denmark, Finland, Italy, Norway, and Sweden where the use of corporal punishment in the home or school is against the law, Canadian law specifically allows for the corporal punishment of children.

Section 43 of the Canadian *Criminal Code* specifies that "[e]very schoolteacher, parent, or person standing in the place of a parent is justified in using force by way of correction toward a pupil or child, as the case may be, who is under his care, if the force does not exceed what is reasonable under the circumstances." However, not all would agree with what Canadian courts have defined to be the "reasonable" use of force. For example, one of the leading decisions used by our courts to interpret section 43 (made by the Quebec Court of Appeal in 1971) specified that "the mere fact that the children disciplined suffered contusions and bruises is not in itself proof of exercise of undue force." The line between "discipline" and "abuse" is not as clearly drawn within Canadian case law as some may suppose.

People use the term **child abuse** to refer to overt acts of aggression, such as excessive verbal derogation, beating, or inflicting physical injury. The term **sexual abuse** refers to forced, tricked, or coerced sexual behaviour—exposure, kissing, fondling of sexual organs, vaginal or anal intercourse, and **incest** (sexual relations between those related by blood such as a brother/sister, mother/son, grandfather/grandson and so on) (Gelles and Conte 1990). The definition of child sexual abuse excludes mutually desired sex play between or among siblings close in age; coerced sex by stronger and/or older siblings is sexual abuse and may be more widespread than parent–child incest (Canavan, Meyer, and Higgs 1992).

Incest is the most emotionally charged form of sexual abuse; it is also the most difficult to detect. The most common forms are father–daughter incest and incest involving a stepfather or older brother. The latter is very probably the most common (Canavan, Meyer, and Higgs 1992). Incest appears to be related to a variety of sexual, emotional, and physical problems among adults who were abused as children (Simons and Whitbeck 1991; Gilgun 1995; Browning and Laumann 1997; Luster and Small 1997; Bell and Belicki 1998). Research by social psychologists find lower self-esteem and greater incidences of depression among adults who have been victims of child abuse (Downs and Miller 1998; Silvern et al. 1995). A study of nearly 43 000 adolescents found that those who had been physically and/or sexually abused were more prone to binge drinking and thoughts of suicide. However, high levels of supportive interest and monitoring from at least one parent decreased the risk for these outcomes among sexually abused adolescents (Luster and Small 1997). Sexual abuse by paid caregivers is also a problem being addressed by policymakers and child-care professionals; sexual exploitation of homeless children is yet another (Shamin and Chowdhury 1993; Hagan and McCarthy 1998).

Child neglect includes acts of omission—failing to provide adequate physical or emotional care. Physically neglected children often show signs of malnutrition, need immunizations, lack proper clothing, attend school irregularly, and need medical attention for such conditions as poor eyesight or bad teeth (Health Canada 1999). Often these conditions are due to economic stress (Baumrind 1994; Kruttschnitt, McLeod, and Dornfeld 1994; Brown et al. 1998), but child neglect can also be willful neglect (Gillham et al. 1998). **Emotional child abuse or neglect** involves a parent's often being overly harsh and critical, failing to provide guidance, or being uninterested in a child's needs. Emotional child abuse might also include allowing children to witness violence between partners (Carlson 1990; Rubiner 1994). Although emotional abuse can occur without physical abuse, physical abuse always results in emotional abuse as well.

HOW EXTENSIVE IS CHILD ABUSE? Although the abuse of children is a complex and serious issue that can have devastating effects, at present in Canada, we lack a national data source on its nature and extent. In the absence of such a source, we are forced to rely on data compiled by police services, hospitals, and provincial/territorial child welfare agencies. These sources of information may well underestimate the prevalence of child abuse in our country. "Despite the existence of mandatory reporting laws in provinces and territories requiring all citizens to report child abuse and neglect to authorities, it has been estimated that as many as 90 percent of cases are not reported to child welfare agencies" (Locke 2000, p. 31).

In 1999, children and youths under the age of 18 were assaulted by family members in 22 percent of the physical assaults and 30 percent of the sexual assaults reported to Canadian police departments. The most common assailant was a parent (Figure 10.10) and the most common victim, a girl (Figure 10.11). "Eighty percent of the child and youth victims sexually assaulted and 53 percent of the victims physically assaulted by their families were girls" (Locke 2000, p. 33).

Research has found that a very small proportion of sexual abusers are female—at most four percent when the victims are girls and 20 percent when the victims are boys (Glaser and Frosh 1988, p. 13). "Especially since contacts with female children occur with at least twice or three times the frequency as male children, the presumption that sexual abusers are primarily men seems clearly supported" (Finkelhor 1984, in Glaser and Frosh 1988, p. 13).[6] Another study (Finkelhor and Baron 1986) found that girls who have been separated from or have poor relationships with their mothers are more likely to be victimized. Although "[t]he data point to the importance of mothers in protecting children from sexually aggressive men" (Gelles and Conte 1990, p. 1052), mothers can also be the perpetrator of childhood sexual abuse (Evert 1992; Vanderbelt 1992).

Abused children live in families of all socioeconomic levels, ethnicities, and religious groups, although child abuse is reported more frequently among poor families (Finkelhor et al. 1996). This may be due to some of the same reasons, discussed earlier, that spouse abuse is reported to police more frequently by the poorer classes. Another reason may be unconscious discrimination on the part of physicians and others who report abuse and neglect (Hampton and Newberger 1988).

6. However, a study (Nelson 1994), which examined how one Canadian police service responded to allegations of child sexual abuse, suggests that this presumption may have a self-fulfilling prophecy effect. Nelson reports that when victims were male, allegations of sexual abuse by an older female were often viewed by police as a "seduction" or a benign "initiation" into sexual activity rather than as a sexual assault.

ABUSE VERSUS "NORMAL" CHILD REARING

One writer has observed that "a culturally defined concept of children as the 'property' of caregivers and of caregivers as legitimate users of physical force appears to be an essential component of child abuse" (Garbarino 1977, p. 725). It is all too easy for parents to go beyond reasonable limits when angry or distraught or to have limits that include as discipline what most observers would define as abuse (Baumrind 1994; Whipple and Richey 1997). Hence, child abuse must be seen as a potential behaviour in many families—even those we think of as "normal" (Gelles and Straus 1988; Straus 1994).

Bearing this in mind, consider the following society-wide beliefs and conditions that, when exaggerated, can encourage even well-intentioned parents to mistreat their children:

- A belief in physical punishment is a contributing (but not sufficient) factor in child abuse. Abusive parents have learned—probably in their own childhood—to view children as requiring physical punishment (Gough and Reavey 1997; Whipple and Richey 1997).

- Parents may have unrealistic expectations about what the child is capable of; often they lack awareness and knowledge of the child's physical and emotional needs and abilities (Gough and Reavey 1997). For example, slapping a bawling toddler to stop her or his crying is completely unrealistic.

- Parents who abuse their children were usually abused or neglected themselves as children. Violent parents are likely to have experienced and thereby learned violence as children. Currently, researchers are focusing on specifically how this tendency toward family violence is transmitted (McNeal and Amato 1998; Fergusson and Horwood 1998). One factor is an inappropriate conception of justice—of deserved consequences for "right" and "wrong" (Blackman 1989).

This does *not* mean that abused children are predetermined to be abusive parents (Gelles and Straus 1988, pp. 48–49). A good estimate is that 25 to 35 percent of abused children grow up to abuse their own children. Although this is not a majority, it is considerably higher than the child abuser rate of two to four percent in the general population (Gelles and Conte 1990).

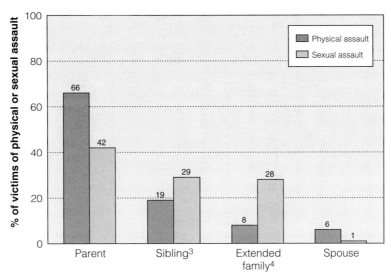

FIGURE   **10.10**

Parents most frequently accused in assaults against children and youth committed by family members, 1999.[1, 2] (Source: Statistics Canada, "Family Violence in Canada: A Statistical Profile," Cat. No. 85-224, July 2000, p. 33.)
Percentages may not total 100% due to rounding.
[1]Data are not nationally representative. Data are based on a sample of 164 police departments, representing 46% of the national volume of crime in 1999.
[2]Includes victims under the age of 18 years where sex of the victim is known.
[3]Sibling includes natural, step, half, foster or adopted siblings.
[4]Extended family includes others related by blood, marriage, adoption, or foster care.

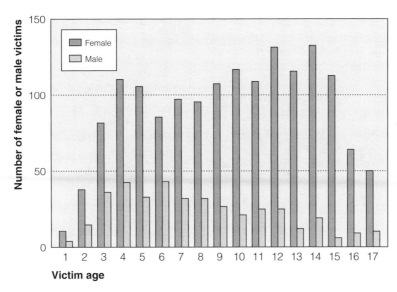

FIGURE   **10.11**

Victims of family-related sexual assaults by age and sex of victims, 1999.[1,2]
(Source: Statistics Canada, "Family Violence in Canada: A Statistical Profile," Cat. No. 85-224, July 2000, p. 34.)
[1]Data are not nationally representative. Data are based on a sample of 164 police departments, representing 46% of the national volume of crime in 1999.
[2]Includes cases where the victim and accused were related by blood, marriage, adoption, or foster care. Excludes cases in which the victim's sex and age are unknown.

- Parental stress and feelings of helplessness play a significant part in child abuse (Rodriguez and Green 1997). Financial problems can cause stress, especially for single mothers; overload, so often related to financial problems, also creates stress that can lead to child abuse (Brown et al. 1998). "Economic adversity and worries about money pervade the typical violent home" (Gelles and Straus 1988, p. 85). Other causes of parental stress are children's misbehaviour, changing lifestyles and standards of living, and the fact that a parent feels under pressure to do a good job but is often perplexed about how to do it.

- Families have become more private and less dependent on kinship and neighbourhood relationships (Berardo 1998). Hence, parents and children are alone together, shut off at home from the "watchful eyes and sharp tongues that regulate parent–child relations in other cultures" (Skolnick 1978, p. 82). In neighbourhoods that have support systems and tight social networks of community-related friends—where other adults are somewhat involved in the activities of the family—child abuse and neglect are much more likely to be noticed and stopped (Gelles and Straus 1988).

RISK FACTORS FOR CHILD ABUSE Circumstances that are statistically related to child maltreatment include parental youth and inexperience, marital discord and divorce, and unusually demanding or otherwise difficult children (Baumrind 1994; Brown et al. 1998). Other risk factors involve parental abuse of alcohol or other substances (Fleming, Mullen, and Bammer 1996), a mother's cohabiting with her boyfriend (who is more likely than a child's male relative to abuse the child) (Margolin 1992), and having a stepfather (because stepfathers are more likely than genetic fathers to abuse their children) (Daly and Wilson 1994).

COMBATING CHILD ABUSE Two approaches to combating child abuse and willful neglect exist: the punitive approach, which views abuse and neglect as crimes for which parents should be punished, and the therapeutic approach, which views abuse as a family problem requiring treatment.

Those who favour the punitive approach believe that one or both parents should be held clearly (that is, legally) responsible for abusing a child. A complicated issue emerging with regard to this approach involves holding battered women criminally responsible either for abusing their children or for failing to act to prevent such abuse at the hands of their male partners.

Research is beginning to uncover a "complexity of connections between spouse [abuse] and child abuse" (Erickson 1991, p. 198). Although some studies have found low correlations between a man's battering his wife and battering his children, other research has found that in about half the cases in which a woman was being battered, the batterer was also abusing the children in the household. Some critics have begun to question whether the law should hold a battered woman responsible for failing to prevent harm to her children when, as a battered woman, she cannot defend even herself. A battered woman is likely to believe that the man of the house has a right to discipline his wife and children and hence is unlikely to challenge him; moreover, by failing to act, the battered woman may be making a reasonable decision under the circumstances:

Perhaps it appears very reasonable to the battered woman to allow the batterer to assault the child as long as she can see that the battering is not "going too far." The alternatives might appear to be worse: interfering and thereby causing an acceleration of the battery so that it does "go too far," or fleeing with the children to an unimaginable life, with no money, no shelter, and no protection from the batterer, should he follow them.... When the law punishes a battered woman for failing to protect her child against a batterer, it may be punishing her for failing to do something she was incapable of doing.... She is then being punished for the crime of the person who has victimized her. (Erickson 1991, pp. 208–209)

Meanwhile, others prefer to hold one or both parents clearly responsible. They reject the family system approach to therapy because it implies a distribution of responsibility for change to all family members, including the child. However, in Canada, sentences in cases of child sexual and physical abuse are not always as harsh as some might like—or believe necessary for the purpose of deterrence.

For example, in her analysis of 1349 cases of child abuse which came before the Winnipeg Family Violence Courts in 1992 and 1997, sociologist Jane Ursel (2000, p. 47) found that:

> [a]mong convicted sexual abuse offenders, 68 percent were sentenced to a jail term compared to 33 percent of physical abuse offenders....Among offenders who received a jail sentence for physically or sexually abusing a child, 43 percent received a sentence of three months or less, 72 percent were sentenced to less than two years while 28 percent were sentenced to more than two years.

Ursel reports that, in cases of child sexual abuse, 68 percent of offenders received a period of incarceration, 30 percent received probation, seven percent, a fine, four percent a conditional sentence and five percent a conditional discharge. Among those convicted of physically abusing a child, while a third were sentenced to some period of incarceration, over half (57 percent) were given probation, 13 percent, a fine, 18 percent a conditional discharge and three percent, an absolute discharge (Ursel 2000, p.47).

The therapeutic approach to combating child abuse involves two interrelated strategies: (1) increasing parents' self-esteem and their knowledge about children and (2) involving the community in child rearing (Goldstein, Keller, and Erne 1985). One voluntary program, Parents Anonymous (PA), for example, holds regular meetings to enhance self-esteem and educate abusive parents.

Involving the community involves getting people other than parents to help with child rearing. Community resources include *supplemental mothers*, who are available to babysit regularly with potentially abused children, and the crisis nursery where parents can take their children when they need to get away for a few hours. Ideally, crisis nurseries are open 24 hours a day and accept children at any hour without pre-arrangement.

Another form of relief for abused or neglected children is to remove them from their parents' homes and place them in foster care. This practice is itself controversial (Ingrassia 1995) as foster parents have themselves been abusive in some cases and in many regions of the country there aren't enough foster parents to go around (Weisman 1994; Gelles 1996). Moreover, sociologist Tanis Das Gupta (2000, p. 155) has noted that until the early 1980s, Native children were vastly overrepresented among those Canadian children placed in foster care and that the majority of these children were placed in non-Native homes. She suggests that this situation stemmed from the devaluation of Native culture and parenting practices by non-Native society in general, and by social workers and child-welfare workers in particular. In the 1990s, she observes, this situation changed somewhat "with more Native empowerment and the growing movement in support of Native people adopting Native children" (p. 155).

We turn now to another topic that is gaining more and more attention: elder abuse and neglect.

Elder Abuse and Neglect

Elder abuse first caught the public's attention in Great Britain in 1975. As with child abuse and neglect, **elder abuse** involves overt acts of aggression, whereas **elder neglect** involves acts of omission or failure to give adequate care. Elder abuse by family members can include physical assault, emotional humiliation, purposeful social isolation (for example, forbidding use of the telephone), or material exploitation and theft (Tatara and Blumerman 1996; Henningson 1997).

The 1999 GSS asked Canadians 65 years of age or over a series of questions in relation to emotional and financial abuse by children, caregivers (individuals paid or unpaid who provide assistance or healthcare in the respondent's home), and spouses (including current and former spouses as well as common-law partners). In addition, it asked questions about possible physical or sexual abuse by children, caregivers, or spouses. Recall that this survey did not include respondents living in institutions (e.g., retirement homes, hospitals) and, as such, cannot provide us with information on the experiences of older Canadians who live in such settings.

This survey found very little physical or sexual violence perpetrated against older Canadians residing in a private household. "[O]nly one percent of this population of seniors indicated that they had been physically or sexually assaulted by a spouse, adult child or caregiver in the five years prior to this survey" (Bunge

2000c, p. 27). Seven percent (or 232 of the total sample of 4324 older Canadians) reported experiencing some type of emotional or financial abuse with spouses identified as the perpetrator in the vast majority of cases. The most common form of emotional abuse reported was being verbally put down or called names (three percent), followed by limiting contact with family or friends (two percent). Men were more likely than women (nine percent versus six percent) to report being victims of emotional or financial abuse by an adult child, caregiver, or spouse. The highest rates of emotional or financial abuse were reported by older adults whose household incomes were between $30 000 and $39 000; were divorced or separated, lived in rural areas, and had some post-secondary education.

According to police-reported statistics, there were 802 cases of violence committed against older adults by family members with the most frequent assailant an adult child (43 percent), followed by a spouse (28 percent) (Figure 10.12). The most common offence committed against an older adult, man or woman, by a family member was common assault (54 percent) followed by uttering threats (22 percent) (Figure 10.13).

The emerging profile of the abused or neglected elderly person is of a female, 70 years or older, who has physical, mental, and/or emotional impairments and is dependent on the abuser-caregiver for both companionship and help with daily living activities.

Studies have found that the neglected elderly are older and have more physical and mental difficulties (and hence are more burdensome to care for) than are elder abuse victims (Pillemer 1986; Whittaker 1995).

There are many parallels between elder abuse and other forms of family violence. In fact, "there is reason to believe that a certain proportion of elder abuse is actually spouse abuse grown old" (Phillips 1986, p. 212). In some cases, marital violence among the elderly involves abuse of a caregiving partner by a spouse who has become ill with Alzheimer's disease (Pillemer 1986). Other causal factors include stress from outside sources, such as financial problems or a caregiver's job conflicts, and social isolation (lack of connectedness with friends and community). As we have seen, these factors are also associated with child abuse. We do not as yet know whether children who neglect or abuse their parents are more likely to have experienced neglectful or violent upbringings (Pillemer 1986, p. 243).

Elder abuse victims, in contrast to the neglected, are relatively healthy and able to meet their daily needs. The common denominators in cases of physical elder abuse are shared living arrangements, the abuser's poor emotional health (often including alcohol or drug problems), and a pathological relationship between victim and abuser (Anetzberger, Korbin, and Austin 1994). Indeed, data from one study of 300 cases of elderly abuse found that abusers

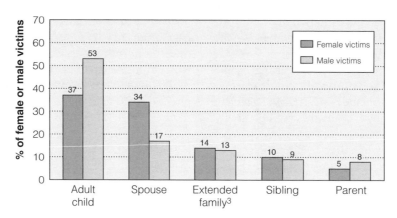

FIGURE 10.12

Older adults most frequently victimized by adult children and spouses, 1999.[1,2] (Source: Statistics Canada, "Family Violence in Canada: A Statistical Profile," Cat. No. 85-224, July 2000, p. 30.)

[1]Data are not nationally representative. Data are based on a sample of 164 police departments, representing 46% of the national volume of crime in 1999.

[2]Includes all violent offences against victims 65 years and older.

[3]Extended family includes grandparents, aunts, uncles, cousins, sister/brother-in-laws, parents-in-law, etc.

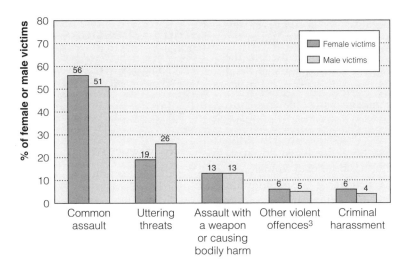

Common assault most frequent offence by family members against older adults, 1999.[1,2] (Source: Statistics Canada, "Family Violence in Canada: A Statistical Profile," Cat. No. 85-224, July 2000, p. 30.)

[1]Data are not nationally representative. Data are based on a sample of 164 police departments, representing 46% of the national volume of crime in 1999.

[2]Includes all violent offences against victims 65 years and older.

[3]Other violent offences includes sexual assault, discharging a firearm with intent, kidnapping, hostage taking, abduction, robbery, extortion, homicide and attempts, criminal negligence, and other offences causing death, unlawfully causing bodily harm, assault against a peace-public officer and other assaults.

(frequently an adult son) were likely to be financially dependent on the elderly victim. As a result, abusive acts may be "carried out by abusers to compensate for their perceived lack or loss of power" (Pillemer 1986, p. 244). "In many instances, both the victim and the perpetrator were caught in a web of interdependency and disability, which made it difficult for them to seek or accept outside help or to consider separation" (Wolf 1986, p. 221; Wolf 1996).

Researching and combating elder abuse generally proceeds from either of two models: the caregiver model and the domestic violence model. The caregiver model views abusive or neglectful caregivers as individuals who are simply overwhelmed with the requirements of caring for their elderly family members. This model tends to focus on differences in mental and physical health and neediness between elderly people who are abused and/or neglected and those who are not. The domestic violence model, in contrast, views elder abuse and neglect as one form of family violence and focuses both on characteristics of abusers and on situations that put potential victims at increased risk (see Finkelhor and Pillemer 1988;

Whittaker 1995). In discussing it here, we have placed elder abuse within the context of family violence. And in addressing family violence in a chapter on power in marriage and families, we have assumed that "all forms of abuse have at their centre the exploitation of a power differential" (Glaser and Frosh 1988, p. 6; Whittaker 1995). We close this chapter with a reminder of everyone's basic right to be respected, and not to be physically, emotionally, or sexually abused—in any relationship.

IN SUM

Power, the ability to exercise one's will, may rest on cultural authority, economic and personal resources that are gender based, love and emotional dependence, interpersonal manipulation, or physical violence.

Although increasing numbers of couples profess to favour egalitarian marriages, most experience a tension between male dominance and egalitarianism. Studies of married couples, cohabiting couples, and gay and lesbian couples illustrate the significance of economic-based power, as well as the possibility for couples to consciously work toward more egalitarian relationships.

Physical violence is most commonly used in the absence of other resources. Although men and women are equally likely to abuse their spouses, the circumstances and outcomes of marital violence indicate that wife abuse is a more crucial social problem. It has received the most programmatic attention. Recently, programs have been developed for male abusers, but less attention has been paid to male victims. Studies indicating that arrest is sometimes a deterrent to further wife abuse illustrate the importance of public policies that meet family needs.

Economic hardships and concerns can lead to physical and/or emotional child abuse—a serious problem in our society and probably far more common than statistics indicate. One difficulty is drawing a clear distinction between "normal" child rearing and abuse.

Elder abuse and neglect is a new area of research, but initial data suggest that abused elderly are often financially independent and abused most frequently by dependent adult children or by elderly spouses. Although some scholars view elder abuse and neglect as primarily a caregiving issue, this chapter presents elder abuse as a form of family violence and as a family power issue.

Key Terms

battered woman syndrome
child abuse
child neglect
coercive power
common couple violence
conjugal power
elder abuse
elder neglect
emotional child abuse or
    neglect
expert power
incest
informational power
legitimate power
marital rape
no-power
objective measure of
    power
patriarchal terrorism

patriarchal violence
power
power politics
principle of least interest
referent power
relative love and need
    theory
resource hypothesis
reward power
sexual abuse
social power
subjective measure of
    fairness
three-phase cycle of
    violence
violence between
    intimates

Study Questions

1. What is Blood and Wolfe's resource hypothesis of conjugal power? Do you agree with this hypothesis? What are your specific agreements and criticisms?

2. How does newer research on conjugal power either confirm or refute the ideas and findings of Blood and Wolfe? Include specific examples of more recent research.

3. What is the principle of least interest? How does it fit into the relative love and need theory? Do you agree with this theory more or less than you agree with the resource hypothesis? Why?

4. How is gender related to power in marriage? How do you think recent social change will affect power in marriage?

5. What does Blumstein and Schwartz's study of four types of couples tell us about power in relationships?

6. How does the relative love and need theory explain wife beating and wives' reactions to the beatings? Do you think that battered women's shelters provide an adequate way out for these women? Why or why not? What about arresting the abuser?

7. How likely do you think it is for a couple to develop a no-power relationship? What are some of the difficulties that you see in trying to develop such a relationship?

8. Should husband abuse receive more attention in the form of social programs? Why or why not?

9. Describe the battered woman syndrome. Do you think it should be used as a defense in homicide cases? In cases of failure to act to protect a child from abuse?

10. Do you think there is a battered husband syndrome? Why or why not?

11. Explain some similarities and differences between same-sex couple violence and heterosexual couple violence.

12. Differentiate between child abuse and child neglect. Do you think that physical abuse is more, or less, or equally damaging to children than emotional abuse?

13. It is not always easy to draw a line between "normal" child rearing and abuse. In your opinion,

at what point can this line be drawn? Where would you draw the line regarding emotional abuse, and why? Be specific; give examples.

14. Discuss some society-wide beliefs and conditions that, when exaggerated, can encourage even well-intentioned parents to mistreat their children.

15. What can we as individuals and as a society do to combat child neglect that is really due to poverty?

16. Explain the therapeutic approach to combating family violence. What about the punitive model and wife beating? Which do you feel is preferable? Why?

17. How is elder abuse and neglect similar to other forms of family violence? How may it be different?

Suggested Readings

Child Abuse and Neglect. A monthly international journal on child maltreatment around the globe.

Duffy, Anne and Julianne Momirov. 1997. *Family Violence: A Canadian Introduction.* Toronto: James Lorimer & Company. A comprehensive, thoughtful, and thought-provoking discussion of the many different theories of family violence.

Journal of Elder Abuse and Neglect. Fairly new journal dedicated to definitions of, and research on, elder maltreatment.

Journal of Family Violence. New York: Plenum Press. Journal, begun in 1985, dedicated to research on family violence.

Renzetti, Claire M., and Charles H. Miley. 1996. *Violence in Gay and Lesbian Domestic Partnerships.* New York: Haworth Press. Theory, research, and practical advice on gay and lesbian battering.

Torr, James D., and Karin Swisher. 1999. *Violence Against Women: Current Controversies.* San Diego, CA: Greenhaven Press. This book presents both sides of various controversies in relation to domestic violence.

On the Net

1) The Costs of Violence: Another Piece of the Puzzle
   http:www.ccsd.ca/vv_puzz.html

2) Elder Abuse
   www.langara.bc.ca/vnc/elder.htm

3) Husband Abuse
   http://www.vix.com/pub/men

4) Life on Brian's Beat: Gay-on-gay Violence
   www.web.apc.org/~jharnick/violence.html

5) Canadian Society for the Prevention of Cruelty to Children
   www.empathicparenting.org

6) National Clearinghouse on Family Violence
   www.hc-sc.gc.ca/hppb/familyviolence/

To Parent or Not to Parent

AND NOW I WANT A CHILD. AND I WANT THAT CHILD TO CARRY ME IN HIS HEAD FOREVER, AND TO LOVE ME FOREVER....

IS THAT A SENTENCE OF LIFE IMPRISONMENT? A LIFETIME OF LOVE? THE WAY THE WORLD IS STRUCTURED?

JOYCE CAROL OATES, DO WITH ME WHAT YOU WILL

There may be someone in your class who's thinking about adopting a child. There may be someone in your class who is thinking about infertility treatment. Or who is thinking about having an abortion. Or about whether to have children ever. Or about having and raising an only child. All these decisions focus on some aspect of whether (or how) to become a parent. They seem like very personal choices, but in this chapter we'll see that they are influenced by the society around us.

A remarkable change has taken place in Canadian childbearing patterns over the past four decades. The total fertility rate[1]—the number of births the typical woman will have over her lifetime—dropped sharply from a high of almost four children per woman in the late 1950s to a previously unprecedented low of 1.58 in 1987. After rising slightly to 1.71 in 1992, it declined again to 1.60 in 1996 and 1.55 in 1997

---

1. Explanation is in order here about birth and fertility rates. The *birthrate*, or **crude birthrate**, as it is technically termed, is the numbers of births per thousand population. The total number of births and the birthrate depend not only on how many births each woman has but also on how many women of childbearing age there are in the population. For example, as the large baby boom cohort (babies born during the post-World War II era, 1946–1959) reached childbearing age, the crude birthrate rose. Now many baby boomers have passed the peak fertility ages, and the crude birthrate has been declining since (Ventura et al. 1995).

A more specific measure is the *general fertility rate*, which is the number of births per thousand women in their childbearing years (generally taken as ages 15–49 in Canada). However, even this statistic does not tell us much about family size.

(Canadian Global Almanac 2000; Vanier Institute of the Family 2000) (Figure 11.1).

Over this time period, cultural attitudes about ideal family size changed, and "[m]any of the baby-boomers who grew up with three or four brothers or sisters chose to have only one or two children" (Vanier Institute of the Family 2000, p. 56). Compared to those born half a century ago, Canadian children today are more likely to be only children. In 1995, 43 percent of the 365 000 babies born in Canada in 1995 were first-born children, 35 percent were second-born children and 22 percent were third-or-more born children. In stark contrast, in 1951, 28 percent were first-born children, 25 percent second-born and 46 percent third-or-more children (Vanier Institute of the Family, p. 59). Put another way, while in 1951, about three-quarters of all Canadian children had older brothers and sisters, "more than two of every five children born near the millennium will be the oldest or only child in the family" (Vanier Institute of the Family 2000, p. 58). Our current fertility rate is significantly below the replacement rate of 2.1 children that is theoretically necessary to ensure the renewal of generations. Moreover, attitudes about whether to have children at all have changed in recent years, so that choosing not to be a parent is more acceptable today.

At the same time that overall fertility[2] levels have dropped, childbearing has increasingly shifted to later ages. Changes in fertility are related to the fact that women are waiting longer to have their first babies, are allowing more time between births, and are choosing to have smaller families. On the edge of the new millenium women were having their first child about three years later, on average, and having fewer children than their counterparts 25 years ago. While in the 1960s and 1970s, first-time Canadian mothers were likely to be 23 or 24 years old, in the 1990s, first-time mothers were, on average, over the age of 26. In addition, increasing numbers of Canadian women are opting to delay childbearing until after their 30th birthday.

> Almost half of the babies born in 1996 were to women 30 years of age or older. In this unprecedented trend over the last quarter of a century, the number of births to women aged 30 to 34 increased by 115 percent. Correspondingly, the number of births to women under the age of 25 declined by 41 percent, and by 42 percent for women under 20 years of age (Vanier Institute of the Family 2000, p. 58).

In 1996, almost one-third (31 percent) of births to women over the age of 30 were first-births. In contrast, in 1951, only 12 percent of births to women over thirty were first-births.

Throughout this chapter we'll be looking at the choices individuals and couples have about whether or not to have children and how many. Among other things we'll see that modern scientific and technological advances have both increased people's options and added new wrinkles to their decision making. We'll see, too, that technological progress does not mean that people can or do exercise complete control over their fertility. To begin, we'll review some fertility trends in Canada. Then we'll examine the decision whether to parent.

FERTILITY TRENDS IN CANADA

Declining Canadian fertility appears to be a sudden change when we compare current birthrates to those of the past. Yolande Lavoie and Jillian Oderkirk (2000, p. 3) observe that "[i]f every 1000 women born in the early 18th century had survived to the end of their reproductive life, they would have given birth to 8200 children, according to the reproductive behaviour prevalent at that time." However, while fertility was high, so too was infant mortality. Moreover, the life expectancy of Canada's

---

The **total fertility rate** for a given year—the rate we will refer to most often in this text—is the number of births that women would have over their reproductive lifetimes if all women at each age had babies at the rate for each age group that year. In reality, this is an artificial figure: the family size that the average woman would have at average childbearing rates provided those rates continued.

A final measure is *completed fertility*—that is, the number of babies per woman of a given cohort (women born in a given year, such as 1946). However, to actually ascertain completed family size, we need to wait until the cohort is age 45 or 50 to know what these women's completed fertility is. So although completed fertility rates might be more accurate, they are long in coming, and the figures most often used to grasp family size is the total fertility rate.

2. The term **fertility** is used by demographers to refer to actual births. Even though everyday language uses fertility to mean ability to reproduce, the technical term for reproductive capacity is **fecundity**. Confusingly, *infertility* and *infecundity* are both used to denote inability to reproduce. *Subfecundity* designates reduced reproductive ability, as for those, for example, who have demonstrated their fecundity (by having children) but who have difficulty bearing more children when they wish to.

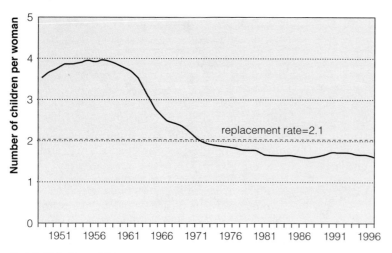

FIGURE **11.1**

Total fertility rate (1951–1996). (Source: based on data from the Statistics Canada publications "Canadian families at the appoach of the year 2000", Catalogue 96-321, March 1999 Marriage and conjugal life in Canada", Catalogue 91-534, 1992, and "The Daily", Catalogue 11-001, October 28, 1999 and January 29, 1998.)

pioneers was short, averaging between 30 to 35 years. In consequence, "every 1000 women born in 1700 bore only 4300 children instead of 8200" (Lavoie and Oderkirk 2000, p. 3).

Nevertheless, prior to the 19th century, fertility levels in Canada were as high or higher than current levels in many of the world's less-developed countries and Canadian women in the 18th and early 19th century could also expect to devote the majority of their adult lives to child-bearing and childrearing. During this period in our history, Canadian women married early (on average, at age 22), conceived their first child a few years after doing so, and, if they lived to age 50, bore approximately 10 children. By the time of their last pregnancies, at around age 40, "these women had exhausted, on average, 70 percent of their expected years of life. For many, responsibilities associated with raising young children continued until their lives ended" (Lavoie and Oderkirk 2000, p. 4).

As Canada underwent the process of transformation from an agrarian to an industrialized society, birthrates declined steadily from their early levels of approximately 50 births per 1000 population. Sociologists Wayne McVey and Warren Kalbach (1995, p. 268) report that while official figures were not collected on an annual basis in Canada until 1921, estimates based on studies of early Canadian census data indicate a "fairly rapid and consistent

decline [in average annual crude birth rates] up to the 1891–1901 decade just prior to the great immigrations of the early 20th century." The estimated average annual number of births per 1000 population in Canada decreased from 45 in 1851–1861 to 30 in 1891–1901 and later, to 29 in 1911–1921.

During the time of the worldwide Depression of the 1930s, "few countries were affected as severely as Canada" (Struthers 1999, p. 1012) and in 1937, Canada's crude fertility rate plunged to a low of 20.1 births per 1000 population (Kalbach 1999, p. 1868). However, improved economic conditions in Canada later reversed the declining trend in fertility rates.

The precise years that mark the baby boom are subject to some dispute. While some authors identify the baby boom period as 1946 to 1959 (McVey and Kalbach 1995, p. 272), others apply this term to the period "from the early 1950s to about 1965" (Krotki 1999, p. 175) or 1951 to 1966 (Kettle 1980, p. 18) or 1947 to 1966 (Foot 1996). Regardless of its precise parameters, there is no doubt that Canada (like the United States, Australia and New Zealand) experienced a significant upsurge in births. In Canada, the birthrate rose to 24.3 per 1000 population in 1945, to 27.2 in 1946 and remained between 27 and 28.5 until 1959 when it gradually began to decline.

A number of factors led to Canada's baby boom. Adie Nelson and Barrie Robinson point out that, "[u]nlike many European countries that had to devote their immediate postwar efforts to physically rebuilding cities and countrysides ravaged by invasion, Canada was able to forge ahead immediately with a peacetime economy buoyed by an optimism....born of victory" (Nelson and Robinson 1999, p. 89). Parents who had grown up during the Great Depression, when family goals were limited by economic factors, found themselves as adults in an affluent economy—one that promised support for their own children. Thus, they were able to fulfill childhood dreams of happy and abundant family life to compensate for deprivations previously suffered as children (Easterlin 1987).

Nelson and Robinson also note that, during this period, the messages emanating from government, manufacturers, and advertisers—assisted by the growing power of the mass media, particularly television, all promoted the Procreation Ethic. This belief system maintained that: marriage was vastly preferable to remaining single; all married couples should become parents; and that having many children was preferable to having an "only" child (Jones 1980, p. 1). For women, marriage and motherhood became exalted as primary cultural goals.

Sociologist Karol Krotki (1999, p. 175) identifies a number of additional factors that were responsible for the baby boom:

> The baby boom began with the births of children who had been postponed during the Depression, but two other factors affected it as well. First, a larger proportion of adults married, and those who did had more children. Taking married and single women together, those born in 1911 and 1912 had an average of 2.9 children, whereas those born between 1929 and 1933 had an average of 3.3....
>
> Second, more than 50 percent of baby-boom births can be attributed to what demographers call "timing phenomena." More young adults married at a younger age (the median age for a woman's first marriage was 23.2 years in 1940 and 21.1 years in 1965), and between the end of the war and 1965, younger couples tended to have their children during the first years of married life.

However, while Canadian woman had, on average, between 3.4 and 3.9 children between 1946 and 1961 (Nelson and Robinson 1999, p. 91), this declined to 2.8 in 1966, 1.8 in 1976 (McVey and Kalbach 1995, p. 270) and, as we have seen, 1.6 more recently. Fertility rates in Canada have declined as a result of: (1) fewer children born to women of child-bearing age following the baby boom (the "baby bust" years), (2) the decline in the size of families; (3) the increase in the average age of women giving birth for the first time; and (4) the increasing popularity of sterilization as a method of contraception (*Canadian Global Almanac 2000*).

The long-term decline in fertility we witness in Canada today also reflects the fact that alternatives to the motherhood role began to open up with the Industrial Revolution and the resulting creation of a "labour force" (see Chapter 13). Women could combine productive work and motherhood in a preindustrial economy, but when that work moved from home to factory, the roles of worker and mother were not so compatible. Consequently, as women's employment increased, fertility declined. Since the 1960s women in general and, married women with children in particular, have entered the labour force in growing proportions, partly in response to an expanding postindustrial economy.

Another cause has been declining infant mortality, as the result of improved health and living conditions. Gradually, it became unnecessary to bear many children to ensure the survival of a few. Changes in values accompanying these transformations in our society (and in other industrialized societies) made large numbers of children more costly economically and less satisfying to parents (Easterlin and Crimmins 1985).

Family Size

Canadian families at the end of the 1990s were much smaller than they were a century before. In 1997, there was an average of only 3.0 persons per family, down from 3.7 in 1971. As you will note from Figure 11.2, the average family size in Canada remained fairly constant in the 1990s, with much of the decline in recent decades occurring between 1971 and 1986.

Although families in Prince Edward Island were slightly above the national average in 1997 and those in Quebec, Nova Scotia, New Brunswick and British Columbia were slightly below the national average, there was little provincial variation in family size in

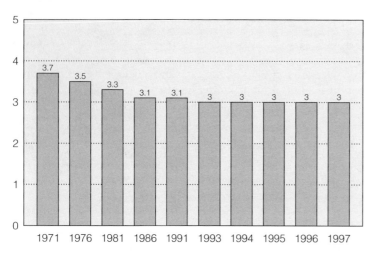

FIGURE   **11.2**

Average number of persons per family, 1971–1997. (Source: Statistics Canada, Catalogue No. 91-213-XPB; and Demography Division.)

Canada. In that year, however, there was some variation in the average size of Canadian families depending on family type. For example, in husband–wife families, there was an average of 3.1 persons compared with 2.5 persons in lone-parent families. Among husband-wife families in that year, married couple families were larger, on average, than common-law families, with 3.2 people per family and 2.8 people per family respectively.

Differential Fertility Rates

Fertility rates and decisions about whether to parent have social, cultural, and economic origins. In general, more highly educated and well-off families have fewer children. Although they have more money, their children are also more costly; these parents expect to send their children to university and to provide them with expensive possessions and experiences. Moreover, people with high education or income have other options besides parenting. For example, they may be involved in demanding careers or enjoy travel, activities they weigh against the greater investment required in parenthood.

There are also rural–urban differentials. Fertility rates of populations living in urban populations have traditionally been higher than among rural-nonfarm and farm populations (McVey and Kalbach 1995, p. 278;

Struthers and Bokemeier 2000). In addition, fertility rates in Canada in the past have differed by the place of birth of the mother, the period of immigration, and the woman's age at the time of immigration. "For younger women, the more recent their immigration to Canada, the lower their cumulative fertility tended to be, while for older women the reverse was true, i.e., the more recent their immigration, the higher their cumulative fertility" (McVey and Kalbach 1995, p. 284). Intermarriage may also influence fertility patterns. For example, in their comparison of the fertility patterns of three husband–wife combinations: husband and wife Aboriginal (HWA), husband Aboriginal and wife non-Aboriginal and wife Aboriginal and husband non-Aboriginal, Travato and Suwal (1998) report that fertility was higher among HWA while non-Aboriginal women had the lowest fertility.

Religion has been another factor influencing fertility in Canada. Consider that for most of the century after Confederation, Quebec was home to about one-third of our nation's population—a fact that some attribute to the teachings of Roman Catholicism and the religious homogeneity of that province (Kalbach and McVey 1995, p. 294). However, as a result of social and economic changes in that province, total births in Quebec have decreased by 25 percent since 1990 and, in 1999, the birth rate in Quebec was at its lowest since 1908, with the drop in the birth rate particularly abrupt among women 20 to 29 (Peritz 1999). Moreover, as Wayne McVey and Warren Kalbach observe, "Fertility differences between Canada's major religious denominations appear to be greatest among the oldest age groups for women, but have significantly lessened with the increasingly younger age groups" (1995, p. 285). They note that even such groups as rural Hutterites and Mennonites, who traditionally have evidenced high fertility, "have not been totally unaffected by the conditions that have led to the long-term decline in fertility, and the post-World War II baby-boom-and-bust cycle" (p. 285).

THE DECISION TO PARENT OR NOT TO PARENT

The variations in birthrates just described reflect values and attitudes about having children. But in traditional society couples didn't decide to have children. Children just came, and preferring not to have any at all was unthinkable. Earlier in the twentieth century, family planning efforts still focused on the timing of children and family size rather than on whether to have them. Now choices include "if" (that is, whether to have children) as well as "when" and "how many."

Not all choices can be realized, whether they reflect a desire to have children or to avoid having children. The extent to which people today consciously choose (or reject) parenthood or experience it as something that simply happens to them is uncertain. Certainly educated and affluent people have more control over their lives generally, so they may be more apt to approach parenthood as a conscious choice. Among others—teenagers, for example—parenthood is usually less thought-out (Henshaw 1998; Kowaleski-Jones and Mott 1998). Some people may be philosophically disinclined to plan their lives generally (Luker 1984). Nevertheless, more so than in the past, our society presents the possibility of choice and decision-making about parenthood. The decision to parent or not to parent (or when to parent) is one in which many couples and individuals invest a great deal of thought and emotion.

Although social change and technology provide more choices, they also present dilemmas. It is not always easy to choose whether to have children, how many to have, and when to have them. In the following pages we'll look more closely at some of the factors involved in an individual's or couple's decision-making about whether to have children: first, the social pressures; then, the personal pros and cons.

Social Pressures

We saw in Chapter 6 that single people in our society often feel strong pressures to conform by marrying. The same kinds of pressures exist for married people who don't want to have children.

Although these pressures are less than in the past, our society still has a **pronatalist bias**: Having children is taken for granted, whereas not having children must be justified (Kling 1996; May 1997). Some of the strongest pressures can come from the couple's parents, who often have difficulty accepting and respecting their children's choices about whether to have children, let alone when and how many. Hopeful prospective grandparents are not always subtle: One gave his wife a grandmother photo album for Christmas, even though his childless daughter and her husband were not aware of any grandchildren on the way!

Although socialization still inclines people toward parenthood, the expectation for married couples to have children is becoming less pronounced. For example, the term *child-free* is often used now instead of the more negative-sounding term *childless*[3]. Some observers, in fact, argue that our society has become antinatalist—that is, against having children or, at least, is not doing all it can to support parents and their children.

IS CANADIAN SOCIETY ANTINATALIST? Some observers have suggested that the social pressures not to have children are becoming too strong, especially for some young, highly educated women. In the late 1970s Betty Friedan expressed concern that the element of choice was being taken away and saw little hope for improvement if some women "have to give up motherhood to keep on in jobs or professions as my generation gave up jobs or professions to make a career of motherhood" (Friedan 1978, pp. 196, 208).

In the years since Friedan voiced these worries, other observers have raised similar—and broader—concerns. They warn that society is characterized by

---

3. Each term conveys an inherent bias. For that reason and because there are no easy-to-use substitute terms, we make equal use of both *childless* and *child-free* in this text.

structural antinatalism (Thomas 1998) inasmuch as "our values, laws, employment policies and culture are inimical to children and disastrous for committed parents" (Leach 1994; Hewlett and West 1998). Sociologists Janet Hunt and Larry Hunt argue that the primary goals of corporate institutions are "power and profit ... over family well-being" (1986, p. 281). Should these values not change, the Hunts predict

> not only a sense of exclusion on the part of those with families, but a widening gap in the standard of living between parents and non-parents.... Those with children will tend to have lower incomes, in addition to absorbing the expenses of children, and will fall further and further behind their child-free counterparts. (Hunt and Hunt 1986, p. 283)

Observers point out that as a nation we have given tax breaks to the wealthy while cutting health, nutrition, social service, financial aid, and education programs directly affecting the welfare of our children (Children's Defense Fund 1998; Hewlett and West 1998). Partly as a result of such cuts—and of the absence of national support for a family wage—"[i]n 1997, 1.4 million Canadian children were living in poverty" (Figure 11.3) (Vanier Institute of the Family 2000).

Although Canada is a signatory to the United Nations Convention on Children's Rights, a treaty that has been described as "the most comprehensive human rights document ever adopted by the international community," and ratified by all but two countries in the world, evidence suggests that we still have some way to go before we achieve a truly "child-friendly" society. This was evident when, in 1999, the Canadian Coalition for the Rights of Children issued its first five-year nongovernmental progress report to the United Nations. Entitled *The UN Convention on the Rights of the Child: How Does Canada Measure Up?*, the report concluded that while Canada met most of its obligations under the UN Convention on the Rights of Children, it had failed to achieve full compliance with the Convention. Among their findings:

- Statistics and information on federal programs and policies for children are unclear and unreliable. For example, there are no national statistics on child abuse and neglect in Canada and there is insuffi-

cient information about how to prevent child maltreatment. This lack of information constrains the development of effective services.

- Canadian legislation rarely recognizes children specifically and there are few redress mechanisms available to them. As such, children's fundamental freedoms are very dependent on the goodwill of adults. Rights education is not part of our schools' core curricula and children's convention rights have not been widely promoted in Canada. In child welfare cases, the child's best interests are weighted against parental rights. In other areas, children's "best interests" are ignored or interpreted without considering the views of children at all. The general principle of maximum survival and development is not assured for our most vulnerable children, such as children with disabilities, Aboriginal children, and children in care of the state.

- Where a child lives often determines the degree to which his or her rights are met. There can be significant differences in the programs and services children receive in different parts of the country. Home care services for families of children with disabilities vary widely and there is no effort to create standards or even to define basic services. Child welfare services are often fragmented and uncoordinated within jurisdictions, with resources unevenly allocated across regions. For Aboriginal children living on reserves, the delivery of services is further complicated by jurisdictional disputes.

- Resources for children's programs and services are often stretched or unstable. Cutbacks to education funding and the closing of schools have undermined access to and the quality of education, especially in special education, citizenship, social studies, and arts education. Child services have taken a back seat to budget cuts in some provinces, despite growing caseloads, chronic waiting lists, and worker burnout. Even with the high number of Aboriginal children affected by disabilities, the delivery of services in Aboriginal communities is generally poor or nonexistent.

- Aboriginal children have a disability rate that is more than twice the national average. Aboriginal children are at greater risk of school failure than other Canadian children. A disproportionate number of Aboriginal children are victims of abuse and neglect compared to non-Aboriginal children. The suicide rate among Aboriginal youth is about five times the national average.

- An estimated 535 000 children and youth under age 20 have some form of disability. Children with disabilities have varying opportunities to live "full and decent lives" and the supports and services they need are not considered an entitlement but a privilege. Many families of children with disabilities do not receive adequate assistance. Early identification and intervention services are not universally available and the right to appropriate education in the most enabling environment is not guaranteed.

- Abused and neglected children continue to fall through the cracks in our child welfare systems. Inquests and inquiries into the deaths of children who were killed by their parents speak of inadequate risk assessments, insufficient training for social workers, a lack of service coordination and information sharing, a shortage of placement facilities, failed foster placements, a crisis orientation, and a lack of long-term planning for children who are in the care of the state.

- The refugee determination system is slow and the long wait unduly prolongs uncertainty in the lives of children and their families. Family reunification is rarely dealt with in a positive and expeditious manner. The interests of children are not taken into account in decisions to deport their parents. Children, even if born in Canada, do not have to be considered in the deportation hearings of their parents.

- Federal and provincial legislation prohibits discrimination against people because of disability but people with disabilities, and children in particular, still experience prejudice. Young people with disabilities experience more abuse and violence than those without disabilities. In addition, many disability issues are examined from the adult perspective and the special needs of children are overlooked. For example, provincial building codes include accessibility standards but they were not designed with children in mind.

- The few complaint mechanisms that are available to children and youth tend to be difficult to access.

Antinatalism may have other, potentially detrimental consequences as well. Psychoanalyst Erik

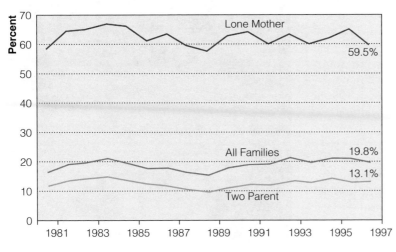

FIGURE **11.3**

Child poverty rates by family type, Canada (1997). (Source: based on data from the Statistics Canada publications "Canadian families at the appoach of the year 2000", Catalogue 96-321, March 1999 Marriage and conjugal life in Canada", Catalogue 91-534, 1992, and "The Daily", Catalogue 11-001, October 28, 1999 and January 29, 1998.)

Erikson, who has focused on adult development in his work, expresses concern that as the birthrate continues to fall (in response to perceived antinatalism or for other reasons) some couples will become self-absorbed and will neglect other outlets that exist to help them take some responsibility for the generations to come. To avoid what he calls stagnation, Erikson advises people who choose not to have children to channel their procreativity "in active pursuits which universally improve the condition of every child chosen to be born" (Erikson 1979).

There are social pressures in our society to have children and not to have children. "I hear two conflicting points of view," explained one child-free woman. "One is that it is terrific to be a mother and the other—you'll regret it; your life will change!" (Boston Woman's Health Book Collective 1998, p. 265). Together, these messages create ambivalence and can act as a source of guilt or self-doubt (Groat et al. 1997). The decisions people make should reflect not only external social pressures but also their own needs, values, and attitudes about becoming parents. In the next three sections we will look at some of the advantages and disadvantages associated with parenthood.

Children's Value to Parents

Traditionally, children were viewed as economic assets; in a farm economy, more hands added to the work that could be produced in the fields and kitchens. We have seen that this pattern of children helping to support their family persists to some extent, especially among immigrant, ethnic minority and farm families (Collins 1999; Keating 1996). Generally, however, the shift from agricultural to industrial society and the development of compulsory education has transformed children from economic assets to economic liabilities. But as their economic value declined, children's emotional significance to parents increased (Zelizer 1985), probably because declining infant mortality rates made it safe to become attached to children, to invest in them emotionally (Rundblad 1990). Parents' quest was for "a child to love" (Zelizer 1985, p. 190).

In a study of 100 working-class and middle-class biological and adoptive parent couples, Mary Ann Lamanna found parents reporting a variety of emo-

tional satisfactions from having children. Many stated that children gave their lives meaning and purpose, a sense of destiny. Children provide a sense of continuity of self—as one parent put it, "the advantage of seeing something of yourself passed on to your children" (although this can be a mixed blessing: "Sometimes you see some bad things in yourself that have been passed on to your children").

Others reported that their satisfaction is in belonging to a close family unit, which they associate with having children, not just with being married. One parent commented: "It gives us one more thing to talk about all the time together.... Since the daughter, we all do things together more than we used to—the zoo, picnics, and things like that."

Many parents in the study enjoyed the satisfaction of nurturing the emotional and physical growth of their children. The challenges involved in child rearing can help fill needs for creativity, achievement, and competence: "It's interesting to see our children reacting to us and our ideas and their response to the way we treat them; it's a challenge" (parent interview,

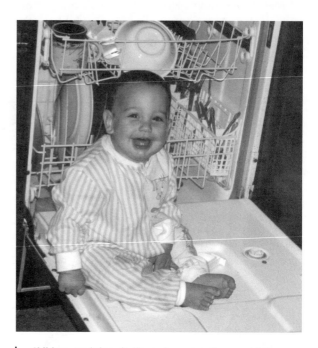

Children can bring vitality and a sense of purpose into a household. Having a child also broadens a parent's role in the world; mothers and fathers become nurturers, advocates, authority figures, counsellors, caregivers, and playmates.

Lamanna 1977). Others spoke of the joy of loving and being loved by their children.

In her study of men's feelings about family and work, sociologist Kathleen Gerson (1993) found that some men value close relationships with their children because they missed having a close emotional bond with their own fathers. Others seemed to find that children offered them an emotional base that work or romantic relationships could not promise (p. 177).

Children provide several other satisfactions: They may represent (though to an ever-lessening degree) a potential means of support and security for parents once parents are no longer able to provide for themselves. This was and is still extremely important in less-modern societies in which government programs of old-age support do not exist. (However, the parents in Gerson's study thought this was *not* a good reason for having children.) Also, even more than completing school, taking a first job, or getting married, having children is tangible evidence that one has reached adulthood.

Parents may perceive rewards in having children that they may not get in jobs they do not find meaningful. Children give parents a chance to influence the course of others' lives and to feel looked up to; they can be symbols of accomplishment, prestige, or wealth; and they attest to the parents' sexuality. Family life also offers an opportunity to exercise a kind of authority and influence that one may not have at a job.

Children can add considerable liveliness to a household, and they have fresh and novel responses to the joys and vexations of life. Focusing on her enjoyment of her grandchildren, one grandmother, whose two grandchildren and daughter have lived with her for about five years, said, "They're fun kids.... I'm less apt to sit down and watch TV; I'm more apt to be sitting down playing Legos" (Jendrick 1993, p. 616). Children provide a sense that something new and different is happening, which may help to relieve the tedium of everyday life. Playing with them can give parents the feeling of reliving their own childhoods. In sum, children "are capable of bringing profound meaning and purpose into people's lives" (Groat et al. 1997, p. 571).

Costs of Having Children

Although the values of having children can be immeasurable, the experience can also be costly. On a purely financial basis, children decrease a couple's level of living considerably.

One estimate of the cost of raising a child to age 18 prepared by Manitoba Agriculture reports that parents could expect to spend about $154 000 (based on 1998 prices for basic goods and services) (Vanier Institute of the Family 2000, p. 136). While the estimated cost of raising a boy ($154 267) was slightly higher than the cost of raising a girl ($153 458), it is evident that the expenses associated with childrearing may create hardship, especially among lone-parent families with children (Figure 11.4). In addition, it should be emphasized that these costs do *not* include the expense associated with financing the costs of a child's higher education—costs that may also be considerable. Consider here that while tuition fees in Canada have grown by 115 percent since 1980, average family income has risen by only one percent (after adjusting for inflation) (Clark 1998). The rising cost of tuition and the associated costs of attending a postsecondary institution will certainly make doing so prohibitive for some families and difficult for many.[4]

Added to the direct costs of parenting are **opportunity costs**: the economic opportunities for wage earning and investments that parents forgo when rearing children. These costs are felt most by mothers. A woman's career advancement may suffer as a consequence of becoming a mother in a society that does not provide adequate day care. A couple in which one partner quits work to stay home with a child or children faces loss of up to half or more of their family income (Longman 1998). The spouse who quits work also faces lost pension and other benefits later (Nelson and Robinson 2002; Townsend 1995). Conversely, the loss of free time is one important cost of trying to lead two lives, as a family person and as a career person (Hochschild 1989; Groat et al. 1997).

Parents in Lamanna's study identified some other costs of having children: They add tension to the household and restrict parents' activities outside the home. Children require a more efficiently organized

---

4. According to Human Resources Development Canada, the typical living costs for an eight-month college or university program was between $10 000 and $13 000 for students living away from home and between $3000 and $6400 for those living in their parents' homes. Based on these figures, the cost of a four-year program for someone living at home would be $25 000 and for someone living away from home, in excess of $50 000 (Clark 1998).

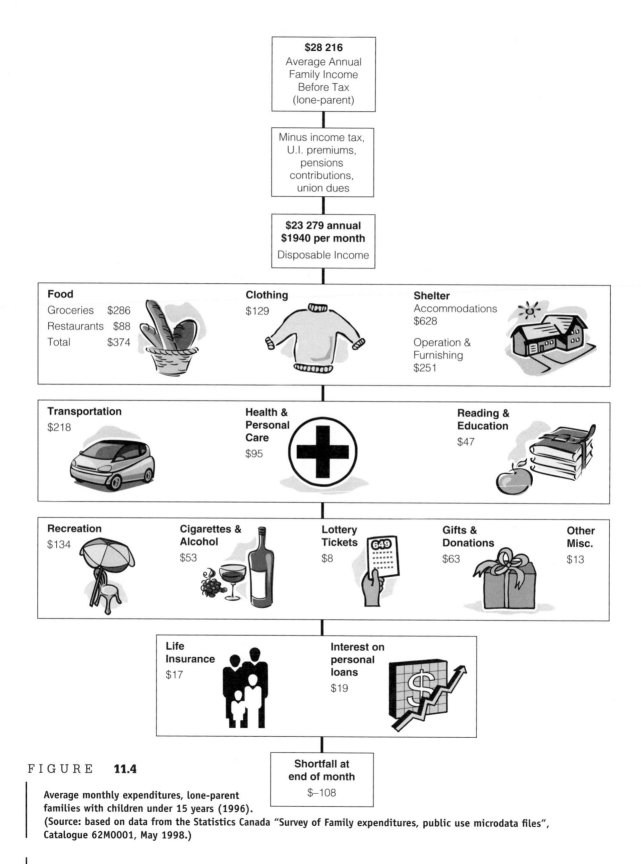

$28 216
Average Annual
Family Income
Before Tax
(lone-parent)

Minus income tax,
U.I. premiums,
pensions
contributions,
union dues

$23 279 annual
$1940 per month
Disposable Income

Food
Groceries $286
Restaurants $88
Total $374

Clothing
$129

Shelter
Accommodations
$628

Operation &
Furnishing
$251

Transportation
$218

**Health &
Personal
Care**
$95

**Reading &
Education**
$47

Recreation
$134

**Cigarettes &
Alcohol**
$53

**Lottery
Tickets**
$8

**Gifts &
Donations**
$63

**Other
Misc.**
$13

**Life
Insurance**
$17

**Interest on
personal
loans**
$19

**Shortfall at
end of month**
$–108

FIGURE   **11.4**

**Average monthly expenditures, lone-parent
families with children under 15 years (1996).**
**(Source: based on data from the Statistics Canada "Survey of Family expenditures, public use microdata files",
Catalogue 62M0001, May 1998.)**

residence and a daily routine that can limit the parents' spontaneity. Children also make for substantial additional work—not only physical care but also the work of parenting: teaching cultural norms, guiding the child's social and emotional growth, and dealing with anxiety about such pitfalls to healthy development as school difficulties and drug use. Adding to these emotional costs is the parent's recognition that once assumed, the parent status is one that a person cannot easily escape.

As a result of all this, having children today is "paradoxical in character—it is potentially oppressive, in terms of limiting other life options," and at the same time the potential source of great joy (Groat et al. 1997, p. 571). As one returning student and mother wrote in an essay on this subject, "When I was in my teens, I did not want to marry or have children. I wanted a fast car and a fast-paced job with no ties, but [now, as a parent] I believe I got a far better deal" (Jones 1998). Still, children are typically a challenge to their parents' couple relationship.

How Children Affect Marital Happiness

A common cost of having children is marital strain. Evidence shows that children—especially in the first year after their birth, or when there are many, or they are of preschool age—stabilize marriage (White 1990, pp. 906–7); that is, such couples are less likely to divorce.[5]

But a stable marriage is not necessarily the same as a happy one. Many, but certainly not all, couples report that the happiest time in marriage was before the arrival of the first child and after the departure of the last. Spouses' reported marital satisfaction tends to decline over time whether they have children or not. But serious conflicts over work, identity, and domestic responsibilities can erupt with the arrival of children (Glenn 1990; Bird 1997).

When they have children, spouses may find that they begin responding to each other more in terms of

more traditional role obligations. Now more than before—and particularly among couples who have children earlier in their marriages (Coltrane 1990)— the husband is responsible for breadwinning and the wife for house and child care. Spouses who as parents are not only busier but also sexually segregated begin to do fewer things together and to share decision making less (Bird 1997). Dissatisfaction with one's marriage after the arrival of the first child seems more pronounced and longer lasting for wives than for husbands (Glenn 1990, p. 825). Meanwhile, one longitudinal study shows that the drop in marital satisfaction is less for couples who were happy before the birth and actively planned for the infant (Cowan and Cowan 1992). And new friendship networks, such as with other parents, may provide some of the social support previously given by one's spouse (Roxburgh 1997).

Studies comparing marriages with and without children consistently report marital happiness to be higher in child-free unions (Glenn and McLanahan 1982; Houseknect 1987; Somers 1993). Even though the addition of a child necessarily influences a household, the arrival of a child is less disruptive when the parents get along well and have a strong commitment to parenting. (Chapter 12 looks more closely at the relationships between parents and their children.) Of course, choices about parenthood involve several options, as we will see in the next section.

THREE EMERGING OPTIONS

We have been discussing several factors that influence the decision to have or not to have children. In this section we will look at three emerging options: choosing to remain childless, postponing parenthood, and having a one-child family.

Remaining Child-Free

Despite some people's beliefs, individuals who choose to remain childless are usually neither frustrated nor unhappy. Voluntarily childless couples typically have vital relationships. Often they believe that adding a third member to their family would change the character of their intense personal relationship (See Box 11.1: "Childless...By Choice").

Child-free women tend to be attached to a satisfying career. Childless couples value their relative

---

5. At least one analysis, in fact, concludes that most of the difference in marital happiness between parents and nonparents is not due to a decline in marital happiness after children are born but to the fact that unhappy parents tend to stay married, whereas unhappy nonparents more often divorce. Therefore, when parents and nonparents are compared in cross-sample studies, still-married nonparents appear happier as a group (White and Booth 1985a).

freedom to change jobs or careers, move around the country, and pursue any endeavour they might find interesting (Dalphonse 1997). A study comparing 74 voluntarily child-free women and men with 127 fathers and mothers found that the child-free couples felt negatively stereotyped by society but meanwhile were more satisfied than the parents were with their relationship as a couple (Somers 1993). One study of childless, older women has found that they have developed a strong network of friends over the years and are not necessarily isolated or regretful (Rubinstein et al. 1991). Indeed, in recent years, various organizations for childless couples have emerged. One such organization, originally started by a Canadian, is "No Kidding!," an "all-volunteer, non-profit social club for couples and singles who, for whatever reason, have never had children" with 68 chapters in Canada (at present, limited to Quebec, Ontario, Alberta and British Columbia), the United States, Seoul, South Korea, and the Ivory Coast (www.nokidding.net).

REMAINING CHILDLESS: DIFFERENCES IN COMMITMENT

There have been very few recent studies on the child-free choice. Research that does exist shows that not all couples are equally committed to remaining child-free. In one study (done more than 20 years ago) of 30 voluntarily childless couples, it was apparent that the degree of resolve varied among the respondents (Nason and Poloma 1976). Some—those who had been sterilized—were irrevocably committed. Others were "strongly committed." They used effective contraception, discussed sterilization, and agreed that if contraception failed, the wife would have an abortion. As a couple they showed no signs of ambivalence about not having children, but they did not entirely rule out the possibility of parenting if their current relationship ended.

The "reasonably committed" couples expressed some minor doubts about the permanence of their decision, but they used contraceptives regularly and effectively and said the wife would probably have an abortion if contraception failed. Some couples were "committed with reservations." They used contraceptives effectively but expressed some doubt about their decision and stated flatly that they would not consider an abortion in the event of unwanted pregnancy.

It is easier to feel strongly committed to remaining childless when in one's 20s or even early 30s. Because people may change their minds, sterilization may not be wise before about age 35.

WOMEN'S AND MEN'S REASONS   From the few studies over the past two decades of couples who decided not to have children, we can draw the following tentative conclusions:

1. It is often the woman who first takes the child-free position (Seccombe 1991). Typically, she is an achievement-oriented only child or a firstborn child who had to help raise her younger brothers or sisters.

2. Men who want to remain childless tend to be more confident about their decision than women, who express more ambivalence. Men in egalitarian marriages may prefer having fewer or no children over sharing the work of raising them (Gerson 1993).

3. When a couple disagrees about having children, substantial conflict may occur before this issue is resolved. It is, of course, possible that it cannot be resolved. A difference in the desire for children is such a serious matter that it ought to be talked out before marriage.

Sometimes partners use prolonged postponement to avoid confronting the issue of permanent childlessness, although they eventually realize that they will not have children. The main disadvantage of not having children earlier in marriage is that, for some couples who want children, a time may arrive when they cannot conceive a child (Hasty and Massey 1997). Fertility tends to diminish with age (Boston Women's Health Book Collective 1998, p. 264)—after about the mid-20s and more so during one's 30s. Many couples, of course, postpone parenthood and do have children before it is too late.

Postponing Parenthood

Delayed parenthood, as Figure 11.5 suggests, is a second available option—and one that increasing numbers of Canadian women are choosing. Later age at marriage, together with the desire of many women to complete their education and become established in a career, appear to be important factors in the high levels of postponed childbearing. Older first-time mothers are better educated and better-off financially than younger mothers (Kobren 1988; Ventura 1988). With the availability of more reliable contraception,

Childless...By Choice

Janet Kurelo is still religiously taking The Pill after 11 years of marriage. "When I was 20, I asked my doctor to tie my tubes, but he wouldn't do it," says the 31-year-old Rogers Cable administrative coordinator, who lives in Oshawa with her husband, Rick, a firefighter. "We realized after just two weeks of dating that we did not want children"....

Yet, despite....more diverse lifestyles, ours is an increasingly child-centred society and childlessness-by-choice is stigmatized. Kurelo has endured unsolicited jibes from friends, family, even her doctor, who said she would be a very lonely senior citizen choosing not to have kids. "The world is so messed-up," she says. "We have too much violence, not enough teachers, racism, no jobs, pedophiles, unreliable, expensive childcare. I can list a thousand reasons why we don't want to bring a child into this world."

Kurelo admits to suffering an occasional attack of "the baby blues" when she sees a mother putting her daughter's hair in a ponytail, as she did last week. "But then I hear about how those two teenage girls were brutally assaulted, raped and one murdered. I don't know how a mother could survive an attack or murder of her child." One of four children raised by a single mother who sacrificed everything she loved to support her family, she says, "I wouldn't want someone else raising my kids so I could work to give them the life they want. We enjoy our freedom and have no regrets."

Sandi Gillis-Huhtala, a 35-year-old retail manager in Ajax, agrees: "I've known I didn't want children since I was a pre-teen. If I had a dollar for every time someone said, 'Oh, you'll change your mind,' I could probably retire." After seven years of marriage, her parents accept her choice, but ironically, her peers don't. "I have people call me selfish or assume I dislike children. And I don't. I love them, they're just not for me," she insists.

"Worse, people have tried to analyze me and come to the absurd conclusion I had a lousy childhood. It seems I'm always on the defensive, forced to justify myself."

Another anonymous woman, 38, who had a tubal ligation 10 years ago, chose a different path of resistance by providing aid to two children in India. "My mother admits she never wanted children, but felt compelled by societal pressures to have four," she confides. "It is supremely sad four children were born to someone who genuinely didn't want any of them." Real wisdom, she says, is admitting you lack a certain calling. At a time when the world population exceeds six billion, "childless people should be applauded and not condemned as is frequently the case."

Going against the cultural flow. What does it mean to be a woman and not have motherhood factored into the equation? Increasingly, women are finding answers that contravene cultural and social trends, says psychologist Mary Ireland, who studied more than 100 socially and culturally diverse women, childless-by-choice. "A significant number are finding they're better, for example, as aunts than as mothers. Others accept they simply don't like children, or prefer the quality of their relationships without children, or want to further their careers in a man's world," says Ireland, 51, childless-by-choice.

Though our culture has trouble understanding what it means to be a woman and not a mother, some years are more neutral. In others, the emphasis is on family values, and childless women are more marginalized, as is the case in a more politically conservative climate, she explains. Our culture has to embrace this identity, so you can feel you don't have to have children, Ireland states. "And it's happening. You can't dismiss it."

Source: Abridged from Naiman 2000.

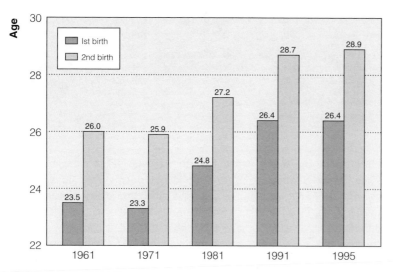

FIGURE **11.5**

Average age of mothers having their first or second born child (1961–1995). (Source: based on data from the Statistics Canada publication "Births and Deaths", Catalogue 84-210, various years.)

the availability of abortion, and the trend toward having only two children, couples can now plan their parenthood earlier or later in their adult lives.

Because fertility declines gradually with age, older couples tend to take longer to conceive. Older women also have higher rates of miscarriage and run a greater risk of conceiving children with certain genetic defects (Winslow 1990). Still, the medical bottom line is that "it is relatively safe for women to postpone child-bearing" into their 30s (Winslow 1990).

POSTPONING PARENTHOOD: A TWO-SIDED COIN   Postponing parenthood is a two-sided coin. Whereas early first-time parents in one study "couldn't remember a time when they weren't parents," postponers reported a sharp sense of before and after (Daniels and Weingarten 1980). The mothers in this study found that combining established careers with parenting created unforeseen problems. Those who set their careers temporarily aside to be full-time mothers met with criticism from their work colleagues and peers. Those who continued to work, even though they reduced their hours, felt they missed important time with their children or were generally overloaded. One special difficulty with choosing late parenthood is that

career commitments may ripen just at the peak of parental responsibilities.

Furthermore, late parents reported their impatience for the empty nest stage of life, when they could return to the personal privacy and freedom from responsibility they enjoyed before their children were born. Early first-time parents, on the other hand, felt they reaped definite pluses later on. One woman, who had been a first-time mother in her early 20s and was now older and a systems analyst, said,

I like the fact that my children are as old as they are, and that I'm as young as I am and my career is so open ahead of me. I'd hate to be in my career position, wanting to have children and not knowing when to make the break. (Daniels and Weingarten 1980, p. 60)

In this respect, postponing parenthood means making a trade-off. More free time before having children means less time after the children are grown. An awareness of this fact—plus an understanding that having children, although rewarding, can cause logistic and emotional complications—is important for people who consciously decide to postpone becoming parents.

Being born to older parents affects children's lives as well. They usually benefit from financial and emotional stability that older parents can provide and the attention given by parents who have waited a long time to have children. "In many ways ... offspring of older parents are children of economic and emotional privilege.... When their playmates' fathers and mothers are thinking about promotions, mortgages, and their own identities, children of older parents are more likely to take centre stage" (Yarrow 1987, p. 17, citing Iris Kern). But children of older parents can also experience anxiety about their parents' health and mortality. Parents may become frail while children are still young. Older parents need to plan for guardianship. And children of older parents may have to assume the burden of caring for their elderly parents before they have established themselves in their adult lives.

The One-Child Family

Throughout this discussion we've been talking about the choice between having no children or waiting to have children. We have used the plural, reflecting an assumption in our society that when a couple become parents, they will have at least two children. Although it is essentially true that there's no such thing as halfway parents, it is also true that there are some differences in degree between having one child and having several children. We'll consider the one-child family as a third option available to couples.

As we have seen, children today are more likely to be only children than in previous decades (Vanier Institute of the Family 2000, p. 58). The proportion of one-child families in Canada appears to be growing because of the high cost of raising a child through college or university, some women's increasing career opportunities and aspirations, and also because the choice to have just one child becomes easier to make as more couples do so. Divorced people may end up with a one-child family because the marriage ended before more children were born.

Negative stereotypes present only children as spoiled, lonely, dependent, and selfish. To find out whether there was any basis for this image, psychologists in the 1970s produced a staggering number of studies. "The overall conclusion: There are no major differences between only children and others; no negative effects of being an only child can be found" (Pines 1981, p. 15). One study interviewed adults

between ages 17 and 62 who had been only children and concluded that despite many people's beliefs, only children turn out to be no more selfish, lonely, or less well-adjusted than those with siblings (Falbo 1976).

Another study (Hawke and Knox 1978) compared the positive and negative aspects of having an only child by interviewing 102 parents of only children and 105 only children. These only children had better verbal skills and higher IQs than children in any other size family, whether eldest, youngest, or whatever. Their grades were as good or better. They displayed more self-reliance and self-confidence than other children and were often the most popular among elementary school students. They were as likely to have successful university experiences and careers, happy marriages, and good parenting experiences as children with brothers and sister.

Since the 1970s, research in this area has sharply diminished. One recent study (Perner, Ruffman, and Leekam 1994), however, has found that children with siblings develop the ability to take another person's perspective earlier than only children do.

ADVANTAGES   Parents with only one child report that they can enjoy parenthood without being overwhelmed and tied down. They have more free time and are better off financially than they would have been with more children (Downey 1995). Researchers have found that family members shared decisions more equally and could afford to do more things together (Hawke and Knox 1978). Then too, a second child presents a new set of family challenges, among them managing an entirely new family relationship—that between siblings (Kreppner 1988).

Research also shows that the child in a one-child family has some advantages over children with siblings. In a study using a national U.S. sample of more than 24 000 eighth graders surveyed in 1988, sociologist Douglas Downey (1995) found that only children were significantly more likely to talk frequently with their parents, to have attended art, music, or dance classes outside of school, and to have visited art, science, or history museums. Furthermore, parents of only children had higher educational expectations for their child, were more likely to know their child's friends and the friends' parents, and had more money saved for their child's post-secondary education. These findings existed even among parents with similar education and income.

DISADVANTAGES   There are disadvantages, too, in a one-child family. For the children, these include the obvious lack of opportunity to experience sibling relationships, not only in childhood but also as adults, and the extra pressure from parents to succeed. They are sometimes under an uncomfortable amount of parental scrutiny, and as adults they have no help in caring for their aging parents. Disadvantages for parents include the constant fear that the only child might be seriously hurt or die and the feeling, in some cases, that they have only one chance to prove themselves good parents.

To this point in the chapter, we have taken for granted a very important factor: the element of choice in having or not having children. Indeed, the extent to which we have this choice is itself remarkable. Until a few decades ago (in some cases a very few years ago), most of the technology on which this ability to choose depends simply didn't exist. The next sections explore some personal and relationship ramifications of fertility technology. We'll look first at some issues surrounding contraception.

PREVENTING PREGNANCY: HISTORY AND ISSUES

Women have long attempted to control pregnancy (see Box 11.2, "The History of Birth Control in Canada"). However, until relatively recently in historical terms, a majority of these methods were relatively ineffective and/or dangerous (Critchlow and Mohr 1998). Although both the condom and the diaphragm were relatively safe and effective, it was not until the 1960s, with the development of the pill, that a significant technological breakthrough in preventing pregnancy was achieved.

With the pill, women could be more certain of controlling fertility; they did not need male cooperation to do so; and they could engage in sexual activity for its own sake, disconnected from reproduction (Luker 1990). At the same time however, it is worth noting that even though the birth control pill has been available in most countries in the West for more than three decades, it was only in the summer of 1999 that Japan's national pharmaceutical regulatory board recommended approval of the pill to the government's ministry of health. Critics of the birth control pill there had long claimed that its use would damage the nation's morals and cause a variety of social ills, including environmental harm from the hormones in the urine of women who took it. Nevertheless, women's groups in Japan intensified their campaign for the pill's approval after the Japanese government gave their swift approval to Viagra, the male anti-impotence pill (*Maclean's* 1999, p. 53).[6]

Although heavy reliance in the twentieth century on the condom and the diaphragm implied male as

Many families choose to have only one child, a decision that can ease time, energy, and economic concerns. There may be extra pressure on only children, and they do not experience sibling relationships. But only children, such as the young woman featured here with her mother, tend to receive more personal attention from parents, and parents may enjoy not feeling so overwhelmed as they might with more offspring to care for.

6. The uneven speed of response to products that may be seen to liberate male versus female sexuality is not unique to Japan. Consider, in this context, that a year after Viagra's 1998 debut, the Constitutional Court in Colombia decreed that state-run health services must reimburse Colombian men needing Viagra to combat impotence due to chronic or terminal diseases. In a country where the public health care system is so overburdened that patients often have to provide their own syringes and people die of gangrene after amputation, at least some questioned the priorities expressed in this high-court ruling that required the government to pay for some men's use of a very expensive drug (*KW Record*, 1999, p. A6).

well as female responsibility for contraception, since the advent of the pill in the sixties contraception has been viewed as mostly the female's responsibility. Writing in *Our Bodies, Ourselves* for the New Century, the Boston Women's Health Book Collective (1998, pp. 290–1) takes the position that placing total responsibility for birth control on women is unfair. The authors add that women may still choose not to use birth control for many reasons, among them their hesitation to inconvenience a partner. But the fear of displeasing him attests to the inequality of the relationship.

This, of course, is the traditional double standard, which assigns women the responsibility for controlling sexual behaviour. The double standard may be in effect here because men can more readily escape the consequences of an unwanted pregnancy. For example, the early research of Stephen Pfohl (1978) on "unwed fathers" observed that a man who impregnates a woman to whom he is not married has the ability to "negotiate from a position of strength." Rather than being seen as "immoral" or "loose"—labels that are still used today to describe unwed mothers—the unwed father is seen, in Pfohl's terms, as a "non-deviant rule breaker." The physical and opportunity costs of children also tend to be higher for women than for men. Further, it is women who physically experience abortion or carry and bear children and who more often relinquish careers and education for parenthood. At the same time, however, the double standard also attests to the still commonly held belief that women do not possess sexual urges that are as powerful as a man's. As a consequence, women are believed to be capable of more rational thinking regarding things sexual.

We have seen that people take many factors into consideration in their decision to have or not to have children. With several methods available both for contraception and for attempting to increase fertility (discussed later in the chapter), people today are more able to make decisions about parenthood than they have ever been. However, as with other kinds of personal choices we have considered throughout this text, people don't always choose knowledgeably about having children. Default decisions are one (but not the only) reason pregnancy and parenthood can profoundly disrupt lives.

Society has a considerable stake in the next generation, and issues related to procreation tend to be central. Pregnancy outside of marriage and abortion are two reproductive issues that are social as well as personal concerns.

PREGNANCY OUTSIDE MARRIAGE

Various images come to mind when we think of pregnancy outside of marriage. One of them may be that of the older professional woman, unmarried, who chooses to bear and rear a child on her own. A contrasting image is that of the teenage mother. Next we will address both childbearing by older single women and teen pregnancy.

Older Single Mothers

Although unwed birthrates are highest among young adult women (ages 20–24), the number of babies born to unwed women over the age of 30 equalled the number born to unwed teenage mothers in 1995 (Figure 11.6) (Vanier Institute of the Family 2000, p. 74). In 1997, just under one-third of first births were to women over the age of 30—up from 19 percent in 1987 (Statistics Canada 1999).

Although some of these pregnancies and births are unintended, others are planned. Both situations are affected by social change. As opportunities grow for women to support themselves, and as the permanence of marriage becomes less certain, the principle of legitimacy becomes less important economically; that is, there is less motivation for a woman to avoid giving birth out of wedlock because she cannot count on lifetime male support for the child even if she is married. Furthermore, stigma and discrimination against unwed mothers have somewhat lessened, and the distinction in legal terms between legitimate and illegitimate children has been virtually eliminated in terms of financial support and inheritance[7] (Dranoff 2001). Nevertheless, the burden of responsibility for support and care of the child remains on the mother, and, in general, "the economic situation of older,

---

7. "Over the past 25 years, all provinces and territories except Alberta and Nova Scotia have enacted legislation to dispense with the distinction between children of married and unmarried parents; now all children born in these jurisdictions generally have the same rights" (Dranoff 2001, p. 105). Moreover, a 1989 case in Nova Scotia ruled that an out-of-wedlock child whose father had died without a will was entitled to inherit and that making a distinction between children inside and outside of marriage was unconstitutional.

11.2 ᴮᴼˣ The History of Birth Control in Canada

Human beings have been trying to control their fertility for a very long time. There is evidence that the first inhabitants of Canada, Aboriginal Canadians, used various types of birth control before the arrival of Europeans. For example, women of the Maliseet band in New Brunswick drank tea brewed from dried beaver testicles to prevent fertilization.

Confederation to the 1930s

Childbearing was very dangerous for women during this period. Many women died in childbirth.... Demographic evidence shows that people were using birth control; however, society did not necessarily approve of its use....

Many methods of preventing pregnancy were employed, with varying degrees of effectiveness. While birth control refers to ways of preventing the birth of children, contraception refers to the prevention of pregnancy. Methods of birth control in use at this time included abstinence, diverse methods of contraception (pessaries, herbal concoctions, vaginal sponges, diaphragms, condoms, withdrawal, douching, prolonged breast feeding and a version of the rhythm method actually based on inaccurate information about the timing of ovulation), sterilization, and abortion. It was not until the 1930s that the correct relationship between ovulation and menstruation was discovered— that ovulation occurred in the middle of the menstrual cycle and not during menstruation.

In 1882, it became a crime to sell or advertise birth control in Canada. The maximum sentence was two years' imprisonment. However, section 207 of the Criminal Code, which made birth control illegal, contained a clause that allowed for the distribution of birth control if it were for the public good. Since the "public good" was not defined, it was left to the courts to interpret the phrase.

Many doctors were reluctant to provide information about contraception, which they saw as suitable only for prostitutes and unmarried women. The theory was that birth control was unnatural [and] constituted a rejection of motherhood by women, and [that] this rejection would in turn harm them. Since it was difficult to receive information from doctors, women looked to other sources....[A] woman from Tecumseh, Ontario....wrote to Marie Stopes, a birth control advocate in England, for information. Other women wrote to Margaret Sanger, an advocate in the United States. Some women in Western Canada wrote to a regional newspaper, *The Western Producer*, for information about birth control. Others turned to family and friends to obtain information....Some forms of contraception could be purchased in drug stores "under the counter."

The 1930s and the Campaign for Birth Control

The campaign for birth control started later in Canada than in either the United States or Great Britain, probably because of Canada's lower rate of industrialization and its higher Roman Catholic population. While the birth control movement was originally started in the 1920s by people associated with "leftist" causes, it gained prominence in the 1930s when it was taken up by more of the population. The movement was successful largely because many people were concerned with the number of children poor women were having during the Great Depression....Also, eugenics (the belief that society could be made smarter and healthier if certain types of people did not produce offspring) was popular during the Depression. Birth control was seen as a way to limit the growth of the "lower classes."

Some women were concerned about reproductive rights and better maternal and infant health, but they were in the minority. The monetary advantages of birth control were stressed; it cost $1500 to give 500 women birth control, while it cost the community $30 000 if each had a child....However, there were limits on who could obtain birth control. It was for married women who wanted to space their children and not for unmarried women who wished to have sex....

During the late 1950s, some forms of contraception were available in drug stores. Condoms were usually kept in drawers behind the pharmacy counters and customers would have to specifically ask for them (and endure the embarrassment).... Since it was illegal to claim a product was a contraceptive, condom manufacturers resorted to promoting their product in other ways. For many years, every tin....of condoms on the market read "sold in drugs stores only for the prevention of contagious diseases." Oral contraceptives, IUDs and diaphragms were prescribed by physicians. Family planning was available to couples who could afford private physicians; otherwise, it was fairly inaccessible....

The Sexual Revolution of the 1960s

The 1960s saw a greater acceptance of birth control. This acceptance was reflected in changes to the law in 1969 which legalized birth control. However, there was still resistance and concern about "sexual immorality," fears that, with the birth rate lowered, immigrants would "take over the country" and that average intelligence would be lowered due to smart people using contraception more effectively. The birth control pill became available in Canada in the early 1960s, but was to be prescribed for therapeutic purposes, such as regulation of the menstrual cycle....

On June 27, 1969, a Liberal government passed a bill which legalized contraception. It became law on July 1, 1969. It also reformed the law surrounding abortion, allowing it if approved by a hospital medical committee as necessary to preserve the pregnant women's life or health. Surprisingly, the Canadian Catholic Conference of the Roman Catholic Church did not oppose the law, stating that Canada was a pluralistic society but that Roman Catholics should not practise birth control.

The Era of Legalized Birth Control (1969 to present)

The legalization of birth control did not ensure that women would be provided with safe and effective contraceptives. By the end of 1974, only three provinces and one territory had policies supporting family planning....

In 1974, the Dalkon Shield, an intrauterine contraceptive device, was pulled from the shelves after three years on the market. It was linked to the deaths of 16 women in the United States and had caused medical problems in numerous other women. The resulting lawsuits bankrupted the manufacturer. In 1986, the Copper 7 IUD was pulled from the shelves in the United States. The manufacturer cited the high costs of defending itself from lawsuits as the reason. It remained on sale in Canada. There were also health concerns over the birth control pill. It is not recommended for smokers or women over 35. In 1986, the Ontario Court of Appeal decided that pill manufacturers had to warn women of the potential side effects....

New ways to deliver spermicides became available. Vaginal Contraceptive Film, Advantage 24(foam), Leah's Shield (a fusion of the diaphragm and cervical cap), and a spermicidal sponge can be purchased in drug stores.... Longer-acting hormonal contraceptives have become available in Canada. Norplant and Depo-Provera were approved in 1994 and 1997 respectively. It took years for each drug to receive Health Canada approval, as there were concerns over their safety. The government faced fierce lobbying from groups concerned about women's safety and, on the other hand, those concerned about women being denied effective, hassle-free contraception. In 1996, the female condom was approved for use in Canada and became available in 1997.

In 1999, the emergency contraceptive pill (ECP) (sometimes called "the morning after pill") was approved by Health Canada. If used within 72 hours of intercourse, research shows that it reduces the risk of

(continued)

(continued)

pregnancy by 75 percent. The most common type of emergency contraception is two high doses of combined estrogen-progestin birth control pills. New progestin-only pills (which produce less nausea) went through clinical trials in Canada in 1999 and became available (by prescription) under the name "Plan B" in 2000.

In May 2000, Wyeth-Ayerst Canada Inc. began airing advertisements for its low estrogen birth control pill Alesse on television station MuchMusic. This marked the first time in Canada that the Pill has been advertised on television. The campaign centres on a theme of "lessons learned" and features young women discussing relationships and birth control. The ads are aimed at women aged 18 to 24. The campaign also includes ads on public transit in 15 cities across Canada and a commercial that will run at 79 Cineplex Odeon cinemas. Federal restrictions govern direct-to-consumer ads for prescription drugs. The Alesse campaign names the drug and talks about what it does, but never in the same commercial.

Future methods or derivations of method expected soon include a single-rod implant which will last for three years....[and] a hormone-release skin patch. Other methods in development include soft silicone vaginal rings that release both estrogen and progesterone slowly over a full month and frameless IUDs. Contraceptive injections, pills, nasal sprays and implants for men are being researched.... However, the outlook for completely new means of birth control is not very promising. The cost of developing drugs is high, governments are providing less money for research and manufacturers are concerned with the costs of lawsuits.

Source: Abridged from Childless by Choice Trust 2000.

---

single mothers is closer to that of teen mothers than that of married childbearers the same age" (Foster, Jones, and Hoffman 1998, p. 163).

Generally, single mothers, by choice, seek out men—or sperm donors—perceived as good biological fathers and expect little or no continued involvement. They consciously establish social networks and carefully plan child care. Research findings are mixed regarding solo mothers' children's outcomes (Gringlas and Weinraub 1995). Some older single mothers are partners in committed lesbian relationships, and research shows that their children are not significantly different from those raised by heterosexuals (Patterson 1992).

A special case of unwed parenthood, presenting especially challenging problems, is that of teen parenthood. The next section discusses teen pregnancy and parenthood.

Teenage Pregnancy

At least among males, hormones in adolescence encourage high levels of sexual activity (Udry 1988). And Canadian females reach puberty earlier now than in the past. The average age of the onset of menstruation was almost 17 in nineteenth-century Europe. In Canada today, the average age for a first period is about 12 1/2, down from age 14 in 1900 (Bueckhert 2000). Moreover, teens have become sexually active at younger ages (Chapter 5). Median age at first intercourse has not only declined in the last 40 years, it is now almost the same for females and

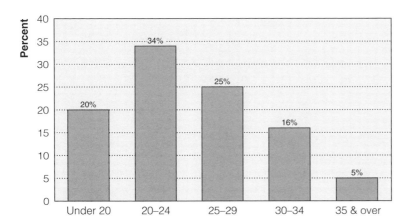

FIGURE **11.6**

Births to not married women: percentage distribution by age of mother (1995). (Source: based on data from the Statistics Canada publication "Births and Deaths", Catalogue 84-210, various years.)

males (Maticka-Tyndale, Barrett and McKay 2000). However, births among 15- to 19-year-old women have actually declined over the past 25 years, "in part because the number of teenagers have declined" but, even more importantly, because of increased access to information, birth control and abortion (Vanier Institute of the Family 2000, p. 74).

In Canada, there were a total of 38 502 teenaged pregnancies in 1995, including live births, abortions, and stillborns. While the pregnancy rate among every other age group of fertile women is decreasing, the teenage pregnancy rate is increasing. From the mid-1970s to 1988, the number of teenage pregnancies declined among 15- to 19-year-olds and then increased somewhat. Among 13- and 14-year-olds, the number of pregnancies declined slowly from the mid-1970s to a low of 573 in 1988; since then, it has hovered at around 600. Although well below their all time highs, rates of teen pregnancies have increased from 41 per 1000 women aged 15 to 19 in 1987 to 47 per 1000 in 1995 to 59.2 in 1997. (Crawford 1997; Health Canada 1999). However, the number of live births to teenagers is down because the proportion of pregnancies ending in abortion is up (Figure 11.7). This proportion almost doubled between 1974 and 1994 (from 26 to 45 percent). From 1987 to 1997, teenagers accounted for 11 percent of first births in Canada (Statistics Canada 1999).

The perception that a teenage pregnancy "epidemic" of "crisis" proportions exists in Canada would seem to be the result of fusing and confusing Canadian rates with U.S. rates. However, the United States has by far the highest teen pregnancy, abortion, and birthrates of any industrialized country (Forrest et al. 1993). The teen pregnancy rate in the U.S. is actually twice as high as the Canadian teen pregnancy rate.

Teenage parents, especially those with more than one child, face a bleaker educational future, a stunted career, and a very good chance of living in poverty, compared with peers who do not become parents as teenagers (Zabin et al. 1992; Solomon and Liefeld 1998; Nock 1998b). Also, teen mothers are less likely than their counterparts to marry later, and teen marriages have higher divorce rates (Manning 1993). It is unclear to what extent these consequences result from teen pregnancy per se and not from various background characteristics such as having lived in poverty (Geronimus 1991). But we can logically assume that the responsibilities of motherhood present further educational and occupational obstacles to already disadvantaged teens (Chase-Lansdale, Brooks-Gunn, and Palkoff 1991; Polakow 1993). Moreover, these negative consequences tend to be passed on to the next generation. Long-term prospects for children of teenage parents include lower academic achievement and a tendency to repeat the cycle of early, unmarried

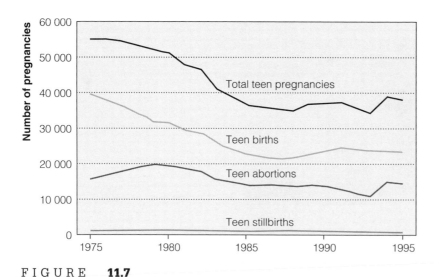

FIGURE **11.7**

Teenage pregnancies, births, and abortions, Canada, 1975–95. (Source: Statistics
Canada, Health Statistics Division, *Health Indications*, 1999 (Cat. No. 82-221-XCB);
and "Births and Deaths", Catalogue 84-210, May 1997.)

pregnancy (Hayes 1987; Alexander and Guyer 1993).[8]

At the same time, researchers argue that teen parents have become too stereotyped as "losers" and that this societal image ignores teen parents' diversity, experiences, and educational and work aspirations (Camarena et al. 1998). One analysis of national data, for instance, shows that teen parents are more responsible than other teenagers. Teen mothers are less likely than other adolescent females to drink alcohol or spend time with friends who do; teen fathers who acknowledge their child are more likely than other adolescent males to be employed or engaged in other "socially productive work," such as volunteering in the community (Kowaleski-Jones and Mott 1998).

Social scientists and others have pointed to the ongoing need for support programs to help young par-

ents and to help their families help them (Leitch 1998). Such programs include health centres, family-planning clinics, nutritional services, primary and preventive health care, mentoring, vocational counselling, and legal and educational services and parental training courses in the public schools (Blinn-Pike et al. 1998; Solomon and Liefeld 1998). Support programs in the schools and programs targeted to teen parents have, in fact, produced good outcomes. Teen parents who remain with their families for a time and who do not marry seem to do better in the long run (Furstenberg, Brooks-Gunn, and Morgan 1987).

Many social workers and policymakers point to the need for including the teen father in programs and services. Some young, unmarried fathers do offer support, but they are often hampered by unemployment, and their involvement with their child tends to decline as the baby gets older and the relationship with the mother grows increasingly distant or strained (Rangarajan and Gleason 1998).

While involving fathers is an important community goal, prevention remains the better option so far as teen pregnancy is concerned. One proposed solution is to encourage "abstinence and responsibility." It is difficult to know how well this approach will work. Another solution is to give teenagers more informa-

8. "However, while early childbearing increases the risk of ill effects for mother and child, it is unclear that the risk is so high as to justify the popular image of the adolescent mother as an unemployed woman living on welfare with a number of poorly cared-for children. To be sure, teenage mothers do not manage as well as women who delay childbearing, but most studies have shown that there is great variation in the effects of teenage childbearing" (Furstenberg, Brooks-Gunn, and Morgan, 1987, p. 142).

tion about contraceptives and increase their availability. This second solution has come under attack by conservative political and religious groups as encouraging nonmarital sex. However, reviews of all the relevant research over the past decade indicate that sex education programs as they currently exist neither hasten nor increase the frequency of teenage intercourse ("Sex Education ..." 1998; Berne and Huberman 1996; Kirby 1995; Franklin et al. 1997). While there is some evidence that such programs actually help to delay the first intercourse, reduce the number of sexual partners, and modestly increase contraception (Kirby 1995; Franklin et al. 1997), research on the effectiveness of such programs in preventing pregnancy is discouraging (Stout and Rivara 1989). Programs that include sex education curricula with easily accessible health clinics, however, do seem to lead to decreases in adolescent pregnancy rates (Jacobs and Wolf 1995).

Reasons for Teenage Nonmarital Pregnancy

Some teens do get pregnant intentionally (Trent and Crowder 1997), but five out of six—and in some samples as many as nine out of ten (Hardy et al. 1989)—teen pregnancies are unintended (Trussell 1988; Daly 1994). For some teenagers, pregnancy may simply be the result of their failure to use birth control during a first episode of sexual intercourse with a current partner. According to the 1998 Canadian Contraception Study, one in five unmarried teenage women aged 15 to 17 said they did not used contraception the first time that they had intercourse with their current partner. Moreover, although oral contraceptives are the most popular method of birth control among teenage women in Canada (Kalagian et al. 1998), some of the other preferred methods used by teenagers may be relatively ineffective as a form of contraception. For example, while withdrawal as a method of contraception was used by nine percent of sexually active women overall, it was used by 22 percent of unmarried 15- to 17-year-olds. Pregnancy may also be the result of failure to use a method of contraception consistently. Within this survey, only 60 percent of 15- to 17-year-old unmarried teenagers reported always using contraception during the past six months (Fisher, Boroditsky and Bridges 1999).

Males may often believe, according to the sexual double standard, that the "real" parent and the one responsible for contraception is the female. In the 1988 U.S. National Survey of Adolescent Males, 76 percent said they agreed "a lot" that men should know whether their partner was using contraception before having sex (Marsiglio 1993). This leaves nearly one-quarter who did not entirely agree.

PARADOXICAL PREGNANCY   Meanwhile, some explanations for the female partner's failure to use contraceptives are provided by a 20-year-old study of 18–19-year-old undergraduate women at Indiana University (Byrne 1977). The term **paradoxical pregnancy** was used to summarize the finding that the more guilty and disapproving these women were about premarital sex, the less likely they were to use contraceptives regularly, if at all. Such paradoxical pregnancies resulted because personal disapproval of premarital sex was often not strong enough to inhibit sexual behaviour, but it did inhibit the use of contraceptives.

The researchers offered some explanations for why such pregnancies happen. First, the sexually negative individual avoids the expectation that intercourse will occur. Because sex is defined as a spontaneous event, he or she is unprepared. A second reason for paradoxical pregnancy is a lack of communication. Sexual partners need to talk to each other about contraception to make sure somebody has done something. Yet partners who disapprove of premarital sex are less likely to talk to each other about either sex or contraception.

OTHER RISK FACTORS   More recent research has explored the relationship between sexual abuse and teen pregnancy. An American study found that for one woman in four, their first experience of intercourse occurred as a rape (Gail Wyatt, in Brody 1989c). Rates of prior sexual molestation among pregnant teens are higher than one in four (Boyer and Fine 1992). Sexual abuse in childhood may lead to lowered self-esteem and less caring and assertiveness about contraception among adolescent females (Small and Kerns 1993; Stock et al. 1997). Then too, forced sexual intercourse is unlikely to be accompanied by contraception and after puberty is the cause of some unplanned pregnancies (Woodman 1995). One recent analysis of national U.S. survey data (Roosa et al. 1997) concluded that sexual abuse alone was unrelated to teen pregnancy. However, sexual abuse was often related to the early onset of intercourse and not using birth control. This research also found sexual abuse by a boyfriend to be a factor in some teen pregnancies.

Other research has found relationships between teen sexual activity and other behaviours of which parents would likely disapprove (Billy, Brewster, and Grady 1994) and between teen pregnancy and risk-taking, having ever moved, run away from home, homelessness among youths, being suspended or expelled from school, being stopped by police, or using illegal drugs (Hagan and McCarthy 1997; Luster and Small 1994; Thornberry, Smith, and Howard 1997; Kowaleski Jones and Mott 1998). One study of single women ages 14–21 has found that being in school or employed increases the likelihood that they will use birth control (Kraft and Coverdill 1994).

Contraception can provide a solution to the potential problems associated with pregnancy outside of marriage. When contraception isn't used, however, many women who don't want to remain pregnant decide to have an abortion. We will look next at this option, which is itself a very controversial social issue.

ABORTION

Abortion is the expulsion of the fetus or embryo from the uterus either naturally (spontaneous abortion or miscarriage) or medically (surgically or drug-induced abortion). This section addresses induced abortion. After amendments to Canada's abortion laws were made in 1969, which allowed for "therapeutic abortion" in hospitals, both the numbers and rates of therapeutic abortions rose significantly. They then began to drop and stablize beginning in 1983 and continuing for some years (Figure 11.8). The number and rates of abortions began to rise substantially again after 1989, when the Supreme Court struck down the 1969 abortion law. Before 1989, abortion clinics operated only in Quebec; by 1995, abortion clinics outside of hospitals operated in all Canadian provinces except Prince Edward Island and Saskatchewan. In 1998, one-third of all therapeutic abortions were performed in clinics and the remaining two-thirds were performed in hospitals. Far fewer Canadian women now obtain abortions in the United States (down from 2757 in 1987 to 297 in 1998). In 1998, 110 331 women obtained therapeutic abortions in Canada. Women in

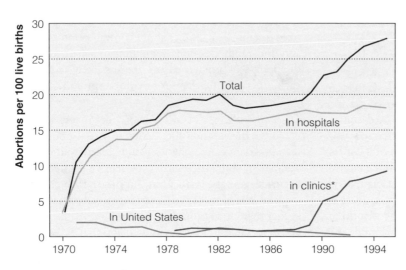

FIGURE **11.8**

Therapeutic abortions, Canadian residents, 1970–1995*.
*For 1978–89, information pertains to Quebec only. For 1990, clinics in Newfoundland, Nova Scotia, Quebec, Ontario, Manitoba, and British Columbia are included. Alberta clinics are added in 1991–95 data, and New Brunswick clinics are included in 1994 and 1995. (Source: Statistics Canada, 1995. *Therapeutic Abortions, 1995*, Cat. No. 82219-XPB, Nov. 1997.)

their 20s accounted for half of all those who obtained abortions in 1998 (Health Canada 1999; Statistics Canada 2000).

The Politics of Abortion

Throughout history, abortion has been a way of preventing birth. However, under section 179c of Canada's Revised Statutes of 1892, any woman who sought or succeeded in inducing her own abortion as well as anyone who assisted such a woman had committed an indictable offence. Until 1988, the Canadian Criminal Act defined any attempt to induce an abortion by any means as a crime for which the maximum penalty was life imprisonment or, if the woman herself was convicted, two years.

Angus McLaren (1999) observes that when an abortion resulting in the death of a married woman wound up in a courtroom, a husband would generally claim that, while he had known of his wife's intention to procure an abortion, he had opposed her intention to do so. The courts, he reports, "tended to downplay the husband's participation." "Husbands were rarely charged as accessories, not because they were less likely than single men to bully their partners into abortion or to support a freely made decision, but because the courts tacitly recognized that as married men they had a 'right' to be so involved" (p. 30). In cases involving an unmarried woman, the police were more likely to lay charges against the woman's partner, with the assumption that the man had been "actively involved" in the process, "usurping the parents' right of surveillance of their unmarried daughters."

On occasion, physicians complained that the criminalization of abortion represented an encroachment by the law on the practice of medicine. However, in voicing this objection, they overlooked the fact that, "in Canada, as elsewhere, physicians, in order to eliminate the competition of midwives and irregular practitioners, had been in the nineteenth century the most vocal proponents of the criminalization of abortion" (McLaren 1999, p. 30). The criminalization of abortion in this country stemmed from a combination of factors including: its mortality risk; its provision by female medical entrepreneurs at a time when physicians sought to establish their own professional respect and control; because many physicians believed that fetal development was a continuous process and that human life should be protected from the time of fer-

tilization; and, because of eugenicist fears that white middle-class women were not reproducing in large enough numbers (and that Canadian society would be overwhelmed by Aboriginals and immigrants of darker skin) (Fox 2001).[9]

Laws prohibiting abortion established during the nineteenth century stood relatively unchallenged until the 1960s, when an abortion reform movement, spearheaded by Canadian physician Dr. Henry Morgentaler, urged the repeal of abortion laws that, in his words, "compelled the unwilling to bear the unwanted" (in Dranoff 2001, p. 17). As we earlier noted, the first such change occurred with the 1969 amendment which allowed for "therapeutic abortion." Consistent with the common law defence of "necessity," abortions were allowed *if* performed by a physician in an accredited hospital and following a three-member committee's certification that the continuance of the pregnancy would be likely to endanger the life or health of the mother.

"In 1988, abortion was decriminalized, and left as a matter of choice between a woman and her physician" (Dranoff 2001, p. 10). In that year, the Supreme Court struck down the law on abortion on the grounds that it contravened a woman's right to control her own reproductive life and, as such, contravened her constitutionally protected guarantees to security of her person (under the equality rights provision of the Canadian Charter of Rights and Freedoms). The Supreme Court also unanimously determined that the civil law in Quebec, the Quebec Charter and the common law do not protect fetal life or interests. In 1989, in the case of *Tremblay v.*

---

9. Later, eugenics fears were to inspire the enactment of Sexual Sterilization Acts in Alberta (in 1928) and in British Columbia (in 1933). The Alberta Sexual Sterilization Act, for example, which was clearly inspired by the belief that certain socially undesirable qualities were inherited, permitted the provincial government's eugenics board to order sterilization when "procreation by the person under consideration (a) would result in the transmission of any mental disability or deficiency to his progeny, or (b) involves the risk of mental injury either to such person or his progeny." During the 33 years in which the Act was in effect, 2822 people were sterilized by order of the Alberta government's eugenics board, to eliminate "the risk of multiplication of the evil by transmission of the disability to progeny." Of this number, "a disproportionate number were eastern European, Catholic or native" (Daisley, 1996, p. 7). Although Alberta and British Columbia were the only provinces to pass sexual sterilization laws, it is believed that hundreds of such operations were also carried out in Ontario. In Alberta, the government finally repealed the Act in 1972. The legislation in B.C., which was used far less frequently than in Alberta, was repealed a year later.

Daigle, the Supreme Court of Canada was to rule that the fetus is not a person in law, and that a father of a fetus has no legal right of veto over the woman's decision with regards to the fetus she is carrying. In 1993, the Supreme Court of Canada was also to strike down legislation that banned abortion clinics.[10]

Although the Criminal Code of Canada specifies that a child only becomes a person after having "completely proceeded in a living state" from his or her mother's body, whether or not the child has taken a breath, has an independent circulation, or has been separated from the umbilical cord, others would argue that life begins at conception. The issue of whether or not the fetus should be extended "legal personhood"—with the protection that this designation conveys under the Charter of Rights and Freedoms—is highly contentious, and it is doubtful that it will become less so in the immediate future. The questions of when life begins, under what circumstances abortion should be regarded as justified, and who should have control over a pregnant woman's body are not simply "legal" questions *per se*. Indeed, the contrasting positions held by pro-choice and pro-life groups seem so intractable that the struggle over meaning in the abortion debate has been termed by one observer as the "clash of absolutes" (Shostak 1991, p. 20). For feminists, "women's struggle for the body" (Currie and Raoul 1992) is of central importance—be it expressed in relation to the abortion debate, efforts over the control of new reproductive technologies, or within the area of health and childcare. That is, "[b]oth metaphorically and literally, the body is at the centre of political life" (Currie and Raoul 1992, p. 21).

Social Attitudes About Abortion

Surveys conducted in both Canada and the United States show that the particular circumstances involved influence people's attitudes about abortion. There is more support for the so-called "hard reasons" of health, genetic defect, and pregnancy resulting from rape and less support for the "soft" reasons of low income, not being married, or simply not wanting more children in the family (Kelly, J. R., 1991).

According to a 1999 poll conducted by Gallup Canada Inc., agreement with the statement that abortion "should be legal under any circumstance" fell from 35 percent in 1995 to 28 percent in 1999 while agreement with the statement that "abortion should be illegal in all circumstances for abortion" rose from 13 percent in 1995 to 15 percent in 1999. In both years, the majority of Canadians were more likely to express agreement with the statement that abortion should be "legal only under certain [undefined] circumstances" (Tun 2000).

Reginald Bibby (2001, pp. 250–251) reports that attitudes towards abortion vary by age, with Canadian teens more likely than Canadians adults to approve of the availability of legal abortion for any reason (55 percent versus 43 percent respectively). He also reports that generational differences exist with young adult "Generation Xers" and adult Baby Boomer parents "who shared in the sexual revolution of the 1960s" showing a slightly higher approval of abortion on demand (46 and 44 percent respectively) than grandparents (36 percent). However, he notes that 90 percent of adults and 84 percent of teens support the availability of legal abortion when rape is involved.

Second-trimester abortions create greater moral problems for many people because they interrupt the fetus's development at a later stage. But only during this period can doctors check for diseased or defective fetuses by taking samples of amniotic fluid. Other second-trimester abortions are obtained by women who may not have realized they were pregnant or who could not make arrangements for a first-trimester abortion (Boston Women's Health Book Collective 1998, p. 403).

Third-trimester, "partial birth," or "late term" abortions have been the focus of heated debate in recent years. Opponents argue that the practice surely constitutes murder because the fetus is viable (i.e., could live outside the womb) and that the procedure itself is cruel. Proponents argue that third-trimester abortions are typically a last resort when a fetus has been recently found to be seriously defective ("Abortion: ..." 1997). What all this public discussion about abortion means for individuals is that women making decisions about abortion today do so in a far more political climate than before (Henshaw 1995) with violence sometimes erupting at abortion clinics and elsewhere (Gegax and Clemetson 1998).

---

10. In 1996, after being penalized under the Canada Health Act for allowing private billing practices at provincial abortion clinics, the Alberta government agreed to fund clinics (Long 1999, p. 6).

The Safety of Abortions

The majority of first-trimester abortions are by vacuum aspiration (the fetus is removed by suction), while the rest are induced with drugs such as RU-486. While illegal and self-induced abortions were accompanied by risk of death or serious injury, including damage to reproductive capacity, abortion is now one of the safest medical procedures when it is performed in a hospital or a clinic in the first trimester, as the vast majority of abortions are. Abortions in the second trimester are about ten times more dangerous than those performed in the first trimester. In addition, "Women seeking second-trimester abortions are often treated as though they are stupid and/or irresponsible and deserve to be punished. The unsupportive atmosphere can make an already emotionally difficult and painful experience that much worse" (Boston Women's Health Book Collective 1998, p. 403).

According to recent and compelling evidence, abortion has no impact on the ability to become pregnant; sterility following abortion is very uncommon and there is virtually no risk to future pregnancies from a first-trimester abortion of a first pregnancy (Boston Women's Health Book Collective 1998, p. 407). But questions of emotional and psychological distress are more often raised regarding abortion.

Emotional and Psychological Impact of Abortion

It's safe to say that for most women (and for many of their male partners) abortion is an emotionally charged, often upsetting, experience (Shostak and McLouth 1984). Some women report feeling guilty or frightened, a situation that can be heightened by demonstrators outside abortion clinics. Other women have reported that the decision to abort actually enhanced their sense of personal empowerment (Boston Women's Health Book Collective 1998, pp. 406–7). For many women, having an abortion probably results in mixed, even unexpected, feelings. The decision to abort is often very difficult to make. But the emotional distress involved in making the decision and having the abortion does not typically lead to severe or long-lasting psychological problems.

Some married couples may consider aborting an unwanted pregnancy if, for example, they feel that they have already completed their family or could not manage or afford to raise another child. Abortion can also be an issue for couples—particularly older ones and those in later stages of pregnancy—who through prenatal diagnosis techniques find out that a fetus has a serious defect. Results of ultrasound and amniocentesis are favourable in 95 to 99 percent of cases, and not all parents choose abortion when they are not. In fact, some parents exclude the possibility of abortion in advance but want the information provided by prenatal testing to prepare themselves to care for a disabled infant. For those faced with evidence of a defective fetus, abortion is not easy, for these are usually wanted pregnancies. "Patients and genetic counsellors alike report that mourning a pregnancy ended because of an abnormality is almost identical to mourning the death of a newborn infant" (Powledge 1983, p. 40).

But abortion decisions are primarily made within the context of unmarried, accidental pregnancy. Research has found positive educational, economic, and social outcomes for teen women who resolve pregnancies by abortion rather than giving birth. In one study, "those who obtained abortions did better economically and educationally and had fewer subsequent pregnancies than those who chose to bear children" (Holmes 1990). These outcomes are related to the reasons women have abortions: educational aspirations or needs or work responsibilities, inability to support a child, being in a poor relationship and/or not wanting to be a single parent (Torres and Forrest 1988).

Several major reviews of extensive research on the emotional and psychological impacts of abortion do not find significant negative consequences. Emotional stress is more pronounced for second-trimester than earlier abortions and for women who are most uncertain about their decision (Boston Women's Health Book Collective 1998, pp. 406–8). Women from ethnic cultures that officially oppose abortion may have more negative and mixed feelings after an abortion, but they are having them and slowly beginning to share their stories with one another (Peterman 1993).

Regardless of predicted outcomes, women (and men) making decisions about abortions are most likely to make them in the context of their values, and a detailed review of the ethical and social issues involved is outside the scope of this text.

INVOLUNTARY INFERTILITY

While society is currently focused on the prevention of conception or birth, a growing minority of individuals and couples face a different problem. They want to have a child, but either they cannot conceive or they cannot sustain a full-term pregnancy.

Involuntary infertility is the condition of wanting to conceive and bear a child but being physically unable to do so. It is usually defined in terms of unsuccessful efforts to conceive for at least 12 months or the inability to carry a pregnancy to full term.[11] (A parallel concept of **subfecundity**, or secondary infertility, indicates the problem of parents who have difficulty having additional children.)

According to sociologist Rona Achilles (1995, p. 348) "[i]nfertility is estimated to affect up to 15 percent of couples and is considered to be on the increase." In about one-third of cases, the problem originates with males, in approximately one-third percent of cases, with females and with both partners or is unknown in the remaining cases (Achilles 1995; Benson 1983). About half of couples defined as infertile will eventually conceive and deliver, either with or without medical intervention (Boston Women's Health Book Collective 1998, p. 532).

The physiology of conception, pregnancy, and childbirth is beyond the scope of this text. However, several factors can contribute to involuntary infertility. A man may have relatively few sperm in his semen (low sperm count) or they may be abnormal. A woman may fail to ovulate, may have a blockage or scarring in her fallopian tubes, or may have a condition called endometriosis, in which uterine tissue migrates to other parts of the abdomen. There are some cases in which each partner might be capable of conceiving with another individual. When both partners have even a minor problem, however, their chances of conceiving together are lowered. Then there are cases of idiopathic infertility—that is, infertility of no known cause. Through advances in health and medicine, the incidence of involuntary infertility declined during most of the twentieth century (Mosher 1990a).

---

11. Miscarriages end almost one-third of pregnancies, for reasons that are largely unknown. Most women who miscarry, however, are fertile and go on to have successful pregnancies (Beck 1988a; Kolata 1988b).

Neither modern contraceptive means (other than possibly the IUD) nor abortion impair fertility. There are new factors contributing to infertility today, however. One is the rising incidence of STDs, which can damage the reproductive systems of women and sometimes men; another is the fairly widespread use of the IUD in the 1970s and 1980s, which can cause uterine infection and scar the fallopian tubes. Exposure to various drugs, chemicals, and radiation can also cause infertility, and smoking and excessive exercise (which inhibits ovulation) can contribute to it. There is also concern that various environmental pollutants are lowering males' sperm counts and generally damaging human reproductive systems (Begley and Glick 1994; Glockner, Gaevert, and Kleinstein 1998). Furthermore, infertility appears to have increased because fecundity (the ability to conceive) declines with age while miscarriages increase with age. The present tendency to postpone childbearing until one's 30s and 40s creates a class of potential parents who are intensely hopeful and also financially able to seek treatment.

When faced with involuntary infertility, an individual or a couple experiences a loss of control over life plans and feels helpless, damaged or defective, angry, and often guilty (Becker 1990). Research shows that this is especially true for women (Abbey, Andrews, and Halman 1991). The cultural "centrality of the motherhood role" tends to render involuntary infertility among women "more central to their lives and more frequently on their minds" (p. 310).

Then too, the psychological burden of infertility may fall especially hard on professional, goal-oriented individuals. These people "have learned to focus all their energies on a particular goal. When that goal becomes a pregnancy that they cannot achieve, they see themselves as failures in a global sense" (Berg 1984, p. 164).

Besides having an effect on each partner's self-esteem, the situation can hurt their relationship and can create a marital crisis (Abbey, Andrews, and Halman 1992). As one wife explained, "We went through a heavy discussion, considering—not considering divorce, but we discussed it. The fact that we'd even discussed it was, to us, pretty far gone. He said to me, 'If you want to get somebody else to do it [impregnate her] ... If you want to get somebody else' ..." (in Becker 1990, p. 79).

For many couples, the partners slowly become aware that they confront a situation "of which they can make no sense." Moreover, this creeping awareness often arises at about the time when other couples they know are publicly planning their pregnancies without apparent difficulty. "It is under these social conditions that most couples embark on the quest for a medical solution to their problem" (Matthews and Matthews 1986, p. 643).

But going through fertility treatment is costly and stressful in itself. For instance, treatment often involves keeping accurate temperature charts, for a woman's body temperature rises after ovulation. Unfortunately, scheduling sexual intercourse in this way is not likely to help a couple relax as they are typically advised to do.[12] Other medical procedures involve drug therapies, include artificial insemination, in vitro fertilization, and related techniques. These treatments can be successful, but sometimes they are not.[13] When they are not, couples are faced with yet another decision—whether, or when to quit. As one woman put it, "It's harder to stop [treatment] than to keep going" (in Begley 1995, p. 45). "For most women and their partners, infertility is a major life crisis" (Boston Women's Health Book Collective 1998, p. 532). Counselling for both partners is recommended (Taylor 1995). These procedures can be successful, but they can be difficult and expensive, and they raise the question of whether and to what extent technology should be involved in human procreation.

Reproductive Technology: Social and Ethical Issues

Reproductive technologies enhance choices for some couples and can reward them with much desired parenthood. But reproductive technologies have tremendous social implications for the family as an institution and raise serious ethical questions as well.

COMMERCIALIZATION OF REPRODUCTION

A general criticism is that the new techniques, performed for profit, commercialize reproduction; prospective parents (or, more specifically their parts—testicles, sperm, ovaries, eggs, wombs, and so on), children, and embryos are treated as products and are thereby dehumanized (Merson 1995; Rothman 1999).

Concern has also been expressed about selective reduction (also called *selective termination*). In **selective reduction**, some (but not all) fetuses in multiple pregnancies resulting from ovulation-stimulating fertility drugs or the GIFT procedure are selectively aborted, usually in the first trimester (Overall 1990). Should more couples refuse to selectively terminate some fetuses, we will see more multiple births resulting in more premature infants with costly medical problems (Cowley and Springer 1997; Kalb 1999).

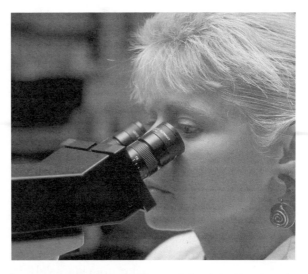

This physician, an infertility specialist, is looking through the microscope to examine a woman donor's eggs, which will be used in treating a couple's infertility. Infertility treatments are increasingly high-tech—and costly.

12. Scheduling sex for the main purpose of contraception can feel depersonalizing (Becker 1990, p. 93) and can also add conflict to a relationship. As one wife explained, "All the things you read about—that men feel like they are just a tool. You have to have an erection and ejaculate at a certain time whether you want to or not. He has said to me in times out of genuine anger, 'I feel that all you want me for is to make a baby. You don't really want me, you just want me to do it'" (in Becker 1990, p. 94).

13. In June 2000, the Canadian Fertility and Andrology Society released the first nation-wide results on assisted reproduction in Canada. Seventeen of Canada's 20 in-vitro fertilization centres voluntarily participated in the collection of this data in 1999. Preliminary analysis suggested a low complication rate and a rate of pregnancy that was on par with other national registries including the United States. Specifically, 4290 in-vitro fertilization cycles were begun in 1999; the overall pregnancy rate was 26 percent per cycle started; and complications occurred in less than three percent of cycles. This study reports that a woman's age has a strong influence on pregnancy rate. While among women under the age of 35 the pregnancy rate was 32 percent, this declined to 26 percent for women 35 to 39 years of age and, for women 40 years and older, to merely 13 percent (CFAS 2000).

Meanwhile, the freezing and saving of embryos raises the possibility not only of posthumous or post-divorce fertility but also of "leftover embryos" (Annas 1991, p. 35). Lawsuits involving the disposition of frozen embryos left by a couple killed in a plane crash and a divorced couple's dispute over the wife's desire to bear children from their frozen embryos are examples (Elson 1989b; Cooper 1992).

MEDDLING WITH NATURE A related issue involves whether unlimited technological meddling with nature is prudent. For example, we are now faced with the question of how old is too old to become a mother. Menopause, which stops ovulation, has traditionally been considered a natural barrier to pregnancy. But using a younger woman's eggs and an embryo transfer, some women past menopause—one as old as 63—have carried and delivered infants. Older mothers who bear children this way are likely to be financially stable, but a mother giving birth in her 50s will be 70 when her child graduates from high school (Kalb 1997). This has always been true for fathers, of course, who can remain fertile into old age.

THE STATUS OF PARENTHOOD More specific issues arise regarding the legal and social status of parenthood when reproductive technologies are involved. For example, who is legally responsible for the infant carried by a surrogate mother should it be born deformed and neither mother wants the baby?

With artificial insemination by a donor (AID), courts have had to address the question, "Who is the father?" According to Rona Achilles (1995, p. 351), in cases involving married couples and third-party sperm donors, "[t]here are, as yet, no laws to protect the participants" in such cases, "except in Quebec, where the child is legally considered to be affiliated with the social father, and in the Yukon, where donors are protected from possible legal suits by offspring or recipients." Problems can arise, as in a Chicago case where the donor was a friend of a lesbian couple and wanted to claim parental rights (Peres 1997). Especially in cases in which the biological father is not an anonymous donor and knows of the child's existence, similar problems may be expected to arise in Canada. In many Canadian provinces, the father of a child born in or out of wedlock has an equal right to make a claim for custody. A biological father may seek a court order declaring his paternity, as well as seek access to the child or custody.

Also, surrogacy, along with embryo transfer technology, creates the possibility that a child could have three mothers: the genetic mother, the gestational mother, and the social (child-raising) mother. In such a situation, how do courts define the "real" mother?

The vast majority of surrogates fulfill the contract they make with the infertile couple. But others do not. In 1993, the Royal Commission on New Reproductive Technologies recommended that all surrogate motherhood be banned in this country, "with breach of this ban to be penalized as a criminal offence against the buyer of surrogacy services, but not against the surrogate mother" (Dranoff 2001, p. 27). Although the federal government first introduced legislation on new reproductive technologies in 1996 that included a prohibition on commercial surrogacy contracts, there is still no law in Canada that prohibits or regulates surrogate motherhood.

INEQUALITY ISSUES Reproductive technologies also raise social class and other inequality issues (Rae 1994; Ragone 1994). Paid surrogates are typically women of relatively low income who hire out their wombs for needed money. The women or couples who hire them are typically wealthy (Rothman 1999). Might a busy, highly paid professional woman hire someone to carry her baby just because she herself doesn't want to? Critics have also pointed to the developing international surrogacy market in which mostly nonwhite, Third World women are encouraged to carry and deliver babies for mostly white, First World mothers (Raymond 1989). Despite all this, it seems possible that, with public and private deliberation, the potential for good in reproductive technologies—reducing involuntary infertility—can be retained without at least some of the negative effects prophesied.

Reproductive Technology: Making Personal Choices

Fertility treatment can be financially, physically, and emotionally complex. Those who are successful are euphoric: "Our son is so gorgeous!" marveled one mother (McCarthy, in Halpern 1989b, p. 151). (Reports of fraud and other professional violations in fertility centres [see, for example, Chartrand 1992; Cowley 1995] make it important to understand that an individual seeking treatment is a consumer and should interview the doctor and investigate the facility.)

Choosing to use reproductive technology depends on one's values and circumstances. For example, religious beliefs may influence decisions. The Catholic Church officially views AID as adultery and argues that reproduction should be kept within the marriage bed (McCormick 1992). The Jewish tradition requires physical union for adultery and hence does not define AID as adulterous. But Judaism does view masturbation as sinful; hence a man's obtaining sperm either to artificially inseminate his wife is morally problematic (Newman 1992). Meanwhile, Protestantism notes that the Bible sees infertility as cause for sorrow and exalts increasing human freedom beyond natural barriers (Meilander 1992).

Costs are also considerable. A couple can spend tens of thousands of dollars to have a high-tech baby (Begley 1995). Furthermore, the need for frequent physicians' visits can interfere with job attendance, and women undergoing infertility treatments report being discriminated against in the workplace (Shellenbarger 1992g).

Then too, infertility treatment can be physically daunting. Women report that artificial insemination can be "very uncomfortable." Other procedures are painful (Halpern 1989c, p. 149).

For some, then, infertility treatment can become the problem instead of the solution (Brant, Springen, and Rogers 1995). Coming to terms with infertility has been likened to the grief process in which initial denial is followed by anger, depression, and ultimate acceptance: "When I finally found out that I absolutely could not have children ... it was a tremendous relief. I could get on with my life" (Bouton 1987, p. 92). Some people gradually choose to define themselves as permanently and comfortably child-free. A second way to get on with life is through adoption. Indeed, some couples explore adoption options even as they continue infertility treatments (Williams, L. S., 1992).

ADOPTION

Once stigmatized, adoption is now more open and culturally supported (Fein 1998). It is estimated

that one in seven Canadians is directly affected by adoption (Welwood 2000). Box 11.3, "Deciding to Relinquish a Baby," explores this option from the birth mother's perspective.

Adoption in Canada falls under provincial jurisdiction and, as a result, adoption laws vary across Canada's provinces and territories.[14] However, certain commonalities do exist. For example, although Aboriginal "custom adoptions" may be recognized in law for various purposes, all Canadian jurisdictions require that adoptions be registered in court in order to register a change of legal parentage. An adoption order permanently alters a child's status and he or she becomes interchangeable with any biological children that his/her adoptive parents may have. For example, an adopted child is entitled to take the family surname, receive financial support and inherit from his/her parents.

Second, all jurisdictions maintain a similar purpose for their adoption regulations even though this purpose is most explicitly stated in British Columbia's Adoption Act. That is, "to provide for new and permanent family ties through adoption, giving paramount consideration in every respect to the child's best interests."

Third, while in the past, secrecy and "confidentiality unless interested parties consent otherwise" was the norm, all Canadian provinces now have some form of adoption disclosure registry and there has been a growing trend towards an assumption of "disclosure unless an interested party registers a veto" (Dranoff 1999; Dranoff 2001 p. 119). For example, in Saskatchewan, the law allows for the release of birth records for adoptions that took place after April 1, 1997; in British Columbia, this situation exists in relation to adoptions that occurred after November 4, 1996. In Nova Scotia, reunions are also facilitated unless such a reunion "would pose a risk to the health, safety or well-being of any person to whom the

14. For example, while some jurisdictions in Canada use a network of children's aid societies, others rely on a central government department. The result can be confusing. In Halifax, for example, adoption is the responsibility of a children's aid society. In Truro (a mere 90 kilometres away), the province does adoption. One may also consider that in Ontario, adoptions are split between 52 children's aid societies and a number of private agencies. As a result, adoption in Canada has been described by one writer as "a helter-skelter system with huge differences in service, depending on where you live" (*KW Record*, September 29, 2001: A6).

reunion relates." However, the most open disclosure policy exists in the Northwest Territories where, since 1998, the adoption registry must provide the names of the adoptee, birth parent(s), all other children, parents and grandparents of the adopting parents and natural parent(s). When the adoptee reaches the legal age of majority (set in NWT at 19), this information can be released, upon request, to any of the above-named persons. This movement to greater openness does, however, present some foreseeable difficulties. For example, a situation may arise where one biological parent does not consent to disclosure of information but the other biological parent does. It is possible, and perhaps likely, that in such situations, an adoptee could obtain the name of the nonconsenting parent from the consenting parent.

While advocacy groups of adoptees support open records, opposition to such developments has been voiced. For example, those who encourage adoption over abortion fear that pregnant women will choose the latter unless they are guaranteed confidentiality, and some adoptive parents find open records threatening.

More open adoption procedures, along with Internet services designed to help adoptees find their biological parents, have resulted in more and more **adoption reunions** (the meeting of birth parents, most often the mother, with the biological child) in recent years. Adoption reunions have various outcomes, some extremely positive and others very negative. They are also characterized by intense emotion (March 1997; Gladstone and Westhues 1998).

The Adoption Process

In Canada, an individual[15] or couple who wishes to adopt a child may pursue a number of different strategies including private relative or stepparent adoptions, adoption of a "Crown ward," that is, children already in the custody of a provincial child welfare agency, or private adoptions through licensed non-profit societies. Several Canadian provinces also permit "private" adoptions. The term "**private adoption**" is used to refer to any adoption that is not arranged by a public agency.

In both "private" and "**public**" **adoptions**, prospective parents typically undergo a home study,

15. All Canadian provinces now allow a single adult to adopt a child, subject to review by the court.

that is, an investigation by a provincial agency that results in an official report on the suitability of the adoptive parent(s). Private adoptions are reputed to involve a shorter waiting period, particularly for a healthy newborn, than do public adoptions. While adoptions through provincial child welfare departments are virtually free of cost, private adoptions "can run anywhere from about $6000 to about $12 000 (Canada Adopts! 2000).

Despite the expense involved in private adoption, Canadian research reports a dramatic increase in private adoptions and a similar decrease in public adoptions between 1981 and 1990 (Sobel and Daly 1992). However, reactions to these developments are mixed. On the one hand, private adoptions may offer the birth and adopting parents more personal control. However, because they can be expensive for an adopting couple, it may become progressively harder for lower-income parents to find children to adopt (Vanier Institute on the Family 1994). Moreover, private adoptions may render both the birth and adoptive parents more vulnerable to exploitation. The birth mother may feel manipulated into relinquishing her baby when she doesn't really want to, for example, even though Canadian laws generally require the "freely given consent" of the natural mother in all cases other than those involving children who are wards of the state. (The biological mother's consent is especially an issue in overseas adoptions because it is more difficult to be sure that the mother has willingly placed her child for adoption [Bogert 1994]).

In Canada, the number of domestic adoptions (i.e., of children born in Canada) peaked in the early 1970s and has sharply declined since. Reasons include the increased availability of abortion; the increased social acceptability of single parenting (which diminished the supply of available white newborns, the preferred choice of many prospective adoptive parents); the rise in infertility; and the rise in intercountry adoption (Welwood 2000). In the 1950s, intercountry adoption was rare. However, beginning with attention directed to Korea's wartime orphans by World Vision and further heightened by the media's coverage of the tragic conditions in Romania's post-Ceausescu orphanages, intercountry adoption increased in the 1990s.

"A reality of intercountry adoption is that the children are available because of some tragedy—war, famine, extreme poverty, racism or some combination of these" (Welwood 2000). In addition, China's "one-child policy" has resulted in thousands of Chinese babies, overwhelmingly female, who have been "abandoned by families who want to meet China's one-child-family policy with a son" (Dranoff 2001, p. 120). At present, the majority of children from other countries and adopted by Canadian parent(s) come from China, Russia, Romania, Vietnam, Haiti, Korea and Latin America (Welwood 2000).[16]

In response to the increase in international adoption, the Intercountry Adoption Act was designed to regulate the adoption of children, ensure that their best interests were served, and prevent the abduction, sale, or traffic in children. This Act was adopted by the Hague Convention on Private International Law. In Canada, this treaty, which currently has 30 signatories, came into effect on April 1, 1997. However only some provinces (e.g., British Columbia, Saskatchewan, Manitoba, New Brunswick and Prince Edward Island) have implemented it.

Intercountry or international adoptions are typically the most expensive to pursue with estimated costs ranging from about $15 000 (Haiti) to approximately $30 000 (Guatemala). In such cases, the prospective parent will face the administrative and legal costs as well as expenses incurred by home studies, translation, notarization and other legal fees, travel, accommodation, medical bills, facilitator fees and donations to orphanages. In addition, intercountry adoptions are generally the most complicated to pursue and involve confronting not only provincial adoption laws but, as well, federal immigration laws and laws surrounding adoption in the child's country of origin. Nevertheless, "[f]or non-traditional applicants such as older couples, gays, singles, couples with children, international adoptions have fewer constraints than other types of adoption" (Canada Adopts! 2000). They also, reportedly, involve shorter waiting periods for the adoption of infants or young children.

While some couples pursue international adoption, another option is to adopt difficult-to-place, or "special needs" children—those who are older, non-white, must come with siblings and/or are disabled.

16. Lorne Welwood (2000) observes that while "[o]ne might think that war-torn and poverty-stricken African countries would be on this list...Canada does not have adoption treaties with them."

Adoption of Minority Children

While the majority of those seeking to adopt are white and middle-class, "it is often easier to find non-white children....because non-whites in our society tend to be poorer than whites, and many non-white women, therefore, find it difficult to raise their children on their own" (Vanier Institute of the Family 1994). However, concern has been voiced about the desirability of trans-racial adoptions (Crook 1999). For example,

> Many activists and social workers with Aboriginal, black and other non-white groups feel that trans-racial adoptions lead to assimilation—the gradual erosion of the cultural identities of their communities. Others see trans-racial adoption as exploitation, "poor women supplying babies for middle-class women." Furthermore, many black and native leaders doubt that white parents can really share the pain and rage provoked by racism. They question whether such parents can provide the pride, appreciation of cultural heritage, culture and sense of identity that a child would gain from parents of the same race. (Vanier Institute of the Family 1994)

Some advocacy groups have charged that agencies do not feel pressed to find homes for minority children, and that prospective minority parents encounter biases in the placement system (Beck 1988b). Over the past two decades, efforts to recruit minority adoptive parents have been only somewhat successful. Such efforts not only require public relations programs but also must address problems that prospective minority adoptive parents often face: middle-class and racial bias, along with sometimes unreasonable eligibility standards and bureaucratic red tape (Kalmuss 1992). Meanwhile, many minority children will remain in foster care indefinitely if not adopted by whites (Simon 1993). The debate over transracial adoption persists, however, as growing numbers of white parents want to adopt and minority children wait in foster care (Hollingsworth 1998; "Foster Parents Fight ..." 1993).

Some transracially adopted children, now in their 20s, relate painful racial experiences. For example, one young woman never wanted to go out to dinner alone with her father because she feared that people might think that she was a prostitute (Nazario

Deciding to Relinquish a Baby

Young women who carry a pregnancy to term can either parent the child themselves, often with help from extended kin such as the baby's grandmother, or place the baby for adoption. Teenage parenting has raised concerns, and some professionals view adoption as the better alternative (Resnick 1984). This views holds that relinquishment enables young women to pursue the developmental tasks of adolescence and early adulthood unencumbered by parenthood. However, clinicians often argue that regret associated with relinquishment can be debilitating and can damage a birth mother psychologically (Watson 1986).

A theme of this text is that making decisions knowledgeably is preferable to making them by default. Although currently there are no national data from which to draw random samples of relinquishers and parenters, two studies help shed light on this subject. A pair of studies on the consequences of relinquishment versus parenting for 190 teenage birth mothers (78 relinquishers and 112 parenters) from one agency found that, after controlling for background variables, relinquishers did better on a variety of sociodemographic outcomes than did those who kept their babies. The two groups were similar on psychological outcomes. The majority in both categories were satisfied with their pregnancy resolution decision, but relinquishers were significantly less satisfied with their decision than were

parenters (McLaughlin, Manninen, and Winges 1988a, 1988b).

In another study (Kalmuss, Namerow, and Bauer 1992), researchers analyzed the short-term effects of relinquishing versus parenting in a sample of 527 unmarried pregnant women (311 of whom parented and 216 of whom placed their babies) ages 21 or younger. The women were interviewed before their baby's birth and again six months after delivery. At the second interview, relinquishers were significantly more likely to be enrolled in school and were more optimistic about achieving positive educational, financial, occupational, and marital outcomes by age 30.

In terms of comfort with the pregnancy resolution choice six months after delivery, relinquishers experienced more regret than parenters and were less likely to say they would make the same decision again. But 56 percent of relinquishers reported little or no regret about their decision, and 78 percent said they would make the same decision again. The researchers concluded that "our findings regarding comfort with the pregnancy resolution decision are not consistent with those from the clinical literature indicating that relinquishers experience a great deal of dissatisfaction with their decision to place the baby for adoption" (Kalmuss, Namerow, and Bauer 1992, p. 89).

1990b). But studies indicate that transracial adoptions are largely successful so far as outcomes to children are concerned. One longitudinal study (Simon and Alstein 1987) observed African-American children in white homes from 1971 and concluded that the children developed a positive sense of black identity and a knowledge of their history and culture. Similar research (McRoy, Grotevant, and Zurcher

1988) found transracially adopted children to have high self-esteem and confidence, although they did struggle with identity issues. Some researchers have suggested that rather than causing serious problems, transracial adoptions may produce individuals with heightened skills at bridging cultures. In the summary words of one researcher, "the message of our findings is that transracial adoption should not be excluded as a permanent placement when no appropriate permanent intraracial placement is available" (Simon 1990).

Adoption of Older Children and of Disabled Children

While some suggest that the trend towards increased intercountry adoption also attests to a shrinking supply of available children in Canada, there is certainly no shortage of children currently in government care in Canada who are available for adoption. Indeed, the Adoption Council of Canada reports that of the approximately 14 000 to 18 000 Canadian children who are currently in foster care and available for adoption, only about 1250 are adopted each year (Welwood 2000). Some are children who have been removed from the homes of abusive biological parents (Lacayo 1989b). Others are "difficult-to-place" children including those who are no longer infants, mixed-race children and children with disabilities or special needs.

Special-needs adoptions occur not only to couples who are infertile but also to those with altruistic motives. Gay men have adopted infants with HIV/AIDS, for example (Morrow 1992). In some cases, lesbian and gay male couples adopt such hard-to-place children because law or adoption agency policies denies or hampers their ability to adopt other children.

The majority of adoptions of older and disabled children work and relatively few end up as **disrupted adoptions** (the child is returned to the agency before the adoption is legally final) or **dissolved adoptions** (the child is returned after the adoption is final). But disruption and dissolution rates rise with the age of the child at the time of adoption: from 10 percent for children older than two to about 25 percent—and perhaps as high as 40 percent—for those between 12 and 17 (Barth and Berry 1988; Sachs 1990).

What causes these high failure rates? For one thing, more children available for adoption are emotionally disturbed or developmentally impaired due to drug- or alcohol-addicted biological parents or to physical abuse from biological or foster parents (Avery 1997). Furthermore, older children have undergone more previously broken attachments, as they have been moved from one foster home to another or through disrupted adoption attempts. Many of these children gradually develop **attachment disorder**, defensively shutting off the willingness or ability to make future attachments to anyone (Barth and Berry 1988). Observers have seen attachment disorder among recent Canadian adoptees from Romanian orphanages (Mainemer, Gilman, and Ames 1998).

Moreover, some parents who had hoped to adopt a healthy infant may be manipulated by agencies into accepting an older or disabled child instead, without being properly advised of potential problems. For example, prospective parents might be told that a child is mildly hyperactive when in truth the problems are much worse, ranging from showing virtually no emotion to destructive rampages—behaviours with which parents are unprepared to cope (Fishman 1992).

According to developmental psychologist Advid Brodzinsky, who has compared adopted with non-adopted children, adopted children often go through a process of emotional turmoil in middle adolescence as they grieve not having been wanted or raised by biological parents (in Fishman 1992). But for adopted children with attachment disorder, emotional and behavioural problems can be extremely difficult to deal with. One father describes the behaviour of his nine-year-old adopted son, Chris, a former victim of severe child abuse:

> [At first] he started making friends with other children in the neighborhood. We read with him faithfully every day and started a tradition of back rubs that he much enjoyed. And while he was still extremely guarded, there were glimpses of trust.... [But as time progressed,] Chris became more and more uncontrollable ... , and his play became both more agitated and more mechanical.... Discipline became less and less effective as he gradually pulled himself outside the orbit of the family.... Games that started innocently enough would escalate in agitation until someone got hurt "accidentally" ... Because of the great difference in age, we began to fear for the safety of our younger children.

> Throughout all this, we struggled to understand what made Chris tick and what was happening to our family. We modified our approach countless times (including home schooling for four months) in the hope of finding a strategy that worked. We searched, ultimately in vain, to find some nugget—an interest, a passion—on which to build a relationship and to foster his development. He seemed,

though, to be stuck at the emotional level of a three-year-old, and we were being drawn, much against our will, into round-the-clock vigilance to protect ourselves and the rest of our family.... (Hotovy 1991, p. 541)

Although Chris' adoption was not dissolved, he was placed in a psychiatric hospital with hopes that eventually he could return to his adoptive home. Adoption professionals point out that parents are willing to adopt all kinds of children, so long as they know what they are getting into and especially if the child's behaviour shows some improvement (Groze 1996).

Any adoption entails both responsibility and risk. To some extent, satisfaction with the decision to adopt is influenced by the attitudes about adoption in one's community and also by the availability of social services and other resources (Miall 1996). Prospective adoptive parents need to think carefully about what they can handle. Prospective parents who imagine themselves accepting the child as she or he is need to know, in as much detail as possible, what that really means in daily life. Agencies are attempting to gather more data, are asking biological mothers about drug usage, heavy drinking, and blood transfusions. Meanwhile, prospective adoptive parents have a responsibility to question case workers thoroughly about a child, perhaps consulting genetic counsellors for testing, information, and advice.

IN SUM

Today, individuals have more choice than ever about whether, when, and how many children to have. Although parenthood has become more of an option, there is no evidence of an embracement of childlessness. The majority of Canadians continue to value parenthood, believe that childbearing should accompany marriage, and feel social pressure to have children. Only a very small percentage view childlessness as an advantage, regard the decision not to have children as positive, believe that the ideal family is one without children, or expect to be childless by choice.

Nevertheless, it is likely that changing values concerning parenthood, the weakening of social norms prescribing marriage and parenthood, a wider range of alternatives for women, the desire to postpone marriage and childbearing, and the availability of modern contraceptives and legal abortion will eventually result in a higher proportion of Canadians remaining childless. Yet, at the same time, our changing society is allowing those who have formerly been denied the opportunity to parent, the chance to do so (see Box 11.4, "Gay Adoption Breaks New Ground").

Children can add a fulfilling and highly rewarding experience to people's lives, but they also impose complications and stresses, both financial and emotional. Couples today are faced with options other than the traditional family of two or more children: remaining childless, postponing parenthood until they are ready, and having only one child. Often, people's decisions concerning having a family are made by default.

For couples who have difficulty in conceiving, reproductive technologies offer both hope and anxiety. These technologies include artificial insemination, in vitro fertilization, embryo transfer, and use of a surrogate mother. There are many social and ethical issues surrounding these procedures. Adoption is a way of becoming a parent without conceiving; some families have both adopted and biological children.

Key Terms

abortion	opportunity costs
adoption reunions	paradoxical pregnancy
attachment disorder	private adoptions
crude birthrate	pronatalist bias
disrupted adoptions	public adoptions
dissolved adoptions	selective reduction
fecundity	structural antinatalism
fertility	subfecundity
involuntary infertility	total fertility rate

Gay Adoption Breaks New Ground

Jared Farrell-Smagata is crying, hot tears drenching his cherubic cheeks and an ear-splitting wail erupting through quivering lips. "Papa," the two year-old toddler sobs, reaching out for the comforting embrace of his father, Paul Farrell, from his safe perch in the burly arms of his father, David Smagata. "I took his potty away," shrugs Mr. Smagata sheepishly, clearly disappointed in his sudden status as the second-string parent.

These two men would be typical first-time parents anxiously treading across the uncharted ground of diapers, baby bottles and nap times were they not, as a gay couple, about as far from typical as any two parents in Canada could be. Partners for the past decade, Mr. Farrell, 35, and Mr. Smagata, 36, became the first same-sex couple to adopt a child jointly from the Children's Aid Society in Toronto—and one of the first to do so anywhere in Canada—when Jared crossed the doorstep of their Toronto house as a nine-month-old baby last year.

"There was a grieving process that I went through, and I know many gay men go through, that parenthood wasn't going to be a possibility," Mr. Farrell said. "We basically had to give up that dream. And to find out it could be realized again was quite exciting." While gays and lesbians have long adopted children as single people, the aftershocks from recent court rulings on gay rights are toppling family-law provisions across Canada that blocked homosexuals from adopting children as couples. At a time when same-sex partners in Canada are still denied the legal right to marry, gay and lesbian couples are winning the right to become parents through adoption in a growing number of provinces...."Marriage is the last frontier [for gays and lesbians]," said Laurie Pawlitza, a family lawyer who argued a groundbreaking Ontario case six years ago that allowed gays and lesbians to adopt their partners' children. "Adoption was second to last...."....

British Columbia was the first province to open the door to same-sex adoption, but others have followed suit, if reluctantly, after courts have forced their hands. A turning point was a landmark Supreme Court of Canada decision two years ago in the case of a lesbian suing her former partner for support after the break-up of their long-standing relationship that found an Ontario law limiting spousal support to opposite-sex couples was unconstitutional. Since that ruling, many provinces have passed omnibus bills rewriting a slew of laws to treat same-sex couples the same as opposite-sex spouses, although a few provinces deliberately left adoption provisions out of the mix.

In conservative Alberta where traditional family values reign, the law was changed after the Supreme Court ruling to allow same-sex partners to adopt jointly as heterosexual couples do. But a spokeswoman for the province's Ministry of Children's Services said the Klein government opposes same-sex adoption nonetheless, and the few cases on the books have involved a step-parent adopting their homosexual partner's child....In Manitoba, an omnibus bill introduced in May to rewrite legislation to reflect the rights for same-sex couples won in the Supreme Court decision sidestepped the province's adoption laws. After clamorous protests outside the legislature in the days that followed, the Justice Minister appointed a judge and lawyer....to study the issue of same-sex adoption and produce a report by the end of the year....

In Ontario, when Mr. Farrell and Mr. Smagata first knocked on the Children's Aid Society door nearly two years ago eager to adopt a boy or girl under two, the law allowed only same-sex adoption of step-children so the two men would have had to choose who would become their adopted child's father. But last year, just as Jared was sweeping into their lives, the law in

(continued)

(continued)

Ontario was changed to allow same-sex couples to adopt jointly. Both would become fathers to their son at the same time, as any other parents would. "It was a relief. A big relief," Mr. Smagata said. "It was nice to have both of our names on [the papers]."....

And now, the two men who told each other they wanted children on the day they met a decade ago are the proud fathers of a rambunctious....boy and they fret and fuss over their son and his stages of development....like all new parents. Mr. Farrell, who speaks only French to Jared, is "Papa." Mr. Smagata is "Daddy." Mr. Farrell [an elementary school teacher] picks Jared up from daycare during the school year, and is home with him over the summer holiday. Mr. Smagata often tucks him into bed.

Both marvel that, as rare as two fathers still may be, no one but a few aging relatives has raised the slightest objection to their unorthodox family...Mr. Farrell and Mr. Smagata can hardly wait to return to the CAS in the fall to start the process over again to adopt a second child. "A brother for Jared," Mr. Smagata says.

Source: Abridged from Philp, 2001: A3.

Study Questions

1. Discuss reasons why there aren't as many large families as there used to be. What accounts for the variation, do you think?

2. How is a pronatalist bias shown in our society? What effect does such a bias have on people who are trying to decide whether to have children? Are there antinatalist pressures in our society?

3. Discuss the advantages and disadvantages of having children. Which do you think are the strongest reasons for having children? Which do you think are the strongest reasons for not having children?

4. What do you see as the major differences among couples choosing to have children soon after marriage, those choosing to remain childless, those postponing parenthood, and those choosing to have only one child?

5. What can cause involuntary infertility? What might account for the recent attention to infertility?

6. What are some important issues surrounding abortion? Do the data on who obtains abortions and on public attitudes on abortion add anything important to the debate?

7. What are some important issues surrounding adoption? How do societywide issues influence personal decisions about adoption? Give examples.

8. How might infertility technologies affect adoption decisions? How might situations regarding adoption affect decisions about whether to begin or continue infertility treatments?

Suggested Readings

Ambert, Anne-Marie. 1997. *Parents, Children, and Adolescents: Interactive Relationships and Development in Context.* New York: Haworth Press. A comprehensive examination of parent–child issues written by one of Canada's most renowned family sociologists.

Benson, J. 1998. *Infertility and IVF: Facts and Feelings from Patients' Perspectives.* London: Scarlet Press. Women and couples' own stories of what it is like to go through in vitro fertilization (IVF) treatment.

Casey, Terri. *Pride and Joy: The Lives and Passions of Women Without Children*. 1998. Hillsboro, Or.: Beyond Words Pub. Collection of interviews with 25 purposefully child-free women who are happy with their decisions.

Nachman, Patricia Ann. 1997. *You and Your Only Child: The Joys, Myths, and Challenges of Raising an Only Child*. New York: Harper Collins. Readable discussion and some advice on parenting an only child.

Ragone, Helena. 1994. *Surrogate Motherhood: Conception in the Heart*. Oxford: Westview Press. An ethnographic study of surrogate mothers that investigates the political economy of surrogate motherhood.

On the Net

1) Final Report of the Royal Commission on New Reproductive Technologies
http://www.cma.ca/cmaj/vol-161/issue-11/1411.htm

2) Child and Family Canada
http://www.cfc-efc.ca

3) Health Canada - New Reproductive and Genetic Technologies
http://www.hc-sc.gc.ca/english/protection/biologics_genetics/reproduction/nrgt/index.htm

4) Adoption Council of Canada
http://www.adoption.ca/

5) Southern Manitoba First Nations Repatriation Program
http://www.wrcfs.org/repat/links.html

6) Technology's Babies
http://canadaonline.about.com/library/weekly/aa050801a.htm

Parents and Children Over the Life Course

IT'S DIFFICULT TO HAVE FAITH IN THE

MIRACLE OF GROWTH WHEN SO MUCH

IS AT STAKE.

EDA LE SHAN

For most of human history, adults raised children simply by living with them and thereby providing example and socialization to eventual adult roles. From a very early age children shared the everyday world of adults, working beside them, dressing like them, sleeping near them. The concept of childhood as different from adulthood did not emerge until about the seventeenth century (Ariès 1962). Children were increasingly assigned the role of student and were gradually drawn away or segregated from the adult world. Although children may continue to do household chores, especially in rural areas and among various race/ethnic minority or recent immigrant families, the move to school has been a move away from participation in the everyday lives of adults. One result is that today we regard children as people who need special training, guidance, and care.

But at the same time, our society does not offer parents or stepparents much psychological or social support. Our society is often indifferent to the needs of parents, including the economic support of families with children. The rate of child poverty now exceeds that of the nation as a whole. And, except for some renewed interest in the nation's schools, the mood of the country and politicians seems not to favour social programs for children (Hewlett and West 1998).

In this chapter we will discuss a limited range of parenting issues. We'll begin by looking at some difficulties of parenting. Next we'll examine the roles of mothers and fathers, and then we'll see that parenting takes place in social contexts that vary with regard to parents' marital status, social class, race/ethnic background, and sexual orientation. (The special concerns of divorced single parents are discussed in Chapter 14; those of stepfamilies are considered in Chapter 15). We will then look at parenting over the life course. We'll discuss some common parenting issues as we go along and consider how parents can make relationships with their children more satisfying.

PARENTS IN MODERN CANADA

Although raising children can be a joyful and fulfilling enterprise, parenting today takes place in a social context that can make child rearing an enormously difficult task. Today's parents face a myriad of questions and dilemmas that parents just a few decades ago would not have imagined: Does my baby need black-and-white toys to stimulate vision? How do I raise nurturing, supportive sons? Does it matter that my daughter loves Barbie? Can I trust my child's babysitter? Should I get a V-chip to limit my child's television access? How do I monitor my child's surfing the Net? Should I let my child walk to school? Should I believe the teacher or doctor who says my child is hyperactive and needs Ritalin? Should I home school my child? Should I allow toy guns in the house? Real ones? What if I find that my child is using marijuana? Or other illegal drugs?

We would not want to point out the difficulties of today's parents without first noting some advantages. Because health conditions are better, parents today are less likely to have to cope with serious childhood illnesses (Bianchi 1990). Parents now have higher levels of education and are likely to have had some exposure to formal knowledge about child development and child-rearing techniques. Many—although assuredly not all—fathers are more emotionally involved than earlier in the twentieth century (Gerson 1997). Many families are smaller, and parents' tasks may be lessened in this respect (Amato and Booth 1997).

Nevertheless, the family ecology theoretical perspective (Chapter 2) leads us to point to ways that the larger environment makes parenting especially difficult today. Here we list eight features of the social context of child rearing that can make modern parenting difficult:

1. In our society the parenting (or stepparenting) role typically conflicts with the working role, and employers place work demands first. Hours for fulltime work seldom coincide with hours when children are in school, so that an employed parent often leaves home in the morning before children leave for school and returns after the children do. Taking time off from work to nurse a sick child at home or keeping in touch by phone with children after school hours may lead to negative job evaluations (Ryan 1999).

The average employed person is now on the job an additional 163 hours a year more than she or he was two decades ago, or the equivalent of an extra month a year. Some executives and professionals find work obligations stretching to eighty or more hours weekly (Schor 1991). And more and more parents are taking second jobs to keep up with inflation. (Chapter 13 presents work–family conflicts in more detail.)

2. Parenting today requires learning attitudes and techniques that are different from those of the past. There is greater emphasis on using positive communication techniques, for example, with corporal punishment often criticized (Straus 1994). Moreover, today's parents are probably judged by higher standards than in the past. Having children's teeth straightened, for instance, or producing offspring who can succeed in university is often an expectation rather than an option.

3. Today's parents raise their children in a pluralistic society, characterized by diverse and conflicting values. Parents are only one of several influences on children. Others are schools, peers, television, movies, music, videos, books, the Internet, travel, and, yes, drug dealers. Even though parents want to pass their own values on, children may reject these for other, quite different ones. Not all parents have the same values, and many communities witness struggles over such things as sex education programs in schools, the books available to children in libraries, and the types of music sold in record stores.

4. The emphasis on the malleability of children tends to make parents feel anxious and guilty about their performance. Even as biologists claim to have found genes that influence a child's aggressiveness, risk-taking, or future addictions, (Wright 1998), psychologists have publicized the fact that parents influence their children's math, language abilities, behaviours, and self-esteem (Nash 1997; Brazelton 1997). Parents may lose confidence, believing that they will make mistakes that have dire consequences.

5. Child-rearing experts sometimes disagree among themselves (Family Science Network 1998). Over the years they have shifted their emphasis from one

child-rearing goal to another, from one best technique to another. Today there is debate among university-based child psychologists concerning disciplinary techniques; which is better: a timeout or reasoning with your child? And given that values shape ideas about what children should be like as young adults, or what parents might do to get them there, psychologists and parents may have conflicting perspectives. As one journalist has commented, "A new theory will change our attitudes about child rearing—we don't know what it is yet, but there always is one" (Adler 1998, p. 57).

6. Parents today are given full responsibility for raising successful or good children, but their authority is often put to question. The state may intervene in parental decisions about schooling, discipline and punishment, and medical care (LeMasters and DeFrain 1989).

7. The fact that people live longer today than in the past means that parents, especially mothers, are responsible not only for working outside the home and child care but also for the needs of aging parents. Middle-aged parents in this **sandwich generation** may find themselves especially pressed as role conflicts arise between parenting and elder care. Caring for aging parents is further addressed in Chapters 13 and 16.

8. Divergent family forms may cause parents special difficulties just because they are different from the idealized norm of the intact, nuclear family. Divorced parents and stepfamilies must cope with different rules at home as children go back and forth between homes or are now living with stepsiblings raised with different rules. There is likely to be lingering emotional distress to cope with (Wallerstein and Blakeslee 1989), and perhaps continued legal struggles as well. Gay male and lesbian parents face the questions of schools, neighbours, and their children's playmates, perhaps legal challenges, and the need to work out their position as child rearers with respect to sexuality and gender role issues (Arnup 1999; Findley 1997; Stacey 1999). And despite growing equality and similarity of the sexes in daily life, our society combines an ambivalent commitment to equality with a continuing sense that the mother's role and father's role are different (Kurz 1997).

MOTHERS AND FATHERS: IMAGES AND REALITY

If we look at men and women as parents, we find a range of ideas and practices.

Old and New Images of Parents

Our cultural tradition stipulates that mothers assume primary responsibility for child rearing. In Canada the mother is expected to be the child's primary psychological parent, assuming the major emotional responsibility for the safety and upbringing of her children (Tavris 1992). The "enduring image of motherhood" includes the ideas that, "A woman enjoys and intuitively knows what to do for her child; she cares for her child without ambivalence or awkwardness" (Thompson and Walker 1991, p. 91).

This traditional image of motherhood persists, even when mom is employed. A recently published children's book, titled *When Mama Comes Home Tonight*, tells it this way:

> When mama comes home from work tonight, she'll cover you with kisses, feed you soup and applesauce and dance you down the hall. [She'll] play a game, hold you at the window, help you count, make three wishes in your name and tell them to the stars. [She'll] put away the blocks...., fix herself a cup of tea and let you have a sip, mend your pajamas, mend her own pink slip, bathe you soft and gentle, brush your hair, read your favorite story.... (Spinelli 1998)

And what about fathers?

GOOD DAD—BAD DAD Fathers were once thought to be mainly providers or breadwinners, neither competent nor desirous of nurturing children on a day-to-day basis (Gerson 1997). Succeeding the breadwinner father of the industrial era, we now have the opposite images of the "good dad" and the "bad dad" (Furstenberg 1991)—the "new father" and the "deadbeat dad" as they are termed in the media.

On the one hand, "'New' fathers are intimately, actively involved with their children; they are responsible and care for their children day-by-day." According to this image, "Both 'new' parents can have it all, including a sense of fairness, respect, and cooperation with one another" (Thompson and Walker

1991, p. 91). However, "Another scenario focuses on ... the growth of 'male rebels' and 'deadbeat dads.' From this vantage point, a growing group of men are eschewing even minimal responsibility for their children (Gerson 1997, p. 119; Blankenhorn 1995). Offering "conflicting views of fathers in the wake of rapid social change in gender relationships and family patterns," these images can foster ambivalence among fathers and mothers alike (Gerson 1997, p. 120).

Moreover, race/ethnic stereotyping continues to give us an exaggerated, negative image of subsets of parents: black matriarchs, aloof or absent black fathers, macho, authoritarian Latino fathers (Gibbs 1993; Cose 1994b). But, because they are exaggerated, these

> images are myths: black couples share childrearing no less, and perhaps more, than white couples, and black husbands are as intimately involved with their children as white husbands, although it is more difficult for them to provide for and protect their children. (Thompson and Walker 1991, p. 91)

With an idea of our varied cultural images of fathers and mothers, we'll look briefly at what mothers and fathers actually do.

Mothers and Fathers: What Do They Do?

Mothers typically engage in more hands-on parenting and take full responsibility for children, whereas fathers are often viewed as helping (Hochschild 1989; Hyde and Texidor 1994). Mothers are more constantly present and available, while fathers come and go. In fact, fathers in married-couple families are not often alone with their children, and the mother serves as a sort of mediator of the parent–child relationship (Thompson and Walker 1991). A recent national survey found that the proportion of teens who report that they receive high levels of enjoyment from their mothers is higher than the proportion who say the same things for fathers (71 percent versus 62 percent, respectively) (Bibby 2001, p. 55). Sociologist Reginald Bibby, who conducted this survey, suggests that one reason for this may be "the limited time many fathers spend 'doing things' with their sons and daughters" (p. 55). (But see Case Study 12.1, "A Full-Time Father's Story," for an exception.)

From the child's point of view, fathers are "novel, unpredictable, physical, exciting [and] engaging." Not surprisingly, children prefer to play with fathers rather than mothers. Mothers' activities include "attentive love ... preserving life, fostering growth, and molding an acceptable person" (Thompson and Walker 1991, pp. 91–92). In fact, Thompson and Walker sum up their review of research on parent roles by terming fathers "playmates" and mothers "caregivers and comfort givers." Mothers view the intense daily contact with children ambivalently: as a source of great life satisfaction but also a source of a great deal of frustration and stress. More involved with their sons than daughters (Harris, Furstenberg, and Marmer 1998), fathers view their still-powerful breadwinning role as an important contribution to their children. As women have entered the labour force in greater numbers, men have been encouraged by their family's need and the redefinition of male roles (see Chapter 13) to want to play a larger part in the day-to-day care of the family (Aldous, Mulligan, and Bjarnason 1998; Hall 1994; Steinberg et al. 2000). They are very emotionally invested in their children, even when they are less active in parenting. They tend to compare themselves favourably to their own fathers (who were much less involved with children), even if they are not yet "new" fathers or 50–50 parents (Adler 1996b, p. 60; Daly 1994, 2000; Morrison 1998). As children grow older, fathers become more involved in instruction and discipline (Thompson and Walker 1991).

At the same time, more and more divorced or unwed fathers are distancing themselves from their children (Blankenhorn 1995)—are not seeing them and not supporting them:

> There are two sides to male liberation. As men have escaped from the excessive burdens of the good provider role, they have been freed to participate more fully in the family. They have also been freed from family responsibilities altogether. (Furstenberg 1992, p. 347)

One result is the recent push by some interest groups to reemphasize "responsible fathering" (Doherty, Kouneski, and Erickson 1998) and the provider role of fathers as valued and necessary (Chira 1994a). Meanwhile, some couples are truly sharing parenthood.

A Full-Time Father's Story

Bob is 31, comes from a working-class background, and has been married seven years. At the time of this interview, he had just gotten out of the military and was collecting unemployment benefits. His wife is a clerical worker. His future goal, he said, is to be a child psychologist. He has two children—Tim, six, and a daughter, Nicole, 18 months. His father deserted his family when Bob was a baby, and he feels he suffered greatly as a result. Here he describes what it's like for him to be a temporary househusband and full-time father.

Today I took a bunch of kids from my son's school to the zoo. Kindergartners. You know I like kids (laughs)....It was something hectic. The kids, they all want to run six different ways. They were climbing over the fences and through the fences to the elephants....

I think fathers should be more involved with their kids when it is possible. In fact, a couple of mothers commented [at the zoo] that they were happy to see a father along for a change. I never had a father....I'm determined that my son and I should have time together—which is tough when I'm working....[But for a while now] I've got the two kids. I fix them lunch and all that. You fix a can of soup, you give her half, you give him half. Hers you don't have any soup in it—just noodles and stuff because she eats with her fingers and you don't want any soup in there. And while they're eating I usually get dressed to take them out. And after they're done eating, I dress them.

I change her diaper and dress her and I dress my kid for school and take him to school. And while the kid's at school, we go somewhere like the park—me and my baby....There aren't too many dads in the park, I'll tell you. Most of them are out working. I get some strange looks once in a while, but it doesn't bother me. It really doesn't. Besides, if some fox comes by, I'll just tell her my wife and I were divorced and I got the kids, right? (laughs)....Then about two thirty, quarter to three, I drive over to the school from the park, and it's time for him to get out. Not the stereotype, you'd think, huh?

Sometimes it's a pain, you know. I can't get anything done. And there's a lot of things I could do, but it's really a chore to keep track of the baby. She's at the age now where she wants outside all the time, and it's really a hassle. I mean I'll bring her in the back door, and while you're locking the back door, she goes out the front. She's one door to the other, and she's out again. Yesterday our son came in, yelling, "She's out walking down the sidewalk!" She was having herself a good old time....

I would do it [though] anytime I was off work because, well, I look at the economical aspects. I can't afford to pay for child care when I'm at home. It's much, much cheaper for me to go ahead and do it myself, and it's not really that much of a hassle ... unless you've gotta go to the library or something like that. You can't drag them with you because—I took them to the library to get some books and I about went nuts chasing the little one around the shelves. She's really too young to understand "Now you stay there!" And she smiles and she's gone by the time you can turn around....

I'm going to keep doing this until my ....[benefits are] up or I find a job. I'm not saying I'm not looking for a job now, but I am saying that I'll probably keep doing this all the ....[eligible] weeks.... I love those kids to pieces. I can just sit there and just look at them, and just smile inwardly at what they do, you know. I don't know if it detracts from my image or anything....

In what ways might Bob and his wife's arrangement be better than day care, do you think? Not as good as day care? As a parent, what would you do differently from Bob? What do you like about Bob's style of fathering? Do you think Bob is a househusband and full-time father now only because of economics? What else might motivate him?

Sharing Parenthood

Diane Ehrensaft (1990) searched for "new" parents to learn more about them. She located, interviewed and observed 40 shared-parenting couples. She defined **shared parenting** not in terms of time, but rather as an identity. Her central question was, "Were both father and mother **primary parents**—a couple "mothering together"—rather than one parent and one helper?

In searching for couples who share parenthood, Ehrensaft encountered many near misses—couples who had decided to share but did not succeed at it. Those couples who chose shared parenting and were able to do it were not distinguished by the wife's work expectations or previous experience with shared housekeeping. Three factors affected both a father's dedication to everyday parenting and the mother's commitment, too.

First, many men and their wives were strongly influenced by the feminist movement or other 1960s ideologies that kept them going during the more difficult times: adapting to breast-feeding, for example, which imposes some difference between the parents. Second, many of the fathers were in occupations related to children, such as academic child psychology. Finally, both parents tended to have good job security, so that they could risk the displeasure of their supervisors in giving time to parenthood.

Nevertheless, there was a tendency to backslide as the husband's income outpaced the wife's. Finally, mothers, more than fathers, engaged in "worrying" (anticipating and coping with problems) and gave more attention to the "psychological management" of children. They seemed to identify more strongly with children and thus to devote more attention to the child's clothing, birthday parties, and other activities from which a father could distance himself. There was a tendency for mothers to "take over" in these areas.

More recent research (McBride and Rane 1998) shows that when fathers believe that their wives have confidence in them as parents, they are more likely to be highly involved. In Ehrensaft's study, fathers tended to have more psychological separation from children, whereas mothers had a communal relationship with them, a sense of shared identification. Men were "intimate" with children, seeking emotional closeness, whereas women's relationships with children could be

better described as "nurturing" and originating from their identification with a child's needs. Occasionally mothers felt squeezed out by an involved father, but by and large mothers felt that their parenting was enhanced. The couples felt that their relationship was strengthened by sharing such an important family activity.

However, Ehrensaft noted some potential strains of shared parenting. Couples had very little time alone. Ehrensaft speculated that this could represent avoidance of the marital relationship, leaving a vacuum that would be difficult to deal with at the empty nest stage of family life.

There were also some important socialization issues. Children tended to switch attachments, and often they were more attached to one parent than to another at any one time. Parents were left with a difficult choice between respecting the child's wishes or imposing their preference for equal parenting (Ehrensaft 1990).

The Parenting Alliance

Recently, researchers have turned their attention from either the separate parenting roles of men and women or the small group of role-sharing parents to the coparenting relationship more generally. Whether or not parents attempt to share parenting, whatever their division of labour is in the home, or whether or not they are married, the relationship between a mother and father affects their parenting. Even though this relationship is different from their relationship as a couple, the dynamics of their couple relationship spill over into parenting effectiveness.

Gable, Belsky, and Crnic (1992) examined the **parenting alliance** of parents of two-year-olds. Observing parents, they noted instances of parents' both supporting each other and undercutting the parental acts of the other, often without awareness. Parents can inadvertently or sometimes intentionally support and undermine one another. Moreover, "[M]arital and interparental relations both pre- and postdivorce, rather than the breakup of the family per se, may be more informative in accounting for children's behaviour problems and adjustment differences" (p. 286). We can expect that the interaction between mothers and fathers as they coparent children will be the subject of much future research.

We have been looking at some differences between mothers and fathers and how they work together as parents. But parents differ by more than gender, and the social context in which they parent is variable. Most obvious are differences in social class and race/ethnic background.

SOCIAL CLASS AND PARENTING

Virtually all life experiences are mediated or influenced by social class, and parenting is no exception (Garrett et al. 1994; Gerris, Dekovic, and Janssens 1997). You'll recall a theme of this text: Decisions are influenced by social conditions that limit or expand a decision maker's options. This section examines some ways in which the conditions of social class—of work, income, and education—affect a parent's decisions and options.

The Family in an Unpredictable Economy

The three decades after the end of World War II were a time of unprecedented economic prosperity and stability in Canada. Throughout the 1950s and 1960s, unemployment and inflation were low and a steady increase in personal incomes financed the growth of the social safety net, including universal health care, the Canadian Pension Plan, unemployment insurance, and inexpensive postsecondary education. By the 1970s however, "stagflation" had set in, with increases in both consumer prices and unemployment levels and a halt in the growth of real income. During this period, many Western countries, including Canada, were pushed into the steepest recession since the time of the Great Depression. Because of economic downturns, economic inequality—the gap between the haves and the have-nots—grew significantly. Since the 1970s, much has changed, beginning with the government's introduction of various tax measures and policy decisions, such as deregulation, privatization, free trade, and monetarism, which reflected a "corporate agenda." These measures have most obviously benefited corporations and those whom John Kenneth Galbraith has referred to as the "contented classes."

While the income gap between high- and low-income families was reduced during the recovery of

the 1980s, the improvement was insufficient to eradicate the inequality increases associated with the 1981–82 recession. Not only has income inequality in Canada been growing in the past decades, "it has been picking up speed" (Barlow and Campbell 1995, p. 76). While high-income families have reaped benefits from very high interest rates on their savings, tax breaks, lower income tax rates, and an increase in both the numbers of those employed within professional and managerial groups and the level of executive earnings, others have fared more poorly. Declines in family income and median real wages, rising unemployment, increases in part-time, temporary, and low-paying jobs, and the accelerated pace of social cuts (designed to make Canada's system of social security more "affordable" and to level the free-trade playing field) have had a huge impact on Canada's poor. Indeed, since 1994, the gap in *after-tax inequality* has also grown, with Statistics Canada reporting that low-income families have been unable to benefit from the latest advances in earnings to the same degree that they did during the economic recovery of the late 1980s (Townson 1998). The gap in after-tax incomes between the richest and poorest families increased after 1995, when the federal government made drastic cuts in social program spending. Cuts to public programs at both the federal and provincial levels have hit poorest families the hardest (Daub and Young 1999).

According to research conducted by the Toronto Centre for Social Justice, the average incomes of the top 10 percent of families with children in 1973 were 8.5 times those of the bottom 10 percent; by 1996, this ratio had increased to 10.2. Although the earned incomes of the wealthiest 10 percent of families rose from $122 000 in 1983 to $138 000 in 1996, the earned incomes of the poorest families with children remained largely unchanged during this time period (approximately $14 001) (Yalnizyan 1998).

Consider as well that over the past decade, a shortage of affordable housing has helped create a significant and visible number of homeless families. Homelessness is a growing problem in Canada. It is estimated that as many as 200 000 Canadians are homeless, including increasing numbers of mothers and children, Aboriginal people, adolescents, and people with mental illnesses (Health Canada 1999). In 1996, almost 26 000 people used Toronto hostels (about 3200 on any given night) with families with children and youths under 18 the fastest-growing groups of hostel users (*Toronto Star* 1999).

Not all homeless families are alike, of course (Glasser and Bridgman 1999). Some homeless parents experience more stress than others—and their children suffer accordingly (Danesco and Holden 1998). One study found that half of homeless women and children were fleeing from abuse ("Domestic Violence and Homelessness" 1998). For those who have been abused within the family home, "homelessness is a problem....but also a strategy for escaping violence" (Novac et al. 1996). Nevertheless, homeless parents, especially those who have been without housing for a longer period of time, have little in the way of a helpful social network (Letiecq, Anderson, and Koblinsky 1996). In any case, it is difficult to imagine raising children while living on the street. For example, carefully monitoring children's homework becomes an impossible expectation for a parent whose concern is finding the children's next meal or keeping them warm (Lindsey 1998).

Sociologist Miles Corak (1998, p. 6) observes:

Parents hope that their children will become successful and self-sufficient adults. But raising children is a complicated affair, and a child's fortune in life is determined not only by parenting strategies, but also by the support available in the community, the resources offered by the State, and sometimes just plain luck. That being said, a prime role in eventual labour market outcomes of children is often attributed to money.

Using income tax information reported by a cohort of approximately 285 000 young Canadian men and women aged 28 to 31 in 1994, Corak related the total market income of these young adults to the incomes of their fathers and mothers in 1982 (when his participants were 16 to 19 years of age and still living at home). Among his findings, he noted that the adult sons and daughters of very low-income fathers (i.e., those in the bottom 10 percent of income earners) "were more likely to follow their father's example than to improve their own position in the income distribution." Approximately 15 percent of adult sons and 14 percent of adult daughters remained in the bottom decile; 14 percent of sons and 11 percent of daughters moved up by only one

decile. Less than six percent of the sons and daughters of very low-income fathers managed to climb to the top 10 percent of the income ladder. Corak points out that, in contrast, over one in five of the adult sons and adult daughters born to fathers in the top 10 decile also occupied this income ranking and less than 7 percent "fell all the way to the bottom."

LOW INCOME AND PARENTING In 1968, Statistics Canada developed the low-income cutoff (LICO) as a measure of poverty. Estimating that poor families or individuals spent approximately 34.7 percent or more of their pre-tax income on such basic needs as food, shelter, and clothing, they then added 20 percentage points to determine the cutoff. In consequence, it was arbitrarily established as a standard that families or individuals who spent 54.7 percent of their pre-tax income on food, clothing, and shelter would be in financial difficulty. Recognizing that the minimum income level necessary to avoid financial hardship also varies according to changes in the cost of living, family size, and place of residence, Statistics Canada calculates different low-income cutoffs for different communities and for families of varying sizes within these communities. For example, in 1997, the low-income cutoff for a family of four living in an urban area with a population of half a million or more was $33 063. For a family of four living in a rural area, it was $22 877. In employing the LICO, "Statistics Canada does not claim to measure poverty; rather, it defines a set of income cutoffs below which people may be said to live in straitened circumstances" (Ross et al 1994). Nevertheless, the LICO provides a useful measure to examine patterns of low income within families within Canada.

FAMILY STRUCTURE AND LOW INCOME Poverty is much more prevalent among female-headed single-parent households than among other types of family structures. In 1995, 48 percent of lone-parent families headed by women fell below the low-income cutoff, compared with only 12 percent of husband-and-wife families, and 24 percent of male lone-parent families (Statistics Canada 1998b). The relationship between family structure and poverty helps to explain why women and children have higher poverty rates than men. "Almost two-thirds of the families headed by single-parent mothers live below the poverty line, and the poorest of all are families with young single-parent mothers" (National Council of Welfare 1999a, p. 89).

Although poverty is often seen as resulting from the rise of solo female-headed families, some have argued that low earnings for fathers continue to be a major determinant of childhood poverty, both because of their direct effect on family income and because of their indirect contribution to mother-only families (Hernandez 1997). In addition, "it is still an open question whether family structure is the cause or the victim of poverty. How many males disappear because they cannot support the children they have fathered? Are single-parent families poor because they are headed by a woman, or because the wage structure allows few mothers to earn their way out of poverty" (Levitan et al. 1998, p. 22).

For example, the National Council of Welfare has observed that, "For minimum-wage workers supporting dependent children, it is simply impossible to rise over the poverty line." They note that while the poverty line for a two-person family (for example, a mother and child) in a large Canadian city in 1998 was $22 452, a person working 40 hours a week for 52 weeks at Ontario's minimum hourly wage of $6.85 would only earn $14 248. Even when supplemented with the Canada Child Tax Benefit of $1625 for one child and a GST refund of $503, the family would only receive a total of $16 376. In British Columbia, a person working full-time in that year at the provincial minimum wage of $7.15 would earn $14 872; with the Canadian Child Tax Benefit, the GST refund, and the additional provincial family benefits available in that province, the family would only receive $17 937. In Newfoundland, an individual working full-time at the minimum wage of $5.25 would earn $10 920 a year. With the Child Tax Benefit and the GST refund, the family's annual income would be $13 048.

Despite a political landscape "littered with political rhetoric about children," Canada has had little success in reducing child poverty and almost one in five Canadian children under the age of 18 lives in a low-income family while almost one of every seven Canadian children under the age of 18 was on welfare as of March 1997 (National Council of Welfare 1999c) (see Figure 12.1).

RACE/ETHNICITY AND LOW INCOME   Based on the findings of the 1996 Canadian census, the incidence of low income is high among visible minorities in Canada and amongst its Aboriginal people (Figure 12.2). Canada's visible minorities population, of which the largest proportion were recent immigrants, had below average employment incomes and an incidence of low income that was significantly above average (36 percent versus 20 percent). In that year, almost half (45 percent) of the children under

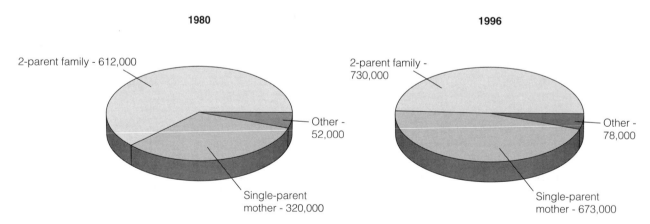

1980

2-parent family - 612,000

Other - 52,000

Single-parent mother - 320,000

1996

2-parent family - 730,000

Other - 78,000

Single-parent mother - 673,000

FIGURE   **12.1**

Number of poor children (under age 18) by family type, Canada, 1980 and 1996. (Source: National Council of Welfare, Poverty Profile 1996, Spring 1998: 79 [Using LICOs].)

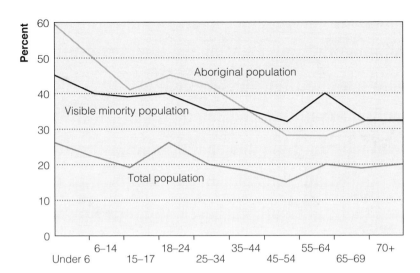

F I G U R E   **12.2**

Percentage of the Aboriginal population, visible minority and total population
with low incomes, by age group, Canada, 1995. (Source: Statistics Canada,
"1996 Census: Sources of Income, Earnings and Total Income and Family
Income," *The Daily*, May 12, 1998 (Statistics Canada, Cat. No. 11-001-XIE).)

the age of six in the visible minority population lived
in low-income families (compared with 26 percent of
all children). Among those who were 65 years of age
or older, the incidence of low income was 32 percent
(compared to a national average of 19 percent).

Excluding the Aboriginal population who lived on
reserves in the Yukon or Northwest Territories,
(where income is generally lower than that of the
Aboriginal population living off reserve), 44 percent
of the Aboriginal population in 1995 was below
Statistics Canada's low-income cutoffs. Among those
who identified themselves as North American
Indians, almost half (48 percent) were in a low-
income situation. Among the Métis (the second
largest group), almost four in 10 (39 percent) were in
a low-income situation. In that year, three out of five
Aboriginal children under the age of six lived in low-
income families. Among those aged six to 14, the
incidence of low income was 48 percent, or more
than twice the national rate of 22 percent (Statistics
Canada 1998b).

DISABILITY AND LOW INCOME   According to
data compiled by the Canadian Council on Social
Development (Fawcett 1999), disability is a strong
indicator of poverty (Figure 12.3). Both women and

men with disabilities are more likely to be sole
providers of family income than their counterparts
without disabilities. However, the situation is particularly bleak among women with disabilities because
they are more likely than other groups to live as lone
parents. In 1996, almost 1 in 10 (9.7 percent) differently-abled woman was a lone parent (compared with
7.6 percent of women without a disability, 2.8 percent of differently-abled men, and 1.1 percent of
men without a disability).

RAISING CHILDREN IN POVERTY   While the
majority of poor parents have homes and are
employed, raising children in poverty is qualitatively
different from doing so otherwise (Garbarino,
Kostelny, and Barry 1997). Items that other
Canadians take for granted (relatively safe neighbourhoods, air conditioning, dental work, music lessons)
are simply not available. Poverty-level parents and
their children have poorer nutrition and more illnesses
such as asthma, which has been associated with household cockroaches, for example (Cowley and
Underwood 1997). Moreover, while the United
Nations' World Health Organization recommends
exclusive breastfeeding of infants for the first six
months of life, babies born to poor mothers are more

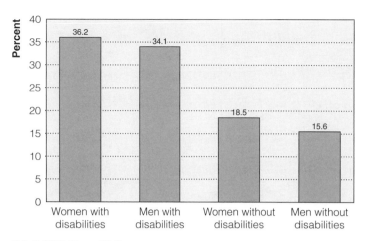

FIGURE **12.3**

Poverty rates for working-age women and men with and without disabilities, Canada, 1995. (Source: Prepared by the Canadian Council on Social Development using data from Statistics Canada's 1996 Census.)

likely to be denied this important start to life. Research has shown that breastfeeding significantly reduces infections, the likelihood of Sudden Infant Death Syndrome (SIDS) and allergies. It also enhances cognitive development and the maintenance of acceptable growth rates (Health Canada 1999). However, poor mothers often fail to breastfeed their babies because of a lack of adequate information and personal supports. A rushed return to work (required, in some provinces, as a condition of welfare), may also force some mothers to wean their babies prematurely (National Council of Welfare 1999b, p. 11).

The ability to parent is also affected by poverty (Canning and Strong 1998). Canada's National Longitudinal Survey of Children and Youth reports that the capacity of parents to care for children and their children's developmental outcomes are better at each step up the income ladder. Low social support, family dysfunction, and parental depression, all of which have significant negative effects on children, are all more common in low-income households. According to this study, 18 percent of children living in low-income households (versus eight percent of children in middle-income households and seven percent of children in higher-income families) lived with parents who had many symptoms of depression (National Council of Welfare 1999c).

Childhood poverty is related to school failure (Fields and Smith 1998), negative involvement with parents (Harris and Marmer 1996), stunted growth, reduced cognitive abilities, limited emotional development (Brooks-Gunn and Duncan 1997; Mayer 1997), and a higher likelihood of dropping out of school (Duncan et al. 1998). The National Longitudinal Survey of Children and Youth found that one quarter of children aged four and five from low-income households (less than $30 000 a year) scored poorly on verbal tests that indicate readiness to learn. In contrast, only 15.6 percent of those children from middle-income households and 9.2 percent of higher-income children scored poorly on these tests. This survey also reported that 14.6 percent of low-income children were in households that were ranked as "dysfunctional." Only 7.5 percent of children in middle-income homes and five percent of children in high-income homes were similarly identified. Similarly, while approximately 15 percent of those in the lowest of four income groups had problems with aggression, depression, anxiety, or hyperactivity, only nine percent of those who were not in the poorest group suffered behavioural problems. Finally, about seven percent of those who were in the poorest groups had failed a grade. Among those who were not in the poorest group, only two percent had failed a grade (Fine 1999b). In various ways, "Economic insecurity, underemployment, and joblessness, on top of years of defeats and dashed hopes, have proven devastating to poor families" (Sugrue 1999, p. 245).

At the same time, a Canadian study, which compared the childrearing practices of the rich and the poor found that "good parenting has a more profound effect on children than [do] poverty or affluence" and that no socio-economic group "has a monopoly on strong childrearing skills—or questionable ones" (Fine 1999a, p. A4). According to researcher Douglas Willms, director of the University of New Brunswick's Atlantic Centre for Policy Research:

> "For too long we've characterized poor families and single-parent families as the source of behaviour problems and low academic achievement....It's really not the case. What really matters is parenting practices: how they parent, how much they've engaged with their children, how responsive they are, how much they monitor behaviour, and so on." (quoted in Fine 1999)

Blue-Collar Parents

Blue-collar, or working-class, families usually take their designation from the husband-father (or stepfather) who is employed in blue-collar work such as manufacturing or construction, for example. However, our economy has increasingly become a service economy over the past few decades, with less need for unskilled labour. "In 1997, for example, 473 000 Canadians worked in construction—139 000 fewer than in 1989—and there were about 1.8 million workers in manufacturing—230 000 fewer than in 1989" (Statistics Canada 1998, p. 377). Blue-collar parents have declined both in number and in resources. Layoffs have become a major concern, along with wage rollbacks and loss of benefits (Rubin 1999, p. 280).

Unlike in the past, today's blue-collar children may not have access to their parents' occupations. Many will move into white-collar jobs; others will take relatively low-paying service jobs. Hence blue-collar parents face problems associated with guiding children into occupational and educational worlds (university, for example, with the unfamiliar language of majors, minors, and credit hours) that they have neither experienced nor fully understand. LeMasters and DeFrain

see blue-collar parents as an emerging minority group: "When all of the social leaders are white collar, when the mass-media idols are white collar, how does a blue-collar father or mother portray his or her way of life as something for a child to emulate or admire?" (1989, p. 108).

Blue-collar parents (and lower middle-class parents)[1] are more likely than upper middle-class parents to be strict disciplinarians, expecting conformity, obedience, neatness, and good manners from their children (Kohn 1977; Luster, Rhoades, and Haas 1989). Middle-class parents, in contrast, tend to emphasize a child's happiness, creativity, ambition, achievement, and independence. They are less restrictive and more "affectionate and responsive" (Belsky 1991, p. 122). But employed wives of blue-collar husbands often have white-collar office or service jobs. Hence, they are exposed to middle-class values. This can make for what LeMasters and DeFrain call a "value stretch" between blue-collar men and their mates: Husbands may value a more restrictive parenting style than do their wives.

Lower Middle-Class Parents

The lower middle-class includes grocery checkers, retail clerks and other lower-level salespeople, small-business owners and managers, secretaries, receptionists and word processors, government clerks, post office workers, and the like. They earn moderate wages. Because employers are cutting back, workers at this level have fewer benefits than in the past and little job security.

Even in two-paycheque marriages, lower middle-class parents often face time and money problems (Rubin 1999). Single mothers in this social class may be working at full-time and part-time jobs in order to meet everyday expenses. LeMasters and DeFrain (1989) suggest that problems for these parents are

1. The line between blue-collar and lower levels of white-collar employment (lower middle-class) blurred in the post-World War II era of rising blue-collar incomes. Also blue-collar men (factory workers, for example), frequently marry lower middle-class women (secretaries, for example). Child development advice literature became widely dispersed across classes through the popular media during this period. Despite a convergence of knowledge about child rearing between white-collar and blue-collar parents, the economically insecure position of blue-collar and lower middle-class parents and their differences in education still leave a gap in parenting values and behaviour between these strata and the upper middle-class.

worsened by their aspiring to an upper middle-class standard of living.

Besides being ambitious for themselves, lower middle-class parents are typically ambitious for their children, encouraging them to go to university even though they themselves usually are not university graduates. This means that their children may eventually adopt different values and behaviours—from how to spend leisure time to political or religious values—and this can create strain between a family's generations.

Upper Middle-Class Parents

Upper middle-class parents do not have considerable family wealth but earn high salaries as corporate executives and professionals: physicians or attorneys, for example. Other professionals, such as professors, accountants, engineers, architects, and psychotherapists, may not earn quite so much money but have a comfortable income that supports an upper middle-class lifestyle.[2] These parents and stepparents have more options than do those in lower social classes. They can choose the neighbourhood in which they want to live and rear their children. They can afford to send their offspring to university and sometimes to private schools. On a different level (but one that points up the myriad of daily-life advantages), upper middle-class parents can hire household help or purchase cars for their adolescent children so that sharing cars is unnecessary.

In general, upper middle-class parents have the material and educational resources to prepare their children for occupational success. Despite this, however, they cannot positively ensure that each child will eventually enjoy a position in the upper middle class. An executive's child will more than likely have to finish university and maybe even attain a higher degree in order to match the parent's occupational status. A concern of parents in the upper middle class, then, is that their adult children not have to move down in social class. Related to this is the problem of how to teach a child raised in affluence to

---

2. The "minor professionals"—teachers, nurses and allied health professionals, social workers and human services personnel, technical specialists, and middle managers—tend to identify with the upper middle-class, although some would classify them as lower middle-class. Perhaps a middle middle-class designation would be most appropriate.

live in less luxurious conditions should she or he be unable to afford luxury in adulthood (LeMasters and DeFrain 1989).

Upper-Class Parents

Upper-class parents not only have disproportionately high shares of wealth and income, but often their families have been established as wealthy for several generations and possess significant power and influence. Wives of the elite class do not usually work outside the home, although they may commit large amounts of time to social activities and volunteer work.

Social scientists have relatively little access to the upper class. Consequently, relatively little is known about them for certain. We do know that their unique challenge is motivating children who are guaranteed a comfortable living no matter what—and whose accomplishments will likely never surpass those of their forebears (Bedard 1992; Rashid 1994; Stanley and Danko 1996).

This section has described various parenting issues that are peculiar to the different social classes, regardless of ethnicity. The next section addresses race/ethnic diversity with regard to parenting issues.

RACE/ETHNIC DIVERSITY AND PARENTING

In the last few decades social scientists began to research ways that various ethnic groups in the United States and in Canada evidence culturally specific parenting styles. One early study, for example, comparing English-speaking and French-speaking Montrealers reported that English-speaking parents were more likely to be traditional and authoritarian in their parenting styles (Taylor et al., 1978). More recently, a study of authoritarian parenting found that Egyptian Canadian men and women scored higher on authoritarianism than Anglo-Canadian men and women (Rudy and Grusec 2001). In addition, a large body of research has focused on the multiple challenges experienced by immigrant and refugee ethnic minority parents and their children (Aycan and Kanungo 1999; Basran 1993; Hyman, Vu and Beiser 2000; Jaurequi 1995; Kulig 1998; Lee and Chen 2000; Ming-Sum 1997; Noivo 1993; Prilleltensky 1993; Salaff et al. 1999; Short and Johnston 1997; Wakil 1994). For example, sociologist Effie

Gavakris' research on Greek immigrant families has suggested how immigrants who cannot communicate with the mainstream population around them may rely on children to act as their "social interpreters," creating a dependency of parent upon child that effectively "redefines the role of the child" (in Alvarez 1995, 2).

Other researchers have focused attention on gender role socialization in various south Asian immigrant families in Canada. Aziz Talbani and Parveen Hasanali (2000) report that even though South Asians tend to integrate secular European cultural elements with their culture, both family structure and community remain male-dominated. Their interviewees (22 adolescent girls aged 15–17 years of age of Indian, Pakistani, and Bangladeshi origin living in Toronto) felt that their parents and communities had more stringent rules for female socialization than any other community in Canada and maintained rigid gender roles through gender segregation, control over the girls' social activities and arranged marriages. They also perceived that a high social cost was attached to protest or dissent. A second study, which used a combination of methods—oral history, interview, survey and participation methods—to examine parent–child interaction patterns in Pakistani-Canadian immigrant families found a difference in the type of interaction and adjustments between immigrant parents and those of their children who had been born and socialized in their country of origin and those who had born since their arrival in Canada. This research reports a substantial schism between immigrant parents and their Canadian-born children in their respective worldviews and their assessment of each others' "attitudes, wishes, intentions and behaviour" (Wakil 1994).

"Astronaut phenomenon" arrangements upon parenting in Hong Kong Chinese families have also been the focus of research. The "**astronaut phenomenon**" is a term used to describe a situation in which one spouse, typically the husband, leaves the family in the country of immigration and returns to Hong Kong to work, with periodic visits with his/her spouse and children. The other spouse remains in Canada and assumes the responsibility for parenting and housework without emotional or physical support from their spouse or other family members (Man 1994; 1995; 1997). Like analyses of the impact of father

absence on Japanese civilian *tanshinfunin* families, in which fathers are required by their work to live away from their families for prolonged periods of time, and research on military families (Harrison and Laliberte 1993), research on the astronaut phenomenon highlights the importance of viewing family life and work as overlapping domains (Hiew 1992).

Social scientists have additionally addressed the need for ethnocultural sensitivity in the delivery of parenting education and early education services to Canadian families (Bernhard et al. 1999; Short and Johnston 1994) and suggested how cultural beliefs can impact on the experience of parenting. For example, in an attempt to develop community-based services for children with disabilities in a Chinese community in Canada, Philip Cook and his colleagues found that Chinese families with a differently-abled child experience a double barrier of disability and culture. Negative attitudes towards children with a disability, they suggest, are grounded in cultural beliefs regarding a child's capacity to contribute to the family, a widespread use of traditional healers in conjunction with a family doctor or hospital, a lack of knowledge about available community supports, and language barriers (Cook et al 1997; see also Ryder, Bean and Dion 2000). We can expect more studies like these in the future.

Although minority parents resemble other parents in their social class, the impact of race or ethnicity remains important. Parents of colour face additional challenges. The status of middle-class black parents does not suffice to protect them from intermittent demeaning or suspicious behaviour on the part of whites, and such incidents may occur in front of children or be directed at them (McClain 1992). Even so simple a matter as buying toys becomes problematic. Black dolls only? Should the child choose? What if the choice is a white Barbie doll?

However, the problems experienced by ethnic/racial minority parents are not mere "child's play." For example, the status of Canada's Native peoples reflects the strains of centuries of cultural "domination, control and exploitation" (Nelson and Fleras 1998, p. 240). Native people suffer the lowest levels of education, income, health, and employment in Canada. Social conditions on many Native reserves, the lands set aside for the exclusive use of status Indians (i.e., those whose names appear on the Indian

Register maintained by the Department of Indian and Northern Affairs pursuant to the *Indian Act*) reflect the historical and political neglect that Canada has shown towards its indigenous peoples. On many reserves, housing fails to meet the most basic structural standards. Less than half of on-reserve homes have sewer or water hook-ups and half can best be described as overcrowded (Frideres 1993). Although the federal budget of February 1999 committed $190 million over three years to new home-care programs and more extensive health monitoring in Aboriginal communities, the infant mortality rate among natives remains 1.7 times the national average. Native men on reserves die, on average, seven years sooner than other Canadians, and the life expectancy for Native women remains six years lower than the national norm (Health Canada 1999). It has been estimated that the suicide rate among the Aboriginal population averages two to seven times that of the Canadian population as a whole (Health Canada 1999).

The rate of accidental death and injury among Aboriginal children is four times that of the non-Aboriginal population; death rates from causes such as birth defects, low birthweight, fetal alcohol syndrome, and respiratory illnesses are consistently and significantly higher among Aboriginal infants and children (Harris et al 1998). Between 1986 and 1990, the suicide rate among Aboriginal children aged 10 to 11 was more than five times the rate found among non-Aboriginal children (National Forum on Health, n.d). Indigenous peoples also experience a heightened risk of violent death that increases from south to north and from east to west, and elevated rates of injury, poisoning, and suicide. In British Columbia, the suicide rate on reserves is twice that found among off-reserve Indians. Among First Nations and Inuit males, the rates of violent death are especially high (Canadian Centre for Substance Abuse 1999).

Indigenous peoples also experience high rates of illicit drug use, with First Nation and Métis youth more likely than non-indigenous youth to use all types of drugs, including solvents (Gfellner 1994). It is estimated that the risk of developing an alcohol problem among First Nations and Métis youths is two to six times greater than that of other Canadians (Scott 1997). The prevalence of daily smoking occurs at about twice the rate found the general Canadian populations (Stephens 1994) and a national survey reported that 76 percent of Inuit women and 54 percent of Indian women smoked during pregnancy (Canadian Centre for Substance Abuse 1999). According to Michael Resnick, Aboriginal "youths have a familiarity and intimacy with death and loss within the family comparable to few other young people in our society" ("Young Indians" 1992, p. D-24).

Parents and Biracial Children

Chapter 7 explores homogamy versus heterogamy in marriage. Here we point out only that raising biracial or multiracial children has challenges peculiar to it, although not without rewards as well. One challenge is that there can be tension between parents—and between parents and children—over cultural values and attitudes. "Black parents may teach their biracial children to grow up to be Black and proud, but society teaches that to be Black is to be an inferior person ... Yet a white parent may have trouble instilling 'white cultural pride' in the child." As one wife put it, "I have nothing against teaching him Black pride, but I am a white person.... In this racist society I'm not even permitted to feel good about being white and teach my child that it's okay that he has a part of whiteness in him as well" (Luke 1994, p. 58, citing Ladner 1984).

> Such contradictory identity positions that parents in fact embody, illustrate the conflicts and paradoxes may interracial parents face. Hence, the complexity of parenting in these contexts is a profoundly different emotional, cultural, and political experience for either parent, particularly when the family includes biracial and monoracial children. (Luke 1994, p. 58)

While few resources exist for understanding the unique challenges that face biracial youth and their families, researchers Stephanie Milan and Margaret Keiley (2000) used data from the U.S. National Longitudinal Survey of Adolescent Health, in which 6058 adolescents were interviewed to compare functioning in biracial youth (n=272) to white adolescents (n=3521) and monoracial minority adolescents (n=1941). Their results suggest that biracial/biethnic youth are a particularly vulnerable group in terms of self-reported delinquency, school problems, internalizing symptoms, and self regard and that, as a group, they are more likely to receive some form of psychological intervention.

For other intermarried parents, the challenge may be about what religion the children will be raised in or how to teach the children one's native tongue.

Religious Minority Parents and Children

Ethnicity is often associated with religious belief. Chinese-Canadians may be Buddhists, for example, and Asian Indian-Canadians, Hindu or Sikh. In a dominant Christian culture, diverse ethno-religious affiliations affect parenting for many Canadians. The Christmas season may be difficult to explain to Jewish or Muslim children, who believe that Jesus was a prophet but not a saviour. For instance, there is a strong tradition in Islam, known as *hadith*, that frowns on singing other than to recite the required Muslim daily prayers; at Christmas time, Muslim children may be invited—at school or in their neighbourhoods—to join in Christmas (or winter) carols (Connell 1993).

Meanwhile, Muslims have their own holy holidays, such as Ramadan, which other Canadians may be unaware of or fail to acknowledge as meaningful. Then too, traditional Muslims, particularly women, dress differently than do the majority of Canadians. Wearing flowing robes and, more often, headscarves, Muslims say they fear ridicule or face discrimination from employers and others (Witt and Roberts 1997; Waugh, McIrvin Abu-Laban, and Qureshi, 1991). Drawing on his survey of 152 Canadian Muslim families, Ahmad Yousif argues that of all the social-psychological challenges that confront Muslims living in a predominantly non-Muslim nation, the most serious is the negative stereotypes of Muslim people and rituals and the discrimination, based on these stereotypes, that follows (Yousif 1994).

Parents of minority religions hope that their children will remain true to their religious heritage, even amid a majority culture that seldom understands (Winston 1998).[3] One solution has been the emer-

gence of religious—and non-Christian—summer camps for children of Jewish, Buddhist, Muslim, Hindu, Sikh, and Zoroastrian parents (Lieblich 1998).

Raising Minority Children in a Racist and Discriminatory Society

For minority parents who are poor, discrimination compounds the circumstances of poverty. However, whatever its social class, the minority family—whether Aboriginal, black, Asian, or multiracial—must serve as an insulating environment, shielding members as much as possible from racial slurs and injustices. Raising children in a white-dominated society creates situations that white families never encounter, regardless of their social class. For example, a parent of a child of colour must decide whether to warn the youngster who is going off to school for the first time about the possibility of classmates' racial slurs (Ambert 1994). As a result, minority parents are acutely concerned about the need to develop high self-esteem in their children, along with pride in their cultural heritage. Some minority parents decide not to discuss racism or discrimination with their children; they do not want them to become unnecessarily bitter or resentful. Instead, these parents prepare to help their offspring cope with racism when it arises (Moore 1993; White 1993). Other minority parents believe it is important to teach their youngsters the history of discrimination against them.

Even parents within the same race/ethnic group do not necessarily agree on the best approach to racial/ethnic issues. About one-third of African-American parents do not attempt any explicit racial socialization. Others differ as to whether they emphasize forewarning or take a more militant position toward the elimination of social inequality (Taylor et al. 1991). Novelist Alex Baldwin, for example, advocates telling children early that blacks "were brought here as a source of cheap labour" and that racism has been "a deliberate policy hammered into place in order to make money from black flesh" (1988, p. 7). Baldwin would assure black youth that the "agonies by which they are surrounded" are "criminal" (p. 11). Some parents in other ethnic minorities would agree.

However, the conservative black author, Shelby Steele, argues that the oppression of slavery "has left us with a dangerously powerful memory of itself that

---

3. The desire that their children maintain their ethno-religious heritage is a principal reason for some immigrant parents' preference that their children marry homogamously, sometimes in arranged marriages (see Chapter 7).

In mosques across Canada Muslims gather for daily prayers at morning, noon, and night. Muslim parents hope that their children will remain true to their religious tradition. Like parents of other minority religions in Canada, meanwhile, they must help their children face fear of ridicule and actual discrimination.

can pull us into warlike defensiveness at a time when there is more opportunity for development than ever before" (1990, p. 327). Putting all this together, we might conclude that,

> In the socialization of children there is some tension between teaching an unclouded knowledge of racism's realities and communicating a sense of personal strength and capability. Black children should be taught that there are major barriers, but they also need to be taught that they can be overcome—a difficult balancing act for parents. (Feagin and Sikes 1994, p. 314)

A dilemma faced by all minority parents is to address the balance between loyalty to one's subculture and individual advancement in the dominant society (See Case Study 12.2, "Parenting Dilemmas in a New Country."). For example, among many Aboriginal families, the wounds inflicted by residential schools and other assimilationist strategies remain raw and painful (Morrissette 1994; Swift 1999). As only one example, those in Native schools who dared to speak their own language were routinely punished by having a sewing needle pushed through their tongue in a practice known as the "needle torture." Eli Taylor, a Dakota-Sioux from Manitoba, has remarked:

> "Our native language embodies a value system about how we ought to live and relate to each other....[I]f you destroy our language, you not only break down these relationships, but you also destroy other aspects of our Indian way of life and culture, especially those that describe man's connection with nature, the Great Spirit, the order of things. Without our language, we will cease to exit as a separate people." (As quoted in Elliott and Fleras 1992, p. 151).

It is reported that, "[d]espite the efforts of Canadian Aboriginal people to maintain their languages, these languages are among the most endangered in the world. Only three of the approximately fifty Aboriginal languages in Canada are in a healthy state; many have already disappeared or are near extinction" (Kendall et al. 2000, p. 75). Concern about the loss of their native Chipewyan language and recognition that the loss of a common language can weaken family bonds led to the creation of the Dene Yatu project in the community of Lutsel'Ke in the Northwest Territories. This program involved extended families and activities such as hunting, fishing, and camping, with the Dene Culture Institute and local school assisting in providing resources and evaluation. According to Joan Barnaby, Executive Director of the Dene Cultural Institute, the children involved not only improved in their proficiency in Dene and spoke more Dene at home, but family members "felt closer to one another and stronger in their culture" (in Kendell et al. 2000, pp. 76–77).

In other ethnic/racial families as well, the dialect or language spoken at home is neither used nor respected in the larger society. Reporting on findings of the 1996 Canadian Census, Jacques Henripin notes that many Canadians, but particularly those whose mother tongue is neither English nor French, have adopted a home language that is different from their mother tongue.

> English has gained at the expense of the French and of the "other" mother tongues....Among adults with "other" mother tongues, 60 percent generally speak a language other than their mother tongue at home. Of adults whose mother tongue is English and who were born in Canada, only one percent do not generally speak English at home, while six percent of those whose mother tongue is French do not generally use their French at home. The long-term ability of the "other" languages to survive thus appears to be weak. (Henripin 1998, p. 1295)

Prior to the passage of Bill 101 *(Charte de la langue francaise* [1977]), which established French as the official language of Quebec and its courts (as well as the normal language of the workplace, of instruction, communications and commerce), about two-thirds of immigrants to that province who choose to learn one of Canada's two official languages selected English. As a result of Bill 101 however, "less than half of those who have come after 1980 have chosen English" (Henripin 1998, p. 1285).

Although only 17 percent of the Canadian population can speak both of Canada's official languages, succeeding in the larger society may be perceived as dependent on learning English and/or French and, in the process, forsaking the language of one's ancestors. Exceptions to this do, of course, exist. Based on the 1996 Census, three languages (Chinese, Italian, and German) were spoken by over 400 000 in each group while seven other languages (Spanish, Portugese, Polish, Punjabi, Ukrainian, Arabic, and Tagalog [Filipino]) were spoken by groups of between 150 000 and 228 000 (Henripin 1998).

Valuing one's cultural heritage while simultaneously being required to deny or "rise above" it in order to advance poses problems both for minority individuals and between minority parents and their children.

Besides social class and race/ethnicity, parents vary in marital status and in sexual orientation. We consider never-married single parenthood in Chapter 11, divorced single parents in Chapter 14, and remarried parents in Chapter 15. Here we look at gay male and lesbian parents.

GAY MALE AND LESBIAN PARENTS

Observing an American study which suggests that there are "between three and eight million gay and lesbian parents in the United States, raising between six and 14 million children," sociologist Katherine Arnup (1995, p. vii) suggests that the proportions in Canada may be equally high. While there are no definitive statistics available as yet, some suggest that a little more than 444 000 families in our country have gay or lesbian parents (Nelson and Robinson 1999, p. 129). The 2001 Canadian census addresses same-sex relationships and explicitly recognizes children being raised in same-sex households, even where the laws of a province or territory do not allow same-sex couples to formally adopt or share guardianship of their children. However, spokespersons for EGALE (Equality for Gays and Lesbians Everywhere), caution that findings of this census will may well underestimate the gay and lesbian parents in Canada. "Many same-sex couples are cautious about providing their personal information to the government. It was only about three decades ago that homosexuality was a criminal offence, and it was not that long ago (1960s–1970s) that the federal government maintained lists of suspected homosexuals in order to fire us from our jobs! As a result, EGALE expects significant under-reporting, this first time that the question is asked" (EGALE Press Release, May 10, 2001).

Gay men and lesbians can become parents in several different ways. A substantial number of gays (about 20 percent) and lesbians (about 33 percent) have been married, and some have children from those marriages (Harry 1983). Lesbian and gay parents of children from previous, heterosexual marriages often face custody issues. While "[n]othing in Canadian law stops a homosexual parent from applying for custody, the courts will often take judicial notice (that is, recognize that it could easily be proven) of the fact that some harm might arise from living with a homosexual parent" (Yogis et al. 1996, p. 56). In consequence, Canadian case law suggests that custody is more likely to be awarded to "discreet, non-militant homosexual parents who do not flaunt their sexual orientation" (p. 56).

To date, gay men have been less likely than heterosexual fathers to be awarded sole or joint custody unless uncontested, and visiting rights have been an

A closer look at family diversity: Parenting Dilemmas in a New Country

The following essay is written by Shashi Assanand, the Executive Director of the Vancouver & Lower Mainland Multicultural Family Support Services Society. Her essay offers advice to parents who, like herself, have emigrated from a traditional culture with values that sometimes clash with the Canadian way of life. In 1974, Assanand and her husband immigrated to Canada with their two young children, having left Uganda as refugees two years earlier. (The original, unabridged version of this article appears on The Vanier Institute of the Family Web site at http://www.vifamily.ca/tm/283/6.htm).

Immigration to Canada presents one of the most difficult challenges to parenting. How can we be effective parents when our survival needs are so demanding, family roles are continuously changing, and the extended family support we are used to is no longer there?

Often in my work with families I have asked parents why they chose to come to Canada. The usual answer is "to have a brighter future for our children." A brighter future means a better education and, as a result, a financially successful and productive life. However, many people who choose to build their family's future in Canada do not consider the effect that a different culture will have on their children's lives....

Children brought up in Canada are exposed to Western values from a very early age. Throughout their school years they learn values such as independence, individuality and making decisions for themselves—values that directly clash with those practised by South Asian people (people from the sub-continent of India). In the South Asian culture, individualism can threaten the existence of the extended family. Since children learn Western values at school (where they spend the better part of their time), expecting them not to be affected by these values is a bit like throwing them into the ocean and expecting them not to get wet.

The complexity of value clashes increases during adolescence, a time of many physical and emotional changes....Besides the usual challenges of adolescence, the teenage daughter or son of immigrant parents has to negotiate a balance between the value systems of two distinctly different cultures. On one side they have parents who expect them to maintain their traditional cultural values, and on the other side there is tremendous peer pressure to conform to Canadian/Western culture....A breakdown in communication often compounds the conflict. The parent's language of communication may be Punjabi, Hindi or one of the many South Asian language while the child's primary language is English or French. Not only do the two generations communicate differently, they even *think* in different languages. The communication necessary for a good relationship has to be at both the mental and verbal levels. If a parent and a teenager think and speak in different languages, how can they communicate in a meaningful way? When communication is poor between the generations of an immigrant family, the children cannot gain a proper understanding of their parents' culture and values. In India, even if there is a lack of communication within a family, the whole environment is constantly teaching youngsters the concepts of South Asian culture.

In Canada, teenagers strive for their own identity. To achieve this they must separate from the parents' identities to which they are attached. This is difficult to do alone, so attachment to peers becomes important. In this country it is normal for teenagers to prefer being with their friends rather than their families, but parents may see this as a rejection of themselves and their culture. They may also fear that their children will acquire bad habits from peers. Parents in these situations sometimes exercise undue control. Adolescents in a rebellious stage of life seldom take this well, and may perceive parental control as a lack of understanding and love on the part of their parents. Pressure from parents to maintain family honour—the "What will people say?" mentality—is likewise not something youngsters can easily comprehend. In the South Asian social system, teenagers do not need to go through a process of separating from their parents' identities because their family *is* their identity. Society recognizes them by the family they belong to, so conflicts with their families are perhaps less common than in North America.

South Asian adolescents living in Canada go through the same stages of separation and individuation as the other teenagers around them. But, because their peers do not understand their family and social systems, it is important for our children to understand who they are in the context of their Canadian identity. If parents do not understand this natural process that their children are going through, it is bound to create a serious crisis. In order to establish their own identity, children may reject their parents' culture. Because of the lack of good communication with their parents, they may miss out on learning in-depth the values of our culture. Similarly, they may lack in-depth understanding of Western culture because they have not been brought up with the norms of this culture.

Many of us come from an environment where the relationship between parents and children is one of ownership. Children must obey, they are to be seen but not heard. Parents make decisions regarding their children's education, friends and marriages. Given that Canadian society teaches children values such as independence and individuality, how can they understand and accept an ownership relationship? When values clash and conflicts occur, teenagers often feel powerless and victimized. They lack a sense of belonging to either culture, and their education—which we hoped

would give them a brighter future—inevitably suffers. They long to break free of tradition, but at the same time they fear losing their family support. Feeling trapped, they may get involved with the wrong people, run away from home, or even attempt suicide....

What can we do? It is very important that children learn their heritage language, but it is an absolute necessity that we, their parents, learn a Canadian language—the language our children are most comfortable with. We need to keep our minds open to the new culture our children are exposed to so that we can understand what they are going through. If we prejudge this culture we may slam shut the door of communication with our children.

Parenting courses are offered in most communities in Canada. Participating in a parents' group—where parents share common concerns and learn from each other's experiences—is also helpful. To resolve conflicts, seeking outside help as a family can make a difference. Your local family services agency is a good place to begin a search for help. If the agency doesn't provide the specific service you're looking for, they can probably tell you who does.

As parents, we need to find creative solutions to the difficult problem of helping our children make the most of their two very different worlds.

How does this essay illustrate the particular challenges facing by parents who are recent immigrants? What other examples or challenges can you think of that might apply here?

issue as well (Knox 1998). Lesbian or bisexual women may also be denied custody of their children on the sole basis of their sexual orientation, despite the fact that research shows that children of lesbian mothers are just as likely to be well-adjusted as those of heterosexual mothers (Patterson 1997; Tasker and Golombok 1997.

Gays and lesbians have also sought parenthood as adoptive parents and as birth parents, as one lesbian partner gives birth to a baby they both parent (Arnup

1999). Artificial insemination by donor (AID), "is largely credited for the 'lesbian baby boom'" since the mid 1970s (Taylor 1997, p. 85). This baby boom includes not only lesbian coparents but an array of combinations of lesbian mothers and biological fathers, surrogate mothers and gay biological fathers (less frequent). In some cases, one lesbian partner is inseminated with the sperm of a male relative of the other partner, genetically linking the baby to both female parents (Salholz 1990).[4] A Family Studies professor describes the diversity apparent in her own lesbian family as follows:

> My partner and I live with our two sons. Our older son was conceived in my former heterosexual marriage. At first, our blended family consisted of a lesbian couple and a child from one partner's previous marriage. After several years, our circumstances changed. My brother's life partner became the donor and father to our second son, who is my partner's biological child. My partner and I draw a boundary around our lesbian-headed family in which we share a household consisting of two moms and two sons, but our extended family consists of additional kin groups. For example, my former husband and his wife have an infant son, who is my biological son's second brother. All four sets of grandparents and extended kin related to our sons' biological parents are involved in all our lives to varying degrees. These kin comprise a diversity of heterosexual and gay identities as well as long-term married, ever-single, and divorced individuals. (Allen 1997, p. 213)

A national Angus Reid Group/CTV/*Globe and Mail* telephone survey of 1500 Canadian adults conducted in May 1999 reports that Canadians are split on the issue of whether or not homosexual couples should be allowed to adopt children. Respondents were asked the question: "And, what do you think about the general issue of homosexual couples—either male or female—who want to adopt kids that are not the biological children of the partners in the relationship? In your opinion, assuming they meet the standards and requirements, should homosexual couples be legally allowed to adopt children?" In response, 47 percent of respondents said "yes," and 50 percent, "no." Support for homosexuals being able to adopt non-biological children was highest in Quebec, British Columbia, and Ontario. Acceptance of homosexual couples adopting children was also inversely related to age and more likely among women than men. Individuals who were university-educated and who reported voting for the Bloc Quebecois or New Democratic Party were the most likely to voice support of homosexuals being allowed to legally adopt children (Angus Reid Group, Inc., June 9, 1999).

Research finds children of gay male and lesbian parents to be well-adjusted, with no noticeable differences from children of heterosexual parents (Patterson 1992; Flaks et al. 1995; Allen 1997). Nor are they more likely to be gay as adults. They may, however, encounter challenges from peers and others. A child's need to blend in may clash with a political parent's desire for activism on gay rights issues. In addition, books depicting same-sex families may be excluded from the school curriculum.

For example, in December 1998, in a landmark case, a Canadian court was asked to rule for the first time on whether a school board could exclude from the curriculum books that depict same-sex families. Controversy arose when the Surrey, B.C. school board, banned three books. In the first, *Asha's Mum*, one of the story's characters told a classmate that it is not wrong to have two mothers "if they're nice to you and you like them." In the second, *One Dad, Two Dads, Brown Dads, Blue Dads*, the dedication read, "To Jacob who has only one mom and one dad" and, in small letters, "But don't feel sorry for him—They are both pretty great parents." The third, *Belinda's Bouquet*, was described as the "most neutral [of the

4. Science may also hold further breakthroughs for gay couples. For example, in September 2000, newspaper headlines reported that gay male couples may, in the near future, be able to sire "motherless" children through cell nuclear replacement, a technique originally seen as a way to treat infertility and metabolic disorders. "Under 'cell nuclear replacement,' scientists replace the nucleus from the egg of a female donor with the nucleus from a sperm cell. The resulting 'male egg,' containing only male DNA, is then fertilized in vitro by sperm from another man" (Honore 2000). Reactions to the prospect of an all-male embryo, which would have DNA solely from its two fathers, and then be implanted in the womb of a surrogate mother who would carry the child to term, were mixed. A spokesperson for Outrage, a gay activist group, called the news "an answer to the prayers of gay couples who want to have children." Others were "appalled by the notion of two men procreating without a woman," a reaction that, for some, was based in homophobia and/or in worries that biotechnologies were "spinning out of control" (Honore 2000).

three books] in its depiction of gays and lesbians" (Joyce 1998). None of the three books explicitly defined the relationship that existed between the two parental figures, nor did the words "gay," "lesbian," "homosexual," or "sex" appear within them. While the school board did not object to housing the books within school libraries, they did ban them from classroom settings. In response, two homosexual teachers, supported by a group of parents, appealed the decision of the school board.

In her 44-page judgment that overturned the ban, Madam Justice Saunders of the B.C. Supreme Court ruled that the boards must reconsider the books it banned kindergarten and grade one students from reading and wrote that her decision was based "upon a very old provision of the *School Act* prohibiting religion or overt religious interference in the conduct of schools." The Act says, in part, that "all schools and provincial schools must be constructed on strictly secular and non-sectarian principles." The decision of Madam Justice Saunders found that the school board had given "significant weight" to "personal and parental concerns that the books would conflict with religious views, contrary to the Act." Paul Ramsey, at the time Minister of Education in B.C., said that the court's decision "sends a very positive signal to those in Surrey and throughout the province who want schools to be inclusive and tolerant places for all our children" (EGALE 1998). However, it would be inaccurate to assume that schools across Canada are always inclusive environments for children from same-sex families.

Concerning parenthood for gays and lesbians, eminent pediatrician T. Berry Brazelton contends that "if the parents really love a child and think about the child's issues rather than their own, there is no reason to shy away from it" (Gross 1991d, p. A-12). There are growing numbers of workshops for lesbians considering parenthood, for lesbians ready to get pregnant, for gays and lesbians who want to parent together, and for new gay parents. There are also discussion groups on rearing children and choosing child care, and there are play groups and organized events for children of gay parents.

What parents of all social contexts have in common is the joy and complexity of parenting, as children progress through various stages of development. We turn next to these stages of parenting.

STAGES OF PARENTING

People are accustomed to thinking of childhood as a developmental process. The early milestones of learning to walk, talk, and think abstractly, for example, are widely recognized. The developmental perspective also applies to adults, and it clearly applies to the parenting role, which is characterized by different tasks and needs at different stages.

Transition to Parenthood

Becoming a parent can be difficult, often more difficult than the parents had anticipated. New fathers and mothers report being bothered by the baby's interruption of such activities as sleeping, going places, and sexual expression. New mothers are distressed about their personal appearance, the additional amount of work required of them, and the need to change plans for their own lives and futures.

Thirty years ago, in what has become a classic analysis that still applies, social scientist Alice Rossi (1968) analyzed the transition to parenthood, comparing the parent role with other adult roles, such as worker or spouse. The transition to parenthood, Rossi asserts, is more difficult than the transition to either of these other roles for several reasons:

1. Cultural pressure encourages adults to become parents even though they may not really want to. But once a baby is born, especially to married couples, there is little possibility of undoing the commitment to parenthood.

2. Most mothers and fathers approach parenting with little or no previous experience in child care. Fantasy often takes the place of realistic training for future parents. Romanticizing leads to disillusionment and often to an emotionally painful cycle of anger, depression, and guilt.

3. Unlike other adult roles, the transition to parenting is abrupt, whether one is tackling it alone or as part of a couple. New parents suddenly are on 24-hour duty, caring for a fragile, mysterious, and utterly dependent infant.

4. Adjusting to parenthood necessitates changes in the couple's relationship. Husbands can expect to receive less attention from their wives. Employed wives who have established fairly egalitarian relationships with

their husbands may find themselves in a different role, particularly if they quit working to become full-time homemakers (see Chapter 11). The transition can be extra difficult when a spouse's expectations for couple involvement in parenting are not fulfilled (Kalmuss, Davidson, and Cushman 1992).

5. Today's parents do not have clear guidelines about what constitutes good parenting. What—exactly—should parents do to guide their children toward adult competency? The proliferation of experts in child rearing can lead parents to believe they could not possibly be competent.

Contemporary research supports the continued validity of Rossi's analysis (Wallace and Gotlib 1990), although investigators are also finding that subgroups of parents with better or poorer adjustment can be identified (Belsky and Rovine 1990; Cowan and Cowan 1992; Levy-Shiff 1994). But a point not mentioned by Rossi (because it was not so true in the 1960s) is that more of today's parents will be caring for fragile infants. Smaller and smaller infants are surviving, thanks to modern technology. But they remain in the hospital in intensive care for some time after birth, may need special care, are likely to suffer some disability, and do not fit easily into a family routine (Rosenthal 1991). Then too, mothers are sent home from the hospital much sooner after delivery than in the past (Begley 1995), and this may make the transition to parenthood more difficult.

Parents with Babies

It is often difficult for new parents to acquire a sense of perspective because their experience is so new and there is little for them to compare it to. It helps to know that babies are different from one another even at birth; the fact that one baby cries a lot does not necessarily mean that he or she is receiving the wrong kind of care. Through the **interactive perspective**, parents can realize that their own ideas and attitudes are affected by the infant's appearance and behaviour, and vice versa.

It is clear the home environment—for example, poverty status, parents' self-esteem and intelligence, and stress levels—affect an infant's irritability (Luster, Boger, and Hannan 1993). Nevertheless, from birth infants have different "readabilities"—that is, varying

clarity in the messages or cues they give to tell caregivers how they feel or what they want (Bell 1974). They also have different temperaments at birth: Some are "easy," responding positively to new foods, people, and situations and transmitting consistent cues (such as tired cry or hungry cry). Other infants are more "difficult." They have irregular habits of sleeping, eating, and elimination, which sometimes extend into childhood; they may adapt slowly to new situations and stimuli; and they may seem to cry endlessly, for no apparent reason. Still other babies, of course, are neither easy nor particularly difficult.

Generally, an "easy" baby contributes to the caregiver's conviction that she or he is a good parent, whereas "difficult" babies may cause the parents to blame themselves. A parent's relationship with a diffi-

From birth, children have different temperaments; some are "easy" while others are more difficult.

cult child may lack many of the expected rewards of parenthood. These parents may be tempted to treat the growing baby as a problem child or to respond by oversheltering the child, two reactions that may cause the child to internalize the sense that he or she is different. Instead, they need to strike a balance between the child's needs for security and predictability and their own needs. These parents may also need more time away from their child than do parents of easier children (Thomas, Chess, and Birch 1968).

All infants have certain needs. Although not all social scientists are in complete agreement (Eyer 1992), there is considerable evidence that infants need to bond, or attach, to one consistent and dependable caregiver to establish the basic human trust that is a prelude to normal development and a protection against psychological harm (Ainsworth 1973; Karen 1994). Like anyone else, they need positive, affectionate, intimate relationships with others in order to develop feelings of self-esteem. They need encouragement, conversation, and variety in their environment in order to develop emotionally and intellectually (Begley 1996; Coutu, Provost and Pelletier 1996). Discipline is never appropriate for babies.

Parents with Preschoolers

Preschool children continue to have many of the same needs they had as infants (Nash 1997). They need opportunities to practise motor development. They also need wide exposure to language, especially when people talk directly to them. And they need to experience consistency in the standards they are trying to learn. (Many parents today worry about whether the standards they set are too harsh or too lenient, but the content of the standards is less important than the consistency.)

During the preschool years, parents and stepparents will establish a parenting style. Psychologist Diana Baumrind (1971, 1978) distinguishes between authoritarian, laissez-faire, and authoritative parenting. **Authoritarian parenting** places all authority to set standards and rules in the parent's hands. The opposite is **laissez-faire parenting**, which is over permissive (Ginott 1965) and allows children to set their own limits with little or no parental guidance. The style preferred by child psychologists is **authoritative**, which means accepting the child's personality, talents, and perhaps goals, while also consciously setting and enforcing rules and limits.

Both parent and child need clear definitions of what behaviour is unacceptable (Dinkmeyer, McKay, and Dinkmeyer 1997). Limits are best set as house rules and stated objectively in third-person terms. A parent can say, for example, "Chairs are for sitting in, not for jumping on." With preschoolers, limits need to be set and stated very clearly: A parent who says "Don't go too far from home" leaves "too far" to the child's interpretation. "Don't go out of the yard at all" is a wiser rule. As the child learns to distinguish what is "too much," limits can be more flexible. Some child psychologists suggest that punishment (time-outs, withholding privileges, slapping hands, spanking) enhances the effectiveness of reasoning with toddlers (Larzelere et al. 1998). (The issue whether spanking is *ever* appropriate is addressed later in this chapter.)

Parents of School-Age Children

School-age children need to be encouraged to accomplish goals appropriate to their abilities. Schools expect parents' cooperation and support in the form of helping the child acquire good study habits, showing interest in his or her work and progress, and assisting with schoolwork (Balli, Demo, and Wedman 1998)—though parents should not do the homework or complete the projects (Dinkmeyer, McKay, and Dinkmeyer 1997). The extracurricular activities of school-age children also demand a significant amount of support and time from parents who are already overloaded.

Children today face demands for achievement from schools, church and recreational organizations, peers, and, of course, parents. This can produce the "hurried child" who is forced to assume too many challenges and responsibilities too soon (Elkind 1988). Hurried children may achieve in adult ways at a young age, but they also acquire the stress induced by the pressure to achieve (Shaw 1997). Or they may "drop out" and abandon goal-directed academic and extracurricular activity. Parents can help not only by checking on whether they have realistic expectations for their children but also by moderating any unreasonable outside demands on the children.

Children also need to feel they are contributing family members. Those who are not given responsibility for their share of household chores may have trouble feeling they belong, or they may become demanding because they have learned to belong as consumers rather than as productive family members (Dinkmeyer, McKay and Dinkmeyer 1997).

Children need to be assigned tasks and taught how to do them. One of the pluses of single-parent families as child-rearing institutions is that children's help is usually genuinely needed if the family is to function successfully.

A further need of school-age children is for increasing recognition of their individuality and emerging autonomy. Like adults, children need some privacy. They can be assigned a spot in the house that is theirs and no one else's, or they can regularly be given some time alone when parents agree not to interrupt them. As growing individuals, children also need to practise making their own decisions. For example, the parent may offer the child a choice between wearing alternative pants or shirts.

Children also need to learn how to get along with others. One particular area of conflict is between siblings. Parents should recognize the inevitability of sibling rivalry and make an effort not to overrespond either by punishing competitiveness or by creating an artificially equal environment (taking one child out for lunch, for instance, because the other has been invited to a birthday party). Children should be encouraged to work out disputes by themselves whenever possible (Felson and Russo 1988). Often, in fact, the dispute loses its momentum when no parents are there to listen.

Having said this, we need to emphasize that physical violence should be kept in check by parents. Research on family violence (Straus, Gelles, and Steinmetz 1980) indicates that violence between siblings, particularly boys, and some of it quite serious, is the most pervasive form of family violence. Parents should provide children with an environment in which nonviolent methods of solving conflicts are learned (Gelles and Straus 1988).

Rather than spankings, or hitting children, time-outs, when all interaction stops for a few minutes, can help. Moreover, unlike spankings, timeouts do not show a child that hitting is an acceptable way to resolve conflict.

The question of care or supervision of school-age children of working parents is addressed in Chapter 13.

Parents of Adolescents

Adolescence is the time when children search for identity—who they are and will be as adults (Collins 1990; Steinberg 1990). While the majority of teenagers do not cause or undergo familial "storm and stress" (Larson and Ham 1993), the teen years do have the special potential for being a time of conflict between parent and child, for in this stage both are involved in periods of transition. Both are experiencing biological shifts: The child is undergoing the physical and hormonal changes accompanying puberty; the parent, those of midlife. From a social-psychological viewpoint, the child is getting ready to move into the adult world, and the parent is increasingly aware of what he or she has yet to accomplish in life. A result may be an increased level of parent–child conflict as they struggle to accommodate the very different needs of each (Hatfield 1985).

Another complicating factor is that our society offers no clear guidelines or prescriptions for relinquishing parental authority: The exact time when authority should be relinquished, or how much, is not culturally specified.[5]

Any struggle between parent (or stepparent) and adolescent over when and how parental authority should be rescinded characteristically involves values. Because our society increasingly requires an adult to display a distinctly personal set of values, adolescents may feel the need to reject their parents' values, at least intellectually and for the time being, to gain adult status.

Research shows that teens and parents conflict more often over everyday matters, such as chores, than over bigger issues like sex and drugs (Barber 1994; Bibby 2001) (See Table 12.1).

Meanwhile, collisions with adolescents over values are especially difficult to negotiate because they usually are not conflicts over specific behaviours.

5. When to relinquish authority is, however, linked to certain economic factors. Upper middle-class families can afford to defer their children's financial independence, paying for some or all of their university education. Working-class parents, however, are experiencing a financial crunch (called the "life cycle crunch" by Valerie Oppenheimer 1974) just at this time. Because blue-collar income typically decreases during late adulthood, children are pushed to earn their own living. It also appears that stepfamilies launch children earlier than intact married-couple families; the exit of an older adolescent may be a way of resolving family conflicts (White and Booth 1985b; Goldscheider and Goldscheider 1989).

TABLE 12.1
Areas of Conflict with Parents

Disagreements "Very Often" or "Fairly Often" Involve...

	Nationally	Males	Females
Jobs around the house	58%	56	60
School	55	61	49
Their reaction to the way you talk to them	52	49	54
Concern about safety (e.g., driving, violence)	49	52	46
Your questioning their authority	44	45	43
The time you come in at night	40	39	40
Money	39	41	37
Concern that you stay out of trouble	36	40	32
Your choice of friends	25	25	25
Concern about drinking	23	26	20
Who you are dating	21	17	25
Concern about drugs	20	24	16
Your appearance (e.g., clothes, hair)	20	20	20
Concern about sex	18	19	17

Source: Bibby 2001, p.64.

Teenagers wonder why they should change what they believe when it does not actually do the parent any harm. If parents insist on having their own way, the adolescent does the same. Parent and child thereby may engage in a power struggle in which the adolescent feels honour-bound to do just the opposite of what the parent demands. Many decisions—whether homework will get finished, what school the youngster will attend, what career choices are available, what the consequences of experimentation with alcohol, other drugs, and premarital sex will be—do of course have far-reaching implications for the young person. These may be viewed by parents as intolerable risks, but by the children as valid choices to make for themselves.

Sociologist Reginald Bibby, reporting on his recent national study of Canadian youth, notes, "today's youth do not generally question the need for discipline. In fact, 56 percent agree with the statement 'Discipline in most homes today is not strict enough.'" According to his research, both teenage males and females believe that the three most appropriate and effective ways for parents to discipline teenagers are to: give them a good talking to; take away privileges; and have a discussion without discipline (Bibby 2001, p. 66) (See Table 12.2).

Parents with Young Adult Children

Parenting does not end when a child reaches 18, 21, or even 25 or older; children benefit from parents' emotional support and encouragement through their 20s and after. Parents typically have had more experience with solving problems and handling complex emotions

TABLE   12.2

How Parents Should Respond to Their Teenagers When They Feel Teens Have Done Something Wrong

	Nationally	Males	Females
Give them "a good talking to"	29%	29	29
Take away privileges	25	25	25
A discussion without discipline	23	22	23
Ground them	5	6	4
A discussion with discipline	5	3	7
Discipline them physically	4	8	2
Combination of responses	8	6	10
Other	1	1	<1

Source: Bibby 2001, p.67.

than their adult children have had. The young adult is facing difficult life tasks—for example, finding meaningful full-time employment or grieving a loss—for the first time and hence without experience. At trying times, the adult child who has moved out may seek a renewed sense of security by touching home base—either by calling often by telephone or in person.

Just listening and using other positive communication skills (described in Chapter 9) can help. (It also helps not to jump to conclusions at a time like this. A child who calls in desperation because his or her marriage is breaking up may not be asking to move home.) Parents can help to replenish self-confidence in frustrated children by reminding them of their past successes and commenting on the strength and skills they demonstrated (Haines and Neely 1987). A parent might say, for example, "I remember your persistence as you worked toward first-chair in band." A grieving young adult will need to be informed that what she or he is feeling is normal.

At times parents may choose to confront their adult children: "It sounds as if drinking is beginning to cause problems for you," or "It sounds as if you feel stuck in a job you don't like." Serious problems, such as dealing with an adult child's chronic depression or chemical addiction, require counselling and/or support groups designed for this purpose.

SHARING THE HOUSEHOLD   More and more young adult children either do not leave the family home or return to it—after college or university, after divorce, or upon finding first jobs unsatisfactory. Unemployment and underemployment, along with a decline in affordable housing, make launching oneself into independent adulthood especially difficult today (Boyd and Norris 2000; Mitchell 1998; Goldscheider 1997).

Parents who anticipated increased intimacy or personal freedom may be disappointed when the nest doesn't empty. Said one widower who is of retirement age but is keeping the large house and his university position so his younger son can live at home and finish university tuition-free:

He seems to think I enjoy working now, that I'd go on forever. I can't find the gratitude in him for the fact that I'm keeping this job just so he can finish school. He's a fifth-year senior. He tells me there're scores of these folks around now. What happened to graduation after four years? He says I'm being unrealistic. He works, and I should be glad about that, I guess. So over Christmas he's driving to Minnesota to visit his girlfriend. He's twenty-two. I guess he doesn't need to ask my permission, but it gripes me anyway. It's a case of his money is his and my money is ours. I buy the food, pay the mortgage and utilities. He puts gas in his car and drives across the country to see his girlfriend! Besides, I thought he'd be around over Christmas.... (Interview with Agnes Riedmann, 1989)

Whether or not parents continue to share their homes with adult children, the relationship will probably be enhanced if they relinquish parental authority, recognizing that their children's attitudes and values may differ from their own (Miller and Glass 1989). Relinquishing parental authority, however, does not mean allowing absolutely any behaviour to go on in the family home. For instance, parents who believe that alcohol or other drug usage is always unwarranted have the right to disallow it under their roof. The relationship will probably be more positive when the adult child is more responsible—older, in school, or employed (White and Rogers 1997). In general, parents should feel comfortable in setting reasonable household expectations. One way to do this is to negotiate a parent–adult child residence-sharing agreement.

PARENT–ADULT CHILD RESIDENCE-SHARING AGREEMENTS   Some issues to address and negotiate are the following:

1. How much money will the adult child be expected to contribute to the household? When is it to be paid? Will there be penalties for late payment?

2. What benefits will the child receive? For example, will the family's laundry soap or anything in the refrigerator be at the child's disposal?

3. Who will have authority over utility usage? Who will decide, for instance, when the weather warrants turning on an air conditioner or where to set the thermostat?

4. What about the telephone? At what time is it too late to call? At what point is a conversation too long? Will telephone rules apply to everyone in the household? (One solution to telephone problems is for the adult child to pay for a second line.)

5. What are the standards for cleanliness and orderliness? For instance, what precisely is the definition of "leaving the bathroom (or kitchen) in a mess"?

6. Who is responsible for cleaning what and when? What about yardwork?

7. Who is responsible for cooking what and when? Will meals be at specified times? Will the adult child provide his or her own food?

8. How will laundry tasks be divided?

9. If the adult child owns a car, where will it be parked? Who will pay the property taxes and insurance?

10. What about noise levels? How loud may music be played and when? If the noise associated with an adult child's coming home late at night disturbs sleeping parents, how will this problem be solved?

11. What about guests? When are they welcome, with how much notice, and in what rooms of the house? Will the home be used for parties? (First, though, what is a party? Three guests? Six? 500?)

12. What arrangement will be made for informing other household members if one will be unexpectedly late? (As an adult, the child should have a right to come and go as he or she pleases. But courtesy requires informing others in the household of the general time when one can be expected home. This avoids unnecessary phone calls to every hospital emergency room in the region.)

13. What about using the personal possessions of other members in the household? Can a mother borrow her adult daughter's clothes without asking, for example?

14. If the adult child has returned home with children, who is responsible for their care? How often, when, and with how much notice will the grandparents babysit? Who in the household may discipline the children? How, when, and for what?

Although a residence-sharing agreement can help temporarily, the goal of the majority of parents is for their adult children to move on. Accomplishing this can be complicated by the fact that ideas differ on just what a parent owes an adult child. Our culture offers few guidelines about when parental responsibility ends or how to withdraw it. The next section examines the parenting process—and parenting styles—more generally.

THE PARENTING PROCESS

Considering the lack of consensus about how to raise children today, it may seem difficult to single out styles of parenting. From one point of view there are as many parenting styles as there are parents. Yet certain elements in relating to children can be broadly classified.

Five Parenting Styles

One helpful grouping is provided in E. E. LeMasters' listing of five parenting styles: the martyr, the pal, the police officer, the teacher-counsellor, and the athletic coach (LeMasters and DeFrain 1989).[6] Individual parents probably combine elements of two or more of these styles in their own personal parenting styles.

MARTYR   Martyring parents believe "I would do anything for my child." Some common examples of martyring are parents who habitually wait on their children or pick up after them, parents who nag children rather than letting them remember things for themselves, parents who buy virtually anything the child asks for, and parents who always do what the children want to do. Child psychologist John Rosemond (1991b) describes the "over-involved parent" who "hovers, assumes responsibility [for the child's tasks], encourages dependence, and sends negative messages" (p. 35). Such parenting undercuts the child's development of his or her own competency and suggests that the parent mistrusts the child's capabilities.

A martyring parenting style presents some problems. First, the goals martyring parents set are impossible to carry out, and so the parent must always feel guilty. Second, as Chapter 4 points out, martyring tends to generate manipulative behaviour.

6. There are some similarities between LeMaster's police officer, pal, and coach and psychologist Diana Baumrind's authoritarian, laissez-faire, and authoritative parenting styles (Baumrind 1971; 1978). The reader who would like a more academic presentation of modes of parental control should pursue Baumrind's articles and related psychological research and theory. Baumrind's typology and sociologist Murray Straus' writings on "parental support and control" (1964) stimulated much social science research and theorizing about parental effectiveness (Patterson 1982; Maccoby and Martin 1983; Parke and Slaby 1983; Peterson and Rollins 1987; Brody 1991). Psychologist Gerald Patterson (1982) has been particularly innovative in pursuing the use of research findings in actual work with parents.

PAL   Some parents, mainly those of older children and adolescents, feel that they should be pals to their children. They adopt a **laissez-faire discipline** policy. Pal parenting is unrealistic. For one thing, parents in our society *are* responsible for guiding their children's development. Children deserve to benefit from the greater knowledge and experience of their parents, and at all ages they need some rules and limits, although these change as children grow older. If parents are too permissive, children do not learn to develop self-control. Much research relates laissez-faire parenting to juvenile delinquency and child behaviour problems (Baumrind 1978; Maccoby and Martin 1983; Loeber and Southhamer-Loeber 1986).

LeMasters and DeFrain point out that there are also relationship risks in the pal-parent model. If things don't go well, parents may want to retreat to a more authoritative parenting style. But once they've established a buddy relationship, it is difficult to regain authority.

POLICE OFFICER   The police officer model is just the opposite of the pal. These parents make sure the child obeys all the rules at all times, and they punish their children for even minor offenses.

Being a police officer as a parent doesn't work very well. **Authoritarian discipline** and parenting have been associated—like laissez-faire parenting—with juvenile delinquency and child behaviour problems (Gove and Crutchfield 1982; Maccoby and Martin 1983).

There are several reasons why the police officer role doesn't work today. For one thing, adolescents are far more likely to be influenced by their parents' knowledge and expertise or a wish to identify with parents' values than by the parents' authority. Even for younger children, parental warmth leads to greater obedience (Brody 1991) and has been positively linked to children's overall social competence (Boyum and Parke 1995).

TEACHER-COUNSELLOR   The parent as teacher-counsellor acts in accord with the **developmental model of child rearing**, in which the child is viewed as an extremely plastic organism with virtually unlimited potential for growth and development. This model conceptualizes the parent(s) as almost omnipotent in guiding children's development. If they do the right things at the right time, their children will more than likely be happy, intelligent, and successful.

The teacher-counsellor approach has many fine features, and children do benefit from environmental stimulation, as well as from parental sensitivity to their needs (Brody 1991). Yet this parenting style also poses problems. For one thing, it puts the needs of the child above those of the parent(s). Also, parents who respond as if each of their child's discoveries is wonderful may give the child the mistaken impression that he or she is the centre of everyone's universe.

Moreover, this view exaggerates the power of the parent and the passivity of children. Children also have inherited intellectual capacities and needs. Instead, many child development experts regard the influence between parent and child as mutual and reciprocal (Peterson and Rollins 1987). The athletic coach model proceeds from this view.

ATHLETIC COACH Athletic coach parenting incorporates aspects of the developmental point of view. The coach (parent) is expected to have sufficient ability and knowledge of the game (life) and to be prepared and confident to lead players (children) to do their best and, it is hoped, to succeed.

This parenting style recognizes that parents, like coaches, have their own personalities and needs. They establish team rules, or house rules (and this can be done somewhat democratically with help from the players), and teach these rules to their children. They enforce the appropriate penalties when rules are broken, but policing is not their primary concern. Children, like team members, must be willing to accept discipline and, at least sometimes, to subordinate their own interests to the needs of the family team.

Coaching parents encourage their children to practise and to work hard to develop their own talents. But they realize that they cannot play the game for their players. LeMasters and DeFrain (1989) recommend the athletic coach parenting style as the most realistic and effective.

The ideal parent is the authoritative parent who demands maturity and effectively punishes forbidden behaviour after having clearly stated the rules, but who listens to the child's point of view, respects the child, and encourages the child's self-development and independence. Such parents tend to have children who are socially competent—that is, with high self-esteem and cooperative, yet independent, personalities.

It is important that parents agree, at least on their basic goals and parenting style. Children can live with minor differences (and in fact learn something about people from these variations), but truly inconsistent discipline results in ineffective socialization into the rules and values of society. Parents who are not married and living together must work especially hard at this (Kutner 1989b, p. 92).

Instead of engaging in power struggles, parents need to recognize that by the very nature of their relationship they exercise decreasing control over what their children choose to do. Parents do continue to influence their adolescents, as well as their younger children, as appropriate models for behaviour.

Values are not just taught; they are caught from those around us whom we admire. That is why it is important for parents to practise what they preach (Dinkmeyer, McKay and Dinkmeyer 1997). (Box 12.1, "Communicating With Children," offers some important advice on parenting.)

As children reach adolescence, all family members can more often have some say in setting rules and consequences for not following them. Rules may be discussed ahead of time, and both parents and children attempt to compromise whenever possible. Moreover, it appears that problem solving is more effective when a parent strives to limit negative emotional blaming and/or outbursts (Forgatch 1989).

Social scientists and counsellors hold that this kind of **authoritative discipline** is more effective with adolescents than is either laissez-faire or autocratic discipline. They also point out that parents need not feel guilty about occasionally setting limits without providing rational explanations. Parents should recognize that it is not always possible to give children watertight explanations for every limit they set. In some situations, a parent has a vague feeling that he or she should not permit something but cannot give a rational explanation why, or the explanation does not stand up to teenagers' rebuttal. I-statements from parent to teenager, as discussed in Chapter 9, can help. For example, "I get angry when you leave the car without gas in it, and I go out to work and find the tank empty." Or, "I was worried because I hadn't heard from you." The next section focuses on the question whether spanking is ever appropriate.

The Best of Times: Communicating With Your Children

As a parent, I want to share the best of times with my kids. A mother's joy is to see her children grow, and be happy. The best of times are, well, the best. We wish they could all be that way. No troubles, no worries, no teenage angst.

In a perfect world, that is the way it would be. If only . . .

But, then, reality sets in. The fears, the anxieties, the lessons learned, and those waiting to be learned. And, then, there are the kids' fears and anxieties. Yes, as parents, we worry more about them than they worry about themselves.

The most important thing is to share all the times with them, the good and the bad. Communication is the key to successful parenting. Great, you are probably thinking, how do we manage that in these busy times?

Okay, it's not always easy, but there are ways to do it.

First, ask questions that require more than a yes or no answer. Instead of "Did you have a good day?" try asking, "What was your day like?" Do this while you are chopping vegetables, jotting down the grocery list, or some other task. Now, it may seem like you are ignoring them, but to the child, it's not quite as intimidating to talk with you if you are not staring at them like this is the Spanish Inquisition. Once the conversation is moving a little bit, you can stop what you are doing, or ask them to join in.

Another great time to talk is when you are tucking them in at night. Sometimes, when they are warm in their bed, safe and secure, surrounded by the dark, they are able to confide their secret fears, their most intimate feelings. It's a great time to share your own thoughts and feelings with them. You can start a conversation out with, "What do you think about just before you fall asleep at night?" Most of the time, you'll get the standard kid reply, "I dunno."

This is your key to open up to them. "Sometimes, I think about what you will be like when you grow up.

What kind of person you will be, what you will do for a living. What do you think you'd like to do?" Still no reply? Try this one: "When I was a kid, I wanted to be President of the United States! Then I found out that Canadians can't be President. But, I could have been the Prime Minister of Canada . . ." Stop, and let the silence surround the two of you.

Silence can be your best friend when talking with your kids. It's easy to forget that we have two ears and only one mouth, which means we should be listening twice as much as we talk. Once you have mastered the listening skills, you will find out far more by reading between the lines.

Another favourite spot to chat is in the car, on the way to school. Once again, you are somewhat occupied with a task that keeps you from making direct eye contact. There are lots of things going on around you, and, you can use things you spot to start a dialogue. "Wow, green hair! What do you think about having your hair green?" Or, "I wonder what it is like to walk around in those baggy pants!" Just give them a chance to start talking, and you'll be amazed at the things they know, or want to know.

The last step in communicating with your kids is to be honest. Make a pact with them that you will be honest if they will. Even if it means telling them the mistakes you made as a kid, you can tell the truth. Just tell them what you learned from it, and how you hope that they can learn from your blunders. After all, isn't that maybe why we made those blunders? To learn a lesson that we can pass along to our own kids? There has to be some kind of reason!

Just spend some time getting to know your kids. They are great people!

©1998 Joanne Keating, all rights reserved.

Is Spanking Ever Appropriate?

Pediatricians and social scientists have conflicting opinions about whether it is appropriate ever to spank a child. Spanking refers to hitting a child with an open hand without causing physical injury. A leading domestic violence researcher, sociologist Murray Straus (1994) advises parents never to hit children of any age under any circumstances. Research by Straus and his colleagues as well as others show that children who have been spanked by their parents—even if infrequently and by parents who are otherwise loving—are more likely later to cheat or tell lies, bully or be cruel or mean to others, disobey in school and misbehave in other ways (Stormshak et al. 2000; Straus 1996; Straus and Mouradian 1998; Straus and Stewart 1999; Straus, Sugarman, and Giles-Sims 1997). Furthermore, being spanked in childhood is linked to depression, suicide, and alcohol or drug abuse in adolescence and to abusing one's own children and beating one's wife in adulthood (Garvey 1999; Turner and Finkelhor 1996; Straus and Kantor 1994). Straus argues that spanking teaches children a "hidden agenda"—that it is all right to hit someone, and that those who love you hit you. This confusion of love with violence sets the stage for spouse abuse (Straus and Yodanis 1996).

However, some researchers contend that Straus and others may be over-simplifying, hence overstating, the case (Gilbert 1997). For example, Robert Larzelere (2000) conducted a review of articles that addressed the outcomes of nonabusive and customary physical punishment by parents. He reports that "the outcomes differ by methodology, child, and subcultural factors as well as by how the physical punishment was used."

> All six studies that used clinical samples and all three sequential-analysis studies found beneficial outcomes, such as reduced noncompliance and fighting, primarily when nonabusive spanking was used to back up milder disciplinary tactics in two- to six-year-olds. Five of eight longitudinal studies that controlled for initial child misbehaviour found predominantly detrimental outcomes of spanking. However, those detrimental outcomes were primarily due to overly frequent use of physical punishment. (Larzelere 2000, p. 199)

Additionally, Larzelere points out that "apparently detrimental outcomes have been found for every alternative disciplinary tactic when investigated with similar analyses" and suggests that "[s]uch detrimental associations of frequent use of any disciplinary tactic may be due to residual confounding from initial child misbehaviour."

Meanwhile, Gunnoe concludes that it is "still fairly muddy whether there are contexts in which spanking could be okay, or at least not deleterious" (Gunnoe, in Gilbert 1997). Agreeing with Gunnoe, prominent psychologist Diana Baumrind (1996) asserts that a "blanket injunction against disciplinary use of spanking is not warranted by the data." She believes that when a child refuses to listen, "The addition of aversive consequences, which can include a couple of smart spanks, may be indicated" (Baumrind, in Gilbert 1997; see also Larzelere 1996 and Larzelere et al. 1998).

Consensus statements drafted at the 1996 Conference of the American Academy of Pediatrics advise that children under two years old and adolescents should *never* be spanked. Spanking can cause physical injury in the former and is known to promote aggression in the latter (Gilbert 1997).

The Resilient Child

This textbook is written for people interested enough in parenting and family life to take a course. But no one is perfect; most parents have failings of one sort or another. Parents may encounter serious problems in their lives, problems that affect their children: poverty, discrimination, divorce, unemployment, legal and financial conflicts, scandal, sudden change of residence, crime victimization, military service, war, death, mental illness, drug or alcohol abuse, or family violence.

The hope that research in child development offers to parents who make mistakes is that children can be surprisingly resilient (Furstenberg and Hughes 1995; Rubin 1997). A long term study was conducted in Hawaii based on a sample of all the children (698) born on the island of Kauai in 1955—one-half of whom were in poverty, and one-sixth of whom were physically or intellectually handicapped. A smaller group of 225 children was identified as being at high risk of poor developmental outcomes. Researchers found that even one-third of this last group "grew into competent young adults who loved well, worked well, played well, and expected well" (Werner 1992, p. 263). The researchers spoke of a "self-righting tendency"

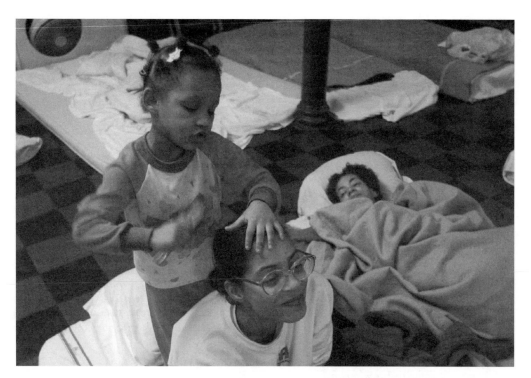

Children have a certain degree of resilience, which is enhanced by strong familial bonds. Although these children experience economic hardship, the self-esteem they gain through their family and friends can help them in becoming self-confident adults.

whereby children lucky enough to have certain characteristics—a sociable personality, self-esteem derived from a particular talent, a support network, and above all, a good relationship with at least one caring adult—emerged into adulthood in good shape (Werner 1992; Werner and Smith 1992). Risk is risk, but hope is not unrealistic (Furstenberg and Hughes 1995). Other research indicates that "[a]dults who acknowledge and seem to have worked through difficulties of their childhood are apparently protected against inflicting them on their children" (Belsky 1991, p. 124).

WHEN PARENTS AND CHILDREN GROW OLDER

Relationships between parents and their children last a lifetime (Kaufman and Uhlenberg 1998). In this section, we examine parent–child—and grandparent—relations as family members grow older.

Adults and Their Parents

In discussing child rearing throughout this chapter, we have taken the perspective of the older generation looking at the younger. But as parents, children, and their children grow older, things change.

Marriage, and then parenthood, redefine the relationship between parents and children. Typically, the parent–child tie moves from one of dependence to interdependence at this point (Cooney 1997, p. 458). For many mothers and daughters, motherhood for the daughter creates a closer bond than had existed in adolescence—perhaps ever—as these women who may have very different views and styles may now have something very important in common (Kutner 1990d).

Adults' relationships with their parents range from tight-knit, to intimate but distant, to nonintimate but sociable, to obligatory, to detached (Silverstein and Bengston 1997). Whether or not parent–child relationships become more egalitarian is debatable. L.

R. Fisher's (1986) study of mothers and daughters found that generally mothers never completely relinquish a parental role and that the adult daughter–mother relationship had both peer and parental elements. But other psychologists have found the contrary. One interviewee described reminding her visiting parents to keep their feet off the couch, a spontaneous remark that symbolized that she was "on the same level as my parents" in their relationship (Kutner 1990d, p. C-8). Even when parents need their adult children for care, however, role reversal is not very likely to occur (Kutner 1988a).

Some parents and children never successfully negotiate the transition to an adult–adult relationship and become estranged. An interesting qualitative study of adults who had moved at least 200 miles from their parents found that some were estranged. The majority, however, were either comfortable with the distance or with their relationships with parents. Others yearned to be reunited. Most kept in touch by telephone (Climo 1992). And now, of course, by e-mail.

In some families, the reality of past abuse, a conflict-filled divorce, or simply fundamental differences in values or lifestyles make it seem unlikely parents and children will spend time together (Kutner 1990a; Kaufman and Uhlenberg 1998). Money matters can also cause tension (Kutner 1990c).

As parents grow old, parent–child relationships might best be characterized by ambivalence (Luescher and Pillemer 1998). Parents may become more controlling as they grow older, a common reaction to loss of bodily and social power with aging and retirement. Parent–child relations enter a new stage when parents become disabled, frail, or suffer cognitive impairment that affects their ability to care for themselves or to live alone (Wolfson et al 1993). Children are often uncertain about when to step in. A study of 242 adult children and 66 elderly parents found that children tended to let parents live independently (usually the parents' preference) as long as it seemed safe (Hansson et al. 1990).

Elderly people are often uncomfortable receiving help, as it represents a threat to self-esteem and autonomy, especially if the caregiver is controlling or if earlier conflicts reemerge (Brubaker, Gorman, and Hiestand 1990; Cicerelli 1990). Adult daughters who, in childhood, were exposed to traditional, extended households tend to have more positive attitudes about taking an aging parent into their own home (Szinovacz 1997). There is some evidence that in Japanese-Canadian families, cultural factors, particularly the value of *oya koh koh* (filial obligation) has a significant effect on adult children's provision and frequency of emotional support, but not on financial or service support (Kobayashi 1998). But assuredly, adult children of all races/ethnicities feel some sense of responsibility to their parents (Eggebeen and Davey 1998) and to their siblings with whom they may share responsibility for aging parents (Stein et al. 1998; Piercy 1998).

The adult child involved in a parent's care is far more likely to be a daughter, or even a daughter-in-law, than a son, raising issues of gender equity similar to those of parenting and domestic work discussed in Arlie Hochschild's *The Second Shift* (1989) (see Chapter 13). In fact, women today spend more years in elder care than in caring for young children (Abel 1991). A fairly large (905) New York sample of individuals over age 40 found that being divorced does not decrease a daughter's help to parents, as some observers had predicted it would (Spitze et al. 1994). Findings from the 1996 General Social Survey indicate that female caregivers are about equally as likely to be living with a spouse and children, living with a spouse only, or living with children only. Female caregivers are also equally likely to be either employed, unemployed, or full-time homemakers, and male caregivers are equally as likely to be either employed or unemployed. Findings from this survey also indicate that, although the percentages reported are small, women (15 percent) today are more likely than are men (9 percent) to change their geographical location to live closer to a person requiring their caregiving aid (Cranswick 1997). Overall, we can conclude that intergenerational relations are varied, "but generally possess the potential to serve their members' needs" (Silverstein and Bengston 1997).

In later life, parents continue to play a vital role in the lives of their adult children and grandchildren, as the next section discusses.

Grandparenting

Surveys show that parents over age 65 prefer to live in their own homes but near their adult children and grandchildren. Middle-aged adult children sometimes return to the geographical area they grew up in to be near their aging parents.

"Approximately three-quarters of older people are grandparents and nearly half are great grandparents" (Larson, Goltz and Munro 2000, p. 280). Because people are living longer, a grandparent spends more time in that role than in the past. Also, grandparenting is less likely to overlap with the parenting role than in previous decades. Besides these demographic changes, this century has seen increased emphasis on love, affection, and companionship with grandparents. Hence many grandparents find the role deeply meaningful: Grandchildren give personal pleasure and a sense of immortality. Some grandfathers see the role as an opportunity to be involved with babies and very young children, an activity discouraged when their own children were young (Cunningham-Burley 1987). Overall, the grandparent role is mediated by the parent; not getting along with the parent dampens the grandparent's contact, hence relationship with his or her grandchildren (Whitbeck, Hoyt, and Huck 1993).

Sociologists Andrew Cherlin and Frank Furstenberg surveyed 510 grandparents (just over one-fifth were under 60 years old). About 20 percent of their sample said they saw their grandchildren less often than every two or three months. One-fourth saw a grandchild once a week or more, although not daily. Another 12 percent saw a grandchild daily; often they lived together (Cherlin and Furstenberg 1986, p. 72). Data collected by the 1990 General Social Survey in Canada indicates that 39 percent of grandchildren with a grandparent still living saw at least one of their grandparents once a month or more, 41 percent saw a grandparent less than once a month, and 20 percent had not seen at least one of their grandparents during the previous year (McDaniel 1993).

Grandparents continue to provide practical help (Cranswick 1997; King and Elder 1995). They may serve as valuable "family watchdogs," ready to provide assistance when needed (Troll 1985). In low-income and minority families, parents and children readily rely on grandparents and other kin. Even among white middle-class families, it is not unusual for grandparents to contribute to the cost of a grandchild's tuition, wedding, or first house. (Grandparents try not to meddle, however. Only 14 percent of Cherlin and Furstenberg's sample said they had helped settle a disagreement between grandchildren and parents.) As we saw in the previous section, divorced parents may turn to their parents for practical and emotional aid. Then, too, when the adult child of a divorced parent divorces, assistance may be more readily available from a grandparent.

Also, race/ethnicity affects grandparenting. In Aboriginal families, for example, grandmothers may assume a parent-like role with their grandchildren and provide crucial assistance to unmarried daughters with children. The increased number of Asians immigrants may also provide a partial explanation for the recent rise in three-generation households in Canada.[7] Janet Che-Alford and Brian Hamm observe that, "People born in Asia are more culturally accustomed to live in a large, extended family system. And because most Asian immigrants are recent arrivals, they are more likely to uphold the traditions of their country than immigrants who have been in Canada longer" (p. 162). They report that in three-generation households with only one "household maintainer" (i.e., the person who paid the rent or mortgage, taxes, electricity, and other expenses for the dwelling), the grandparent was most often identified (55 percent of the time in 1996). In situations with more than one maintainer, "the contribution of grandparents was also considerable. At least one grandparent helped out with household payments in about 55 percent of three-generation households in 1991 and 54 percent in 1996" (p. 164).

Grandparenting styles vary and are shaped by health, employment status, and personality (Troll 1985). Grandparents often adopt a grandparenting style similar to the one they experienced as grandchildren with their own grandparents (King and Elder

---

7. Although still relatively uncommon in Canada, the number of three-generation households increased by almost 40 percent in the last decade and a half and in 1995, almost three-quarters of a million Canadians lived in three-generation households. In 31 percent of such households, there was one grandparent, two parents and their children; in 24 percent, one grandparent resided with one parent and his/her children; in 21 percent, there were two grandparents, two parents and their children; and in 24 percent, there were two grandparents, one parent and his/her children (Vanier Institute of the Family 2000, p. 29).

1997). Cherlin and Furstenberg's study (1986) identified three general styles of grandparenting among more conventionally situated grandparents: remote, companionate, and involved. About 30 percent of Cherlin and Furstenberg's respondents had "remote" relationships with their grandchildren. Usually this was because they lived far away. About 55 percent of the relationships were "companionate." These grandparents did things with their grandchildren but exercised little authority over the child and allowed the parent to control access to the youth. Companionate grandparents are often involved in work, leisure, or social activities of their own. Another 15 percent of the respondents were more "involved." Some lived with their grandchildren. (In most of these cases, the grandparent is household head with an adult child and his or her children having moved in, rather than vice versa.) Involved grandparents who do not reside with their grandchildren tend to frequently initiate interaction with a grandchild.

Of course, a grandparent may have different relationship styles with different grandchildren. In general, grandparents are most actively involved with preadolescents, particularly preschoolers (although 8 percent of Cherlin and Furstenberg's sample preferred teenagers). Preschoolers are more available and respond most enthusiastically to a grandparent's attention. There is evidence that, after a typically disinterested adolescence, adults renew relationships with grandparents (Cherlin and Furstenberg 1986, p. 89).

How does an adult child's divorce affect the grandparent relationship? Evidence suggests that the news hits hard, and grandparents worry over whether to intervene on behalf of the grandchildren. As might be expected, effects of the divorce are different for the **custodial grandparent** (parent of the custodial parent) than for the **noncustodial grandparent** (parent of the noncustodial parent) (Spitze et al. 1994). According to Cherlin and Furstenberg's study, during the marital breakup only six percent of custodial grandparents saw their grandchildren less often, compared with 41 percent of noncustodial grandparents (1986, pp. 142–48). This pattern persists. Several years after the divorce, 37 percent of custodial and 58 percent of noncustodial grandparents were seeing their grandchildren less often than before the breakup. With the current trends in child custody, the most common situation is for maternal grandparent relationships to be maintained or enhanced while paternal ones diminish. Because divorce appears to strengthen maternal intergenerational ties, children of divorced parents may develop stronger bonds with some of their grandparents than do other youngsters (Cherlin and Furstenberg 1986, p. 164).

Then, too, remarriages create stepgrandparents. There is very little information on stepgrandparents, but what data there are suggest that younger stepgrandchildren and those who live with the grandparent's adult child are more likely to develop ties with the stepgrandparent. Meanwhile, stepgrandparents typically distinguish their "real" grandchildren from those of remarriages (Cherlin and Furstenberg 1986, pp. 156–57).

GRANDPARENTS AS PARENTS Drugs and alcohol, particularly crack, along with the spread of AIDS—combined with teen pregnancy, abuse, neglect, abandonment, incarceration, and sometimes murder—are some of the factors that result in grandparent families (Jendrick 1993; Holloway 1994; Toledo and Brown 1995, p. 13).

According to Sylvie de Toledo, a social worker whose nephew was raised by her mother after her sister's suicide and who founded a support group, Grandparents as Parents (GAP) as a result:

Sometimes the call comes at night, sometimes on a bright morning. It may be your child, the police, or child protective services. "Mama, I've messed up ..." "We're sorry. There has been an accident ..." "Mrs. Smith, we have your grandchild. Can you take him?" Sometimes you make the call yourself—reporting your own child to the authorities in a desperate attempt to protect your grandchild from abuse or neglect. Often the change is gradual. At first your grandchild is with you for a day, then four days, a month, and then two months as the parents slowly lose control of their lives. You start out babysitting. You think the arrangement is temporary. You put off buying a crib or moving to a bigger apartment. Then you get a collect call from jail—or no call at all. (Toledo and Brown 1995, p. 9)

At other times the change is more sudden, as when a grandchild's parents are killed in an auto accident, for example, or when the state removes children from their parent's home because of abuse or neglect, and places them with a grandparent who officially acts as foster parent.

Research on grandparents as parents is just beginning (Jendrick 1993), but we do know a few things. For instance, we know that residing with a grandparent can be better than living with only one's single mother, at least in some cases (Manning and Smock 1997). A study of Baltimore elementary children found that black children of single mothers living in grandmother-headed households got higher reading grades than did black children in mother-only—or even in mother-father—households (Entwisle and Alexander 1996).

We also know that becoming a primary parent requires adjustment for grandparents. For example, the grandparent's finances may suffer. Because they are older, grandparents may be concerned that they will not be able to care for their children as long as will be needed. In some cases, grandparents have set up custodial or caretaker trusts so that their grandchildren will be taken care of in the event that something happens to the grandparent(s) (Rosenfeld 1997, p. 181).

Furthermore, grandparents make more than just financial adjustments. Their circle of friends may change or dwindle because no one else in the grandparent's peer group has children, and the grandparent is older than parents with children. And living with children in the house is an adjustment after years of not doing so. "For Grandma, it's a distinct feeling of *deja vu*. For Grandpa, who may have seen little of his own children while they were growing up, having kids around for 24 hours a day can be quite a shock. For a single grandparent, it's twice as hard" (Toledo and Brown 1995, pp. 25–26). Moreover, a grandmother's work life may change. She may retire early, reduce her work hours, or try to negotiate more flexible ones. On the other hand, she may return to work to have money to raise the child.

Toledo points out that **grandparents as primary parents** can expect to feel isolation, grief, anger and guilt, fear, and doubt. Toledo suggests, among other

things, that grandparents who are serving as parents prioritize (decide what is most important and handle it first), take one thing at a time, set limits with their grandchildren, and take time for themselves. A grandparent's assuming the role of primary parent is a family crisis; handling family crises creatively is addressed in Chapter 16.

The next section explores some ways that all parents can improve their relationships with their children.

TOWARD BETTER PARENT–CHILD RELATIONSHIPS

Studies generally show that good parenting involves at least three factors: (1) adequate economic resources, (2) being involved in a child's life and school, and (3) using supportive, rather than negative, communication in the family (DuBois, Eitel, and Felner 1994; Klebanov, Brooks-Gunn, and Duncan 1994; Simons, Johnson, and Conger 1994). At the same time, parents today need to work to build their confidence and self-esteem. Important to this is a parent's learning to accept his or her limitations and mistakes as inevitable and human. Instead of feeling guilty about how poorly he handled a fight between his children, for example, a father can praise himself for the patience he showed in helping his child with a homework assignment.

As parents gain self-acceptance, they will also become more accepting of their children. When parents make positive attributions to their children, such as "She [or he] wants to do the right thing," children internalize them. This sense of respect contributes to better parent–child relationships and improved self-images for both parents and children.

Over the past 30 years, various organizations have emerged to help parents with the parent–child relationship. One program is Thomas Gordon's Parent Effectiveness Training (PET), which applies the guidelines for no-win intimacy to the parent–child relationship. Another is Systematic Training for Effective Parenting (STEP). Both STEP and PET combine instruction on effective communication techniques with emotional support for parents. These programs are offered in many communities, and related books are also available (e.g., Kennedy 2001). In addition, countless local and community programs have emerged that teach various facets of parent education, particularly to teen and low-income parents (Bogenschneider and Stone 1997; Warren and Cannan 1997). Groups such as Parents, Family, and Friends of Lesbians and Gays (PFLAG) are also politically active in their efforts to achieve equal rights for the families of gays, lesbians, bisexuals, and transgendered persons.

Furthermore, parents need to be willing to seek professional help when their efforts seem to be unsuccessful. Problems are best addressed early in the child's life, when intervention or the changes parents make in response to advice will have the most effect (research evidence supports this truism; Brody 1991). Psychotherapists are now prepared to help with problems of children still in infancy (Gelman 1990).

In addition to gaining self-acceptance, self-esteem, and knowledge of good parenting techniques, parents can involve other members of their communities in child rearing. "Pediatrics is politics," the late pediatrician Benjamin Spock once said (Maier 1998). He meant that good parenting makes for better communities—and more supportive communities make for better parents. The first step, perhaps, is to insist that society recognize the positive achievements of conscientious parents, and not just criticize parents and children for inadequacies.

Then, too, parents can encourage more cooperation among friends and neighbours. For instance, parents might exchange homework help—"I'll help Johnny with math on Tuesday evenings if you'll help Mary with English"—and of course form car pools for children's lessons and activities. Such practical exchanges provide the occasion for children to form supportive relationships with other adults, and they are also a basis for shared parenting.

Another source of support is the community itself: teachers, school counsellors and principals, police officers, adolescents' employers, the library, and the public in general (Warren and Cannan 1997). Parents and stepparents are encouraged to seek general information, answers to specific questions, and avenues for assistance from local agencies or counsellors, in books, or in parent advocacy organizations. Programs such as Big Brothers/Big Sisters and Foster Grandparents involve volunteers who care about and can help with child rearing. If children learn to relate well to other human beings and to take some personal responsibility for these relationships, they will be prepared to have good relationships as adults.

IN SUM

Raising children is both exciting and frustrating. The family ecology theoretical perspective reminds us that societywide conditions influence the relationship, and these factors can place extraordinary emotional and financial strains on parents. Formerly, children were expected to become more help and less trouble as they grew older; today, it is different. Most of what children need costs more as they grow: clothes, transportation, leisure activities, and schooling.

This chapter began by presenting some reasons why parenting and stepparenting can be difficult today. Some things noted are that work and parent roles often conflict. Middle-aged parents, especially mothers, may be sandwiched between dependent children on one hand and increasingly dependent, aging parents on the other.

Not only mothers' but fathers' roles can be difficult, especially in a society like ours in which attitudes have changed so rapidly and in which there is no consensus about how to raise children and how mothers and fathers should parent. In addition, both children's and parents' needs change over the course of life. One thing that does not change as children mature is their need for supportive communication from a parent. Grandparents, particularly companionate and involved ones, can be helpful.

The need for supportive—and socially supported—parenting transcends social class and race or ethnicity. At the same time, we have seen that parenting differs in some important ways, according to economic resources, social class, and whether parent and child suffer discrimination due to minority status or sexual orientation of the parents.

To have better relationships with their children, parents need to recognize their own needs and to avoid feeling unnecessary guilt; to accept help from others (friends and the community at large as well as professional caregivers); and finally, to try to build and maintain flexible, intimate relationships using techniques suggested in this chapter, along with those suggested in Chapter 9.

Key Terms

astronaut phenomenon
authoritarian discipline
authoritarian parenting
authoritative discipline
authoritative parenting
custodial grandparent
developmental model of child rearing
grandparents as primary parents
interactive perspective
laissez-faire discipline
laissez-faire parenting
noncustodial grandparent
parenting alliance
primary parents
sandwich generation
shared parenting

Study Questions

1. Describe reasons why parenting can be difficult today. Can you think of others besides those presented in this chapter?

2. Describe some historical and contemporary images of mothers and fathers in Canada. How well, in your opinion, do these images reflect reality?

3. How does parenting differ according to social class? Race or ethnicity? How would you prepare a minority child to face racial discrimination?

4. Compare these three parenting styles: authoritarian, authoritative, and laissez-faire. What are some empirical outcomes of each? Which one is recommended by most experts? Why?

5. Compare the advantages and disadvantages of the five parenting styles discussed by LeMasters and Defrain.

6. Why might the transition to parenthood be more difficult than the transition to other adult roles, such as worker or spouse?

7. Compare the parenting challenges of parents with babies, preschoolers, school-age children, teenagers, and young adult children. Which stage do you think would be the most challenging? The least? Why?

8. What have you observed about the relationships of adult children and their parents? What do they enjoy? What are areas of conflict?

Suggesting Readings

Arnup, Katherine (ed.). 1995. *Lesbian Parenting: Living With Pride & Prejudice*. Charlottetown, P.E.I.: gynergy books. A rich collection of articles edited by a leading Canadian scholar working in the areas of lesbian parenting and reproductive rights for women.

Kazemipur, Abdolmohammad and Shiva S. Halli. 2000. *The New Poverty in Canada: Ethnic Groups and Ghetto Neighbourhoods*. Toronto: Thompson Educational Publishing, Inc. Examines the relationship between poverty and ethnicity in Canada and compares the Canadian experience with that of the United States and European countries.

McMahon, Martha. 1995. *Engendering Motherhood: Identity and Self-Transformation in Women's Lives*. New York: The Guilford Press. An important work which uses symbolic interaction as an analytical tool to suggest how class, marital status and work shape the ways in which women create identities for themselves as mothers.

Poussaint, Alvin F. and James P. Comer. 1992. *Raising Black Children: Questions and Answers for Parents and Teachers*. New York: NAL/Dutton. Advice to parents from two African-American psychiatrists at Harvard and Yale. Or, see James P. Comer and Alvin F. Poussaint. 1992. *Raising Black Children*. New York: Penguin Books/Plume.

Rubin, Lillian B. 1997. *The Transcendent Child: Tales of Triumph over the Past*. New York: HarperPerennial. Well-known sociologist Rubin talks about her own childhood, where she was raised in poverty by an abusive mother, and addresses factors—using much empirical evidence besides her own—that effect children's ability to transcend difficult pasts, i.e. to be "resilient" children.

On the Net

1) Parenting psychology, advice, and tips from Girls and Boys Town psychologists. Features such as "Parenting Questions & Answers" and "Common Sense skill of the Week."
http://www.parenting.org

2) National Council of Welfare
Statistics, research reports, policy issues, and general information on poverty's effects on the family.
http://www.ncwcnbes.net

3) Canadian Council on Social Development
Provides statistics and research reports on such

issues as education, poverty, and disability.
http://www.ccsd.ca

4) Existing Government of Canada Programs
Related to the Homeless
http://www.cmhc-schl.gc.ca/en/prfias/otaspr/
otaspr_002.cfm

5) Raising the Roof
A national charity devoted to finding solutions to
the problem of homelessness in Canada.
http://www.communitygates.com/raisetheroof/
under.htm

Work and Family

WHAT YOU GET FROM THE ROMANCE OF LOVE AND MARRIAGE IS IN FACT NOT SIMPLY A FAMILY, BUT A HOUSE-HOLD, AND THAT'S QUITE ANOTHER MATTER.

SOCIOLOGIST RAYNA RAPP, 1999

In a survey of 22 000 Canadian workers, 40 percent of mothers and 25 percent of fathers reported that they experienced high levels of conflict between their work and family lives (Higgins, Duxbury and Lee 1993). In 1998, among married parents, aged 25 to 44 and employed full-time time, one in three reported dissatisfaction with the balance between their work and family life. "Not having enough time for family, including their spouses and children, was the main reason for their dissatisfaction" (Statistics Canada 2000). "Where do you work?" is a new question in human history. Until recently, cooperative labour for survival was the primary purpose of marriage (Tilly and Scott 1978). Providing and caring for all family members, including dependent children and the old, is integral to our definition of families and to the functional theoretical perspective on families as well (see Chapter 2). Only since the Industrial Revolution, however, has working been considered separate from family living (Robinson 1995), and only since then have the concepts "employed" and "unemployed" emerged.

For those who stayed home (usually middle- and upper-class wives and mothers), working in the public sphere was beyond their experience and took on an aura of mystery. For those who laboured outside the home and earned money (mainly husbands), partners who stayed at home seemed unproductive; they were not "employed." "His" work was in the public sphere, for money; "her" work was in the private sphere of the household, for free. Spouses' work roles were quite distinct (see Chapter 3).

Today, although occupational segregation and sex discrimination in employment persist, the trend is away from distinguishing work based on sex. A majority of married women work outside the home.

Many chapters in this book discuss social changes and how they affect people's attitudes and family life. This chapter looks at one aspect of modern living that is profoundly affecting marriages and families. We'll explore traditional employment patterns that have characterized our society until recently, then look at newer patterns and the interrelationship of work and family roles for both women and men. We'll see that the trend toward women's working outside the home offers new options for families. With new options come new responsibilities for making knowledgeable decisions. To begin, we will examine the concept of "labour force" as a social invention.

THE LABOUR FORCE—A SOCIAL INVENTION

Although human beings have always worked, it was not until the industrialization of the workplace in the nineteenth century that people characteristically became wage earners, hiring out their labour to someone else and joining a so-called **labour force**. The labour force, then, is a social invention.

The Labour Force in Postindustrial Society

Gradually throughout the twentieth century, our society has moved from an industrial one that manufactured products to a postindustrial one that transmits information and offers other services. In such a service society, production is transferred to the office, hospital restaurant, store, telemarketing centre and so on.

Many of the new jobs created by the service economy pay less than did industrial work. Many are part-time and offer few or no employee benefits such as extended medical, dental and pension plans (Taylor 1997; Booth, Crouter, and Shanahan 1999). Although other factors are involved, Canadian workers' average hourly wages, when adjusted for inflation, have generally declined or stagnated since the 1980s (Morisette 1997; Statistics Canada 2000). One way families have adapted to this decline is for both wives and husbands to be employed.

At the same time, however, employees are increasingly aware that they are replaceable, if not dispensable. Partly in order to compete with foreign markets and partly to maintain corporate profits in a generally constricting economy, employers have dedicated themselves to reducing costs by streamlining operations. One way they have done that has been to let some workers go. By the 1990s, job security had become an issue even for highly educated managerial employees (Ehrbar 1993). Even in the rebounding economy of the late 1990s, "downsizing" or job cuts continued (Uchitelle 1998b; Ryan 1999). Fully one-third of Canada's workers believe that their jobs are not secure (Statistics Canada 1998a).

Many Canadians find their positions or careers challenging and satisfying, not only in their professions or the corporate world, but in manufacturing and related economic sectors. Some jobs that were formerly manual or craft jobs in manufacturing or construction design have been computerized in a way that makes them more mentally challenging and less physically demanding (Gans 1996). But a significant (and growing) proportion of workers have difficulty finding personal satisfaction or security in their jobs. Between 1991 and 1994–95, the proportion of working Canadians who were very satisfied with their jobs declined (Health Canada 1999, p. 64). This is not only true at lower occupational levels, but also in such professions as medicine, because the opportunity for independent decision-making is receding; in nursing, where short staffing places pressure on floor nurses; and in law, where the "best" jobs require a 60–80 hour work week and "part-time" is a 40-hour work week (Abelson 1998; Ryan 1999).

Overall, men in Canada are more likely than women to be satisfied with their jobs. "Women are disadvantaged relative to men in terms of job satisfaction because they are more likely to work in situations affording them little control over the pace and content of their tasks" (Health Canada 1999, p. 64). According to the National Population Health Survey, job satisfaction increased with age, with those men and women aged 15 to 24 the least likely to report that they were satisfied with their work. Marked variation also existed among the provinces in relation to job satisfaction. Those in the Atlantic provinces were more likely than Canadians in general to report high satisfaction with their jobs (e.g., 58 percent in New

Brunswick), while those in Canada's three largest provinces were the least likely to do so (47 percent in Quebec, and 50 percent in both Ontario and British Columbia) (Health Canada 1999).

Moreover, especially in single-parent families and in unions in which both partners are employed and have dependents, the separation of the labour force from family living creates role conflict and tension. Increasingly, stressed and overloaded workers juggle what have become conflicting obligations: providing for and caring for family members. Approximately two-thirds of full-time employed parents report that they are dissatisfied with the balance between their job and family life; "26 percent of married fathers, 38 percent of married mothers and 38 percent of single mothers report severe time stress" (Canadian Council on Social Development 2001) (Table 13.1).

It is in this context (which flows from the family ecology theoretical perspective described in Chapter 2) that we explore the relationship between work and family. We will look first at what has been the traditional work model in industrialized society.

THE TRADITIONAL MODEL: PROVIDER HUSBANDS AND HOMEMAKING WIVES

As discussed in Chapter 3, competing for success in a chosen occupation has been essential to the traditional masculine gender role. A husband has been culturally and legally expected to be his family's principal breadwinner (Coltrane 1996). Meanwhile, wives have been culturally and legally bound to husband care, house care, and child care (Hertz 1997).

Husbands and the Provider Role

What sociologist Jessie Bernard terms the **good provider role** for men emerged in both Canada and the United States during the 1830s. Before then a man was expected to be "a good steady worker," but "the idea that he was *the* provider would hardly ring true" (Bernard 1986, p. 126; Booth and Crouter 1998). The good provider role lasted into the late 1970s. Its end was officially marked in this country when the 1981 Census of Canada no longer automatically assumed the male to be head of the household. Indeed, "[o]ver the past two decades, the proportion of single-earner husband-wife families with children at

TABLE 13.1

"...many families today are just exhausted, living with very frenetic schedules."

Women whose youngest child is under age 10	
Severely time crunched	34.3%
Time crunched	39.0%
Time-stress free	26.7%
Other women	
Severely time crunched	25.1%
Time crunched	32.3%
Time-stress free	42.6%
Men whose youngest child is under age 10	
Severely time crunched	16.3%
Time crunched	35.5%
Time-stress free	48.2%
Other men	
Severely time crunched	15.2%
Time crunched	35.0%
Time-stress free	49.8%

Source: Statistics Canada, <http://www.statcan.ca/english/ads/11-008-XIE/family.html>

home has decreased from 59 pecent to 31 percent" (Marshall 1998, p. 9) (see Figure 13.1).

Although the role of family wage earner is no longer reserved for husbands, and the prevalence of wives as primary earners in dual-earner families rose rapidly in Canada during the 1990–1992 recession with many women becoming the family's main breadwinner by default (Crompton and Geran 1995), many Canadians still believe that the man should be the *principal* provider for his family (Bibby 1995, 2001; Crowley 1998; Ghalam 2000). Sociologist Jane Hood (1986) identified three provider role systems in dual-worker marriages. They vary according to the couples' attitudes toward husbands' and wives' responsibilities. Some working couples see their roles in terms of a main provider/secondary provider division. For the **main/secondary provider couple**, providing is the man's responsibility; the home, the

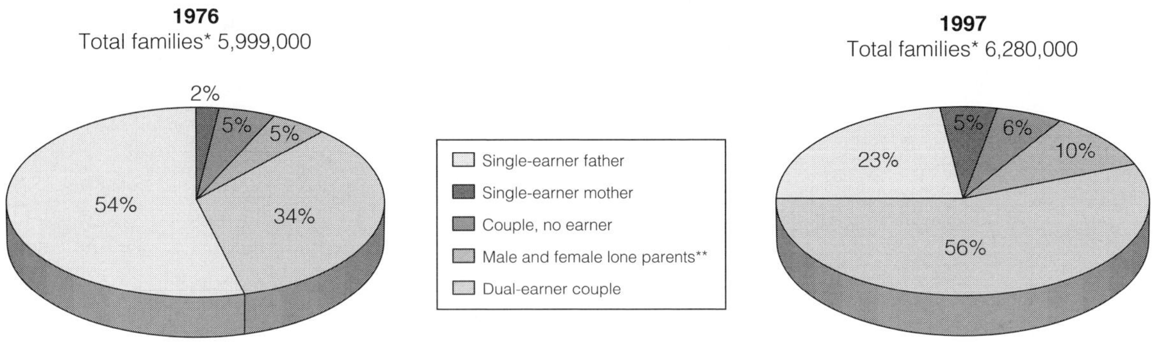

1976
Total families* 5,999,000

2%
5% 5%
54%
34%

1997
Total families* 6,280,000

23%
5% 6%
10%
56%

- Single-earner father
- Single-earner mother
- Couple, no earner
- Male and female lone parents**
- Dual-earner couple

FIGURE **13.1**

The family structure has changed considerably over the past two decades.
(Source: Statistics Canada, "Perspectives on labour and Income, Cat. No. 75-001, Winter 2000, p. 15.)
*Couples and lone parents with at least one child under 16 at home.
**Includes both employed and not employed.

woman's. Whatever wages her employment brings in are nice, but extra. In the two other models, the wife's income is recognized as essential to the couple's finances. In a **coprovider couple**, both partners are seen as equally responsible for providing. In the **ambivalent provider couple**, the wife's providing responsibilities are not clearly acknowledged. To these we should add **role-reversed couples** in which the husband is mainly responsible for homemaking and child care while the wife is the principal breadwinner (Johnson et al. 1992; Marshall 1998). Research suggests that coprovider couples, although emerging, are a statistical minority—about 15 percent of all two-earner unions (Potuchek 1992).

Table 13.2 shows the average number of hours per week spent, by Canadian men and women at different ages, in paid and unpaid work. As Katherine Marshall (2000, p. 15) suggests, despite a "blending" of the roles of breadwinner and homemaker, the paid and unpaid work roles of contemporary Canadian men and women reflect their legacy.

Findings from the 1995 Survey of Work Arrangements suggests that striking a balance between work and family commitments tends to result in different outcomes for men and women. Among the findings of this survey that reiterate the centrality of men's assumption of the good provider role are:

- In November 1995, most married fathers were in the labour force, regardless of the age of their children at home.

- Among lone parents with children under age 16, a higher proportion of fathers than mothers were in the labour force (85 percent, compared with 63 percent).

- Almost all men in families were working full time—ranging from 94 percent to 98 percent.

- Men in single-earner families, on average, worked slightly more hours per day and more days per week than all women or other men. They worked even longer hours when they had children at home. For example, men in single-earner families with all children aged six to 15 worked an average of 5.2 days per week; 84 percent usually worked 40 or more hours a week. Furthermore, 12 percent with preschoolers at home worked six or more days, compared with just nine percent of dual-earner men and five percent or less of all women.

- One in 10 women and one in five men put in regular overtime at their jobs, regardless of the presence or age of children at home.

- Given the choice, more men than women would have worked more hours for more pay whether they were employed full time (22 percent, compared with 16 percent) or part time (63 percent, compared with 43 percent).

- The desire for more hours was highest for men with preschool aged children at home and, conversely, lowest for women. For example, 83 percent

TABLE 13.2

Average work hours per week

Age		Total	Paid	Unpaid
15 to 24	Men	31	22	9
	Women	34	18	17
35 to 44	Men	65	43	22
	Women	64	27	38
55 to 65	Men	46	23	23
	Women	47	13	34

Source: Statistics Canada, "Perspectives on Labour and Income," Cat. No. 75-001, Vol. 12, No. 04, Dec. 2000.

of men working part time with preschoolers at home preferred more hours compared with 63 percent of men overall; on the other hand, only 38 percent of women in a similar situation preferred more hours, compared with 43 percent of women overall.

- In 72 percent of dual-earner couples both partners worked full time in November 1995. In 25 percent, the husband worked full time and the wife part time; in two percent, this situation was reversed. In the remaining one percent, both partners worked part-time (Marshall 1998, pp. 73–75).

Reporting on her qualitative study of dual-career spouses who shared parenting roles, sociologist Rosanna Hertz (1997) notes that fathers did not mention feeling guilty about working full-time, although mothers did—a situation that "underscores the cultural symmetry in the emphasis placed on the unique role of the mother/child dyad" (p. 377).

REWARDS AND COSTS The good provider role entailed both rewards and costs for men. Rewards included social status and reinforcement of the husband's authority in the family. Moreover, the traditional exchange, described in Chapter 7, meant that the male exchanged breadwinning for the female's homemaking, child rearing, sexual availability, and more general husband care.

A serious cost was that the good provider role encouraged a man to put all of his "gender-identifying eggs into one psychic basket"; that is, "Men were judged as men by the level of living they provided.... The good provider became a player in the male competitive macho game" (Bernard 1986, p. 130). Consequently, failure (or even mediocre performance) in the role meant one had failed *as a man*, indeed *as a* (male) *person* (Bernard 1986; Crowley 1998). What can feel like personal failure as a breadwinner, of course, is actually a result of having to cope with societal expectations that do not mesh with the reality of economic opportunities. This situation is especially applicable to blue-collar, minority, and post-retirement husbands (Gerson 1993; Grimm-Thomas and Perry-Jenkins 1994).

Meanwhile, social scientist Joseph Pleck has argued that "the most obvious and direct effect" of the male's breadwinning role is "the restricting effect of the male occupational role on men's family role" (1977, p. 420; Coltrane 1996). As a result, husbands who want to share household work and child care will not find it easy (Brayfield 1995). "The male feels not just conflicts, but intense pressures," said a lawyer and father. "Society hasn't lowered its level of job performance, but it has raised its expectations of our roles in our children's lives" (Gregg 1986, p. 48; Berry and Rao 1997). For this reason, partners who want to create new options for themselves need to work for changes in the public and corporate spheres, an option explored later in this chapter.

NEW OPTIONS FOR MEN While the role of "stay-at-home dad" may be a response to such factors as unemployment and, as such, less than truly voluntary, some husbands today are rejecting the idea that dedication to one's job or occupational achievement is the ultimate indicator of success (Booth and Crouter 1998). Some are choosing less competitive careers and are spending more time with their families. Such men place the needs of their families and their own desire for time with their families ahead of career success (Gerson 1993).

While some husbands persist in fighting to decrease the demands of the workplace in order to participate more at home, a very small minority are relinquishing breadwinning completely to become **househusbands**: husbands who stay home to care for the house and

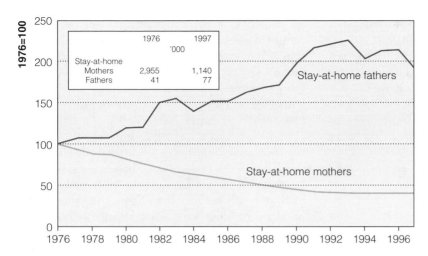

FIGURE   **13.2**

More fathers are opting to stay home with their children. (Source: Statistics Canada, "Perspectives on labour and Income," Cat. No. 75-001, Vol. 10, No. 01, March 1998.)

family while their wives work (Figure 13.2). Between 1976 and 1997, the proportion of Canadian families with stay-at-home fathers increased from one percent to six percent (Marshall 1998, p. 11).

Families with a stay-at-home dad are less likely than those with a stay-at-home mother to have a pre-school aged child at home (40 percent versus 59 percent). Compared to their female counterparts, stay-at-home dads are older, on average, than stay-at-home mothers

(42 compared with 35). Stay-at-home dads also devoted less hours per day on average to such unpaid work as child care, housework (e.g., meal preparation and clean-up, laundry), shopping and volunteer work than stay-at-home mothers (Marshall 1998) but spent more hours at these tasks than single-earner mothers and single-earner fathers (Figure 13.3).

In Canada, the Atlantic region has a disproportionately high rate (12 percent) of families with stay-at-

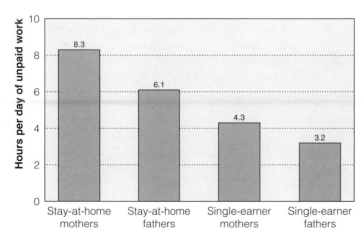

FIGURE   **13.3**

Stay-at-home mothers do the most unpaid work. (Source: Statistics Canada, "Perspectives on labour and Income," Cat. No. 75-001, Vol. 10, No. 01, March 1998.)

home dads (versus seven percent or less in all other regions of the country). About one in four stay-at-home-dad families resides in a rural area (compared with one in five stay-at-home-mother families). Stay-at-home dads in the Atlantic and rural regions are more likely than those elsewhere to be "discouraged workers," persons "not in the labour force who wanted to have a job, but... not looking for one in the belief that no work was available" (Marshall 1998, p. 10).

Reasons househusbands give for staying home include unemployment, poor health, disillusionment or dissatisfaction with the competitive grind, the desire to spend more time with their children, and their wives' desire to pursue full-time careers. These situations are still considered role reversal rather than normal family situations. But acceptance may be growing. (See Case Study 12.1, "A Full-Time Father's Story" on p. 366.)

The various options for men who would like to give more time to families are limited by the simple fact that in our society men typically earn more than women do, a point explored more fully later in this chapter. Consequently, whatever their values, many families find themselves needing to encourage the husband's dedication to his job or career in the interests of the family's overall financial well-being (Casper and O'Connell 1998). Thus, our society's gender system places constraints on family choices.

The next section examines wives' traditional work role.

Wives as Full-Time Homemakers

Historically, the homemaker, or housewife—the married woman who remains in the home to do housework and rear children—is a relatively modern role. Before industrialization, women produced goods and income by working on the family farm or, for example, by taking in boarders. As the Industrial Revolution removed employment from the household, women could less easily "combine employment with care of the home. At the same time, the increase in real income made it feasible for most wives to devote their time solely to housekeeping. Things have changed markedly since then. As a result, while in 1931, only 3.5 percent of married women were in the paid labour force, by 1996, 61.6 of Canadian wives were employed" (Nelson and Robinson 1999, p. 245). Looking more narrowly at those aged 25 to 54 years of

age, in 1998, 77 percent of married women, 79 percent of wives with school-aged children, and 69 percent of wives with pre-schoolers worked outside of the home. Among lone-parent mothers, 55 percent of those with pre-schoolers and 75 percent of those with school-aged children were in the labour force (Vanier Institute of the Family 2001).

Although traditional legal assumptions minimize the value and importance of housework (Ahlander and Bahr 1995), the economic benefits of a full-time homemaker to her family have been evaluated in many ways.[1] One way is to figure the value of her projected earnings were she to join the labour force. Another is to calculate the replacement cost of the homemaker's services. Economists conclude that a full-time housewife with at least one child under age six contributes household services equal to more than 100 percent of mean family income.

Even these calculations ignore important economic benefits to society provided by homemakers. For example, older wives often provide nursing services for their husbands or other relatives.[2] But work that is directly productive (and paid for) is more highly valued and rewarded in most industrialized societies. It is therefore not surprising to find that the job of homemaker has ambiguous status and low economic rewards. An essential feature of the housewife role is constant availability to meet others' needs, and female houseworkers report a lower sense of being in control of their lives than do employed women (Bird and Ross 1993).

One study investigated the hypothesis that the homemaker role is particularly stressful in societies which emphasizes individual achievement—but that this may not be so in more traditional, familistic societies in which the homemaker role is more highly valued (Ross, Mirowsky, and Ulrich 1983). Mexican

1. Economists have interested themselves in this issue, often as a service to insurance companies or personal injury trial attorneys who want to establish the projected value of a disabled homemaker's loss of services.

2. Among some business, professional, and political families, wives are expected to help their husbands professionally by cultivating appropriate acquaintances and by being charming hostesses and companions. These wives are part of a **two-person single career**; their contributions advance their husbands' careers and benefit the spouses' employers. Wives in two-person single careers typically do volunteer work in the arts and for charitable organizations; they may also provide their husbands career support services such as word-processing, bookkeeping, researching, and writing.

According to traditional roles, wives are the principal homemakers, and husbands the primary economic providers. Even though the majority of wives are employed outside the home today, they continue to do the lion's share of the housework.

culture, for example, places more importance on the family than on work for both sexes. And "the Mexican female, as the centre of the family, is accorded honour and prestige" (p. 672) that is not generally extended to her counterparts in the United States or Canada. It is therefore not surprising that data from a survey of 330 married people conducted in El Paso, Texas, and Juarez, Mexico, suggested that women of Mexican ethnic identity were somewhat less psychologically distressed by the homemaker role than were Anglo women.

ECONOMIC COMPENSATION? Social scientist Jessie Bernard once suggested that housewives be paid for their job of keeping the work force motivated and in good condition (Bernard 1982). Presently, homemaking is not formal employment; no financial compensation is associated with this position.

Sociologists Adie Nelson and Barrie Robinson (1999, p. 285) have observed that, "Attaching a dollar value to household and child care has long been resisted within our society, which insists that housework is a personal service, a 'labour of love'....willingly and selflessly done as a testimony of women's fundamental nature." Since 1972, the Wages for Housework Campaign (WFH) "has been working internationally to make visible women's 'double day" (WHFC Campaign 2000). However, this movement has met with only limited success.

HOMEMAKERS BY CHOICE In a study of 317 mothers of infants, researchers interviewed mothers whose babies had just been born and had them complete questionnaires three months later. The majority of new mothers sampled believed that they alone could best meet their children's needs. At the first interview almost 70 percent of the mothers said that they would rather stay home with the baby than seek outside employment; after three months this proportion had risen to 75 percent (Hock, Gnezda, and McBride 1984).

Clearly, a significant proportion of homemakers enjoy their work (Glass 1992). And a number of employed women would rather be full-time homemakers but, presumably because of financial constraints, do not have this option. The critical difference between full-time homemakers who enjoy their work and those who don't is choice (Klein et al. 1998). Satisfied homemakers are women who are exercising their preference to work in the home.

As full-time homemaking has become a minority pattern rather than the taken-for-granted role of adult women, reasons for this preference are more consciously thought through. One small study of housewives elicited two major themes. These mothers, university-educated women who had been employed prior to parenting, wished to stay deeply involved in their children's daily lives and did not anticipate that this would change as the children grew older. They wanted to help out at their children's schools and to be home when the children returned from school. They had also assessed their situations and were pessimistic about the chances of getting their husbands to share housework and child care in the event they went to work. Staying at home is one response to our society's pervasive lack of support for working mothers. And although these women exhibited considerable confidence about their ability to reenter the labour market successfully, they saw paid employment as unsatisfying, preferring to pursue other activities, such as arts and crafts, as a supplement to domesticity (Milner 1990).

Some contemporary housewives consider this role a stage (Hertz 1997). Meanwhile, not everything is perfect, even among satisfied full-time homemakers who have freely chosen that role. A survey of nearly 18 000 readers of *Parents* magazine found 62 percent of full-time mothers answering that their biggest stress was not having enough time with other adults or that their role was not valued by society (Louv 1996). Their answers may point to reasons that many women are not choosing this role. We turn now to newer work-family patterns.

WOMEN IN THE LABOUR FORCE

Women's participation in the labour force increased greatly since the turn of the twentieth century. Industrialization gave rise to bureaucratic corporations, which depended heavily on paperwork. Clerical workers were needed, and not enough men were available. Some industries, such as textiles, were considered to require a dexterity thought to be possessed by women. The expanding economy needed more workers, and women were drawn into the labour force in significant numbers beginning around 1890.

This trend accelerated during World War I and the Great Depression, then slowed following World War II. As soldiers came home to jobs, the government encouraged women to return to their kitchens and disbanded and repealed special services and legislation that had been created to facilitate the entry of wives and mothers into the labour force. The Income Tax Act, which had been changed during World War II to allow husbands a full tax exemption for working wives, regardless of the amount of income their wives earned, was rescinded and men were only allowed to claim as dependent those wives who earned below a minimum income level. The Nurseries Agreement, passed during World War II, which saw the federal and provincial governments split the costs of nursery care, foster care, and day care for children from infancy to age 16 (so that mothers could work full-time) was also rescinded and these places of child care disbanded. All of these measures reinforced the notion of husbands as providers and encouraged men and women to return to their "normal" spheres of work and home, respectively. As part of this process,

the full-time homemaker and mother was also idealized in movies and magazines.

Despite the cultural pressure against employment of women, the number of wage-earning women continued to slowly increase during the 1950s and 1960s with the greatest increases occurring among married women whose paid-labour force participation rates increased from 11.2 percent in 1951 to 22.1 percent in 1961 to 37.0 in 1971. However, throughout most of this period, the largest group of wage-earning women was young (ages 15–24), and relatively few women worked during the typical child-bearing and child-rearing years between 25–34. The pattern was fairly consistent:

> With the impending or actual arrival of their first child, these women tended, in overwhelming numbers, to drop out of the labour force and concentrate their energies upon household management....and childrearing. Existing social beliefs stressed the crucial importance of mothers being physically present for their children....[and] [o]nly severe financial hardship was considered sufficient grounds for a married woman with children present in the home to remain in or to re-enter the labour market. Following the real or imminent departure of their children, a small proportion of married women then re-entered the labour force. (Nelson and Robinson 1999, p. 93)

The picture has changed in recent decades with labour force participation rates rising substantially for women of all marital statuses (Table 13.3). The last women to move into employment outside the home, mothers of young children, have also been entering the labour force in increasing numbers. By 1999, 61 percent of Canadian women with children less than three years of age were employed—more than double the figure in 1976 (Statistics Canada 2000). Formerly, mothers of small children were likely to work only in situations of objective economic hardship, but the recent trend toward working for pay has extended to women whose husbands are in the highest income quartile (Leibowitz and Klerman 1995).

Women's Market Work

The pronounced tendency for men and women to be employed in different types of jobs is termed **occupa-**

TABLE   13.3

Percentage of the Population 15 Years of Age and Over in the Labour Force by Marital Status and Sex, Canada: 1971, 1981, 1991, 1996

Sex and Marital Status	1971*	1981*	1991**	1996**
Males:				
Single	63.5	69.6	72.9	69.7
Married	84.4	83.6	79.6	75.5
Separated/Divorced	—	—	76.9	73.0
Widowed	46.8	57.5	22.9	17.6
Total	76.4	78.2	76.4	72.4
Females:				
Single	53.5	61.8	66.4	63.6
Married	37.0	51.9	63.2	61.6
Separated/Divorced	—	—	68.2	64.7
Widowed	26.6	31.3	14.5	11.4
Total	39.9	51.8	59.9	57.6

*1971 and 1981: Separated are listed with married; figures listed for widowed include both widowed and divorced combined.

** 1991 and 1996: Married includes persons in common-law unions.

Source: Nelson and Robinson 1999, p.245.

tional sex segregation. Although more and more women are working, women are still heavily represented in low-prestige, low wage **pink-collar jobs** that offer few benefits. Consider, for example, that in 1995, women accounted for about three out of every five persons who worked full year, full time in the 25 lowest paying occupations in Canada. The average earnings of women in these occupations was $16 564 (Statistics Canada 1998d). Moreover, women in higher paying jobs are often confronted by a glass ceiling—an invisible barrier that prevents women and other minorities from moving into top corporate positions. A recent study of Fortune 500 companies found that women hold less than 11 percent of all seats on the Fortune 500 company boards (Klein 1998). Interestingly, Cianni and Romberg's investigation (1997) of visible minority women and men in Fortune 500 companies indicates that gender has more of a role in "organizational treatment" than race.

Figure 13.4 depicts the top 10 most frequent occupations of women in the labour force in Canada in 1996. Changes in hiring patterns and in women's aspirations over the past decades have improved the situation for women compared to 1961, when the 10 most frequent occupations for women accounted for just under two-thirds (62.7 percent) of employed women (Wilson 1996, p. 106). But female workers remain concentrated in low-paying occupations. In 1996, 52 percent of all employed women were clerical, sales or service workers.

Women-dominated professions tend to be service or support professions: clerical work, health, teaching, social work, library work, or recreation. In medicine, women tend to be in pediatrics, anesthesiology, and psychiatry. In academia, in which women have also made gains, they are more apt to occupy the especially low-paid, part-time positions (Roos and Jones 1993, CAUT 2000). As was discussed in Chapter 3, despite

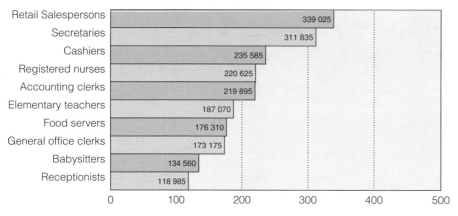

FIGURE **13.4**

The ten most frequent jobs for women in Canada, 1996. (Source: adapted from Statistics Canada, *The Daily*, Catalogue no. 11-001, March 17, 1998.)

demands of the women's movement for equal pay for equal work and the passage of pay equity legislation in most Canadian provinces, discrepancy in pay for employed men and women persists (Figure 13.5).

Economists have explored the reasons for the persistent wage gap between full-time men and women workers (Wellington 1994; Morgan 1998). The concentration of women in lower-paying occupations and lower-status positions within a broad occupational category plays a major role. Researchers disagree on why females remain segregated in a limited number of

occupations and earn less income (Tam 1997). One explanation is sexual harassment and other forms of discrimination on the part of blue-collar (Padavic 1992) and other employers (Women's Research and Education Institute 1990) and employees who fear the prestige of their profession will be lessened with the entrance of women, or who simply believe that "the ideal worker is normatively masculine" (Martin 1992, p. 220). Employers in business and the professions continue to stereotype all women as lacking in career commitment (Shellenbarger 1992i; Burke 1994).

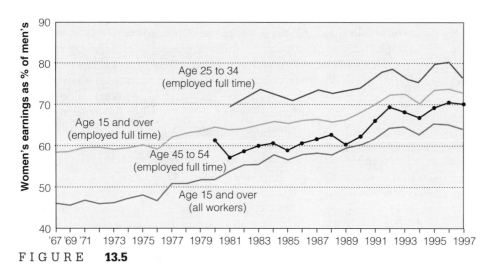

FIGURE **13.5**

Women's average earnings still lag behind men's. (Source: Statistics Canada, "Perspectives on Labour and Income," Cat. No. 75-001, Vol. 12, No. 04, Dec. 2000.)

Moreover, women may aspire to traditionally female occupations because they believe these are the only ones open to them, or they may consciously trade off higher wages and advancement for the reduced demands that traditional female occupations sometimes make. (As an indication of male dominance explored in Chapter 3, jobs that are considered masculine have higher salaries and occupational prestige [Glick 1991].)

The future is difficult to predict (Wellington 1994). On the one hand, women's increased entry into professional and managerial tracks suggests a more substantial future presence in those jobs (Oppenheimer 1994), perhaps even parity with men. Younger men and women have relatively equal pay rates. A recent study found that a gender gap remains in earnings at career entry, and this gap is not accounted for by differences in human capital (that is, years of education, college major, knowledge about the job, mental aptitude, or self-esteem) (Marini and Fan 1997). Moreover, even comparable wages in entry-level jobs do not necessarily predict future occupational status and earnings. Finally, the difficulty of combining work and family responsibilities, a burden that most often falls unevenly on women, still seems to present a formidable barrier to equal occupational status and income (Shelton 1992). According to one Canadian survey, 85 percent of working women said that there were not enough hours in the day to accomplish everything they needed to do; more than one-quarter had thought about quitting their jobs because the effort of balancing work and family life was so stressful (Lee et al. 1994).

TWO-EARNER MARRIAGES—NEWER PROVIDER-CAREGIVING OPTIONS

Today, **two-earner marriages** in which both partners are in the labour force have become the statistical norm with dual-earner families outnumbering single-earner families more than three to one (Marshall 1998, p.72). Moreover, an employed wife contributes a significant amount to her family's income (Ingrassia 1995), while a growing number earn more than their husbands do (Crompton and Geran 1995; Lawlor 1997). As we have seen, however, even among two-earner couples, the majority consider providing financially to be the husband's main role; the unpaid work of family caregiving (house care, child care, and perhaps elderly care) is the wife's principal obligation (Shelton 1992). Even though we may tend to think of two-earner couples as ones in which both partners are employed nine to five, spouses evidence considerable flexibility in how they design their two-earner unions. In this section we examine several two-earner patterns: two-career marriages, self- and part-time employment, shift work, and temporarily leaving the labour force.

Two-Career Marriages

Careers differ from jobs in that they hold the promise of advancement, are considered important in themselves and not just a source of money, and demand a high degree of commitment. Although the majority of women work in pink-collar jobs, career women hope to climb the occupational ladder. Career women work in occupations such as medicine, law, politics, banking, and company management that usually require education beyond the bachelor's degree.

The vast majority of two-paycheque marriages can hardly be classified as dual career. Indeed, we have already noted that occupational segregation remains strong (Statistics Canada 1998). Nevertheless, most of today's university students view the **two-career marriage** as an available and workable option. Increasingly, however, experts are pointing out—both from research and from personal experience—that expecting to have it all in a two-career marriage, particularly one with children, may be unrealistic.

For two-career couples with children, family life is hectic and often tense as partners juggle schedules, chores, and child care. "Career and family involvement have never been combined easily in the same person" (Hunt and Hunt 1986, p. 280). Career wives, in particular, often find themselves in a Catch-22 situation. The career world tends to view the person who splits time between work and family as being less than professional, yet society encourages working women to do exactly this (Hochschild 1997).

Part-Time Employment

Of the 18 000 mothers surveyed by *Parents* magazine, nearly two-thirds (61 percent) said that, if they could do anything they wished, they would have a part-time job (Louv 1996). Research shows that mothers employed part-time are more traditional and similar to full-time homemakers than to full-time employed mothers in their attitudes about wife and mother roles (Glass 1992; Muller 1995). However, while Canadian women are still more likely than Canadian men to work full-year, part-time, not all of them are doing so voluntarily. Some women are channeled into part-time work because they cannot find full-time jobs and/or adequate child care. For example, in 1998, about 30 percent of adult women working part-time were doing so involuntarily because they could not obtain full-time employment. An additional 20 percent worked part-time so that they could provide care for their children (Statistics Canada 1999).

Although greater family and personal time is a clear benefit of part-time employment, there are costs. As it exists now, part-time work seldom offers job security or other benefits such as employer pensions. And part-time pay is rarely proportionate to that for full-time jobs. For example, a part-time teacher or secretary usually earns well below the wage paid to regular staff. In higher level professional/managerial jobs, a different problem appears. To work "part-time" as an attorney, accountant, or aspiring manager is to forego the salary, status, and security of a full-time position and to put in 40 hours a week or more (Abelson 1998). Despite these drawbacks, James White (1999) reports that his analysis of 2757 cases collected by Statistics Canada as part of their annual General Social Survey indicates that "mothers who worked over 20 hours a week are less satisfied with the balance between work and family time than fathers and mothers who work less than 20 hours or are at home full time" and that "[p]art-time dual earner families show relatively high satisfaction with work-family balance for both genders."

Shift Work

Sometimes one or both spouses engage in **shift work** (evening, night, rotating or split). According to the 1995 Survey of Work Arrangements, one in four husbands and one in five wives in full-time dual-earner couples worked shift (Marshall 1998b, p. 13). This survey found that although the majority of both husbands and wives reported that doing so was a requirement of the job, women were more likely than men to identify another factor—generally caring for children and other family members—as their main reason for doing so.

Some spouses work shift for higher wages or to ease child-care arrangements (Hertz 1997). For example, in November 1995, dual-earner couples with children under the age of 16 at home were somewhat more likely than others to have at least one earner working shift. "Some 26 percent of couples who both worked shift had at least one preschool aged child at home, compared with only 23 percent of non-shift work couples" (Marshall 1998b, p. 12). But shift work reduces the overlap of family members' shared time and leisure time. In November 1996, "shift couples had an average four hours and 20 minutes less shared time off each day, because their employment overlap was less, and their average workdays were longer" (Marshall 1998b, p. 11).

In addition, research based on in-depth interviews with 90 predominantly male newsprint mill shiftworkers and their spouses living in three communities in different regions of Canada, supplemented with questionnaire data from 130 workers, found that the onus for adjusting to shifts fell mainly on the spouses of workers. Spouses also felt constrained by their partners' shift schedules in making decisions about child care and/or whether to continue with their own paid employment. In the vast majority of these households, a traditional division of labour predominated with respect to both child care and domestic work (Preston et al 2000). Analysis of responses of 1668 individuals in a national American survey designed to examine the relationship between labour force participation and marital quality (White and Keith 1990) found that—after controlling for education, race, age, number of children, years married, wife's employment, and family income—a partner's doing shift work reduced satisfaction with the sexual relationship and increased the probability of divorce.

Home-Based Work

In 1996, almost six out of 10 employed Canadians working at home (58 percent) were self-employed; the rest were paid by employers located elsewhere (Statistics Canada 1998b). In that year, more Canadian women than men usually worked at home. Approximately 36 percent of Canadian women who worked at home were employed in sales and service, with over one-third of this group working as nannies or babysitters. Another one-third of women who worked at home were employed in business, finance or administrative positions or, less commonly, worked as clerks, bookkeepers and secretaries. The occupations of men who worked at home were more diverse. Compared to non-home-based workers, home-based workers are more likely to work part-time, with women especially likely to do so (Statistics Canada 1999b).

Although more and more older retirees are starting home-based businesses (Shaver 1991), parents with children at home are doing so as well (Alexander 1991). Home-based work (working from home, either for oneself or for an employer) mushroomed over the past decade as a way to integrate work and family activities. This situation is largely due to the advent of tele-working, or telecommuting—connecting to the office, customers, clients, or others by Internet. Based on the findings of the 1996 Census, working at home appears to be slightly more popular in the Western provinces, even when farming occupations are excluded from consideration (Statistics Canada 1998b).

For some, working at home may represent an attempt to integrate work with "competing domestic demand, such as taking care of children or household chores" ("Both Sexes" 1990). As an example, one mother's

> highly spirited teenage daughter took an emotional nosedive and attempted suicide three years ago. Fortunately, [the mother] had just landed a work-at-home post.... That gave her flexibility to closely manage her daughter's treatment and supervise her and her friends after school, all while getting her work done. (Shellenbarger 1998, p. B1)

Besides combining work with parenting, another possible advantage of home-based employment is to "knit neighbourhoods together" as at-home neighbours interact frequently, taking more interest in their communities (Shellenbarger 1998).

One study (Hill, Hawkins, and Miller 1996) compared 157 home-based teleworkers for a major corporation with 89 office workers from the same company. Almost three-quarters of the teleworkers reported benefiting from the arrangement. Remarking on the advantages of flexibility, mothers of young children were the most likely to be favourable: "I can take care of the sick child and get my work done. A win-win situation" (p. 297).

However, home-based work is not an entirely rosy picture. Both worker categories reported putting in about 52 hours a week, with those at home working slightly more than the office-based employees. Teleworkers were no more likely than the office workers to feel they had enough time for family life. Some said that they tended to work more hours than they would otherwise, "instead of taking time to enjoy the family" (p. 297). Indeed, work-family flexibility may be a double-edged sword. The families of some teleworkers "struggled because workplace and schedule flexibility blurred the boundaries between work and family life" (p. 293). As one teleworker said, "I am always at work.... Between 5:00 A.M. and midnight, seven days a week" (p. 298).

Interestingly, the researchers discovered that teleworkers who had a home office with a closing door were even less likely than others to report having enough family time.

> One possible explanation is that this dedicated home work environment may lead to longer hours of work at home. Having a home office with a door that closes enables ... teleworkers to work with fewer external cues about when it is time for work to stop and may make it less likely that they would be available to interaction with their family. (pp. 297–298)

Then too, mothers employed at home report interruptions. Like full-time homemakers, they are often asked to do chores for extended kin and others—to run errands for relatives, for example, to watch neighbours' children when bad weather closes the school, or keep an eye out for the older kids (Kutner 1988b). Last, but certainly not least, an additional problem is that those home-based workers who are self-employed—the majority of home-based workers in 1996—receive neither benefits nor pensions (Schetagne 2000).

Leaving the Labour Force and Reentry

A common work pattern among marrieds has been for the wife to be employed full-time until shortly before the birth of her first child and then to leave the full-time labour force either permanently or temporarily. "The 'homecoming' movement is a way of living life to the fullest," explained one mother. "It's a move that protects ... marriages. It gives the couple time to strategize, time to get things done, and time for sex" (in Richardson 1988, p. C-10). However, this "homecoming" period is increasingly likely to be of short duration. Fast and Da Pont (1997) find that women in Canada are less likely to interrupt their paid work today and, when interruptions do occur, they return to paid employment more quickly than women did in the past—despite the entrenchment of paid maternity leave policies.

In 2001, Canada doubled the length of its paid maternity/parental leave to eligible claimants through the Employment Insurance (EI) program from six months to one year. Employment Insurance (EI) allows 15 weeks (the first two of which are unpaid) of *maternity benefits* provided that the pregnant woman has worked at least 600 hours during the previous year. These benefits provide women with 55 percent of their normal weekly pay to a maximum amount of $413 dollars a week (gross). Fathers or mothers may also apply for *parental benefits* for an additional 35 weeks following the birth or adoption of a child. While women who claim maternity benefits are prohibited from employment, those who receive parental benefits are allowed to work part-time and earn 25 percent of their wage up to a set maximum.

Results from the longitudinal Survey of Labour and Income Dynamics (SLID) indicate the absence of maternity leave and self-employment are linked to quick returns to the paid workplace. "The odds of the mother's returning to work by the end of the first month [following a child's birth] were almost six times higher when she did *not* receive maternity leave benefits. Also, the odds of returning early were almost eight times higher for the self-employed than for employees" (Marshall 1999, p. 22). In general, however, women evidenced a strong attachment to participation in the paid labour force.

> Of the 367 000 employed Canadian women who gave birth in 1993 or 1994, some 76 000 or 21 percent were back to work by the end of the first month after childbirth—15 percent of paid workers (50 000) and 76 percent of the self-employed (26 000). In other words, almost one in five mothers took very little time off. Some 19 percent of women returned after six months, while another 12 percent did so after five, and 11 per-

cent after seven....Within a year's time, 86 percent of mothers had returned to work, and by two years a full 93 percent were back to paid work. (Marshall 1999, p. 20)

According to this survey, only seven percent of all Canadian women who gave birth in the early 1990s did not return to paid work after two years. Compared to those who did, non-returnees were more likely to have been employed in part-time work (38 percent versus 28 percent) and less likely to have held, prior to giving birth, a unionized job (16 percent versus 33 percent) or a professional job (30 percent versus 40 percent). In addition, non-returnees had, on average, spent less time at their last job than those who returned and earned lower median salaries ($16 700 versus $25 600). Non-returnees were also younger and more unlikely to be married "Some 30 percent of non-returnees were on their own (living without a partner), compared with just four percent of the women who returned to work" (Marshall 1999, p. 23). It may be that those who return to paid employment quickly after childbirth perceive that they have more to gain and more to lose than those who do not.

Yet there are costs associated with leaving the labour force even temporarily. Anne Machung, research associate for a study of graduating women, describes her respondents:

> Almost all plan to have careers and children at the same time.... There is enormous confusion among young women about how they're going to do this. They have this fantasy that they can get their careers established by age 28 or 29, have children, then re-enter the labour force. They're not aware of the difficulties of staying home and then re-entering the work force. They don't realize there are consequences. (in Rimer 1988b, p. 30)

For one thing, women who leave the labour force face lost pension and other job-related benefits ("Poverty Looms" 1991). Moreover, after years of being at home, reentering women find that they have lost job or professional contacts, confidence, and, in some cases, skills. "Other costs of not returning to paid employment include the depreciation of job-related skills and/or lost opportunities for building further skills, both of which may affect future earnings" (Marshall 1999, p. 25). Potential employers may also question the career or work commitment of reentering women (Gideonse 1998).

All this results in decreased earning power and, in the case of professional women, reduced potential career advancement (Waldfogel 1997). As one mother who had graduated in the top 10 percent of her law school class and left a high position in a law firm to stay home for 10 years said, "I'll probably never achieve the pay scale or the prestige I would have had if I'd kept working those 10 years" (in Waldman 1992).

This discussion of ways that two-earner couples organize their provider and family roles illustrates that unpaid family work is indeed a factor to be considered. The following section examines unpaid family work.

UNPAID FAMILY WORK

Unpaid family work involves the necessary tasks of attending both the emotional needs of all family members and the practical needs of dependent members (such as children or elderly parents) as well as maintaining the family domicile. In Canada, the 1996 Census was the first to include questions on unpaid household work: providing care or assistance to seniors, housework or home maintenance, and unpaid child care. "While men, on average, spent more time than women on paid employment...women performed significantly more unpaid work in all three categories" of unpaid work (Statistics Canada, 1998). We'll examine these three forms of unpaid work in turn.

Caring for Dependent Family Members

As discussed in Chapter 12, our cultural tradition and social institutions give women principal responsibility for raising children. This situation has not changed even as more and more mothers have entered the labour force. Even in two-career marriages, wives are far more likely to make the child-care arrangements (Health Canada, 1999, Peterson and Gerson 1992; Statistics Canada, 1998c).

Moreover, our culture designates women as "kin-keepers" (Rosenthal 1985) whose job it is to keep in touch with—and, if necessary, care for—adult siblings and other relatives.

THE SANDWICH GENERATION The vast majority of informal elderly care is provided by female relatives, usually daughters and (albeit less often) daughters-in-law (Keith 1995; Globerman 1996). One small, qualitative study (Aronson 1992) of women over 35 who were caring for aging mothers pointed to the power of the stereotypical link between femininity and caregiving in our society (see Chapter 3). Women, more so than men, feel obliged to care for frail parents and experience guilt when they do not (McGrew 1998). One woman said she had "yelled at" her brothers, "and they did go down and visit [her ailing mother], ... but not one of them go down and clean or bring laundry" (p. 17). Respondents cited men's primary commitment to employment and relative inability to anticipate their mothers' needs as explanations for their husbands' and brothers' lesser sense of obligation and involvement.

As defined for the purposes of the 1996 Census, providing unpaid care or assistance to seniors included such activities as "providing personal care to a senior family member, visiting seniors, talking with them on the telephone, and helping them with shopping, banking or with taking medication." More women than men (19 percent versus 14 percent) reported providing unpaid care to seniors.

Besides gender, feeling responsible to personally care for aging parents (one aspect of filial responsibility, an adult child's felt responsibility to parents) differs by ethnicity (Ishii-Kuntz 1997), how well adult children get along with their parents (Bromley and Blieszner 1997), and whether one's family adheres to more individualistic or collectivist values (see Box 2.1, "Marriages and Families Across Cultures," and footnote 7.2), among other things (Pyke and Bengston 1996).

Helping an elderly parent can have a profound effect on the primary caregiver, who is often a middle-aged mother in the "sandwich generation"—that is, sandwiched between simultaneously caring for dependent children and aging parents. (The sandwich generation, also mentioned in Chapter 12, is more fully addressed in Chapter 16.) In fact, just when many mothers whose children who are getting older "thought they could get back to their careers, some are finding themselves on an even longer 'Daughter Track,' with their parents, or their husband's parents, growing frail" (Beck 1990, p. 49). Typically, caregivers to disabled parents give up leisure activities and contacts with friends in order to fulfill work and family responsibilities (Burnley 1987; Roots 1998). At home a wife can feel torn between caring for her children, her husband, and her aging parent (Kleban et al. 1989)—not to mention the housework ("Loving Care ..." 1997).

Housework

Utopians and engineers alike shared a hope that advancing technology and changed social arrangements would make obsolete the need for families to cook, clean, or mind children (Hayden 1981). But instead, middle-class women spend more time on housework today than they did at the turn of the twentieth century. Collective arrangements proposed by utopians and feminists never caught on. Housewives were left alone in their free-standing suburban homes, as the postwar economy thrived on the construction of houses and automobiles (Wright 1981). Servants, who did much of the work for earlier middle-class housewives, entered factory work or took more challenging jobs, eventually benefiting from changed roles for women.

Technology seems merely to have raised the standards; instead of changing clothes at infrequent intervals, we now do so daily (Cowan 1983). At the same time, however, "disappearing, except from all but the wealthiest homes today, are butlers, maid, nannies, governesses, charwomen, kitchen and scullery aides, gardeners and groundskeepers, and that general class of workers once common to even the most average of middle-class homes—the domestic" (Nelson and Robinson 1999, p. 284). It is evident that only a minority of households can afford the expense entailed by hiring live-in housekeepers or daily housekeeping service providers. In consequence, contemporary women typically spend as much time on housework as did women in earlier times.

WHO DOES HOUSEWORK? Despite changing attitudes among couples (Ferree 1991) and media portrayals of two-earner couples who share housework, women in fact continue to do the bulk of it. Whether or not they are employed outside the home, Canadian women bear a disproportionate burden of unpaid housework (Figure 13.6). Among those who worked full-time (30 or more hours per week) outside the home, about one in two wives (51 percent) but

less than one in four husbands (23 percent) reported spending 15 hours per week doing unpaid housework. Among those with no paid employment, 70 percent of wives, but only 36 percent of husbands reported spending 15 or more hours of housework. The number of children in the family is associated with both women's and, to extent, men's household work. While approximately 37 percent of wives who were employed full-time but had no children reported spending 15 hours or more on housework, this increased to 60 percent for those with at least one child less than 15 years of age at home. The comparable figures for husbands were 19 percent and 26 percent, respectively.

An earlier study (Brayfield 1992) found that, independent of employment patterns and family characteristics, French-Canadian couples generally allocate housework more equitably than do either English-Canadian or recently arrived non-French, non-English, immigrant couples. It has been suggested that this reflects a greater emphasis placed by Francophone feminists, since the time of Quebec's Quiet Revolution, on implementing changes simultaneously, to both the public and private spheres. In contrast, "only recently have anglophone feminists acknowledged that housework itself and the nexus between the private world of housework and the public world of paid work hold the key to producing a more equitable division of labour between women and men in our society" (Nelson and Robinson 1999, p. 306). In addition, within some ethnic groups, such as Vietnamese and Laotian, for example, housework is significantly shared by household members other than the wife/mother, even if not by her husband (Johnson, P. 1998).

THE DIFFERENTLY-ABLED AND HOUSEWORK
Both men and women with disabilities spend more time doing housework than those who do not have disabilities. "Women with disabilities are clearly more likely than any other group to spend more time on unpaid household tasks, regardless of their living arrangements, leaving them with less time and energy to pursue paid employment" (Fawcett 1998). Diane Fawcett's research reports that men and women with disabilities generally displayed different attitudes towards housework. For example, men adopted a very practical attitude, with one differently-abled man observing, "For a person with a physical disability like

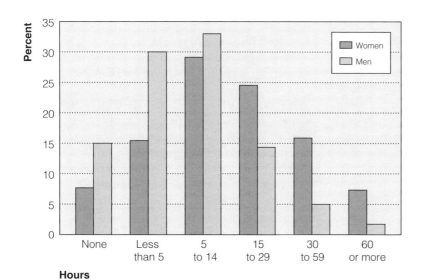

FIGURE **13.6**

Women report more hours of housework than men, 1996. (Source: Statistics Canada 1998d.)

mine, the best use of my time is not housework. I'm better off having an able-bodied person do that while I use my intellect—that's my strength." In contrast, women with disabilities typically felt obliged to perform housework tasks themselves, even when they acknowledged that doing so threatened their physical well-being: "I get exhausted working and doing things around the house. Then I am more likely to get really sick again" (in Fawcett 1998).

THE SECOND SHIFT   Many employed wives (and just a few husbands) put in a **second shift** in unpaid family work that amounts to an extra month of work each year (Hochschild 1989).

The second shift for women means a "leisure gap" between husbands and wives, as the latter sacrifice avocational activities (Schnittger and Bird 1990), leisure—and sleep—to accomplish unpaid family work (Hochschild 1989; Shelton 1992). As a result,

> women tend to talk more intently about being overtired, sick, and "emotionally drained." Many women I know could not tear away from the topic of sleep.... These women talked about sleep the way a hungry person talks about food." (Hochschild 1989, p. 9)

Women's revolutionary entry into the labour force ought to mean a concurrent restructuring of household labour. As we saw earlier in this chapter, husbands are doing somewhat more around the house than 20 years ago. But "women, rather than men, continue to adjust their time to accomplish both paid and unpaid work" (Shelton 1990, p. 132; see also McFarlane, Beaujot and Haddad, 2000; Spitze and Ward 1995; Kurz 1997). Hochschild (1989) calls this situation a **stalled revolution**.

Ways in which individual families manage during this stalled revolution vary. Some wives scale back their paid work, and others quit entirely (Hochschild 1989). (These may seem the best choices, given the options. But the reality is that "no-fault divorce laws combined with rising divorce rates have substantially increased the risks for women [who do so].... Divorced women are now expected to be able to support themselves" [Peterson 1989, p. 2].) Many busy spouses lower housework standards and food preparation time after a wife becomes employed (Shelton 1990). Some two-earner couples hire household help (Ferree 1991), although usually it is the wife who ends up coordinating things (Thompson 1991). Especially in single-parent families, older children help (Fassinger 1990), but children's contributions are limited (Berk 1988),

CHAPTER 13   Work and Family

and they actually do little to lessen the load (Piotrkowski, Rapoport, and Rapoport 1987).

Several studies have found that when family size and the wife's employment hours increase to the point that she can no longer do it all, wives may become dissatisfied with the level of cleanliness at home (Robinson and Milkie 1998) and her husband does pitch in (Peterson and Gerson 1992)—but often only to do some of the "nicer" tasks such as playing with the kids while she makes dinner (Berk 1985; Hochschild 1989). Wives get more help when their earnings are considered essential to family finances (Perry-Jenkins and Crouter 1990). The larger the share of family income provided by a wife and the longer she has been employed, the more household work her husband does (Kelly 1990; Pittman and Blanchard 1996). When a wife is thought to be working mainly for self-fulfillment, household help is less likely (Hochschild 1989).

Husbands who telecommute or have other kinds of flexible schedules do more housework (Kelly 1990). Generally, husbands follow "the path of least resistance" (Peterson and Gerson 1992, p. 532): To secure her spouse's help with the second shift a wife generally must take the initiative, in essence

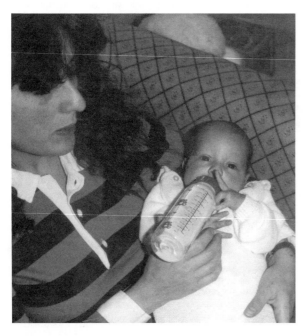

Our cultural tradition and social institutions give women principal responsibility for raising children.

demanding his participation (Hochschild 1989; Guelzow, Bird, and Koball 1991).

Our cultural tradition and social institutions give women principal responsibility for raising children.

WHY WOMEN DO THE HOUSEWORK For some homemakers, the perception of "home" as "the world where we carry out the private search for intimacy.... And expect to explore and create selves there" (Nippert-Eng 1996, p. 22) gives housekeeping tasks meaning. However, those doing housework generally find the tasks boring, while getting them done in today's busy family is stressful (Barnett and Shen 1997). In any case, household labour is of keen interest to social scientists because struggles over who does it are central to analyses of class and gender.[3] We might apply the conflict and feminist theoretical perspectives discussed in Chapter 2 to this question. Doing so would mean arguing that women are more likely than men to do housework—and other unpaid family labour—because they have less power in their families than do men. Meanwhile, a number of related perspectives on the division of household labour have emerged.

The **ideological perspective** points to the effects of cultural expectations on household labour (Hiller and Philliber 1986; Hardesty and Bokemeier 1989). In this view, who does the housework at least partly reflects stereotypes and normative scripts about "who should do what" (Berk 1985). Some research has found that more highly educated husbands are more willing to do housework, a finding in support of the ideological perspective inasmuch as more education results in less traditional gender attitudes (Ross 1987). As discussed in Chapter 3, girls are socialized to do housework more often than boys are. Researchers (see, for example, Blair and Lichter 1991; Shelton 1992) have found that wives do the vast majority of traditionally feminine household tasks, or "women's work." Wives do more than 96 percent of making beds, for example, and 94 percent of diapering children. Husbands, who do 86 percent of household repairs, 75 percent of the grass cutting, and 77 percent of

3. All the perspectives on who does the housework assume, of course, that the household division of labour is not natural but socially constructed and subject to change. Moreover, current perspectives differ from the 1950s approach, which assumed that women's roles were simply expressive and housework was not real family labour. Hence, researchers now examine what was once taken for granted.

snow shoveling, spend most of their household labour time on chores considered masculine (Berk 1985). In a study of 382 two-earner marriages in 1989 (Ferree 1991), wives were more likely to cook, clean, and do laundry, whereas husbands helped clean up after meals or shopped for groceries.

As pointed out in Chapter 3, however, adults do not simply live out cultural scripts learned in childhood. Rather, people weave the fabric of their lives with many threads, among them opportunities and chance (Gerson 1985). For example, a woman who is experiencing career success, or who is divorced, or whose husband is unemployed may gradually come to see herself as a primary breadwinner. At the same time, a wife with children and a higher-earning husband is less likely to redefine formerly learned gender boundaries (Potuchek 1992).

A second view holds simply that the partner with more time does the housework (England and Farkas 1986). Expanding on this idea, the **rational investment perspective** argues that couples attempt to maximize the family economy by trading off between time and energy investments in paid market work and unpaid household labour (Becker 1991). Spouses agree that each partner will spend more time and effort in the activities at which she or he is more efficient. Similarly, the **resource hypothesis**, proposed by Blood and Wolfe (1960) and described in Chapter 10, suggests that one spouse's household labour is a consequence of her or his resources compared to those of the other. Thus, the partner with higher resources (such as greater income or long-term earning potential) will have more power and hence spend less time on housework.

In principle, both the rational investment perspective and the resource hypothesis are gender neutral: Either husband or wife might invest more time and energy in the labour force and less in housework. But as we have already seen, husbands are likely to be receiving higher salaries than are their wives even within the professions and in sales and management positions. It follows that men and not women invest relatively more time in the labour force. Furthermore, as was discussed in Chapter 10, resources are unevenly distributed between women and men. As a result, husbands are likely to have more status and power in marriages and can therefore resist housework demands (Coverman 1985).

It is evident that "divisions of household labour are, in fact, the result of multiple causal forces. Who does what around the house is shaped by time availability, relative resources, and ideology" (Coltrane and Ishii-Kuntz 1992, p. 53; Zvonkovic et al. 1996).

A REINFORCING CYCLE   When we consider men's and women's paid and unpaid work, it becomes apparent that a **reinforcing cycle** emerges: For a number of reasons, which we have already explored, men employed full-time average higher earnings than do women employed full-time. Because most husbands actually or potentially earn more than their wives, couples allow her paid work role to be more vulnerable to family demands than his. This situation, in turn, has the effects of lowering the time and energy a wife spends in the labour force and of giving employers reason to pay women less than men. This lower pay, coupled with society's devaluation of family in favour of job demands, encourages husbands to see their wives' work (paid and unpaid) as less important than their own—and to conclude that they really shouldn't be asked to take responsibility for homemaking. Disproportionately burdened with household labour, wives find it difficult to invest themselves in the labour force to the same degree that husbands do (Zvonkovic et al. 1996). This situation remains true even for the majority of two-career couples, including, for example, physicians married to one another (Grand et al. 1990).

Given the general finding of disparity between husbands' and wives' contributions to household labour, "it is important to keep in mind that there is considerable variability in the amount of housework that men do, and that there are men who make significant contributions to the work of the household" (Blair and Johnson 1992, p. 575). In the next section we will examine how partners juggle household labour demands.

JUGGLING EMPLOYMENT AND UNPAID FAMILY WORK

The concept of juggling implies a hectic and stressful situation. Virtually all research and other writings on the subject suggest that today's typical family is a hectic one (Schor 1993). This is particularly true when there are children in the home.

The Speed-Up of Family Life

For one thing, working people are spending significantly more hours at work now than 20 years ago (Bond 1997). According to data obtained in the 1998 General Social Survey, Canadian men aged 25 to 44 averaged 48.6 hours of paid work and work-related activities per week, and women in this age group averaged 38.4 hours—an increase of two hours per week for both men and women since 1992 (Canadian Press 1999). In an unpredictable economy characterized by "the pervasive fear of dismissal" (O'Boyle 1990), professionals, managers, and lower-level workers as well feel compelled to demonstrate their skills and job commitment by working more hours (Michaels and Willwerth 1989).

For example, in 1997, about one in 10 Canadian workers put in overtime without being reimbursed for it with either extra pay or time off. In that year, such unpaid overtime was most common for white-collar workers, particularly those who were teachers or manufacturers. In addition, in the past two decades, the number of Canadians who "moonlight" or hold down more than one job has tripled. In 1996, there were approximately 700 000 Canadians who did so (Statistics Canada, 1998a).

To measure work stress, the 1996–97 National Population Health Survey used a scale composed of 12 questions describing working conditions that were answered on a five-point scale of agree or disagree. The minimum score on the test was 0 and the maximum was 45; "high stress" was defined as a score of 30 or higher. The survey found that more women reported high stress levels than men did in every age category, with women aged 20 to 24 almost three times as likely to report high work stress than the average Canadian worker (Health Canada 1999). Notable differences in high work stress occurred among persons in different types of households. Single parents were twice as likely as Canadians in couple relations without children to report high work stress (Figure 13.7).

The 1998 General Social Survey also found that Canadians are increasingly likely to feel time-crunched. According to this survey, 21 percent of women over 15 years of age complained about time stress in 1998, compared with 15 percent in 1992. The proportion of men complaining about time stress rose to 16 percent from 12 percent. Time-stress levels were highest for married men and women aged 25 to 44 who were employed full-time with children at home. Among these individuals, the "struggle to juggle" could be acute. Working parents report chronic fatigue and being at "the breaking point" (Hancock 1995; Gibbs and Duffy 1996; Morin and Rosenfeld 1998). In short,

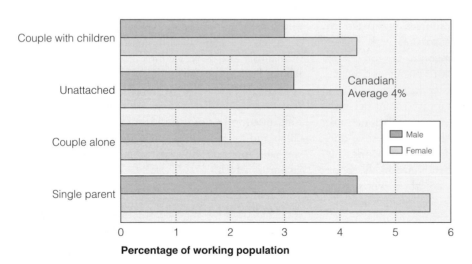

FIGURE **13.7**

High work stress, by household type (age-standardized), employed persons aged 15+, Canada, 1994–1995. (Source: Statistics Canada, <http://www.statcan.ca/Daily/English/980317/d980317.htm>)

"Today more than ever before, family life has become impoverished for want of time, adding another threat to the already fragile bonds that hold families together" (Rubin 1999, p. 283).

Among families following the traditional model, this added workload translates into greater father absence. "The 5 o'clock Dad of the 1950s and '60s has been replaced by an 8 or 9 o'clock Dad, who very likely also attends to his job on Saturday or Sunday, if he's not holding down an altogether different weekend job" (Schor, in Coston 1992).

Sociologist Arlie Hochschild's (1989) qualitative study of 500 two-earner couples points to the frantic pace and sense of pressure for everyone involved, but especially for mothers and for children, whose harried mothers often rush them: "Hurry up! It's time to go," "Finish your cereal now," "You can do that later," "Let's go!" ... "Let's see who can take their bath the quickest!" (Hochschild 1989, pp. 9–10).

We will look now at how children in two-earner marriages are doing more generally.

 Focusing on Children

How Are Children Faring?

Before women with children entered the paid work force in large numbers, working mothers were considered problematic by child development experts. Now they are taken for granted (Brazelton 1989b). But the psychological development of children without a parent at home full-time is frequently a subject of concern.

Early research supported the notion that working mothers were not detrimental and might even be advantageous to their children's development (Hoffman and Nye 1974). Overall, this continues to be the prevailing view. Several studies show that, contrary to common assumptions, employed mothers spend almost as much time in direct interaction with their children and in visiting their children's schools as other mothers do, and no significant difference exists in the quality of care provided by employed mothers and full-time homemakers (Chira 1994b; Muller 1995; Bryant and Zick 1996; Holmes 1998). Employed mothers foster independence in their children and are especially good role models for adoles-

cent daughters, who have better social and personality adjustment and higher academic motivation and accomplishment than do daughters of homemakers (Wilkie 1988). Furthermore, the economic benefit to children of working mothers cannot be overlooked. Family income tends to be favourably associated with various child outcome measures (National Council of Welfare 1999).

Important for parents, though, is keeping their child's needs in the forefront in the face of daily pressures. Recent studies, in fact, have found that mothers who work part-time are better at this than those who work full-time—and may indeed spend more time helping their children with homework than even full-time homemakers (Muller 1995).

While granting the importance and equity of women's current opportunities for work achievement, many experts caution about eclipsing children's needs in the process. Hochschild seemed astonished to hear one mother talk about her nine-month-old daughter's need for independence; clearly, a child's needs were being minimized to benefit the mother's schedule (1989, p. 198). A recent study suggests that "the time-squeeze felt by parents trying to juggle the demands of work and family is increasingly being transferred to their children's lives.... [A]s parents' lives have become more hectic, those of their children are becoming more tightly organized," and children are spending more time on school, organized sports, chores, and going with their parents on errands rather than engaging in unstructured play or organizing their own activities with other children (Holmes 1998).

Eminent pediatrician T. Berry Brazelton urges parents to respect the process of attachment to a new infant. "When new parents do not have the time and freedom to face this process and live through it successfully, they may indeed escape emotionally. In running away, they may miss the opportunity to develop a secure attachment to their baby and never get to know themselves as real parents" (Brazelton 1989b, p. 68). Discipline, sleep issues, feeding, competition with the caregiver, and perfectionism are other issues Brazelton sees as possible pitfalls for working families. But "understand that there is no perfect way to be a parent. The myth of the supermom serves no real purpose except to increase the parents' guilt" (Brazelton 1989b, p. 69). Brazelton urges the same policy measures we outline later in this chapter, and Box 13.1, "Bringing Up Baby: A Doctor's

Prescription for Busy Parents," presents his guidelines for individual parents. We turn now to the question of how parents are faring as they juggle paid and unpaid work.

How Are Parents Faring?

This chapter focuses on work and family in marriages for two reasons. First, the vast majority of research on the interface between paid employment and family labour concerns marrieds (Crouter and Helms-Erikson 1997); second, single parenting is addressed in some detail in Chapter 14. But here for a moment we want to point to the work–family conflict for the single custodial parent.

WORK, FAMILY, AND THE SINGLE PARENT
The following experience captures the work-family conflict for single parents well:

> I shut off the engine [of my car]; I have not moved for twenty minutes. The minutes and then the hours tick by. My heart beats faster and louder as I stare at the dashboard clock. I was due to pick up my four-year-old son at five o'clock. The hands are crawling past six o'clock, seven o'clock, eight o'clock. Finally the cars break free and I race to the baby-sitter's house. She primly informs me that she had no idea where I was and she has called the police to take my son. Choking with anxiety, I drive to the police station. The cruel-mouthed sergeant tells me that my son has been sent to his father. The police have determined that I am clearly not a fit mother and will no longer be allowed to take care of him.
>
> This is my recurring nightmare. It is founded in a real incident which occurred ten years ago when I was living through a painful divorce and trying to learn the difficult role of single-parent working mother. The real-life incident did not end disastrously; the baby-sitter was merely annoyed. But clearly the sharp anxiety and profound feelings of inadequacy which were evoked by that very troubled period have not yet been put to rest. (Mason 1988, pp. 11–12)

An American study found that single-parent mothers spend nine hours weekly in parent–child activities, while two-earner parent-families spend about 19 hours in combined time and two-parent, breadwinner–housewife families spend 22 hours (Holmes 1998). Trying to do everything involved in parenting—in half the time—takes its toll on employed single parents in general and single parents with disabilities in particular (Table 13.5). Meanwhile, family law scholar Cheri Wood (1995) argues that single mothers are up against "the new Catch-22": "Mothers who do not take financial responsibility for their children are 'bad.' Conversely, mothers who are away from their children because they work are 'bad.'"

Although the rough edges of the work-family conflict may be particularly sharp for single parents with disabilities, non-disabled, two-earner marriages assuredly have them also. A student (Vance 1998) wrote the following in response to Box 13.1, "Bringing Up Baby: A Doctor's Prescription for Busy Parents":

> I wanted to comment on T. Berry Brazelton's [advice]. I personally tried to imagine how his ideas could fit into my life. The only problem I see is that being a full-time student, and parent, most of [Brazelton's suggestions] are hard to comply with.... A student, like myself, has homework and projects that need many more hours to complete than time allotted. How can I save up energy at school to be ready for homecoming, or compartmentalize as Brazelton mentions? He says to let yourself feel guilty. I feel guilty because I cannot give my children the attention they need. I try to lend half of myself to them and half to my school work. This does not include time for my husband....

Whether single or married, "career and family involvement have never been combined easily in the same person" (Hunt and Hunt 1986, p. 280; Schor 1993).

The media have given us the new man, the baby boom era (or younger) husband who shares wage-earning and family responsibilities on an egalitarian basis and relates warmly to his children. Indeed, more fathers are taking off work following the birth of a child, and they are more visible in parenting classes, in pediatricians' offices, and dropping off and picking up children in day-care centres (Levine, in Lawson 1990). But "the image of the new man is like the image of the supermom: it obscures the strain" (Hochschild 1989, p. 31). Indeed, the man who gives family priority may have to deal with challenges to his masculinity. In her most recent book on work-family tensions and corporate family policies, sociologist Arlie Hochschild gave her chapter on men who took paternity leave the sardonic title: "Catching Up on the Soaps" (1997, p. 115) to capture the pressures these men felt from workmates as well as supervisors.

The primary source of strain is apparently role conflict: Employers consciously and unconsciously fail to see unpaid family work as important and do not believe that employees, especially males, should allow family responsibilities to interfere with labour force involvement (Hochschild 1997). As a result, some husbands report having lied to bosses or taking other evasive steps at work to hide conflicts between job and family. One man told his boss that he has "another meeting" so that he can leave the office each day at 6 P.M.; "I never say it's a meeting with my family." Another man said he parked his car in the back lot to avoid having to pass his boss at 5:30 P.M. while leaving for the child-care centre. The fact that "men are not supposed to feel these sorts of conflicts," according to Families and Work Institute researcher James Levine, makes matters worse, increasing personal stress (Shellenbarger 1991a; Windle and Dumenci 1997). This discussion applies to all two-earner couples and families. In the next section we will look at some stresses peculiar to two–*career* marriages.

Two-Career Marriages—Juggling Even Faster

Twenty years ago, Hunt and Hunt (1977) noted that dual-career families require a support system of child care providers and household help that depends heavily on ability to pay, which is inherently limited to a small number of families. Today's two-career union is premised on the existence of a labour pool of low-paid, but highly dependable, household help. The vast majority of such help is provided by women, many of whom have their own families to worry about (Romero 1992). (See Box 13.2, "A Nanny's Life.") Even parents who can afford to pay for it find that locating such help can be difficult.

Two-career couples with children may find themselves juggling even faster than spouses in other two-earner marriages. For example, two careers requiring travel can present added problems as parents "scramble to patch things together" for overnight child care (Shellenbarger 1991b). Two-career partners need the dexterity to balance not only career and family life but also her and his careers so that both spouses prosper professionally in what they see as a fair way.

The balance between partners can be upset by career fluctuations as well as family time allocations. The contrast between one career that is going well and one that is not can be hard on the partner on the down side. But the marriage can "operate as a buffer, cushioning the negative impacts of failures or reversals in one or the other career" (Hertz 1986, p. 59). When the marriage is rewarding, compromises such as turning down opportunities that would require relocation are acceptable because of the importance given to marriage as well as career.

Hertz (1986) found that the two-career couples she studied were realistic, though sometimes regretful, about some benefits of the traditional relationships they are giving up. Although men acknowledged that their wives provided less husband care, they appreciated the excitement, and also the status, associated with an achieving wife. Some of them had considered or made career changes that would not have been possible if wives had not been successful wage earners. Both partners claimed fulfillment from and assigned emotional meaning to an egalitarian dual-career marriage: "'She has a sense of a full partnership and she should'" (p. 75).

Commitment was perceived as truer: "'Working ... has decreased my dependence.... That makes it into much more of a voluntary relationship than an involuntary one of my staying with him because I need to stay with him. He's not staying with me because he's obligated to somehow, and it just makes it into a much clearer situation'" (p. 75). Very visible to Hertz was the way in which communication was enhanced by similar lives, making possible a higher level of mutual support than in conventional couples. "These couples ... [had] a different level of understanding about each other's lives, a level that is intimate and empathic" (p. 77).

The couples studied by Hertz did report conflict over balancing time, commitment, and career moves. Indeed, the geography of two careers presents a significant challenge to couples.

THE GEOGRAPHY OF TWO CAREERS   Because career advancement often requires geographic mobility—and even international transfers—juggling

Bringing Up Baby: A Doctor's Prescription for Busy Parents

Juggling work and family life can often seem overwhelming. Dr. Brazelton offers some practical advice for easing the strain on harried parents:

1. Learn to compartmentalize—when you work, be there, and when you are at home, be at home.

2. Prepare yourself for separating each day. Then prepare the child. Accompany him [sic] to his [sic] caregiver.

3. Allow yourself to grieve about leaving your baby—it will help you find the best substitute care, and you'll leave the child with a passionate parting.

4. Let yourself feel guilty. Guilt is a powerful force for finding solutions.

5. Find others to share your stress—peer or family resource groups.

6. Include your spouse in the work of the family.

7. Face the reality of working and caring. No supermom or superbaby fantasies.

8. Learn to save up energy in the workplace to be ready for homecoming.

9. Investigate all the options available at your workplace—on-site or nearby day care, shared-job options, flexible-time arrangements, sick leave if your child is ill.

10. Plan for children to fall apart when you arrive home after work. They've saved up their strongest feelings all day.

11. Gather the entire family when you walk in. Sit in a big rocking chair until everyone is close again. When the children squirm to get down, you can turn to chores and housework.

12. Take children along as you do chores. Teach them to help with the housework, and give them approval when they do.

13. Each parent should have a special time alone with each child every week. Even an hour will do.

14. Don't let yourself be overwhelmed by stress. Instead, enjoy the pleasures of solving problems together. You can establish a pattern of working as a team.

Source: T. Berry Brazelton, M.D., in *Newsweek*, Feb. 13, 1989, pp. 68–69. Courtesy *Newsweek* Magazine.

two careers can prove difficult for marrieds. A career move for one partner can make the other a **trailing spouse** who relocates to accommodate the other's (but not one's own) career. Increasingly, couples turn down transfers because of two-career issues. As a result, some large companies now offer career-opportunity assistance to a trailing spouse, such as hiring a job search firm, intercompany networking, attempts to locate a position for the spouse in the same institution, or career counselling (Lublin 1992).

Although wives still move for their husband's careers more often than the reverse (Shihadeh 1991), the number of trailing husbands has increased in recent years, perhaps to 10 to 30 percent of all trailing spouses. Counsellors who work with trailing husbands note that these men have few role models and must confront norms and social pressures that conflict with their decisions. Financial pressures when a trailing spouse cannot find a job may intensify the strain. But more two-career marriages today are based on a conscious mutuality to which partners have become accustomed by the time a career move presents itself. Such couples are less likely to have problems with a female-led relocation than are more traditional marrieds. For many spouses, trailing is preferable to commuting, another solution to the problem of opportunities in two locations.

TO COMMUTE OR NOT TO COMMUTE? Social scientists have called marriages in which spouses live apart **commuter marriages** or **two-location families**. The vast majority of commuting couples would rather not do so but endure the separation for the sake of career or other goals. Since research began on commuter marriages in the early 1970s, social scientists have drawn different conclusions. Some studies suggest that the benefits of such marriages—greater economic and emotional equality between spouses and the potential for better communication—counter its drawbacks. Other research suggests a different view, focusing on difficulties in managing the lifestyle. One conclusion to be drawn from the research is that commuters who are able to have frequent reunions are happier with the lifestyle than those who cannot.

One study (Bunker et al. 1992) compared life satisfaction for 90 commuting and 133 single-resident, two-career couples. Almost three-fourths of the commuters saw their partner weekly. The researchers were surprised to find that commuters experienced less stress and overload then the single-residence couples. "Perhaps there is some restructuring in the commuting two-residence couple that simplifies life or perceptions of it. Perhaps short separations facilitate compartmentalization, allowing commuters to keep work life and family life in well-separated spheres, and to confront the demands of each role in alternation rather than simultaneously" (p. 405). Then too, the commuter couples had significantly fewer babies and young children than did single-resident couples; commuter marriages probably work better in the absence of dependent children (Stern 1991).

Generally, the researchers concluded that commuting has both rewards and costs. Commuters reported more satisfaction with their work life than did single-residence, two-career respondents, but commuters were significantly less satisfied with their partner relationships and family life (Bunker et al. 1992). Some commuters say they can put their respective careers first for only so long before their relationship frays: "Career-wise it was absolutely fantastic," said one spouse who had given it up. "Personally, it was absolutely horrible" (in Stern 1991, p. B3). Consider the following example:

Michael and Judy Casper intended to celebrate their 25th wedding anniversary last month with a three-week vacation in Alaska. But their conflicting careers scotched the trip.

Michael couldn't get away from his new job—as a Gulf Bank general manager in Kuwait City. He says he spent the anniversary watching a rented videotape.

Judy lives 7700 miles away in Houston, where she owns a thriving home-interior shop—her first paid job after following her husband around the world for 17 years. She celebrated the anniversary by going out for Italian food with their three college-age children. Later, she cried. (Lublin 1992, p. B1)

"Perhaps reflecting the strong influence of these relationship issues on overall quality of life," commuters were less satisfied with life as a whole than were single-residence couples (Bunker et al. 1992, p. 405).

Couples who have been married for shorter periods of time seem to have more difficulties with commuter marriages. Younger couples who are simultaneously beginning their careers and their relationship often lack not only experience but also information about managing a two-career marriage. Perhaps because of their history of shared time, more "established" couples in commuter marriages have a greater "commitment to the unit" (Gross 1980).

This general discussion of juggling paid and unpaid labour points to the fact that despite the benefits of employment to women and their families, and despite the broad societal pressures and gender role changes leading to high female employment rates, neither families nor public policy have fully adapted to this change. The next section examines policy issues regarding work and family.

SOCIAL POLICY, WORK, AND FAMILY

Our discussions so far show that employment and household labour conflict; that is, "time spent in one sphere means less time spent in another. If commitments to paid labour and household labour call for full-time participation in both, that time must come either at the expense of leisure or else some of the demands of paid labour and household labour must go unmet" (Shelton 1992, p. 143; Vannoy and Dubeck 1998). Corporate policy expert Ellen

A Nanny's Life

Eleven years ago, Nelia Guzman was sitting in a park in Hong Kong with other Filipino nannies....But....a discarded newspaper and a gust of wind brought Nelia to a new life. Incredibly, the classified section of a recent *Toronto Star* blew across the park and landed at her feet. She picked it up and read that an employment agency wanted qualified women to work as nannies....Nelia answered the ad. Three months later, she was looking after a handicapped child in a house in Whitby....

In Forest Hill mansions and Annex duplexes, in parks and playgrounds across the city, Filipino women like Nelia are taking care of Toronto's middle-class children. Daisy, the four-year-old daughter of Tecca Crosby and Allan Kling, has been cared for most of her life by one Filipino woman, Christie Arrubio....A couple of generations ago, only wealthy families hired nannies, preferably those trained in Britain or Switzerland, housekeeping was often done by local girls from poor homes. Women's work has never been highly paid, and those willing to do it were usually scarce.....

In 1981, the federal government....passed the Foreign Domestic Movement program; its replacement, the Live-In Caregiver program, established in 1992, is still in effect. It's open to English- or French-speaking prospective nannies who have a high school education and six months of fulltime job training or 12 months paid experience in a related field. It offers, at the end of the road, Canadian citizenship. During the last 15 years it has attracted more than 90 000 women, the vast majority from the Philippines. About 70 percent live in Ontario, and close to 60 000 settled in the Toronto area....

When Lynn Mendelson was ready to hire a nanny, her sister suggested she visit the local park. "See what the nanny network looks like," she advised. "If they look like they're from the Islands, get someone from the Islands. If they look like they're from the Philippines, get someone from the Philippines." Her sister knew from experience that if you wanted your children to play with neighbourhood children it was easier if their nannies were friends.... After the first round of interviewing "about a million people" sent by an agency, Lynn settled on Tess because "she felt right." Vacuuming was important, yes. How she treated the children, certainly. But in the end, because Lynn was a stay-at-home mother, it came down to "finding somebody who could be with me but apart, who knew not to talk to me when I just wanted to be alone"....

When Allan Kling and his wife, Tecca Crosby, started looking for a nanny, they hooked up with a network recommended by friends. Christie lived with them for three years. "It's tough to consider her an employee," Allan observes, "when she's seen you unshaven and in your bathrobe." The line between worker and boss was blurred even more when Christie insisted on making weekend birthday parties for Daisy in a friend's....apartment, inviting other nannies, as well as Tecca and Allan, as guests....It isn't only Daisy's birthday that Christie insists on celebrating; for Tecca's birthday she takes them all for a Chinese dinner. Over the years, Allan has learned not to say, "Oh, you can't afford it. We'll pay. It offends her, so we don't argue any more"....

Salaries in the Philippines remain pitifully low—a few dollars a day for agricultural workers, a few thousand a year for professionals... As a result, the Philippines is the largest exporter of labour in Asia—more than four million Filipino migrants are scattered in 43 countries. About 70 percent are domestics. Workers sending home billions of dollars a year are the country's largest source of foreign currency. "Once we exported our coconut products and our sugar," says Florchita ("Chit") Bautista, a former nun who runs Aware, a program set up to help Catholic Filipinos in Toronto. "Now the No. 1 export of the Philippines is human labour."

So, in the 1980s, when the Canadian economy was growing and baby boomers were starting two-career families, thousands of Filipinas came to Canada, sponsored by individual families who needed live-in nannies. Employers were required to use a model contract devised by Ottawa that reflected provincial employment standards. Such a contract today in Ontario—based on a 44-hour work week, a minimum wage of $6.85 an hour, less deductions for accommodations and benefits—would leave a nanny with a net monthly salary of about $677. Long-time nannies make far more, as much as $1300 net. For live-out nannies, take-home pay ranges between $300 and $350 a week....

In the early days, when there were fewer nannies and they all had live-in jobs, many were badly treated. Intercede, a Toronto organization for domestic workers' rights was set up more than a dozen years ago to give them advice. "When the workplace and the home place were the same," says Columbia... Tarape-Diaz, an Intercede counsellor, "nannies were more subject to abuse—long hours, no privacy, isolation, living in cold, damp basements—extensions of the laundry room, really, or the playroom."....

[Evelyn] stayed for three-and-a-half years as a live-in nanny. She loved the children she worked with, she was never mistreated, and yet she understands, with heartbreaking clarity, the ambiguous situation of the nanny. "I know a lot of Filipino nannies have a beautiful relationship with their employers, but still they are employers. You have to respect them, to have reservations. They can't really be your equals. If I'm paid, I cannot be like family"....

Lydia Taguiam, Lynn Mendelson's current nanny, was recommended to her by her former nanny, Delia. Lydia lives out because she has a child of her own to look after. One of seven children, Lydia was born in the provinces [of the Philippines], a country girl. She began working when she was 15, first in Italy—with the same family for eight years—then in Canada in 1992. Ten years ago she married a man in the Philippines, and until recently, sent money home to her parents, her siblings, and her husband. After her last trip to the Philippines, Lydia, who's now 43, returned to Canada pregnant....

"I can't send any money back home any more," Lydia says. "I didn't work for almost a year and I need my money for my apartment, my baby, and my cousin who is my babysitter." Lydia lives within walking distance of Lynn's house. "I get up at six o'clock to prepare things. I change my daughter and by eight o'clock we leave the apartment and go to the babysitter. I get here about 8:30 and I start to work." Nine hours later, she picks up her daughter and goes home.

Lynn Mendelson has mixed feelings about this arrangement. She worked away from home herself until her third child was born and understands Lynn's difficulties. "I feel bad that she's here taking care of my kids while someone else is taking care of her kid. Ultimately it's a choice. She was actually able to stay with her daughter until she was 13 months old, and to me that's great."

Although they have a verbal contract requiring Lydia to work until seven P.M., Lydia tries to let her go by five. Some of Lynn's friends think she's a bit soft. "Their nannies stay until the dinner dishes are done and they always say, 'That's the hardest part of the day and your nannies always leave before dinner. It's ridiculous!'"... In the best of all possible worlds Lynn would hire two nannies to work around the clock, and another for weekends....

Lydia, now a landed immigrant, has been preparing for the arrival of her husband in Canada. He's a security guard in the Philippines. She looked slightly wistful as she said she didn't know what he'd do here. The experience of friends has taught her that bringing a husband to Canada is perilous.

"'Too much liberation,' they say, is clashing with Filipino culture," according to Florchita Bautista. "Many of the men, and the women, have had affairs with other people. They have to begin their lives together all over again. The man insists, 'I am the head of the family,' because in the Philippines he *is* the head of the family.

(continued)

A Closer Look at Family Diversity: A Nanny's Life

(continued)

'I want you to respect me. I want you to spend some time in the house with me and with the children,' and so on. She says, 'No, I have to go and do my work' and it becomes a clash."

The situation can be complicated by children. "Often the children were left behind when they were babies or toddlers. Now they are teenagers. The children have become independent of the control of the mother—and in the Philippines it is the mother who takes control of the children, the discipline, everything. Now she can no longer control them. They say, 'We have been existing without you and now you tell us what to do?' It's very difficult."

In May, Christie's family arrived at Toronto airport—Pablo; her son, King, who is 20; and two teenaged daughters, Mary Jane and Jeniel. Two children could not come because they're too old to qualify as dependents. When Christie left the Philippines 15 years ago, Jeniel was an infant. She hasn't seen her more than half-a-dozen times since them. As Allan King says, "She's missed the whole thing."

To demonstrate sufficient income for immigration purposes, Christie wanted to work eight hours a day for Allan and Tecca and then work from midnight to eight A.M. at a nursing home. "I frankly don't think that Daisy would have suffered even though this would have meant that Christie virtually wouldn't have slept," Allan says. But they felt they had to say no, and Christie

began working in nursing homes fulltime and taking care of Daisy on weekends and some weekday evenings. "I bet she hasn't taken off more than six days in the six years that she's been working in Canada," says Allan.

Allan knows that in Christie's case, the real motivator was always the children. Unfortunately, they are much older than she wants them to be. "She was under a lot of pressure—almost a version of a biological clock: 'If I don't get these kids over soon they're not going to know who the hell I am, and it's going to be an even harder transition to this freezing cold country.' That's why she was so desperate to get this thing to happen."

Her family is here now....but they don't see much of Christie. She's taken a different live-in nanny job, does weekend work, and grabs all the overtime she can. She says her family needs the money. Their house is small and they've rented the basement. Only half a house is left, so for practical reasons it's better to free up a bed.

Christie's reasons for not living at home are probably more complex. Although she says that having her family in Toronto is "like a dream," they are mainly strangers to her...."In terms of her relationship with her husband," says Allan, "you sometimes get a stoical grin from her." How do you re-establish a life of daily intimacy after 15 years of separation?....

Source: Abridged from Geraldine Sherman. "A Nanny's Life." The unedited article, which originally appeared in the September 1996 issue of *Toronto Life,* can be found on the Web at http://geraldinesherman.com/Nanny.html.

Galinsky recounts the following not unusual episode from the life of a working family:

> One father told of a morning when his four-year-old daughter lost her shoes. Amid all the other normal complications of getting two young children dressed, fed, and ready for daycare, he and his wife searched everywhere but the shoes were nowhere to be found. The mother began to go through the house a second time while the father made calls to find someone to take over his carpool to the metal factory where he worked. Because his

factory had strict time policies (warnings were issued; after several warnings a worker could be fired), he felt frantic, as did his wife who also had a job tied to the time clock. Eventually they settled for last year's too small shoes, put them on their daughter, and they all rushed out the door. Both parents were late for work, and were censored by their supervisors. When they got home from work, they found a note from their daughter's teacher—it asked them please to buy shoes for their child that fit. (Galinsky 1986, pp. 109–10)

"Ten years ago, people thought [situations like the one described above were] temporary," according to a Harvard professor of family law. But now, "It is no longer possible to pretend it will go away" (Minow, in Smolowe 1996c). This section examines public or social policy issues as society responds (or fails to respond) to today's work–family conflicts. Policy issues centre on two questions: "What is needed?" and "Who will provide it?"

What Is Needed to Resolve Work–Family Issues?

Researchers and other work-family experts are in general agreement that single-parent and two-earner families are in need of more adequate provisions for child and elder care, family leave, and more flexible employment scheduling. We will examine each of these separately.

CHILD CARE   Policy researchers define **child care** as the full-time care and education of children under age six, care before and after school and during school vacations for older children, and overnight care when employed parents must travel. Child care may be paid or unpaid and provided by relatives or others. "Informal care by relatives, neighbours, and paid caregivers (sitters) is the most prevalent form of child care used in Canada for children whose parents work for pay" (Baker and Lero 1996, p. 95).

Paid care may be provided in the child's home by a caregiver who comes to the house daily or lives in (see Box 13.2). The term **family day care** refers to care provided in a caregiver's home, often by an older woman or a mother who has chosen to remain out of the labour force to care for her own children. Family day care is the most widely used type of care by non-

relatives for toddlers and infants (Atkinson 1992). Parents who prefer family day care seem to be seeking a family-like atmosphere, with a smaller scale, less routinized setting. Perhaps they also desire social similarity of caregiver and parent to better ensure that their children are socialized according to their own values. **Centre care** provides group care for a larger number of children in day-care centres. Currently, non-parental child care is provided to 40 percent of all Canadian children under the age of five. Of these children, 56 percent are cared for in someone else's home, 22 percent are cared for in their own home and 20 percent are cared for within a daycare centre (Vanier Institute of the Family, 2001).

In both Canada and the United States, the use of day-care centres has increased (Shellenbarger 1992e). Increased centre-care use is due, in part, to the perception that centre day care offers greater safety and a strong preschool curriculum. About half of parents using paid care change their arrangements each year because a caregiver quit, the cost was too high, the hours or location were inconvenient, the child was

Grandparents and other relatives may be asked to provide child care, especially when parents' work involves travel, shift work, or night-time employment.

unhappy, or the parent disliked the caregiver (Shellenbarger 1991d).

Although "[c]hild care is a fact of life for Canadian children and their families," it has been noted that "very little regulated child care even exists in Canada," and that "there are regulated child care spaces for only 8.4 percent of the children who need them" (National Council of Welfare 1999, p. 17). While the costs of child care in general, and for preschoolers in particular, are high and rising, the federal, provincial and territorial governments have cut funding for social programs, cut or frozen fee subsidies to low-income families, and made eligibility criteria for subsidies more restrictive (Doherty et al. 1998). The National Council of Welfare (1999) observes that although parents who are able to do so may pay as much as $850 a month per child for high-quality care in downtown Toronto or Ottawa, most parents are forced to rely on unregulated care "where the quality of care is completely unpredictable." It is argued that this situation "creates unconscionable risks for children's health and safety, and unnecessary anxiety for their parents." For parents of children with special needs as well as those parents who work irregular hours or shift-work, "child care is often completely unavailable" (p. 17).

In 1997, Quebec introduced a comprehensive family policy that attempts to integrate family benefits, paid parental leave, child care, and kindergarten. Its child care component heralded universally available, affordable child care in that province. The aim was to make every child in Quebec, by 2001, able to receive child care for $5 a day (and for as little as $2 a day for certain low-income families). This nominal fee would entitle a child to a maximum of 10 hours a day of child care, one meal and two snacks, and use of all educational materials. As of September 1997, all five-year-olds in Quebec whose families desired it became entitled to receive free full-time kindergarten with $5-a-day after-school care organized by the educational authorities. Similarly, all four-year-olds have part-time or full-time junior kindergarten or child care for $5 a day, with additional free early intervention services available for those whose parents receive welfare. As of September 1998, all three-year-olds became eligible for $5-a-day child care. In 2000, Quebec additionally launched 10 pilot projects offering evening, weekend and even overnight daycare—all available at the same

$5-a-day rate charged under Quebec's government-financed daycare system (Dougherty and Jelowicki 2000). While the costs of providing such a comprehensive child care system are significant, Quebec's family policy has been lauded by some as "a pioneering approach to family supports in North America" (National Council of Welfare 1999, p. 44).

In March, 2000, the provincial budget of British Columbia committed that government to working towards the creation of publicly funded child care in B.C. In doing so, the province of B.C. became the second jurisdiction in North American to move towards publicly funded child care for all families "rich, poor, and the large majority in between" (Canadian Council on Social Development 2001, p.6). From January 1, 2001, families in British Columbia who seek before- and after-school care for their children will be able to access licensed spaces on and off school sites at a cost to parents of $7 a day during the school year and $14 a day during school holidays. Provincial grants will be given to non-profit and for-profit child organizations that maintain and expand existing spaces for children from grade one to age 12. "The province has budgeted $14 million for 2000/01 and $30 million for 2001/02 to fund over 20 000 spaces for school-aged children around the province under this initiative" (Government of British Columbia 2001).

The provision of child care elsewhere in Canada, however, "continues to be provided with no clear sense of direction" and is "severely compromised on three fronts: the availability of spaces to meet the needs of children and their families, the affordability of care and the quality of services provided" (National Council of Welfare 1999c, p. 44).

Talk to employed parents of young children for any length of time, and the subject turns to the difficulty of finding day care. Some parents pay providers months in advance to reserve space for babies not yet born. Other couples may work at timing pregnancies to correspond with rare day-care vacancies. Day care is even more difficult to find for mildly ill youngsters too sick to go to their regular day-care facility (Galinsky and Stein 1990). Then too, family day care and day-care centres are usually open weekdays only and close by 7 P.M. (if not earlier). Some parents, such as single parents on shift work or those who travel, need access to 24-hour care centres (Curtis 1997). For

Selecting a Day-Care Facility

The demand for day-care facilities has grown steadily in the past decade as more mothers join the labour force. "In a wave of fundamental social change, day care is becoming a basic need of the ...family" (Watson, 1984, p. 14). Although some employers offer child care, finding quality facilities at an affordable cost has become a serious problem for many parents.

Most child-care experts agree that when day-care facilities are clean, safe, and adequately staffed, and when children are allowed to play together comfortably with some respect for individual needs, such environments are as healthy for children as home care. Besides these general considerations, parents should look for the following criteria in a day-care facility:

- A *stable staff*. Some research indicates that children do best when cared for consistently by the same people. Ask about staff turnover. Because some turnover is inevitable, ask how the situation is handled. How are children informed of and prepared for upcoming staff changes?

- *Low staff-to-child ratio*. Although experts disagree on ideal staff-to-child ratios, some recommend ratios of 1:3 for infants, 1:4 for toddlers, and 1:8 for three- to six-year-olds. For home-based facilities, recommended ratios are 1:5 for children under two years old and 1:6 for youngsters between two and six years.

- *A well-trained staff*. Because day-care workers are poorly paid, it is difficult to find centres with highly educated staff. Nevertheless, the ideal situation is for staff to be specifically trained in such fields as child development and psychology.

- *The right kind of attention*. Babies need a responsive adult who coos and talks to them. One-year-olds need a staff member who will name things for them. Two-year-olds need someone who reads to them. Older children need adults as well but can also profit from supervised exchanges (such as games) with other children.

- *Appropriate activities*. Learning the alphabet is fine, but children don't need to be immersed only in academics. Look for a facility that also fosters play and community activities, such as trips to the zoo or fire station.

- *A role for parents*. Any day-care facility should welcome parental involvement. Be wary of centres that do not allow unannounced visits.

- *References*. Ask for names and phone numbers of other parents who have children enrolled there and talk with them about the facility. Be wary of a centre that refuses to give you this information.

- *Visits*. Visit the daycare centre as often as possible—and, if possible, unannounced—both before and after selecting a facility.

Source: Adapted from Watson, 1984.

parents who rely on accessible transit, coordinating transportation to the workplace with child care schedules may require booking two buses—one to take the child to child care and another to take the differently-abled parent to work—"with up to an hour of waiting time in between." One woman, interviewed by Diane Fawcett (1999), observed, "I can't use Wheel Trans to take my son to day care because the day care hours are so inflexible that it just wouldn't work with my schedule."

Adding to the difficulty of finding and accessing day care is the fact that parents are looking for *quality* day care, and some facilities are of better quality than others (Glass and Estes 1997). Some research points to concern that infants in their first year who are in nonparental care for 20 or more hours per week "are at elevated risk of being classified as insecure in their attachments to their mothers at 12 or 18 months of age and of being more disobedient and aggressive when they are from three to eight years old" (Belsky 1990, p. 895). Meanwhile, studies have generally supported the conclusion that children in day care and children cared for by their own parents differ little in development and emotional stability (Chira 1996). "The consensus at recent conferences has been that good day care—that is, day care with adequate staffing by trained responsive adults—not only has no ill effects, but can be beneficial" (Lewin, 1989b, p. 91; and see Booth 1992 for a comprehensive presentation of research in this area).[4]

Nevertheless, as we have earlier noted, "day care with adequate staffing by trained responsive adults" does not describe all day care in this country. For example, family day-care providers can be unusually stressed due to high demands and limited family and financial resources (Atkinson 1992). It is widely assumed among experts that high provider turnover and repeated staff departures associated with day-care centres can result in a child's emotional withdrawal and can otherwise interfere with development. Staff turnover is high; low pay for workers is an important factor (Shellenbarger 1992e; Alter 1997). Keeping centre day care affordable may result in caregiver-child ratios that are too low for quality care (Lewin 1989b; Jenson 2000). (Box 13.3, "Selecting a Day-Care Facility," discusses things parents should look for in choosing day care.)

Meanwhile, paid child care is expensive for parents (Anderson and Vail 1999). According to the Canadian National Child Care Survey, if child care costs rose by 10 percent, the employment rate of single-parent mothers would drop by about six percent. Nearly 40 percent of single-parent mothers who were working and paying for child care reported that if their child care costs were to rise by 25 percent, they would quit their jobs (National Council of Welfare 1999b).

---

4. Despite a smattering of confirmed cases, concerns about abuse of children in day care have largely proved to be unfounded; studies indicate that children are at greater risk of abuse in their own homes (Finkelhor, Hotaling, and Sedlak 1991).

As they struggle to find quality, affordable child care, many parents must make more than one arrangement for each child (Folk and Yi 1994). As they patch together a series of child-care arrangements, the system becomes increasingly unpredictable and is inclined to fall apart (Galinsky and Stein 1990; Blau and Robins 1998). This same situation very probably applies to elder care.

ELDER CARE   **Elder care** involves providing assistance with daily living activities to an elderly relative who is chronically frail, ill, or disabled (Galinsky and Stein 1990). Increasingly, employees will need forms of elder care, such as day care for the elderly (Ettner 1995). The fact that more and more people now live longer means that middle-aged children (especially daughters) are increasingly responsible not only for working outside the home and for child care but also for the needs of aging parents. Employees in this sandwich generation are especially pressed as conflicts arise among roles as employee, parent, and adult child of aging parent (Roots 1998). Research consistently finds that primary elder caregivers are most likely to be women, in their roles as wives, daughters, or daughters-in-law (Cranwswick 1997; Dumas and Belanger 1994; Piercy 1998).

The strains of elder caregiving are showing up in the workplace. Findings from the 1996 General Social Survey indicate that just over half (55 percent) of women caregivers and just less than half (45 percent) of men caregivers report that caregiving responsibilities have affected their employment situations in the form of coming in later, leaving early, or missing days of paid work (Cranswick 1997, p. 5). Research in one company indicated that one of every four employees responsible for the care of elderly relatives had problems with the cost of services needed, and one employee in five worried about the relative while at work (Galinsky and Stein 1990). In addition, those caregivers who provide care to an elder suffering from a cognitive-behavioural problem associated with some form of dementia tend to experience greater stress than those who provide care for an elder who only experiences some form of physical impairment (Starrels et al. 1997).

FLEXIBLE SCHEDULING   **Flexible scheduling** includes options such as job sharing, working at home or telecommuting, compressed work weeks, flextime, and personal days. Compressed work weeks allow an employee to concentrate the work week into three or four, sometimes slightly longer, days. With **job sharing**, two workers share the responsibility of one job. In Canada, job-sharers are most likely to be well-educated individuals in good jobs. In 1995, for example, about half had a college or university education and about four of 10 were professionals. In that year, about 171 000 Canadians shared their jobs with other workers, with women in general and nurses and teachers in particular most likely to do so (Statistics Canada 1998a). **Flextime** involves flexible starting and ending times with required core hours, usually 10 A.M. to 3:30 P.M.

Flexible scheduling, although not a panacea, can help parents share child care or be at home before and after an older child's school hours (Glass 1998). Some types of work do not lend themselves to flexible scheduling (Christensen and Staines 1990), but the practice has begun to catch on, partly because it offers employee-recruiting advantages and prevents turnover (Trost 1992). Another important reason that companies are now offering some workers flexible scheduling is that it saves the company money. For example, 20 employees at one firm who work at home two days each week saved their employer thousands of dollars in leasing costs by sharing office space. As another example, it is not uncommon for employees on compressed work weeks to accomplish their entire job for reduced pay (Shellenbarger 1992d). Some union officials charge that moves toward flexible schedules may actually be corporate ploys to replace most costly full-time jobs with part-time work offering fewer benefits (Christensen and Staines 1990).

Companies are finding that employees on flexible schedules like them and "will do almost anything" to make them work (Shellenbarger 1992d). Yet jobs with flexible schedules often pay less, and there are proportionately fewer takers in today's weak economy (Trost 1992). Moreover, although flextime has gained currency as one solution to work–family conflicts, research shows that it is not as beneficial as often hoped. Employees who get flextime report enhanced job satisfaction—possibly due to greater feelings of autonomy—but do not find that flextime alleviates all or even most family–work conflicts (Christensen and Staines 1990).

A MOMMY—OR PARENT—TRACK? To meet the needs of women who wished to devote more time to their families during the childbearing and early child-rearing years, corporate career consultant Felice Schwartz has proposed that business (and by extension, professions such as law) create positions that demand less time and overall involvement. "Career and family women" would elect that track while "career primary women" continued to meet the heavy demands of the "fast track." Schwartz acknowledged that "career and family women" would most likely not make it to the top ranks of management or the professions. But they could enjoy middle-management jobs while maintaining their families with less stress, a trade-off many might welcome (Schwartz 1989a).

Schwartz herself did not use the term **mommy track**, although this was the instant label given to her proposal by the press. But concern (not to mention distress) was expressed that such a policy would reinforce society's assigning to women (but not men) primary social responsibility for child care. By assuming that they would likely have problems combining work and family, the proposal also risked condemning women in general to continued second-class employment status (Kantrowitz 1989; Lewin 1989a). In reply, Schwartz argued that

> the danger of charting our direction on the basis of wishful thinking is clear. Whether or not men play a greater role in child rearing, companies must reduce the family-related stresses on working women. The flexibility companies provide for women now will be a model in the very near future for men—thus women will not be forced to continue to take primary responsibility for child care.... What I advocate is that companies create options that allow employees to set their own pace. (Schwartz 1989b, p. 27).

In her subsequent book written with corporation managers in mind, Schwartz (1992) argued again that "as things stand now, the business world must enlarge its infrastructure to support the family needs of employees." To that end, Schwartz recommended that the corporate world should:

• Accept the fact that you must be flexible and must provide family supports. The alternatives include unacceptable rates of turnover, terrible losses in productivity, and exclusion from the leadership pool of high-potential, high-performing women (and, increasingly, men) who want to be involved in their children's lives.

- Provide the full range of ongoing benefits to women on disability and maternity leave and to those who return part-time.

- Let women who have babies return when they're ready. By "ready" I mean when they feel well psychologically and physically, when they're getting enough sleep to function effectively during the day, when they feel they've bonded with their babies, and when they have located, tested, and are satisfied with whatever kind of child care they've chosen.

- Let women return from maternity leave on less than full-time or other alternative schedules—part-time, shared, telecommuticating arrangements—for as long as they want.

- Permit new fathers to take parental leaves, sequencing them with those of their wives.

- Establish a policy that permits parents to cut back to half-time (at prorated pay) and reenter the competition for senior management levels, partnership, or tenure if they choose. (Translation: Don't put them on a "mommy track.")

- When a woman (or a man) is out on leave or working part-time for a significant period, provide the additional heads and hands that are necessary to get the work done.

- Take responsibility—in partnership with parents, communities, and governments—for making high-quality, affordable child care available for every child.

- Find every opportunity you can to enable parents (and other executives who need uninterrupted time to think and work) to work at home.

- Contract out as much work as you can.

- Finally, the *sine qua non* for all of the above: Learn how to measure productivity instead of time in the office and put systems in place to do so (Schwartz 1992, pp. 203–4).

In sum, Schwartz argued for what we might call a *parent track*, supportive to parents of either gender. A few companies have begun to make "family-friendly" policies, such as those listed above, explicitly available to both male and female employees (Shellenbarger 1992f). Robert Glossop, the Executive Director of Programs for the Vanier Institute of the Family, and Nora Spinks, President of Work-Life Harmony Enterprise, point out that the conflict experienced between juggling work work and family responsibilities is responsible for much of today's stress. They observe that "with employees' stress-related disorders costing Canadian businesses an estimated 12 billion dollars a year, enlightened business owners and managers are looking for ways to help their staff solve what used to be discounted as a purely personal problem" (1998).

THE LIFE COURSE SOLUTION One policy analyst (Moen 1992) has offered the radical suggestion that all of us—parents, educators, corporate executive officers (CEOs), middle managers, and regular employees—push for a complete redefinition of the individual life course. According to Moen's **life course solution**, policymakers and the rest of us would rethink "the lockstep pattern of education, employment, and retirement." Doing so

> could lead to a variety of arrangements, including a return to school at various ages and a continuation of paid work well beyond the usual age of retirement. It could also encourage both men and women to cut back on their working hours or to take extended sabbaticals while their children are young. The changes we as a society are experiencing call loudly for a thoughtful reappraisal of existing life patterns. This could lead to a reconfiguration of the life course in ways that create more options and a greater diversity for both men and women in youth, early adulthood, mid-life, and the later years. (Quarm 1984, p. 129)

The life course solution assumes that all Canadians need changed social policies with regard to work-family conflicts. Who will lead in making policy changes is a matter of debate.

Who Will Provide What Is Needed to Resolve Work–Family Issues?

Social commentators hotly disagree over whose ultimate responsibility it is to provide what is needed regarding various work–family solutions. A principal conflict concerns whether solutions such as child care or family leave constitute employees' rights, or privileges for which a worker must negotiate (Burstein, Bricher, and Einwohner 1995; Gilbert 1998; see also Elison 1997; Marks 1997).

The countries of northwestern Europe, have generally adopted a pronatalist and social-welfare orientation, and viewed family concerns as a right. There is "the pervasive belief … that children are a precious national resource for which society has collective responsibility … to help develop and thrive" (Clinton 1990, p. 25). Putting this belief into practice, most European countries are committed to *paid* maternity leave for up to a year or longer (Aldous and Dumon 1980). In 1974, the Swedish government extended its one-year paid maternity leave to men and changed the term to *parental leave*, arguing that the move was "an important sign that the father and mother share the responsibility for the care of the child" (Haas 1990, p. 402). More recently, Sweden, which "leads the world in parental leave policies, child care, women's labour force and so on" launched an advertising campaign to encourage men to take paternity leave. "One ad depicts a naked man, spread-eagled and seemingly pinned to a machine gear. 'A man whose work is his life becomes trapped by it,' says the ad. 'It's not that men want this, but that the world expects it'" (Glossop and Theilheimer 2000).

A comparison of government-sponsored maternity, paternity, and parental leave programs in Canada, Belgium, the United Kingdom, Finland, Germany, Sweden and the United States is provided in Table 13.4. As you will note, Canada's maternity and parental leaves are more generous than those in the United States (which offers no paid leave programs) or the United Kingdom (which does not currently provide parental leave) but fall short of those offered in Finland, Germany, and Sweden.

As we have already noted, some large corporations demonstrate interest in effecting **family-friendly workplace policies** that are supportive of employee efforts to combine family and work commitments. Such policies include on-site day-care centres, sick-child-care facilities, other organizationally or financially assisted child-care services, flexible schedules, parental or family leaves, workplace seminars and counselling programs, and support groups for employed parents (Galinsky and Stein 1990). In addi-

tion, unions, such as the Canadian Auto Workers, have managed to negotiate contracts with such family-friendly benefits as on-site daycares, compressed work weeks, and personal care days (Glossop and Spinks 1998). Research on family-friendly outcomes for employers is currently inadequate (Raabe 1990), but what there is suggests that such programs help in recruitment, reduce employee stress, absenteeism and job turnover, and enhance morale and thus increase productivity (Galinsky and Stein 1990; Shellenbarger and Trost 1992b).

But family-friendly policies are hardly available to all workers, of course (Trczinski and Finn-Stevenson 1991; Shellenbarger 1993). Companies that help provide or subsidize child care are likely to be large and in service industries rather than in, for example, manufacturing. And employees at corporate headquarters typically have greater access to on-site day care than do workers in branch offices (Shellenbarger 1992b). Furthermore, family-friendly policies are not necessarily available to all employees even within a company that offers them. Professionals and managers are much more likely than technical and clerical workers to have access to leave policies, telecommuting, or other forms of flexible scheduling (Christensen and Staines 1990)—or to be able to afford tuition at corporate, on-site day-care centres. "Just as top managers get more stock options and nicer offices, they get better child-care deals than the working class" (Guyon 1992).

Moreover, companies have tended to leave the administration of work–family policies to the discretion of individual managers or supervisors. Although some aggressively promote work-family benefits, others view them less favourably (Galinsky and Stein 1990; Hochschild 1997). Thus, many employees are reluctant to lobby for child-care benefits or request time off to attend to family needs (Auerbach 1990; Beck 1990; Hochschild 1997). "Some women are so nervous that they try to appear biologically correct at all times," according to one vice-president for human resources (in Guyon 1992). Some employees say that "even discussing child care issues at work is freighted with potential for embarrassment, censure and career-limiting exposure" (Guyon 1992; see also Daly 1994; Schwartz 1992, pp. 39–62).

A few experts point to family-friendly companies as indicative of positive future trends. But many analysts warn that voluntary programs and benefits

TABLE 13.4

Government-sponsored maternity, paternity and parental paid leave programs for selected jurisdictions*

	Canada	Belgium	United Kingdom	Finland	France	Germany	Sweden	United States
Maternity leave								
Eligibility	Previous employment with contributions	Previous employment with contributions	Previous employment with contributions	Universal	Previous employment with contributions	Previous employment with contributions	Falls under Parental leave unless sick	na
Duration	15 weeks	14 weeks	18 weeks	18 weeks	16–26 weeks**	14 weeks	up to 15 wks sick leave	na
Compensation	55% of previous earnings	75%–80% of previous earnings	90% of previous earnings for 6 weeks, then flat rate	80% of previous earnings or flat rate	84% of previous earnings	100% of previous earnings	80%–90% of previous earnings	na
Paternity leave								
Eligibility	na	na	na	Universal	na	na	Universal	na
Duration	na	na	na	1–2 weeks	na	na	10 days	na
Compensation	na	na	na	80% of previous earnings or flat rate	na	na	90% of previous earnings or flat rate	na
Parental leave								
Eligibilty	Either parent, previous employment with contributions	Both parents, previous employment	na	Either parent, universal	Either parent, previous employment	Both parents, universal	Either parent, universal	na
Duration	10 weeks	6–12 months	na	6 months	24 months	24 months	15 months	na
Compensation	55% of previous earnings	18% of average industrial earnings	na	80% of previous earnings or flat rate	46% of base wage for 9 months***	About 15% of median industrial earnings	90% of previous earnings or flat rate	na

* In 2001, Canada doubled the length of its paid maternity/parental leave to eligible claimants through the Employment Insurance (EI) program from six months to one year.

** 16 weeks for those with fewer than three children and 26 weeks for those with three or more.

*** Means-tested thereafter.

Na Not applicable.

Source: Statistics Canada, Canadian Social Trends, Cat. No. 11-008, Summer 1998.

depend on cost constraints and corporate self-interest (Kingston 1990) and are not likely to become widespread (Aldous 1990; Shellenbarger 1993). Moreover, it is evident that

> we cannot leave to a few progressive business leaders the problem of easing the well-documented conflicts between fulfilling job requirements and caring for family members. Governmental action requiring businesses to give these benefits and subsidies to fund them is necessary. (Aldous 1990, p. 365)

One important step in realizing a more satisfying balance between work and family lives is to recognize the full scope of the challenge" (Kingston 1990, p. 453).

This challenge extends to the workers themselves. Sociologist Arlie Hochschild conducted a three-year field study of a company that prided itself on its family friendly policies. She found a not-unusual unevenness in implementation of the policy for different kinds of workers and across supervisors. What was truly surprising, however, was the degree to which workers did not take advantage of the policies. Their most common reason was that they preferred to be at work.

For many, "work becomes home and home becomes work" (Hochschild, 1997, title page). The "second shift" of home chores and child care was not only onerous but also a source of emotional tension and conflict between married or cohabiting partners. Moreover, a "third shift" of emotion work was needed to smooth out the hostility and tension of children and partners who were distressed about the lack of family time. (A national U.S. survey cited by Hochschild [p. 281, fn. 4] reported that 35 percent of children of employed parents were in child care 41 hours a week or more, often much more. Some children in Hochschild's study were spending 10 hours a day in child care.)

Not only did parents spend long hours at work, but they often brought additional work home. What time remained for family life was strictly programmed rather than spontaneous, and children were quick to see that their questions and needs were being compressed into certain limited time slots. "Part of modern parenthood now includes coping with children's resistance to the tight-fitting temporal uni-

forms required when home becomes work and work becomes home" (p. 217).

Meanwhile, contemporary modifications of work settings have made work more attractive and pleasant. Workers felt competent and successful on the job compared to their uncertainties about how their families were doing. Strong friendships developed at work, and workers also had "a sense of being cared for" (p. 208) by a familial and appreciative company or office team. People felt more relaxed at work than at home, where the time press required family activities and conversation to be tightly scheduled. At home, multi-tasking was common, as worker-parents took care of voice mail, for example, while allegedly spending quality time with children. At work, one could sit down and have a cup of coffee with a coworker.

We have devoted considerable attention to work–family policy because these issues so strongly influence the options and choices of individual families. Working in the political arena toward the kinds of changes we want is one aspect of creating satisfying marriages and families. Given social constraints, employed couples want to know what *they* can do to maintain happy marriages. We turn to that topic now.

THE TWO-EARNER MARRIAGE AND THE RELATIONSHIP

We have been addressing problems associated with two-earner marriages. But research shows that—provided there is enough time to accomplish things—a person's having multiple roles (such as employee/spouse/parent) does not add to stress and in fact can enhance personal happiness (O'Neil and Greenberger 1994; Roxburgh 1997). Research also points to the heightened satisfaction, excitement, and vitality that two-earner couples can have because these partners are more likely to have common experiences and shared worldviews than are more traditional spouses, who often lead very different everyday lives (Chafetz 1989; Hughes, Galinsky, and Morris 1992). At the same time, however, conflict can arise in two-earner marriages as couples negotiate the division of household labour, and more generally adjust to changing roles (Orbuch and Custer 1995; Hondagneu-Sotelo and Messner 1999; Johnson, P. 1998).

Negotiating the Second Shift

How a couple allocates paid and unpaid work represents a combination of each partner's **gender strategy**—a way of working through everyday situations that takes into account an individual's beliefs and deep feelings about gender roles, as well as her or his employment commitments (Hochschild 1989). In today's changing society, one's beliefs and deeper feelings about gender may conflict. For example, a number of men in Hochschild's study articulated egalitarian sentiments but clearly had traditional gut-level feelings.

Even when each spouse's feelings correspond with his or her beliefs, partners may disagree with one another. Tensions exhibited by many of Hochschild's respondents were a consequence of "faster-changing women and slower-changing men" (1989, p. 11). These couples often engaged in prolonged struggles, which did not always end happily. Some husbands distanced themselves to avoid pressure; some justified their reluctance to participate, claiming no time, incompetence, fatigue, clumsiness, squeamishness, and inexperience (Thompson 1991). Some wives in Hochschild's study mentioned divorce statistics, clearly seeing that to press husbands too hard was to risk divorce (Hochschild 1989). Some gave up efforts to get husbands to share, but did so with a resentment that poisoned the marriage.

Moreover, even when spouses share similar attitudes about gender, circumstances may not allow them to act accordingly (Zvonkovic et al. 1996). In one couple interviewed by Hochschild (1989) for example, both partners held the traditional belief that a wife should be a full-time homemaker. Yet because the couple needed the wife's income, she was employed and they shared housework on a nearly equal basis. How couples manage their everyday lives in the face of these various contradictions reflects a consciously or unconsciously negotiated gender strategy (Zvonkovic et al. 1996).

One gender strategy noted by Hochschild (1989) involves a husband's consistently praising his wife's homemaking skills rather than actually sharing the tasks. A more recent study of two-earner couples (Wilkie, Ferree, and Ratcliff 1998) found that a wife's receiving credit for homemaking, and a husband's receiving credit for bread-winning, contribute to both spouses' sense of fairness in their marriage. As another

example, Hochschild observed that some wives who earned more than their husbands "made up" for their mate's possible loss of self-esteem by doing more of the second shift than their proportionate income would have predicted. Still another gender strategy, used by wives who would like a husband to do more but are reluctant to insist, is to compare their husbands to other men "out there" who apparently are doing even less (Hochschild 1989). Some men suggest an even more favourable comparison: They compare themselves to their father or grandfathers (Thompson 1991). Ironically perhaps, one study that used national survey data found that the more a husband relies on his wife's income, the less housework he does. The author argues that, when being principal breadwinner is in jeopardy, a husband demonstrates his manhood by not doing "women's work" (Brines 1994; see also Kroska 1997).

A fairly common gender strategy, according to Hochschild (1989), is to develop **family myths**—"versions of reality that obscure a core truth in order to manage a family tension" (p. 19). For example, when a husband shares housework in a way that contradicts his traditional beliefs and/or feelings, couples may develop a myth alleging the wife's poor health or incompetence in order to protect the man's image of himself. A common family myth defines the wife as an organized and energetic superwoman who has few needs of her own, requires little from her husband, and congratulates herself on how much she can accomplish (Thompson 1991).

Meanwhile, there are couples who equally share work, family, and parenting roles (Coltrane 1996). Sociologists (Risman and Johnson-Sumerford 1998) located 15 of them and interviewed them extensively, visiting them at home after work and remaining until the children were asleep. Having "described people who have freed themselves from most of the contemporary constraints of gender inequality in their family lives," the researchers concluded that:

> Although gender exists at the institutional, interactional, and individual levels in our society, the existence of these couples shows us that the consequences of gender are far from deterministic.... The women and men in this sample.... [D]o not consider that wifehood involves a script of domestic service or that breadwinning is an aspect of successful masculinity. (p. 38)

It is possible, then—should both individuals in a couple want to—to move "beyond gender" (Risman and Johnson-Sumerford 1998).

Maintaining Intimacy during Role Changes

Study after study show that marital satisfaction is greater when wives feel that husbands share fairly in the household work (Pina and Bengtson 1993; Barnett 1994; Perry-Jenkins and Folk 1994; Suitor and Pillemer 1994; Ahlander and Bahr 1995). For example, one study of 452 married couples concluded that

> the factor which most strongly affects the marital quality experienced by both spouses appears to be the ability to give and receive support. Husbands with sensitive personalities experience higher quality marriages and produce higher quality marriages for their wives. Women also experience higher marital quality the more egalitarian she believes her husband's expectations to be. (Vannoy and Philliber 1992, p. 397)

Women who perceive their housework load as fair also experience higher psychological well-being (Lennon and Rosenfield 1994; Roxburgh 1997). Meanwhile, the majority of two-earner couples today can be characterized as what Hochschild (1989) terms transitional. Transitional couples may be at the highest risk for conflict over work and family roles (McHale and Crouter 1992).

While husbands may carry a good share of the responsibility for family work (Ferree 1990; Risman and Johnson-Sumerford 1998), getting comfortable with transitional marital roles is not a quick and easy process. One of Hochschild's points is that not only do women suffer from overload when men don't share the second shift; so do husbands, "through the resentment their wives feel toward them and through their need to steel themselves against that resentment" (1989, p. 7). As pointed out in Chapter 10, however, when the transition proceeds from a mutual commitment to achieve an equitable, no-power relationship, the result can be greater intimacy. As discussed in Chapter 9, a first step is to address the conflict.

ACCEPT CONFLICT AS A REALITY   The idea that mates can sometimes have competing interests and needs departs from the more romanticized view that sees marriages and families as integrated units with shared desires and goals. Nevertheless, as a first step toward maintaining intimacy during role changes, partners need to recognize their possibly competing interests and to expect conflict (Paden and Buehler 1995).

Sociologists Janet and Larry Hunt (1986), two of the first to research two-career marriages, argue that the low status of household work makes it symbolically unattractive to most husbands, who have become used to greater conjugal power. Furthermore, women have moved into and thereby altered one sphere of men's lives, the workplace. As a result, men may press for stability, resisting change in another sphere—at home. Moreover, research on one small sample of 314 dual-income spouses found that women cope with overload by talking about it, while for men, talking about it only seemed to make them feel worse (Paden and Buehler 1995). Clearly, today's domestic stage is set for conflict.

ACCEPT AMBIVALENCE   After accepting conflict as a reality, the next step in maintaining intimacy as spouses adjust to two-earner marriages is for both to recognize that each will have ambivalent feelings. The following excerpt from one young husband's essay for his English composition class is illustrative: "I'm in school six days a week. My wife works between 40 to 50 hours a week. So I do the majority of the cooking, cleaning, and laundry. To me this is not right. But am I wrong to think so? I'm lost in my own mind."

Women may also be ambivalent. Conflicting feelings become evident: They want their husbands to be happy; they want their husbands to help and support them; they feel angry about past inequalities; and they feel guilty about their declining interest in housekeeping and husband care and their decreasing willingness to accommodate to their husbands' preferences. Furthermore, men who participate have opinions about how child rearing or housework should be done. As a husband begins to pitch in, his wife may resent his intrusion into her traditional domain.

EMPATHIZE   A next step is to empathize. This can be difficult, for it is tempting instead to retaliate for past or current hurts. But partners who retaliate rather than empathize are trying to win or "show" the other. If couples are to maintain intimacy, they must make sure *both* partners win (see Chapter 9).

It has been suggested that as wives empathize, they try to recognize that a husband's lack of participation is very likely "due to insensitivity, not malice" (Crosby 1991, p. 167). Partly because many wives do much of the housework when their mates are not home (Thomas 1991), most husbands underestimate the number of hours that household labour takes (Wilkie, Ferree, and Ratcliff 1998). It is never easy to adjust to new roles, and men especially may feel they have a lot to lose. A man who has enjoyed being emotionally cared for by his wife may feel threatened by her choosing to invest energy in school, a job, or a career. In the words of one observer, "Fear can close even the most open mind; and vague, ill-defined fears can make us all mulish" (Crosby 1991, p. 162). A wife's pressing for role changes may threaten a man with the loss of authority and privilege, of a unilateral helpmate, of the "hero-at-home" status of the "good provider," and of the promise of a dependable listener (pp. 159–77).

Men gain, too, of course: They develop domestic skills, their marriage is enhanced, there is more money, and they benefit from spending time with their children (Crosby 1991). In Hochschild's study (1989) some fathers who felt they had been emotionally deprived in relationships with their own fathers took great pleasure in creating more satisfying family relationships with and for their children.

As husbands empathize, they need to be aware that their willingness to participate in household tasks is vitally important to wives, especially perhaps to employed wives (McHale and Crouter 1992). For one thing, wives doing a second shift value having a "down time" due to a responsive mate's freeing them from overload or from specific tasks they dislike (Thompson 1991; Blair and Johnson 1992). On another level, a husband's sharing carries a symbolic meaning for a wife, indicating that her work is recognized and appreciated and that her husband cares (Thompson 1991). Indeed, wives are more inclined to see the division of household labour as fair when their work is obviously appreciated (Blair and Johnson 1992). A husband's participation becomes

caring; his resistance, carelessness and inattentiveness (Thompson 1991, p. 187).

STRIKE AN EQUITABLE BALANCE   Researchers who studied 153 couples with school children concluded the following: "Our data imply that the adjustment of individual family members, as well as harmonious family relationships, requires a *balance* among the very different and often conflicting needs and goals of different family members" (McHale and Crouter 1992, pp. 545–46, italics in original). Once equity is habitual, calculation and constant comparison are no longer necessary; some observers point out that the balance need not be an exactly calculated 50-50 split. Such an arrangement, complete with rules and his-and-her chore lists, may seem too impersonal: People find it alienating and hurtful when others treat them according to some fixed rule rather than as individuals with particular needs and desires. We do not feel so much cared for when others' responsiveness is routinized and rulebound (Thompson 1991, p. 188).

SHOW MUTUAL APPRECIATION   Once partners have committed themselves to striking a balance, they need to create ways to let each know the other is loved. Traditional role expectations were relatively rigid and limiting, but they sometimes let mates know they were cared for. When a wife cooked her husband's favourite meal, for example, he felt cared about. As spouses relinquish some traditional behaviours, they need to create new ways of letting each other know they care, rather than succumbing completely to the time pressures of today's hectic family life.

Many people have noted the potential of shared work and of shared provider and caregiving roles for enriching a marriage (Beeghley 1996; Risman and Johnson-Sumerford 1998). Hochschild (1989) holds out this hope also, if the present transition from a traditional division of labour to an egalitarian one can be negotiated successfully. Integrating work and family is a significant challenge to family members today. The next two chapters examine other, related, family challenges: divorce and stepfamilies. All of these challenges entail stress. The final chapter in this text discusses stress and coping more generally.

IN SUM

The labour force is a social invention. Traditionally, marriage has been different for men and women: The husband's job has been as breadwinner, the wife's as homemaker. These roles are changing as more and more women enter the work force. Women still remain very segregated occupationally and earn lower incomes than men, on the average.

We distinguished between two-earner and two-career marriages. In the latter, wives and husbands both earn high wages and work for intrinsic rewards. Even in such marriages, the husband's career usually has priority. Responsibility for housework falls largely on wives. Many wives would prefer shared roles, and negotiation and tension over this issue cast a shadow on many marriages. An incomplete transition to equality at work and at home affects family life profoundly.

We have emphasized that both cultural expectations and public policy affect people's options. As individuals come to realize this, we can expect pressure on public officials to meet the needs of working families by providing supportive policies: parental leave, child care, and flextime.

We have seen that paid work is not usually structured to allow time for household responsibilities and that women, rather than men, continue to adjust their time to accomplish both paid and unpaid work. "If we can't return to traditional marriage, and if we are not to despair of marriage altogether, it becomes vitally important to understand marriage as a magnet for the strains of the stalled revolution" (Hochschild 1989, p. 18). To be successful, two-earner marriages will require social policy support and workplace flexibility. But there are some things the couple themselves can keep in mind that will facilitate their management of a working-couple family. Recognition of both positive and negative feelings and open communication between partners can help working couples cope with an imperfect social world.

Household work and child care are pressure points as the two-earner marriage continues to be the norm. To make it work, either the structure of work must be changed, social policy must support working families, or women and men must change their household role patterns—and very probably all three.

Key Terms

ambivalent provider couple
centre care
child care
commuter marriages
coprovider couple
elder care
family day care
family-friendly workplace policies
family myths
flexible scheduling
flextime
gender strategy
good provider role
househusbands
ideological perspective
job sharing
labour force
life course solution
main/secondary provider couple
mommy track
occupational sex segregation
pink-collar jobs
rational investment perspective
reinforcing cycle
resource hypothesis
role-reversed couple
second shift
shift work
stalled revolution
trailing spouse
two-career marriage
two-earner marriages
two-location families
two-person single career
unpaid family work

Study Questions

1. Discuss whether or to what extent distinctions between husbands' and wives' work are disappearing.

2. What do you see as the advantages and disadvantages of men being househusbands? Discuss this from the points of view of both men and women.

3. Discuss the advantages and the disadvantages of full-time homemaking for wives, for husbands, and for children.

4. What are some advantages and disadvantages of home-based work? Why are mothers more likely to choose this arrangement, when possible, than fathers?

5. What are some differences between career wives and husbands and other categories of wives and husbands?

6. Discuss the problems inherent in two-earner and two-career families. What influence does the social environment have on these families?

7. What is meant by work–family conflict? Interview some married or single-parent friends of yours for concrete examples and for some suggestions for resolving such conflicts.

8. What is unpaid family labour, and why is it called "labour"? Discuss social policy regarding work-family conflicts.

9. How can husbands and wives negotiate decisions about job opportunities in two locations?

10. How does gender help to explain why women, and not men, are most often in the "sandwich generation"?

Suggested Readings

Beeghley, Leonard. 1996. *What Does Your Wife Do?: Gender and the Transformation of Family Life.* Boulder, CO: Westview Press. Analysis of social change in women's work–family roles.

Coltrane, Scott. 1996. *Family Man: Fatherhood, Housework, and Gender Equity.* New York: Oxford University Press. Readable, scholarly, supportive, research-based analysis of men's family roles today.

Daly, Kerry J. 1996. *Families and Time: Keeping Pace in a Hurried World.* Thousand Oaks, Calif: Sage Publications. Informative discussion of the decisions and strategies made by families in order to manage time.

Kobayashi, Audrey. 1994. *Women, Work and Place.* Montreal: McGill-Queen's University Press. Brings together a diverse selection of readings which collectively illustrate the legacy of the "separate spheres" ideology upon contemporary families.

Vannoy, Dana, and Paula Dubeck. 1998. *Challenges for Work and Family in the Twenty-First Century.* New York: Aldine de Gruyter. Explores issues and changes as the family moves into the future.

On the Net

1) Working Mom's Internet Refuge
Covers topics from home/family to pay and women's career advancement. Includes a "rant board" for venting frustrations.
http://www.momsrefuge.com

2) Fatherhood
Discussions of issues and experiences among fathers involved in combining work with active, involved parenting.
http://www.fatherhood.org

3) Government of Canada's Collective Reflections on the Changing Workplace
http://www.reflection.gc.ca

4) Bringing Down the Barriers: The Labour Market and Women with Disabilities, Human Resources Development Canada
http://www.ccsd.ca/pubs/2000/wd/figlist.htm

5) "Left Poor by the Market: A Look at Family Poverty and Earnings," by Grant Schellenberg and David P. Ross (executive summary)
http://www.ccsd.ca/es_left.htm

Divorce

FOCUSING ON CHILDREN: DIVORCE AND CHILDREN

HER AND HIS DIVORCE

FORMING FAMILIES: THE NEXT GENERATION

SHOULD DIVORCES BE HARDER TO GET?

You cannot imagine how much

we hoped in the beginning.

Liv Ullmann,

Changing

Divorce has become a common experience in Canada, in all social classes, age categories, and religious and ethnic groups (see Table 14.1). In this chapter we'll look at divorce in broad terms and analyze why so many couples divorce in our society today. At the more personal level, we'll examine factors that affect people's decisions to divorce, the experience itself, and ways the experience can be made less painful and become the prelude to the future, alone or in a new marriage (remarriages are discussed in Chapter 15). This chapter ends with an examination of the policy debate, whether a divorce should be harder to get than it is today. We'll begin by looking at current divorce rates in Canada.

TODAY'S DIVORCE RATE

Sociologist Anne-Marie Ambert (1998) observes that there are at least four reasons why Canadians may be misinformed about divorce in our society:

> To begin with, much of the media that informs us is American. As a result, we often accept American facts and erroneously apply them to the Canadian situation.... Second, official statistics about divorce are sometimes confusing and erroneously interpreted, even by a few scientists themselves.... [T]hird, when research information and official statistics are published, radio, TV, and newspaper people often....report on some selected pieces of information and consequently may inadvertently blow them out of proportion. Furthermore, media people may neither have the time nor the space to provide the necessary appreciation of the context and other important facts which are essential in the interpretation of the information they selectively provide.

Before we examine the divorce rate today, we need to understand how divorce rates are reported.

TABLE   14.1

Divorce Rates by Number of Divorces, Rates per 100 000 Population and Rates per 100 000 Married Couples, Canada, 1921–1998

Years	# of divorces	Rates per 100,000 population	Rates per 100,000 Married couples
1921	558	6.4	N/A
1941	2,462	21.4	N/A
1961	6,563	36.0	N/A
1968*	11,343	54.8	N/A
1969	26,093	124.2	N/A
1981	67,980	271.8	1,174.4
1985**	61,980	253.6	1,103.3
1986	78,304	298.8	1,301.3
1987***	96,200	362.3	1,575.5
1990	80,998	295.8	1,311.5
1994	78,880	269.7	1,246.3
1995	77,636	262.2	1,221.9
1997	67,408	222.6	
1998	69,088	228.4	

*   Reform of Divorce Laws

** Divorce Act ("no fault")

*** Peak Year

Source: Adapted from Ambert, 1998 with additions from Statistics Canada, 1999, 2000e

How Divorce Rates Are Reported

Divorce rates are reported in many forms, some of which are more useful than others.

- *Number of divorces per year.* The number of divorces recorded per year is not an accurate measure of the rate because it does not take into account the general increase in population. There may be more divorces in a population simply because there are more people.

- *Ratio of current marriages to current divorces.* This measure is faulty because the marriages reported in the media have all taken place in the current year, whereas the divorces reported are of marriages that took place in many different years. The divorce rate then comes to depend on the marriage rate;

that is, if the number of marriages goes down, the divorce rate will appear to rise, even if the number of divorces remains constant.

- *Crude divorce rate.* The crude divorce rate is the number of divorces per 100 000 population. This measure takes into account changes in size of population but includes portions of the population—children and the unmarried—not at risk for divorce.

- **Refined divorce rate.** This is the number of divorces per 1000 or 100 000 legally married couples. This measure compares the number of divorces with the total number of women eligible for divorce and hence is a more valid indicator of the propensity for divorce. It does not, however, predict one's chances either of divorcing over a lifetime or of divorcing at any particular age. Age-specific divorce rates (number of divorces per 1000 married couples in each age group) are available, but they do not provide an overall rate.

Ideally, a cohort of married couples would be followed over a lifetime and their rate of divorce calculated. This sort of longitudinal study has never been done on a large scale and is unlikely ever to be done because of the expense and the length of time necessary for collecting data and ascertaining results. Of course, any rate calculated on this basis would be applicable only to those who married in the same year because socio-historical conditions (which affect divorce rates) would have changed over time.

On balance, the most useful and valid divorce rate appears to be the refined divorce rate. However, as Anne-Marie Ambert (1998) has emphasized, three important points should be borne in mind: first, statistics on divorce provide us with estimates and projections about important social trends. However, as she remarks, divorce "projections depend on many 'ifs'":

> Whether they will go up or down in the future largely depends on demographic factors and on people's lifestyle as well as values. For instance, as more and more young couples choose to cohabit before marriage and as the "children of divorce" who are at a higher risk of divorcing enter into marriage themselves...there are chances that divorce rates could go up again one day...The truth is that no one can accurately predict the future. For instance, if the rates of women bearing children out-of-wedlock—what we call "never-married" mothers—skyrocketed, divorce rates would go down as these never-married mothers have far fewer chances of ever marrying. (Ambert 1998, p. 5.)

Second, some of the divorces that occur each year involve previously married and divorced persons. The proportion of individuals who divorce at some time during their lifetime is increased by those who divorce for a second or third time. Third, demographers argue that marital dissolution, including informal or non-legal separation is underreported. For example, when a cohabiting couple breaks up, the dissolution of their union is not recorded in statistics on divorce. While

the break up of cohabiting unions could be considered as "hidden divorces" (Ambert 1998, p. 3), their incidence remains invisible within divorce statistics, which focus solely on terminations of legal marriage. As a result, real dissolution rates are higher than official divorce statistics indicates. In addition, it is evident that an unknown proportion of married couples separate but never initiate formal divorce proceedings. Once again, although "this type of conjugal dissolution may be as real as a divorce...it does not appear in divorce statistics either" (Ambert 1998, p.3).

Our Current Divorce Rate

Between 1968 and 1987, Canada experienced a seven-fold increase in divorce; from 1968 to 1995 the increase was five-fold (Ambert 1998, p. 4). However, divorce rates in Canada peaked in 1987 and have generally declined since then (see Figure 14.1).

One reason for the general decline in the Canadian divorce rate is that fewer people are marrying at the vulnerable younger ages. Among both men and women, divorce declines as people get older. From 1976 to 1987, marriages among Canadian teenagers were the most likely to result in divorce. During this time period, "the annual divorce rate for every 10 000 first marriages of men who were aged 15–19 at the time of their marriage was more than 5000 every year except 1985 when it was 4700" (Oderkirk 2000, p. 97). Among Canadian women who married between the ages of 15 and 19, the annual divorce rates were more than 4000 each year. The divorce rates among those 25 years of age and older at the time of their first marriage was much lower. Continuing this pattern, Canadians in their twenties are most susceptible to divorce (Gentleman and Park 1997). "[B]etween 1990 and 1992, the rate of divorce per 1000 married women was 2.2; but it was only 1.1 for women aged 45–49, and 0.65 for women 75–87 (versus 0.85 among older men)" (Ambert 1998, p. 5).

In addition, increasing numbers of Canadians are choosing common-law relationships as their first unions. This is particularly true for those whose first language is French, regardless of where in Canada they reside (Turcotte and Belanger 1997). The proportion of all first unions that were common-law rose, in Canada, from 17 percent in 1970–1974 to 41 percent in 1980–1984 and 57 percent in 1990–1995 (Ambert

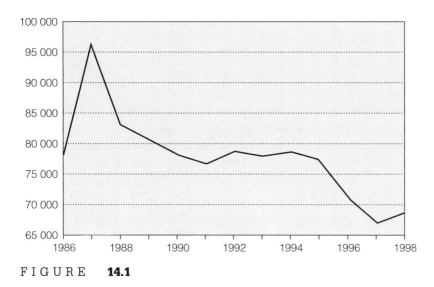

FIGURE **14.1**

Number of divorces in Canada, 1986 to 1998. (Source: Statistics Canada, <http://www.statcan.ca/Daily/English/001218/d001218.htm>)

1998, p. 7). In Quebec, cohabitation has become the norm, with 80 percent of all first unions being common-law unions. In 1995, common-law couples accounted for one in four couples in Quebec and 14 percent of all Canadian couples. "Between 1981 and 1995, the number of couples living in common-law unions tripled to over one million" (Ambert 1998, p. 7). While cohabiting unions are less stable than marriages, their dissolutions, as we have already noted, are not included within divorce statistics.

The aftermath of divorce and separation is nevertheless apparent in the prevalence of single-parent families. In 1996, a lone parent headed 14.5 percent of all Canadian families (Statistics Canada 1997c). While lone-parent families in the first half of the twentieth century were primarily the product of the death of a parent (Oderkirk and Lochhead 1992) occasioned by wars, mortalities associated with childbirth, and generally more hazardous living conditions, widowed people raising children alone accounted for only 20 percent of lone-parent families in 1996 (Statistics Canada 1996). While one in four children living with a lone mother parent in that year had a never-married mother (Ambert 1998, p. 6), solo parenting in Canada is currently most likely to be the product of marital dissolution (either separation or divorce), after which child custody is typically

granted, either formally or informally, to one parent only (mothers overwhelmingly). In 1996, there were 1.1 million lone-parent families in Canada, the vast majority (83 percent) of them headed by women, and the majority having separated/divorced parents, raising 1 740 485 children (Statistics Canada 1998).

Anne-Marie Ambert suggests that although headlines in the popular press suggest that "40 to 50 percent of children will experience the divorce of their parents," such projections must be treated cautiously:

If we consider that only about 30 percent of all marriages may end in divorce and that a proportion of these marriages, perhaps 40 percent, do not include children, then this prediction is far too high. Including older children who are adults, current rates would lead to an estimate closer to 30 percent. (1998, pp. 6–7)

At the same time, she acknowledges that if we consider all Canadian children who are affected by the dissolution of their parents' relationship and note the higher dissolution rate of common-law unions, it is evident that "a substantial proportion of these children will also experience the dissolution of their parents' common-law 'marriage' at some point and will become members of a single-parent family" (Ambert 1998, p. 7).

Such findings do not mean that Canadians have given up on marriage; it means that they find an unhappy marriage intolerable and hope to replace it with a happier one (Glenn 1996). Meanwhile, an emerging trend is **redivorce**. Redivorces take place more rapidly than first divorces. In both Canada and the United States, "[t]he more frequently people divorce and remarry, the shorter each subsequent remarriage" (Ambert 1998, p. 6). For example, among men 65–87 who divorced in 1990 to 1992, "the average duration of their first marriage was 37.8 years, while second and subsequent divorces occurred after an average of 14.4 years of marriage" (Ambert 1998, p. 6). Consequently, many who divorce—and their children—can expect several rapid and emotionally significant transitions in lifestyle and the family unit. They will experience stress and the need for adjustment. The stability of remarriages is addressed in greater detail in Chapter 15, and the general topic of family stress is the focus of Chapter 16.

WHY MORE COUPLES ARE DIVORCING

Various factors can bind marriages and families together: economic interdependence; legal, social, and moral constraints; and the spouses' relationship. The binding strength of some of these factors has lessened, however. We'll examine how these changes affect the divorce rate.

Decreased Economic Interdependence

Traditionally, as we've seen, the family was a self-sufficient productive unit. Survival was far more difficult outside of families, so members remained economically bound to one another. But today, because family members no longer need each other for basic needs, they are freer to divorce than they once were (Coontz 1997b).

Families are, however, still somewhat interdependent economically. As long as marriage continues to offer practical benefits, economic interdependence will help hold marriages together. The economic practicality of marriages varies according to several conditions. We'll look briefly at two: income and how it relates to divorce, and wives' employment.

DIVORCE AND INCOME A positive relationship usually exists between marital stability and education and income; that is, up to a certain level, the higher the income, the less likely a couple is to divorce (Raschke 1987). A relative loss or lack of socioeconomic status seems important, too; men who are downwardly mobile—with less education than their parents—are more likely to divorce, as are those who fail to complete university. Both the stress of living with inadequate finances and the failure to meet one's expectations for economic or educational attainment seem to contribute to marital instability (White 1990). This situation, together with the tendency of low-income groups to marry relatively early, helps explain why less well-off families have the highest rates of marital disruption, including divorce, separation, and desertion.

Although economic stress is less in high-income marriages, the higher the income, the less economic impediment there is to divorce. This relative economic independence, plus the fact that the pursuit of occupational success can erode marital intimacy, contributes to the divorce rate among high-income couples.

WIVES IN THE LABOUR FORCE AND DIVORCE Statistics show that divorce rates have risen as women's employment opportunities have increased and women have entered the labour force in large numbers (Richardson 1996; Ruggles 1997). But many other changes have occurred during the same time period. How directly does women's employment affect divorce rates?

In general, employed women, especially those working more hours (Greenstein 1990), do have higher divorce rates than do nonemployed women (Heckert, Nowak, and Snyder 1998).

Sociologist Charles Hobart (1996, p. 17) claims:

[P]aid employment has greatly reduced the time available to wives for domestic work, and having paycheques has empowered them, giving them increased influence and independence. Conflict has resulted, over (1) husbands' reluctance to share the domestic work fairly, and (2) wives' refusal to be traditionally subservient.

But research indicates that wives' employment *per se* makes no difference in marital quality—although, as Chapter 13 points out, whether husbands are supportive of their wives' employment and share in housework does relate to wives' marital satisfaction. In any case, although it may not make marriages less happy, employment may nevertheless contribute to a divorce by giving an *unhappily* married woman the economic power, the increased independence, and the self-confidence to help her decide on divorce (Booth, Johnson, and White 1984; Hiedemann, Suhomlinova, and O'Rand 1998).

The relationship between employment and divorce may also run in the other direction; that is, it is also possible that women whose marriages are not going well will enter employment in anticipation of the need to be self-supporting (Spitze 1988; Wilkie 1988).

Finally, recent research suggests that, among low-income couples, a wife's earnings may actually help to hold the marriage together by counteracting the negative effects of poverty on marital stability (Ono 1998; Heckert, Nowak, and Snyder 1998).

High Expectations: The Ideal Marriage

People increasingly expect marriage to provide a happy, emotionally supportive relationship. This is an essential family function; yet high expectations for intimacy between spouses push the divorce rate upward (Glenn 1996). Research has found that couples whose expectations are more practical are more satisfied with their marriages than are those who expect more loving and expressive relationships (Troll, Miller, and Atchley 1979; see also White and Booth 1991). Indeed, many observers attribute our divorce rate to the fact that our expectations about marital happiness are too high. Although many couples part for serious reasons, others may do so because of unrealized (often unrealistic) expectations and general discontent.

The Changed Nature of Marriage Itself

To say that there are *no* societal constraints against divorce any more is an overstatement; nevertheless, as we have seen, they have weakened. A related issue is the changed nature of marriage itself. In Chapter 1 we noted that marriage has been redefined as a nonpermanent—or, at best, a semi-, maybe, or hopefully permanent—relationship. We have also noted that marriage was originally perceived as a social institution for the practical purposes of economic support and responsible child rearing. But we have come to equate marriage with ongoing love, with *relationship*. Emphasis on the relationship itself over the institutional benefits of marriage results in its being defined as not necessarily permanent (Glenn 1996; Cowan and Cowan 1998). As Frederick Engels, a colleague of Karl Marx and an early family theorist, noted near the turn of the twentieth century, "If only the marriage based on love is moral, then also only the marriage in which love continues." Engels went on to argue—as have some counsellors and others over the past three decades—that "if affection definitely comes to an end or is supplanted by a new passionate love, separation is a benefit for both partners as well as for society" (Engels 1942, p. 73).

SELF-FULFILLING PROPHECY Defining marriage as semipermanent becomes a self-fulfilling prophecy. Increasingly, spouses may enter the union with reservations, making "no definitive gift" of themselves. But, "just as the person makes no definitive gift of himself, he [sic] has definitive title to nothing" (Durkheim 1951, p. 271). If partners behave as if their marriage could end, it is more likely that it will. Experts on the family who had at first remained optimistic even as divorce rates rose are now concerned about what they see as eroding family commitment (Glenn 1991; 1996).

MARITAL CONVERSATION—MORE STRUGGLE AND LESS CHITCHAT Besides being visibly less permanent, marriage has changed in another way. No longer are the rules or normative role prescriptions for wives, husbands, or children taken for granted (Cowan and Cowan 1998, p. 172). Consequently, marriage entails continual negotiation and renegotiation among members about trivial matters as well as important ones. When family roles were culturally agreed on, members were likely to "share the indifferent 'intimacies' of the day" (Simmel 1950, p. 127), to engage in relatively inconsequential conversation about events outside the family. Today, however, as family roles are less precisely defined, "marital conversation is more struggle and less chitchat.... The conversation turns inward, to the question of defining the makeup of the family, ... [to the] forging and fighting for identities" (Wiley 1985, pp. 23, 27). As one divorced woman put it:

It had taken Howard and me only about ten minutes to pronounce the "I do's," but we would spend the next ten years trying to figure out who, exactly, was supposed to do what: Who was responsible for providing child care, finding babysitters and tutors, driving car pools, for which periods and where? (Blakely 1995, p. 37)

One result is that, increasingly, marriage and family living feel like work, and living alone may look restful by comparison.

Decreased Social, Legal, and Moral Constraints

Another important influence on the divorce rate has been the change in cultural values and attitudes (Glenn 1996): The social constraints that once kept unhappy partners from separating operate less strongly now, and divorce is generally more acceptable.

No-fault divorce grounds, first introduced into Canadian divorce law by the 1968 Divorce Act, allow couples to divorce without requiring them to stipulate their specific reason(s) for doing so. They also may be seen as a symbolic representation of how our society now views divorce. The official posture of many—though not all—religions in Canada has also changed to be less critical of divorce than in the past.

A related factor may be the rise of individualistic values (Popenoe 1996). We increasingly value personal freedom and happiness—gained, if necessary, at the cost of a marriage—over commitment to the family (Glenn 1996). Many Canadians—perhaps most—believe marriages ought to be happy if they are to continue. The definition of marriage as an emotional relationship rather than a practical one is modern (Shorter 1975; Stone, 1980). For all societies undergoing the transition from traditional to modern, divorce has become increasingly easy to obtain (Fine and Fine 1994), and divorce rates have increased (Coontz 1997a, 1997b).

Meanwhile, as we saw in Chapter 8, at least two states (Louisiana and Arizona) in the United States have enacted laws allowing covenant marriage

designed to counteract the trend toward decreased social, legal, and moral constraints regarding divorce. Issues involved in making divorce harder are addressed later in this chapter.

Other Factors Associated with Divorce

So far in this section we have looked at socio-historical and cultural factors that encourage rising divorce rates. Another way to think about causes for divorce is to recognize that certain social or demographic factors are related to divorce rates. These include the following (White 1990, pp. 906–907):

- As we have already seen, remarried mates are more likely to divorce.

- Cohabitation, as discussed in Chapter 7, is associated with higher probability of divorce.

- Marrying young, also discussed in Chapter 7, increases the likelihood of divorce (Wu and Penning 1997).

- Premarital childbearing increases the risk of divorce in a subsequent marriage. (Premarital conception, by itself, does not.)

- As discussed in Chapter 11, a married couple's having young children stabilizes marriage—that is, decreases the possibility of divorce. Hence, remaining childfree is associated with a higher likelihood of divorce.

- A growing literature suggests that having parents who divorced increases the likelihood of divorcing (Amato 1996). Reasons for this are hypothetical. It is possible that divorcing parents model divorce as a solution to marital problems, or that children of divorced parents are more likely to marry inappropriate partners and to exhibit personal behaviours that interfere with maintaining a happy marriage (Amato 1996). There is also evidence that children of divorced parents marry at younger ages and are more likely to experience premarital births, and both factors are associated with higher divorce rates.

- Those who irregularly or never attend religious services are more likely to divorce than those who do. Findings from the 1995 General Social Survey indicates that while religious people are "just as unwilling as those who never attended religious services to forgive a spouse's abusive or unfaithful behaviour, they were less likely to view lack of love and respect, and a partner's drinking too much as grounds for divorce. Religious couples were also more likely to state that they would stay married for the sake of their children" (Clark 2000, p. 110).

So far we have been discussing social factors that are associated with divorce. Now we will look at some of the common marital complaints voiced by divorcing couples.

Common Marital Complaints

Marital complaints given by the divorced include infidelity, alcoholism, drug abuse, jealousy, moodiness, family violence, and, much less often, homosexuality (White 1990; Amato and Rogers 1997). But knowing this tells us little about the extent to which these factors are actually associated with divorce. Indeed, it is "striking ... that so few empirical studies of divorce take these individual complaints seriously" (White 1990, p. 908).

Recognizing that "little is known about why some marriages succeed and others fail," Judith A. Frederick and Jason Hamel (1998) sought to explore sociodemographic characteristics that affect Canadians' beliefs about the conditions that justify divorce. To do so, they used data collected by the 1995 General Social Survey on family and social support. This survey sampled approximately 11 000 Canadians aged 15 and older and living in the 10 provinces, excluding full-time residents of institutions. They focused their research on a question which asked whether "...you think the following reasons are sufficient for splitting up a marriage or common-law relationship" (see Table 14.2). The 10 reasons that followed this question fell into three broad categories: (1) abusive or disrespectful behaviour toward a partner; (2) "experiential issues" such as conflict over money, household chores, and raising the children; and (3) issues related to fertility (e.g., an inability to have children or disagreement about the specific number of children desired). Respondents were also asked if they would stay in a union "for the sake of their children."

Adopting the three broad age grouping used earlier by Michael Adams (1997), these researchers used the term "Elders" to refer to respondents born before 1946, "Boomers," for those born between 1946 and 1965, and "Gen-Xers" for those born after 1965. In his earlier work, Adams had suggested that gender, age, and income largely determine the values of Elders and that their society tended to be supportive of such well-established institutions as marriage. In contrast to Elders, Boomers were more affluent, educated, well travelled, and informed. They were also more likely to challenge then venerate the institution of marriage and the values that it represents. Finally, Gen-Xers were seen as less affluent than their parents were and more likely than other groups to view marriage as irrelevant.

Frederick and Hamel report that most Canadians (over 95 percent), regardless of their age, agree that abusive behaviour, infidelity, and disrespect toward a partner justify divorce. Indeed, Elders, Boomers, and Gen-Xers displayed near unanimity on this issue. In relation to a partner who drank too much, the level of agreement declined. However, nearly three out of four felt this situation would be sufficient grounds for divorce. In addition, the majority of Canadians (approximately 60 percent) reported that they would not stay in a bad marriage for the sake of their children, with Boomers the least likely to say that they would do so. Men were more likely than women to report that they would remain married for the sake of their children (almost 60 percent of men versus less than a third of women).

The three age groups were found to differ most in relation to experiential issues—"that is, dealing with finances, sexual relationships, household chores, and raising children." With increasing age (and experience of such problems), the less tolerant Canadians are. In addition, Frederick and Hamel found that marital history influences Canadians' views about divorce with people who have remained in their first marriage taking a less liberal view than those who had not. Those who had only been married once and remained married and those who were widowed were the least likely to view any of the issues presented to them as sufficient to justify divorce. Predictably enough, those who were separated, divorced, in a common-law union, or remarried were more likely to view divorce as a viable option.

Meanwhile, a general (and perhaps obvious) conclusion drawn from research is that deficiencies in the

TABLE   14.2

What Justifies Divorce?

Fundamental Issues	Gen-Xers 15–20	Boomers 30–49	Elders 50 and over	Total % of population aged 15 and over
Abusive behaviour from the partner	95	95	94	95
Unfaithful behaviour from the partner	89	85	89	88
Lack of love and respect from the partner	86	86	87	88
Partner drinks too much	68	73	80	74
Experiential Issues				
Constant disagreements about how the family finances should be handled	28	40	49	40
Unsatisfactory sexual relationship with the partner	21	37	45	35
Unsatisfactory division of household tasks with the partner	12	16	21	17
Conflict about how the children are raised	14	17	12	17
Fertility Issues				
Inability to have children with the partner	8	12	17	13
Disagreement about the number of children to have	3	6	11	7
Would stay for the children	44	39	32	43

Source: Statistics Canada, "Canadian Social Trends," Cat. No 11-008, Spring 1998, No. 48.

emotional quality of the marriage lead to divorce (Martin and Luke 1991). In one study (Spanier and Thompson 1987) of 210 separated people, 56 percent of the women were dissatisfied with their husband's contribution to household tasks. For 40 percent of the women and 20 percent of the men, their spouse had not lived up to their expectations as a parent. Many were unhappy with their partner as a leisure-time companion, as someone with whom to talk things over, or as a sex partner. Subsequent research finds marital stability to be positively associated with a wife's perception that household tasks are shared fairly (Greenstein 1995).

Financial and job-related problems can contribute to marital deterioration. The greatest source of strain in working- and lower-class marriages often is vulnerability to economic difficulties. A husband's provision of adequate financial support is important to his and

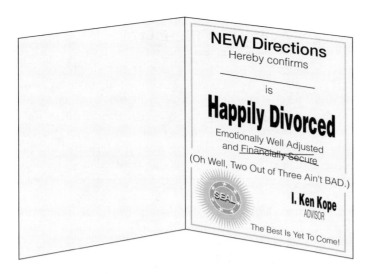

With greeting cards like this one in our everyday, or popular, culture it is clear that divorce has decreased stigma associated with it than in the past. Consumer items such as this are marketed to the divorced (and their friends), but their presence in the culture also helps to legitimize divorce.

his wife's marital satisfaction, with a husband's unemployment having a definite negative effect (Aldous and Tuttle 1988; Blakely 1995). Along with obvious economic hardships, loss of identity and increased time on their hands impose stress on unemployed husbands, one result of which can be diminished displays of affection and increased hostility (Conger et al. 1990). Unions in which one or both partners work night or unusual shifts are more vulnerable to divorce (White and Keith 1990). Some spouses may enjoy their careers more than family life; in two-career marriages, conflicting interests and ambitions can cause problems (Hochschild 1997).

In many cases, thinking about divorce is apparently precipitated by third-party involvement. In the Spanier and Thompson study, more than 60 percent of the respondents had had extramarital sexual relationships. In-laws may also have a negative influence, especially if they disapprove of the marriage (Burns 1984). Counsellors suggest that some common problems—with money, sex, and in-laws, for example— are really arenas for acting out deeper conflicts, such as who will be the more powerful partner. Problems can become routine, as we saw in Chapter 8, resulting in devitalized or conflict-habituated marriages. The personal decision about divorce involves a process of balancing alternatives against the practical and emotional satisfactions of one's present union.

THINKING ABOUT DIVORCE: WEIGHING THE ALTERNATIVES

Not everyone who thinks about divorce actually gets one. As divorce becomes a more available option, spouses continually compare the benefits of their union with the projected consequences of not being married (Kurdek 1998).

Marital Happiness, Barriers to Divorce, and Alternatives to the Marriage

One model (Levinger 1965) derived from the exchange theory (see Chapter 2) argues that spouses weigh their marital happiness against both alternatives to the marriage (possibilities for remarriage or fashioning a satisfying single life) and barriers to divorce (for example, religious beliefs against divorce, parental pressure to stay married, common friendship networks, joint economic investments, and children to consider).

There is considerable research evidence spanning the past three decades to indicate that young children serve as a barrier to divorce. Because research also shows that children are likely to lessen marital happiness, we can conclude that affection for their children, along with economic and other concerns about children's welfare after divorce, discourages some parents from dissolving their marriage.

One important analysis (Waite and Lillard 1991) found that children increase marital stability through their preschool years. (Older children and those born before the marriage actually increase chances for dissolution.) "The initially stabilizing and later destabilizing effects of children combine over the course of the marriage to give parents only a modestly higher chance than childless couples of reaching their twentieth anniversary" (Waite and Lillard 1991, p. 930). These authors argue that young children's high requirements for parental time and effort (and their expense) stabilize marriages because single parenting seems too costly compared to remaining married. As children grow older, however, they require less constant care and their presence lessens their parents' marital happiness—a situation resulting in children's later destabilization of marriages.

Most divorces occur relatively early in marriage (Clarke 1995b). In Canada, the highest rate of divorces per 1000 population occurs at year five of marriage (with over 3.5 divorces per 1000 population) and then "swiftly diminishes each year thereafter" (Ambert 1998, p. 5). The proportion of divorces for couples married 20 years or more has increased, however (Wu and Penning 1997). This situation may be partly related to dissatisfaction with one's marital relationship at the onset of the empty nest, when the couple's grown children leave home (Hiedemann, Suhomlinova, and O'Rand 1998). Nevertheless, long marriages are less likely to end in divorce even though empirical evidence consistently shows that marital happiness declines over time. One reason for this is that barriers to divorce, such as common economic interests and friendship networks, increase over time (White and Booth 1991; Kurdek 1998). One study (Black et al. 1991) that compared spouses who had initiated the divorce (the "leavers") with the "left" found that the two groups did not differ on marital satisfaction or barriers to divorce, but leavers saw more alternatives to their marriage.

Our discussion of weighing the alternatives suggests that one of the first questions married people ask themselves is whether they would be happier if they were to divorce.

"Would I Be Happier?"

This is not an easy question to answer. Deciding whether one would be happier after divorce requires one to hypothesize about future alternatives. Some people may prefer to stay single after divorce, but many partners probably weigh their chances for a remarriage. According to national U.S. surveys over the past two decades, divorced and separated individuals have lower levels of life satisfaction and a more negative general mood than married people (Stack and Eshleman 1998). Divorced people also have poorer physical health than marrieds, are more often depressed (Menaghan and Lieberman 1986; Wineberg 1994), and are somewhat more inclined to suicide (Stack 1990). Analysis of 6573 respondents from the U.S. National Survey of Families and Households found that even though factors such as income and education were more important, people in first marriages reported greater happiness and less depression than those who had ever divorced. Furthermore, people who had divorced just once were less depressed than those with a history of two or more divorces. Those currently married reported greater happiness and less depression than cohabitors, who in turn reported greater well-being on these two scores than those who lived without another adult (Kurdek 1991b).

One study of 1755 individuals found an interesting wrinkle, however. Higher levels of depression among the divorced were *not* apparent among those who saw themselves as escaping marriages with serious, long-term problems (Aseltine and Kessler 1993). Other research (Ross 1995) used data from a national U.S. sample of 2031 adults to compare depression levels among those with no partners and those in relationships of varying quality. Their results showed that persons without a partner are likely to be more depressed than average—but those in unhappy relationships are likely to be even more depressed.

Then too, some (but not all) depression effects may mean that people who divorce are more inclined to unhappiness anyway (Gove, Style, and Hughes 1990). Counsellors advise that in some cases partners might be happier trying to improve their relationship than divorcing. They warn that frequently one's motive for divorce is really to solve an *individual* problem—one that stems from a period of transition, perhaps, or some personal inadequacies. If this is true, deciding to divorce will not be a solution unless personal growth also occurs (Counts and Sacks 1991).

Marriage can and often does provide emotional support, sexual gratification, companionship, and economic and practical benefits. But unhappy marriages do not provide all (or in some cases, any) of these benefits (Wickrama et al. 1997). Compared with unhappily married people, divorced individuals display generally better physical and emotional health and higher morale. "In short, it appears that at any particular point in time most marriages are 'good marriages' and that such marriages have a strong positive effect on well-being and that 'bad marriages' have a strong negative effect on well-being" (Gove, Style, and Hughes 1990, p. 14).

One must decide whether divorce represents a healthy step away from an unhappy relationship that cannot be satisfactorily improved or is an illusory way to solve what in reality are personal problems. Going to a marriage counsellor can help partners become more aware of the consequences of divorce so that they can make this decision more knowledgeably. However, at the same time, we emphasize that counselling is not a cure-all.

GETTING THE DIVORCE

One of the reasons it feels so good to be engaged and newly married "is the rewarding sensation that out of the whole world, you have been selected. One of the reasons that divorce feels so awful is that you have been de-selected" (Bohannan 1970b, p. 33).

Sociologist Paul Bohannan (1970b) analyzed the divorce experience in terms of six different facets, or "stations": the emotional, the legal, the community, the psychic, the economic, and the co-parental divorce. Experience in each of these realms varies from one individual to another; some stations, such as the coparental, do not characterize every divorce. Yet they capture the complexity of the divorce experience. In this section, we will examine the first four stations; the economic and co-parental aspects of divorce will be explored in greater detail later in this chapter.

The Emotional Divorce

Emotional divorce involves withholding positive emotions and communications from the relationship (Vaughan 1986), typically replacing these with alienating feelings and behaviour. Partners no longer reinforce but rather undermine each other's self-esteem through endless large and small betrayals: responding with blame rather than comfort to a spouse's disastrous day, for instance, or refusing to go to a party given by the spouse's family, friends, or colleagues. As emotional divorce intensifies, betrayals become greater.

In a failing marriage, both spouses feel profoundly disappointed, misunderstood, and rejected (Brodie 1999). Because the other's very existence and presence is a symbol of failure and rejection, the spouses continually grate on each other. The couple may want the marriage to continue for many reasons—continued attachment, fear of being alone, obligations to children, the determination to be faithful to marriage vows—yet they can hurt one another as they communicate their frustration by look, posture, and tone of voice.

Not all divorced people wanted or were ready to end their marriage, of course. It may have been their spouses' choice. Not surprisingly, research shows that the degree of trauma a divorcing person suffers usually depends on whether that person or the spouse wanted the dissolution (Hopper 1993; Pettit and Bloom 1984), at least partly because the one feeling "left" experiences a greater loss of control (Wilder and Chiriboga 1991; but see also Rossiter 1991). Even for those who actively choose to divorce, however, divorce and its aftermath can be unexpectedly painful.

The Legal Divorce

A **legal divorce** is the dissolution of the marriage by the state through a court order terminating the marriage. The principal purpose of the legal divorce is to dissolve the marriage contract so that emotionally divorced spouses can conduct economically separate lives and be free to remarry.

Two aspects of the legal divorce itself make marital breakup painful. First, divorce, like death, creates the need to grieve. But the usual divorce in court is a rational, unceremonial exchange that takes only a few minutes. And lawyers have been trained to solve problems rationally and to deal with clients in a detached, businesslike manner. Although divorcing spouses might need and want them to, very few divorce attorneys view their role as helping with the grieving process.

A second aspect of the legal divorce that aggravates the misery is the adversarial system. Under our judicial system a lawyer advocates his or her client's interest only. Eager to "get the most for my client" and "protect my client's rights," opposing attorneys are not trained to and ethically are not even supposed to balance the interests of the parties and strive for the outcome that promises most mutual benefit. Also, the divorcing individuals can feel frustrated by their lack of control over a process in which the lawyers are the principals. In one study of divorced women, virtually all had complaints about their lawyers and the legal system (Arendell 1986).

DIVORCE MEDIATION **Divorce mediation** is an alternative, nonadversarial means of dispute resolution by which the couple, with the assistance of a mediator or mediators (frequently a lawyer–therapist team), negotiate the terms of their settlement of custody, support, property, and visitation issues. The couple work out a settlement best suited to the needs of their family. In the process it is hoped that they learn a pattern of dealing with each other that will enable them to work out future disputes.

Divorce mediation is a fairly recent development, having emerged over the past thirty years (Greatbatch and Dingwall 1997). Research indicates that couples who use divorce mediation have less relitigation, feel more satisfied with the process and the results, and report better relationships with ex-spouses (Marlow and Sauber 1990) and children (Beck and Blank 1997). Children of mediated divorces also adjust better to the divorce than children of litigated divorces do (Marlow and Sauber 1990). However, various women's task groups have noted that mediation as it is currently practised may be biased against females, who report being labeled "unladylike" or "vindictive" if they refuse to give in on a point (Lonsdorf 1991; Woo 1992b). Canadian family lawyer Linda Silver Dranoff also cautions that mediation is not always feasible and that "[s]pouses who have been bullied or dominated during the marriage may not be capable of holding their own in mediation, while rigid or abusive spouses may not be capable of the necessary flexibility and compromise" (2001, p. 254). Moreover, sociologist Judith

Wallerstein (1999) points out that the positive effects of divorce mediation *for children* may be overdrawn. In her words:

> What protects children in the divorced family is cooperative, civilized coparenting. The resolution of conflict may represent a necessary step along the road, but resolution of legally defined conflict, alone, which has been the central concern of the courts and the mediation movement, is not sufficient to protect the child. (p. 79)

NO-FAULT DIVORCE Prior to the turn of the century, divorce was a complex, drawn-out legal process in Canada. "In some provinces, a 'parliamentary' divorce, was the only option: a private member's bill had to pass first reading in both the Commons and the Senate; after second reading in the House of Commons, it could be heard by a special divorce committee" (Boyd 1998, p. 229). In consequence, as might it be expected, divorce was a rarity at that time.

In his study of divorce in Canada between 1900 and 1940, James Snell observes that:

> Divorce in Canada was squarely founded on a belief in innocence and guilt, which meshed nicely with the moral pathology of divorce. The process itself, through mandatory confrontation, always and with impressive assurance assigned those attributes to the participating parties. Few divorces were granted through either the judicial or the legislative process, and the matter was not of particular concern in the dominion. (in Boyd 1998, p. 224)

Consistent with this emphasis on assigning blame, prior to 1968, adultery was the only grounds for divorce in Canada, except in Nova Scotia, where cruelty was sufficient grounds even before Confederation (Morrison 1987).

The Divorce Act of 1968, the first federal divorce statute, expanded the "fault grounds" under which a divorce could be granted. In addition to adultery, proof that one's partner had engaged in prohibited activities such as mental or physical cruelty, rape, gross addiction to alcohol or other drugs, sodomy, bestiality, or homosexual acts, entitled the petitioner to an immediate divorce. This Act, as we have previously noted, also took a first step toward "**no-fault**" **divorce**. The dissolution of a marriage also was permitted on grounds of unspecified "marital break-down," if couples had lived "separate and apart" for a three-year period before applying for a divorce and jointly consented to being divorced. In the event that one party did not wish to be divorced, the court required that five years pass from the time of the separation before applying for divorce. This Act actually represented a compromise position that sought to satisfy those who felt that marriage should not be regarded as a terminal condition and those who felt that divorce was unacceptable on moral or religious grounds. However, in seeking to satisfy everyone, the Act satisfied virtually no one.

The 1968 Divorce Act placed a strong emphasis on the virtues of reconciliation, with the lawyers for each spouse legally obliged to discuss reconciliation with their client. Divorce trial judges were also required to determine whether the couple's reconciliation was possible. However, for those who felt that the law should support marriage, the availability of no-fault provisions for divorce was seen as unduly liberal. In contrast, others charged that the fault grounds were too narrow and noted that the disparate degrees of access to divorce provided by fault cases and no-fault cases encouraged a degree of fraud among those who did not wish to wait three years before they were legally divorced. For example, it has been noted that during this time period in Canada, "most fault divorces were adultery cases and...these cases were really consent divorces disguised to allow the spouses to avoid the three-year waiting period" (Morton 1990, p. 213). In addition, a judge could deny a divorce if s/he felt there was insufficient evidence of matrimonial misconduct. For example, in one 1976 case, divorce was denied to a woman whose husband refused to let her work outside of the home; in a 1980 case, a husband whose wife had undergone an abortion without his knowledge was denied a divorce. In both cases, the judge felt that insufficient grounds existed for a divorce to be granted on the grounds of "mental cruelty" (Dranoff 2001, p. 249–250).

With the amendment of Canada's Divorce Act in 1985, there is only one ground available for divorce—marital breakdown—but this is defined in three ways: (1) the spouses have lived apart for one year; (2) one of the spouses has committed an act of adultery; (3) one spouse has treated the other with mental or physical cruelty. While proof of fault entitles couples to an immediate divorce, those opting for a one-year separation "may apply for a divorce any time after separation to ensure that their case is heard soon after the year is up" (Morton 1990, p. 214).

Today, a partner seeking divorce no longer has to prove grounds. Instead, a marriage is legally "dissolved" because the relationship is "irretrievably broken." No-fault divorce legally abolishes the concept of the "guilty party." But learning to think in terms of no-win/no-lose is difficult even for people in good marriages. One result, some observers suspect, is that divorcing spouses who are bent on publicly determining guilt or innocence fight the same court battle, but as a child-custody suit instead; we'll address this issue when we discuss coparental divorce.

The Community Divorce

Marriage is a public announcement to the community that two individuals have joined their lives. Marriage usually also joins extended families and friendship networks and simultaneously removes individuals from the world of dating and mate seeking. Divorce occasions reverse changes in social networks, which are sometimes disappointing or embittering, often confusing. Divorce also provides the opportunity for forming new ties.

KIN NO MORE?   Given the frequency of divorce, most extended families find themselves touched by it. Grandparents fear losing touch with grandchildren, and this does happen. However, in Newfoundland, the law specifically provides that a grandparent may apply for custody or access to a child and in other provinces, such as New Brunswick, Nova Scotia, Ontario, Prince Edward Island, and Saskatchewan, as well as the Yukon Territory, the law allows for access and custody orders to be made to persons other than the child's parents (Dranoff 2001, p. 257).

In some cases, grandparents become closer to grandchildren, as adult children turn to grandparents for help (Coleman, Ganong, and Cable 1997) or grandchildren seek emotional support (Spitze et al. 1994). Researchers and therapists have concluded that

these relationships work best when family members do not take sides in the divorce and make their primary commitment to the children.

Grandparents can play a particular role, especially if their marriages are intact: symbolic generational continuity and living proof to children that relationships can be lasting, reliable, and dependable. Grandparents also convey a sense of tradition and a special commitment to the young that extends beyond and over the parents' heads. Their encouragement, friendship, and affection has special meaning for children of divorce; it specifically counteracts the children's sense that all relationships are unhappy and transient.

For the fortunate children in our study who could rely on their extended families, the world seemed a more stable, predictable place. (Wallerstein and Blakeslee 1989, p. 111)

Of course, more and more grandparents' marriages are not intact today. Nevertheless, one can assume that even a loving, divorced grandparent could help make the world seem "a more stable, predictable place" for a grandchild of divorce.

Women are more likely to retain in-law relationships after divorce, particularly if they had been in close contact before the divorce and if the in-law approves of the divorce (Serovich, Price, and Chapman 1991). Relationships between former in-laws are more likely to continue when children are involved. One study looked at the general character of postdivorce extended-kin relationships. This study found that in half of the cases, the kinship system included **relatives of divorce** (Johnson 1988, p. 168; see also Stacey 1990). This was most likely to occur with paternal relatives, who, of course, needed to keep in touch in order to see grandchildren living with custodial mothers. When fathers had custody, they too were likely to have contact with their former spouse's extended family (Ambert 1988). But the most commonly retained tie was between a grandmother and her former daughter-in-law. Still, relationships between former in-laws frequently deteriorate or vanish (Ambert 1988).

Adult children's relationships with their own parents may change after the children's divorce. According to one study, after an adult child's divorce:

Members of both generations had to revise their expectations of the other, and members of the older generation found themselves in a situation of having to give more of themselves to a child than they had expected to do at their stage of life. They were often forced into a parenting role, and this greater involvement provided more opportunity to observe and comment on their adult child's life....

Even so, there was extensive contact between generations, which did not decrease over time.... Nevertheless, there appeared to be incongruity in their expectations. Adult children were more likely to feel that parents should be available to help them with their emotional problems than their parents felt was appropriate. Divorcing children did not want their parents to interfere in childrearing or offer unsolicited advice, while their parents felt they could voice their concerns. (Johnson 1988, pp. 190–91)

There was considerable variation in these relationships within the sample of 52 adult–child dyads followed over several years in Johnson's study. But most older parents espoused "modern values of personal freedom and self-fulfillment" (p. 191); that is, they did not criticize the decision to divorce from a traditional perspective.

Couples who divorce later in life and/or after long marriages often find socioemotional support from their adult children (Gander 1991), but this is not always the case and may be truer for mothers than for fathers (Wright and Maxwell 1991).

FRIENDS NO MORE?   Important changes in one's lifestyle almost invariably mean changes in one's community of friends. When they marry, people usually replace their single friends with couple friends, and couples also change communities when they divorce. Separating from one's former community of friends and in-laws is part of the pain of divorce. Over three-quarters of the women in one study reported losing friends during or after the divorce (Arendell 1986).

Divorced people often feel uncomfortable with their friends who are still married because activities are done in pairs. Conversely, a married couple may find that a friend's divorce challenges them to take another look at their own marriage, an experience that can cause them to feel anxious and uncomfortable with the divorced friend. Also, couple friends may be reluctant to become involved in a conflict over allegiances and often experience their own sense of loss and grief. A common outcome is a mutual withdrawal, during which the divorced person feels heightened loneliness.

Like many newly married people, those who are newly divorced must find new communities to replace old friendships that are no longer mutually satisfying. The initiative for change may in fact come not only from rejection or awkwardness in old friendships but also from the divorced person's finding or wanting to find friends who share with him or her the new concerns and emotions of the divorce experience. Priority may also go to new relationships with people of the opposite sex; for the majority of divorced and widowed people, building a new community involves dating again.

The Psychic Divorce

Psychic divorce refers to the regaining of psychological autonomy through emotional separation from the personality and influence of the former spouse. In the process, one learns to feel whole and complete again and to have faith in one's ability to cope with the world (Brodie 1999). In psychic divorce, one must distance oneself from the still-loved aspects of the spouse, from the hated aspects, and "from the baleful presence that led to depression and loss of self-esteem" (Bohannan 1970b, p. 53).

Not all divorced people fully succeed at psychic divorce. "The 'graph' of divorce recovery is typically jagged rather than straight, and each forward step is likely to be matched by a retreat" (Sprenkle 1989, p. 175). But counsellors point out that this stage is a necessary prerequisite to a satisfying remarriage. Box 14.1, "Fifteen Suggestions for Healing," provides some guidelines.

To be successful, a psychic divorce requires a period of mourning. The experience of loss is real (Brodie 1999). Just as a gradual process of emotional estrangement starts long before the actual legal event of divorce, the partners' emotional involvement often continues long after. This "persistence of attachment" (Weiss 1975) is real for both spouses and should be understood and addressed.

There are at least three stages in the mourning process. The first, which typically occurs before the legal divorce, is denial. Sometimes, a person's inability to accept the divorce manifests itself in physical illnesses, accidents, or even suicide attempts. Eventually, however, the frustration of emotional divorce leads partners to face facts. They may say to each other, "We can't go on like this."

A second stage, characterized by anger and depression, follows this realization. These feelings often alternate, so that recently divorced people feel confused. Sometimes one's feelings resemble those of an ex-wife, who asked a counsellor, "How come I miss so terribly someone I couldn't stand?" (Framo 1978, p. 102). Unfortunately, many former partners vent their anger in the coparental arena (Masheter 1991).

In the third stage, ex-spouses take responsibility for their own part in the demise of the relationship, forgive themselves and the mate, and proceed with their lives: The psychic divorce is then complete. As long as one views the ex-spouse as an enemy or object of ongoing anger, however, the psychic divorce has not been accomplished, because preoccupation with one's ex-spouse (Masheter 1991), along with bitterness and hate, are emotions of a continuing relationship.

Counselling can help; increasingly, communities and religious groups are providing workshops (such as "BE," or Beginning Experience) that can be helpful as well (Byrne and Overline 1992).

Deciding knowledgeably whether to divorce means weighing what we know about the consequences of divorce. The next section examines the economic consequences of divorce.

THE ECONOMIC CONSEQUENCES OF DIVORCE

Increasingly social scientists and policymakers worry about the economic consequences of divorce, especially for children.

Divorce, Single-Parent Families, and Poverty

> Divorce is a direct cause of poverty for a large proportion of women and their children. Many will experience the consequences of poverty in the short term following divorce, and many will suffer its effects for several years. (Ambert 1998, p. 9)

While child poverty in Canada is not restricted to single-parent families, a far higher proportion of children of single parents and, in particular, lone-parent mothers, live in low-income circumstances (Figure 14.2). The younger the age of children at the time of

Fifteen Suggestions for Healing

Separation by divorce, like death, inflicts a painful emotional wound that must heal. A little book entitled *How to Survive the Loss of a Love: 58 Things to Do When There Is Nothing to Be Done* suggests some ways to facilitate the healing process.

1. Do your mourning *now*. Don't pretend, deny, cover up, or run away from the pain. Everything else can wait. The sooner you allow yourself to be with your pain, the sooner it will pass. Resisting the mourning only postpones healing, and grief can return months or even years later to haunt you.

2. Be gentle with yourself. Accept the fact that you have an emotional wound, that it is disabling, and that it will take a while before you are completely well. Treat yourself with the same care, consideration, and affection you would offer a good friend in a similar situation.

3. If possible, don't take on new responsibilities. When appropriate, let employers and co-workers know you're healing.

4. Don't blame yourself for any mistakes (real or imagined) you may have made that brought you to this loss. You can acknowledge mistakes later, when the healing process is further along.

5. Remember that it's okay to feel depressed. Let the healing process run its full course. A time of convalescence is very important. Just follow your daily routine and let yourself heal.

6. For a while, don't get involved in an all-consuming passionate romance or a new project that requires great time and energy.

7. Don't try against obvious odds to rekindle the old relationship. Futile attempts at reconciliation are painful and a waste of recuperative energy, and they slow healing and growth.

8. If you find photographs and mementos helpful to the mourning process, use them. If you find they bind you to a dead past, get rid of them. Put them in the attic, sell them, give them away, or throw them out.

9. Remember that it's okay to feel anger toward God, society, or the person who left you (even if through death). But it is not okay or good for you to hate yourself or to act on your anger in a destructive way. Let the anger out safely: hit a pillow, kick the bed, sob, scream. Practise screaming as loudly as you can. A car with the windows up makes a great scream chamber.

10. Use addictive prescription drugs like Valium wisely. Take them only if prescribed by your personal physician and only for a short period of time. Don't take them to mask your grief because your friends have grown tired of it.

11. Watch your nutrition. Take vitamins, eat good foods, and try to get plenty of rest.

12. Don't overindulge in alcohol, marijuana, or other recreational chemicals, or cigarettes.

13. Pamper yourself a little. Get a manicure, take a trip, bask in the sun, sleep late, see a good movie, visit a museum, listen to music, take a long bath instead of a quick shower. As healing progresses, remember that it's okay not to feel depressed.

14. You might find keeping a journal or diary helpful. This way you can see your progress as you read past entries.

15. Heal at your own pace. The sadness comes and goes—though it comes less frequently and for shorter lengths of time as healing proceeds.

Source: Colgrove, Bloomfield, and McWilliams 1978.

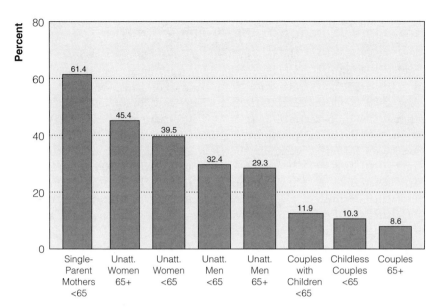

FIGURE **14.2**

Poverty rates by family types, 1996. (Source: Kendall et al. 2000, p. 263.)

divorce or dissolution of a common-law relationship, the more likely they are to be living in a low-income situation (Ambert 1998, p. 9).

In response, some have argued that single-parent families are the major cause of poverty and hence should virtually always be discouraged. Opponents of this view argue that financial privation exists (albeit to a lesser extent) even in married-couple families and point out that between 1990 and 1995, the percentage of married couples with children in low-income situations rose from 9.5 to 13 percent (a total of about 460 000 families) (Health Canada 1999, p. ix). They also emphasize that race/ethnic discrimination and low wages, particularly for women, account for poverty (Mauldin 1990; Lichter and Eggebeen 1994; Lichter and Landale 1995). Still others point out that for many individuals—those who have experienced family violence, for example—divorce is the lesser of two evils. Here, the primary concern is the economic betterment of single-parent families.

Meanwhile, a consistent and unequivocal research finding is that divorce is inversely related to a woman's (but not necessarily to a man's) economic status (Arditti 1997; Ross 1995; Vanier Institute of the Family 1994). Indeed, "the longer the period of

divorce (or widowhood) of a woman, the more she is likely to be poor" (Choi 1992, p. 40). Why is this the case?

Husbands, Wives, and Economic Divorce

Upon divorce, a couple undergoes an **economic divorce** in which they become distinct economic units, each with its own property, income, control of expenditures, and responsibility for taxes, debts, and so on. The laws in Canada that govern the division of marital assets have shifted dramatically in the past decades. In the early 1970s, Irene Murdock, a farm wife, claimed that her labours over the course of 15 years had earned her a proprietary share in the family farm. In rejecting Mrs. Murdock's claim, the Supreme Court of Canada agreed with the trial judge that "haying, raking, swapping, moving, driving trucks and tractors and teams, quieting horses, taking cattle back and forth to the reserve, dehorning, vaccinating, and branding" were no more than an ordinary farm wife would do. The court ruled that Mrs. Murdock did not make a compensable contribution to the accumulation of marital assets and was therefore, not entitled to share in the property that she and her husband had accumulated (Dranoff 2001, p. 237; Steel 1986, p. 159). "Until 1978, spouses had no right anywhere in Canada to claim, by virtue of their marital status, a share of any property accumulated during their marriage" (Dranoff 2001, p. 272).

There is no federal property law that applies throughout Canada. Under constitutional law, property is under provincial jurisdiction. While all Canadian provinces and territories have laws requiring spouses to share assets in the event of marital breakdown, the precise definition of what constitutes a "family asset" varies and creates inconsistencies across jurisdictions (Dranoff 2001, p. 273). Debates can also occur between divorcing spouses as to what actually constitutes the sum total of "marital property" to be divided.

In theory, the so-called family assets that all spouses generally share on separation are those assets used and enjoyed by both spouses and/or their children including, for example, the family home and its contents, cars and other recreational vehicles, bank accounts normally used for family purposes and other tangible assets accrued jointly over the course of a marriage. However, given provincial variation in relation to the division of "non-family" or business assets, gifts and inheritances, the matrimonial home, employment-related assets, lottery winnings, and private pensions, it would be extremely simplistic—and misleading—to say that "sharing" always results in a 50/50 division.

In addition, while property consists of such tangible items as a house or money in the bank, the valuable "new property" (Glendon 1981) for all but a few very wealthy people in today's society is the earning power of a professional degree, a business or managerial position, work experience, a skilled trade, or other "human capital." When property is legally divided in divorce, the wife may get an equal share of tangible property, such as a house or savings, but that usually does not put her on an equal footing with her former husband. An even split of the marital property may not be truly equitable if one partner has stronger earning power and benefits such as pensions but the other does not, and if the parent with custody of the children has a heavy child-support burden. Put another way, dividing property may be easy compared with ensuring that both partners and their children will have enough to live on comfortably after divorce.

About 15 years ago, sociologist Lenore Weitzman addressed the plight of divorced women and their children in her book *The Divorce Revolution* (1985). She reported a 42 percent increase in the standard of living for ex-husbands, compared with a 73 percent decline for ex-wives with minor children. Others, including sociologist Richard R. Peterson (1996), disputed these figures (see also Smock 1993). Peterson's research shows a 27 percent income decline for divorced women, together with a 10 percent increase in the amount ex-husbands have to spend on themselves. In Canada, research indicates that in the first year following divorce, the income of Canadian women declines by about 50 percent while men's household income decreases by about 25 percent (Finnie 1993). However, Ambert (1998, p. 9) observes that:

> *when the figures are adjusted for family size, women's income drops by 40 percent while men's increases slightly.* Women's poverty rises from 16 percent before divorce to 43 percent after divorce. Even three years after divorce, women's income remains far below what they had during marriage and far below their ex-husbands' current income. (emphasis in original)

What accounts for this situation? A fundamental reason for the income disparity between ex-husbands and their former wives is men's and women's unequal wages (Smock 1993), a situation discussed in Chapters 3 and 13. But factors associated with the divorce itself—attitudes about alimony, for example, and difficulties collecting adequate child support—make financial matters worse for women (Weitzman 1996). We will look at both of these factors in some detail.

Attitudes About Alimony

Popular myth once had it that ex-wives lived comfortably on high **alimony** awards, now generally called "maintenance" or **spousal support**. (The word alimony comes from the Latin verb that means "to nourish." Historically, alimony stemmed from the assumption that the contract of marriage includes a husband's life-time obligation to support his wife and children.) "It was not uncommon in divorce granted prior to 1968 in Canada for a husband to be ordered to pay a monthly sum of alimony to his wife, either in perpetuity (i.e., until the death of either spouse) or until she remarried, when the obligation of financially provision would be transferred legally to her new husband" (Nelson and Robinson 1999, p. 388). Much more rarely, a husband would be awarded alimony from a former wife.

With the introduction of property-sharing laws in the 1970s and 1980s, and the introduction of the concepts of "maintenance" in 1968 and "support" in 1985, the courts began to act on the premise that women and men have—or would quickly achieve—equal earning power to attain economic self-sufficiency soon after the divorce—even when and if a spouse had never worked outside of the home. "Spousal support" was redefined as **rehabilitative alimony**, an interim measure that provided spouses with a limited period of support (typically four to five years) in which to initiate significant steps (through education, training or retraining) toward economic self-sufficiency.

Full-time homemakers, often older, who suddenly found themselves divorced and without adequate support (called **displaced homemakers**) were particularly disadvantaged by this system (Coontz 1997a, 23). When they married, they expected the conditions and assumptions of the basic exchange to last for life. Many had few or no marketable skills, no employment record, and no pension. Nor were they in a position to pursue education or job training followed by long-term employment.

In reaching a landmark decision in the 1992 case of *Moge v. Moge*, the Supreme Court of Canada held that it was unreasonable to expect total self-sufficiency from a long-term homemaker (generally the wife), and that compensatory spousal support, in the form of periodic or lump-sum support, could be awarded when marriage responsibilities have eroded a spouse's earning ability. A major theme of spousal support following *Moge* was the compensatory model of support. The roles assumed during marriage (and their effect on a spouse's economic position after marriage), career sacrifice, career contribution, and duration of marriage were to be held as important considerations in determining spousal support. In the 1999 case of *Bracklow v. Bracklow*, the duration of cohabitation was important in determining how long the obligation to provide support based on need or hardship was to last. While a long-term relationship involving a differently-abled spouse could result in an indefinite support order, in a relationship of relatively short duration (in this case, 7.5 years), support would not be indefinite.

Nevertheless, it should be noted that "only 16 percent of divorcing women in Canada request spousal support and only six percent are actually awarded such support" (Nelson and Robinson 1999, p. 388). This situation may change, however, as a result of a recent court decision.

Although Canadian courts have generally held to a "deal is a deal" position and been extremely reluctant to revisit or alter final spousal support agreements, a recent decision by the Ontario Court of Appeal suggests that there is no "final" settlement on spousal support. In April 2001, in the case of *Miglin v. Miglin*, the Ontario Court of Appeal ruled that courts may override final divorce settlements if "a former spouse's financial circumstances change 'materially' after divorce" (Schmitz 2001). In 1994, Eric Miglin agreed to pay his former spouse $60 000 a year in child support and his wife permanently waived spousal support. However, in February 2000, she petitioned for, and received $4400 a month in spousal support for five years with the court reducing the amount of child support to $36 000 a year. The husband appealed the decision of the lower court to the Ontario Court of Appeal, arguing that this judgment made him responsible for paying $28 000 a year more than had been specified in the couple's original agreement.

In a unanimous decision on this case, delivered in April 2001, the Ontario Court of Appeal ruled that "Often, dependent spouses are in unequal bargaining positions as a result of the family dynamics. As well, a dependent spouse may misapprehend his or her needs after separation and be unaware of the real cost of post-separation life." The Court removed the five-year time limit on the spousal support order and ordered the 51-year-old husband to pay his 49-year-old former wife $4000 monthly for an indefinite period. It was noted that although the husband had originally agreed to share responsibility for the couple's children, he had failed to do so, leaving his wife to shoulder the bulk of child care responsibilities. In addition, and contrary to their original separation agreement, the husband had ceased to pay his wife $15 000 annually. In the opinion of the Court, while a spousal support agreement should be given "significant weight," a former spouse who desired to

Child Support

Child support involves money paid by the noncustodial to the custodial parent in order financially to support the children of a separated marital, cohabiting, or sexual relationship. Under the Divorce Act, either parent may be ordered to pay child support. However, because mothers retain custody in the vast majority of cases—and because women are more likely to be economically disadvantaged in employment—the vast majority of those ordered to pay child support are fathers.

Every jurisdiction in Canada requires parents to support their children following separation or divorce. However, until relatively recently, "child support has not always been consistent or adequate" (Dranoff 2001, p. 289). In 1991, a federal Justice Department report on child support noted that judges, lawyers and parents themselves often seriously underestimated the costs of raising children, that the work provided by custodial parents went unrecognized in financial terms and that when support payments were not made, approximately three-quarters lived in low-income situations. It was additionally noted that when support payments were made, about two-thirds of divorced women and children lived in low-income situations (in Dranoff 2001, p. 289).

In 1994, a five-judge panel of the Albert Court of Appeal released a landmark decision in the case of *Levesque v. Levesque* which gave priority to maintaining the lifestyle of a couple's children. Specifically, the court decided "that it was reasonable to spend 20 percent of the parents' gross income on one child or 32 percent on two children. Each parent was to contribute in proportion to his or her income" (Dranoff 2001, p. 290). In 1997, the federal government introduced standardized formula guidelines, based on the income of the noncustodial parent only and the number of children involved, to establish the amount of mandatory payment for child-support orders granted from May 1 1997 onwards under the Divorce Act. While the intent of these guidelines is to provide more consistency across support orders, slight variations are permitted to exist between provinces to reflect cost-of-living differences, including provincial income taxes and sales. In addition, judges may increase support payments to accommodate the costs of childcare for preschool children, medical costs not covered under provincial healthcare plans, educational expenditures, and "extraordinary" expenses

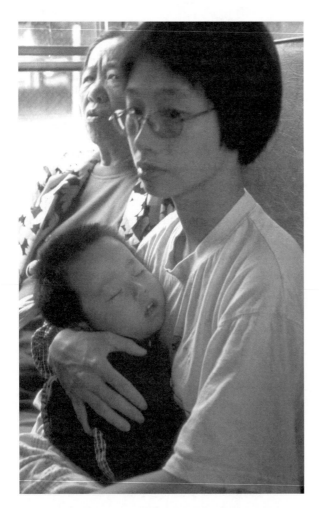

Ex-husbands often complain that "she took me to the cleaners," but research and statistics show otherwise. Ex-wives' standard of living typically declines after divorce, while ex-husbands' does not.

reopen a "final" settlement on spousal support could do so if s/he was able to prove that a "material change of circumstance" had occurred since the time of the agreement or divorce order "which if known at the time, would likely have resulted in a different order."

Although newspaper editorials predicted that this ruling would result in "tens of thousands of peoples who believed they had agreed to a 'final' divorce settlement" facing increased demands (Schmitz 2001), it is too early to assess the effects of this ruling. However, it is undeniable that families of women and children would be much better off after divorce if they received the child support due them.

(e.g., extracurricular activities). Payments may be decreased in joint custody cases where the noncustodial parent is responsible for a child at least 40 percent of the time. Court orders in themselves, however, do not always guarantee that child support will be paid. In practice, orders for child and spousal support have often been difficult to enforce and there has been very high default rates.

In February 1997, Bill C-41 received Royal assent and became law in May of that year. This legislation included amendments to the Divorce Act to establish a framework for the use of child support guidelines; amendments to the Family Orders and Agreements Enforcement Assistance Act (FOAEA) that added Revenue Canada to the list of federal departments whose databanks can be searched to locate persons who have breached family support orders; new provisions in the FOAEA to establish a new federal license denial scheme that will also authorize the suspension of passports and certain federal transport licenses when a payer of child support has persistently breached support obligations, amendments to the Garnishment, Attachment and Pensions Diversion Act to expand access to federal public service employee pension benefits to satisfy support arrears, and amendments to the Shipping Act to allow for the wages of a person working at sea to be garnisheed to support a family obligation. All Canadian provinces now have their own programs to protect against the nonpayment of child support (e.g., Alberta Maintenance, Ontario Family Responsibilities Office, Family Maintenance of B.C.). For example, under Ontario's Family Support Plan, all support payments are registered and paid to the Family Support office and then distributed to the receiving spouse—a system that allows the province to track and enforce payment. Unlike other debt obligations, which are only enforced through private initiatives, provinces have moved from private enforcement of support obligations to public enforcement strategies.

Despite such measures, the problem of "deadbeat parents" remains significant. Indeed, one Canadian organization, Families Against Deadbeats (FAAD), which maintains a Web site featuring "Wanted Posters" of those who have never paid court-ordered child support or are seriously in arrears, reports that "over two billion dollars in child support arrears is owned" in Canada (FAD 2000).

Some research suggests that the principal reason for a noncustodial parent's failure to pay is unemployment or underemployment (Meyer and Bartfeld 1996). Among families in which the absent parent has been employed during the entire previous year, payment rates are 80 percent or more. Hence,

> coercive child-support collection policies, such as automatic wage withholding, will have only limited success. Divorced fathers (perhaps in distinction to never married fathers) appear to pay quite well if they are fully employed.... The key to reducing poverty thus appears to be the old and unglamorous one, of solving un- and underemployment, both for the fathers and the mothers. (Braver, Fitzpatrick, and Bay 1991, pp. 184–85)

The child support issue is complex. Some noncustodial fathers provide support in ways other than money (Teachman 1991), such as child care, for example. "In some cases attempts to locate and require payments from such fathers may result in severing these ties" (Peterson and Nord 1990, p. 539).

One suggested alternative has been guaranteed child support. With **guaranteed child support**, used in France and Sweden, the government sends to the custodial parent the full amount of support awarded to the child, even though this sum may not have been received from the noncustodial parent. It then becomes the government's responsibility to collect the money from the parent that owes it (Salt 1991).

 Focusing on Children

DIVORCE AND CHILDREN

How do separation and divorce affect children? Experts disagree, and the situation may be changing as well, so we cannot give a definitive answer to this question. It also depends on what comparison is being made. Children's self-concepts are affected not so much by family structure as by the quality of familial relationships (Demo and Acock 1996a). Living in an intact family characterized by unresolved tension and alienating conflict can cause as great or greater emotional stress and lower self-esteem in children than living in a supportive single-parent family

(Peterson and Zill 1986; Kline, Johnston, and Tschann 1991; L'Heureux-Dube 1998).

Nevertheless, the divorce experience is both psychologically stressful and, in most cases, financially disadvantageous for children.

The Various Stresses for Children of Divorce

During and for a period of time after divorce, children typically feel guilty, depressed, and anxious (Hetherington 1973; Wallerstein and Kelly 1980). In the only longitudinal study of children's postdivorce adjustment, psychologists Judith Wallerstein and Joan Kelly interviewed all of the members of some 60 families with one or more children in counselling at the time of the parents' separation in 1974. Wallerstein and her colleagues reinterviewed children at one year, two years, five years, 10 years, and in some cases, 15 years later. Children appeared worst in terms of their psychological adjustment at one year after separation, many having declined significantly since their parents' separation. By two years postdivorce, households had generally stabilized. At five years, many of the 131 children seemed to have come through the experience fairly well; 63 percent were either in excellent or reasonably good psychological health. Another 37 percent, however, were not coping well, with anger playing a significant part in the emotional life of 23 percent.

By 1984, after following her sample of children of divorce for 10 years, Wallerstein and colleagues found the majority to be approaching economic self-sufficiency, enrolled in educational programs, and in general, to be responsible young adults. Still, the overall impression left by Wallerstein's research is one of loss. Children may lose fathers, who become disinterested and detached; they may lose mothers, who are overwhelmed by the task of supporting the family and managing a household alone and who either see little chance of happiness for themselves or else are busy pursuing their "second chance" (Wallerstein and Blakeslee 1989).

One of Wallerstein's major findings is that girls, who seemed, as in other studies, far better adjusted than boys in the early postdivorce years, evidenced a "sleeper effect," which surfaced as they reached adolescence and young adulthood (Wallerstein and Lewis 1998). They were beset with "lingering sorrow" and

seemed hesitant about marriage and childbearing. Said one of Wallerstein's respondents, "How can you expect commitment when anyone can change his mind?" The "sleeper effect" described by Wallerstein has not been generally supported by subsequent, long-term studies, however (Coontz 1997).

Children of divorce do experience the loss of their identity as a member of an intact family, along with the loss of daily interaction with one of their parents (Hetherington 1988, 1989). They get less help with homework (Astone and McLanahan 1991), and at school and elsewhere they may suffer from the cultural stigma of being from a "broken home" (Amato 1991), although this is lessening as more families get divorces (Coontz 1997) and many schools have instituted programs to help children cope with their parents' divorce (Peres and Pasternack 1991).

CHILDREN OF REDIVORCE   In some cases, but certainly not all, a new stepparent can prove a stabilizing and supportive influence. Counsellors—who now see children who have experienced divorce more than once—encourage divorced stepparents to maintain contact with their former stepchildren. Wallerstein found that half of the children in her study had experienced a second divorce of one or both parents. According to psychiatrist Clifford Sager, the dangers to the emotional health of both the stepchild and the stepparent when a remarriage breaks up have been overlooked—"woefully underestimated." In Sager's words,

> we have given too little thought to what kind of values we are demonstrating when we just walk away from these relationships or cut them off. The child is left with the fear that nobody can be trusted and perhaps he wasn't worth the love anyway. The stepparents must realize that after making all kinds of motions about being a caring loving parent or friend they can't suddenly disappear. They have a moral obligation. It's something the biological parent must understand too. (Brooks 1984b, p. 46)

LESS MONEY AND LESS EDUCATION   Children whose parents have divorced will more than likely have noticeably less money to live on, and the chances are fairly good that they will suffer economic deprivation. This is especially significant because some of the negative impact of divorce can be attributed to economic deprivation (Garfinkel and McLanahan 1986; McLanahan and Booth 1989).

We may think here in terms of children at the lower end of the socioeconomic scale, but one researcher found considerable deprivation among middle-class children compared to what they could have expected had their parents remained married (Wallerstein and Blakeslee 1989).

Because divorce settlements seldom include arrangements for how parents will pay for children's postsecondary education—and because family savings are often eroded by the costs involved with divorcing—financing the costs of higher education for children of divorced parents can be especially problematic. Some children of divorced parents who would otherwise have attended college or university may find that they cannot afford it, whereas others who would have gone away to university may find themselves attending a local school (Powers 1997).

Wallerstein, who followed her sample into young adulthood, was surprised at the extent of their educational downward mobility. Sixty percent of the study children were likely to receive less education than their fathers; 45 percent, less than their mothers. This phenomenon is connected to the financial marginality of most divorced mothers and the defection of many fathers (Stern 1994; Amato, Rezac, and Booth 1995). Even divorced fathers who had retained close ties, who had the money or could save it, and who ascribed importance to education, seemed to feel less obligated to support their children through college or university.

> Children of divorce feel less protected economically; unlike children from intact families, whose parents usually continue to support them through college or university and sometimes even beyond, the children of divorce face an abrupt, premature end to an important aspect of their childhood.... [Moreover,] nowhere is it written that psychological or emotional support stops at age eighteen, but many children of divorce cannot help but feel that when child support stops, something else stops in the social contract between parent and child. (Wallerstein and Blakeslee 1989, p. 157)

While many children do adapt to their parents' divorce, they often express a great sense of loss, no matter how rationally a divorce is handled. Holidays, in particular, can be stressful for divorced families.

Along with this may came a favouring of boys over girls. In Wallerstein's sample, fathers who helped with university were twice as likely to help sons.

Because the Wallerstein study is based on a small sample of children once in counselling, it has been challenged by studies with more representative samples and that reach somewhat less pessimistic conclusions. The absence of a comparison group to tell us how children in intact homes are faring these days also renders the study inconclusive (although whenever possible, Wallerstein referred to other studies including relevant national sample data).

SURVEY VERSUS CLINICAL FINDINGS One analysis (Dawson 1991) from a nationally representative U.S. sample of 17 110 children under age 18 found that those living with single mothers or stepfathers were more likely to have school, behavioural, and health problems than were those living with both biological parents (see also Pong 1997; Bankston and Caldas 1998). A second (Ambert 1998) reports that "[a]t all age levels, children of divorced parents have higher rates of emotional, behavioural, social and academic problems than children in two-parent families."

In a nutshell, children whose parents are divorced (and even after they are remarried) are far more likely than children whose parents remain together to:
- suffer from depression, anxiety and other emotional disorders;
- exhibit behavioural problems including hyperactivity, aggressiveness, fighting, hostility;
- become young offenders...;
- do less well in school, stay less long in school, and achieve a lower educational level throughout their entire life span;
- have more social problems in part due to their behavioural problems, fewer friends, lower popularity, and less involvement in extra-curricular activities. (Ambert, 1998)

She observes that adult children, whose parents divorced during their teen or, particularly, their childhood years, are also more likely than those from intact, two-parent families, to: have had a child out of wedlock more often, especially during adolescence; have left home earlier; have achieved lower educational levels; have experienced unemployment more frequently and done less well economically (a point

disputed by Corak and Heisz 1999); have had more marital problems and divorces.

There is evidence that adolescents in single-parent families are at greater risk for substance abuse and premarital sex (Flewelling and Bauman 1990; Needle, Su, and Doherty 1990). The latter may result from these teenagers' more liberal attitudes toward nonmarital sex as a result of their divorced parents' dating behaviour (Whitbeck, Simons, and Kao 1994). This situation may also reflect diminished parenting. Simply put, when one parent attempts to do the job of two, they may have less time to monitor and supervise the behaviour of their children. "Unsupervised children are far more likely than others to engage in delinquent acts and premature sex" (Ambert 1998, p. 12).

Meanwhile, sociologists Paul Amato and Bruce Keith have conducted two important, systematic reviews and statistical analyses of virtually all studies of children's and young adults' postdivorce adjustment through the 1980s. After analyzing 92 studies of children, Amato and Keith (1991a) concluded that parental divorce is associated with negative outcomes in academic achievement, conduct, psychological adjustment, self-esteem, and social relations. A similar review of 33 studies found that adults who had experienced parental divorce as children, compared with those from continuously intact families, have poorer psychological adjustment, lower socioeconomic attainment, and greater marital instability (Amato and Keith 1991b). "The cumulative picture that emerges from the evidence suggests that parental divorce (or some factor connected with it) is associated with lowered well-being among both children and adult children of divorce" (Amato 1993, p. 23).

Still, the differences are small, and smaller today than in the past, when divorce was less common. Clinical studies (such as Wallerstein's, previously described) found stronger negative effects than studies using representative samples. "This is due to the fact that a great deal of variability is present among children of divorce, with some experiencing problems and others adjusting well or even showing improvements in behaviour" (Amato 1993, p. 23). Overall, Amato and Keith concluded that, at least for effects-of-divorce research, "clinical studies should not be generalized to the larger community" (1991b, p. 55).

REASONS FOR NEGATIVE EFFECTS OF DIVORCE ON CHILDREN Amato (1993) has summarized five theoretical perspectives found in the literature concerning the reasons for negative outcomes among children of divorced parents. These are as follows:

1. The **life stress perspective** assumes that, just as divorce is known to be a stressful event for adults, it must also be so for children. Furthermore, divorce is not one single event but a process of associated events (Morrison and Cherlin 1995; Lorenz et al. 1997)—moving, changing schools, giving up pets, loss of contact with grandparents and other relatives—that may be distressing to children. This perspective holds that an accumulation of negative stressors results in problems for children of divorce.

2. The **parental loss perspective** assumes that a family with both parents living in the same household is the optimal environment for children's development. Both parents are important resources, providing children with emotional support, practical assistance, information, guidance, and supervision, as well as modeling social skills like cooperation, negotiation, and compromise. Accordingly, the absence of a parent from the household is problematic for children's socialization.

3. The **parental adjustment perspective** notes the importance of the custodial parent's psychological adjustment. Supportive and appropriately disciplining parents facilitate their children's well-being. However, the stress of divorce is compounded for parents by the associated stressors that follow, such as lower economic well-being. Such stress can lead to parental depression (Lorenz et al. 1997), which can impair a parent's child-rearing skills, with probable negative consequences for children.

4. The **economic hardship perspective** assumes that economic hardship brought about by marital dissolution is primarily responsible for the problems faced by children whose parents divorce (Entwisle and Alexander 1995).

5. The **interparental conflict perspective** holds that conflict between parents prior to, during, and after the divorce is responsible for the lowered well-being of children of divorce. Although the literature offers only modest support for the first four perspectives stated, research strongly supports this fifth perspective (Amato 1993). Many studies indicate that much of what appear to be negative results for children of divorce are probably not simply the results of divorce per se but also of parental and family conflict before, during, and after the divorce (Amato and Booth 1996; Dawson 1991; Morrison and Cherlin 1995; Cherlin, Chase-Lansdale, and McRae 1998; Hetherington 1999).

FAMILY RELATIONS VERSUS FAMILY STRUCTURE It is important to note that the interparental conflict explanation (described above) finds family relations and communication patterns more important to children's well-being than any particular family form or structure (Wenk et al. 1994; Amato and Booth 1996, 1997; Demo and Acock 1996). As an example, one survey analysis of 1291 Michigan adolescents found that teens in intact families who described their fathers as not interested in them had lower self-esteem than did those in mother-headed, single-parent families (Clark and Barber 1994). Perhaps what matters, the authors surmise,

> are not only adolescents' perceptions of how parents think and behave but adolescents' accounts to themselves of why parents behave as they do. A lack of paternal interest following divorce, when it occurs, could conceivably be attributed to one or more divorce-related factors, such as a father's wish to avoid conflictual situations with his ex-wife. It may be that in two-parent families, a low level of paternal interest is harder for an adolescent to "explain away" or view as beyond his or her control than would be the case for an adolescent whose parents are divorced. (p. 613)

Our overall conclusion is that in choosing to divorce, parents are not necessarily enhancing their children's development—although they may be preventing more damaging experiences—but they are not necessarily condemning them to a disastrous and disappointing life either.

Even Wallerstein, whose research presents the most negative view of children's postdivorce adjustment, says:

When people ask whether they should stay married for the sake of the children, I have to say, "Of course not." All our evidence shows that children turn out less well adjusted when exposed to open conflict, where parents terrorize or strike one another, than do children from divorced families. And while we lack systematic studies comparing unhappily married families and divorced families, I do know that it is not useful to provide children with a model of adult behaviour that avoids problem solving and that stresses martyrdom, violence, or apathy. A divorce undertaken thoughtfully and realistically can teach children how to confront serious life problems with compassion, wisdom, and appropriate action.... Our findings do not support those who would turn back the clock. (Wallerstein and Blakeslee 1989, p. 305; see also Coontz 1997)

From studies that reach different conclusions about overall outcome, we can still learn much that is potentially useful about what postdivorce circumstances are most beneficial to children's development and what pitfalls to avoid. Wallerstein and Blakeslee consider a good mother–child (or, custodial parent–child) bond to be the most significant factor (see also Tschann et al. 1989). Another highly important factor in children's adjustment to divorce is the divorced parents' relationship with each other (Wallerstein 1998).

FIGHTING THROUGH THE CHILDREN In some divorces, "children are handed a hunting license by one parent to go out and take shots at the other" (Wallerstein and Blakeslee 1989, p. 188). In the Wallerstein study, more than half of 8- and 12-year-old children were asked by one parent to spy on the other—to go through bureau drawers and the like. Even though married partners may be angry and feel vindictive, they do not usually draw children openly into the spousal wars in the way that ex-spouses do.

Visitation is one frequent arena of paternal disputes: The child isn't ready to go when visitation time starts or the visiting parent brings the child home late, for instance. Visitation can be an arena in which ex-spouses continue the basic conflicts they experienced before the divorce (Kelly and Wallerstein 1990). Counsellors urge ex-spouses to work out irritations and conflict directly with each other rather than

through their children. Parents need to communicate as openly as possible about their divorce without speaking negatively about the ex-spouse. Counsellors encourage the attitude "We had our problems, but that doesn't mean he (or she) is bad or that I'm bad."

Experts agree that adjusting to divorce is easier for children and parents when former spouses cooperate (Brody and Forehand 1990; Ahrons and Miller 1993; Bronstein et al. 1994). The child's maintaining ties with the noncustodial parent can be important also (Kline, Johnston, and Tschann 1991). We turn now to custody issues.

Custody Issues

About half of Canadian couples who divorce have dependent children (Nelson and Robinson 1999, p. 407). A basic issue for them is determining which parent will take **custody**, or assume primary responsibility for making decisions about the children's upbringing and general welfare. Available alternatives include sole custody to one parent, joint custody, split custody (i.e., dividing up of the children, generally along sex lines), or custody to neither parent. If parents are unable to make this decision among themselves, a court-ordered solution through litigation may be the only alternative.

At present, the guiding rule in determining child custody is what arrangement will be in "the best interests of the child." In making this determination, the court will review a number of factors including, but not limited to, both parents' proposals for the children's upbringing and daily patterns of living, the child's emotional relationship with each parent and the extent and nature of each parent's previous involvement in child care, the physical and mental capacity of the parents to meet their children's needs, whether the custodial parent will facilitate access by the non-custodial parent, the career commitment of both parents and the amount of time each working parent will have available for the children.

In the past and continuing, child custody is usually an extension of the basic exchange: Divorced fathers have legal responsibility for financial support while divorced mothers continue the physical, day-to-day care of their children. Prior to the mid-to-late 1800s, fathers were automatically given custody in Canada, but from the beginning of the twentieth century until recently, courts have presumed that maternal custody was virtually always in the child's best interest (Grych and Fincham 1992). While joint custody is becoming more popular, it remains the case that custody is awarded to mothers in the vast majority of cases (Figure 14.3). For example, in 1995, mothers were awarded custody of children in almost seven out of 10 (68 percent) divorce cases involving children settled in court. In contrast, custody was awarded to the fathers in just over one in 10 (11 percent) cases (Statistics Canada 2000). In 1998, among cases with a custody order, custody was granted to the wife in 60 percent cases of these cases, "far ahead of joint custody to both husband and wife (30 percent) or to the husband only (10 percent)" (Statistics Canada 2000).

Custody, we should note, is not always settled in the courts. Indeed, the number of children affected by custody orders decreased between 1982 and 1995 from 65 000 children to 48 000 children. In 1998, less than a third (31 percent) of divorces granted involved a custody order for dependent children (Statistics Canada 2000).

With worsening economic prospects, and changing attitudes and gender roles, however, a few mothers are voluntarily relinquishing custody and more fathers are seeking custody. Today, a small number of fathers are awarded both custody and child support from ex-wives. The odds of father custody are slightly higher when the children are older, especially when the eldest child is male and when the father is the plaintiff in the divorce (Fox and Kelly 1995).

Under current laws a father and a mother who want to retain custody have theoretically equal chances, and judges try to assess the relationship between each parent and the child. However, because mothers are typically the ones who have physically cared for the child, and because many judges still have traditional attitudes about gender, some courts give preference to mothers (Dranoff 2001, p. 259; Robinson and Barret 1986, p. 87). Generally, studies have found nothing to preclude father custody (Rosenthal and Kesher 1980) and, according to sociologist John Conway (1997, p. 29) "studies of single parent fathers suggest they are quite successful at parenting, and they express more satisfaction than single-parent mothers." These findings may reflect the fact that, when compared to solo mothers, solo fathers tend to be older, better off financially, more likely to be parenting older children and more likely to spend fewer years as single parents (Nelson and Robinson 1999, p. 421; Conway 1997, p. 29).

In a study of noncustodial mothers based on interviews with over 500 women, over 90 percent reported that the process of becoming noncustodial was stressful. Most commonly, money (30 percent),

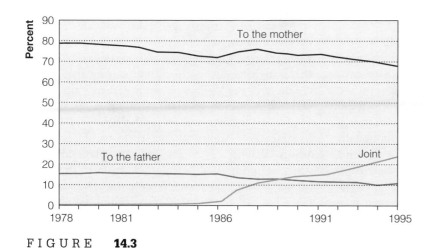

FIGURE **14.3**

Custody awards of children involved in divorce cases settled by the courts, 1978–1995. (Source: Statistics Canada, Catalogue 84-213; and Health Statistics Division.)

child's choice (21 percent), difficulty in handling the children (12 percent), avoidance of moving the children (11 percent), and self-reported instability or problems (11 percent) were given as reasons. Only nine percent reported losing their children in a court battle or ceding custody to avoid a custody fight (Greif and Pabst 1988, p. 88).

Judith Fisher, who also studied noncustodial mothers, believes that women should not relinquish custody because they feel inadequate in comparison to their successful husbands. At the same time, she strongly supports the freedom of men and women to make choices about custody—including the woman's choice to live apart from her children—without guilt or stigma. She urges

> (1) the negation of the unflattering stereotypes of noncustody mothers; (2) sensitivity to the demands society places on mothers (as opposed to parents) and to the needs of all family members; (3) supportiveness of the woman's choice when it appears to have been well thought out; and (4) ... prohibitions against blaming the mother when others (the children, the children's father, the courts) decide that the children should live apart from her. (Fisher 1983, p. 357)

Children living with fathers typically have more contact and are emotionally closer to noncustodial parents, that is, their mothers (Greif and Pabst 1988; Lewin 1990a).

THE VISITING PARENT Almost all of the research and discussion to date on visiting parents have been about fathers, but some research suggests that the same findings apply to visiting mothers (Spanier and Castro 1979, p. 249). Fathers without custody experience a sense of extreme loss. There is some evidence that, ironically, more emotionally involved fathers may cope with this loss by visiting their children *less* often than fathers with less emotional involvement before the divorce (Kruk 1991). This can also be true for stepfathers and men who have cohabited with women and their children (Brooks 1984b; Dullea 1987b).

Early visits may display what has been called the Disneyland Dad syndrome, in which the father indulges his child to make the visit as happy as possible. As time goes by, this phase generally passes.

Often fathers become increasingly frustrated with their loss of influence over the children's upbringing, and they let themselves drift away from the children (Wallerstein 1998, p. 75). Visiting typically declines over time (Seltzer 1991a) and often becomes episodic. This lack of divorced father–child contact persists into and throughout the child's adulthood, eventually reducing the probability that a divorced father can think of his children as potential sources of support in times of need (Amato 1994; Aquilino 1994b; Cooney 1994; Lawton, Silverstein, and Bengston 1994).

Research is inconclusive regarding the relationship of a father or father figure to a child's overall development and well-being (Hawkins and Eggebeen 1991). In some cases, such as verbal, physical, or sexual abuse, father contact may actually be damaging to children (King 1994). We've seen that some divorces are precipitated by alcoholism, drug abuse, or domestic violence; in such cases visitation is not necessarily in the best interest of a child. In some cases, access is made subject to supervision. In such cases, parent–child contact occurs only in the presence of a third party, such as a social worker or a court employee. The hope is that, "By facilitating contact, **supervised visitation** centres may provide a safe, supportive environment for families to change from a path of abuse and violence toward one of success" (Perkins and Ansay 1998, p. 258). Electronic monitors have also been used to monitor visits between children and potentially abusive or otherwise troublesome noncustodial parents (Garofoli 1996).

Meanwhile, studies generally indicate that an involved, caring father benefits his children in many ways (Harris, Furstenberg, and Marmer 1998) and that a father's decreased visiting can be painful for children. In the Wallerstein study, fathers visited their children with more regularity than other research has found, but they were often psychologically detached. In one case, "Almost always, there would be other adults around or adult activities planned. Carl watched hundreds of hours of television at his father's house, feeling more and more alone and removed from his earlier visions of family life" (Wallerstein and Blakeslee 1989, p. 79). Children often forgave geographically distant fathers who did not appear frequently but were very hurt by those nearby fathers who rarely visited. Some fathers managed to retain a fantasy image of themselves and their children relating happily in the face of a quite different reality.

Other studies have found fathers to have vanished even more thoroughly. A study by Furstenberg and Harris followed 1000 children from 1976 to 1987 (and included children of unwed as well as divorced parents). Forty-two percent had not seen their fathers in the previous year, and over half had never been in the father's home. "Men regard marriage as a package deal. They cannot separate their relations with their children from their relations to their former spouse. When that relationship ends, the paternal bond usually withers within a few years too" (Furstenberg, in Lewin 1990a, p. A18; Furstenberg and Cherlin 1991).[1] According to Canada's National Child Survey, following parental separation, about one-third of children have very little contact with their fathers (i.e., either irregular visits or no visits at all) with children born of common-law unions even less likely to see their fathers than are children born to married parents (Figure 14.4). "Since fathers who have low levels of contact with their children are least likely to pay child support, these findings indicate that many, many Canadian children are at a high risk of losing both the personal and financial support of their fathers when their parents separate" (National Council of Welfare 1999b, p. 5).

CHILD SNATCHING   At the other extreme is **child snatching**: kidnapping one's children from the other parent. According to Patricia Chisholm and Mary Nemeth (2001):

> While abductions by strangers draw the headlines, there were only 42 in Canada last year [2000], compared with 416 parental abduction cases listed on the data bases of the Canadian Police

Information Centre. Those are mostly cases where charges have been laid. There are many more instances of parental abduction that are either unreported or that go through the civil courts, so the actual number of abductions is unknown.

According to Rhonda Morgan, executive director of the Missing Children Society of Canada's Calgary headquarters, of the 179 cases her office has dealt with, 112 abductions were by mothers and 67 were by fathers (in Chisholm and Nemeth 2001).

Child snatching is frightening and confusing for the child, can be physically dangerous, and is usually detrimental to the child's psychological development (Wallerstein and Blakeslee 1989; Fass 1998). Yet it is only recently that parental abduction has been regarded as a crime and "some officers believe abducted children are in no real danger because they are with a parent" (Chisholm and Nemeth 2001). At least in theory, a parent who abducts a child under the age of 14 can be charged with kidnapping if they: refuse to return the child after an access visit; take and detain a child out of the jurisdiction in which the child resides, contrary to an access agreement; or remove the child from the custodial parent's charge without consent. Unless the abducting parent can prove, for example, that s/he took the child in order to protect the child from "danger of imminent harm" or took the child with the other parent's consent, the abducting parent can be punished with a prison sentence of up to ten years. However, depending on where the abductor flees, Canadian police may be stymied in their attempts to locate an abducted child. For example, most countries in the Middle East are not signatories to The Hague Convention on the Civil Aspects of International Child Abduction.

Child snatching is an extreme act, but it points up the frustration involved in arrangements regarding sole custody and visiting parents. An alternative is joint custody.

JOINT CUSTODY   When parents live close to each other and when both are committed to the arrangement, joint custody or shared living arrangements, or both, can bring the experiences of both parents closer together, providing advantages to each. In **joint custody**, both divorced parents continue to take equal responsibility for important decisions regarding the child's general upbringing. In 1995, 21 percent of all

---

1. While not a majority, there are noncustodial fathers who do retain contact with their children, and at least some are angry that their efforts seem to go unrecognized. For example, one noncustodial father wrote the following in a letter to "Dear Abby":

I'm concerned that [some noncustodial] fathers (including myself) are getting a bad rap. I take my children to weekly counseling sessions, due in part to an ex-wife who constantly tells them what a "jerk" their father is. Not only do I send the required child-support payments on time, I send an amount over the required legal minimum. I also help their mother with religious-school tuition, summer-camp expenses and assorted other child-care expenses—gifts, sports and extracurricular activities....I attend my kid's school and extracurricular activities with enthusiasm (when I'm notified about them) and call the kids regularly. Regrettably, I have only the legally minimum visitation opportunities, which their mother tried to deny me.... ("Divorced Dad Tries..." 1996, p. E7).

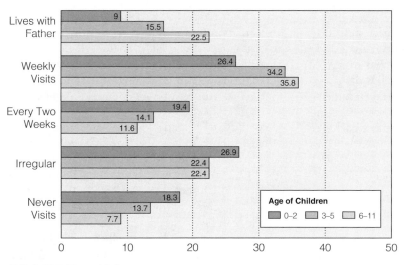

F I G U R E **14.4**

Contact with father after separation, by age group of children. (Source: National Council of Welfare 1999b.)

custody cases decided in court resulted in an award of joint custody (up from merely one percent in 1986) (Statistics Canada 2000).

There are two variations in joint custody agreements. One is joint legal and physical custody, in which parents or children move periodically (usually weekly, biweekly, or monthly) to reside with the children. The second variation, recommended by some policy experts (see, for example, Furstenberg and Cherlin 1991), is *joint legal custody*—in which both parents still have the right to participate in important decisions and retain a symbolically important legal authority—with *physical custody* (that is, residential care of the child) going to one parent. Parents with higher incomes and education are more likely to have joint custody (Seltzer 1991b; Wallerstein 1998).

An important predictor of mothers' choice for joint custody is faith in their ex-husband's parenting competence (Wilcox, Wolchik, and Braver 1998). There are several advantages to arrangements for joint legal and physical custody. (Table 14.3 lists advantages and disadvantages of joint custody from a father's perspective.) Shared custody gives children the chance for a more realistic and normal relationship with each parent (Arditti and Keith 1993). Furthermore, both parents may feel they have the opportunity to pass their own beliefs and values on to

their children. In addition, neither parent is overloaded with sole custodial responsibility and its concomitant loss of personal freedom.

One study (Maccoby, Depner, and Mnookin 1990) of divorced families compared coparental interaction among parents with joint physical custody (170 families) to those with mother custody (420 families) and to those with father custody (74 families). Eighteen months after the divorce, just one-fifth of parents with father custody and one-fourth of those with mother custody described their postdivorce relationship as cooperative. More—but still only one-third—of those with joint custody said their coparental relationship was cooperative. Of the families with joint custody, nearly 50 percent said they discussed their children once a week or more, but only 34 percent said they consciously tried to coordinate rules about bedtime, TV, or homework in the two households.

Another difficulty with joint physical custody is today's high rate of geographic mobility. When ex-mates move to separate regions, it would be difficult, and very likely harmful, for the children to divide the year between two different schools and communities. Even without the problems of geographic mobility, some children who have experienced joint custody report feeling "torn apart," particularly as they get older (Simon 1991). Although some youngsters

TABLE 14.3

Advantages and Disadvantages of Joint Custody from a Father's Perspective

Advantages	Disadvantages
Fathers can have more influence on the child's growth and development—a benefit for men and children alike.	Children lack a stable and permanent environment, which can affect them emotionally.
Fathers are more involved and experience more self-satisfaction as parents.	Children are prevented from having a relationship with a "psychological parent" as a result of being shifted from one environment to another.
Parents experience less stress than sole-custody parents.	Children have difficulty gaining control over and understanding of their lives.
Parents do not feel as overburdened as sole-custody parents.	Children have trouble forming and maintaining peer relationships.
Generally, fathers and mothers report more friendly and cooperative interaction in joint custody than in visitation arrangements, mostly because the time with children is evenly balanced and agreement exists on the rules of the system.	Long-term consequences of joint custody arrangements have not been systematically studied.
Joint custody provides more free social time for each single parent.	
Relationships with children are stronger and more meaningful for fathers.	
Parental power and decision making are equally divided, so there is less need to use children to barter for more.	

Source: Robinson and Barret 1986, p.89.

appreciate the contact with both parents and even the "change of pace," others don't and find the experience to be disruptive (Krementz 1984).

Joint custody is also expensive. Each parent must maintain housing, equipment, toys, and often a separate set of clothes for the children and must sometimes pay for travel between homes. Mothers, more than fathers, would find it difficult to maintain a family household without child support, which is often not awarded when custody is shared.

Research does not support the presumption that joint custody is best for children of divorced parents, but neither does it indicate that it is more harmful than traditional sole custody; several studies have found no difference between joint and sole custody (Coysh et al. 1989; Kline et al. 1989; Wallerstein 1998, p. 82).

Joint custody parents recognize that they are in the minority, and as yet experts are unclear on what advice to give. School-age children seem to adjust better than preschoolers, perhaps because their more

sophisticated cognitive skills allow them to place the frequent changes in routine in perspective (Steinman 1981). One thing is clear: "[J]oint residence should not be ordered by the court or proposed by the mediator for the purpose of resolving disputes between parents" (Wallerstein 1998, p. 84).

Parent Education for Ex-Spouses

Earlier in this chapter we saw that much of the pain and disorganization suffered by children of divorce results from parents' hostility toward each other before the divorce and continuing thereafter. According to Wallerstein:

We have seen shocking examples of this, clinically, for many years.... [I]ntense conflict between the parents can impair the parent's most rudimentary judgment in caregiving. [Therapists have] reported parental conflict running so counter to parental intuition that, for example, a mother was described as repeatedly ramming her car against the father's car, while the terrified child, who was the object of the custody dispute, was clinging to the seat beside her. (1998, p. 80)

Parenting programs for divorcing parents (Shapiro and Schrof 1995) represent a new trend aimed at strengthening postdivorce families. Such programs emphasize that it is very important for both parents to remain involved in their children's lives. Such programs also teach parents skills to help their children adjust to the divorce and advise parents to avoid expressing hostility or criticism toward the ex-spouse in front of the children. For example, in Canada, the B.C. Ministry of the Attorney-General is piloting a "Parenting after Separation" program for separated and divorced couples with children.

Parent education programs for divorcing parents usually involve a series of lectures or workshops offered by a mediator or mental health professional and are sometimes followed by small-group discussions. In some communities the children also meet in groups with a teacher or mental health professional (Geasler and Blaisure 1998).

Although many parents have been reluctant to participate, evaluation forms completed after the sessions have shown predominantly positive responses. "At this time, however, there has been no evaluation of whether the information provided is actively employed by parents in their relationship with each other or with the child or whether, indeed, there is any change in the child's well-being" (Wallerstein 1998, p. 85).

This discussion of mothers' and fathers' custody issues suggests that being divorced is in many ways a very different experience for men and women. Just as sexually segregated or traditional roles can lead to "his" and "her" marriages (Bernard 1982), so also can they result in "his" and "her" divorces.

HER AND HIS DIVORCE

We have seen that gender roles diminish communication and understanding between women and men. Perhaps nowhere is the lack of understanding more evident than in the debate over which partner—the ex-wife or the ex-husband—is the victim of divorce. Both are victims (Ross 1995). The first year after divorce is especially stressful for both ex-spouses. Divorce wields a blow to each one's self-

esteem. Both feel they have failed as spouses and, if there are children, as parents (Brodie 1999). They may question their ability to get along well in a remarriage. Yet each has particular difficulties that are related to societal expectations.

Her Divorce

Women who were married longer, particularly those oriented to traditional gender roles, lose the identity associated with their husband's status. Getting back on their feet may be particularly difficult for women in this group. Older women have few opportunities for meaningful career development and limited opportunities to remarry (Choi 1992; Nelson and Robinson 1999).

Divorced mothers who retain sole custody of their children also experience difficulties. They often undergo severe overload as they attempt to provide not only for their financial self-support but also for the day-to-day care of their children (Campbell and Moen 1992; Dandurand 1994). Their difficulties are aggravated by discrimination in promotion and salaries, by the high cost of child care, and often by their less extensive work experience and training. All in all, custodial mothers frequently feel alone as they struggle with money, scheduling, and discipline problems. Objective difficulties are reflected in decreased psychological well-being (Ambert 1998; Doherty, Su, and Needle 1989; Ross 1995).

His Divorce

Ex-husbands' anger, grief, and loneliness may be aggravated by the traditional male gender role, which discourages them from sharing their pain with other men (Arendell 1995). Sociologist Catherine Ross (1995) compared levels of psychological distress for men and women in four different categories: marrieds, cohabitors, those who were dating, and those with no partner. As part of her analysis, Ross found that divorced men had the lowest levels of emotional support of any group, while emotional support among divorced women was "not that much lower than married women's" (p. 138).

Meanwhile, divorced men miss their families and children. At least one therapist maintains that divorced, noncustodial fathers have more radical readjustments to make in their lifestyles than do custodial mothers. In return for the responsibilities and loss of freedom associated with single parenthood, custodial mothers escape much of the loneliness the loss of family status might otherwise offer and are somewhat rewarded by social approval for rearing their children (see Myers 1989).

Noncustodial fathers often retain the financial obligations of fatherhood while experiencing few of its joys (Arendell 1995). Whether it takes place in the children's home, the father's residence, or at some neutral spot, visitation is typically awkward and superficial. And the man may worry that if his ex-wife remarries, he will lose even more influence over his children's upbringing. For many individuals, parenthood plays an important role in adult development. "Removed from regular contact with their children after divorce, many men stagnate" (Wallerstein and Blakeslee 1989, p. 143).

Many ex-husbands feel shut out and lost because women may control access to emotional nurturance and may also have a stronger influence on children (Thomas and Forehand 1993). Yet for most women, men still hold the keys to economic security, and ex-wives suffer financially more than do ex-husbands. This interrelationship also applies to women's and men's separate experiences in divorce. The fact is that both men's and women's grievances could be at least somewhat alleviated by eliminating the economic discrimination toward women and the gender role expectations that create husbands' and wives' divorces. This leads us to some consideration of how divorce affects the families of the future.

FORMING FAMILIES: THE NEXT GENERATION

We have talked about the general impact of divorce on children, but what do we know specifically about how a parental divorce affects adult children's married and family lives? Sociologists have paid particular attention to the effects of parental divorce on two broad areas regarding adult children's family lives: (1) the quality of intergenerational relationships between adult children and their divorced parents, and (2) the marital stability for adult children of divorced parents.

Adult Children of Divorced Parents and Intergenerational Relationships

There is evidence that adult children of divorced parents have probably come to accept their parents'

divorce as a desirable alternative to ongoing family conflict (Amato and Booth 1991). Nevertheless, several recent studies point to one conclusion: Ties between adult children and their parents are generally weaker (less close or supportive) when the parents are highly conflicted and "divorce prone," even if they are still together (Booth and Amato 1994b), or when the parents are divorced (Aquilino 1994a, 1994b; Cooney 1994; White 1994; Furstenberg, Hoffman, and Shrestha 1995; Lye et al. 1995; Marks 1995; Szinovacz 1997). The effect for divorced parents is stronger for fathers, who were usually the noncustodial parent, but the relationship has been found for mothers as well.

Sociologist Lynn White (1994) analyzed data from 3625 National (U.S.) Survey of Families and Households respondents to examine the long-term consequences of childhood family divorce for adults' relationships with their parents. Using a broad array of indicators of family solidarity—relationship quality, contact frequency, and perceived and actual social support (doing favours, lending and giving money, feeling that one can call on the parent for help in an emergency)—White found that adults raised by single parents reported lowered solidarity with them. They saw their parents less often, had poorer quality relationships, felt less able to count on parents for help and emotional support, and actually received less support. White found these negative effects to be stronger regarding, but not limited to, the noncustodial parent (usually the father).

In another study, sociologist William Aquilino (1994a) analyzed the U.S. National Survey of Families and Households data from 3281 young adults between ages 19 and 34 who grew up in intact families and had therefore lived with both biological parents from birth to age 18. Aquilino separated his sample into three categories: those whose parents were still married, those whose parents had divorced (about 20 percent of the sample), and those whose parent had been widowed. Aquilino found that parental divorce did not reduce the amount of help adult children gave their parents, but it did reduce the amount of help and money that the divorced parents gave their sons (though not their daughters). Furthermore, Aquilino found that even when parents divorce after the child is 18, the divorce seems to negatively affect the quality of their relationship. Children of divorced parents were in contact with their parents less often and reported lower relationship quality overall. These findings applied to both mothers and fathers, although the effect was much stronger for fathers. At the conclusion of still another analysis of different national survey data from adults, about 20 percent of whom had experienced the divorce of their parents, demographer Frank Furstenberg and his colleagues went so far as to pronounce that "marital disruption is altering the organization of kinship" and that "When men relinquish ties to their children during childhood, they rarely resume those ties in later life" (Furstenberg, Hoffman, and Shrestha 1995, p. 330).

Generally, evidence suggests that adult children of divorced parents feel less obligation to remain in contact with them and are less likely to receive help from them or to provide help to them. Social scientists (Lye et al. 1995) have posited four reasons for these findings:

1. Children raised in divorced, single-parent families may have received fewer resources from their custodial parents than did their friends in intact families, and thus they may feel less obliged to reciprocate.

2. Strain in single-parent families, deriving from the custodial parent's emotional stress and/or economic hardship, may weaken subsequent relations between adult children and their parents.

3. The reciprocal obligations of family members in different generations may be less clear in single-parent, postdivorce families—a situation that may also tend to weaken intergenerational relations in later life.

4. Adult children raised in divorced, single-parent families may still be angry, feeling that their parents failed to fulfill their obligation to provide a stable, two-parent household.

Marital Stability for Adult Children of Divorced Parents

Studies show that children of divorced parents do, in fact, have higher divorce rates than children from stable households. On average, adult children of divorced parents leave home earlier, acquire less education, marry sooner, and are more likely to cohabit and/or to have children before marriage (Ambert 1998; Boyd and Norris 1995; Keith and Finlay 1988; McLanahan and Bumpass 1988). All these factors are associated with the increased likelihood of divorce (Bumpass, Martin, and Sweet 1991; Thornton 1991).

But not all studies find parental divorce to be the long-term family handicap that we might expect. Although adult children whose parents divorced may be more negative about their families of origin, they seem little different from children of intact marriages in their goals and attitudes toward marriage and families—only perhaps a little more realistic (Amato and Booth 1991). They value marriage, believe that it should be forever, that partners should be monogamous, and that one's truly important relationships are in families. At the same time, they are "aware of [marriage's] limitations and tolerant toward its alternatives" (Amato 1988, pp. 453, 460). Moreover, although adult children of divorced parents express more accepting attitudes toward divorce, adult children from intact families that were characterized by conflict express this attitude also (Amato and Booth 1991).

Graham Spanier stresses the resilience of children and families in unpromising circumstances. "Many children who experience abuse, family disruption, or poverty nevertheless reach adulthood, against great odds, with a strong commitment to family life" (1989, p. 3). "Some widely held beliefs about the negative impact on children of divorce or parental absence may be overstated, if not wrong" (p. 10). Spanier also suggests that individuals can move on from difficult childhoods to create a satisfying family life:

> Hope stems from the evidence that much childhood trauma has the prospect of being left behind; that some of the setbacks of childhood are short-lived; that we should be skeptical about any intellectual conviction about the superiority of the intact nuclear family; that growing insight into protective favors may help us help children to negotiate risk situations better; that individual and family resilience, or hardiness, exists and can be learned or enhanced; that ... [responsible individuals in extended family networks] can forge continuity out of chaos; and that the intergenerational dynamics of the future may dictate stronger familial bonds. (Spanier 1989, p. 10)

It would be nice to conclude here. At the same time, family scholars and policymakers increasingly express concern that the rising number and proportion of single-parent families are causally related to rising childhood poverty rates (Ambert 1997, 1998;

Eggebeen and Lichter 1991). Both optimistic and pessimistic views of the impact of divorce on children are grounded in current research, and there seems no way of reconciling the diverse perspectives one encounters in the sociology of divorce. We end this chapter with attention to the current debate whether divorces should be more difficult to get than they are.

SHOULD DIVORCES BE HARDER TO GET?

Some family scholars argue that our divorce rate signals "the decline of the family" (see Chapter 1). This situation is "cause for alarm" (Popenoe 1993, 1996) because our future generations, increasingly growing up without fathers, will be "lost" (Blankenhorn 1995; Gairdner 1991; Gill 1997). To address this situation, some have proposed changes in divorce laws so that divorces would be more difficult to get. An assumption behind this movement is that making divorces harder to get would foster a renewed "culture of marriage" (Council on Families in America 1996) and "encourage people to take marriage more seriously" (Wagner 1998).

For example, as an effort to make divorce harder, at least two states in the United States have enacted marriage covenant laws (see Chapter 8). As an alternative to standard marriage, covenant marriage requires divorcing spouses to prove fault and requires a significantly longer-waiting period between filing for divorce and its being granted in court. Others have called for longer mandatory separation periods for couples with dependent children (Galston 1996).

Critics of such divorce "reform" portray family decline as a "myth" and insist that we need to better "understand ... families in a world of rapid social change" (Kain 1990). Arguments centre around two points: First, divorce is not always or necessarily bad for children; and second, making divorce harder to get is simply unrealistic. "We can watch *Ozzie and Harriet* reruns as long as we like, but we cannot return to the world it evokes, even if we wish to" (Stacey 1999, p. 489). Given this situation, what can be done to address the negative consequences of divorce for children?

Is Divorce Necessarily Bad for Children?

In his book on the subject, sociologist David Popenoe (1996) argues that there is "compelling new evidence

that fatherhood and marriage are indispensable for the good of children and society." Popenoe's critics characterize his book as "scientific half-truths" in the "family values debate" (Coltrane 1997). Why half-truths?

Having thoroughly reviewed the literature and conducted his own longitudinal research on the subject, sociologist Paul Amato (Amato and Keith 1991a, 1991b; Amato and Booth 1997), concludes that children whose parents were continuously and happily married are indeed the most successful in adulthood. Children of divorce or those whose parents remained unhappily married were less successful. The quality of the parents' relationship is what is most important. Disturbingly, this research also concludes that marital-relationship quality is declining today. However, making divorce more difficult would not be the solution because the cause of negative outcomes for children is not divorce per se but parental conflict (Amato and Booth 1997; Hetherington 1999).

Furthermore, sociologist Richard Gelles (1996), an expert on domestic violence, warns that, when child abuse is present, preserving families can cost children their lives. More generally, divorce is justified because it provides an escape from marital behaviours, such as a parent's alcoholism or drug abuse, for example, that can be more harmful than divorce itself (Riley 1991; Coontz 1997). Family sociologist Arlene Skolnick sums up the argument:

> Few family social scientists would disagree with the mantra that "Two parents are better than one." But the statement needs qualification: "Two allied parents are better than one."... The harm done by conflict between parents ... is well-documented, whether the family is intact or not.... The proper question is, "Are children better off in a marriage that has broken down?" ... The evidence suggests that other factors—especially economic and emotional stress, and the quality of the child's relationship with the primary parent—are more important. (1997, p. 220)

What Can be Done to Address the Negative Consequences of Divorce for Children?

Wallerstein's research on the long-term negative impact of divorce for children (reviewed earlier in this chapter) is often cited in support for making divorces harder to get. But Wallerstein herself generally opposes legal restrictions on divorce (Coontz 1997a; Wallerstein 1998).

Meanwhile, an important cross-cultural study gives insight into what the wider society might do to help. Sociologists Sharon Houseknecht and Jaya Sastry (1996) conducted research to examine the relationship between family "decline" and child well-being in four industrialized countries: Sweden, the United States, the former West Germany, and Italy. The researchers' measure of family decline included nonmarital birth and divorce rates, the proportion of one-parent households with children, and the percent of employed mothers with children under three years old. Child well-being was measured by six factors: educational performance, percent of children in poverty, infant deaths from child abuse, teenage suicide rates, juvenile delinquency rates, and juvenile drug offense rates.

The researchers found the following:

Sweden, which has the highest family decline score, does not demonstrate a high level of negative outcomes for children compared with other countries with lower levels of family decline. It looks much better than the U.S., which ranks the lowest on child well-being. Having said this, though, we must acknowledge that Italy, ranking lowest on family decline, looks the best of all the countries as far as child well-being is concerned. (p. 736)

What accounts for the difference in child well-being? The answer seems to be Sweden's "egalitarian and generous" welfare policies (p. 737). Swedes' society-wide willingness to support children's needs by paying relatively high taxes translates into significantly less child poverty, fewer working hours for parents, and more family support programs (see Chapter 13). This situation results in relatively high levels of child well-being, despite high proportions of non-marital births, mother employment, divorces, and single-parent households.

As sociologist Robert Glossop has observed:

An awful lot of people figure the only reason that we face the tragedy of child poverty is because we have so many lone-parent families.... The majority of poor kids are, in fact, living with poor mothers and dads. That means the question of how you deal with child poverty is not confined only to questions of absent fathers and support payment enforcement procedures. It raises questions about the working poor, about good jobs and bad jobs, and about minimum wages, which have decreased dramatically in their real purchasing power in the last 15 years. It also raises questions about the tax treatment of low- and modest-income families.... If you're going to resolve the questions of child poverty generally, you are going to need income security for families in general, within which you then have special targeted provisions for lone-parent families. (1994, p. 6)

Researchers on both sides of this debate do agree on one thing: The opposing interpretations of the consequences of family change have polarized some family scholars. Meanwhile, "most people, the general public as well as those who teach, research and write about families, are in the ambivalent middle—welcoming some changes, worrying about others" (Skolnick 1997, p. 221).

We turn in Chapter 15 to a consideration of a next step for many divorced people: remarrying.

IN SUM

Reasons why more people are divorcing now than in past decades have to do with changes in society: economic interdependence and legal, moral, and social constraints are lessening; expectations for intimacy are increasing; and expectations for permanence are declining. People's personal decisions to divorce, or to redivorce, involve weighing marital complaints—most often problems with communication or the emotional quality of the relationship—against the possible consequences of divorce. Two consequences that receive a great deal of consideration are how the divorce will affect children, if there are any, and whether it will cause serious financial difficulties.

Bohannan has identified six ways in which divorce affects people. These six stations of divorce are the emotional divorce, the legal divorce, the community divorce, the psychic divorce, the economic divorce, and the coparental divorce. The psychic divorce involves a healing process that individuals must complete before they can fully enter new intimate relationships.

The economic divorce is typically more disastrous for women than for men, and this is especially so for custodial mothers. Over the past 20 years, child support policies have undergone sweeping changes, and results seem to be positive, with more child support being collected.

Researchers have proposed five possible theories to explain negative effects of divorce on children. These include the life stress perspective, the parental loss perspective, the parental adjustment perspective, the economic hardship perspective, and the interparental conflict perspective. The interparental conflict perspective, which asserts that conflict between parents before, during, and after divorce is responsible for children's lowered well-being, is most strongly supported by research.

Husbands' and wives' divorce experiences, like husbands' and wives' marriages, are different. Both the overload that characterizes the wife's divorce and the loneliness that often accompanies the husband's divorce, especially when there are children, can be lessened in the future by more androgynous settlements. Joint custody offers the opportunity of greater involvement by both parents, although its impact is still being evaluated. Meanwhile, heated debate has emerged among family scholars and policymakers concerning whether today's divorce rate represents family "decline" and is therefore "cause for alarm," or whether it is an effect of broad social change, the implications of which must be addressed in ways other than hoping to turn back the clock.

Key Terms

alimony/spousal support	joint custody
child snatching	legal divorce
child support	life stress perspective
custody	no-fault divorce
displaced homemakers	parental adjustment
divorce mediation	perspective
economic divorce	parental loss perspective
economic hardship	psychic divorce
perspective	redivorce
emotional divorce	refined divorce rate
guaranteed child support	rehabilitative alimony
interparental conflict	relatives of divorce
perspective	supervised visitation

Study Questions

1. What three factors bind marriages and families together? How have these factors changed, and how has the divorce rate been affected?

2. Discuss the relationship of economics to marital stability.

3. Two reasons for divorce in Canada are the myth of the ideal relationship and the rise of individualistic values. Can we promote these and at the same time support the present institution of marriage?

4. What are the consequences of divorce for children? When is divorce a better alternative for the children than maintaining the marriage? A worse alternative?

5. Describe the six stations of divorce, and speculate on how each station might be made less difficult.

6. Describe the five perspectives that explain the possible negative effects of divorce on children. Do any of these theories seem plausible? Why or why not?

7. How is "his" divorce different from "her" divorce? How are these differences related to societal expectations?

8. Differentiate between joint custody and shared living arrangements. How can these narrow the gap between his and her divorces and help lessen the pain of divorce for some couples with children?

9. Discuss family policy measures with regard to child support and women's and children's poverty. Is the support of children ultimately the responsibility of their parents, or of society in general?

10. Discuss the impact of parental divorce on adult children. What are some research findings in this regard? How might individuals make personal, knowledgeable choices that might result in improved consequences?

11. When, in your opinion, would divorce be the lesser of two evils? When would it not?

Suggested Readings

Arendell, Terry. 1995. *Men and Divorce.* Thousand Oaks, CA: Sage. Qualitative research on men's experiences of divorce. Based on interviews with 75 men, with integration of expert sources in law, medicine, and mental health.

Brodie, Deborah. 1999. *Untying the Knot: Ex-husbands, Ex-wives, and Other Experts on the Passage of Divorce.* New York: St. Martin's Press. Sometimes with humour, everyday people tell about their experiences with divorce.

Conway, John. 1997. *The Canadian Family in Crisis,* 3rd edition. Toronto: James Lorimer & Company Ltd. Considers the implications of divorce as well as the implications of social changes on men, women, and children. Also examines how these issues might be dealt with through family policy.

Gold, Lois. 1992. *Between Love and Hate.* New York: Plenum. Written by a social worker, this book is mainly a guide for divorcing adults on "facing the crisis of separation constructively"; discusses healing, custody, conflict, negotiating, mediation, and other relationship issues of families involved in divorce or separation; gives practical advice, exercises, and rituals for such tasks as letting go and forgiving.

Sammons, William and Jennifer M. Lewis. 1999. *Don't Divorce Your Children: Protecting Their Rights and Happiness.* Chicago, IL: Contemporary Books. Sound advice for parenting your own children of divorce.

On the Net

1) Divorce Wizards
   Various experts give advice and answer questions about divorce.
   http://www.divorcewizards.com/askexperts.html

2) Divorce Law in Canada
   http://www.duhaime.org/ca-divor.htm

3) Divorce Info
   http://www.divorceinfo.com/

4) Divorce Online
   http://www.divorce-online.com

5) *Divorce Magazine*
   http://www.divorcemag.com/

Remarriages

THE STEPFAMILY FUNCTIONS DIFFER-

ENTLY FROM OTHER FORMS OF FAMI-

LIES AND HAS ITS OWN STRENGTHS.

STEPFAMILY THERAPISTS MALA S.

BURT AND ROGER B. BURT

IT'S A DIFFERENT SORT OF HAPPINESS

NOW, ... LESS INNOCENT, MORE PRO-

FOUND, LESS CAREFREE, MORE WISE.

REMARRIED WOMAN

Marrying again, usually after being divorced, is an alternative that many Canadians choose. Today, about one-quarter of all marriages involve at least one person who has been married before (Nelson and Robinson 1999, p. 391). Remarriages are now common enough that you can buy congratulatory greeting cards for remarrying parents.

Until about 25 years ago, research and advice concerning remarriages were sparse, but social scientists, counsellors, and journalists have now given remarriage considerable attention. Their findings show that many remarried people are generally satisfied with their relationships and lives. At the same time, remarriages are often beset with special challenges. **Remarried families** are different from—but not necessarily better or worse than—first-marriage families (Visher and Visher 1996).

This chapter explores remarriages. We will discuss choosing a remarriage partner, noting some social factors that influence that choice. We'll examine happiness and stability in remarriage, as well as the adjustment and well-being of children in stepfamilies. We'll see that no consistent cultural or legal model exists to guide interactions among the often complex networks of kin. We'll focus on two particularly difficult problem areas in remarriages: stepchildren and finances. Finally, we will explore the writing of a remarriage agreement. We'll begin with an overview of remarriage in Canada today.

REMARRIAGE: SOME BASIC FACTS

Remarriage (a marriage in which at least one partner has previously been divored or widowed) is not a "new" phenomenon. However, until the end of World War II, remarriages were most likely to involve widowed persons rather than those who were divorced. "In 1994, over seven times as many divorced as widowed men and women married again" (Ward 1998, p. 220). In 1971, about one in 10 marriages was a remarriage for at least one partner; by the early 1990s, one-third of all marriages were remarriages for one or both partner. "In two out of three marriages in 1997, both spouses were marrying for the first time. A first-time partner married a divorced partner 18 percent of the time and both partners had been divorced in 12 percent of the marriages. Very few marriages in 1997 involved a widow (under five percent)" (Statistics Canada 1999).

The remarriage rate (the number of marriages per 1000 of previously married [widowed or divorced] population) declined somewhat from 1955 until 1961. It then began to rise to an all time-time high in 1962 for both women and men (respectively, 136 and 148). However, from 1967 and continuing, the remarriage rate plummeted (Wu 1998). Since the time period covered in Figure 15.1, the remarriage rates among both men and women and for all marital statuses have continued to decline. "Among all Canadians aged 15 and over, marriages per 1000 population for previously divorced people has declined from 148.0 in 1975 to 40.5 in 1995, and for the previously widowed from 13.5 to 6.0" (Nelson and Robinson 1999, p. 391). While in the early 1970s, about eight out of 10 divorced men (85 percent) and women (79 percent) remarried, by the mid-1980s, 76 percent of men and 64 percent of women did so. As Figure 15.1 indicates, the remarriage rates for men have typically been higher than those for women.

In 1991, the incidence of remarriage outside of Quebec was 69 percent for divorced men and 58 percent for divorced women. In the province of Quebec, 46 percent of divorced men and 34 percent of divorced women remarried. A large proportion of this decline in remarriage is due to the increasing popularity of cohabitation (Dumas and Peron 1992; Wu and Balakrishnan 1994). The decline may also be due, in part, to the economic uncertainties of recent years, which discourage people, particularly divorced

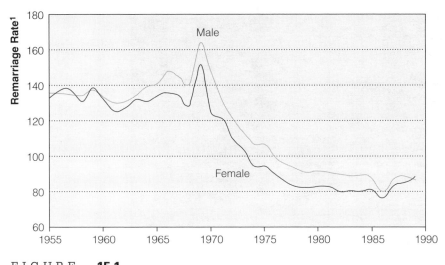

FIGURE **15.1**

Remarriage rates in Canada, 1955–1989. (Source: Wu 1998, p.4.)
[1] Number of marriages per 1,000 previously married population.

men who may already be paying child support, from assuming financial responsibility for a new instant family.

Nevertheless, "remarriage is still the most frequent likelihood following divorce, for both men and women, everywhere in Canada except in Quebec" (Nelson and Robinson 1999, p. 391). "It may be that eventually the majority of people will be married more than once during their lifetime if the rate of divorce for first marriages continues at the present rate" (Ihinger-Tallman and Pasley 1997, p. 24).

Some divorce lawyers and counsellors report having begun to see "regulars"—people who divorce, remarry, redivorce, then remarry and perhaps redivorce yet again (Leerhsen 1985). But a large majority of remarriages are second marriages.

Single-parent and remarried families are still stereotyped as not as normal or functional as first-marriage, nuclear families (Ganong and Coleman 1997; Gamache 1997). But there is no question that the increased incidence of divorce and remarriage has led to greater cultural tolerance of these families.

In both the United States and Canada, the average divorced person who remarries does so within less than three years after divorce (Nault 1996; U.S. National Center for Health Statistics 1991b, p. 5). Rapidity—and overall probability—of remarriage varies, however, for women and men. Research in

both Canada (Nault 1996) and the United States (Glick and Lin 1987) notes that men have been and are more likely than women to remarry and to do so more quickly after a divorce. We will examine reasons for this later in this chapter.

Remarriages have always been fairly common in Canada. However, while early in the 20th century, the majority of remarriages followed widowhood, today, the largest proportion of the remarried population involves divorced people. Remarriage is much more likely to occur, age for age, among divorced women than among widowed women (Talbott 1998).

Remarriage and Children's Living Arrangements

One result of the significant number of remarriages today is that more Canadians are parenting other people's children—and more children are living with other than their biological parents. In 1995, approximately one in 10 Canadian families composed of a couple with children (approximately 430 000 families) were stepfamilies (Figure 15.2). Just over half of these families consisted of couples who were currently married, with the rest, common-law couples.

Although stepfamilies have also become increasingly diverse, we can distinguish three basic kinds. The first, and most common form, are stepfamilies in

In Canada, stepfamilies have become increasingly common.

which the children are the biological offspring of the mother and stepchildren of the father. In 1995, slightly more than 50 percent of stepfamilies took this form. The second type, consisting of a biological father, his children, and a stepmother accounted for 13 percent of all stepfamilies. The third type, referred to as a **blended family** or "reconstituted" or "recombined" family, involves "a mix of children that both parents brought to the family from previous union, or...a mix of children from previous unions and the current one" (Statistics Canada 1996). In 1995, over a third of all stepfamilies (approximately 161 000) were blended families (Figure 15.3).

Figure 15.3 points up the fact that stepfamilies are not all alike: A stepparent can be mother or father (although usually it is the father), and a stepfamily may or may not contain biological children of both remarried parents. Moreover, in some stepfamilies both parents are stepparents to their spouse's biological children.

The remainder of this chapter explores what family life is like for children—and their parents— who are living in stepfamilies. We begin with a question about courtship. Do people choose partners differently the second (or third) time around?

CHOOSING PARTNERS THE NEXT TIME: VARIATIONS ON A THEME

It may go without saying that spouses are older at the time of remarriage than at first marriage. While in 1997, grooms averaged about 33.5 years of age, while brides averaged 30.9 years, for those remarrying in that year, previously married and divorced grooms and brides averaged 43.4 and 39.8 years of age respectively while widowed men and women averaged 62.1 and 55.5 years of age respectively (Statistics Canada 1999).

Counsellors often add that people who ended troubled first marriages through divorce often are still experiencing personal conflicts, which they must resolve before they can expect to succeed in a second marriage. Consequently, many counsellors advise waiting at least two years after divorce before entering into another serious relationship.

Meanwhile, courtship before remarriage may differ in many respects from courtship before first marriage. It may proceed much more rapidly, with the people involved viewing themselves as mature adults who know what they are looking for—or it may be more

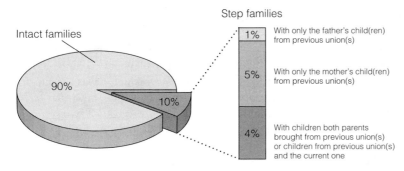

**Number of couples
with children 4,165,000**

Intact families

Step families

90%

10%

1% — With only the father's child(ren) from previous union(s)

5% — With only the mother's child(ren) from previous union(s)

4% — With children both parents brought from previous union(s) or children from previous union(s) and the current one

FIGURE **15.2**

Couples with children, 1995. (Source: Statistics Canada, "The Daily," Cat. No. 11-001, June 19, 1996.)

cautious, with the partners needing time to recover from, or being wary of repeating, their previous marital experience. It is likely to have an earlier, more open sexual component—which may be hidden from the children through a series of complex arrangements. It may include both outings with the children and evenings at home as partners seek to recapture their accustomed domesticity.

Courtship for remarriage has not been a major topic for research. Canadian sociologists Roy Rodgers and Linda Conrad have posed several hypotheses for future testing. Generally, the hypotheses point up the complicated interrelationships between courting parents, their respective children, and their ex-spouses. For example, if one ex-spouse begins courtship while the other does not, conflict between the former spouses may escalate. Moreover, the noncourting partner may try to interfere with the ex-spouse's new relationship. Not only ex-spouses but children, too, may react negatively to a parent's dating. Generally, "the more the custodial parent's new partner displaces the child as a source of emotional support for the parent, the greater the probability of a negative reaction of the child to the new partner" and the more problems are likely to arise (Rodgers and Conrad 1986, p. 771).

All of this suggests that courtship toward remarriage differs from that for first marriages in important ways. Nevertheless, the basic structure of the remarriage process has much in common with initial marriage. We'll look at two significant factors that we first examined in Chapter 7 with regard to first marriages: the traditional exchange and homogamy.

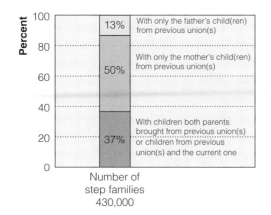

FIGURE **15.3**

Stepfamilies by type, 1995. (Source: Statistics Canada, "The Daily," Cat. No. 11-001, June 19, 1996.)

The Traditional Exchange in Remarriage

Economists and other social scientists point out that in general ex-wives, but not ex-husbands, are likely to gain financially by being remarried. Indeed, U.S. research notes that "stepfamily relationships are important in lifting single-parent families out of poverty. When single or divorced mothers remarry, the household income increases by more than three-fold, rising to roughly the same level as nuclear families" (Mason 1998, p. 114).

One extensive longitudinal study by Pamela Smock (1993) used three large national American data sets to monitor the financial well-being of women as they married, divorced, and then remarried over the years. She reports that the situation of women who separated or divorced during the 1980s was essentially the same as those who did so in the late 1960s and 1970s. In constant 1987 dollars, the median annual income of married white women before they divorced was approximately $24 000–$25 000. With divorce or separation, annual income dropped by more than 40 percent. With remarriage, the women's annual family income returned to what it had been prior to their divorce. This same pattern was found for African-American women, with the exception that overall their annual family earnings were lower than for whites. However, black women who remarried in the 1980s had annual family incomes higher than their white counterparts ($28 722 compared with $24 801). This situation may reflect the somewhat higher proportion of African-American wives in the U.S. labour force.

In Canada, research has used longitudinal data to investigate whether the movement of children in and out of low income was primarily associated with changes in the parents' labour market status or their marital status. The results of this investigation found that marriage had a much greater impact than a change in the parent's job status.

Virtually all (99 percent) children with a single parent who married or formed a common-law union were able to climb out of low income, compared with only 21 percent of children in families where there was no such union. Changes in the parent's job had a significant, but less profound effect. (For example, a $117 increase in weekly earnings increased the probability of climbing out of low income from 22 percent to 46 percent.) However, only seven percent of children were in a lone-parent family in which a marriage occurred (Statistics Canada 1999e). Chapter 14 addresses the economic plight of divorced women in more detail.

Meanwhile, the following account by a single male in his late 20s illustrates that women typically have more to gain financially from being remarried than men do:

She was eyeing me and eyeing my house as a nice place to live with her son. It was the first thing she did. We went to my house one night and she says, "Boy, you've really got a nice backyard and a nice house here." And I'm thinking, "Why is she saying that?" It didn't click at the time, but she told this buddy of mine that her plan was to move in here with her kid—whatever his name was. Jason, that was the name, Jason. I could not stand that kid at all. So when I found this out, that I was her meal ticket, I thought, "Hea-a-a-vy." And that was the last time I saw her. She had great plans for me, but then I thought "Nah." (personal interview)

From the discussion in Chapter 7 of the traditional marriage exchange, you will remember that homemaking services are largely available to single men today whereas women, especially older women and those who have been out of the labour force for a number of years, can find it difficult to get well-paying jobs and support themselves. This situation is one reason that women's remarriage rate is less than half of men's. In part, that statistic is a consequence of the very low remarriage rate of widows, for whom few partners are available in later life. But even comparing only divorced people, men's remarriage rates are substantially higher, particularly at older ages. Two factors influencing the exchange work against women remarrying.

CHILDREN AND THE ODDS OF REMARRIAGE

One factor that works against women in the remarriage market is the presence of dependent children (Buckle, Gallup, and Rodd 1996). As we saw in Chapter 14, the woman usually retains custody of children from a previous marriage. As a result, a prospective second husband may look on her family as a financial—and also an emotional and psychological—liability. Furthermore, according to one qualitative study of 30 single-parent women employed outside the home, the independent and assertive attitudes and behaviours necessary for single parenthood are contradictory to those they assumed they should exhibit in order to remarry (Quinn and Allen 1989). Then too, children are often strongly loyal to the first family and may oppose or have strong reservations about the divorce for as long as five years afterward.

In general, the more children a woman has, the less likely she is to remarry (Glick and Lin 1986b).

AGE AND THE ODDS OF REMARRIAGE A second factor, age, works against women in several ways. As discussed in Chapters 6 and 7, women live longer, on the average, than men do: by age 65 there are only 72.9 men for every 100 women (McVey 1998). The *double standard of aging* works against women in the remarriage market. In our society, women are considered to be less physically attractive with age, and they may also be less interested in fulfilling traditional gender role expectations.

Research conducted in Canada in the 1980s and 1990s reports that while the probability of a divorced woman remarrying declines sharply after age 35, no similar decline exists among men (Adams and Nagnur 1988). Anne-Marie Ambert (1998, p. 7) observes:

> About 75 percent and 65 percent, respectively, of divorced men and women remarry. The probability of remarriage between the years of 35–50 for women is 48 percent compared to 61 percent for men. For younger women between 25 and 35, the probability is 66 percent and closer to 80 percent among men. Therefore, it is obvious that age discriminates against women the older they are; the older they are, the lower their chances of remarrying. But this is not the case for men. Such is the double standard.

Table 15.1 reflects both greater female longevity and the greater likelihood of previously widowed men remarrying. As you will note, while the majority of Canadian men between the ages of 50 and 89 are legally married and living with a spouse (and it is only among men age 90 and over that less than 50 percent of men are married), the proportions of females currently married drops dramatically with age.

Age works against both women's and men's remarriage in another way; older people often face considerable social opposition to remarriage from their friends and children. Grown children may feel that remarriage is inappropriate, or may be concerned about the biological parent's continued interest in them or, ultimately, the estate (Rosenfeld 1997).

Homogamy in Remarriage

Homogamy has traditionally been a second important factor influencing marriage choices. We saw in Chapter 7 that homogamy can be important in both the choice of a first marriage partner and the degree to which couples live happily ever after. Does it affect second marriages in the same way? The answer to that question is, on the whole, no. Older people, particularly those who are widowed, are likely to remarry homogamously. Sometimes the new partner is someone who reminds them of their first spouse or is someone they've known for years. This rule does not apply to middle-aged or younger people who choose second marriage partners.

Choosing a remarriage partner differs from making a marital choice the first time inasmuch as there is a smaller pool of eligibles with a wider range of any given attribute. As prospective mates move from their late 20s into their 30s, they affiliate in occupational circles and interest groups that assemble people from more diverse backgrounds. There is also some evidence that divorced people tend more toward heterogamy than nondivorced people the first time around and that they simply accentuate this tendency when they remarry. As a result, remarriages are less homogamous than first marriages with partners varying in age, educational background (U.S. National Center for Health Statistics 1990b), and religious background. Some observers note that homogamy increases the likelihood for marital stability and point to this preference for and increase in heterogamy as a partial explanation for the fact that the divorce rate is higher for second than for first marriages. The next section discusses stability and happiness in marriage.

SPOUSES' HAPPINESS AND STABILITY IN REMARRIAGE

As pointed out elsewhere in this text, marital happiness and stability are not the same. Marital happiness refers to the quality of the marital relationship whether or not it is permanent; stability refers simply to the duration of the union. We'll look at both ways of evaluating remarriage.

TABLE 15.1

Legal Marital Status*, By Selected Five-Year Age Groups, in Percentage, Canada: 1996

Age	Never Married		Legally Married**		Separated***		Divorced		Widowed	
	Male	Female	Male	Female	Male	Female	Male	Female	Male	Female
50–54	8.4	7.0	73.8	69.2	4.1	4.1	12.5	14.5	1.3	5.2
55–59	7.2	5.9	76.4	69.4	3.6	3.4	10.7	11.8	2.2	9.5
60–64	6.8	5.6	77.7	66.0	3.1	2.8	8.5	9.2	3.8	16.3
65–69	6.9	5.8	77.4	58.8	2.8	2.4	6.5	6.8	6.4	26.1
70–74	6.6	6.1	76.1	48.4	2.5	1.9	4.6	4.8	10.2	38.8
75–79	6.1	6.9	73.0	35.4	2.2	1.5	3.2	3.2	15.5	53.0
80–84	6.6	8.4	65.6	22.2	2.1	1.1	2.4	2.0	23.4	66.4
85–89	6.9	9.4	54.7	11.9	2.1	0.7	1.7	1.3	34.6	76.8
90+	7.7	10.3	38.7	4.8	1.7	0.4	1.4	0.8	50.4	83.9

Note: * Individuals in common-law arrangements are listed by their legal marital status.

** Legally married and still living together.

*** Physically living apart but still legally married.

Source: Statistics Canada, "1991 Census of Canada," Cat. No. 92-915, 1984, 1993, 1997.

Happiness in Remarriage

Researchers consistently find little difference in partners' overall well-being (Demo and Acock 1996b) or in marital happiness between first and later marriages (Ihinger-Tallman and Pasley 1997). In fact, not only is there little difference generally in marital satisfaction, but there also appears to be little difference in marital quality for remarriages of men compared to those of women; stepfathers compared to stepmothers; double remarriages (both parties were previously married) compared to single ones; or single compared to blended stepfamily households (with both parties bringing children to the marriage). The effect of stepchildren on marital satisfaction is minimal, with one national U.S. sample study finding a slight negative effect (in unions where both spouses are remarried) (White and Booth 1985b), whereas a number of studies found a minimal positive effect (Vermer et al. 1989; MacDonald and DeMaris 1995). Despite the challenges peculiar to remarriages (discussed later in this chapter), remarriages tend to be as happy as first marriages (Coleman and Ganong 1990, pp. 931–32; Ihinger-Tallman and Pasley 1997).

Some writers have suggested that older, more experienced mates in remarriages are likely to be more mature than when they began their first marriages. Then too, we saw in Chapters 10 and 13 that wives' satisfaction with the division of household labour is important to marital satisfaction. There is some evidence that remarried husbands contribute slightly more to housework than do husbands in first marriages. Interestingly, this finding appears to have more to do with an ex-wife's less-than-satisfactory experience in her first marriage, and subsequent partner selection for remarriage, than with remarried men's resolution to do more around the house (Sullivan 1997). However, while

[r]emarried men describe themselves as being less assertive and more accomodating than they were in their previous marriage [and] [c]ouples gener-

ally agree that decision-making and overall participation levels in decision-making are more egalitarian in remarriages...remarriages are not more egalitarian, with wives still bearing the brunt of responsibilities and actual participation in housework and childrearing. (Nelson and Robinson 1999, p. 392)

NEGATIVE STEREOTYPES AND REMARRIEDS' HAPPINESS   To use the family ecology theoretical perspective, one way that remarital satisfaction is influenced by the wider society is through the negative stereotyping of remarriages (Ganong and Coleman 1997). Historically (Phillips 1997), and today, society is beset with such potentially harmful myths as, "A stepfamily can never be as good as a family in which children live with both natural parents" (Kurdek and Fine 1991, p. 567). In one study of 31 white, middle-class spouses in stepfather families, researchers found, especially among the wives, that believing in none or very few of these negative myths and having high optimism about the remarriage were related to high family, marital, and personal satisfaction (Kurdek and

Fine 1991). Another study (Kurdek 1989a) that compared relationship quality between remarrieds and first marrieds found that high satisfaction with social support from friends and families of origin, together with high expressiveness in partners, were more important to marital satisfaction than whether the union was a first marriage or a remarriage.

The Stability of Remarriages

Even though remarriages are about as likely to be happy as intact first marriages, they differ somewhat in the likelihood of their stability, with one estimate suggesting that remarriages are about 20 percent more likely to end in divorce than first marriages (Martin and Bumpass 1989). Other projections predict eventual convergence of divorce rates for first and subsequent marriages (Dumas and Peron 1992; Norton and Moorman 1987). In fact, some scholars consider the current divergence between divorce rates for first and subsequent marriages to be relatively minimal (Clarke and Wilson 1997; Furstenberg 1987). Research conducted in the United States concludes that "marrying

As Canadians live longer, many of them are finding that love and intimacy can occur at any age. People tend to choose partners differently the second time around and, although remarriage rates are relatively low for those over 65, some do find happiness in a late remarriage.

at a young age was a stronger determinant of divorce than was a previous marriage of either or both spouses" (Wilson and Clarke 1992, p. 123; Clarke and Wilson 1994).

Nevertheless, remarriages are somewhat less likely to be stable. Furthermore, people tend to get a subsequent divorce in less time than it took them to obtain their initial divorce—about six years for a second and four years for a third divorce versus seven years for a first divorce.

There are several reasons for the lower overall stability of remarriages. First, people who divorce in the first place are disproportionately from lower middle- and lower-class groups, which generally have higher divorce rates.

Second, people who remarry after divorce are, as a group, more accepting of divorce (White and Booth 1985b; Booth and Edwards 1992) and may have already demonstrated that they are willing to choose divorce as a way of resolving an unsatisfactory marriage.

Third, remarrieds receive less social support from their families of origin and are generally less integrated with parents and in-laws (Booth and Edwards 1992), a situation that may serve to encourage divorce.

Fourth, remarriages present some special stresses on a couple, stresses that are not inherent in first marriages. Our culture has not yet fully evolved norms or traditions that provide remarried partners and their families with models for appropriate behaviour (Mason 1998). As we gain experience with the special challenges of remarriage, which are discussed throughout this chapter, remarriages may become more stable.

Perhaps the most significant factor in the comparative instability of remarriages is the presence of stepchildren. Sociologists Lynn White and Alan Booth explored the puzzling question of why remarried couples are as happy as couples in their first marriages, yet have higher divorce rates. They interviewed a national U.S. sample of over 2000 married people (under age 55) in 1980 and reinterviewed four-fifths of them in 1983. During that interval, **double remarriages**, in which both partners had been married before, were twice as likely to have broken up as those of people in their first marriages. **Single remarriages**, in which only one partner had been previously married, did not differ significantly from first marriages in their likelihood of divorce.

Double remarriage increased the probability of divorce by 50 percent over what it would otherwise have been, and having stepchildren in the home increased it an additional 50 percent.[1] Although the presence of stepchildren did not make so much difference in single remarriages, double remarriages involving stepchildren have a very elevated risk of dissolution. Of course, these are the most complex family types in a society that has not yet developed a normative structure for stepfamilies.

Nevertheless, White and Booth found that marital quality does not vary greatly between first marriages and single or double remarriages. It is satisfaction with family life generally that is affected. Individuals in families with stepchildren are more likely to report that they have problems with the children, that they are unhappy with the way the spouse gets along with their children, that they would enjoy living apart from their children, that marriage has a negative effect on their relationships with their children, and that, if they had it to do over again, they would not remarry. "Since they report only modestly lower marital happiness, we interpret this evidence that the stepfamily, rather than the marriage, is stressful.... These data suggest that ... if it were not for the children these marriages would be stable. The partners manage to be relatively happy despite the presence of stepchildren, but they nevertheless are more apt to divorce because of child-related problems" (White and Booth 1985b, p. 696).

Focusing on Children

CHILDREN'S WELL-BEING IN STEPFAMILIES

How does membership in a stepfamily affect children's well-being? Just as social scientists debate on whether the family is in "decline" (see Chapters 1 and 14), they disagree on how to interpret findings about stepchildren's well-being. "In recent years, a new

---

1. In presenting their findings, White and Booth take into account the fact that divorce occurs earlier in remarriages.

rationale for the superiority of the nuclear family model has emerged" (Ganong and Coleman 1997, p. 87). Sociobiologists and evolutionary psychologists (see Chapters 3 and 5) argue that biological forces make genetically-related families more functional for children than other family types (Popenoe 1994, 1996). According to this view, bioevolutionary forces encourage parents to favour their genetic offspring. This situation puts stepchildren at risk and perhaps even jeopardizes their safety. For instance, there is evidence that the incidence of child abuse, including sexual abuse, is higher for stepfathers than for biological fathers (Daly and Wilson 1994; Giles-Sims 1997). From this perspective, the formation of stepfamilies should be discouraged (Popenoe 1994, 1998).

However, the vast majority of social scientists reject the idea that stepfamily formation should be discouraged. Sociologist Jean Giles-Sims (1997) points out that, although child abuse rates are higher among stepfamilies, this situation assuredly "does not mean that all stepfamilies are at risk" (p. 227). In fact, "a low percent of stepchildren are physically or sexually abused" (p. 220). Indeed,

> The factors that increase risk in stepfamilies likely include the same factors that put other children at risk, plus some individual and group characteristics that are more common in stepfamilies, and also a general lack of understanding and training for parental care and a morality which stresses the needs of children .... All families would benefit from raising awareness and commitment to children. (p. 227)

Meanwhile, considerable research has found that stepchildren, on average, do less well in school (Zill 1994), may experience more family conflict (Hanson, McLanahan, and Thomson 1996), and are somewhat less well-adjusted than children in first-marriage families (Ihinger-Tallman and Pasley 1997; Coleman and Ganong 1997). In one important study, child development expert E. Mavis Hetherington (1993, 1999) followed a group of nine- through 11-year-old children in nondivorced, divorced single-mother, and stepfather families over a period of 26 months. Hetherington found that children in both divorced and remarried families had more behaviour problems than those in first-marriage families.

However, sociologist Paul Amato (1994) has pointed out that the differences found in these and other studies are fairly small. Since many of the small, negative outcomes for stepchildren are also associated with divorce (see Chapter 14),

> it is difficult to know the relative contribution of parental remarriage to poor child adjustment. It may well be that most of the negative effects can be attributed to predivorce conditions ... or post-divorce effects (e.g., reduced income, multiple transitions that accompany divorce), of which parental remarriage is only one. (Ihinger-Tallman and Pasley 1997, p. 31)

Some social scientists have asked whether remarriage can lessen some of the negative effects of divorce for children. One researcher has concluded that, "Children of stepfamilies don't do better than children of mothers who never marry" (McLanahan and Sandefur 1994, p. 51). However, in a Canadian study (Pagani et al. 1997), children of divorce were more anxious and hyperactive, but a custodial parent's remarriage somewhat lessened these effects. Other researchers (Zill, Morrison, and Coiro 1993) have concluded that remarriage lessens some negative effects for children—but only for those who experienced their parents' divorce at an early age and when the remarriage has remained intact (see also Arendell 1997b, pp. 186–188). Other research shows that younger children adjust better to a parent's remarriage than do older children, especially adolescents (Hetherington 1993, 1999; Gamache 1997; Ihinger-Tallman and Pasley 1997).

In sum, research findings can hardly be characterized as rosy, but we can still conclude that most children "eventually adapt to life in a stepfamily and emerge as reasonably competent individuals" (Hetherington and Jodl 1994, p. 76). Erica De'Ath, of the National Stepfamily Association, notes that, "Understanding how families manage change and supporting all families to provide good enough parenting is likely to be a better investment for children than cataloguing disadvantages and difficulties and denigrating different family structures" (1996, p. 82). Meanwhile, an important reason that stepfamilies may not be as supportive for children as intact first marriages is that, although they are increasingly prevalent, remarried families remain a "normless norm."

REMARRIED FAMILIES: A NORMLESS NORM

When neither spouse in a remarriage has children, the couples' union is usually very much like a first marriage. This is probably also true for the estimated 18 percent of remarried parents who have all their children after the remarriage (see Glick 1989, p. 25). But when at least one spouse has children from a previous marriage, family life often differs sharply from that of first marriages. A primary reason for this is the fact that our society offers members of remarried families no **cultural script**, or set of socially prescribed and understood guidelines for relating to each other or for defining responsibilities and obligations. Social Work Professor Irene Levin (1997) argues that "the nuclear family has a kind of model monopoly when it comes to family forms" (p. 123). According to this **nuclear-family model monopoly**, the first-marriage family is the "real" model for family living, with all other family forms "seen as deficient alternatives." This "prejudice" affects everyone's understanding of stepfamilies—researchers and stepfamily members alike—so that we incorrectly think of a second marriage as "more or less the same as the first" (p. 124).

Although society tends to broadly apply to second marriages the rules and assumptions of first marriages, these rules often ignore the complexities of remarried families and leave many questions unanswered (Kheshgi-Genovese and Genovese 1997). Three areas in which these shortcomings are most apparent are within the remarried families, in relationships with kin, and in family law.

Characteristics of Remarried Families

The complexity of stepfamily structure, which affects family relationships, is illustrated in Table 15.2. It compares stepfamilies with the original nuclear family and with the single-parent family, which generally is a stage between marriages and remarriages. The sequential transitions from one family structure to another create a prolonged period of upheaval and stress. Yet, enough adjustment to a single-parent household is likely to have occurred so that a new adaptation to a two-parent remarried family is all the more difficult.

STEPFAMILIES ARE OF VARIOUS TYPES Despite these important differences between remarriages and first marriages, remarried families are of various types. The simplest is one in which a divorced or widowed spouse with one child remarries a never-married childless spouse. In the most complex, both remarrying partners bring children in from previous unions and also have a mutual child or children together. If a remarriage is followed by redivorce and a subsequent remarriage, the new remarried family structure is even more complex (Trost 1997). Moreover,

> ex-spouses remarry, too, to persons who have spouses by previous marriages, and who also have mutual children of their own. This produces an extraordinarily complicated network of family relationships in which adults have the roles of parent, stepparent, spouse, and ex-spouse; some adults have the role of custodial parent and others have the role of noncustodial, absent parent. The children all have roles as sons or daughters, siblings, residential stepsiblings, nonresidential stepsiblings, residential half-siblings, and nonresidential half-siblings. There are two subtypes of half-sibling roles: those of children related by blood to only one of the adults, and the half-sibling role of the mutual child. Children also have stepgrandparents and exstepgrandparents as well as grandparents. (Beer 1989, p. 8)

DIFFERENCES BETWEEN FIRST MARRIAGES WITH CHILDREN AND STEPFAMILIES We can point to the following differences between stepfamilies and first marriages with children (Visher and Visher 1996, pp. 41–2):

1. There are different structural characteristics (see Table 15.2). Therefore, the first-married, nuclear family model is not valid.

2. There is a complicated "supra family system," including family members from one or more previous marriages.

3. Children may have more than two parenting figures.

4. There may be less family control because of an influential parent elsewhere or in memory.

5. There may be preexisting parent–child coalitions.

TABLE 15.2

Major Structural Characteristics of Three Family Patterns

Stepfamilies	Nuclear (Intact) Families	Single-Parent Families
Biological parent is elsewhere.	Both biological parents are present.	Biological parent is elsewhere.
Virtually all members have recently sustained a primary relationship loss.	_____	All members have recently sustained a primary relationship loss.
An adult couple is in the household.	An adult couple is in the household.	_____
Relationship between one adult (parent)and child pre-dates the marriage.	Spousal relationship predates parental ones.	Parental relationship is the primary family relationship.
Children are members in more than one household.	Children are members in only one household.	Children may be members in more than one household.
One adult (stepparent) is not legally related to a child (stepchild).	Parents and child(ren) are legally related.	Parents and child(ren) are legally related.

Source: Visher and Visher 1979.

6. There have been many losses for all individuals.

7. There are ambiguous family boundaries with little—and little agreement about—shared family history.

8. At least initially, there is little or no family loyalty.

9. There is a long integration period.

10. Prior to possible integration, family members must recover from previous transitional stresses.

11. Because society compares stepfamilies negatively to first-married families, individuals need validation as members of a worthwhile family unit.

12. The balance of power is different: Stepparents have relatively little authority initially and children generally wield more power than in first-married families.

13. A good couple relationship does not necessarily make for good stepparent-stepchild relationships. In later sections of this chapter, we will further address many of these characteristics and what can be done to meet the challenges that they create.

Kin Networks in the Remarried Family

Relationships with kin outside the immediate remarried family are complex and uncharted as well (Ganong and Coleman 1997). Two decades ago, an anthropologist observed that:

> Many people are married to people who have been married to other people who are now married to still others to whom the first parties may not have been married, but to whom somebody has likely been married. (Tiger 1978, p. 14)

The observation also describes a large segment of Canadian families today, and the complexity it portrays is striking in several respects. One is the fact that our language has not yet caught up with the proliferation of new family roles. As family members separate and then join new families formed by remarriage, the new kin do not so much *replace* as *add* to kin from the first marriage (White and Riedmann 1992). What are the new relatives to be called? There may be stepparents, stepgrandparents, and stepsiblings, but what, for instance, does a child call the new wife that her or his noncustodial father has married? (Ganong and

Coleman 1997, pp. 89–90). Or if a child alternates between the new households or remarried parents in a joint custody arrangement, what does he or she call "home," and where is his or her "family"? According to sociologist William Beer, "I began my in-depth interviewing of one stepfamily with a question about who the family members were. The response was a confused look and the question, 'Well, when do you mean?'" (1989, p. 9).

Anthropologist Paul Bohannan suggests a new term to define another previously unnamed relationship, the person one's former spouse remarries. He calls this person one's **quasi-kin** (Bohannan 1970a). But he and other observers point to another way in which our culture has not yet caught up with the needs of the new remarried family: We have few mutually accepted ways of dealing with these new relationships. Interaction takes place between these families, often on a regular basis, yet there are no set ways of dealing with quasi-kin. In many cases there is little meaningful interaction between former spouses (Spanier and Furstenberg 1987, p. 57; see also Lewin 1990a).

The Binuclear Family Research Project collected data from 98 pairs of Wisconsin families at one, three, and five years after divorce. At three years, only nine percent of divorced spouses continued to engage in **coparenting**—shared decision making and parental supervision in such areas as discipline and schoolwork or shared holidays and recreation. But conflict and mutual support had not declined. Satisfaction declined for fathers, but not for mothers. Tentative data indicate that the coparental relationship deteriorated if one parent remarried, especially the man.

Biological parents and their new partners had high rates of coparenting, with 62 percent of stepmothers and 73 percent of stepfathers reporting joint involvement in seven of 10 areas of child rearing. Researchers Ahrons and Wallisch (1987) pose, but do not answer, the question of whether stepparents are "substitute" or "alternative" parents, but other research suggests that it is often the former (Wallerstein and Blakeslee 1989). Today, experts conclude simply that, "The roles and positions of stepparents vary widely" (Arendell 1997b, p. 183). Cultural norms do not clearly indicate which role the stepparents should play (Coleman and Ganong 1997; Visher and Visher 1996).

Because of the cultural ambiguity of remarried family relationships, social scientist Andrew Cherlin

calls the remarried family an **incomplete institution** (1978).[2] A second symptom of its incompleteness stems from the laws surrounding remarriage.

Family Law and the Remarried Family

"Remarriage presents its own set of legal issues and concerns" (Dranoff 2001, p. 304). Research suggests that remarried people may be reluctant to commit all of their economic resources to a second marriage and take care to protect their individual interests and those of their biological children (Fishman 1983). However, honouring financial obligations to first and/or subsequent spouses as well as children from current and previous marriages can sometimes become a "legal minefield" (Dranoff 2001, p. 305).

Upon marriage to a formerly married person, a new partner does not incur a legal obligation to assume or share his/her spouse's financial obligations to a former spouse and/or children from a previous marriage. That is, the court will not order new partners to pay monies directly to their spouses' former spouses or children to support their financial needs. However, "the court will probably consider a new spouse's current and potential financial circumstances when recalculating the remarried partner's support obligations" (Dranoff 2001, p. 307). For example, if a new spouse receives income from paid employment, or simply possesses the capacity to work, this will be seen as potentially enabling some portion of his or her spouse's income to be freed up for purposes of paying support payments.

While parents retain the primary obligation of supporting their children from prior or current marriages, on occasion, a new spouse will voluntarily assume the position of parent and financial provider for his/her stepchild. Doing so may create a legal obligation to continue supporting the child if the new marital relationships ends—a form of support referred to as "in loco parentis." In determining whether or not such a responsibility exists, emphasis is placed on evidence that suggests that the stepparent "intended" to treat the child as his/her own during

2. Sociologist Gary Grizzle (1996) argues that there is insufficient empirical evidence to support Cherlin's concept, incomplete institution, and that "further examination of Cherlin's views should begin at once" (p. 198).

the course of the marriage. Having a friendly relationship with a child or taking a child to school or on various outings would not, in and of themselves, provide evidence that the stepparent stood "in loco parentis" to his/her stepchild.

Provincial laws on the division of marital property are additionally complex in the case of remarriages and inconsistent across jurisdictions. For example, if a remarried spouse owns, prior to his/her remarriage, a home that subsequently becomes the remarried couple's matrimonial home, the entire value of that home will be equally shared between the spouses, should their marriage break down, in B.C., Saskatchewan, Ontario, New Brunswick, Nova Scotia, Newfoundland, the N.W.T., and the Yukon. In contrast, in the provinces of Alberta, Manitoba, Quebec, and P.E.I., simply the value accumulated during the course of the marriage would be shared.

Rights on death of one of the new spouses are additionally complicated. For example, in a 1995 case in British Columbia,

> Pursuant to a separation agreement, the husband agreed to maintain his first wife as beneficiary of his pension by designating her as "spouse." Unfortunately, his pension was governed by the Canadian Forces Superannuation Act, which provides that a former spouse cannot be designated as a beneficiary. This left the second wife as the recipient on the husband's death. The first wife asked the court to order the second wife to act as trustee for the first wife and to pass on the pension payments when the cheques arrived in the mail. The court rejected this proposal and denied the first wife any claim to the pension. The second wife received the entire pension as the surviving spouse. (Dranoff 2001, p. 305)

If one spouse dies without a will ("intestate"), only the current legal spouse (and/or the individual's children) will benefit from the estate. However, if a spouse dies without ensuring support for either first or second family, the dependants may sue the estate for support (Dranoff 2001, p. 311).

In the event that a custodial parent remarries and subsequently dies, "there is no clear-cut rule as to whether the step-parent or the non-custodial parent gets custody" (Dranoff 2001, p. 309). She observes:

> In any custody fight between the surviving natural parent and the step-parent, the key issue is the child's relationship with each. The natural parent has no ownership rights to the child, and the step-parent has no possessory rights. The parental figure who is a more integral part of the child's emotional and daily life is likely to get custody. Regardless of which parent wins the case, the other is likely to have the right of access to the child. (p. 309)

Among factors that the court will take into consideration in determining whether the stepparent or natural parent will obtain custody are, (in no particular order of importance): blood ties (which, though important, are not assumed to always create a close bond between child and natural parent); the child's wishes; which relationship would minimize disruption and maximize continuity and stability in the child's life; the family setting and whether a connection to a large extended family or siblings exists; and preservation of a religious or bilingual heritage.

Margaret Mead (1972) pointed out that incest taboos serve the important function of allowing children to develop affection for and identification with other family members without risking sexual exploitation. However, the legal prohibition of "incest" under the Canadian Criminal Code focuses solely on sexual intercourse between blood relatives (e.g., mothers/ fathers with daughters/sons, siblings, grandparents and grandchildren, etc.). As such, it is not, by definition, applicable to equivalent behaviour committed by stepparents or stepsiblings (Giles-Sims 1997).[3]

---

3. It should be noted, however, that stepparents, like all others in Canada, can be charged with sexual assault, *sexual interference* (direct or indirect touching for a sexual purpose) of a person under the age of 14 years using a part of the body or an object; *invitation to sexual touching* (inviting, counselling, or inciting a person under the age of 14 years to touch (for a sexual purpose) the body of any person directly or indirectly with a part of the body or with an object; or *sexual exploitation*, committed when a person in a position of trust or authority towards a young person (i.e., a person between 14 and 18 years of age) or a person with whom the young person is in a relationship of dependency, engages in an act(s) of sexual interference or sexual touching.

STEPPARENTING: A CHALLENGE IN REMARRIAGE

For most first-married couples, the biggest problems are immaturity, sexual difficulties, and personal lack of readiness for marriage. For a remarried spouse, in contrast, stepchildren and finances present the greatest challenges (Visher and Visher 1996). One important study on a national American sample of black and white couples concluded that stepchildren are not necessarily associated with more frequent marital conflict. Moreover, the negative impact of stepchildren declines with the length of the remarriage (MacDonald and DeMaris 1995). Case Study 15.1 "My (Remarried) Family," illustrates these points. But even though stepchildren may not cause undue family conflict and can turn out to be well adjusted, being a stepparent (or married to one) often poses problems for the marriage.

Meanwhile, remarried couples often go on to have children together. This is more likely to occur if the woman has no children or only one from the first marriage. Because remarried women with two or more children are not so likely to have another child, researchers infer that the assumption that partners have children to validate their relationship is not true. Rather, women seem to be completing a family of desired size (Wineberg 1990).

However, Canadian research which used data from the General Social Survey and the National Longitudinal Survey of Children and Youth reports that "[t]he number of children already present has a negligible effect on the decision to have another child in a stepfamily. According to this research, "[t]he lower the age of the mother and of the youngest child in the step-family, the more likely a birth is to occur in the new union" (Statistics Canada, 2001).

Some experts have expressed concern about the impact on remarriage of having a child early in what is bound to be a complex adjustment (Bernstein 1997). Yet, the children a couple have from their new marriage seem to be associated with both increased happiness and stability (White and Booth 1985b). According to Cherlin:

> This is what we would expect, since children from a previous marriage expand the family across households and complicate the structure of family roles and relationships. But children born into the new marriage bring none of these complications.

Consequently, only children from a previous marriage should add to the special problems of families in remarriage. (1978, p. 645)

Some Reasons Stepparenting Is Difficult

One study investigating children's contact with absent parents found such contact to be significantly less likely when the biological parent had been succeeded by a stepparent or adoptive parent. "The interpretation [of the data] implies that noncustodial parents discard ties to their biological children with divorce, and ties are replaced through remarriage" as men become stepparents in another family (Seltzer and Bianchi 1988, p. 674).

"Crucial to children's overall well-being and development in remarriage and stepparent families, as in divorced and intact families as well, is the quality of parenting" (Arendell 1997b, p. 187). Meanwhile, there are special difficulties associated with bringing families together under the same roof. Stepsiblings may not get along because they resent sharing their room or possessions, not to mention their respective parents (Beer 1989; Bernstein 1997). Over the past 25 years, researchers and family therapists have consistently reported an array of challenges specific to stepfamilies. For instance, ties with the noncustodial parent may create a triangle effect that makes the spouse's previous marriage seem "more real" than the second union. The children, upset after visits with the noncustodial parent, can make life difficult for everyone else. Stepchildren in joint-custody arrangements (see Chapter 14) may regularly move back and forth between two households with two sets of rules. Family-rule differences, along with disruptions associated with one or more family members' coming and going, can be stressful (Kheshgi-Genovese and Genovese 1997). And the biological parents may feel caught between loyalties to the biological child and their desire to please their partner (Messinger 1976; Visher and Visher 1996; Bray 1999). More specifically, three major problem areas can be identified in remarried families: financial burdens, role ambiguity, and negative feelings of the children, who often don't want the new family to work (Kheshgi-Genovese and Genovese 1997).

FINANCIAL STRAINS Observers point out that the particular challenges that characterize remarriages

My (Remarried) Family

The following essay was written for a marriage and family course by a young student named David.

I'm writing this paper about my family. My family is made up of my family that I reside with and then my dad, stepmother, and half-sister that I visit. My family I reside with is who I consider my real family. We are made up of five girls and three boys, a cat and a dog, my mom and stepfather. The oldest is Harry, then down the line goes Diane, Barbara Ann, Kathy, Debi, Mel, Sharon, and myself. My sister Debi and I are the only kids from my mom's original marriage, so as you can see my mom was taking a big step facing six new kids. (My mom has guts!)

I still consider my dad "family", but I don't come into contact with him that much now. I would like to concentrate on my new "stepfamily," but I really don't like that word for it. My family is my family. My brothers and sisters are all my brothers and sisters whether they are step or original. My stepfather, although I don't call him "dad," is my father. My grandparents, step or original, are my grandparents. I can honestly say I love them all the same.

It all began when I was four. I don't remember much about my parents' divorce. The one real memory I have is sleeping with my dad downstairs while my sister slept upstairs with my mom....

My mom met my stepfather, Harry, through mutual friends who went to our church. I was in first grade, and I don't really remember much about their dating. All I knew was either these strange kids came over to my house or I went over to theirs. They were married in March 1976. I was five. At the reception I got to see all my relatives, old and new. When my parents left for their honeymoon, I began to cry. My aunt did a good job of consoling me.

After my parents got married, we moved. We didn't move into my stepfather's and his kids' house but to a new house altogether for everyone. I still live there. I love it there and probably will live in that area all my life.

I remember when we first went to look at the house. We live on a golf course. Mel, my brother (step), and sister (step), and I went out on this big sand trap to get a look around. The next thing I remember is getting pushed off and swallowing sand and not being able to breathe. I don't know if this was just an older brother thing or a new stepbrother thing. In any event, Mel came over and helped me get my breath back and all was fine. That was just the first of our many childhood altercations. There were lots of other fights over things from broken toys to slap shots in the face.

Well, we moved into our new house, and I had to change schools. I had to leave all my old friends and make some new ones. I did make new friends, and what was neat was that our two football teams played each other every year. So I got to play against my old friends with my new friends. When I got into high school, we were all united again. So I had gotten a new family, a new house, and a new school with new friends. I would have to say it was a major life transition.

As I grew up there were some tough times. I got picked on, but the youngest always does. But as I got older, it got to be less and less. And by the time I made it into high school, my long-time adversary, Mel, was beginning to be my best friend. I owe him a lot. During my childhood, my stepfather was extremely busy with work, and my dad was seldom around. It was Mel who taught me how to ride a bike and play basketball, baseball, and football. He also watched out for the younger kids, me and Sharon. I owe him a lot and would do anything for him.

Both my parents agreed about most issues (discipline, for example), and this led to smooth communication between our parents and us kids. The only thing detrimental I can think of that came out of being in a large family was that I had poor study habits as a young child. The problem was my stepfather can watch TV, listen to the radio, and prepare a balance sheet all at the same time. So he let his kids listen to the radio or watch TV while they did their homework. My mom didn't agree with

(continued)

My (Remarried) Family

(continued)

this, but it was too hard for her to enforce not watching TV with so many kids already used to doing it....

I love all my brothers and sisters very much and would do anything for them. It is neat to see them get married and have kids. I have three nieces and five nephews. It is very exciting to get the whole family together. A lot of my family, nuclear and extended, live in our area. My grandparents, aunts, and uncles, cousins, three sisters and their kids all live within 20 minutes of our house. Having roots and strong family connections are two things I'm very thankful for. These are things I received from my stepfather because if I lived with my dad, I would be on what I consider his nomadic journey: he moves about every three years.

I think I'm very lucky. I had a solid upbringing and relatively few problems. I owe my stepfather a lot. He has given me clothes and food, taught me important lessons, instilled in me a good work ethic, and seen to it that I get a good education—all the way through college. Without him a lot of these things would not be possible; I am grateful for everything he has done for me. I'm happy with the way things turned out, and I love my family dearly.

What might be a reason that David does not like to apply the term stepfamily to his own family? How does David's essay illustrate some potential problems specific to stepfamilies? Do you think David's parents have a stable marriage? Why or why not? Divorce and remarriage can be thought of as transitions and/or crises, the subject matter of Chapter 14. In what ways does David's essay illustrate meeting crises creatively, as discussed in that chapter? If you live in a stepfamily, how does David's experience compare with your own?

frequently begin with the previous divorce. This is particularly evident in the case of finances (Mason 1998). Frequently, money problems arise because of obligations left over from first marriages.

A remarried spouse (usually the husband) may end up financially accountable by law for children from the first marriage and responsible, although not legally, for supporting stepchildren. "Against the backdrop of laws requiring no financial contribution, many stepparents do in fact help to support the stepchildren with whom they reside, either through direct contributions to the child's personal expenses or through contributions to general household expenses such as food and shelter" (Mahoney 1997, p. 236).

Even though disproportionately more second wives are employed outside their homes than are first wives, remarried husbands report feeling caught between the often impossible demands of their former family and their present one. Some second wives also feel resentful about the portion of the husband's income that goes to his first wife to help support his children from that marriage. Or a second wife may feel guilty about the burden of support her own children place on their stepfather.

The emotional impact of the previous divorce also causes money problems. In one early study, some remarried wives reported stashing money away in case of a second divorce, and some remarried husbands refused to revise their wills and insurance policies for the same reason. For many couples, money became a sensitive issue that neither partner talked about (Messinger 1976).

ROLE AMBIGUITY   Another challenge to remarried families is that roles of stepchild and stepparent are neither defined nor clearly understood (Fine, Coleman, and Ganong 1999; Bray 1999). As one stepfamily expert explains, the role of the stepparent is precarious....The only way for a person to cement his or her legal tie to stepchildren is by adopting them, but this requires the cooperation of the noncustodial parent, which may not always be forthcoming. (Beer 1989, p. 11; Mahoney 1997)

Legally, the stepparent is a nonparent with no prescribed rights or duties (Mason 1998). Indeed, the term stepparent originally meant a person who replaced a dead parent, not an acquired quasi-kin who becomes an additional parent.

Uncertainties arise when the role of parent is shared between stepparent and the noncustodial natural parent (Beer 1992). What Bohannan pointed out over 25 years ago remains true today: Stepparents aren't "real" parents, but "the culture so far provides no norms to suggest how they are different" (Bohannan 1970a, p. 119; Fine, Coleman, and Ganong 1999). Not surprisingly, relatively low role ambiguity has been associated with higher remarital satisfaction, especially for wives, and with greater parenting satisfaction, especially for stepfathers (Kurdek and Fine 1991).

One result of role ambiguity is that society seems to expect stepparents and children to love each other in much the same way as biologically related parents and children do. In reality, however, this is not often the case, and therapists increasingly point out that stepparents and stepchildren should not necessarily expect to feel the same, as if they were biologically related (Visher and Visher 1996; Pasley et al. 1996).

Then too, stepchildren often don't react to their new stepparent as though he or she were the "real" parent. The irony of expecting "real" parent–child love between acquired kin is further compounded by the fact that stepparents are not generally "equal" in disciplining their stepchildren (Beer 1992). Actually, therapists advise that a stepparent's waiting through a period of family adjustment before becoming an active disciplinarian is usually a good idea (Visher and Visher 1996).

Moreover, adolescent stepchildren may have considerable family power (Kurdek and Fine 1995; Visher and Visher 1996). Our discussion of power in Chapter 10 focused on marital power, but children are a force to be reckoned with in any family. Giles-Sims' research on stepfamilies found mothers to have more power on both major and everyday decisions than did either stepfathers or adolescents. But in 12 percent of the

families, adolescents had more power than either parent, particularly in everyday decision making. "It is possible that the disruptive influence of adolescents on remarriage [citations omitted] is related to their power position" (Giles-Sims and Crosbie-Burnett 1989, p. 1076). Adolescents had less power in stepfamilies of greater longevity, reflecting either the breakup of the most troubled families or a gradual consolidation of the new stepfamily, which is evident over time in some (though not all) research (Papernow 1993). Of course, children's attitudes as well as their power can have an impact on the new marriage.

STEPCHILDREN'S HOSTILITY A third reason for the difficulty in stepparent–child relationships lies in children's lack of desire to see them work. After age two or three (Gamache 1997), children often harbour fantasies that their original parents will reunite (Burt and Burt 1996; Bray 1999). Wallerstein and colleagues' longitudinal research showed that five years after divorce, 30 percent of children or adolescents still strongly disapproved of their parents' divorce, and another 42 percent had reservations (Wallerstein and Kelly 1980). Children who want their natural parents to remarry may feel that sabotaging the new relationship can help achieve that goal (Kheshgi-Genovese and Genovese 1997). In the case of remarriage after widowhood, children may have idealized, almost sacred, memories of the parent who died and may not want another to take his or her place. "Stepchildren may feel they are betraying their biological parent of the same sex as the stepparent if they form a friendly relationship with the stepparent" (Kheshgi-Genovese and Genovese 1997, p. 256). As a result, stepchildren can prove hostile adversaries. This is especially true for adolescents.

For a young teenager, a parent's remarriage may prove more difficult to accept than was the divorce (Krementz 1984). At puberty, when children are discovering their own sexuality, it is remarkable how conservative they can expect their parents to be with regard to *their* sexuality. Adolescence can be a trying time for parents; teens can be impatient, self-centred, and argumentative. They can be especially distrustful, suspicious, and resentful toward a new parent, and they are sometimes verbally critical of a stepparent's goals, values, or personal characteristics. Anger displacement, described in Chapter 9, may also play a part in the stepparent's difficulty. Many adolescents blame their parents or themselves, or both, because the first marriage broke up. The stepparent becomes a convenient scapegoat for their hostilities. Then too, therapists point out that the desire of the remarried parents to create a cohesive family may conflict with an adolescent's normal need to express independence (Visher and Visher 1996; Kheshgi-Genovese and Genovese 1997).

Sociologists Lynn White and Alan Booth's (1985b) analysis of stability in remarriages, discussed earlier, considered one additional point: that family tension can be resolved by the child's rather than the partner's exit from the home. Speculating that children might be moved out by sending them to live with the other parent or forcing them to become independent, White and Booth found that indeed teenage children in stepfamilies leave home at significantly lower ages than do teens in intact families. For example, of teens age 16 and over in the first wave of the study, 65 percent of stepchildren were no longer living at home three years later, compared to 44 percent of children in intact families. White and Booth were working from the perspective of the married parents; qualitative data from Wallenstein's study of divorced families suggest that stepchildren often feel excluded and out of place in their new household, shut out by the tight bond between the remarried couple. They frequently report a sense of rejection, as they perceive the largest share of the parent's attention and energy going to the new marriage (Wallerstein and Blakeslee 1989). The following, from a student essay, helps to illustrate this process:

> I grew up with my biological mother and stepfather without much happiness. As I grew up, I never felt my stepfather ever showed me any love nor spent any time with me and I feel he influenced my mother to act the same. I can still remember only feeling like a financial burden to this man, and perhaps this is why I moved out of their house at 19 as opposed to 22 or 23 or after college like many of my friends.

Subsequent research (Goldscheider and Goldscheider 1998) supports the finding that stepchildren are likely to move away from home at younger ages than do children in first-marriage families, "especially to independence, cohabitation, or relatively early marriage."

Although virtually all stepchildren and stepparents are uncomfortable with some aspects of their family role, certain difficulties are more likely to trouble stepmothers, and others are more common to stepfathers. We'll look at each of these roles and the problems associated with them in more detail.

The Stepmother Trap

Clinicians and parents consider the role of stepmother to be more difficult than that of stepfather (Coleman and Ganong 1997). Some research by sociologists points to the same conclusion (White and Riedmann 1992; Aquilino 1994b; White 1994). One important reason for this is a contradiction in expectations for the role of stepmother:

> Whether mothers or stepmothers, ... the women's roles are very similar. Irrespectively, they take care of children and housework. The stepparent role does not expect her to do such tasks. On the contrary; the stepparent role expects a certain distance, the female role the opposite. Between the two roles there is a dilemma. One cannot be distant and close at the same time. (Levin 1997, p. 187)

Other explanations for the greater difficulty of the *residential* stepmother role include the fact that stepmother families, more than stepfather families, may begin after difficult custody battles and/or have a history of particularly troubled family relations. Then too, a remarried wife, more often than a remarried husband, may suddenly find herself a full-time stepmother, even though she had never anticipated this (Ihinger-Tallman and Pasley 1987, pp. 100–101). Phyllis Raphael (1978) refers to it as the **stepmother trap**: On the one hand, society seems to expect romantic, almost mythical loving relationships between stepmothers and children (Smith 1990). On the other hand, stepmothers are seen and portrayed as cruel, vain, selfish, competitive, and even abusive (remember Snow White's, Cinderella's, and Hansel and Gretel's?). Stepmothers are accused of giving preferential treatment to their own children (Coleman and Ganong 1997). As a result, writes Lucile Duberman, in our society "a stepmother must be exceptional before she is considered acceptable. No matter how skillful and patient she is, all her actions are suspect" (1975, p. 50). Consequently, stepmothers tend to be more stressed, anxious, and depressed than other mothers (Santrock and Sitterle 1987) and also more stressed than stepfathers (Pasley and Ihinger-Tallman 1988).

Conflicting expectations seem to come with the stepmother role, and relations between stepmothers and daughters seem particularly troubled. Some researchers find that stepmothers behave more negatively toward stepchildren than do stepfathers, and children in stepmother families seem to do less well in terms of their behaviour (Pasley and Ihinger-Tallman 1988). Yet, other studies indicate that stepmothers can and do have a positive impact on stepchildren (Santrock and Sitterle 1987; Smith 1990).

Still, some stepmothering situations often make the role especially complicated (Coleman and Ganong 1997). For example, special problems accompany the role of part-time or weekend stepmother when women are married to noncustodial fathers who see their children regularly. The part-time stepmother may try to establish a loving relationship with her husband's children only to be openly rejected, or she may feel left out by the father's ongoing relationship with his offspring.

Part-time stepmothers can feel left out not only by the father's relationship with his children but also by his continued relationship with his ex-wife. Noncustodial fathers can spend long hours on the telephone with their ex-wives discussing their children's school problems, orthodontia, illnesses, and even household maintenance and repairs.

One stepmother summed up the feelings of many others in her role: "I heard my stepson on the phone to his mother say to her, 'I love you,' and it hurt so much! You think you've come to terms with the whole situation, and then some tiny thing can make you feel completely thrown out again, after [several] years" (in Smith 1990, p. 62). (Box 15.1, "Some Stepparenting Tips," contains some evidence that may make stepparenting easier.)

Stepfathering

Men who decide to marry a woman with children come to their new responsibilities with varied emotions. The motivations may be far different from those that make a man assume responsibility for his biological children. "I was really turned on by her," said one stepfather of his second wife. "Then I met her kids." This sequence is fairly common, and a new husband may have both positive and negative reactions, ranging from admiration to fright to contempt. Research into the stepfather role suggests that stepfathers tend to view themselves as less effective than natural fathers view themselves (Beer 1992). Research also shows that stepfathers are more likely to feel positive about their parenting when their role expectations are clear and when their parenting behaviour meets these expectations (Fine, Ganong, and Coleman 1997). Meanwhile, stepfathers' relatively low appraisal of their own performance may reflect the special problems and discomforts they experience in the stepfathering role. We'll look at a few of these.

ODD MAN OUT IN AN IN-GROUP   A new stepfather typically enters a household headed by a mother. When a mother and her children make up a single-parent family, the woman tends to learn autonomy and self-confidence, and her children may do more work around the house and take more responsibility in family decisions than do children in two-parent households. These are positive developments, but to enter such a family, a man must work his way into a closed group (Cherlin and Furstenberg 1994). For one thing, the mother and children share a common history, one that does not yet include a new stepfather.

Living arrangements can cause a new husband to feel like the odd man out. One stepfather moved into his wife's house because she didn't want to move her children to a new school and neighbourhood. But, he said, he "never felt at home there.... I'd sit someplace, and then I'd move someplace else. I didn't have a place there. I couldn't find a place there for the first few months" (in Bohannan and Erickson 1978, p. 59). In fact, stepfathers do have less power relative to adolescent stepchildren when they move into the mother-child home (Giles-Sims and Crosbie-Burnett 1989).

THE HIDDEN AGENDA   The new husband-father may feel out of place not only because of his different background but also because he has a different perspective on family life. After years of living as a single-parent family, for instance, both the mother and children are likely to have developed a heightened concern over the fairness of chore allocation. A newcomer, especially if he assumes the traditional male role in a two-earner remarriage, may draw complaints that he is not contributing enough. This last bone of

Some Stepparenting Tips

Preparing to Live in Step

In a stepfamily at least three (and usually more) individuals find themselves struggling to form new familial relationships while still coping with reminders of the past. Each family member brings to the situation expectations and attitudes that are as diverse as the personalities involved. The task of creating a successful stepfamily, as with any family, will be easier for all concerned if each member tries to understand the feelings and motivations of the others as well as his or her own.

It is important to discuss the realities of living in a stepfamily before the marriage, when problems that are likely to arise can be foreseen and examined theoretically. If you are contemplating entering a steprelationship, here are some key points to consider:

1. Plan ahead! Some chapters of Parents Without Partners conduct "Education for Remarriage" workshops. Contact your local chapter or write to Parents Without Partners.

2. Examine your motives and those of your future spouse for marrying. Get to know him or her as well as possible under all sorts of circumstances. Consider the possible impact of contrasting lifestyles.

3. Discuss the modifications that will be required in bringing two families together. Compare similarities and differences in your concepts of child rearing.

4. Explore with your children the changes remarriage will bring: new living arrangements, new family relationships, and the effect on their relationship with their noncustodial parent.

5. Give your children ample opportunity to get to know your future spouse well. Consider your children's feelings, but don't allow them to make your decision about remarriage.

6. Discuss the disposition of family finances with your future spouse. An open and honest review of financial assets and responsibilities may reduce unrealistic expectations and resultant misunderstandings.

7. Understand that there are bound to be periods of doubt, frustration, and resentment.

Living in Step

Any marriage is complex and challenging, but the problems of remarriage are more complicated because more people, relationships, feelings, attitudes, and beliefs

contention is part of another source of potential conflict: the hidden agenda.

The **hidden agenda** is one of the first difficulties a stepfather encounters: The mother or her children, or both, may have expectations about what the stepfather will do but may not think to give the new husband a clear picture of what those expectations are. The stepfather may have a hidden agenda of his own. For example, he may see his new stepchildren as unruly and decide they need discipline.

A part of the stepchildren's hidden agenda involves the extent to which they will let the new husband play the father role. Children may be adamant in their distaste for or jealousy of the stepfather, or they may be ready and anxious to accept the stepfather as a new daddy. This last is particularly true of young children.

Stepfathers tend to be more distant and detached than stepmothers, especially when they have biological children of their own (Coleman and Ganong 1997). "It has been suggested by clinicians that such detached parenting behaviours are essential for improved relationships of stepparent and stepchild, especially during the early years of remarriage" (Pasley and Ihinger-Tallman 1988, p. 210), and stepfathers

are involved than in a first marriage. The two families may have differing roles, standards, and goals. Because its members have not shared past experiences, the new family may have to redefine rights and responsibilities to fit the individual and combined needs.

Time and understanding are key allies in negotiating the transition from single-parent to stepfamily status. Consideration of the following points may ease the transition process:

1. Let your relationship with stepchildren develop gradually. Don't expect too much too soon from the children or yourself. Children need time to adjust, accept, and belong. So do parents.

2. Don't try to replace a lost parent; be an additional parent. Children need time to mourn the parent lost through divorce or death.

3. Expect to deal with confusing feelings—your own, your spouse's, and the children's. Anxiety about new roles and relationships may heighten competition among family members for love and attention; loyalties may be questioned. Your children may need to understand that their relationship with you is valued but different from that of your relationship with your spouse and that one cannot replace the other. You love and need them both, but in different ways.

4. Recognize that you may be compared with the absent partner. Be prepared to be tested, manipulated, and challenged in your new role. Decide, with your mate, what is best for your children and stand by it.

5. Understand that stepparents need support from natural parents on child-rearing issues. Rearing children is tough; rearing someone else's is tougher.

6. Acknowledge periods of cooperation among stepsiblings. Try to treat stepchildren and your own with equal fairness. Communicate! Don't pretend that everything is fine when it isn't. Acknowledge problems immediately and deal with them openly.

7. Admit that you need help if you need it. Don't let the situation get out of hand. Everyone needs help sometimes. Join an organization for stepfamilies; seek counselling.

Source: U.S. Department of Health, Education, and Welfare 1978; Van Pelt 1985.

with such a parenting style do have better relationships with their stepchildren (citing Hetherington 1987). Young adult children may be mature enough to think of the new addition to the family primarily as their mother's husband rather than as a stepfather.

Discipline is likely to be a particularly tricky aspect of both the children's and the parents' hidden agendas. One study that compared university students' perceptions of stepfathers with biological fathers found that the students had "a less positive perception of stepfathers carrying out a disciplinary role than of [biological] fathers" (Claxton-Oldfield 1992, p. 386). A few problem areas are notable. There are now two parents rather than one to establish house rules and to influence children's behaviour, but the parents may not agree. A second problem can be the holdover influence of the biological father. To the new father, there may sometimes seem to be three parents instead of two—especially if the noncustodial father sees the children regularly—with the biological father wielding more influence than the stepfather. A third problem can be the development of children's responsibility and participation in decision making in single-parent families. The children may be unwilling to go back to being "children"—that is, dependent on and subject to adult direction. The new parent may view them as spoiled and undisciplined rather than mature.

A stepfather can react to these difficulties in finding a place in a new family in one of four ways. First, the stepfather can be driven away. Second, he may take control, establishing himself as undisputed head of the household, and force the former single-parent family to accommodate to his preferences. Third, he may be assimilated into a family with a mother at its head and have relatively little influence on the way things are done. And fourth, the stepfather, his new wife, and her children can all negotiate new ways of doing things (Isaacs, Montalvo, and Abelsohn 1986, 248–64). This is the most positive alternative for everyone, and it is best achieved by writing a personal remarriage agreement, addressed in the final section of this chapter. First, though, we'll review what family therapists can tell us about creating supportive stepfamilies.

CREATING SUPPORTIVE STEPFAMILIES

Therapists agree that creating a supportive stepfamily "is one of the most difficult tasks that families can face" (Wark and Jobalia 1998, p. 69). The task is difficult for two reasons. First, establishing a supportive stepfamily is a developmental process that takes time—from four to seven years (Papernow 1993; Gamache 1997). The unrealistic "urge to blend the two biological families as quickly as possible" can lead to disappointment when one or more adult or child members "resist connecting" (Wark and Jobalia 1998, p. 70).[4]

The second cause for difficulty in creating supportive stepfamilies stems from society's nuclear-family model monopoly, discussed earlier in this chapter. Remarrieds might try to approximate the nuclear-family model, but "this model does not work for most remarried families" (Wark and Jobalia 1998, p. 70) because stepfamilies are different from first-marriage families (Kelly 1996; Ganong and Coleman 1997). For instance, satisfying stepfamilies often evidence less loyalty and more permeable family boundaries than the nuclear-family model prescribes (Ihinger-Tallman and Pasley 1997; Visher and Visher 1996).

Moreover, the nuclear-family model monopoly can have a negative impact on adjustment to the stepparent role (Gamache 1997). "Few stepparents are truly prepared for the challenge the stepparenting role presents because it is not a role for which people are socialized. In the absence of such socialization, most stepparents assume they will function as [biological] parents" (Coleman and Ganong 1997, p. 109). However, a stepchild may not agree that the stepparent should behave as a biological parent (Fine, Ganong, and Coleman 1997).[5]

In fact, relatively low parental involvement by a stepparent characterizes many supportive stepfamilies. The key is not so much the level of stepparental involvement with a stepchild (for example, whether a stepparent sees him- or herself more as "parent" or as "friend"), but whether that level is mutually satisfactory (Ihinger-Tallman and Pasley 1997).

Meanwhile, counsellors remind remarrieds not to forget their couple relationship. Because stepfamilies—once called "instant families" (Phillips 1997)—have children from the start, spouses have little time or privacy to adjust to each other as partners. Furthermore, the relationship between biological parent and child predates the remarriage and may be stronger than the marital relationship. Therefore, "the couple relationship needs to be a priority in the family's life" (Kheshgi-Genovese and Genovese 1997, p. 260). Time away from the children can help, as can writing a remarriage agreement.

---

4. Papernow (1993) suggested a seven-stage model of the stepfamily development: (1) Fantasy—adults expect a smooth and quick adjustment while children expect that the stepparent will disappear and their parents will be reunited; (2) Immersion—tension-producing conflict emerges between the stepfamily's two biological "subunits"; (3) Awareness—family members realize that their early fantasies are not becoming reality; (4) Mobilization—family members initiate efforts toward change; (5) Action—remarried adults decide to form a solid alliance, family boundaries are better clarified, and there is more positive stepparent-stepchild interaction; (6) Contact—the stepparent becomes a significant adult family figure and the couple assumes more control; (7) Resolution—stepfamily achieves integration and appreciates its unique identity as a stepfamily.

5. Remarrieds and their children may have negative stereotypes of stepfamilies that result from our cultural view of the first-marriage family as best. "Avoidance of terms with negative connotations may help to reduce negative attitudes and expectations. The term 'stepchild' used as a metaphor for something that is unwanted or abused should be considered as inappropriate to use to illustrate a point as a racial or ethnic slur would be" (Ganong and Coleman 1997, p. 101).

Writing a Personal Remarriage Agreement

Reasons for writing a personal marriage agreement were discussed in Chapter 8. To varying degrees, these reasons also apply to remarriage agreements. But additional reasons make it useful to negotiate a personal remarriage agreement or at least to talk over the issues involved. (In many locations, prospective spouses can participate in remarriage preparatory courses to alert remarrying couples to common problems and to help them find ways to discuss inevitable conflicts.)

A second reason for negotiating a remarriage agreement is that, when not openly acknowledged, past rejection, loss, and guilt can undermine a new intimate relationship without either partner understanding what is happening. One way to counteract this situation is to share negative feelings about oneself, then to try to negotiate a relationship in which each partner feels as secure, as positive about himself or herself, and as comfortable as possible.

A third, related reason for writing a remarriage agreement is that, in their desire to make their marriage work, divorced and remarried spouses may feel too battle-scarred to open a can of worms. Accordingly, they may gloss over differences that need airing and resolution. As Chapter 9 points out, avoiding important conflicts is a serious mistake.

Finally, remarriage agreements are important because, as we have seen, society has not yet evolved an effective cultural model for these complex relationships. Unless they discuss their expectations, new mates may be unrealistic. Furthermore, the legal issues involved in remarriage are best given careful consideration before the marriage (Mason 1998). Inheritance is one: Do you want your money, property and/or joint survivor pension to go to your new spouse or your children? What does the law in your jurisdiction permit on this? (Mahoney 1997).

Custodial parents may want their new spouse to adopt the children. This involves a waiver of parental rights by the biological parent, who may not wish to do so. Recent court cases have addressed this issue; without the natural parent's consent, the court will usually only proceed in extreme circumstances (e.g., if the children do not know the natural parent at all, if the natural parent is insane, incompetent, has disappeared from his/her children's lives for a long time period, etc.).[6] The consent of the custodial parent (the potential adoptive parent's spouse) is also required in all Canadian provinces. As well, in most provinces, child welfare authorities may conduct a home study and prepare a submission to the court on whether or not the placement is in the child's best interests. In the event that adoption takes place, most statutes include a statement specifying that, for all purposes, including but not limited to rights of inheritance, the relationship between the adopted child and parent becomes "as if the child had been born to that parent in lawful wedlock" (Dranoff 2001, p. 309).

Rights of stepparents to visitation or even custody of a stepchild in the event of death or divorce from the child's parent is also a crucial issue, when so many people become closely attached to stepchildren. It is important to indicate in a will or other statement that the biological parent would like his/her children's relationship with a stepparent preserved through visitation, if that is the case (Mahoney 1997).

The most general point here is that people who remarry should not assume that they can do some of these things without checking with a lawyer. Individuals may also want to become active in relevant public policy areas that concern them.

Chapter 8 suggests some questions to address when creating a personal marriage agreement; the majority of these apply to second marriages as well. Remarriage agreements, like other marriage agreements, should be revised as situations and partners change.

Divorce and remarriage have become commonplace in our society. As families becomes more and more diverse, "it is becoming increasingly important [for family therapists and policy makers] to be able to respond to social change in a way that does not pathologize an ever increasing number of families in our communities" (Gamache 1997, p. 65). Moreover, therapists generally agree that "it is neither the structural complexity nor the presence/absence of children in the home *per se* that impacts the marital relationship. Rather, the ways in which couples interact around

---

6. In Newfoundland and the Yukon, the law would view the following as evidence that a parent was a "concerned" parent and that the adoption should not proceed without that parent's consent: s/he has regularly exercised visitation rights or, at least, attempted to do so; s/he has regularly provided child support.

these issues are the key to understanding marital relationships in general and marital relationships in remarriages specifically" (Ihinger-Tallman and Pasley 1997, p. 25). Interacting in positive ways in remarriages and stepfamilies involves making knowledgeable choices. Then too, we have seen that living in a stepfamily can be stressful. The next, and final, chapter explores family stress, and coping with it, in detail.

IN SUM

Although remarriages have always been fairly common in Canada, patterns have changed. Remarriages now more frequently follow divorce rather than widowhood. The courtship process by which people choose remarriage partners has similarities to courtship preceding first marriages, but the basic exchange often weighs more heavily against older women, and homogamy tends to be less important.

Second marriages are usually about as happy as first marriages, but they tend to be slightly less stable. An important reason is the lack of a cultural script. Relationships in immediate remarried families and with kin are often complex, yet there are virtually no social prescriptions and few consistent legal rules to clarify roles and relationships.

The lack of cultural guidelines is clearest in the stepparent role. Stepparents are often troubled by financial strains, role ambiguity, and stepchildren's hostility. Marital happiness and stability in remarried families are greater when the couple have strong social support, high expressiveness, a positive attitude about the remarriage, low role ambiguity, and little belief in negative stereotypes and myths about remarriages or stepfamilies. Personal remarriage agreements can help to establish an understanding where few social norms exist. "Stepfamily therapists now use a model that assumes that stepfamilies are normal and can be successful in a variety of ways, enriching the lives of their members" (Burt and Burt 1996, p. 182).

Key Terms

blended family
coparenting
cultural script
double remarriages
hidden agenda
incomplete institution
nuclear-family model
    monopoly

quasi-kin
remarriage
remarried families
single remarriages
stepmother trap

Study Questions

1. Discuss the similarities and differences between courtship before remarriage and courtship before first marriage.

2. How is the basic exchange in remarriage tipped against women? Compare this with the basic exchange in first marriages.

3. How might remarriage rates be different if divorced women were not at such an economic disadvantage, compared with married women?

4. Why are remarriages somewhat less stable than first marriages even though they are about as likely to be happy as are intact first marriages?

5. The remarried family has been called an incomplete institution. What does this mean? How does this affect the people involved in a remarriage? Include a discussion of kin networks and family law. Do you think this situation is changing?

6. What evidence can you gather from observation and/or your own personal experience to show that stepfamilies: (a) may be more culturally acceptable today than in the past, and (b) remain negatively stereotyped as not as functional or as normal as first-marriage, nuclear families?

7. What are some problems faced by both stepmothers and stepfathers? What are some problems particularly faced by stepfathers? Why might the role of stepmother be more difficult than that of stepfather? How might these problems be resolved or alleviated?

8. What are some reasons for writing a personal remarriage agreement? Is it more or less important to write a remarriage agreement than a first marriage agreement? Why? Discuss some topics that could be important to consider in a remarriage agreement but not in a first marriage agreement.

Suggested Readings

Booth, Alan, and Judy Dunn, eds. 1994. *Stepfamilies: Who Benefits? Who Does Not?* Hillsdale, NJ: Lawrence Erlbaum. A collection of papers on stepfamilies by recognized authorities in the field.

_____. (Ed.). 1997. *Divorce and Remarriage: International Studies.* New York: Haworth Press. A collection of articles from Australia, Chile, Israel, Japan, and Norway, among other countries.

Ganong, Lawrence H. and Marilyn Coleman. 1994. *Remarried Family Relationships.* Thousand Oaks, CA: Sage. The authors have done significant research on remarriage and stepfamilies. Part of a series on "close relationships," this book presents a comprehensive view of remarried families and includes recent research.

Hetherington, E. Mavis. (Ed.). 1999. *Coping with Divorce, Single Parenting, and Remarriage: A Risk and Resiliency Perspective.* Mahwah, NJ: Lawrence Erlbaum. Edited collection of research reports and literature reviews by prominent pioneer of longitudinal research in this field.

On the Net

1) The Stepfamily Foundation
   Statistics, research reports, policy issues, general information, and advice for professionals and stepfamily members alike.
   http://www.stepfamily.org

2) Family Help in Canada:
   http://www.focusas.com/Canada.html

3) For a 9-step approach to building healthy stepfamilies see:
   http://www.weber.edu/chfam/topics/nine.steps.html

4) B.C. Council for Families Parenting:
   http://www.bccf.bc.ca/learn/par_stepfam.html

5) The Stepfamily Foundation: Resources
   http://www.stepfamily.ca/resources.htm

Managing Family Stress and Challenges

GOD, GRANT ME THE SERENITY
ACCEPT THE THINGS I C
CHANGE, THE CO
THE THI

... TO

... ANNOT

... OURAGE TO CHANGE

... GS I CAN, AND THE WISDOM

TO KNOW THE DIFFERENCE.

THE SERENITY PRAYER

amilies are more likely to be happy when they work toward mutually supportive relationships, and when they have the resources to do so. Nowhere does this become more apparent than in a discussion of how families manage stress and challenges.

Family stress is a state of tension that arises when demands tax a family's resources. Responding to the needs of aging parents while simultaneously negotiating children's adolescent years is stressful for a family. Especially for women, being a member of the "sandwich generation" with both children and aging parents to care for is a source of family stress. Families experience financial pressures, like finding adequate housing on a poverty budget or financing children's education on a middle-class income. Managing full-time jobs while parenting children (discussed in Chapter 13) is a common source of family stress.

Family stress calls for family adjustment. In response to financial pressures, middle-class family members might adjust their budget, cutting back spending on clothing, recreation, travel, or eating out. They might cope with time pressures by reducing their responsibilities or by arranging for someone outside the immediate family to help. Many times, though, there is no easy way to remove pressures of time, money, or responsibilities. If solving the problem by adding resources or helpers or by subtracting responsibilities is not possible, family coping takes a more social psychological form: expressing feelings, doing things that give the family pleasure or establishing rituals that offset tension, even using humour. But constant stress can be wearing to family members and family harmony.

There is another kind of family stress that is not so much the chronic challenge of demands on a family, but rather an event that changes things. Each such event is a **crisis**—a crucial change in the course of events, a turning point, an unstable condition in affairs. A crisis is a sharper trauma to a family.

The definition of crisis encompasses three interrelated ideas:

1. Crises necessarily involve change.

2. A crisis is a turning point with the potential for either positive or negative effects, or both.

3. A crisis is a time of relative instability.

Family crises share these characteristics. They are turning points that require some change in the way family members think and act in order to meet a new situation (Hansen and Hill 1964; McCubbin and McCubbin 1991).

When people live together over a period of time, they develop patterns of relating to one another. Family members are fairly well aware of where each fits in and what each is expected to do; the family functions smoothly (or, at least, predictably) when each member behaves according to the expectations of the others. Any change that disrupts these expectations marks the onset of a crisis. Sometimes, the event that precipitates a crisis is dramatic, unexpected, and unfortunate. The death of a child or a spouse, diagnosis of a serious illness, a breadwinner's loss of employment, a nonmarital pregnancy, a family member's imprisonment—all of these require major alterations in the way family members think, feel, and act.

Positive changes can precipitate crises, too. Suddenly getting rich by winning the lottery or, much more commonly, moving to another city or another province because of a promotion are examples.

Family **transitions**—expected or predictable changes in the course of family life—precipitate family stress and/or crises. Having a first baby or sending the youngest child off to university, for example, tax a family's resources and bring about significant changes in family relationships and expectations. Throughout the course of family living all families are faced with stress, crises, and transitions.

This chapter examines how families cope with stress and challenges. We'll look at family transitions, along with some ways families can face stress and crises more creatively. We'll discuss how families define or interpret stressful situations and how their definitions affect the course of such events. To begin, we'll ask what precipitates family stress or crisis?

WHAT PRECIPITATES FAMILY STRESS?

Something must happen to precipitate a crisis. That something is what social scientists call a **stressor**, a precipitating event that creates stress. Stressors vary in both kind and degree, and their nature is one factor that affects how a family responds to crisis.

Types of Stressors

There are several types of stressors, as Figure 16.1 shows. Some involve the *loss of a family member* either permanently, such as through death or desertion, or temporarily, such as through hospitalization or imprisonment. (Box 16.1, "Death of a Child," discusses this family stressor.) A family member can be lost through divorce but can still remain a part of the family psychologically, socially, and economically (Boss 1999). The ambiguity of the boundaries of a postdivorce family can be stressful in itself, as Chapters 14 and 15 illustrate.

A precipitating event can also involve the *addition of a member* or members to the family through birth, adoption, or marriage. Not only are in-laws (and increasingly stepparents and stepsiblings) added through marriage but also a whole array of *their* kin. Sociologist Pauline Boss (1980) described these additions and losses as *family boundary changes*; that is, family boundaries are shifting or contracting to include or exclude certain members. The addition of family members can bring into intimate social contact people who are very different from one another in values and life experiences.

Sudden change in the family's income or social status can also be a stressor. Most people think of stressors as being negative, and some sudden changes are, such as traffic accidents. But positive changes, such as a move to a better neighbourhood or a promotion can cause stress too. One author of this text knows a family that became wealthy suddenly when a product they had invented and manufactured on a small scale became popular nationally. This family hired a consultant to teach them how to behave in their new social circumstances. Deciding such matters as whether it would be appropriate for the children to continue to take babysitting jobs occupied a great deal of family energy.

Ongoing *unresolved conflict* among members over *familial roles* can be a stressor. As husbands' and wives' roles change, conflicts can arise over child-care responsibilities, for example, or over division of household labour. This point is well illustrated in Chapters 10 and 13. Deciding how adolescents should be disciplined for rules violations can bring to the surface divisive differences over parenting roles. The role of an adult child living with parents is often ambiguous and can be a source of unresolved conflict. If children of teenagers or of divorced adult children are involved, the situation becomes even more challenging. Watching a married child go through family conflict can be a stressor (Hall and Cummings 1997).

Caring for a dependent or differently-abled family member is a stressor. Being responsible for an adult sibling with mental illness or retardation is an example (Seltzer et al. 1997a). Parents' raising a mentally or physically disabled child is another example. Due mainly to advancing medical technology, the number of dependent people and the severity of their disabil-

Loss of a family member

Addition of a family member

Sudden change

Conflict over family roles

Caring for a disabled or dependent family member

Demoralizing event

Daily family hassles

FIGURE **16.1**

| Types of stressors.

The likelihood of death in our society influences how we define a death in the family. In a society such as ours in which death is statistically infrequent, not all deaths, but only unnecessary, preventable, or "premature" ones, are highly problematic (Parsons and Lidz 1967). Under the mortality conditions that existed in this country in the 1800s, parents defined the loss of a child, social historians believe, as an almost natural or **predictable crisis** and, consequently, suffered less pain than do parents today. Today, in comparison, the probability of a child dying is small. To illustrate this change, demographer Robert Wells asks readers to imagine themselves on a village street in 1750:

> As you sit by the roadside, you notice a [funeral procession] coming toward you.... The coffin is ... that of a child. This, also, you learn is not unusual, because children commonly died during this time period. The second thing that surprises you is that the individuals following the coffin to the graveyard seem to accept their loss relatively calmly. You will later learn that since so many children die at a relatively early age, parents do not invest significant amounts of emotional energy in their children until they have survived the first five or ten years of life. In addition, their religious beliefs encourage many colonists to view death not as an ending, but as a release from earthly miseries and sins.
>
> As you watch the procession go by, you realize that about half the people in the procession are children, including several you later learn are brothers and sisters of the deceased. (Wells 1985, pp. 1–2)

Family members who lose a child today, by comparison, have not had much opportunity to witness death, dying, or grieving (Kübler-Ross 1979). The death—defined as unnatural, irrational, uncalled-for—is an uncommonly painful event, especially in a rational progress- and action-oriented society such as ours. The long-term effects of grieving such a loss can negatively affect marital intimacy (Gottlieb, Lang, and Amsel 1996). When an only child dies, parents must adjust to the sudden loss of an important role as well as grieving their child (Talbott 1996, 1997).

Loss of potential children through miscarriage, still-birth, or infant death has the added strain of ambiguity. Attachment to the fetus or newborn may vary greatly so that the loss may be grieved greatly or little. Add to that the generally minimal display of bereavement customary in Canada and the omission of funerals or support rituals for perinatal (birth process) loss, and "all these ambiguities mean that a family may have to cope with sharply different feelings among family members ... [and] the family as a whole may have to cope with the fact that they as a family have a very different reaction to loss than do the people around them" (Rosenblatt and Burns 1986, p. 238). In fact, a study of 55 instances of perinatal loss found that grief was still felt by some parents 40 years later, whereas the majority reported no long-run grief and some had always defined their loss as a medical problem rather than a child death. Men and women may have different reactions to their pregnancy loss and a different sensibility about the expression of feelings (Stinson et al. 1992).

This study, because it dealt with an especially ambiguous situation, discovered a truth about death that is probably more general: "Loss through death may represent more than the person who has died" (p. 251). Here, "what is grieved may be the child, but it may also be subsequent childlessness, the absence of a desired additional child, an unpleasant medical or marital experience associated with the loss, a loss of innocence, the end to feelings of invulnerability, a loss of faith that life is fair, or something else" (p. 251).

Many of the frail elderly depend upon, or live with, family members. While care is often given with fondness and love, it also can bring stress, conflicting emotions, and great demands on time, energy, and finances.

ities have steadily increased over recent decades. For example, more babies survive birth defects, and more people survive serious accidents; but they may require ongoing care and medical attention. Parents may need to see their children through bone marrow, kidney, or liver transplants, sometimes requiring several months' residence at a medical centre away from home. Adults with advanced AIDS may return home to be taken care of by family members. Caring for a terminally ill or differently-abled family member is, of course, another stressor—for young children, who may exhibit behaviour problems as a response—as well as for other adults in the household (LeClere and Kowalewski 1994; Seltzer and Heller 1997).

Stressors can be *demoralizing events*—those that signal some loss of family morale. Demoralization can accompany the stressors already described. But this category also includes job loss, unwanted pregnancy, poverty, homelessness, having one's child placed in foster care, juvenile delinquency or criminal prosecution, scandal, family violence, mental illness, alcoholism and drug abuse, and suicide, among others. Chapter 12 addresses grandparents' raising grandchildren as often associated with demoralizing events.

Physical illness can be demoralizing if it carries attributions of family dysfunction (anorexia nervosa or bulimia, for example) or is socially stigmatized (AIDS, for example). Sexually transmitted diseases with less serious health implications may nevertheless present a threat to the marriage. Alzheimer's disease or head injury, in which a beloved family member seems to have become a different person, is heartbreaking.

Finally, *daily family* hassles are stressors (Fisher, Fagot, and Leve 1998). Here are some examples:

- Tension between two or more family members, not involving you.

- Not enough money needed to buy something for the family.

- Looking for a job—calling, applying, interviewing, etc.

- Work situation is stressful.

- Someone in the family is in a bad mood.

- Disagreement with children over homework.

- Child comes home very upset.

- Child's school contacts you because of poor work, bad behaviour, tardiness, or truancy.

- Family member did not do fair share of work around the house.

- Did not receive expected money or had an unexpected bill.

- Children's quarreling among themselves.

- Someone criticized how you are handling your children.

- Not have enough money to pay the bills.

- Family schedule disrupted because of something unexpected.

- You feel overworked at home.

Daily family hassles can pile up, increasing family stress.

Stressor Overload

A family can be stressed not just by one serious, chronic problem but also by a series of small, unrelated stressors that build on each other too rapidly for the members to cope effectively (McCubbin, Thompson, and McCubbin 1996). Sociologist and marriage counsellor Carlfred Broderick explains:

> Even small events, not enough by themselves to cause any real stress, can take a toll when they come one after another. First an unplanned pregnancy, then a move, then a financial problem that results in having to borrow several thousand dollars, then the big row with the new neighbours over keeping the dog tied up, and finally little Jimmy breaking his arm in a bicycle accident, all in three months, finally becomes too much. (Broderick 1979b, p. 352)

Even though it may be difficult to point to any single precipitating factor, an unremitting series of relatively small stressors can add up to a major demoralizing crisis. In today's economy, characterized by longer working hours, two paycheque marriages and less job security, **stressor overload** may be more common than in the past. (Box 16.3 "Stressor Pile-Up Among Single-Mother Families in Homeless Shelters," illustrates stressor overload.)

Characteristically, stressor overload creeps up on people without their realizing it.

In general, stressors are less difficult to cope with when they are expected, brief in duration, and gradually improve over time. We will look next at family transitions as stressors.

FAMILY TRANSITIONS AS STRESSORS

The transitions that individuals and families make over time have been explored throughout this text. Over the course of family living, people may form cohabiting relationships, marry, become parents, divorce, remarry, redivorce, remarry again, and make transitions to retirement and widow- or widowerhood. All these transitions are stressors. Many are discussed in detail elsewhere in this text, and we won't repeat those discussions here. This section focuses on family transitions that occur mostly in life's second half: transitions to the sandwich generation and to the empty nest, retirement, and widow- or widowerhood.

The Sandwich Generation

Several years ago journalists and social scientists began to write about the **sandwich generation**: middle-aged (or older) individuals, usually women—although not always (Harris and Bichler 1997)—who are sandwiched between the simultaneous responsibilities of caring for their dependent (sometimes young adult) children and aging parents. The sandwich generation experiences all the hectic task juggling discussed in Chapter 13 on work and family. Motivated by both filial responsibility and, often, affection, middle-aged children care for their aging parents "because they're my parents" (Stein et al. 1998). However, stress builds as family members handle not only employment and child care but also parent care.

We can expect that responsibility for attending elderly parents will become an increasingly common experience for several reasons. First, the number of elderly in our population is growing. In 1951, there were slightly more than a million Canadians 65 years of age and over, compared to 3.5 million in 1996. As well, in 1996, there were about three-quarters of a million Canadians over the age of 80—double the level of a quarter of a century ago. Consider as well that while in 1991 there were 3700 Canadians a 100 years of age or over, this number—which is the triple that reported in 1971—is expected to double by 2021. According to estimates prepared by Statistics Canada, there could be as many as 25 000 centenarians in Canada by 2031! (Statistics Canada 1998).

Not just the number of elderly, but also their proportion of the total population is growing. In 1951, about eight percent of Canada's total population was 65 or older. By 1996, the proportion was 12 percent. Projections are that by the year 2011, seniors aged 75 and over will represent almost seven percent of Canada's population and over 46 percent of the population aged 65 and over (Health Canada 1999, p. 164). By 2031, it is estimated that the proportion of seniors will be more than 20 percent of the total Canadian population (Statistics Canada 1998, p. 72).

Because individuals are living longer (with estimates suggesting that by 2016, life expectancy will be 78.5 years for men and 84 years for women), and because the majority of families are smaller than in the past, the ratio of middle-aged adult children to elderly parents is declining. In other words, there are fewer adult siblings available to share in the care of their elderly parents.

As we noted in an earlier chapter, until the ages of 90 and above, most men are married. At age 85 to 89, about half (54.7 percent) of the men are married versus 11.9 percent of women. At 75 to 79 years old, about three-quarters (73.0 percent) of the men and just over a third (35.4 percent) of the women are married (Statistics Canada 1997). One implication of these data is that most elderly men will have a spouse for assistance if their health fails, while the majority of elderly women will not (Nelson and Robinson 2002, pp. 421–422).

As people live longer, long-term chronic illness, disability, and dependency become more likely. In 1995, about a quarter of a million Canadians lived in long-term health care institutions, the majority 65 years of age or older (Statistics Canada 1998). Although the elderly live in a variety of contexts, depending on their health and financial status and only a small minority of elderly Canadians reside in long-term health care institutions (e.g., about one-quarter of men and slightly more than a third of women over the age of 85), a family member's decision to move an elderly parent there is often a crisis situation in itself (Seltzer et al. 1997b; Bromley and Blieszner 1997). Nursing home residents are not typical of the elderly—they are likely to be widowed, or quite ill, or over 80, or without family to take care of them (Kinsella and Taeuber 1993).

An estimated seven percent of Canada's 3 795 123 seniors currently require institutional care and 10.3 percent require some form of home care. However, the demand for both publicly funded long-term care beds and home care exceeds their supply. In 1999, for example, there were about 7000 seniors on waiting lists for long-term care beds at publicly funded institutions in the province of British Columbia. In that year in Ontario there were 11 000 seniors on waiting lists for publicly funded home care (Arnold 1999). In Canada, seniors are the "largest consumers of publicly-funded home-care services"; in 1996–97, five percent of seniors aged 65 to 75 and 17 percent of those aged 75 and over used home-care services (Health Canada 1999, p. 166).

In 1997, Canadians aged 45 to 54 were most likely to provide some unpaid senior care and Canadians aged 55 to 64 most likely to provide 10 hours or more unpaid hours of care to seniors (Health Canada 1999). Women, as we noted earlier, are more likely than men are to provide some senior care (19 percent versus 14 percent) with the largest disparity found among those providers aged 45 to 54 (27 percent of women and 19 percent of men) (Health Canada 1999). As such, it is relatives—usually daughters, although among Asians the eldest son may be designated by custom (Kamo and Zhou 1994)—who themselves are often in their 50s and 60s, who face the difficulties of providing care (Atchley 1997, pp. 217–19; Chappell 1990).

In fact, a trend today is for the dependent and differently-abled of all ages to be cared for at home, if possible (Freedman 1993). Families take responsibility for complicated care regimens (such as administering intravenous drugs) that have traditionally been handled only in hospitals by health care professionals. This situation places added demands on family members' time, energy, emotional commitment, and other resources. This is particularly true for the primary caregiver, who averages seven to nine hours per day in caregiving (Mehdizadeh and Atchley 1992) and often exhibits symptoms of depression (Gerstel and Gallagher 1993; Dwyer, Lee, and Jankowski 1994). With budget cutbacks resulting in the closing of hospital beds, an increase in the number of day surgeries, a decrease in the number of days that patients stay at public hospitals, and an increase in outpatient treatments (Health Canada 1999), the sandwich generation may face added stresses.

The Postparental Period

The postparental stage of family life first came to attention about 30 years ago through the value-laden term **empty nest**. It was assumed that mothers would feel lonely and depressed once their children had grown and left home.[1] However, changes in our society that offer middle-aged women opportunities

---

1. The empty nest problem was highlighted in 1972 by sociologist Pauline Bart's study of women who were hospitalized for depression. She found that many of these women had invested much of their lives in being mothers and that they felt lost, unneeded, and depressed once the youngest child left home. Bart also found that women who devoted their time and energy to alternative roles or activities, such as employment, school, volunteer work, or their marital relationship, were better able to adjust (Bart 1972).

to return to work or school have made this a satisfying period of life for many. Current cohorts of women are likely to have continuous work patterns, or close to it. Indeed, now, having young-adult children who do not leave the nest as early as their parents had anticipated—or who return—can be viewed as a potential crisis. The old stereotype of the depressed empty nest mother is also ironic because fathers can have transition pains, too (Nelson and Robinson 1999; Robinson and Barret 1986).

The postparental period is a time when couples can return their attention to each other and reorganize their lives. But these couple relationships differ from newly married ones because family history plays an important role in giving meaning to their married lives. Intergenerational and other kin contacts are usually very satisfying to middle-aged and older people (Atchley 1997). But the older generation is sometimes at a loss concerning how to maintain affectionate and open communication with children and to deal with practical matters while avoiding interfering in their children's lives (Brubaker 1991).

In any case, the need to readjust the couple's relationship and roles after parenthood is a challenging situation. The outcome is more positive when parents have other meaningful roles, such as work, school, or other activities, to turn to. In fact, this is a transition with a high likelihood of a positive outcome because marital satisfaction often increases when couples have time, energy, and financial resources to invest in their couple relationship (Ishii-Kuntz and Secombe 1989; Binstock and George 1996). Still, a frequent strain on couples during this period is imposed by the failing health of their aging parents. So even if their children have left home—and assuming they have no differently-abled dependents to care for—the psychic and economic costs of caring for one's parents may make the empty nest stage far from a period of new freedom. It may instead be a period of new family responsibilities.

Later in life, spouses may be caregivers to their mates, with women particularly likely to provide such care to their spouses. Caregiving for a spouse recuperating from a hospital stay or other health condition creates stress. A qualitative study of 75 spouse caregivers found that those in longer, emotionally close marriages with little ongoing conflict evidenced better overall well-being (Townsend and Franks 1997). Some studies that examined sex differences find men to be less stressed, perhaps because their socialization prepares them to distance themselves somewhat or because they receive more help from relatives, whereas women are more burdened and depressed (Brubaker 1991). Other studies find few gender differences in stress, social support, time spent in caregiving, or emotional strain, although women do experience some strain to their health (Miller 1990).

Some couples divorce in middle age or later. Consequently, there may be less income and fewer contacts with friends and kin; divorced men are especially likely to be isolated from family (Keith 1989; Brubaker 1991). Divorce (and/or remarriage) of older parents can disrupt family rituals, such as celebrations of religious holidays, weddings, births, and birthdays (Pett, Lang, and Gander 1992).

During later life, morale and well-being frequently derive from nonfamily contacts—from friends and neighbours. Health is an important factor in morale in later life, and it has a substantial impact on marital quality (Wickrama et al. 1997; Booth and Johnson 1994), family and other social contacts (Atchley 1997).

Retirement

While most older people retire, some do not—and many of those who don't are employed into their 70s and 80s. Having a negative attitude toward retirement is one reason for continuing to work. Another reason, particularly applicable to single women, is being unable to afford to retire (Atchley 1997).

Some—although not all—retired couples experience financial deprivation, finding themselves in tighter straits than are their children and grandchildren. In 1996, the elderly and children were the groups most likely in Canada to be classified as low income. However, this was not true for elderly people living in families. In that year, the elderly in families were actually the *least* likely to be classified as low income (eight percent), while children under the age of 18 were the most likely.

In the last four decades, seniors in Canada have benefited from rising incomes. While in 1951, the average senior earned slightly more than half the income of Canadians of working age, in 1995, the average senior earned $20 400 or almost $84 for every $100 earned by working-aged Canadians (Statistics Canada 1998). Because of income security programs such as the Guaranteed Income Supplement, the Old Age Security pension, and the Spouse's Allowance, very few Canadian seniors have to rely on welfare. Between 1980 and 1996, the number of older Canadians who fell below Statistics Canada's low-income cutoff dropped substantially. However, one in five seniors (mostly unattached women) is still likely to be living in a low-income situation (National Council of Welfare 1998). Women are far more likely to be the surviving spouse (Barringer 1992a) and far less likely than men to have access to additional private-sector (i.e., nongovernmental) pensions such as those provided by employers to employees (Boyd 1995; Townson 1995). In 1997, among Canadians 65 to 68 years of age, about 50 percent of Canadian men—but only 25 percent of women—received some income from a private pension (Marshall 2000, p. 11) (see Figure 16.2). "Certain groups, such as First Nations women and women with disabilities, are particularly unlikely to be covered by private pension plans, and the likelihood of poverty is particularly pronounced among elderly women with disabilities" (Nelson and Robinson 1999, p. 483).

We tend to think of retirement as an abrupt event, but many people retire gradually by steadily reducing their work hours (Atchley 1997). A study of well-educated men over age 65 found that today many of them leave and return to the labour force several times before retiring permanently (Elder and Pavalko 1993). Even when it is not an abrupt event, retirement represents a great change for individuals and couples, particularly for males who have embraced the traditional masculine gender role. But retirement will soon be an event experienced by men who are, on the whole, less traditional in their roles. Women in their traditional roles do not mark a sharp change of activities in their 60s, but in the future the vast majority of women will take the formal step from employment to nonemployment. One small study of 228 couples (Smith and Moen 1998) found that, both for employed wives and husbands, the decision to retire is influenced by one's spouse. However, wives are more often motivated by their husband's decision to do so than the other way around (Townson 1995).

We know most about the retirement experience of employed men who were unlikely to be sharing domestic roles. Accustomed to seeing himself as principal breadwinner and head of the family, the traditional retired husband faced a major role loss. A retired husband might devote more attention to family roles such as being a companionate husband and grandparent and might spend more time in homemaking tasks. Doing this can be problematic, however, for men who cling to the traditional masculine role that

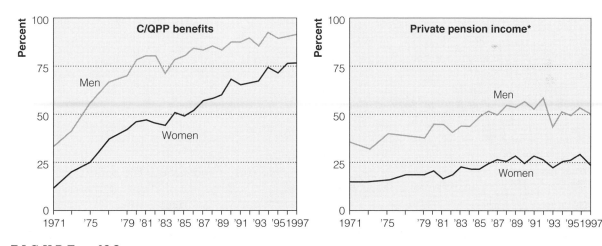

FIGURE 16.2

Despite improvements, proportionately fewer women receive pension benefits. (Source: Statistics Canada, "Perspectives on Labour and Income," Cat. No. 75-001, Vol. 12, No. 04, Dec. 2000.)

highly values work and achievement (Aldous 1978). Role flexibility is important to successful adjustment.

A husband's retirement forces homemaking wives to adjust as well. Full-time homemakers may find it difficult to share the house that has become their exclusive territory during the day. In this situation, role flexibility for women is also important, and "both husbands and wives are happier in the aging period when they emphasize mutual help, companionship, and affection rather than trying to maintain the segregation of daily role activities characteristic of the preretirement period" (Aldous 1978, p. 204). Mutuality and continuity of sharing support seem to predict good adjustment for all couples, including traditional ones (Brubaker 1991).

There seems to be no overall relationship between retirement and marital satisfaction. Research to date suggests that simultaneous retirement or the retirement of the wife before the husband goes most smoothly in terms of the marital relationship (Lee and Shehan 1989; Brubaker 1991). Ironically, the better a couple adjusts to retirement together, the more painful may be a forthcoming transition to widow- or widowerhood.

Widowhood and Widowerhood

Adjustment to widow- or widowerhood is an important family transition that often must be faced in later life. Because women's life expectancy is longer and because older men remarry far more often than women do, widowhood is significantly more common in our society than is widowerhood. Nevertheless, we are reminded that, "Widowhood is often thought to be something that happens primarily to women, yet in 1996 about one-quarter of the male population aged 80 to 84 was widowed" (Statistics Canada 1997). Widowhood is usually a permanent status for older women. Indeed, for some women, widowhood may last longer than the child-rearing stage of life.

Typically, widow- and widowerhood begin with **bereavement**, a period of mourning, followed by gradual adjustment to the new, unmarried status and to the loss. Mates who lose a partner suddenly and without warning tend to have more difficulty adjusting to the loss than do those who had warning, such as with a long illness (Newman 1979; Novak 1997). If the spouse's dying has been prolonged,

much of the mourning may have preceded the actual death, so that grieving after the death is less intense. In an early study of widows, about half said they had recovered from their husband's death within a year, although 20 percent said they had never gotten over it and did not expect to (Lopata 1973).

> If all widowed women must attempt to come to terms with living without a partner with whom they have shared daily living....those women whose identity has been forged in the "Wife of" role....will feel particularly unsettled by the death of a spouse....For these women, widowhood alters their identity now to being a "Former Wife of." Other women must grapple with defining themselves as an independent person in their own right. (Nelson and Robinson 1999, p. 488)

Bereavement manifests itself in physical, emotional, and intellectual symptoms (Figley et al. 1998). Recently widowed people perceived their health as declining and reported depressive symptoms (Brubaker 1991). Emotional reactions include anger, guilt, sadness, anxiety, and preoccupation with thoughts of the dead spouse. These responses tend to diminish over time and are characteristic of both men and women. Social support and activities with friends, children, and sometimes siblings facilitate adjustment (Atchley 1997, pp. 324–333).

Although research reveals few differences in other realms, there is some evidence that being single in old age is more detrimental, physically and emotionally, for men than for women (DiGiulio 1992; McPherson 1994; Peters and Liefbroer 1997). Women more often have social support outside the family, whereas men are typically more dependent on family for support. But

> men and women experience similar physical and emotional difficulties initially, but after a time seem to cope with the loss of a spouse.... [B]oth establish new [single] lifestyles based on their past patterns of interaction. For both, their financial [and health] situation is related to their feelings of well-being. (Brubaker 1991, p. 233)

A spouse's death brings the conjugal unit to an end—often a profoundly painful event—yet, widow- and widowerhood and the other family transitions we have been discussing are stressors that can often be anticipated and planned for. As we will see, anticipating and planning ahead for crises whenever possible is an important aid to meeting them effectively and creatively. First, however, we will examine the course of a family crisis.

THE COURSE OF A FAMILY CRISIS

A family crisis ordinarily follows a fairly predictable course, similar to the truncated roller coaster shown in Figure 16.3. Three distinct phases can be identified: the event that causes the crisis, the period of disorganization that follows, and the reorganizing or recovery phase after the family reaches a low point. Families have a certain level of organization before a crisis; that is, they function at a certain level of effectiveness—higher for some families, lower for others. In the period of disorganization following the crisis, family functioning declines from its initial level. Families reorganize, and after the reorganization is complete (1) they may function at about the same level as before; (2) they may have been so weakened by the crisis that they function only at a reduced level; or (3) they may have been stimulated by the crisis to reorganize in a way that makes them more effective.

At the onset of a crisis, it may seem that no adjustment is required at all. Family members may be numbed by the new or sudden stress and, in a process of denial, go about their business as if the event had not occurred.

Gradually, however, they begin to assimilate the reality of the crisis and to appraise the situation. Then the **period of disorganization** sets in.

The Period of Disorganization

At this time, family organization slumps, habitual roles and routines become nebulous and confused, and members carry out their responsibilities with less enthusiasm. Typically, and legitimately, they begin to feel angry and resentful.

Expressive relationships within the family change, some growing stronger and more supportive perhaps, and others more distant. Sexual activity, one of the most sensitive aspects of a relationship, often changes sharply and may temporarily cease. Parent–child relations may also change.

Relations between family members and their outside friends, as well as extended kin network, may also change during this phase. Some families withdraw from all outside activities until the crisis is over; as a result, they may become more private or isolated than before the crisis began. As we shall see, withdrawing from friends and kin often weakens rather than strengthens a family's ability to meet a crisis.

At the nadir, or low point, of family disorganization, conflicts may develop over how the situation should be handled. For example, in families with a seriously ill member, the healthy members are likely either to overestimate or to underestimate the sick person's incapacitation and, accordingly, to act either more sympathetically or less tolerantly than the ill member wants (Strauss and Glaser 1975; Pyke and Bengtson 1996). Reaching the optimal balance between nurturance and encouragement of the ill person's self-sufficiency may take time, sensitivity, and judgment.

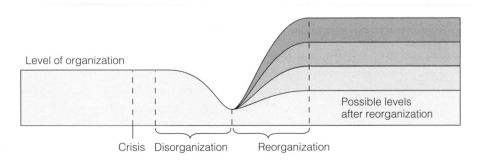

F I G U R E **16.3**

Patterns of family adaptation to crisis. (Source: Adapted from Hansen and Hill 1964, p. 810.)

During the period of disorganization, family members face the decision of whether to express or to smother any angry feelings they may have. As Chapter 9 points out, people can express their anger either in primarily bonding or in alienating ways. Expressing anger as blame will almost always sharpen hostilities. When family members opt to repress their anger, they risk converting it into destructive "anger insteads" or allowing it to smolder, thus creating tension and increasingly strained relations. How members cope with conflict at this point will greatly influence the family's overall level of recovery.

Recovery

Once the crisis hits bottom, things often begin to improve. Either by trial and error or (when possible) by thoughtful planning, family members usually arrive at new routines and reciprocal expectations. They are able to look past the time of crisis to envision a return to some state of normalcy and to reach some agreements about the future.

Some families do not recover intact, and end in divorce. Divorce can be seen both as an adjustment to family crisis and as a family crisis in itself (Figure 16.4).

Other families stay together, although at lower levels of organization or mutual support than before the crisis. As Figure 16.3 showed, some families remain at a very low level of recovery, with members continuing to interact much as they did at the low point of disorganization. This interaction often involves a series of circles in which one member is viewed as deliberately causing the trouble and the others blame and nag him or her to stop. This is true of many families in which one member is an alcoholic or otherwise chemically dependent, an overeater, or a chronic gambler, for example. Rather than directly expressing anger about being blamed and nagged, the offending member persists in the unwanted behaviour. (Box 16.2, "Alcoholism as a Family Crisis," defines stages in the response of an alcoholic's family to the crisis.)

Some families match the level of organization they had maintained before the onset of the crisis, whereas others rise to levels above what they experienced before the crisis (McCubbin 1995). For example, a family member's attempted suicide might motivate all family members to reexamine their relationships. With the help of professional mental health and marriage therapists, they might develop a personal marriage contract that is more supportive to both.

Reorganization at higher levels of mutual support can also result from less dramatic crises. For example, partners in midlife might view their boredom with their relationship as a challenge and revise their lifestyle to add some zest—by traveling more or planning to spend more time together rather than in activities with the whole family, for example.

Now that we have examined the course of family crises, we will turn our attention to a theory of family crisis and adaptation.

THEORIES OF FAMILY CRISIS AND ADAPTATION

Some years ago sociologist Reuben Hill proposed the ABC-X family crisis model, and much of what we've already noted about stressors is based on Hill's insights and research (Hill 1958; Hansen and Hill 1964). The **ABC-X model** (Figure 16.5) states that A

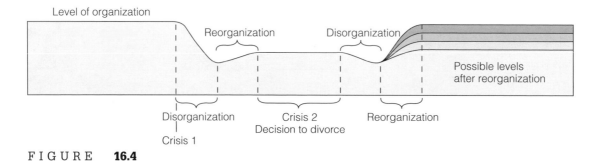

FIGURE **16.4**

Divorce as a family adjustment to crisis and as a crisis in itself
(Source: Adapted from Hansen and Hill 1964.)

(the stressor event) interacting with B (the family's ability to cope with a crisis, their crisis-meeting resources) interacting with C (the family's appraisal of the stressor event) produces X (the crisis) (see Sussman, Steinmetz, and Peterson 1999).

Building on this ABC-X model, Hamilton McCubbin and Joan Patterson (1983) advanced the double ABC-X model to better describe family adjustment to crises. In Hill's original model the "a" factor was the stressor event; in the **double ABC-X model**, "a" factor becomes "Aa," or "family pile-up." **Pile-up** includes not just the stressor but also previous family strains (Olson and McCubbin 1983) and hardships induced by the stressor event. A parent's losing a job, for example, would be a stressor; it would soon be accompanied by hardships as bills begin to accumulate. Prior strains are the residuals of family tension that linger from unresolved stressors or that are inherent in ongoing family roles such as being a single parent or a spouse in a two-career family. Stressors and strain are connected to the family life cycle stage, as are the family resources available to cope with the stressor event (McCubbin and McCubbin 1991; Florian and Dangoor 1994).

When a family experiences a new stressor, prior strains that may have gone unnoticed come to the fore. For example, ongoing-but-ignored family conflict may intensify when parents or stepparents must deal with a child who has joined a criminal gang or is abusing drugs. As another example, financial and time constraints typical of single-parent families may assume crisis-inducing importance with the addition of a stressor, such as caring for an injured child.

Stressors and hardships call for family coping and management skills. When family members do not have adequate resources for coping and managing— either because of prior strains or because of the character of the stressor event itself—stress emerges.

The pile-up concept of family-life stressors and strains (similar to the concept of stressor overload described earlier) is important in predicting family adjustment over the course of family life. Social scientists have hypothesized that an excessive number of life changes and strains occurring within a brief time, perhaps a year, are more likely to disrupt a family (Olson and McCubbin 1983, p. 120). Pile-up renders a family more vulnerable to emerging from a crisis at a lower level of effectiveness (McCubbin and McCubbin 1989). (See Box 16.3, "Stressor Pile-up Among Single-Mother Families in Homeless Shelters.")

We have examined various characteristics of A, the stressor event, in the double ABC-X model. Next we will look at C, how the family defines or appraises stressor(s). We'll look at B, the family's crisis-meeting resources, after that.

Appraising the Situation

The way in which a family interprets a crisis-precipitating event can, at times, have as much or more to do with members' ability to cope as with the character of the event itself (Patterson and Garwick 1994; McCubbin and McCubbin 1991). For example, a study of families faced with caring for an aging family member (Pyke and Bengston 1996) found that some families (more individualistic ones) felt more ambivalent or negative about having to provide care. More collectivist-oriented families, however, saw caregiving as one more chance to bring the family together. Several factors influence how family members define a crisis.[2] One is the nature of the precipitating event itself. Another is the degree of hardship or the kind of problems the stressor creates. Temporary unemployment is less a hardship than is a layoff in an area where there are few job prospects or a loss of a job at age 55. Being victimized by a crime is always a stressful event, but coming home to find one's house burglarized is certainly less traumatic than being robbed at gunpoint or raped.

A third factor that influences appraisal of a stressor is the family's previous successful experience with crises, particularly those of a similar nature. If family members have had experience in nursing a sick member back to health, they will feel less bewildered and more capable of handling a new, similar situation.

2. While we are discussing the family's definition of the situation, it is important to remember the possibility that each family member experiences a stressful event in a unique way. "These unique meanings may enable family members to work together toward crisis resolution or they may prevent resolution from being achieved. That is, an individual's response to a stressor may enhance or impede the family's progress toward common goals, may establish or reduce family cohesion, may encourage or interfere with collective efficacy. From this perspective, what is important is not the 'family's' definition of the stressor but an understanding of individual perspectives regarding stressful situations, how these perspectives relate to behaviour, and the influences of members' perspectives in combination" (Walker 1985, pp. 832–33).

When a family member becomes an alcoholic, the course of the crisis is similar to that described in this chapter. One authority, Joan Jackson, has described seven stages in the course of alcoholism. Not all alcoholic families move through all seven stages; instead, many become mired in the early stages.

Stage 1: Attempts to Deny the Problem

Alcoholism rarely emerges full blown overnight. It is usually heralded by widely spaced incidents of excessive drinking, each of which sets off a small family crisis. The alcoholic may arrive home late with a ticket for reckless driving, for instance. Both mates try to account for such an episode as perfectly normal.

Between drinking episodes, both mates feel guilty about the alcoholic's behaviour. (It is common for nonalcoholic family members to blame themselves either consciously or unconsciously for the alcoholic's drinking.) Gradually, the drinking problem and any other problems in the marriage may be side-stepped.

It takes some time for the sober spouse to realize that his/her partner's drinking is neither normal nor controllable. Meanwhile, to protect themselves from embarrassment, the family may begin to eliminate outside activities and to become socially isolated.

Stage 2: Attempts to Eliminate the Problem

This stage begins when the family finally defines the drinking as not normal and tries to stop it alone. Lacking clear-cut guidelines, the nonalcoholic partner makes trial-and-error efforts. The family gradually becomes so preoccupied with finding ways to keep the alcoholic sober that they lose sight of all other family goals. Almost all thought becomes centred on alcohol. Meanwhile, family isolation peaks.

Stage 3: Disorganization

This is a stage of "What's the use?" Nothing seems effective in stabilizing the alcoholic, and efforts to change the situation become sporadic. The family gives up trying to understand the alcoholic. The children may no longer be required to show the alcoholic parent affection or respect. The sober partner, recognizing his or her own inconsistent behaviour, may become concerned about his or her sanity.

Stage 4: Attempts to Reorganize in Spite of the Problem

Here the sober partner takes sole family leadership. The alcoholic is ignored or assigned the status of a recalcitrant child and is increasingly excluded from family activities. Hostility diminishes and is replaced by feelings of pity, exasperation, and protectiveness.

The sober mate seeks assistance from public agencies and self-help groups such as Al-Anon. With an emerging new support network, the sober partner gradually regains his or her sense of worth. Some families remain at this stage indefinitely. But despite greater stabilization, subsidiary crises multiply. The alcoholic may become violent or get arrested for drunken driving. Each crisis temporarily disrupts the new family organization, but the realization that the events are caused by alcoholism often prevents the complete disruption of the family.

Stage 5: Efforts to Escape the Problem

When some major subsidiary crisis occurs—desertion or unemployment, for example—the family feels forced to take survival action. At this point many couples separate or divorce. First, however, the sober partner has to resolve the mental conflicts about deserting a sick mate. Separating from the alcoholic is further complicated by the fact that when the decision is about to be made, the alcoholic often gives up drinking for a while.

Some other events have made separation possible, however. By this time the sober partner has learned that the family runs more smoothly without the alcoholic. Taking over control has bolstered the sober mate's self-confidence, and his or her orientation has shifted from inaction to action.

Stage 6: Reorganization of the Family

Here the family reorganizes without the alcoholic. For the most part this goes relatively smoothly. The family has long ago closed ranks against the alcoholic and now feels free of the minor disruptions the drinker created in the family. Reorganization is impeded, however, if the alcoholic continues to attempt reconciliation or believes she or he must "get even" with the family for leaving or "kicking me out."

Stage 7: Reorganization with Sobriety

If the partners have not divorced by the time the alcoholic recognizes that he or she has a drinking problem and makes serious efforts to stop drinking, hope is mobilized. The family attempts to open ranks again to give the alcoholic the maximum chance for recovery.

If treatment is successful, the couple can expect many other problems to appear, however. Both mates may have unrealistic expectations; the family may harbour built-up resentments; and it may require a major adjustment for both the spouse and the children to again respect the alcoholic as a responsible adult. Gradually, perhaps through counselling or membership in groups such as Alcoholics Anonymous and Al-Anon, the difficulties may be overcome and family adjustment and reorganization with sobriety can be achieved.

Source: Jackson 1958, pp. 90–98.

Believing from the start that a crisis is surmountable makes adjustment somewhat easier. Family members' interpretations of a crisis event shape their responses in subsequent stages of the crisis. Meanwhile, the family's crisis-meeting resources affect its appraisal of the situation.

Crisis-Meeting Resources

A family's crisis-meeting resources (B) comprise its abilities to prevent a stressor from creating severe disharmony or disruption.

The personal resources of each family member (for example, intelligence, problem-solving skills, physical and emotional health) are important here. At the same time, the family *as family* or family system has a level of resources, including bonds of trust, appreciation, and support (family harmony); sound finances and financial management and health practices; positive communication patterns; healthy leisure activities; and overall satisfaction with the family and quality of life (McCubbin and McCubbin 1989). Rituals can be family resources. A study of alcoholic families found that adult children of alcoholics who came from families that had maintained family dinner and other rituals (or who married into families that did) were less likely to become alcoholics themselves (Bennett, Wolin, and Reiss 1988; Goleman 1992a).

All of these factors are components in the **resiliency model of family stress, adjustment, and adaptation** (see Figure 16.5). Although this model does not use the ABC-X designations, it has the same elements: a stressor event, family appraisal of the stressor event, and the family's resources for coping with a stress, strain, or transition (McCubbin and McCubbin 1991).

The resiliency model is a more complex model, adding an analysis of the family system and a typology of families to the basic elements. Simplifying the McCubbins' detailed analyses, which appear in various publications, we can say that family systems and types can be low or high in vulnerability (McCubbin and McCubbin 1991). Families that cope well with stress are **resilient families**, who emphasize mutual accep-

Stressor Pile-up Among Single-Mother Families in Homeless Shelters

There are many causes of homelessness among single-mother families. Some are created when mothers flee abusive relationships. Other causes include job loss, eviction due to inability to pay rent or other conflicts with landlords, a partner's substance abuse, and conflict with relatives or friends with whom the family was staying prior to becoming homeless.

The average age of children in homeless families is six years. While the majority are preschoolers, many school-age children are homeless as well. Many homeless mothers have not graduated from high school and have inconsistent work histories, along with high rates of depression. Typically, they have had traumatic childhoods: Homeless mothers are more likely than other low-income women to have lived in foster care, a group home or institution; run away from home; been physically or sexually abused; and lived on the street or other public places. "They also tend to have small social networks that they turn to and exhaust before entering shelters" (Lindsey 1998, p. 244).

Social scientist Elizabeth Lindsey (1998) analyzed interviews from 17 Georgia and North Carolina mothers who had stayed in a homeless shelter with at least one of their children. "The sample size was determined by the criterion of redundancy, that is, interviewing stopped when additional interviews ceased to generate new data" (p. 245).

Participants ranged in age from 19 to 52 years. Twelve were African-American and five, white. The families had from one to five children, between six months and 16 years of age; they had stayed in shelters between two weeks and eight months. Some had been homeless more than once.

Lindsey noted that, while these families had many past and present stressors, they also evidenced important strengths: pride, determination, a positive orientation, clarity of focus, commitment to parenting and other personal relationships, finding purpose in helping others, and a moral structure used to guide their lives. "It is also important to note that women who enter shelters with their children have managed to maintain enough stability to avoid having the children placed into foster care" (p. 244).

These families obviously benefited from being sheltered. However, shelter life itself often added stress, partly because shelters usually hold families to the same rules as singles. For example, the mothers objected strongly to requirements that they and their children leave the shelter during the day, regardless of the weather: "How can this mother go out and look for a job or even look for a place to live when she's got three kids, and it's raining, or it's cold?" (p. 248).

Other problematic rules involved bedtimes, mealtimes, keeping their children quiet, and the requirement that children be with their parents at all times:

> They have a bedtime for the children, 8:00.... And if you can't get them in the bed, they require that you put them in the room if you can, and keep them occupied until they're sleepy. [T]hey need those rules with that many people (p. 249)

> We had to eat the main meal at 4:00 ... [and you] couldn't bring any food in there.... Little boys eat all the time, and they don't eat their main meal of the day at 4:00, 4:30 in the evening. (p. 248)

tance, respect, and shared values. Family members rely on one another for support. Generally accepting difficulties, they work together to solve problems with members, feeling they have input into major decisions. Resilient families foster predictable family routines, rituals, and other times together (McCubbin and McCubbin 1989).

Vulnerable families are more prone to negative outcomes from crisis-provoking events than are resilient families. Having a lower sense of common

[My son] was more or less suffocated because you couldn't really be a child.... You could sit there and play with their toys, look at their books, and watch TV up to a point, but just to get wild, like a child likes to do, you couldn't do it.... Basically, they were to be seen and not heard. (p. 248)

It was tough on him, it was real tough on him. My son's ADD [diagnosed with Attention Deficit Disorder], and there he had to be quiet and still, play quietly in the bedrooms, no running around. (p. 250)

The kids is [sic] supposed to be with you at all times. [Even] at 15, they supposed to be with you at all times. ... You're supposed to know where your kid is at all times, but it's very hard to do, ... to keep your child 24-7 when you're here (p. 247)

Other stressors occurred as well. One mother told of a single male resident's "getting fresh with my older girl" (p. 249). Another mother expressed concern about changes in her son:

My 12-year-old, oh gosh! He was so depressed.... His personality changed, and I had to learn how to deal with that. And it was so tough because he had always been such a sweet child ... but his attitude became rotten. He was fed up with the rules.... (p. 250)

However, Lindsey found that perhaps the most troublesome aspect of shelters for the mothers was the prohibition against any type of corporal punishment. "Parents were expected to make their children behave but were not allowed to use their main form of discipline. At times, shelter staff corrected the mothers in front of their children, undermining their parental authority" (p. 248).

Some mothers described the stress they felt. One said she was:

in a daze.... I really didn't know where to turn. My nerves were gone. I couldn't sleep. I was about afraid to close my eyes, and I didn't feel safe when I first got there.... I had a three-year-old, and I was like panicking. "What am I going to do?" (p. 249)

Beginning in their own childhoods, these mothers' stresses had gradually piled-up, or accumulated.

Lindsey's findings were not all negative. Many of the younger children liked the security and attention they received from shelter residents and staff. Some mothers said that they and their children had grown closer at the shelter. Nevertheless, this research shows that shelter life itself can add to stressor pile-up for homeless families.

Suggestions for lessening family stress while at homeless shelters include allowing parents as much control as possible over bedtimes and eating arrangements, as well as offspring day care and keeping shelters open to families during the day. Furthermore, since "punitive approaches toward parents who rely on corporal punishment do not necessarily prevent parents from spanking," shelter staff need to be supportive in helping parents learn and use other forms of discipline (Lindsey 1998, p. 251).

purpose and feeling less in control of what happens to them, they often cope with problems by showing diminished respect or understanding for one another. Hesitant to depend on the family for support and understanding, members may avoid one another.

Vulnerable families are also less experienced in shifting responsibilities among family members and are more resistant to compromise. There is little emphasis on family routines or predictable time together (McCubbin and McCubbin 1989). As

This family has survived a flood that greatly damaged their home. Families with strong crisis-meeting resources work together so as not to make the crisis they are experiencing even worse.

described in Chapter 15, a main task in stepfamilies is to move from vulnerability to resiliency.

Noting that a family's typology and the family system affect how positively it faces a crisis enables us to predict or explain its good ("bonadjustment") or bad ("maladjustment") adjustment to the stressor event. At the end point of the resiliency model, the family either successfully adapts or becomes exhausted and vulnerable to continuing crisis. The next section discusses factors that help families to meet crises creatively.

MEETING CRISES CREATIVELY

Meeting crises creatively means that after reaching the nadir in the course of the crisis, the family rises to a level of reorganization and emotional support that is equal to or higher than that which preceded the crisis. Most families have some handicaps in meeting crises creatively, however.

The typical family is under a high level of stress at all times. Providing family members with emotional security in an impersonal and unpredictable society is difficult even when things are running smoothly.

Family members are trying to do this while holding jobs and managing other activities and relationships.

Determining Factors

For some families, breaking up is the most beneficial (and perhaps the only workable) way to reorganize. Other families stay together and find ways to meet crises effectively. What differentiates families that reorganize creatively from those that do not?

A POSITIVE OUTLOOK   In times of crisis, family members make many choices, one of the most significant of which is whether to blame one member for the hardship (Judge 1998). Casting blame, even when it is deserved, is less productive than viewing the crisis primarily as a challenge.

Put another way, choosing a positive outlook helps a person or a family to meet a crisis constructively. Electing to work toward developing more open, supportive family communication—especially in times of conflict—also helps individuals and families meet crises constructively. Families that meet a crisis with an accepting attitude, focusing on the positive aspects

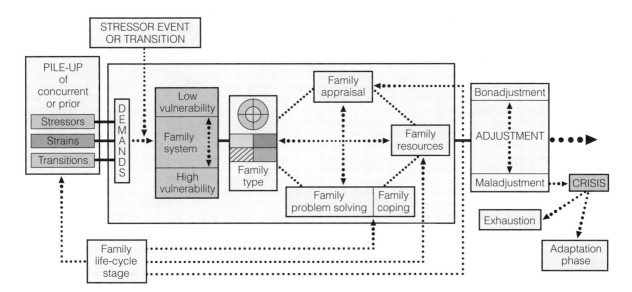

FIGURE 16.5

The resiliency model of family stress, adjustment, and adaptation. This model elaborates on an earlier family crisis model, the double ABC-X model of family stressors and strains. Components of the double ABCX model include: a stressor event (A); the family's appraisal of the stressor event (B); the family's crisis-meeting resources (C); the doubling of these components through pile-up; and the experience or avoidance of crisis (X).

In the resiliency model these letters no longer identify components. Family system characteristics and typology are added concepts, and the family's resilient adjustment or its experience of crisis have been developed in greater detail. Demands on the family from prior or concurrent stressors and strains and family life-cycle transitions have been included to better predict and understand the family's vulnerability to the stressor event. (Source: Adapted from Figure 1.2, Components of the Adjustment Phase of the Resiliency Model, McCubbin and McCubbin 1991, p. 5; see their article for more detail including other components added in a Family Adaptation Phase, Figure 1.5, p. 16.)

of their lives, do better than those that feel they have been singled out for misfortune. For example, many chronic illnesses have downward trajectories, so that both partners can realistically expect that the ill mate's health will only grow worse. Some couples are remarkably able to adjust to this, "either because of immense closeness to each other or because they are grateful for what little life and relationship remains" (Strauss and Glaser 1975, p. 64). Ironically, it is often easier for family members to focus on the positive when they accept their own and each other's negative feelings.

SPIRITUAL VALUES AND SUPPORT GROUPS Some researchers have found that strong religious faith is related to high family cohesiveness (Bahr and Chadwick 1985) and helps people meet crises, partly

because it provides a positive way of looking at suffering. A spiritual outlook can be fostered in many ways, including Buddhism, Judaism, Christianity, Islam, and other religious or philosophical traditions. Self-help groups, such as Al-Anon for families of alcoholics, can also help people take a positive approach to family crises.

OPEN, SUPPORTIVE COMMUNICATION Families whose members interact openly and supportively meet crises more creatively. For one thing, freeflowing communication opens the way to understanding. For example, divorcing parents who interact cooperatively do their children—and themselves—a great favour as Chapter 14 points out. As another example, a study of husbands with multiple sclerosis showed that the better-adjusted husbands believed

From Stepfather to Father: Meeting Crises Creatively

At the groom's dinner the night before my marriage to Jack, there was much good-natured bantering. My children were happy that my grief over the death of their father had finally run its course. They savoured the sight of their mother filled with joy over a new love.

Jack, a genuine, never-been-married bachelor, received their mock gratitude for taking me off their hands. They congratulated him on his good fortune in acquiring them as family now that they were all grown up rather than during their teen years when they had been really rotten. I laughed with them, remembering those earlier times. At the nuptial Mass the next morning, I thanked God for this man and all he would bring to the family.

Honeymoon's End

Jack was elated over this new family of his—a wife, four children aged 19 to 24, a son-in-law, and two grandchildren—though he did wince the first few times the little ones called him "Grumpa." That discomfort eased when I reminded him that he would now be sharing his life with a grandmother.

The new relationship between Jack and his step-family began smoothly enough. We left the offspring behind at their various apartments and campuses when we relocated.... because of Jack's job. But a series of harried phone calls caused the rosy family picture to fade. One of the brood had spent tuition money repairing a car that she had not maintained. Then another neglected to wrap water pipes at the family homestead before a fierce storm. The frozen lines ruptured, requiring major replacement work.

Another's car died. Though I would have preferred to send flowers, a loan was more to the point. We weren't optimistic about repayment. As each new problem unfolded, I saw the light dim in Jack's eyes. These kids he had gotten so easily were not all grown up.

Meanwhile, the tales he brought home about co-workers' children bore a common thread: achievement!

One father, with all due modesty, reported on the winning touchdown made by his high school junior, whose coach, of course, saw potential for the pros. Another's daughter had graduated Phi Beta Kappa and was breezing through a prestigious M.B.A. program.

Before Jack became part of the "Dad Derby," such tales hadn't affected him. But as a new parent, he was listening to the daily achievement litany as other parents paraded the most recent honours bestowed upon brilliant kids. And Jack had no one to brag about. I felt responsible both for my kids' failures and for his disillusionment.

The Truth

In despondent moments I thought about family friends back home. They had all had problems similar to mine with nearly-adult children. How did I know that? I wondered. Ah, yes, I'd heard the misadventures from other mothers—not fathers.

The next time we dined with friends of Jack's, I paid close attention. It was the men who reported accomplishments. Mothers mostly remained quiet or cautiously changed the subject. On another dinner date, the conversation predictably progressed to children, theirs then mine—"our children," I hastily corrected. But what wondrous tale could I spin about my splendid, overachieving children? What story could I tell that would make Jack glow with pride over his new heirs?

A little voice in my heart said, "Forget it, Mary. It won't work." So I told the truth—the latest dumb thing that had happened back home.

There was just the briefest moment of silence, a collective sigh, and then came the response. "You think that's bad? Well, wait till you hear about our kids' latest exploits." I sat back and enjoyed watching Jack's stunned expression as the stories spilled across the table. See, I wanted to say, mine aren't so bad. At least they're normal. I finally felt vindicated.

Family Triangle

There was still a bumpy road ahead for this family. My kids were my kids. Jack was accepting them as that and was beginning to acknowledge that they really were pleasant young people. And they thought he was great as Mom's husband. But there remained distance.

Toward the end of the first year, one son quit college and decided that ...where Mom and Jack lived had better job potential than the old hometown. He was taking us up on the promise that our home would always be his. This was the kid who had quit talking to the family for five years when he reached 13. The same one who couldn't wait to be old enough to get away from his parents.

Now there was a triangle in the house, a disruption of the still-delicate relationship Jack and I were working out together. I felt caught between the two males, serving as a messenger, carrying subtle little missives between them.

When the star boarder found a good job within a few weeks, I was relieved. But, of course, he had to stay on for a bit to build financial reserves. I finally gave him a little nudge; it was time he settled into a place of his own. I had been struggling on the family bridge long enough.

Trial by Fire

Two years later the same son was stricken with a rare form of meningitis. It was scary watching his body and his mind atrophy while neurologists struggled to diagnose him. Meanwhile, I fell into near despair, terrified that his brain would be destroyed before they found a treatment.

Jack, a fitness buff, decided that disuse had caused the wasting away of his stepson's body and mind. "He needs to get out of that hospital bed and move around to regain strength in his muscles." But he was unable to stand or sit unsupported. "He needs to make himself eat to rebuild his stamina." But he couldn't hold a fork anymore; he vomited whatever he could swallow.

We were with him and his future bride the evening his neurologist came in with the final test results, which we all hoped would bring an answer. But the tests hadn't isolated his specific kind of meningitis.

"We have come to the wall," the doctor said. "We have no choice but to schedule a cranial biopsy for tomorrow morning." We were stunned. The surgery would involve drilling a hole the size of a quarter through his skull to reach the meninges, the membranes surrounding the brain, for tissue samples.

After reading and signing the papers, I looked at Jack. He had moved to the bedside. He was looking down, oblivious to the tears dripping off his cheeks, at my son—*our* son. I saw nothing short of pure love in his face, his touch, his heart. Jack became a dad that night.

Real Love

The surgery solved the mystery, and medication miraculously brought on a quick return of full brain function, though it was several years before our son's body returned to normal. Meanwhile, there were other minor crises with each child. And each time, sharing both the problem and the solution created deeper bonds. Through these experiences, Jack has learned and taught both of our sons that it is okay to cry and to hug another man—their stepdad and each other, for starters.

The whole gang has learned to trust this man, knowing they can rely on him without doubt or fear. We know that Jack loves us all, even with our many warts.

We are a family.

What principles discussed in this chapter are illustrated in this woman's essay? What points addressed in Chapter 15, Remarriages, are illustrated in this essay? What factors helped to make this remarried family a resilient one?

Source: Mary Zimmeth Schomaker, "From Stepfather to Father," *Liguorian.* June 1994: 54–56.

that—despite being embarrassed when they fell in public or were incontinent—they could freely discuss these situations with their families and feel confident that their families understood (Power 1979). And as a final example, talking openly and supportively with an elderly parent who is dying about what that parent wants, in terms of medical treatment, hospice, and burial, can help (Fein 1997).

Some research indicates that families who have difficulty coping with crises are far more inadequate in communicating with and supporting each other than they are in dealing with practical problems. For example, the prolonged disruption or isolation that families experience after a geographical move is often a result of strained relationships and inadequate supportive communication rather than of problems associated with the move itself (McAllister, Butler, and Kaiser 1973).

Knowing how to indicate the specific kind of support one needs is important at stressful times. For example, differentiating between—and knowing how to request—just listening as opposed to problem-solving discussion can help reduce misunderstandings among family members—and between family members and others as well (Perlman and Rook 1987). Box 16.4, "From Stepfather to Father," addresses open, supportive communication as one element in meeting crises creatively.

ADAPTABILITY   Adaptable families are better able to respond effectively to crises (Kosciulek and Lustig 1998). And families are more adaptable when they are more democratic and when conjugal power is fairly egalitarian (Patterson and McCubbin 1984). In families in which one member wields authoritarian power, the whole family suffers if the authoritarian leader does not make effective decisions during a crisis—and allows no one else to move into a position of leadership (Hansen and Hill 1964; McCubbin and McCubbin 1994).

Often, family power relations change in response to crisis. An ineffective leader tends to be replaced eventually by another family member—the spouse or an older child—if she or he does not solve the problem effectively (Bahr and Rollins 1971). Men who feel comfortable only as family leaders may resent their loss of power, and this resentment may continue to cause problems when the crisis is over.

When wives took over all family decisions in the absence of husbands serving in military, marital strife was sometimes the outcome upon the husband's return (Mercier and Mercier 2000).

Just as traditional gender roles continue to affect most areas of family life, so, too, do they influence family crises. Social scientists Bryan Robinson and Robert Barret, in their book *The Developing Father* (1986), argue that fathers, more often than mothers, have more difficulty coping with their severely retarded children; they are especially vulnerable to social stigma. Differences between fathers and mothers in coping can cause problems in their marriage. For example, a mother's using community and social support could increase the father's stress over potential social stigma and invasion of privacy (pp. 198–99). Women who adapted to husbands' unemployment by seeking emotional support from relatives and friends found that their husbands often viewed this as disloyalty (Roberton et al. 1991).

Family adaptability in aspects other than leadership is also important (Burr, Klein, and McCubbin 1995). Families who can adapt their schedules and use of space, their family activities and rituals, and their connections with the outside world to the limitations and possibilities posed by the crisis will cope more effectively than families that are committed to preserving sameness. For example, a study of mothers of children with developmental disabilities found that mothers who worked part time had less stress than those who worked full time or were not employed at all (Gottlieb 1997). Having multiple roles, along with time flexibility, seemed to help.

INFORMAL SOCIAL SUPPORT   It's easier to cope with crises when a person doesn't feel alone (see, for example, Turner and Avison 1985; Suarez and Baker 1997). It may go without saying that spouses do better when they feel supported by their mates (Suitor and Pillemer 1994; Owens and Qualls 1997). Families can find helpful support in times of crisis from kin, good friends, neighbours, and even acquaintances such as work colleagues. These various relationships provide a wide array of help—from lending money in financial emergencies to helping with child care to just being there for emotional support. Even continued contact with more casual acquaintances can be helpful as often they offer useful information, along with enhancing one's sense of community (Milardo 1989).

AN EXTENDED FAMILY Kin networks are a valuable source of support in times of crisis. Grandparents, aunts, or other relatives may help with child rearing in two-career families. Families going through divorce often fall back on relatives for practical help and financial assistance. In other crises, kin provide a shoulder to lean on—someone who can be asked for help without causing embarrassment—which can make a crucial difference in a family's ability to recover. Indeed, with current divorce rates and difficult economic circumstances, adults may increasingly find that their more permanent kin ties are with their families of origin rather than with their mates. They may rely more on kin for emotional support, financial assistance, and exchange of services.

Many turn to their extended family in times of stress. Kin may provide emotional support, monetary support, practical help, and a strong shoulder to lean on without embarrassment.

Put another way, we may increasingly see a *vertical family* (attachment to parents and family of origin) as opposed to the *horizontal family* (stressing priority and permanence of the marital bond).

Even though extended families as residential groupings represent a small proportion of family households, kin ties remain salient and may become more so. One aspect of all this that is just beginning to get research attention is reciprocal friendship and support among adult siblings (White and Riedman 1992; Horwitz 1993).

We need to be aware, though, of the dark side of helping (Fisher, Nadler, and Alagne 1982; Staub et al. 1984; Worchel 1984). Sometimes the recipient's discomfort or perceived vulnerability to control attempts on the part of the helper can cloud the relationship or discourage the person in need (Saks and Krupat 1988; Brigham 1991).

Although in most cases the extended family is viewed as a resource in times of trouble, some clinicians argue that, at least in some cases, having the family find out about your distress may be the problem rather than the solution (Hines et al. 1992). Then too, among some recent immigrant groups, as we have seen, expectations of the extended family may clash with the more individualistic values of more Westernized family members (Kamo and Zhou 1994).

COMMUNITY RESOURCES The success with which families meet crises also depends on the community resources available to help:

> Community-based resources are all of those characteristics, competencies and means of persons, groups and institutions outside the family which the family may call upon, access, and use to meet their demands. This includes a whole range of services, such as medical and health care services. The services of other institutions in the family's … environment, such as schools, churches, employers, etc. are also resources to the family. At the more macro level, government policies that enhance and support families can be viewed as community resources. (McCubbin and McCubbin 1991, p. 19)

Among others, community resources include government social workers and family welfare agencies; foster child care; church programs that provide food, clothing, or shelter to poor or homeless families; 12-step and other support programs for substance abusers and their families; programs for crime or abuse victims and their families; support groups for persons with serious diseases such as cancer or AIDS; support groups for parents and other relatives of differently-abled or terminally ill children; support groups for caregivers of differently-abled family members or those with cancer or Alzheimer disease; and community pregnancy prevention and/or parent education programs.

One such community resource is marriage and family counselling. Counselling can help families after a crisis occurs; it can also help when families foresee a family change or crisis. For instance, a couple might visit a counsellor when expecting or adopting a baby, when deciding about work commitments and family needs, when the youngest child is about to leave home, or when the husband or wife is about to retire. Marriage counsellors now offer premarital counselling to help partners anticipate some of the problems associated with the transition to married life. Marriage counselling is not just for marriages that are in trouble but a resource that can help relationships.

MEETING CHALLENGES: DISASTER OR OPPORTUNITY?

A family crisis is a turning point in the course of family living that requires members to change how they have been thinking and acting (McCubbin and McCubbin 1991, 1994). The word *crisis* actually comes from the Greek word for *decision*. Although we cannot control the occurrence of many crises, we can decide how to cope with them.

Every challenge that confronts us—even the most unfortunate ones—has the potential for positive as well as negative effects. One therapist cites cases in which death in a family with longstanding problems precipitated counsellor-supported change, enabling family members to function more effectively than they ever had functioned previously (Gelcer 1986). Whether a family emerges from a crisis with a greater capacity for supportive family interaction depends largely on how family members choose to define the crisis. A major theme of this text is that, given the opportunities and limitations posed by society, people create their marriages and families based on the choices they make. Families whose members choose to be flexible in roles and leadership meet crises creatively.

Even though they have options and choices, however, family members do not have absolute control over their lives (Kleber et al. 1997). Many family troubles are really the results of public issues (Coontz 1997b). The serious family disorganization that results from poverty, for example, is as much a social as a private problem. In this text we have often suggested that the tension between individualistic and family values in our society creates personal and family conflict. And the society-wide movement toward equality and greater self-actualization may spark family challenges as wives and children move toward independence. Moreover, many family challenges are more difficult to bear because communities lack adequate resources to help families meet them (Coontz 1997b; Mason, Skolnick, and Sugarman 1998). Families must act collectively to obtain the social resources they need for effective crisis management in everyday living.

IN SUM

Family challenges may be expected, as when a baby is born or adopted, or they may be unexpected. In either case the event that causes the crisis is called a stressor. Stressors are of various types and have varied characteristics. Generally, stressors that are expected, brief, and improving are less difficult to cope with.

The predictable changes of individuals and families—parenthood, midlife transitions, postparenthood, retirement, and widow- and widowerhood—are all family transitions that can be viewed as stressors. During transitions, spouses can expect their relationship to follow the course of a family crisis.

A common pattern can be traced in families' reactions. Three distinct phases of a crisis can be identified: the event that causes the crisis, the period of disorganization that follows, and the reorganizing or recovery phase after the family reaches a low point. The eventual level of reorganization a family reaches depends on a number of factors, including the type of stressor, the degree of stress it imposes, whether other stressors accompany it, and the family's definition of the crisis situation. Various models of family crisis and reorganization try to capture this process in an analytical way, to pursue through research useful knowledge about coping with crisis.

Meeting challenging events creatively means resuming daily functioning at or above the level that existed before the crisis. Several factors can help: a positive outlook, spiritual values, the presence of support groups, high self-esteem, open and supportive communication within the family, adaptability, counselling, and the presence of a kin network.

Key Terms

ABC-X model
bereavement
crisis
double ABC-X model
empty nest
family stress
period of disorganization
pile-up
predictable crisis

resiliency model of family
stress, adjustment, and
adaptation
resilient families
sandwich generation
stressor
stressor overload
transitions
vulnerable families

Study Questions

1. Define crisis and explain how family transitions fit this definition.

2. Describe the three phases of a family crisis. Use an example to illustrate each phase.

3. Differentiate among the types of stressors. How are these single events different from stressor overload?

4. Discuss concrete ways that living in poverty can create stressor overload.

5. Discuss issues addressed in other chapters of this text (e.g., work–family issues, parenting, divorce, and remarriage) in terms of the ABC-X model of family crisis.

6. Discuss the factors that influence how family members appraise a crisis. How does the family's appraisal relate to the members' ability to adjust to the crisis?

7. Describe the period of disorganization in a family crisis situation. How can this phase of a crisis pull a family apart? How can it bring a family together?

8. What factors help some families recover from crisis while others remain in the disorganization phase?

9. Are family transitions, which are at least somewhat expected, easier to adjust to than unexpected crises? Why or why not?

10. Compare the transitions of sandwich generation, empty nest, retirement, and widow- or widower-hood. Are there similarities? Any differences? What factors would encourage adjustment to each transition? What factors would inhibit adjustment?

11. Discuss the advantages and the drawbacks of relying on help from an extended family.

12. What should government do to help families in crisis?

Suggested Readings

Family Relations 46(4). 1997. Special issue on family caregiving for persons with disabilities.

Figley, Charles R. and Hamilton T. McCubbin (eds.). 1983. *Stress and the Family, Vol. II: Coping with Catastrophe*. New York: Brunner/Mazel. Part of a two-volume book on stress, covering current research in this field. Stressful family situations are divided into the transitions in family stages that are widely shared (Vol. I) and crises of various sorts that only some families experience (Vol. II).

Fowler, Ruth. 1998. *As We Grow Old: How Adult Children and Their Parents Can Face Aging with Candor and Grace*. Valley Forge, PA: Judson Press. Realistic, positive advice on this subject.

Harris, Phyllis B., and Joyce Bichler. 1997. *Men Giving Care: Reflections of Husbands and Sons*. New York: Garland Press. Report of a qualitative study of 30 husbands and 30 sons who are caregivers to a relative with dementia.

Journal of Health and Social Behavior. Academic journal that reports many studies of relationships between life events, stress, social supports, and other coping mechanisms, and physical and mental health.

On the Net

1) Canadian Health Network
   Health Canada has set up this site that gives access to over 400 Canadian health organizations.
   http://www.canadian-health-network.ca

2) The Alzheimer's Association
   http://www.alz.org

3) PFLAG (Parents and Friends of Lesbians and Gays)
   http://www.pflag.ca

4) Canadian Association of Retired Persons
   http://www.50plus.com/

5) For research on the lingering effects of child abuse and a number of useful Web links see:
   http://www.jimhopper.com/abstats

Glossary

(Numbers in parentheses refer to the chapter(s) containing the main discussion of the term.)

A

ABC-X model   A model of family crisis in which A (the stressor event) interacts with B (the family's resources for meeting a crisis) and with C (the definition the family formulates of the event) to produce X (the crisis). See also *double ABC-X model, resiliency model, stressor*. (16)

abortion   The expulsion of the fetus or embryo from the uterus either naturally (spontaneous abortion or miscarriage) or medically (induced abortion). (11)

abstinence   The standard that maintains that regardless of the circumstances, nonmarital intercourse is wrong for both women and men. Many religions espouse abstinence as a moral imperative. See also *double standard, permissiveness with affection, permissiveness without affection*. (5)

adoption reunions   The meeting of birth parents, most often the mother, with the biological child. (11)

A-frame relationship   A relationship style (symbolized by the capital letter A) in which partners have a strong couple identity but little self-esteem; therefore, they are dependent on each other rather than interdependent. See also *H-frame relationship, M-frame relationship*. (4)

agape   The love style that emphasizes unselfish concern for the beloved in which one attempts to fulfill the other's needs even when that means some personal sacrifice. See also *eros, ludus, mania, pragma, storge*. (4)

age expectations   Societal expectations about how people should think and behave because of their age. For instance: Women over ___ (you fill in the blank) should not wear bikinis; men over ___ should not wear tank tops. (1)

agreement reality   What members of a society agree is true and what comes to be the taken-for-granted truth that "everybody knows." (2)

alienating fight tactics   Tactics in fighting that tend to create distance between intimates: They don't resolve conflict; they increase it. See also *stonewalling* and *gaslighting*; compare with *bonding fighting*. (9)

alimony/spousal support   Derived from the Latin verb meaning "to nourish" or "to give food to;" the traditional condition in which the breadwinning husband undertook the obligation to support his dependent wife and children even after divorce. With the advent of no-fault divorce laws, the term "alimony" was replaced by "spousal support" or "maintenance." The change in terminology reflects a departure from the obligation of lifetime support, which was premised on wifely economic dependency in a lifelong contractual relationship. Spousal support is presumed to be temporary, a practical means of meeting a spouse's economic needs during a period of readjustment. (14)

ambivalent provider couple   The wife's income is essential to the family, but her responsibility as an economic provider is not acknowledged. (13)

androgyny   The social and psychological condition in which individuals can think, feel, and behave in ways that express both instrumental and expressive character traits. Androgyny is the combination of both masculine and feminine qualities in one individual. Androgynous people will probably be better equipped to deal with industrial society. Moreover, androgynous partners may find greater intimacy in marriage than do more traditional spouses. (3)

anger "insteads"   Ways people deal with their anger rather than expressing it directly. Some substitutes for open anger are overeating, boredom, depression, physical illness, and gossip. (9)

archival family function   The creating, storing, preserving, and passing on of particular objects, events, or rituals that family members consider relevant to their personal identities and to maintaining the family as a unique existential reality or group. (1)

arranged marriage   Marriages arranged by parents rather than by prospective marital partners themselves. Includes the sororate and/or levirate arrangements. (7)

assortive mating   A process of filtering out persons from among a pool of potentially eligible partners. (7)

astronaut phenomenon   A term used to describe a situation in which one immigrant spouse, typically the husband, leaves the family in the country of immigration and returns to their country of origin to work, with periodic visits made to his/her spouse and children. (12)

attachment disorder   An emotional disorder in which a person defensively shuts off the willingness or ability to make future attachments to anyone. (11)

attachment theory   A psychological theory that holds that during infancy and childhood a young person develops a general style of attaching to others; Once an individual's attachment style is established, she or he unconsciously applies that style to later, adult relationships. The three basic styles are *secure, insecure/anxious,* and *avoidant*. (4)

attribution   Assigning or attributing character traits to other people. Attributions can be positive or negative, such as when a spouse is told he or she is an interesting or a boring person. (9)

authoritarian discipline   A form of discipline in which parents make sure that the child obeys all the rules at all times. Children are punished for even minor offences. (12)

authoritarian parenting   All decision making is in parents' hands and the emphasis is on compliance with rules and directives. Parents are more punitive than supportive, and use of physical punishment is likely. (12)

authoritative discipline   A form of discipline in which the parent demands maturity and effectively punishes forbidden behaviour after having clearly stated the rules, but who listens to the child's point of view, respects the child, and encourages the child's self-development and independence. (12)

authoritative parenting   Parents accept the child's personality and talents and are emotionally supportive. At the same time, they consciously set and enforce rules and limits, whose rationale is usually explained to the child. Parents provide guidance and direction and state expectations for the child's behaviour. Parents are in charge, but the child is given responsibility and must take the initiative in completing schoolwork and other tasks and in solving child-level problems. (12)

avoidant attachment style   One of three attachment styles in attachment style theory, this style avoids intimacy either by evading relationships altogether or establishing considerable distance in intimate situations. See also *insecure/anxious attachment style, secure attachment style.* (4)

B

balanced connection   As described within Stephen Mark's model, partners with this type of connection move their focus from one corner of each individual's triangular self to another. See also *couple-centred connection, family-centred connection, loose connection.* (8)

battered woman syndrome   A circumstance in which a battered woman feels incapable of making any change in her way of living. (10)

belligerence   Defined by John Gottman and his colleagues as one of the "Four Horsemen of the Apocalypse": behaviour by a spouse that is provocative and that challenges the other spouse's power and authority. (9)

bereavement   A period of mourning after the death of a loved one. (16)

blended family   A term used interchangeably with the term "reconstituted" or "recombined family" to indicate a family in which there is a mix of children that both parents brought to the family from previous unions or a mix of children from previous unions and the current one. (15)

bonding fighting   Fighting that brings intimates closer together rather than leaving them just as far apart or pushing them even farther apart. Compare with *alienating fight tactics.* (9)

borderwork   Interaction rituals that are based on and reaffirm boundaries and differences between girls and boys. (3)

bride price   Money or property that the future groom pays the future bride's family so that he can marry her. (7)

C

case study   A written summary and analysis of data gained by psychologists, psychiatrists, counsellors, and social workers when working directly with individuals and families. Case studies are often used as sources in scientific investigation. (2)

census family   A now-married couple (with or without never-married sons and/or daughters of one or both spouses), a couple living common law (again, with or without never-married sons and/or daughters of either or both parents), or a lone parent of any marital status, with at least one never-married son or daughter living in the same dwelling. (1)

centre care   Group child care provided in day-care centres for a relatively large number of children. (13)

checking-it-out   A communication or fighting technique in which a person asks the other whether her or his perceptions of the other's feelings or thoughts are correct. (9)

child abuse   Overt acts of aggression against a child, such as excessive verbal derogation, beating, or inflicting physical injury. Sexual abuse is a form of physical child abuse. See also *emotional child abuse or neglect.* (10)

child care   As defined by policy researchers, the full-time care and education of children under age six, care before and after school and during vacations for older children, and overnight care when employed parents must travel. (13)

child neglect   Failure to provide adequate physical or emotional care for a child. See also *emotional child abuse or neglect.* (10)

child snatching   Kidnapping one's own children from the other parent after divorce. (14)

child support   Money paid by the noncustodial to the custodial parent to financially support children of a separated marital, cohabiting, or sexual relationship. (14)

Chodorow's theory of gender   A theory of gender socialization that combines psychoanalytic ideas about identification of children with parents with an awareness of what those parents' social roles are in our society. (3)

choosing by default   Making semiconscious or unconscious choices when one is not aware of all the possible alternatives or when one pursues the path of least resistance. From this perspective, doing nothing about a problem or issue, or making no choice, is making a serious choice—that is, the choice to do nothing. (1)

choosing knowledgeably   Making choices and decisions after (1) recognizing as many options or alternatives as possible; (2) recognizing the social pressures that can influence personal choices; (3) considering the consequences of each alternative; and (4) becoming aware of one's own values. (1)

coercive power   One of the six power bases, or sources of power. This power is based on the dominant person's ability and willingness to punish the partner either with psychological-emotional or physical violence, or with more subtle methods of withholding affection. See also *expert power, informational power, legitimate power, referent power, reward power.* (10)

cohabitation   Living together in an intimate, sexual relationship without traditional, legal marriage. Sometimes referred to as living together or marriage without marriage. Cohabitation can be a courtship process or an alternative to legal marriage, depending on how partners view it. (6, 7)

collectivist society   A society in which people identify with and conform to the expectations of their relatives or clan, who look after their interests in return for their loyalty. (2)

commitment (to intimacy)   The determination to develop relationships in which experiences cover many areas of personality, problems are worked through, conflict is expected and seen as a normal part of the growth process, and there is an expectation that the relationship is basically viable and worthwhile. (4)

commitment (Sternberg's triangular theory of love)   The short-term decision that one loves someone and the long-term aspect—the commitment to maintain that love; one dimension of the triangular theory of love. See also *intimacy, passion*. (4)

common couple violence Mutual violence between partners that tends to be less severe in terms of injuries. (10)

common-law relationship A legal concept whereby cohabiting partners are considered legally married if certain requirements are met, such as showing intent to enter into a marriage and living together as husband and wife for a certain period of time. (6)

commune A group of adults and perhaps children who live together, sharing aspects of their lives. Some communes are group marriages, in which members share sex; others are communal families, with several monogamous couples, who share everything except sexual relations, and their children. (6)

commuter marriage A marriage in which the two partners live in different locations and commute to spend time together. Also called "two-location family." (13)

conflict-habituated marriage A marital relationship characterized by ongoing tension and unresolved conflict. See also *devitalized marriage, passive-congenial marriage, total marriage, vital marriage*. (8)

conflict taboo The cultural belief that conflict and anger are wrong, which thereby discourages people from dealing with these negative emotions openly. (9)

conjugal kin The term used to define relationships acquired through marriage (spouses and in-laws), as opposed to consanguineous relatives (parents and grandparents), who are blood related. Compare with *consanguineous kin*. (8)

conjugal power Power exercised between spouses. (10)

consanguineous kin The term used to define blood-related kin (parents and grandparents), as opposed to conjugal kin (spouses and in-laws), who are related through marriage. Compare with *conjugal kin*. (8)

consensual validation The process whereby people depend on others, especially significant others, to help them affirm their definitions of and attitudes and feelings about reality. Consensual validation is important in modern society because social reality is no longer just taken for granted as the way things are. Compare with *gaslighting*. (9)

consummate love A complete love, in terms of Sternberg's triangular theory of love, in which the components of *passion, intimacy,* and *commitment* come together. (4)

contempt Defined by John Gottman and his colleagues as one of the "Four Horsemen of the Apocalypse": behaviour that indicates that one regards one's partner as inferior or undesirable. (9)

continuum of social attachment A conception of social attachment developed by Catherine Ross that emphasizes the quality of the attachment and its relationship to happiness or depression. Her research found that singles are not all socially unattached, isolated, or disconnected, and that people who are in relationships that are unhappy are more depressed than people who are alone and without a partner. (6)

convenience One of four forms of cohabitation identified by Carl Ridley and his colleagues. This form of cohabiting relationship involves partners who live together sexually more for practical reasons than for intimacy. See also *emancipation, "Linus blanket," testing*. (7)

coparenting Shared decision making and parental supervision in such areas as discipline and schoolwork or shared holidays and recreation. (15)

coprovider couple Both partners have a primary responsibility for the family's economic support. (13)

couple-centred connection As described within Stephen Mark's model, in relationships with this type of connection, the spouses retain elements of all three corners of the self but the couple is more romantically fused, focusing mainly on their relationship. See also *balanced connection, family-centred connection, loose connection*. (8)

courtly love Popular during the twelfth century and later, courtly love is the intense longing for someone other than one's marital partner—a passionate and sexual longing that ideally goes unfulfilled. The assumptions of courtly love influence our modern ideas about romantic love. (7)

courtship The process whereby a couple develops a mutual commitment to marriage. (7)

covenant marriage A new type of legal marriage in which the bride and groom agree to be bound by a marriage contract that will not let them get divorced as easily as is allowed presently. (8)

crisis A crucial change in the course of events, a turning point, an unstable condition in affairs. (16)

criticism Defined by John Gottman and his colleagues as one of the "Four Horsemen of the Apocalypse": involves making disapproving judgments or evaluations of one's partner. (9)

cross-cultural researchers Researchers who compare cultures around the world. (2)

crude birthrate The number of births per thousand population. See also *total fertility rate*. (11)

cultural deviant A theoretical framework that emphasizes those features that minority families exhibit that distinguish them from white mainstream families. These qualities are viewed as negative or pathological. (2)

cultural equivalent A theoretical framework that emphasizes those features that minority families have in common with mainstream white families. (2)

cultural script A set of socially prescribed and understood guidelines for relating to each other and for defining responsibilities and obligations. (15)

cultural variant A theoretical approach that calls for making contextually relevant interpretations of minority families. Minority families are studied on their own terms (as opposed to favourably or unfavourably with regard to mainstream white families) and comparisons are made within those groups. (2)

custodial grandparent A parent of a divorced, custodial parent. (12)

custody Responsibility for making decisions about the children's upbringing and general welfare. (14)

cyberadultery A new brand of marital infidelity: adultery on the Internet. May be limited to flirtations in chat rooms or result in in-person meetings. (8)

D

date rape (acquaintance rape) Forced or unwanted sexual contact between people who are on a date. (7)

defensiveness Defined by John Gottman and his colleagues as one of the "Four Horsemen of the Apocalypse": defined as preparing to defend oneself against what one presumes is an upcoming attack. (9)

dependency-distancing couple A term used by Stephen Marks to refer to a couple in which one partner focuses on the marriage while the other partner puts most of his/her energy outside of the relationship. See also *romantically fused couple, separate couple*. (8)

dependence The general reliance on another person or on several others for continuous support and assurance, coupled with subordination to that other. A dependent partner probably has low self-esteem and is having illegitimate needs met by the partner on whom he or she is dependent. See also *independence, interdependence.* (4)

developmental model of child rearing Popularized by many child-rearing experts, this view sees the child as an extremely plastic organism with virtually unlimited potential that the parent is called on to tap and encourage. The model ignores or deemphasizes parents' personal rights. (12)

devitalized marriage A marital relationship in which a couple have lost the original zest, intimacy, and meaningfulness that were once a part of their relationship. See also *conflict-habituated marriage, passive-congenial marriage, total marriage, vital marriage.* (8)

displaced homemaker A full-time housewife who, through divorce or widowhood, loses her means of economic support. (14)

displacement A passive-aggressive behaviour in which a person expresses anger with another by being angry at or damaging people or things the other cherishes. See also *passive-aggression, sabotage.* (9)

disrupted adoptions Adoptions in which the child to be adopted is returned to the agency before the adoption is legally final. See also *dissolved adoptions.* (11)

dissolved adoptions Adoptions in which the adopted child is returned after the adoption is final. See also *disrupted adoptions.* (11)

divorce mediation A nonadversarial means of dispute resolution by which the couple, with the assistance of a mediator or mediators (frequently a lawyer–therapist team), negotiate the terms of their settlement of custody, support, property, and visitation issues. (14)

dominant dyad A centrally important twosome that symbolizes the culture's basic values and kinship obligations. (8)

double ABC-X model A variation of the *ABC-X model* of family crises that emphasizes the impact of unresolved prior crises. In this model, A becomes Aa and represents not only the current stressor event but also family pile-up, or residual strains from prior crises. (16)

double remarriage A remarriage in which both partners were previously married. Compare with *single remarriage.* (15)

double standard The standard according to which premarital sex is more acceptable for males than for females. Reiss subdivided the double standard into orthodox and transitional. See also *abstinence, permissiveness with affection, permissiveness without affection.* (5)

double standard of aging A sociological concept describing the situation in which men are not considered old or sexually ineligible as early in their lives as women are. (6)

dowry A sum of money or property brought to the marriage by the female. (7)

E

economic divorce The separation of the couple into separate economic units, each with its own property, income, control of expenditures, and responsibility for taxes, debts, and so on. (14)

economic hardship perspective One of the five theoretical perspectives concerning the negative outcomes among children of divorced parents. From the economic hardship perspective, the marital dissolution is primarily responsible for the problems faced by children. See also *life stress perspective, parental adjustment perspective, parental loss perspective, interparental conflict perspective.* (14)

elder abuse Overt acts of aggression toward the elderly, in which the victim may be physically assaulted, emotionally humiliated, purposefully isolated, or materially exploited. (10)

elder care The provision of assistance with daily living activities for an elderly relative who is chronically frail, ill, or disabled. (13)

elder neglect Acts of omission in the care and treatment of the elderly. (10)

emancipation One of four forms of cohabitation identified by Carl Ridley and his colleagues. In this form, cohabitation is used to gain independence from parental values and influence. See also *convenience, "Linus blanket," testing.* (7)

emotion A strong feeling arising without conscious mental or rational effort, such as joy, reverence, anger, fear, love, or hate. Emotions are neither bad nor good and should be accepted as natural. People can and should learn to control what they *do* about their emotions. (4)

emotional child abuse or neglect A parent or other caregiver's being overly harsh and critical, failing to provide guidance, or being uninterested in a child's needs. See also *child abuse.* (10)

emotional divorce Withholding any bonding emotions and communication from the relationship, typically replacing these with alienating feelings and behaviour. (14)

empty nest An old (some say outdated) sociological term referring to the postparental stage of family life. With the contracting economy, the trend to stay single longer, and the rising divorce rate, more and more parents are complaining that their nests won't seem to empty. (16)

endogamy Marrying within one's own social group. See also *exogamy.* (7)

eros The love style characterized by intense emotional attachment and powerful sexual feelings or desires. See also *agape, ludus, mania, pragma, storge.* (4)

evolutionary psychology A school of psychology which argues that humans have an evolutionary biological origin that affects their sexual relations. (5)

exchange theory Theoretical perspective that sees relationships as determined by the exchange of resources and the reward–cost balance of that exchange. This theory predicts that people tend to marry others whose social class, education, physical attractiveness, and even self-esteem are similar to their own. (2, 7)

exogamy Marrying a partner from outside one's own social group. See also *endogamy.* (7)

expectations of permanence The expectation of permanent, life-long commitment. See also *primariness, marriage premise.* (8)

experiential reality Knowledge based on personal experience. (2)

experiment One tool of scientific investigation, in which behaviours are carefully monitored or measured under controlled conditions; also called "laboratory observation." (2)

expert power One of the six power bases, or sources of power. This power stems from the dominant person's superior judgment, knowledge, or ability. See also *coercive power, informational power, legitimate power, referent power, reward power.* (10)

expressive character traits Such traits as warmth, sensitivity to the needs of others, and the ability to express tender feelings, traditionally associated with women. Expressive character traits and roles complement *instrumental character traits.* (3)

expressive sexuality The view of human sexuality in which sexuality is basic to the humanness of both women and men; all individuals are free to express their sexual selves; and there is no one-sided sense of ownership. (5)

extended family   Family including relatives besides parents and children, such as aunts or uncles. See also *family, nuclear family*. (2)

externalizing   Behavioural problems in children that occur as a result of growing up exposed to a conflict-habituated parental relationship. Includes aggression, lying, cheating, running away from home, disobeying at school, delinquency, and so on. Compare with *internalizing*. (8)

extramarital sex   Adultery; sexual relations between a married person and another who is not his/her spouse. (8)

F

family   Any sexually expressive or parent–child or other kin relationship in which people live together with a commitment, in an intimate interpersonal relationship. Family members see their identity as importantly attached to the group, which has an identity of its own. Families today take several forms: single-parent, remarried, dual-career, communal, homosexual, traditional, and so forth. See also *extended family, nuclear family*. (1)

family-centred connection   As described within Stephen Mark's model, a relationship in which spouses focus on a shared third-corner, such as parenting or relations with extended kin. See also *balanced connection, couple-centred connection, loose connection*. (8)

family cohesion   That intangible emotional quality that holds groups together and gives members a sense of common identity. (9)

family day care   Child care provided in a day-care worker's home. (13)

family development perspective   Theoretical perspective that gives attention to changes in the family over time. (2)

family ecology perspective   This theoretical perspective explores how a family influences and is influenced by the environments that surround it. A family is interdependent first with its neighbourhood, then with its social–cultural environment, and ultimately with the physical–biological environment. All parts of the model are interrelated and influence one another. (2)

family-friendly workplace policies   Workplace policies that are supportive of employee efforts to combine family and work commitments. (13)

family life cycle   Stages of family development defined by the addition and subtraction of family members, children's stages, and changes in the family's connection with other social systems. (2)

family myths   Versions of reality that obscure a core truth in order to manage a family's tension. (13)

family of orientation   The family in which an individual grows up. Also called "family of origin." (8)

family of procreation   The family that is formed when an individual marries and has children. (8)

family policy   All the actions, procedures, regulations, attitudes, and goals of government that affect families. (2)

family stress   State of tension that arises when demands tax a family's resources. (16)

family systems theory   An umbrella term for a wide range of specific theories. This theoretical perspective examines the family as a whole. It looks to the patterns of behaviour and relationships within the family, in which each member is affected by the behaviour of others. Systems tend toward equilibrium and will react to change in one part by seeking equilibrium by restoring the old system or creating a new one. (2)

family values (familism)   Values that focus on the family group as a whole and on maintaining family identity, loyalty, and cohesiveness. (1)

fecundity   The technical term for biological reproductive capacity. See also *fertility*. (11)

feedback   The communication technique of stating in different words what another person has said or revealed nonverbally. (9)

female-demand/male-withdrawal pattern   A phrase used to describe the differing response of men and women to negative effect in close relationships. When faced with a complaint from their partner, men tend to withdraw emotionally while women do not. (9)

female genital mutilation (FGM)   An umbrella term used to refer to a set of practices including female circumcision (excision), clitoridectomy, infibulation, and labiadectomy. (5)

femininities   A term used to recognize that there are different variants of "femininity." (3)

feminist theory   Umbrella term used to refer to a wide range of theories that consider the issue gender to be of fundamental importance to understanding the position of men and women in society. Feminist theories are conflict theories. While many different types of feminist theorizing exist, they share a commitment to ending the oppression of women (and/or related patterns of subordination based on social class, race/ethnicity, age, or sexual orientation) by developing knowledge that confronts this disparity. (2)

fertility   In everyday language, the ability to reproduce biologically. See also *fecundity*. (11)

flexible marriage   One that allows and encourages partners to grow and change both as individuals and in the relationship. A synonym is "open marriage." (8)

flexible scheduling   A type of employment scheduling that includes scheduling options such as job sharing or flextime, among others. See also *flextime, job sharing*. (13)

flextime   A policy that permits an employee some flexibility to adjust working hours to suit family needs or personal preference. See also *flexible scheduling, job sharing*. (13)

Four Horsemen of the Apocalypse   Four processes identified by John Gottman and his colleagues as predictive of divorce. Includes *belligerence, contempt, criticism,* and *defensiveness*. (9)

free-choice culture   A culture in which people freely choose their mates. (7)

G

gaslighting   An alienating tactic in which one partner chips away at the other's perception of her- or himself and at the other's definitions of reality. Gaslighting can literally drive people insane. Compare with *consensual validation*. (9)

gender   Attitudes and behaviour associated with and expected of the two sexes. The term "sex" denotes biology; "gender" refers to social role. (3)

gendered   The way every aspect of people's lives and relationships are influenced by gender, by whether we are male or female. (3)

gender identity   The degree to which an individual sees her- or himself as feminine or masculine based on society's definition of appropriate gender roles. (3)

gender-linked characteristics and roles   Societal attitudes and behaviours expected of and associated with men and women. (3)

gender roles   Masculine and feminine prescriptions for behaviour. The masculine gender role demands *instrumental character traits* and behaviour, whereas the feminine gender role demands *expressive character traits* and behaviour. Traditional gender roles are giving way to *androgyny*, but they're by no means gone. (3)

gender schema   A framework of knowledge about what girls/boys, men/women actually do that is used to interpret information and think about gender. (3)

gender strategy   A way of working through everyday family situations that takes into account an individual's beliefs and deep feelings about gender roles, as well as her or his employment and other non-family commitments. (13)

getting together   A courtship process different from dating, in which groups of women and men congregate at a party or share an activity. (7)

good provider role   A specialized masculine role that emerged in the 1830s in Canada and the United States and that emphasizes the husband as the only or the primary economic provider for his family. (13)

grandparents as primary parents   Grandparents who assume the responsibility for parenting their grandchildren. (12)

guaranteed child support   Type of child support, used in France and Sweden, in which the government sends to the custodial parent the full amount of support awarded to the child, even though this sum may not have been received from the noncustodial parent. It then becomes the government's responsibility to collect the money from the parent who owes it. (14)

gunnysacking   An alienating fight tactic in which a person saves up, or gunnysacks, grievances until the sack gets too heavy and bursts, and old hostilities pour out. (9)

H

habituation   The decreased interest in sex that results from the increased accessibility of a sexual partner and the predictability in sexual behaviour with that partner over time. (5)

hermaphrodite   A person whose genitalia cannot be clearly identified as either female or male at birth. Attending physicians assign a sex identity to hermaphrodites at birth or shortly thereafter. (3)

heterogamy   Marriage between partners who differ in race, age, education, religious background, or social class. Compare with *homogamy*. (7)

heterosexism   The taken-for-granted system of beliefs, values, and customs that places superior value on heterosexual behaviour (as opposed to homosexual) and denies or stigmatizes nonheterosexual relations. This tendency also sees the heterosexual family as standard. (2, 5)

heterosexuals   Individuals who prefer sexual partners of the opposite sex. (5)

H-frame relationship   Relationships that are structured like a capital H: Partners stand virtually alone, each self-sufficient and neither influenced much by the other. An example would be a *devitalized, two-career marriage*. See also *A-frame relationship, M-frame relationship*. (4)

hidden agenda   Associated with stepfathers who, with remarriage, assume functioning single-parent families of a mother and her children. The family may have a hidden agenda, or assumptions and expectations about how the stepfather will behave—expectations and assumptions that are often not passed on to the new stepfather. (15)

HIV/AIDS   Human immunodeficiency virus, the virus that causes AIDS. AIDS (acquired immune deficiency syndrome) is a sexually transmitted disease involving breakdown in the manufacture of white blood cells, which resist viruses, bacteria, and fungi. (5)

holistic view of sex   The view that conjugal sex is an extension of the whole marital relationship, which is not chopped into compartments, with sex reduced to a purely physical exchange. (5)

homogamy   Marriage between partners of similar race, age, education, religious background, and social class. Compare with *heterogamy*. (7)

homophobia   Fear, dread, aversion to, and often hatred of homosexuals. (5)

homosexuals   People who prefer same-sex partners. (5)

horizontally extended family   Family members from the same generation or other related lines such as uncles, brothers, sisters, and aunts who live and work together. Compare with *vertically extended family*. (2)

hormones   Chemical substances secreted into the bloodstream by the endocrine glands; they influence the activities of cells, tissues and body organs. (3)

househusband   A man who takes a full-time family care role, rather than being employed; the male counterpart to a housewife. (13)

hypergamy   A marriage in which a person gains social rank by marrying someone of higher rank. Compare with *hypogamy*. (7)

hypogamy   Lowering one's social and/or economic status by marrying down. Compare with *hypergamy*. (7)

I

identity   A sense of inner sameness developed by individuals throughout their lives. They know who they are throughout their various endeavours and pursuits, no matter how different these may be. (2)

ideological perspective   A perspective used in explaining the division of household labour in families that points to the impact of cultural expectations on household labour. (13)

illegitimate needs   Needs that arise from feelings of self-doubt, unworthiness, and inadequacy. Loving partners cannot fill each other's illegitimate needs no matter how much they try. One fills one's illegitimate needs best by personally working to build one's self-esteem. A first step might be doing something nice for oneself rather than waiting for somebody else to do it. (4)

imaging   Choosing to look and behave in ways that one imagines one's partner will consider attractive. An imaging partner complements a romanticizing one. Imaging is the opposite of authenticity. (7)

incest   Sexual relations between related individuals. (10)

incomplete institution   A term used by Andrew Cherlin in reference to remarried family relationships and to highlight the cultural ambiguity of such relationships. (15)

independence   Self-reliance and self-sufficiency. To form lasting intimate relationships, independent people must choose to become interdependent. See also *dependence, interdependence*. (4)

individualistic orientation   An orientation in which people think in terms of seeking primarily personal—as opposed to communal, or group—happiness and goals. (1)

individualistic society   Societies in which the main concern is with one's own interests and those of one's immediate family. (2)

individualistic (self-fulfillment) values   Values that encourage self-fulfillment, personal growth, doing one's own thing, autonomy, and independence. Individualistic values can conflict with *family values*. (1)

informational power   One of the six power bases, or sources of power. This power is based on the persuasive content of what the dominant person tells another individual. See also *coercive power, expert power, legitimate power, referent power, reward power*. (10)

insecure/anxious attachment style   One of three attachment styles in attachment style theory, this style entails concern that the beloved will disappear, a situation often characterized as "fear of abandonment." See also *avoidant attachment style, secure attachment style*. (4)

instrumental character traits   Traits that enable one to accomplish difficult tasks or goals—for example, rationality, leadership. Traditionally, people thought men were born with instrumental character traits. See also *expressive character traits*. (3)

interactional relationship pattern   A pattern noted by sociologist Jessie Bernard among middle-class marriages (as opposed to the parallel relationship pattern among working-class marriages) in which partners expect companionship, intimacy, and practical benefits. See also *parallel relationship pattern*. (8)

interactionist perspective   Theoretical perspective that focuses on internal family dynamics; the ongoing action and response of family members to each other. (2)

interactionist perspective on human sexuality   Maintains that how we are sexual—where, when, how often, with whom, and why—has to do with cultural learning, with meaning transmitted in a cultural setting. (5)

interactive perspective   A perspective of parenting that considers the influence between parent and child reciprocal rather than flowing from parent to child. (12)

interdependence   A relationship in which people who have high self-esteem make strong commitments to each other, choosing to help fill each other's legitimate, but not illegitimate, needs. See also *dependence, independence*. (4)

internalize   The process of making a cultural belief, value, or attitude one's own. When internalized, an attitude becomes a part of us and influences how we think, feel, and act. Internalized attitudes become valued emotionally and therefore are difficult to change. When people do begin to change them, they can expect to go through a period of ambivalence. (3)

internalizing   A response on the part of children to growing up in a conflict-habituated parental relationship. Includes withdrawal, depression, and anxiety. Compare with *externalizing*. (8)

interparental conflict perspective   One of the five theoretical perspectives concerning the negative outcomes among children of divorced parents. From the interparental conflict perspective, the conflict between parents prior to, during, and after the divorce is responsible for the lowered well-being of the children of divorce. This perspective is strongly supported by research on the effects of divorce on children. See also *economic hardship perspective, life stress perspective, parental adjustment perspective, parental loss perspective*. (14)

interracial marriages   Unions between partners of different "races." (7)

intimacy   Committing oneself to a particular other and honouring that commitment in spite of some personal sacrifices while sharing one's inner self with the other. Intimacy requires *interdependence*. (4)

intimacy (Sternberg's triangular theory of love)   Close, connected, and bonded feelings in loving relationships, including sharing oneself with the loved one; one dimension of the triangular theory of love. See also *commitment, passion*. (4)

intrinsic marriage   A marriage in which the emphasis is on the intensity of feelings about each other and the centrality of the spouse's welfare in each mate's scale of values. Intrinsic marriages are primary, intimate relationships. Compare with *utilitarian marriage*. (8)

involuntary infertility   The condition of wanting to conceive and bear a child but being physically unable to do so. (11)

involuntary stable singles   Older divorced, widowed, and never-married people who wanted to marry or remarry, but have not found a mate and have come to accept being single as a probable life situation. (6)

involuntary temporary singles   Singles who would like, and expect, to marry. These can be younger never-marrieds who do not want to be single and are actively seeking mates, as well as somewhat older people who had not previously been interested in marrying but are now seeking mates. (6)

J

jealousy   Emotional pain, anger, and uncertainty arising when a valued relationship is threatened or perceived to be threatened. Research has shown that men and women experience and react differently to jealousy. (8)

job sharing   Two people sharing one job. See also *flexible scheduling, flextime*. (13)

joint custody   A situation in which both divorced parents continue to take equal responsibility for important decisions regarding their child's general upbringing. (14)

K

kin scripts framework   A theoretical framework for studying ethnic minority families that includes three culturally relevant family concepts: kin-work, kin-time, and kin-scription. Kin scripts theorizing helps to make theory and research less biased and more relevant to minority families. In addition, it can be applied to mainstream families. (2)

L

labour force   A social invention that arose with the industrialization of the nineteenth century when people characteristically became wage earners, hiring out their labour to someone else. (13)

laissez-faire discipline   Discipline in which parents let children set their own goals, rules, and limits. (12)

laissez-faire parenting   Overly permissive parenting. Children set their own standards for behaviour, with little or no parental guidance or authority. Parents are indulgent, but not necessarily involved in a supportive way with the child's everyday activities and problems. (12)

legal divorce   The dissolution of a marriage by the state through a court order terminating the marriage. (14)

legitimate needs   Needs that arise in the present rather than out of the deficits accumulated in the past. (4)

legitimate power   One of the six power bases, or sources of power. This power stems from the more dominant individual's ability to claim authority, or the right to request compliance. See also *coercive power, expert power, informational power, referent power, reward power*. (10)

leveling   Being transparent, authentic, and explicit about how one truly feels, especially concerning the more conflictive or hurtful aspects of an intimate relationship. Among other things, leveling between intimates implies *self-disclosure* and *commitment (to intimacy)*. (9)

liberal feminism   A branch of feminist theorizing that is grounded on the assumption that a society based upon the principles of equality of opportunity and freedom will provide the most positive environment for all persons to achieve the best of their potential. (2)

life course solution   A policy proposal designed to ease work/family tension in which policymakers and employers would rethink the traditionally accepted pattern of education, then full-time employment, then retirement. (13)

life stress perspective   One of the five theoretical perspectives concerning the negative outcomes among children of divorced parents. From the life stress perspective, divorce involves the same stress for children as for adults, and divorce is not one single event but a process of stressful events—moving, changing schools, and so on. See also *economic hardship perspective, interparental conflict perspective, parental adjustment perspective, parental loss perspective*. (14)

"Linus blanket"   One of four forms of cohabiting identified by Carl Ridley and his colleagues. This form of cohabiting relationship develops from the dependence or insecurity of one of the partners, who prefers a relationship with anyone to being alone. See also *convenience, emancipation, testing*. (7)

listener backchannels   Brief vocalizations, head nods, and facial movements that convey to the speaker that the listener is paying attention to what the speaker is saying. (9)

longitudinal study   One technique of scientific investigation, in which researchers study the same individuals or groups over an extended period of time, usually with periodic surveys. See also *survey*. (2)

looking-glass self   The concept that people gradually come to accept and adopt as their own the evaluations, definitions, and judgments of themselves that they see reflected in the faces, words, and gestures of those around them. (9)

loose connection   As described within Stephen Mark's model, a relationship in which both partners focus on their individual third-corners, such as careers or friends. See also *balanced connection, couple-centred connection, family-centred connection*. (8)

love   A deep and vital emotion resulting from significant need satisfaction, coupled with a caring for and acceptance of the beloved, and resulting in an intimate relationship. Love may make the world go 'round, but it's a lot of work too. (4)

love style   A distinctive character or personality that loving or love-like relationships can take. One social scientist has distinguished six: *agape, eros, ludus, mania, pragma,* and *storge*. (4)

ludus   The love style that focuses on love as play and on enjoying many sexual partners rather than searching for one serious relationship. This love style emphasizes the recreational aspect of sexuality. See also *agape, eros, mania, pragma, storge*. (4)

M

main/secondary provider couple   Husband provides family's primary economic support; wife contributes to the family income, but her earnings are seen as inessential. She takes primary responsibility for homemaking. (13)

male dominance   The cultural idea of masculine superiority; the idea that men exercise the most control and influence over society's members. (3)

mania   The love style that combines strong sexual attraction and emotional intensity with extreme jealousy and moodiness, in which manic partners alternate between euphoria and depression. See also *agape, eros, ludus, pragma, storge*. (4)

manipulating   Seeking to control the feelings, attitudes, and behaviour of one's partner or partners in underhanded ways rather than by assertively stating one's case. (4)

marital rape   A husband's compelling a wife against her will to submit to sexual contact that she finds offensive. (10)

marriage gradient   The sociological concept that men marry down in educational and occupational status and women marry up. As a result, never-married women may represent the cream of the crop, whereas never-married men may be the bottom of the barrel. The marriage gradient is easy to observe in the way Canadian couples match their relative heights and ages, with the men slightly taller and older. (7)

marriage market   The sociological concept that potential mates take stock of their personal and social characteristics and then comparison shop or bargain for the best buy (mate) they can get. (7)

marriage premise   By getting married, partners accept the responsibility to keep each other primary in their lives and to work hard to ensure that their relationship continues. See also *expectations of permanence, primariness*. (8)

marriage squeeze   Used to refer to a situation where sex ratios create an "excess of women." (7)

martyring   Doing all one can for others while ignoring one's own legitimate needs. Martyrs often punish the person to whom they are martyring by letting her or him know "just how much I put up with." (4)

Marxist feminism   A branch of feminist theorizing that insists that the entire structure of our society must be changed before true gender equality can be attained. Argues that the only solution to eliminating women's oppression is to radically transform the economic institution from one based on capitalism to one based on socialism and, eventually, communism. (2)

masculinities   A term used to recognize that there are different "types" of masculinity. (3)

M-frame relationship   Relationship based on couple interdependence. Each partner has high self-esteem, but they mutually influence each other and experience loving as a deep emotion. See also *A-frame relationship, H-frame relationship*. (4)

mixed, or double, messages   Two simultaneous messages that contradict each other; also called a double message. For example, society gives us mixed messages regarding family values and individualistic values and about premarital sex. People, too, can send mixed messages, as when a partner says, "Of course I always like to talk with you" while turning up the TV. (9)

modern family   Throughout most of this century, the traditional nuclear family—husband, wife, and children living in one household. See also *postmodern family, nuclear family*. (1)

mommy track   Term applied to Felice Schwartz's proposal that corporations should develop a separate career ladder for women who wish to work fewer hours so that they may have more time for their families. In return, they would not expect to advance as far or as fast as full-time career women (and men). (13)

monogamy   The sexually exclusive union of a couple. (2)

N

narcissism   Characterized by an exaggerated concern with one's own self-image. (4)

naturalistic observation   A technique of scientific investigation in which a researcher lives with a family or social group or spends extensive time with them, carefully recording their activities, conversations, gestures, and other aspects of everyday life. (2)

no-fault divorce   The legal situation in which a partner seeking a divorce no longer has to prove grounds. (14)

noncustodial grandparent   A parent of a divorced, noncustodial parent. (12)

no-power   A situation in which partners are equally able to influence each other and, at the same time, are not concerned about their relative power vis-à-vis each other. No-power partners negotiate and compromise instead of trying to win. (10)

nuclear family   A family group comprising only the wife, the husband, and their children. See also *family, extended family, modern family, postmodern family.* (1)

nuclear-family model monopoly   Viewing the first-marriage family as the "real" model for family living, with all other family forms seen as deficient. (15)

O

objective measure of power   Identification of which partner in a relationship actually makes more important—or more—decisions, does more housework, and/or feels freer to raise complaints. Compare with *subjective measure of fairness.* (10)

occupational sex segregation   The distribution of men and women into substantially different occupations. Women are overrepresented in clerical and service work, for example, whereas men dominate the higher professions and the upper levels of management. (13)

opportunity costs (of children)   The economic opportunities for wage earning and investments that parents forgo when rearing children. (11)

P

paradoxical pregnancy   The concept that the more guilty and disapproving a sexually active woman is about premarital sex, the less likely she is to use contraceptives regularly, if at all. (11)

parallel relationship pattern   A pattern noted by sociologist Jessie Bernard among working-class marriages (as opposed to the interactional pattern among middle-class marriages) in which the husband was expected to be a hard-working provider and the wife a good housekeeper and cook. See also *interactional relationship pattern.* (8)

parental adjustment perspective   One of the five theoretical perspectives concerning the negative outcomes among children of divorced parents. From the parental adjustment perspective, the parent's child-rearing skills are impaired as a result of the divorce, with probable negative consequences for the children. See also *economic hardship perspective, interparental conflict perspective, life stress perspective, parental loss perspective.* (14)

parental loss perspective   A perspective which assumes that a family with both parents living in the same household is the optimal environment for children's development, and which views the absence of a parent from the household as problematic for the socialization of children. See also *economic hardship perspective, interparental conflict perspective, life stress perspective, parental adjustment perspective.* (14)

parenting alliance   The relationship between mothers and fathers or gay and lesbian parents as they coparent children, whether or not they are married or living together. (12)

passion (Sternberg's triangular theory of love)   The drives that lead to romance, physical attraction, sexual consummation, and so on in a loving relationship; one dimension of the triangular theory of love. See also *commitment, intimacy.* (4)

passive-aggression   Expressing anger at some person or situation indirectly, through nagging, nitpicking, or sarcasm, for example, rather than directly and openly. See also *displacement, sabotage.* (9)

passive-congenial marriage   A marital relationship in which spouses accent things other than emotional closeness; unlike devitalized partners, passive-congenial spouses have always done so. See also *conflict-habituated marriage, devitalized marriage, total marriage, vital marriage.* (8)

patriarchal sexuality   The view of human sexuality in which men own everything in the society, including women and women's sexuality, and males' sexual needs are emphasized while females' needs are minimized. (5)

patriarchal terrorism   A type of wife abuse that stems from a man's attempt to compensate for general feelings of powerlessness or inadequacy in their jobs, their marriages, or both. (10)

patriarchal violence   Refers specifically to wife abuse that results in more severe forms of injuries. (10)

patriarchy   A societal organization based on the supremacy of fathers and inheritance through the male line. (2)

period of disorganization   That period in a family crisis, after the stressor event has occurred, during which family morale and organization slump and habitual roles and routines become nebulous. (16)

permissiveness with affection   The standard that permits premarital sex for women and men equally, provided they have a fairly stable, affectionate relationship. See also *abstinence, double standard, permissiveness without affection.* (5)

permissiveness without affection   The standard that allows premarital sex for women and men regardless of how much stability or affection there is in their relationship. Also called the "recreational standard." See also *abstinence, double standard, permissiveness with affection.* (5)

personal marriage agreement   An articulated, negotiated agreement between partners about how each will behave in many or all aspects of the marriage. Personal marriage contracts need to be revised as partners change. A synonym is *relationship agreement.* (8)

pile-up   Concept from family stress and crisis theory that refers to the accumulation of family stressors and prior hardships. (16)

pink-collar jobs   Low-status, low-pay jobs still reserved primarily for women. The pink-collar job ghetto includes secretaries, beauticians, clerks, domestic workers, bookkeepers, waitresses, and so forth. (13)

pleasure bond   The idea, from Masters and Johnson's book by the same name, that sexual expression between intimates is one way of expressing and strengthening the emotional bond between them. (5)

pleasuring   Spontaneously doing what feels good at the moment during a sexual encounter; the opposite of *spectatoring.* (5)

polygamy A marriage system in which a person takes more than one spouse. "Polygyny" describes one man with multiple wives, while a marriage of a woman with plural husbands is termed "polyandry." (2)

pool of eligibles A group of individuals who, by virtue of background or birth, are most likely to make compatible marriage partners. (7)

postmodern family As a result of progressively increasing family diversity, today's family has little or no objective reference to a particular structure. In the postmodern perspective, there is tremendous variability of family forms in contemporary society, leading some theorists to conclude that the concept of "family" no longer has any objective meaning. See also *modern family, nuclear family* (1, 2)

power The ability to exercise one's will. Personal power, or autonomy, is power exercised over oneself. Social power is the ability to exercise one's will over others. (10)

power politics Power struggles between spouses in which each seeks to gain a power advantage over the other; the opposite of a no-power relationship. (10)

pragma The love style that emphasizes the practical, or pragmatic, element in human relationships and involves the rational assessment of a potential (or actual) partner's assets and liabilities. See also *agape, eros, ludus, mania, storge.* (4)

predictable crises Fairly predictable transitions over the course of family living that can be considered crises or critical opportunities for creatively reorganizing a family's values, attitudes, roles, or relationships. (16)

primariness Commitment to keeping one's partner the most important person in one's life. See also *expectations of permanence, marriage premise.* (8)

primary group A group, usually relatively small, in which there are close, face-to-face relationships. The family and a friendship group are primary groups. Compare with *secondary group.* (1)

primary parent Parent who takes full responsibility for meeting a child's physical and emotional needs by providing the major part of the child's care directly and/or managing the child's care by others. (12)

principle of least interest The postulate that the partner with the least interest in the relationship is the one who is more apt to exploit the other. See also *relative love and need theory.* (10)

private adoption Also called independent adoptions, private adoptions are those arranged directly between adoptive parent(s) and the biological mother, usually through an attorney. See also *public adoption.* (11)

pronatalist bias A cultural attitude that takes having children for granted. (11)

psychic divorce Regaining psychological autonomy after divorce; emotionally separating oneself from the personality and influence of the former spouse. (14)

psychic intimacy The sharing of people's minds and feelings. Psychic intimacy may or may not involve *sexual intimacy.* (4)

public adoption Adoptions that take place through licensed agencies that place children in adoptive families. See also *private adoption.* (11)

Q

quasi-kin Anthropologist Paul Bohannan's term for the person one's former spouse remarries. The term is also used more broadly to refer to former in-laws and other former and added kin resulting from divorce and remarriage. (15)

R

radical feminism A branch of feminist theorizing which suggest that the oppression of women is ultimately based on a system of ideas, referred to as patriarchy, that promotes the belief in male superiority. (2)

rapport talk In Deborah Tannen's terms, this is conversation engaged in by women aimed primarily at gaining or reinforcing rapport or intimacy. See also *report talk.* (9)

rational investment perspective Theory arguing that couples attempt to maximize the family economy by trading off between time and energy investments in paid market work and unpaid household labour. (13)

redivorce Redivorces take place more rapidly than first divorces so that many who divorce (and their children) can expect several rapid and emotionally significant transitions in lifestyle and family unit. (14)

referent power One of the six power bases, or sources of power. This power is based on the less dominant person's emotional identification with the more dominant individual. See also *coercive power, expert power, informational power, legitimate power, reward power.* (10)

refined divorce rate Number of divorces per 1000 married women over age 15. (14)

registered partnerships Laws that permit an unmarried couple to register their partnership and then receive some of the legal benefits of marriage, such as joint health or auto insurance or bereavement leave. (8)

rehabilitative alimony A plan under which a man pays his former wife support for a limited period after their divorce while she goes to school or otherwise gets retraining and finds a job. (14)

reinforcing cycle A cycle regarding women's earnings and paid and unpaid family work in which cultural expectations and persistent discrimination result in employed males receiving higher average earnings than women employed full-time, and hence in women's doing more unpaid family work. (13)

relationship agreement See *personal marriage agreement.* (8)

relative love and need theory Theory of conjugal power that holds that the spouse with the least to lose if the marriage ends is the more powerful in the relationship. See also *principle of least interest.* (10)

relatives of divorce Kinship ties established by marriage, but retained after the marriage is dissolved. For example, the relationship of a former mother-in-law and daughter-in-law. (14)

remarriages Marriages in which at least one partner has already been divorced or widowed. Remarriages are becoming increasingly common for Canadians. (15)

remarried family A family consisting of a husband and wife, at least one of whom has been married before, and one or more children from the previous marriage of either or both spouses. There are more remarried families in Canada today, and they usually result from divorce and remarriage. (15)

report talk In Deborah Tannen's terms, this is conversation engaged in by men aimed primarily at conveying information. See also *rapport talk.* (9)

representative sample Survey samples that reflect, or represent, all the people about whom social scientists want to know something. (5)

resiliency model of family stress, adjustment, and adaptation Complex model of family stress and adaptation developed from the *double ABC-X model*. (16)

resilient families Families that emphasize mutual acceptance, respect, and shared values; members rely on each other for emotional support. (16)

resource hypothesis Hypothesis by Blood and Wolfe that because conjugal power was no longer distributed according to sex, the relative power between wives and husbands would result from their relative resources (for example, age, education, job skills) as individuals. (10, 13)

reward power One of the six power bases, or sources of power. This power is based on an individual's ability to give material or nonmaterial gifts and favours. See also *coercive power, expert power, informational power, legitimate power, referent power*. (10)

role making Improvising a course of action and fitting it to that of others. In role making we use our acts to alter the traditional expectations and obligations associated with a role. (8)

role-reversed couples Couples in which the woman is the provider and the man assumes responsibility for childrearing/housework. (13)

romantically-fused couple A term used by Stephen Marks to refer to a couple in which "enormous energy" fuses the couple together. See also *dependancy-distancing couple, separate couple*. (8)

S

sabotage A passive-aggressive action in which a person tries to spoil or undermine some activity another has planned. Sabotage is not always consciously planned. See also *displacement, passive-aggression*. (9)

safer sex The use of latex condoms and the selective limiting of number of sex partners as a precaution against contracting or spreading *HIV/AIDS* or other sexually transmitted diseases. (5)

sandwich generation Middle-aged (or older) individuals, usually women, who are sandwiched between the simultaneous responsibilities of caring for their dependent children (sometimes young adults) and aging parents. (12, 16)

scapegoating A negative family interaction behaviour in which one family member is consistently blamed for everything that goes wrong in the household. (9)

scientific investigation The systematic gathering of information—using surveys, experiments, naturalistic observation, and case studies—from which it often is possible to generalize with a significant degree of predictability. (2)

secondary group A group, often large, characterized by distant, practical relationships. An impersonal society is characterized by secondary groups and relations. Compare with *primary group*. (1)

second shift Sociologist Arlie Hochschild's term for the domestic work that employed women must perform after coming home from a day on the job. (13)

secure attachment style One of three attachment styles in attachment style theory, this style involves trust that the relationship will provide necessary and ongoing emotional and social support. See also *avoidant attachment style, insecure/anxious attachment style*. (4)

selective reduction Also called "selective termination," a process involved in reproductive technology in which some (but not all) fetuses in multiple pregnancies (resulting from ovulation-stimulating fertility drugs or the GIFT procedure) are selectively aborted, usually in the first trimester. (11)

self-concept The basic feelings people have about themselves, their abilities, and their worth; how people think of or view themselves. (2)

self-disclosure Letting others see one as one really is. Self-disclosure demands authenticity. (4)

self-esteem Feelings and evaluations people have about their own worth. (4)

self-identification theory A theory of gender socialization, developed by psychologist Lawrence Kohlberg, that begins with a child's categorization of self as male or female. The child goes on to identify sex-appropriate behaviours in the family, media, and elsewhere, and to adopt those behaviours. (3)

separate couple A term used by Stephen Marks to refer to a couple type in which both individuals are focused outside the marriage and distance themselves from their spouses. See also *dependancy-distancing couple, romantically-fused couple*. (8)

sex The different chromosomal, hormonal, and anatomical components of males and females at birth. (3)

sex ratio The ratio of men to women in a given society or subgroup of society. (6, 7)

sexual abuse A form of child abuse that involves forced, tricked, or coerced sexual behaviour—exposure, unwanted kissing, fondling of sexual organs, intercourse, and incest—between a young person and an older person. (10)

sexual exclusivity Expectations for strict monogamy in which a couple promise or publicly vow to have sexual relations only with each other. (8)

sexual intimacy A level of interpersonal interaction in which partners have a sexual relationship. Sexual intimacy may or may not involve *psychic intimacy*. (4)

sexual orientation The attraction an individual has for a sexual partner of the same or opposite sex. (5)

sexual responsibility The assumption by each partner of responsibility for his or her own sexual response. (5)

sexually open marriage A marriage agreement in which spouses agree that each may have openly acknowledged sexual relationships with others while keeping the marriage relationship primary. (8)

shared parenting Mother and father (or two homosexual parents) who both take full responsibility as parents. (12)

shift work Any work schedule in which more than half an employee's hours are before 8 A.M. or after 4 P.M. (13)

significant others People whose opinions about one are very important to one's self-esteem. Good friends are significant others, as are family members. (9)

single remarriage A remarriage in which only one of the partners was previously married. Compare with *double remarriage*. (15)

social institution A system of patterned and predictable ways of thinking and behaving—beliefs, values, attitudes, and norms—concerning important aspects of people's lives. The five major social institutions are family, religion, government or politics, economics, and education. (2)

socialist feminism A branch of feminist theorizing which combines both the Marxist and radical feminist perspectives. Argues that it is the historical combination of the capitalist economic and political system and patriarchal ideology that leads to the oppression of women. (2)

socialization The process by which society influences members to internalize attitudes, beliefs, values, and expectations. (3)

social learning theory   According to this theory, children learn gender roles as they are taught by parents, schools, and the media. (3)

social power   The ability to exercise one's will over others. (10)

spectatoring   A term Masters and Johnson coined to describe the practice of emotionally removing oneself from a sexual encounter in order to watch oneself and see how one is doing. Compare with *pleasuring*. (5)

stalled revolution   As used by sociologist Arlie Hochschild, the juxtaposition of women's entry into the paid labour force but without men's doing more unpaid family work. (13)

static (closed) marriage   A marriage that does not change over the years and does not allow for changes in the partners. Static marriage partners rely on their formal, legal bond to enforce permanence and sexual exclusivity. Static marriages are more inclined to become *devitalized* than are *flexible marriages*. (8)

stepmother trap   The conflict between two views: Society sentimentalizes the stepmother's role and expects her to be unnaturally loving toward her stepchildren but at the same time views her as a wicked witch. (15)

Sternberg's triangular theory of love   Psychologist Robert Sternberg's formulation of love, in which a variety of types of love are constructed from the three basic dimensions of *passion, intimacy,* and *commitment*. (4)

SVR (Stimulus-values-roles)   A three-stage filtering sequence in *assortive mating*. (7)

stonewalling   Tactics designed to evade or avoid a fight. Refusing to engage with a partner's attempts to raise disputed or tension-producing issues. (9)

storge   An affectionate, companionate style of loving. See also *agape, eros, ludus, mania, pragma*. (4)

stressor   A precipitating event that causes a crisis—it is often a situation for which the family has had little or no preparation. See also *ABC-X model, double ABC-X model*. (16)

stressor overload   A situation in which an unrelenting series of small crises adds up to a major crisis. (16)

structural antinatalism   The structural, or societal, condition in which bearing and rearing children is discouraged either overtly or covertly through subtle economic discrimination against parents. (11)

structural-functionalist perspective   Theoretical perspective that looks to the functions that institutions perform for society and the structural form of the institution. (2)

subfecundity   Also called "secondary infertility," the condition in which parents who have at least one child have difficulty having additional children. (11)

subjective measure of fairness   Perceptions of whether or not a relationship is fair. Compare with *objective measure of power*. (10)

supervised visitation   A situation in which contact between a child and a visiting noncustodial parent occurs only in the presence of a third party, such as a social worker or a court employee. (14)

suppression of anger   Repression—the involuntary, unconscious blocking of painful thoughts, feelings, or memories from the conscious mind—as it applies to anger. Repressed feelings of anger often come out in other ways, such as overeating and feeling bored or depressed. (9)

survey   A technique of scientific investigation using questionnaires or brief face-to-face interviews or both. An example is the Canadian census. See also *longitudinal study*. (2)

survival of the fittest   Proposed by Charles Darwin, a theory that suggests that only the strongest, more intelligent and adaptable of a species survive to reproduce. (5)

swinging   A marriage agreement in which couples exchange partners in order to engage in purely recreational sex. (8)

symbiotic relationship   A relationship, based on the mutual meeting of *illegitimate needs*, in which each partner depends on the other for a sense of self-worth. See also *legitimate needs*. (4)

T

testing   One of four patterns of cohabition identified by Carl Ridley and his colleagues. In this pattern, cohabitation is viewed as a "trial marriage." See also *convenience, emancipation, "Linus blanket."* (7)

theoretical perspective   A way of viewing reality, or a lens through which analysts organize and interpret what they observe. Researchers on the family identify those aspects of families that are of interest to them, based on their own theoretical perspective. (2)

theory of complementary needs   Theory developed by social scientist Robert Winch suggesting that we are attracted to partners whose needs complement our own. In the positive view of this theory, we are attracted to others whose strengths are harmonious with our own so that we are more effective as a couple than either of us would be alone. (7)

three-phase cycle of violence   A relationship-violence cycle in which (1) tension builds between two parties; (2) the situation escalates, exploding in a violent episode; and (3) the violent person becomes contrite, apologizing and treating the other lovingly. Predictably, the cycle continually repeats itself. (10)

total fertility rate   For a given year, the number of births that women would have over their reproductive lifetimes if all women at each age had babies at the rate for each age group that year. See also *crude birthrate*. (11)

total marriage   A marital relationship in which partners are intensely bound together psychologically; an *intrinsic* rather than a *utilitarian marriage*. Total relationships are similar to vital relationships but are more multifaceted. See also *conflict-habituated marriage, devitalized marriage, passive-congenial marriage, vital marriage*. (8)

trailing spouse   The spouse of a relocated employee who moves with him or her. (13)

transitions   Predictable changes in the course of family life. (16)

two-career marriage   A marriage in which both partners have a strong commitment to the lifetime development of careers. (13)

two-earner marriage   Both partners are in the paid labour force. (13)

two-location families   See *commuter marriage*. (13)

two-person single career   The situation in which one spouse, usually the wife, encourages and participates in the other partner's career without direct recognition or personal remuneration. (13)

two-stage marriage   An alternative to more formal dating proposed by the late anthropologist Margaret Mead. Individuals would first enter into individual marriages involving no children but a serious though not necessarily lifelong commitment. Couples who were compatible in individual marriages might choose to move into the second stage, parental marriage, which would presume lifelong commitment and the ability to cooperatively support and care for a child or children. (7)

U

unpaid family work   The necessary tasks of attending to both the emotional needs of all family members and the practical needs of dependent members, such as children or elderly parents, and maintaining the family domicile. (13)

utilitarian marriage   A union begun or maintained for primarily practical purposes. Compare with *intrinsic marriage*. (8)

V

vertically extended family   Three or more generations sharing houses and resources. Compare with *horizontally extended family*. (2)

violence between intimates   Murders, sexual assaults, robberies, or assaults committed by spouses, ex-spouses, boyfriends, or girlfriends. (10)

vital marriage   A marital relationship in which partners are intensely bound together psychologically; an *intrinsic* rather than a *utilitarian marriage*. See also *conflict-habituated marriage, devitalized marriage, passive-congenial marriage, total marriage*. (8)

voluntary stable singles   Singles who are satisfied to have never married, divorced people who do not want to remarry, cohabitants who do not intend to marry, and those whose lifestyles preclude marriage, such as priests and nuns. (6)

voluntary temporary singles   Younger never-marrieds and divorced people who are postponing marriage or remarriage. They are open to the possibility of marriage, but searching for a mate has a lower priority than do other activities, such as career. (6)

vulnerable families   Families that have a low sense of common purpose, feel in little control over what happens to them, and tend to cope with problems by showing diminished respect and/or understanding for each other. (16)

W

wheel of love   An idea developed by Ira Reiss in which love is seen as developing through a four-stage, circular process, including rapport, self-revelation, mutual dependence, and personality need fulfillment. (4)

References

A

AAMFT (American Association for Marital and Family Therapy). <http://www.aamft.org/>

AAUW (American Association of University Women). 1992. *The AAUW Report: How Schools Shortchange Girls.* New York: Marlowe & Company.

Abbey, Antonia, Frank M. Andrews, and L. Jill Halman. 1991. "Gender's Role in Responses to Infertility." *Psychology of Women Quarterly* 15:295–316.

———. 1992. "Infertility and Subjective Well-Being: The Mediating Roles of Self-Esteem, Internal Control, and Interpersonal Conflict." *Journal of Marriage and the Family* 54 (2) (May):408–17.

Abel, Emily K. 1991. *Who Cares for the Elderly? Public Policy and the Experiences of Adult Daughters.* Philadelphia: Temple University Press.

Abella, Irving. 1999. "Anti-Semitism." P. 90 in *Canadian Encyclopedia: Year 2000 Edition* edited by James H. Marsh. Toronto: McClelland & Stewart Inc.

Abelson, Reed. 1998. "Part-Time Work for Some Adds up to Full-Time Job." *New York Times.* November 2:A1–A16.

Abizadeh, Sohrab and Nancy Zukewich Ghalam. 1994. "Immigrants and Canadian-born: A Consumptive Behaviour Assessment." *Social Indicators Research* 32 (1) May:49–72.

"Abortion: 'Partial Birth' Ground Zero." 1997. *Newsweek* 129 (21):34.

Abu-Rabia, Salim. 1997. "Gender Differences In Arab Students' Attitudes Toward Canadian Society And Second Language Learning." *Journal of Social Psychology* 137 (2) (Feb.):125–128.

Achilles, R. 1995. "Assisted Reproduction: The Social Issues." Pp. 346–364 in *Gender in the 1990s: Images, Realities and Issues,* edited by E.D. Nelson and B.W. Robinson. Toronto: Nelson.

Acker, M. and M. H. Davis. 1992. "Intimacy, Passion, and Commitment in Adult Romantic Relationships: A Test of the Triangular Theory of Love." *Journal of Social and Personal Relationships* 9:21–30.

Acock, Alan C. and David C. Demo. 1994. *Family Diversity and Well-Being.* Thousand Oaks, CA: Sage.

Adams, Karen L. and Norma C. Ware. 1995. "Sexism and the English Language: The Linguistic Implications of Being a Woman." Pp. 331–346 in *Women: A Feminist Perspective.* 5th ed., edited by Jo Freeman. Mountain View, CA: Mayfield.

Adams, Michael. 1997. *Sex in the Snow.* Toronto: Viking Press.

Adams, Owen and Dhruva Nagnur. 1990. "Marrying and Divorcing: A Status Report for Canada." Pp. 142–145 in *Canadian Social Trends,* edited by Craig McKie and Keith Thompson.

Adams, O.B. and D.N. Nagnur. 1988. *Marriage, Divorce and Mortality: A Life Table Analysis for Canada and Regions.* Ottawa: Statistics Canada.

Adler, Jerry. 1993. "Sex in the Snoring '90s." *Newsweek.* (April) 26:55–57.

———. 1996a. "Adultery: A New Furor Over an Old Sin." *Newsweek.* September 30:54–60.

———. 1996b. "Building a Better Dad." *Newsweek.* June 17:58–64.

———. 1997b. "How Kids Mourn." *Newsweek.* September 22:58–61.

———. 1998. "Tomorrow's Child." *Newsweek.* November 2:54–64.

Adler, Nancy E., Henry P. David, Brenda N. Major, Susan H. Roth, Nancy F. Russo, and Gail E. Wyatt. 1990. "Psychological Responses After Abortion," *Science* 248:41–44.

Ahlander, Nancy Rollins and Kathleen Slaugh Bahr. 1995. "Beyond Drudgery, Power, and Equity: Toward an Expanded Discourse on the Moral Dimensions of Housework in Families." *Journal of Marriage and the Family* 57 (1) (Feb.):54–68.

Ahlburg, Dennis A. and Carol J. De Vita. 1992. *New Realities of the American Family. Population Bulletin* 47 (2). Washington, DC: Population Reference Bureau.

Ahmed, Ashraf Uddin. 1993. "Marriage and Its Transition in Bangladesh." Pp. 74–83 in *Next of Kin: An International Reader on Changing Families,* edited by Lorne Tepperman and Susannah J. Wilson. Englewood Cliffs, NJ: Prentice Hall.

Ahrons, Constance R. and Richard B. Miller. 1993. "The Effect of the Post-Divorce Relationship on Paternal Involvement: A Longitudinal Analysis." *American Journal of Orthopsychiatry* 63 (3) (July):462–79.

Ahrons, Constance R. and Lynn Wallisch. 1987. "Parenting in the Binuclear Family: Relationships Between Biological and Stepparents." Pp. 225–56 in *Remarriage and Stepparenting,* edited by Kay Pasley and Marilyn Ihinger-Tallman. New York: Guilford.

Ahuvia, Aaron C. and Mara B. Adelman. 1992. "Formal Intermediaries in the Marriage Market: A Typology and Review." *Journal of Marriage and the Family* 54 (May):452–63.

"AIDS Front: Good News and Grim News." 1995. *U.S. News & World Report.* Feb. 13.

Ainsworth, M. D. S. 1973. "The Development of Infant–Mother Attachment." In *Review of Child Development Research,* vol. III, edited by B. M. Caldwell and H. N. Ricuiti. Chicago: University of Chicago Press.

Albrecht, Carol M., Mark A. Fossett, Cynthia M. Cready, and K. Jill Kiecolt. 1997. "Mate Availability, Women's Marriage Prevalence, and Husbands' Education." *Journal of Family Issues* 18 (4):429–52.

Albrecht, Don E. and Stan L. Albrecht. 1996. "Family Structure among Urban, Rural and Farm Populations: Classic Sociological Theory Revisited." *Rural Sociology* 61 (3):446–63.

Alden, Paulette Bates. 1998. *Crossing the Moon: A Journey through Infertility.* New York: Penguin Books.

Aldous, Joan. 1978. *Family Careers: Developmental Change in Families.* New York: Wiley.

———. 1990. "Specification and Speculation Concerning the Politics of Workplace Family Policies." *Journal of Family Issues* 11 (4) (Dec.):355–67.

Aldous, Joan, and Wilfried Dumon, eds. 1980. *The Politics and Programs of Family Policy.* Notre Dame, IN: University of Notre Dame Press.

Aldous, Joan, Lawrence Marsh, and Scott Trees. 1985. "Families and Inflation." Paper prepared for presentation at the 80th Annual Meeting of the American Sociological Association, Aug. 26–30.

Aldous, Joan, Gail M. Mulligan, and Thoroddur Bjarnason. 1998. "Fathering over Time: What Makes the Difference?" *Journal of Marriage and the Family* 60 (4):809–20.

Aldous, Joan and Robert C. Tuttle. 1988. "Unemployment and the Family." Pp. 17–41 in *Employment and Economic Problems: Families in Trouble,* vol. 1, edited by Catherine S. Chilman, Elam W. Nunnally, and Fred M. Cox. Newbury Park, CA: Sage.

Alexander, C. S., and B. Guyer. 1993. "Adolescent Pregnancy: Occurrence and Consequences." *Pediatric Annals* 22:85–88.

Alexander, Pamela C., Sharon Moore, and Elmore R. Alexander III. 1991. "What Is Transmitted in the Inter-

generational Transmission of Violence?" *Journal of Marriage and the Family* 53 (3) (Aug.):657–68.

Alexander, Suzanne. 1991. "More Working Mothers Opt for Flexibility of Operating a Franchise from Home." *The Wall Street Journal,* Jan. 13, p. B1.

Allen, Katherine R. 1993. "The Dispassionate Discourse of Children's Adjustment to Divorce." *Journal of Marriage and the Family* 55 (1) (Feb.):46–49.

———. 1997. "Lesbian and Gay Families." Pp. 196–218 in Terry Arendell (ed.). *Contemporary Parenting: Challenges and Issues.* Thousand Oaks, CA: Sage.

Allen, Katherine R. and David H. Demo. 1995. "The Families of Lesbians and Gay Men: A New Frontier in Family Research." *Journal of Marriage and the Family* 57 (1) (Feb.):111–27.

Allen, Robert L. and Paul Kivel. 1994. "Men Changing Men." *Ms.* Sept./Oct.:50–53.

Allen, W. 1978. "The Search for Applicable Theories of Black Family Life." *Journal of Marriage and the Family* 40 (1):117–31.

Allgeier, E. R. 1983. "Sexuality and Gender Roles in the Second Half of Life." Pp. 135–37 in *Changing Boundaries: Gender Roles and Sexual Behavior,* edited by Elizabeth Rice Allgeier and Naomi B. McCormick. Palo Alto, CA: Mayfield.

Almeida, David M., Maggs, Jennifer L., Galambos, Nancy L. 1993. "Wives' Employment Hours and Spousal Participation in Family Work." *Journal of Family Psychology* 7 (2) (Sept.):233–244.

Almond, Brenda and Carole Ulanowsky. 1990. "HIV and Pregnancy." *Hastings Center Report* (Mar./Apr.). 16–21.

Alter, Jonathan. 1997. "Making Child Care Macho." *Newsweek.* November 3:70.

Altman, I. and W. W. Haythorn. 1965. "Interpersonal Exchange in Isolation." *Sociometry* 28:411–26.

Altman, Irwin and Dalmas A. Taylor. 1973. *Social Penetration: The Development of Interpersonal Relations.* New York: Holt, Rinehart & Winston.

Alvardo, Donna. 1992. "Children Having Children." *San Jose Mercury News,* July 1, pp. 1D, 6D.

Alvarez, Lizette. 1995. "Pint-Size Interpreters of World for Parents." *New York Times,* Oct. 1, p. A16.

Alvi, Shahid, Walter DeKeseredy and Desmond Ellis. 2000. *Contemporary Social Problem in North American Society.* Don Mills, ON: Addison-Wesley.

Alwin, Duane, Philip Converse, and Steven Martin. 1985. "Living Arrangements and Social Integration." *Journal of Marriage and the Family* 47:319–34.

Amato, Paul R. 1988. "Parental Divorce and Attitudes Toward Marriage and Family Life." *Journal of Marriage and the Family* 50:453–61.

———. 1991. "The 'Child of Divorce' as a Person Prototype: Bias in the Recall of Information About Children in

Divorced Families." *Journal of Marriage and the Family* 53 (1) (Feb.):59–70.

———. 1993. "Children's Adjustment to Divorce Theories, Hypotheses, and Empirical Support." *Journal of Marriage and the Family* 55 (1) (Feb.):23–28.

———. 1994a. "Father-Child Relations, Mother-Child Relations, and Offspring Psychological Well-Being in Early Adulthood." *Journal of Marriage and the Family* 56 (4) (Nov.):1031–42.

———. 1994b. "The Implications of Research Findings on Children in Stepfamilies." Pp. 81–88 in *Stepfamilies: Who Benefits? Who Does Not?* Edited by Alan Booth and Judy Dunn (Eds.). Hillsdale, NJ: Lawrence Erlbaum Associates.

———. 1996. "Explaining the Intergenerational Transmission of Divorce." *Journal of Marriage and the Family* 58 (3):628–40.

Amato, Paul R. and Alan Booth. 1991. "The Consequences of Divorce for Attitudes Toward Divorce and Gender Roles." *Journal of Family Issues* 12 (3) (Sept.):306–22.

———. 1996. "A Prospective Study of Divorce and Parent-Child Relationships." *Journal of Marriage and the Family* 58 (2):356–65.

———. 1997. *A Generation at Risk: Growing Up in an Era of Family Upheaval.* Cambridge, MA: Harvard University Press.

Amato, Paul R. and Bruce Keith. 1991a. "Parental Divorce and the Well-Being of Children: A Meta-analysis." *Psychological Bulletin* 110:26–46.

———. 1991b. "Parental Divorce and Adult Well-Being: A Meta-analysis." *Journal of Marriage and the Family* 53 (1) (Feb.):43–58.

Amato, Paul R., Sandra J. Rezac, and Alan Booth. 1995. "Helping Between Parents and Young Adult Offspring: The Role of Parental Marital Quality, Divorce, and Remarriage." *Journal of Marriage and the Family* 57 (2) (May):363–74.

Amato, Paul R. and Stacy J. Rogers. 1997. "A Longitudinal Study of Marital Problems and Subsequent Divorce." *Journal of Marriage and the Family* 59 (3):612–24.

Ambert, Anne-Marie. 1988. "Relationships with Former In-laws After Divorce: A Research Note." *Journal of Marriage and the Family* 50:679–86.

———. 1994. "A Qualitative Study of Peer Abuse and Its Effects: Theoretical and Empirical Implications." *Journal of Marriage and the Family* 56 (1) (Feb.):119–30.

———. 1997. *Parents, Children, and Adolescents: Interactive Relationships and Development in Context.* New York: Haworth Press.

———. 1998. "Divorce: Facts, Figures and Consequences." Vanier Institute of the Family. <http://www.vifamily.ca/cft/divorce/divorce.htm>

Ambroz, Juliann R. 1995. "Keeping Love Alive: How Couples Counseling Can Work for You." *Mothering* (Fall):75–80.

American Psychological Association. Public Interest Directorate. 1987. *Research Review: The Psychological Sequelae of Abortion.* Washington, DC: American Psychological Association.

Ames, Katherine. 1992. "Extramarital Bliss." *Newsweek.* March 23.

Andersen, Margaret L. 1988. *Thinking About Women: Sociological Perspectives on Sex and Gender,* 2d ed. New York: Macmillan.

Anderson, Kristin L. 1997. "Gender, Status, and Domestic Violence: An Integration of Feminist and Family Violence Approaches." *Journal of Marriage and the Family* 59 (3):655–69.

Anderson, Tamara, and Beth Vail. 1999. "Child-Care Dilemmas in Contemporary Families." Pp. 359–70 in *American Families: A Multicultural Reader,* edited by Stephanie Coontz . New York: Routledge.

Anderssen, Erin. 1999. "Gay-Bashing Preacher Calls Off Protest." *Globe and Mail,* June 29. <www.egale.ca/archives/press/9906299gm.htm>

Andrews, Bernice and Chris R. Brewin. 1990. "Attributions of Blame for Marital Violence: A Study of Antecedents and Consequences." *Journal of Marriage and the Family* 52 (3) (Aug.):757–67.

Andrews, Lori B. and Nanette Elster. 2000. "Regulating Reproductive Technologies." *Journal of Legal Medicine* 21(1) (March):35–65.

Anetzberger, Georgia, Jill Korbin, and Craig Austin. 1994. "Alcoholism and Elder Abuse." *Journal of Interpersonal Violence* 9 (2):184–93.

Angier, Natalie. 1998. "Men. Are Women Better Off with Them, or without Them?" *New York Times.* June 21.

Angus Reid Group, Inc. 1999. "Majority (55%) Agree with Supreme Court Decision That Definition of 'Spouse' Apply to Same-Sex Couples." Press release date: Wednesday June 9.

Ankney, C. D. 1995. "Sex Differences in Brain Size and Mental Abilities: Comments on R. Lynn and D. Kimura." *Personality and Individual Differences* 18:423–24.

Annas, George J. 1991. "Crazy Making: Embryos and Gestational Mothers." *Hastings Center Report* (Jan./Feb.):35–38.

Annuziata, Jane. 1998. *Why Am I an Only Child?* Washington, DC: Magination Press.

Anson, Ofra. 1989. "Marital Status and Women's Health Revisited: The Importance of a Proximate Adult." *Journal of Marriage and the Family* 51:185–94.

Antill, J. K. 1987. "Parents' Beliefs and Values about Sex Roles, Sex Differences, and Sexuality." Pp. 294–328 in

Sex and Gender, edited by P. Shaver and C. Hendrick. Newbury Park, CA: Sage.

Aquilino, William S. 1994a. "Later Life Parental Divorce and Widowhood: Impact on Young Adults' Assessment of Parent–Child Relations." *Journal of Marriage and the Family* 56 (4) (Nov.):908–22.

———. 1994b. "Impact of Childhood Family Disruption on Young Adults' Relationships with Parents." *Journal of Marriage and the Family* 56 (2) (May):295–313.

———. 1997. "From Adolescent to Young Adult: A Prospective Study of Parent-Child Relations During the Transition to Adulthood." *Journal of Marriage and the Family* 59:670–86.

Arafat, I. and Betty Yorburg. 1973. "On Living Together Without Marriage." *Journal of Sex Research* 9:21–29.

Arditti, Joyce A. 1997. "Women, Divorce, and Economic Risk." *Family and Conciliation Courts Review* 35 (1):79–92.

Arditti, Joyce A. and Timothy Z. Keith. 1993. "Visitation Frequency, Child Support Payment, and the Father–Child Relationship Postdivorce." *Journal of Marriage and the Family* 55 (3) (Aug.):699–712.

Arendell, Terry. 1986. *Mothers and Divorce: Legal, Economic, and Social Dilemmas.* Berkeley: University of California Press.

———. 1995. *Fathers and Divorce.* Thousand Oaks, CA: Sage.

———. 1997a. "A Social Constructionist Approach to Parenting." Pp. 1–44 in *Contemporary Parenting: Challenges and Issues* edited by Terry Arendell. Thousand Oaks, CA: Sage.

———. 1997b. "Divorce and Remarriage." Pp.154–95 in *Contemporary Parenting: Challenges and Issues* edited by Terry Arendell. Thousand Oaks, CA: Sage.

Ariès Phillipe. 1962. *Centuries of Childhood: A Social History of Family Life.* New York: Knopf.

Arnold, Tom. (1999, November 30) "Older Heart Attack Patients Less Likely to Get Vital Drugs." *National Post,* p. A5.

———. 2000. "Youth Ignorant of Morning-after Pill, Study Finds." *National Post,* August 23, 2000.

———. 2001. "B.C. Court Says No to Gay Marriage." *National Post,* October 4: A1, A15.

Arnup, Katherine (ed.) 1995. *Lesbian Parenting: Living with Pride and Prejudice.* Charlottetown, PEI: gynergy books.

———. 1999. "Out in This World: The Social and Legal Context of Gay and Lesbian Families." *Journal of Gay & Lesbian Social Services* 10 (1):1–25.

Arond, Miriam and Samuel L. Pauker, M.D. 1987. *The First Year of Marriage.* New York: Warner.

Aronson, Jane. 1992. "Women's Sense of Responsibility for the Care of Old People: But Who Else Is Going to Do It?" *Gender & Society* 6 (1) (Mar.):8–29.

Armstrong, Pat. 1999. Pp. 813–815 in *The Canadian Encyclopedia: Year 2000 Edition,* edited by James H. Marsh. Toronto: McClelland & Stewart Inc.

Aseltine, Robert H. Jr., and Ronald C. Kessler. 1993. "Marital Disruption and Depression in a Community Sample." *Journal of Health and Social Behavior* 34 (Sept.):237–51.

Associated Press. 2000. "Canada Court: Polygamy Ban is Invalid." <http://www.polygamyinfo.com/past_media%20plyg%2030ap.htm>

Astone, Nan Marie and Sara S. McLanahan. 1991. "Family Structure, Parental Practices and High School Completion." *American Sociological Review* 56 (June):309–20.

Astor, Gerald. 1996. "Computer Marriage: The Mouse that Roared." *Cosmopolitan.* April:218–21.

Atchley, Robert C. 1997. *Social Forces and Aging.* Belmont, CA: Wadsworth.

Atkin, David J., Jay Moorman, and Carolyn A. Lin. 1991. "Ready for Prime Time: Network Series Devoted to Working Women in the 1980s." *Sex Roles* 25 (11/12):677–83.

Atkinson, Alice M. 1992. "Stress Levels of Family Day Care Providers, Mothers Employed Outside the Home, and Mothers at Home." *Journal of Marriage and the Family* 564 (2) (May):379–86.

———. 1994. "Rural and Urban Families' Use of Child Care." *Family Relations* 43:16–22.

Atkinson, Maxine P. and Stephen P. Blackwelder. 1993. "Fathering in the 20th Century." *Journal of Marriage and the Family* 55:975–86.

Atlas, James. 1997. "Making the Grade: Going to Private School is Increasingly Hard Work—for the Parents." *The New Yorker.* April 14:34–39.

Auerbach, Judith D. 1990. "Employer-Supported Child Care as a Women-Responsive Policy." *Journal of Family Issues* 11 (4) (Dec.):384–400.

Aulette, Judy. 1994. *Changing Families.* Belmont, CA: Wadsworth.

Avery, Rosemary J. 1997. *Adoption Policy and Special Needs Children.* Westport, CT: Auborn House.

Aycan, Zeynep and Rabindra N. Kanungo. 1998. "Impact of Acculturation on Socialization Beliefs and Behavioral Occurrences among Indo-Canadian Immigrants." *Journal of Comparative Family Studies* 29 (3) (autumn):451–467.

Axinn, William G. and Jennifer S. Barber. 1997. "Living Arrangements and Family Formation Attitudes in Early Adulthood." *Journal of Marriage and the Family* 59:595–611.

Axinn, William G. and Arland Thornton. 1992. "The Relationship Between Cohabitation and Divorce: Selectivity or Casual Influence?" *Demography* 29 (3) (Aug.):357–74.

———. 1993. "Mothers, Children, and Cohabitation: The Intergenerational Effects of Attitudes and Behavior." *American Sociological Review* 58 (2) (Apr.):233–45.

B

Babbie, Earl. 1992. *The Practice of Social Research*, 6th ed. Belmont, CA: Wadsworth.

———. 1998. *The Practice of Social Research,* 8th ed. Belmont, CA: Wadsworth.

Bach, George R. and Ronald M. Deutsch. 1970. *Pairing.* New York: Avon.

Bach, George R. and Peter Wyden. 1970. *The Intimate Enemy: How to Fight Fair in Love and Marriage.* New York: Avon.

Bachman, Ronet and Linda S. Saltzman. 1995. "Violence Against Women: Estimates from the Redesigned Survey August 1995." *U.S. Department of Justice Special Report NCJ-154348.* Washington, DC: U.S. Bureau of Justice Statistics Clearinghouse. <www.ojp.usdoj.gov>

Backhouse, Constance. 1999. "White Female Help and Chinese-Canadian Employers: Race, Class, Gender, and Law in the Case of Yee Clun, 1924." Pp. 3–22 in *Law in Society: Canadian Readings,* edited by Nick Larsen and Brian Burtch (eds.). Toronto: Harcourt Brace.

Bahr, Howard M. and Bruce A. Chadwick. 1985. "Religion and Family in Middletown, USA." *Journal of Marriage and the Family* 47 (2):407–14.

Bahr, Stephen J. and Boyd C. Rollins. 1971. "Crisis and Conjugal Power." *Journal of Marriage and the Family* 33:360–67.

Bailey, Martha. 2000. *Marriage and Marriage-Like Relationships.* <http://www.lcc.gc.ca/cgi-bin/repere_en.c...y%2C+Martha&language=en&range=1&numdoc>

Bailey, Sue. 2001. "Ex-NBA Star Loses Custody Battle." *KW Record*, September 29: A12.

Baker, James N. 1989. "Lesbians: Portrait of a Community." *Newsweek*, Mar. 12, p. 24.

Baker, M. and D. Lero. 1996. "Division of Labour: Paid Work and Family Structure." Pp. 78–103 in *Families: Changing Trends in Canada*, 3rd edition, edited by Maureen Baker. Toronto: McGraw-Hill Ryerson.

Baker, Maureen. 1996. "Introduction to Family Studies: Cultural Variation and Family Trends." Pp. 3–34 in *Families: Changing Trends in Canada*, 3rd edition, edited by Maureen Baker. Toronto: McGraw-Hill Ryerson.

Bala, Nicholas. 1996. "Spousal Abuse and Children of Divorce: A Differentiated Approach." *Canadian Journal of Family Law* 13(2):215–285.

———. 1994. "The Evolving Canadian Definition of the Family: Towards a Pluralistic and Functional Approach." *International Journal of Law and the Family* 8 (3) (Dec.):293–318.

Balakrishnan, T.R., K. Krotki and E. Lapierre-Adamcyk. 1985. "Contraceptive Use in Canada." *Family Planning Perspectives* 17:209–15.

Baldwin, James. 1988. "A Talk to Teachers." Pp. 3–12 in *Multicultural Literacy*, edited by Rick Simonson and Scott Walker. St. Paul, MN: Graywolf Press.

Balli, Sandra J., David H. Demo, and John F. Wedman. 1998. "Family Involvement with Children's Homework: An Intervention in the Middle Grades." *Family Relations* 47 (2):149–57.

Bandura, A. 1986. *The Social Foundations of Thought and Action: A Social Cognitive Theory.* Englewood Cliffs, NJ: Prentice-Hall.

Bankston, Carl L. III. 1998. "Sibling Cooperation and Scholastic Performance among Vietnamese-American Secondary School Students: An Ethnic Social Relations Theory." *Sociological Perspectives* 41 (1):167–84.

Bankston, Carl L. III and Stephen J. Caldas. 1998. "Family Structure, Schoolmates, and Racial Inequalities in School Achievement." *Journal of Marriage and the Family* 60 (3):715–23.

Barber, Brian K. 1994. "Cultural, Family, and Personal Contexts of Parent–Adolescent Conflict." *Journal of Marriage and the Family* 56 (2) (May):375–86.

Bardwick, Judith M. 1971. *Psychology of Women: A Study of Biocultural Conflicts.* New York: Harper & Row.

Baril, Alain and George A. Mori. 1991. "Leaving the Fold: Declining Church Attendance." *Canadian Social Trends* 22:21–24.

Barlow, Maude and Bruce Campbell. 1995. *Straight Through The Heart.* Toronto: HarperCollins Publishers Ltd.

Barnett, Rosalind C. 1994. "Home-to-Work Spillover Revisited: A Study of Full-Time Employed Women in Dual-Earner Couples." *Journal of Marriage and the Family* 56 (3) (Aug.):647–56.

Barnett, Rosalind C. and Grace K. Baruch. 1987. "Social Roles, Gender, and Psychological Distress." Pp. 122–43 in *Gender and Stress*, edited by Rosalind C. Barnett, Lois Biener, and Grace K. Baruch. New York: Free Press.

Barnett, Rosalind C., Nancy L. Marshall, and Joseph H. Pleck. 1992. "Men's Multiple Roles and Their Relationship to Men's Psychological Distress." *Journal of Marriage and the Family* 54 (2) (May):358–67.

Barnett, Rosalind C. and Yu-Chu Shen. 1997. "Gender, High- and Low-Schedule-Control Housework Tasks, and Psychological Distress." *Journal of Family Issues* 18 (4):403–28.

Barnett, R.C. and C. Rivers. 1998. *She Works, He Works: How Two Income Families are Happy, Healthy and Thriving.* Cambridge, Mass.: Harvard Unversity Press.

Barringer, Felicity. 1992a. "Among Elderly, Men's Prospects Are the Brighter." *New York Times*, Nov. 10.

———. 1992c. "Rate of Marriage Continues Decline." *New York Times*, July 19.

Bart, Pauline. 1972. "Depression in Middle-Aged Women." Pp. 163–86 in *Women in Sexist Society: Studies in Power and Powerlessness,* edited by Vivian Gornick and Barbara K. Moran. New York: New American Library.

Barth, Richard P. and Marianne Berry. 1988. *Adoption and Disruption: Rates, Risks, and Responses.* New York: Aldine de Gruyter.

Bartholomew, K. 1993. "From Childhood to Adult Relationships: Attachment Theory and Research." Pp. 30–62 in *Learning about Relationships,* edited by S.W. Duck. Newbury Park, CA: Sage.

Basavarajappa, K.G. and S.S. Halli. 1997. "A Comparative Study of Immigrant and Non-Immigrant Families in Canada with Special Reference to Income, 1986." *International Migration* 35 (2):225–252.

Basow, Susan H. 1991. "The Hairless Ideal: Women and Their Body Hair." *Psychology of Women Quarterly* 15:83–96.

———. 1992. *Gender: Stereotypes and Roles.* 3d ed. Pacific Grove, CA: Brooks/Cole.

Basran, G.S. 1993. "Indo-Canadian Families: Historical Constraints and Contemporary Contradictions." *Journal of Comparative Family Studies* 24 (3) (autumn):339–352.

Baucom, Donald H. and Paige K. Besch. 1985. "Personality Processes and Individual Differences." *Journal of Personality and Social Psychology* 48 (5):1218–26.

Baumrind, Diana. 1971. "Current Patterns of Parental Authority." *Developmental Psychology Monographs* 4:1–102.

———. 1978. "Parental Disciplinary Patterns and Social Competence in Children." *Youth and Society* 9:239–76.

———. 1994. "The Social Context of Child Maltreatment." *Family Relations* 43 (4) (Oct.):360–68.

———. 1996a. "The Discipline Controversy Revisited." *Family Relations* 45 (4):405–17.

———. 1996b. "Response: A Blanket Injunction against Disciplinary Use of Spanking Is Not Warranted by the Data." *Pediatrics* 98:828–42.

Beach, Frank A. 1977. "Cross-Species Comparisons and the Human Heritage." Pp. 296–316 in *Human Sexuality in Four Perspectives,* edited by Frank A. Beach. Baltimore: Johns Hopkins University Press.

Beattie, Melody. 1987. *Codependent No More: How to Stop Controlling Others and Start Caring for Yourself.* New York: Harper/Hazelden.

Beaujot, Roderic. 1997. "Parental Preferences for Work and Childcare." *Canadian Public Policy* 23 (3) (Sept.):276–288.

Beck, Melinda. 1988. "Miscarriages." *Newsweek*, Aug. 15, pp. 46–52.

———. (1990, July 16). "Trading Places." *Newsweek*, 48–54.

Beck, Peggy and Nancee Blank. 1997. "Broadening the Scope of Divorce Mediation to Meet the Needs of Children." *Mediation Quarterly: Journal of the Academy of Family Mediators* 14 (3):179–85.

Becker, Gary S. 1991. *A Treatise on the Family.* 2d ed. Cambridge, MA: Harvard University Press.

Becker, Gay. 1990. *Healing the Infertile Family.* New York: Bantam.

Bedard, Marcia E. 1992. *Breaking With Tradition: Diversity, Conflict, and Change in Contemporary Families.* Dix Hills, NY: General Hall.

Beeghley, Leonard. 1996. *What Does Your Wife Do? Gender and the Transformation of Family Life.* Boulder, CO: Westview Press.

Beer, William R. 1989. *Strangers in the House: The World of Stepsiblings and Half Siblings.* New Brunswick, NJ: Transaction.

———. 1992. *American Stepfamilies.* New Brunswick, NJ: Transaction.

Begay, Eugene A. 1998. Keynote Speech to the American Indian Leadership Spring Forum, May 29. Broadcast on SPNN, July 23.

Begley, Sharon. 1995a. "Deliver, Then Depart." *Newsweek,* July 10, p. 62.

———. 1995b. "The Baby Myth." *Newsweek.* September 4:38–47.

———. 1996. "Your Child's Brain." *Newsweek.* February 19:55–61.

———. 1998. "You're OK, I'm Terrific: 'Self-Esteem' Backfires." *Newsweek.* July 13:69.

Begley, Sharon and Daniel Glick. 1994. "The Estrogen Complex." *Newsweek*, March 21:76–77.

Begley, Sharon and Pat Wingert. 1997. "Teach Your Parents Well." *Newsweek.* April 28:72.

Belanger, Alain. 2000. "Trends in Contraceptive Sterilization." Pp. 126–129 in *Canadian Social Trends: Volume 3.* Toronto: Thompson Educational Publishing, Inc.

Belcastro, Philip A. 1985. "Sexual Behavior Differences Between Black and White Students." *The Journal of Sex Research* 21(1):56–67.

Bell, Alan P., Martin S. Weinberg, and Sue Kiefer Hammersmith. 1981. *Sexual Preference: Its Development in Men and Women.* Bloomington: University of Indiana Press.

Bell, Diane and Kathy Belicki. 1998. "A Community-Based Study of Well-Being in Adults Reporting Childhood Abuse." *Child Abuse & Neglect* 22 (7):681–85.

Bell, Richard Q. 1974. "Contributions of Human Infants to Caregiving and Social Interaction." Pp. 11–19 in *The Effect of the Infant on Its Care Giver: Origins of Behavior Series,* vol. 1, edited by Michael Lewis and Leonard A. Rosenblum. New York: Wiley.

Bellah, Robert N., Richard Madsen, William M. Sullivan, Ann Swidler, and Steven M. Tipton. 1985. *Habits of the*

Heart: Individualism and Commitment in American Life. Berkeley and Los Angeles: University of California Press.

Belle, Marilyn and Kevin McQuillan. 2000. "Births Outside Marriage." Pp. 115–118 in *Canadian Social Trends: Volume 3.* Toronto: Thompson Educational Publishing, Inc.

Belsky, J. 1990. "Parental and Occupational Child Care and Children's Socioemotional Development: A Decade in Review." *Journal of Marriage and the Family,* 52 (4) (November):885–903.

Belsky, Jay. 1990. "Parental and Nonparental Child Care and Children's Socioemotional Development: A Decade in Review." *Journal of Marriage and the Family* 52 (4) (Nov.):885–903.

———. 1991. "Parental and Non-parental Child Care and Children's Socioemotional Development." Pp. 122–40 in *Contemporary Families: Looking Forward, Looking Back,* edited by Alan Booth. Minneapolis: National Council on Family Relations.

Belsky, Jay and Michael J. Rovine. 1990. "Patterns of Marital Change Across the Transition to Parenthood: Pregnancy to Three Years Postpartum." *Journal of Marriage and the Family* 52:5–19.

Bem, Sandra Lipsitz. 1975. "Androgyny vs. the Tight Little Lives of Fluffy Women and Chesty Men." *Psychology Today* 9:58–62.

———. 1981. "Gender Schema Theory: A Cognitive Account of Sex Typing." *Psychological Review* 88:354–64.

———. 1993. *The Lenses of Gender: Transforming the Debate on Sexual Inequality.*

Benenson, Harold. 1984. "Women's Occupation and Family Achievement in the U.S. Class System: A Critique of the Dual-Career Family Analysis." *British Journal of Sociology* 35:19–41.

Bengtson, Vern L. and Dale Dannefer. 1987. "Families, Work and Aging: Implications of Disordered Cohort Flow for the Twenty-First Century." Pp. 256–89 in *Health and Aging: Sociological Issues and Policy Directions,* edited by Russell A. Ward and Sheldon S. Tobin. New York: Springer.

Benin, Mary and Verna M. Keith. 1995. "The Social Support of Employed African American and Anglo Mothers." *Journal of Family Issues* 16 (3) (May):275–97.

Bennett, Linda A., Steven J. Wolin, and David Reiss. 1988. "Deliberate Family Process: A Strategy for Protecting Children of Alcoholics." *British Journal of Addiction* 83:821–29.

Bennett, Linda A., Steven J. Wolin, David Reiss, and Martha A. Teitelbaum. 1987. "Couples at Risk for Transmission of Alcoholism: Protective Influences." *Family Process* 26:111–29.

Bennett, Neil G., David E. Bloom, and Cynthia K. Miller. 1995. "The Influence of Nonmarital Childbearing on the Formation of First Marriages." *Demography* 32 (1) (Feb.):47–62.

Benoit, D. and K. Parker. 1994. "Stability and Transmission of Attachment across Three Generations." *Child Development* 65:1444–56.

Benson, Jo. 1998. *Infertility and IVF: Facts and Feelings from Patients' Perspectives.* London: Scarlet Press.

Benson, R. C. 1983. *Handbook of Obstetrics and Gynecology.* Los Altos, CA: Large Medical Publishers.

Berardo, Felix M. 1998. "Family Privacy." *Journal of Family Issues* 19 (1):4–19.

Berg, Barbara. 1984. "Early Signs of Infertility." *Ms.,* May, pp. 68ff.

Berger, Peter L., Brigitte Berger, and Hansfried Kellner. 1973. *The Homeless Mind: Modernization and Consciousness.* New York: Random House.

Berger, Peter L. and Hansfried Kellner. 1970. "Marriage and the Construction of Reality." Pp. 49–72 in *Recent Sociology No. 2,* edited by Hans Peter Dreitzel. New York: Macmillan.

Berger, Peter L., and Thomas Luckmann. 1966. *The Social Construction of Reality: A Treatise in the Sociology of Knowledge.* New York: Doubleday.

Berger, Roni. 1997. "Immigrant Stepfamilies." *Contemporary Family Therapy* 19 (3):361–70.

Berk, Richard A. and Phyllis J. Newton. 1985. "Does Arrest Really Deter Wife Battery? An Effort to Replicate the Findings of the Minneapolis Spouse Abuse Experiment." *American Sociological Review* 50:253–62.

Berk, Richard A., Phyllis J. Newton, and Sarah Fenstermaker Berk. 1986. "What a Difference a Day Makes: An Empirical Study of the Impact of Shelters for Battered Women." *Journal of Marriage and the Family* 48:481–90.

Berk, Sarah Fenstermaker. 1985. *The Gender Factory: The Apportionment of Work in American Households.* New York: Plenum.

———. 1988. "Women's Unpaid Labor: Home and Community." Pp. 287–302 in *Women Working.* 2d ed., edited by Ann Helton Stromberg and Shirley Harkess. Mountain View, CA: Mayfield.

Berke, Richard L. 1998. "Chasing the Polls on Gay Rights." *New York Times,* Sunday. August 2–3.

Bernard, Jessie. 1964. "The Adjustment of Married Mates." Pp. 675–739 in *The Handbook of Marriage and the Family,* edited by Harold T. Christensen. Chicago: Rand McNally.

———. 1982 [1972]. *The Future of Marriage,* 2d ed. New York: Bantam.

———. 1986. "The Good-Provider Role: Its Rise and Fall." Pp. 125–44 in *Family in Transition: Rethinking Marriage, Sexuality, Child Rearing, and Family Organization.* 5th ed., edited by Arlene S. Skolnick and Jerome H. Skolnick. Boston: Little, Brown.

Berne, Linda A. and Barbara K. Huberman. 2000. "Lessons Learned: European Approaches to Adolescent Sexual Behavior and Responsibility." *Journal of Sex Education Therapy* 25 (2-3):189–199.

Bernhard, Judith K., Marie Louise Lefebvre, Kenise Murphy Kilbride, Gyda Chud and Rika Lange. 1999. "Troubled Relationships in Early Childhood Education: Parent-Teacher Interactions in Ethnoculturally Diverse Child Care Settings." *Early Education & Development*, 9 (1) (Jan.):5–28.

Bernstein, Anne C. 1997. "Stepfamilies from Siblings' Perspectives." Pp. 153–75 in *Stepfamilies: History, Research, and Policy*, edited by Irene Levin and Marvin B. Sussman. New York: Haworth Press.

Berry, Dawn Bradley. 1998. *The Divorce Recovery Sourcebook*. Los Angeles: Lowell House.

Berry, Judy O. and Julie Meyer Rao. 1997. "Balancing Employment and Fatherhood." *Journal of Family Issues* 18 (4):386–402.

Besharov, Douglas J. 1993. "Truth and Consequences: Teen Sex." *The American Enterprise* (Jan./Feb.):52–59.

Best, D.L. and J.E. Williams. 1998. "Masculinity and Femininity in the Self and Ideal Self Descriptions of University Students in 14 Countries." Pp. 106–116 in *Masculinity and Femininity: The Taboo Dimensions of National Cultures*, edited by G. Hofstede et al. Thousand Oaks, CA: Sage.

Beutel, Ann M. and Margaret Mooney Marini. 1995. "Gender and Values." *American Sociological Review* 60 (3) (June):436–49.

Bhargava, Gura. 1988. "Seeking Immigration Through Matrimonial Alliance: A Study of Advertisements in an Ethnic Weekly." *Journal of Comparative Family Studies*, 19:245–9.

Bianchi, S.M. 1990. "America's Children: Mixed Prospects." *Population Bulletin*, 45:3–41.

Bianchi, Suzanne and Daphne Spain. 1996. "Women, Work, and Family in America." *Population Bulletin* 51 (3). Washington, DC: Population Reference Bureau, Inc.

Bianchi, Suzanne M., Lynne M. Casper, and Pia K. Peltola. 1999. "A Cross-National Look at Married Women's Earnings Dependency." *Gender Issues* 17(3) (summer):3–33.

Bibby, Reginald W. 2001. *Canada's Teens: Today, Yesterday, and Tomorrow*. Toronto: Stoddart Publishing Co. Ltd.

———. 1997. "The Persistence of Christian Religious Identification in Canada." *Canadian Social Trends* 44:24–28.

———. 1995. *The Bibby Report: Social Trends Canadian Style*. Toronto: Stoddart.

———. 2000. "The Persistence of Christian Religious Identification in Canada." Pp. 197–201 in *Canadian Social Trends: Volume 3*. Toronto: Thompson Educational Publishing, Inc.

Bigler, Rebecca S. 1997. "Conceptual and Methodological Issues in the Measurement of Children's Sex Typing." *Psychology of Women Quarterly* 21 (1):53–69.

Billy, John O. G., Karin L. Brewster and William R. Grady. 1994. "Contextual effects of the sexual behavior of adolescent women." *Journal of Marriage & the Family*, 56(2), May: 387–404.

Binkley, Marian. 1996. "Nova Scotian Fishing Families Coping with the Fisheries Crisis." *Anthropologica* 38(2):197–219.

Binstock, Robert H. and Linda K. George. 1996. *Handbook of Aging and the Social Sciences*, 4th ed. San Diego: Academic Press.

Bird, Chloe E. 1997. "Gender Differences in the Social and Economic Burdens of Parenting and Psychological Distress." *Journal of Marriage and the Family* 59 (4):809–23.

Bird, Chloe E. and Catherine E. Ross. 1993. "Houseworkers and Paid Workers: Qualities of the Word and Effects on Personal Control." *Journal of Marriage and the Family* 55 (Nov.):913–25.

"Births to Women in Their Late 30s Have Risen Among Both Blacks and Whites Since 1980." 1992. *Family Planning Perspectives* 24:91–92.

Black, Leora E., Matthew M. Eastwood, Douglas H. Sprenkle, and Elaine Smith. 1991. "An Exploratory Analysis of Leavers Versus Left as It Relates to Levinger's Social Exchange Theory of Attractions, Barriers, and Alternative Attractions." *Journal of Divorce and Remarriage* 15 (1/2):127–40.

Blackman, Julie. 1989. *Intimate Violence: A Study of Injustice*. New York: Columbia University Press.

Blackstone, William. 1809. *Commentaries on the Laws of England*, 15th edition, Vol. 1.

Blackwell, Debra L. 1998. "Marital Homogamy in the United States: The Influence of Individual and Paternal Education." *Social Science Research* 27 (2):159–64.

Blain, Jenny. 1993. "'I Can't Come In Today, The Baby Has Chickenpox!' Gender and Class Processes in How Parents in the Labour Force Deal with the Problem of Sick Children." *Canadian Journal of Sociology* 18 (4) (fall):405–429.

Blair, Sampson Lee and Michael P. Johnson. 1992. "Wives' Perceptions of the Fairness of the Division of Household Labor: The Intersection of Housework and Ideology." *Journal of Marriage and the Family* 54 (3) (Aug.):570–81.

Blair, Sampson Lee and Daniel T. Lichter. 1991. "Measuring the Division of Household Labor: Gender Segregation of Housework Among American Couples." *Journal of Family Issues* 12 (1) (Mar.):91–113.

Blaisure, Karen and Katherine R. Allen. 1995. "Feminists and the Ideology and Practice of Marital Equality." *Journal of Marriage and the Family* 57 (1) (Feb.):5–19.

Blake, Judith. 1974. "Can We Believe Recent Data on Birth Expectations in the U.S.?" *Demography* 11:25–44.

Blakely, Mary Kay. 1995. "An Outlaw Mom Tells All." *Ms. Magazine.* (January/February):34–45.

Blankenhorn, David. 1995. *Fatherless America: Confronting Our Most Urgent Social Problem.* New York: Basic Books.

Blau, David M. and Philip K. Robins. 1998. "A Dynamic Analysis of Turnover in Employment and Child Care." *Demography* 35 (1):83–96.

Blee, Kathleen M. and Ann R. Tickamyer. 1995. "Racial Differences in Men's Attitudes About Women's Gender Roles." *Journal of Marriage and the Family* 57 (1) (Feb.):21–30.

Blinn-Pike, Lynn, Diane Kuschel, Annette McDaniel, Suzanne Mingus, and Megan Poole Mutti. 1998. "The Process of Mentoring Pregnant Adolescents: An Exploratory Study." *Family Relations* 47 (2):119–27.

Blood, Robert O., Jr. and Donald M. Wolfe. 1960. *Husbands and Wives: The Dynamics of Married Living.* New York: Free Press.

Blumberg, Rae Lesser and Marion Tolbert Coleman. 1989. "A Theoretical Look at the Gender Balance of Power in the American Couple." *Journal of Family Issues* 10:225–50.

Blumstein, Philip and Pepper Schwartz. 1983. *American Couples: Money, Work, Sex.* New York: Morrow.

Bly, Robert. 1990. *Iron John: A Book About Men.* Reading, MA: Addison-Wesley.

Bogenschneider, Karen and Margaret Stone. 1997. "Delivering Parent Education to Low and High Risk Parents of Adolescents via Age-Paced Newsletters." *Family Relations* 46 (2):123–34.

Bohannan, Paul. 1970a. "Divorce Chains, Households of Remarriage, and Multiple Divorces." Pp. 113–23 in *Divorce and After,* edited by Paul Bohannan. New York: Doubleday.

———. 1970b. "The Six Stations of Divorce." Pp. 29–55 in *Divorce and After,* edited by Paul Bohannan. New York: Doubleday.

Bohannan, Paul and Rosemary Erickson. 1978. "Stepping In." *Psychology Today* 12:53–54.

Bogert, Carroll. (1994, Nov. 21). "Bringing Back Baby." *Newsweek,* 78–9.

Bollier, David. 1982. *Liberty and Justice for Some.* New York: Frederick Ungar.

Bond, James T., Ellen Galinsky and Jennifer E. Swanberg. 1997. *The 1997 National Study of the Changing Workplace.* New York: Families and Work Institute.

Booth, Alan. 1977. "Wife's Employment and Husband's Stress: A Replication and Refutation." *Journal of Marriage and the Family* 39:645–50.

———. 1992. *Child Care in the 1990s: Trends and Consequences.* Hillsdale, NJ: L. Erlbaum Associates.

Booth, Alan and Paul R. Amato. 1994a. "Parental Gender Role Nontraditionalism and Offspring Outcomes." *Journal of Marriage and the Family* 56 (4) (Nov.):865–77.

———. 1994b. "Parental Marital Quality, Parental Divorce, and Relations with Parents." *Journal of Marriage and the Family* 56 (1) (February):21–34.

Booth, Alan and Ann C. Crouter. 1998. *Men in Families: When Do They Get Involved? What Difference Does It Make?* Mahwah, NJ: Lawrence Erlbaum Associates.

Booth, Alan, Ann C. Crouter, and Nancy Landale. 1997. *Immigration and the Family: Research and Policy on U.S. Immigrants.* Mahway, NJ: Lawrence Erlbaum Associates.

Booth, Alan, Ann C. Crouter, and Michael J. Shanahan. 1999. *Transitions to Adulthood in a Changing Economy: No Work, No Family, No Future?* Westport, CT: Praeger.

Booth, Alan and James Dabbs. 1993. "Testosterone and Men's Marriages." *Social Forces* 72:463–77.

Booth, Alan and Judy Dunn. (Eds.). 1994. *Stepfamilies: Who Benefits? Who Does Not?* Hillsdale, NJ: Lawrence Erlbaum Associates.

Booth, Alan and John Edwards. 1985. "Age at Marriage and Marital Instability." *Journal of Marriage and the Family* 47 (1):67–75.

———. 1992. "Starting Over: Why Remarriages Are More Unstable." *Journal of Family Issues* 13 (2) (June):179–94.

Booth, Alan and David Johnson. 1988. "Premarital Cohabitation and Marital Success." *Journal of Family Issues* 9:255–72.

———. 1994. "Declining Health and Marital Quality." *Journal of Marriage and the Family* 56 (1):218–23.

Booth, Alan, David R. Johnson, Ann Branaman, and Alan Sico. 1995. "Belief and Behavior: Does Religion Matter in Today's Marriage?" *Journal of Marriage and the Family* 57 (3) (Aug.):661–71.

Booth, Alan, David R. Johnson, and Lynn K. White. 1984. "Women, Outside Employment, and Marital Instability." *American Journal of Sociology* 90 (3):567–83.

Borello, Gloria M. and Bruce Thompson. 1990. "A Note Regarding the Validity of Lee's Typology of Love." *Journal of Psychology* 124:639–44.

Boroditsky, R., W.A. Fisher and M. Sand. 1996. "Condoms: Attitudes and Practices of Canadian Women: The 1995 Canadian Contraception Study." *Journal of the Society of Obstetrics and Gynaecology,* special supplement, December.

Boss, Pauline G. 1980. "Normative Family Stress: Family Boundary Changes Across the Lifespan." *Family Relations* 29:445–52.

———. 1999. *Ambiguous Loss: Learning to Live with Unresolved Grief.* Cambridge, MA: Harvard University Press.

Boss, Pauline G., William J. Doherty, Ralph LaRossa, Walter R. Schumm, and Suzanne K. Steinmetz, Eds. 1993. *Sourcebook of Family Theories and Methods: A Contextual Approach.* New York: Plenum.

Bossard, James H., and E. S. Boll. 1943. *Family Situations.* Philadelphia: University of Pennsylvania Press.

Boston University Medical School. <http://med-amsa.bu.edu>

Boston Women's Health Book Collective. 1998. *Our Bodies, Ourselves for the New Century.* New York: Touchstone/Simon & Schuster.

Bould, Sally. 1993. "Familial Caretaking: A Middle-Range Definition of Family in the Context of Social Policy." *Journal of Family Issues,* 14 (1):133–151.

"Both Sexes Are Drawn to Working at Home." 1990. *The Wall Street Journal,* May 24.

Boulding, Elise. 1976. "Familial Constraints on Women's Work Roles." Pp. 95–117 in *Women and the Workplace,* edited by Martha Blaxall and Barbara Reagan. Chicago: University of Chicago Press.

Bouton, Katherine. 1987. "Fertility and Family." *Ms. Magazine,* Apr., p. 92.

Bower, Bruce. 1995. "Depression: Rates in Women, Men ... and Stress Effects Across Sexes." *Science News* 147 (22) (June 3):346.

Bowlby, John. 1969. *Attachment and Loss.* New York: Basic Books.

Boyd, Susan B. 1987. "Child Custody and Working Mothers." Pp. 168–183 in Sheilah L. Martin and Kathleen E. Mahoney (eds.) *Equality and Judicial Neutrality.* Toronto: Carswell.

Boyd, Monica. 2000. "Canada's Refugee Flows: Gender Inequality." Pp. 84–87 in *Canadian Social Trends: Volume 3.* Toronto: Thompson Educational Publishing, Inc.

———. 1995. "Gender Inequality: Economic and Political Aspects." Pp. 3.1–3.29 in *New Society: Brief Edition,* edited by Robert J. Brym. Toronto: Harcourt Brace & Company.

——— and Doug Norris. 1995. "Leaving the Nest? The Impact of Family Structure." *Canadian Social Trends* 38:14–19.

——— and Doug Norris. 2000. "Crowded Nest? Young Adults At Home." Pp. 157–160 in *Canadian Social Trends: Volume 3.* Toronto: Thompson Educational Publishing, Inc.

——— and Edward T. Pryor. 1989. "The Cluttered Nest: The Living Arrangements of Young Canadian Adults." *Canadian Journal of Sociology* 14:461–477.

——— and Edward T. Pryor. 1989. "Young Adults Living in their Parents' Home." *Canadian Social Trends* (summer):17–20.

Boyd, Neil. 1998. *Canadian Law: An Introduction.* Toronto: Harcourt Brace Canada.

Boyer, Debra and David Fine. 1992. "Sexual Abuse as a Factor in Adolescent Pregnancy and Child Maltreatment." *Family Planning Perspectives* 24 (1) (Jan./Feb.):4–11.

Boyer, King David, Jr. 1981. "Changing Male Sex Roles and Identities." Pp. 158–65 in *Men in Difficult Times,* edited by Robert A. Lewis. Englewood Cliffs, NJ: Prentice-Hall.

Boyum, Lisa Ann and Ross D. Parke. 1995. "The Role of Family Emotional Expressiveness in the Development of Children's Social Competence." *Journal of Marriage and the Family* 57 (3) (Aug.):593–608.

Bradsher, Keith. 1989. "Young Men Pressed to Wed for Success." *New York Times,* Dec. 13.

———. 1990b. "Modern Tale of Woe: Being Left at the Altar." *New York Times,* Mar. 7.

Braithwaite, John. 1989. *Crime, Shame and Reintegration.* Melbourne, Australia: Cambridge University Press.

Brand, Dionne. 1999. "Black Women and Work: The Impact of Racially Constructed Gender Roles on the Sexual Division of Labour." Pp. 83–96 in *Scratching the Surface: Canadian Anti-Racist Feminist Thought* edited by Enakshi Dua and Angela Robertson. Toronto: Women's Press.

Branden, Nathaniel. 1980. *The Psychology of Romantic Love.* Los Angeles: J. P. Tarcher.

———. 1988. "A Vision of Romantic Love." Pp. 218–31 in *The Psychology of Love,* edited by Robert J. Sternberg and Michael L. Barnes. New Haven, CT: Yale University Press.

———. 1994. *Six Pillars of Self-Esteem.* New York: Bantam.

Brandwein, Ruth A. 1999. *Battered Women, Children, and Welfare Reform: The Ties That Bind.* Thousand Oaks, CA: Sage.

Brannon, L. 1995. *Gender: Psychological Perspectives.* Boston: Allyn & Bacon.

Brant, Martha, Karen Springen, and Adam Rogers. 1995. "The Baby Myth." *Newsweek,* Sept. 4, pp. 38–47.

Braver, Sanford L., Pamela J. Fitzpatrick, and R. Curtis Bay. 1991. "Noncustodial Parent's Report of Child Support Payments." *Family Relations* 40 (2) (Apr.):180–85.

Bray, James H. 1999. "From Marriage to Remarriage and Beyond." Pp. 253–71 in *Coping with Divorce, Single Parenting and Remarriage,* edited by E. Mavis Hetherington. Mahwah, NJ: Lawrence Erlbaum Associates.

Brayfield, April. 1995. "Juggling Jobs and Kids: The Impact of Employment Schedules on Fathers' Caring for Children." *Journal of Marriage and the Family* 57 (2) (May):321–32.

Brazelton, T. Berry. 1989a. "Bringing Up Baby: A Doctor's Prescription for Busy Parents." *Newsweek,* Feb. 13, pp. 68–69.

———. 1989b. "Working Parents." *Newsweek,* Feb. 13, pp. 66–69.

———. 1997. "Building A Better Self-Image." *Newsweek* Special Issue. (Spring/Summer):76–79.

Breidenbach, Susan. 1997. "Where are all the Women?" *Network World* 14 (41):68–69.

Brigham, John C. 1991. *Social Psychology*. 2d ed. New York: HarperCollins.

Brines, Julie. 1994. "Economic Dependency, Gender, and the Division of Labor at Home." *American Journal of Sociology* 100 (3) (Nov.):652–88.

Bringle, Robert G. and Diane Byers. 1997. "Intentions to Seek Marriage Counseling." *Family Relations* 46 (3):299–304.

British Columbia (Ministry of Social Development and Economy Security). 2000. *Child Care for British Columbia*. April. <http://www.sdes/gov.bc.ca/PUBLICAT/CC_BC_report.html>

Broderick, Carlfred B. 1979a. *Couples: How to Confront Problems and Maintain Loving Relationships*. New York: Simon & Schuster.

———. 1979b. *Marriage and the Family*. Englewood Cliffs, NJ: Prentice-Hall.

Brodie, Deborah. 1999. *Untying the Knot: Ex-Husbands, Ex-Wives, and Other Experts on the Passage of Divorce*. New York: St. Martin's Griffin.

Brody, Charles J. and Lala Carr Steelman. 1985. "Sibling Structure and Parental Sex-Typing of Children's Household Tasks." *Journal of Marriage and the Family* 47 (2) (May):265–73.

Brody, Gene H. and Rex Forehand. 1990. "Interparental Conflict, Relationship with the Noncustodial Father, and Adolescent Post-Divorced Adjustment." *Journal of Applied Psychology* 11 (2) (April–June):312–36.

Brody, Jane E. 1989a. "Personal Health: Research Casts Doubt on Need for Many Caesarean Births as Their Rate Soars." *New York Times*, July 27.

———. 1989b. "Who's Having Sex? Data Are Obsolete, Experts Say." *New York Times*, Feb. 18.

———. 1991. "Better Conduct? Train Parents, Then Children." *New York Times*, Dec. 3.

Broman, Clifford L. "Race Differences in Marital Well-Being." *Journal of Marriage and the Family* 55 (3) (Aug.):724–32.

Bromley, Mark C. and Rosemary Blieszner. 1997. "Planning for Long-Term Care: Filial Behavior and Relationship Quality of Adult Children with Independent Parents." *Family Relations* 46 (2):155–62.

Bronfenbrenner, Urie. 1979. *The Ecology of Human Development*. Cambridge, Mass.: Harvard University Press.

Bronstein, Phyllis, Miriam F. Stoll, JoAnn Clauson, Craig Abrams, and Maria Briones. 1994. "Fathering After Separation or Divorce: Factors Predicting Children's Adjustment." *Family Relations* 43:469–79.

Brooke, James. 1998. "Utah Struggles With A Revival of Polygamy." *New York Times*, August 23.

Brooks, Andrée. 1984a. "Child-Care Homes Divide Communities." *New York Times*, July 19.

———. 1984b. "Stepparents and Divorce: Keeping Ties to Children." *New York Times*, July 29.

———. 1985. "Trial Separation as a Therapy Technique." *New York Times* Style, Sept. 6.

Brooks-Gunn, Jeanne and Greg Duncan. 1997. "The Effects of Poverty on Children." *Future of Children* 17 (2):55–70.

Brophy, Julia. 1985. "Child Care and the Growth of Power: The Status of Mothers in Custody Disputes." Pp. 97–116 in *Women in Law: Explorations in Law, Family, and Sexuality*, edited by Julia Brophy and Carol Smart. London: Routledge & Kegan Paul.

Brown, E.M. 1999. *Affairs: A Guide to Working Through the Repercussions of Infidelity*. New York: Jossey-Bass.

Brown, Jocelyn, Patricia Cohen, Jeffrey G. Johnson, and Suzanne Salzinger. 1998. "A Longitudinal Analysis of Risk Factors for Child Maltreatment: Findings of a 17-Year Prospective Study of Officially Recorded and Self-Reported Child Abuse and Neglect." *Child Abuse & Neglect* 22 (11):1065–78.

Brown, Pamela D., K. Daniel O'Leary, and Shari R. Feldbau. 1997. "Dropout in a Treatment Program for Self-Referring Wife Abusing Men." *Journal of Family Violence* 12 (4):365–87.

Browning, Christopher R. and Edward O. Laumann. 1997. "Sexual Contact Between Children and Adults: A Life Course Perspective." *American Sociological Review* 62:540–60.

Brubaker, Ellie, Mary Anne Gorman, and Michele Hiestand. 1990. "Stress Perceived by Elderly Recipients of Family Care." Pp. 267–81 in *Family Relationships in Later Life*. 2d ed., edited by Timothy H. Brubaker. Newbury Park, CA: Sage.

Brubaker, Timothy H. 1991. "Families in Later Life: A Burgeoning Research Area." Pp. 226–48 in *Contemporary Families: Looking Forward, Looking Back*, edited by Alan Booth. Minneapolis: National Council on *Family Relations*.

Brush, Lisa D. 1990. "Violent Acts and Injurious Outcomes in Married Couples: Methodological Issues in the National Survey of Families and Households." *Gender and Society* 4:56–67.

Bryant, S. and Demian. 1990. "National Survey Results of Gay Couples in Long-Lasting Relationships." *Partners: Newsletter for Gay & Lesbian Couples* (May/June):1–16.

Bryant, W. Keith and Cathleen D. Zick. 1996. "An Examination of Parent–Child Shared Time." *Journal of Marriage and the Family* 58 (1):227–37.

Bryon, Peg. 1998. "Affirmative Marriage Statement." Lambda Legal Defense and Education Fund. <http://www.ftm.org/archive/lldef/affirmative.html>

Bubolz, Margaret M. and M. Suzanne Sontag. 1993. "Human Ecology Theory." Pp. 419–48 in *Sourcebook of Family Theories and Methods: A Contextual Approach*, edited by Pauline G. Boss, William J. Doherty, Ralph LaRossa, Walter R. Schumm, and Suzanne K. Steinmetz. New York: Plenum.

Buchanan, Patrick J. 1983. "Nature Exacts Awful Penalty from Gays." *Omaha World-Herald*, May 25, p. 36.

Buckle, Leslie, Gordon G. Gallup Jr., and Zachary A. Rodd. 1996. "Marriage as a Reproductive Contract: Patterns of Marriage, Divorce, and Remarriage." *Ethology and Sociobiology* 17:363–77.

Bueckhert, H. 2000. "Age of menstruation getting younger." <http://www.people.virginia.edu/~rjhau/gnrh.html>

Buehler, Cheryl. 1995. "Divorce Law in the United States." Pp. 99–120 in *Families and Law,* edited by Lisa J. McIntyre and Marvin B. Sussman (eds.). New York: Hayworth.

Buehler, Cheryl, Ambika Krishnakumar, Gaye Stone, Christine Anthony, Sharon Pemberton, Jean Gerard and Brian K. Barber. 1998. "Interpersonal Conflict Styles and Youth Problem Behaviors." *Journal of Marriage and the Family* 60(1): 119–32.

Bulcroft, Kris, Linda Smeins, and Richard Bulcroft. 1999. *Romancing The Honeymoon: Consummating Marriage in Modern Society.* Thousand Oaks, CA: Sage.

Bulcroft, Richard A. and Kris A. Bulcroft. 1993. "Race Differences in Attitudinal and Motivational Factors in the Decision to Marry." *Journal of Marriage and the Family* 55 (2) (May):338–55.

Bumpass, Larry L. 1990. "What's Happening to the Family? Interactions Between Demographic and Institutional Change." *Demography* 27:483–98.

Bumpass, Larry L., Teresa Castro Martin, and James E. Sweet. 1991. "The Impact of Family Background and Early Marital Factors on Marital Disruption." *Journal of Family Issues* 12 (1) (Mar.):22–42.

Bumpass, Larry L., R. K. Raley, and J. Sweet. 1995. "The Changing Character of Stepfamilies: Implications of Cohabitation and Nonmarital Childbearing." *Demography* 32 (3) (Aug.):425–36.

Bumpass, Larry L., and James A. Sweet. 1989. "Children's Experience in Single-Parent Families: Implications of Cohabitation and Marital Transitions." *Family Planning Perspectives* 21:256–61.

———. 1995. "Cohabitation, Marriage, Nonmarital Childbearing, and Union Stability: Preliminary Findings from NSFH2." Population Association of America Annual Meeting, San Francisco, April.

Bumpass, Larry L., James A. Sweet and Andrew Cherlin. 1991. "The Role of Cohabitation in Declining Rates of Marriage." *Journal of Marriage and the Family* 53 (4) (Nov.):913–27.

Bunge, Valerie Pottie. 2000. "Spousal Violence." Pp. 11–21 in Statistics Canada, *Family Violence in Canada: A Statistical Profile 2000.* Catalogue no. 85-224-XIE. Ottawa: Minister of Industry.

———. 2000a. "Police-Reported Spousal Violence." Pp. 21–26 in Statistics Canada, *Family Violence in Canada: A Statistical Profile 2000.* Catalogue no. 85-224-XIE. Ottawa: Minister of Industry.

———. 2000b. "Abuse of Older Adults by Family Members." Pp. 27–30 in Statistics Canada, *Family Violence in Canada: A Statisitcal Profile 2000.* Catalogue no. 84-24-XIE. Ottawa: Minister of Industry.

Bunker, Barbara B., Josephine M. Zubek, Virginia J. Vanderslice, and Robert W. Rice. 1992. "Quality of Life in Dual-Career Families: Commuting Versus Single-Residence Couples." *Journal of Marriage and the Family* 54 (3) (May):399–407.

Burchell, R. Clay. 1975. "Self-Esteem and Sexuality." *Medical Aspects of Human Sexuality* (Jan.):74–90.

Bureau of Justice Assistance. 1993. *Family Violence: Interventions for the Justice System.* Washington, DC: U.S. Department of Justice.

Burgess, Ernest and Harvey Locke. 1953 [1945]. *The Family: From Institution to Companionship.* New York: American Book Co.

Burke, Peter J. and Alicia D. Cast. 1997. "Stability and Change in the Gender Identities of Newly Married Couples." *Social Psychology Quarterly* 60 (4):277–90.

Burke, R.J. 1994. "Canadian Business Students' Attitudes Towards Women as Managers." *Psychological Reports* 75: 1123–9.

Burnley, Cynthia S. 1987. "The Impact of Emotional Support for Single Women." *Journal of Aging Studies* 1 (3) (fall):253–64.

Burns, A. 1984. "Perceived Causes of Marriage Breakdown and Conditions of Life." *Journal of Marriage and the Family* 46:551–62.

Burns, A. and R. Homel. 1989. "Gender Division of Tasks by Parents and Their Children." *Psychology of Women Quarterly* 13:113–25.

Burns, David D. 1989. *The Feeling Good Handbook.* New York: Penguin.

Burr, Wesley R., Shirley Klein, and Marilyn McCubbin. 1995. "Reexamining Family Stress: New Theory and Research." *Journal of Marriage and the Family* 57 (3):835–46.

Burstein, Paul, R. Marie Bricher, and Rachel L. Einwohner. 1995. "Policy Alternatives and Political Change: Work, Family, and Gender on the Congressional Agenda, 1945–1990." *American Sociological Review* 60 (1):67–83.

Burt, Marla S. and Roger B. Burt. 1996. *Stepfamilies: The Step by Step Model of Brief Therapy.* New York: Brunner/Mazel.

Buscaglia, Leo. 1982. *Living, Loving, and Learning.* New York: Holt, Rinehart & Winston.

Buschman, Joan K. and Silvo Lenart. 1996. "'I Am Not A Feminist, But...': College Women, Feminism and Negative Experiences." *Political Psychology* 17(1) (March):59–75.

Bushman, Brad J. and Roy F. Baumeister. 1998. "Threatened Egotism Narcissism, Self-Esteem, and Direct and Displaced Aggression: Does Self-Love or Self-Hate Lead to Violence?" *Journal of Personality and Social Psychology* 75 (1):219–30.

Buss, D. M. 1994. *The Evolution of Desire: Strategies of Human Mating.* New York: Basic Books.

Buss, D. M. and D. T. Kenrick. 1998. "Evolutionary Social Psychology." Pp. 982–1026 in *The Handbook of Social Psychology,* vol. 2, edited by D. T. Gilbert, T. Fiske and G. Lindzey. New York: McGraw-Hill.

Buunk, Bram. 1982. "Strategies of Jealousy: Styles of Coping with Extramarital Involvement of the Spouse." *Family Relations* 31:13–18.

———. 1991. "Jealousy in Close Relationships: An Exchange Theoretical Perspective." Pp. 148–77 in *The Psychology of Jealousy and Envy,* edited by Peter Salovey. New York: Guilford.

Buxton, Amity Pierce. 1991. *The Other Side of the Closet: The Coming-Out Crisis for Straight Spouses.* Santa Monica, CA: IBS Press.

———. 1992. "Don't Forget the Abandoned Spouses of Gays." *New York Times,* Aug. 15.

Buzawa, Eve S. and Carl G. Buzawa. 1990. *Domestic Violence: The Criminal Justice Response.* Newbury Park, CA: Sage.

———. 1992. *Domestic Violence: The Criminal Justice Response.* Westport, CT: Auburn House.

Byrne, Donn E. 1977. "A Pregnant Pause in the Sexual Revolution." *Psychology Today* 11:67–68.

Byrne, Robert C. and Harry M. Overline. 1992. "A Study of Divorce Adjustment Among Paraprofessional Group Leaders and Group Participants." *Journal of Divorce and Remarriage* 17 (1/2):171–92.

Byrne, W. 1994. "The Biological Evidence Challenged." *Scientific American,* May.

C

Caldera, Y. M., A. C. Huston, and M. O'Brien. 1989. "Social Interactions and Play Patterns of Parents and Toddlers with Feminine, Masculine, and Neutral Toys." *Child Development* 60:70–76.

Caldwell, John, Indra Gajanayake, Bruce Caldwell, and Pat Caldwell. 1993. "Marriage Delay and the Fertility Decline in Sri Lanka." Pp. 140–46 in *Next of Kin: An International Reader on Changing Families,* edited by Lorne Tepperman and Susannah J. Wilson. Englewood Cliffs, NJ: Prentice Hall.

Call, Vaughn, Susan Sprecher, and Pepper Schwartz. 1995. "The Incidence and Frequency of Marital Sex in a National Sample." *Journal of Marriage and the Family* 57 (3) (Aug.):639–52.

Callaghan, K. A. (Eds.). 1994. *Ideals in Feminine Beauty.* Westport, CT: Greenwood Press.

Camarena, Phame M., Kris Minor, Theresa Melmer, and Cheryl Ferrie. 1998. "The Nature and Support of Adolescent Mothers' Life Aspirations." *Family Relations* 47 (2):129–37.

Campbell, Bernadette, E. Glenn Schellenberg, and Charlene Y. Senn. 1997. "Evaluating Measures of Contemporary Sexism." *Psychology of Women Quarterly* 1 (1):89–102.

Campbell, Marian L. and Phyllis Moen. 1992. "Job–Family Role Strain Among Employed Single Mothers of Preschoolers." *Family Relations* 41 (2) (Apr.):205–11.

Campbell, Susan. 1991. "Male Day-Care Workers Face Prejudice." *Omaha World-Herald,* July 14.

———. 1996. "Online Romance a Threat to Some Marriages." *San Francisco Examiner.* April 7: E11.

Campaign 2000. 2001. *Child Poverty in Canada: Report Card 2000.* Toronto: Campaign 2000.

Canadian Centre on Substance Abuse. 1999. *Canadian Profile: Alcohol, Tobacco, and Other Drugs, 1999.* Ottawa: Canadian Centre on Substance Abuse and Centre for Addiction and Mental Health.

Canadian Coalition for the Rights of the Child. 1999. *How Does Canada Measure Up?* Ottawa: Canadian Coalition for the Rights of the Child.

Canadian Council on Social Development. 2001. *The Progress of Canada's Children 2001–Highlights.* March. <http://www.ccsd.ca/pubs/2001/pcc2001.hl.htm>

———. 2000. *The Progress of Canada's Children 2000: At-a-Glance.* <http://www.ccsd.ca/pubs/pcc00/glance.htm>

———. 2000a "Unequal Access: A Report Card on Racism." *Perception* (24) (3) (December). <http://www.ccsd.ca/perception/243/racism.htm>

———. 1999. *Thinking Ahead: Trends Affecting Public Education in the Future.* <http://www.ccsd.ca/pubs/gordon/toc.htm>

Canadian Federation of Students. 2001. "No Means No: Campaign Against Sexual Assault, 2001 Fact Sheet." <http://www.city.vancouver.bc.ca/police/InvesServDiv/sos-dvach/soscfs.htm>

———. 2001a "Date Rape: No Means No." <http://www.cfs-fcee.ca/action/nmn.shtml>

Canadian Global Almanac 2000 (Susan Girvan, Publisher and Editor-in-Chief). Toronto: Macmillan Canada.

Canadian Press. 2000. "Viagra's First Year Perks Up Sex Lives for Thousands, Leaves Many Others Wanting, as Canucks Spend Millions." March 8 <3/lwysiwyg://41/http://healthcentralsympatic...text.cfm?id=29041&StoryType=CanadianPress>

Canadian Press. 2001. "Canadians Just as Unfaithful Online as Off, Survey Says." *National Post,* February 7:A3.

Canary, D. J. and K. Dindia. 1998. *Sex Differences and Similarities in Communication.* Mahaw, NJ: Lawrence Erlbaum and Associates.

Canavan, Margaret M., Walter J. Meyer, III, and Deborah C. Higgs. 1992. "The Female Experience of Sibling Incest." *Journal of Marital and Family Therapy* 18 (2) (Apr.):129–42.

Cancian, Francesca M. 1985. "Gender Politics: Love and Power in the Private and Public Spheres." Pp. 253–64 in *Gender and the Life Course*, edited by Alice S. Rossi. New York: Aldine de Gruyter.

———. 1987. *Love in America: Gender and Self-Development*. New York: Cambridge University Press.

Canning, Patricia M. and Charlotte Strong. 1998. "Families Adapting to the Cod Moratorium." International Sociological Association (ISA).

Cano, Annmarie and K. Daniel O'Leary. 1997. "Romantic Jealousy and Affairs: Research and Implications for Couple Therapy." *Journal of Sex & Marital Therapy* 23 (4):249–75.

Caplow, Theodore, Howard M. Bahr, Bruce A. Chadwick, Reuben Hill, and Margaret Holmes Williamson. 1982. *Middletown Families: Fifty Years of Change and Continuity*. Minneapolis: University of Minnesota Press.

Capulet, Nancy. 1998. *Putting Your Heart Online*. Oakland, CA: Variable Symbols, Inc.

Carder, J., Jaenicke, D. and D.A. Seamands. 1995. *Torn Asunder: Recovering From Extramarital Affairs*. New York: Moody Press.

Carey, Elaine. 2000. "Race, Income Splits Toronto, Study Warns." *Toronto Star*, July 7. <wysiwyg://60/http://www.geocities.com/CapitalHill/6174/racepoor.html>

Cargan, Leonard and Matthew Melko. 1982. *Singles: Myths and Realities*. Newbury Park, CA: Sage.

Carlson, Bonnie. 1990. "Adolescent Observers of Marital Violence." *Journal of Family Violence* 5 (4):285–99.

Carlson, Margaret. 1994. "Old Enough to Be Your Mother." *Time*, Jan. 10, p. 41.

Carol, Arthur. 1983. "Pay Gaps: Worry Not for Women But Humdrum Households." *Wall Street Journal*, Aug. 12.

Carter, B. 1991. "Children's TV, Where Boys Are King." *New York Times*, May 1, pp. A1, C18.

Carver, Karen Price and Jay D. Teachman. 1993. "Female Employment and First Union Dissolution in Puerto Rico." *Journal of Marriage and the Family* 55 (3) (Aug.):686–98.

Casey, Terri. 1998. *Pride and Joy: The Lives and Passions of Women without Children*. Hillsboro, OR: Beyond Words Publications.

Casper, Lynne M. and Martin O'Connell. 1998. "Work, Income, the Economy, and Married Fathers as Child-Care Providers." *Demography* 35 (2):243–50.

Cassidy, B., R. Lord and N. Mandell. 1998. "Silenced and Forgotten Women: Race, Poverty and Disability." Pp. 26–54 in *Feminist Issues: Race, Class and Sexuality*, 2nd edition, edited by Nancy Mandell. Scarborough: Prentice Hall Allyn and Bacon Canada.

Cate, Rodney M. and Sally A. Lloyd. 1992. *Courtship*. Newbury Park, CA: Sage.

CAUT (Canadian Association of University Teachers). 1999. "Women Granted Doctorates by Major Discipline, Canada, 1995–1998." *CAUT Bulletin*, SWC Supplement:8.

Cazenave, N. A. 1984. "Race, Socioeconomic Status, and Age: The Social Context of American Masculinity." *Sex Roles* 11:639–56.

CBC Trust. n.d. "History of Birth Control in Canada." <http://www.cbctrust.com/birth.html>

Celis, William, 3d. 1992. "Hispanic Youths Quitting School at a High Rate." *New York Times*, Oct. 14.

CFAS (Canadian Fertility and Andrology Society) 2000. "First Time In Canada—Assisted Reproductive Pregnancy Rates Now Available." June 8. <http://www.veritascanada.com/documents/media_room/releases_2000/000608_cfas_ivf.html>

Chafetz, Janet Saltzman. 1988. "The Gender Division of Labor and the Reproduction of Female Disadvantage: Toward an Integrated Theory." *Journal of Family Issues* 9:108–31.

———. 1989. "Marital Intimacy and Conflict: The Irony of Spousal Equality." Pp. 149–56 in *Women: A Feminist Perspective*, 4th ed., edited by Jo Freeman. Mountain View, CA: Mayfield.

Chandra, Anjani and Elizabeth Hervey Stephen. 1998. "Impaired Fecundity in the United States: 1982–1995." *Family Planning Perspectives* 30 (1):35–42.

Chappell, Crystal Lee Hyun Joo. 1996. "Korean-American Adoptees Organize for Support." *Minneapolis Star Tribune*. December 29:E7.

Chappell, Nina. 1990. *Aging of the Canadian Population*. Ottawa: Department of the Secretary of State of Canada.

"Charge in Fetus's Death Spawns Battle over Drug-Using Mothers." 1992. *The Wall Street Journal*, June 18.

Chartrand, Sabra. 1992. "Parents Recall Ordeal of Prosecuting in Artificial-Insemination Fraud Case." *New York Times*, Mar. 15, p. 10.

Chase-Lansdale, P. Lindsay, Jeanne Brooks-Gunn, and Roberta L. Palkoff. 1991. "Research and Programs for Adolescent Mothers: Missing Links and Future Promises." *Family Relations* 40 (4) (Oct.):396–403.

Che-Alford, Janet and Brian Hamm. 2000. "Three Generations Living Together." Pp. 161–164 in *Canadian Social Trends: Volume 3*. Toronto: Thompson Educational Publishing, Inc.

Chen, Kathy. 1995. "Women Pack Up After Fractious Meeting." *The Wall Street Journal*, Sept. 18, p. B1.

Cherlin, Andrew J. 1978. "Remarriage as Incomplete Institution." *American Journal of Sociology* (84):634–50.

———. 1990. "Recent Changes in American Fertility, Marriage and Divorce." Pp. 145–54 in *World Population: Approaching the Year 2000,* edited by Samuel H. Preston. Newbury Park, CA: Sage.

———. 1997. "A Reply to Glenn: What's Most Important in a Family Textbook?" *Family Relations* 46 (3):209–11.

Cherlin, Andrew J. and Aphichat Chamratrithirong. 1993. "Variations in Marriage Patterns in Central Thailand." Pp. 84–89 in *Next of Kin: An International Reader on Changing Families,* edited by Lorne Tepperman and Susannah J. Wilson. Englewood Cliffs, NJ: Prentice Hall.

Cherlin, Andrew J. and Frank F. Furstenberg Jr. 1986. *The New American Grandparent: A Place in the Family, A Life Apart.* New York: Basic Books.

———. 1994. "Stepfamilies in the United States: A Reconsideration." *Annual Review of Sociology* 20:359–81.

Cherlin, Andrew J., P. Lindsay Chase-Lansdale, and Christine McRae. 1998. "Effects of Parental Divorce on Mental Health Throughout the Life Course." *American Sociological Review* 63 (2):239–49.

Chesley, L., D. MacAulay and J.L. Ristock. 1991. *Abuse in Lesbian Relationships: A Handbook of Information and Resources.* Toronto: Counselling Centre for Lesbians and Gays.

Chilly Collective (eds.). 1995. *Breaking Anonymity: The Chilly Collective for Women Faculty.* Waterloo, ON: Wilfrid Laurier University Press.

Chilman, Catherine Street. 1978. "Families of Today." Paper presented at the Building Family Strengths Symposium, University of Nebraska, Lincoln, May.

———. 1993. "Hispanic Families in the United States." Pp. 141–63 in *Family Ethnicity: Strength in Diversity,* edited by Harriette Pipes McAdoo. Newbury Park, CA: Sage.

Chira, Susan. 1991. "Poverty's Toll on Health Is Plague of U.S. Schools." *New York Times,* Oct. 5.

———. 1994a. "Push to Revamp Ideal for American Fathers." *New York Times,* June 19.

———. 1994b. "Role of Parents Diminishes as Pupils Age, Report Says." *New York Times,* Sept. 5.

———. 1996. "Study Says Babies in Child Care Keep Secure Bonds to Mothers: Federal Research Counters Some Earlier Reports." *New York Times.* April 21.

Chisholm, Patricia and Mary Nemeth. 2001. "Missing." *Maclean's,* June 4. <http://www.macleans.ca/xta-asp/storyview...print&vpath=/2001-06/04/cover/51881.shtml>

Chodorow, Nancy. 1978. *The Reproduction of Mothering: Psychoanalysis and the Sociology of Gender.* Berkeley: University of California Press.

Choi, Namkee G. 1992. "Correlates of the Economic Status of Widowed and Divorced Elderly Women." *Journal of Family Issues* 13 (1) (Mar.):38–54.

Choice, Pamela and Leanne K. Lamke. 1997. "A Conceptual Approach to Understanding Abused Women's Stay/Leave Decisions." *Journal of Family Issues,* 18(31), May: 290–314.

Chojnack, Joseph T. and W. Bruce Walsh. 1990. "Reliability and Concurrent Validity of the Sternburg Triangular Love Scale." *Psychological Reports* 67:219–24.

Chow, E. N. 1985. "The Acculturation Experience of Asian American Women." Pp. 238–51 in *Beyond Sex Roles,* 2d ed., edited by A. Sargent. St. Paul, MN: West.

Christ, Grace. 1982. "Dis-synchrony of Coping Among Children with Cancer, Their Families, and the Treating Staff." Pp. 85–96 in *Psychosocial Interventions in Chronic Pediatric Illness,* edited by Adolph E. Christ and Kalmen Flamenhaft. New York: Plenum.

Christensen, A. and C.K. Heavey. 1993. "Gender Differences in Marital Conflict: The Demand-Withdraw Interaction Pattern." Pp. 113–141 in *Gender Issues in Contemporary Society,* edited by S. Oskamp and M. Constanzo. Newbury Park, CA: Sage.

Christensen, Carole Pigler and Morton Weinfeld. 1993. "The Black Family in Canada: A Preliminary Exploration of Family Patterns and Inequality." *Canadian Ethnic Studies* 25(3):26–44.

Christensen, Kathleen E. and Graham L. Staines. 1990. "FlexTime: A Viable Solution to Work/Family Conflict?" *Journal of Family Issues* 11 (4) (Dec.):455–76.

Christensen, Kimberly. 1997. " 'With Whom Do You Believe Your Lot Is Cast?' White Feminists and Racism." *Signs: Journal of Women in Culture and Society* 22 (3):617–48.

Church, Elizabeth. 1999. "Who Are the People in Your Family? Stepmothers' Diverse Notions of Kinship." *Journal of Divorce and Remarriage* 31 (1-2):83–105.

Cianni, M. and B. Romberger. 1997. "Life in the Corporation: A Multi-Method Study of the Experiences of Male and Female Asian, Black, Hispanic and White Employees." *Gender, Work and Organization,* 4(2) (April):116–129.

Cicerelli, Victor G. 1990. "Family Support in Relation to Health Problems of the Elderly." Pp. 212–28 in *Family Relations in Later Life.* 2d ed., edited by Timothy H. Brubaker. Newbury Park, CA: Sage.

Clark, Jennifer and Bonnie L. Barber. 1994. "Adolescents in Postdivorce and Always-Married Families: Self-Esteem and Perceptions of Fathers' Interest." *Journal of Marriage and the Family* 56 (3) (Aug.):608–14.

Clark, L. and D. Lewis. 1977. *Rape: The Price of Coercive Sexuality.* Toronto: Women's Educational Press.

Clark, Warren. 1999. "Paying off Student Loans." *Canadian Social Trends* (51) (winter):24–28.

———. 2000. "Religious Observance, Marriage and Family." Pp. 109–114 in *Canadian Social Trends: Volume 3.* Toronto: Thompson Educational Publishing, Inc.

Clarke, Sally C. 1995a. "Advance Report of Final Marriage Statistics, 1989 and 1990." *Monthly Vital Statistics Report* 43 (12), July 14. U.S. Department of Health and Human Services, National Center for Health Statistics.

———. 1995b. "Advance Report of Final Divorce Statistics, 1989 and 1990." *Monthly Vital Statistics Report* 43 (9). Supp., March 22.

Clarke, Sally C. and Barbara F. Wilson. 1994. "The Relative Stability of Remarriages: A Cohort Approach Using Vital Statistics." *Family Relations* 43:305–10.

Clatworthy, Nancy M. 1975. "Living Together," Pp. 67–89 in *Old Family/New Family*, edited by Nona Glazer-Malbin. New York: Van Nostrand.

Clavan, Sylvia. 1978. "The Impact of Social Class and Social Trends on the Role of Grandparent." *Family Coordinator* 27:351–57.

Claxton-Oldfield, Stephen and Paula Kavanagh. 1999. "The Effect of Stepfamily Status On Impressions of Children's Report Card Information." *Journal of Divorce and Remarriage* 32(1-2):145–153.

Claxton-Oldfield, Stephen. 1992. "Perceptions of Stepfathers: Disciplinary and Affectionate Behavior." *Journal of Family Issues*, 13(3) (Sept.):378–389.

Clements, Marcelle. 1998. *The Improvised Woman: Single Women Reinventing Single Life*. New York: W. W. Norton.

Cleveland, G. and M. Krashinsky. 1998. *The Costs and Benefits of Good Child Care: The Economic Rationale for Public Investment in Young Children*. Toronto: Canadian Childcare Research Unit.

Climo, Jacob. 1992. *Distant Parents*. New Brunswick, NJ: Rutgers University Press.

"Clinton Attacks Teen Pregnancy." 1997. *Associated Press*. January 5.

Clinton, Hillary Rodham. 1996. *It Takes a Village: and Other Lessons Children Teach Us*. New York: Simon and Schuster.

———. (1990, Apr. 7). "In France, Day Care is Every Child's Right." *New York Times*.

Cobb, Chris. 1997. "East is Best When it Comes to Sex." *Ottawa Citizen*, December 19: A1.

Cobb, Nathan. 1997. "More Singles Are Settling into Suburbia." *Boston Globe*. October 21.

Cogan, Karen Beth. 2000. *Inside Intermarriage: The Experience of Gentile People Married to Jewish Spouses*. Unpublished dissertation, University of Alberta.

Cohen, Joyce S. and Anne Westhues. 1995. "A Comparison Of Self-Esteem, School Achievement, And Friends Between Intercountry Adoptees And Their Siblings." *Early Child Development & Care. Special Issue: Social Work Practice with Children*, 106:205–224.

Cohen, Rina. 1991. "Women Of Color In White Households: Coping Strategies Of Live-In Domestic Workers." *Qualitative Sociology* 14(2) (summer):197–215.

Cole, Thomas. 1983. "The 'Enlightened' View of Aging." *Hastings Center Report* 13:34–40.

Coleman, Marilyn. 1997. "Not Necessarily the Brady Bunch." *Contemporary Psychology* 42 (6):541–42.

Coleman, Marilyn and Lawrence H. Ganong. 1990. "Remarriage and Stepfamily Research in the 1980s: Increased Interest in an Old Family Form." *Journal of Marriage and the Family* 52:925–40.

———. 1997. "Stepfamilies from the Stepfamily's Perspective." Pp. 107–22 in *Stepfamilies: History, Research, and Policy* Irene Levin and Marvin B. Sussman (Eds.). New York: Haworth Press.

Coleman, Marilyn, Lawrence H. Ganong, and Susan M. Cable. 1997. "Beliefs about Women's Intergenerational Family Obligations to Provide Support before and after Divorce and Remarriage." *Journal of Marriage and the Family* 59 (1):165–76.

Colgrove, Melba, Harold Bloomfield, and Peter McWilliams. 1978. *How to Survive the Loss of a Love: 58 Things to Do When There Is Nothing to Be Done*. New York: Bantam.

Collins, J. A., J. B. Garner, E. H. Wilson, W. Wrixon, and R. F. Casper. 1984. "A Proportional Hazard's Analysis of the Clinical Characteristics of Infertile Couples." *American Journal of Obstetrics and Gynecology* 148:527–32.

Collins, Patricia Hill. 1991. *Black Feminist Thought: Knowledge, Consciousness, and the Politics of Empowerment*. New York: Routledge.

———. 1999. "Shifting the Center: Race, Class, and Feminist Theorizing about Motherhood." Pp. 197–217 in Stephanie Coontz (Ed.). *American Families: A Multicultural Reader*. New York: Routledge.

Collins, Randall. 1995. *Sociology of Marriage and the Family: Gender, Love, and Property*, 4th ed. Chicago: Nelson-Hall.

———. 1979. *The Credential Society: An Historical Look at Education*. New York: Academic Press.

Collins, Rebecca L. 1998. "Social Identity and HIV Infection: The Experiences of Gay Men Living With HIV." Pp. 30–55 in *HIV and Social Interaction*, edited by Valerian J. Derlega and Anita P. Barbee. Thousand Oaks, CA: Sage.

Collins, W. A. 1990. "Parent-Child Relationships in the Transition to Adolescence: Continuity and Change in Interaction, Affect and Cognition." Pp. 85–106 in *From Childhood to Adolescence: A Transitional Period? Advances in Adolescent Development*, vol. 2, edited by R. Montemayor, G. R. Adams, and T. P. Gullotta. Newbury Park, CA: Sage.

Coltrane, Scott. 1990. "Birth Timing and the Division of Labor in Dual-Earner Families: Exploratory Findings and Suggestions for Further Research." *Journal of Family Issues* 11:157–81.

———. 1996. *Family Man: Fatherhood, Housework, and Gender Equity.* New York: Oxford University Press.

———. 1997. "Scientific Half-Truths and the Postmodern Parody Parody in the Family Values Debate." *Contemporary Sociology* 26:7–10.

Coltrane, Scott and Michele Adams. 1997. "Children and Gender." Pp. 219–53 in *Contemporary Parenting: Challenges and Issues* edited by Terry Arendell. Thousand Oaks, CA: Sage.

Coltrane, Scott and Masako Ishii-Kuntz. 1992. "Men's Housework: A Life Course Perspective." *Journal of Marriage and the Family* 54 (2) (Feb.):43–57.

Comfort, Alex. 1972. *The Joy of Sex.* New York: Crown.

Commission on Lesbian and Gay Concerns of the American Psychological Association. 1991. "Avoiding Heterosexual Bias in Language." *American Psychologist* 46:973–74.

"Communal Living Returns, This Time with Yuppie Flair." 1998. *Associated Press.* February 19.

Conger, Rand D., Glen H. Elder, Jr., Frederick O. Lorenz, Katherine J. Conger, Ronald L. Simons, Les B. Whitbeck, Shirley Huck, and Janet N. Melby. 1990. "Linking Economic Hardship to Marital Quality and Instability." *Journal of Marriage and the Family* 52 (3) (Aug.):643–56.

Connell, Joan. 1993. "For Some Muslims, the Holiday Is Difficult." *Newhouse News Service.* December 18.

Connidis, Ingrid Arnet. 1997. "Family Ties and Aging in Canada: Continuity and Change over the Past Three Decades." *Lien Social et Politiques–RIAC* 38(78) (autumn):133–143.

Connor, Michael E. 1986. "Some Parenting Attitudes of Young Black Fathers." Pp. 159–68 in *Men in Families,* edited by Robert A. Lewis and Robert E. Salt. Newbury Park, CA: Sage.

Connor, Steve. 1994. "Downward Spiral in Quality of Sperm." *San Francisco Chronicle,* Aug. 28, p. A2.

Conway, John F. 1990. *The Canadian Family in Crisis.* Toronto: James Lorimer.

———. 1997. *The Canadian Family in Crisis, 3rd edition.* Toronto: James Lorimer.

Cook, Philip, Michele Cook, Lien Tran and Wei Tu. 1997. "Children Enabling Change: A Multicultural, Participatory, Community-Based Rehabilitation Research Project Involving Chinese Children With Disabilities And Their Families." *Child & Youth Care Forum* 26(3) (June):295–219.

Cooley, Charles Horton. 1902. *Human Nature and the Social Order.* New York: Scribner's.

———. 1909. *Social Organization.* New York: Scribner's.

Cooney, Rosemary, Lloyd H. Rogler, Rose Marie Hurrel and Vilma Ortiz. 1982. "Decision Making in Intergenerational Puerto Rican Families." *Journal of Marriage and the Family* 44: 621–31.

Cooney, Teresa M. 1994. "Young Adults' Relations with Parents: The Influence of Recent Parental Divorce." *Journal of Marriage and the Family* 56 (1) (Feb.):45–56.

———. 1997. "Parent–Child Relations across Adulthood." Pp. 451–68 in *Handbook of Personal Relationships: Theory, Research, and Interventions,* 2nd edition, edited by Steve Duck. New York: John Wiley & Sons.

Cooney, Teresa M. and Dennis P. Hogan. 1991. "Marriage is an Institutionalized Life Course: First Marriage Among American Men in the Twentieth Century." *Journal of Marriage and the Family* 53:178–90.

Cooney, Teresa M. and Peter Uhlenberg. 1991. "Changes in Work-Family Connections Among Highly Educated Men and Women." *Journal of Family Issues* 12 (1) (Mar.):69–90.

Coontz, Stephanie. 1992. 1996. *The Way We Never Were: American Families and the Nostalgia Trap.* New York: Basic Books.

———. 1997a. "Divorcing Reality." *The Nation.* November 17:21–24.

———. 1997b. *The Way We Really Are: Coming to Terms with America's Changing Families.* New York: Basic Books.

Cooper, Helene. 1992. "Tennessee Court Refuses to Give Custody of 7 Embryos to Mother." *The Wall Street Journal,* June 2, p. B8.

Cooper, M., R. Corrado, A.M. Karlberg and L.P. Adams. 1992. "Aboriginal Suicide in British Columbia: An Overview." *Canada's Mental Health* (September):19–23.

Coopersmith, Stanley. 1967. *The Antecedents of Self-Esteem.* San Francisco: Freeman.

Copenhaver, Stacey and Elizabeth Grauerholz. 1991. "Sexual Victimization Among Sorority Women: Exploring the Link Between Sexual Violence and Institutional Practices." *Sex Roles* 24 (1/2):31–41.

Corak, Miles. 1998. "Getting Ahead in Life: Does Your Parents' Income Count?" *Canadian Social Trends* 49:6–15.

Corak, Miles and Andrew Heisz. 1999. *Death And Divorce: The Long-Term Consequences Of Parental Loss On Adolescents.* Analytic Studies Branch research paper series, June 9, Cat. 11F0019MPE99135.

Cordon, Juan Antonio Fernandez. 1997. "Youth-Residential Independence and Autonomy: A Comparative Study." *Journal of Family Issues* 18(6):576–607.

Cose, Ellis. 1994a. "Truths About Spouse Abuse." *Newsweek,* Aug. 8, p. 49.

———. 1994b. "The Year of the Father." *Newsweek,* Oct. 31, p. 61.

———. 1995. "Black Men and Black Women." *Newsweek,* June 15, pp. 66–69.

Coston, Charisse. 1992. "Worries about crime: Rank-ordering survival concerns among urban transient females." *Deviant Behavior,* 19(4), Oct.-Dec: 365–76.

Cottrell, Ann Baker. 1993. "Cross-National Marriages." Pp. 96–103 in *Next of Kin: An International Reader on Changing Families,* edited by Lorne Tepperman and Susannah J. Wilson. New York: Prentice Hall.

Council on Families in America. 1996. "Marriage in America: A Report on the Nation." Pp. 293–318 in *Promises to Keep: Decline and Renewal of Marriage in America,* edited by D. Popenoe, J. B. Elshtain, and D. Blankenhorn. Lanham, MD: Rowman and Littlefield.

Counts, Robert M. and Anita Sacks. 1991. "Profiles of the Divorce Prone: The Self-Involved Narcissist." *Journal of Divorce and Remarriage* 15 (1/2):51–74.

"Couple Sues a County Agency for Barring a Transracial Adoption." 1990. *The Wall Street Journal,* Nov. 5.

Court of Appeal for British Columbia. 2000. *Van de Perre v. Edwards.* <http://qsilver.queensu.ca/law/restrict/bala/law520/vandeperrevedwards.htm>

Coutu, Sylvain, March Provost and Daniel Pelletier. 1996. "Mother-Child Relations and Quality of Fraternal Interactions in Preschool Children." *Canadian Journal of Behavioural Science* 28(1)(January):1–11.

"Covenant Marriages Ministry." 1998. <http://www.covenantmarriages.com/index2.html>

"Covenant Marriages Tie a Firm Knot." 1997. *American Civil Liberties Union News Wire.* <http://www.aclu.org/news/w081897b.html>

Coverman, Shelly. 1985. "Explaining Husbands' Participation in Domestic Labor." *Sociological Quarterly* 26 (1):81–97.

Covey, Stephen R. 1997. *The 7 Habits of Highly Effective Families.* New York: Golden Books.

Cowan. C. P. and P. A. Cowan. 1992. *When Partners Become Parents: The Big Life Change for Couples.* New York: Basic Books.

———. 1998. "New Families: Modern Couples as New Pioneers." Pp. 169–92 in *All Our Families: New Policies for a New Century,* edited by Mary Ann Mason, Arlene Skolnick, and Stephen D. Sugarman. New York: Oxford University Press.

Cowan, Ruth Schwartz. 1983. *More Work for Mother: The Ironies of Household Technology from the Open Hearth to the Microwave.* New York: Basic Books.

Coward, Raymond T., Claydell Horne, and Jeffrey W. Dwyer. 1992. "Demographic Perspectives on Gender and Family Caregiving." Pp. 18–33 in *Gender, Families, and Elder Care,* edited by J. W. Dwyer and R. T. Coward. Newbury Park, CA: Sage.

Cowley, Geoffrey. 1995. "Ethics and Embryos." *Newsweek,* June 12, pp. 66–67.

———. 1996. "The Biology of Beauty." *Newsweek.* June 3:61–66.

———. 1998a. "Is Sex a Necessity?" *Newsweek.* May 11:62–63.

———. 1998b. "Sobering Up about AIDS." *Newsweek.* June 29:60.

Cowley, Geoffrey and Karen Springer. 1997. "Multiplying the Risks." *Newsweek.* December 1:66.

Cowley, Geoffrey and Anne Underwood. 1997. "Why Ebonie Can't Breathe." *Newsweek.* May 26:57–64.

Coysh, William S., Janet R. Johnston, Jeanne M. Tschann, Judith S. Wallerstein, and Marsha Kline. 1989. "Parental Postdivorce Adjustment in Joint and Sole Physical Custody Families." *Journal of Family Issues* 10:52–71.

Craig, Pat. 1996. "Net Satisfaction." *San Ramoan Valley Times.* February 27: A1.

Craig, Stephen. 1992. "The Effect of Television Day Part on Gender Portrayals in Television Commercials: A Content Analysis." *Sex Roles* 26 (5/6):197–211.

Cramer, James C. 1995. "Racial and Ethnic Differences in Birthweight: The Role of Income and Financial Assistance." *Demography* 32 (2) (May):231–47.

Cranswick, Kelly. 1997. "Canada's Caregivers." *Canadian Social Trends* 47(winter):2–6.

———. 2000. "Who Needs Short-Term Help?" Pp. 51–54 in *Canadian Social Trends: Volume 3.* Toronto: Thompson Educational Publishing, Inc.

———. 2000. "Canada's Caregivers." Pp. 121–125 in *Canadian Social Trends: Volume 3.* Toronto: Thompson Educational Publishing, Inc.

Cravens, Hamilton. 1997. "Postmodernist Psychobabble: The Recovery Movement for Individual Self-Esteem in Mental Health Since World War II." *Journal of Policy History* 9 (1):141–53.

Crawford, M. 1995. *Talking Difference: On Gender and Language.* London: Sage.

Crawford, Maria, Rosemary Gartner and Myrna Dawson. 1997. *Intimate Femicide in Ontario.* Toronto: Ontario Women's Directorate.

Crawford, Trish. 1997. "Sexual Health Programs Are At Risk." *The Toronto Star,* August 23:M1.

Cready, Cynthia M., Mark Fossett, and K. Jill Kiecolt. 1997. "Mate Availability and African American Family Structure in the U.S. Nonmetropolitan South, 1960–1990." *Journal of Marriage and the Family* 59:192–203.

Critchlow, Donald T. and James C. Mohr. 1998. "The Politics of Abortion and Birth Control in Historical Perspective." *Bulletin of the History of Medicine* 72 (1):151–83.

Critelli, Joseph W., Emilie J. Myers, and Victor E. Loos. 1986. "The Components of Love: Romantic Attraction and Sex Role Orientation." *Journal of Personality* 54:354–76.

Crohan, Susan E. 1992. "Marital Happiness and Spousal Consensus on Beliefs About Marital Conflict: A Longitudinal Investigation." *Journal of Social and Personal Relationships* 9:89–102.

Crompton, Susan and Michael Vickers. 2000. "One Hundred Years of Labour Force." *Canadian Social Trends* (summer):2–6.

Crompton, Susan and Leslie Geran. 1995. "Women As Main Wage-Earners." *Perspectives on Labour and Income* 7(4)(winter):26–29. Statistics Canada, Catalogue 75-001-XPE.

Crompton, Susan and Anna Kemeny. 2000. "In Sickness and in Health: The Well-Being of Married Seniors." Pp. 45–50 in *Canadian Social Trends: Volume 3.* Toronto: Thompson Educational Publishing, Inc.

Crook, Joanne F. 1999. "The Best Interests of the First Nations Child." *Law Now* 24(2)(October/November):18–19.

Crosby, Faye J. 1991. *Juggling: The Unexpected Advantages of Balancing Career and Home for Women and Their Families.* New York: The Free Press.

Crosby, John F. 1985 [1976]. *Illusion and Disillusion: The Self in Love and Marriage.* 2d, 3d eds. Belmont, CA: Wadsworth.

———. 1991. *Illusion and Disillusion: The Self in Love and Marriage.* 4th ed. Belmont, CA: Wadsworth.

Crouter, Ann C. and Heather Helms-Erikson. 1997. "Work and Family from a Dyadic Perspective: Variations in Inequality." Pp. 487–503 in *Handbook of Personal Relationships: Theory, Research, and Interventions*, 2nd ed., edited by Steve Duck. New York: John Wiley & Sons.

Crowley, Kathleen. 1998. "Making Room for Many Feminisms: The Dominance of the Liberal Political Perspective in the Psychology of Women." *Psychology of Women Quarterly.* Special Issue: Integrating Gender and Ethnicity into Psychology Courses 22(1), (March):113–130.

Crowley, M. Sue. 1998. "Men's Self-perceived Adequacy as the Family Breadwinner: Implications for Their Psychological, Marital, and Work–Family Well-Being." *Journal of Family and Economic Issues* 19 (1):7–23.

Cuber, John and Peggy Harroff. 1965. *The Significant Americans.* New York: Random House. (Published also as *Sex and the Significant Americans*, Baltimore: Penguin, 1965.)

Cue, Kelly L., William H. George, and Jeanette Norris. 1996. "Women's Appraisals of Sexual-Assault Risk in Dating Situations." *Psychology of Women Quarterly* 20:487–504.

Cunningham-Burley, Sarah. 1987. "The Experience of Grandfatherhood." Pp. 91–105 in *Reassessing Fatherhood: New Observations on Fathers and the Modern Family*, edited by Charles Lewis and Margaret O'Brien. Newbury Park, CA: Sage.

"Cupid's Arrows Strike at Random." 1981. *St. Louis Post-Dispatch*, Feb. 15, p. 2-B.

Currie, Dawn H. and Valerie Raoul. 1992. "The Anatomy of Gender: Dissecting Sexual Differences in the Body of Knowledge." Pp. 1–36 in *Anatomy of Gender: Women's Struggle for the Body*, edited by Dawn Currie and Valerie Raoul. Ottawa: Carleton University Press.

Curry, Hayden, Denis Clifford, and Robin Leonard. 1998. *A Legal Guide for Lesbian and Gay Couples*, 10th edition. Berkeley, CA: Nolo Press.

Curtis, Carla M. 1997. "Factors Influencing Parents' Perceptions of Child Care Services." *Journal of Black Studies* 27 (6):768–82.

D

Dahms, Alan M. 1976. "Intimacy Hierarchy." Pp. 85–104 in *Process in Relationship: Marriage and Family.* 2d ed., edited by Edward A. Powers and Mary W. Lees. New York: West.

Daisley, B. 1996. "Foreign Domestic Wins Sexual Harassment Suit Against Boss." *The Lawyers' Weekly* 15 (47)(April):21–26.

Dalphonse, Sherri. 1997. "Childfree by Choice." *The Washingtonian* 32 (5):48–57.

Daly, Kerry. 2000. "It Keeps Getting Faster: Changing Patterns of Time in Families." <http://www.vifamily.ca/cft/dalye.htm>

———. 1996. *Families and Time: Keeping Place in a Hurried Culture.* Thousand Oaks, CA: Sage.

———. 1994. "Uncertain Terms: The Social Construction of Fatherhood." Pp. 170–185 in *Doing Everyday Life: Ethnography As A Human Lived Experience*, edited by M. Lorenz Dietz, R. Prus and W. Shaffir. Mississauga: Copp Clark Longman.

———. 1994. "Adolescent Perceptions of Adoption: Implications for Resolving an Unplanned Pregnancy." *Youth & Society* 25(3)(March):330–350.

Daly, M. and M. I. Wilson. 1994. "Some Differential Attributes of Lethal Assaults on Small Children by Stepfathers versus Genetic Fathers." *Ethology and Sociobiology* 15:207–17.

Dandurand, Renee B. 1994. "Women and Families: Under the Sign of Paradox." *Recherches féministes*, 7(1):1–22.

Daniels, Pamela and Kathy Weingarten. 1980. "Postponing Parenthood: The Myth of the Perfect Time." *Savvy Magazine* (May):55–60.

Danesco, Evangeline R. and E. Wayne Holden. 1998. "Are There Different Types of Homeless Families?" *Family Relations* 47 (2):159–65.

D'Antonio, William V., James Davidson, Dean Hoge, and Ruth Wallace. 1996. Laity: *American and Catholic: Transforming the Church.* Kansas City, MO: Sheed and Ward.

"The Dark Side of Cyber Romance." 1997. <http.//www.cvp.com/cyber/badlove.html>

Darling, Carol A. 1987. "Family Life Education." Pp. 815–34 in *Handbook of Marriage and the Family*, edited by Marvin B. Sussman and Suzanne K. Steinmetz. New York: Plenum.

Darling, Carol A., David J. Kallen, and Joyce E. VanDusen. 1984. "Sex in Transition, 1900–1980." *Journal of Youth and Adolescence* 13 (5):385–99.

Darroch, Gordon. 1987. "Urban Ethnicity in Canada: Personal Assimilation and Personal Communities." *Canadian Review of Sociology and Anthropology* 30:93–100.

Darroch, Gordon and Marston, Wilfrid G. 1987. "Patterns of Urban Ethnicity: Toward a Revised Ecological World." In Noel Iverson (Ed.), *Urbanism and Urbanization: Views, Aspects and Dimensions* (pp. 127-162). London: E.J. Brill.

Das Gupta, Tanis. 1996. *Racism and Paid Work*. Toronto: Garamond Press.

———. 1999. "The Effects of Transitions in Marital Status on Men's Performance of Housework." *Journal of Marriage and the Family* 61:700–711.

———. 1999. "The Politics of Multiculturalism: 'Immigrant Women' and the Canadian State." Pp. 187–206 in *Scratching The Surface: Canadian Anti-Racist Feminist Thought*, edited by Enakshi Dua and Angela Robertson. Toronto: Women's Press.

———. 2000. "Families of Native People, Immigrants, and People of Colour." Pp. 146–187 in *Canadian Families: Diversity, Conflict, and Change*, edited by Nancy Mandell and Ann Duffy. Toronto: Harcourt Brace Canada.

Daub, Shannon and Margaret Young. 1999. "Families Need More than Tax Fairness." <www.policyalternatives.ca>

David, Deborah S. and Robert Brannon, Eds. 1976. *The Forty-Nine Percent Majority; The Male Sex Role*. Reading, MA: Addison-Wesley.

David, Miriam. 1998. "Home-School Relations Or Families, Parents And Education." *British Journal of Sociology of Education* 19(2)(June):255–261.

Davidson, Bernard, Jack Balswick, and Charles Halverson. 1983. "Affective Self-Disclosure and Marital Adjustment: A Test of Equity Theory." *Journal of Marriage and the Family* 45:93–102.

Davidson, Jeannette R. 1992. "Theories about Black–White Interracial Marriage: A Clinical Perspective." *Journal of Multicultural Counseling and Development* 20 (4):150–57.

Davidson-Harden, Jennifer, William Fisher and Paul Davidson. 2000. "Attitudes Toward People In Exclusive Dating Relationships Who Initiate Condom Use." *The Canadian Journal of Human Sexuality* 9:1–14.

Davis, Angela. 1989. *Women, Culture, and Politics*. New York: Random House.

Davis, Bob and Dana Milbank. 1992. "If the U.S. Work Ethic Is Fading, Alienation May Be Main Reason." *The Wall Street Journal*, Feb. 7, pp. A1, A5.

Davis, Fred. 1991. [1963]. *Passage Through Crisis: Polio Victims and Their Families*. 2d ed. New Brunswick, NJ: Transaction.

———. 1961. "Deviance Disavowal: The Management of Strained Interaction by the Visibly Handicapped." *Social Problems*, 9:121–132.

Davis, James. 1991. *Who Is Black? One Nation's Definition*. University Park, PA: The Pennsylvania State University Press.

Davis, J.A. 1980. "General Social Surveys, 1972–1980 Cumulative Data." Chicago: National Opinion Research Centre.

Davis, K.R. and S.C. Weller. 1999. "The Effectiveness Of Condoms In Reducing Heterosexual Transmission Of HIV." *Family Planning Perspectives* 31:272–279.

Davis, Nanciellen. 1995. "French-British Marriages, Gender And Cultural Orientation: An Example From Nineteenth Century New Brunswick." *Canadian Ethnic Studies*, 27(1):123–141.

———. 1985. *Ethnicity and Ethnic Group Persistence in an Acadian Village in the Maritimes Canada*. New York: AMS Press.

Dawson, Deborah A. 1991. "Family Structure and Children's Health and Well-Being: Data from the 1988 National Health Interview Survey on Child Health." *Journal of Marriage and the Family* 53 (3) (Aug.):573–84.

Day, Randal D., Gary W. Peterson, and Coleen McCracken. 1998. "Predicting Spanking of Younger and Older Children by Mothers and Fathers." *Journal of Marriage and the Family* 60 (1):79–94.

De'Ath, Erica. 1996. "Family Change: Stepfamilies in Context." *Children & Society* 10:80–82.

DeBuono, Barbara A., Stephen H. Zinner, Maxim Daamen, and William M. McCormack. 1990. "Sexual Behavior of College Women in 1975, 1986, and 1989." *New England Journal of Medicine* 222:821–25.

Deenen, A. A., L. Gijs, and A. X. van Naerssen. 1994. "Intimacy and Sexuality in Gay Male Couples." *Archives of Sexual Behavior* 23 (4):421–31.

DeKeseredy, Walter and Katherine Kelly. 1993. "The Incidence and Prevalence of Woman Abuse in Canadian University and College Dating Relationships." *Canadian Journal of Sociology* 18(2)(spring):137–159.

——— and D. Ellis. 1995. "Intimate Male Violence Against Women In Canada." Pp. 97–125 in *Violence In Canada: Sociopolitical Perspectives*, edited by I. Ross. Don Mills, ON: Oxford University Press.

DeLamater, John D. and Janet Shibley Hyde. 1998. "Essentialism vs. Social Constructionism in the Study of Human Sexuality." *The Journal of Sex Research* 35 (1):10–18.

De Lisi, R. and L. Soundranayagam. 1990. "The Conceptual Structure of Sex Stereotypes in College Students." *Sex Roles* 23:593–611.

DeLoach, C. and B.G. Greer. 1981. *Adjustment to Severe Physical Disability: A Metamorphosis*. New York: McGraw-Hill.

del Pinal, Jorge and Audrey Singer. 1997. *Generations of Diversity: Latinos in the United States.* Population Bulletin 52 (3).

DeMaris, Alfred and William MacDonald. 1993. "Premarital Cohabitation and Marital Instability: A Test of the Unconventionality Hypothesis." *Journal of Marriage and the Family* 55 (2) (May):399–407.

DeMaris, Alfred, Meredith D. Pugh, and Erika Harman. 1992. "Sex Differences in the Accuracy of Recall of Witnesses of Portrayed Dyadic Violence." *Journal of Marriage and the Family* 54 (2) (May):335–45.

DeMaris, Alfred and Steven Swinford. 1996. "Female Victims of Spousal Violence: Factors Influencing Their Level of Fearfulness." *Family Relations* 45 (1):98–106.

D'Emilio, John and Estelle B. Freedman. 1988. *Intimate Matters: A History of Sexuality in America.* New York: Harpers.

Demo, David H. and Alan C. Acock. 1996a. "Family Structure, Family Process, and Adolescent Well-Being." *Journal of Research on Adolescence* 6 (4):457–88.

———. 1996b. "Singlehood, Marriage, and Remarriage: The Effects of Family Structure and Family Relationships on Mothers' Well-Being." *Journal of Family Issues* 17 (3):388–407.

Department of Justice Canada. 1997. "Selected Statistics On Canadian Families And Family Law." November. <http://canada.justice.gc.ca/en/ps.sup/stat.htm>

de Santis, Marie. 1990. "Hate Crimes Bill Excludes Women." *Off Our Backs,* June.

Desai, S. and L. J. Waite. 1991. "Women's Employment During Pregnancy And After The First Birth: Occupational Characteristics And Work Commitment." *American Sociological Review* 56(4)(August):551–566.

Desrosiers, Helene, Celine Le Bourdais and Benoit Laplante. 1995. "The Breakup Of Reconstituted Families: The Experience Of Canadian Women." *Recherches Sociographiques,* 36(1)(Jan-Apr):47–64.

Deziel, A. 2000. "Gender Bender 101: Life in an Ovary Tower." *Maclean's,* June 10:19.

Dhruvarajan, Vanaja. 1993 "Ethnic Cultural Retention and Transmission Among First Generation Hindu Asian Native Canadians in a Canadian Prairie City." *Journal of Comparative Family Studies* 224(1):63–80.

———. 1996. "Hindo-Indo-Canadian Families." Pp. 301–328 in *Voices: Essays on Canadian Families,* edited by Marion Lynn. Scarborough: Nelson.

Dickinson, Harley D. 1993. "Scientific Parenthood: The Mental Hygiene Movement And The Reform Of Canadian Families, 1925–1980." *Journal of Comparative Family Studies* 24(3):387–402.

Di Giulio, R.C. 1992. "Beyond Widowhood." Pp. 457–469 in *Marriage and Family in a Changing Society,* 4th edition, edited by J.M. Henslin. New York: Free Press.

Dill, Bonnie Thornton. 1999. "Fictive Kin, Paper Sons, and Compadrazgo: Women of Color and the Struggle for Family Survival." Pp. 2–29 in *American Families: A Multicultural Reader,* edited by Stephanie Coontz. New York: Routledge.

Dilworth-Anderson, Peggye, Linda M. Burton, and Eleanor Boulin Johnson. 1993. "Reframing Theories for Understanding Race, Ethnicity, and Families." Pp. 627–46 in *Sourcebook of Family Theories and Methods: A Contextual Approach*, edited by Pauline G. Boss, William J. Doherty, Ralph LaRossa, Walter R. Schumm, and Suzanne K. Steinmetz. New York: Plenum.

Dinkmeyer, Don Sr., Gary D. McKay, and Don Dinkmeyer Jr. 1997. *The Parent's Handbook: Systematic Training for Effective Parenting.* Circle Pines, MN: American Guidance Service, Inc.

Dion, Karen K. and Kenneth L. Dion. 1988. "Romantic Love: Individual and Cultural Perspectives." Pp. 264–89 in *The Psychology of Love,* edited by Robert J. Sternberg and Michael L. Barnes. New Haven, CT: Yale University Press.

———. 1991. "Psychological Individualism and Romantic Love." *Journal of Social Behavior and Personality* 6:17–33.

———. 1993. "Individualistic and Collectivist Perspectives on Gender and the Cultural Context of Love and Intimacy." *Journal of Social Issues* 49:53–69.

"The Divorce Dilemma." 1996. *U.S. News & World Report.* September 30:58–62.

"Divorced Dad Tries to Give Children His Full Support." 1996. *Dear Abby. Minneapolis Star Tribune.* January 8:E7.

Dobash, Russell P., R. Emerson Dobash, Margo Wilson, and Martin Daly. 1992. "The Myth of Sexual Symmetry in Marital Violence." *Social Problems* 39 (1) (Feb.):71–91.

Dobkin, Patricia L., Richard E. Tremblay, Lyse Desmarais-Gervais and Louise Depelteau. 1994. "Is Having An Alcoholic Father Hazardous For Children's Physical Health?" *Addiction* 89(12)(Dec.): 1619–1627.

Doherty, Gillian, Martha Friendly, and Mab Oloman. 1998. *Women's Support, Women's Work: Child Care in an Era of Deficit Reduction, Downsizing and Deregulation.* Ottawa: Status of Women Canada.

Doherty, William J., Edward F. Kouneski, and Martin Erickson. 1998. "Responsible Fathering: An Overview and Conceptual Framework." *Journal of Marriage and the Family* 60 (2):277–92.

Doherty, William, J., Susan Su, and Richard Needle. 1989. "Marital Disruption and Psychological Well-Being: A Panel Study." *Journal of Family Issues* 10:72–85.

Dolgin, Janet L. 1997. *Defining the Family: Law, Technology, and Reproduction in an Uneasy Age.* New York: New York University Press.

Doudna, Christine. 1981. "Where Are the Men for the Women at the Top?" Pp. 21–34 in *Single Life,* edited by Peter J. Stein. New York: St. Martin's Press.

Dougherty, Kevin and Amanda Jelowicki. 2000. "Night Daycare To Make Debut." *The Montreal Gazette*, August 31. <http://www.childcarecanada.org/ccin/2000/ccin8_31_00.html>

Douglas, Susan. 1995. "Sitcom Women: We've Come a Long Way. Maybe." *Ms. Magazine* (Nov./Dec.):76–80.

Doyle, J. 1989. *The Male Experience*. Dubuque, IA: William C. Brown.

Downey, Douglas B. 1995. "When Bigger Is Not Better: Family Size, Parental Resources, and Children's Educational Performance." *American Sociological Review* 60:746–61.

Downs, Donald A. 1996. *More Than Victims: Battered Women, the Syndrome Society, and the Law*. Chicago: University of Chicago Press.

Downs, William R. and Brenda A. Miller. 1998. "Relationships between Experiences of Parental Violence during Childhood and Women's Self-Esteem." *Violence and Victims* 13 (1):63–74.

Drachman, D. et al 1996. "Migration and Resettlement Experiences of Dominican and Korean Families." *Families in Society: The Journal of Contemporary Human Services* 77(10):626–638.

Drakes, Shellene. 1999. "Recent Immigrants Have Tougher Time Finding Good Jobs. " *Toronto Star*, November 24:A1.

Dranoff, Linda Silver. 2001. "Adoption." <wysiwyg://67/http://www.chatelaine.com/article/jsp?/page=read&cid=2722>

———. 2001. *Everyone's Guide to the Law*. Toronto: HarperCollins Publishers Ltd.

Driedger, Dianne. 1993. "Discovering Disabled Women's History." Pp. 173–188 in *And Still We Rise,* edited by L. Carty. Toronto: Women's Press.

Dua, Enakshi. 1999. "Canadian Anti-Racist Feminist Thought: Scratching the Surface of Racism." Pp. 7–31 in *Scratching The Surface: Canadian Anti-Racist Feminist Thought*, edited by Enakshi Dua and Angela Robertson. Toronto: Women's Press.

Duberman, Lucile. 1975. *The Reconstituted Family: A Study of Remarried Couples and Their Children*. Chicago: Nelson-Hall.

DuBois, David L., Susan K. Eitel, and Robert D. Felner. 1994. "Effects of Family Environment and Parent–Child Relationships on School Adjustment During the Transition to Early Adolescence." *Journal of Marriage and the Family* 56 (2) (May):405–14.

Dubois, Stephanie L. 1997. "Gender Differences In The Emotional Tone Of Written Sexual Fantasies." *The Canadian Journal of Human Sexuality* 6:307–316.

Duck, Steve. 1998. *Human Relationships*, 3rd ed. Thousand Oaks, CA: Sage.

———. 1998. "In India, an Arranged Marriage of 2 Worlds." *New York Times*. July 20:A1, A10.

Duffy, Anne and Julian Momirov. 1997. *Family Violence: A Canadian Introduction*. Toronto: James Lorimer & Company.

Dugger, Karen. 1996. "Social Location and Gender-Role Attitudes: A Comparison of Black and White Women." Pp. 32–51 in *Race, Class, and Gender,* edited by Esther Ngan-Ling Chow, Doris Wilkinson, and Maxine Baca Zinn. Newbury Park, CA: Sage.

Dullea, Georgia. 1987a. "AIDS and Divorce: A New Legal Arena." *New York Times*, Sept. 21.

———. 1987b. "Divorces Spawn Confusion Over Stepparents' Rights." *Omaha World-Herald*, Mar. 18.

———. 1987c. "False Child-Abuse Charges Seem to Be on the Increase." *New York Times*, reprinted in *Omaha World-Herald*, Jan. 19.

———. 1987d. "When Illness Destroys a Marriage." *New York Times*, Sept. 21.

———. 1988a. "Gay Couples' Wish to Adopt Grows, Along with Increasing Resistance." *New York Times*, Feb. 7.

Dumas, Jean (adapted by Jillian Oderkirk). 2000. "Marriage in Canada: Changing Beliefs and Behaviours, 1600–1990." Pp. 93–98 in *Canadian Social Trends: Volume 3*. Toronto: Thompson Educational Publishing.

Dumas, J. and A. Belanger. 1997. *Report on the Demographic Situation in Canada*. Cat. 91-2090XPE. Ottawa: Statistics Canada, Minister of Industry.

Dumas, J. and Y. Peron. 1992. *Marriage and Conjugal Life in Canada*. Cat. 91-534. Ottawa: Statistics Canada.

Duncan, Greg and Willard Rodgers. 1987. "Single-Parent Families: Are Their Economic Problems Transitory or Persistent?" *Family Planning Perspectives* 19:171–78.

Duncan, Greg, W. Jean Yeung, Jeanne Brooks-Gunn, and Judith Smith. 1998. "How Much Does Childhood Poverty Affect the Life Chance of Children?" *American Sociological Review*, 63:402–423.

Duncan, Stephen F., Gabrielle Box, and Benjamin Silliman. 1996. "Racial and Gender Effects on Perceptions of Marriage Preparation Programs among College Educated Young Adults." *Family Relations* 45 (1):80–90.

Dunlap, David W. 1996. "In AIDS Age, Love Can Add Risk." *New York Times* National Saturday. July 27.

Dunning, Jennifer. 1986. "Women and AIDS: Discussing Precautions." *New York Times*, Nov. 3.

Durkheim, Emile. 1933 [1893]. *Division of Labor in Society*, translated by George Simpson. New York: Macmillan.

———. 1951. *Suicide*, translated by John A. Spaulding and George Simpson. Glencoe, IL: Free Press.

Durm, Mark W., Angela Giddens, and Melissa Blankenship. 1997. "Parental Marital Status and Self-esteem of Boys and Girls." *Psychological Reports* B1 (1):125–37.

Durrant, Joan E. 1993/1994. "Sparing The Rod: Manitoban's Attitudes Toward The Abolition Of Physical Discipline And Implications For Policy Change." *Canada's Mental Health* 41(4)(winter):2–6.

Durrant, Joan E., Anders G. Broberg, and Linda Rose-Krasnor. 1999. "Predicting Mother's Use Of Physical Punishment During Mother-Child Conflicts In Sweden And Canada." Pp. 25–41 in *Conflict As A Context For Understanding Maternal Beliefs About Child Rearing And Children's Misbehavior,* edited by Caroline C. Piotrowski and Paul D. Hastings. New Directions for Child and Adolescent Development, No. 86. San Francisco, CA: Jossey-Bass Inc.

Dutton, Donald G. and James J. Browning. 1988. "Concern for Power, Fear of Intimacy, and Aversive Stimuli for Wife Assault." Pp. 163–75 in *Family Abuse and Its Consequences: New Directions in Research,* edited by Gerald T. Hotaling, David Finkelhor, John T. Kirkpatrick, and Murray A. Straus. Newbury Park, CA: Sage.

Duvall, E. M. 1957. *Family Development.* Philadelphia: Lippincott.

Dwyer, Jeffrey W. and Karen Seccombe. 1991. "Elder Care as Family Labor: The Influence of Gender and Family Position." *Journal of Family Issues* 12 (2) (June):229–47.

Dwyer, Jeffrey W., Gary R. Lee, and Thomas B. Jankowski. 1994. "Reciprocity, Elder Satisfaction, and Caregiver Stress and Burden: The Exchange of Aid in the Family Caregiving Relationship." *Journal of Marriage and the Family* 56 (1) (Feb.):35–43.

E

Eagly, Alice H. 1995. "The Science and Politics of Comparing Women and Men." *American Psychologist* 50 (1):164–68.

Easterlin, Richard. 1987. *Birth and Fortune: The Impact of Numbers on Personal Welfare.* 2d rev. ed. Chicago: University of Chicago Press.

Easterlin, Richard A. and Eileen M. Crimmins. 1985. *The Fertility Revolution: A Supply-Demand Analysis.* Chicago: University of Chicago Press.

Eberstadt, Nicholas. 1992. "America's Infant Mortality Problem: Parents." *The Wall Street Journal,* Jan. 20, p. A12.

Eby, Lillian T., Jacquelyn S. DeMatteo and Joyce E.A. Russell. 1997. "Employment Assistance Needs Of Accompanying Spouses Following Relocation." *Journal of Vocational Behavior,* Special Issue on Work and Family Balance, 50(2)(April):291–307.

Economic Report of the President. 1989. Washington: U.S. Government Printing Office. Jan.

Edmonds, Scott. 2001. "Manitoba Announces Study Of Gay And Lesbian Adoptions And Other Rights Issues." *Canadian Press,* June 23. <wysiwyg:// 36/http://www.canada.com/cgi-bi.../cp/stories/ 20010619/national-512022.html>

Edwards, John N. 1987. "Changing Family Structure and Youthful Well-Being." *Journal of Family Issues* 8 (4):355–72.

———. 1991. "New Conceptions: Biosocial Innovations and the Family." *Journal of Marriage and the Family* 53:349–60.

EGALE. 2001. "Press Release: 2001 Census To Recognize Same-Sex Couples." May 10. <http://www.egale.ca/ pressrel/010510-e.html>

———. 2001. "Census Kit." <http://www.egale.ca/ documents/census-kit-e.htm>

———. 1999. "Poll Supports Gay Marriages." *Globe and Mail,* June 10. <www.egale.ca/pressrel/990611.htm>

———. 1999a. "Employers Offering Same-Sex Benefits." April10. <www.egale.ca/features/employers.htm>

———. 1999b. "Press Release." June 7. <www.egale.ca/politics.motion.htm>

———. 1999c. "Press Release." June 7. <www.egale.ca/archives/press/990610poll.htm>

———. 1999d. "BC Introduces New Same Sex Laws, Commits to Omnibus Legislation." July 9. <www.egale.ca/pressrel/990709.htm>

Eggebeen, David J. and Adam Davey. 1998. "Do Safety Nets Work? The Role of Anticipated Help in Times of Need." *Journal of Marriage and the Family* 60 (4):939–50.

Eggebeen, David J. and Daniel T. Lichter. 1991. "Race, Family Structure, and Changing Poverty Among American Children." *American Sociological Review* 56 (Dec):801–17.

Ehrbar, Al. 1993. "Pride of Progress." *The Wall Street Journal,* Mar. 16, Pp. A1, A11.

Ehrenreich, Barbara. 1983. *The Hearts of Men: American Dreams and the Flight from Commitment.* Garden City, NY: Anchor/Doubleday.

Ehrensaft, Diane. 1990. *Parenting Together: Men and Women Sharing the Care of Their Children.* Urbana: University of Illinois Press.

Eisenberg, Susan. 1998. *We'll Call You If We Need You: Experiences of Women Working Construction.* Ithaca, NY: ILR Press.

Elder, Glen H., Jr. 1974. *Children of the Great Depression.* Chicago: University of Chicago Press.

———. 1977. "Family History and the Life Course." *Journal of Family History* 2:279–304.

Elder, Glen H., Jr. and Eliza K. Pavalko. 1993. "Work Careers in Men's Later Years: Transitions, Trajectories, and Historical Change." *Journal of Gerontology: Social Sciences* 48 (4):S180–91.

Elison, Sonja Klueck. 1997. "Policy Innovation in a Cold Climate." *Journal of Family Issues* 18 (1):30–54.

Elkin, Larry M. 1994. *First Comes Love, Then Comes Money.* New York: Doubleday.

Elkind, David. 1988. *The Hurried Child: Growing Up Too Fast Too Soon.* Reading, MA: Addison–Wesley.

Elliott, Jean Leonard and Augie Fleras. *Unequal Relations: An Introduction to Race and Ethnic Dynamics in Canada*, 2nd edition. Scarborough: ON: Prentice Hall Canada.

Ellis, Walter L. 1991. "The Effects of Background Characteristics of Attorneys and Judges on Decision Making in Domestic Relations Court: An Analysis of Child Support Awards." *Journal of Divorce and Remarriage* 16 (1/2):107–20.

Ellman, Ira Mark. 1996. "The Place of Fault in a Modern Divorce Law." *Arizona State Law Journal* 28 (3):773–92.

Elmer-Dewitt, Philip. 1991a. "How Safe Is Sex?" *Time*, Nov. 25, p. 72.

———. 1991b. "Making Babies." *Time*, Sept. 30, pp. 56–63.

Elson, John. 1989. "The Rights of Frozen Embryos." *Time*, July 24, p. 63.

Emmons, R. A. 1987. "Narcissism: Theory and Measurement." *Journal of Personality and Social Psychology* 52 (1):11–17.

Enda, Jodi. 1998. "Women Have Made Gains, Seek More." Washington Bureau in St. Paul, Minneapolis Pioneer Press, Early Edition, July 19:1A, 4A.

Engels, Friedrich. 1942 [1884]. *The Origin of the Family, Private Property, and the State.* New York: International.

England, Paula and George Farkas. 1986. *Households, Employment and Gender: A Social, Economic and Demographic View.* New York: Aldine de Gruyter.

Entwisle, Doris R. and Karl L. Alexander. 1995. "A Parent's Economic Shadow: Family Structure Versus Family Resources as Influences on Early School Achievement." *Journal of Marriage and the Family* 57 (2) (May):399–409.

———. 1996. "Family Type and Children's Growth in Reading and Math Over the Primary Grades." *Journal of Marriage and the Family* 58 (2):341–55.

Epstein, Cynthia Fuchs. 1988. *Deceptive Distinctions: Sex, Gender, and the Social Order.* New Haven and New York: Yale University Press and Russell Sage Foundation.

Epstein, Norma, Lynda Evans, and John Evans. 1994. "Marriage." Pp. 115–25 in *Encyclopedia of Human Behavior*, vol. 3, edited by V.S. Ramachandran. New York: Academic.

Erel, O. and B. Burman. 1995. "Interrelatedness of Marital Relations and Parent–Child Relations: A Meta-Analytic Review." *Psychological Bulletin* 118:108–32.

Erickson, Nancy S. 1991. "Battered Mothers of Battered Children: Using Our Knowledge of Battered Women to Defend Them Against Charges of Failure to Act." *Current Perspectives in Psychological, Legal, and Ethical Issues*, vol. 1A: Children and Families: Abuse and Endangerment:197–218.

Erickson, Rebecca J. 1993. "Reconceptualizing Family Work: The Effect of Emotion Work on Perceptions of Marital Quality." *Journal of Marriage and the Family* 55 (3) (Nov.):888–900.

Erikson, Erik. 1979. Interview in *Omaha World-Herald*, Aug. 5.

Espiritu, Yen. 1997. *Asian American Women and Men.* Thousand Oaks, CA: Sage Publications.

Estess, Patricia Schiff. 1996. *Money Advice for Your Successful Remarriage: Handling Delicate Financial Issues with Love and Understanding.* Cincinnati, OH: Betterway Books.

Etaugh, C. and M.B. Liss. 1992. "Home, School, and Playroom: Training Groups for Adult Gender Roles." *Sex Roles*, 26:129–147.

Ettelbrick, Paula L. 1989. "Since When Is Marriage a Path to Liberation?" *OUT/LOOK, National Gay and Lesbian Quarterly* 6 (Fall).

Ettner, Susan L. 1995. "The Impact of 'Parent Care' on Female Labor Supply Decisions." *Demography* 32 (1) (Feb.):63–80.

Evans, Sara. 1978. *Personal Politics.* New York: Knopf.

Everett, Craig A. (Ed.). 1995. *Understanding Stepfamilies: Their Structure and Dynamics.* New York: Haworth Press.

———. (Ed.). 1997. *Divorce and Remarriages: International Studies.* New York: Haworth Press.

Evert, Kathy. 1987. *When You're Ready: Women Healing from Physical and Sexual Abuse.* Maryland: Launch Press.

Eyer, Diane E. 1992. *Mother–Infant Bonding: A Scientific Fiction.* New Haven, CT: Yale University Press.

Eyre, Linda and Richard Eyre. 1994. *Teaching Your Children Joy. Teaching Your Children Responsibility. Teaching Your Children Values.* 3 books. New York: Simon & Schuster, Fireside Books.

F

FAD (Families Against Deadbeats). 2000. <www.wantedposters.com>

Fagot, B. I. 1978. "Reinforcing Contingencies for Sex Role Behaviors: Effects of Experience with Children." *Child Development* 49:30–36.

Falbo, T. 1976. "Does the Only Child Grow Up Miserable?" *Psychology Today* 9:60–65.

Faludi, Susan. 1991. *Backlash.* New York: Crown.

Family Science Network. 1998. "Corporal Punishment Debate: The Play of Values and Perspectives." familysci@lsv.uky.edu.

Farber, Bernard. 1959. "Effects of a Severely Mentally Retarded Child on Family Integration." *Monographs of the Society for Research in Child Development* 24 (71):80–94.

———. 1964. *Family Organization and Interaction.* San Francisco: Chandler.

Farver, Jo Ann M., Barbara Welles-Nystrom, Dominick L. Frosch, Supra Wimbarti, and Sigfried Hoppe-Graff. 1997. "Toy Stories: Aggression in Children's Narratives in the United States, Sweden, Germany, and Indonesia." *Journal of Cross-Cultural Psychology* 28 (4):393–420.

Fass, Paula S. 1998. "A Sign of Family Disorder? Changing Representations of Parental Kidnapping." Pp. 144–68 in *All Our Families: New Policies for a New Century,* edited by Mary Ann Mason, Arlene Skolnick, and Stephen D. Sugarman. New York: Oxford University Press.

Fassinger, Polly. 1990. "The Meanings of Housework for Single Parents: Insights into Gender Strategies." Paper presented at the annual meeting of the Midwest Sociological Society, Chicago, Apr. 13.

Fast, Janet and Moreno Da Pont. 2000. "Changes in Women's Work Continuity." Pp. 78–83 in *Canadian Social Trends: Volume 3.* Toronto: Thompson Educational Publishing, Inc.

Fast, Janet E. and Judith A. Frederick. 2000. "Working Arrangements and Time Stress." Pp. 151–156 in *Canadian Social Trends: Volume 3.* Toronto: Thompson Educational Publishing, Inc.

Fawcett, Diane. 1999. "Disability in the Labour Market: Barriers and Solutions." *Perception,* 23(3) December. <www.ccsd.ca/perception/233/disab.htm>

Fawcett, Gail. 2000. "Bringing Down the Barriers: The Labour Market and Women with Disabilities in Ontario." *Canadian Council on Social Development.* <http://www.ccsd.ca/pubs/2000/wd/sect2b.htm>

———. 1999. "Disability in the Labour Market: Barriers and Solutions." *Perception* 23(3)(December). Canadian Council on Social Development. <www.ccsd.ca/perception/233/disab.htm>

Feagin, Joe R. and Melvin P. Sikes. 1994. *Living with Racism: the Black Middle-Class Experience.* Boston: Beacon Press.

Federal Court of Canada. 1999. *Ali v. Canada (Minister of Citizenship and Immigration).* <http://www.fja.gc.ca/documents.cfm?org=greffe&greffe=IMM-613-97&doc=9549&start=1>

Fedorowycz, Orest. 1999. "Homicide in Canada, 1998." *Juristat* 19(10). Canadian Centre for Justice Statistics. Cat. 85-002-XIE.

Fein, Esther B. 1997. "Failing to Discuss Dying Adds to Pain of Patient and Family." *New York Times.* March 5:A1, A14.

———. 1998. "Secrecy and Stigma No Longer Clouding Adoptions." *New York Times* National Sunday. October 25:1, 18–19.

Feingold, Alan. 1994. "Gender Differences in Personality: A Meta-analysis." *Psychological Bulletin* 116:429–56.

Fejgin, Naomi. 1995. "Factors Contributing to the Academic Excellence of American Jewish and Asian Students." *Sociology of Education* 68 (1):18–30.

Felson, Richard B. and Natalie Russo. 1988. "Parental Punishment and Sibling Aggression." *Social Psychology Quarterly* 51 (1):11–18.

Ferguson, Susan J. 1995. "Marriage Timing of Chinese American and Japanese American Women." *Journal of Family Issues* 16 (3) (May):314–43.

Fergusson, David M. and L. John Horwood. 1998. "Exposure to Interparental Violence in Childhood and Psychosocial Adjustment in Young Adulthood." *Child Abuse & Neglect* 22 (5):339–57.

Ferrari, J. R. and R. A. Emmons. 1994. "Procrastination As Revenge: Do People Report Using Delays As a Strategy for Vengeance?" *Personality and Individual Differences* 17 (4):539–42.

Ferree, Myra Marx. 1990. "Beyond Separate Spheres: Feminism and Family Research." *Journal of Marriage and the Family* 52:866–84.

———. 1991. "The Gender Division of Labor in Two-Earner Marriages: Dimensions of Variability and Change." *Journal of Family Issues* 12 (2) (June):158–80.

Festy, Patrick. "Children in the Family: A Demographic Analysis." *Education et societes,* 2:149–167.

Fields, Jason and Kristin Smith. 1998. "Poverty, Family Structure, and Child Well-Being." Population Division. Washington, DC: U.S. Bureau of Census.

Fiese, Barbara H., Karen A. Hooker, Lisa Kotary, and Janet Schwagler. 1993. "Family Rituals in the Early Stages of Parenthood." *Journal of Marriage and the Family* 55 (3) (Aug.):633–42.

Figley, Charles, Brian Bride, Nicholas Mazza, and Marcia Egan. 1998. "Death and Trauma: The Traumatology of Grieving." *Health and Social Work* 23 (1):186–98.

Findley, Barbara. 1997. "All In The Family Values." *Canadian Journal of Family Law* 14(2):129–196.

Fine, Mark A., Marilyn Coleman, and Lawrence H. Ganong. 1999. "A Social Constructionist Multi-Method Approach to Understanding the Stepparent Role." Pp. 273–94 in *Coping with Divorce, Single Parenting, and Remarriage,* edited by E. Mavis Hetherington. Mahway, NJ: Lawrence Erlbaum Associates.

Fine, Mark A. and David R. Fine. 1994. "An Examination and Evaluation of Recent Changes in Divorce Laws in Five Western Countries: The Critical Role of Values." *Journal of Marriage and the Family* 56(2) (May): 249-63.

Fine, Mark A., Lawrence H. Ganong, and Marilyn Coleman. 1997. "The Relation between Role Constructions and Adjustment among Stepfathers." *Journal of Family Issues* 18 (5):503–25.

Fine, Sean. 1999. "Child Development More Affected by Parenting than Social Class." *Globe and Mail,* October 4:A4.

———. 1999b. "How Canada Broke Its Pledge to Poor Children." *The Globe and Mail,* November 24:A14.

Fineman, Martha Albertson and Roxanne Mykitiuk. 1994. *The Public Nature of Private Violence: The Discovery of Domestic Abuse*. New York: Routledge.

Finkelhor, David and Larry Baron. 1986. "High Risk Children." Pp. 60–88 in *A Sourcebook on Child Sexual Abuse*, edited by David Finkelhor. Newbury Park, CA: Sage.

Finkelhor, David and Karl Pillemer. 1988. "Elder Abuse: Its Relationship to Other Forms of Domestic Violence." Pp. 244–54 in *Family Abuse and Its Consequences: New Directions in Research*, edited by Gerald T. Hotaling, David Finkelhor, John T. Kirkpatrick, and Murray A. Straus. Newbury Park, CA: Sage.

Finkelhor, David and Kersti Yllo. 1985. *License to Rape: Sexual Abuse of Wives*. New York: Holt.

Finkelhor, David, Gerald Hotaling, and Andrea Sedlak. 1991. "Children Abducted by Family Members: A National Household Survey of Incidence and Episode Characteristics." *Journal of Marriage and the Family* 53 (3) (Aug.):805–17.

Finkelhor, David, David Moore, Sherry L. Hamby, and Murray A. Straus. 1996. "Sexually Abused Children in a National Survey of Parents: Methodological Issues." *Child Abuse & Neglect* 21 (1):1–9.

Finnie, Ross. 1993. "Women, Men and the Economic Consequences of Divorce: Evidence from Canadian Longitudinal Data." *Canadian Review of Sociology and Anthropology* 30(2):205–241.

Fisher, Jeffrey D., Arie Nadler, and S. Alagne. 1982. "Recipient Reactions to Aid." *Psychological Bulletin* 91:25–54.

Fisher, Judith L. 1983. "Mothers Living Apart from Their Children." *Family Relations* 32:351–57.

Fisher, Lucy R. 1986. *Linked Lives: Adult Daughters and Their Mothers*. New York: Harper.

Fisher, Philip A., Beverly I. Fagot, and Craig S. Leve. 1998. "Assessment of Family Stress across Low-, Medium-, and High-Risk Samples Using the Family Events Checklist." *Family Relations* 47:215–19.

Fisher, William A., Richard Boroditsky and Martha L. Bridges. 1999. "The 1998 Canadian Contraception Study." *The Canadian Journal of Human Sexuality* 8(3):161–216.

Fishman, Barbara. 1983. "The Economic Behavior of Stepfamilies." *Family Relations* 32:359–66.

Fishman, Katherine Davis. 1992. "Problem Adoptions." *The Atlantic Monthly*, 270(3) (Sept.)37–69.

Fiske, S.T. 1998. "Stereotyping, Prejudice, and Discrimination." Pp. 357–411 in *The Handbook of Social Psychology*, edited by D.T. Gilbert, S.T. Fiske and G. Lindsey. New York: McGraw-Hill.

Fitzgerald, Louise R. and Sandra L. Shullman. 1993. "Sexual Harassment: A Research Analysis of Agenda for the '90s." *Journal of Vocational Behavior*, 40:5–27.

Fitzgerald, Robin. 1999. "Assaults Against Children and Youth in the Family, 1996." Pp. 185–96 in *Canadian Centre for Justice Statistics, The Juristat Reader: A Statistical Overview of the Canadian Justice System*. Toronto: Thompson Educational Publishing Inc.

Fitzpatrick, Mary Anne. 1988. *Between Husbands and Wives: Communication in Marriage*. Newbury Park, CA: Sage.

———. 1992. *AIDS: A Communication Perspective*. Hillsdale, NJ: Lawrence Erlbaum Associates.

———. 1995. *Explaining Family Interactions*. Thousand Oaks, CA: Sage.

Fivush, Robyn. 1999. "The stories we tell: How language shapes autobiography." *Applied Cognitive Psychology*, 12(5), October: 483-7.

Flaks, D. K., I. Ficher, F. Masterpasqua, and G. Joseph. 1995. "Lesbians Choosing Motherhood: A Comparative Study of Lesbians and Heterosexual Parents and Their Children." *Developmental Psychology* 31 (1):105–14.

Flanery, James Allen. 1992. "Siblings May Suffer from Fetal Abuse." *Omaha World-Herald*, June 17.

Fleming, Julian, Paul Mullen, and Cabriele Bammer. 1996. "A Study of Potential Risk Factors for Sexual Abuse in Childhood." *Child Abuse & Neglect* 21 (1):49–58.

Fleras, Augie and Jean Leonard Elliott. 1996. *Unequal Relations: An Introduction to Race, Ethnicity and Indigeneity in Canada*, 2nd edition. Scarborough, Ontario: Prentice Hall.

Flewelling, Robert L. and Karl E. Bauman. 1990. "Family Structure as a Predictor of Initial Substance Use and Sexual Intercourse in Early Adolescence." *Journal of Marriage and the Family* 52 (1) (Feb.):171–81.

Florian, Victor and Nira Dangoor. 1994. "Personal and Familial Adaptation of Women with Severe Physical Disabilities: A Further Validation of the Double ABCX Model." *Journal of Marriage and the Family* 56 (3) (Aug.):735–46.

Flynn, Clifton P. 1990. "Relationship Violence by Women: Issues and Implications." *Family Relations* 39 (2) (Apr.):194–98.

Foley, Lara and James Fraser. 1998. "A Research Note on Post-Dating Relationships." *Sociological Perspectives* 41 (1):209–19.

Folk, Karen and Yunae Yi. 1994. "Piecing Together Child Care with Multiple Arrangements: Crazy Quilt or Preferred Pattern for Employed Parents of Preschool Children?" *Journal of Marriage and the Family* 56 (3) (Aug.):669–80.

Fong, Colleen and Judy Yung. 1995. "In Search of the Right Spouse: Interracial Marriage among Chinese and Japanese Americans." *Amerasia Journal* 21 (3):77–84.

Foot, D. with D. Stoffman. 1996. *Boom, Bust, and Echo: How to Profit from the Coming Demographic Shift*. Toronto: Macfarlane, Water and Ross.

Foote, Nelson. 1954. "Sex as Play." *Social Problems* 1:159–63.

Ford, Clellan A. and Frank A. Beach. 1971. "Human Sexual Behavior in Perspective." Pp. 155–71 in *Family in Transition: Rethinking Marriage, Sexuality, Child Rearing, and Family Organization,* edited by Arlene S. Skolnick and Jerome H. Skolnick. Boston: Little, Brown.

Forgatch, Marion S. 1989. "Patterns and Outcome in Family Problem Solving: The Disrupting Effect of Negative Emotion." *Journal of Marriage and the Family* 51:115–24.

Forman, Robert. 1996. *Drug Induced Infertility and Sexual Dysfunction.* Cambridge, MA: Cambridge University Press.

Forrest, Jacqueline Darroch. 1987. "Unintended Pregnancy Among American Women." *Family Planning Perspectives* 19:76–77.

Forrest, Jacqueline Darroch, Noreen Goldman, Stanley Henshaw, Richard Lincoln, Jeannie Rosoff, Charles Westoff, and Deidre Wulf. 1993. "Teenage Pregnancy in Industrial Countries." Pp. 135–39 in *Next of Kin: An International Reader on Changing Families,* edited by Lorne Tepperman and Susannah J. Wilson. New York: Prentice Hall.

Forste, Renata and Koray Tanfer. 1996. "Sexual Exclusivity among Dating, Cohabiting, and Married Women." *Journal of Marriage and the Family* 58:33–47.

Forste, Renata, Koray Tanfer, and Lucky Tedrow. 1995. "Sterilization Among Currently Married Men in the United States, 1991." *Family Planning Perspectives* 27 (3) (May/June):100–107, 122.

Foster, E. Michael, Damon Jones, and Saul D. Hoffman. 1998. "The Economic Impact of Nonmarital Childbearing: How Are Older, Single Mothers Faring?" *Journal of Marriage and the Family* 60 (1):163–74.

"Foster Parents Fight for Interracial Adoptions." 1993. *The Congressional Quarterly* Researcher 3 (44):1093–97.

Fowler, Ruth. 1998. *As We Grow Old: How Adult Children and Their Parents Can Face Aging with Candor and Grace.* Valley Forge, PA: Judson Press.

Fox, Greer L. and Robert F. Kelly. 1995. "Determinants of Child Custody Arrangements at Divorce." *Journal of Marriage and the Family* 57 (3) (Aug.):693–708.

Fox-Genovese, E. 1991. *Feminism Without Illusions: A Critique of Individualism.* Chapel Hill: University of North Carolina Press.

Fracher, Jeffrey and Michael S. Kimmel. 1992. "Hard Issues and Soft Spots: Counseling Men About Sexuality." Pp. 438–50 in *Men's Lives.* 2d ed. edited by Michael S. Kimmel and Michael A. Messner. New York: Macmillan.

Framo, James L. 1978. "The Friendly Divorce." *Psychology Today* 11:77–80, 99–102.

Francoeur, Robert T. 1987. "Human Sexuality." Pp. 509–34 in *Handbook of Marriage and the Family,* edited by Marvin B. Sussman and Suzanne K. Steinmetz. New York: Plenum.

———. Ed. 1994. *Taking Sides: Clashing Views on Controversial Issues in Human Sexuality.* 4th ed. New York: Dushkin.

Franklin II, Clyde W. 1988. *Men and Society.* Chicago: Nelson-Hall.

Franklin, Cynthia, Darlene Grant, Jacqueline Corcoran, Pamela Miller, and Linda Bultman. 1997. "Effectiveness of Prevention Programs for Adolescent Pregnancy: A Meta-Analysis." *Journal of Marriage and the Family* 59:551–67.

Frederick, J.A. and J. Hamel. 1998. "Canadian Attitudes to Divorce." *Canadian Social Trends*, 48:6–11. Reprinted in *Canadian Social Trends: Volume 3.* Toronto: Thompson Educational Publishing, Inc., 2000, pp. 99–104.

Fredrickson, Barbara L. and Tomi-Ann Roberts. 1997. "Objectification Theory: Toward Understanding Women's Lived Experiences and Mental Health Risks." *Psychology of Women Quarterly* 21 (2):173–206.

Freedman, Samuel G. 1986. "New York Offers Help to Unmarried Fathers." *New York Times,* reprinted in *Omaha World-Herald,* Dec. 7.

Freedman, Vicki A. 1993. "Kin and Nursing Home Lengths of Stay: A Backward Recurrence Time Approach." *Journal of Health and Social Behavior* 34 (June):138–52.

Freeman, William J. 1994. "Letters." *U.S. News & World Report,* Nov. 14, p. 8.

French, J. R. P., and Bertram Raven. 1959. "The Basis of Power." In *Studies in Social Power,* edited by D. Cartwright. Ann Arbor: University of Michigan Press.

Frideres, J.S. 1993. "Health Promotion and Indian Communities: Social Support or Social Disorganization." Pp. 269–295 in *Racial Minorities: Medicine and Health,* edited by B. Singh Bolaria and R. Bolaria. Halifax, NS: Fernwood.

Friedan, Betty. 1963. *The Feminine Mystique.* New York: Dell.

———. 1978. "Where Are Women in 1978?" *Cosmopolitan,* Aug., pp. 196, 206–11.

Friedman, D., M. Hechter, and S. Kanazawa. 1994. "A Theory of the Value of Children." *Demography* 31:375–401.

Friedman, Joel, Marcia M. Boumil, and Barbara Ewert Taylor. 1992. *Date Rape: What It Is, What It Isn't, What It Does to You, What You Can Do About It.* Deerfield Beach, FL: Health Communications.

Friedrich, William. 1998. "Normal Sexual Behavior in Children." *Journal of Pediatrics* 104, Electronic Version. April.

Fromm, Erich. 1956. *The Art of Loving.* New York: Harper & Row.

Frye, Marilyn. 1992. "Lesbian 'Sex.'" Pp. 109–19 in *Essays in Feminism 1976–1992,* edited by Marilyn Frye. Freedom, CA: Crossing Press.

Fuller, T. L., and F. D. Fincham. 1997. "Attachment Style in Married Couples: Relation to Current Marital Functioning, Stability over Time, and Method of Assessment." *Personal Relationships* 2:17–34.

Furman, W., and A. S. Flanagan. 1997. "The Influence of Earlier Relationships on Marriage: An Attachment Perspective." Pp. 179–202 in *Clinical Handbook of Marriage and Couples Interventions,* edited by W. K. Halford and H. J. Markman. Chichester, UK: Wiley.

Furstenberg, Frank F., Jr. 1987. "The New Extended Family: The Experience of Parents and Children after Remarriage." Pp. 42–61 in *Remarriage and Stepparenting,* edited by Kay Pasley and Marilyn Ihinger-Tallman. New York: Guilford.

———. 1991. "As the Pendulum Swings: Teenage Childbearing and Social Concern." *Family Relations* 40:127–38.

———. 1992. "Good Dads—Bad Dads: Two Faces of Fatherhood." Pp. 342–62 in *Families in Transition.* 7th ed., edited by Arlene S. and Jerome H. Skolnick. New York: Harper.

Furstenberg, Frank F., Jr. and Andrew J. Cherlin. 1991. *Divided Families: What Happens to Children When Parents Part.* Cambridge, MA: Harvard University Press.

Furstenberg, Frank F., Jr. and Mary Elizabeth Hughes. 1995. "Social Capital and Successful Development Among At-Risk Youth." *Journal of Marriage and the Family* 57 (3) (Aug.):580–92.

Furstenberg, Frank F., Jr., J. Brooks-Gunn, and S. Philip Morgan. 1987. *Adolescent Mothers in Later Life.* New York: Cambridge University Press.

Furstenberg, Frank F., Jr. Saul D. Hoffman, and Laura Shrestha. 1995. "The Effect of Divorce on Intergenerational Transfers: New Evidence." *Demography* 32 (3) (Aug.):319–33.

G

Gable, Sara, Jay Belsky, and Keith Crnic. 1992. "Marriage, Parenting, and Child Development: Progress and Prospects." *Journal of Family Psychology* 5:276–94.

Gagnon, John H. 1977. *Human Sexualities.* Glenview, IL: Scott, Foresman.

Gairdner, William. 1992. *The War Against the Family: A Parent Speaks Out.* Toronto: Stoddart.

Galambos, Nancy L. and Heather A. Sears. 1998. "Adolescents' Perceptions Of Parents' Work And Adolescents' Work Values In Two-Earner Families." *Journal of Early Adolescence* 18(4)(November):397–420.

Galen, Michele. 1994. "White, Male, and Worried." *Business Week,* Jan. 31, pp. 50–55.

Galinsky, Ellen. 1986. "Family Life and Corporate Policies." Pp. 109–45 in *In Support of Families,* edited by Michael W. Yogman and T. Berry Brazelton. Cambridge, MA: Harvard University Press.

Galinsky, Ellen and Peter J. Stein. 1990. "The Impact of Human Resource Policies on Employees: Balancing Work/Family Life." *Journal of Family Issues* 11 (4) (Dec.):368–83.

Gallagher, Maggie. 1996. *The Abolition of Marriage: How We Destroy Lasting Love.* Washington, DC: Regnery.

"Gallup Poll Shows More Americans Say Premarital Sex Is Wrong, Reversing Trend of Last 20 Years." 1988. *Family Planning Perspectives* 20:180–81.

Galston, William A. 1996. "Children Are Victims of No-fault Divorce: Law Needs to Make It More Difficult for Mom and Dad To Call It Quits." *Minneapolis Star Tribune.* January 3:A11.

Gamache, Susan J. 1997. "Confronting Nuclear Family Bias in Stepfamily Research." *Marriage and Family Review* 26 (1–2):41–50.

Gander, Anita Moore. 1991. "After the Divorce: Familial Factors that Predict Well-Being for Older and Younger Persons." *Journal of Divorce and Remarriage* 15 (1/2):175–92.

Ganguly-Scrase, Ruchira and Roberta Julian. 1998. "Minority women and the experiences of migration." *Women's Studies International Forum* 21 (6)(Nov.-Dec.):633–48.

———. 1997. "The Gendering of Identity: Minority Women in Comparative Perspective." *Asian and Pacific Migration Journal* 6(3/4):415–38.

Ganong, Lawrence H. and Marilyn Coleman. 1992. "Gender Differences in Expectations of Self and Future Partner." *Journal of Family Issues* 13 (1) (Mar.):55–64.

———. 1994. *Remarried Family Relationships.* Thousand Oaks, CA: Sage.

———. 1997. "How Society Views Stepfamilies." Pp. 85–106 in *Stepfamilies: History, Research, and Policy,* edited by Irene Levin and Marvin B. Sussman. New York: Haworth Press.

Ganong, Lawrence H., Marilyn Coleman and Dennis Mapes. 1990. "A Meta-analytic Review of Family Structure Stereotypes." *Journal of Marriage and the Family* 52 (2) (May):287–97.

Gans, Herbert J. 1996. *The War against the Poor.* New York: Basic Books.

Garbarino, James. 1977. "The Human Ecology of Child Maltreatment: A Conceptual Model for Research." *Journal of Marriage and the Family* 39:721–35.

Garbarino, James, Kathleen Kostelny, and Frank Berry. 1997. "Value Transmission in an Ecological Context: The High-Risk Neighborhood." Pp. 307–32 in *Parenting and Children's Internalization of Values,* edited by Joan E. Grusee and Leon Kuczynski. New York: John Wiley & Sons.

Garcia, Luis T. 1999. "The Certainty Of The Sexual Self-Concept." *The Canadian Journal of Human Sexuality* 8:263–270.

Gardner, Arthur. 2000. "Their Own Boss: The Self-Employed in Canada." Pp. 188–191 in *Canadian Social Trends: Volume 3*. Toronto: Thompson Educational Publishing, Inc.

Gardner, Richard A. 1993. "Modern Witch Hunt—Child Abuse Charges." *The Wall Street Journal*, Feb. 22, p. A-10.

Garfinkel, Irwin and Sara S. McLanahan. 1986. *Single Mothers and Their Children: A New American Dilemma*. Washington, DC: Urban Institute Press.

Garofoli, Joe. 1996. "By Order of the Court: Monitors Supervise Visitations during Sensitive Custody Battles." *Contra Costa Times*. February 18.

Garrett, Patricia, John Ferron, Nicholas Ng'Andu, Donna Dryant, and Gloria Harbin. 1994. "A Structural Model for the Development Status of Young Children." *Journal of Marriage and the Family* 56 (1) (Feb.):147–63.

Garvey, Christine Ann. 1999. "The Intergenerational Transmission of Discipline." *Dissertation Abstracts International*, Section A: The Sciences and Engineering, 60(3-B), Sept: 1027

Gauthier, Eric. 1999. "The Identity Dynamic in a Migratory Situation: About the Young Born to Hmong Immigrants." *Cahiers de Sociologie Economique et Culturelle, Ethnopsychologie* 31(June):73–99.

Geasler, Margie J. and Karen R. Blaisure. 1998. "A Review of Divorce Education Program Materials." *Family Relations* 47 (2):167–75.

Gegax, T. Trent and Lynette Clemetson. 1998. "The Abortion Wars Come Home." *Newsweek*. November 9:34–35.

Geist, William E. 1987. "In AIDS Era, a New Club for Singles." *New York Times*, Apr. 15.

Gelcer, Esther. 1986. "Training in Family Therapy." *Journal of Strategic and Systemic Therapies*, 6(3), Fall:42–56.

Gelles, Richard J. 1994. "Ten Risk Factors." *Newsweek*, July 4, p. 29.

———. 1996. *The Book of David: How Preserving Families Can Cost Children's Lives*. New York: Basic Books.

———. 1997. *Intimate Violence in Families*, 3rd ed. Thousand Oaks, CA: Sage.

Gelles, Richard J. and Jon R. Conte. 1990. "Domestic Violence and Sexual Abuse of Children: A Review of Research in the Eighties." *Journal of Marriage and the Family* 52 (4) (Nov.):1045–58.

Gelles, Richard J. and Donileen R. Loseke. 1993. *Current Controversies on Family Violence*. Newbury Park, CA: Sage.

Gelles, Richard J. and Murray A. Straus. 1988. *Intimate Violence: The Definitive Study of the Causes and Consequences of Abuse in the American Family*. New York: Simon & Schuster.

Gelman, David. 1990. "A Is for Apple, P Is for Shrink." *Newsweek*. Dec. 24, pp. 64–66.

———. 1992. "Born or Bred?" *Newsweek*, Feb. 24, pp. 46–57.

Genovese, Eugene D. 1999. "The Myth of the Absent Family." Pp. 25–31 in *The Black Family: Essays and Studies*, edited by Robert Staples. Belmont, CA: Wadsworth.

Gentleman, Jane F. and Evelyn Park. 1997. "Divorce in the 1990s." *Health Reports*, 9(2):53–58.

Georgas, James, John W. Berry, Alex Shaw, Sophia Christakopoulou. 1996. "Acculturation of Greek Family Values." *Journal of Cross-Cultural Psychology* 27(3)(May):329–338.

Gerhard, Susan. 1994. "Cybersex: The New Abstinence." *San Francisco Bay Guardian*, Aug. 24, pp. 23–4.

Geronimus, Arline T. 1991. "Teenage Childbearing and Social and Reproductive Disadvantage: The Evolution of Complex Questions and the Demise of Simple Answers." *Family Relations* 40 (4) (Oct.):463–71.

Gerris, Jan R., Maja Dekovic, and Jan M. A. M. Janssens. 1997. "The Relationship between Social Class and Childrearing Behaviors: Parents' Perspective Taking and Value Orientations." *Journal of Marriage and the Family* 59 (4):834–47.

Gerson, Kathleen. 1985. *Hard Choices: How Women Decide About Work, Career, and Motherhood*. Berkeley: University of California Press.

———. 1993. *No Man's Land: Men's Changing Commitments to Family and Work*. New York: Harper-Collins, Basic Books.

———. 1997. "The Social Construction of Fatherhood." Pp. 119–53 in *Contemporary Parenting: Challenges and Issues*, edited by Terry Arendell. Thousand Oaks, CA: Sage.

Gerstel, Naomi and Sally K. Gallagher. 1993. "Kinkeeping and Distress: Gender, Recipients of Care, and Work–Family Conflict." *Journal of Marriage and the Family* 55 (3) (Aug.):598–607.

Geschwender, James A. 1994. "Married Women's Waged Labor and Racial/Ethnic Stratification in Canada." *Canadian Ethnic Studies*, 26(3):53–73.

Gfellner, Barbara M. 1994. "A Matched-Group Comparison Of Drug Use And Problem Behavior Among Canadian Indian And White Adolescents." *Journal of Early Adolescence* 14(1)(Feb.):24–48.

Gfellner, B.M. and J.D. Hundelby, 1995. "Patterns of Drugs Use Among Native and White Adolescents: 1990–1995." *Canadian Journal of Public Health* 86:95–7.

Ghalam, Nancy Zukewich. 1997. "Attitudes Toward Women, Work and Family." *Canadian Social Trends* 46,(autumn):14–17.

———. 2000. "Attitudes Towards Women, Work and Family." Pp. 68–72 in *Canadian Social Trends: Volume 3*. Toronto: Thompson Educational Publishing, Inc.

Gibbs, Nancy R. 1989. "The Baby Chase." *Time*, Oct. 9, pp. 86–89.

———. 1991. "Marching Out of the Closet." *Time*, Aug. 19, pp. 14–15.

———. 1993. "Bringing Up Father." *Time*, June 28, pp. 53–61.

Gibbs, Nancy R. and Michael Duffy. 1996. "Desperately Seeking Lori." *Time*. October 14:45–52.

Gideonse, Theodore. 1998. "Mommy Track at the *Times*." *Newsweek*. June 1:61.

Gilanshah, Farah. 1994. "The Effects of Immigration on Hmong Women in La Crosse, Wisconin." Pp. 95–103 in *Ethnic Women: A Multiple Status Reality*, edited by Vasilike Demos and Marcia Hexler Segal. Dix Hills, NY: General Hall, Inc.

Gilbert, Neil. 1998. "Working Families: Hearth to Market." Pp. 193–216 in *All Our Families: New Policies for a New Century*, edited by Mary Ann Mason, Arlene Skolnick, and Stephen D. Sugarman. New York: Oxford University Press.

Gilbert, Susan. 1993. "The Waiting Game." *New York Times Magazine*. April 25:68, 71–72, 92.

———. 1997. "2 Spanking Studies Indicate Parents Should Be Cautious." *New York Times*. August 20.

Giles-Sims, Jean. 1984. "The Stepparent Role: Expectations, Behavior, and Sanctions." *Journal of Family Issues* 5:116–30.

———. 1997. "Current Knowledge about Child Abuse in Stepfamilies." Pp. 215–30 in *Stepfamilies: History, Research, and Policy*, edited by Irene Levin and Marvin B. Sussman. New York: Haworth.

Giles-Sims, Jean and Margaret Crosbie-Burnett. 1989. "Adolescent Power in Stepfather Families: A Test of Normative Resource Theory." *Journal of Marriage and the Family* 52:1065–78.

Gilgun, Jane E. 1995. "We Shared Something Special: The Moral Discourse of Incest Perpetrators." *Journal of Marriage and the Family* 57 (2) (May):265–81.

Gill, Dhara S. and Bennett Matthews. 1995. "Changes in the Breadwinner Role: Punjabi Families in Transition." *Journal of Comparative Family Studies* 26(2):255–263.

Gill, Richard T. 1997. *Posterity Lost: Progress, Ideology, and the Decline of the American Family*. Lanham: Rowman & Littlefield Publishers.

Gillespie, Dair. 1971. "Who Has the Power? The Marital Struggle." *Journal of Marriage and the Family* 33:445–58. Reprinted in *Women: A Feminist Perspective,* edited by Jo Freeman. Mountain View, CA: Mayfield.

Gillham, Bill, Gary Tanner, Bill Cheyne, Isobel Freeman, Martin Rooney, and Allan Lambie. 1998. "Unemployment Rates, Single Parent Density, and Indices of Child Poverty: Their Relationship to Different Categories of Child Abuse and Neglect." *Child Abuse & Neglect* 22 (2):79–90.

Gillis, J. Roy, Heino F.L. Meyer-Bahlburg, Theresa M. Exner and Anke A. Ehrhardt. 1998. "The Predictive Utility Of An Expanded AIDS Risk Reduction Model (ARRM) Among Adult Gay And Bisexual Men." *The Canadian Journal of Human Sexuality* 7:31–50.

Gilmore, David D. 1990. *Manhood in the Making: Cultural Concepts of Masculinity*. New Haven, CT: Yale University Press.

Ginott, Haim G. 1965. *Between Parent and Child*. New York: Macmillan.

Gladstone, James and Anne Westhues. 1998. "Adoption Reunions: A New Side to Intergenerational Family Relationships." *Family Relations* 47 (2):177–84.

Glaser, Danya and Stephen Frosh. 1988. *Child Sexual Abuse*. Chicago: Dorsey.

Glass, Jennifer. 1992. "Housewives and Employed Wives: Demographic and Attitudinal Change, 1972–1986." *Journal of Marriage and the Family* 54 (Aug.):559–69.

———. 1998. "Gender Liberation, Economic Squeeze, or Fear of Strangers: Why Fathers Provide Infant Care in Dual-Earner Families." *Journal of Marriage and the Family* 60 (4):821–32.

Glass, Jennifer and Sarah Beth Estes. 1997. "Employment and Child Care." Pp. 254–88 in *Contemporary Parenting: Challenges and Issues*, edited by Terry Arendell. Thousand Oaks, CA: Sage.

Glasser, Irene and Rae Bridgman. 1999. *Braving the Street: The Anthropology of Homelessness*. New York: Berghahn.

Glazer, Nona. 1990. "The Home as Workshop: Women as Amateur Nurses and Medical Care Providers." *Gender and Society* 4:479–99.

Gleick, Elizabeth. 1996. "Scandal in the Military." *Time*. November 25:28–31.

Glendon, Mary Ann. 1981. *The New Family and the New Property*. Toronto: Butterworths.

———. 1987. *Abortion and Divorce in Western Law*. Cambridge, MA: Harvard University Press.

———. 1989. *The Transformation of Family Law: State, Law, and Family in the United States and Western Europe*. Chicago: University of Chicago Press.

Glenn, Norval D. 1982. "Interreligious Marriage in the United States: Patterns and Recent Trends." *Journal of Marriage and the Family*, 44: 555–68.

———. 1987. "Continuity Versus Change, Sanguineness Versus Concern: Views of the American Family in the Late 1980s." Introduction to a special issue of the *Journal of Family Issues* 8:348–54.

———. 1990. "Quantitative Research on Marital Quality in the 1980s: A Critical Review." *Journal of Marriage and the Family* 52 (Nov.):818–31.

———. 1991. "The Recent Trend in Marital Success in the United States." *Journal of Marriage and the Family* 53 (2) (May):261–70.

———. 1993. "A Plea for Objective Assessment of the Notion of Family Decline." *Journal of Marriage and the Family* 55 (3) (Aug.):542–44.

———. 1996. "Values, Attitudes, and the State of American Marriage." Pp. 15–33 in *Promises to Keep: The Decline and Renewal of Marriage in America*, edited by David Popenoe, Jean Bethke Elshtain, and David Blankenhorn. Lanham, MD: Rowman and Littlefield.

———. 1997a. "A Reconsideration of the Effect of No-Fault Divorce on Divorce Rates." *Journal of Marriage and the Family* 59 (4):1023–30.

———. 1997b. "A Critique of Twenty Family and Marriage and Family Textbooks." *Family Relations* 46 (3):197–208.

Glenn, Norval D. and Sara McLanahan. 1982. "Children and Marital Happiness: A Further Specification of the Relationship." *Journal of Marriage and the Family* 44:63–72.

Glenn, Norval D. and Charles N. Weaver. 1988. "The Changing Relationship of Marital Status to Reported Happiness." *Journal of Marriage and the Family* 50:317–24.

Glick, Jennifer E., Frank D. Bean, and Jennifer Van Hook. 1997. "Immigration and Changing Patterns of Extended Family Household Structure in the United States: 1970–1990." *Journal of Marriage and the Family* 59:177–91.

Glick, Paul C. 1988. "Fifty Years of Family *Demography*: A Record of Social Change." *Journal of Marriage and the Family* 50 (4):861–73.

———. 1989. "Remarried Families, Stepfamilies, and Stepchildren: A Brief Demographic Profile." *Family Relations* 38 (Jan.):24–27.

Glick, Paul C. and Sung-Ling Lin. 1986a. "More Young Adults Are Living With Their Parents: Who Are They?" *Journal of Marriage and the Family* 48:107–12.

———. 1986b. "Recent Changes in Divorce and Remarriage." *Journal of Marriage and the Family* 48 (4):737–47.

Glick, Paul C. and Arthur J. Norton. 1979. "Marrying, Divorcing, and Living Together in the U.S. Today." *Population Bulletin* 32 (5). Washington, DC: Population Reference Bureau.

Glick, Paul C. and Graham Spanier. 1980. "Married and Unmarried Cohabitation in the United States." *Journal of Marriage and the Family* 42:19–30.

Glick, Peter. 1991. "Trait-Based and Sex-Based Discrimination in Occupational Prestige, Occupational Salary, and Hiring." *Sex Roles* 25 (5/6):351–78.

Glick, Peter and Susan T. Fiske. 1997. "Hostile and Benevolent Sexism: Measuring Ambivalent Sexist Attitudes Toward Women." *Psychology of Women Quarterly* 21 (1):119–36.

Globerman, Judith. 1996. "Motivations to Care: Daughters- and Sons-in-Law Caring for Relatives with Alzheimer's Disease." *Family Relations* 45 (1):37–45.

Glockner, D., K. Gaevert, and J. Kleinstein. 1998. "Declining Sperm Quality in Men of Childless Couples." *Andrologia* 30 (1):55–67.

Glossop, Robert and Ish Theilheimer. 2000. "Does Society Support Involve Fathering?" *Child & Family Canada*. <http://www.cfc-efc.ca/docs/0000003.htm>

Glossop, R. 1994. "Robert Glossop on the Canadian Family." *Canadian Social Trends* 35:2–10.

Glossop, Robert and Nora Spinks. 1998. "Can Canadian Businesses Afford Work-Family Conflict? Tackling a multi-billion-dollar problem." *Vanier Institute of the Family News Release Communique*, October 28 <http://www.vifamily.ca/work/tkpr.htm>

Goffman, Erving. 1959. *The Presentation of Self in Everyday Life*. Garden City, NY: Doubleday.

———. 1963. *Stigma: Notes on the Management of Spoiled Identity*. Englewood Cliffs, N.J.: Prentice-Hall.

Gold, J. M., and J. D. Rogers. 1995. "Intimacy and Isolation: A Validation Study of Erikson's Theory." *Journal of Humanistic Psychology* 35 (1):78–86.

Gold, Steven J. 1993. "Migration and Family Adjustment: Continuity and Change Among Vietnamese in the United States." Pp. 300–14 in *Family Ethnicity: Strength in Diversity*, edited by Harriette Pipes McAdoo. Newbury Park, CA: Sage.

Goldberg, Carey. 1998a. "Rhode Island Moves to End Sodomy Ban." *New York Times*. May 10.

Goldberg, Herb. 1987. *The Inner Male: Overcoming Roadblocks to Intimacy*. New York: New American Library.

Goldberg, Steven. 1973. *The Inevitability of Patriarchy*. New York: Morrow.

Goldner, Virginia. 1993. "Feminist Theories." Pp. 623–25 in *Sourcebook of Family Theories and Methods: A Contextual Approach*, edited by Pauline G. Boss, William J. Doherty, Ralph LaRossa, Walter R. Schumm, and Suzanne K. Steinmetz. New York: Plenum.

Goldscheider, Frances K. 1997. "Recent Changes in U.S. Young Adult Living Arrangements in Comparative Perspective." *Journal of Family Issues* 18 (6):708–24.

Goldscheider, Frances K. and Calvin Goldscheider. 1989. "Family Structure and Conflict: Nest-leaving Expectations of Young Adults and Their Parents." *Journal of Marriage and the Family* 51:87–97.

———. 1994. "Leaving and Returning Home in 20th Century America." *Population Bulletin* 48 (4) (Mar.)

———. 1998. "Effects of Childhood Family Structure on Leaving and Returning Home." *Journal of Marriage and the Family* 60:745–56.

Goldstein, Arnold P., Harold Keller, and Diane Erne. 1985. *Changing the Abusive Parent*. Champaign, IL: Research Press.

Goleman, Daniel. 1985. "Patterns of Love Charted in Studies." *New York Times*, Sept. 10.

———. 1986. "Two Views of Marriage Explored: His and Hers." *New York Times*, Apr. 1.

———. 1988a. "Adding the Sounds of Silence to the List of Health Risks." *New York Times*, Aug. 4.

———. 1988b. "The Lies Men Tell Put Women in Danger of AIDS." *New York Times*, Aug. 14.

———. 1989. "For a Happy Marriage, Learn How to Fight." *New York Times*, Feb. 21.

———. 1990a. "Aggression in Men: Hormone Levels Are a Key." *New York Times*, July 17.

———. 1990b. "Anger over Racism Is Seen as a Cause of Blacks' High Blood Pressure." *New York Times*, Apr. 24.

———. 1992. "Family Rituals May Promote Better Emotional Adjustment." *New York Times*, Mar. 11.

———. 1992. "Gay Parents Called No Disadvantage." *New York Times*, Dec. 21.

Goode, William J. 1959. "The Theoretical Importance of Love." *American Sociological Review* 24:38–47.

———. 1963. *World Revolution and Family Patterns.* New York: Free Press.

———. 1982. "Why Men Resist." Pp. 131–50 in *Rethinking the Family: Some Feminist Questions*, edited by Barrie Thorne and Marilyn Yalom. New York: Longmans.

Goodman, Ellen. 1987. "M Is for Money, Not Mother." Boston Globe Newspaper Company/Washington Post Writers Group. In *The Daily Nebraskan*, Feb. 17.

Goodstein, Laurie and Marjorie Connelly. (1998, Apr. 30). "Teenage Poll Finds a Turn to the Traditional." *The New York Times*, A10.

Gordon, Leland J. and Stewart M. Lee. 1977. *Economics for Consumers.* New York: Van Nostrand.

Gordon, Linda. 1988. *Heroes of Their Own Lives: The Politics and History of Family Violence.* New York: Viking.

———. 1997. "Killing in Self-Defense." *The Nation.* March 24:25–28.

Gordon, Thomas. 1970. *Parent Effectiveness Training.* New York: Wyden.

Gore, Susan. 1978. "The Effect of Social Support in Moderating the Health Consequences of Unemployment." *Journal of Health and Social Behavior* 19:157–65.

Gore, Susan and Thomas W. Mangione. 1983. "Social Roles, Rex Roles, and Psychological Distress: Addictive and Interactive Models of Sex Differences." *Journal of Health and Social Behavior* 24:300–12.

Gorman, Christine. 1991. "Returning File Against AIDS." *Time*, June 24, p. 44.

———. 1992. "Sizing Up the Sexes." *Time*, Jan. 20, pp. 42–51.

———. 1993. "When AIDS Strikes Parents." *Time*, Nov. 18, pp. 76–77.

———. 1996a. "A New Attack on AIDS." *Time*. July 8:52–3.

Gorman, Jean Cheng. 1998. "Parenting Attitudes and Practices of Immigrant Chinese Mothers of Adolescents." *Family Relations* 47 (1):73–80.

Gottfried, Adele E. and Allen W. Gottfried, Eds. 1994. *Redefining Families: Implications for Children's Development.* New York: Plenum.

Gottlieb, Alison Stokes. 1997. "Single Mothers of Children with Developmental Disabilities: The Impact of Multiple Roles." *Family Relations* 46 (1):5–12.

Gottlieb, Annie. 1979. "The Joyful Marriage." *Redbook*, Nov., pp. 29, 194–96.

Gottlieb, Laurie N., Ariella Lang, and Rhonda Amsel. 1996. "The Long-Term Effects of Grief on Marital Intimacy Following an Infant's Death." *Omega* 33 (1):1–9.

Gottman, John M. 1979. *Marital Interaction: Experimental Investigations.* New York: Academic.

———. 1994. *Why Marriages Succeed or Fail.* New York: Simon and Schuster.

———. 1996. *What Predicts Divorce? The Measures.* Hillsdale, NJ: Lawrence Erlbaum Associates.

Gottman, John M. and L. J. Krokoff. 1989. "Marital Interaction and Satisfaction: A Longitudinal View." *Journal of Consulting and Clinical Psychology* 57:47–52.

Gottman, John M. and R. W. Levinson. 1988. "The Social Psychophysiology of Marriage." Pp. 182–200 in *Perspectives on Marital Interaction*, edited by P. Noller and M. A. Fitzpatrick. Philadelphia: Multilingual Matters.

Gottman, John M., James Coan, Sybil Carrere, and Catherine Swanson. 1998. "Predicting Marital Happiness and Stability from Newlywed Interactions." *Journal of Marriage and the Family* 60 (1):5–22.

Gough, Brendan and Paula Reavey. 1997. "Parental Accounts Regarding the Physical Punishment of Children: Discourses of Dis/empowerment." *Child Abuse & Neglect* 21 (5):417–30.

Gove, Walter R., and Robert D. Cruchfield. 1982. "The Family and Juvenile Delinquency." *The Sociological Quarterly* 23:301–19.

Gove, Walter R., Carolyn Briggs Style, and Michael Hughes. 1990. "The Effect of Marriage on the Well-Being of Adults." *Journal of Family Issues* 11 (1) (Mar.):4–35.

Grant, Linda, Layne A. Simpson, Xue Lan Rong, and Holly Peters-Golden. 1990. "Gender, Parenthood, and Work Hours of Physicians." *Journal of Marriage and the Family* 52 (2) (Feb.):39–49.

Government of Canada. 2001. "Women—Federal Political Representation." <http://www.parl.gc.ca/information/about/p.../StandingsWomen.asp?Language=E&Source=hoc>

Grant, Linda, Layne A. Simpson, Xue Lan Rong, and Holly Peters-Golden. 1990. "Gender, Parenthood, and Work

Hours of Physicians." *Journal of Marriage and the Family* 52(2) (Feb.): 39–49.

Grauerholz, Elizabeth. 1987. "Balancing the Power in Dating Relationships." *Sex Roles* 17:563–71.

Gray, John. 1995. *Mars and Venus in the Bedroom.* New York: HarperCollins.

Gray-Little, Bernadette. 1982. "Marital Quality and Power Processes Among Black Couples." *Journal of Marriage and the Family* 44:633–46.

Greatbatch, David and Robert Dingwall. 1997. "Argumentative Talk in Divorce Mediation Sessions." *American Sociological Review* 62 (1):151–70.

Greeley, Andrew. 1989. "Protestant and Catholic." *American Sociological Review* 54:485–502.

———. 1991. *Faithful Attraction: Discovering Intimacy, Love and Fidelity in American Marriage.* New York: Tom Doherty Associates.

Greenblatt, Cathy Stein. 1983. "The Salience of Sexuality in the Early Years of Marriage." *Journal of Marriage and the Family* 45:289–99.

Greenfield, Sidney J. 1969. "Love and Marriage in Modern America: A Functional Analysis." *Sociological Quarterly* 6:361–77.

Greeno, Cherri. 2000. "Stalking rate high in K-W." *KW Record*, December 1:A1–A2.

Greenstein, Theodore N. 1990. "Marital Disruption and the Employment of Married Women." *Journal of Marriage and the Family* 52 (3) (Aug.):657–76.

———. 1995. "Gender Ideology, Marital Disruption, and the Employment of Married Women." *Journal of Marriage and the Family* 57 (1) (Feb.):31–42.

Gregg, Gail. 1986. "Putting Kids First." *New York Times Magazine*, Apr. 13, pp. 47ff.

Green, Melvyn. 1986. "The History of Canadian Narcotics Control: The Formative Years." Pp. 22–40 in *The Social Dimensions of Law*, edited by Neil Boyd. Scarborough, Ont.: Prentice Hall.

Greif, Gepffreu and Mary S. Pabst. 1988. *Mothers Without Custody.* Lexington, MA: Heath.

Grey, Julius. 1999. "Family Law." P. 816 in *Canadian Encyclopedia:Year 2000 Edition*, edited by James Marsh. Toronto: McClelland & Stewart Inc.

Grimes, Ronald L. 1995. *Marrying and Burying: Rites of Passage in a Man's Life.* Boulder, CO: Westview.

Grimm-Thomas, Karen and Maureen Perry-Jenkins. 1994. "All in a Day's Work: Job Experiences, Self-Esteem, and Fathering in Working-Class Families." *Family Relations* 43:174–81.

Gringlas, Marcy and Marsha Weinraub. 1995. "The More Things Change ... Single Parenting Revisited." *Journal of Family Issues* 16 (1) (Jan.):29–52.

Griswold, Robert L. 1993. *Fatherhood in America: A History.* New York: Basic Books.

Grizzle, Gary L. 1996. "Remarriage as an Incomplete Institution: Cherlin's (1978) Views and Why We Should Be Cautious about Accepting Them." *Journal of Divorce & Remarriage* 26 (1/2):191–201.

Groat, Theodore, Peggy Giordano, Stephen Cernkovich, M.D. Puch, and Steven Swinford. 1997. "Attitudes toward Childbearing among Young Parents." *Journal of Marriage and the Family* 59:568–81.

Gross, Harriet Engel. 1980. "Dual-Career Couples Who Live Apart: Two Types." *Journal of Marriage and the Family* 42:567–76.

Gross, Jane. 1991a. "A Milestone in the Fight for Gay Rights: A Quiet Suburban Life." *New York Times*, June 30.

———. 1991b. "More Young Single Men Clinging to Apron Strings." *New York Times*, June 16.

———. 1991c. "New Challenge of Youth: Growing Up in a Gay Home." *New York Times*, Feb. 11.

———. 1992a. "Collapse of Inner-City Families Creates America's New Orphans." *New York Times*, Mar. 29.

———. 1992b. "Divorced, Middle-Aged and Happy: Women, Especially, Adjust to the 90's." P. 10 in The *New York Times, Themes of the Time*s. Englewood Cliffs, NJ: Prentice-Hall.

———. 1994. "After a Ruling, Hawaii Weighs Gay Marriages." *New York Times*, April 25: A1, C12.

Groze, V. 1996. *Successful Adoptive Families: A Longitudinal Study.* Westport, CT: Praeger.

Grubb, W. Norton and Robert H. Wilson. 1989. "Sources of Increasing Inequality in Wages and Salaries, 1960–80." *Monthly Labor Review* 112:3–13.

Grych, John H. and Frank D. Fincham. 1992. "Interventions for Children of Divorce: Toward Greater Integration of Research and Action." *Psychological Bulletin* 111 (3):434–54.

Guelzow, Maureen G., Gloria W. Bird, and Elizabeth H. Koball. 1991. "An Exploratory Path Analysis of the Stress Process for Dual-Career Men and Women." *Journal of Marriage and the Family* 53 (1) (Feb.):151–64.

Guerin, P.J., Fay, L.F., Burden, S.L. and Kautto, J.G. 1987. *The Evaluation And Treatment Of Marital Conflict.* New York: Basic.

Gurian, Michael. 1996. *The Wonder of Boys: What Parents, Mentors and Educators Can Do to Shape Boys into Exceptional Men.*

Gutis, Philip S. 1989a. "Family Redefines Itself, and Now the Law Follows." *New York Times*, May 28.

———. 1989b. "What Is a Family? Traditional Limits Are Being Redrawn." *New York Times*, Aug. 31.

Guyon, Janet. 1992. "Inequality in Granting Child-Care Benefits." *The Wall Street Journal*, Oct. 23, pp. A1, A5.

Guy-Sheftall, B. and P. Bell-Scott. 1989. "Finding a Way: Black Women Students and the Academy." Pp. 47–56 in *Educating the Majority: Women Challenge Tradition in*

Higher Education, edited by C. S. Pearson, D. L. Savlik, and J. G. Touchton. New York: American Council on Education/Macmillan.

Gwyn, Richard. 2001. "Little Elijah is Canadian of This Century." *Toronto Star*, June 17.

H

Haas, Kurt and Adalaide Haas. 1993. *Understanding Sexuality*, 3d ed. St. Louis: Mosby.

Haas, Linda. 1990. "Gender Equality and Social Policy: Implications of a Study of Parental Leave in Sweden." *Journal of Family Issues* 11 (4) (Dec.):401–23.

Haddad, Y. and J. Smith. 1996. "Islamic Values Among American Muslims." Pp. 19–40 in *Family and Gender Among American Muslims*, edited by B. Asswad and B. Bilge. Philadelphia: Temple University Press.

Hafen, Elder Bruce C. 1998. "Covenant Marriage." July 7. <http://www.mormons.org/conferences/96_oct/Hafen_Marriage.html>

Hagan, John and Bill McCarthy. 1997. *Mean Streets: Youth Crime and Homelessness*. Cambridge: Cambridge University Press.

Hagar, Laura. 1995. "Why Has AIDS Education Failed?" *Express: The East Bays' Weekly*, June 23, pp. 1, 10–16.

———. 1997. "The American Family Is Dead!" *Bay Area Express* 19 (20). February 21:1, 6–13.

Haines, Michael R. 1996. "Long-Term Marriage Patterns in the United States from Colonial times to the Present." *The History of the Family: An International Quarterly* 1(1):15–39.

Haines, James and Margery Neely. 1987. *Parents' Work Is Never Done*. Far Hills, NJ: New Horizon Press.

Hale-Benson, J. E. 1986. *Black Children: Their Roots, Culture, and Learning Styles*. Provo, UT: Brigham Young University Press.

Hall, Edie Jo and E. Mark Cummings. 1997. "The Effects of Marital and Parent–Child Conflicts on Other Family Members: Grandmothers and Grown Children." *Family Relations* 46 (2):135–43.

Hall, Wendy A. 1994. "New Fatherhood: Myths and Realities." *Public Health Nursing* 11(4), August:219–228.

Hallenbeck, Phyllis N. 1966. "An Analysis of Power Dynamics in Marriage." *Journal of Marriage and the Family* 28:200–203.

Haller, Max. 1981. "Marriage, Women, and Social Stratification: A Theoretical Critique." *American Journal of Sociology* 86:766–95.

Halpern, Sue. 1989a. "AIDS: Rethinking the Risk." *Ms. Magazine*, May, pp. 80–87.

———. 1989b. "And Baby Makes Three." *Ms. Magazine*, Jan.-Feb., p. 151.

———. 1989c. "Infertility: Playing the Odds." *Ms. Magazine*, Jan.-Feb., pp. 147–56.

Hamachek, Don E. 1971. *Encounters with the Self*. New York: Holt, Rinehart & Winston.

———. 1992. *Encounters with the Self*, 4th ed. New York: Holt, Rinehart & Winston.

Hamby, Sherry L., Valerie C. Poindexter, and Bernadette Gray-Little. 1996. "Four Measures of Partner Violence: Construct Similarity and Classification Differences." *Journal of Marriage and the Family* 58 (1):127–39.

Hamer, Dean and Peter Copeland. 1994. *The Science of Desire: The Search for the Gay Gene and the Biology of Behavior*. New York: Simon & Schuster.

———. 1998. *Living with Our Genes*. New York: Doubleday.

Hamilton, Kendall and Claudia Kalb. 1995. "They Log On, But They Can't Log Off." *Newsweek*. December 18:60–1.

Hampton, Robert L. and Eli H. Newberger. 1988. "Child Abuse Incidence and Reporting by Hospitals: Significance of Severity, Class and Race." In Gerald T. Hotaling, David Finkelhor, John T. Kirkpatrick and Murray A. Straus (Eds.), *Coping with Family Violence: Research and Policy Perspectives* (pp. 212–23). Newbury Park, CA: Sage.

Hanash, Kamal A. 1994. *Perfect Lover: Understanding and Overcoming Sexual Dysfunction*. New York: SPI Books.

Hanawalt, Barbara. 1986. *The Ties that Bound: Peasant Families in Medieval England*. New York: Oxford University Press.

Hancock, LynNell. (1995, March 6). "Breaking Point." *Newsweek*, 56–62.

Haney-Lopez, Ian F. 1997. *White By Law: The Legal Construction of Race*. New York: New York University Press.

Hansen, Donald A. and Reuben Hill. 1964. "Families Under Stress." Pp. 782–819 in *The Handbook of Marriage and the Family*, edited by Harold Christensen. Chicago: Rand McNally.

Hansen, Gary L. 1985. "Perceived Threats and Marital Jealousy." *Social Psychology Quarterly* 48 (3):262–68.

Hanson, Thomas L., Sara McLanahan, and Elizabeth Thomson. 1996. "Double Jeopardy: Parental Conflict and Stepfamily Outcomes for Children." *Journal of Marriage and the Family* 58 (1):141–54.

Hansson, Robert O., R. Eric Nelson, Margaret D. Carver, David H. NeeSmith, Elsie M. Dowling, Wesla L. Fletcher, and Peter Suhr. 1990. "Adult Children with Frail Elderly Parents: When to Intervene?" *Family Relations* 39:153–58.

"Happiest Couples in Study Have Sex after 60." 1992. *New York Times* National Sunday. October 4:13.

Haraway, Donna. 1989. *Primate Visions: Gender, Race, and Nature in the World of Modern Science*. New York: Routledge, Chapman and Hall.

Hardcastle, James R. 1995. "Singles in Northern Virginia's Condos." *New York Times*, Aug. 20, p. Y25.

Hardesty, C. and J. Bokemeier. 1989. "Finding Time and Making Do: Distribution of Household Labor in Nonmetropolitan Marriages." *Journal of Marriage and the Family* 51:253–67.

Hardwick, Deborah and Dianne Patychuk. 1999. "Geographic Mapping Demonstrates The Association Between Social Inequality, Teen Births And STDS Among Youth." *The Canadian Journal of Human Sexuality* 8:77–90.

Hardy, Janet B., Anne K. Duggan, Katya Masnyk, and Carol Pearson. 1989. "Fathers of Children Born to Young Urban Mothers." *Family Planning Perspectives* 21 (4) (July/Aug.):159–87.

Harkins, Elizabeth B. 1978. "Effects of Empty Nest Transition on Self-Report of Psychological and Physical Well-Being." *Journal of Marriage and the Family* 40:549–56.

Harris, Kathleen M., Frank F. Furstenberg Jr., and Jeremy K. Marmer. 1998. "Paternal Involvement with Adolescents in Intact Families: The Influence of Fathers over the Life Course." *Demography* 35 (2):201–16.

Harris, Kathleen and Jeremy Marmer. 1996. "Poverty, Parental Involvement and Adolescent Well-Being." *Journal of Family Issues* 17(5):614–640.

Harris, Phyllis B. and Joyce Bichler. 1997. *Men Giving Care: Reflections of Husbands and Sons.* New York: Garland.

Harris, S.B., R. Glazier, K. Eng and J. McMurray. 1998. "Disease Patterns Among Canadian Aboriginal Children: Study In A Remote Rural Setting." *Canadian Family Physician* 44(September):1869–1877.

Harrison, Deborah and Lucie Laliberte. 1993. "How Combat Identity Structures Military Wives' Domestic Labour." *Studies in Political Economy* 40(autumn):45–80.

Harrison, Michelle. 1999. "Social Construction of Mary Beth Whitehead." Pp. 425–37 in *American Families: A Multicultural Reader,* edited by Stephanie Coontz. New York: Routeledge.

Harrist, Amanda W. and Ricardo C. Ainslie. 1998. "Marital Discord and Child Behavior Problems." *Journal of Family Issues* 19 (2):140–63.

Harry, Joseph. 1983. "Gay Male and Lesbian Relationships." In Eleanor D. Macklin and Roger H. Rubin (Eds.), *Contemporary Families and Alternative Lifestyles: Handbook in Research and Theory* (pp. 216–34). Newbury Park, CA: Sage.

Hart, Mitchell Bryan. 2000. *Social Science and the Politics of Modern Jewish Identity.* Stanford, Calif: Stanford University Press.

Harvey, Andrew S, Bobby Siu, Kathleen Reil and John Blakely. 1999. "Socioeconomic Status of Immigrant Men and Women in Selected Ethnocultural Groups in Canada." Paper prepared for the 3rd National Metropolish Conference, January 14-15-16, Vancouver, B.C.

Hasty, L. A., and J. B. Massey. 1997. "Infertility Risks Associated with Postponing Pregnancy." *Journal of the Medical Association of Georgia* 86 (3):228–32.

Hatcher, Robert A., Felicia Stewart, James Trussell, Deborah Kowal, Felicia Guest, Gary K. Stewart, and Willard Cates. 1992. *Contraceptive Technologies 1990–1992,* 15th rev. ed. New York: Irvington.

———. 1998. *Contraceptive Technology* (17th revised edition). New York: Ardent Media, Inc.

Hatfield, E. and S. Sprecher. 1986. *Mirror, Mirror … The Importance of Looks in Everyday Life.* Albany, NY: State University of New York Press.

Hatfield, Julie. 1985. "Adolescents Have Need to Try Their Wings." *Boston Globe,* reprinted in *Omaha World-Herald,* May 6.

Hatfield, Larry D. (1996, May 8). "Same-Sex Marriages Assailed in Congress." *San Francisco Examiner,* p. A1.

Haveman, Robert H. and Barbara Wolfe. 1994. *Succeeding Generations: On the Effects of Investments in Children.* New York: Russell Sage Foundation.

Hawa, Roula, Brenda E. Munro and Maryanne Doherty-Poirier. 1998. "Information, Motivation And Behaviour As Predictors Of AIDS Risk Reduction Among Canadian First Year University Students." *The Canadian Journal of Human Sexuality* 7:9–18.

Hawke, Sharryl and David Knox. 1978. "The One-Child Family: A New Life-style." *Family Coordinator* 27:215–19.

Hawkesworth, Mary. 1997. "Confounding Gender." *Signs* 22 (3):649–86.

Hawkins, Alan J. and David J. Eggebeen. 1991. "Are Fathers Fungible? Patterns of Coresident Adult Men in Maritally Disrupted Families and Young Children's Well-being." *Journal of Marriage and the Family* 53 (4) (Nov.):958–72.

Hayden, Dolores. 1981. *The Grand Domestic Revolution: A History of Feminist Designs for American Homes, Neighborhoods, and Cities.* Cambridge, MA: MIT Press.

Hayes, Arthur S. 1991. "Courts Concede the Sexes Think in Unlike Ways." *The Wall Street Journal.,* May 28: B1, B5.

Hayes, Cheryl D., ed. 1987. *Risking the Future: Adolescent Sexuality, Pregnancy, and Childbearing,* vol. 1. Washington, DC: National Academy Press.

Hazen, C. and P. Shaver. 1994. "Attachment As an Organizing Framework for Research on Close Relationships." *Psychological Inquiry* 5:1–22.

Health Canada. 2001. "AIDS." <http://www.hc-sc.gc.ca/english/aids.htm>

———. 2000. "HIV Testing Among Canadians: 15,000 Current HIV Infections May Not Be Diagnosed." Bureau of HIV/AIDS, STD and TB Update Series, *HIV/AIDS Epi Update,* Centre for Infectious Disease Prevention and Control. <http://www.hc-sc.gc.ca/hpb/lcdc/bah/epi/hivtest_e.html>

———. 2000. "The AIDS/HIV FIles." April 26, 2000 <www.hc-sc.gc.ca/real/aids/state.html>

———. n.d. "HIV/AIDS and Aboriginal People in Canada." December 28, 1999 <www.hc-sc.gc.ca/hppb/hiv_aids/programs/aboriginal.html>

———. 1999. *Toward a Healthy Future: Second Report on the Health of Canadians.* Prepared by the Federal, Provincial and Territorial Advisory Committee on Population Health for the Meeting of Ministers of Health. Charlottetown, PEI, September.

———. 1999b. *Statistical Report on the Health of Canadians.* <www.hc-sc.gc.ca/hpph/phdd/report/state/englover.html>

Heaton, Tim B. 1984. "Religious Homogamy and Marital Satisfaction Reconsidered." *Journal of Marriage and the Family* 46:729–33.

Heaton, Tim B. and Stan L. Albrecht. 1996. "The Changing Pattern of Interracial Marriage." *Social Biology* 43 (3–4):203–15.

Heaton, Tim B. and Edith L. Pratt. 1990. "The Effects of Religious Homogamy on Marital Satisfaction and Stability." *Journal of Family Issues* 11 (2) (June):191–207.

Heaton, Tim B., S. L. Albrecht, and T. K. Martin. 1985. "The Timing of Divorce." *Journal of Marriage and the Family* 47:631–39.

Heaton, Tim B. and Cardell K. Jacoboson. 2000. "Intergroup Marriage: An Examination Of Opportunity Structures." *Sociological Inquiry* 70:30–41.

Heckert, D. Alex, Thomas C. Nowak, and Kay A. Snyder. 1998. "The Impact of Husbands' and Wives' Relative Earnings on Marital Disruption." *Journal of Marriage and the Family* 60 (3):690–703.

Hedges, Larry V. and Amy Nowell. 1995. "Sex Differences in Mental Test Scores, Variability, and Numbers of High-Scoring Individuals." *Science* 269 (5220) (July 7):41–46.

Heiss, Jerold. 1991. "Gender and Romantic Love Roles." *The Sociological Quarterly* 32:575–92.

Helgeson, Vicki S. 1994. "Relation of Agency and Communion to Well-Being: Evidence and Potential Explanations." *Psychological Bulletin* 116 (3) (Nov.):412–29.

Heller, P.E. and B. Wood. 2000. "The Influences of Religious and Ethnic Differences on Marital Intimacy: Intermarriage Versus Intramarriage." *Journal of Marital and Family Therapy* 26(2):241–252.

Hellstrom, Wayne J. 1997. *Male Infertility and Sexual Dysfunction.* New York: Springer Press.

Hendrick, Clyde and Susan S. Hendrick. 1989. "Research on Love: Does It Measure Up?" *Journal of Personality and Social Psychology* 56:784–94.

———. 1986. "A Theory and Method of Love." *Journal of Personality and Social Psychology* 50:392–402.

Hendrick, S. 1988. "A Generic Measure of Relationship Satisfaction." *Journal of Marriage and the Family* 50:93–8.

Henley, Nancy and Jo Freeman. 1989. "The Sexual Politics of Interpersonal Behavior." Pp. 457–69 in *Women: A Feminist Perspective*, 4th ed., edited by Jo Freeman. Mountain View, CA: Mayfield.

———. 1995. "The Sexual Politics of Interpersonal Behavior." Pp. 79–91 in *Women: A Feminist Perspective.* 5th ed. Mountain View, CA: Mayfield.

Henningson, Ellen. 1997. "Financial Abuse of the Elderly." *Wisconsin Department of Health and Family Services.* <www.dhrs.state.wi.us>

Henripin, Jacques. 1999. "Baby Boom." Pp. 175 in *The Canadian Encyclopedia: Year 2000 Edition*, edited by James Marsh. Toronto: McClelland & Stewart Inc.

Henshaw, Stanley K. 1987. "Characteristics of U.S. Women Having Abortions, 1982–1983." *Family Planning Perspectives* 19:5–9.

———. 1990. "Induced Abortion: A World Review, 1990." *Family Planning Perspectives* 22:76–89.

———. 1995. "Factors Hindering Access to Abortion Services." *Family Planning Perspectives* 27 (2) (Mar./Apr.):54–9.

———. 1998. "Unintended Pregnancy in the United States." *Family Planning Perspective*, 30(1): 24–9.

Henshaw, Stanley K., Jacqueline Darroch Forrest, and Jennifer Van Vort. 1987. "Abortion Services in the United States, 1984 and 1985." *Family Planning Perspectives* 19:63–70.

Henslin, James and Adie Nelson. 1995. *Sociology: A Down-To-Earth Approach: First Canadian Edition.* Scarborough: Allyn and Bacon.

Herbert, Tracy Bennett, Roxane Cohen Silver, and John H. Ellard. 1991. "Coping with an Abusive Relationship: I. How and Why Do Women Stay?" *Journal of Marriage and the Family* 53 (2) (May):311–25.

Hering, Peter. 1997. "Internet Romances Don't Work." *The Arachnet Journal on Virtual Culture* 26 (2). <http://homepage.seas.up...f/bulkpak/netlove.html>

Hernandez, Donald J. 1997. "Poverty Trends." Pp. 18–34 in *Consequences of Growing Up Poor*, edited by Greg J. Duncan and Jeanne Brooks-Gunn. New York: Russell Sage Foundation.

Herscher, Elaine. 1998. "Same-Sex Marriage Suffers Setback." *San Francisco Chronicle.* November 5:A2.

Hershey, Robert D., Jr. 1989. "Unemployment Rate Drops to 4.9%, Lowest Mark Since '73." *New York Times*, Apr. 8.

Hertz, Rosanna. 1986. *More Equal than Others: Women and Men in Dual Career Marriages.* Berkeley: University of California Press.

———. 1997. "A Typology of Approaches to Child Care." *Journal of Family Issues* 18 (4):355–85.

——— . 1988. *More Equal Than Others: Women and Men in Dual-Career Marriages.* Berkeley, CA: University of California Press.

Hetherington, E. Mavis, 1973. "Girls Without Fathers." *Psychology Today* 6:47–52.

——— . 1987. "Family Relations Six Years After Divorce." Pp. 185–205 in *Remarriage and Stepparenting,* edited by Kay Pasley and Marilyn Ihinger-Tallman. New York: Guilford.

——— . 1988. "Parents, Children, and Siblings Six Years After Divorce." Pp. 311–31 in *Relationships within Families,* edited by R. Hinde and J. Stevenson-Hinde. Cambridge: Cambridge University Press.

——— . 1989. "Coping with Family Transitions: Winners, Losers, and Survivors." *Child Development* 60:1–14.

——— . 1993. "An Overview of the Virginia Longitudinal Study of Divorce and Remarriage with a Focus on Early Adolescence." *Journal of Family Psychology* 7:39–56.

——— . (Ed.). 1999. *Coping with Divorce, Single Parenting, and Remarriage: A Risk and Resiliency Perspective.* Mahwah, NJ: Lawrence Erlbaum Associates.

Hetherington, E. Mavis and K. M. Jodl. 1994. "Stepfamilies as Settings for Child Development." Pp. 55–80 in *Stepfamilies: Who Benefits? Who Does Not?,* edited by Alan Booth and J. Dunn (Eds.). Hillsdale, NJ: Lawrence Erlbaum Associates.

Hewlett, Sylvia Ann. 1986. *A Lesser Life: The Myth of Women's Liberation in America.* New York: Morrow.

Hewlett, Sylvia Ann and Cornell West. 1998. *The War Against Parents: What We Can Do for America's Beleaguered Moms and Dads.* Boston: Houghton Mifflin.

Hevesi, Dennis. 1994. "U.S. Court Faults a New York List on Child Abusers." *New York Times,* Mar. 6, p. A-1.

Hicks, S. 1980. "Relationship and Sexual Problems of the Visually Handicapped." *Sexuality and Disability,* 2:293–300.

Hiedemann, Bridget, Olga Suhomlinova and Angela M. O'Rand. 1998. "Economic Independence, Economic Status, and Empty Nest in Midlife Marital Disruption." *Journal of Marriage and the Family* 60 (1):219–31.

Hiew, Chok C. 1992. "Separated By Their Work: Families With Fathers Living Apart." *Environment and Behavior* 24(2)(March):206–225.

Higgins, C., L. Duxbury and C. Lee. 1993. *Balancing Work and Family: A Study of the Canadian Private Sector.* London, ON: National Centre for Research, Management and Development, University of Western Ontario.

Hill, Jeffrey E., Alan J. Hawkins, and Brent C. Miller. 1996. "Work and Family in the Virtual Office: Perceived Influences of Mobile Telework." *Family Relations* 45 (3):293–301.

Hill, Martha S. 1992. "The Role of Economic Resources and Remarriage in Financial Assistance for Children of Divorce." *Journal of Family Issues* 13 (2) (June):158–78.

Hill, Reuben. 1958. "Generic Features of Families Under Stress." *Social Casework* 49:139–50.

Hill, Shirley A. and Mary K. Zimmerman. 1995. "Valiant Girls and Vulnerable Boys: The Impact of Gender and Race on Mothers' Caregiving for Chronically Ill Children." *Journal of Marriage and the Family* 57 (1) (Feb.):43–53.

Hiller, Dana V. and William W. Philliber. 1986. "The Division of Labor in Contemporary Marriage: Expectations, Perceptions, and Performance." *Social Problems* 33 (3):191–201.

Hines, Paulette M., Nydia Garcia-Preto, Monlea McGoldrick and Rhea Almedia. 1992. "Intergenerational Relationships Across Cultures." *Families in Society. Special Issue: Multicultural Practice,* 73(6), June: 323–38.

Hobart, Charles. 1990. "Relationships Between The Formerly Married." *Journal of Comparative Family Studies* 21(1)(spring):81–97.

——— . 1996. "Intimacy and Family Life: Sexuality, Cohabitation and Marriage." Pp. 143-173 in *Families: Changing Trends in Canada,* third edition, edited by Maureen Baker. Toronto: McGraw-Hill Ryerson.

Hobart, Charles W. and Frank Grigel. 1992. "Cohabitation Among Canadian Students at the End of the Eighties." *Journal of Comparative Family Studies,* 23: 311–337.

Hochschild, Arlie. 1979. "Emotion Work, Feeling Rules, and Social Structure." *American Journal of Sociology* 85:551–75.

——— . 1983. *The Managed Heart: Commercialization of Human Feeling.* Berkeley: University of California Press.

——— . 1989. *The Second Shift: Working Parents and the Revolution at Home.* New York: Viking/Penguin.

——— . 1997. *The Time Bind: When Work Becomes Home and Home Becomes Work.* New York: Holt.

Hochswender, Woody. 1990. "For Today's Fathers, Their Holiday Seems a Bit Set in Its Ways." *New York Times,* June 17.

Hock, Ellen, M. Therese Gnezda, and Susan L. McBride. 1984. "Mothers of Infants: Attitudes Toward Employment and Motherhood Following Birth of the First Child." *Journal of Marriage and the Family* (May):425–31.

Hoffman, Lois W. and F. Ivan Nye, Eds. 1974. *Working Mothers.* San Francisco: Jossey-Bass.

Hofstede, G. 1980. *Culture's Consequences: International Differences in Work-Related Values.* Beverly Hills, CA: Sage.

Hogan, Dennis P. and Nan Marie Astone. 1986. "The Transition to Adulthood." *Annual Review of Sociology* 12:109–30.

Hogue, Carol J. Rowland, Willard Cates, Jr., and Christopher Tietze. 1983. "Impact of Vacuum Aspiration on

Future Childbearing: A Review." *Family Planning Perspectives* 15:119–26.

Hollingsworth, Leslie Doty. 1998. "Promoting Same-Race Adoption for Children of Color." *Social Work* 43 (2):104–16.

Holloway, Lynette. 1994. "A Grandmother Fights for Her 2d Generation." *New York Times*, Dec. 12, p. 59.

Holmes, Ivory H. 1983. *The Allocation of Time by Women Without Family Responsibilities*. Lanham, MD: University Press of America.

Holmes, Jeremy. 1997. "Attachment, Autonomy, Intimacy: Some Clinical Implications of Attachment Theory." *British Journal of Medical Psychology* 70 (3):231–43.

Holmes, J. G. and S. L. Murray. 1996. "Conflict in Close Relationships." Pp. 622–54 in *Social Psychology: Handbook of Basic Principles*, edited by E. T. Higgins and A. Kruglanski. New York: Guilford.

Hoff Sommers. C. 2000. *The War Against Boys*. New York: Simon & Schuster.

Holmes, Steven A. 1990. "Day Care Bill Marks a Turn Toward Help for the Poor." *New York Times*, Jan. 25.

———. 1998. "Children Study Longer and Play Less, A Report Says." *New York Times*. November 11.

Hondagneu-Sotelo, Pierrette. 1992. "Overcoming Patriarchal Constraints: The Reconstruction of Gender Relations Among Mexican Immigrant Women and Men." *Gender and Society* 6 (3) (Sept.):393–415.

Hondagneu-Sotelo, Pierrette and Michael A. Messner. 1999. "Gender Displays and Men's Power: The 'New Man' and the Mexican Immigrant Man." Pp. 342–58 in *American Families: A Multicultural Reader*, edited by Stephanie Coontz. New York: Routeledge.

Honoré, Carl. 2000. "'Male Egg' Could Enable Two Men To Conceive a Child." *National Post*, September 26:A1, A12.

Hood, Jane C. 1986. "The Provider Role: Its Meaning and Measurement." *Journal of Marriage and the Family* 48:349–59.

Hopfensperger, Jean. 1990. "A Day for Courting, Hmong Style." *Minneapolis Star Tribune*, Nov. 24, p. 1B.

Hopkins, June and Priscilla White. 1978. "The Dual-Career Couple: Constraints and Supports." *Family Coordinator* 27:253–59.

Hopper, Joseph. 1993. "The Rhetoric of Motives in Divorce." *Journal of Marriage and the Family* 55 (4) (Nov.):801–13.

Horwith, Melvin and Julianne Imperato-McGinley. 1983. "The Medical Evaluation of Disorders of Sexual Desire in Males and Females." Pp. 183–95 in *The Evaluation of Sexual Disorders: Psychological and Medical Aspects*, edited by Helen Singer Kaplan. New York: Brunner/Mazel.

Horwitz, Allan. V. 1993. "Adult Siblings as Sources of Social Support for the Seriously Mentally Ill: A Test of the Serial Model." *Journal of Marriage and the Family* 55 (3) (Aug.):623–32.

Hotovy, Steven. 1991. "Adopting the Older Child: A Personal Reflection." *America*, May 18, pp. 541–49.

Houseknect, Sharon K. 1987. "Voluntary Childlessness." Pp. 369–418 in *Handbook of Marriage and the Family*, edited by Marvin B. Sussman and Suzanne K. Steinmetz. New York: Plenum.

Houseknect, Sharon K. and Jaya Sastry. 1996. "Family 'Decline' and Child Well-Being: A Comparative Assessment." *Journal of Marriage and the Family* 58 (3):726–39.

Houts, Renate M., Elliot Robins, and Ted L. Huston. 1996. "Compatibility and the Development of Premarital Relationships." *Journal of Marriage and the Family* 58:7–20.

Howard, J. A. 1988. "Gender Differences in Sexual Attitudes: Conservatism or Powerlessness?" *Gender and Society* 2:103–14.

Howard, Marion and Judith Blamey McCabe. 1990. "Helping Teenagers Postpone Sexual Involvement." *Family Planning Perspectives* 22:21–26.

Howell, Nancy. 1996. "Families and Ethnicity." Pp. 119–139 in Maureen Baker (ed.) *Families: Changing Trends in Canada*, 3rd edition. Toronto: McGraw Hill Ryerson.

Hoy, Claire. 1995. *The Truth About Breast Cancer*. Toronto: Stoddart.

Hrdy, Sara Blaffer. 1981. *The Woman That Never Evolved*. Cambridge, MA: Harvard University Press.

Hsu, F. L. K. 1971. *Kinship and Culture*. Chicago: Aldine.

Huber, Joan. 1973. "From Sugar and Spice to Professor: Ambiguities in Identity Transformation." Pp. 125–35 in *Academic Women on the Move*, edited by Alice S. Rossi and Ann Calderwood. New York: Russell Sage Foundation.

———. 1986. "Trends in Gender Stratification, 1970–1985." *Sociological Forum* 1:476–95.

———. 1989. "A Theory of Gender Stratification." Pp. 110–19 in *Feminist Frontiers II*, edited by Laurel Richardson and Verta Taylor. New York: Random House.

Huber, Joan and Glenna Spitze. 1983. *Sex Stratification*. New York: Academic.

Hudson, Margaret F. 1986. "Elder Mistreatment: Current Research." Pp. 125–66 in *Elder Abuse: Conflict in the Family*, edited by Karl A. Pillemer and Rosalie S. Wolf. Dover, MA: Auburn.

Hueschler, Anne (*YWCA: Women Against Violence*). 1989. *Personal communication*, Apr. 15.

Hughes, Diane, Ellen Galinsky, and Anne Morris. 1992. "The Effects of Job Characteristics on Marital Quality: Specifying Linking Mechanisms." *Journal of Marriage and the Family* 54 (1) (Feb.):31–42.

Hughes, Kathleen A. 1991. "Pregnant Professionals Face Subtle Bias at Work as Attitudes Toward Them Shift." *The Wall Street Journal*, Feb. 6, pp. B1, B6.

Hughes, Michael and Walter R. Gove. 1989. "Explaining the Negative Relationship Between Social Integration and Mental Health: The Case of Living Alone." Paper presented at the annual meeting of the American Sociological Association, San Francisco, Aug.

Hughes, Robert Jr. and Maureen Perry-Jenkins. 1996. "Social Class Issues in Family Life Education." *Family Relations* 45 (2):175–82.

Hunt, Janet G. and Larry L. Hunt. 1977. "Dilemmas and Contradictions of Status: The Case of the Dual-Career Family." *Social Problems* 24:407–16.

———. 1986. "The Dualities of Careers and Families: New Integrations or New Polarizations?" Pp. 275–89 in *Family in Transition: Rethinking Marriage, Sexuality, Child Rearing, and Family Organization.* 5th ed., edited by Arlene S. Skolnick and Jerome H. Skolnick. Boston: Little, Brown.

Hunt, Morton. 1974. *Sexual Behavior in the Seventies.* Chicago: Playboy Press.

Hunter, Andrea G. and Sherill L. Sellers. 1998. "Feminist Attitude among African American Women and Men." *Gender and Society* 12:81–99.

Hurd, Burton W. 1964. *Ethnic Origin and Nativity of the Canadian People.* 1941 Census Monograph. Dominion Bureau of Statistics. Ottawa: Queen's Printer.

Hussein, Lula J. 1995. *Report on the Ottawa Consultations on Female Genital Mutilation Held for Representatives of the Somali Community.* March. <http://129.128.19.162/docs/fgmdoj.html>

Hutchinson, Earl Ofari. 1992. *Black Fatherhood: The Guide to Male Parenting.* Los Angeles: Middle Passage Press.

Hutchinson, Janice. 1997. *Adolescent Maltreatment: Youth as Victims of Abuse and Neglect.* Arlington, VA: National Center for Maternal and Child Health.

Hutchinson, Ray and Miles McNall. 1994. "Early Marriage in a Hmong Cohort." *Journal of Marriage and the Family* 56 (3) (Aug.):579–90.

Hwang, Sean-Shong and Benigno E. Aguirre. 1997. "Structural and Assimilationist Explanations of Asian American Intermarriage." *Journal of Marriage and the Family* 59:758–72.

Hwang, Sean-Shong and Rogelio Saenz. 1997. "Fertility of Chinese Immigrants in the U.S.: Testing a Fertility Emancipation Hypothesis." *Journal of Marriage and the Family* 59:50–61.

Hyde, Barbara L. and Margaret Texidor. 1994. "A Description of the Fathering Experience Among Black Fathers." Pp. 157–164 in *The Black Family: Essays and Studies.* 5th ed., edited by Robert Staples. Belmont, CA: Wadsworth.

Hyde, Janet Shibley, Elizabeth Fennema, and Susan Lamon. 1990. "Gender Differences in Mathematics Performance: A Meta-analysis." *Psychological Bulletin* 106:139–55.

Hyde, Janet Shibley and Elizabeth Ashby Plant. 1995. "Magnitude of Psychological Gender Differences: Another Side to the Story." *The American Psychologist* 50 (3) (Mar.):159–62.

Hyman, Ilene, Nhi Vu and Morton Beiser. 2000. "Post-Migration Stresses Among Southeast Asian Refugee Youth In Canada: A Research Note." *Journal of Comparative Family Studies* 31(2)(spring):281–293.

Hyman, Michael R. 1997. "Internet Romances—They Can Succeed." *The Arachnet Journal on Virtual Culture* 2 (3). <http://homepage.seas.up...f/bulkpak/netlove. html>

I

Ihinger-Tallman, Marilyn and Kay Pasley. 1987. *Remarriage.* Newbury Park, CA: Sage.

———. 1997. "Stepfamilies in 1984 and Today—A Scholarly Perspective." Pp. 19–40 in *Stepfamilies: History, Research, and Policy*, edited by Irene Levin and Marvin B. Sussman. New York: Haworth Press.

Inciardi, James A. and Lana D. Harrison. 1997. "HIV, AIDS, and Drug Abuse in the International Sector." *Journal of Drug Issues*, 27:1–8.

Ingoldsby, Bron B. 1995a. "Mate Selection and Marriage." Pp. 143–60 in *Families in Multicultural Perspective*, edited by Bron B. Ingoldsby and Suzanna Smith. New York: Guilford Press.

Ingoldsby, Bron B. and Suzanna Smith. 1995. *Families in Multicultural Perspective.* New York: Guilford Press.

Ingrassia, Michele. 1995b. "On the Side of the Child." *Newsweek.* February 20:63.

Irvine, Jane A. 1997. "Parental Responsibility Versus Custody: the Linguistic Precipitation of Conflict." *American Journal of Family Law* 11 (3):155–72.

Isaacs, Marla Beth, Braulio Montalvo, and David Abelsohn. 1986. *The Difficult Divorce: Therapy for Children and Families.* New York: Basic Books.

Isaacs, Stephen L. and Renee J. Holt. 1987. *Redefining Procreation: Facing the Issues.* Population Bulletin 42. Washington, DC: Population Reference Bureau.

Isaacs, S., S. Keogh, C. Menard et al. 1998. "Suicide in the Northwest Territories: A Descriptive Review." *Chronic Diseases in Canada* 19 (4):152–156.

Ishii-Kuntz, Masako. 1997. "Intergenerational Relationships among Chinese, Japanese, and Korean Americans." *Family Relations* 46 (1):23–32.

Ishii-Kuntz, Masako and Karen Seccombe. 1989. "The Impact of Children upon Social Support Networks Throughout the Life Course." *Journal of Marriage and the Family* 51 (3):777–90.

Island, David and Patrick Letellier. 1991. *Men Who Beat the Men Who Love Them: Battered Gay Men and Domestic Violence.* New York: Haworth.

J

"J" (Joan Garrity). 1977. *Total Living*. New York: Simon & Schuster.

Jackson, Andrew. 2001. "Poverty and Racism." *Perception*, 24(spring). <http://www.ccsd.ca/perception/244/racism.htm>

Jackson, E. and S. Persky. 1982. *Flaunting It: A Decade of Gay Journalism from the Body Politic*. Toronto: Pink Triangle Press.

Jackson, James S., Wayne R. McCullough, and Gerald Gurin. 1988. "Family, Socialization, Environment, and Identity Development in Black Americans." Pp. 242–56 in *Black Families*, edited by Harriette Pipes McAdoo. Newbury Park, CA: Sage.

Jackson, Joan J. 1958. "Alcoholism and the Family." *Annals of the American Academy of Political and Social Science* 315:90–98.

Jacobs, C.D. and E.M. Wolf. 1995. "School Sexuality Education and Adolescent Risk-Taking Behavior." *Journal of School Health*, 65:91–5.

Jacobson, N. S. and A. Christensen. 1996. *Integrative Couple Therapy: Promoting Acceptance and Change*. New York: W. W. Norton.

Jacobvitz, Deborah and Neil F. Bush. 1996. "Reconstructions of Family Relationships: Parent-Child Alliances, Personal Distress, and Self-Esteem." *Developmental Psychology* 32 (4):732–43.

Jain, Anju and Jay Belsky. 1997. "Fathering and Acculturation: Immigrant Indian Families with Young Children." *Journal of Marriage and the Family* 59 (4):873–83.

Jain, Arvind K and Annamma Joy. 1997. "Money Matters: An Exploratory Study of the Socio-cultural Context of Consumption, Saving, and Investment Patterns." *Journal of Economic Psychology* 18 (6)(November):649–675.

Janus, S. and C. Janus. 1993. *The Janus Report on Sexual Behaviour*. New York: Wiley.

Jasso, Guillermina. 1985. "Marital Coital Frequency and the Passage of Time: Estimating the Separate Effects of Spouses' Ages and Marital Duration, Birth and Marriage Cohorts, and Period Influences." *American Sociological Review* 50:224–41.

Jaurequi, Immculada. 1995. "Psychological Aspects Of Delinquency And Behavior Disorders In Adolescents Of Ethnic Minorities." *Revue Canadienne de Psycho-Education* 24(1):31–54.

Jendrick, Margaret Platt. 1993. "Grandparents Who Parent Their Grandchildren: Effects on Lifestyle." *Journal of Marriage and the Family* 55 (3) (Aug.):609–21.

Jezl, D. R., C. E. Molidor, and T. L. Wright. 1996. "Physical, Sexual and Psychological Abuse in High School Dating Relationships: Prevalence Rates and Self-Esteem Issues." *Child and Adolescent Social Work Journal* 13 (1):69–74.

Joesch, J.M. 1994. "Children And The Timing Of Women's Paid Work After Childbirth: A Further Specification Of The Relationship." *Journal of Marriage and the Family* 56(2), May:429–440.

Joffe, Carole. 1997. "Abortion as Single-Issue Politics." *Society* 34 (5):25–37.

Johann, Sara Lee. 1994. *Domestic Abusers: Terrorists in Our Homes*. Springfield, IL: Thomas.

Johannson, Melanie A. and Leslie M. Tutty. 1998. "An Evaluation of After-Treatment Couples' Groups for Wife Abuse." *Family Relations* 47 (1):27–35.

Johnson, Colleen L. 1975. "Authority and Power in Japanese-American Marriage." Pp. 182–96 in *Power in Families*, edited by Ronald E. Cromwell and David H. Olson. Newbury Park, CA: Sage.

———. 1988. *Ex Familia: Grandparents, Parents, and Children Adjust to Divorce*. New Brunswick, NJ: Rutgers University Press.

Johnson, Dirk. 1990. "Chastity Organizations: Starting Over in Purity." *New York Times*, Jan. 28.

———. 1991. "Polygamists Emerge from Secrecy, Seeking Not Just Peace but Respect." *New York Times*, Apr. 9.

Johnson, Elizabeth M. and Ted L. Huston. 1998. "The Perils of Love, or Why Wives Adapt to Husbands During the Transition to Parenthood." *Journal of Marriage and the Family* 60 (1):195–204.

Johnson, Fenton. 1996. "Wedded to an Illusion: Do Gays and Lesbians Really Want the Right to Marry?" *Harper's*. November:41–50.

Johnson, Holly. 1996. *Dangerous Domains: Violence Against Women in Canada*. Scarborough: Nelson Canada.

———. 2000. "Trends in Victim-Reported Wife Assault." Pp. 20–21 in Statistics Canada, *Family Violence in Canada: A Statistical Profile 2000*. Catalogue no. 85-224-XIE. Ottawa: Minister of Industry.

Johnson, Kirk. 1998. "Self-Image Is Suffering from Lack of Esteem." *New York Times*. May 5:B12.

Johnson, Michael P. 1995. "Patriarchal Terrorism and Common Couple Violence: Two Forms of Violence Against Women." *Journal of Marriage and the Family* 57 (2) (May):283–94.

Johnson, Michael P., Ted L. Huston, Stanley D. Gaines, Jr., and George Levinger. 1992. "Patterns of Married Life among Young Couples." *Journal of Social and Personal Relationships* 9:343–64.

Johnson, Phyllis J. 1998. "Performance of Household Tasks by Vietnamese and Laotian Refugees." *Journal of Family Issues* 10 (3):245–73.

Johnson, Tanya. 1986. "Critical Issues in the Definition of Elder Maltreatment." Pp. 167–96 in *Elder Abuse: Conflict in the Family*, edited by Karl A. Pillemer and Rosalie S. Wolf. Dover, MA: Auburn House.

Johnson, Walter R. and D. Michael Warren. 1994. *Inside the Mixed Marriage: Accounts of Changing Attitudes, Patterns, and Perceptions of Cross-Cultural and Interracial Marriages.* New York: University Press of America.

Johnston, Ann Dowsett. 1999. "Welcome to the Gender Wars." *Maclean's,* September 27:39.

Johnston, Janet R., Marsha Kline, and Jeanne M. Tschann. 1988. "Ongoing Post-Divorce Conflict in Families Contesting Custody: Does Joint Custody and Frequent Access Help?" Paper presented at the annual meeting of the American Orthopsychiatric Association, San Francisco, Mar. Cited in Judith Wallerstein and Sandra Blakeslee, *Second Chances* (New York: Ticknor and Fields, 1989), p. 321.

Jones, Ann. 1994. "Where Do We Go from Here?" *Ms. Magazine.* (Sept./Oct.):56–63.

Jones, Laren Renee. 1998. "Reaction Paper for Chapter 11." Unpublished Student Essay.

Joseph, Elizabeth. 1991. "My Husband's Nine Wives." *New York Times,* May 23.

Joshi, Mary Sissons and Meena Krishna. 1998. "English and North American Daughters-in-law in the Hindy Joint Family." Pp. 171–191 in *Cross-cultural Marriage: Identity and Choice,* edited by Rosanna Hill. New York: Berg.

Jourard, Sidney M. 1976. "Reinventing Marriage." Pp. 231–37 in *Process in Relationship: Marriage and Family.* 2d ed., edited by Edward A. Powers and Mary W. Lees. New York: West.

———. 1979. "Marriage Is for Life." Pp. 230–37 in *Choice and Challenge: Contemporary Readings in Marriage.* 2d ed., edited by Carl E. Williams and John F. Crosby. Dubuque, IA: Wm. C. Brown.

Joyce, Gregg. 1998. "Court Overturns School Board Ban on Same-Sex Books." *Canadian Press,* December 16. <www.egale.ca/archives/press/9812cp.htm>

Judge, Sharon L. 1998. "Parental Coping Strategies and Strengths in Families of Young Children with Disabilities." *Family Relations* 47 (3):263–68.

Judis, John B. 1994. "Crosses to Bear: The Many Faces of the Religious Right." *The New Republic* 211 (11) (Sept. 12):21–26.

Julian, Teresa W., Patrick C. McKenry, and Mary W. McKelvey. 1994. "Cultural Variations in Parenting." *Family Relations* 43:30–37.

K

Kaestner, Robert. 1997. "The Effects of Cocaine and Marijuana Use on Marriage and Marital Stability." *Journal of Family Issues* 18 (2):145–73.

Kagan, Jerome. 1994. *Galen's Prophecy.* New York: Basic Books.

Kain, Edward L. 1990. *The Myth of Family Decline: Understanding Families in a World of Rapid Social Change.* Lexington, MA: Lexington Books.

Kalagian, Wyn, Terry Delmore, Irene Loewen, and Cheryl Busca. 1998. "Adolescent Oral Contraceptive Use: Factors Predicting Compliance At 3 And 12 Months." *The Canadian Journal of Human Sexuality* 7:1–8.

Kalb, Claudia. 1997. "How Old Is Too Old?" *Newsweek.* May 5:64.

———. 1998. "Now, a Scary Strain of Drug-Resistant HIV." *Newsweek.* July 13:63.

———. 1999. "The Octuplet Question." *Newsweek.* January 11:33.

Kalbach, Madeline A. 2000. "Ethnicity and the Altar." Pp. 111–121 in *Perspectives on Ethnicity in Canada: A Reader,* edited by Madeline A. Kalbach and Warren E. Kalbach. Toronto: Harcourt Canada.

Kalbach, Warren E. 1999. "Population." Pp. 1867–1869 in *The Canadian Encyclopedia: Year 2000 Edition,* edited by James Marsh. Toronto: McClelland & Stewart Inc.

Kalish, Susan. 1994. "Rising Costs of Raising Children." *Population Today* 22 (7/8) (July/Aug.):4–5.

Kalmijn, Matthijs. 1991. "Status Homogamy in the United States." *American Journal of Sociology* 97 (2) (Sept.):496–523.

———. 1998. "Differentiation and Stratification—Intermarriage and Homogamy: Causes, Patterns, and Trends." *Annual Review of Sociology* 24:395–427.

Kalmuss, Debra. 1992. "Adoption and Black Teenagers: The Viability of a Pregnancy Resolution Strategy." *Journal of Marriage and the Family* 54 (3) (Aug.):485–95.

Kalmuss, Debra, Andrew Davidson, and Linda Cushman. 1992. "Parenting Expectations, Experiences, and Adjustment to Parenthood: A Test of the Violated Expectations Framework." *Journal of Marriage and the Family* 54 (3) (Aug.):516–26.

Kalmuss, Debra, Pearila B. Namerow, and Ursula Bauer. 1992. "Short-Term Consequences of Parenting Versus Adoption Among Young Unmarried Women." *Journal of Marriage and the Family* 54 (1) (Feb.):80–90.

Kalof, Linda and Timothy Cargill. 1991. "Fraternity and Sorority Membership and Gender Dominance Attitudes." *Sex Roles* 25 (7/8):417–23.

Kamat, Leena. 2000. "Arranged Marriages: A True Family Affair." *The Gazette: The Daily Student Newspaper at the University of Western Ontario,* 94, 38. <http://www.gazette.uwo.ca/2000/November/7/Campus_and_Culture1.htm>

Kamateros, Melpa. 1998. "The Isolated Immigrant Family." *Transition Magazine* 28(3) (September). <http://www.vifamily.ca/htm/293/4.htm>

Kamo, Yoshinori and Min Zhou. 1994. "Living Arrangements of Elderly Chinese and Japanese in the United States." *Journal of Marriage and the Family* 56 (3) (Aug.):544–58.

Kane, Rosalie. 1995. *Family Caregiving in an Aging Society: Policy Perspectives.* Newbury Park, CA: Sage.

Kann, Mark E. 1986. "The Costs of Being on Top." *Journal of the National Association for Women Deans, Administrators, and Counselors* 49:29–37.

Kanter, R.M. 1989. *When Giants Learn to Dance: Mastering the Challenges of Strategy, Management, and Careers in the 1990s.* New York: Simon and Schuster.

Kantor, David and William Lehr. 1975. *Inside the Family: Toward a Theory of Family Process.* San Francisco: Jossey-Bass.

Kantrowitz, Barbara. 1987. "The Year of Living Dangerously." *Newsweek on Campus,* Apr., pp. 12–21.

———. 1989. "Advocating a 'Mommy Track.' " *Newsweek,* Mar. 13, p. 45.

———. 1992. "Teenagers and AIDS." *Newsweek,* Aug. 3, pp. 45–49.

———. 1996. "Gay Families Come Out." *Newsweek.* November 4:50–57.

Kantrowitz, Barbara and Claudia Kalb. 1998. "Boys Will Be Boys." *Newsweek.* May 11:54–60.

Kaplan, Helen Singer. 1974. "No-Nonsense Therapy for Six Sexual Malfunctions." *Psychology Today* 8:132–38.

———. 1983. *The Evaluation of Sexual Disorders: Psychological and Medical Aspects.* New York: Brunner/Mazel.

———. 1995. *The Sexual Desire Disorders: Dysfunctional Regulation of Sexual Motivation.* New York: Brunner/Mazel.

Kaplan, Marion A., Ed. 1985. *The Marriage Bargain: Women and Dowries in European History.* New York: Harrington Park Press.

Kaplan, David A. and Daniel Klaidman. (1996, June 3). "A Battle, Not the War." *Newsweek,* 24–30.

Karen, R. 1994. *Becoming Attached: Unfolding the Mystery of the Infant–Mother Bond and Its Impact on Later Life.* New York: Warner.

Kassel, V. 1966. "Polygyny after 60." *Geriatrics* 21:214–18.

Kassorla, Irene. 1973. *Putting It All Together.* New York: Brut Publications; Hawthorn/Dutton.

Katz, Lillian G. 1998. *Distinction between Self-Esteem and Narcissism: Implications for Practice.* <http://ericps.ed.uiuc.edu/eeec/pubs./books/selfe.html>

Katz, Stan J. and Aimee E. Liu. 1988. *False Love and Other Romantic Illusions: Why Love Goes Wrong and How to Make It Right.* New York: Ticknor & Fields.

Kaufman, Gayle and Peter Uhlenberg. 1998. "Effects of Life Course Transitions on the Quality of Relationships between Adult Children and Their Parents." *Journal of Marriage and the Family* 60 (4):924–38.

Kazemipur, A. and S.S. Halli. 1997. "Plight of Immigrations: The Spatial Concentration of Poverty in Canada." *Canadian Journal of Regional Science* 20(1/2):29–48.

Keating, Joanne. 1998. "The Best of Times: Communicating With Your Children." http://www.canadianparents.com/articles/feature88c.htm

Keating, Norah C. 1996. "Legacy, Aging and Succession in Farm Families." *Generations* 20 (3) (fall):61–64.

Keith, Carolyn. 1995. "Family Caregiving Systems: Models, Resources, and Values." *Journal of Marriage and the Family* 57 (1) (Feb.):179–89.

Keith, Pat M. 1989. *The Unmarried in Later Life.* New York: Praeger.

Keith, Verna M. and Barbara Finlay. 1988. "The Impact of Parental Divorce on Children's Educational Attainment, Marital Timing, and Likelihood of Divorce." *Journal of Marriage and the Family* 51:797–809.

Kelly, James R. 1990. "The Koop Report and a Better Politics of Abortion." *America* 162 (21):542–46.

Kelly, Joan Berlin and Judith S. Wallerstein. 1990. *Surviving the Breakup.* New York: Basic Books.

Kelly, Karen, Linda Howatson-Leo and Warren Clark. 2000. "I Feel Overqualified for My Job." Pp. 182–187 in *Canadian Social Trends: Volume 3.* Toronto: Thompson Educational Publishing, Inc.

Kelly, Mary E. 1990. "Choice and Constraint: Nurturing Behavior in Women and Men." Paper presented at the annual meeting of the Midwest Sociological Society, Chicago, Apr. 13.

Kelly, Patricia. 1996. "Family-Centered Practice with Stepfamilies." *Journal of Contemporary Human Services* 77 (9):535–44.

Kempe, C. Henry, Frederic N. Silverman, Brandt F. Steele, William Droegemueller, and Henry K. Silver. 1962. "The Battered-Child Syndrome." *Journal of the American Medical Assn.* 181 (July 7):17–24.

Kendall, Diana, Jane Lothian Murray, Rick Linden. 2000. *Sociology In Our Times: Second Canadian Edition.* Toronto: Nelson Thomson Learning.

Kennedy, Rod Wallace. 2001. *The Encouraging Parent: How To Stop Yelling At Your Kids And Start Teaching Them Confidence, Self-Discipline, And Joy.* New York: Three Rivers Press.

Kephart, William. 1971. "Oneida: An Early American Commune." Pp. 481–92 in *Family in Transition: Rethinking Marriage, Sexuality, Child Rearing, and Family Organization,* edited by Arlene S. Skolnick and Jerome H. Skolnick. Boston: Little, Brown.

Kern, Louis J. 1981. *An Ordered Love: Sex Roles and Sexuality in Victorian Utopias—the Shakers, the Mormons, and the Oneida Community.* Chapel Hill: University of North Carolina Press.

Kerr, R. and J. McLean. 1996. *Paying for Violence: Some of the Ccosts of Violence Against Women in B.C.* Prepared for the Ministry of Women's Equality, Province of British

Columbia. <http://www.weq.gov.bc.ca/stv/payingforviolence.html>

Kettle, J. 1980. *The Big Generation.* Toronto: McClelland & Stewart.

Kheshgi-Genovese, Zareena and Thomas A. Genovese. 1997. "Developing the Spousal Relationship within Stepfamilies." *Families in Society* 78 (3):255–64.

Kiecolt, K. Jill and Mark A. Fossett. 1995. "Mate Availability and Marriage among African Americans: Aggregate and Individual Level Analyses." Pp. 121–35 in *The Decline in Marriage among African Americans: Causes, Consequences, and Policy Implications,* edited by Belinda Tucker and Claudia Mitchell-Kernan. New York: Russell Sage.

Kilborn, Peter T. 1992a. "Lives of Unexpected Poverty in Center of a Land of Plenty." *New York Times,* July 7.

Kilbourne, Jean. 1994. " 'Gender Bender' Ads: Same Old Sexism." *New York Times.* May 15, p. F–13.

Kimmel, Michael S. 1989. "From Pedestals to Partners: Men's Responses to Feminism." Pp. 581–94 in *Women: A Feminist Perspective.* 4th ed., edited by J. Freeman. Mountain View, CA: Mayfield.

———. 1995a. "Misogynists, Masculinist Mentors, and Male Supporters: Men's Responses to Feminism." Pp. 561–72 in *Women: A Feminist Perspective.* 5th ed., edited by Jo Freeman. Mountain View, CA: Mayfield.

———. 1995b. *Manhood in America: A Cultural History.* Berkeley: University of California Press.

Kimura, D. 1992. "Sex Differences in the Brain." *Scientific American.* September.

Kindlon, Dan and Michael Thompson. 1998. *Raising Cain: Protecting the Emotional Life of Boys.* London: Michael Joseph Publishers.

King, Valerie. 1994. "Variation in the Consequences of Nonresident Father Involvement for Children's Well-Being." *Journal of Marriage and the Family* 56 (3) (Nov.):963–72.

King, Valerie and Glen H. Elder, Jr. 1995. "American Children View Their Grandparents: Linked Lives Across Three Rural Generations." *Journal of Marriage and the Family* 57 (1) (Feb.):165–78.

———. 1997. "The Legacy of Grandparenting: Childhood Experiences with Grandparents and Current Involvement with Grandchildren." *Journal of Marriage and the Family* 59 (4):848–59.

Kingsbury, Nancy and John Scanzoni. 1993. "Structural-Functionalism." Pp. 195–217 in *Sourcebook of Family Theories and Methods: A Contextual Approach,* edited by Pauline G. Boss, William J. Doherty, Ralph LaRossa, Walter R. Schumm, and Suzanne K. Steinmetz. New York: Plenum.

Kingston, Paul W. 1990. "Illusions and Ignorance: About the Family-Responsive Workplace." *Journal of Family Issues* 11(4) (Dec.):438–54.

Kinsella, K. and C.M. Taeuber. 1993. *An Aging World.* Washington, D.C.: U.S. Bureau of the Census.

Kinsey, Alfred, Wardell B. Pomeroy, and Clyde E. Martin. 1948. *Sexual Behavior in the Human Male.* Philadelphia: Saunders.

———. 1953. *Sexual Behavior in the Human Female.* Philadelphia: Saunders.

Kirby, Douglas. 1995. "Sex Education." *Atlantic Monthly.* June:10–11.

Kitano, Harry and Roger Daniels. 1995. *Asian Americans: Emerging Minorities.* 2d ed. Englewood Cliffs, NJ: Prentice-Hall.

Kite, M. E. and K. Deaux. 1987. "Gender Belief Systems: Homosexuality and the Implicit Inversion Theory." *Psychology of Women Quarterly* 11:83–96.

Kleban, Morton H., Elaine M. Brody, Claire B. Schoonover, and Christine Hoffman. 1989. "Family Help to the Elderly: Perceptions of Sons-in-law Regarding Parent Care." *Journal of Marriage and the Family* 51 (2):303–12.

Klebanov, Pamela Kato, Jeanne Brooks-Gunn, and Greg Duncan. 1994. "Does Neighborhood and Family Poverty Affect Mothers' Parenting, Mental Health, and Social Support?" *Journal of Marriage and the Family* 56 (2) (May):441–55.

Kleber, Rolf J., Charles R. Figley, P. R. Barthold, and John P. Wilson. 1997. "Beyond Trauma: Cultural and Societal Dynamics." *Contemporary Psychology* 42 (6):516–27.

Klein, David M. and James K. White. 1996. *Family Theories: An Introduction.* Thousand Oaks, CA: Sage.

Klein, Marjorie H., Janet S. Hyde, Marilyn J. Essex, and Roseanne Clark. 1998. "Maternity Leave, Role Quality, Work Involvement, and Mental Health One Year after Delivery." *Psychology of Women Quarterly* 22 (2):239–66.

Klein, Matthew. 1998. "Women's Trip to the Top." *American Demographics,* February:22.

Klein, R. C. and M. P. Johnson. 1997. "Strategies of Couple Conflict." Pp. 14–39 in *Handbook of Personal Relationships: Theory, Research, and Interventions,* 2nd ed., edited by S. Duck. New York: Wiley.

Klein, Robert J. 1989. "Cutting Your Debt." Pp. 16–19 in *Money Guide: Basics of Personal Finance,* edited by Money Magazine. Spring.

Kline, Jennie, Zena Stein, Mervyn Susser, and Dorothy Warburton, eds. 1986. "Induced Abortion and the Chromosomal Characteristics of Subsequent Miscarriages (Spontaneous Abortions)." *American Journal of Epidemiology* 123:1066–79.

Kline, Marsha, Janet R. Johnston, and Jeanne M. Tschann. 1991. "The Long Shadow of Marital Conflict: A Model of Children's Postdivorce Adjustment." *Journal of Marriage and the Family* 53 (2) (May):297–309.

Kline, Marsha, Jeanne M. Tschann, Janet R. Johnston, and Judith Wallerstein. 1989. "Children's Adjustment in Joint and Sole Physical Custody Families." *Developmental Psychology* 25:430–38.

Klinetob, N.A. and C. D.A. Smith. 1996. "Demand-Withdraw Communication in Marital Interaction: Tests of Interspousal Contingency and Gender Role Hypothesis." *Journal of Marriage and the Family*, 56:945–957.

Kling, Cynthia. 1996. "Childless by Choice." *Harper's Bazaar*. June 1:134–42.

Knox, David. 1998. *The Divorced Dad's Survival Book: How to Stay Connected with Your Kids*. New York: Insight Books.

Knox, David H., Jr. 1975. *Marriage: Who? When? Why?* Englewood Cliffs, NJ: Prentice-Hall.

Knudson-Martin, Carmen and Anne Rankin Mahoney. 1998. "Language and Processes in the Construction of Equality in New Marriages." *Family Relations* 47 (1):81–91.

Kobayashi, Karen Midori. 1998. "The Nature of Support in Older Parent-Adult Child Relationships in Japanese Canadian Families." International Sociological Association (ISA).

Kobren, Gerri. 1988. "Older First-Time Moms Better Educated, Secure." *Omaha-World Herald*, Dec. 30.

Koch, Joanne and Lew Koch. 1976. "A Consumer's Guide to Therapy for Couples." *Psychology Today* 9:33–38.

Kohlberg, Lawrence. 1966. "A Cognitive-Developmental Analysis of Children's Sex-Role Concepts and Attitudes." Pp. 82–173 in *The Development of Sex Differences*, edited by Eleanor E. Maccoby. Palo Alto, CA: Stanford University Press.

Kohn, M. L. 1977. *Class and Conformity: A Study in Values*. Chicago: University of Chicago Press.

Kolata, Gina. 1987. "Tests of Fetuses Rise Sharply Amid Doubts." *New York Times*, Sept. 22.

———. 1988. "Researchers Report Miscarriages Occurring in 31% of Pregnancies." *New York Times*, July 27.

———. 1989a. "Growing Movement Seeks to Help Women Infected with AIDS Virus." *New York Times*, May 4.

———. 1989b. "Lesbian Partners Finding the Means to Be Parents." *New York Times*, Jan. 30.

Komter, A. 1989. "Hidden Power in Marriage." *Gender and Society* 3:187–216.

Kong, Rebecca. 1997. "Criminal Harassment in Canada." *Canadian Social Trends* 45 (autumn):29–33.

———. 1999. "Criminal Harassment." Pp. 213–224 in Canadian Centre for Justice Statistics, *The Juristat Reader: A Statistical Overview of the Canadian Justice System*. Toronto: Thompson Educational Publishing, Inc.

———. 2000. "Stalking: Criminal Harassment in Canada." Pp. 232–236 in *Canadian Social Trends: Volume 3*. Toronto: Thompson Educational Publishing, Inc.

Konner, Melvin. 1990. "Women and Sexuality." *New York Times Magazine*, Apr. 29, pp. 24, 26.

Kornfein, Madeleine, Thomas S. Weisner, and Joan C. Martin. 1979. "Women into Mothers: Experimental Family Life-Styles." Pp. 259–91 in *Women into Wives: The Legal and Economic Impact of Marriage*, edited by Jane Roberts Chapman and Margaret Gates. Newbury Park, CA: Sage.

Korte, Diana. 1995. "Midwives on Trial." *Mothering* (fall):52–63.

Kosciulek, J. F. and D. C. Lustig. 1998. "Predicting Family Adaptation from Brain Injury-Related Family Stress." *Journal of Applied Rehabilitation Counseling* 29 (1):8–19.

Kotsopoulos, Sotiris, Selena Walker, Winona Copping, Andre Cote et al. 1993. "A Psychiatric Follow-Up Study of Adoptees." *Canadian Journal of Psychiatry* 38(6)(August):381–396.

Kowaleski-Jones, Lori and Frank L. Mott. 1998. "Sex, Contraception and Childbearing among High-Risk Youth: Do Different Factors Influence Males and Females?" *Family Planning Perspectives* 30(4): 163–9.

Kozol, Jonathan. 1995. *Amazing Grace: The Lives of Children and The Conscience of a Nation*. New York: HarperPerennial.

Kraft, Joan Marie and James E. Coverdill. 1994. "Employment and the Use of Birth Control by Sexually Active Single Hispanic, Black, and White Women." *Demography* 31 (4) (Nov.):593–602.

Kramarow, Ellen A. 1995. "The Elderly Who Live Alone in the United States: Historical Perspectives on Household Change." *Demography* 32 (3) (Aug.):335–52.

Kraus, L. A., M. H. Davis, D. Bazzini, M. B. Church, and C. M. Kirchman. 1993. "Personal and Social Influences on Loneliness: The Mediating Effect of Social Provisions." *Social Psychology Quarterly* 56:37–53.

Krementz, Jill. 1984. *How It Feels When Parents Divorce*. New York: Knopf.

Kreppner, Kurt. 1988. "Changes in Parent–Child Relationships with the Birth of the Second Child." *Marriage and Family Review* 12 (3–4):157–81.

Krieger, Lisa M. 1995. "AIDS Loses Urgency in Nation's List of Worries." *San Francisco Examiner*, Jan. 29, pp. A1, A9.

Krokoff, Lowell J. 1987. "The Correlates of Negative Affect in Marriage: An Exploratory Study of Gender Differences." *Journal of Family Issues* 8:111–35.

Krolewiec, Stanislaw.n.d. "First European Christian Polygamy Page: Polygamy in Canada." <http://www.nccg.org/fecpp/canada.html>

Kroska, Amy. 1997. "The Division of Labor in the Home: A Review and Reconceptualization." *Social Psychology Quarterly* 60 (4):304–22.

Krotki, Karol J. 1999. Baby Boom. In *The Canadian Encyclopedia: Year 2000 Edition* (p. 173). Toronto: McClelland & Stewart Inc.

Krotki, Karol J. and Colin Reid. 1994. "Demography of Canadian Population by Ethnic Group." Pp. 17–59 in

Ethnicity and Culture in Canada: The Research Landscape, edited by J.W. Berry and J.A. Laponce. Toronto: University of Toronto Press.

Kruk, Edward. 1991. "Discontinuity Between Pre- and Post-Divorce Father–Child Relationships: New Evidence Regarding Paternal Disengagement." *Journal of Divorce and Remarriage* 16 (3/4):195–227.

Kruttschnitt, Candace, Jane D. McLeod, and Maude Dornfeld. 1994. "The Economic Environment of Child Abuse." *Social Problems* 41 (2) (May):299–315.

Ku, Leighton, Freya L. Sonnenstein and Joseph H. Pleck. 1995. "When We Use Condoms and Why We Stop." *Population Today* (March): 3.

Kübler-Ross, Elisabeth. 1979. *On Death and Dying*. New York: Macmillan.

Kuczynski, Leon. 1998. "Corporal Punishment Debate: The Play of Values and Perspective." *Family Science Network*. November 7. famlysci@lsv.uky.edu.

Kuhn, Manfred. 1955. "How Mates Are Sorted." *In Family, Marriage, and Parenthood*, edited by Howard Becker and Reuben Hill. Boston: Heath.

Kulig, Judith C. 1998. "Family Life Among El Salvadorans, Guatemalans and Nicaraguans: A Comparative Study." *Journal of Comparative Family Studies* 29(3)(autumn):469–479.

Kunz, Jean Lock, Anne Milan and Sylvain Schetagne. 2001. *Unequal Access: A Canadian Profile of Racial Differences in Education, Employment, and Income*. Ottawa: Canadian Race Relations Foundation.

Kunz, Jean Lock, Anne Milan and Sylvain Schetage. 2000. "Unequal Access: A Report Card on Racism." *Perception* 24(3)(December). <http://www.ccsd.ca/perception/243.racism.htm>

Kurdek, Lawrence A. 1989a. "Relationship Quality for Newly Married Husbands and Wives: Marital History, Stepchildren, and Individual-Difference Predictors." *Journal of Marriage and the Family* 51 (4) (Nov.):1053–64.

———. 1989b. "Relationship Quality in Gay and Lesbian Cohabiting Couples: A 1-Year Follow-up Study." *Journal of Social and Personal Relationships* 6:35–59.

———. 1991. "The Relations Between Reported Well-being and Divorce History, Availability of a Proximate Adult, and Gender." *Journal of Marriage and the Family* 53 (1) (Feb.):71–78.

———. 1994. "Areas of Conflict for Gay, Lesbian, and Heterosexual Couples: What Couples Argue About Influences Relationship Satisfaction." *Journal of Marriage and the Family* 56 (4) (Nov.):923–34.

———. 1995a. "Assessing Multiple Determinants of Relationship Commitment in Cohabiting Gay, Cohabiting Lesbian, Dating Heterosexual, and Married Heterosexual Couples." *Family Relations* 44:261–66.

———. 1995b. "Predicting Change in Marital Satisfaction from Husbands' and Wives' Conflict Resolution Styles." *Journal of Marriage and the Family* 57 (1) (Feb.):153–64.

———. 1996. "The Deterioration of Relationship Quality for Gay and Lesbian Cohabiting Couples: A Five-year Prospective Longitudinal Study." *Personal Relationships* 3:417–42.

———. 1998. "Relationship Outcomes and Their Predictors: Longitudinal Evidence from Heterosexual Married, Gay Cohabiting, and Lesbian Cohabiting Couples." *Journal of Marriage and the Family* 60 (3):553–68.

Kurdek, Lawrence A. and Mark A. Fine. 1991. "Cognitive Correlates of Satisfaction for Mothers and Stepfathers in Stepfather Families." *Journal of Marriage and the Family* 53 (3) (Aug.):565–72.

———. 1995. "Mothers, Fathers, Stepfathers, and Siblings as Providers of Supervision, Acceptance, and Autonomy to Young Adolescents." *Journal of Family Psychology* 9 (1):95–9.

Kurz, Demie. 1993. "Physical Assaults by Husbands: A Major Social Problem." Pp. 88–103 in *Current Controversies on Family Violence*, edited by Richard J. Gelles and Donileen R. Loseke. Newbury Park, CA: Sage.

———. 1997. "Doing Parenting: Mothers, Care Work, and Policy." Pp. 68–91 in *Contemporary Parenting: Challenges and Issues*, edited by Terry Arendell. Thousand Oaks, CA: Sage.

Kutner, Lawrence. 1988a. "Parent & Child: Parents Change: Children Must Too." *New York Times*, Mar. 24.

———. 1988b. "Parent and Child: Working at Home; or, The Midday Career Change." *New York Times*, Dec. 8.

———. 1989a. "Parent & Child: 'The Forgotten Mourners': Help for Adults Whose Sibling Has Died." *New York Times*, Dec. 21.

———. 1989b. "Parent & Child: When Mom and Dad Do Not Agree on Discipline, the Child May Take Advantage of the Confusion." *New York Times*, Sept. 21.

———. 1990a. "Parent & Child: Chasms of Pain and Growth: When Generation Gaps Are Too Wide to Leap." *New York Times*, Mar. 8.

———. 1990b. "Parent & Child: Confronting Mother and Father About Their Battles and the Effect It Has on the Family." *New York Times*, Mar. 29.

———. 1990c. "Parent & Child: Money Matters, for Some as Confidential as Sex, Are Often A Stressful Subject." *New York Times*, Jan. 11.

———. 1990d. "Parent & Child: When a Child Marries: The Pride and the Pitfalls." *New York Times*, May 10.

———. 1991. "Parent & Child: First Comes the Baby, Then Anger and Frustration When Not All Goes According to Expectations." *New York Times*, Nov. 7.

K-W Record. 1999. "What's Up With Viagra Decision?" November 25: A16.

———.2001. "Adoption is rarely an option." September 29: A1, A6.

L

Lacayo, Richard. 1989a. "Whose Life Is It?" *Time*, May 1, pp. 20–24.

Lackey, Chad and Kirk R. Williams. 1995. "Social Bonding and the Cessation of Partner Violence Across Generations." *Journal of Marriage and the Family* 57 (2) (May):295–305.

Ladner, Joyce A. 1977. "Mixed Families: White Parents and Black Children." *Society* (Sept./Oct.):70–78.

———. 1984. "Providing a Healthy Environment for Interracial Children." *Interracial Books for Children Bulletin* 15 (6):7–9.

Lafrance, Marianne, Hiram Brownell and Eugene Hahn. 1997. "Interpersonal Verbs, Gender, and Implicit Causality." *Social Psychology Quarterly* 60 (2):138–52.

Laing, Ronald D. 1971. *The Politics of the Family*. New York: Random House.

Lally, Catherine F. and James W. Maddock. 1994. "Sexual Meaning Systems of Engaged Couples." *Family Relations* 43:53–60.

Lamanna, Mary Ann. 1977. "The Value of Children to Natural and Adoptive Parents." Ph.D. dissertation, Department of Sociology, University of Notre Dame.

Lambert, Marjorie E. 1998. *Constructing Ethnic Identity in Canada: The Case of Kurds From Turkey*. Unpublished MA thesis, Department of Sociology, University of Waterloo.

Lambert, Ronald D. and James E. Curtis. 1984. "Quebecois and English Canadian Opposition to Racial and Religious Intermarriage, 1968-1983." *Canadian Ethnic Studies*, 16(2):30–46.

Langan, P. and C. Innes. 1986. *Preventing Domestic Violence Against Women*. Bureau of Justice Statistics. Washington, DC: Department of Justice.

Langhinrichsen-Rohling, Jennifer, Natalie Smutzler, and Dina Vivian. 1994. "Positivity in Marriage: The Role of Discord and Physical Aggression Against Wives." *Journal of Marriage and the Family* 56 (1) (Feb.):69–79.

Langley, Patricia. 1988. Reproductive Technology Fact Sheet. Unpublished.

LaRossa, Ralph. 1979. *Conflict and Power in Marriage: Expecting the First Child*. Newbury Park, CA: Sage.

Lapierre-Adamcyk, Evelyne, Le Bourdais, Celine, and Nicole Marcil-Gratton. 1999. "Living As A Couple For The First Time: The Significance Of The Choice Of Cohabitation In Quebec And Ontario." *Cahiers quebecois de demographie* 28 (1-2)(spring-autumn):199–227.

Laroche, M. 1998. "In and Out of Low Income." *Canadian Social Trends* 40:20–24.

Laroche, M. et al. 1996. "An Empirical Study Of Multidimensional Ethnic Change: The Case Of The French Canadians In Quebec." *Journal of Cross-Cultural Psychology* 27 (1):114–31.

LaRossa, Ralph and Donald C. Reitzes. 1993. "Symbolic Interactionism and Family Studies." Pp. 135–63 in *Sourcebook of Family Theories and Methods: A Contextual Approach*, edited by Pauline G. Boss, William J. Doherty, Ralph LaRossa, Walter R. Schumm, and Suzanne K. Steinmetz. New York: Plenum.

Larson, D. 1991. "Grandparent: Redefining the Role." *Modern Maturity*. December/January:31–38.

Larson, Jeffry H., Shannon M. Anderson, Thomas B. Holman, and Brand K. Niemann. 1998. "A Longitudinal Study of the Effects of Premarital Communication, Relationship Stability, and Self-Esteem on Sexual Satisfaction in the First Year of Marriage." *Journal of Sex & Marital Therapy* 24:193–206.

Larson, Lyle, J. Walter Goltz and Brenda E. Munro. 2000. *Families in Canada: Social Contexts, Continuities, and Changes*. 2nd ed. Toronto: Prentice Hall.

Larson, R. and M. Ham. 1993. "Stress and 'Storm and Stress' in Early Adolescence: The Relationship of Negative Events with Dysphoric Affect." *Developmental Psychology* 29:130–40.

Larzelere, Robert E. 1993. "Response to Oosterhuis: Empirically Justified Uses of Spanking: Toward a Discriminating View of Corporal Punishment." *Journal of Psychology and Theology* 21 (2):142–59.

———. 1996. "Presentation: Implications of the Strongest Studies for Discriminating Effective versus Counterproductive Corporal Punishment." *Pediatrics* 98:824–27.

Larzelere, Robert E. and Jack A. Merenda. 1994. "The Effectiveness of Parental Discipline for Toddler Misbehavior at Different Levels of Child Distress." *Family Relations* 43 (4):480–89.

Larzelere, Robert E., Paul R. Sather, William N. Schneider, David B. Larson, and Patricia L. Pike. 1998. "Punishment Enhances Reasoning's Effectiveness As a Disciplinary Response to Toddlers." *Journal of Marriage and the Family* 60 (2):388–403.

Larzelere, Robert E., William N. Schneider, David B. Larson, and Patricia L. Pike. 1996. "The Effects of Discipline Responses in Delaying Toddler Misbehavior Recurrences." *Child and Family Behavior Therapy* 18 (3):35–51.

Larzelere, Robert E. 2000. "Child Outcomes of Nonabusive and Customary Physical Punishment by Parents: An Updated Literature Review." *Clinical Child & Family Psychology Review*, vol. 3 (4) (December):199–221.

Larzelere, Robert E. and Byron Johnson. 1999. "Evaluations Of The Effects Of Sweden's Spanking Ban On Physical Child Abuse Rates: A Literature Review." *Psychological Reports* 85 (2)(October):381–392.

Lasch, Christopher. 1977. *Haven in a Heartless World: The Family Besieged*. New York: Basic Books.

———. 1980. *The Culture of Narcissism.* New York: Warner.

Laslett, Peter. 1971. *The World We Have Lost: England Before the Industrial Age.* 2d ed. New York: Scribner's.

Lauer, Jeanette and Robert Lauer. 1985. "Marriages Made to Last." *Psychology Today,* June.

Laumann, Edward O., John H. Gagnon, Robert T. Michael, and Stuart Michaels. 1994. *The Social Organization of Sexuality: Sexual Practices in the United States.* Chicago: University of Chicago Press.

Lauritzen, Paul. 1990. "What Price Parenthood?" *Hastings Center Report* (Mar./Apr.):38–46.

Lavoie, Yolande and Jillian Oderkirk. 2000. "Social Consequences of Demographic Change." Pp. 2–5 in *Canadian Social Trends: Volume 3.* Toronto: Thompson Educational Publishing, Inc.

Lawlor, Julia. 1997. "The New Breadwinner." *Working Mother.* June:12–17.

Lawson, Carol. 1990. "Fathers, Too, Are Seeking a Balance Between Their Families and Careers." *New York Times,* Apr. 12.

Lawson, Erma Jean. 2000. *Black Men and Divorce.* Thousand Oaks, CA: Sage.

Lawton, Leora, Merril Silverstein, and Vern Bengston. 1994. "Affection, Social Contact, and Geographic Distance Between Adult Children and Their Parents." *Journal of Marriage and the Family* 56 (1) (Feb.):57–68.

Layton-Tholl, Debbie. 1998. "Extramarital affairs: What is the Allure?" <members.aol.com/affairlady/affair.html>

Leach, Penelope. 1994. *Children First.* New York: Knopf.

Leaper, C. 1994. "Exploring the Consequences of Gender Segregation on Social Relationships." In *Childhood Gender Segregation: Causes and Consequences.* San Francisco: Jossey-Bass.

Leary, Warren E. 1988. "Experts Caution Against Repeated Caesareans and Recommend Natural Deliveries." *New York Times,* Oct. 27.

———. 1991. "Hypertension Among Blacks Tied to Bias, Poverty, and Diet." *New York Times,* Feb. 6.

———. 1999. A Contraceptive Returns to the Market." *New York Times,* March 30.

Le Bourdais, Celine, Ghyslaine Neill and Nicole Marcil-Gratton. 2000. "The Effect Of Type Of Union On The Stability Of So-Called 'Intact' Families." *Recherches Sociographiques* 41 (4)(Jan-April):53–74.

Le Bourdais, Celine, Ghyslaine Neill and Pierre Turcotte. 2000. "The Changing Face Of Conjugal Relationships." *Canadian Social Trends* (Spring):14–17. Statistics Canada, Catalogue No. 11-008.

Le Bourdais, C. and N. Marcil-Gratton. 1996. "Family Transformations across the Canadian-American Border: When the Laggard becomes the Leader." *Journal of Comparative Family Studies* 27 (2):415–36.

Le Bourdais, Celine, Gyslaine Neill and Nathalie Vachon. 2000. "Family Disruption In Canada: Impact Of The Changing Patterns Of Family Formation And Of Female Employment." *Canadian Studies in Population* 27 (1):85–105.

LeClere, Felicia B. and Brenda M. Kowalewski. 1994. "Disability in the Family: The Effects on Children's Well-Being." *Journal of Marriage and the Family* 56 (2) (May):457–68.

Lee, Betty Kaman and Ling Chen. 2000. "Cultural Communication Competence And Psychological Adjustment: A Study Of Chinese Immigrant Children's Cross-Cultural Adaptation In Canada." *Communication Research* 27 (6)(December):764–792.

Lee, Gary R., Julie K. Netzer, and Raymond T. Coward. 1994. "Filial Responsibility Expectations and Patterns of Intergenerational Assistance." *Journal of Marriage and the Family* 56 (3) (Aug.):559–65.

Lee, Gary R., Chuck W. Peek, and Raymond T. Coward. 1998. "Race Differences in Filial Responsibility Expectations among Older Parents." *Journal of Marriage and the Family* 60 (2):404–12.

Lee, Gary R., Karen Seccombe and Constance L. Shehan. 1991. "Marital Status and Personal Happiness: An Analysis of Trend Data." *Journal of Marriage and the Family* 55: 839–44.

Lee, Gary R. and Constance L. Shehan. 1989. "Retirement and Marital Satisfaction." *Journal of Gerontology* 44:S226–30.

Lee, John Alan. 1973. *The Colours of Love.* Toronto: New Press.

———. 1981. "Forbidden Colors of Love: Patterns of Gay Love." Pp. 128–39 in *Single Life: Unmarried Adults in Social Context,* edited by Peter J. Stein. New York: St. Martins.

———. 1999. "Homosexuality." Pp. 1095–1096 in *The Canadian Enclobedia: Year 2000 Edition,* edited by James Marsh. Toronto: McClelland & Stewart Inc.

Leerhsen, Charles. 1985. "Reading, Writing and Divorce." *Newsweek,* May 13, p. 74.

Lehrer, Evelyn L. and Carmel U. Chiswick. 1993. "Religion as a Determinant of Marital Stability." *Demography,* 30:385–403.

Leibowitz, Arleen and Jacob Alex Klerman. 1995. "Explaining Changes in Married Mothers' Employment over Time." *Demography* 32 (3) (Aug.):365–78.

Leitch, M. Laurie. 1998. "Contextual Issues in Teen Pregnancy and Parenting: Refining Our Scope of Inquiry." *Family Relations* 47 (2):145–47.

Leiter, Michael P and Marie Josette Durup. 1996. "Work, Home And In-Between: A Longitudinal Study Of Spillover." *The Journal of Applied Behavioral Science* 32 (1)(March):29–47.

Leland, John. 1995. "Bisexuality." *Newsweek*, July 17, pp. 44–50.

———. 1996. "The End of AIDS?" *Newsweek*. December 2:64–73.

———. 1997. "A Pill for Impotence?" *Newsweek*. November 17:62–8.

Leland, Nancy Lee, Donna Petersen, Mary Braddock, and Greg Alexander. 1995. "Variations in Pregnancy Outcomes by Race among 10–14-Year-Old Mothers in the United States." *Public Health Reports* 110 (1)(Jan.-Feb.):53–8.

LeMasters, E. E. and John DeFrain. 1989. *Parents in Contemporary America: A Sympathetic View*, 5th ed. Belmont, CA: Wadsworth.

Lennon, Mary Clare and Sarah Rosenfield. 1994. "Relative Fairness and the Division of Housework: The Importance of Options." *American Journal of Sociology* 100 (2) (Sept.):506–31.

Lenz, Elinor and Barbara Myerhoff. 1985. *The Feminization of America*. Los Angeles: Tarcher (St. Martin's).

Leslie, Leigh A. and Bethany Letiecq. 1999. "Marital Quality of Interracial Couples." Paper presented at the 61st Annual Conference of the National Council on Family Relations, Irvine, CA, Nov. 12–15.

Letiecq, Bethany L., Elaine A. Anderson, and Sally A. Koblinsky. 1996. "Social Support of Homeless and Permanently Housed Low-Income Mothers with Young Children." *Family Relations* 45 (3):265–72.

Levay, Alexander N., Lawrence Sharpe, and Arlene Kagel. 1981. "The Effects of Physical Illness on Sexual Functioning." Pp. 169–90 in *Sexual Problems in Medical Practice*, edited by Harold I. Lief, M.D. Monroe, WI: American Medical Association.

LeVay, S. and D. H. Hamer. 1994. "Evidence for a Biological Influence in Male Homosexuality." *Scientific American* (May).

Lever, Janet. 1995. "Bringing the Fundamentals of Gender Studies into Safer-Sex Education." *Family Planning Perspectives* 27 (4):170–74.

Levin, Irene. 1997. "Stepfamily as Project." Pp. 123–33 in *Stepfamilies: History, Research, and Policy*, edited by Irene Levin and Marvin B. Sussman. New York: Haworth Press.

Levine, Elizabeth. 2001. "Living Together Can Double Separation Risk: Statscan Finding Applies To Couples Who Have Children." *National Post*, June 23. *Canada.com.* <wysiwyg://13/http://www.canada.com/cgi-bi...nationalpost/stories/200106 12/599934.html?>

Levine, Robert, Suguru Sato, Tsukasa Hashimoto, and Jyoti Verma. 1995. "Love and Marriage in Eleven Cultures." *Journal of Cross-Cultural Psychology* 26 (5):554–71.

Levine, Stephen B. 1998. "Extramarital Sexual Affairs." *Journal of Sex & Marital Therapy* 24:207–16.

Levinger, George. 1965. "Marital Cohesiveness and Dissolution: An Integrative Review." *Journal of Marriage and the Family* 27:19–28.

Levinson, David. 1989. *Family Violence in Cross-Cultural Perspective*. Newbury Park, CA: Sage.

Levinson, D.J. 1996. *The Seasons of a Woman's Life*. New York: Alfred A. Knopf.

Levitan, Sar A., Garth L. Mangum, and Stephen L. Mangum. 1998. *Programs in Aid of the Poor*, 7th edition. Baltimore: John Hopkins University Press.

Levy, Barrie, ed. 1991. *Dating Violence: Young Women in Danger*. Seattle, WA: Seal Press.

Levy-Shiff, R. 1994. "Individual and Contextual Correlates of Marital Change Across the Transition to Parenthood." *Developmental Psychology* 30:591–601.

Lewin, Tamar. 1989a. "Family or Career? Choose, Women Told." *New York Times*, Mar. 8.

———. 1989b. "Small Tots, Big Biz." *New York Times Magazine*, Jan. 29, pp. 30–31, 89–92.

———. 1990. "Father's Vanishing Act Called Common Drama." *New York Times*, June 4.

———. 1992. "Rise in Single Parenthood Is Reshaping U.S." *New York Times*, Oct. 5.

Lewis, Robert A., Phillip J. Freneau, and Craig L. Roberts. 1979. "Fathers and the Postparental Transition." *Family Coordinator* 28:514–20.

L'Heureux-Dubé, Claire. 1998. "A Response to Remarks by Dr. Judith Wallerstein on the Long-Term Impact of Divorce on Children." *Family and Conciliation Courts Review* 36 (3):384–86.

Libby, Roger W. 1976. "Social Scripts for Sexual Relationships." In *Sexuality Today and Tomorrow*, edited by Sol Gordon and Roger W. Libby. North Scituate, MA: Duxbury.

Lichter, Daniel T., Robert N. Anderson, and Mark D. Hayward. 1995. "Marriage Markets and Marital Choice." *Journal of Family Issues* 16 (4) (July):412–31.

Lichter, Daniel T. and David J. Eggebeen. 1994. "The Effect of Parental Employment on Child Poverty." *Journal of Marriage and the Family* 56 (3) (Aug.):633–45.

Lichter, Daniel T. and Nancy S. Landale. 1995. "Parental Work, Family Structure, and Poverty Among Latino Children." *Journal of Marriage and the Family* 57 (2) (May):346–54.

Lichter, Daniel T., Felicia B. LeClere, and Diane K. McLaughlin. 1991. "Local Marriage Markets and the Marital Behavior of Black and White Women." *American Journal of Sociology* 96 (4) (Jan.):843–67.

Lieberson, Stanley and Mary Waters. 1988. *From Many Strands*. New York: Russell Sage Foundation.

Lieblich, Julia. 1998. "Non-Christian Summer Camps for Kids Combine Fun, Faith." *Saint Paul Pioneer Press*. July 19:3G.

Liebow, Elliot. 1967. *Tally's Corner*. Boston: Little, Brown.

Lillard, L.A., M.J. Brien and L.J. Waite. 1995. "Premarital Cohabitation and Subsequent Marital Dissolution: A Matter of Self-Selection?" *Demography*, 32(3):437–57.

Lillard, Lee Al. and Linda J. Waite. 1995. "Til Death Do Us Part: Marital Disruption and Mortality." *American Journal of Sociology*, 110:1131–1156.

Lin, Chien and William T. Liu. 1993. "Relationships Among Chinese Immigrant Families." Pp. 271–86 in *Family Ethnicity: Strength in Diversity*, edited by Harriette Pipes McAdoo. Newbury Park, CA: Sage.

Lindberg, Laura Duberstein. 1996. "Women's Decisions about Breastfeeding and Maternal Employment." *Journal of Marriage and the Family* 58 (1):239–51.

Lindsey, Elizabeth W. 1998. "The Impact of Homelessness and Shelter Life on Family Relationships." *Family Relations* 47 (3):243–52.

Linton, Sally. 1971. "Woman the Gatherer: Male Bias in Anthropology." In *Women in Cross-Cultural Perspective*, edited by Lenore Jacobs. Champaign-Urbana: University of Illinois Press.

Lipman, Ellen L. and David R. Offord. 1997. "Psychosocial Morbidity Among Poor Children in Ontario." Pp. 239–287 in *Consequences of Growing Up Poor*, edited by Greg J. Duncan and Jeanne Brooks-Gunn. New York: Russell Sage Foundation.

Lipman, Joanne. 1993. "The Nanny Trap." *The Wall Street Journal*, April 14, pp. A1, A8.

Lipmen-Blumen, Jean. 1984. *Gender Roles and Power*. Englewood Cliffs, NJ: Prentice-Hall.

Lips, Hilary M. 1995. "Gender-Role Socialization: Lessons in Femininity." Pp. 128–48 in *Women: A Feminist Perspective*. 5th ed., edited by Jo Freeman. Mountain View, CA: Mayfield.

———. 1999. *A New Psychology of Women: Gender, Culture and Ethnicity*. Mountain View, CA: Mayfield Publishing Company.

Lloyd, Kim M. and Scott J. South. 1996. "Contextual Influences on Young Men's Transition to First Marriage." *Social Forces* 74:1097–1119.

Locke, Daisy. 2000. "Violence Against Children and Youth by Family Members." Pp. 31–37 in Statistics Canada, *Family Violence in Canada: A Statistical Profile 2000*. Catalogue no. 84-225-XIE. Ottawa: Minister of Industry.

———. 2000a. ""Family Homicide." Pp. 39–44 in Statistics Canada, *Family Violence in Canada: A Statistical Profile 2000*. Catalogue 84-225-XIE. Ottawa: Minister of Indsutry.

Lockhart, L.L., White, B.W., V. Causby and A. Issac. 1994. "Letting Out the Secret: Violence in Lesbian Relationships." *Journal of Interpersonal Violence*, 9 (4):469–492.

Loeber, Rolf and Magda Stouthamer-Loeber. 1986. "Family Factors as Correlates and Predictors of Juvenile Conduct Problems and Delinquency." Pp. 29–149 in *Crime and Justice*, vol. 7, edited by Michael Tonry and Normal Morris. Chicago: University of Chicago Press.

Lofas, Jeannette. 1998. *Family Rules: Helping Stepfamilies and Single Parents Build Happy Homes*. New York: Kensington Books.

London, Kathryn A. 1991. *Advance Data Number 194: Cohabitation, Marriage, Marital Dissolution, and Remarriage: United States, 1988*. U.S. Department of Health and Human Services: Vital and Health Statistics of the National Center, Jan. 4.

Long, Linda. 1999. "Abortion." Pp.3–4 in *The Canadian Encyclopedia: Year 2000 Edition*, edited by James Marsh. Toronto: McClelland & Stewart Inc.

Longman, Philip J. (1998, March 30). "The Cost of Children." *U.S. News & World Report*, p. 51–8.

Longmore, Monica A. 1998. "Symbolic Interactionism and the Study of Sexuality." *The Journal of Sex Research* 35 (1):44–57.

Longmore, Monica A. and Alfred Demaris. 1997. "Perceived Inequality and Depression in Intimate Relationships: The Moderating Effect of Self-Esteem." *Social Psychology Quarterly* 60 (2):172–81.

Lonsdorf, Barbara J. 1991. "The Role of Coercion in Affecting Women's Inferior Outcomes in Divorce: Implications for Researchers and Therapists." *Journal of Divorce and Remarriage* 16 (1/2):69–106.

Lopata, Helan Znaniecki. 1973. "Living Through Widowhood." *Psychology Today* 7:87–92.

Lopez, Frederick G. 1995. "Contemporary Attachment Theory: An Introduction with Implications for Counseling Psychology." *The Counseling Psychologist* 23 (3):395–412.

Lorenz, Frederick O., Ronald L. Simons, Rand D. Conger, and Glen H. Elder Jr. 1997. "Married and Recently Divorced Mothers' Stressful Events and Distress: Tracing Change across Time." *Journal of Marriage and the Family* 59 (1):219–32.

Losh-Hesselbart, Susan. 1987. "Development of Gender Roles." Pp. 535–64 in *Handbook of Marriage and the Family*, edited by Marvin B. Sussman and Suzanne K. Steinmetz. New York: Plenum.

Louv, Richard, 1996. "What Do Mothers Really Want." *Parents*. May:38–40.

"Loving Care." 1997. *Modern Maturity*. May/June:92.

Lowen, A. 1985. *Narcissism: Denial of the True Self*. New York: Macmillan.

Lowinsky, Naomi Ruth. 1992. *Stories from the Motherline: Reclaiming the Mother-Daughter Bond, Finding Our Feminine Souls*. Los Angeles: Jeremy P. Tarcher.

Lublin, Joann S. 1992. "Spouses Find Themselves Worlds Apart as Global Commuter Marriages Increase." *The Wall Street Journal*, Aug. 19, pp. B1, B6.

Luciano, Lani. 1989. "Saving for Retirement." Pp. 84–87 in *Money Guide: Basics of Personal Finance*, edited by Money Magazine. Spring.

Luescher, Kurt and Karl Pillemer. 1998. "Intergenerational Ambivalence: A New Approach to the Study of Parent–Child Relations in Later Life." *Journal of Marriage and the Family* 60 (2):413–25.

Luke, Carmen. 1994. "White Women in Interracial Families: Reflections on Hybridization, Feminine Identities, and Racialized Othering." *Feminist Issues* 14 (2):49–72.

Luker, Kristin. 1984. *Abortion and Politics of Motherhood*. Berkeley: University of California Press.

———. 1990. Interviewed by Margo Adler on "Morning Edition." *National Public Radio*, May 14.

———. 1997. *Dubious Conceptions: The Politics of Teenage Pregnancy*. Cambridge: Harvard University Press.

Luster, Tom, Robert Boger, and Kristi Hannan. 1993. "Infant Affect and Home Environment." *Journal of Marriage and the Family* 55 (3) (Aug.):651–61.

Luster, Tom, Kelly Rhoades, and Bruce Haas. 1989. "The Relation Between Parental Values and Parenting Behavior: A Test of the Kohn Hypothesis." *Journal of Marriage and the Family* 51:139–47.

Luster, Tom and Stephen A. Small. 1994. "Factors Associated with Sexual Risk-Taking Behaviors Among Adolescents." *Journal of Marriage and the Family* 56 (3) (Aug.):622–32.

———. 1997. "Sexual Abuse History and Problems in Adolescence: Exploring the Effects of Moderating Variables." *Journal of Marriage and the Family* 59 (1):131–42.

Lye, Diane N., Daniel H. Klepinger, Patricia Davis Hyle, and Anjanette Nelson. 1995. "Childhood Living Arrangements and Adult Children's Relations with Their Parents." *Demography* 32 (2) (May):261–80.

Lynd, Robert S. and Helen Merrell Lynd. 1929. *Middletown: A Study in American Culture*. New York: Harcourt & Brace.

Lytton, H. and D. M. Romney. 1991. "Parents' Differential Socialization of Boys and Girls: A Meta-analysis." *Psychological Bulletin* 109:267–96.

M

MacCharles, Tonda. 2001. "Ex-NBA Player Accuses 'Racist' Lover." *Toronto Star*, June 15.

———. 2001a. "Top Court Set to Decide Custody of Mixed-Race Boy: White, Single Mother Fighting Rich, Black Father." *Toronto Star*, July 13: A1.

Maccoby, Eleanor E., Charlene E. Depner, and Robert H. Mnookin. 1990. "Coparenting in the Second Year after Divorce." *Journal of Marriage and the Family* 52 (1) (Feb.):141–55.

Maccoby, Eleanor E. and Carol Nagy Jacklin. 1974. *The Psychology of Sex Differences*. Stanford, CA: Stanford University Press.

Maccoby, Eleanor E. and J. A. Martin. 1983. "Socialization in the Context of the Family: Parent–Child Interaction." Pp. 1–101 in *Handbook of Child Psychology*, vol. 4, *Socialization, Personality, and Social Development*, edited by E. Mavis Hetherington. New York: Wiley.

MacDonald, Cameron L. 1998. "Manufacturing Motherhood: The Shadow Work of Nannies and Au Pairs." *Qualitative Sociology* 21 (1):25–53.

MacDonald, William L. and Alfred DeMaris. 1995. "Remarriage, Stepchildren, and Marital Conflict: Challenges to the Incomplete Institutionalization Hypothesis." *Journal of Marriage and the Family* 57 (2) (May):387–98.

Macionis, John J., Juanne Nancarrow Clarke and Linda M. Gerber. 1997. *Sociology: Second Canadian Edition*. Scarborough: Prentice Hall Allyn and Bacon Canada.

Mackey, Richard A. 1997. *Gay and Lesbian Couples: Voices from Lasting Relationships*. Westport, CT: Praeger.

Mackey, Richard A. and Bernard A. O'Brien. 1995. *Lasting Marriages: Men and Women Growing Together*. Westport, CT: Praeger.

———. 1998. "Marital Conflict Management: Gender and Ethnic Differences." *Social Work* 43 (2):128–41.

Macklin, Eleanor D. 1983. "Nonmarital Heterosexual Cohabitation: An Overview." Pp. 49–74 in *Contemporary Families and Alternative Lifestyles: Handbook on Theory and Research*, edited by Eleanor D. Macklin and Roger H. Rubin. Newbury Park, CA: Sage.

———. 1987. "Nontraditional Family Forms." Pp. 317–53 in *Handbook of Marriage and the Family*, edited by Marvin B. Sussman and Suzanne K. Steinmetz. New York: Plenum.

———. 1988. "AIDS: Implications for Families." *Family Relations* 37 (Apr.):141–49.

MacNeil, Sheila and E. Sandra Byers. 1997. "The Relationship Between Sexual Problems, Communication, And Sexual Satisfaction." *The Canadian Journal of Human Sexuality* 6:277–284.

Maddock, J. W., M. J. Hogan, A. L. Antonove, and M. S. Matskovsky,Eds. 1993. *Peristroika and Family Life: Post-USSR and US Perspectives*. New York: Guilford.

Magdol, Lynn, Terrie E. Moffitt, Avshalom Caspi, and Phil A. Silva. 1998. "Hitting Without a License: Testing Explanations for Differences in Partner Abuse between Young Adult Daters and Cohabitors." *Journal of Marriage and the Family* 60 (1):41–55.

Mahoney, Margaret M. 1997. "Stepfamilies from a Legal Perspective." Pp. 231–47 in *Stepfamilies: History, Research, and Policy*, edited by Irene Levin and Marvin B. Sussman. New York: Haworth Press.

Maier, Thomas. 1998. "Everybody's Grandfather." *U.S. News & World Report*. March 30:59.

Mainemer, Henry, Lorraine C. Gilman, and Elinor W. Ames. 1998. "Parenting Stress in Families Adopting Children from Romanian Orphanages." *Journal of Family Issues* 19 (2):164–80.

Majors, Richard G. and Janet M. Billson. 1992. *Cool Pose: The Dilemmas of Black Manhood in America.* Lexington, MA: Heath.

Makepeace, James M. 1981. "Courtship Violence Among College Students." *Family Relations* 30:97–102.

———. 1986. "Gender Differences in Courtship Violence Victimization." *Family Relations* 35:383–88.

Malcolm, Andrew H. 1991. "Helping Grandparents Who Are Parents Again." *New York Times*, Nov. 19.

Man, Guida. 1996. "The Experience of Middle-Class Women in Recent Hong Kong Chinese Immigrant Families in Canada." In *Voices: Essays on Canadian Families*, edited by Marion Lynn, pp. 271–300. Scarborough, Ontario: Nelson Canada.

———. 1995. "The Experience of Women in Chinese Immigrant Families: An Inquiry into Institutional and Organizational Processes." *Asian and Pacific Migration Journal* 4 (2-3):303–326.

———. 1994. "The Astronaut Phenomenon: Consequences of the Diaspora of the Hong Kong Chinese." *Sociology*Express.* (email:info@mail.socabs.com)

Mancini, Jay A. and Rosemary Bleiszner. 1989. "Aging Parents and Adult Children: Research Themes in Intergenerational Relations." *Journal of Marriage and the Family* 51 (2):275–90.

Mandel, Michele. 1999. "Threesome Or What's Your Sexual Fantasy?" *Toronto Sun*, September 22:56–60.

———. 1999a. "Hotbed Of Risks." *Toronto Sun*, September 21:44–48.

Mandell, Louise. 1987. "Native Culture on Trial." Pp. 358–365 in *Equality and Judicial Neutrality,* edited by Sheilah L. Martin and Kathleen E. Mahoney. Toronto: Carswell.

Mandell, Nancy. 1995. "Introduction." Pp. vii–xxi in *Feminist Issues: Race, Class and Sexuality.* Scarborough, ON: Prentice Hall.

Maneker, Jerry S. and Robert P. Rankin. 1993. "Religious Homogamy and Marital Duration among Those Who File for Divorce in California, 1966–1971." *Journal of Divorce and Remarriage* 19 (1–2):233–41.

Manke, Beth, Brenda L. Seery, Ann C. Crouter, and Susan M. McHale. 1994. "The Three Corners of Domestic Labor: Mothers,' Fathers,' and Children's Weekday and Weekend Housework." *Journal of Marriage and the Family* 56 (3) (Aug.):657–68.

Mann, P.S. 1995. "Cyborgean Motherhood and Abortion." In J.K. Gardiner (Ed.), *Provoking Agents: Gender and Agency in Theory and Practice* (pp. 133–151). Chicago: University of Chicago Press.

Manning, Wendy D. 1993. "Marriage and Cohabitation Following Premarital Conception." *Journal of Marriage and the Family* 55 (3) (Nov.):839–50.

Manning, Wendy D. and Pamela J. Smock. 1997. "Children's Living Arrangements in Unmarried-Mother Families." *Journal of Family Issues* 18 (5):526–44.

Marano, Hara Estroff. 1997. "Puberty May Start at 6 as Hormones Surge." *New York Times.* July 1:B1, B12.

March, Karen. 1997. "The Dilemma of Adoption Reunion: Establishing Open Communication between Adoptees and Their Birth Mothers." *Family Relations* 46 (2):99–105.

Marcil-Gratton, Nicole. 1999. "Growing Up With Mom And Dad? The Intricate Family Life Courses Of Canadian Children." Ottawa: Minister of Industry, Catalogue no. 89-566-XIE.

Marcus, Amy Dockser. 1990. "Medical, Social Changes May Spur Courts to Reformulate Definition of Parenthood." *The Wall Street Journal*, Sept. 18, pp. B1, B13.

Mare, Robert D. 1991. "Five Decades of Educational Assortive Mating." *American Sociological Review*, 56 (Feb.): 15–32.

Marecek, Jeanne. 1995. "Gender, Politics, and Psychology's Ways of Knowing." *The American Psychologist* 50 (3) (Mar.):162–64.

Margolin, Leslie. 1989. "Gender and the Prerogatives of Dating and Marriage: An Experimental Assessment of a Sample of College Students." *Sex Roles* 20 (1/2):91–101.

———. 1992. "Child Abuse by Mothers' Boyfriends: Why the Overrepresentation?" *Child Abuse & Neglect* 16:541–51.

Marin, Peter. 1991. "The Prejudice Against Men." *The Nation*, 8 July.

Marini, Margaret Mooney and Pi Ling Fan. 1997. "The Gender Gap in Earnings at Career Entry." *American Sociological Review* 62:588–604.

Markman, Howard, Scott Stanley, and S. L. Blumberg. 1994. *Fighting for Your Marriage.* San Francisco: Josey-Bass.

Marks, Michelle Rose. 1997. "Party Politics and Family Policy." *Journal of Family Issues* 18 (1):55–70.

Marks, Nadine F. 1995. "Midlife Marital Status Differences in Social Support Relationships with Adult Children and Psychological Well-Being." *Journal of Family Issues* 16 (1) (Jan.):5–28.

Marks, Stephen R. 1989. "Toward a Systems Theory of Marital Quality." *Journal of Marriage and the Family* 51:15–26.

Marlow, Lenard and S. Richard Sauber. 1990. *The Handbook of Divorce Mediation.* New York: Plenum.

Marshall, Katherine. 2000. "Incomes Of Younger Retired Women: The Past 30 Years." *Perspectives on Labour and Income* 12(4)(winter):9–17. Catalogue no. 75-001-XPE.

————. 1998a. "Balancing Work and Family." *Perspectives on Labour and Income*. (Statistics Canada, Catalogue no. 71-535-MPB) 8:72–80.

————. 1998b. "Stay-At-Home Dads." *Perspectives on Labour and Income* (spring):9–15. Cat.75-001-XPE.

————. 1998c. "Couples Working Shift." *Perspectives on Labour and Income* (autumn):9– 13. Statistics Canada, Catalogue no. 75-001-XPE.

————. 1999. "Employment After Childbirth." *Perspectives on Labour and Income* (autumn):16–25. Catalogue 75-001-XPE.

Marshall, Susan E. 1995. "Keep Us on the Pedestal: Women Against Feminism in Twentieth-Century America." Pp. 547–60 in *Women: A Feminist Perspective.* 5th ed., edited by Jo Freeman. Mountain View, CA: Mayfield.

Marshall, Victor. 1986. "A Sociological Perspective on Aging and Dying." Pp. 125–46 in *Later Life: The Social Psychology of Aging*, edited by Victor M. Marshall. Newbury Park, CA: Sage.

————. 1992. "Stepfathers with Minor Children Living at Home." *Journal of Family Issues* 13 (2) (June):195–214.

———— and William Marsiglio. 1993. "Adolescent Males' Orientation Toward Paternity and Contraception." *Family Planning Perspectives* 25 (1) (Jan./Feb.):22–31.

Marsiglio, William. 1992. "Adolescent Males' Orientation Toward the Reproductive Realm: Paternity, and Contraception." Paper presented at the annual meeting of the Population Association of America. Denver. May 1.

Marsiglio, William and Denise Donnelly. 1991. "Sexual Relations in Later Life: A National Study of Married Persons." *Journal of Gerontology: Social Sciences* 46 (6):5338–44.

Martin, April. 1993. *The Lesbian and Gay Parenting Handbook: Creating and Raising Our Families.* New York: HarperCollins.

Martin, C. L. 1989. "Children's Use of Gender-Related Information in Making Social Judgments." *Developmental Psychology* 25:80–88.

Martin, C.L., L. Eisenbud and H. Rose. "Children's Gender-Based Reasoning About Toys." *Child Development* 66:1453–1471.

Martin, Douglas. 1990. "Odd Man Out: Helping Big Boys Feel Like Fathers." *New York Times*, Apr. 7.

Martin, George T. Jr. 1997. "An Agenda for Family Policy in the United States." Pp. 289–324 in *Contemporary Parenting: Challenges and Issues,* edited by Terry Arendell. Thousand Oaks, CA: Sage.

Martin, Jean-Claude. 1997. "The Elderly, Their Families And Others, Or The Local Community As A Living Environment." *Lein Social et Politiques—RIAC* 38 (78)(autumn):159–164.

Martin, Patricia Yancey. 1992. "Gender, Interaction, and Inequality in Organizations." Pp. 208–231 in *Gender, Interaction, and Inequality*, edited by Cecilia Ridgeway. New York: Springer-Verlag.

Martin, Peter and Landy Luke. 1991. "Divorce and the Wheel Theory of Love." *Journal of Divorce and Remarriage* 15 (1/2):3–22.

Martin, Philip and Elizabeth Midgley. 1994. *Immigration to the United States: Journey to an Uncertain Destination. Population Bulletin* 49 (2) (Sept.). Washington DC: Population Reference Bureau.

Martin, Teresa Castro and Larry Bumpass. 1989. "Trends in Marital Disruption." *Demography* 26:37–52.

Martin Matthews, A. and C. Rosenthal. 1993. "Balancing Work and Family in An Aging Society: The Canadian Experience." Pp. 96–119 in *Annual Review of Gerontology and Geriatrics*, edited by G.L. Maddox and M.P. Lawton. New York: Springer.

Masheter, Carol. 1991. "Postdivorce Relationships Between Ex-spouses: The Roles of Attachment and Interpersonal Conflict." *Journal of Marriage and the Family* 53 (1) (Apr.):103–10.

Maslow, Abraham H. 1943. "A Theory of Human Motivation." *Psychological Review* 50:370–96.

Mason, Mary Ann. 1988. *The Equality Trap.* New York: Simon & Schuster.

————. 1998. "The Modern American Stepfamily: Problems and Possibilities." Pp. 95–116 in *All Our Families: New Policies for a New Century*, edited by Mary Ann Mason, Arlene Skolnick, and Stephen D. Sugarman. New York: Oxford University Press.

Mason, Mary Ann, Arlene Skolnick, and Stephen D. Sugarman. 1998. *All Our Families: New Policies for a New Century.* New York: Oxford University Press.

Masters, William H. and Virginia E. Johnson. 1966. *Human Sexual Response.* Boston: Little, Brown.

————. 1970. *Human Sexual Inadequacy.* Boston: Little, Brown.

————. 1973. "Orgasm, Anatomy of the Female." In *The Encyclopedia of Sexual Behavior*, edited by Albert Ellis and Albert Abarbanel. New York: Aronson.

————. 1976. *The Pleasure Bond: A New Look at Sexuality and Commitment.* New York: Bantam.

Masters, William H., Virginia E. Johnson, and Robert C. Kolodny. 1994. *Heterosexuality.* New York: HarperCollins.

Maticka-Tyndale, Eleanor, Michael Barrett and Alexander McKay. 2000. "Adolescent Sexual And Reproductive Health In Canada: A Review Of National Data Sources And Their Limitations." *Canadian Journal of Human Sexuality* 9:41–65.

Maticka-Tyndale, Eleanor and Edward Herold. 1997. "The Scripting Of Sexual Behaviour: Canadian University Students On Spring Break In Florida." *The Canadian Journal of Human Sexuality* 6:317–328.

Mattessich, Paul and Reuben Hill. 1987. "Life Cycle and Family Development." Pp. 437–69 in *Handbook of Marriage and the Family*, edited by Marvin B. Sussman and Suzanne K. Steinmetz. New York: Plenum.

Matthews, Ralph and Anne Martin Matthews. 1986. "Infertility and Involuntary Childlessness: The Transition to Nonparenthood." *Journal of Marriage and the Family* 48:641–49.

Maugh, Thomas H. 1998. " 'Honey, just be a yes man'—Study: Marriage Lasts if Husband Gives In." *Los Angeles Times*. February 21.

Mauldin, Teresa A. 1990. "Women Who Remain Above the Poverty Level in Divorce: Implications for Family Policy." *Family Relations* 39 (2) (Apr.):141–46.

Mauldon, Jane and Suzanne Delbanco. 1997. "Public Perceptions about Unplanned Pregnancy." *Family Planning Perspectives* 29 (1):25–29.

May, Elaine Tyler. 1997. *Barren in the Promised Land: Childless Americans and the Pursuit of Happiness*. Cambridge, MA: Harvard University Press.

May, Rollo. 1969. *Love and Will*. New York: Norton.

———. 1975. "A Preface to Love." Pp. 114–19 in *The Practice of Love*, edited by Ashley Montagu. Englewood Cliffs, NJ: Prentice-Hall.

Mayer, Susan E. 1997. *What Money Can't Buy: Family Income and Children's Life Chances*. Cambridge, Mass: Harvard University Press.

McAllister, Ronald J., Edgar W. Butler, and Edward J. Kaiser. 1973. "The Adaptation of Women to Residential Mobility." *Journal of Marriage and the Family* 35:197–204.

McAninch, C.B., R. Milich, G.B. Crumbo and M.N. Funtowicz. 1996. "Children's Perceptions of Gender-Role-Congruent and -Incongruent Behavior in Peers: Fisher-Price Meets Price Waterhouse." *Sex Roles* 35 (9/10):619–638.

McBride, Brent A. and Thomas R. Rane. 1998. "Parenting Alliance as a Predictor of Father Involvement: An Exploratory Study." *Family Relations* 47:229–36.

McCabe, Marita P. 1999. "The Interrelationist Between Intimacy, Relationship Functioning, And Sexuality Among Men And Women In Committed Relationships." *The Canadian Journal of Human Sexuality* 8:31–38.

McCarthy, Barry W. 1998. *Couple Sexual Awareness: Building Sexual Happiness*. New York: Carroll & Graf Publishers.

McClain, Leanita. 1992. "The Middle Class Black's Burden." Pp. 120–22 in *Race, Class, and Gender: An Anthology*, edited by Margaret L. Andersen and Patricia Hill Collins. Belmont, CA: Wadsworth.

McClelland, David C. 1986. "Some Reflections on the Two Psychologies of Love." *Journal of Personality* 54:334–53.

McCormick, Naomi B. and Clinton J. Jessor. 1983. "The Courtship Game: Power in the Sexual Encounter." Pp. 64–86 in *Changing Boundaries: Gender Roles and Sexual Behavior*, edited by Elizabeth Rice Allgeier and Naomi B. McCormick. Mountain View, CA: Mayfield.

McCormick, Richard A., S. J. 1992. "Christian Approaches: Catholicism." Paper presented at the Surrogate Motherhood and Reproductive Technologies Symposium, Creighton University, Jan. 13.

McCubbin, Hamilton I. and Marilyn A. McCubbin. 1991. "Family Stress Theory and Assessment: The Resiliency Model of Family Stress, Adjustment and Adaptation." Pp. 3–32 in *Family Assessment Inventories for Research and Practice*, 2d ed. Edited by Hamilton I. McCubbin and Anne I. Thompson. Madison: University of Wisconsin, School of Family Resources and Consumer Services.

———. 1994. "Families Coping with Illness: The Resiliency Model of Family Stress, Adjustment, and Adaptation." Chapter 2 in *Families, Health, and Illness*. St. Louis: Mosby Press.

McCubbin, Hamilton I. and Joan M. Patterson. 1983. "Family Stress and Adaptation to Crisis: A Double ABCX Model of Family Behavior." Pp. 87–106 in *Family Studies Review Yearbook*, vol. 1, edited by David H. Olson and Brent C. Miller. Newbury Park, CA: Sage.

McCubbin, Hamilton I., Anne I. Thompson, and Marilyn A. McCubbin. 1996. *Family Assessment: Resiliency, Coping and Adaptation: Inventories for Research and Practice*. Madison, WI: University of Wisconsin Publishers.

McCubbin, Marilyn A. 1989. "Family Stress and Family Strengths: A Comparison of Single- and Two-Parent Families with Handicapped Children." *Research in Nursing and Health* 12:101–10.

———. 1995. "The Typology Model of Adjustment and Adaptation: A Family Stress Model." *Guidance and Counseling* 10 (4):31–39.

McCubbin, Marilyn A. and Hamilton I. McCubbin. 1989. "Theoretical Orientations to Family Stress and Coping." Pp. 3–43 in *Treating Families Under Stress*, edited by Charles Figley. New York: Brunner/Mazel.

McDaniel, Susan A. 1993. "Single Parenthood: Policy Apartheid in Canada." Pp. 203–211 in *Single Parent Families: Canadian Perspectives on Research and Policy*, edited by Burt Galloway and Joe Hudson. Toronto: Thompson Educational Publishing.

McDaniel, Susan A. 1993a. "The Changing Canadian Family: Women's Roles and the Impact of Feminism." Pp. 422–451 in *Changing Patterns: Women in Canada*, 2nd edition, edited by Sandra Burt and Lorraine Code. Toronto: McClelland & Stewart.

———. and E. Roosmalen. 1992. "Sexual Harassment in Canadian Academe: Explorations of Power and Privilege." *Atlantis* 17(1):3–19.

McDonald, Gerald W. and Marie Withers Osmond. 1980. "Jealousy and Trust: Unexplored Dimensions of Social

Exchange Dynamics." Paper presented at the National Council on Family Relations Workshop on Theory Construction and Research Methodology, Portland, OR, Oct. 21.

McFarlane, Seth, Beaujot, Roderic, Haddad, Tony. 2000. "Time Constraints And Relative Resources As Determinants Of The Sexual Division Of Domestic Work." *Canadian Journal of Sociology/Cahiers canadiens de sociologie* 25 (1)(winter):61–82.

McGill, Michael E. 1985. *The McGill Report on Male Intimacy.* New York: Holt, Rinehart & Winston.

McGrew, Kathryn B. 1998. "Daughters' Caregiving Decisions: From an Impulse to a Balancing Point of Care." *Journal of Women and Aging* 10 (2):49–65.

McGrew, W. C. 1981. "The Female Chimpanzee as a Human Evolutionary Prototype." Pp. 35–74 in *Woman the Gatherer*, edited by Frances Dahlberg. New Haven, CT: Yale University Press.

McHale, Susan M., W. T. Bartko, Ann C. Crouter, and M. Perry-Jenkins. 1990. "Children's Housework and Psychological Functioning: The Mediating Effects of Parents' Sex-Role Behaviors and Attitudes." *Child Development* 61:1413–26.

McHale, Susan M. and Ann C. Crouter. 1992. "You Can't Always Get What You Want: Incongruence Between Sex-Role Attitudes and Family Work Roles and Its Implications for Marriage." *Journal of Marriage and the Family* 54 (3) (Aug.):537–47.

McIvoy, Anne. 1999. "Most in Poll Want Gay Marriages Legalized." *The Globe and Mail*, June 10. <www.egale.ca/archives/press.190610poll.htm>

McKay, Alexander, Mary-Anne Pietrusiak and Philippa Holowaty. 1998. "Education in the Schools." *The Canadian Journal of Human Sexuality* 7:134–146.

McKay, Alexander and Michael Barrett. 1999. "Pre-Service Sexual Health education Training of Elementary, Secondary, and Physical Health Education Teachers in Canadian Faculties of Education." *The Canadian Journal of Human Sexuality*, 8:91–101.

McLanahan, Sara S. and Karen Booth. 1989. "Mother-Only Families: Problems, Prospects, and Politics." *Journal of Marriage and the Family* 51:557–80.

McLanahan, Sara S. and Larry Bumpass. 1988. "Intergenerational Consequences of Family Disruption." *American Journal of Sociology* 94:130–52.

McLanahan, Sara S. and Gary Sandefur. 1994. *Growing Up with a Single Parent.* Cambridge, MA: Harvard University Press.

McLaren, Angus. 1999. "Illegal Abortions: Women, Doctors, and Abortion, 1886–1939." Pp. 22–38 in *Law in Society: Canadian Readings*, edited by Nick Larsen and Brian Burtch (eds.). Toronto: Harcourt Brace Canada.

McLaughlin, Diane K. and Daniel T. Lichter. 1997. "Poverty and the Marital Behavior of Young Women." *Journal of Marriage and the Family* 59:582–94.

McLaughlin, S. D., D. L. Manninen, and L. D. Winges. 1988. "The Consequences of the Relinquishment Decision Among Adolescent Mothers." *Social Work* 33:320–24.

McLeod, Jane D. 1995. "Social and Psychological Bases of Homogamy for Common Psychiatric Disorders." *Journal of Marriage and the Family* 57 (1) (Feb.):201–14.

McNab, Miriam. 1999. Pp. 1598–1599 in *The Canadian Encyclopedia: Year 2000 Edition*, edited by James Marsh. Toronto: McClelland & Stewart Inc.

McNeal, Cosandra and Paul R. Amato. 1998. "Parents' Marital Violence: Long-Term Consequences for Children." *Journal of Family Issues* 19 (2):123–39.

McPherson, B.D. 1994. "Aging: The Middle and Later Years." Pp. 230–266 in *Sociology*, edited by Lorne Tepperman, James Curtis and James Richardson. Toronto: McGraw Hill Primus.

McQuillan, Kevin and Marilyn Belle. 1999. *Lone-Father Families in Canada, 1971–1996.* Population Studies Centre Discussion Paper, No. 99-8, June 1999. University of Western Ontario, Population Studies Centre, London, ON.

McQuire, Randall. 1992. "Archeology and the First Americans." *American Anthropologist*, 94(4): 816-36.

McRoy, Ruth G., Harold D. Grotevant, and Louis A. Zurcher, Jr. 1988. *Emotional Disturbance in Adopted Adolescents: Origins and Development.* New York: Praeger.

McVey, Wayne. 1998. "Population by Single Years of Age, Showing Sex, for Canada, Provinces, and Census Metropolitan Areas: 1996." Statcan 6.1 (prepared by Demografics, Ltd.).

McVey, Wayne W. Jr. and Warren E. Kalbach. 1995. *Canadian Population.* Scarborough, Ontario: Nelson.

Mead, George Herbert. 1934. *Mind, Self, and Society.* Chicago: University of Chicago Press.

Mead, Margaret. 1949. *Male and Female: A Study of the Sexes in a Changing World.* New York: Morrow.

———. 1966. "Marriage in Two Steps." *Redbook,* July.

Means, Marianne. 1997. "Another Try for Legal Rights for Women." *Hearst Newspapers.* March 27.

Mehdizadeh, S.A. and R.C. Atchley. 1992. "The Economics of Long-Term Care in Ohio." <casnov1.cas/muohio.edu/scripps/NewFiles/New%20frm%20economicsLTC.html>

Meilander, Gilbert. 1992. "Christian Approaches: Protestantism." Paper presented at the Surrogate Motherhood and Reproductive Technologies Symposium, Creighton University, Jan. 13.

Melli, Marygold S. 1986. "Constructing a Social Problem: The Post-Divorce Plight of Women and Children." *American Bar Foundation Research Journal* 1986:759–72.

Menaghan, Elizabeth and Morton Lieberman. 1986. "Changes in Depression Following Divorce: A Panel Study." *Journal of Marriage and the Family* 48:319–28.

Mendola, Mary. 1980. *The Mendola Report: A New Look at Gay Couples*. New York: Crown.

Mensch, Barbara and Denise B. Kandel. 1992. "Drug Use as a Risk Factor for Premarital Teen Pregnancy and Abortion in a National Sample of Young White Women." *Demography* 29 (3) (Aug.):409–29.

Mercier, Peter J. and Judith D. Mercier (eds.). 2000. *Battle Cries On The Home Front: Violence In The Military Family*. Springfield, Illinois: Charles C. Thomas Publisher Ltd.

Meredith, William H., Douglas A. Abbott, Mary Ann Lamanna, and Gregory Sanders. 1989. "Rituals and Family Strengths: A Three Generation Study." *Family Perspectives* 23:75–83.

Merson, Julie. (1995, May 10). "Eggs for Sale." *The San Francisco Bay Guardian*, p. 14–5.

Messinger, Lilian. 1976. "Remarriage Between Divorced People with Children from Previous Marriages: A Proposal for Preparation for Remarriage." *Journal of Marriage and Family Counseling* 2:193–200.

Messner, Michael A. 1992. *Power at Play: Sports and the Problem of Masculinity*. Boston: Beacon.

Meston, Cindy M., Paul D. Trapnell, and Boris B. Gorzalka. 1998. "Ethnic, Gender, and Length-of-Residency Influences on Sexual Knowledge and Attitudes." *The Journal of Sex Research* 35 (2):176–88.

Meyer, Daniel R. and Judi Bartfield. 1996. "Compliance with Child Support Orders in Divorce Cases." *Journal of Marriage and the Family* 58 (1):201–12.

Meyer, Daniel R., Elizabeth Phillips, and Nancy L. Maritato. 1991. "The Effects of Replacing Income Tax Deductions for Children with Children's Allowances." *Journal of Family Issues* 12 (4) (Dec.):467–91.

Meyer, Thomas J. 1984. " 'Date Rape': A Serious Campus Problem That Few Talk About." *Chronicle of Higher Education*, Dec. 5, pp. 1, 12.

Miall, Charlene E. 1996. "The Social Construction of Adoption: Clinical and Community Perspectives." *Family Relations* 45 (3):309–17.

Michaels, Marguerite and James Willwerth. 1989. "How America Has Run Out of Time." *Time*, Apr. 24, pp. 58–67.

Milan, Stephanie and Margaret K. Keiley. 2000. "Biracial Youth And Families In Therapy: Issues And Interventions." *Journal of Marital and Family Therapy* 2 (6):305–315.

Milano, Elyce and Stephen F. Hall. 1986. "Sex-Roles in Dating: Paying vs. Putting Out." Unpublished paper.

Milardo, Robert M. 1989. "Theoretical and Methodological Issues in the Identification of the Social Networks of Spouses." *Journal of Marriage and the Family* 51 (1):165–74.

Miller, Baila. 1990. "Gender Differences in Spouse Caregiver Strain: Socialization and Role Explanations." *Journal of Marriage and the Family* 52:311–21.

Miller, Richard B. and Jennifer Glass. 1989. "Parent–Child Attitude Similarity Across the Life Course." *Journal of Marriage and the Family* 51:991–97.

Miller, Vernon D., and Mark L. Knapp. 1986. "Communication Paradoxes and the Maintenance of Living Relationships with the Dying." *Journal of Family Issues* 7:255–76.

Mills, C. Wright. 1973 [1959]. *The Sociological Imagination*. New York: Oxford University Press.

Mills, D. M. 1984. "A Model for Stepfamily Development." *Family Relations* 33:365–72.

Mills, Rabia. n.d. "Polygamy: Punishing Honesty and Rewarding Deception." <http://www.muslim-canada.org/polygamy.html>

Milner, Jan. 1990. "Strangers in a Strange Land: Housewives in the 1980's." Paper presented at the annual meeting of the Midwest Sociological Society, Chicago, Apr. 14.

Ming-Sum, Tsui. 1997. "A Child's Conception Of Another World: A Chinese Boy's View Of Canada." *Child & Adolescent Social Work Journal* 14 (2)(April):79–93.

Minkowitz, Donna. 1995. "In the Name of the Father." *Ms. Magazine*. November/December:64–71.

Minister of Citizenship and Immigration. 1999. *Ali v. Canada (Minister of Citizenship and Immigration)*. Federal Court of Canada. <http://www.fja.gc.ca/fc/1000/fic/v1/1999fc23488.html>

Misovich, Stephen E., Jeffrey D. Fisher and William A. Fisher. 1999. "Belief In A Cure For HIV Infection Associated With Greater HIV Risk Behaviour Among HIV Positive Men Who Have Sex With Men." *The Canadian Journal of Human Sexuality* 8:241–248.

Mitchell, Barbara A. 1998. "Too Close for Comfort? Parental assessments of 'Boomerang Kid' Living Arrangements." *Canadian Journal of Sociology* 23 (1)(winter):21–46.

———. 1994. "Family Structure and Leaving the Nest: A Social Resource Perspective." *Sociological Perspectives* 37 (4)(winter):651–671.

Mitchell, Juliet and Ann Oakley, Eds. 1986. *What Is Feminism?* New York: Pantheon.

Mitchell, K. 1983. "The Price Tag of Responsibility: A Comparison of Divorced and Remarried Mothers." *Journal of Divorce* 6:33–42.

Moen, Phyllis. 1992. *Women's Two Roles: A Contemporary Dilemma*. New York: Auburn House.

Moir, A. and D. Jessel. 1991. *Brain Sex: The Real Difference Between Men and Women*. New York: Delta.

Money, John. 1995. *Gendermaps: Social Constructionism, Feminism, and Sexosophical History*. New York: Continuum.

Money, John and Anke A. Ehrhardt. 1974. *Man and Woman, Boy and Girl: Differentiation and Dimorphism of*

Gender Identity from Conception to Maturity. New York: New American Library/Mentor.

"Monogamy: Is It for Us?" 1998. *The Advocate.* June 23:29.

Monroe, Michael, Richard C. Baker, and Samuel Roll. 1997. "The Relationship of Homophobia to Intimacy in Heterosexual Men." *Journal of Homosexuality* 33 (2):23–37.

Montgomery, Marilyn J. and Gwendolyn T. Sorell. 1997. "Differences in Love Attitudes across Family Life Stages." *Family Relations* 46:55–61.

Moore, Kristin A., Margaret C. Simms, and Charles L. Betsey. 1986. *Choice and Circumstance: Racial Differences in Adolescent Sexuality and Fertility.* New Brunswick, NJ: Transaction.

Moore, Teresa. 1993. "Pain of Color-Coded Child Rearing." *San Francisco Chronicle*, Feb. 15, p. B3.

Moorman, Jeanne E. and Donald J. Hernandez. 1989. "Married Couple Families with Step, Adopted, and Biological Children." *Demography* 26:267–78.

Moreau, J. 1991. "Employment Equity." *Canadian Social Trends* 22 (autumn):26–28.

Morgan, Laurie A. 1998. "Glass-Ceiling Effect or Cohort Effect? A Longitudinal Study of the Gender Earnings Gap for Engineers, 1982 to 1989." *American Sociological Review* 63 (4):479–83.

Morin, Richard and Megan Rosenfeld. 1998. "The Politics of Fatigue." *The Washington Post National Weekly Edition.* April 20:6–7.

Morris, Marika. 2000. "Women and Poverty." <http://www.vtiaw-icref.ca/Poverty_fact_sheet.htm>

Morrison, Bradley Thomas. 1998. *Being There: A Qualitative Study of How Fathers Overcome Obstacles To Intimacy With Their Children.* Unpublished dissertation, Wilfrid Laurier University, Waterloo, Ontario, Canada.

Morrison, Donna R. and Andres J. Cherlin. 1995. "The Divorce Process and Young Children's Well-Being: A Prospective Analysis." *Journal of Marriage and the Family* 57 (3) (Aug.):800–12.

Morrison, Nancy. 1987. "Separation and Divorce." Pp. 125–143 in M.J. Dymond (ed.) *The Canadian Woman's Legal Guide.* Toronto: Doubleday.

Morrissette, Patrick J. 1994. "The Holocaust Of First Nation People: Residual Effects On Parenting And Treatment Implications." *Contemporary Family Therapy: An International Journal* 16 (5)(October):381–392.

Morisette, R. 1997. "Declining Earnings of Young Men." *Canadian Social Trends*, 46 (autumn):8–12.

Morrow, Lance. 1992. "Family Values." *Time*, Aug. 31, pp. 22–27.

Morton, Mildred. 1990. "Controversies Within Family Law." Pp. 216–240 in *Families: Changing Trends in Canada*, edited by Maureen Baker. Toronto: McGraw-Hill Ryerson.

Mosher, William D. 1990. "Fecundity and Infertility in the United States, 1965–1988." *Advance Data.* 192. U.S. Department of Health and Human Services.

Mosher, William D. and Willim F. Pratt. 1993. "AIDS-Related Behavior Among Women 15–44 Years of Age: United States, 1988 and 1990." *Advance Data* No. 239. Dec. 22. Hyattsville, MD: U.S. Department of Health and Human Services, National Center for Health Statistics.

Mugford, Jane and Stephen Mugford. 1991. "Shame and Reintegration in the Punishment and Deterrence of Spouse Assault." Paper presented at the annual meeting of the American Society of Criminology, San Francisco.

Muhajarine, N. and C. D'Arcy. 1999. "Physical Abuse During Pregnancy: Prevalence and Risk Factors." *CMAJ* 160 (7)(April 6):1022–3.

Mulcahy, John J. 1997. *Diagnosis and Management of Male Sexual Dysfunction.* New York: Igaku-Shoin.

Muller, Chandra. 1995. "Maternal Employment, Parent Involvement, and Mathematics Achievement Among Adolescents." *Journal of Marriage and the Family* 57 (1) (Feb.):85–100.

Munsil, Len. 1998. *Center for Arizona Policy Family Fax.* May 21. <http.//www.cenazpol.org/fax/u.html.>

Murdock, George. 1949. *Social Structure.* New York: Free Press.

Murnen, Sarah K., Annette Perot, and Don Byrne. 1989. "Coping with Unwanted Sexual Activity: Normative Responses, Situational Determinants, and Individual Differences." *Journal of Sex Research* 26:85–106.

Murphy, John E. 1988. "Date Abuse and Forced Intercourse Among College Students." Pp. 285–96 in *Family Abuse and Its Consequences: New Directions in Research*, edited by Gerald T. Hotaling, David Finkelhor, John T. Kirkpatrick, and Murray A. Straus. Newbury Park, CA: Sage.

Murphy, Lisa. 2000. "The Facts On Female Genital Mutilation." <http://www.chatelaine.com/read/news+views/fgn4.html>

Murphy, Mike, Karen Glaser, and Emily Grundy. 1997. "Marital Status and Long-Term Illness in Great Britain." *Journal of Marriage and the Family* 59:156–64.

Murstein, Bernard I. 1980. "Mate Selection in the 1970s." *Journal of Marriage and the Family* 42:777–92.

———. 1986. *Paths to Marriage.* Newbury Park, CA: Sage.

Murstein, Bernard I. and E. R. Adler. 1997. "Gender Differences in Power and Self-Disclosure in Dating and Married Couples." *Personal Relationships* 2:199–209.

Myaskovsky, Larissa and Michele Andrisin Wittig. 1997. "Predictors of Feminist Social Identity Among College Women." *Sex Roles* 37 (11/12) (December):861–883.

Myers, Michael F. 1989. *Men and Divorce.* New York: Guilford.

Myers, Ted, Dan Allman, Liviana Calzavara, Ken Morrison, Rick Marchand and Carol Major. 1999. "Gay And Bisexual Men's Sexual Partnerships And Variations In Risk Behaviour." *The Canadian Journal of Human Sexuality* 8:115–126.

N

Nachman, Patricia Ann. 1997. *You and Your Only Child: The Joys, Myths, and Challenges of Raising an Only Child.* New York: HarperCollins.

Naiman, Sandy. 2000. "Childless...by Choice." *Toronto Sun*, August 24. <http:www.canoe.ca/Health0008/24_child.html>

Nakonezny, P. A., R. D. Shull, and J. L. Rodgers. 1995. "The Effect of No-fault Divorce Law on the Divorce Rate across the 50 States and Its Relation to Income, Education, and Religiosity." *Journal of Marriage and the Family* 57 (2):477–88.

Nanji, Azim A. 1993. "The Muslim Family in North America." Pp. 229–42 in *Family Ethnicity: Strength in Diversity*, edited by Harriette Pipes McAdoo. Newbury Park, CA: Sage.

Nasar, Sylvia. 1992. "More College Graduates Taking Low-Wage Jobs." *New York Times*, Aug. 7.

Nash, J. Madeleine. 1997. "Special Report: Fertile Minds." *Time*. February 3:48–56.

Nason, Ellen M. and Margaret M. Poloma. 1976. *Voluntarily Childless Couples: The Emergence of a Variant Life Style.* Newbury Park, CA: Sage.

National Commission on the Role of the Schools and the Community in Improving Adolescent Health. 1990. Code Blue: Uniting for Healthier Youth. Washington DC: National Association of State Boards of Education/American Medical Association.

National Council of Welfare. 1999. *Children First: A Pre-Budget Report by the National Council of Welfare.* <http://www.ncwcnbes.net.htmdocument/reportchildfirst.htm>

National Forum on Health. n.d. *The Need for An Aboriginal Health Institute in Canada.* Synthesis Reports and Issues Paper, Final Report, Vol. 11. <www.hc-sc.gc.ca/publicat/involv2/aborig/idsabo/html>

National Gay & Lesbian Task Force (NGLTF) flyer. n.d. Washington DC: National Gay & Lesbian Task Force.

National Institute of Mental Health. 1985. *Plain Talk About Wife Abuse.* Rockville, MD: U.S. Department of Health and Human Services.

National Library of Canada. 2001. "Women in Canadian Legislatures." <http://www.nlc-bnc.ca/digiproj/women/women97/ewomen97.htm>

National Post. 2001. "A Deal is a Deal." June 11. *National Post Online.* <wysiwyg://Network_Page 26/http://www.nati...20010611/587976.html&qs=spousal%20support>

National Report Card of Child Poverty-Campaign 2000.

Nault, F. 1996. "Twenty Years of Marriages." *Health Reports* 8 (2):39–46.

"Navaho Tribal Court Supported by Utah Court in Adoption Case." 1988. *New York Times*, Dec. 15.

Nave-Herz, Rosemarie. 1997. "Still in the Nest: The Family and Young Adults in Germany." *Journal of Family Issues* 18 (6):671–689.

Nazario, Sonia L. 1990a. "Midwifery Is Staging Revival as Demand for Prenatal Care, Low-Tech Births Rises." *The Wall Street Journal*, Sept. 25.

———. 1990b. "Identity Crisis: When White Parents Adopt Black Babies, Race Often Divides." *The Wall Street Journal*, Sept. 20.

Needle, Richard H., S. Susan Su, and William J. Doherty. 1990. "Divorce, Remarriage, and Adolescent Substance Use: A Prospective Longitudinal Study." *Journal of Marriage and the Family* 52 (1) (Feb.):157–59.

Neisen, Joseph H. 1990. "Heterosexism: Redefining Homophobia for the 1990s." *Journal of Gay and Lesbian Psychotherapy* 1:21–35.

Nelson, Adie and Augie Fleras. 1998. *Social Problems in Canada.* Scarborough: Prentice-Hall.

Nelson, A. and B.W. Robinson. 1994. *Gigolos and Madames Bountiful: Illusions of Gender, Power and Intimacy.* Toronto: University of Toronto Press.

Nelson, E.D. 1991. "'Employment Equity' and the Red Queen's Hypothesis: Recruitment and Hiring in Western Canadian Municipal Police Department." *Canadian Police College Journal* 10 (3):184–203.

———. 1994. "Females Who Sexually Abuse Children: A Discussion of Gender Stereotypes and Symbolic Assailants." *Qualitative Sociology* 17 (1):63–88.

———. 1993. "'Sugar Daddies' The Concept and Code of the Gentleman." *Qualitative Sociology* 16 (1):43–68.

——— and Barrie W. Robinson. 1995. "The Quest for Intimacy." In E.D. Nelson and Barrie W. Robinson (eds.) *Gender in the 1990s: Images, Realities and Issues.* Scarborough: ON: Nelson.

——— and Barrie W. Robinson. 1999. *Gender in Canada.* Scarborough: Prentice Hall.

Nelson, Geoffrey. 1993. "Risk, Resistance, And Self-Esteem: A Longitudinal Study Of Elementary School-Aged Children From Mother Custody And Two-Parent Families." *Journal of Divorce & Remarriage* 19 (1-2):99–119.

Nelson, Marissa. 2001. "Stepfamilies Becoming Common, Report Finds." *Globe and Mail*, June 23:A2.

Nelson (Nelson Political Science). 2001. "Women in Politics in Canada." <http://polisci.nelson.com/women.html>

Nevid, Jeffrey S. 1995. *Human Sexuality in a World of Diversity.* 2d ed. Boston: Allyn & Bacon.

Newcomb, Paul R. 1979. "Cohabitation in America: An Assessment of Consequences." *Journal of Marriage and the Family* 41:597–603.

"New Fathers: Trend or Phenomenon." 1991. *Family Affairs* 4, p. 13.

Newman, Katherine S. 1988. *Falling from Grace: The Experience of Downward Mobility in the American Middle Class.* New York: Random House.

Newman, Louis. 1992. "Jewish Approaches." Paper presented at the Surrogate Motherhood and Reproductive Technologies Symposium, Creighton University, Jan. 13.

Newman, Robert. 1979. "For Women Only: Warning of Widowhood Eases Adjustment Period." *United Feature Syndicate,* in *Omaha World-Herald,* Apr. 11.

Nieves-Squires, Sarah. 1991. *Hispanic Women: Making Their Presence on Campus Less Tenuous.* Washington, D.C.: Project on the Status and Education of Women. Association of American Colleges.

Niezen, Ronald. 1993. "Power And Dignity: The Social Consequences Of Hydro-Electric Development For The James Bay Cree." *Canadian Review of Sociology & Anthropology* 30 (4)(Nov.):510–529.

Nign, Mary E. 1995. "Intrigue on the Internet." *McCalls.* September:102–104.

Nikoforuk, Andrew. 1999. "A Question of Style." *Time,* May 31:58–59.

Nippert-Eng, Christena E. 1996. *Home and Work: Negotiating Boundaries Through Everyday Life.* Chicago: University of Chicago Press.

Nock, Steven L. 1995. "A Comparison of Marriages and Cohabiting Relationships." *Journal of Family Issues* 16 (1) (Jan.):53–76.

———. 1998a. "Too Much Privacy?" *Journal of Family Issues* 19 (1):101–18.

———. 1998b. "The Consequences of Premarital Fatherhood." *American Sociological Review* 63 (2):250–63.

Noivo, Edite. 1993. "Ethnic Families And The Social Injuries Of Class, Migration, Gender, Generation And Minority Group Status." *Canadian Ethnic Studies* 25 (3):66–75.

Noller, Patricia and Mary Anne Fitzpatrick. 1991. "Marital Communication in the Eighties." Pp. 42–53 in *Contemporary Families: Looking Forward, Looking Back,* edited by Alan Booth. Minneapolis: National Council on Family Relations.

Normand, Jose. 1995. "Education of Women in Canada." *Canadian Social Trends* 39 (winter):17–21.

Norton, Arthur J. and L. F. Miller. 1992. *Marriage, Divorce, and Remarriage in the 1990s. Current Population Reports,* Series P–23, No. 180. Washington, DC: U.S. Government Printing Office.

Norton, Arthur J. and Jeanne E. Moorman. 1987. "Current Trends in Marriage and Divorce Among American Women." *Journal of Marriage and the Family* 49:3–14.

Novac, S., J. Brown and C. Bourbonnais. 1996. *No Room Of Her Own: A Literature Review on Women and Homelessness.* Canadian Mortgage and Housing Corporation. <www.cmhc-schl.gc.ca/cmhc.html>

Novak, Mark. 1997. *Aging and Society: A Canadian Perspective,* 3rd ed. Scarborough: Nelson.

Nova Scotia Department of Health and Dalhousie University. 1998. *Nova Scotia Drug Use 1998: Technical Report.*

Nye, F. Ivan. 1979. "Choice, Exchange, and the Family." Pp. 1–41 in *Contemporary Theories about the Family,* vol. 2, edited by Wesley Burr, Reuben Hill, F. Ivan Nye, and Ira Reiss.

Nyrop, R. E. 1985. *India: A Country Study.* Washington, DC: U.S. Government Printing Office.

O

Obejas, Achy. 1994. "Women Who Batter Women." *Ms. Magazine.* (Sept./Oct.):53.

O'Boyle, Thomas F. 1990. "Fear and Stress in the Office Take Toll." *The Wall Street Journal,* Nov. 6, pp. B1, B16.

O'Brien, Patricia. 1980. "How to Survive the Early Years of Marriage." Pp. 51–54 in *Marriage and Family* 80/81, edited by Robert H. Walsh and Ollie Pocs. Guilford, CT: Dushkin.

Oderkirk, J. 1994. "Marriage in Canada: Changing Beliefs and Behaviours 1600–1990." *Canadian Social Trends* (summer):2–7.

——— and C. Lochhead. 1992. "Lone Parenthood: Gender Differences." *Canadian Social Trends* 27 (spring):16–19.

Odgers, S. 1979. "Five Types of Men Disabled Women Should Avoid." *Accent on Living,* 24:72–76.

Ogrodnik, Lucie and Cathy Trainor. 1997. *An Overview of the Differences between Police-Reported and Victim-Reported Crime, 1997.* Catelogue 85-542-XPE. Canadian Centre for Justice Statistics. Ottawa: Minister of Industry.

Oh, Susan. (2000, June 12). "Just Like a Virgin." *Maclean's,* 44.

Olson, David H. 1994. *Prepare, Enrich: Counselor's Manual.* Minneapolis, MN: Prepare-Enrich, Inc.

———. 1998. *Making Our Marriage Last a LifeTime.* Appleton, WI: Aid Association for Lutherans.

Olson, David H. and Hamilton I. McCubbin. 1983. *Families: What Makes Them Work.* Newbury Park, CA: Sage.

Olson, Walter. 1998. "Free To Commit." *Reason Online Magazine.* October. <http://www.reasonmag.com/9710/col.olson.html.>

O'Neal, Glenn. (1998, March 10). "Girls Often Dropped from Computer Equation." *USA Today,* p. D4.

O'Neil, Robin and Ellen Greenberger. 1994. "Patterns of Commitment to Work and Parenting: Implications for Role Strain." *Journal of Marriage and the Family* 56 (1) (Feb.):101–18.

O'Neill, Nena and George O'Neill. 1972. *Open Marriage: A New Life Style for Couples*. New York: M. Evans.

———. 1974. *Shifting Gears: Finding Security in a Changing World*. New York: M. Evans.

Ono, Hiromi. 1998. "Husbands' and Wives' Resources and Marital Dissolution." *Journal of Marriage and the Family* 60 (3):674–89.

Oppenheimer, Valerie Kincaide. 1974. "The Life Cycle Squeeze: The Interaction of Men's Occupational and Family Life Cycles." *Demography* 11:227–45.

———. 1994. "Women's Rising Employment and the Future of the Family in Industrial Societies." *Population and Development Review* 20 (2) (June):293–342.

Oostindie, Irwin. n.d. "Domestic Worker Support in Canada." <http://www.spunk.org/library/pubs/lr/sp001716/labside.html>

Orbuch, Terri L. and Lindsay Custer. 1995. "The Social Context of Married Women's Work and Its Impact on Black Husbands and White Husbands." *Journal of Marriage and the Family* 57 (2) (May):333–45.

Orenstein, Peggy. 1994. *School Girls: Young Women, Self-Esteem, and the Confidence Gap*. New York: Doubleday.

Orentlicher, David. 1998. "Spanking and Other Corporal Punishment of Children by Parents: Overvaluing Pain, Undervaluing Children." *Houston Law Review* 35 (1):147–61.

Ortega, Suzanne T., Hugh P. Whitt, and J. Allen Williams. 1988. "Religious Homogamy and Marital Happiness." *Journal of Family Issues* 9:224–39.

O'Sullivan, Lucia F. and Elizabeth Rice Allgeier. 1998. "Feigning Sexual Desire: Consenting to Unwanted Sexual Activity in Heterosexual Dating Relationships." *Journal of Sex Research* 35 (3):234–43.

Otten, Alan L. 1990. "Who Cares for Kids Depends on Their Status." *The Wall Street Journal*, Nov. 29, p. B1.

Overall, Christine. 1990. "Selective Termination of Pregnancy and Women's Reproductive Autonomy." *Hastings Center Report* (May/June):6–11.

Owens, Stephen J. and Sara H. Qualls. 1997. "Family Stress at the Time of a Geopsychiatric Hospitalization." *Family Relations* 46 (2):179–85.

P

Padavic, Irene. 1992. "White-Collar Work Values and Women's Interest in Blue-Collar Jobs." *Gender & Society* 6 (2) (June):215–30.

Paden, Shelley L. and Cheryl Buehler. 1995. "Coping with Dual-Income Lifestyle." *Journal of Marriage and the Family* 57 (1) (Feb.):101–10.

Pagani, Linda, Bernard Boulerice, Richard E. Tremblay, and Frank Vitaro. 1997. "Behavioural Development in Children of Divorce and Remarriage." *Journal of Child Psychology and Psychiatry and Allied Disciplines* 38 (7):769–81.

Pagani-Kurtz, Linda and Jeffrey L. Derevensky. 1997. "Access By Noncustodial Parents: Effects Upon Children's Postdivorce Coping Resources." *Journal of Divorce & Remarriage* 27(1-2):34–55.

Page, Jessica R., Heather B. Stevens, and Shelley L. Galvin. 1996. "Relationships between Depression, Self-Esteem, and Self-Silencing Behavior." *Journal of Social and Clinical Psychology* 15 (4):381–90.

Paludi, M. A., Ed. 1990. *Ivory Power: Sexual Harassment on Campus*. Albany: State University of New York Press.

Papanek, Hanna. 1973. "Men, Women, and Work: Reflections on the Two-Person Career." Pp. 90–110 in *Changing Women in A Changing Society*, edited by Joan Huber. Chicago: University of Chicago Press.

Papernow, P. 1993. *Becoming a Stepfamily: Patterns of Development in Remarried Families*. San Francisco: Josey-Bass.

Parke, Ross D. and Ronald G. Slaby. 1983. "The Development of Aggression." Pp. 547–641 in *Handbook of Child Psychology*, vol. 4, *Socialization, Personality, and Social Development*, edited by E. Mavis Hetherington. New York: Wiley.

Parsons, Talcott. 1943. "The Kinship System of the Contemporary United States." *American Anthropologist* 45:22–38.

Parsons, Talcott and Robert F. Bales. 1955. *Family, Socialization, and Interaction Process*. Glencoe, IL: Free Press.

Parsons, Talcott and Renee Fox. 1952. "Illness, Therapy, and the Modern American Family." *Journal of Social Issues* 8:31–44.

Parsons, Talcott and Victor Lidz. 1967. "Death in American Society." Pp. 133–70 in *Essays on Self-Destruction*, edited by Edwin Scheidman. New York: Science House.

Paset, Pamela S. and Ronald D. Taylor. 1991. "Black and White Women's Attitudes toward Interracial Marriage." *Psychological Reports* 69:753–54.

Pasley, Kay and Marilyn Ihinger-Tallman. 1988. "Remarriage and Stepfamilies." Pp. 204–21 in *Variant Family Forms*, edited by Catherine S. Chilman, Elam W. Nunnally, and Fred M. Cox. Newbury Park, CA: Sage.

Pasley, Kay, Lyn Rhoden, Emily B. Visher, and John S. Visher. 1996. "Successful Stepfamily Therapy: Clients' Perspectives." *Journal of Marital and Family Therapy* 22 (3):343–57.

Passell, Peter. 1991. "Chronic Poverty, Black and White." *New York Times*, Mar. 6.

Patterson, Charlotte. 1992. "Children of Lesbian and Gay Parents." *Child Development* 63:1025–42.

———. 1997. "Children of Lesbian and Gay Parents: Summary of Research Findings." Pp. 146–154 in *Same-Sex Marriage: Pro and Con*, edited by A. Sullivan. New York: Vintage Books.

Patterson, Gerald R. 1982. *Coercive Family Process.* Eugene, OR: Castalia.

Patterson, Joan. M. and A. W. Garwick. 1994. "Levels of Meaning in Family Stress Theory." *Family Process* 33 (3):287–95.

Patterson, Joan M. and Hamilton I. McCubbin. 1984. "Gender Roles and Coping." *Journal of Marriage and the Family* 46 (1):95–104.

Payn, Betsy, Koray Tanfer, John O. G. Billy and William R. Grady. 1997. "Men's Behavior Change Following Infection with a Sexually Transmitted Disease." *Family Planning Perspectives* 29 (4):152–57.

Pear, Robert. 1991. "5.5 Million Children in U.S. Are Hungry, a Study Finds." *New York Times*, Mar. 27.

Pearlin, Leonard I. 1975. "Status Inequality and Stress in Marriage." *American Sociological Review* 40:344–57.

Peck, M. Scott, 1978. *The Road Less Traveled: A New Psychology of Love, Traditional Values and Spiritual Growth.* New York: Simon & Schuster.

Peele, S. and R. DeGrandpre. 1995. "My Genes Made Me Do It." *Psychology Today*, 28 (4) (July/August):50–53.

Peplau, Letitia A. 1981. "What Homosexuals Want in Relationships." *Psychology Today* 15:28–38.

Peplau, Letitia A. and Steven L. Gordon. 1983. "The Intimate Relationships of Lesbians and Gay Men." Pp. 226–44 in *Changing Boundaries: Gender Roles and Sexual Behavior*, edited by Elizabeth Rice Allgeier and Naomi B. McCormick. Palo Alto, CA: Mayfield.

Peplau, Letitia A. and Susan Miller Campbell. 1989. "The Balance of Power in Dating and Marriage." Pp. 121–37 in *Women: A Feminist Perspective.* 4th ed., edited by Jo Freeman. Mountain View, CA: Mayfield.

Peres, Judy. 1997. "Sperm-Donor's Case Challenges Old Laws." *Chicago Tribune.* August 12:1, 8.

Peres, Yochanan and Rachel Pasternack. 1991. "To What Extent Can the School Reduce the Gaps Between Children Raised by Divorce and Intact Families?" *Journal of Divorce and Remarriage* 15 (3/4):143–58.

Peritz, Ingrid. 1999. "Birth Rate in Quebec Lowest Since 1908." *The Globe and Mail*, October 4:A1.

Perkins, Daniel F. and Sylvia J. Ansay. 1998. "The Effectiveness of a Visitation Program in Fostering Visits with Noncustodial Parents." *Family Relations* 47 (3):253–58.

Perkins, Daniel F., Sylvia J. Ansay, Tom Luster, Francisco A. Villarruel, and Stephen Small. 1998. "An Ecological, Risk-Factor Examination of Adolescents' Sexual Activity in Three Ethnic Groups." *Journal of Marriage and the Family* 60 (3):660–73.

Perlman, Daniel and Karen S. Rook. 1987. "Social Support, Social Deficits, and the Family." Pp. 17–44 in *Family Processes and Problems: Social Psychological Aspects.* Applied Social Psychology Annual, vol. 7, edited by Stuart Oskamp. Newbury Park, CA: Sage.

Perlman, Robert, Ed. 1983. *Family Home Care: Critical Issues for Services and Policies.* New York: Haworth Press.

Perner, J., T. Ruffman, and S. R. Leekam. 1994. "Theory of Mind Is Contagious: You Catch It from Your Sibs." *Child Development* 65:1228–38.

Perry, Charlotte. 1999. "Extended Family Support among Older Black Females." Pp. 70–76 in *The Black Family: Essays and Studies*, 6th ed, edited by Robert Staples. Belmont, CA: Wadsworth.

Perry-Jenkins, Maureen and Ann C. Crouter. 1990. "Men's Provider Role Attitudes: Implications for Household Work and Marital Satisfaction." *Journal of Family Issues* 11:136–56.

Perry-Jenkins, Maureen and Karen Folk. 1994. "Class, Couples, and Conflict: Effects of the Division of Labor on Assessments of Marriage in Dual-Earner Families." *Journal of Marriage and the Family* 56 (1) (Feb.):165–80.

Peterman, Jean. 1993. "Puerto Rican Women Deciding to Get an Abortion: Beginning a Collective Story." *Latino Studies Journal* 4 (3):44–59.

Peters, Arnold and Aart C. Liefbroer. 1997. "Beyond Marital Status: Partner History and Well-Being in Old Age." *Journal of Marriage and the Family* 59 (3):687–99.

Peters, Marie Ferguson. 1988. "Parenting in Black Families with Young Children." Pp. 228–41 in *Black Families,* 2d ed., edited by Harriette Pipes McAdoo. Newbury Park, CA: Sage.

Peters, Marie Ferguson and Harriette P. McAdoo. 1983. "The Present and Future of Alternative Lifestyles in Ethnic American Cultures." Pp. 288–307 in *Contemporary Families and Alternative Lifestyles: Handbook on Research and Theory*, edited by Eleanor D. Macklin and Roger H. Rubin. Newbury Park, CA: Sage.

Petersen, Larry R. 1994. "Education, Homogamy, and Religious Commitment." *Journal for the Scientific Study of Religion* 33 (2):122–28.

Petersen, Larry R. and G. V. Donnenwerth. 1997. "Secularization and the Influence of Religion on Beliefs about Premarital Sex." *Social Forces* 75:1071–89.

Peterson, Gary W. and Boyd C. Rollins. 1987. "Parent–Child Socialization." Pp. 471–507 in *Handbook of Marriage and the Family*, edited by Marvin B. Sussman and Suzanne K. Steinmetz. New York: Plenum.

Peterson, James L. and Christine Winquist Nord. 1990. "The Regular Receipt of Child Support: A Multistep

Process." *Journal of Marriage and the Family* 52 (2): (May):539–51.

Peterson, James L. and Nicholas Zill. 1986. "Marital Disruption, Parent–Child Relationships, and Behavioral Problems in Children." *Journal of Marriage and the Family* 48:295–307.

Peterson, Oliver. 1991. "Many Older People Are Richer Than Other Americans." *New York Times*, Oct. 30.

Peterson, Richard R. 1989. *Women, Work, and Divorce*. New York: State University of New York Press.

———. 1996. "A Re-Evaluation Of The Economic Consequences Of Divorce." *American Sociological Review* 61:528–536.

Peterson, Richard R. and Kathleen Gerson. 1992. "Determinants of Responsibility for Child Care Arrangements Among Dual-Earner Couples." *Journal of Marriage and the Family* 54 (3) (Aug.):527–36.

Peterson, Sharyl Bender and Traci Kroner. 1992. "Gender Biases in Textbooks for Introductory Psychology and Human Development." *Psychology of Women Quarterly* 16:17–36.

Pett, Marjorie A., Nancy Lang, and Anita Gander. 1992. "Late-Life Divorce: Its Impact on Family Rituals." *Journal of Family Issues* 13:526–53.

Pettit, Ellen J. and Bernard L. Bloom. 1984. "Whose Decision Was It? The Effects of Initiator Status on Adjustment to Marital Disruption." *Journal of Marriage and the Family* 46 (3):587–95.

Peyser, Marc. 1997. "A Deadly Dance." *Newsweek*. September 29:76–77.

Pfuhl, E.H. 1978. "The Unwed Father: A Non-Deviant Rule Breaker." *The Sociological Quarterly* 19:113–128.

Phillips, Linda R. 1986. "Theoretical Explanations of Elder Abuse: Competing Hypotheses and Unresolved Issues." Pp. 197–217 in *Elder Abuse: Conflict in the Family*, edited by Karl A. Pillemer and Rosalie S. Wolf. Dover, MA: Auburn House.

Phillips, Roderick. 1997. "Stepfamilies from a Historical Perspective." Pp. 5–18 in *Stepfamilies: History, Research, and Policy*, edited by Irene Levin and Marvin B. Sussman. New York: Haworth Press.

Philp, Margaret. 2001. "Gay Adoption Breaks New Ground." *The Globe and Mail*, July 9: A3.

Phipps, S., P. Burton and L. Lethbridge. 1998. *In and Out of the Labour Market: Long-term Income Consequences of Interruptions in Paid Work*. Halifax: Department of Economics, Dalhousie University.

Picard, Michele. 1997. "Get Back to Work: Employers' Efforts to Be 'Family Friendly' Have Left Some Childless Workers Feeling Excluded, Overworked, and Resentful." *Training* 34 (9):33–37.

Piche, Lyne, Gilles Trudel and Jean Belanger. 2000. "La Determination Du Degre De Relation Entre L'estime De Soi Et Quatre Elements De L'experience Sexuelle." *Canadian Journal of Human Sexuality*, 9:31–40.

Picot, Garnett, Wendy Pyper and Myles Zyblock. 1999. "Why Do Children Move Into And Out Of Low Income: Changing Labour Market Conditions Or Marriage And Divorce?" *Analytic Studies Branch Research Paper Series* April 21. Catalogue No.11FOO19MPE99132.

Picot, Garnett and John Myles. 2000. "Children in Low-Income Families." Pp. 130–134 in *Canadian Social Trends: Volume 3*. Toronto: Thompson Educational Publishing.

Piercy, Kathleen W. 1998. "Theorizing about Family Caregiving: The Role of Responsibility." *Journal of Marriage and the Family* 60 (1):109–18.

Pietropinto, Anthony and Jacqueline Simenauer. 1977. *Beyond the Male Myth: What Women Want to Know About Men's Sexuality, A National Survey*. New York: Times Books.

Pillard, Richard C. and J. Michael Bailey. 1998. "Human Sexuality Has A Heritable Component." *Human Biology* 70 (April):347–365.

Pillemer, Karl A. 1986. "Risk Factors in Elder Abuse: Results from a Case-Control Study." Pp. 239–64 in *Elder Abuse: Conflict in the Family*, edited by Karl A. Pillemer and Rosalie S. Wolf. Dover, A: Auburn House.

Pina, Darlene L. and Vern L. Bengtson. 1993. "The Division of Household Labor and Wives' Happiness: Ideology, Employment, and Perceptions of Support." *Journal of Marriage and the Family* 55 (4) (Nov.):901–12.

Pines, Maya. 1981. "Only Isn't Lonely (or Spoiled or Selfish)." *Psychology Today* 15:15–19.

Piotrkowski, Chaya S., Robert N. Rapoport, and Rhona Rapoport. 1987. "Families and Work." Pp. 251–83 in *Handbook of Marriage and the Family*, edited by Marvin S. Sussman and Suzanne K. Steinmetz. New York: Plenum.

Pitman, Sara. 1997. "From Keyboards to Human Contact: Love Relationships Through Computer-Mediated Communications." *Internet* 26. <http://edie.cprost.sfu.ca/~chiklink/sarticle.html>

Pittman, F. 1990. *Private lies: Infidelity and Betrayal of Intimacy*. New York: Norton.

Pittman, Joe F. and David Blanchard. 1996. "The Effects of Work History and Timing of Marriage on the Division of Household Labor: A Life-Course Perspective." *Journal of Marriage and the Family* 58 (1):78–90.

Pitts, Patty. 1995. "Dating Difficult In The Middle Ages." *The Ring* 21(1), July 14. <http://communications.uvic.ca/Ring/95jul14/Veevers.html>

Pleck, Joseph H. 1977. "The Work–Family Role System." *Social Problems* 24:417–27.

———. 1985. *Working Wives/Working Husbands*. Newbury Park, CA: Sage.

———. 1992. "Prisoners of Manliness." Pp. 98–107 in *Men's Lives.* 2d ed, edited by Michael S. Kimmel and Michael A. Messner. New York: Macmillan.

Plous, S. and Dominique Neptune. 1997. "Racial and Gender Biases in Magazine Advertising." *Psychology of Women Quarterly* 21 (4):627–44.

Podnieks, E. and Karl Pillemer. 1990. *National Survey of Abuse of the Elderly in Canada.* Ottawa: National Clearinghouse on Family Violence. Health and Welfare Canada.

Polakow, Valerie. 1993. *Single Mothers and Their Children in the Other America.* Chicago: University of Chicago Press.

Pollack, William. 1998. *Real Boys: Rescuing Our Sons from the Myths of Boyhood.* New York: Random House.

Pollard, Michael and Zheng Wu. 1998. *Economic Circumstances And The Stability Of Nonmarital Cohabitation.* Statistics Canada Income Research Paper Series, Catalogue no. 75F0002M1E98010.

"Polygamy, the Quaranic Way." 1997. <http://www.submission.org>

Pomerleau, A., D. Bolduc, G. Malcuit, and L. Cossetts. 1990. "Pink or Blue: Environmental Stereotypes in the First Two Years of Life." *Sex Roles* 22:359–67.

Pong, Suet-Ling. 1997. "Family Structure, School Context, and Eighth-Grade Math and Reading Achievement." *Journal of Marriage and the Family* 59 (3):734–46.

Popenoe, David. 1988. *Disturbing the Nest: Family Change and Decline in Modern Societies.* New York: Aldine De Gruyter.

———. 1993. "American Family Decline, 1960–1990: A Review and Appraisal." *Journal of Marriage and the Family* 55 (3) (Aug.):527–55.

———. 1994. "The Evolution of Marriage and the Problem of Stepfamilies: A Biosocial Perspective." Pp. 3–28 in *Stepfamilies: Who Benefits? Who Does Not?,* edited by Alan Booth and Judy Dunn. Hillsdale, NJ: Lawrence Erlbaum Associates.

———. 1996. *Life without Father: Compelling New Evidence that Fatherhood and Marriage Are Indispensable for the Good of Children and Society.* New York: Martin Kessler Books.

———. 1998. "The Decline of Marriage and Fatherhood." Pp. 312–19 in *Seeing Ourselves: Classic, Contemporary, and Cross-Cultural Readings in Sociology,* 4th edition, edited by John J. Macionis and Nijole V. Benokraitis. Upper Saddle River, NJ: Prentice Hall.

Popenoe, David, Andrew Norton, and Barry Maley (Eds.). 1994. *Shaping the Social Virtues. Centre for Independent Studies: CIS Policy Monographs* 28.

Population Information Program. The Johns Hopkins University. 1984. "After Contraception: Dispelling Rumors About Later Childbearing." *Population Reports,* Series 1, No. 28.

Population Reference Bureau. 1998. "1998 World Population Data Sheet of the Population Reference Bureau, Inc." Washington, DC: Population Reference Bureau.

Porter, Sylvia. 1976. *Sylvia Porter's Money Book.* New York: Avon.

Porterfield, Ernest. 1982. "Black-American Intermarriages in the United States." Pp. 17–34 in *Intermarriages in the United States,* edited by Gary Crester and Joseph J. Leon. New York: Haworth.

Potuchek, Jean L. 1992. "Employed Wives' Orientation to Breadwinning: A Gender Theory Analysis." *Journal of Marriage and the Family* 54 (3) (Aug.):548–58.

Power, Paul W. 1979. "The Chronically Ill Husband and Father: His Role in the Family." *Family Coordinator* 28:616–21.

Powers, Mike. 1997. "The Hidden Costs of Divorce." *Human Ecology Forum* 25 (1):4–15.

Powledge, Tabitha M. 1983. "Windows on the Womb." *Psychology Today* 17:37–42.

Pozzetta, George E., Ed. 1991. *Immigrant Family Patterns: Demography, Fertility, Housing, Kinship, and Urban Life.* New York: Garland.

Prager, Karen and Janice Steil. 1997. "The Psychology of Intimacy." *Contemporary Psychology* 42 (4):302–11.

Presser, Harriet B. 1988. "Shift Work and Child Care Among Young Dual-Earner American Parents." *Journal of Marriage and the Family* 50:133–48.

Preston, Valerie, Rose Damaris, Glen Norcliffe, and John Holmes. 2000. "Shift Work, Childcare and Domestic Work: Divisions of Labour in Canadian Paper Mill Communities." *Gender, Place and Culture* 7 (1) (March):5–29.

Prilleltensky, Isaac. 1993. "The Immigration Experience Of Latin American Families: Research And Action On Perceived Risk And Protective Factors." *Canadian Journal of Community Health, Special Issue: Cultural Diversity: Voice, Access, and Involvement.* 12(2) (fall):101–116.

Pruchino, Rachel, Christopher Burant, and Norah D. Peters. 1994. "Family Mental Health: Marital and Parent–Child Consensus as Predictors." *Journal of Marriage and the Family* 56 (3) (Aug.):747–58.

Purdum, Todd S. (1996, Sept. 22). "Heat on Clinton for Gay Marriage Ruling." *San Francisco Examiner,* p. A-2.

Puri, Deepika. 2000. *Gift of a Daughter: Change and Continuity in Marriage Patterns among Two Generations of North Indians in Toronto and Delhi.* Unpublished dissertation, University of Toronto.

Purnine, Daniel M. and Michael P. Carey. 1998. "Age and Gender Differences in Sexual Behavior Preferences: A Follow-Up Report." *Journal of Sex & Marital Therapy* 24:93–102.

Pyke, Karen D. 1997. "Class-Based Masculinities: The Interdependence of Gender, Class, and Interpersonal Power." *Gender and Society* 10:527–49.

Pyke, Karen D. and Vern L. Bengston. 1996. "Caring More or Less: Individualistic and Collectivist Systems of Family Eldercare." *Journal of Marriage and the Family* 58 (2):379–92.

Q

Qian, Zhenchao. 1998. "Changes in Assortive Mating: The Impact of Age and Education, 1970–1970." *Demography*, 35(3): 279–92.

Quarm, Daisy. 1984. "Sexual Inequality: The High Costs of Leaving Parenting to Women." Pp. 187–208 in *Women in the Workplace: Effects on Families*, edited by Kathryn M. Borman, Daisy Quarm, and Sarah Gideonse. Norwood, NJ: Ablex.

Queen, Stuart A., Robert W. Habenstein, and Jill Quadagno (Eds.). 1985. *The Family in Various Cultures*, 5th edition. New York: Harper & Row.

Quindlen, Anna. 1990. "Men at Work." *New York Times*, Feb. 18.

Quinn, Peggy and Katherine R. Allen. 1989. "Facing Challenges and Making Compromises: How Single Mothers Endure." *Family Relations* 28 (Oct.):390–95.

Qvortrup, M. B., G. Sgritta, and H. Wintersberger, eds. 1994. *Childhood Matters: Social Theory, Practice, and Politics*. Vienna: European Centre for Social Welfare Policy and Research.

R

Raabe, Phyllis Hutton. 1990. "The Organizational Effects of Workplace Family Policies." *Journal of Family Issues* 11 (4) (Dec.):477–91.

Rae, Scott B. 1994. *The Ethics of Commercial Surrogate Motherhood: Brave New Families?* Westport, CT: Praeger.

Ragone, Helena. 1994. *Surrogate Motherhood: Conception in the Heart*. Oxford: Westview.

Raley, Gabrielle. 1999. "No Good Choices: Teenage Childbearing, Concentrated Poverty, and Welfare Reform." Pp. 258–72 in *American Families: A Multicultural Reader*, edited by Stephanie Coontz. New York: Routeledge.

Raley, R. Kelly. 1995. "Black-White Differences in Kin Contact and Exchange Among Never Married Adults." *Journal of Family Issues* 16 (1):77–103.

Rangarajan, Anu and Philip Gleason. 1998. "Young Unwed Fathers of AFDC Children: Do They Provide Support?" *Demography* 35 (2):175–86.

Raphael, Phyllis. 1978. "The Stepmother Trap." *McCall's*, Feb., pp. 188–94.

Rapp, Rayna. 1999. "Family and Class in Contemporary America: Notes toward an Understanding of Ideology." Pp. 180–96 in *American Families: A Multicultural Reader*, edited by Stephanie Coontz. New York: Routledge.

Raschke, Helen C. 1987. "Divorce." Pp. 597–624 in *Handbook of Marriage and the Family*, edited by Marvin B. Sussman and Suzanne K. Steinmetz. New York: Plenum.

Rashid, Abdul. 1994. "High Income Families." *Perspectives on Labour and Income* 6 (4) (winter):46–57.

Raven, Bertram, Richard Centers, and Arnoldo Rodrigues. 1975. "The Bases of Conjugal Power." Pp. 217–32 in *Power in Families*, edited by Ronald E. Cromwell and David H. Olson. Beverly Hills: Sage.

Ravo, Nick. 1993. "With a New Kind of Housing, Togetherness Is Built Right In." *New York Times*, Feb. 25.

Rawlings, Steve W. 1994. *Household and Family Characteristics: March 1993*. U.S. Bureau of the Census, Current Population Reports, P20–477. Washington, DC: U.S. Government Printing Office.

Raymond, Janice G. 1989. "The International Traffic in Women: Women Used in Systems of Surrogacy and Reproduction." *Reproductive and Genetic Engineering* 2 (1):51–57.

———. 1991. "Women as Wombs." *Ms. Magazine*. 1 (6), May/June, pp. 28–33.

Razack, Sherene. 1993. "Exploring the Omissions and Silences in Law Around Race." Pp. 37–48 in *Investigating Gender Bias: Laws, Courts and the Legal Profession*, edited by Joan Brockman and Dororthy E. Chunn. Toronto: Thompson Education Publishing, Inc.

———. 1994. "What Is To Be Gained By Looking White People In The Eye? Culture, Race, and Gender in Cases of Sexual Violence." *Signs* 19 (4):894–923.

Reagan, Pamela. 1999. "Hormonal Correlates And Causes Of Sexual Desire: A Review." *The Canadian Journal of Human Sexuality* 8:1–16.

Real, Terrence. 1997. *I Don't Want to Talk about It: Overcoming the Secret Legacy of Male Depression*. New York: Scribner.

Reese, Thomas J. 1992. "Bishops Meet at Notre Dame." *America*, July 4–11, pp. 4–6.

Register, Cheri. 1991. *"Are Those Kids Yours?": American Families with Children Adopted from Other Countries*. New York: Free Press.

Reid, John. 1982. *Black America in the 1980s*. Population Bulletin 37. Washington, DC: Population Reference Bureau.

Reimann, Renate. 1997. "Does Biology Matter?: Lesbian Couples' Transition to Parenthood and Their Division of Labor." *Qualitative Sociology* 20 (2):153–85.

Reinisch, J. 1990. *The Kinsey Institute New Report on Sex: What You Must Know To Be Sexually Literate*. New York: St. Martin's.

Reiss, David, Sandra Gonzalez, and Norman Kramer. 1986. "Family Process, Chronic Illness, and Death: On the Weakness of Strong Bonds." *Archives of General Psychiatry* 43:795–804.

Reiss, Ira L. 1976. *Family Systems in America.* 2d ed. Hinsdale, IL: Dryden.

———. 1986. *Journey into Sexuality: An Exploratory Voyage.* Englewood Cliffs, NJ: Prentice-Hall.

Reiss, Ira L. and G. L. Lee. 1988. *The Family System in America.* 4th ed. New York: Holt, Reinhart & Winston.

Reitz, Jeffrey. 1997. "Institutional Structure and Immigrant Earnings: A Comparison of American, Canadian and Australian Cities." *American Sociological Association Paper.*

———. 2000a. *Warmth of the Welcome.* Boulder, CO: Westview Press.

———. 2000b. "Immigrant Success in the Knowledge Economy: Institutional Change and the Immigrant Experience in Canada, 1970–1995." Paper prepared for presentation at the meetings of the Canadian Ethnic Studies Association, Toronto, March 25–6.

——— and Janet Lum. 2000. "Immigration and Diversity in a Changing Canadian City: Social Bases of Inter-group Relations in Toronto." Unpublished paper.

ReligiousTolerance.org 2000a. "Female Genital Mutilation (Female Circumcision)" <http://www.religious tolerance.org/fem_cirm.htm>

ReligiousTolerance.org 2000b. "Female & Intersexual Genital Mutilation In North America & Europe." <wysiwyg://19/http://www.religioustolerance.org/fem_cir a.htm>

Renaud, Cheryl A. and E. Sandra Byers. 1999. "Exploring The Frequency, Diversity, And Content Of University Students' Positive And Negative Sexual Cognitions." *The Canadian Journal of Human Sexuality* 8:17–30.

Renzetti, Claire M. 1992. *Violent Betrayal: Partner Abuse in Lesbian Relationships.* Newbury Park, CA: Sage.

Renzetti, Claire M. and Charles H. Miley. 1996. *Violence in Gay and Lesbian Domestic Partnerships.* New York: Haworth Press.

Resnick, M. 1984. "Studying Adolescent Mothers' Decision Making About Adoption and Parenting." *Social Work* 29:4–10.

Reuters Health. 2001. "Cyber Sexual Revolution Continues: Survey." April 18. <4/18/20wysiwyg://36/ http://healthcentralsympatic...ext.cfm>

Reuters. 2001. "Over 70 Countries Consider Homosexuality a Crime." June 23 <wysiwyg://80/http:// www.canada.com/cig-bi.../international-rights-homosexuals-dc.html>

Rice, G., C. Anderson, N. Risch and G. Ebers. 1999. "Male Homosexuality: Absence of Linkage to Microsatellite Markers at Xq28." *Science* 23 April, 284 (5414):665–667.

Richard, Madeline A. 1991. *Ethnic Groups and Marital Choices.* Vancouver: University of British Columbia Press.

Richardson, Brenda Lane. 1988. "Working Women Do Go Home Again." *New York Times*, Apr. 20.

Richardson, J. 1997. *Gender Differences in Human Cognition.* New York: Oxford University Press.

Richardson, L. 1996. "Gender Stereotyping in the English Language." In K.E. Rosenblum and T.M.C. Travis (Eds.), *The Meaning of Difference: American Constructions of Race, Sex and Gender and Sexual Orientation.* New York: McGraw-Hill.

Richardson, Laurel Walum. 1985. *The New Other Woman: Contemporary Single Women in Affairs with Married Men.* New York: Free Press.

Richmond, Anthony H. 1993. "Education and Qualifications Of Caribbean Migrants In Metropolitan Toronto." *New Community* 19 (2) (Jan):273–280.

Ridgeway, Cecilia L. 1997. "Interaction and the Conservation of Gender Inequality: Considering Employment." *American Sociological Review* 62:218–35.

Ridley, Carl, Dan J. Peterman and Arthur W. Avery. 1978. "Cohabitation: Does It Make for a Better Marriage?" *Family Coordinator* 27:129–36.

Rigdon, Joan E. 1991. "Exploding Myth: Asian-American Youth Suffer a Rising Toll for Heavy Pressure." *The Wall Street Journal*, July 10.

Riggs, D. S. 1993. "Relationship Problems and Dating Aggression: A Potential Treatment Target." *Journal of Interpersonal Violence* 8:18–35.

Riley, Glenda. 1991. *Divorce: An American Tradition.* New York: Oxford University Press.

Riordan, Teresa and Sue Kirchhoff. 1995. "Women on the Hill: Can They Make a Difference?" *Ms. Magazine.* (Jan./Feb.):85–89.

Rimer, Sara. 1988a. "Child Care at Home: 2-Women, Complex Roles." *New York Times*, Dec. 26.

Risman, Barbara J. and Danette Johnson-Sumerford. 1998. "Doing It Fairly: A Study of Postgender Marriages." *Journal of Marriage and the Family* 60 (1):23–40.

Ristock, J.L. 1991. "Beyond Ideologies: Understanding Violence In Lesbian Relationships." *Canadian Woman Studies* 12 (1):74–79.

Rivera, Carla. 1996. "Welfare Reform Hits Grandparents." *Los Angeles Times*, reprinted in *San Jose Mercury News.* December 24:A13.

Roberts, Jillian. 1999. "Canadian Families with HIV/AIDS: Quality of Life Experiences in Public Schools." Unpublished dissertation, University of Calgary.

Roberts, Robert E. L. and Vern L. Bengston. 1993. "Relationships with Parents, Self-Esteem, and Psychological Well-Being in Young Adulthood." *Social Psychology Quarterly* 56 (4):263–77.

Roberts, Siobhan. 2001. "Same-Sex Couples Preparing to Tie Knot." *The Globe and Mail*, January 13: A8.

Robertson, Elizabeth B., Glen H. Elder, Jr., Martie L. Skinner, and Rand D. Conger. 1991. "The Costs and

Benefits of Social Support in Families." *Journal of Marriage and the Family* 53:403–16.

Robertson, Joan F. 1978. "Women in Mid-Life: Crisis, Reverberations, and Support Networks." *Family Coordinator* 27:375–82.

Robinson, Bryan E. and Robert L. Barret. 1986. *The Developing Father: Emerging Roles in Contemporary Society.* New York: Guilford.

Robinson, Bryan, Patsy Skeen, and Lynda Walters. 1987. "The AIDS Epidemic Hits Home." *Psychology Today* (Apr.):48–52.

Robinson, Ira, B. Ganza, S. Katz, and E. Robinson. 1991. "Twenty Years of the Sexual Revolution, 1965–1985: An Update." *Journal of Marriage and the Family* 53:216–20.

Robinson, Ira E. and Davor Jedlicka. 1987. "Fear Of Venereal Disease And Other Presumed Restraints On The Occurrence Of Premarital Coitus." *Journal of Sex Research* 23 (3) (August):391–396.

———. 1982. "Change in Sexual Attitudes and Behavior of College Students from 1965 to 1980." *Journal of Marriage and the Family*, 44 (1) (February):237–240.

Robinson, John P. and Melissa A. Milkie. 1998. "Back to the Basics: Trends in and Role Determinants of Women's Attitudes toward Housework." *Journal of Marriage and the Family* 60 (1):205–18.

Robinson, Robert V. 1995. "Family Economic Strategies in Nineteenth- and Early Twentieth-Century Indianapolis." *Journal of Family History* 20 (1):1–22.

Robson, Ruthann and S. E. Valentine. 1990. "Lov(h)ers: Lesbians as Intimate Partners and Lesbian Legal Theory." *Temple Law Review* 63:511–41.

Rodgers, Joseph Lee and David C. Rowe. 1990. "Adolescent Sexual Activity and Mildly Deviant Behavior." *Journal of Family Issues* 11 (3) (Sept.):274–93.

Rodgers, Karen. 2000. "Wife Assault in Canada." Pp. 237–242 in *Canadian Social Trends: Volume 3.* Toronto: Thompson Educational Publishing, Inc.

——— and Garry MacDonald. "Canada's Shelters for Abused Women." Pp. 248–252 in *Canadian Social Trends: Volume 3.* Toronto: Thompson Educational Publishing, Inc.

Rodgers, Roy H. and Linda M. Conrad. 1986. "Courtship for Remarriage: Influences on Family Reorganization After Divorce." *Journal of Marriage and the Family* 48:767–75.

Rodgers, Roy H. and James M. White. 1993. "Family Development Theory." Pp. 225–54 in *Sourcebook of Family Theories and Methods: A Contextual Approach,* edited by Pauline G. Boss, William J. Doherty, Ralph LaRossa, Walter R. Schumm, and Suzanne K. Steinmetz. New York: Plenum.

Rodriguez, Christina M. and Andrea J. Green. 1997. "Parenting Stress and Anger Expression As Predictors of

Child Abuse Potential." *Child Abuse & Neglect* 21 (4):367–77.

Rogers, David. 1995. "House Votes to Ban Late-Term Abortion in Challenges to Supreme Court Decision." *The Wall Street Journal,* Nov. 2.

Rogers, Fred. 1997. *Stepfamilies.* New York: G. P. Putnam's Sons.

Rogers, Patrick. 1994. "Surviving the Second Wave." *Newsweek,* Sept. 19, pp. 50–51.

Rogers, S.J. 1999. "Wives' Income and Marital Quality: Are There Reciprocal Effects?" *Journal of Marriage and the Family* 61:123–132.

Rogers, Susan M. and Charles F. Turner. 1991. "Male–Male Sexual Contact in the U.S.A.: Findings from Five Sample Surveys, 1970–1990." *The Journal of Sex Research* 28 (4):491–519.

Rohland, Pamela. 1995. "Choosing to be Childless." *The San Francisco Bay Guardian.* January 4:18–24.

Romano, Lois and Jacqueline Trescott. 1992. "Love in Black & White." *Redbook,* Feb., pp. 88–94.

Romero, Mary. 1992. *Maid in the U.S.A.* New York: Routledge.

Ronfeldt, Heidi M., Rachel Kimerling, and Ilena Arias. 1998. "Satisfaction with Relationship Power and the Perpetuation of Dating Violence." *Journal of Marriage and the Family* 60(1), Feb.:70–78.

Roos, Patricia A. and Catherine W. Jones. 1993. "Shifting Gender Boundaries. Women's Inroads into Academic Sociology." *Work and Occupations* 20:395–428.

Roosa, Mark W., Jenn-Yun Tein, Cindy Reinholtz, and Patricia Jo Angelini. 1997. "The Relationship of Childhood Sexual Abuse to Teenage Pregnancy." *Journal of Marriage and the Family* 59:119–30.

Roosens, Eugene. 1991. *Creating Ethnicity: The Process of Ethnogenesis,* 2nd edition. Newbury Park: Sage Publications Inc.

Roots, Charles R. 1998. *The Sandwich Generation: Adult Children Caring for Aging Parents.* New York: Garland.

Rose, Jerry. 1976. *Peoples: The Ethnic Dimension in Human Relations.* Chicago: Rand McNally Publishing Company.

Rosen, Ruth. 2000. *The World Split Open: How the Modern Women's Movement Changed America.* New York: Viking.

Rosenberg, Elinor B. 1992. *The Adoption Life Cycle: The Children and Their Families Through the Years.* New York: Free Press.

Rosenberg, Janet, Harry Perlstadt and William Phillips. 1997. "Now That We Are Here: Discrimination, Disparagement and Harassment at Work and the Experience of Women Lawyers." Pp. 247–259 in *Workplace/Women's Place,* edited by Dana Dunn. Los Angeles: Roxbury.

Rosenblatt, Paul C. and Linda Hammer Burns. 1986. "Long-Term Effects of Perinatal Loss." *Journal of Family Issues* 7:237–54.

Rosenthal, A. M. 1987. "Individual Ethics and the Plague." *New York Times*, May 28.

Rosenthal, Andrew. 1990. "President Signs Laws on Hate Crimes." *New York Times*, Apr. 24.

Rosenthal, C.J. 1987. "The Comforter: Providing Personal Advice and Emotional Support to Generations in the Family" *Canadian Journal on Aging* 6 (3):228–239.

Rosenthal, Carolyn T. 1985. "Kinkeeping in the Familial Division of Labor." *Journal of Marriage and the Family*, 47: 965–74.

Rosenthal, Elisabeth. 1991. "As More Tiny Infants Live, Choices and Burdens Grow." *New York Times*, Sept. 29.

Rosenthal, Kristine and Harry F. Keshet. 1978. "The Not Quite Stepmother." *Psychology Today* 12:82–86.

———. 1980. *Fathers Without Partners*. New York: Rowman & Littlefield.

Rosenbluth, Susan C. 1997. "Is Sexual Orientation a Matter of Choice?" *Psychology of Women Quarterly* 21:595–610.

Rosenbluth, Susan C., Janice M. Steil, and Juliet H. Whitcomb. 1998. "Marital Equality: What Does It Mean?" *Journal of Family Issues* 19 (3):227–44.

Rosenfeld, Jeffrey P. 1997. "Will Contests: Legacies of Aging and Social Change." Pp. 173–91 in *Inheritance and Wealth in America,* by Robert K. Miller, Jr. and Stephen J. McNamee. New York: Plenum Press.

Ross, Catherine E. 1987. "The Division of Labor at Home." *Social Forces* 65 (3):816–33.

———. 1995. "Reconceptualizing Marital Status as a Continuum of Social Attachment." *Journal of Marriage and the Family* 57 (1) (Feb.):129–40.

Ross, Catherine E., John Mirowsky, and Patricia Ulrich. 1983. "Distress and the Traditional Female Role." *American Journal of Sociology* 89:670–82.

Ross, David P., E. Richard Shillington and Clarence Lochhead. 1994. *The Canadian Fact Book on Poverty*. Ottawa: Canadian Council on Social Development.

Rossi, Alice S. 1968. "Transition to Parenthood." *Journal of Marriage and the Family* 30:26–39.

———, Ed. 1973. *The Feminist Papers*. New York: Bantam.

———. 1984. "Gender and Parenthood." *American Sociological Review* 49:1–19.

———, Ed. 1994. *Sexuality Across the Life Course*. Chicago: University of Chicago Press.

Rossiter, Amy B. 1991. "Initiator Status and Separation Adjustment." *Journal of Divorce and Remarriage* 15 (1/2):141–56.

Rotenberg, Ken J., George B. Schaut, and Brian O'Connor. 1993. "The Roles of Identity Development and Psychosocial Intimacy in Marital Success." *Journal of Social and Clinical Psychology* 12 (2):198–213.

Rothblum, Esther and Ellen Cole, Eds. 1989. *Loving Boldly: Issues Facing Lesbians*. New York: Harrington Park.

Rothman, Barbara Katz. 1982. *In Labor: Women and Power in the Birthplace*. New York: Norton.

———. 1984. "The Meaning of Choice in Reproductive Technology." Pp. 1–33 in *Test-Tube Women*, edited by Rita Arditti, Renate Duelli Klein, and Shelley Minden. London: Routledge & Kegan Paul.

———. 1989. *Recreating Motherhood: Ideology and Technology in a Patriarchal Society*. New York: Norton.

———. 1999. "Comment on Harrison: The Commodification of Motherhood." Pp. 435–38 in *American Families: A Multicultural Reader*, edited by Stephanie Coontz . New York: Routledge.

"Routine Circumcisions Under Increasing Scrutiny." 1999. *Omaha World Herald* (AP). April 19.

Rowland, Mary. (1994, May 22). "Hurdles for Unmarried Parents." *New York Times*.

Roxburgh, Susan. 1997. "The Effect of Children on the Mental Health of Women in the Paid Labor Force." *Journal of Family Issues* 18 (3):270–89.

Royal Commission on Aboriginal Peoples. 1996. *Looking Forward, Looking Back: Report of the Royal Commission on Aboriginal Peoples*, vol. 1. Ottawa: Supply and Services Canada.

Royal Commission on New Reproductive Technologies. 1993. (Patricia Baird, Chairperson). *Proceed With Caution: Final Report of the Royal Commission on New Reproductive Technologies*. Ottawa: Canadian Communications Groups.

Rozovsky, L.F. and F.A. Rozovsky 1998. *Legal Sex*. Toronto: Doubleday Canada.

"RU-486 ... Again." 1991. *Hastings Center Report*. July–Aug., p. 45.

Rubin, Lillian B. 1976. *Worlds of Pain: Life in the Working-Class Family*. New York: Basic Books.

———. 1979. *Women of a Certain Age: The Midlife Search for Self*. New York: Harper & Row.

———. 1983. *Intimate Strangers: Men and Women Together*. New York: Harper & Row.

———. 1990. *Erotic Wars: What Happened to the Sexual Revolution?* New York: Farrat, Straus, and Giroux.

———. 1992. *Worlds of Pain: Life in the Working-Class Family*. New York: Basic Books.

———. 1994. *Families on the Fault Line: America's Working Class Speaks About the Family, the Economy, Race, and Ethnicity*. New York: HarperCollins.

———. 1997. T*he Transcendent Child: Tales of Triumph over the Past*. New York: HarperPerrenial.

———. 1999. "Excerpts from Families on the Fault Line: America's Working Class Speaks about the Family, the Economy, Race, and Ethnicity." Pp. 273–86 in *American Families: A Multicultural Reader*, edited by Stephanie Coontz. New York: Routeledge.

Rubiner, Betsy. 1994. "The Hidden Damage." *The Des Moines Register*, Oct. 9, p. 2E.

Rubinstein, Robert L., Baine B. Alexander, Marcene Goodman, and Mark Luborsky. 1991. "Key Relationships of Never Married, Childless Older Women: A Cultural Analysis." *Journal of Gerontology* 46 (5):270–81.

Rudy, Duane and Joan E. Grusec. 2001. "Correlates Of Authoritarian Parenting In Individualist And Collectivist Cultures And Implications For Understanding The Transmission Of Values." *Journal of Cross-Cultural Psychology, Special Issue: Perspectives on Cultural Transmission* 32 (2) (March):202–212.

Ruefli, Terry, Olivia Yu, and Judy Barton. 1992. "Brief Report: Sexual Risk Taking in Smaller Cities." *The Journal of Sex Research* 29 (1):95–108.

Rugel, Robert P. 1992. "Self-Esteem Maintenance in 'Accepting-Open' and 'Devaluing-Closed' Marital Systems." *American Journal of Family Therapy* 20 (1):36–51.

Rugel, Robert P. and Zoran Martinovich. 1997. "Dealing with the Problem of Low Self-Esteem: Common Characteristics and Treatment in Individual, Marital/Family and Group Psychotherapy." *Contemporary Psychotherapy* 42 (1):69–76.

Ruggles, Steven. 1987. *Prolonged Connections: The Rise of the Extended Family in 19th-century England and America.* Madison: University of Wisconsin Press.

———. 1997. "The Rise of Divorce and Separation in the United States, 1880–1990." *Demography* 34(4): 455–66.

Rundblad, Georganne. 1990. "Talking Stones: An Examination of the Effects of Declining Mortality on Expression of Sentiment." Paper presented at the annual meeting of the Midwest Sociological Society, Chicago, Apr. 13.

Runkel, Gunter. 1998. "Sexual Morality of Christianity." *Journal of Sex and Marital Therapy* 24:103–22.

Russell, Diana E. H. 1982. *Rape in Marriage.* New York: Macmillan.

Russo, Francine. 1997. "Can the Government Prevent Divorce?" *Atlantic Monthly.* October. <http://www.theatlantic.com/issues/97oct/divorce.html>

Russo, Nancy Felipe. 1997. "Editorial: Forging New Directions in Gender Role Measurement." *Psychology of Women Quarterly* 21 (1):i–ii.

Ryan, Barbara and Eric Plutzer. 1989. "When Married Women Have Abortions: Spousal Notification and Marital Interaction." *Journal of Marriage and the Family* 51:41–50.

Ryan, Jim and Anne Ryan. 1995. "Dating in the Nineties: Courtship Makes a Comeback." *Focus on the Family.* November:11–12.

Ryan, John. 1999. "Hutterites." Pp. 1124–1125 in *The Canadian Encyclopedia: Year 2000 Edition,* edited by James Marsh. Toronto: McClelland & Stewart Inc.

Ryan, Kenneth J. 1988. "Giving Birth in America, 1988." *Family Planning Perspectives* 20:298–301.

Ryan, Sarah. 1999. "Management By Stress: The Reorganization of Work Hits Home in the 1990s." Pp. 332–41 in *American Families: A Multicultural Reader,* edited by Stephanie Coontz. New York: Routeledge.

Ryder, Andrew G., Graham Bean and Kenneth L. Dion. 2000. "Caregiver Responses To Symptoms Of First-Onset Psychosis: A Comparative Study Of Chinese- And Euro-Canadian Families." *Transcultural Psychiatry* 37 (2) (June):255–265.

Rye, B.J. 1998. "Impact Of An AIDS Prevention Video On AIDS-Related Perceptions." *The Canadian Journal of Human Sexuality* 7:19–30.

S

Saad, Lydia. 1995. "Children, Hard Work Taking Their Toll on Baby Boomers." *The Gallup Poll Monthly.* April:21–24.

Sachs, Andrea. 1990. "When the Lullaby Ends." *Time,* June 4, p. 82.

Sadker, M., and D. Sadker. 1986. "Sexism in the Classroom: From Grade School to Graduate School." *Phi Delta Kappan* (Mar.):512–15.

———. 1994. *Failing at Fairness: How America's Schools Cheat Girls.* New York: Charles Scribner's Sons.

Sadler, A. E. 1996. *Family Violence.* San Diego, CA: Greenhaven Press.

Safilios-Rothschild, Constantina. 1967. "A Comparison of Power Structure and Marital Satisfaction in Urban Greek and French Families." *Journal of Marriage and the Family* 29:345–52.

———. 1970. "The Study of Family Power Structure: A Review 1960–1969." *Journal of Marriage and the Family* 32:539–43.

———. 1979. *The Sociology and Social Psychology of Disability and Rehabilitation.* New York: Random House.

———. 1983. "Toward a Social Psychology of Relationships." Pp. 306–12 in *Family in Transition: Rethinking Marriage, Sexuality, Child Rearing, and Family Organization,* 4th ed., edited by Arlene S. Salaff, Janet. 1999. "Networks and Transnationalization of Asian Immigrants." American Sociological Association.

Salaff, Janet, Eric Fong and Siu-lun Wong.1999. "Using Social Networks to Exit Hong Kong." In Barry Wellman (Ed.), *Networks in the Global Village* (pp. 299–329). Boulder, CO: Westview.

Salamon, Edna. 1984. *Kept Women: Mistresses of the '80s.* London: Orbis.

Salholz, Eloise. 1992. "The Future of Gay America." Pp. 81–85 in *Human Sexuality 92/93,* edited by Ollie Pocs. Guilford, CT: Dushkin.

Saks, Michael J. and Edward Krupat. 1988. *Social Psychology and Its Applications.* New York: Harper & Row.

Salholz, Eloise. 1990. "The Future of Gay America." *Newsweek*, Mar. 12, pp. 20–25.

———. 1993. "For Better or For Worse." *Newsweek*, May 24, p. 69.

Salt, Robert. 1991. "Child Support in Context: Comments on Rettig, Christensen, and Dahl." *Family Relations* 40 (2) (Apr.):175–78.

Sammons, William and Jennifer Lewis. 1999. *Don't Divorce Your Children: Protecting Their Rights and Your Happiness.* Chicago: Contemporary Books.

Samuelson, Robert J. 1992. "How Our American Dream Unraveled." *Newsweek*, Mar. 2, pp. 32–39.

———. 1995. "RIP: The War on Poverty." *Newsweek*, Oct. 9, p. 59.

Sanders, Douglas. 1999. "Constructing Lesbian and Gay Rights." Pp. 158–193 in *Law in Society: Canadian Readings*, edited by Nick Larsen and Brian Burtch. Toronto: Harcourt Brace Canada.

Sangi-Haghpeykar, Haleh, Alfred N. Poindexter 3rd, and Louise Bateman. 1997. "Consistency of Condom Use among Users of Injectable Contraceptives." *Family Planning Perspectives* 29 (2):67–69, 75.

Santelli, John S., Charles W. Warren, Richard Lowry, Ellen Sogolow, Janet Collins, Laura Cann, Rachel B. Kaufmann and David D. Celentano. 1997. "The Use of Condoms with Other Contraceptive Methods among Young Men and Women." *Family Planning Perspectives* 29 (6):261–67.

Santrock, John W. and Karen A. Sitterle. 1987. "Parent-Child Relationships in Stepmother Families." Pp. 273–99 in *Remarriage and Stepparenting*, edited by Kay Pasley and Marilyn Ihinger-Tallman. New York: Guilford.

Satir, Virginia. 1972. *Peoplemaking*. Palo Alto, CA: Science and Behavior Books.

Satzewich, Vic. 1993. "Migrant and Immigrant Families in Canada: State Coercion and Legal Control in the Formation of Ethnic Families." *Journal of Comparative Family Studies*, 24 (3) (autumn):315–338.

Saunders, D. B. 1988. "Wife Abuse, Husband Abuse, or Mutual Combat?" Pp. 90–113 in *Feminist Perspectives on Wife Abuse*, edited by K. Yllo and M. Bograd. Newbury Park, CA: Sage.

Savin-Williams, Ritch C. and Eric M. Dube. 1998. "Parental Reactions to Their Child's Disclosure of a Gay/Lesbian Identity." *Family Relations* 47 (1):7–14.

Saxton, Lloyd. 1996. *The Individual, Marriage, and the Family*. Belmont, CA: Wadsworth Publishing Company.

Scanzoni, John H. 1970. *Opportunity and the Family*. New York: Free Press.

———. 1972. *Sexual Bargaining: Power Politics in the American Marriage*. Englewood Cliffs, NJ: Prentice-Hall.

———. 1997. "A Reply to Glenn: Fashioning Families and Policies for the Future—Not the Past." *Family Relations* 46 (3):213–17.

Scanzoni, John H. and William Marsiglio. 1993. "New Action Theory and Contemporary Families." *Journal of Family Issues* 14:105–32.

Scarf, Maggie. 1995. *Intimate Worlds: Life Inside the Family.* New York: Random House.

Schafer, Robert B. and Patricia M. Keith. 1981. "Equity in Marital Roles Across the Family Life Cycle." *Journal of Marriage and the Family* 43:359–67.

Schafer, Robert B., K. A. S. Wickrama and Patricia M. Keith. 1996. "Self-Concept Disconfirmation, Psychological Distress, and Marital Happiness." *Journal of Marriage and the Family* 58:167–77.

Scheffler, Tanya S. and Peter J. Naus. 1999. "The Relationship Between Fatherly Affirmation And A Woman's Self-Esteem, Fear Of Intimacy, Comfort With Womanhood And Comfort With Sexuality." *Canadian Journal of Human Sexuality* 8:39–46.

Schetagne, Sylvain. 2000. "Maternity Leave, Parental Leave, And Self-Employed Workers: Time for Action!" *Perception*, 24(4) (March). <http://www.ccsd.ca/perception/234/ml.htm>

Scheuble, Laurie and David R. Johnson. 1993. "Marital Name Change: Plans and Attitudes of College Students." *Journal of Marriage and the Family* 55 (3):747–54.

Schlesinger, Ben. 1998. "Contemporary Family Trends: Strengths in Families: Accentuating the Positive." *Vanier Institute of the Family.*

Schmalz, Jeffrey. 1993. "Poll Finds an Even Split on Homosexuality's Cause.' *New York Times: Themes of the Year*, Fall, 1, 11.

Schmidt, William E. 1990. "Valentine in a Survey: Fidelity Is Thriving." *New York Times*, Feb. 12.

Schmitt, Eric. 1992. "Wall of Silence Impedes Inquiry into a Rowdy Navy Convention." *New York Times*, June 14, pp. 1, 20.

———. 1993. "In Fear, Gay Soldiers Marry for Camouflage." *New York Times*, July 12, p. A7.

Schmitz, Christin. 2001. "Divorce Deals Never Final: Court: 1994 Settlement Reopened: 'It Means A Lot Of Litigation In The Family Law Arena'." *National Post Online*, April 28. <http:www.nationalpost.com/scripts/print...inter.asp?f=/stories/20010428/547137.html>

Schneider, Margaret and Susan Phillips. 1997. "A Qualitative Study of Sexual Harassment of Female Doctors by Patients." *Social Science and Medicine* 45:669–676.

Schnittger, Maureen H. and Gloria W. Bird. 1990. "Coping Among Dual-Career Men and Women Across the Family Life-Cycle." *Family Relations* 39 (2) (Apr.):199–205.

Schoen, Robert. 1992. "First Unions and the Stability of First Marriages." *Journal of Marriage and the Family* 54 (May): 281–84.

Schoen, Robert and Robin M. Weinick. 1993. "Partner Choice in Marriages and Cohabitations." *Journal of Marriage and the Family* 55 (2) (May):408–14.

Schomaker, Mary Zimmeth. 1994. "From Stepfather to Stepfather." *Liguorian*. June:54–56.

Schor, Juliet B. 1991. *The Overworked American: The Unexpected Decline of Leisure.* New York: Basic Books.

———. 1993. *The Overworked American: The Unexpected Decline of Leisure.* New York: Basic Books.

———. 1998. *The Overspent American: Upscaling, Downshifting, and the New American Consumer.* New York: Basic Books.

Schrof, Joannie M. 1994. "Sex in America." *U.S. News & World Report*, Oct. 17, pp. 74–81.

Schwartz, Felice N. 1989a. "Management Women and the New Facts of Life." *Harvard Business Review* 67:65–76.

———. 1989b. "The 'Mommy Track' Isn't Anti-Woman." *New York Times*, Mar. 22.

———. 1992. *Breaking with Tradition: Women and Work, the New Facts of Life.* New York: Warner.

Schwartz, Pepper. 1994. *Peer Marriage: How Love between Equals Really Works.* New York: Free Press.

Schwartz, Richard D. 1954. "Social Factors in the Development of Legal Control." *Yale Law Journal* 63:471–91.

Schwebel, Andrew I., Mark A. Fine, and Maureen A. Renner. 1991. "A Study of Perceptions of the Stepparent Role." *Journal of Family Issues* 12 (1) (Mar.):43–57.

Scott, Joseph W. 1980. "Black Polygamous Family Formulation." *Alternative Lifestyles* 3:41–64.

———. 1991. "From Teenage Parenthood to Polygamy: Case Studies in Black Family Formation." Pp. 278–88 in *The Black Family: Essays and Studies*, edited by Robert Staples. Belmont, CA: Wadsworth.

———. 1999. "From Teenage Parenthood to Polygamy: Case Studies in Black Polygamous Family Formation." Pp. 339–38 in *The Black Family: Essays and Studies*, edited by Robert Staples, 6th ed. Belmont, CA: Wadsworth.

Scott, Julie Kay. 1992. *Traditional and Postmodern Family Images: A Content and Comparative Analysis of Contemporary American Films.* Illinois State University, Department of Sociology, Anthropology, and Social Work. Masters Thesis.

Scott, K. 1997. "Indigenous Canadians." In *Canadian Profile: Alcohol, Tobacco and Other Drugs 1997*, edited by D. McKenzie, R. William and E. Single. Ottawa: Canadian Centre on Substance Abuse.

Scott, Niki. 1992. "Irate Husband Vents His Side of the Story." *Working Woman*, Apr. 13.

Scott, Sarah. 2000. "The Deepest Cut Of All." <wysiwyg://49http://www.chatelaine.com/read/news+views.fgm.html>

Seals, Brenda. 1990. *Personal communication.*

Seccombe, Karen. 1991. "Assessing the Costs and Benefits of Children: Gender Comparisons Among Childfree Husbands and Wives." *Journal of Marriage and the Family* 53 (1) (Feb.):191–202.

Segal, Lynne. 1994. *Straight Sex: Rethinking the Politics of Pleasure.* Berkeley: University of California Press.

Segers, Mary C. and Timothy A. Byrnes, Eds. 1995. *Abortion Politics in American States.* Armonk, NY: M. E. Sharpe.

Seidler, Victor J. 1992. "Rejection, Vulnerability, and Friendship." Pp. 15–34 in *Men's Friendships: Research on Men and Masculinities,* edited by Peter M. Nardi. Newbury Park, CA: Sage.

Seidman, Steven. 1991. *Romantic Longings: Love in America, 1830–1980.* New York: Routledge.

Seltzer, Judith A. 1991a. "Relationships Between Fathers and Children Who Live Apart: The Father's Role After Separation." *Journal of Marriage and the Family* 53 (1) (Feb.):79–101.

———. 1991b. "Legal Custody Arrangements and Children's Economic Welfare." *American Journal of Sociology* 96:895–929.

Seltzer, Judith A. and Suzanne M. Bianchi. 1988. "Children's Contact with Absent Parents." *Journal of Marriage and the Family* 50:663–77.

Seltzer, Marsha and Tamar Heller. (Eds.). 1997. "Family Caregiving for Persons with Disabilities." *Family Relations* Special Issue 46 (4). October.

Seltzer, Marsha, Jan Greenberg, Wyngaarden Krauss, Rachel Gordon, and Katherine Judge. 1997. "Siblings of Adults with Mental Retardation or Mental Illness: Effects on Lifestyle and Psychological Well-Being." *Family Relations* 46 (4):395–405.

Seltzer, Marsha, Jan Greenberg, Wyngaarden Krauss, and Jinkuk Hong. 1997. "Predictors and Outcomes of the End of Co-Resident Caregiving in Aging Families of Adults with Mental Retardation or Mental Illness." *Family Relations* 46 (1):13–22.

Sengupta, Somini. (1997, Jan. 13). "College Freshmen Adopting Stricter Views, Survey Finds." *New York Times*.

Senn, Charlene Y., Serge Desmarais, Norine Verberg and Eileen Wood. 2000. "Predicting Coercive Sexual Behavior Across The Lifespan In A Random Sample Of Canadian Men." *Journal of Social and Personal Relationships* 17 (1) (Feb):95–113.

Sennett, Richard and Jonathan Cobb. 1974. *The Hidden Injuries of Class.* New York: Random House.

Serovich, Julianne M., Judy A. Kimberly, and Kathryn Greene. 1998. "Perceived Family Member Reaction to Women's Disclosure of HIV-Positive Information." *Family Relations* 47 (1):15–22.

Serovich, Julianne M., Sharon J. Price, and Steven F. Chapman. 1991. "Former In-Laws as a Source of Support." *Journal of Divorce and Remarriage* 17 (1/2):17–26.

"Sex Education Does Not Increase Sexual Activity in Young People." 1998. *Population Today*. May 8.

"Sex Education in Classroom Found to Bring Few Changes." 1989. *New York Times*, Mar. 16.

"Sex Partners Often Silent about H.I.V." 1998. *New York Times*. February 9.

Shahan, Lynn. 1981. *Living Alone and Liking It!: A Complete Guide to Living on Your Own*. New York: Stratford Press (dist. by Harper & Row).

Shain, A. 1995. "Employment of People with Disabilities." *Canadian Social Trends* 38 (autumn):8–13.

Shamin, Ishrat and Quamrul Ahsan Chowdhury. 1993. *Homeless and Powerless: Child Victims of Sexual Exploitation*. Dhaka, Bangladesh: University of Dhaka Press.

Shapiro, Johanna. 1983. "Family Reactions and Coping Strategies in Response to the Physically Ill or Handicapped Child: A Review." *Social Science and Medicine* 17:913–31.

Shapiro, Joseph and Joanna M. Schrof. (1995, Feb. 27). "Honor Thy Children." *U.S. News and World Report*, pp. 39–49.

Shapiro, Laura. 1990. "Guns and Dolls." *Newsweek*, May 26, pp. 56–65.

———. 1997. "The Myth of Quality Time." *Newsweek*. May 12:62–71.

Shatzmiller, Maya. 1996. "Marriage, Family, and the Faith: Women's Conversion to Islam." *Journal of Family History* 21 (3):235–46.

Shaver, Katherine. 1991. "Retirees Decide to Mind Their Own Businesses." *The Wall Street Journal*, July 18, pp. B1–B2.

Shaw, Elizabeth. 1997. "Is This What Life's About?" *Newsweek*. May 5:22.

Shaywitz, B. A. 1995. "Sex Differences in the Functional Organization of the Brain for Language." *Nature* 373:607–609.

Sheehan, Constance L., E. Wilbur Bock, and Gary R. Lee. 1990. "Religious Heterogamy, Religiosity, and Marital Happiness: The Case of Catholics." *Journal of Marriage and the Family* 52 (Feb.):73–79.

Shellenbarger, Sue. 1991a. "Child-Care Setups Still Fall Apart Often." *The Wall Street Journal*, Sept. 26.

———. 1991b. "Companies Team Up to Improve Quality of Their Employees' Child-Care Choices." *The Wall Street Journal*, Oct. 17, pp. B1, B4.

———. 1991c. "Leaving Infants for Work Boosts Child-Care Costs." *The Wall Street Journal*, July 22.

———. 1991e. "Work & Family: Business Travel's Toll on Parents Grows." *The Wall Street Journal*, Nov. 13.

———. 1991f. "Work & Family: Firms' On-Site Day Care Proves Too Expensive." *The Wall Street Journal*, Aug. 16, p. B1.

———. 1991g. "Work & Family: Men Become Evasive About Family Demands." *The Wall Street Journal*, Aug. 16, p. B1.

———. 1992a. "Ads Urge Careful Shopping for Day Care." *The Wall Street Journal*, July 6, pp. B1, B18.

———. 1992b. "Averting Career Damage from Family Policies." *The Wall Street Journal*, June 24, p. B1.

———. 1992c. "Concerns Seek Help from Public Agencies." *The Wall Street Journal*, Sept. 2.

———. 1992d. "Employees Take Pains to Make FlexTime Work." *The Wall Street Journal*, Aug. 18.

———. 1992f. "Indicators of Quality in Day Care Worsen." *The Wall Street Journal*, May 6, p. B1.

———. 1992g. "Infertile Employees Seek Firms' Support." *The Wall Street Journal*, May 12, pp. B1, B5.

———. 1992h. "Work & Family: Employers Try to See If Family Benefits Pay." *The Wall Street Journal*, Apr. 3.

———. 1992i. "Work & Family: Flexible Policies May Slow Women's Careers." *The Wall Street Journal*, Apr. 22.

———. 1992j. "Work & Family: States Create Patchwork of Family-Leave Laws." *The Wall Street Journal*, July 28.

———. 1993. "So Much Talk, So Little Action." *The Wall Street Journal*, June 21.

———. 1998. "Families, Communities Can Benefit from Rise in Home-Based Work." The *Wall Street Journal*. May 13:B1.

Shellenbarger, Sue and Cindy Trost. 1992a. "Annual List of Family-Friendly Firms Is Issued by Working Mother Magazine." *The Wall Street Journal*, Sept. 22, pp. A2, A4.

———. 1992b. "Partnership of 109 Companies Aims to Improve Care Nationwide for Children and the Elderly." *The Wall Street Journal*, Sept. 11, p. A12.

Shelton, Beth Anne. 1990. "The Distribution of Household Tasks: Does Wife's Employment Status Make a Difference?" *Journal of Family Issues* 11 (2) (June):115–35.

———. 1992. *Women, Men and Time*. New York: Greenwood.

Shelton, Beth Anne and Daphne John. 1993. "Ethnicity, Race, and Difference: A Comparison of White, Black, and Hispanic Men's Household Labor Time." Pp. 131–50 in *Men, Work, and Family*, edited by Jane C. Hood. Newbury Park, CA: Sage.

Sher, Julian. *White Hoods: Canada's Klu Klux Klan*. Vancouver: New Star Books.

Sherman, Lawrence W. 1992. *Policing Domestic Violence: Experiments and Dilemmas*. New York: Free Press.

Sherman, Lawrence W. and Richard A. Berk. 1984. "Deterrent Effects of Arrest for Domestic Assault." *American Sociological Review* 49:261–72.

Sherman, Paul J. and Janet T. Spence. 1997. "A Comparison of Two Cohorts of College Students in Responses to the Male–Female Relations Questionnaire." *Psychology of Women Quarterly* 21 (2):26–278.

Sherman, Suzanne, Ed. 1992. *Lesbian and Gay Marriage: Private Commitments, Public Ceremonies.* Philadelphia: Temple University Press.

Shields, Nancy M. and Christine R. Hanneke. 1988. "Multiple Sexual Victimization: The Case of Incest and Marital Rape." Pp. 255–69 in *Family Abuse and Its Consequences: New Directions in Research*, edited by Gerald T. Hotaling, David Finkelhor, John T. Kirkpatrick, and Murray A. Straus. Newbury Park, CA: Sage.

Shihadeh, Edward S. 1991. "The Prevalence of Husband-Centered Migration: Employment Consequences for Married Mothers." *Journal of Marriage and the Family* 53 (2) (May):432–44.

Short, Kathryn H. and Charlotte Johnston. 1994. "Ethnocultural Parent Education in Canda: Current Status and Directions." *Canadian Journal of Community Mental Health* 13 (1) (spring):43–54.

———. 1997. "Stress, Maternal Distress, and Children's Adjustment Following Immigration: The Buffering Role of Social Support." *Journal of Consulting & Clinical Psychology* 65 (3) (June):494–503.

Shorter, Edward. 1975. *The Making of the Modern Family.* New York: Basic Books.

Shostak, Arthur. 1987. "Singlehood." Pp. 355–67 in *Handbook of Marriage and the Family*, edited by Marvin B. Sussman and Suzanne K. Steinmetz. New York: Plenum.

Shostak, Arthur and Gary McLouth. 1984. *Men and Abortion: Lessons, Losses, and Love.* New York: Praeger.

Shostak, Arthur. 1991. "Abortion in America: Ten Cautious Forecasts." *The Futurist* (July/August):20–24.

Siddique, C.M. 1977. "Changing Family Patterns: A Comparative Analysis of Immigrant Indian and Pakistani Families of Saskatoon, Canada." *Journal of Comparative Family Studies* 179–199.

Signorella, M. L. and W. Jamison. 1986. "Masculinity, Feminity, Androgyny, and Cognitive Performance: A Meta-Analysis." *Psychological Bulletin* 100:227–228.

Silverman, Jason H. 1985. *Unwelcome Guests: Canada West's Response to American Fugitive Slaves, 1800–1865.* Millwood, N.Y.: Associated Faculty Press.

Silvern, Louise, Jane Karyl, Lynn Waelde, William F. Hodges, and Joanna Starek. 1995. "Retrospective Reports of Parental Partner Abuse: Relationships to Depression, Trauma Symptoms and Self-Esteem among College Students." *Journal of Family Violence* 10 (2):177–86.

Silverstein, Merril and Vera L. Bengston. 1997. "Intergenerational Solidarity and the Structure of Adult Child–Parent Relationships in American Families." *American Journal of Sociology* 103 (2):429–60.

Simmel, Georg. 1950. *The Sociology of Georg Simmel,* translated and edited by Kurt H. Wolfe. Glencoe, IL: Free Press.

Simon, Barbara Levy. 1987. *Never Married Women.* Philadelphia: Temple University Press.

Simon, Rita J. 1990. "Transracial Adoptions Can Bring Joy: Letters to the Editor." *The Wall Street Journal*, Oct. 17.

———. 1993. "Should White Families Be Allowed to Adopt African American Children?" *Health* (July/Aug.):22.

Simon, Rita J. and Howard Alstein. 1987. *Transracial Adoptees and Their Families: A Study of Identity and Commitment.* New York: Praeger.

Simon, Stephanie. 1991. "Joint Custody Loses Favor for Increasing Children's Feeling of Being Torn Apart." *The Wall Street Journal*, July 15, p. B1.

Simons, Ronald L., Christine Johnson, Jay Beaman, and Rand D. Conger. 1993. "Explaining Women's Double Jeopardy: Factors that Mediate the Association Between Harsh Treatment as a Child and Violence by a Husband." *Journal of Marriage and the Family* 55 (3) (Aug.):713–23.

Simons, Ronald L., Christine Johnson, and Rand D. Conger. 1994. "Harsh Corporal Punishment Versus Quality of Parental Involvement as an Explanation of Adolescent Maladjustment." *Journal of Marriage and the Family* 56 (3) (Aug.):591–607.

Simons, Ronald L., Kuei-Hsiu Lin, and Leslie C. Gordon. 1998. "Socialization in the Family of Origin and Male Dating Violence: A Prospective Study." *Journal of Marriage and the Family* 60:467–78.

Simons, Ronald L. and Les B. Whitbeck. 1991. "Sexual Abuse as a Precursor to Prostitution and Victimization Among Adolescent and Adult Homeless Women." *Journal of Family Issues* 12 (3) (Sept.):361–79.

Singer, Bennett L. and David Deschamps, eds. 1994. *Gay & Lesbian Stats.* New York: New Press.

Singer v. Hara. 1974. 11 Wash. App. 247, 522 P 2d 1187.

Singh, Gopal K., T. J. Matthews, Sally C. Clarke, Trina Yannicos, and Betty L. Smith. 1995. "Annual Summary of Births, Marriages, Divorces, and Deaths: United States, 1994." *Monthly Vital Statistics Report* 43 (13). National Center for Health Statistics, U.S. Department of Health and Human Services, Oct. 23.

Skolnick, Arlene S. 1978. *The Intimate Environment: Exploring Marriage and Family,* 2d ed. Boston: Little, Brown.

———. 1997. "A Response to Glenn: The Battle of the Textbooks: Bringing in the Culture Wars." *Family Relations* 46 (3):219–22.

Slater, Philip. 1976. *The Pursuit of Loneliness: American Culture at the Breaking Point.* 2d ed. Boston: Beacon.

Slater, Suzanne. 1995. *The Lesbian Family Life Cycle.* New York: Free Press.

Small, Stephen A. and Donell Kerns. 1993. "Unwanted Sexual Activity Among Peers During Early and Middle Adolescence: Incidence and Risk Factors." *Journal of Marriage and the Family* 55 (3) (Nov.):941–52.

Small, Stephen A. and Tom Luster. 1994. "Adolescent Sexual Activity: An Ecological, Risk-Factor Approach." *Journal of Marriage and the Family* 56 (1) (Feb.):181–92.

Small, Stephen A. and Dave Riley. 1990. "Toward a Multidimensional Assessment of Work Spillover into Family Life." *Journal of Marriage and the Family* 52:51–61.

Smith, Daniel Scott. 1981. "Historical Change in the Household Structure of the Elderly in Economically Developed Societies." In *Aging*, edited by James C. March. New York: Academic.

Smith, Deborah B. and Phyllis Moen. 1998. "Spousal Influence on Retirement: His, Her, and Their Perceptions." *Journal of Marriage and the Family* 60 (3):734–44.

Smith, Donna. 1990. *Stepmothering.* New York: St. Martin's Press.

Smith, Gregory C. 1995. *Strengthening Aging Families: Diversity in Practice and Policy.* Thousand Oaks, CA: Sage.

Smith, Lee. 1988. "Who Is the Family of the Adolescent Mother?" Panel presentation at the annual meeting of the National Council on Family Relations, New Orleans, Nov. Custom Audio Tape No. 8866. Bridgeport, IL.

Smith, Marguerite T. 1989. "Saving." Pp. 12–15 in *Money Guide: Basics of Personal Finance,* edited by Money Magazine. New York: Time Inc. Magazines.

Smith, Thomas A. 1992. "Family Cohesion in Remarried Families." *Journal of Divorce and Remarriage* 17 (1/2):49–66.

Smith-Rosenberg, Carroll. 1975. "The Female World of Love and Ritual: Relations Between Women in Nineteenth Century America." *Signs* 1:1–29.

Smits, Jeroen, Wout Ultee, and Jan Lammers. 1998. "Educational Homogamy in 65 Countries: An Explanation of Differences in Openness Using Country-Level Explanatory Variables." *American Sociological Review* 63 (2):264–75.

Smock, Pamela J. 1993. "The Economic Costs of Marital Disruption for Young Women over the Past Two Decades." *Demography* 30 (3) (Aug.):353–71.

Smolowe. Jill. 1996. "The Stalled Revolution." *Time.* May 6:63.

———. 1996a. "The Unmarrying Kind. *Time,* April 29:68–69.

———. 1996b. "Parenting On Trial." *Time,* May 20:50.

———. 1996c. "The Stalled Revolution." *Time,* May 6:63.

Sobel, Michael and Kerry J. Daly. 1992. "The Adoption Alternative for Pregnant Adolescents: Decision-making, Consequences, and Policy Implications." *Journal of Social Issues* 48(3):143–161.

Soldo, Beth J. and Emily M. Agree. 1988. *America's Elderly. Population Bulletin* 43 (3). Washington, DC: Population Reference Bureau.

Sollors, Werner. 2000. *Interracialism: Black-White Intermarriage in American History, Literature and Law.* Oxford, New York: Oxford University Press.

Soloman, Richard and Cynthia Pierce Liefeld. 1998. "Effectiveness of a Family Support Center Approach to Adolescent Mothers: Repeat Pregnancy and School Drop-Out Rates." *Family Relations* 47 (2):139–44.

Somers, Marsha D. 1993. "A Comparison of Voluntarily Childfree Adults and Parents." *Journal of Marriage and the Family* 55 (3) (Aug.):643–50.

Sonkin, Daniel Jay, Del Martin, and Lenore E. Auerbach Walker. 1985. *The Male Batterer: A Treatment Approach.* New York: Singer.

Sontag, Susan. 1976. "The Double Standard of Aging." Pp. 350–66 in *Sexuality Today and Tomorrow,* edited by Sol Gordon and Roger W. Libby. North Scituate, MA: Duxbury.

Sorensen, Elaine Shaw. 1993. *Children's Stress and Coping: A Family Perspective.* New York: Guilford Press.

South, Scott J. 1993. "Racial and Ethnic Differences in the Desire to Marry." *Journal of Marriage and the Family* 55 (2) (May):357–70.

———. 1995. "Do You Need to Shop Around?" *Journal of Family Issues* 16 (4) (July):432–49.

South, Scott J. and Kim M. Lloyd. 1992a. "Marriage Markets and Non-Marital Fertility in the U.S." *Demography* 29:247–64.

———. 1992b. "Marriage Opportunities and Family Formation: Further Implications of Imbalanced Sex Ratios." *Journal of Marriage and the Family* 54 (May):440–51.

Spanier, Graham B. 1976. "Measuring Dyadic Adjustment: New Scales for Assessing the Quality of Marriage and Similar Dyads." *Journal of Marriage and the Family* 38:15–28.

———. 1989. "Bequeathing Family Continuity." *Journal of Marriage and the Family* 51:3–13.

Spanier, Graham B. and Robert F. Castro. 1979. "Adjustment to Separation and Divorce: An Analysis of 50 Case Studies." *Journal of Divorce* 2:241–53.

Spanier, Graham B. and Frank F. Furstenberg, Jr. 1982. "Remarriage After Divorce: A Longitudinal Analysis of Well-Being." *Journal of Marriage and the Family* 44:709–20.

———. 1987. "Remarriage and Reconstituted Families." Pp. 419–34 in *Handbook of Marriage and the Family,* edited by Marvin B. Sussman and Suzanne K. Steinmetz. New York: Plenum.

Spanier, Graham B. and Linda Thompson. 1987. *Parting: The Aftermath of Separation and Divorce,* updated edition. Newbury Park, CA: Sage.

Spence, Janet T., R. Helmreich, and J. Stapp. 1973. "A Short Version of the Attitudes Toward Women Scale (AWS)." *Bulletin of Psychonomic Society.*219–20.

Spence, Janet T. and Eugene D. Hahn. 1997. "The Attitudes Toward Women Scale and Attitude Change in College Students." *Psychology of Women Quarterly* 21 (1):17–34.

Sperling, Susan. 1991. "Baboons with Briefcases: Feminism, Functionalism, and Sociobiology in the Evolution of Primate Gender." *Signs: Journal of Women in Culture and Society* 17 (11):1–27.

Spinelli, Eileen. 1998. *When Mama Comes Home Tonight.* New York: Simon & Schuster.

Spiro, Melford. 1956. *Kibbutz: Venture in Utopia.* New York: Macmillan.

Spitze, Glenna. 1988. "Women's Employment and Family Relations: A Review." *Journal of Marriage and the Family* 50:585–618.

Spitze, Glenna, John R. Logan, Glenn Deane, and Suzanne Zerger. 1994. "Adult Children's Divorce and Intergenerational Relationships." *Journal of Marriage and the Family* 56 (2) (May):279–93.

Spitze, Glenna and Russell Ward. 1995. "Household Labor in Intergenerational Households." *Journal of Marriage and the Family* 57 (2) (May):355–61.

Sprecher, Susan. 1989. "Premarital Sexual Standards for Different Categories of Individuals." *Journal of Sex Research* 26:232–48.

Sprecher, Susan and Kathleen McKinney. 1993. *Sexuality.* Newbury Park, CA: Sage.

Sprecher, Susan, Kathleen McKinney, and Terri Orbuch. 1987. "Has the Double Standard Disappeared?: An Experimental Test." *Social Psychology Quarterly* 50:24–31.

Sprecher, Susan, Kathleen McKinney, Robert Walsh, and Carrie Anderson. 1988. "A Revision of the Reiss Premarital Sexual Permissiveness Scale." *Journal of Marriage and the Family* 50:821–28.

Sprecher, Susan and Pepper Schwartz. 1994. "Equity and Balance in the Exchange of Contributions in Close Relationships." Pp. 89–116 in *Entitlement and the Affectional Bond: Justice in Close Relationships*, edited by M. J. Lerner and G. Mikula. New York: Plenum.

Sprecher, Susan, Quintin Sullivan, and Elaine Hatfield. 1994. "Mate Selection Preferences: Gender Differences Examined in a National Sample." *Journal of Personality and Social Psychology* 66 (6) (June):1074–81.

Sprenkle, Douglas H. 1989. "The Clinical Practice of Divorce Therapy." Pp. 171–95 in *The Divorce and Divorce Therapy Handbook*, edited by Martin Textor. Northvale, NJ: Jason Aronson.

Spring, J.A. 1997. *After The Affair: Healing The Pain And Rebuilding Trust When A Partner Has Been Unfaithful.* New York: Harper/Perennial.

Springer, S. and G. Deutsch. 1994. *Left Brain/Right Brain,* 4th edition. New York: Freeman.

Sreenivasan, Jyotsna. 1997. "Woman Are 11 Percent of New Congress." *Feminist Majority Newsletter* 8 (4). <http://feminist.org/research/report/84_five.html>

Stacey, Judith. 1990. *Brave New Families: Stories of Domestic Upheaval in Late Twentieth Century America.* New York: Basic Books.

———. 1993. "Good Riddance to 'The Family': A Response to David Popenoe." *Journal of Marriage and the Family* 55 (3) (Aug.):545–47.

———. 1996. *In the Name of the Family: Rethinking Family Values in the Postmodern Age.* Boston: Beacon Press.

———. 1999. "The Family Values Fable." Pp. 487–90 in *American Families: A Multicultural Reader*, edited by Stephanie Coontz. New York: Routledge.

Stacey, William A., Lonnie R. Hazlewood, and Anson Shupe. 1994. *The Violent Couple.* Westport, CT: Praeger.

Stack, Carol B. 1974. *All Our Kin: Strategies for Survival.* New York: Harper & Row.

Stack, Steven. 1990. "New Micro-level Data on the Impact of Divorce on Suicide, 1959–1980: A Test of Two Theories." *Journal of Marriage and the Family* 52 (1) (Feb.):119–27.

———. 1994. "The Effect of Geographic Mobility on Premarital Sex." *Journal of Marriage and the Family* 56 (1) (Feb.):204–8.

Stack, Steven and J. Ross Eshleman. 1998. "Marital Status and Happiness: A 17-Nation Study." *Journal of Marriage and the Family* 60 (2):527–36.

Stack, Steven and Ira Wasserman. 1993. "Marital Status, Alcohol Consumption, and Suicide: An Analysis of National Data." *Journal of Marriage and the Family* 55:1018–24.

Staheli, L. 1998. *Affair Proof Your Marriage: Understanding, Preventing, And Surviving And Affair.* New York: Harper-Collins.

Stanley, Thomas J. and William D. Danko. 1996. *The Millionaire Next Door: The Surprising Secrets of America's Wealthy.* Atlanta, GA: Longstreet Press.

Staples, Robert. 1972. "The Sexuality of Black Women." *Sexual Behavior* 2:4–15.

———. 1981. "Black Singles in America." Pp. 40–51 in *Single Life,* edited by Peter J. Stein. New York: St. Martin's.

———. 1985. "Changes in Black Family Structure: The Conflict Between Family Ideology and Structural Conditions." *Journal of Marriage and the Family* 47:1005–13.

———. 1991. "Changes in Black Family Structure: The Conflict Between Family Ideology and Structural Conditions." Pp. 28–36 in *The Black Family: Essays and Studies.* 4th ed., edited by Robert Staples. Belmont, CA: Wadsworth.

———. 1994. *The Black Family: Essays and Studies.* 5th ed. Belmont, CA: Wadsworth.

———. 1999a. *The Black Family: Essays and Studies.* 6th ed. Belmont, CA: Wadsworth.

————. 1999b. "Sociocultural Factors in Black Family Transformation: Toward a Redefinition of Family Functions." Pp. 18–23 in *The Black Family: Essays and Studies,* 6th ed, edited by Robert Stapes. Belmont, CA: Wadsworth.

————. 1999c. "Interracial Relationships: A Convergence of Desire and Opportunity." Pp. 129–36 in *The Black Family: Essays and Studies,* 6th ed, edited by Robert Stapes. Belmont, CA: Wadsworth.

Staples, Robert and Leanor Boulin Johnson. 1993. *Black Families at the Crossroads: Challenges and Prospects.* San Francisco: Jossey-Bass.

Staples, Robert and Alfredo Mirande. 1980. "Racial and Cultural Variations Among American Families: A Decennial Review of the Literature on Minority Families." *Journal of Marriage and the Family* 42:887–903.

Stark, Steven. 1997. "Alliance Sees Pure Sense in Abstaining from Sex." *Chicago Tribune.* July 26:1–5.

Starrels, M.E., B.Ingersoll-Dayton, D.W. Dowler and M.B. Neal. 1997. " Stress of Caring for a Parent Effects of the Elder's Impairment on an Employed, adult Child." *Journal of Marriage and the Family,* 59:860–72.

Statistics Canada. 1996. "Canadian families: Diversity and Change, 1995." *The Daily,* June 19. <http://collection.nlc-bnc.ca/100/201/301/daily/daily-h/1996/96-06/960619/d960619.htm>

Statistics Canada. 1997. *Labour Force Update: Hours of Work* 1(2) (summer, July). Statistics Canada, Household Surveys Division, Catalogue no. 71-005-XPB.

Statistics Canada. 1997. "1996 Census: Marital Status, Common-Law Unions And Families." *The Daily,* October 14. <http://www.statcan.ca/Daily/English/971014/d971014.htm>

Statistics Canada. 1997. *Earnings of Men and Women.* Annual. Cat. 13-217-XPB.

Statistics Canada. 1997. *Labour Force Update: The Self-Employed.* Autumn, vol. 1, no. 3. Catalogue no. 71-005-XPB. Statistics Canada Household Surveys Division.

Statistics Canada. 1998. *Canada Yearbook 2000.* Ottawa: Minister of Industry.

Statistics Canada. 1998. *Work Arrangements in the 1990s.* Analytic Report No. 8. May. Catalogue no. 71-535-MPB.

Statistics Canada. 1998. "1996 Census: Sources of Income, Earnings And Total Income, And Family Income." *The Daily,* May 12. <http:www.statcan.ca/daily/english/980512/d90512.html>

Statistics Canada. 1998. "1996 Census: Labour Force Activity, Occupation And Industry, Place Of Work, Mode Of Transportation To Work, Unpaid Work." *The Daily,* March 17. <http://www.statcan.ca/Daily/English/980317/d980317.htm>

Statistics Canada. 1998. "What is Happening to Earnings Inequality in the 1990s?" <www.statcan.ca>

Statistics Canada. 1998. "Multiple-Risk Behavior In Teenagers And Young Adults." *The Daily,* October 29. <http:www.statcan.ca/daily/english/981029/d981029.htm>

Statistics Canada. 1998. "1996 Census: Aboriginal data." *The Daily,* January 13. <http://www.statcan.ca/Daily/English/980113/d980113.htm>

Statistics Canada. 1998. "1996 Census: Ethnic Origin, Visible Minorities." *The Daily,* February 17. <www.statcan.ca/daily/English/980217/d980217.htm>

Statistics Canada. 1998. "1996 Census: Sources of Income, Earnings and Total Income, and Family Income." *The Daily,* May 12. <www.statcan.ca:80/Daily/English/980512/d980512.htm>

Statistics Canada. 1999. "Low Income among Children." *The Daily,* April 29. <http://www.statcan.ca/Daily/English/990429/d990429b.htm>

Statistics Canada. 1999. "Vital Statistics Compendium, 1996." *The Daily,* November 25. <http://www.statcan/Daily/English/991125/d991125d.htm>

Statistics Canada. 1999. "Divorces 1997." *The Daily,* May 18. <http://www.statcan.ca/Daily/English/990518/d990518b.htm>

Statistics Canada. 1999. *Work Absence Rates, 1987 to 1998.* Labour and Household Surveys Analysis Division, Analytic Report No. 10, July. Ottawa: Minister of Industry.

Statistics Canada. 1999. "Vital Statistics Compendium." *The Daily,* November 25. <http:www.statcan.ca/Daily/English/991125/d991125d.htm>

Statistics Canada. 1999. "Births 1997." *The Daily,* June 16. <http://www.statcan.ca/Daily/English/990616/d990616b.htm>

Statistics Canada. 1999. *Income After Tax, Distribution by Size in Canada.* Annual. Cat. 13-217XPB.

Statistics Canada. 1999. "General Social Survey: Time Use." *The Daily,* November 9. <http:www.statcan.ca/Daily/English/991109/d991109a.htm>

Statistics Canada. 1999. *Age, Sex, Marital Status and Common-law Status.* 1996 Census Technical Report. April. Catalogue: 92-353-XIE. Ottawa: Minister of Industry.

Statistics Canada. 1999. "Marriages." *The Daily,* October 28. <http:www.statcan.ca/Daily/English/991028/d991028c.htm>

Statistics Canada 2000. "Women in Canada 2000." *The Daily,* September 14. <http://www.statcan.ca/Daily/English/000914/d000914c.htm>

Statistics Canada. 2000. "Full-time university faculty." *The Daily,* August 8. <http://www.statcan.ca/Daily/English/000808/d000808a.htm>

Statistics Canada. 2000. "Time Spent With Children." *The Daily,* June 13. <http://www.statcan.ca/Daily/English/000613/d000613a.htm>

Statistics Canada. 2000. "Divorces, 1998." *The Daily*, September 28. <http:www.statcan.ca/Daily/English/000928/d000926.htm>

Statistics Canada. 2000. "Therapeutic Abortions 1998." *The Daily*, December 18. <http://www.statcan.ca/Daily/English/001218/d001218d.htm>

Statistics Canada. 2000. "Canadian social trends: The changing face of conjugal relationships, 1995." *The Daily*, March 16. <http://www.statcan.ca/Daily/English/000316/d000316a.htm>

Statistics Canada. 2000. *Family Violence in Canada: A Statistical Profile 2000.* Catalogue no. 885-224-XIE. Ottawa: Minister of Industry.

Staub, Debbie, Ilene S. Schwartz, Chryson Gallucci and Charles A. Peck. 1994. "Four portraits of Friendship At an Inclusive School." *Journal of the Association for Persons with Severe Handicaps*, 19(4), Winter: 314–25.

Steel, Freda M. 1987. "Alimony and Maintenance Orders." Pp. 155–167 in *Equality and Judicial Neutrality*, edited by Sheilah L. Martin and Kathleen E. Mahoney. Toronto: Carswell.

Steele, Shelby. 1990. "The Memory of Enemies: On the Black Experience in America." *Dissent*. (summer):326–32.

Steil, J. M. 1997. *Marital Equality: Its Relationship to the Well-Being of Husbands and Wives*. Thousand Oaks, CA: Sage.

Stein, Catherine H., Virginia A. Wemmerus, Marcia Ward, Michelle E. Gaines, Andrew L. Freeberg, and Thomas C. Jewell. 1998. " 'Because They're My Parents': An Intergenerational Study of Felt Obligation and Parental Caregiving." *Journal of Marriage and the Family* 60 (3):611–22.

Stein, Peter J. 1976. *Single*. Englewood Cliffs, NJ: Prentice-Hall.

———. (Ed.) 1981. *Single Life: Unmarried Adults in Social Context*. New York: St. Martin's.

Steinberg, L. 1990. "Interdependency in the Family: Autonomy, Conflict, and Harmony in the Parent–Adolescent Relationship." In *At the Threshold: The Developing Adolescent*, edited by S. Feldman and G. Elliot. Cambridge, MA: Harvard University Press.

Steinberg, Susanne, Laurence Kruckman and Stephanie Steinberg. 2000. "Reinventing Fatherhood in Japan and Canada." *Social Science and Medicine* 50(9) (May):1257–1272.

Steinem, Gloria. 1992. *Revolution from Within: A Book of Self-Esteem*. Boston: Little, Brown.

Steinhauer, Jennifer. 1995. "Living Together without Marriage or Apologies." *New York Times*. July 6.

Steinman, Susan B. 1981. "The Experience of Children in a Joint Custody Arrangement: A Report of a Study." *American Journal of Orthopsychiatry* 51:403–14.

Steinmetz, Suzanne K. 1977. *The Cycle of Violence: Assertive, Aggressive, and Abusive Family Interactions*. New York: Praeger.

Stephen, Timothy D. 1985. "Fixed Sequence and Circular-Causal Models of Relationship Development: Divergent Views on the Role of Communication in Intimacy." *Journal of Marriage and the Family* 47:955–63.

Stephens, William N. 1963. *The Family in Cross-Cultural Perspective*. New York: Holt, Rinehart & Winston.

Stephens. T. 1994. *Smoking among Aboriginal People in Canada 1991*. Ottawa: Health Canada.

Stern, Gabriella. 1991. "Young Women Insist on Career Equality, Forcing the Men in Their Lives to Adjust." *The Wall Street Journal*, Sept. 16, pp. B1, B3.

Stern, Linda. 1994. "Money Watch: Divorce." *Newsweek*, June 6, p. 58.

Sternberg, Robert J. 1988a. "Triangulating Love." Pp. 119–38 in *The Psychology of Love*, edited by Robert J. Sternberg and Michael L. Barnes. New Haven, CT: Yale University Press.

———. 1988b. *The Triangle of Love: Intimacy, Passion, Commitment*. New York: Basic Books.

Sternberg, Robert J. and Mahzad Hojjat (Eds.). 1997. *Satisfaction in Close Relationships*. New York: Guilford Press.

Stets, Jan E. 1991. "Cohabiting and Marital Aggression: The Role of Social Isolation." *Journal of Marriage and the Family* 53 (3) (Aug.):669–80.

Stevens, Amy and Milo Geyelin. 1990. "Surrogate Mother Denied Parental Rights." *The Wall Street Journal*, Oct. 23.

Stevens, Gillian. 1991. "Propinquity and Educational Homogamy." *Sociological Forum* 6 (4):715–26.

Stevenson, Winona. 1999. "Colonialism and First Nations Women in Canada." Pp. 49–80 in Enakshi Dua and Angela Robertson (eds.) *Scratching the Surface: Canadian Anti-Racist Feminist Thought*. Toronto: Women's Press.

Stewart, Dana G. 1991. "Single Custodial Females and Their Families: Housing and Coping Strategies After Divorce." *International Journal of Law and the Family*, 5 (3) (December):296–317.

Stewart, Mary White. 1984. "The Surprising Transformation of Incest: From Sin to Sickness." Paper presented at the annual meeting of the Midwest Sociological Society, Chicago, Apr. 18.

Stinnett, Nick. 1979. *Building Family Strengths: Blueprints for Action*. Lincoln, NE: University of Nebraska Press.

———. 1979. "In Search of Strong Families." Pp. 23–30 in *Building Family Strengths: Blueprints for Action*, edited by Nick Stinnett, Barbara Chesser, and John DeFrain. Lincoln: University of Nebraska Press.

———. 1983. "Strong Families." Pp. 27–38 in *Prevention in Family Services*, edited by David R. Mace. Newbury Park, CA: Sage.

———. 1985. *Secrets of Strong Families.* New York: Little, Brown.

———. 1996. *Good Kids: How You and Your Kids Can Successfully Navigate the Teen Years.* New York: Doubleday.

———. 1997. *Good Families.* New York: Doubleday.

Stinson, Kandi M., Judith N. Lasker, Janet Lohmann, and Lori J. Toedter. 1992. "Parents' Grief Following Pregnancy Loss: A Comparison of Mothers and Fathers." *Family Relations* 41:218–23.

Stock, Jacqueline L., Michelle A. Bell, Debra K. Boyer, and Frederick A. Connell. 1997. "Adolescent Pregnancy and Sexual Risk-Taking among Sexually Abused Girls." *Family Planning Perspectives* 29 (5):200–03.

Stock, Robert W. 1997. "When Older Women Contract the AIDS Virus." *New York Times.* July 31:B1.

Stoddard, Thomas B. 1989. "Why Gay People Should Seek the Right to Marry." *OUT/LOOK, National Gay and Lesbian Quarterly* 6 (Fall).

Stokes, Joseph P., Robin L. Miller and Rhonda Mundhenk. 1998. "Toward an Understanding of Behaviourally Bisexual Men: The influence of Context and Culture." *The Canadian Journal of Human Sexuality,* 7:101–114.

Stone, Lawrence. 1980. *The Family, Sex, and Marriage in England, 1500–1800.* New York: Harper & Row.

Stormshak, Elizabeth A., Karen L. Bierman, Robert J. McMahon and Liliana J. Lengua. 2000. "Parenting Practices and Child Disruptive Behavior Problems in Early Elementary School." *Journal of Clinical Child Psychology,* 29(1) (March):17–29.

Stout, Hilary. 1992. "Adequacy of Spending on AIDS Is an Issue Not Easily Resolved." *The Wall Street Journal,* Apr. 22, pp. A1, A6.

Stout, Madeleine Dion. 1996. "Aboriginal Canada: Women and Health." <http://www.hc-sc.gc.ca/canusa/papers/canada/english>

Straus, Murray A. 1964. "Power and Support Structures of the Family in Relation to Socialization." *Journal of Marriage and the Family* 26:318–26.

———. 1993. "Physical Assaults by Wives: A Major Social Problem." Pp. 67–87 in Richard J. Gelles and Donileen R. Loseke (Eds.). *Current Controversies on Family Violence.* Newbury Park, CA: Sage.

———. 1994. *Beating the Devil Out of Them: Corporal Punishment in American Families.* New York: Lexington Books.

———. 1996. "Presentation: Spanking and the Making of a Violent Society." *Pediatrics* 98:837–49.

Straus, Murray A. and Denise A. Donnelly. 1993. "Corporal Punishment of Adolescents by American Parents." *Youth and Society* 24 (4):419–28.

Straus, Murray and Richard Gelles. 1995. *Physical Violence in American Families: Risk Factors and Adaptations to Violence in 8,145 Families.* New Brunswick, NJ: Transaction Publishers.

Straus, Murray A. and Glenda Kaufman Kantor. 1994. "Corporal Punishment of Adolescents by Parents: A Risk Factor in the Epidemiology of Depression, Suicide, Alcohol Abuse, Child Abuse, and Wife Beating." *Adolescence* 29 (115):543–56.

Straus, Murray A. and Vera E. Mouradian. 1998. "Impulsive Corporal Punishment by Mothers and Antisocial Behavior and Impulsiveness of Children." *Behavioral Sciences & the Law* 16 (3):353–62.

Straus, Murray, Richard Gelles and Susan K. Steinmetz. 1980. *Behind Closed Doors: Violence in the American Family.* New York: Doubleday.

Straus, Murray A. and Julie H. Stewart. "Corporal Punishment By American Parents: National Data On Prevalence, Chronicity, Severity, And Duration, In Relation To Child And Family Characteristics." *Clinical Child & Family Psychology Review* 2 (2) (June):55–70.

Straus, Murray A., David B. Sugarman, and Jean Giles-Sims. 1997. "Spanking by Parents and Subsequent Antisocial Behavior of Children." *Archives of Pediatrics & Adolescent Medicine* 151 (8):761–73.

Straus, Murray A. and Carrie L. Yodanis. 1996. "Corporal Punishment in Adolescence and Physical Assaults on Spouses Later in Life: What Accounts for the Link?" *Journal of Marriage and the Family* 58 (4):825–924.

Strauss, Anselm and Barney Glaser. 1975. *Chronic Illness and the Quality of Life.* St. Louis, Mosby.

Strobe, W. and M. Strobe. 1996. "The Social Psychology of Social Support." Pp. 597–621 in *Social Psychology: Handbook of Basic Principles,* edited by E. T. Higgins and A. Kruglanski (Eds.). New York: Guilford.

Struthers, Cynthia B. and Janet L. Bokemeier. 2000. "Myths and Realities of Raising Children and Creating Family Life in a Rural County." *Journal of Family Issues* 21 (1) (January):17–46.

Struthers, James. 1999. "Great Depression." Pp. 1012–1013 in *The Canadian Encyclopedia: Year 2000 Edition,* edited by James Marsh. Toronto: McClelland & Stewart Inc.

Stubblefield, P. G., R. R. Monson, S. C. Schoenbaum, C. E. Wolfson, D. J. Cookson, and K. C. Ryan. 1984. "Fertility After Induced Abortion: A Prospective Follow-up Study." *Obstetrics and Gynecology* 62:186.

"Study Sees Little Distress After Abortion." 1990. *New York Times,* Apr. 6.

Suarez, Liza M. and Bruce L. Baker. 1997. "Child Externalizing Behavior and Parents' Stress: The Role of Social Support." *Family Relations* 46 (4):373–81.

Sugarman, Stephen D. 1998. "Single-Parent Families." Pp. 13–38 in *All Our Families: New Policies for a New Century,* edited by Mary Ann Mason, Arlene Skolnick, and Stephen D. Sugarman. New York: Oxford University Press.

Sugrue, Thomas J. 1999. "Poor Families in an Era of Urban Transformation: The 'Underclass' Family in Myth and

Reality." Pp. 243–57 in *American Families: A Multicultural Reader*, edited by Stephanie Coontz. New York: Routledge.

"Suicides Tied with AIDS on the Rise." 1990. *Omaha World-Herald*, Apr. 5.

Suitor, J. Jill and Karl Pillemer. 1994. "Family Caregiving and Marital Satisfaction: Findings from a 1-Year Panel Study of Women Caring for Parents with Dementia." *Journal of Marriage and the Family* 56 (3) (Aug.):681–90.

Sullivan, Andrew. 1995. *Virtually Normal: An Argument About Homosexuality*. New York: Knopf.

Sullivan, Oriel. 1997. "The Division of Housework among Remarried Couples." *Journal of Family Issues* 18 (2):205–23.

Sullivan, Ronald. 1992. "Judge Says Lesbian Can Adopt Companion's Child." *New York Times*, Jan. 31.

Sunseri, Linda. 2000. "Moving Beyond the Feminism versus Nationalism Dichotomy: An Anti-Colonial Feminist Perspective on Aboriginal Liberation Struggles." *Canadian Woman Studies* 20 (2):143–148.

Surra, Catherine A. 1990. "Research and Theory on Mate Selection and Premarital Relationships in the 1980s." *Journal of Marriage and the Family* 52 (Nov.):844–65.

Surra, Catherine A. and Debra K. Hughes. 1997. "Commitment Processes in Accounts of the Development of Premarital Relationships." *Journal of Marriage and the Family* 59:5–21.

Sussman, Marvin B., Suzanne K. Steinmetz, and Gary W. Peterson. 1999. *Handbook of Marriage and the Family*, 2nd ed. New York: Plenum Press.

Suwal, J. and F. Travato. 1998. "Canadian Aboriginal Fertility." *Canadian Studies in Population* 25 (1):69–86.

Swanson, J. 1986. "Ethnicity, Marriage and Role Conflict." In B. Asswad and B. Bilge (Eds.), *Family and Gender Among American Muslims* (pp. 241–9). Philadelphia: Temple University Press.

Swartz, Mimi. 1992. "Love and Hate at Texas A & M." *Texas Monthly*, Feb., pp. 64–71.

Sweet, James, Larry Bumpass, and Vaughn Call. 1988. *The Design and Content of the National Survey of Families and Households* (Working Paper NSFH-1). Madison: University of Wisconsin, Center for Demography and Ecology.

Swift, Shelley. 1999. "One of the Those Kids: AFN and Others Try to Restore Faded Tribal Ties for Canada's Native Adoptees." *American Indian Report*, 15 (1) (October):22–24.

Swim, Janet K. and Laurie L. Cohen. 1997. "A Comparison Between the Attitudes Toward Women and Modern Sexism Scales." *Psychology of Women Quarterly* 21 (1):103–18.

Swim, Janet K. 1994. "Perceived Versus Meta-analytic Effect Sizes: An Assessment of the Accuracy of Gender Stereotypes." *Journal of Personality and Social Psychology* 66 (1) (Jan.):21–37.

Swim, Janet K., K. J. Aikin, W. S. Hall, and B. A. Hunter. 1995. "Sexism and Racism: Old-Fashioned and Modern Prejudices." *Journal of Personality and Psychology* 68:199–214.

Szasz, Thomas S. 1976. *Heresies*. New York: Doubleday/Anchor.

Szinovacz, Maximiliane. 1997. "Adult Children Taking Parents into Their Homes: Effects of Childhood Living Arrangements." *Journal of Marriage and the Family* 59:700–17.

T

Tait, H. 1999. "Educational Achievement of Young Aboriginal Adults." *Canadian Social Trends* 52:6–10.

Talbani, Aziz and Parveen Hasanali. 2000. "Adolescent Females Between Tradition and Modernity: Gender Role Socialization in South Asian Immigrant Culture." *Journal of Adolescence* 23 (5) (October):615–627.

Talbot, Kay. 1996. "Transcending a Devastating Loss: the Life Attitude of Mothers Who Have Experienced the Death of Their Only Child." *The Hospice Journal* 11 (4):67–74.

———. 1997. "Mothers Now Childless: Survival after the Death of an Only Child." *Omega* 34 (3):177–86.

Talbott, Maria M. 1998. "Older Widows' Attitudes Towards Men and Remarriage." *Journal of Aging Studies* 12 (4):429–49.

Tam, Tony. 1997. "Sex Segregation and Occupational Gender Inequality in the United States: Devaluation or Specialized Training?" *American Journal of Sociology* 102 (6):1652–92.

Tanaka, Jennifer. 1996. "No Boys Allowed." *Newsweek*. October 28:82–84.

Tanfer, Koray and Lisa A. Cubbins. 1992. "Coital Frequency Among Single Women: Normative Constraints and Situational Opportunities." *The Journal of Sex Research* 29 (2):221–50.

Tannen, Deborah. 1990. *You Just Don't Understand*. New York: Morrow.

Tasker, Fiona L. and Susan Golombok. 1997. *Growing Up in a Lesbian Family: Effects on Child Development*. New York: Guilford.

Tatara, Tochio and Lisa Blumerman. 1996. *Summaries of the Statistical Data on Elder Abuse in Domestic Settings: An Exploratory Study of State Statistics for FY93 and FY94*. Washington, DC: National Center on Elder Abuse.

Tavris, Carol. 1992. *The Mismeasure of Woman*. New York: Simon & Schuster.

Taylor, D.M., N. Frasure-Smith and W.E. Lambert. 1978. "Psychological Development of French and English Canadian Children: Child-rearing Attitudes and Ethnic Identity." Pp. 153–168 in *The Canadian Ethnic Mosaic: A Quest for Identity*, edited by Leo Driedger. Toronto: McClelland & Stewart.

Taylor, Ericka. 1995. "The Stress of Infertility." *Human Ecology Forum* 23 (4):12–20.

Taylor, John. 1997. "Groups: Some Midlands Jobs Lack 'Livable Wage.'" *Omaha World-Herald.* December 10:39.

Taylor, Robert J. 1986. "Receipt of Support from Family Among Black Americans: Demographic and Familial Differences." *Journal of Marriage and the Family* 48:67–77.

Taylor, Robert J., Linda M. Chatters, M. Belinda Tucker, and Edith Lewis. 1990. "Developments in Research on Black Families: A Decade Review." *Journal of Marriage and the Family* 52 (Nov.):993–1014.

———. 1991. "Developments in Research on Black Families: A Decade Review." Pp. 274–96 in *Contemporary Families Looking Forward, Looking Back*, edited by Alan Booth. Minneapolis: National Council on Family Relations.

Taylor, Ronald L. 1997. "Who's Parenting? Trends and Patterns." Pp. 68–91 in *Contemporary Parenting: Challenges and Issues*, edited by Terry Arendell. Thousand Oaks, CA: Sage.

Teachman, Jay D. 1983. "Early Marriage, Premarital Fertility, and Marital Dissolution." *Journal of Family Issues* 4:105–26.

———. 1991. "Who Pays? Receipt of Child Support in the United States." *Journal of Marriage and the Family* 53 (3) (Aug.):759–72.

Teachman, Jay D. and Karen A. Polonko. 1990. "Cohabitation and marital stability in the United States." *Social Forces* 79: 207–20.

Tepperman, Lorne and Susannah J. Wilson (Eds.). 1993. *Next of Kin: An International Reader on Changing Families.* New York: Prentice Hall.

Terrelonge, Pauline. 1995. "Feminist Consciousness and Black Women." Pp. 607–16 in *Women: A Feminist Perspective.* 5th ed., edited by Jo Freeman, Mountain View, CA: Mayfield.

Teti, Douglas M. and Michael Lamb. 1989. "Socioeconomic and Marital Outcomes of Adolescent Marriage, Adolescent Childbirth, and Their Co-occurrence." *Journal of Marriage and the Family* 51:203–12.

Textor, Martin R. 1989. *The Divorce and Divorce Therapy Handbook.* Northvale, NJ: Jason Aronson.

Thibaut, John W. and Harold H. Kelley. 1959. *The Social Psychology of Groups.* New York: Wiley.

Thomas, Alexander, Stella Chess, and Herbert G. Birch. 1968. *Temperament and Behavior Disorders in Children.* New York: New York University Press.

Thomas, Amanda and Rex Forehand. 1993. "The Role of Paternal Variables in Divorced and Married Families." *American Journal of Orthopsychiatry* 63 (1) (Jan.):154–68.

Thomas, Darwin and Jean Edmondson Wilcox. 1987. "The Rise of Family Theory: A Historical-Critical Analysis." Pp. 103–24 in *Handbook of Marriage and the Family,* edited by Marvin B. Sussman and Suzanne K. Steinmetz. New York: Plenum.

Thomas, Evan and Gregory L. Vistica. 1997. "A Question of Consent." *Newsweek.* April 28:41.

Thomas, Rich. 1991. "Middle-Class Blessings: Another View." *Newsweek,* Nov. 4, p. 25.

Thomas, Susan L. 1998. "Race, Gender, and Welfare Reform: The Antinatalist Response." *Journal of Black Studies* 28 (4):419–46.

Thomas, Veronica G. 1990. "Determinants of Global Life Happiness and Marital Happiness in Dual-Career Black Couples." *Family Relations* 39 (2) (Apr.):174–78.

Thompson, Linda. 1991. "Family Work: Women's Sense of Fairness." *Journal of Family Issues* 12 (2) (June):181–96.

Thompson, L. 1993. "Conceptualizing Gender in Marriage: The Case of Marital Care." *Journal of Marriage and the Family,* 55:557–569.

Thompson, Linda and Alexis J. Walker. 1991. "Gender in Families." Pp. 76–102 in *Contemporary Families: Looking Forward, Looking Back*, edited by Alan Booth. Minneapolis: National Council on Family Relations.

Thomson, Elizabeth and Ugo Colella. 1992. "Cohabitation and Marital Stability: Quality or Commitment?" *Journal of Marriage and the Family* 54 (May):259–67.

Thomson, Elizabeth, Sara S. McLanahan, and Roberta Braun Curtin. 1992. "Family Structure, Gender, and Parental Socialization." *Journal of Marriage and the Family* 54 (2) (May):368–78.

Thornberry, Terence P., Carolyn A. Smith, and Gregory J. Howard. 1997. "Risk Factors for Teenage Fatherhood." *Journal of Marriage and the Family* 59:505–22.

Thorne, Barrie. 1992. "Girls and Boys Together ... But Mostly Apart: Gender Arrangements in Elementary School." Pp. 108–23 in *Men's Lives.* 2d ed., edited by Michael S. Kimmel and Michael A. Messner. New York: Macmillan.

Thornton, Arland. 1991. "Influence of the Marital History of Parents on the Marital and Cohabitational Experiences of Children." *American Journal of Sociology* 96 (4) (Jan.):868–94.

Thornton, Arland, William G. Axinn, and Jay D. Teachman. 1995. "The Influence of School Enrollment and Accumulation on Cohabitation and Marriage in Early Adulthood." *American Sociological Review* 60:762–74.

Thurman, Judith. 1982. "The Basics: Chodorow's Theory of Gender." *Ms. Magazine* (Sept.):35–36.

Tien, Jenn-Yun, Mark W. Roosa, and Marcia Michaels. 1994. "Agreement between Parent and Child Reports on Parental Behaviors." *Journal of Marriage and the Family* 56 (May):341–55.

Tiger, Lionel. 1969. *Men in Groups.* New York: Vintage.

———. 1978. "Omnigamy: The New Kinship System." *Psychology Today* 12:14.

Tilly, Louise A. and Joan W. Scott. 1978. *Women, Work, and Family*. New York: Holt, Rinehart & Winston.

Tjaden, P. and N. Thoennes. 2000. "Prevalence and Consequences of Male-to-Female and Female-to-Male Partner Violence as Measured by the National Violence Against Women Survey." *Violence Against Women* 6 (2):142–161.

Toledo, Sylvie de and Doborah Edler Brown. 1995. *Grandparents as Parents: A Survival Guide for Raising a Second Family*. New York: Guilford Press.

Tolstoy, Leo. 1886. *Anna Karenina*. New York: Crowell.

Tomaskovic-Devey, Donald. 1993. "The Gender and Race Composition of Jobs and the Male/Female White/Black Pay Gap." *Social Forces* 72 (1):45–76.

Tong, Rosemarie. 1989. *Feminist Theory: A Comprehensive Introduction*. Boulder: Westview Press.

Tongas, F., R. Brown, A. M. Beaton, and S. Joly. 1995. "Neosexism: Plus ca change, plus c'est pareil." *Personality and Social Psychology Bulletin* 21:842–49.

Toronto Star. 1999. "A Picture of Poverty." January 15: B3.

Torr, James D. and Karin Swisher. 1999. *Violence Against Women*. San Diego, CA: Greenhaven Press.

Torres, Aida and Jacqueline Darroch Forrest. 1988. "Why Do Women Have Abortions?" *Family Planning Perspectives* 20:169–76.

Torres, Zenia. 1997. "Interracial Dating." Unpublished student paper.

Totten, Mark Douglas. 2001. *Guys, Gangs and Girlfriend Abuse*. Peterborough, Ontario: Broadview Press.

Toufexis, Anastasia. 1990. "Sex Lives and Videotape." *Time*, Oct. 20, p. 104.

———. 1996. "Romancing the Computer." *Time*. February 19:53.

Townsend, Aloen L. and Melissa M. Franks. 1997. "Quality of the Relationship between Elderly Spouses: Influence on Spouse Caregivers' Subjective Effectiveness." *Family Relations* 46 (1):33–39.

Townson, Monica. 1995. *Financial Futures: Mid-Life Prospects for a Secure Retirement*. Ottawa: Canadian Advisory Council on the Status of Women.

———. 1998. "Canada's Record." *CCPA Monitor* (October). <www.policyalternatives.ca>

Trainor, Cathy. 1999. "Canada's Shelters For Abused Women." *Juristat: Canadian Centre for Justice Statistics*, Catalogue no. 85-002-XIE, 19, 6.

Travers, Robb and Dino Paoletti. 1999. "Responding To The Support Needs Of HIV Positive Lesbian, Gay And Bisexual Youth." *The Canadian Journal of Human Sexuality* 8:271–284.

Treas, Judith. 1995. "Older Americans in the 1990s and Beyond." *Population Bulletin* 50 (2) (May).

Trent, Katherine and Kyle Crowder. 1997. "Adolescent Birth Intentions, Social Disadvantage, and Behavioral Outcomes." *Journal of Marriage and the Family* 59:523–35.

Triandis, H. C. 1995. *Individualism and Collectivism*. Boulder, CO: Westview.

Tribe, Lawrence H. 1990. *Abortion: The Clash of Absolutes*. New York: Horton.

Trocme, N. and R. Brison. 1997. "Homicide, Assault and Abuse and Neglect: Patterns and Opportunities for Action." In Health Canada, *For the Safety of Canadian Children and Youth: From Injury Data to Preventive Measures*. Ottawa: Minister of Public Works and Government Services Canada.

Troiden, Richard R. 1988. *Gay and Lesbian Identity: A Sociological Analysis*. New York: General Hall.

Troll, Lillian E. 1985. "The Contingencies of Grandparenting." Pp. 135–50 in *Grandparenthood,* edited by Vern L. Bengston and Joan F. Robertson. Newbury Park, CA: Sage.

Troll, Lillian E., Sheila J. Miller, and Robert C. Atchley. 1979. *Families in Later Life*. Belmont, CA: Wadsworth.

Troost, Kay Michael and Erik Filsinger. 1993. "Emerging Biosocial Perspectives on the Family." Pp. 677–710 in *Sourcebook of Family Theories and Methods: A Contextual Approach,* edited by Pauline G. Boss, William J. Doherty, Ralph LaRossa, Walter R. Schumm, and Suzanne K. Steinmetz. New York: Plenum.

Troper, Harold. 1999. "Immigration." In *The Canadian Encyclopedia: Year 2000 Edition*, edited by James H. Marsh, pp. 1139–1141. Toronto: McClelland & Stewart Inc.

Trost, Cathy. 1992. "To Cut Costs and Keep the Best People, More Concerns Offer Flexible Work Plans." *The Wall Street Journal*, Feb. 18, p. B1.

Trost, Cathy and Carol Hymowitz. 1990. "Careers Start Giving in to Family Needs." *The Wall Street Journal*, June 18, p. B1.

Trost, Jan. 1997. "Step-Family Variations." Pp. 71–84 in *Stepfamilies: History, Research, and Policy*, edited by Irene Levin and Marvin B. Sussman. New York: Haworth Press.

Trovato, Frank and Gloria Lauris. 1989. "Marital Status and Mortality in Canada: 1951–1981." *Journal of Marriage and the Family* 51:907–912.

Trussell, James. 1988. "Teenage Pregnancy in the United States." *Family Planning Perspectives* 20:262–72.

Trzcinski, Eileen and Matia Finn-Stevenson. 1991. "A Response to Arguments Against Mandated Parental Leave: Findings from the Connecticut Survey of Parental Leave Policies." *Journal of Marriage and the Family* 53 (2) (May):445–60.

Tsang, David. 2001. "Gay Pride, Asian Proud." *Banana: Asian-Canadian Lifestyle and Culture Magazine*, Summer 2001, vol. 1(1), 24–25.

Tschann, Jeanne M., Janet R. Johnston, Marsha Kline, and Judith S. Wallerstein. 1989. "Family Process and Children's Functioning During Divorce." *Journal of Marriage and the Family* 51 (2) (May):431–44.

Tucker, Jennifer. 1994. *Defining Work and Family Issues: Listening to the Voices of Women of Color.* Washington, DC: Center for Women Policy Studies.

Tucker, Judith E., Ed. 1993. *Arab Women: Old Boundaries, New Frontiers.* Bloomington: Indiana University Press.

Tun, Paul. 2000. "Polls Show Canadians Not Settled On Abortion." *The Interim*, August. <http://www.lifesite.net/interim/2000/aug/09pollsshow.html>

Turcotte, Pierre and Alain Belanger.1996–1997. "The Dynamics of Formation and Dissolution of First Common-Law Unions in Canada." <http://www.statscan.ca/english/research.htm>

———. 2000. "Moving In Together: The Formation of First Common-Law Unions." Pp. 105–108 in *Canadian Social Trends: Volume 3.* Toronto: Thompson Educational Publishing, Inc.

Turner, Barbara F. and Catherine Adams. 1988. "Reported Change in Adult Sexual Activity over the Adult Years." *Journal of Sex Research* 25:289–303.

Turner, Heather A. and David Finkelhor. 1996. "Corporal Punishment as a Stressor among Youth." *Journal of Marriage and the Family* 58 (1):155–66.

Turner, Ralph H. 1976. "The Real Self: From Institution to Impulse." *American Journal of Sociology* 81 (5):989–1016.

Turner, R. Jay and William R. Avison. 1985. "Assessing Risk Factors for Problem Parenting: The Significance of Social Support." *Journal of Marriage and the Family* 47 (4):881–92.

Twaite, James A., Daniel Silitsky, and Anya K. Luchow. 1998. *Children of Divorce: Adjustment, Parental Conflict, Custody, Remarriage, and Recommendations for Clinicians.* Northvale, NJ: Jason Aronson.

Twenge, Jean M. 1997a. "Attitudes Toward Women, 1970–1995: A Meta-Analysis." *Psychology of Women Quarterly* 21 (1):35–51.

———. 1997b. " 'Mrs. His Name': Women's Preferences for Married Names." *Psychology of Women Quarterly* 21 (3):417–30.

———. and Alyssa N. Zucker. 1999. "What is a Feminist? Evaluations and Stereotypes in Closed- And Open-End Responses." *Psychology of Women Quarterly* 23 (3) (September):594–605.

Tyyska, Vappu. 2001. *Women, Citizenship and Canadian Child Care Policy in the 1990s.* March. Unpublished paper.

Tzeng, Jessie M. 2000. "Ethnically Heterogamous Marriages: The Case Of Asian Canadians." *Journal of Comparative Family Studies* 31 (3):321–337.

U

Uchino, Bert N. and John T. Cacioppa. 1996. "The Relationship between Social Support and Physiological Processes: A Review with Emphasis on Underlying Mech-

anisms and Implications for Health." *Psychological Bulletin* 119 (3):488–503.

Uchitelle, Louis. 1998a. "Even the Rich Can Buffer from Income Inequality." *New York Times.* November 15.

———. 1998b. "Downsizing Comes Back, but the Outcry Is Muted." *New York Times.* December 7.

Udry, J. Richard. 1974. *The Social Context of Marriage.* 3d ed. Philadelphia: Lippincott.

———. 1988. "Biological Predispositions and Social Control in Adolescent Sexual Behavior." *American Sociological Review* 53:709–22.

———. 1994. "The Nature of Gender." *Demography* 31 (4) (Nov.):561–73.

Uhlenberg, Peter. 1980. "Death and the Family." *Journal of Family History* 5 (fall):313–20.

Umberson, Debra, Kristin Anderson, Jennifer Glick, and Adam Shapiro. 1998. "Domestic Violence, Personal Control, and Gender." *Journal of Marriage and the Family* 60 (2):442–52.

Umberson, Debra, Meichu D. Chen, James S. House, Kristine Hopkins, and Ellen Slaten. 1996. "The Effect of Social Relationships on Psychological Well-Being: Are Men and Women Really So Different?" *American Sociological Review* 61:837–857.

Upchurch, Dawn M., Lene Levy-Storms, Clea A. Sucoff, and Carol S. Aneshensel. 1998. "Gender and Ethnic Differences in the Timing of First Sexual Intercourse." *Family Planning Perspectives* 30 (3):121–27.

Urchins, B. N., and J. T. Cacioppo. 1996. "The Relationship between Social Support and Physiological Processes: A Review with Emphasis on Underlying Mechanisms and Implications for Health." *Psychological Bulletin* 119:488–531.

Ursel, Jane. 2000. "Family Violence Courts." Pp. 45–48 in Statistics Canada, *Family Violence in Canada: A Statistical Profile 2000.* Catalogue 85-224-XIE. Ottawa: Minister of Industry.

U.S. Bureau of the Census. 1998. *Statistical Abstract of the United States, 1998.* Washington, DC: U.S. Government Printing Office.

U.S. Centers for Disease Control and Prevention. 1992. *HIV/AIDS Surveillance: First Quarter Edition.* (Apr.) Atlanta: U.S. Department of Health and Human Services, Centers for Disease Control.

———. 1993. "1993 Sexually Transmitted Diseases Treatment Guidelines." Atlanta: U.S. Department of Health and Human Services, Centers for Disease Control.

U.S. Department of Justice. 1998b. "Stalking and Domestic Violence: The Third Annual Report to Congress under the Violence Against Women Act." Washington, DC: Violence Against Women Grants Office.

V

Van den Haag, Ernest. 1974. "Love or Marriage." Pp. 134–42 in *The Family: Its Structures and Functions*. 2d ed., edited by Rose Laub Coser. New York: St. Martin's.

Van Pelt, Nancy L. 1985. *How to Turn Minuses into Pluses: Tips for Working Moms, Single Parents, and Stepparents*. Washington, DC: Review and Herald, Better Living Series.

Van Yperen, N. W. and Bram P. Buunk. 1990. "A Longitudinal Study of Equity and Satisfaction in Intimate Relationships." *European Journal of Social Psychology* 20:287–309.

———. 1994. "Social Comparison and Social Exchange in Marital Relationships." Pp. 89–116 in *Entitlement and the Affectional Bond: Justice in Close Relationships*, edited by M. J. Lerner and G. Mikula. New York: Plenum.

Vance, Lisa M. 1998. "Reaction Paper, Chapter 13." Unpublished Student Paper.

Vander Zanden, James W. 1981. *Social Psychology*. 2d ed. New York: Random House.

Vanderbelt, H. 1992. "Incest." *Lear's*, February:49–77.

Vanier Institute of the Family. 1996. *Canada's Familes: They Count*. Neapean, Ontario: Vanier Institute of the Family.

———. n.d. "Adoption in Canada: A Summary of the Important Issues." <http://www.canadianparents.com/articles/feature28e.htm>

———. 1998. "Older Canadians: Facts and Trends." *Transition Magazine* (December). <http://www.vifamily.ca/htm/284/3.htm>

———. 1998b. "Immigration Facts." *Transition Magazine* (September). <http://www.vifamily/ca/tm/283/2.htm>

———. 1998. "Family Facts." <http://www.vifamily.ca/faqs.faq.htm>

VanLear, C. Arthur. 1992. "Marital Communication Across the Generations: Learning and Rebellion, Continuity and Change." *Journal of Social and Personal Relationships* 9:103–23.

Vannoy, Dana. 1991. "Social Differentiation, Contemporary Marriage, and Human Development." *Journal of Family Issues* 12:251–67.

Vannoy, Dana and Paula Dubeck. 1998. *Challenges for Work and Family in the Twenty-First Century*. New York: Aldine de Gruyter.

Vannoy, Dana and William W. Philliber. 1992. "Wife's Employment and Quality of Marriage." *Journal of Marriage and the Family* 54 (2) (May):387–98.

Vannoy-Hiller, Dana and William W. Philliber. 1989. *Equal Partners: Successful Women in Marriage*. Newbury Park, CA: Sage.

Vaugh, P. 1998. *The Monogamy Myth: A Personal Handbook For Recovering From Affairs*. New York: Newmarket Press.

Vaughan, Diane. 1986. *Uncoupling: Turning Points in Intimate Relationships*. New York: Oxford University Press.

Vaughan, Peggy. 1998. "Dear Peggy.com" <http://www.dearpeg.com/index.html>

Vermer, Elizabeth, Marilyn Coleman, Lawrence H. Ganong, and Harris Cooper. 1989. "Marital Satisfaction in Remarriage: A Meta-analysis." *Journal of Marriage and the Family* 51:713–25.

Ventura, Stephanie J. 1988. "Births of Hispanic Parentage, 1985." *Monthly Vital Statistics Report* 36 (11), Suppl., Feb. 26.

Ventura, Stephanie J., Robert N. Anderson, Joyce A. Martin, and Betty L. Smith. 1998. "Births and Deaths: Preliminary Data for 1997." *National Vital Statistics Reports* vol. 47, No. 4. Hyattsville, MD: National Center for Health Statistics.

Ventura, Stephanie J., T.J. Mathews, and Sally C. Curtin. 1998b. "Declines in Teenage Birth Rates, 1991–97: National and State Patterns." *Monthly Vital Statistics Report* vol. 47, No. 12. Hyattsville, MD: National Center for Health Statistics.

Verkuyten, Maykel and Barbara Kinket. 1999. "The Relative Importance Of Ethnicity: Ethnic Categorization Among Older Children." *International Journal of Psychology* 34 (2):107–118.

Viscott, David, 1976. *How to Live with Another Person*. New York: Random House.

Visher, Emily B. and John S. Visher. 1979. *Stepfamilies: A Guide to Working with Stepparents and Stepchildren*. New York: Brunner/Mazel.

———. 1996. *Therapy with Stepfamilies*. New York: Brunner/Mazel.

Vogel, Ezra F. and Norman W. Bell. 1960. "The Emotionally Disturbed Child as Family Scapegoat." Pp. 382–97 in *Modern Introduction to the Family*, edited by Norman W. Bell and Ezra F. Vogel. Glencoe, IL: Free Press.

W

Wade, Nicholas. 1994. "How Men and Women Think." *New York Times* Magazine, June 12, p. 32.

Wages for Housework Campaign. n.d. "Wages for Housework Campaign." <http://www.payequity.net/WFHCampaign/wfhcpgn.htm>

Wagner, David G. and Joseph Berger. 1997. "Gender and Interpersonal Task Behaviors: Status Expectation Accounts." *Sociological Perspectives* 40 (1):1–32.

Wagner, David M. 1998. "Divorce Reform: New Directions." *Current*. February 1:7–10.

Wagner, R. M. 1988. "Changes in Extended Family Relationships for Mexican American and Anglo Single Mothers." Pp. 158–73 in *Minority and Ethnic Issues in the Divorce Process*, edited by C. A. Everett. New York: Haworth Press.

Waite, Linda J. 1995. "Does Marriage Matter?" *Demography* 32 (4) (November):483–507.

Waite, Linda J., Frances Kobrin Goldscheider, and Christina Witsberger. 1986. "Nonfamily Living and the Erosion of Traditional Family Orientations Among Young Adults." *American Sociological Review* 51:541–54.

Waite, Linda J. and Lee A. Lillard. 1991. "Children and Marital Disruption." *American Journal of Sociology* 96 (4) (Jan.):930–53.

Wakil, P. "Profiles in Conflict, Time Perspectives and Parent-Children Interaction Patterns: Case of the Pakistani-Canadian Immigrant Families." Unpublished paper.

Wakil, Parvez S., C.M. Siddique and F.A. Wakil. 1981. "Between Two Cultures: A Study in Socialization of Children of Immigrants." *Journal of Marriage and the Family* 43 (November):929–940.

Waldfogel, Jane. 1997. "The Effect of Children on Women's Wages." *American Sociological Review* 62:209–17.

Walker, Lenore E. 1988. "The Battered Woman Syndrome." Pp. 139–48 in *Family Abuse and Its Consequences: New Directions in Research,* edited by Gerald T. Hotaling, David Finkelhor, John T. Kirkpatrick, and Murray A. Straus. Newbury Park, CA: Sage.

Walker, Lou Ann. 1985. "When a Parent Is Disabled." *New York Times*, June 20.

Wallace, Michele. 1995. "For Whom the Bell Tolls: Why America Can't Deal with Black Feminist Intellectuals." *Village Voice Literary Supplement.* November:19–24.

Wallace, Pamela M. and Ian H. Gotlib. 1990. "Marital Adjustment During the Transition to Parenthood: Stability and Predictors of Change." *Journal of Marriage and the Family* 52:21–29.

Waller, Willard. 1937. "The Rating and Dating Complex." *American Sociological Review* 2:727–34.

———. 1951. *The Family: A Dynamic Interpretation.* New York: Dryden. (Revised by Reuben Hill.)

Wallerstein, Judith S. 1998. "Children of Divorce: A Society in Search of Policy." Pp. 66–94 in *All Our Families: New Policies for a New Century,* edited by Mary Ann Mason, Arlene Skolnick, and Stephen D. Sugarman. New York: Oxford University Press.

Wallerstein, Judith S. and Sandra Blakeslee. 1989. *Second Chances: Men, Women, and Children a Decade After Divorce.* New York: Ticknor & Fields.

———. 1995. *The Good Marriage: How and Why Love Lasts.* Boston: Houghton Mifflin.

Wallerstein, Judith S. and Joan Kelly. 1980. *Surviving the Break-Up: How Children Actually Cope with Divorce.* New York: Basic Books.

Wallerstein, Judith S. and Julia Lewis. 1998. "The Long-Term Impact of Divorce on Children: A First Report from a 25-Year Study." *Family and Conciliation Courts Review* 36 (3):368–79.

Wallis, Claudia. 1989. "Onward, Women!" *Time*, Dec. 4, pp. 80–89.

Walster, Elaine H. 1965. "The Effects of Self-Esteem on Romantic Liking." *Journal of Experimental and Social Psychology* 1:184–97.

Walster, Elaine H., E. Aronson, D. Abrams, and L. Rottman. 1966. "Importance of Physical Attractiveness in Dating Behavior." *Journal of Personality and Social Psychology* 4:508–16.

Walster, Elaine H. and G. William Walster. 1978. *A New Look at Love.* Reading, MA: Addison-Wesley.

Walster, Elaine H., G. William Walster, and Ellen Berscheid. 1978. *Equity: Theory and Research.* Boston: Allyn and Bacon.

Walter, Bernd, Janine Alison Isenegger and Nicholas Bala. 1995. "'Best Interests' In Child Protection Proceedings: Implications And Alternatives." *Canadian Journal of Family Law* 12 (2):367–439.

Ward, Angela. 1988. "A Feminist Mystique." *Newsweek*, Sept. 12, pp. 8–9.

Ward, Margaret. 1997. "Family Paradigms and Older-Child Adoption: A Proposal for Matching Parents' Strengths to Children's Needs." *Family Relations* 46 (3):257–62.

———. 1998. *The Family Dynamic: A Canadian Perspective,* 2nd edition. Toronto: I.T.P. Nelson

——— and G. Spitze. 1996. "Will the Children Ever Leave? Parent-Child Coresidence: History and Plans." *Journal of Family Issues,* 17:514–539.

——— and G. Spitze. 1996. "Gender Differences in Parent-Child Coresidence Experiences." *Journal of Marriage and the Family,* 58:718–725.

Waring, E. M., B. Schaefer, and R. Fry. 1994. "The Influence of Therapeutic Self-Disclosure on Perceived Marital Intimacy." *Journal of Sex and Marital Therapy* 20 (2):135–41.

Wark, Linda and Shilpa Jobalia. 1998. "What Would it Take to Build a Bridge? An Intervention for Stepfamilies." *Journal of Family Psychotherapy* 9 (3):69–77.

Warner, Gary A. 1992. "Statistics Needed to Determine Scope of Military Rape Problem." *The Orange County Register*, reprinted in *Omaha World-Herald*, July 13, p. 8.

Warren, Chris and Crescy Cannan. 1997. *Social Action with Children and Families: A Community Approach to Child and Family Welfare.* New York: Routledge.

Warshaw, Robin. 1995. *I Never Called It Rape: The Ms. Report on Recognizing, Fighting and Surviving Date and Acquaintance Rape.* New York: HarperCollins.

Waterman, C., L. Dawson and M. Bologna. 1989. "Sexual Coercion In Gay And Lesbian Relationships: Predictors And Implications For Support Services." *Journal of Sex Research* 26:118–124.

Watson, K. 1986. "Birth Families: Living with the Adoption Decision." *Public Welfare*, pp. 5–10.

Watson, Roy E. L. and Peter W. DeMeo. 1987. "Premarital Cohabitation Versus Traditional Courtship and Subsequent Marital Adjustment: A Replication and Follow-Up." *Family Relations* 36:193–97.

Watson, Russell. 1984. "What Price Day Care?" *Newsweek*, Sept. 10, pp. 14–21.

Waugh, Earle H. Waugh, Sharon McIrvin Abu-Laban and Regula Bruckhardt Qureshi. 1991. *Muslim Families in North America*. Calgary: University of Alberta Press.

Wax, Amy L. 1998. "Bargaining in the Shadow of the Market: Is There a Future for Egalitarian Marriage?" *Virginia Law Review* 84 (4):509–36.

Weaver, Sally. 1992. "First Nations Women and Government Policy, 1970–92: Discrimination and Conflict." Pp. 92–150 in *Changing Patterns: Women in Canada*, 2nd edition, edited by S. Burt, L. Code, and L. Dorney. Toronto: McClelland & Stewart.

Weber, Max. 1948. *The Theory of Social and Economic Organization,* edited by Talcott Parsons. New York: Free Press.

Weeks, John R. 1992. *Population: An Introduction to Concepts and Issues.* 5th ed. Belmont, CA: Wadsworth.

———. 1996. *Population*, 6th ed. Belmont, CA: Wadsworth.

Weigert, Andrew and Ross Hastings. 1977. "Identity Loss, Family and Social Change." *American Journal of Sociology* 28:1171–85.

Weiner, Nan. 2001. "Employment Barriers Still Block Aboriginals & Visible Minorities." *CAUT BULLETIN ACPPU* (April): A9.

Weingarten, Helen R. 1985. "Marital Status and Well-Being: A National Study Comparing First-Married, Currently Divorced, and Remarried Adults." *Journal of Marriage and the Family* 47:653–62.

Weisman, Mary-Lou. 1994. "When Parents Are Not in the Best Interests of the Child." *The Atlantic Monthly.* July:43–63.

Weiss, Robert S. 1975. *Marital Separation: Managing After a Marriage Ends.* New York: Basic Books.

———. 1987. "Men and Their Wives' Work." Pp. 109–21 in *Spouse, Parent, Worker: On Gender and Multiple Roles,* edited by F. J. Crosby. New Haven, CT: Yale University Press.

Weitzman, Lenore J. 1981. *The Marriage Contract: Spouses, Lovers, and the Law.* New York: Free Press.

———. 1985. *The Divorce Revolution: The Unexpected Social and Economic Consequences for Women and Children in America.* New York: Free Press.

———. 1996. "The Economic Consequences of Divorce Are Still Unequal: Comment on Peterson." *American Sociological Review* 61 (3):537–39.

Wellington, Alison J. 1994. "Accounting for the Male/ Female Wage Gap Among Whites: 1976 and 1985." *American Sociological Review* 56 (6) (Dec.):839–49.

Welwood, Lorne. 2000. "Adoption in Canada." <http://www.mbconf.ca/mb/mbh3622/lorne.htm>

Wenk, DeeAnn and Patricia Garrett. 1992. "Having a Baby: Some Predictions of Maternal Employment Around Childbirth." *Gender & Society* 6 (1) (Mar.):49–65.

Wenk, DeeAnn, Constance L. Hardesty, Carolyn S. Morgan, and Sampson Lee Blair. 1994. "The Influence of Parental Involvement on the Well-Being of Sons and Daughters." *Journal of Marriage and the Family* 56 (1) (Feb.):229–34.

Werking, Kathy. 1997. *We're Just Good Friends: Men and Women in Non-Romantic Relationships.* New York: Guilford.

Werner, Emmy E. 1992. "The Children of Kauai: Resilience and Recovery in Adolescence and Adulthood." *Journal of Adolescent Health* 13:262–68.

Werner, Emmy E. and Ruth S. Smith. 1992. *Overcoming the Odds: High Risk Children from Birth to Adulthood.* Ithaca, NY: Cornell University Press.

West, Traci C. 1999. *Spirit-Wounding Violence against Black Women: Unleashing Resistance Ethics.* New York: New York University Press.

Westfall, A. 1989. "Extramarital Sex: The Treatment of the Couple." In G. Weeks (ed.) *Treating Couples: The Intersystem Model of the Marriage Council of Philadelphia.* New York: Brunner/Mazel.

Weston, Kath. 1991. *Families We Choose: Lesbians, Gays, Kinship.* New York: Columbia University Press.

Wexler, Richard. 1991. "Child-Abuse Hysteria Snares Innocent Victims." *The Wall Street Journal*, June 4.

Whipple, Ellen E. and Cheryl A. Richey. 1997. "Crossing the Line from Physical Discipline to Child Abuse: How Much Is Too Much?" *Child Abuse & Neglect* 21 (5):431–44.

Whitbeck, Les. B., Danny R. Hoyt, and Shirley M. Huck. 1993. "Family Relationship History, Contemporary Parent–Grandparent Relationship Quality, and the Grandparent–Grandchild Relationship." *Journal of Marriage and the Family* 55 (4) (Nov.):1025–35.

Whitbeck, Les B., Ronald L. Simons, and Meei-Ying Kao. 1994. "The Effects of Divorced Mothers' Dating Behaviors and Sexual Attitudes on the Sexual Attitudes and Behaviors of Their Adolescent Children." *Journal of Marriage and the Family* 56 (3) (Aug.):615–21.

White, Carol Wayne. 1995. "Toward an Afra-American Feminism." Pp. 529–46 in *Women: A Feminist Perspective.* 5th ed., edited by Jo Freeman. Mountain View, CA: Mayfield.

White, Gregory L. and Paul E. Mullen. 1989. *Jealousy: Theory, Research, and Clinical Strategies.* New York: Guilford.

White, Jack E. 1993. "Growing Up in Black and White." *Time*, May 17, pp. 48–49.

White, James M. 1999. "Work-family Stage and Satisfaction with Work-family Balance." *Journal of Comparative Family Studies* 30 (2) (spring):163–175.

———. 1992. "Marital Status and Well-Being in Canada: An Anlysis of Age Group Variations." *Journal of Family Issues*, 13:390–409.

White, J. W., and M. P. Koss. 1991. "Courtship Violence: Incidence in a National Sample of Higher Education Students." *Violence and Victims* 6:247–56.

White, Lynn K. 1987. "Freedom Versus Constraint: The New Synthesis." *Journal of Family Issues* 8 (4):468–70.

———. 1990. "Determinants of Divorce: A Review of Research in the Eighties." *Journal of Marriage and the Family* 52 (Nov.):904–12.

———. 1994. "Growing Up with Single Parents and Stepparents: Long-Term Effects on Family Solidarity." *Journal of Marriage and the Family* 56 (4) (Nov.):935–48.

———. 1985a. "The Transition to Parenthood and Marital Quality." *Journal of Family Issues* 6 (4):435–49.

———. 1985b. "The Quality and Stability of Remarriages: The Role of Stepchildren." *American Sociological Review* 50:689–98.

———. 1991. "Divorce Over the Life Course: The Role of Marital Happiness." *Journal of Family Issues* 12 (1) (Mar.):5–21.

White, Lynn K., Alan Booth, and John N. Edwards. 1986. "Children and Marital Happiness." *Journal of Family Issues* 7 (2):131–47.

White, Lynn K. and Bruce Keith. 1990. "The Effect of Shift Work on the Quality and Stability of Marital Relations." *Journal of Marriage and the Family* 52:453–62.

White, Lynn K. and Agnes Riedmann. 1992. "When the Brady Bunch Grows Up: Step/Half- and Full-sibling Relationships in Adulthood." *Journal of Marriage and the Family* 54 (1) (Feb.):197–208.

White, Lynn K. and Stacy J. Rogers. 1997. "Strong Support But Uneasy Relationships: Coresidence and Adult Children's Relationships with Their Parents." *Journal of Marriage and the Family* 59 (1):62–76.

Whiting, B. and C. P. Edwards. 1988. *Children of Different Worlds: The Formation of Social Behavior.* Cambridge, MA: Harvard University Press.

Whitla, W. 1995. "A Chronology of Women in Canada." Pp. 315–353 in *Feminist Issues: Race, Class and Sexuality,* edited by Nancy Mandell. Scarborough, ON: Prentice Hall Canada.

Whitman, David. 1997. "Was It Good for Us?" *U.S. News & World Report.* May 19:56–64.

Whittaker, Terri. 1995. "Violence, Gender and Elder Abuse: Towards a Feminist Analysis and Practice." *Journal of Gender Studies* 4 (1):35–45.

"Why Interracial Marriages Are Increasing." 1996. *Jet.* June 3:12–15.

Whyte, Martin King. 1990. *Dating, Mating, and Marriage.* New York: Aldine de Gruyter.

Wickrama, K. A. S., Frederick O. Lorenz, Rand D. Conger, and Glen H. Elder. 1997. "Marital Quality and Physical Illness: A Latent Growth Curve Analysis." *Journal of Marriage and the Family* 59 (1):143–55.

Wiederman, Michael W. 1997. "Extramarital Sex: Prevalence and Correlates in a National Survey." *Journal of Sex Research* 34 (2):167–74.

Wiederman, Michael W. and Shannon R. Hurst. 1998. "Body Size, Physical Attractiveness, and Body Image among Young Adult Women: Relationships to Sexual Experience and Sexual Esteem." *Journal of Sex Research* 35 (3):272–81.

Wiederman, Michael W. and Lisa LaMar. 1998. " 'Not with Him You Don't!': Gender and Emotional Reactions to Sexual Infidelity During Courtship." *Journal of Sex Research* 35 (3):288–97.

Wilcox, Kathryn L., Sharlene A. Wolchik, and Sanford L. Braver. 1998. "Predictors of Maternal Preference for Joint or Sole Legal Custody." *Family Relations* 47 (1):93–101.

Wilder, H. B. and David A. Chiriboga. 1991. "Who Leaves Whom: The Importance of Control." Pp. 224–47 in *Divorce: Crisis, Challenge or Relief?,* edited by David A. Chiriboga and Linda S. Catron. New York: New York University Press.

Wiley, Norbert F. 1985. "Marriage and the Construction of Reality: Then and Now." Pp. 21–32 in *The Psychosocial Interior of the Family.* 3d ed., edited by Gerald Handel. Hawthorne, NY: Aldine de Gruyter.

Wilkie, Jane Riblett. 1988. "Marriage, Family Life, and Women's Employment." Pp. 149–66 in *Women Working.* 2d ed., edited by Ann Helton Stromberg and Shirley Harkess. Mountain View, CA: Mayfield.

———. 1991. "The Decline in Men's Labor Force Participation and Income and the Changing Structure of Family Economic Support." *Journal of Marriage and the Family* 53 (1) (Feb.):111–22.

Wilkie, Jane Riblett, Myra Marx Ferree, and Kathryn Strother Ratcliff. 1998. "Gender and Fairness: Marital Satisfaction in Two-Earner Couples." *Journal of Marriage and the Family* 60 (3):577–94.

Wilkins, R. 1998. "Mortality by Neighbourhood Income in Canada, 1986 to 1991." Paper presented at the Conference of the Canadian Society for Epidemiology and Biostatistics, St. John's Newfoundland, August.

Wilkinson, Doris. 1993. "Family Ethnicity in America." Pp. 15–59 in *Family Ethnicity: Strength in Diversity,* edited by Harriette Pipes McAdoo. Newbury Park, CA: Sage.

Williams, J.E., R.C. Satterwhite and D.L. Best. 1999. "Pancultural Gender Stereotypes Revisited: The Five Factor Model." *Sex Roles* 40 (7/8) (April):513–525.

Williams, Joan C. 1991. "Deconstructing Gender." Pp. 95–123 in *Feminist Legal Theory: Readings in Law and Gender*, edited by Katharine T. Bartlett and Rosanne Kennedy. San Francisco: Westview.

Williams, Karen. 1995. "The Good Mother." Pp. 98–110 in *Lesbian Parenting: Living with Pride and Prejudice*, edited by Katherine Arnup. Charlottetown, PEI: gynergy books.

Williams, Kirk R. 1992. "Social Sources of Marital Violence and Deterrence: Testing an Integrated Theory of Assaults Between Partners." *Journal of Marriage and the Family* 54 (3) (Aug.):620–29.

Williams, Lena. 1989. "Teen-Age Sex: New Codes Amid Old Anxiety." *New York Times*, Feb. 27.

Williams, Linda S. 1992. "Adoption Actions and Attitudes of Couples Seeking In Vitro Fertilization." *Journal of Family Issues* 13 (1) (Mar.):99–113.

Williams, Mary E., Brenda Stalcup, and Karin Swisher. 1998. *Working Women: Opposing Viewpoints*. San Diego: Greenhaven Press.

Williams, Richard and Michele Andrisin Wittig. 1997. "'I'm Not A Feminist, But...': Factors Contributing to the Discrepancy Between Pro-Feminist Orientation and Feminist Social Identity." *Sex Roles* 37 (11/12) (December):885–904.

Willie, Charles Vert. 1986. "The Black Family and Social Class." Pp. 224–31 in *The Black Family: Essays and Studies*, edited by Robert Staples. Belmont, CA: Wadsworth.

Wills, T. A. 1991. "Social Support and Interpersonal Relationships." *Review of Personality and Social Psychology* 12:265–89.

Wilson, Barbara Foley and Sally Cunningham Clarke. 1992. "Remarriages: A Demographic Profile." *Journal of Family Issues* 13 (2) (June):123–41.

Wilson, Margo and Martin Daly. 1994. "Spousal Homicide." *Juristat*, March, 14(8). Ottawa: Ministry of Industry, Science and Technology. Castalogue 85-002-XPE.

Wilson, Margo, Holly Johnson and Martin Daly. 1995. "Lethal and Non-Lethal Violence Against Wives." *Canadian Journal of Criminology* 37 (3):331–361.

Wilson, S.J. 1996. *Women, Families and Work*, 4th edition. Toronto: McGraw-Hill Ryerson.

Winch, Robert F. 1958. *Mate Selection: A Study of Complementary Needs*. New York: Harper & Row.

Windle, Michael and Levent Dumenci. 1997. "Parental and Occupational Stress as Predictors of Depressive Symptoms among Dual-Income Couples: A Multilevel Modeling Approach." *Journal of Marriage and the Family* 59 (3):625–34.

Wine, J.D. and J.L. Ristock. 1991. "Introduction: Feminist Activist Activism in Canada." Pp. 1–18 in *Women and Social Change: Feminist Activism in Canada*, edited by J.D. Wine and J.L. Ristock. Toronto: James Lorimer.

Wineberg, Howard. 1990. "Childbearing After Remarriage." *Journal of Marriage and the Family* 52:31–38.

———. 1994. "Marital Reconciliation in the United States: Which Couples Are Successful?" *Journal of Marriage and the Family* 56 (1) (Feb.):80–88.

Wineberg, Howard and James McCarthy. 1998. "Living Arrangements after Divorce: Cohabitation versus Remarriage." *Journal of Divorce & Remarriage* 29 (1/2):131–46.

Winslow, Ron. 1990. "Study Is Good News for People Waiting to Have Children." *The Wall Street Journal*, Mar. 8.

———. 1991. "C-Sections Tied to Economic Factors in Study." *The Wall Street Journal*, Jan. 2.

Winston, Kimberly. 1998. "A Test of Faith." *San Francisco Chronicle*. April 5:A–1, A–11.

Winton, Chester A. 1995. *Frameworks for Studying Families*. Guilford, CT: Dushkin.

Witt, April and Dennis Roberts. 1997. "Mission for Islam: Muslims Try to Educate Americans about their Religious Practices." *The Modesto Bee*. January 25:G–1, G–2.

Wolf, N. 1993. *Fire with Fire: The New Female Power and How It Will Change the 21st Century*. New York: Random House.

Wolf, Rosalie S. 1986. "Major Findings from Three Model Projects on Elderly Abuse." Pp. 218–38 in *Elder Abuse: Conflict in the Family*, edited by Karl A. Pillemer and Rosalie S. Wolf. Dover, MA: Auburn House.

———. 1996. "Elder Abuse and Family Violence: Testimony Presented before the U.S. Senate Special Committee on Aging." *Journal of Elder Abuse & Neglect* 8 (1):81–96.

Wolfson, C., R. Handfield-Jones, K.C., K.C. Glass, J. McClaran and E. Keyserlingk. 1993. "Adult Children's Perceptions of Their Responsibility to Provide Care for Dependent Elderly Parents." *The Gerontologist*, 13(3): 315–23.

Women Federal Political Representation. 20001. "Women-Federal Political Representation: Current List." <http://www.parl.gc.ca/information/about/p.../StandingsWomen.asp?Language=E&Source=hoc>

Women's Research and Education Institute. 1990. "The American Woman 1990–91." In *Bias, Tradition Seen in Pay Lag of U.S. Women*." *Omaha World-Herald*, Apr. 26.

Wong, Paul, Chienping Faith Lai, Richard Nagazawa, and Tieming Lin. 1998. "Asian Americans as a Model Minority: Self-Perceptions and Perceptions by Other Racial Groups." *Sociological Perspectives* 41 (1):95–118.

Woo, Junda. 1992. "Mediation Seen as Being Biased Against Women." *The Wall Street Journal*, Aug. 4, pp. B1, B9.

Wood, Cheri L. 1995. "Childless Mothers?—The New Catch-22: You Can't Have Your Kids and Work for Them Too." *Loyola of Los Angeles Law Review* 29 (1):383–402.

Woodman, Sue. (1995, Jan./Feb.). "How Teen Pregnancy Has Become a Political Football." *Ms. Magazine*, pp. 90–1.

Woodward, Kenneth L. 1992. "Better Than a Gold Watch: Sex after 60 Turns Out to be Good and Plentiful." *Newsweek*. August 24:71.

———. 1997. "Was the Pope Wrong?" *Newsweek*. June 16:48.

Worchel, Stephen. 1984. "The Darker Side of Helping: The Social Dynamics of Helping and Cooperation." Pp. 379–418 in *Development and Maintenance of Prosocial Behavior: International Perspectives on Positive Morality*, edited by E. Staub et al. New York: Plenum.

Wrangham, Richard and Dale Peterson. 1996. *Demonic Males*. New York: Houghton Mifflin.

Wright, Carol L. and Joseph W. Maxwell. 1991. "Social Support During Adjustment to Later-Life Divorce: How Adult Children Help Parents." *Journal of Divorce and Remarriage* 15 (3/4):21–48.

Wright, Eric Olin, James Baxter and Elizabeth Birkelund Gunn. 1995. "The Gender-Gap in Workplace Authority: A Cross-National Study." *American Sociological Review*, 60:407–435.

Wright, Gwendolyn. 1981. *Building the Dream: A Social History of Housing in America*. New York: Pantheon.

Wright, Robert. 1994a. *The Moral Animal: Evolutionary Psychology and Everyday Life*. New York: Pantheon.

———. 1994b. "Our Cheating Hearts." *Time*. August 15:44–52.

Wright, William. 1998. *Born That Way*. New York: Knopf.

Wu, Zheng. 2000. *Cohabitation: An Alternative Form of Family Living*. Don Mills, ON: Oxford University Press.

———. 1998. "Recent Trends in Marriage Patterns in Canada." *Policy Options* (September):3–11.

———. 1995. "The Stability of Cohabitation Relationships: The Role of Children." *Journal of Marriage and the Family* 57 (1) (Feb.):231–36.

——— and T.R. Balakrishnan. 1994. "Cohabitation After Marital Dissolution in Canada." *Journal of Marriage and the Family* 56:723–734.

——— and T.R. Balakrishnan. 1995. "Dissolution Of Premarital Cohabitation in Canada." *Demography* 32 (4):521–532.

——— and Margaret J. Penning. 1997. "Marital Instability after Midlife." *Journal of Family Issues* 18 (5):459–78.

Wulf, Steve. 1995. "Generation Excluded." *Newsweek*, Oct. 23, p. 86.

Wyatt, Gail Elizabeth and Gloria Johnson Powell, eds. 1988. *Lasting Effects of Child Sexual Abuse*. Newbury Park, CA: Sage.

Wyman, Hastings, Jr. 1994. "When the Love Boat Sails for Honolulu." *The Washington Blade*, Mar. 9, p. 35.

Y

Yalnizyan, A. 1998. *The Growing Gap*. Toronto: Centre for Social Justice.

Yancey, George and Sherelyn Yancey. 1998. "Interracial Dating." *Journal of Family Issues* 19 (3):334–48.

Yankelovich, Daniel A. 1981. *New Rules: Searching for Self-Fulfillment in a World Turned Upside Down*. New York: Random House.

Yarrow, Andrew L. 1987. "Older Parents' Child: Growing Up Special." *New York Times*, Jan. 26.

Yee, M. 1993. "Finding The Way Home Through Issues of Gender, Race and Glass." Pp. 3–44 in *Returning the Gaze: Essays on Racism, Feminism and Politics*, edited by H. Bannerji. Toronto: Star Vision Press.

Yllo, Kersti and Michele Bograd, eds. 1988. *Feminist Perspectives on Wife Abuse*. Newbury Park, CA: Sage.

Yoachum, Susan and Louis Freedberg. 1995. "Boxer Finds Herself in Media Spotlight." *San Francisco Chronicle*, Sept. 8, p. A14.

Yogis, J.A., R.R. Duplak and J.R. Trainor. 1996. *Sexual Orientation and Canadian Law: An Assessment of the Law Affecting Lesbian and Gay Persons*. Toronto: Emond Montgomery Publications Limited.

Yoshihama, Mieko, Asha L. Parekh, and Doris Boyington. 1991. "Dating Violence in Asian/Pacific Communities." Pp. 184–95 in *Dating Violence: Young Women in Danger*, edited by Barrie Levy. Seattle: Seal Press.

Young, Michael, George Denney, Raffy Luquis and Tamara Young. 1998. "Correlates Of Sexual Satisfaction In Marriage." *The Canadian Journal of Human Sexuality* 7:115–128.

Young-Hee, Yoon and Linda J. Waite. 1994. "Converging Employment Patterns of Black, White, and Hispanic Women: Return to Work After First Birth." *Journal of Marriage and the Family* 56 (Feb.):209–17.

Yousif, Ahmad F. 1994. "Family Values, Social Adjustment and Problems of Identity: The Canadian Experience." *Journal Institute of Muslim Minority Affairs* 15 (1-2) (Jan-July):108–120.

Z

Zabin, Laurie Schwab, Rebeca Wong, Robin M. Weinick, and Mark R. Emerson. 1992. "Dependency in Urban Black Families Following the Birth of an Adolescent's Child." *Journal of Marriage and the Family* 54 (3) (Aug.):496–507.

Zablocki v. Redhail. 1978. 434 U.S. 374, 54 L.Ed.2d 618, 98 S.Ct. 673.

Zahn-Waxler, Carolyn, Ed. 1995. *Sexual Orientation and Human Development*. Special issue of *Developmental Psychology*, vol. 31.

Zak, A. 1998. "Individual Differences in Perception of Fault in Intimate Relationships." *Personality and Individual Differences* 24:131–33.

Zelizer, Viviana K. 1985. *Pricing the Priceless Child: The Changing Social Value of Children.* New York: Basic Books.

Zicklin, Gilbert. 1997. "Deconstructing Legal Rationality: The Case of Lesbian and Gay Family Relationships." Pp. 55–76 in *Families and Law*, edited by Lisa J. McIntyre and B. Sussman. New York: Haworth Press.

Zilbergeld, Bernie. 1992. *The New Male Sexuality.* New York: Bantam.

Zill, Nicholas. 1994. "Understanding Why Children in Step-families Have More Learning and Behavior Problems Than Children in Nuclear Families." Pp. 97–106 in *Step-families: Who Benefits? Who Does Not?,* edited by Alan Booth and Judy Dunn. Hillsdale, NJ: Lawrence Erlbaum Associates.

Zill, Nicholas, D. R. Morrison, and M. J. Coiro. 1993. "Long-Term Effects of Parental Divorce on Parent-Child Relationships, Adjustment, and Achievement in Young Adulthood." *Journal of Family Psychology* 7:91–103.

Zvonkovic, Anisa M., Kathleen M. Greaves, Cynthia J. Schmiege, and Leslie D. Hall. 1996. "The Marital Construction of Gender through Work and Family Decisions: A Qualitative Analysis." *Journal of Marriage and the Family* 58 (1):91–100.

Credits

Photo Credits

1 © C. Ikeda-Blazys; **16** PhotoDisc; **26** ©R. Lambert; **28**
©R. Lambert; **33** ©R. Lambert; **39** PhotoDisc; **40**
©R. Lambert; **49** PhotoDisc; **57** ©Adie Nelson; **58** © Courtesy
of Canadian Space Agency; **60** ©Adie Nelson; **68** Sault
Star/Keith Stephen/CP Picture Archive; **87** PhotoDisc; **89**
PhotoDisc; **91** Bluestone Productions/SuperStock; **96**
PhotoDisc; **114** Kevin Frayer/CP Picture Archive; **129**
PhotoDisc; **135** Fred Chartrand/CP Picture Archive; **143**
PhotoDisc; **149** PhotoDisc; **158** SuperStock; **174** Eyewire; **177**
PhotoDisc; **186** Eyewire; **205 Left** © S. Mehta, **Right** ©J.
Waterson; **221** © Corel Corporation; **238** PhotoDisc; **243**
©R. Lambert; **253** PhotoDisc; **259** PhotoDisc; **269** PhotoDisc;
274 © Myrleen Ferguson Cate/Photo Edit; **279** CORBIS RF;
283 PhotoDisc; **293** PhotoDisc; **319** ©R. Lambert; **328** ©Adie
Nelson; **336** ©Adie Nelson; **349** © Corel Corporation; **361**
©Adie Nelson; **378** PhotoDisc; **384** ©Adie Nelson; **394** AP
Photo/Michael S. Green/CP Picture Archive; **403** Eyewire; **411**
Francisco Cruz/SuperStock; **422** ©Adie Nelson; **433** ©Adie
Nelson; **447** CORBIS RF/MAGMA; **468** © Spencer
Grant/Photo Edit; **471** PhotoDisc; **487** PhotoDisc; **490**
© M. DeCambra; **495** PhotoDisc; **515** ©R. Lambert; **519**
CORBIS RF/MAGMA; **532** Halifax Daily News/Tony
Caldwell/CP Picture Archive; **537** Eyewire

Text Credits

These pages constitute an extension of the copyright page. We
have made every effort to trace the ownership of all copyrighted
material and to secure permission from copyright holders. In the
event of any question arising as to the use of any material, we
will be pleased to make the necessary corrections in future
printings.

Chapter 1

3 Box 1.1 David M. Klein and James K. White, *Family
Theories: An Introduction,* p. 24. Copyright © 1996 by
Sage Publications. Reprinted by Permission of Sage
Publications, Inc.

4 Box 1.2 Questions # 5 and #6, from the Statistics
Canada publication "2001 Canadian Census
Questionnaire." Statistics Canada information is used
with the permission of the Minister of Industry, as
Minister responsible for Statistics Canada. Information
on the availability of the wide range of data from
Statistics Canada can be obtained from Statistics Canada's
Regional Offices, its World Wide Web site at
http://www.statcan.ca, and its toll-free access number
1/800/263-1136.

7 Figure 1.1 "Changing Family Structures," from the
Statistics Canada publication "Canada Year Book 1999,"
Cat. No. 11-204, p. 188.

12 Figure 1.2 "Aboriginal and Visible Minority Children (0-
14 years) More Likely to be Poor," from Statistics Canada,
custom tabulations.

13 Excerpt Reprinted with permission of Martha Bailey.

14–15 Excerpt "2001 Race Report" by Kuntz, Milan, and
Schetagne in *Perspectives,* June 20, 2001. Reprinted with
permission of the Canadian Race Relations Foundation.

15 Figure 1.3 "Employment Rates by Racial Groups, People
Aged 25-64, 1996" by Kuntz, Milan, and Schetagne in
Perspectives, June 20, 2001. Reprinted with permission of
the Canadian Race Relations Foundation.

17 Box 1.4 Excerpts from *Canada's Teens: Today, Yesterday
and Tomorrow* copyright © 2001 Reginald W. Bibby.
Excerpts from *The Bibby Report: Social Trends Canadian
Style* copyright © Reginald W. Bibby. Reprinted by
permission of Stoddart Publishing, Toronto.

19 Excerpt From *Campaign 2000 Publication: Child Poverty in
Canada Report Card 2000.*

20 Figure 1.4 "Percentage Distribution of Total Income of
Families and Unattached Individuals by Quintiles, Canada,
1951–1996," from the Statistics Canada publication
"Income Distribution by Size in Canada," Cat. No. 13-
207, 1996.

20 Figure 1.5 From *Campaign 2000 Publication: Child
Poverty in Canada Report Card 2000.*

25 Figure 1.6 Figure adapted from *Shifting Gears,* by Nena
O'Neill, p. 167, 1974. Copyright © 1974 by Nena
O'Neill and George O'Neill. Reprinted by permission of
the publisher, M. Evans and Company, New York, NY.

Chapter 2

35 Figure 2.1 Adapted from "Human Ecology Theory" by Margaret M. Bubolz and M. Suzanne Sontag, 1993, p. 432. In Pauline G. Boss, William J. Doherty, Ralph La Rossa, Walter R. Schumm & Suzanne K. Seinmetz (eds.), *Sourcebook of Family Theories and Methods: A Contextual Approach.* Copyright © 1993 Plenum Publishers, Inc. Adapted by permission of both the publisher and the authors.

37–38 Case Study 2.1 Reprinted by permission from *Maclean's*, June 25, 2001.

42 Figure 2.2 "Family Structure 1996," from the Statistics Canada publication "Canadian Families: Diversity and Change," Cat. No. 12F0061, June 1996.

Chapter 3

64–65 Table 3.1 "Average Earnings of Full-Year, Full-Time Workers in the 25 Highest Paying and 25 Low Paying Occupations, by Sex, Canada, 1995," from the Statistics Canada Web Site http://www.statcan.ca/Daily/English/980512/d980512.htm.

78 Excerpt Excerpt from *Hard Choices: How Women Decide about Work, Career, and Motherhood*, by Kathleen Gerson, 1985, pp. 18–19. University of California Press Copyright © 1985. The Regents of the University of California. Reprinted by permission.

81 Excerpt Excerpt from "The Costs of Being on Top," by Mark E. Kann, *Journal of National Association for Women Deans, Administrators and Counselors*, 14 (summer). Copyright © 1986 by the National Association for Women Deans, Administrators and Counselors. Reprinted with permission.

82 Box 3.1 Madeleine Dion Stout, a Cree woman, builds the critique on Aboriginal feminism. Reprinted with permission.

Chapter 4

94 Figure 4.1 Adapted from *The Psychology of Love* by Sternberg and Barnes (eds.). Copyright © 1988. Reprinted by permission of Yale University Press.

99 Box 4.1 "Self-esteem Checklist," from *Encounters with the Self*, 1st edition by Hamachek. Reprinted with permission.

100 Box 4.2 "Learning to Love Yourself More," from *Encounters with the Self*, 1st edition by Hamachek. Reprinted with permission.

102 Figure 4.2 "Reiss Theory of the Development of Love," from *The Family System in America*, 1st edition by Reiss, 1988, p. 103. Reprinted with permission.

Chapter 5

119–120 Box 5.1 Reprinted with permission from "Lesbian Sex," [pp. 109-119] in *Willful Virgin: Essays in Feminism* by Marilyn Frye, © 1992. Published by the Crossing Press. Reprinted with permission.

120 Excerpt Excerpt from *School Girls: Young Women, Self-esteem Generation gap*, 1994, p. 61. Copyright © 1994 by Peggy Orenstein. Reprinted by permission of Doubleday, a division of Bantam Doubleday Dell.

124 Figure 5.1 From "Reconceptualizing Marital Status as a Continuum of Social Attachment" by C. E. Ross, 1995. *Journal of Marriage and the Family 57(1)*, pp. 129-140, Figure 2. Copyrighted © 1995 by the National Council on Family Relations, 3989 Central Ave. NE, Suite 550, Minneapolis, MN 55421. Reprinted by permission.

127 Figure 5.2 Excerpts from *Canada's Teens: Today, Yesterday and Tomorrow* copyright © 2001 Reginald W. Bibby. Excerpts from *The Bibby Report: Social Trends Canadian Style* copyright © Reginald W. Bibby. Reprinted by permission of Stoddart Publishing, Toronto.

131 Figure 5.3 Reprinted with permission of Health Canada and the Minister of Public Works of Canada, 2002.

133 Table 5.1 William A. Fisher, Richard Boroditsky and Martha Bridges, 1999. "Condom Use Among Canadian Women: Practices and Opinions." *The Canadian Journal of Human Sexuality 8(3)*, Fall, p. 190. Reprinted by permission of SIECCAN.

133 Figure 5.4 William A. Fisher, Richard Boroditsky and Martha Bridges, 1999. "Condom Use Among Canadian Women: Practices and Opinions." *The Canadian Journal of Human Sexuality 8(3)*, Fall, p. 91. Reprinted by permission of SIECCAN.

Chapter 6

144 Figure 6.1 based on data from the Statistics Canada Census of Population 1901.

145 Figure 6.2 based on data from the Statistics Canada publications "Population by five-year age groups", Catalogue 93F0022, October 1997, and 1992, and "Population 15 years and over living in common-law unions by five-year age groups", Catalogue 95F0188, January 1998.

145 Excerpt Reprinted by permission of the Vanier Institute of the Family.

146 Table 6.1 based on data from the Statistics Canada publications "Population by five-year age groups", Catalogue 93F0022, October 1997, and 1992, and "Population 15 years and over living in common-law unions by five-year age groups", Catalogue 95F0188, January 1998.

147 Table 6.2 adapted from the Statistics Canada publication "Incidence of low income," Cat. 93F0029, The Nation Series 1996 Census, May 1998.

148 Figure 6.3 "Average Age at First Marriage," from the Statistics Canada publications "Marriage and Conjugal Life in Canada," Cat. No. 91-534, 1992, and "The Daily," Cat. 11-001, Oct. 28, 1999 and Jan. 29, 1998.

151 Box 6.1: Excerpt from a student. Reprinted by permission of Judith Harazin.

154–156 Box 6.2 Harlan Hahn, "The Social Component of Sexuality and Disability: Some Problems and Proposals,"

Sexuality and Disability, vol.4, no. 4, Fall, 1981. Reprinted by permission of Plenum Publishers.

157 Table 6.3 Excerpt from Peter J. Stein (ed.) *Single Life: Unmarried Adults in Social Context*, 1981, p. 11. Copyright © 1981 by St. Martin's Press. Reprinted with permission of the publisher.

158 Table 6.4 "Incidence of Low Income for Selected Types of Families, 1997," adapted from the Statistics Canada publication "Incidence of low income," Cat. 93F0029, The Nation Series 1996 Census, May 1998.

160 Table 6.5 "The Proportion of Young Adults Living at Home Has Been Rising Over the Past 15 Years," from the Statistics Canada publication "Canadian Social Trends," Cat. No. 11-008, September 1995, No. 38.

162 Figure 6.4 From *Cohabitation: An Alternative Form of Family Living* by Zheng Wu. Copyright © Oxford University Press Canada 2000. Reprinted by permission of Oxford University Press Canada.

163 Table 6.6 From *Cohabitation: An Alternative Form of Family Living* by Zheng Wu. Copyright © Oxford University Press Canada 2000. Reprinted by permission of Oxford University Press Canada.

163–164 Excerpt Reprinted by permission of the Vanier Institute of the Family.

165–166 Box 6.3 From *Everyone's Guide to the Law* Published by HarperCollins *Publishers Ltd.* Copyright 1997, 2001 by Linda Silver Dranoff.

168 Figure 6.5 "Living Alone," from the Statistics Canada publication "Canada Year Book 1999," Cat. No. 11-204, p. 183.

173 Case Study 6.1 "Gay Pride, Asian Proud," by David Tsang in *Banana: Asian-Canadian Lifestyle and Culture Magazine*, Summer 2001, vol. 1(1): pp. 24-25. Reprinted with permission.

Chapter 7

178 Excerpt From "Separated" by Len Gasparini. Reprinted by permission of the author.

180–181 Box 7.1 "Arranged Marriages: a True Family Affair" by Leena Kamat in *The Gazette*, November 7, 2000. Reprinted with permission by *The Gazette* at the University of Western Ontario.

182 Figure 7.1 Robert Levine, Suguru Sato, Tsukasa Hashimoto, and Jyoti Verma. *Journal of Cross-Cultural Psychology 26(5)*: pp. 554-71. Copyright © 1995 by Sage Publications. Reprinted by Permission of Sage Publications, Inc.

191–192 Box 7.2 "Proportion of All Women Experiencing," excerpt from the Statistics Canada publication "Canadian Social Trends," Cat. No. 11-008, March 2000, No. 56.

193 Table 7.1 "Proportion of All Women Experiencing," from the Statistics Canada publication "Canadian Social Trends," Cat. No. 11-008, March 2000, No. 56.

193 Figure 7.2 From *Cohabitation: An Alternative Form of Family Living* by Zheng Wu. Copyright © Oxford University Press Canada 2000. Reprinted by permission of Oxford University Press Canada.

194 Figure 7.3 based on data from the Statistics Canada publications "Population by five-year age groups….", Catalogue 93F0022, October 1997, and 1992, and "Population 15 years and over living in common-law unions by five-year age groups….", Catalogue 95F0188, January 1998.

194 Figure 7.4 based on data from the Statistics Canada publications "Population by five-year age groups….", Catalogue 93F0022, October 1997, and 1992, and "Population 15 years and over living in common-law unions by five-year age groups….", Catalogue 95F0188, January 1998.

195 Figure 7.5 based on data from the Statistics Canada publication "Population 15 years and over living in common-law unions by five-year age groups….", Catalogue 95F0188, January 1998.

195 Excerpt From *Cohabitation: An Alternative Form of Family Living* by Zheng Wu. Copyright © Oxford University Press Canada 2000. Reprinted by permission of Oxford University Press Canada.

196 Table 7.2 From *Cohabitation: An Alternative Form of Family Living* by Zheng Wu. Copyright © Oxford University Press Canada 2000. Reprinted by permission of Oxford University Press Canada.

198–199 Table 7.3 From "Cohabitation: Does it Make for a Better Marriage?" by Carl A. Riley, Dan J. Peterman and Arthur W. Avery, 1978. *Family Coordinator 27,* pp. 129-136. Copyrighted © 1978 by the National Council on Family Relations, 3989 Central Ave. NE, Suite 550, Minneapolis, MN 55421. Reprinted by permission.

202 Box 7.3 Reprinted with permission of Simon & Schuster, Inc. from TOTAL LOVING by "J" by Joan Garrity. Copyright © 1977 by Joan Garrity.

206 Table 7.4 Adapted from Wayne W. McVey and Warren E. Kalbach, *Canadian Population.* Toronto: Nelson, 1995.

208–209 Box 7.4 From "Formal Intermediaries in the Marriage Market: A Typology and Review" by Aaron C. Ahuvia and Mara B. Adelman, 1992. *Journal of Marriage and the Family 54 (May)*, pp. 452-463. Copyrighted © 1992 by the National Council on Family Relations, 3989 Central Ave. NE, Suite 550, Minneapolis, MN 55421. Reprinted by permission.

212 Table 7.6 Excerpts from *Canada's Teens: Today, Yesterday and Tomorrow* copyright © 2001 Reginald W. Bibby. Excerpts from *The Bibby Report: Social Trends Canadian Style* copyright © Reginald W. Bibby. Reprinted by permission of Stoddart Publishing, Toronto.

213 Table 7.7 "Racially Homogeneous and Racially Heterogeneous Couples," based on data from the Statistics Canada 1996 Census of Population, the Nation Series.

Chapter 8

223 Excerpt   From "Introduction to Family Studies: Cultural Variations and Family Trends" by Maureen Baker in *Families: Changing Trends in Canada*, 3rd edition. Copyright © 1996. Reprinted with permission of McGraw-Hill Ryerson.

225 Figure 8.1   From "Towards a Systems Theory of Marital Quality" by Stephen R. Marks, 1989. *Journal of Marriage and the Family 51*, pp. 15-26. Copyrighted © 1989 by the National Council on Family Relations, 3989 Central Ave. NE, Suite 550, Minneapolis, MN 55421. Reprinted by permission.

226 Figure 8.2   From "Towards a Systems Theory of Marital Quality" by Stephen R. Marks, 1989. *Journal of Marriage and the Family 51*, pp. 15-26. Copyrighted © 1989 by the National Council on Family Relations, 3989 Central Ave. NE, Suite 550, Minneapolis, MN 55421. Reprinted by permission.

230 Table 8.1   Excerpts from *Canada's Teens: Today, Yesterday and Tomorrow* copyright © 2001 Reginald W. Bibby. Excerpts from *The Bibby Report: Social Trends Canadian Style* copyright © Reginald W. Bibby. Reprinted by permission of Stoddart Publishing, Toronto.

231, 237, 239 Excerpts   Reprinted with permission of Martha Bailey.

245 Table 8.2   J. M. Twenge, "Mrs. His Name, Women's Preferences" in *Psychology of Women Quarterly 21*, 1997, pp. 417-430. Reprinted with permission by Blackwell Publishing Inc.

Chapter 9

266 Excerpt   Reprinted with the permission of Simon & Schuster from COUPLES by Carlfred B. Broderick. Copyright © 1979 by Dr. Carlfred B. Broderick.

275 Table 9.1   "Religious People Tend to Place Greater Importance on Marriage, Family, and Children," from the Statistics Canada publication "Canadian Social Trends," Cat. No. 11-008, September 1998, No. 50.

Chapter 10

289 Box 10.1   Reprinted with the permission of Simon & Schuster from COUPLES by Carlfred B. Broderick. Copyright © 1979 by Dr. Carlfred B. Broderick.

295 Figure 10.2   "Homicides by Type of Relationship, Canada, 1979-1998," from the Statistics Canada publication "Family Violence in Canada: A Statistical Profile," Cat. No. 85-224, July 2000, p. 39.

295 Figure 10.3   "Spousal Homicides in Canada, 1979-1998," from the Statistics Canada publication "Family Violence in Canada: A Statistical Profile," Cat. No. 85-224, July 2000, p. 40.

297 Table 10.1   "Solved Homicides of Victims Under Age 18 by Accused-Victim Relationship, 1998," from the Statistics

Canada publication "Family Violence in Canada: A Statistical Profile," Cat. No. 85-224, July 2000, p. 43.

298 Figure 10.4   "Women More Likely Than Men to Experience Spousal Violence in Most Provinces, Past 5 Years," from the Statistics Canada publication "Family Violence in Canada: A Statistical Profile," Cat. No. 85-224, July 2000, p. 12.

299 Figure 10.5   "Slight Decline in the Most Serious Violence Against Wives," from the Statistics Canada publication "Family Violence in Canada: A Statistical Profile," Cat. No. 85-224, July 2000, p. 21.

300 Figure 10.6   "Change in Severity of Assaults on Wives," from the Statistics Canada publication "Family Violence in Canada: A Statistical Profile," Cat. No. 85-224, July 2000, p. 11.

304 Figure 10.8   "A Conceptual Approach to Understanding Abused Women's Stay/Leave Decisions," by Pamela Choice and Leanne K. Lamke, 1997. *Journal of Family Issues* 18(3):290–314.

305 Box 10.2   From *Family Violence Against Women with Disabilities*, Health Canada, *1993*. © Minister of Public Works and Government Services Canada, 2001.

307 Figure 10.9   "Motivations for Involving the Police Somewhat Different for Women and Men, Past 5 Years," from the Statistics Canada publication "Family Violence in Canada: A Statistical Profile," Cat. No. 85-224, July 2000, p. 11.

311 Figure 10.10   "Parents Most Frequently Accused in Assaults Against Children and Youth Committed by Family Members, 1999," from the Statistics Canada publication "Family Violence in Canada: A Statistical Profile," Cat. No. 85-224, July 2000, p. 33.

311 Figure 10.11   "Victims of Family-Related Sexual Assaults by Age and Sex of Victims, 1999," from the Statistics Canada publication "Family Violence in Canada: A Statistical Profile," Cat. No. 85-224, July 2000, p. 34.

314 Figure 10.12   "Older Adults Most Frequently Victimized by Adult Children and Spouses, 1999," from the Statistics Canada publication "Family Violence in Canada: A Statistical Profile," Cat. No. 85-224, July 2000, p. 30.

315 Figure 10.13   "Common Assault Most Frequent Offence by Family Members Against Older Adults, 1999," from the Statistics Canada publication "Family Violence in Canada: A Statistical Profile," Cat. No. 85-224, July 2000, p. 30.

Chapter 11

321 Excerpt   Reprinted by permission of the Vanier Institute of the Family.

322 Figure 11.1   based on data from the Statistics Canada publications "Canadian families at the approach of the year 2000", Catalogue 96-321, March 1999 Marriage and conjugal life in Canada", Catalogue 91-534, 1992, and "The Daily", Catalogue 11-001, October 28, 1999 and January 29, 1998.

324 Figure 11.2 "Average Number of Persons Per Family, 1971-1997," from the Statistics Canada publication "Annual Demographics Statistics," Cat. No. 91-213, February 1998.

326–327 Excerpt Canadian Coalition for the Rights of Children, "How Does Canada Measure Up?" CCRC, 1999.

327 Figure 11.3 based on data from the Statistics Canada publications "Canadian families at the approach of the year 2000", Catalogue 96-321, March 1999 Marriage and conjugal life in Canada", Catalogue 91-534, 1992, and "The Daily", Catalogue 11-001, October 28, 1999 and January 29, 1998.

330 Figure 11.4 based on data from the Statistics Canada "Survey of Family Expenditures, public use microdata files", Catalogue 62M0001, May 1998.

334 Figure 11.5 based on data from the Statistics Canada publication "Births and Deaths", catalogue 84-210, various years.

338–340 Box 11.2 "History of Birth Control in Canada," by Childbirth by Choice Trust, http://www.cbctrust.com. Reprinted with permission.

341 Figure 11.6 based on data from the Statistics Canada publication "Births and Deaths", Catalogue 84-210, various years.

342 Figure 11.7 "Teenage Pregnancies, Births, and Abortions, 1975-1995," from the Statistics Canada publications "Heath Indicators," Cat. No. 82-221, July 1999 and "Births and Deaths," Cat. 84-210, May 1997.

344 Figure 11.8 "Therapeutic Abortions, Canadian Residents, 1970–95 ," from the Statistics Canada publication "Therapeutic Abortions," Cat. No. 82-219, Nov. 1997.

355–356 Excerpt From "Adopting the Cider Child: A Personal Reflection" by Steven Hotovy in *America*, May 15, 1991. Reprinted with permission of American Press, Inc. All rights reserved. www.americamagazine.org

357–358 Box 11.4 Reprinted with permission from *The Globe and Mail*.

Chapter 12

370 Figure 12.1 "Number of Poor Children" in *Poverty Profile 1996*, Spring 1998, National Council of Welfare. Reprinted with permission of the Minister of Public Works and Government Services Canada, 2002.

371 Figure 12.2 "Percentage of Aboriginal Population, Visible Minority and Total Populations with Low Incomes, by Age Group, Canada, 1995," from the Statistics Canada publication "The Daily," Cat. No. 11-001, May 12, 1998.

372 Figure 12.3 Reproduced with permission of the Canadian Council on Social Development.

380–381 Case Study 12.2 Reprinted with permission of the Vanier Institute of the Family.

387 Table 12.1 Excerpts from *Canada's Teens: Today, Yesterday and Tomorrow* copyright © 2001 Reginald W. Bibby. Excerpts from *The Bibby Report: Social Trends Canadian Style* copyright © Reginald W. Bibby. Reprinted by permission of Stoddart Publishing, Toronto.

388 Table 12.2 Excerpts from *Canada's Teens: Today, Yesterday and Tomorrow* copyright © 2001 Reginald W. Bibby. Excerpts from *The Bibby Report: Social Trends Canadian Style* copyright © Reginald W. Bibby. Reprinted by permission of Stoddart Publishing, Toronto.

392–393 Box 12.1 Reprinted with permission of the author.

Chapter 13

406 Table 13.1 "Many Families Today are Just Exhausted, Living with Very Frenetic Schedules," from the Statistics Canada Web Site: http://www.statcan.ca/english/ads/11-008-XIE/family.html.

407 Figure 13.1 "The Family Structure has Changed Considerably Over the Past 2 Decades," from the Statistics Canada publication "Perspectives on Labour and Income," Cat. No. 75-001, Winter 2000, p. 15.

407–408 Excerpt "Balancing Work and Family," from the Statistics Canada publication "Perspectives on Labour and Income," Cat. No. 75-001, March 1994.

408 Table 13.2 "Average Work Hours Per Week," from the Statistics Canada publication "Perspectives on Labour and Income," Cat. No. 75-001, Vol. 12, No. 04, Dec. 2000.

409 Figure 13.2 "More Fathers are Opting to Stay Home with Their Children," from the Statistics Canada publication "Perspectives on Labour and Income," Cat. No. 75-001, Vol. 10, No. 01, March 1998.

409 Figure 13.3 "Stay-at-home Mothers Do Most of the Work," from the Statistics Canada publication "Perspectives on Labour and Income," Cat. No. 75-001, Vol. 10, No. 01, March 1998.

413 Table 13.3 "Percentage of the Population 15 Years of Age and Over in the Labour Force by Marital Status and Sex, Canada," from the Statistics Canada publication "Historical – Labour Force for Canada and Provinces, 1911-1971 (3, 1-2)," Cat. No. 94-702.

414 Figure 13.4 "Ten Most Frequent Jobs for Women in Canada, 1996" from the Statistics Canada publication "The Daily," Cat. No. 11-001, March 17, 1998.

414 Figure 13.5 "Women's Average Earnings Still Lag Men's," from the Statistics Canada publication "Perspectives on Labour and Income," Cat. No. 75-001, Vol 12, No. 04, Dec. 2000.

421 Figure 13.6 "Women Report More Hours of Housework than Men, 1996," from the Statistics Canada Web Site: <http://www.statcan.ca/Daily/English/980317/d980317.htm>

424 Figure 13.7 "High Work Stress by Household Type (age-standardized), Employed Persons Age 15+, Canada, 1994-

1995," from the Statistics Canada Web Site: <http://www.statcan.ca/english/freepub/82-570-XIE/free.htm>

428 Box 13.1 From "Bringing Up Baby: A Doctor's Prescription for Busy Parents," by T. Berry Brazelton, M.D., in *Newsweek*, February 13, 1989, pp. 68-69. Reprinted with permission of T. Berry Brazelton.

440 Table 13.4 "Government Sponsored Maternity, Paternity, and Parental Paid Leave Programs for Selected Jurisdictions," from the Statistics Canada publication "Canadian Social Trends," Cat. No. 11-008, summer 1998.

Chapter 14

448, 450 Excerpts Reprinted with permission of the Vanier Institute of the Family.

449 Table 14.1 Reprinted with permission of the Vanier Institute of the Family.

451 Figure 14.1 "Number of Divorces in Canada, 1986 to 1998," from the Statistics Canada Web Site: http://www.statcan.ca/Daily/English/001218/d001218.htm.

456 Table 14.2 "What Justifies Divorce?" from the Statistics Canada publication "Canadian Social Trends," Cat. No. 11-008, Spring 1998, No. 48.

462 Excerpt Excerpts from *Ex Familia: Grandparents and Children Adjust to Divorce*, by Colleen Leahy Johnson, 1988, pp. 190-191. Copyright © 1988 by Rutgers, The State University. Used by permission of Rutgers University Press.

464 Box 14.1 Abridged from *How to Survive the Loss of Love: 58 Things to Do When There is Nothing to be Done*, by Melba Colgrove, Harold Bloomfield & Peter McWilliams, 1978. Copyright © 1978. Used by permission of Bantam Books.

465 Figure 14.2 "Poverty Rates by Family Types" in *Poverty Profile 1996*, Spring 1998, National Council of Welfare. Reprinted with permission of the Minister of Public Works and Government Services Canada, 2002.

475 Figure 14.3 "Custody Awards of Children (involved in divorce cases settled by the courts, 1978-1995)," from the Statistics Canada publication "Divorces," Cat. No. 84-213, January 1997.

478 Figure 14.4 From *Preschool Children: Promises to Keep* (Spring 1999), Figure 14.9. Reproduced by permission of the Minister of Public Works and Government Services Canada, 2001.

479 Table 14.3 Adapted from *The Developing Father: Emerging Roles in Contemporary Society*, by B. E. Robinson and R. L. Barret, 1986, p. 89. Copyright © 1986 Guilford Publications. Adapted by permission.

Chapter 15

489 Figure 15.1 From *Cohabitation: An Alternative Form of Family Living* by Zheng Wu. Copyright © Oxford University Press Canada 2000. Reprinted by permission of Oxford University Press Canada.

491 Figure 15.2 "Couples with Children, 1995," from the Statistics Canada publication "The Daily," Cat. No. 11-001, June 19, 1996.

491 Figure 15.3 "Stepfamilies by Type, 1995," from the Statistics Canada publication "The Daily," Cat. No. 11-001, June 19, 1996.

494 Table 15.1 "Legal Marital Status by Selected Five-Year Age Groups in Percentage, Canada," from the Statistics Canada publication "1991 Census of Canada," Cat. No. 92-915, 1984, 1993, 1997.

498–499 Excerpt Copyright © 1997 from Therapy with Stepfamilies by E.B. Visher and J.S. Visher. Reproduced by permission of Taylor & Francis Inc., http://www.routledge.ny.com.

499 Table 15.2 Adapted by *Stepfamilies: A Guide to Working with Stepparents and Stepchildren*, by Emily B. Visher and John S. Visher, 1979. Copyright © 1979 by Brunner/Mazel. Used by permission.

501 Excerpt From *Everyone's Guide to the Law* Published by HarperCollins *Publishers Ltd.* Copyright 1997, 2001 by Linda Silver Dranoff.

Chapter 16

523 Figure 16.2 "Despite Improvements, Proportionately Fewer Women Receive Pension Benefits," from the Statistics Canada publication "Perspectives on Labour and Income," Cat. No. 75-001, Vol. 12, No. 04, Dec. 2000.

525 Figure 16.3 Adapted from "Families Under Stress" by Donald A. Hansen and Reuben Hill, p. 810. In Harold Christensen (ed.) *The Handbook of Marriage and the Family*. Copyright © 1964 by Rand McNally & Company. Reprinted by permission.

528–529 Box 16.2 Abridgement of "Alcoholism and the Family" by Joan J. Jackson, pp. 90-98, 1958, *Annals of the American Academy of Political and Social Science, 315.* Copyright © 1958 by the American Academy of Political and Social Science. Reprinted with permission.

530–531 Box 16.3 Excerpts from "The Impact of Homelessness and Shelter Life on Family Relationships," by E.W. Lindsey, 1998, *Family Relations, 47 (3)*, 243–252. Copyright © 1998 National Council on Family Relations.

533 Figure 16.5 Adapted from "Family Stress Theory and Assessment" by H.I. McCubbin and M.A. McCubbin, figure 1.5, p. 16, 1991. In H.I. McCubbin and Annie I. Thompson, *Family Assessment Inventories for Research and Practice*, University of Wisconsin-Madison. Adapted by permission.

534–535 Box 16.3 Excerpts from "The Impact of Homelessness and Shelter Life on Family Relationships," by E.W. Lindsey, 1998, *Family Relations, 47 (3)*, 243–252. Copyright © 1998 National Council on Family Relations.

Name Index

Note: Page numbers followed by letters refer to the following: *b* = box, *c* = case study, *f* = figure, *n* = footnote, and *t* = table.

Chen, Kathy, 63
Chen, Ling, 374
Cherlin, Andrew J., 148, 150, 152, 162, 180, 396, 397, 473, 477, 478, 502, 507
Chesley, L.D., 306
Chess, Stella, 385
Childless by Choice Trust, 340*b*
Children's Defense Fund, 326
Chilly Collective, 80
Chilman, Catherine Street, 28, 223
Chira, Susan, 365, 425, 436
Chiriboga, David A., 459
Chisholm, Patricia, 477
Chiswick, Carmel U., 210
Chodorow, Nancy, 73
Choi, Namkee G., 465, 480
Choice, Pamela, 303, 304*f*
Chojnack, Joseph T., 94
Chow, E.N., 59
Chowdhury, Quamrul Ahsan, 309
Christensen, A., 262, 269
Christensen, Kathleen E., 437, 439
Christensen, Kimberly, 80
Cianni, M., 413
Cicerelli, Victor G., 395
Clark, Jennifer, 473
Clark, L., 300
Clark, Warren, 455
Clark, Wayne, 274*b*
Clarke, Sally, 458, 495, 496
Clatworthy, Nancy M., 225
Claxton-Oldfield, Stephen, 509
Clemetson, Lynette, 346
Climo, Jacob, 395
Clinton, Hillary Rodham, 439
Cobb, Chris, 123*n*, 124, 126
Cobb, Jonathan, 185
Cobb, Nathan, 159
Cohen, Laurie L., 66
Coiro, M.J., 497
Cole, Thomas, 125
Colella, Ugo, 196, 197
Coleman, Marilyn, 203, 461, 489, 494, 495, 497, 499–500, 504, 505, 506, 507, 508, 510, 510*n*
Coleman, Marion Tolbert, 282, 283, 284, 285, 287, 290, 302
Coleman, Valerie, 306
Colgrove, Melba, 464*b*
Collins, Patricia Hill, 328
Collins, Randall, 152, 282
Collins, W.A., 386

Coltrane, Scott, 283, 331, 406, 408, 423, 442, 483
Comfort, Alex, 139
Commission on Lesbian and Gay Concerns of the American Psychological Association, 109
"Communal Living ...", 161
Conger, Rand D., 398, 457
Connell, Joan, 377
Connelly, Marjorie, 117
Conrad, Linda, 491
Conte, Jon R., 304, 309, 310
Converse, Philip, 169
Conway, John F., 16, 475
Cook, Philip, 375
Cooley, Charles Horton, 3, 42, 254
Cooney, Rosemary, 284
Cooney, Teresa M., 146, 394, 476, 481
Coontz, Stephanie, 16, 452, 454, 467, 470, 474, 483, 484, 538
Cooper, Helene, 350
Coopersmith, Stanley, 98
Copeland, Peter, 109, 110
Copenhaver, Stacey, 77
Corak, Miles, 369, 472
Cose, Ellis, 304, 365
Coston, Charisse, 425
Cottrell, Ann Baker, 182
Council on Families in America, 483
Counts, Robert M., 459
Coutu, Sylvain, 385
"Covenant Marriages Ministry," 231
"Covenant Marriages Tie a Firm Knot," 231
Coverdill, James E., 344
Coverman, Shelly, 423
Cowan, C.P., 331, 384, 453
Cowan, P.A., 331, 384, 453
Cowan, Ruth Schwartz, 420
Cowley, Geoffrey, 125, 131, 183, 349, 351, 371
Coysh, William S., 479
Craig, Pat, 235
Craig, Stephen, 72
Cranswick, Kelly, 395, 396, 436
Cravens, Hamilton, 97*n*
Crawford, M., 71
Crawford, Trish, 8*b*, 341
Crimmins, Eileen M., 323
Critchlow, Donald T., 336
Critelli, Joseph W., 90
Crnic, Keith, 367
Crohan, Susan E., 257

Crompton, Susan, 406, 415
Crook, Joanne F., 353
Crosbie-Burnett, Margaret, 505, 507
Crosby, Faye J., 89, 444
Crosby, John, 97, 99, 100, 224*n*, 247, 249, 256, 257, 258, 265
Crouter, Ann C., 405, 406, 408, 422, 426, 443, 444
Crowder, Kyle, 343
Crowley, Kathleen, 406, 408
Cruchfield, Robert D., 390
Cubbins, Lisa A., 120
Cuber, John, 128, 129, 223, 225, 226, 227, 228, 246
Cue, Kelly L., 188
Cummings, E. Mark, 517
Cunningham-Burley, Sarah, 396
Currie, Dawn H., 346
Curtis, Carla M., 434
Curtis, James E., 212
Cushman, Linda, 384
Custer, Lindsay, 441

D
Dabbs, James, 71
Dahms, Alan M., 89, 101
The Daily, 414*f*
Daisley, B., 345*n*
Dalphonse, Sherri, 332
Daly, Kerry, 343, 352, 365, 439
Daly, M., 312, 497
Daly, Martin, 296
Dandurand, Renee B., 480
Danesco, Evangeline R., 369
Dangoor, Nira, 527
Daniels, Pamela, 334
Daniels, Roger, 208
Danko, William D., 374
D'Antonio, William V., 21
Da Pont, Moreno, 418
"The Dark Side ...", 235
Darling, Carol A., 112, 118
Darroch, Gordon, 19
Darwin, Charles, 110
Das Gupta, Tanis, 63
Daub, Shannon, 368
Davey, Adam, 395
David, Deborah, 60
Davidson, Andrew, 384
Davidson, Bernard, 91
Davidson, Jeannette R., 213
Davidson-Harden, Jennifer, 134
Davis, Fred, 52, 155*b*

Subject Index

Note: Page numbers followed by letters refer to the following: *b* = box, *c* = case study, *f* = figure, *n* = footnote, and *t* = table.

defined, 91
empathy, 443–444
vs. imaging, 185
making time for, 129–131
mutual appreciation, 444
and persons with disabilities,
    154*b*–156*b*
psychic, 91
and role changes, 443–444
sexual, 91
triangular theory of love, 91–94,
    94*f*
intimacy reduction affairs, 235
intrinsic marriage, 223, 225
invitro fertilization. *See* reproductive
    technology
involuntary infertility, 348–351
involuntary stable singles, 156
involuntary temporary singles, 156
I-statements, 268

J

jealousy, 236
job sharing, 437
joint custody, 477–479
Joy of Sex (Comfort), 139

K

kin scripts framework, 50*b*
Kinsey reports, 122
kinship
    defined, 222
    and divorce, 461–462
    extended family, 223
    obligations of, 223–224
    and stepfamilies, 499–500
knowledgeable choices, 24–26, 25*f*

L

laboratory observation, 51–52
labour force, 405–406, 412–415
laissez-faire discipline, 390
laissez-faire parenting, 385
language, 378–379
Layland v. Ontario, 237–239
legal divorce, 459–460
legal reforms, 36
legitimate needs, 89
legitimate power, 281, 284
lesbians
    see also same-sex couples; sexual
        orientation
    domestic arrangements, 163–166

vs. gay male behaviours, 116–117
    homophobia and, 113
    parenting and, 379–383
    "sex," 119*b*–120*b*
    sexual identities, 113
leveling, 267
Levesque v. Levesque, 468
levirate arrangements, 179*n*
liberal feminism, 46
life course solution, 438
life cycle crunch, 384*n*
life expectancy, 17*n*
life stress perspective, 473
"Linus blanket" relationship, 190
listener backchannels, 267
listening, 266–267
loneliness
    vs. aloneness, 169–171
    as reason for marriage, 218
lone-parent families
    average monthly expenditures,
        330*f*
    employment of mothers, 410
    homelessness, 530*b*–531*b*
    number of children in, 11
    poverty, 463–465
    prevalence, 451
    statistics, 9
    work and family issues, 426
longitudinal studies, 53
long-term affairs, 234
looking-glass self, 254
loose connection, 224
love
    acceptance, 89–90, 101
    battered wives, 301–302
    caring, 89–90
    and conflict, 256–258
    consummate, 94
    courtly (romantic), 182
    definitions of, 88–90
    as discovery, 101–102
    as emotion, 88
    and emotional interdependence,
        99–101
    illegitimate needs, 89
    and intimacy, 91–94
    legitimate needs, 89
    maintaining, 103–104
    vs. manipulation, 97
    vs. martyring, 96–97
    rediscovering after 25 years,
        92*c*–93*c*

relative love and need theory, 285
self-esteem as prerequisite, 97–99
styles, 94–95
triangular theory, 91–94
wheel of love, 102–103, 102*f*
"love" marriages, 180, 182–183
lower middle-class parents, 373–374
low income. *See* poverty and low
    income
low-income cutoff, 369
ludus, 95

M

M. v. H., 115
main/secondary provider couple,
    406–407
maintenance, 466–468
male dominance
    defined, 61
    economic, 63–64
    political, 62
    religion, 62–63
mania, 95–96
manipulating, 97
marital conflict. *See* conflict
marital rape, 300
marital satisfaction
    children and, 331
    cohabitation and, 196–197
    common marital complaints,
        455–457
    communication and, 258–260
    early marriages, 242
    premarital pregnancy and, 217
    remarriages, 494–495
    rules for, 259*b*
    unpaid family work, sharing of,
        443
marital sex
    boredom, 126, 130
    fewer good weeks, 123
    frequency, 123–124, 126
    habituation, 126
    middle-aged spouses, 124–125
    older spouses, 125–126
    sex surveys, 122–123
    young spouses, 124
marital stability
    adult children of divorced parents,
        482–483
    early marriages, 215–216
    heterogamy and, 214–215
    late marriages, 215–216

maturity, 216
remarriages, 495–496
marital status
    by age, 147*t*, 194*f*
    continuum of social attachment, 171
    divorced, 145
    figures, 144*f*, 145*f*
    by province, 146*t*
    widowed, 145
marriage
    agreements, 247–251, 511
    alternatives to, 458
    arranged, 179–182
    changing attitudes towards, 149–153
    changing nature of, 453–454
    closed, 246–247
    common-law. *See* common-law relationships
    commuter, 429
    conflict-habituated, 225–226, 228*b*–229*b*
    covenant, 231
    devitalized, 226–227, 258
    early. *See* early marriages
    first, 148*f*
    first years of, 242–243
    flexible, 246–247
    group, 167*n*
    and health care, 170
    homosexuality and. *See* same-sex couples
    individual, 189
    interclass, 211
    interethnic, 214
    interracial, 211–213
    interreligious, 210–211
    intrinsic, 223, 225
    and kinship, 222–225
    "love," 180, 182–183
    name change, 244*b*–245*b*
    negotiation and renegotiation, 453–454
    opposite-sex friends, 238*b*
    passive-congenial, 227
    percentage of conjugal unions, 194*f*
    postponement of, 7–8, 148
    practical need, 283
    preparation, 241–242
    reasons for marrying, 216–219
    and religion, 274*b*–275*b*

sexually open, 232–233
static, 246–247
swinging, 232
total, 228–229
"trial." *See* common-law relationships
two-career, 415, 427–429
two-earner, 415–419, 441–444
two-stage, 189
utilitarian, 223, 225, 246
vital, 227–228
marriage counsellors, 293–294
Marriage Encounter weekends, 272*c*
marriage gradient, 205–206
marriage maintenance affairs, 234–235
marriage market
    bride price, 201
    exchange theory, 201
    intermediaries, 208*b*–209*b*
    optimistic view, 203
    pessimistic view, 203–204
    sex ratio, 204–205
    traditional exchange, 201–203
marriage premise
    covenant marriage, 231
    defined, 229
    expectation of permanence, 229–231
    primariness, 231–233
marriage relationships
    conflict-habituated marriage, 225–226, 228*b*–229*b*
    devitalized marriage, 226–227
    outside interests, 224–225
    passive-congenial marriage, 227
    total marriage, 228–229
    vital marriage, 227–228
"marriage squeeze," 205
Married Women's Property Act, 5
martyring, 96–97, 266, 390
Marxist feminism, 46
masculinists, 81
masculinities, 60–61
maternity leave, 418
maturity, 216
media, and stereotypes, 72
men
    see also fathers; gender differences
    ambivalence and confusion, 83
    anger, 83
    antifeminists, 81
    breadwinner revolt, 152

child-free choice, 332
divorce experience, 480–481
double standard, 118–121
good provider role, 406–410
househusbands, 408–410
masculinists, 81
profeminists, 81
retirement, 523–524
role conflict, 427
unemployment, and divorce, 457
unpaid family work, 422
withdrawal pattern, 262–263
work and family issues, 426–427
Mendola Report (Mendola), 241
men's movements, 69*n,* 81
M-frame relationships, 100
micropolitics, 286
middle-aged spouses, 124–125
Miglin v. Miglin, 467–468
mixed messages, 268
modern family, 4
Modernization of Benefits and Obligations Act, 4–5
modern sexism, 66
mommy track, 437–438
monogamy, 43
mothers
    see also women
    age of first-time mothers, 8–9
    average age, at first or second born child, 334*f*
    employment, 9
    noncustodial, 475–476
    older single, 337–340
    old *vs.* new images, 364
    part-time employment, 415–416
    responsibilities, 365
    single mothers. *See* lone-parent families
    stay-at-home, 409, 409*f,* 410–412
    stepmother trap, 506–507
    supplemental, 313
    as visiting parent, 476–478
Murdock v. Murdock, 465–466
mutual appreciation, 444
mutual dependency, 103

N

name change, 244*b*–245*b*
nannies, 430*b*–432*b*
narcissism, 98
National Child Survey, 477

National Opinion Research Center study, 122–123
National Survey of Families and Households, 123*n*
naturalistic observation, 52–53
needs
  complementary, 184
  illegitimate, 89
  legitimate, 89
  relative love and need theory, 285
negative affect, 260
neosexism, 66
never-married, 146–149
  see also singlehood; singles
"no-fault" divorce, 460–461
noncustodial grandparent, 397
nonmarital sex
  abstinence, 117–118
  double standard, 118–121
  four standards of, 117–121
  permissiveness with affection, 118
  permissiveness without affection, 118
non-official languages, 11
no-power relationships, 288, 292–293
normative answers, 51
nuclear family, 4
nuclear-family model monopoly, 498, 510

O

obligation, 218
occupational sex segregation, 412–413
older spouses, 125–126
old-fashioned sexism, 66
one-child family, 335–336
open-coupled relationships, 153
open-ended questions, 49
opportunity costs, 329
opposite-sex friends, 238*b*
Organization for Economic Co-operation and Development, 19
Origin of the Species (Darwin), 110
Our Bodies, Ourselves (Boston Women's Health Book Collective), 337

P

paradoxical pregnancy, 343
parallel relationship pattern, 223
parental abduction, 477
parental adjustment perspective, 473

parental loss perspective, 473
parent–child relationships, 394–399
parenting
  adult children, 394–395
  alliance, 367–368
  "astronaut phenomenon," 375
  authoritarian, 385
  authoritative, 385
  bi-racial children, 376–377
  blue-collar, 373
  conflicts with children, 387*t*
  difficulties, 363–364
  discipline, 385, 386
  discrimination, approach to, 377–379
  education for divorcing parents, 479–480
  and ethnicity and race, 374–379
  fragile infants, 384
  gay and lesbian parents, 379–383
  gender of children, 74
  grandparenting, 395–398
  by grandparents, 397–398
  immigrant families, 380*c*–381*c*
  laissez-faire, 385
  lower middle-class, 373–374
  and low income, 369
  minority children, 377–379
  mistakes, and resilient children, 393–394
  older parents, 335
  religious minorities, 377
  shared, 367
  and social class, 368–374
  stages, 383–389
  in stepfamilies. *See* stepparenting styles, 390–391
  time-stress, 9–10
  tips for working parents, 428*b*
  upper-class, 374
  upper middle-class, 374
parenting decision
  child-free option, 331–332
  children's value to parents, 328–329
  costs of having children, 329–331
  marital satisfaction, effect on, 331
  one-child family, 335–336
  postponement of parenthood, 332–335
  social pressures, 325–328
parenting stages
  adolescents, 386–387

babies, 384–385
  preschoolers, 385
  school-age children, 385–386
  transition to parenthood, 383–384
  young adults, 387–389
parenting styles
  athletic coach, 391
  communication with children, 392*b*
  developmental model of child rearing, 390–391
  martyr, 390
  pal, 390
  police officer, 390
  spanking, 393
  teacher-counsellor, 390–391
parent track, 437–438
passion, 93, 94
passive-aggression, 267–268
passive-congenial marriage, 227
patriarchal sexuality, 110
patriarchal terrorism, 300–301
patriarchal violence, 304
patriarchy, 47
period of disorganization, 525–526
permanence, expectation of, 229–231
permissiveness with affection, 118
permissiveness without affection, 118
personality need fulfillment, 103
personal marriage agreements, 247–251
personal power, 280
personal remarriage agreement, 511
persons with disabilities
  adoption of children with disabilities, 355
  children, 326–327
  housework and, 420–421
  low income, 371
  obstacles to intimacy, 154*b*–156*b*
  social conventions, 154*b*–156*b*
  suitability of partners, 156*b*
  violence and women with disabilities, 305*b*
physical attraction, 183, 218
pile-up, 527
pink-collar jobs, 413
pity, 218
play and games, 75
pleasure bond of sex, 126–131
pleasuring, 127
politics
  abortion, 345–346

and male dominance, 62
sex education, 138
sexuality and, 137–138
polyandry, 167, 167*n*
polygamy, 43, 167, 167*n*, 232
pool of eligibles, 206
positive affect, 261
postmodern family, 4
postmodern family condition, 48
postparental period, 521–522
postponement of parenthood, 332–335
postsecondary education, and women, 76–77
poverty and low income
children and, 11–12, 20*f,* 327, 327*f,* 371–373, 463–465
divorce, 463–465
and ethnicity, 370–371
family structure and, 369–370
and parenting, 369
persons with disabilities, 371
rates, 465*f*
visible minorities, 12
power
bases of, 281
coercive, 281
conjugal. *See* conjugal power
in courtship, 187–189
defined, 280
egalitarian, 281–282
expert, 281
informational, 281
legitimate, 281, 284
objective measures, 280
personal, 280
referent, 281
relative love and need theory, 285
reward, 281
social, 280
subjective measure of fairness, 280
power politics
alternatives, 290–293
case study, 291*c*–292*c*
in marriage, 288–290
vs. no-power relationships, 288–292
pragma, 95
predictable crisis, 518*b*
pregnancy
older single mothers, 337–340
outside marriage, 337–344
paradoxical, 343

premarital, 217
prevention. *See* contraception
unmarried women, 341*f*
premarital pregnancy, 217
prenuptial contracts, 249
preschoolers, 385
Presentation of Self in Everyday Life (Goffman), 186*n*
primariness, 231–233
primary group, 3
primary parents, 367
principle of least interest, 285
"private" adoption, 352
profeminists, 81
pronatalist bias, 325
propinquity, 207
psychic divorce, 463
psychic intimacy, 91
"public" adoption, 352

Q

quasi-kin, 500
Quebec
civil law system, 5
cohabitation in, 161, 190
immigration, 23*b*
remarriages, 488

R

race. *See* ethnicity and race
racially homogenous and heterogenous couples, 213*t*
radical feminists, 46–47
rapport, 102, 183
rapport talk, 261
rational investment perspective, 423
reactive affairs, 235
rebellion, 217
rebound, 217
recovery from crises, 526
redivorce, 452
referent power, 281
refined divorce rate, 449–450
refusing-to-accept-influence, 261
registered partnerships, 239–240
rehabilitative alimony, 467
reinforcing cycle, 423
relationship agreements, 248
relationship-driven couples, 184
relative love and need theory, 285
relatives of divorce, 462
religion
HIV/AIDS and, 137–138

importance of marriage, family and children, 275*t*
and male dominance, 62–63
and marriage, 274*b*–275*b*
religious minorities, 377
sexuality and, 137–138
remarriages
see also stepfamilies
age and, 490, 493
children and. *See* stepfamilies
courtship and, 490–491
dependent children, presence of, 492–493
double, 496
facts about, 488–490
family law and, 500–501
gender differences, 489
homogamy, 493
incomplete institution, 500
marital satisfaction, 494–495
marital stability, 495–496
odds of, 492–493
personal remarriage agreement, 511
rate, 488
redivorce, 452
single, 496
statistics, 10
stepgrandparents, 397
stereotypes, 495
traditional exchange in, 491–492
remarried families, 488
see also stepfamilies
report talk, 261
representative sample, 51, 122
reproductive technology
choices, 350–351
commercialization, 349–350
costs, 351
gay couples and, 382*n*
inequality issues, 350
nature and, 350
parenthood status, 350
selective reduction, 349
statistics, 349*n*
surrogacy, 350
research. *See* scientific investigation
resiliency model of family stress, adjustment and adaptation, 529, 533*f*
resilient children, 393–394
resilient families, 529–530
resources
cohabitation, 288

resiliency model of family stress, adjustment and adaptation, 529, 533f
responsibility for others, 517–519
stressor overload, 519–520
stressors, 517–520
sudden changes, 517
time, and parenting, 9–10
transitions, 516, 520–525
unresolved conflict over roles, 517
work, 424f
stressor overload, 519–520
stressors, 517–520
structural antinatalism, 326
structural-functionalist perspective, 39–41
subfecundity, 348
subjective measure of fairness, 280
suburban singles, 158–159
suicides
    Aboriginal peoples, 376
    AIDS-related, 135
supervised visitation, 476
support
    child support, 468–469
    common-law couples, 165b
    and family crises, 536–537
    groups, 533
    networks, and singlehood, 172–174
supportive communication, 260–266
suppression of anger, 258
Survey of Labour and Income Dynamics, 418
Survey of Work Arrangements, 407–408
surveys, 49–51
swinging, 232
symbiotic relationships, 97
systems theory, 45

T

teachers, 75–76
teenage pregnancy
    consequences, 341–342
    educational goals and, 217
    increase in rate, 8
    paradoxical pregnancy, 343
    prevalence, 341
    prevention, 342–343
    reasons for, 343–344
    risk factors, 343–344
teenagers
    marital stability, 215

parents of, 386–387
puberty, 340–341
and safer sex, 132–133
in stepfamilies, 505–506
telecommuting, 417
testing mode of cohabitation, 190
theoretical perspectives
    defined, 34
    exchange theory, 44–45
    family development perspective, 36–38
    family ecology perspective, 34–36, 35f
    family systems theory, 45
    feminist perspectives, 45–48
    human sexuality, 110–113
    interactionist perspective, 42–44
    structural-functionalist perspective, 39–41
theory of complementary needs, 184
three-generation households, 396n
three-phase cycle of violence, 300
time-stressed parents, 9–10
total fertility rate, 321n, 322f
total marriage, 228–229
traditional exchange, 201–203, 203f, 204f, 491–492
traditional family model, 406–412
trailing spouse, 428
transitions, 516
    postparental period, 521–522
    retirement, 522–524
    sandwich generation, 520–521
    the widowed, 524–525
trans-racial adoptions, 353–355
Tremblay v. Daigle, 345–346
triangular theory of love, 91–94, 94f
two-career marriages, 415, 427–429
two-earner marriages, 415–419, 441–444
two-location families, 429
two-person single career, 410n
two-stage marriage, 189

U

UN Convention on the Rights of the Child: How Does Canada Measure Up, 326
United Nations Convention on Children's Rights, 326
unmarried. *See* singlehood
unpaid family work

balance with employment, 423–425
defined, 419
dependent family members, care of, 419–420
economic compensation, 411
equitable balance, 442–443, 444
gender strategy, 442
housework, 420–423
ideological perspective, 422
and marital satisfaction, 443
men, 422
rational investment perspective, 423
reinforcing cycle, 423
resource hypothesis, 423
sandwich generation, 419–420
second shift, 421–422, 442–443
stalled revolution, 421
women, 420, 421t, 422–423
upper-class parents, 374
upper middle-class parents, 374
urban singles, 158–159
utilitarian marriage, 223, 225, 246

V

values
    family, 26, 29
    individualistic (self-fulfillment), 27
    spiritual, 533
Van de Perre v. Edwards, 37b–38b
verbal skills, 71
vertical family, 537
vertically extended family, 43
Viagra, 125
victimization surveys, 294, 296
video dating, 208b
violence
    accused-victim relationship in solved homicides, 297t
    in arranged marriages, 181b
    child abuse, 308–313
    common couple, 304
    counselling and group therapy, 308
    courtship, 187–188
    elder abuse and neglect, 313–315
    husband abuse, 303–306
    infant homicides, 296
    intervention, 307–308
    between intimates, 294
    legal arrest, 307–308
    patriarchal, 304